Freedom and Responsibility

READINGS IN PHILOSOPHY AND LAW

Edited by
HERBERT MORRIS

STANFORD UNIVERSITY PRESS
STANFORD, CALIFORNIA
1961

Stanford University Press
Stanford, California

© 1961 by the Board of Trustees of the
Leland Stanford Junior University

Library of Congress Catalog Card Number: 61–8469
Printed in the United States of America

PREFACE

Everyone knows that many philosophical problems interest few people other than professional philosophers. Questions like "Does the external world exist?" and "Is time real?" or "Do we really know how another feels?" and "Are we awake or dreaming?" are bread and butter to philosophers. Most other people, believing they have better things to do with their time, consider such questions tedious or inconsequential. It is different with problems related to freedom and responsibility. Questions like "What am I responsible for?" and "To what extent are we free?" and "Is it right to blame or punish anyone?" interest many people, not just philosophers. Answers to such questions influence our social behavior. Legal systems embody principles of responsibility; children are reared in accord with those principles. Quite literally, these are philosophical problems that touch the purse strings. They have a practical urgency: we have to come to terms with them.

There are periods when a whole society's attitude toward responsibility is uncertain and changing, when issues of praise and blame, reward and punishment, are being reflected upon anew, and people wonder about what is being done and why it is being done. Ezekiel lived in such a period of ferment:

> The word of the Lord came unto me again, saying,
> What mean ye, that ye use this proverb concerning
> the land of Israel, saying,
> The fathers have eaten sour grapes, and the
> children's teeth are set on edge?
> As I live, saith the Lord God, ye shall not have
> occasion any more to use this proverb in Israel.
>
> * * *
>
> The son shall not bear the iniquity of the
> father, neither shall the father bear the
> iniquity of the son: the righteousness of the
> righteous shall be upon him, and the
> wickedness of the wicked shall be upon him.

Ours is a period like his. Our notions of responsibility are in flux, especially in the law, and we have serious reservations about our conceptual apparatus. We wonder whether or not basic attitudes need serious revision. Simple, everyday, rock-bottom kinds of human activities are called into question, and we feel unsure of ourselves. We dread that we may not be doing what should be done.

Among other things we need carefully and systematically to re-assess the principles by which we praise or blame, reward or punish. We need to improve our understanding of the concepts that enter into our judgments on these matters. It is the aim of this collection to promote just such an inquiry.

Although there is a sizable body of legal and philosophical literature on freedom and responsibility, much of the best work is known only to specialists. Moreover, there is little exchange of ideas between specialists: it is as if philosophers had never heard of the law and lawyers of philosophy. In this book I have assembled materials from both disciplines, and some from psychology as well. As things turned out, philosophers are more in evidence than lawyers, and lawyers than psychologists, but this is perhaps inevitable. The selections as a whole have only one thing in common: they are all relevant in one way or another to questions that are raised when one thinks about moral and legal responsibility.

I have excluded literary works from this collection with some regret, for such works have provided many of our most profound insights into ethical problems. I had hoped also to include material on primitive conceptions of responsibility, but could not, to my dismay, discover any treatment of the subject that served my particular purposes. There are a number of fine works on primitive law, several of which are listed in the bibliography for the first chapter, but in none of them could I find passages of suitable length and content for this collection.

The first chapter is a potpourri. It is designed to suggest the main legal and philosophical questions that arise in connection with freedom and responsibility. The remaining nine chapters are organized around concepts that play a crucial role when responsibility is in some manner at issue. These concepts, which may be regarded as the lowest common denominators of freedom and responsibility, are interrelated, so that a discussion of one will necessarily involve consideration of most of the others. In each chapter, consequently, we sweep over the whole area, but we do so each time from a slightly different point of view and with a different emphasis.

The chapter introductions are designed to accomplish two things: first, to clarify the role assumed by the concepts in question when issues of responsibility arise; and second, to prepare the reader for certain important specific questions that are raised by the selections included in each chapter. Occasionally, I have given way to temptation and raised some questions of my own.

I wish to express my appreciation to the authors and publishers who have kindly given permission to reprint the selections in this volume. I am indebted to various members of Stanford University Press and to Professor

Norman Abrams of the UCLA Law School for many valuable suggestions. I want also to acknowledge the fine secretarial assistance provided by the Stanford Philosophy Department, the UCLA Law School, and Mary Howard of the UCLA Philosophy Department.

J. L. Austin's "A Plea for Excuses" (pp. 6–19) from *Aristotelian Society Proceedings,* LVII (1956–57), 1–30, is reprinted by special permission of the Editor of the Aristotelian Society. Professor Austin's Collected Papers are about to be published by Oxford University Press on behalf of his literary executors, whose general policy is that his papers cannot otherwise be reproduced. Permission in this case was only granted because by the time the general policy of the literary executors and their publishers had been made known through the Editor of the Aristotelian Society, very heavy pre-publication expenses had been already incurred.

HERBERT MORRIS

CONTENTS

V · NEGLIGENCE, RECKLESSNESS, AND STRICT LIABILITY · 231

VI · CAUSATION · 282

VII · IGNORANCE AND MISTAKE · 343

VIII · LEGAL INSANITY · 392

RESPONSIBILITY

"Mother, little heart of mine," he said (he had begun using such strange caressing words at that time), "little heart of mine, my joy, believe me, everyone is really responsible to all men for all men and for everything. I don't know how to explain it to you, but I feel it is so, painfully even. And how is it we went on then living, getting angry and not knowing."

DOSTOYEVSKY, *The Brothers Karamazov*

Suppose that your treasured antique clock lies shattered upon the floor. You are told that the repairman is responsible. He is said to have dropped it, and you must now determine whether or not he was in fact responsible, and if so whether or not he was at fault, and if so how seriously at fault. If he has dropped the clock as a result of an unexpected muscle spasm, you will normally not censure him, blame him, or hold him responsible or accountable. The muscle spasm and not *he* was responsible for the incident. Bad luck, a matter for regret, but there the matter ends unless you are off to another antique shop.

If he has dropped the clock purposely, however, your attitude will be completely different. You will hold him accountable. Before you pass critical judgment, however, you may wish to consider his reasons, and if these should be convincing, you may excuse him or perhaps you may even find his behavior under the circumstances justifiable. All well and good. We all surely recognize this type of situation. We were still infants when we tried to avoid punishment or at least to soften the blow by saying "I didn't mean it!" It is this basic situation that provides us with the serious and difficult philosophical problems that are principally to concern us in this volume.

In the case I have described a person has acted in a certain way. He has dropped something, relaxed his grip. Persons, however, are held responsible, not just for doing things or for the consequences of what they do, but for omitting and for failing to do things; for example, to file tax returns, to pass examinations. And, of course, a person may be held responsible for simply possessing something; for example, narcotics. Is possessing something "doing" something? Again, people hold others responsible for being the kind of person they are: he is criticized for being vain; she is praised for being modest. And certain judgments of responsibility extend even further, for there are those who would have us answer for our thoughts, our feelings, our desires. "But I say unto you, That whosoever looketh on a woman to lust after her hath committed adultery with her already in his heart." Freud has argued that we are morally responsible for the content of our dreams.[1] And Dostoyevsky would, it seems, be prepared to censure us, not just for our own lustful desires, but for the desires of other men as well.

There are those, then, who would have us responsible when others would say that we cannot be, that "it is nonsense even to suggest we are." Thus a major question is "For what may one be held responsible?" And connected with it : "Why is it that one is responsible for such things and not for others?" Some say we are responsible for our intentions only; some, for our choices. Some say we are responsible for our desires, be they conscious or unconscious; some only for what we attempt to do; some, only for what we in fact do or for the consequences of what we do. Is there, perhaps, some fundamental agreement underlying these divergent views, an agreement, perhaps, that a man must have some control over what he is held responsible for? Freud writes, "Obviously one must hold oneself responsible for the evil impulses of one's dreams. In what other way can one deal with them?"[2] Does it make any difference whether we are thinking of moral or legal responsibility? And why should this make a difference?

We shall want also to examine questions that arise once it is settled that some person is responsible. Determining responsibility may be only the beginning of our inquiry. Does it follow, because a certain person is responsible for some occurrence, that we are going to blame him, or make him "pay up"? Clearly not. He might have done it by mistake, or he may have some other excuse. Thus, there may be a difference between "being responsible" and "being held responsible" for some occurrence, the latter phrase perhaps implying the appropriateness of some kind of censure. When we say that a person is "morally" or "legally" responsible for something that has happened, we are "holding" him responsible; it is our judgment that he may properly be praised or blamed, or that the legal system will hold him answerable. The readings in this book are concerned with problems of determining when someone is responsible, and to what extent a person found to be responsible may properly be blamed or praised.

We are not concerned with questions like "What is the responsibility of a lawyer to his client?" "What is the responsibility of a parent to his child?" "What is the responsibility of a corporation director to the shareholders, to the public, to the consumer?" In such cases, the word responsibility involves a consideration of the *specific* things for which someone is or should be made answerable: it may be replaced with no loss of meaning by words like duty and obligation, and it lends itself easily to the plural form, "responsibilities,"

---

[1] "Moral Responsibility for the Content of Dreams," *Collected Papers* (London: The Hogarth Press, 1957), V, 154–57.
[2] *Ibid.*, p. 156.

which, in our context of moral and legal responsibility, makes no sense. We are not at all concerned in this volume with the specific responsibilities or duties of any person, or class of persons, or office, but rather with those conditions that must be satisfied if one is ever to be held answerable. The matters of concern to us bear on whether or not a parent, for example, can be blamed for failing to fulfill his responsibilities to his child, whatever one might believe those responsibilities to be.

It should be apparent, too, that the scope of these materials is not limited to the subject of responsibility conceived as an inquiry into the defense of legal insanity. In legal literature the topic of criminal responsibility is frequently viewed in this restricted way. Thus the requirement of an "overt act," together with what constitutes one and what justifies requiring one before a person may be held civilly or criminally liable, would be viewed by many in the law as a question, not of responsibility, but of liability. These readings, of course, involve questions other than those of legal insanity.

The readings in this first chapter are designed to suggest the range of different problems and philosophical attitudes in this broad area we have carved out and labeled "freedom and responsibility." There are at least three major types of problems: (1) By what principles do we hold a person responsible or absolve a person of responsibility? And by what principles do we determine degrees of praise and blame? (2) Are these principles justifiable? (3) What analysis can be offered of the concepts that enter into these principles? Let me elaborate briefly each of these.

(1) Aristotle and Gabriel de Tarde, for example, are concerned with making explicit the conditions they believe must be satisfied before someone can be praised or blamed. Aristotle holds the view that a person must have acted voluntarily, at least at some point, if he is to be justly praised or blamed. Tarde believes that there are difficulties with the concept of freedom and makes responsibility rest upon two conditions: personal identity and social similarity. The person who is held responsible must be the self-same person who did the deed and he must share certain features with those who are holding him responsible. Now an inquiry of this kind has a number of different aspects, for we may be interested in both the relevant moral principles and the relevant legal principles (and the different ones for different areas of the law) and the relationship between them.

Let us first direct our attention to the moral sphere. Serious questions may arise over what today appears to be an obviously agreed-upon moral principle, namely, "no moral responsibility without fault." Have all societies been committed to such a principle? It would seem that they have not. What, after all, was Ezekiel objecting to if not vicarious or familial responsibility? And yet, it may not be quite so simple a matter. When a society adopts what appears to us to be vicarious responsibility, is the principle "no responsibility without fault" being rejected, or is it, rather, that different cultures have different conceptions of the person and the group, so that where we would say "one person" has done something, another culture would be prepared to say that "others" had done it as well? Indeed, we see in Holmes's treatment of early forms of liability that the problem arises even with inanimate objects, which are blamed in some cultures. Are there any cultures that disregard completely the distinctions we make between voluntary and involuntary actions, between intentional and unintentional harms?

Some argue that morality is concerned not with the deed but only with the thought behind the deed, and that a person is praised or blamed for what he wills and not for what he does. Is this in fact the principle underlying our moral judgments? Strictly, then, we should blame a person not, say, for breaking a promise or shooting a policeman, but rather for his state of mind at a certain time. Some hold, to the contrary, that will is unessential.

When we turn to legal systems, we find principles underlying judgments of liability and responsibility that seem clearly to differ from the principles involved in moral judgments. Motive, for example, which some consider essential to assessing moral blameworthiness or praiseworthiness, plays an insignificant role in legal judgments; in the law the deed counts more than the thought behind the deed. Some writers have attempted to make out a general distinction between law and morals along these lines. Kant and Kantorowicz, for example, argue that "law prescribes external conduct" and morality "prescribes internal conduct." Is their distinction too simple? If not, what accounts for this difference between morality and law?

We must, of course, exercise caution in thinking of "the law," for there are many kinds of law. The principles involved in providing compensation to the injured may differ pronouncedly from those involved in punishing the guilty. The law of torts may be different in certain respects from criminal law. Attempts have been made to define the limits of different areas of the law. Some argue, for example, that in a crime, but not in a tort, moral culpability is essentially involved. Are there legal principles that underlie the whole of the law, a principle such as "there must be a voluntary act," and other principles limited to special areas? And if this is so, can we account for its being so?

(2) The next major question is this: Are our principles justifiable? To answer this question, we must first make explicit the criteria we use in evaluating different principles.

If there are differences between legal and moral principles, can these differences be justified? A person may, of course, be legally responsible and morally above reproach. For example, a man may be required to pay damages for injuries that he has caused despite his having done his very best to avoid those injuries. Many theorists think that the law of torts rightly ignores moral blameworthiness. They claim that where two morally innocent parties are involved, one of whom has been injured by the other, it is justifiable under certain circumstances to shift the burden of repairing the injury from the person who has suffered it to the person who has caused it. What principles justify shifting losses from one person to another?

Legal systems distinguish between criminal attempts that fail through some fortuity and those that succeed. The former are punished less severely than the latter. Is this justifiable? Is it perhaps justifiable only on the ground that the public would simply not tolerate any other principle? Is that a *moral* justification?

What justifies certain defenses in the law such as ignorance or mistake of fact, insanity, and duress? Some think that to punish persons who do wrong under such circumstances has no deterrent effect on others. If we could show that punishing the insane has a greater deterrent value than not punishing them, would we believe ourselves justified in doing away with the defense plea of insanity? Why are children excused? Can we believe that they do not intentionally injure others and that they cannot be deterred?

Persons are not usually blamed in our culture for having diseases as they were in Butler's *Erewhon*. Is there a defensible distinction between those who succumb to temptation and those who succumb to diseases? Some claim that in neither case can a person do anything to prevent what takes place; they acknowledge no "free will," and doubt whether we are justified in blaming or punishing anyone. If no one had "free will," whatever that might be, would we still perhaps be justified in punishing within a legal system? And if praise and blame, reward and punishment, continued in societies where there was no belief in free will, would such judgments there have some fundamentally different meaning?

These and many other questions concerning justifiability are raised by these readings. Hovering above them all is some anxiety that perhaps all our notions of praise and blame, reward and punishment, are carry-overs from a less "scientific" era. Perhaps they should be junked. What should we gain and what should we lose by junking them?

(3) Finally, in setting out the different legal and moral principles we use words like "voluntarily," "act," "desire," "intention," "motive," "negligence," "cause," and "punishment." These are common enough words, and we are normally quite comfortable with them. And yet we can be made uncomfortable by the philosopher who asks, "Well, then, what *is* an act?" "What *is* it to do something intentionally?" "What *are* the differences between wishing, wanting, desiring, hoping, expecting, intending, willing?" The philosopher wants to discover what is common and peculiar to situations labeled one way rather than another. He is engaged in conceptual analysis. When he asks such questions he is after something we can call "an explanatory definition." Aristotle and Austin introduce us to such a philosophical inquiry.

These are some of the chief problems raised in a discussion of freedom and responsibility. There are others, big and small, many of which are taken up in our first essay, a contemporary philosopher's brilliant plea for a close and precise examination of the very matters with which this collection deals.

A Plea for Excuses*

The subject of this paper, *Excuses,* is one not to be treated, but only to be introduced, within such limits. It is, or might be, the name of a whole branch, even a ramiculated branch, of philosophy, or at least of one fashion of philosophy. I shall try, therefore, first to state *what* the subject is, *why* it is worth studying, and *how* it may be studied, all this at a regrettably lofty level: and then I shall illustrate, in more congenial but desultory detail, some of the methods to be used, together with their limitations, and some of the unexpected results to be expected and lessons to be learned. Much, of course, of the amusement, and of the instruction, comes in drawing the coverts of the microglot, in hounding down the minutiae, and to this I can do no more here than incite you. But I owe it to the subject to say, that it has long afforded me what philosophy is so often thought, and made, barren of—the fun of discovery, the pleasures of cooperation, and the satisfaction of reaching agreement.

What, then, is the subject? I am here using the word "excuses" *for a title,* but it would be unwise to freeze too fast to this one noun and its partner verb: indeed for some time I used to use "extenuation" instead. Still, on the whole "excuses" is probably the most central and embracing term in the field, although this includes others of importance— "plea," "defense," "justification," and so on. When, then, do we "excuse" conduct, our own or somebody else's? When are "excuses" proffered?

In general, the situation is one where someone is *accused* of having done something, or (if that will keep it any cleaner) where someone is *said* to have done something which is bad, wrong, inept, unwelcome, or in some other of the numerous possible ways untoward. Thereupon he, or someone on his behalf, will try to defend his conduct or to get him out of it.

One way of going about this is to admit flatly that he, X, did do that very thing, A, but to argue that it was a good thing, or the right or sensible thing, or a permissible thing to do, either in general or at least in the special circumstances of the occasion. To take this line is to *justify* the action, to give reasons for doing it: not to say, to brazen it out, to glory in it, or the like.

A different way of going about it is to admit that it wasn't a good thing to have done, but to argue that it is not quite fair or correct to say *baldly* "X did A." We may say it isn't fair just to say *X* did it; perhaps he was under somebody's influence, or was nudged. Or, it isn't fair to say baldly he *did* A; it may have been partly accidental, or an unintentional slip. Or, it isn't fair to say he did simply *A*—he was really doing something quite different and A was only incidental, or he was looking at the whole thing quite differently. Naturally these arguments can be combined or overlap or run into each other.

In the one defense, briefly, we accept responsibility but deny that it was bad: in the other, we admit that it was bad but don't accept full, or even any, responsibility.

By and large, justifications can be kept distinct from excuses, and I shall not be so anxious to talk about them because they have enjoyed more than their fair share of philosophical attention. But the two certainly can be confused, and can *seem* to go very near to each other, even if they do not perhaps actually do so. You dropped the tea-tray: Certainly, but an emotional storm was about to break out: or, Yes, but there was a wasp. In each case the defense, very soundly, insists on a fuller description of the event in its context; but the first is a justification, the second an excuse. Again, if the objection is to the use of such a dyslogistic verb as "murdered," this may be on the ground that the killing was done in battle (justification) or on the ground that it was only accidental if reckless (excuse). It is arguable that we do not use the terms justification and excuse as carefully as we might; a miscellany of even less clear terms, such as "extenuation," "palliation," "mitigation," hovers uneasily between partial justification and partial excuse; and when we plead, say, provocation, there is genuine uncertainty or ambiguity as to what we mean—is *he* partly responsible, because he roused a violent impulse or passion in me, so that it wasn't truly or merely me acting "of

* J. L. Austin, *Aristotelian Society Proceedings,* LVII (1956–57), 1–30, reprinted by special permission of the Editor of The Aristotelian Society, London (see Preface). Footnotes have been renumbered.

my own accord" (excuse)? Or is it rather that, he having done me such injury, I was entitled to retaliate (justification)? Such doubts merely make it the more urgent to clear up the usage of these various terms. But that the defenses I have for convenience labeled "justification" and "excuse" are in principle distinct can scarcely be doubted.

This then is the sort of situation we have to consider under "excuses." It will only further point out how very wide a field it covers. We have of course to bring in the opposite numbers of excuses—the expressions that *aggravate,* such as "deliberately," "on purpose," and so on, if only for the reason that an excuse often takes the form of a rebuttal of one of these. But we have also to bring in a large number of expressions which at first blush look not so much like excuses as like accusations—"clumsiness," "tactlessness," "thoughtlessness," and the like. Because it has always to be remembered that few excuses get us out of it *completely*: the average excuse, in a poor situation, gets us only out of the fire into the frying pan—but still, of course, any frying pan in a fire. If I have broken your dish or your romance, maybe the best defense I can find will be clumsiness.

Why, if this is what "excuses" are, should we trouble to investigate them? It might be thought reason enough that their production has always bulked so large among human activities. But to moral philosophy in particular a study of them will contribute in special ways, both positively toward the development of a cautious, latter-day version of conduct, and negatively toward the correction of older and hastier theories.

In ethics we study, I suppose, the good and the bad, the right and the wrong, and this must be for the most part in some connection with conduct or the doing of actions. Yet before we consider what actions are good or bad, right or wrong, it is proper to consider first what is meant by, and what not, and what is included under, and what not, the expression "doing an action" or "doing something." These are expressions still too little examined on their own account and merits, just as the general notion of "saying something" is still too lightly passed over in logic. There is indeed a vague and comforting idea in the background that, after all, in the last analysis, doing an action must come down to the mak-

ing of physical movements with parts of the body; but this is about as true as that saying something must, in the last analysis, come down to making movements of the tongue.

The beginning of sense, not to say wisdom, is to realize that "doing an action," as used in philosophy,[1] is a highly abstract expression—it is a stand-in used in the place of any (or almost any?) verb with a personal subject, in the same sort of way that "thing" is a stand-in for any (or when we remember, almost any) noun substantive, and "quality" a stand-in for the adjective. Nobody, to be sure, relies on such dummies quite implicitly quite indefinitely. Yet notoriously it is possible to arrive at, or to derive the idea for, an oversimplified metaphysics from the obsession with "things" and their "qualities." In a similar way, less commonly recognized even in these semisophisticated times, we fall for the myth of the verb. We treat the expression "doing an action" no longer as a stand-in for a verb with a personal subject, as which it has no doubt some uses, and might have more if the range of verbs were not left unspecified, but as self-explanatory, ground-level description, one which brings adequately into the open the essential features of everything that comes, by simple inspection, under it. We scarcely notice even the most patent exceptions or difficulties (is to think something, or to say something, or to try to do something, to do an action?), any more than we fret, in the *ivresse des grandes profondeurs,* as to whether flames are things or events. So we come easily to think of our behavior over any time, and of a life as a whole, as consisting in doing now action A, next action B, then action C, and so on, just as elsewhere we come to think of the world as consisting of this, that, and the other substance or material thing, each with its properties. All "actions" are, as actions (meaning what?), equal, composing a quarrel with striking a match, winning a war with sneezing: worse still, we assimilate them one and all to the supposedly most obvious and easy cases, such as posting letters or moving fingers, just as we assimilate all "things" to horses or beds.

If we are to continue to use this expression in sober philosophy, we need to ask such questions as: Is to sneeze to do an action? Or is to breathe, or to see, or to checkmate, or each

[1] This use has little to do with the more down-to-earth occurrences of "action" in ordinary speech.

one of countless others? In short, for what range of verbs, as used on what occasions, is "doing an action" a stand-in? What have they in common, and what do those excluded severally lack? Again we need to ask how we decide what is the correct name for "the" action that somebody did—and what, indeed, are the rules for the use of "the" action, "an" action, "one" action, a "part" or "phase" of an action, and the like. Further, we need to realize that even the "simplest" named actions are not so simple—certainly are not the mere makings of physical movements, and to ask what more, then, comes in (intentions? conventions?) and what does not (motives?), and what is the detail of the complicated internal machinery we use in "acting"—the receipt of intelligence, the appreciation of the situation, the invocation of principles, the planning, the control of execution, and the rest.

In two main ways the study of excuses can throw light on these fundamental matters. First, to examine excuses is to examine cases where there has been some abnormality or failure: and as so often, the abnormal will throw light on the normal, will help us to penetrate the blinding veil of ease and obviousness that hides the mechanisms of the natural successful act. It rapidly becomes plain that the breakdowns signalized by the various excuses are of radically different kinds, affecting different parts or stages of the machinery, which the excuses consequently pick out and sort out for us. Further, it emerges that not *every* slip-up occurs in connection with *every*-thing that could be called an "action," that not every excuse is apt with every verb—far indeed from it: and this provides us with one means of introducing some classification into the vast miscellany of "actions." If we classify them according to the particular selection of breakdowns to which each is liable, this should assign them their places in some family group or groups of actions, or in some model of the machinery of acting.

In this sort of way, the philosophical study of conduct can get off to a positive fresh start. But by the way, and more negatively, a number of traditional cruces or mistakes in this field can be resolved or removed. First among these comes the problem of Freedom. While it has been the tradition to present this as the "positive" term requiring elucidation, there is little doubt that to say we acted "freely" (in the philosopher's use, which is only faintly related to the everyday use) is to say only that we acted *not* un-freely, in one or another of the many heterogeneous ways of so acting (under duress, or what not). Like "real," "free" is only used to rule out the suggestion of some or all of its recognized antitheses. As "truth" is not a name for a characteristic of assertions, so "freedom" is not a name for a characteristic of actions, but the name of a dimension in which actions are assessed. In examining all the ways in which each action may not be "free," i.e., the cases in which it will not do to say simply "X did A," we may hope to dispose of the problem of Freedom. Aristotle has often been chidden for talking about excuses or pleas and overlooking "the real problem": in my own case, it was when I began to see the injustice of this charge that I first became interested in excuses.

There is much to be said for the view that, philosophical tradition apart, Responsibility would be a better candidate for the role here assigned to Freedom. If ordinary language is to be our guide, it is to evade responsibility, or full responsibility, that we most often make excuses, and I have used the word myself in this way above. But in fact "responsibility" too seems not really apt in all cases: I do not exactly evade responsibility when I plead clumsiness or tactlessness, nor, often, when I plead that I only did it unwillingly or reluctantly, and still less if I plead that I had in the circumstances no choice: here I was constrained and have an excuse (or justification), yet may accept responsibility. It may be, then, that at least two key terms, Freedom and Responsibility, are needed: the relation between them is not clear, and it may be hoped that the investigation of excuses will contribute toward its clarification.[2]

So much, then, for ways in which the study of excuses may throw light on ethics. But there are also reasons why it is an attractive subject methodologically, at least if we are

[2] Another well-flogged horse in these same stakes is Blame. At least two things seem confused together under this term. Sometimes when I blame X for doing A, say for breaking the vase, it is a question simply or mainly of my disapproval of A, breaking the vase, which unquestionably X did: but sometimes it is, rather, a question simply or mainly of how far I think X responsible for A, which unquestionably was bad. Hence if somebody says he blames me for something, I may answer by giving a *justification*, so that he will cease to disapprove of what I did, or else by giving an *excuse*, so that he will cease to hold me, at least entirely and in every way, responsible for doing it.

to proceed from "ordinary language," that is, by examining *what we should say when,* and so why and what we should mean by it. Perhaps this method, at least as *one* philosophical method, scarcely requires justification at present—too evidently, there is gold in them thar hills : more opportune would be a warning about the care and thoroughness needed if it is not to fall into disrepute. I will, however, justify it very briefly.

First, words are our tools, and, as a minimum we should use clean tools : we should know what we mean and what we do not, and we must forearm ourselves against the traps that language sets us. Secondly, words are not (except in their own little corner) facts or things : we need therefore to prise them off the world, to hold them apart from and against it, so that we can realize their inadequacies and arbitrarinesses, and can re-look at the world without blinkers. Thirdly, and more hopefully, our common stock of words embodies all the distinctions men have found worth drawing, and the connections they have found worth marking, in the lifetimes of many generations : these surely are likely to be more numerous, more sound, since they have stood up to the long test of the survival of the fittest, and more subtle, at least in all ordinary and reasonably practical matters, than any that you or I are likely to think up in our armchairs of an afternoon—the most favored alternative method.

In view of the prevalence of the slogan "ordinary language," and of such names as "linguistic" or "analytic" philosophy or "the analysis of language," one thing needs specially emphasizing to counter misunderstandings. When we examine what we should say when, what words we should use in what situations, we are looking again not *merely* at words (or "meanings," whatever they may be) but also at the realities we use the words to talk about : we are using a sharpened awareness of words to sharpen our perception of, though not as the final arbiter of, the phenomena. For this reason I think it might be better to use, for this way of doing philosophy, some less misleading name than those given above—for instance, "linguistic phenomenology," only that is rather a mouthful.

Using, then, such a method, it is plainly preferable to investigate a field where ordinary language is rich and subtle, as it is in the pressingly practical matter of Excuses, but certainly is not in the matter, say, of Time. At the same time we should prefer a field which is not too much trodden into bogs or tracks by traditional philosophy, for in that case even "ordinary" language will often have become infected with the jargon of extinct theories, and our own prejudices too, as the upholders or imbibers of theoretical views, will be too readily, and often insensibly, engaged. Here too, Excuses form an admirable topic ; we can discuss at least clumsiness, or absence of mind, or inconsiderateness, even spontaneousness, without remembering what Kant thought, and so progress by degrees even to discussing deliberation without for once remembering Aristotle or self-control without Plato. Granted that our subject is, as already claimed for it, neighboring, analogous, or germane in some way to some notorious center of philosophical trouble, with these two further requirements satisfied, we should be certain of what we are after : a good site for *field work* in philosophy. Here at last we should be able to unfreeze, to loosen up and get going on agreeing about discoveries, however small, and on agreeing about how to reach agreement.[3] How much it is to be wished that similar field work will soon be undertaken in, say, aesthetics ; if only we could forget for a while about the beautiful and get down instead to the dainty and the dumpy.

There are, I know, or are supposed to be, snags in "linguistic" philosophy, which those not very familiar with it find, sometimes not without glee or relief, daunting. But with snags, as with nettles, the thing to do is to grasp them—and to climb above them. I will mention two in particular, over which the study of excuses may help to encourage us. The first is the snag of Loose (or Divergent or Alternative) Usage ; and the second the crux of the Last Word. Do we all say the same, and only the same, things in the same situations ? Don't usages differ ? And, Why should what we all ordinarily say be the only or the best or final way of putting it ? Why should it even be true ?

Well, people's usages do vary, and we do talk loosely, and we do say different things apparently indifferently. But first, not nearly

---

[3] All of which was seen and claimed by Socrates, when he first betook himself to the way of Words.

as much as one would think. When we come
down to cases, it transpires in the very great
majority that what we had thought was our
wanting to say different things and in *the
same* situation was really not so—we had
simply imagined the situation *slightly* differently: which is all too easy to do, because of
course no situation (and we are dealing with
imagined situations) is ever "completely" described. The more we imagine the situation
in detail, with a background of story—and
it is worth employing the most idiosyncratic
or, sometimes, boring means to stimulate and
to discipline our wretched imaginations—the
less we find we disagree about what we should
say. Nevertheless, *sometimes* we do ultimately
disagree: sometimes we must allow a usage
to be, though appalling, yet actual; sometimes
we should genuinely use either or both of two
different descriptions. But why should this
daunt us? All that is happening is entirely
explicable. If our usages disagree, then you
use "X" where I use "Y," or more probably
(and more intriguingly) your conceptual system is different from mine, though very likely
it is at least equally consistent and service-
able: in short, we can find *why* we disagree—
you choose to classify in one way, I in another.
If the usage is loose, we can understand the
temptation that leads to it, and the distinctions
that it blurs: if there are "alternative" descriptions, then the situation can be described
or can be "structured" in two ways, or perhaps it is one where, for current purposes, the
two alternatives come down to the same. A
disagreement as to what we should say is not
to be shied off, but to be pounced upon: for
the explanation of it can hardly fail to be
illuminating. If we light on an electron that
rotates the wrong way, that is a discovery,
a portent to be followed up, not a reason for
chucking physics: and by the same token, a
genuinely loose or eccentric talker is a rare
specimen to be prized.

As practice in learning to handle this bogey,
in learning the essential *rubrics,* we could
scarcely hope for a more promising exercise
than the study of excuses. Here, surely, is
just the sort of situation where people will
say "almost anything," because they are so
flurried, or so anxious to get off. "It was a
mistake," "It was an accident"—how readily
these can *appear* indifferent, and even be used
together. Yet, a story or two, and everybody
will not merely agree that they are completely

different, but even discover for himself what
the difference is and what each means.[4]

Then, for the Last Word. Certainly ordinary language has no claim to be the last
word, if there is such a thing. It embodies,
indeed, something better than the metaphysics
of the Stone Age, namely, as was said, the
inherited experience and acumen of many generations of men. But then, that acumen has
been concentrated primarily upon the practical
business of life. If a distinction works well
for practical purposes in ordinary life (no
mean feat, for even ordinary life is full of
hard cases), then there is sure to be something
in it, it will not mark nothing: yet this is
likely enough to be not the best way of ar-
ranging things if our interests are more extensive or intellectual than the ordinary. And
again, that experience has been derived only
from the sources available to ordinary men
throughout most of civilized history: it has
not been fed from the resources of the microscope and its successors. And it must be
added too, that superstition and error and
fantasy of all kinds do become incorporated
in ordinary language and even sometimes
stand up to the survival test (only, when they
do, why should we not detect it?). Certainly,
then, ordinary language is *not* the last word:
in principle it can everywhere be supplemented and improved upon and superseded.
Only remember, it *is* the *first* word.

For this problem too the field of Excuses
is a fruitful one. Here is matter both contentious and practically important for everybody, so that ordinary language is on its toes:
yet also, on its back it has long had a bigger
flea to bite it, in the shape of the Law, and
both again have lately attracted the attentions
of yet another, and at least a healthily growing, flea, in the shape of psychology. In the
law a constant stream of actual cases, more
novel and more tortuous than the mere imagination could contrive, are brought up *for decision*—that is, formulae for docketing them

---

[4] You have a donkey, so have I, and they graze in
the same field. The day comes when I conceive a
dislike for mine. I go to shoot it, draw a bead on it,
fire: the brute falls in its tracks. I inspect the victim, and find to my horror that it is *your* donkey.
I appear on your doorstep with the remains and say—
what? "I say, old sport, I'm awfully sorry, etc., I've
shot your donkey *by accident*"? Or "*by mistake*"?
Then again, I go to shoot my donkey as before, draw
a bead on it, fire—but as I do so, the beasts move,
and to my horror yours falls. Again the scene on the
doorstep—what do I say? "By mistake"? Or "by
accident"?

must somehow be found. Hence it is necessary first to be careful with, but also to be brutal with, to torture, to fake and to override, ordinary language: we cannot here evade or forget the whole affair. (In ordinary life we dismiss the puzzles that crop up about time, but we cannot do that indefinitely in physics.) Psychology likewise produces novel cases, but it also produces new methods for bringing phenomena under observation and study: moreover, unlike the law, it has an unbiased interest in the totality of them and is unpressed for decision. Hence its own special and constant need to supplement, to revise, and to supersede the classifications of both ordinary life and the law. We have, then, ample material for practice in learning to handle the bogey of the Last Word, however it should be handled.

Suppose, then, that we set out to investigate excuses, what are the methods and resources initially available? Our object is to imagine the varieties of situation in which we make excuses, and to examine the expressions used in making them. If we have a lively imagination, together perhaps with an ample experience of dereliction, we shall go far, only we need system: I do not know how many of you keep a list of the kinds of fool you make of yourselves. It is advisable to use systematic aids, of which there would appear to be three at least. I list them here in order of availability to the layman.

First we may use the dictionary—quite a concise one will do, but the use must be *thorough*. Two methods suggest themselves, both a little tedious, but repaying. One is to read the book through, listing all the words that seem relevant; this does not take as long as many suppose. The other is to start with a widish selection of obviously relevant terms, and to consult the dictionary under each: it will be found that, in the explanations of the various meanings of each, a surprising number of other terms occur, which are germane though of course not often synonymous. We then look up each of *these,* bringing in more for our bag from the "definitions" given in each case; and when we have continued for a little, it will generally be found that the family circle begins to close, until ultimately it is complete and we come only upon repetitions. This method has the advantage of grouping the terms into convenient clusters— but of course a good deal will depend upon the comprehensiveness of our initial selection.

Working the dictionary, it is interesting to find that a high percentage of the terms connected with excuses prove to be *adverbs,* a type of word which has not enjoyed so large a share of the philosophical limelight as the noun, substantive or adjective, and the verb: this is natural because, as was said, the tenor of so many excuses is that I did it but only *in a way,* not just flatly like that—i.e., the verb needs modifying. Besides adverbs, however, there are other words of all kinds, including numerous abstract nouns, "misconception," "accident," "purpose," and the like, and a few verbs too, which often hold key positions for the grouping of excuses into classes at a high level ("couldn't help," "didn't mean to," "didn't realize," or again "intend" and "attempt"). In connection with the nouns another neglected class of words is prominent, namely, prepositions. Not merely does it matter considerably which preposition, often of several, is being used with a given substantive, but further the prepositions deserve study on their own account. For the question suggests itself, Why are the nouns in one group governed by "under," in another by "on," in yet another by "by" or "through" or "from" or "for" or "with," and so on? It will be disappointing if there prove to be no good reasons for such groupings.

Our second sourcebook will naturally be the law. This will provide us with an immense miscellany of untoward cases, and also with a useful list of recognized pleas, together with a good deal of acute analysis of both. No one who tries this resource will long be in doubt, I think, that the common law, and in particular the law of tort, is the richest storehouse; crime and contract contribute some special additions of their own, but tort is altogether more comprehensive and more flexible. But even here, and still more with so old and hardened a branch of the law as crime, much caution is needed with the arguments of counsel and the dicta or decisions of judges: acute though these are, it has always to be remembered that, in legal cases—

(1) there is the overriding requirement that a decision be reached, and a relatively black or white decision—guilty or not guilty—for the plaintiff or for the defendant;

(2) there is the general requirement that the charge or action and the pleadings be brought under one or another of the heads and

procedures that have come in the course of history to be accepted by the Courts. These, though fairly numerous, are still few and stereotyped in comparison with the accusations and defenses of daily life. Moreover contentions of many kinds are beneath the law, as too trivial, or outside it, as too purely moral—for example, inconsiderateness;

(3) there is the general requirement that we argue from and abide by precedents. The value of this in the law is unquestionable, but it can certainly lead to distortions of ordinary beliefs and expressions.

For such reasons as these, obviously closely connected and stemming from the nature and function of the law, practicing lawyers and jurists are by no means so careful as they might be to give to our ordinary expressions their ordinary meanings and applications. There is special pleading and evasion, stretching and strait-jacketing, besides the invention of technical terms, or technical senses for common terms. Nevertheless, it is a perpetual and salutary surprise to discover how much is to be learned from the law; and it is to be added that if a distinction drawn is a sound one, even though not yet recognized in law, a lawyer can be relied upon to take note of it, for it may be dangerous not to—if he does not, his opponent may.

Finally, the third sourcebook is psychology, with which I include such studies as anthropology and animal behavior. Here I speak with even more trepidation than about the Law. But this at least is clear, that some varieties of behavior, some ways of acting or explanations of the doing of actions, are here noticed and classified which have not been observed or named by ordinary men and hallowed by ordinary language, though perhaps they often might have been so if they had been of more practical importance. There is real danger in contempt for the "jargon" of psychology, at least when it sets out to supplement, and at least sometimes when it sets out to supplant, the language of ordinary life.

With these sources, and with the aid of the imagination, it will go hard if we cannot arrive at the meanings of large numbers of expressions and at the understanding and classification of large numbers of "actions." Then we shall comprehend clearly much that, before, we only made use of *ad hoc*. Definition, I would add, explanatory definition, should stand high among our aims: it is not enough to show how clever we are by showing how obscure everything is. Clarity, too,

I know, has been said to be not enough: but perhaps it will be time to go into that when we are within measurable distance of achieving clarity on some matter.

So much for the cackle. It remains to make a few remarks, not, I am afraid, in any very coherent order, about the types of significant result to be obtained and the more general lessons to be learned from the study of Excuses.

(1) *No modification without aberration.* When it is stated that X did A, there is a temptation to suppose that given some, indeed perhaps *any,* expression modifying the verb we shall be entitled to insert either it or its opposite or negation in our statement: that is, we shall be entitled to ask, typically, "Did X do A Mly or not Mly?" (e.g., "Did X murder Y voluntarily or involuntarily?"), and to answer one or the other. Or as a minimum it is supposed that if X did A there must be at least *one* modifying expression that we could, justifiably and informatively, insert with the verb. In the great majority of cases of the use of the great majority of verbs ("murder" perhaps is not one of the majority) such suppositions are quite unjustified. The natural economy of language dictates that for the *standard* case covered by any normal verb—not, perhaps, a verb of omen such as "murder," but a verb like "eat" or "kick" or "croquet"—no modifying expression is required or even permissible. Only if we do the action named in some *special* way or circumstances, different from those in which such an act is naturally done (and of course both the normal and the abnormal differ according to what verb in particular is in question) is a modifying expression called for, or even in order. I sit in my chair, in the usual way—I am not in a daze or influenced by threats or the like: here, it will not do to say either that I sat in it intentionally or that I did not sit in it intentionally,[5] nor yet that I sat in it automatically or from habit or what you will. It is bedtime, I am alone, I yawn: but I do not yawn involuntarily (or voluntarily!), nor yet deliberately. To yawn in any such peculiar way is just not to just yawn.

(2) *Limitation of application.* Expressions modifying verbs, typically adverbs, have lim-

---

[5] Caveat or hedge: of course we can say "I did *not* sit in it 'intentionally'" as a way simply of repudiating the suggestion that I sat in it intentionally.

ited ranges of application. That is, given any adverb of excuse, such as "unwittingly" or "spontaneously" or "impulsively," it will not be found that it makes good sense to attach it to any and every verb of "action" in any and every context: indeed, it will often apply only to a comparatively narrow range of such verbs. Something in the lad's upturned face appealed to him, he threw a brick at it—"spontaneously"? The interest then is to discover why some actions can be excused in a particular way but not others, particularly perhaps the latter.[6] This will largely elucidate the meaning of the excuse, and at the same time will illuminate the characteristics typical of the group of "actions" it picks out: very often too it will throw light on some detail of the machinery of "action" in general (see (4)), or on our standards of acceptable conduct (see (5)). It is specially important in the case of some of the terms most favored by philosophers or jurists to realize that at least in ordinary speech (disregarding back-seepage of jargon) they are not used so universally or so dichotomistically. For example, take "voluntarily" and "involuntarily": we may join the army or make a gift voluntarily, and the more we consider further actions which we might naturally be said to do in either of these ways, the more circumscribed and unlike each other do the two classes become, until we even doubt whether there is *any* verb with which both adverbs are equally in place. Perhaps there are some such; but at least sometimes when we may think we have found one it is an illusion, an apparent exception that really does prove the rule. I can perhaps "break a cup" voluntarily, *if* that is done, say, as an act of self-impoverishment: and I can perhaps break another involuntarily *if,* say, I make an involuntary movement which breaks it. Here, plainly, the two acts described each as "breaking a cup" are really very different, and the one is similar to acts typical of the "voluntary" class, the other to acts typical of the "involuntary" class.

(3) *The importance of Negations and Opposites.* "Voluntarily" and "involuntarily," then, are not opposed in the obvious sort of way that they are made to be in philosophy or jurisprudence. The "opposite," or rather "opposites," of "voluntarily" might be "under

constraint" of some sort, duress or obligation or influence:[7] the opposite of "involuntarily" might be "deliberately" or "on purpose" or the like. Such divergences in opposites indicate that "voluntarily" and "involuntarily," in spite of their apparent connection, are fish from very different kettles. In general, it will pay us to take nothing for granted or as obvious about negations and opposites. It does not pay to assume that a word must have an opposite, or one opposite, whether it is a "positive" word like "willfully" or a "negative" word like "inadvertently." Rather, we should be asking ourselves such questions as why there is no use for the adverb "advertently." For above all it will not do to assume that the "positive" word must be around to wear the trousers; commonly enough the "negative" (looking) word marks the (positive) abnormality, while the "positive" word, *if* it exists, merely serves to rule out the suggestion of that abnormality. It is natural enough, in view of what was said in (1) above, for the "positive" word not to be found at all in some cases. I do an act A_1 (say, crush a snail) *inadvertently* if, in the course of executing by means of movements of my bodily parts some other act A_2 (say, in walking down the public path) I fail to exercise such meticulous supervision over the courses of those movements as would have been needed to ensure that they did not bring about the untoward event (here, the impact on the snail.)[8] By claiming that A_1 was inadvertent we place it, where we imply it belongs, on this special level, in a class of incidental happenings which must occur in the doing of any physical act. To lift the act out of this class, we need and possess the expression "not . . . inadvertently": "advertently," if used for this purpose, would suggest that, if the act was not done inadvertently, then it must have been done noticing what I was

---

[6] For we are sometimes not so good at observing what we *can't* say as what we can, yet the first is pretty regularly the more revealing.

[7] But remember, when I sign a check in the normal way, I do *not* do so *either* "voluntarily" or "under constraint."

[8] Or analogously: I do an act A_1 (say, divulge my age, or imply you are a liar) *inadvertently* if, in the course of executing by the use of some medium of communication some other act A_2 (say, reminiscing about my war service), I fail to exercise such meticulous supervision over the choice and arrangement of the signs as would have been needed to ensure that . . . . It is interesting to note how such adverbs lead parallel lives, one in connection with physical actions ("doing") and the other in connection with acts of communication ("saying"), or sometimes also in connection with acts of "thinking" ("inadvertently assumed").

doing, which is far from necessarily the case (e.g., if I did it absent-mindedly), or at least that there is *something* in common to the ways of doing all acts not done inadvertently, which is not the case. Again, there is no use for "advertently" at the *same* level as "inadvertently": in passing the butter I do not knock over the cream-jug, though I do (inadvertently) knock over the teacup—yet I do not bypass the cream-jug *advertently*: for at this level, below supervision in detail, *anything* that we do is, if you like, inadvertent, though we only call it so, and indeed only call it something we have done, if there is something untoward about it.

A further point of interest in studying so-called "negative" terms is the manner of their formation. Why are the words in one group formed with *un-* or *in-*, those in another with *-less* ("aimless," "reckless," "heedless," etc.), and those in another with *mis-* ("mistake," "misconception," "misjudgment," etc.)? Why care*less*ly but *in*attentively? Perhaps care and attention, so often linked, are rather different. Here are remunerative exercises.

(4) *The machinery of action*. Not merely do adverbial expressions pick out classes of actions, they also pick out the internal detail of the machinery of doing actions, or the departments into which the business of doing actions is organized. There is for example the stage at which we have actually to *carry out* some action upon which we embark—perhaps we have to make certain bodily movements or to make a speech. In the course of actually *doing* these things (getting, weaving) we have to pay (some) attention to what we are doing and to take (some) care to guard against (likely) dangers: we may need to use judgment or tact: we must exercise sufficient control over our bodily parts: and so on. Inattention, carelessness, errors of judgment, tactlessness, clumsiness, all these and others are ills (with attendant excuses) which affect one specific stage in the machinery of action, the *executive* stage, the stage where we *muff* it. But there are many other departments in the business too, each of which is to be traced and mapped through its cluster of appropriate verbs and adverbs. Obviously there are departments of intelligence and planning, of decision and resolve, and so on: but I shall mention one in particular, too often overlooked, where troubles and excuses abound. It happens to us, in military life, to

be in receipt of excellent intelligence, to be also in self-conscious possession of excellent principles (the five golden rules for winning victories), and yet to hit upon a plan of action which leads to disaster. One way in which this can happen is through failure at the stage of *appreciation* of the situation, that is at the stage where we are required to cast our excellent intelligence into such a form, under such heads and with such weights attached, that our equally excellent principles can be brought to bear on it properly, in a way to yield the right answer.[9] So too in real, or rather civilian, life, in moral or practical affairs, we can know the facts and yet look at them mistakenly or perversely or not fully realize or appreciate something, or even be under a total misconception. Many expressions of excuse indicate failure at this particularly tricky stage: even thoughtlessness, inconsiderateness, lack of imagination, are perhaps less matters of failure in intelligence or planning than might be supposed, and more matters of failure to appreciate the situation. A course of E. M. Forster and we see things differently: yet perhaps we know no more and are no cleverer.

(5) *Standards of the unacceptable*. It is characteristic of excuses to be "unacceptable": given, I suppose, almost any excuse, there will be cases of such a kind or of such gravity that "we will not accept" it. It is interesting to detect the standards and codes we thus invoke. The extent of the supervision we exercise over the execution of any act can never be quite unlimited, and usually is expected to fall within fairly definite limits ("due care and attention") in the case of acts of some general kind, though of course we set very different limits in different cases. We may plead that we trod on the snail inadvertently: but not on a baby—you ought to look where you're putting your great feet. Of course it *was* (*really*), if you like, inadvertence: but that word constitutes a plea, which isn't going to be allowed, because of standards. And if you try it on, you will be subscribing to such dreadful standards that your last state will be worse than your first. Or again, we set different standards, and will accept different

---

[9] We know all about how to do quadratics: we know all the needful facts about pipes, cisterns, hours, and plumbers: yet we reach the answer "3¾ men." We have failed to cast our facts correctly into mathematical form.

excuses, in the case of acts which are rule-governed, like spelling, and which we are expected absolutely to get right, from those we set and accept for less stereotyped actions: a wrong spelling may be a slip, but hardly an accident, a winged beater may be an accident, but hardly a slip.

(6) *Combination, dissociation, and complication.* A belief in opposites and dichotomies encourages, among other things, a blindness to the combinations and dissociations of adverbs that are possible, even to such obvious facts as that we can act at once on impulse and intentionally, or that we can do an action intentionally yet for all that not deliberately, still less on purpose. We walk along the cliff, and I feel a sudden impulse to push you over, which I promptly do: I acted on impulse, yet I certainly intended to push you over, and may even have devised a little ruse to achieve it: yet even then I did not act deliberately, for I did not (stop to) ask whether to do it or not.

It is worth bearing in mind, too, the general rule that we must not expect to find simple labels for complicated cases. If a mistake results in an accident, it will not do to ask whether "it" was an accident or a mistake, or to demand some briefer description of "it." Here the natural economy of language operates: if the words already available for simple cases suffice in combination to describe a complicated case, there will be need for special reasons before a special new word is invented for the complication. Besides, however well-equipped our language, it can never be forearmed against all possible cases that may arise and call for description: fact is richer than diction.

(7) *Regina v. Finney.* Often the complexity and difficulty of a case is considerable. I will quote the case of *Regina v. Finney* :[10]

Shrewsbury Assizes. 1874   12 Cox 625.
Prisoner was indicted for the manslaughter of Thomas Watkins.
The Prisoner was an attendant at a lunatic asylum. Being in charge of a lunatic, who was bathing, he turned on hot water into the bath, and thereby scalded him to death. The facts appeared to be truly set forth in the statement of the prisoner made before the committing magistrate, as follows: "I had bathed Watkins, and had loosed the bath out. *I intended putting in a clean bath,* and asked Watkins if he would get out. At this time *my attention was drawn* to the next bath by the new attend-

[10] The italics are mine.

ant, who was asking me a question; and *my attention was taken from the bath* where Watkins was. I put my hand down to turn water on in the bath where Thomas Watkins was. *I did not intend to turn the hot water, and I made a mistake in the tap. I did not know what I had done until* I heard Thomas Watkins shout out; and *I did not find my mistake out till* I saw the steam from the water. You cannot get water in this bath when they are drawing water at the other bath; but at other times it shoots out like a water gun when the other baths are not in use. . . ."

(It was proved that the lunatic had such possession of his faculties as would enable him to understand what was said to him, and to get out of the bath.)

A. YOUNG (for Prisoner). The death *resulted from accident.* There was no such *culpable negligence* on the part of the prisoner as will support this indictment. A *culpable mistake,* or some degree of *culpable negligence,* causing death, will not support a charge of manslaughter; unless the *negligence* be so gross as to be *reckless.* (*R. v. Noakes.*)

LUSH, J. To render a person liable for *neglect of duty* there must be such a degree of culpability as to amount to *gross negligence* on his part. If you accept the prisoner's own statement, you find no such amount of *negligence* as would come within this definition. It is not every little *trip or mistake* that will make a man so liable. It was the duty of the attendant not to let hot water into the bath while the patient was therein. According to the prisoner's own account, *he did not believe that* he was letting the hot water in while the deceased remained there. The lunatic was, we have heard, a man capable of getting out by himself and of understanding what was said to him. He was told to get out. A new attendant who had come on this day, was at an adjoining bath, and he *took off the prisoner's attention.* Now, if the prisoner, knowing that the man was in the bath, had turned on the tap, and turned on the hot instead of the cold water, I should have said there was gross negligence; for he ought to have looked to see. But from his own account he had told the deceased to get out, and *thought he had got out.* If you think that indicates gross *carelessness,* then you should find the prisoner guilty of manslaughter. But if you think it *inadvertence* not amounting to culpability—e.g., what is properly an accident—then the prisoner is not liable.

Verdict, Not guilty.

In this case there are two morals that I will point: (8 ff.) Both counsel and judge make very free use of a large number of terms of excuse, using several as though they were, and even stating them to be, indifferent or equivalent when they are not, and presenting as alternatives those that are not. (11) It is constantly difficult to be sure, *what* act it is that counsel or judge is suggesting might be qualified by what expression of excuse.

The learned judge's concluding direction is a paradigm of these faults.[11] Finney, by contrast, stands out as an evident master of the Queen's English. He is explicit as to each of his acts and states, mental and physical; he uses different, and the correct, adverbs in connection with each: and he makes no attempt to boil down.

(8) *Small distinctions, and big too.* It should go without saying that terms of excuse are not equivalent, and that it matters which we use: we need to distinguish inadvertence not merely from (save the mark) such things as mistake and accident, but from such nearer neighbors as, say, aberration and absence of mind. By imagining cases with vividness and fullness we should be able to decide in which precise terms to describe, say, Miss Plimsoll's action in writing, so carefully, "DAIRY" on her fine new book: we should be able to distinguish between sheer, mere, pure, and simple mistake or inadvertence. Yet unfortunately, at least when in the grip of thought, we fail not merely at these stiffer hurdles. We equate even—I have seen it done—"inadvertently" with "automatically": as though to say I trod on your toe inadvertently means to say I trod on it automatically. Or we collapse succumbing to temptation into losing control of ourselves—a bad patch, this, for telescoping.[12]

All this is not so much a *lesson* from the study of excuses as the very object of it.

(9) *The exact phrase and its place in the*

---

[11] Not but what he probably manages to convey his meaning somehow or other. Judges seem to acquire a knack of conveying meaning, and even carrying conviction, through the use of a pithy Anglo-Saxon which sometimes has literally no meaning at all. Wishing to distinguish the case of shooting at a post in the belief that it was an enemy, as *not* an "attempt," from the case of picking an empty pocket in the belief that money was in it, which *is* an "attempt," the judge explains that in shooting at the post "the man is never on the thing at all."

[12] Plato, I suppose, and after him Aristotle, fastened this confusion upon us, as bad in its day and way as the later, grotesque, confusion of moral weakness with weakness of will. I am very partial to ice cream, and a bombe is served divided into segments corresponding one to one with the persons at High Table: I am tempted to help myself to two segments and do so, thus succumbing to temptation and even conceivably (but why necessarily?) going against my principles. But do I lose control of myself? Do I raven, do I snatch the morsels from the dish and wolf them down, impervious to the consternation of my colleagues? Not a bit of it. We often succumb to temptation with calm and even with finesse.

sentence. It is not enough, either, to attend simply to the "key" word: notice must also be taken of the full and exact form of the expression used. In considering mistakes, we have to consider seriatim "by mistake," "owing to a mistake," "mistakenly," "it was a mistake to," and so on: in considering purpose, we have to consider "on," "with the," "for the," etc., besides "purposeful," "purposeless," and the like. These varying expressions may function quite differently—and usually do, or why should we burden ourselves with more than one of them?

Care must be taken too to observe the precise position of an adverbial expression in the sentence. This should of course indicate what verb it is being used to modify: but more than that, the position can also affect the *sense* of the expression, i.e., the way in which it modifies that verb. Compare, for example:—

a_1. He clumsily trod on the snail.

a_2. Clumsily he trod on the snail.

b_1. He trod clumsily on the snail.

b_2. He trod on the snail clumsily.

Here, in a_1 and a_2 we describe his treading on the creature at all as a piece of clumsiness, incidental, we imply, to his performance of some other action: but with b_1 and b_2 to tread on it is, very likely, his aim or policy, what we criticize is his execution of the feat.[18] Many adverbs, though far from all (not, e.g., "purposely") are used in these two typically different ways.

(10) *The style of performance.* With some adverbs the distinction between the two senses referred to in the last paragraph is carried a stage further. "He ate his soup deliberately" may mean, like "He deliberately ate his soup," that his eating his soup was a deliberate act, one perhaps that he thought would annoy somebody, as it would more commonly if he deliberately ate *my* soup, and which he decided to do: but it will often mean that he went through the performance of eating his soup in a noteworthy manner or style—pause after each mouthful, careful choice of point of entry for the spoon, sucking of moustaches, and so on. That is, it will mean that he ate *with* deliberation rather than *after* deliberation. The

---

[18] As a matter of fact, most of these examples *can* be understood the other way, especially if we allow ourselves inflections of the voice, or commas, or contexts. a_2 might be a poetic inversion for b_2: b_1, perhaps with commas round the "clumsily," might be used for a_1: and so on. Still, the two senses are clearly enough distinguishable.

style of the performance, slow and unhurried, is understandably called "deliberate" because each movement has the typical *look* of a deliberate act : but it is scarcely being said that the making of each motion *is* a deliberate act or that he is "literally" deliberating. This case, then, is more extreme than that of "clumsily," which does in both uses describe literally a manner of performing.

It is worth watching out for this secondary use when scrutinizing any particular adverbial expression : when it definitely does not exist, the reason is worth enquiring into. Sometimes it is very hard to be sure whether it does exist or does not : it does, one would think, with "carelessly," it does not with "inadvertently," but does it or does it not with "absent-mindedly" or "aimlessly"? In some cases a word akin to but distinct from the primary adverb is used for this special role of describing a style of performance : we use "purposefully" in this way, but never "purposely."

(11) *What modifies what?* The Judge in *Regina v. Finney* does not make clear what event is being excused in what way. "If you think that indicates gross carelessness, then . . . But if you think it inadvertence not amounting to culpability i.e., what is properly called an accident—then . . ." Apparently he means that Finney may have *turned on the hot tap* inadvertently :[14] does he mean also that the tap may have been turned accidentally? And was the carelessness in turning the tap or in thinking Watkins had got out? Many disputes as to what excuse we should properly use arise because we will not trouble to state explicitly *what* is being excused.

To do so is all the more vital because it is in principle always open to us, along various lines, to describe or refer to "what I did" in so many different ways. This is altogether

too large a theme to elaborate here. Apart from the more general and obvious problems of the use of "tendentious" descriptive terms, there are many special problems in the particular case of actions." Should we say, are we saying, that he took her money, or that he robbed her? That he knocked a ball into a hole, or that he sank a putt? That he said "Done," or that he accepted an offer? How far, that is, are motives, intentions, and conventions to be part of the description of actions? And more especially here, what is *an* or *one* or *the* action? For we can generally split up what might be named as one action in several distinct ways, into different *stretches* or *phases* or *stages*. Stages have already been mentioned : we can dismantle the machinery of the act, and describe (and excuse) separately the intelligence, the appreciation, the planning, the decision, the execution, and so forth. Phases are rather different : we can say that he painted a picture or fought a campaign, or else we can say that first he laid on this stroke of paint and then that, first he fought this action and then that. Stretches are different again : a single term descriptive of what he did may be made to cover either a smaller or a larger stretch of events, those excluded by the narrower description being then called "consequences" or "results" or "effects" or the like of his act. So here we can describe Finney's act *either* as turning on the hot tap, which he did by mistake, with the result that Watkins was scalded, *or* as scalding Watkins, which he did *not* do by mistake.

It is very evident that the problems of excuses and those of the different descriptions of actions are throughout bound up with each other.

(12) *Trailing clouds of etymology.* It is these considerations that bring us up so forcibly against some of the most difficult words in the whole story of Excuses, such words as "result," "effect," and "consequence," or again as "intention," "purpose," and "motive." I will mention two points of method which are, experience has convinced me, indispensable aids at these levels.

One is that a word never—well, hardly ever —shakes off its etymology and its formation. In spite of all changes in and extensions of and additions to its meanings, and indeed rather pervading and governing these, there will still persist the old idea. In an *accident*

[14] What Finney says is different: he says he "made a mistake in the tap." This is the basic use of "mistake," where we simply, and not necessarily accountably, take the wrong one. Finney here attempts to account for his mistake, by saying that his attention was distracted. But suppose the order is "Right turn" and I turn left: no doubt the sergeant will insinuate that my attention was distracted, or that I cannot distinguish my right from my left—but it wasn't and I can; this was a simple, pure mistake. As often happens. Neither I nor the sergeant will suggest that there was any accident, or any inadvertence either. If Finney had turned the hot tap inadvertently, then it would have been knocked, say, in reaching for the cold tap: a different story.

something befalls: by *mistake* you take the wrong one: in *error* you stray: when you act *deliberately* you act after weighing it up (*not* after thinking out ways and means). It is worth asking ourselves whether we know the etymology of "result" or of "spontaneously," and worth remembering that "unwillingly" and "involuntarily" come from very different sources.

And the second point is connected with this. Going back into the history of a word, very often into Latin, we come back pretty commonly to pictures or *models,* of how things happen or are done. These models may be fairly sophisticated and recent, as is perhaps the case with "motive" or "impulse," but one of the commonest and most primitive types of model is one which is apt to baffle us through its very naturalness and simplicity. We take *some very simple action,* like shoving a stone, usually as done by and viewed by oneself, and use *this,* with the features distinguishable in it, as our model in terms of which to talk about other actions and events: and we continue to do so, scarcely realizing it, even when these other actions are pretty remote and perhaps much more interesting to us in their own right than the acts originally used in constructing the model ever were, and even when the model is really distorting the facts rather than helping us to observe them. In primitive cases we may get to see clearly the differences between, say, "results," "effects," and "consequences," and yet discover that these differences are no longer clear, and the terms themselves no longer of real service to us, in the more complicated cases where we had been bandying them about most freely. A model must be recognized for what it is. "Causing," I suppose, was a notion taken from a man's own experience of doing simple actions, and by primitive man every event was construed in terms of this model: every event has a cause, that is, every event is an action done by somebody—if not by a man, then by a quasi-man, a spirit. When, later, events which are *not* actions are realized to be such, we still say that they must be "caused," and the word snares us: we are struggling to ascribe to it a new, unanthropomorphic meaning, yet constantly, in searching for its analysis, we unearth and incorporate the lineaments of the ancient model. As happened even to Hume, and consequently to Kant. Examining such a word historically, we may well find that it

has been extended to cases that have by now too tenuous a relation to the model case, that it is a source of confusion and superstition.

There is too another danger in words that invoke models, half-forgotten or not. It must be remembered that there is no necessity whatsoever that the various models used in creating our vocabulary, primitive or recent, should all fit together neatly as parts into one single, total model or scheme of, for instance, the doing of actions. It is possible, and indeed highly likely, that our assortment of models will include some, or many, that are overlapping, conflicting, or more generally simply *disparate.*[15]

(13) In spite of the wide and acute observation of the phenomena of action embodied in ordinary speech, modern scientists have been able, it seems to me, to reveal its inadequacy at numerous points, if only because they have had access to more comprehensive data and have studied them with more catholic and dispassionate interest than the ordinary man, or even the lawyer, has had occasion to do. I will conclude with two examples.

Observation of animal behavior shows that regularly, when an animal is embarked on some recognizable pattern of behavior but meets in the course of it with an insuperable obstacle, it will betake itself to energetic, but quite unrelated, activity of some wild kind, such as standing on its head. This phenomenon is called "displacement behavior" and is well identifiable. If now, in the light of this, we look back at ordinary human life, we see that displacement behavior bulks quite large in it: yet we have apparently no word, or at least no clear and simple word, for it. If, when thwarted, we stand on our heads or wiggle our toes, then we aren't exactly *just* standing on our heads, don't you know, in the ordinary

---

[15] This is by way of a general warning in philosophy. It seems to be too readily assumed that if we can only discover the true meanings of each of a cluster of key terms, usually historic terms, that we use in some particular field (as, for example, "right," "good," and the rest in morals), then it must without question transpire that each will fit into place in some single, interlocking, consistent, conceptual scheme. Not only is there no reason to assume this, but all historical probability is against it, especially in the case of a language derived from such various civilizations as ours is. We may cheerfully use, and with weight, terms which are not so much head-on incompatible as simply disparate, which just don't fit in or even on. Just as we cheerfully subscribe to, or have the grace to be torn between, simply disparate ideals—why *must* there be a conceivable amalgam, the Good Life for Man?

way, yet is there any convenient adverbial expression we can insert to do the trick? "In desperation"?

Take, again, "compulsive" behavior, however exactly psychologists define it, compulsive washing for example. There are of course hints in ordinary speech, that we do things in this way—"just feel I have to," "shouldn't feel comfortable unless I did," and the like:

but there is no adverbial expression satisfactorily pre-empted for it, as "compulsively" is. This is understandable enough, since compulsive behavior, like displacement behavior, is not in general going to be of great practical importance.

Here I leave and commend the subject to you.

Aristotle, *Nicomachean Ethics**

BOOK III

Chapter 1

Since virtue is concerned with passions and actions, and on voluntary passions and actions praise and blame are bestowed, on those that are involuntary pardon, and sometimes also pity, to distinguish the voluntary and the involuntary is presumably necessary for those who are studying the nature of virtue, and useful also for legislators with a view to the assigning both of honors and of punishments.

Those things, then, are thought involuntary, which take place under compulsion or owing to ignorance; and that is compulsory of which the moving principle is outside, being a principle in which nothing is contributed by the person who is acting or is feeling the passion, e.g., if he were to be carried somewhere by a wind, or by men who had him in their power.

But with regard to the things that are done from fear of greater evils or for some noble object (e.g., if a tyrant were to order one to do something base, having one's parents and children in his power, and if one did the action they were to be saved, but otherwise would be put to death), it may be debated whether such actions are involuntary or voluntary. Something of the sort happens also with regard to the throwing of goods overboard in a storm; for in the abstract no one throws goods away voluntarily, but on condition of its securing the safety of himself and his crew any sensible man does so. Such actions, then, are mixed, but are more like voluntary actions; for they are worthy of choice at the time when they are done, and the end of an action

is relative to the occasion. Both the terms, then, voluntary and involuntary, must be used with reference to the moment of action. Now the man acts voluntarily; for the principle that moves the instrumental parts of the body in such actions is in him, and the things of which the moving principle is in a man himself are in his power to do or not to do. Such actions, therefore, are voluntary, but in the abstract perhaps involuntary; for no one would choose any such act in itself.

For such actions men are sometimes even praised, when they endure something base or painful in return for great and noble objects gained; in the opposite case they are blamed, since to endure the greatest indignities for no noble end or for a trifling end is the mark of an inferior person. On some actions praise indeed is not bestowed, but pardon is, when one does what he ought not under pressure which overstrains human nature and which no one could withstand. But some acts, perhaps, we cannot be forced to do, but ought rather to face death after the most fearful sufferings; for the things that "forced" Euripides' Alcmaeon to slay his mother seem absurd. It is difficult sometimes to determine what should be chosen at what cost, and what should be endured in return for what gain, and yet more difficult to abide by our decisions; for as a rule what is expected is painful, and what we are forced to do is base, whence praise and blame are bestowed on those who have been compelled or have not.

What sort of acts, then, should be called compulsory? We answer that without qualification actions are so when the cause is in the external circumstances and the agent contributes nothing. But the things that in themselves are involuntary, but now and in return

* Reprinted from Aristotle, *Nicomachean Ethics,* trans. W. D. Ross (Oxford: Clarendon Press, 1925), chaps. 1–5 and 8, by permission of the publishers.

for these gains are worthy of choice, and whose moving principle is in the agent, are in themselves involuntary, but now and in return for these gains voluntary. They are more like voluntary acts; for actions are in the class of particulars, and the particular acts here are voluntary. What sort of things are to be chosen, and in return for what, it is not easy to state; for there are many differences in the particular cases.

But if someone were to say that pleasant and noble objects have a compelling power, forcing us from without, all acts would be for him compulsory; for it is for these objects that all men do everything they do. And those who act under compulsion and unwillingly act with pain, but those who do acts for their pleasantness and nobility do them with pleasure; it is absurd to make external circumstances responsible, and not oneself, as being easily caught by such attractions, and to make one's self responsible for noble acts but the pleasant objects responsible for base acts. The compulsory, then, seems to be that whose moving principle is outside, the person compelled contributing nothing.

Everything that is done by reason of ignorance is *not* voluntary; it is only what produces pain and repentance that is *in*voluntary. For the man who has done something owing to ignorance, and feels not the least vexation at his action, has not acted voluntarily, since he did not know what he was doing, nor yet involuntarily, since he is not pained. Of people, then, who act by reason of ignorance he who repents is thought an involuntary agent, and the man who does not repent may, since he is different, be called a not voluntary agent; for, since he differs from the other, it is better that he should have a name of his own.

Acting by reason of ignorance seems also to be different from acting in ignorance; for the man who is drunk or in a rage is thought to act as a result not of ignorance but of one of the causes mentioned, yet not knowingly but in ignorance.

Now every wicked man is ignorant of what he ought to do and what he ought to abstain from, and it is by reason of error of this kind that men become unjust and in general bad; but the term "involuntary" tends to be used not if a man is ignorant of what is to his advantage—for it is not mistaken purpose that causes involuntary action (it leads rather to wickedness), nor ignorance of the universal

(for *that* men are *blamed*), but ignorance of particulars, i.e., of the circumstances of the action and the objects with which it is concerned. For it is on these that both pity and pardon depend, since the person who is ignorant of any of these acts involuntarily.

Perhaps it is just as well, therefore, to determine their nature and number. A man may be ignorant, then, of who he is, what he is doing, what or whom he is acting on, and sometimes also what (e.g., what instrument) he is doing it with, and to what end (e.g., he may think his act will conduce to someone's safety), and how he is doing it (e.g., whether gently or violently). Now of all of these no one could be ignorant unless he were mad, and evidently also he could not be ignorant of the agent; for how could he not know himself? But of what he is doing a man might be ignorant as for instance people say "it slipped out of their mouths as they were speaking," or "they did not know it was a secret," as Aeschylus said of the mysteries, or a man might say he "let it go off when he merely wanted to show its working," as the man did with the catapult. Again, one might think one's son was an enemy, as Merope did, or that a pointed spear had a button on it, or that a stone was pumice-stone; or one might give a man a draught to save him, and really kill him; or one might want to touch a man, as people do in sparring, and really wound him. The ignorance may relate, then, to any of these things, i.e., of the circumstances of the action, and the man who was ignorant of any of these is thought to have acted involuntarily, and especially if he was ignorant on the most important points; and these are thought to be the circumstances of the action and its end. Further, the doing of an act that is called involuntary in virtue of ignorance of this sort must be painful and involve repentance.

Since that which is done under compulsion or by reason of ignorance is involuntary, the voluntary would seem to be that of which the moving principle is in the agent himself, he being aware of the particular circumstances of the action. Presumably acts done by reason of anger or appetite are not rightly called involuntary. For in the first place, on that showing none of the other animals will act voluntarily, nor will children; and secondly, is it meant that we do not do voluntarily *any* of the acts that are due to appetite or anger, or that we do the noble acts voluntarily and the base acts involuntarily? Is not this absurd, when one and the same thing is the cause? But it would surely be odd to describe as involuntary the things one ought to desire; and we ought both to be angry at certain things and to have an appetite for certain things, e.g., for health and for learning. Also what is involuntary is thought to be painful, but what is in accordance with appetite is thought to be pleasant. Again, what is the difference in respect of involuntariness between errors committed upon calculation and those committed in anger? Both are to be avoided, but the irrational passions are thought not less human than reason is, and therefore also the actions which proceed from anger or appetite are the man's actions. It would be odd, then, to treat them as involuntary.

Chapter 2

Both the voluntary and the involuntary having been delimited, we must next discuss choice; for it is thought to be most closely bound up with virtue and to discriminate characters better than actions do.

Choice, then, seems to be voluntary, but not the same thing as the voluntary; the latter extends more widely. For both children and the lower animals share in voluntary action, but not in choice, and acts done on the spur of the moment we describe as voluntary, but not as chosen.

Those who say it is appetite or anger or wish or a kind of opinion do not seem to be right. For choice is not common to irrational creatures as well, but appetite and anger are. Again, the incontinent man acts with appetite, but not with choice; while the continent man on the contrary acts with choice, but not with appetite. Again, appetite is contrary to choice, but not appetite to appetite. Again, appetite relates to the pleasant and the painful, choice neither to the painful nor to the pleasant.

Still less is it anger; for acts due to anger are thought to be less than any others objects of choice.

But neither is it wish, though it seems near to it; for choice cannot relate to impossibles, and if anyone said he chose them he would be thought silly; but there may be a wish even for impossibles, e.g., for immortality. And wish may relate to things that could in no way be brought about by one's own efforts, e.g., that a particular actor or athlete should win in a competition; but no one chooses such things, but only the things that he thinks could be brought about by his own efforts. Again, wish relates rather to the end, choice to the means; for instance, we wish to be healthy, but we choose the acts which will make us healthy, and we wish to be happy and say we do, but we cannot well say we choose to be so; for, in general, choice seems to relate to the things that are in our own power.

For this reason, too, it cannot be opinion; for opinion is thought to relate to all kinds of things, no less to eternal things and impossible things than to things in our own power; and it is distinguished by its falsity or truth, not by its badness or goodness, while choice is distinguished rather by these.

Now with opinion in general perhaps no one even says it is identical. But it is not identical even with any kind of opinion; for by choosing what is good or bad we are men of a certain character, which we are not by holding certain opinions. And we choose to get or avoid something good or bad, but we have opinions about what a thing is or whom it is good for or how it is good for him; we can hardly be said to opine to get or avoid anything. And choice is praised for being related to the right object rather than for being rightly related to it, opinion for being truly related to its object. And we choose what we best know to be good, but we opine what we do not quite know; and it is not the same people that are thought to make the best choices and to have the best opinions, but some are thought to have fairly good opinions, but by reason of vice to choose what they should not. If opinion precedes choice or accompanies it, that makes no difference; for it is not this that we are considering, but whether it is *identical* with some kind of opinion.

What, then, or what kind of thing is it, since it is none of the things we have mentioned? It seems to be voluntary, but not all that is voluntary to be an object of choice. Is it, then, what has been decided on by previous deliberation? At any rate choice involves a rational principle and thought. Even the name seems to suggest that it is what is chosen before other things.

Chapter 3

Do we deliberate about everything, and is everything a possible subject of deliberation, or is deliberation impossible about some things? We ought presumably to call not what a fool or a madman would deliberate about, but what a sensible man would deliberate about, a subject of deliberation. Now about eternal things no one deliberates, e.g., about the material universe or the incommensurability of the diagonal and the side of a square. But no more do we deliberate about the things that involve movement but always happen in the same way, whether of necessity or by nature or from any other cause, e.g., the solstices and the risings of the stars; nor about things that happen now in one way, now in another, e.g., droughts and rains; nor about chance events, like the finding of treasure. But we do not deliberate even about all human affairs; for instance, no Spartan deliberates about the best constitution for the Scythians. For none of these things can be brought about by our own efforts.

We deliberate about things that are in our power and can be done; and these are in fact what is left. For nature, necessity, and chance are thought to be causes, and also reason and everything that depends on man. Now every class of men deliberates about the things that can be done by their own efforts. And in the case of exact and self-contained sciences there is no deliberation, e.g., about the letters of the alphabet (for we have no doubt how they should be written); but the things that are brought about by our own efforts, but not always in the same way, are the things about which we deliberate, e.g., questions of medical treatment or of money-making. And we do so more in the case of the art of navigation than in that of gymnastics, inasmuch as it has been less exactly worked out, and again about other things in the same ratio, and more also in the case of the arts than in that of the sciences; for we have more doubt about the former. Deliberation is concerned with things that happen in a certain way for the most part, but in which the event is obscure, and with things in which it is indeterminate. We call in others to aid us in deliberation on important questions, distrusting ourselves as not being equal to deciding.

We deliberate not about ends but about means. For a doctor does not deliberate whether he shall heal, nor an orator whether he shall persuade, nor a statesman whether he shall produce law and order, nor does anyone else deliberate about his end. They assume the end and consider how and by what means

it is to be attained; and if it seems to be produced by several means they consider by which it is most easily and best produced, while if it is achieved by one only they consider how it will be achieved by this and by what means *this* will be achieved, till they come to the first cause, which in the order of discovery is last. For the person who deliberates seems to investigate and analyze in the way described as though he were analyzing a geometrical construction (not all investigation appears to be deliberation—for instance mathematical investigations—but all deliberation is investigation), and what is last in the order of analysis seems to be first in the order of becoming. And if we come on an impossibility, we give up the search, e.g., if we need money and this cannot be got; but if a thing appears possible we try to do it. By "possible" things I mean things that might be brought about by our own efforts; and these in a sense include things that can be brought about by the efforts of our friends, since the moving principle is in ourselves. The subject of investigation is sometimes the instruments, sometimes the use of them; and similarly in the other cases—sometimes the means, sometimes the mode of using it or the means of bringing it about. It seems, then, as has been said, that man is a moving principle of actions; now deliberation is about the things to be done by the agent himself, and actions are for the sake of things other than themselves. For the end cannot be a subject of deliberation, but only the means; nor indeed can the particular facts be a subject of it, as whether this is bread or has been baked as it should; for these are matters of perception. If we are to be always deliberating, we shall have to go on to infinity.

The same thing is deliberated upon and is chosen, except that the object of choice is already determinate, since it is that which has been decided upon as a result of deliberation that is the object of choice. For everyone ceases to inquire how he is to act when he has brought the moving principle back to himself and to the ruling part of himself; for this is what chooses. This is plain also from the ancient constitutions, which Homer represented; for the kings announced their choices to the people. The object of choice being one of the things in our own power which is desired after deliberation, choice will be deliberate desire of things in our own power; for when we have decided as a result of deliberation, we desire in accordance with our deliberation.

We may take it, then, that we have described choice in outline, and stated the nature of its objects and the fact that it is concerned with means.

Chapter 4

That *wish* is for the end has already been stated; some think it is for the good, others for the apparent good. Now those who say that the good is the object of wish must admit in consequence that that which the man who does not choose aright wishes for is not an object of wish (for if it is to be so, it must also be good; but it was, if it so happened, bad); while those who say the apparent good is the object of wish must admit that there is no natural object of wish, but only what seems good to each man. Now different things appear good to different people, and, if it so happens, even contrary things.

If these consequences are unpleasing, are we to say that absolutely and in truth the good is the object of wish, but for each person the apparent good; that that which is in truth an object of wish is an object of wish to the good man, while any chance thing may be so to the bad man, as in the case of bodies also the things that are in truth wholesome are wholesome for bodies which are in good condition, while for those that are diseased other things are wholesome—or bitter or sweet or hot or heavy, and so on; since the good man judges each class of things rightly, and in each the truth appears to him? For each state of character has its own ideas of the noble and the pleasant, and perhaps the good man differs from others most by seeing the truth in each class of things, being as it were the norm and measure of them. In most things the error seems to be due to pleasure; for it appears a good when it is not. We therefore choose the pleasant as a good, and avoid pain as an evil.

Chapter 5

The end, then, being what we wish for, the means what we deliberate about and choose, actions concerning means must be according to choice and voluntary. Now the exercise of the virtues is concerned with means. Therefore virtue also is in our own power, and so

too vice. For where it is in our power to act it is also in our power not to act, and *vice versa*; so that, if to act, where this is noble, is in our power, not to act, which will be base, will also be in our power, and if not to act, where this is noble, is in our power, to act, which will be base, will also be in our power. Now if it is in our power to do noble or base acts, and likewise in our power not to do them, and this was what being good or bad meant, then it is in our power to be virtuous or vicious.

The saying that "no one is voluntarily wicked nor involuntarily happy" seems to be partly false and partly true; for no one is involuntarily happy, but wickedness *is* voluntary. Or else we shall have to dispute what has just been said, at any rate, and deny that man is a moving principle or begetter of his actions as of children. But if these facts are evident and we cannot refer actions to moving principles other than those in ourselves, the acts whose moving principles are in us must themselves also be in our power and voluntary.

Witness seems to be borne to this both by individuals in their private capacity and by legislators themselves; for these punish and take vengeance on those who do wicked **acts** (unless they have acted under compulsion or as a result of ignorance for which they are not themselves responsible), while they honor those who do noble acts, as though they meant to encourage the latter and deter the former. But no one is encouraged to do the things that are neither in our power nor voluntary; it is assumed that there is no gain in being persuaded not to be hot or in pain or hungry or the like, since we shall experience these feelings none the less. Indeed, we punish a **man** for his very ignorance, if he is thought responsible for the ignorance, as when penalties are doubled in the case of drunkenness; for the moving principle is in the man himself, since he had the power of not getting drunk and his getting drunk was the cause of his ignorance. And we punish those who are ignorant of anything in the laws that they ought to know and that is not difficult, and so too in the case of anything else that they are thought to be ignorant of through carelessness; we assume that it is in their power not to be ignorant, since they have the power of taking care.

But perhaps a man is the kind of man not

to take care. Still they are themselves by their slack lives responsible for becoming men of that kind, and men make themselves responsible for being unjust or self-indulgent, in the one case by cheating and in the other by spending their time in drinking bouts and the like; for it is activities exercised on particular objects that make the corresponding character. This is plain from the case of people training for any contest or action; they practice the activity the whole time. Now not to know that it is from the exercise of activities on particular objects that states of character are produced is the mark of a thoroughly senseless person. Again, it is irrational to suppose that a man who acts unjustly does not wish to be unjust or a man who acts self-indulgently to be self-indulgent. But if *without* being ignorant a man does the things which will make him unjust, he will be unjust voluntarily. Yet it does not follow that if he wishes he will cease to be unjust and will be just. For neither does the man who is ill become well on those terms. We may suppose a case in which he is ill voluntarily, through living incontinently and disobeying his doctors. In that case it was *then* open to him not to be ill, but not now, when he has thrown away his chance, just as when you have let a stone go it is too late to recover it; but yet it was in your power to throw it, since the moving principle was in you. So, too, to the unjust and to the self-indulgent man it was open at the beginning not to become men of this kind, and so they are unjust and self-indulgent voluntarily; but now that they have become so it is not possible for them not to be so.

But not only are the vices of the soul voluntary, but those of the body also for some men, whom we accordingly blame; while no one blames those who are ugly by nature, we blame those who are so owing to want of exercise and care. So it is, too, with respect to weakness and infirmity; no one would reproach a man blind from birth or by disease or from a blow, but rather pity him, while everyone would blame a man who was blind from drunkenness or some other form of self-indulgence. Of vices of the body, then, those in our own power are blamed, those not in our power are not. And if this be so, in the other cases also the vices that are blamed must be in our own power.

Now someone may say that all men desire the apparent good, but have no control over the appearance, but the end appears to each man in a form answering to his character. We reply that if each man is somehow responsible for his state of mind, he will also be himself somehow responsible for the appearance; but if not, no one is responsible for his own evil-doing, but everyone does evil acts through ignorance of the end, thinking that by these he will get what is best, and the aiming at the end is not self-chosen but one must be born with an eye, as it were, by which to judge rightly and choose what is truly good, and he is well endowed by nature who is well endowed with this. For it is what is greatest and most noble, and what we cannot get or learn from another, but must have just such as it was when given us at birth, and to be well and nobly endowed with this will be perfect and true excellence of natural endowment. If this is true, then, how will virtue be more voluntary than vice? To both men alike, the good and the bad, the end appears and is fixed by nature or however it may be, and it is by referring everything else to this that men do whatever they do.

Whether, then, it is not by nature that the end appears to each man such as it does appear, but something also depends on him, or the end is natural but because the good man adopts the means voluntarily virtue is voluntary, vice also will be none the less voluntary; for in the case of the bad man there is equally present that which depends on himself in his actions even if not in his end. If, then, as is asserted, the virtues are voluntary (for we are ourselves somehow partly responsible for our states of character, and it is by being persons of a certain kind that we assume the end to be so and so), the vices also will be voluntary; for the same is true of them.

With regard to the virtues in *general* we have stated their genus in outline, viz., that they are means and that they are states of character, and that they tend, and by their own nature, to the doing of the acts by which they are produced, and that they are in our power and voluntary, and act as the right rule prescribes. But actions and states of character are not voluntary in the same way; for we are masters of our actions from the beginning right to the end, if we know the particular facts, but though we control the beginning of our states of character the gradual progress is not obvious, any more than it is in illnesses; because it was in our power, however, to act in this way or not in this way, therefore the states are voluntary.

Let us take up the several virtues, however, and say which they are and what sort of things they are concerned with and how they are concerned with them; at the same time it will become plain how many they are. And first let us speak of courage.

. . .

BOOK V

Chapter 8

Acts just and unjust being as we have described them, a man acts unjustly or justly whenever he does such acts voluntarily; when involuntarily, he acts neither unjustly nor justly except in an incidental way; for he does things which happen to be just or unjust. Whether an act is or is not one of injustice (or of justice) is determined by its voluntariness or involuntariness; for when it is voluntary it is blamed, and at the same time is then an act of injustice; so that there will be things that are unjust but not yet acts of injustice, if voluntariness be not present as well. By the voluntary I mean, as has been said before, any of the things in a man's own power which he does with knowledge, i.e., not in ignorance either of the person acted on or of the instrument used or of the end that will be attained (e.g., whom he is striking, with what, and to what end), each such act being done not incidentally nor under compulsion (e.g., if A takes B's hand and therewith strikes C, B does not act voluntarily; for the act was not in his own power). The person struck may be the striker's father, and the striker may know that it is a man or one of the persons present, but not know that it is his father; a similar distinction may be made in the case of the end, and with regard to the whole action. Therefore that which is done in ignorance, or though not done in ignorance is not in the agent's power, or is done under compulsion, is involuntary (for many natural processes, even, we knowingly both perform and experience, none of which is either voluntary or involuntary; e.g., growing old or dying). But in the case of unjust and just acts alike the injustice or justice may be only incidental; for a man might return a deposit unwillingly and from fear, and then he must not be said either to do what is just

or to act justly, except in an incidental way. Similarly the man who under compulsion and unwillingly fails to return the deposit must be said to act unjustly, and to do what is unjust, only incidentally. Of voluntary acts we do some by choice, other not by choice; by choice those which we do after deliberation, not by choice those which we do without previous deliberation. Thus there are three kinds of injury in transactions between man and man; those done in ignorance are *mistakes* when the person acted on, the act, the instrument, or the end that will be attained is other than the agent supposed; the agent thought either that he was not hitting anyone or that he was not hitting with this missile or not hitting this person or to this end, but a result followed other than that which he thought likely (e.g., he threw not with intent to wound but only to prick), or the person hit or the missile was other than he supposed. Now when (1) the injury takes place contrary to reasonable expectation, it is a *misadventure*. When (2) it is not contrary to reasonable expectation, but does not imply vice, it is a *mistake* (for a man makes a mistake when the fault originates in him, but is the victim of accident when the origin lies outside him). When (3) he acts with knowledge but not after deliberation, it is an *act of injustice*— e.g., the acts due to anger or to other passions necessary or natural to man; for when men do such harmful and mistaken acts they act unjustly, and the acts are acts of injustice, but this does not imply that the doers are unjust or wicked; for the injury is not due to vice. But when (4) a man acts from choice, he is an *unjust man* and a *vicious man*.

Hence acts proceeding from anger are rightly judged not to be done of malice aforethought; for it is not the man who acts in anger but he who enraged him that starts the mischief. Again, the matter in dispute is not whether the thing happened or not, but its justice; for it is apparent injustice that occasions rage. For they do not dispute about the occurrence of the act—as in commercial transactions where one of the two parties *must* be vicious—unless they do so owing to forgetfulness; but, agreeing about the fact, they dispute on which side justice lies (whereas a man who has deliberately injured another cannot help knowing that he has done so), so that the one thinks he is being treated unjustly and the other disagrees.

But if a man harms another by choice, he acts unjustly; and *these* are the acts of injustice which imply that the doer is an unjust man, provided that the act violates proportion or equality. Similarly, a man *is just* when he acts justly by choice; but he *acts justly* if he merely acts voluntarily.

Of involuntary acts some are excusable, others not. For the mistakes which men make not only in ignorance but also from ignorance are excusable, while those which men do not from ignorance but (though they do them *in* ignorance) owing to a passion which is neither natural nor such as man is liable to, are not excusable.

Introduction to the Science of Right*

GENERAL DEFINITIONS AND DIVISIONS

A. What the Science of Right Is

The Science of Right has for its object the Principles of all the Laws which it is possible to promulgate by external legislation. . . .

B. What Is Right?

The question may be said to be about as embarrassing to the Jurist as the well-known question "What is Truth?" is to the Logician. It is all the more so, if, on reflection, he strives to avoid tautology in his reply, and recognize the fact that a reference to what holds true merely of the laws of some one country at a particular time, is not a solution of the general problem thus proposed. It is quite easy to state what may be right in particular cases (*quid sit juris*), as being what the laws of a certain place and of a certain time say or may have said; but it is much more difficult to determine whether what they have enacted is right in itself, and to lay down a universal Criterion by which Right and Wrong in general, and what is just and unjust, may be recognized. All this may remain entirely hidden even from the practical Jurist until he abandon his empirical principles for a time, and search in the pure Reason for the sources of such judgments, in order to lay a real foundation for actual positive Legislation. In this search his empirical Laws may, indeed, furnish him with excellent guidance; but a merely empirical system that is void of rational principles is, like the wooden head in the fable of Phaedrus, fine enough in appearance, but unfortunately it wants brain.

1. The conception of Right—as referring to a corresponding Obligation which is the moral

* Immanuel Kant, *Philosophy of Law,* trans. W. Hastie (Edinburgh: T. & T. Clark, 1887), pp. 43–47.

aspect of it—in the *first* place, has regard only to the external and practical relation of one Person to another, in so far as they can have influence upon each other, immediately or mediately, by their *Actions* as facts. 2. In the *second* place, the conception of Right does not indicate the relation of the action of an individual to the *wish* or the mere desire of another, as in acts of benevolence or of unkindness, but only the relation of his free *action* to the freedom of action of the other. 3. And, in the *third* place, in this reciprocal relation of voluntary actions, the conception of *Right* does not take into consideration the *matter* of the act of Will in so far as the end which anyone may have in view in willing it, is concerned. In other words, it is not asked in a question of Right whether anyone on buying goods for his own business realizes a profit by the transaction or not; but only the *form* of the transaction is taken into account, in considering the relation of the mutual acts of Will. Acts of Will or Voluntary Choice are thus regarded only in so far as they are *free,* and as to whether the action of one can harmonize with the Freedom of another, according to a universal law.

Right, therefore, comprehends the whole of the conditions under which the voluntary actions of any one Person can be harmonized in reality with the voluntary actions of every other Person, according to a universal Law of Freedom.

C. Universal Principle of Right

"Every Action is *right* which in itself, or in the maxim on which it proceeds, is such that it can coexist along with the Freedom of the Will of each and all in action, according to a universal Law."

If, then, my action or my condition generally can coexist with the freedom of every other, according to a universal Law, any one does me a wrong who hinders me in the performance of this action, or in the maintenance of this condition. For such a hindrance or obstruction cannot coexist with Freedom according to universal Laws.

It follows also that it cannot be demanded as a matter of Right, that this universal Principle of all maxims shall itself be adopted as my maxim, that is, that I shall make it the *maxim* of my actions. For anyone may be free, although his Freedom is entirely indifferent to me, or even if I wished in my heart to infringe it, so long as I do not actually violate that freedom by my external action. Ethics, however, as distinguished from Jurisprudence, imposes upon me the obligation to make the fulfillment of Right a *maxim* of my conduct.

The universal Law of Right may then be expressed, thus: "Act externally in such a manner that the free exercise of the Will may be able to coexist with the Freedom of all others, according to a universal Law." This is undoubtedly a Law which imposes obligation upon me; but it does not at all imply and still less command that I ought, merely on account of this obligation, to limit my freedom to these very conditions. Reason in this connection says only that it is restricted

thus far by its Idea, and may be likewise thus limited in fact by others; and it lays this down as a Postulate which is not capable of further proof. As the object in view is not to teach Virtue, but to explain what Right is, thus far the Law of Right, as thus laid down, may not and should not be represented as a motive-principle of action.

D. Right Is Conjoined with the Title or Authority to Compel

The resistance which is opposed to any hindrance of an effect, is in reality a furtherance of this effect, and is in accordance with its accomplishment. Now, everything that is wrong is a hindrance of freedom, according to universal Laws; and Compulsion or Constraint of any kind is a hindrance or resistance made to Freedom. Consequently, if a certain exercise of Freedom is itself a hindrance of the Freedom that is according to universal Laws, it is wrong; and the compulsion or constraint which is opposed to it is right, as being a *hindering of a hindrance of Freedom,* and as being in accord with the *Freedom* which exists in accordance with universal Laws. Hence, according to the logical principle of Contradiction, all Right is accompanied with an implied Title or warrant to bring compulsion to bear on anyone who may violate it in fact.

Law and Morals*

I. LEGAL AND MORAL RULES

We have proposed to understand by law a body of rules; we have seen that rules refer to human conduct and are best expressed as prescriptions; we have therefore implicitly proposed to understand by law a body of rules prescribing a certain conduct. This corresponds to the most usual definitions, but disagreement begins as soon as we ask "What conduct?" In attempting to find an answer we must again keep in mind that it must prove useful for enabling us clearly to distinguish legal thought and legal science from kinds of thought and science concerned

* Hermann Kantorowicz, *The Definition of Law* (Cambridge, Eng.: Cambridge University Press, 1958), pp. 41–51, reprinted by permission of the publishers. Footnotes are omitted.

with rules prescribing a different conduct. The first question which presents itself concerns the distinction between legal and moral rules, no matter whether the latter are religious or secular in content or origin. Here too it could be shown that a classification of moral rules into commands, precepts, and dogmas would be useful for the understanding of morals and ethics, but what interests us at the moment is how to distinguish all kinds of moral from all kinds of legal rules. It is true that totalitarian jurists have contended that their countries have succeeded in establishing harmony between law and morals, or even in making them identical, but these theories do not interest us here, as the adherents of harmony openly presuppose the distinction between law and morals while the adherents of identity do the same though less openly: they are in the position of a mathematician who should argue that, since all equilateral triangles are equiangular and conversely, equilateral is the same as equiangular. If two concepts refer to the same thing it is all the more necessary to distinguish them.

It is more serious if, as we are often told, there is no such distinction in primitive law and oriental law is always mixed up with morals. The meaning of these statements is not in every respect clear, but an analogy will be helpful. If we find a mass of bones in a prehistoric graveyard we may be told on good grounds (a) that of some bones it cannot be predicated with certainty whether they were a man's or a woman's, (b) that other bones which are certainly men's are intermixed with those of women, (c) that others are bones neither of men nor of women but of animals. But if we were told that some bones were at the same time bones of a man and of a woman, we should not believe it, however venerable the bones might be. Of course it may happen that the same legal rule occurs in two distinct systems of law, or that the same individual act complies with the relevant rules of morals as well as with the relevant rules of law; but it is impossible that the rules of law should belong at the same time to that other great social system, morals, once we have decided to define morals in a way which permits of their being regarded as a distinctive body of rules. And we are bound so to define morals, if for no other reason than for the sake of analyzing those tragical conflicts in the history of States and Churches in which the same act has been felt to be legal but immoral, or moral but illegal.

II. LAW: "PRESCRIBING EXTERNAL CONDUCT"

The best-known distinction is the one first suggested by the Stoa, chiefly developed by Thomasius (d. 1728) and Kant, and still prevailing: law is concerned with *external* conduct, morals with *internal*. This distinction seems to be too shallow and too little qualified to be fruitful but it can and must be maintained provided it is rightly understood. This has unfortunately seldom been the case, and the adherents of this doctrine have therefore not been able to deal with the misunderstandings on which the chief objection is based. Croce, in agreement with many eminent jurists and legal philosophers such as Le Fur, Somlò, and even Max Weber, believed that it was possible and sufficient to object: "Is there a law condemning a man who has killed another by accident or negligence as a murdered?" The answer is simply that there are certainly many mental phenomena, each of them representing some internal conduct, which are of the deepest relevance for the application of law, such as will, intention, guilty mind, malice, good faith, knowledge, error, and consensus of minds; it is for these reasons that even some of the most barbarous legal systems have different rules for damage done by infants and for that done by adults. This nobody ever denied; what the adherents of the distinction which is here advocated meant, unfortunately without stressing this all-important point, was something quite different, as may be concluded from the usual connection of this doctrine with another one (which is *not* advocated here), namely, "external conduct can be *enforced,* internal conduct cannot." What was meant is therefore evidently this: all the various ethical systems *prescribe* internal conduct consisting of volitions, and deem the resulting inner attitude virtuous (as for instance pride or meekness, pugnacity or peacefulness, self-assertion or self-abnegation), whereas the rule of law never *prescribes* internal conduct, either good faith, due care, or the will to forbear from committing a crime, from having a guilty mind, from bearing malice, or from being negligent.

Let us look at the requirements of the law in the light of what was said about its prescriptive function and the conception of legal rights and duties. If a possessor of a thing is to acquire property by usucaption, the law may require him to be or to have been in good faith as to his right to possess the thing as his (Inst. 2.6 pr.); but this does not mean that certain people are to have, or should be presumed to have good faith. This would indeed be preaching morals. What is meant is that everybody should in his external conduct respect certain cases of possession as tantamount to ownership if (*inter alia*) the possessor has complied with the requirement of good faith, and that in this the court will protect him, if his possession is not so respected. The law may prescribe that the borrower of a thing, where it is borrowed both in the interest of the borrower and the lender, must show the care shown in his own affairs (D. 13.6.18. pr.) ; but this does not threaten any sanctions however careless he be in mind, provided he does not in fact cause damage to the thing by *external acts* such as he would be careful to avoid in his own affairs. If I board an omnibus the law requires me to conclude a contract of carriage with the company running the omnibuses, and this, according to the accepted doctrine, requires two internal acts constituting a consensus of minds ; but if I pay my usual fare absent-mindedly because I am reading a novel I have nevertheless done all that the law requires me to do and the conductor cannot turn me out on the ground that I have not made a payment in the legal sense of a willed transaction, but merely made external movements of my fingers.

The theory leads to satisfactory results even in those extreme cases in which ethical rules of religious or secular origin have been embodied in the law. The place in which a rule is to be found written down does not, of course, decide its original nature. If this were so, even rules of the multiplication table would become legal if embodied in, let us say, an Act of Parliament containing a tariff of taxes. Thus in several of the North American States the constitution embraces the Ten Commandments ; the governor's oath of office therefore covers also the observance of the fifth commandment. Can he be impeached if in his heart he refuses to honor his father, a notorious rascal, but treats him externally with complete respect? Would any court answer in the affirmative? Here an ethico-religious rule has become legal, at the price, however, of losing its characteristic internality. We need not be surprised to find the same rule inserted in a purely legal document, the Swiss Civil Code of 1907 (art. 275, s. I). An opposite example is provided by modern Roman Catholic Church law. Heresy is still a matter of internal conduct and punished quite independently of its external manifestation : it is the crime of obstinately denying or doubting any of the tenets of faith by persons calling themselves Christians ; the sanctions are certain penalties and incapacities. This leaves no doubt that according to canon law the struggle against heretical ideas is required as the duty of a Christian, but this duty is originally religious and has not changed its character by being legally recognized.

What the law really prescribes is, therefore, nothing but external conduct, i.e., certain movements of the human body, its muscles, organs of speech, etc., or the forbearance from performing such movements. These movements must as a rule be capable of being performed consciously and voluntarily ; but in certain circumstances the conduct may be mechanical and unconscious without losing its legal significance. These movements are usually not described in detail though in archaic law they often are : such "formalities" are not infrequent even in developed law, as, e.g., the position of fingers in taking an oath, the attitude of the body in giving a military salute, the rites to be performed in religious ceremonies with legal effect such as enthronements of bishops and kings, the procedure in capital executions, and so on. Usually, however, law contents itself with prescribing the results of the movements and does not care whether, e.g., the signature is made with the right or the left hand, in sitting or standing position, or whether a person forbears from committing a tort or a crime by remaining passive or by making such movements as are incompatible with the committing of the illegal act.

III. EXTERNALITY IN JUSTICE AND QUASI-MORALITY

This leads to interesting consequences. We may accept a well-known and well-founded attempt to solve one of the problems of the mind-body relation, namely that the life of the body consists of an uninterrupted causal chain of purely physiological changes ruled by the principle of the conservation of energy and therefore in no way caused by, or causing, the corresponding mental phenomena. We could then imagine theoretically that a mechanical model could be constructed which, although deprived of any mental life, could behave exactly like a human being. The response of the mechanism to the appropriate external stimuli would be exactly the response prescribed by the law and this *homme-machine* would be a perfect, perhaps the only perfect, law-abiding citizen.

Morally viewed, however, his conduct would be quite indifferent, neither bad nor good. All systems of morals, those preached as well as those practiced, whether religious or secular in origin, however different in form and substance, require some kind of motive causing, or at least some kind of consciousness accompanying, the prescribed acts, or even treat this internal conduct as sufficient without requiring any kind of external manifestation of the will. But in law a person may act from the meanest, or at least from a purely selfish, motive and yet comply with his legal duties. A money-lender who promises his client to lend him a certain sum at the legal rate of interest and keeps his promise has acted correctly from the standpoint of modern law, which protects his claim without inquiring into his motive. Ethics would judge differently. If his motive were purely selfish, it would be regarded as morally indifferent by the utilitarian systems of ethics, whereas asceticism would condemn it; if the motive were malicious, if, let us say, he advanced the sum with the intention of accustoming his client to ruinous spending and finally of exploiting him financially, the payment would be judged highly immoral by all systems, though primitive and tribal ethics would make the qualification that the debtor must be the creditor's "neighbor."

This is again not one of those terminological statements such as writers on ethics indulge in when they assert that what is "called" moral does not cover purely selfish or malicious acts; what we mean is, that it *ought* not to be called moral if we wish to provide the science of ethics—and at the same time related disciplines such as general jurisprudence and social philosophy—with a criterion enabling them safely to distinguish law from morals and important enough to justify such distinction. Hitherto important parts of what should be counted as law and legal science have often been considered parts of morals and ethics; this limitation is anything but fruitful and results in serious practical dangers. Our distinction of law and morals would make it impossible to regard, as Austin did, the law of nations as "positive international *morality*," or to admit with Gray that "the doctrines of *morality* are largely . . . a most important source from which the judges draw and ought to draw the rules which make the law," or to remark with Pound that when a court seeks an interpretation which will yield a "satisfactory" result, "satisfactory" will almost always mean in practice *morally* satisfactory. All this means playing into the hands of those who would like to reduce legal science to a mechanical exposition of State law in force, although nobody could have been more adverse to this conception than these three leaders of juristic thought themselves. If we feel that justice demands a change of the income-tax law to the effect that bachelors' incomes should be taxed higher than incomes of married persons, and if we agitate in this sense, we are acting under the dictation of our conscience; but we do not propose that bachelors should be forced by law to feel in conscience bound to pay the additional tax or should be exempt from paying it if they feel unable, as many probably would do, to make their conscience dictate such a duty. It will be sufficient for them to pay, no matter for what reason, in order to satisfy both law and justice. If a law is observed by a person, his action is so far not only legal but also just, though the person may be anything but a just man in the moral sense. Thus Kant's theory that law, as opposed to morals, requires nothing but "legality," i.e., mere conformity of external conduct with the law regardless of the underlying motive, is correct, not only as to the law in force, but also as to the law that ought to be, viz., justice.

Justice in this legalistic sense belongs to a sphere of what we propose to call "quasi-morality." By this word we mean a purely external conduct which as to its content complies with moral rules and which therefore would be moral if it were dictated by a good motive. If, for instance, a rich man is obliging to his neighbors, fair to his competitors, helpful to his friends, generous to charities, he may be considered a valuable citizen, even if it be known that his behavior is dictated purely by calculation, or fear of reproach or vanity, or even a desire to fill others with envy. This phenomena is of great social importance: quasi-morality is all that can be achieved by social reform, practical politics, and the pressure of public opinion, though it is true that genuine morality may follow in its wake through the familiar process whereby internal conduct is, at the bidding of self-respect, adjusted to external conduct.

Conceptual distinctions, however, do not imply actual separation. At least one moral precept has a fundamental importance for law: Thou shalt abide by the law. It is true that ethical systems may allow illegal acts in exceptional situations in which legal rules clash with extra-legal rules of great dignity, particularly rules of a religious nature, and sometimes glorify such acts. But the law it- self can often deal with these exceptions, as in the modern case of conscientious objectors, and provide special institutions for them, like reprieve, pardon, amnesty. There are indeed ethical systems such as radical anarchism and certain forms of asceticism which deny value to law or to any matters secular, and therefore do not recognize the moral dignity of law at all. Should any society accept these doctrines, law would cease to function. "Legalism" alone could not uphold it; if selfish motives, e.g., fear of the regular enforcement of the law, were the only ones to recommend its observ- ance, there would be so many ready to take a chance of its nonenforcement that there would soon be no enforcement at all. No selfish motive can replace the sense of moral duty, which is the only guardian of law not itself needing a guardian. Thus the prevail- ing theory contrasting law and morals as externally and internally binding forces has stood the test of usefulness.

Of other theories we shall mention only that of L. Petrazycki, the well-known Rus- sian jurist, since it has recently found many adherents in Western Europe. He recognizes duties in both law and morals, but rights in law only. This distinction between the bilat- eral or, as he calls it, "imperative-attributive" character of the law, and the unilateral,

"purely imperative," character of morals, does not correspond to elementary facts of moral consciousness: certainly not all systems of ethics have room for the concept of moral rights, but there are many that do. It may even be argued that every moral duty implies the subject's moral right that he be not pre- vented by others from complying with his duty. In vain Petrazycki analyzes the Ser- mon on the Mount to prove the contrary. The evil-doer of course has no right "that ye resist not evil," but there are more parties than two in ethico-religious relations. Religious mor- als, if claiming to be based on a revelation of divine will, must necessarily regard sin as disobedience, which presupposes a Being endowed with a right to obedience. Secular morals too may be clearly bilateral. Mutual promises to be faithful to each other between lovers and friends are usually of a definitely nonlegal, purely moral character, but they are felt to be contractually binding, as is shown by the violent reaction if they are broken. "England expects that every man will do his duty" does not purport to give a psychological description but to state Eng- land's right to claim dutiful conduct. It is this endowment of a dimly conceived person- ality with imperative rights which accounts for the mystical thrill still caused by the plain words of the immortal signal.

The Common Law*

LECTURE I. EARLY FORMS OF LIABILITY

The object of this book is to present a gen- eral view of the Common Law. To accomplish the task, other tools are needed besides logic. It is something to show that the consistency of a system requires a particular result, but it is not all. The life of the law has not been logic: it has been experience. The felt necessities of the time, the prevalent moral and political the- ories, intuitions of public policy, avowed or unconscious, even the prejudices which judges share with their fellow-men, have had a good deal more to do than the syllogism in deter- mining the rules by which men should be gov-

---

* Oliver Wendell Holmes, Jr., *The Common Law* (Boston: Little, Brown and Company, 1923), pp. 1– 113, reprinted by permission of the publishers. Foot- notes are omitted.

erned. The law embodies the story of a na- tion's development through many centuries, and it cannot be dealt with as if it contained only the axioms and corollaries of a book of mathematics. In order to know what it is, we must know what it has been, and what it tends to become. We must alternately consult his- tory and existing theories of legislation. But the most difficult labor will be to understand the combination of the two into new products at every stage. The substance of the law at any given time pretty nearly corresponds, so far as it goes, with what is then understood to be convenient; but its form and machinery, and the degree to which it is able to work out desired results, depend very much upon its past.

In Massachusetts today, while, on the one

hand, there are a great many rules which are quite sufficiently accounted for by their manifest good sense, on the other, there are some which can only be understood by reference to the infancy of procedure among the German tribes, or to the social condition of Rome under the Decemvirs.

I shall use the history of our law so far as it is necessary to explain a conception or to interpret a rule, but no further. In doing so there are two errors equally to be avoided both by writer and reader. One is that of supposing, because an idea seems very familiar and natural to us, that it has always been so. Many things which we take for granted have had to be laboriously fought out or thought out in past times. The other mistake is the opposite one of asking too much of history. We start with man full grown. It may be assumed that the earliest barbarian whose practices are to be considered, had a good many of the same feelings and passions as ourselves.

The first subject to be discussed is the general theory of liability civil and criminal. The Common Law has changed a good deal since the beginning of our series of reports, and the search after a theory which may now be said to prevail is very much a study of tendencies. I believe that it will be instructive to go back to the early forms of liability, and to start from them.

It is commonly known that the early forms of legal procedure were grounded in vengeance. Modern writers have thought that the Roman law started from the blood feud, and all the authorities agree that the German law began in that way. The feud led to the composition, at first optional, then compulsory, by which the feud was bought off. The gradual encroachment of the composition may be traced in the Anglo-Saxon laws, and the feud was pretty well broken up, though not extinguished, by the time of William the Conqueror. The killings and house-burnings of an earlier day became the appeals of mayhem and arson. The appeals *de pace et plagis* and of mayhem became, or rather were in substance, the action of trespass which is still familiar to lawyers. But as the compensation recovered in the appeal was the alternative of vengeance, we might expect to find its scope limited to the scope of vengeance. Vengeance imports a feeling of blame, and an opinion, however distorted by passion, that a wrong has been done. It can hardly go very far beyond the case of

a harm intentionally inflicted: even a dog distinguishes between being stumbled over and being kicked.

Whether for this cause or another, the early English appeals for personal violence seem to have been confined to intentional wrongs. Glanvill mentions melees, blows, and wounds —all forms of intentional violence. In the fuller description of such appeals given by Bracton it is made quite clear that they were based on intentional assaults. The appeal *de pace et plagis* laid an intentional assault, described the nature of the arms used, and the length and depth of the wound. The appellor also had to show that he immediately raised the hue and cry. So when Bracton speaks of the lesser offenses, which were not sued by way of appeal, he instances only intentional wrongs, such as blows with the fist, flogging, wounding, insults, and so forth. The cause of action in the cases of trespass reported in the earlier Year Books and in the Abbreviatio Placitorum is always an intentional wrong. It was only at a later day, and after argument, that trespass was extended so as to embrace harms which were the defendant's act. Thence again it extended to unforeseen injuries.

It will be seen that this order of development is not quite consistent with an opinion which has been held, that it was a characteristic of early law not to penetrate beyond the external visible fact, the *damnum corpore corpori datum*. It has been thought that an inquiry into the internal condition of the defendant, his culpability or innocence, implies a refinement of juridical conception equally foreign to Rome before the Lex Aquilia, and to England when trespass took its shape. I do not know any very satisfactory evidence that a man was generally held liable either in Rome or England for the accidental consequences even of his own act. But whatever may have been the early law, the foregoing account shows the starting-point of the system with which we have to deal. Our system of private liability for the consequences of a man's own acts, that is, for his trespasses, started from the notion of actual intent and actual personal culpability.

The original principles of liability for harm inflicted by another person or thing have been less carefully considered hitherto than those which governed trespass, and I shall therefore devote the rest of this Lecture to discussing them. I shall try to show that this liability also had its root in the passion of revenge, and to point out the changes by which it reached its present form. But I shall not confine myself strictly to what is needful for that purpose, because it is not only most interesting to trace the transformation throughout its whole extent, but the story will also afford an instructive example of the mode in which the law has grown, without a break, from barbarism to civilization. Furthermore, it will throw much light upon some important and peculiar doctrines which cannot be returned to later.

A very common phenomenon, and one very familiar to the student of history, is this. The customs, beliefs, or needs of a primitive time establish a rule, or a formula. In the course of centuries the custom, belief, or necessity disappears, but the rule remains. The reason which gave rise to the rule has been forgotten, and ingenious minds set themselves to inquire how it is to be accounted for. Some ground of policy is thought of, which seems to explain it and to reconcile it with the present state of things; and then the rule adapts itself to the new reasons which have been found for it and enters on a new career. The old form receives a new content, and in time even the form modifies itself to fit the meaning which it has received. The subject under consideration illustrates this course of events very clearly.

I will begin by taking a medley of examples embodying as many distinct rules, each with its plausible and seemingly sufficient ground of policy to explain it.

A man has an animal of known ferocious habits, which escapes and does his neighbor damage. He can prove that the animal escaped through no negligence of his, but still he is held liable. Why? It is, says the analytical jurist, because, although he was not negligent at the moment of escape, he was guilty of remote heedlessness, or negligence, or fault, in having such a creature at all. And one by whose fault damage is done ought to pay for it.

A baker's man, while driving his master's cart to deliver hot rolls of a morning, runs another man down. The master has to pay for it. And when he has asked why he should have to pay for the wrongful act of an independent and responsible being, he has been answered from the time of Ulpian to that of Austin, that it is because he was to blame for employing an improper person. If he answers, that he used the greatest possible care in choosing his driver, he is told that that is no excuse; and then perhaps the reason is shifted, and it is said that there ought to be a remedy against someone who can pay the damages, or that such wrongful acts as by ordinary human laws are likely to happen in the course of the service are imputable to the service.

Next, take a case where a limit has been set to liability which had previously been unlimited. In 1851, Congress passed a law, which is still in force, and by which the owners of ships in all the more common cases of maritime loss can surrender the vessel and her freight then pending to the losers; and it is provided that, thereupon, further proceedings against the owners shall cease. The legislators to whom we owe this act argued that, if a merchant embark a portion of his property upon a hazardous venture, it is reasonable that his stake should be confined to what he puts at risk—a principle similar to that on which corporations have been so largely created in America during the last fifty years.

It has been a rule of criminal pleading in England down into the present century, that an indictment for homicide must set forth the value of the instrument causing the death, in order that the king or his grantee might claim forfeiture of the deodand, "as an accursed thing," in the language of Blackstone.

I might go on multiplying examples; but these are enough to show the remoteness of the points to be brought together. As a first step toward a generalization, it will be necessary to consider what is to be found in ancient and independent systems of law.

There is a well-known passage in Exodus, which we shall have to remember later: "If an ox gore a man or a woman, that they die: then the ox shall be surely stoned, and his flesh shall not be eaten; but the owner of the ox shall be quit." When we turn from the Jews to the Greeks, we find the principle of the passage just quoted erected into a system. Plutarch, in his Solon, tells us that a dog that had bitten a man was to be delivered up bound to a log four cubits long. Plato made elaborate provisions in his Laws for many such cases. If a slave killed a man, he was to be given up to the relatives of the deceased. If he wounded a man, he was to be given up to the injured party to use him as he pleased. So if he did damage to which the injured party did not contribute as a joint cause. In either case, if the owner failed to surrender the slave, he was bound to make good the loss. If a beast killed a man, it was to be slain and cast beyond the borders. If an inanimate thing caused death, it was to be cast beyond the borders in like manner, and expiation was to be made. Nor was all this an ideal creation of merely imagined law, for it was said in one of the speeches of Aeschines, that "we banish beyond our borders stocks and stones and steel, voiceless and mindless things, if they chance to kill a man; and if a man commits suicide, bury the hand that struck the blow afar from its body." This is mentioned quite as an everyday matter, evidently without thinking it at all extraordinary, only to point an antithesis to the honors heaped upon Demosthenes. As late as the second century after Christ the traveler Pausanius observed with some surprise that they still sat in judgment on inanimate things in the Prytaneum. Plutarch attributes the institution to Draco.

In the Roman law we find the similar principles of the *noxae deditio* gradually leading to further results. The Twelve Tables (451 B.C.) provided that, if an animal had done damage, either the animal was to be surrendered or the damage paid for. We learn from Gaius that the same rule was applied to the torts of children or slaves, and there is some trace of it with regard to inanimate things.

The Roman lawyers, not looking beyond their own system or their own time, drew on their wits for an explanation which would show that the law as they found it was reasonable. Gaius said that it was unjust that the fault of children or slaves should be a source of loss to their parents or owners beyond their own bodies, and Ulpian reasoned that *a fortiori* this was true of things devoid of life, and therefore incapable of fault.

This way of approaching the question seems to deal with the right of surrender as if it were a limitation of a liability incurred by a parent or owner, which would naturally and in the first instance be unlimited. But if that is what was meant, it puts the cart before the horse. The right of surrender was not introduced as a limitation of liability, but, in Rome and Greece alike, payment was introduced as the alternative of a failure to surrender.

The action was not based, as it would be nowadays, on the fault of the parent or owner. If it had been, it would always have been brought against the person who had control of the slave or animal at the time it did the

harm complained of, and who, if anyone, was to blame for not preventing the injury. So far from this being the course, the person to be sued was the owner at the time of suing. The action followed the guilty thing into whosesoever hands it came. And in curious contrast with the principle as inverted to meet still more modern views of public policy, if the animal was of a wild nature, that is, in the very case of the most ferocious animals, the owner ceased to be liable the moment it escaped, because at that moment he ceased to be owner. There seems to have been no other or more extensive liability by the old law, even where a slave was guilty with his master's knowledge, unless perhaps he was a mere tool in his master's hands. Gaius and Ulpian showed an inclination to cut the *noxae deditio* down to a privilege of the owner in case of misdeeds committed without his knowledge; but Ulpian is obliged to admit, that by the ancient law, according to Celsus, the action was noxal where a slave was guilty even with the privity of his master.

All this shows very clearly that the liability of the owner was merely a way of getting at the slave or animal which was the immediate cause of offense. In other words, vengeance on the immediate offender was the object of the Greek and early Roman process, not indemnity from the master or owner. The liability of the owner was simply a liability of the offending thing. In the primitive customs of Greece it was enforced by a judicial process, expressly directed against the object, animate or inanimate. The Roman Twelve Tables made the owner, instead of the thing itself, the defendant, but did not in any way change the ground of liability, or affect its limit. The change was simply a device to allow the owner to protect his interest.

But it may be asked how inanimate objects came to be pursued in this way, if the object of the procedure was to gratify the passion of revenge. Learned men have been ready to find a reason in the personification of inanimate nature common to savages and children, and there is much to confirm this view. Without such a personification, anger toward lifeless things would have been transitory, at most. It is noticeable that the commonest example in the most primitive customs and laws is that of a tree which falls upon a man, or from which he falls and is killed. We can conceive with comparative ease how a tree might have been put on the same footing with animals.

It certainly was treated like them, and was delivered to the relatives, or chopped to pieces for the gratification of a real or simulated passion.

In the Athenian process there is also, no doubt, to be traced a different thought. Expiation is one of the ends most insisted on by Plato, and appears to have been the purpose of the procedure mentioned by Aeschines. Some passages in the Roman historians which will be mentioned again seem to point in the same direction.

Another peculiarity to be noticed is, that the liability seems to have been regarded as attached to the body doing the damage, in an almost physical sense. An untrained intelligence only imperfectly performs the analysis by which jurists carry responsibility back to the beginning of a chain of causation. The hatred for anything giving us pain, which wreaks itself on the manifest cause, and which leads even civilized man to kick a door when it pinches his finger, is embodied in the *noxae deditio* and other kindred doctrines of early Roman law. There is a defective passage in Gaius, which seems to say that liability may sometimes be escaped by giving up even the dead body of the offender. So Livy relates that, Brutulus Papius having caused a breach of truce with the Romans, the Samnites determined to surrender him, and that, upon his avoiding disgrace and punishment by suicide, they sent his lifeless body. It is noticeable that the surrender seems to be regarded as the natural expiation for the breach of treaty, and that it is equally a matter of course to send the body when the wrong-doer has perished.

. . .

It will readily be imagined that such a system as has been described could not last when civilization had advanced to any considerable height. What had been the privilege of buying off vengeance by agreement, of paying the damage instead of surrendering the body of the offender, no doubt became a general custom. The Aquilian law, passed about a couple of centuries later than the date of the Twelve Tables, enlarged the sphere of compensation for bodily injuries. Interpretation enlarged the Aquilian law. Masters became personally liable for certain wrongs committed by their slaves with their knowledge, where previously they were only bound to surrender the slave. If a pack-mule threw off his burden upon a passer-by because he had been improperly overloaded, or a dog which might have been restrained escaped from his master and bit anyone, the old noxal action, as it was called, gave way to an action under the new law to enforce a general personal liability.

Still later, shipowners and innkeepers were made liable as if they were wrong-doers for wrongs committed by those in their employ on board ship or in the tavern, although of course committed without their knowledge. The true reason for this exceptional responsibility was the exceptional confidence which was necessarily reposed in carriers and innkeepers. But some of the jurists, who regarded the surrender of children and slaves as a privilege intended to limit liability, explained this new liability on the ground that the innkeeper or shipowner was to a certain degree guilty of negligence in having employed the services of bad men. This was the first instance of a master being made unconditionally liable for the wrongs of his servant. The reason given for it was of general application, and the principle expanded to the scope of the reason.

The law as to shipowners and innkeepers introduced another and more startling innovation. It made them responsible when those whom they employed were free, as well as when they were slaves. For the first time one man was made answerable for the wrongs of another who was also answerable himself, and who had standing before the law. This was a great change from the bare permission to ransom one's slave as a privilege. But here we have the history of the whole modern doctrine of master and servant, and principal and agent. All servants are now as free and as liable to a suit as their masters. Yet the principle introduced on special grounds in a special case, when servants were slaves, is now the general law of this country and England, and under it men daily have to pay large sums for other people's acts, in which they had no part and for which they are in no sense to blame. And to this day the reason offered by the Roman jurists for an exceptional rule is made to justify this universal and unlimited responsibility.

. . .

We will now follow the history of that branch of the primitive notion which was least likely to survive—the liability of inanimate things.

It will be remembered that King Alfred ordained the surrender of a tree, but that the later Scotch law refused it because a dead thing could not have guilt. It will be remembered, also, that the animals which the Scotch law forfeited were escheat to the king. The same thing has remained true in England until well into this century, with regard even to inanimate objects. As long ago as Bracton, in case a man was slain, the coroner was to value the object causing the death, and that was to be forfeited as deodand *"pro rege."* It was to be given to God, that is to say to the Church, for the king, to be expended for the good of his soul. A man's death had ceased to be the private affair of his friends as in the time of the barbarian folk-laws. The king, who furnished the court, now sued for the penalty. He supplanted the family in the claim on the guilty thing, and the Church supplanted him.

In Edward the First's time some of the cases remind us of the barbarian laws at their rudest stage. If a man fell from a tree, the tree was deodand. If he drowned in a well, the well was to be filled up. It did not matter that the forfeited instrument belonged to an innocent person. "Where a man killeth another with the sword of John at Stile, the sword shall be forfeit as deodand, and yet no default is in the owner." That is from a book written in the reign of Henry VIII, about 1530. And it has been repeated from Queen Elizabeth's time to within one hundred years, that if my horse strikes a man, and afterwards I sell my horse, and after that the man dies, the horse shall be forfeited. Hence it is, that, in all indictments for homicide, until very lately it has been necessary to state the instrument causing the death and its value, as that the stroke was given by a certain penknife, value sixpence, so as to secure the forfeiture. It is said that a steam-engine has been forfeited in this way.

I now come to what I regard as the most remarkable transformation of this principle, and one which is a most important factor in our law as it is today. I must for the moment leave the common law and take up the doctrines of the Admiralty. In the early books which have just been referred to, and long afterwards, the fact of *motion* is adverted to as of much importance. A maxim of Henry Spigurnel, a judge in the time of Edward I, is reported, that "where a man is killed by a cart, or by the fall of a house, or in other like manner, and the thing in motion is the cause of the death, it shall be deodand." So it was

said in the next reign that "omne illud quod movet cum eo quod occidit homines deodandum domino Regi erit, vel feodo clerici." The reader sees how motion gives life to the object forfeited.

The most striking example of this sort is a ship. And accordingly the old books say that, if a man falls from a ship and is drowned, the motion of the ship must be taken to cause the death, and the ship is forfeited—provided, however, that this happens in fresh water. . . .

A ship is the most living of inanimate things. Servants sometimes say "she" of a clock, but everyone gives a gender to vessels. And we need not be surprised, therefore, to find a mode of dealing which has shown such extraordinary vitality in the criminal law applied with even more striking thoroughness in the Admiralty. It is only by supposing the ship to have been treated as if endowed with personality, that the arbitrary seeming peculiarities of the maritime law can be made intelligible, and on that supposition they at once become consistent and logical.

By way of seeing what those peculiarities are, take first a case of collision at sea. A collision takes place between two vessels, the *Ticonderoga* and the *Melampus,* through the fault of the *Ticonderoga* alone. That ship is under a lease at the time, the lessee has his own master in charge, and the owner of the vessel has no manner of control over it. The owner, therefore, is not to blame, and he cannot even be charged on the ground that the damage was done by his servants. He is free from personal liability on elementary principles. Yet it is perfectly settled that there is a lien on his vessel for the amount of the damage done, and this means that that vessel may be arrested and sold to pay the loss in any admiralty court whose process will reach her. If a livery-stable keeper lets a horse and wagon to a customer, who runs a man down by careless driving, no one would think of claiming a right to seize the horse and wagon. It would be seen that the only property which could be sold to pay for a wrong was the property of the wrong-doer. . . .

It may be admitted that, if this doctrine were not supported by an appearance of good sense, it would not have survived. The ship is the only security available in dealing with foreigners, and rather than send one's own citizens to search for a remedy abroad in strange courts, it is easy to seize the vessel and satisfy the claim at home, leaving the foreign owners to get their indemnity as they may be able. I dare say some such thought has helped to keep the practice alive, but I believe the true historic foundation is elsewhere. The ship no doubt, like a sword, would have been forfeited for causing death, in whosesoever hands it might have been. So, if the master and mariners of a ship, furnished with letters of reprisal, committed piracy against a friend of the king, the owner lost his ship by the admiralty law, although the crime was committed without his knowledge or assent. It seems most likely that the principle by which the ship was forfeited to the king for causing death, or for piracy, was the same as that by which it was bound to private sufferers for other damage, in whose hands soever it might have been when it did the harm.

If we should say to an uneducated man today, "She did it and she ought to pay for it," it may be doubted whether he would see the fallacy, or be ready to explain that the ship was only property, and that to say, "The ship has to pay for it," was simply a dramatic way of saying that somebody's property was to be sold, and the proceeds applied to pay for a wrong committed by somebody else.

It would seem that a similar form of words has been enough to satisfy the minds of great lawyers. The following is a passage from a judgment by Chief Justice Marshall, which is quoted with approval by Judge Story in giving the opinion of the Supreme Court of the United States: "This is not a proceeding against the owner; it is a proceeding against the vessel for an offence committed by the vessel; which is not the less an offence, and does not the less subject her to forfeiture, because it was committed without the authority and against the will of the owner. It is true that inanimate matter can commit no offence. But this body is animated and put in action by the crew, who are guided by the master. The vessel acts and speaks by the master. She reports herself by the master. It is, therefore, not unreasonable that the vessel should be affected by this report." And again Judge Story quotes from another case: "The thing is here primarily considered as the offender, or rather the offence is primarily attached to the thing."

In other words, those great judges, although of course aware that a ship is no more alive than a mill-wheel, thought that not only the law did in fact deal with it as if it were alive, but that it was reasonable that the law should do so. The reader will observe that they do not say simply that it is reasonable on grounds of policy to sacrifice justice to the owner to security for somebody else, but that it is reasonable to deal with the vessel as an offending thing. Whatever the hidden ground of policy may be, their thought still clothes itself in personifying language.

. . .

But none of the foregoing considerations, nor the purpose of showing the materials for anthropology contained in the history of the law, are the immediate object here. My aim and purpose have been to show that the various forms of liability known to modern law spring from the common ground of revenge. In the sphere of contract the fact will hardly be material outside the cases which have been stated in this Lecture. But in the criminal law and the law of torts it is of the first importance. It shows that they have started from a moral basis, from the thought that someone was to blame.

It remains to be proved that, while the terminology of morals is still retained, and while the law does still and always, in a certain sense, measure legal liability by moral standards, it nevertheless, by the very necessity of its nature, is continually transmuting those moral standards into external or objective ones, from which the actual guilt of the party concerned is wholly eliminated.

LECTURE II. THE CRIMINAL LAW

The desire for vengeance imports an opinion that its object is actually and personally to blame. It takes an internal standard, not an objective or external one, and condemns its victim by that. The question is whether such a standard is still accepted either in this primitive form, or in some more refined development, as is commonly supposed, and as seems not impossible, considering the relative slowness with which the criminal law has improved.

It certainly may be argued, with some force, that it has never ceased to be one object of punishment to satisfy the desire for vengeance. The argument will be made plain by considering those instances in which, for one reason or another, compensation for a wrong is out of the question.

Thus an act may be of such a kind as to make indemnity impossible by putting an end to the principal sufferer, as in the case of murder or manslaughter.

Again, these and other crimes, like forgery, although directed against an individual, tend to make others feel unsafe, and this general insecurity does not admit of being paid for.

Again, there are cases where there are no means of enforcing indemnity. In Macaulay's draft of the Indian Penal Code, breaches of contract for the carriage of passengers, were made criminal. The palanquin-bearers of India were too poor to pay damages, and yet had to be trusted to carry unprotected women and children through wild and desolate tracts, where their desertion would have placed those under their charge in great danger.

In all these cases punishment remains as an alternative. A pain can be inflicted upon the wrong-doer, of a sort which does not restore the injured party to his former situation, or to another equally good, but which is inflicted for the very purpose of causing pain. And so far as this punishment takes the place of compensation, whether on account of the death of the person to whom the wrong was done, the indefinite number of persons affected, the impossibility of estimating the worth of the suffering in money, or the poverty of the criminal, it may be said that one of its objects is to gratify the desire for vengeance. The prisoner pays with his body.

The statement may be made stronger still, and it may be said, not only that the law does, but that it ought to, make the gratification of revenge an object. This is the opinion, at any rate, of two authorities so great, and so opposed in other views, as Bishop Butler and Jeremy Bentham. Sir James Stephen says, "The criminal law stands to the passion of revenge in much the same relation as marriage to the sexual appetite."

The first requirement of a sound body of law is, that it should correspond with the actual feelings and demands of the community, whether right or wrong. If people would gratify the passion of revenge outside of the law, if the law did not help them, the law has no choice but to satisfy the craving itself, and thus avoid the greater evil of private retribution. At the same time, this passion is not one which we encourage, either as private individuals or as law-makers. Moreover, it does not cover the whole ground. There are crimes

which do not excite it, and we should naturally expect that the most important purposes of punishment would be coextensive with the whole field of its application. It remains to be discovered whether such a general purpose exists, and if so what it is. Different theories still divide opinion upon the subject.

. . .

For the most part, the purpose of the criminal law is only to induce external conformity to rule. All law is directed to conditions of things manifest to the senses. And whether it brings those conditions to pass immediately by the use of force, as when it protects a house from a mob by soldiers, or appropriates private property to public use, or hangs a man in pursuance of a judicial sentence, or whether it brings them about mediately through men's fears, its object is equally an external result. In directing itself against robbery or murder, for instance, its purpose is to put a stop to the actual physical taking and keeping of other men's goods, or the actual poisoning, shooting, stabbing, and otherwise putting to death of other men. If those things are not done, the law forbidding them is equally satisfied, whatever the motive.

Considering this purely external purpose of the law together with the fact that it is ready to sacrifice the individual so far as necessary in order to accomplish that purpose, we can see more readily than before that the actual degree of personal guilt involved in any particular transgression cannot be the only element, if it is an element at all, in the liability incurred. So far from its being true, as is often assumed, that the condition of a man's heart or conscience ought to be more considered in determining criminal than civil liability, it might almost be said that it is the very opposite of truth. For civil liability, in its immediate working, is simply a redistribution of an existing loss between two individuals; and it will be argued in the next Lecture that sound policy lets losses lie where they fall, except where a special reason can be shown for interference. The most frequent of such reasons is, that the party who is charged has been to blame.

It is not intended to deny that criminal liability, as well as civil, is founded on blameworthiness. Such a denial would shock the moral sense of any civilized community; or, to put it another way, a law which punished conduct which would not be blameworthy in the average member of the community would be too severe for that community to bear. It is only intended to point out that, when we are dealing with that part of the law which aims more directly than any other at establishing standards of conduct, we should expect there more than elsewhere, to find that the tests of liability are external, and independent of the degree of evil in the particular person's motives or intentions. The conclusion follows directly from the nature of the standards to which conformity is required. These are not only external, as was shown above, but they are of general application. They do not merely require that every man should get as near as he can to the best conduct possible for him. They require him at his own peril to come up to a certain height. They take no account of incapacities, unless the weakness is so marked as to fall into well-known exceptions, such as infancy or madness. They assume that every man is as able as every other to behave as they command. If they fall on any one class harder than on another, it is on the weakest. For it is precisely to those who are most likely to err by temperament, ignorance, or folly, that the threats of the law are the most dangerous.

The reconciliation of the doctrine that liability is founded on blameworthiness with the existence of liability where the party is not to blame, will be worked out more fully in the next Lecture. It is found in the conception of the average man, the man of ordinary intelligence and reasonable prudence. Liability is said to arise out of such conduct as would be blameworthy in him. But he is an ideal being, represented by the jury when they are appealed to, and his conduct is an external or objective standard when applied to any given individual. That individual may be morally without stain, because he has less than ordinary intelligence or prudence. But he is required to have those qualities at his peril. If he has them, he will not, as a general rule, incur liability without blameworthiness.

· · ·

LECTURE III. TORTS.—TRESPASS AND
NEGLIGENCE

· · ·

The business of the law of torts is to fix the dividing lines between those cases in which a man is liable for harm which he has done, and those in which he is not. But it cannot enable him to predict with certainty whether a given act under given circumstances will make him liable, because an act will rarely have that effect unless followed by damage, and for the most part, if not always, the consequences of an act are not known, but only guessed at as more or less probable. All the rules that the law can lay down beforehand are rules for determining the conduct which will be followed by liability if it is followed by harm—that is, the conduct which a man pursues at his peril. The only guide for the future to be drawn from a decision against a defendant in an action of tort is that similar acts, under circumstances which cannot be distinguished except by the result from those of the defendant, are done at the peril of the actor; that if he escapes liability, it is simply because by good fortune no harm comes of his conduct in the particular event.

If, therefore, there is any common ground for all liability in tort, we shall best find it by eliminating the event as it actually turns out, and by considering only the principles on which the peril of his conduct is thrown upon the actor. We are to ask what are the elements, on the defendant's side, which must all be present before liability is possible, and the presence of which will commonly make him liable if damage follows.

The law of torts abounds in moral phraseology. It has much to say of wrongs, of malice, fraud, intent, and negligence. Hence it may naturally be supposed that the risk of a man's conduct is thrown upon him as the result of some moral shortcoming. But while this notion has been entertained, the extreme opposite will be found to have been a far more popular opinion; I mean the notion that a man is answerable for all the consequences of his acts, or, in other words, that he acts at his peril always, and wholly irrespective of the state of his consciousness upon the matter.

· · ·

The general principle of our law is that loss from accident must lie where it falls, and this principle is not affected by the fact that a human being is the instrument of misfortune. But relatively to a given human being anything is accident which he could not fairly have been expected to contemplate as possible, and therefore to avoid. In the language of the late Chief Justice Nelson of New York: "No case or principle can be found, or if found can be maintained, subjecting an individual to liability for an act done without fault on his part. . . . All the cases concede that an injury arising from inevitable accident, or, which in law or reason is the same thing, from an act that ordinary human care and foresight are unable to guard against, is but the misfortune of the sufferer, and lays no foundation for legal responsibility." If this were not so, any act would be sufficient, however remote, which set in motion or opened the door for a series of physical sequences ending in damage; such as riding the horse, in the case of the runaway, or even coming to a place where one is seized with a fit and strikes the plaintiff in an unconscious spasm. Nay, why need the defendant have acted at all, and why is it not enough that his existence has been at the expense of the plaintiff? The requirement of an act is the requirement that the defendant should have made a choice. But the only possible purpose of introducing this moral element is to make the power of avoiding the evil complained of a condition of liability. There is no such power where the evil cannot be foreseen. Here we reach the argument from policy, and I shall accordingly postpone for a moment the discussion of trespass upon land, and of conversions, and will take up the liability for cattle separately at a later stage.

A man need not, it is true, do this or that act—the term *act* implies a choice—but he must act somehow. Furthermore, the public generally profits by individual activity. As action cannot be avoided, and tends to the public good, there is obviously no policy in throwing the hazard of what is at once desirable and inevitable upon the actor.

The state might conceivably make itself a mutual insurance company against accidents, and distribute the burden of its citizens' mishaps among all its members. There might be a pension for paralytics, and state aid for those who suffered in person or estate from tempest or wild beasts. As between individuals it might adopt the mutual insurance principle *pro tanto,* and divide damages when both were in fault, as in the *rusticum judicium* of the admiralty, or it might throw all loss upon the actor irrespective of fault. The state does none of these things, however, and the prevailing view is that its cumbrous and expensive machinery ought not to be set in motion unless some clear benefit is to be derived from disturbing the *status quo.* State interference is an evil, where it cannot be shown to be a good. Universal insurance, if desired, can be better and more cheaply accomplished by private enterprise. The undertaking to redistribute losses simply on the ground that they resulted from the defendant's act would not only be open to these objections, but, as it is hoped the preceding discussion has shown, to the still graver one of offending the sense of justice. Unless my act is of a nature to threaten others, unless under the circumstances a prudent man would have foreseen the possibility of harm, it is no more justifiable to make me indemnify my neighbor against the consequences, than to make me do the same thing if I had fallen upon him in a fit, or to compel me to insure him against lightning.

. . .

Supposing it now to be conceded that the general notion upon which liability to an action is founded is fault or blameworthiness in some sense, the question arises, whether it is so in the sense of personal moral shortcoming, as would practically result from Austin's teaching. The language of Rede, J., which has been quoted from the Year Book, gives a sufficient answer. "In trespass the intent" (we may say more broadly, the defendant's state of mind) "cannot be construed." Suppose that a defendant were allowed to testify that, before acting, he considered carefully what would be the conduct of a prudent man under the circumstances, and, having formed the best judgment he could, acted accordingly. If the story was believed, it would be conclusive against the defendant's negligence judged by a moral standard which would take his personal characteristics into account. But supposing any such evidence to have got before the jury, it is very clear that the court would say, Gentlemen, the question is not whether the defendant thought his conduct was that of a prudent man, but whether you think it was.

Some middle point must be found between the horns of this dilemma.

The standards of the law are standards of general application. The law takes no account of the infinite varieties of temperament, intellect, and education which make the internal character of a given act so different in different men. It does not attempt to see men as

God sees them, for more than one sufficient reason. In the first place, the impossibility of nicely measuring a man's powers and limitations is far clearer than that of ascertaining his knowledge of law, which has been thought to account for what is called the presumption that every man knows the law. But a more satisfactory explanation is, that, when men live in society, a certain average of conduct, a sacrifice of individual peculiarities going beyond a certain point, is necessary to the general welfare. If, for instance, a man is born hasty and awkward, is always having accidents and hurting himself or his neighbors, no doubt his congenital defects will be allowed for in the courts of Heaven, but his slips are no less troublesome to his neighbors than if they sprang from guilty neglect. His neighbors accordingly require him, at his proper peril, to come up to their standard, and the courts which they establish decline to take his personal equation into account.

The rule that the law does, in general, determine liability by blameworthiness, is subject to the limitation that minute differences of character are not allowed for. The law considers, in other words, what would be blameworthy in the average man, the man of ordinary intelligence and prudence, and determines liability by that. If we fall below the level in those gifts, it is our misfortune; so much as that we must have at our peril, for the reasons just given. But he who is intelligent and prudent does not act at his peril, in theory of law. On the contrary, it is only when he fails to exercise the foresight of which he is capable, or exercises it with evil intent, that he is answerable for the consequences.

There are exceptions to the principle that every man is presumed to possess ordinary capacity to avoid harm to his neighbors, which illustrate the rule, and also the moral basis of liability in general. When a man has a distinct defect of such a nature that all can recognize it as making certain precautions impossible, he will not be held answerable for not taking them. A blind man is not required to see at his peril; and although he is, no doubt, bound to consider his infirmity in regulating his actions, yet if he properly finds himself in a certain situation, the neglect of precautions requiring eyesight would not prevent his recovering for an injury to himself, and, it may be presumed, would not make him liable for injuring another. So it is held that, in cases

where he is the plaintiff, an infant of very tender years is only bound to take the precautions of which an infant is capable; the same principle may be cautiously applied where he is defendant. Insanity is a more difficult matter to deal with, and no general rule can be laid down about it. There is no doubt that in many cases a man may be insane, and yet perfectly capable of taking the precautions, and of being influenced by the motives, which the circumstances demand. But if insanity of a pronounced type exists, manifestly incapacitating the suffered from complying with the rule which he has broken, good sense would require it to be admitted as an excuse.

Taking the qualification last established in connection with the general proposition previously laid down, it will now be assumed that, on the one hand, the law presumes or requires a man to possess ordinary capacity to avoid harming his neighbors, unless a clear and manifest incapacity be shown; but that, on the other, it does not in general hold him liable for unintentional injury, unless, possessing such capacity, he might and ought to have foreseen the danger, or, in other words, unless a man of ordinary intelligence and forethought would have been to blame for acting as he did. The next question is, whether this vague test is all that the law has to say upon the matter, and the same question in another form, by whom this test is to be applied.

Notwithstanding the fact that the grounds of legal liability are moral to the extent above explained, it must be borne in mind that law only works within the sphere of the senses. If the external phenomena, the manifest acts and omissions, are such as it requires, it is wholly indifferent to the internal phenomena of conscience. A man may have as bad a heart as he chooses, if his conduct is within the rules. In other words, the standards of the law are external standards, and, however much it may take moral considerations into account, it does so only for the purpose of drawing a line between such bodily motions and rests as it permits, and such as it does not. What the law really forbids, is the act on the wrong side of the line, be that act blameworthy or otherwise.

Again, any legal standard must, in theory, be one which would apply to all men, not specially excepted, under the same circumstances. It is not intended that the public force should fall upon an individual accidentally, or at the whim of any body of men. The standard, that is, must be fixed. In practice, no doubt, one man may have to pay and another may escape, according to the different feelings of different juries. But this merely shows that the law does not perfectly accomplish its ends. The theory or intention of the law is not that the feeling of approbation or blame which a particular twelve may entertain should be the criterion. They are supposed to leave their idiosyncrasies on one side, and to represent the feeling of the community. The ideal average prudent man, whose equivalent the jury is taken to be in many cases, and whose culpability or innocence is the supposed test, is a constant, and his conduct under given circumstances is theoretically always the same.

Finally, any legal standard must, in theory, be capable of being known. When a man has to pay damages, he is supposed to have broken the law, and he is further supposed to have known what the law was.

If now, the ordinary liabilities in tort arise from failure to comply with fixed and uniform standards of external conduct, which every man is presumed and required to know, it is obvious that it ought to be possible, sooner or later, to formulate these standards at least to some extent, and that to do so must at last be the business of the court. It is equally clear that the featureless generality, that the defendant was bound to use such care as a prudent man would do under the circumstances, ought to be continually giving place to the specific one, that he was bound to use this or that precaution under these or those circumstances. The standard which the defendant was bound to come up to was a standard of specific acts or omissions, with reference to the specific circumstances in which he found himself. If in the whole department of unintentional wrongs the courts arrived at no further utterance than the question of negligence, and left every case, without rudder or compass, to the jury, they would simply confess their inability to state a very large part of the law which they required the defendant to know, and would assert, by implication, that nothing could be learned by experience. But neither courts nor legislatures have ever stopped at that point.

From the time of Alfred to the present day, statutes and decisions have busied themselves with defining the precautions to be taken in certain familiar cases; this is, with substituting for the vague test of the care exercised by a prudent man, a precise one of specific acts or omissions. The fundamental thought is still the same, that the way prescribed is that in which prudent men are in the habit of acting, or else is one laid down for cases where prudent men might otherwise be in doubt.

It will be observed that the existence of the external tests of liability which will be mentioned, while it illustrates the tendency of the law of tort to become more and more concrete by judicial decision and by statute, does not interfere with the general doctrine maintained as to the grounds of liability. The argument of this Lecture, although opposed to the doctrine that a man acts or exerts force at his peril, is by no means opposed to the doctrine that he does certain particular acts at his peril. It is the coarseness, not the nature, of the standard which is objected to. If, when the question of the defendant's negligence is left to a jury, negligence does not mean the actual state of the defendant's mind, but a failure to act as a prudent man of average intelligence would have done, he is required to conform to an objective standard at his peril, even in that case. When a more exact and specific rule has been arrived at, he must obey that rule at his peril to the same extent. But, further, if the law is wholly a standard of external conduct, a man must always comply with that standard at his peril.

. . .

The Vulgar Notion of Responsibility in Connection with the Theories of Free Will and Necessity*

What is *not* the scope of this essay? We must begin with that, for round the phrases which appear in our title there exist "perverse associations," which may lead our readers to expect, some this, and others that. And, because we think that some of these expectations will be disappointed, we will start with saying what it is that we do not propose to treat of.

The scope of this essay might have been the solution of one, or both, of two difficult problems. We might have asked what responsibility at bottom is; whether it implies necessity or freedom, and what these mean; and then we should have come to questions of abstract metaphysic. Or again, our task might have been the limitation of our accountability with reference to legal imputation, and here we should have had a juridical inquiry. But our object is not the solution of either one or the other of these questions.

What then is the end which we do set before us? It is a threefold undertaking: to ascertain first, if possible, what it is that, roughly and in general, the vulgar mean when they talk of being responsible; to ask, in the second place, whether either of the doctrines of Freedom and Necessity (as current among ourselves) agrees with their notions; and, in case they do not agree, lastly to inquire in what points or respects they are incompatible with them.

And, at first sight, this undertaking may seem to the reader both easy and worthless; easy, because what everyone thinks must be known by all men; and worthless, because the theories of philosophers do not stand and fall with the opinions of the people. To a more thoughtful consideration, however, it will appear to be neither.

It is not so easy to say what the people mean by their ordinary words, for this reason, that the question is not answered until it is asked; that asking is reflection, and that we reflect in general not to find the facts, but to prove our theories at the expense of them. The ready-made doctrines we bring to the work color whatever we touch with them;

and the apprehension of the vulgar mind, at first sight so easy, now seems, because *we* are not vulgar, to present a difficulty. And to know the signification of popular phrases is, in the second place, not worthless. Not all our philosophy professes its readiness to come into collision with ordinary morality. On the subject of responsibility this is certainly the case; the expounders of "Free Will" believe their teaching to be thoroughly at one with popular ideas, and even to be the sole expression and interpretation of them. So much does this weigh with many men, that their belief in vulgar moral accountability is the only obstacle to their full reception of Necessitarianism. And not to all of the disciples of Necessity has been given that strength of mind, which still survives in our Westminster Reviewers, and for which "responsibility or moral desert in the vulgar sense" are terms which stand for "horrid figments of the imagination" (*West. Rev.,* Oct. 1873, p. 311). But, if to any philosophy what we call responsibility is not yet a figment, then it cannot be without interest to know, on the one side, the conclusions of that philosophy; on the other side, the beliefs of the vulgar; and whether the two can be reconciled with one another. This is the limit of our present essay. Beyond us lie the fields of metaphysic, which the reader must remember we are, so far as possible, not to enter but merely to indicate.

So much by way of preface; what we have now to do is, first, to enter on a question of fact. What is the popular notion of responsibility? The popular notion is certainly to be found in the ordinary consciousness, in the mind of the plain or non-theoretical man, the man who lives without having or wishing for opinions of his own, as to what living is or ought to be. And, to find this plain man, where are we to go? For nowadays, when all have opinions, and too many also practice of their own; when every man knows better, and does worse, than his father before him; when to be enlightened is to be possesssed by some wretched theory, which is our own just so far as it separates us from others; and to be cultivated is to be aware that doctrine means narrowness, that all truths are so true

* F. H. Bradley, *Ethical Studies* (London: Oxford University Press, 1927), pp. 1–8, reprinted by permission of the publishers.

that any truth must be false; when "young pilgrims," at their outset, are "spoiled by the sophistry" of shallow moralities, and the fruit of life rots as it ripens—amid all this "progress of the species" the plain man is by no means so common as he once was, or at least is said to have been. And so, if we want a moral sense that has not yet been adulterated, we must not be afraid to leave enlightenment behind us. We must go to the vulgar for vulgar morality, and there what we lose in refinement we perhaps are likely to gain in integrity.

Betaking ourselves, therefore, to the uneducated man, let us find from him, if we can, what lies at the bottom of his notion of moral responsibility.

What in his mind is to be morally responsible? We see in it at once the idea of a man's appearing to answer. He answers for what he has done, or (which we need not separately consider) has neglected and left undone. And the tribunal is a moral tribunal; it is the court of conscience, imagined as a judge, divine or human, external or internal. It is not necessarily implied that the man does answer for all or any of his acts; but it is implied that he might have to answer, that he is liable to be called upon—in one word (the meaning of which, we must remember, we perhaps do not know), it is *right* that he should be subject to the moral tribunal; or the moral tribunal has a *right* over him, to call him before it, with reference to all or any of his deeds.

He must answer, if called on, for *all* his deeds. There is no question of lying here; and, without lying, he can disown none of his acts—nothing which in his heart or his will has ever been suffered to come into being. They are all his, they are part of his substance; he cannot put them on one side, and himself on the other, and say, "It is not mine; I never did it." What he ever at any time has done, that he *is* now; and, when his name is called, nothing which has ever been his can be absent from that which answers to the name. . . .

And he must account for all. But to give an account to a tribunal means to have one's reckoning settled. It implies that, when the tribunal has done with us, we do not remain, if we were so before, either debtors or creditors. We pay what we owe; or we have that paid to us which is our due, which is owed to us (what we deserve). Further, because the court is no civil court between man and man, that which is owed to us is what *we pay* (alas for the figments of the unenlightened mind). In short, there is but one way to settle accounts; and that way is punishment, which is due to us, and therefore is assigned to us.

Hence, when the late Mr. Mill said, "Responsibility means punishment," what he had in his mind was the vulgar notion, though he expressed it incorrectly, unless on the supposition that all must necessarily transgress. What is really true for the ordinary consciousness; what it clings to, and will not let go; what marks unmistakably, by its absence, a "philosophical" or a "debauched" morality, is the necessary connection between responsibility and liability to punishment, between punishment and desert, or the finding of guiltiness before the law of the moral tribunal. For practical purposes we need make no distinction between responsibility, or accountability, and liability to punishment. Where you have the one, there (in the mind of the vulgar) you have the other; and where you have not the one, there you cannot have the other. And, we may add, the theory which will explain the one, in its ordinary sense, will also explain the other; and the theory which fails in the one, fails also in the other; and the doctrine which conflicts with popular belief as to one, does so also with regard to the other.

So far we have seen that subjection to a moral tribunal lies at the bottom of our answering for our deeds. The vulgar understand that *we* answer; that we answer not for everything, but only for what is ours; or, in other words, for what can be imputed to us. If now we can say what is commonly presupposed by *imputability,* we shall have accomplished the first part of our undertaking, by the discovery of what responsibility means for the people. And at this point again we must repeat our caution to the reader, not to expect from us either law or systematic metaphysics; and further to leave out of sight the slow historical evolution of the idea in question. We have one thing to do, and one only, at present—to find what lies in the mind of the ordinary man.

Now the first condition of the possibility of my guiltiness, or of my becoming a subject for moral imputation, is my self-sameness; I must be throughout one identical person. We do say, "He is not the same man that he was," but always in another sense, to signify that the character or disposition of the person is altered. We never mean by it, "He is not the same *person*," strictly; and, if that were our meaning, then we (the non-theoretical) should also believe, as a consequence, that the present person could not rightly be made to answer for what (not his self, but) another self had done. If, when we say, "I did it," the I is not to be the one I, distinct from all other I's; or if the one I, now here, is not the same I with the I whose act the deed was, then there can be no question whatever but that the ordinary notion of responsibility disappears.

In the first place, then, I must be the very same person to whom the deed belonged; and, in the second place, it must have belonged to me—it must have been *mine*. What then is it which makes a deed mine? The question has been often discussed, and it is not easy to answer it with scientific accuracy; but here we are concerned simply with the leading features of the ordinary notion. And the first of these is, that we must have an act, and not something which cannot be called by that name. The deed must issue from my will . . . Where I am forced, there I do nothing. I am not an agent at all, or in any way responsible. Where compulsion exists, there my will, and with it accountability, do not exist. So far the ordinary consciousness is clear, and on this point we must not press it further. To fix the limits of compulsion; to say where force ends, and where will begins; to find the conditions, under which we may say, "There was no possibility of volition, and there could have been none"[1]—is no easy matter, and fortunately one which does not concern us.

Not only must the deed be an act, and come from the man without compulsion, but, in the second place, the doer must be supposed intelligent; he must know the particular circumstances of the case. . . . If the man is ignorant, and if it was not his duty to know (for, supposing that to be his duty, the act, done in ignorance, is imputed to the will through the ignorance itself, which is criminally imputable), then the deed is not his act. A certain amount of intelligence, or "sense,"

is thus a condition of responsibility. No one who does not possess a certain minimum of general intelligence can be considered a responsible being; and under this head come imbecile persons, and, to a certain extent, young children. Further, the person whose intellect is eclipsed for a time—such eclipse being not attributable to himself—cannot be made accountable for anything. He can say, and say truly, "I was not myself"; for he means by his self an intelligent will.

Thirdly, responsibility implies a *moral*[2] agent. No one is accountable, who is not capable of knowing (not, who *does* not know) the moral quality of his acts. Wherever we cannot presume upon a capacity for apprehending (not, an actual apprehension of) moral distinctions, in such cases, for example, as those of young children and some madmen, there is, and there can be, no responsibility, because there exists no moral will. Incapacity, however, must not be imputable to act or willful omission.

No more than the above is, I believe, contained in the popular creed. There are points which that creed has never encountered, and others again where historical development has, to some extent, been the cause of divergences.

If we asked the plain man, What is an act? he could not possibly tell us what he meant by it. The problem, In what does an act consist? has never come home to his mind. To some extent we shall see the opinions of that mind, when we see (as we shall) what are *not* its opinions. For the present we may say, that what seems to lie at the bottom of its notion is this, that an act translates mere thoughts into corresponding external existence; that, by the mediation of the body, it carries what was only in the mind into the world outside the mind, in such a way that the changes thereby produced in the outer world are, on the other side, alterations in itself; and that in that quality they all form

---

[1] If, through my bad habits, it is my fault that what presumably would not have been compulsion amounted to it in my case, then I am responsible for what I do under such compulsion. The degree is of course another matter.

[2] *If* there are in fact any adult sane persons, of whom it can be said that (capacity or no capacity) they not only are without any notions of good and bad, but have never had any the smallest chance of having them, and so are incapable, and whose fault it therefore in no sense is that they are what they are, *then* such persons must be considered as out of the moral sphere, and therefore, in the court of conscience, irresponsible and lunatic (whatever they have to be in law). But what standard a man is to be *morally* judged by, is quite another question, which we do not discuss.

part of, and are all forever preserved in, the self.[3]

And there are points again, where ordinary morality shows divergences of opinion. In the absence of intelligence and moral capacity responsibility cannot exist. A beast or an idiot is not accountable. But the vulgar could not tell us beforehand the amount of sense which is required, and, even in particular

[3] If we act "without thinking," are we responsible? I am not concerned to decide whether we ever do so; but, given a case where thinking in no sense was, yet responsibility may be even there. The act may come from presence or absence of habits of mind, for the creation, or non-creation, or non-suppression of which we certainly are responsible. Our self means thought, and the act is the outcome and issue of our self. Let us take an instance: a man of violent disposition, accustomed to handle weapons, is insulted at table by another man. A knife is in his hand, with which he at once stabs. Is he responsible? Yes; the deed came not merely from his disposition—a man is more than his disposition; it came from his character, the habits which his acts have formed. These acts have issued from the thinking self, and the thinking self is therefore responsible for the outcome of the habits. Hence for our dreams, and for what may seem to be merely physical, we *may* be accountable. The description in the text, let me remark, applies only to an *overt* act.

cases, would often be found to disagree amongst themselves. If we asked again about the relation of act to intent, we should find little more than confusion. What consequences are, and what are not, contained in the act itself, and how far are they contained? What, in such cases, is the degree of moral responsibility? Does a criminal state (e.g., drunkenness) make a man accountable for what he does in that state, and, if so, to what degree? How far, again, does a wrong act, done for an object innocent in itself, make the doer responsible for consequences issuing contrary to his intention? With regard to such points we should find a sterner and a softer view. One section would emphasize the act, and the other the (actual or possible) intention. The one sees crime committed, and is prone to neglect the mind of the doer; while the other is always ready to narrow the field of criminality, to see incapacity rather than guilt, and to make absence of crime in the intent carry its quality into the act.

The Theory of Responsibility*

What is the result of the preceding chapters? A conclusion which does not appear to be very encouraging. As we have seen, responsibility made to depend on free will adjudged to be in actual existence is ruined at its very base by the progress of scientific determinism; responsibility made to depend on free will looked upon as an ideal to be realized is nothing more than an illusion, and responsibility based on social utility to the exclusion of everything else has nothing in common with responsibility as understood in the preceding senses except its name; while its name is refused it, and justly so, by the more rigorous of the utilitarians.

Does it follow from all this that it is impossible to find a rational foundation for an idea which is plainly visible to all of humanity, which enlightens every man coming into the social world, and which is no superstition

* Gabriel de Tarde, *Penal Philosophy*, trans. Howell (Boston: Little, Brown and Company, 1912), pp. 83–89, reprinted by permission of Lawrence J. Knapp, trustee for John H. Wigmore, editor. Footnotes are omitted.

in process of receding before the advance of civilization, but an exact conception, spreading as civilization increases and expands? We do not believe so. The best means, as we look at it, by which to combat or to acquire control over the various theories hereinbefore set forth, is to oppose to them some theory which has in it nothing scholastic, but which evolves itself and ought to formulate itself, if one closely scrutinizes what men in fact have always meant when they say that in their opinion one of themselves is responsible, either civilly or criminally. Have they thought that he was responsible for some action because in carrying it out he, through his voluntary decision, through his freedom of choice, made necessary a mere possibility which, previous to this decision born "ex nihilo," would have had not one of the characteristics of a necessity? Never has human common sense entered into such subtleties. From all time a being has been adjudged to be responsible for an act when it was thought that he and no one else was the author, the willing and conscious author, be it understood, of this very act. The problem solved by means of this judgment is one dealing with causality and identity and not with freedom. Just as soon as free will shall be a truth and not a hypothesis, the fact alone that its existence is denied almost universally by the learned men of our time and an ever-increasing proportion of educated people should make us feel the urgency of seeking elsewhere for the support of responsibility. In fact, when consulted by justice on the point of whether an accused is responsible in the classical interpretation of the word, the medico-legal expert ought always to reply, and as a matter of fact does more and more reply in the negative; and from this arise acquittals as scandalous as they are logical. Our utilitarians have indeed felt this danger and they have endeavored to avert it. But they have not been successful in doing so. By reason of the obligation which they believe to be imposed upon them after having denied the existence of free will, of defining responsibility as being a thing apart from any idea of morality, that is to say of decapitating and destroying it, they appear to justify this pretension, so often advanced by the partisans of free will, that, their principle having been destroyed, morality falls to the ground. There is in this a prejudice so dear to the spiritual conscience, and so eloquently propagated and supported by the noblest minds, that we cannot hope to see broken up this association of ideas entirely opposed to morality, as long as we limit ourselves to the undermining of the pretended foundation of the latter without having carved out or unearthed some new foundation on which to rest it. The importance of and the opportunity for this attempt should be an excuse for its very boldness. So we are going to take the liberty of outlining in the following pages, in a theoretical way, our way of looking at the matter . . .

The problem of responsibility is connected with the philosophical search for causes and is but an application of the latter, but a very arduous one, to the study of the facts relative to man living in society.

It is just because of this slim connection between the two problems that the conception of free will came into existence. In fact it came into existence, and it must logically have come into existence, at a time when the idea of the unlimited and absolute guilt of the

sinner was the rule. If being guilty of an act means primarily being the cause of the same, it follows that being guilty of it absolutely and without limit, in the opinion of everybody and without any restriction, as is necessary in order to justify the notion of eternal damnation, must indeed mean being its absolute and first cause, in other words, the free cause, beyond which it is impossible for us to go back along the chain of the series of causes. Liberty used in this sense is an "ex nihilo" creative power, a divine attribute conferred upon man. The free agent resists and is able to check God; he is in reality a little god opposed to a great one. To refuse to man this creative power, this privilege of suspending the divine laws by means of a sort of incomprehensible *veto,* and at the same time to judge him to be deserving of punishments without end for having placed an obstacle in the path of the will of God, would unquestionably be to contradict oneself. But if, instead of an absolute and unlimited liability, henceforth left out of the discussion, the only question is one of a relative and limited liability similar to every real and positive thing, a causality itself relative and limited, a *secondary* causality, so to speak, will suffice. Consequently liberty becomes a useless postulate. We have arrived at that point. The question is to know finally whether, in order to be simply a stitch of the tissue bound about by phenomena and woven by necessity, the "myself" has lost all right to be called a cause, and whether there is no true cause excepting the first cause which is hypothetical and imperceptible. The question is to find out whether, instead of being founded upon the supposed indeterminateness of the act, responsibility will not be conditioned upon the special nature of its very determination, its internal determinism.

. . .

However, we must recognize the fact that there is nothing more obscure than the idea of a cause and the relation of causality, nothing has given rise to more discussion among the philosophers. Hume and Kant, the positivists, and the critical philosophers, scarcely agree on this subject; and if the question had to remain unsolved until they had reached some agreement thereon, one might look upon it as impossible of solution. But human consciousness is not engaged in this debate; it has never here asked itself, what is the cause? Taking this word in its most obvious and practical meaning, it has merely asked itself, *where* is the cause? It has replied, in various ways according to the period of time, by circumscribing the more or less narrow circle of reality judged to be indivisible, within which the cause should be found enclosed. We say when we see an assassin who has just committed a crime, it is in this brain, in this soul that the cause of this homicide lies. A few centuries ago we would have said in a more vague way, it is within this individual, and at a time still more remote, when the individual was bound to his family as the member is to the body, we would rather have said, it is within this family. The essential thing is not to mistake one family for another, one individual for another, one soul, one brain for another; let us now add, for this progress continues, one "myself" for another. A family changes during the course of time and is renewed, an organism is transformed, a "soul" is modified, a "myself" is altered; but as long as the family, the body, or the person endures, the transformations taking place in them are variations upon a theme which remains more or less identical and whose identity, attenuated but not destroyed, gives us the right to look upon these circles of reality as always enclosing the cause of an act previously committed, the same cause or very nearly the same. Psychologists have attached far too great an importance to the feeling which we have of our liberty and not enough to the feeling, firm in every other respect, which we have of our identity. Moralists have expended treasures of analysis as a loss simply, in setting up the scale of the degrees of liberty; and the degrees of identity have escaped their vigilance. It is, however, easy enough to say at a certain moment of time, when one scrutinizes a person very closely, to what extent that person has remained the same as at a previous date; but no one can say just to what extent that person was a free agent. Let us admit free will, be it so; but at least we ought to recognize the fact that there is a most incontestable practical advantage in making responsibility rest upon identity which is a patent fact, rather than upon liberty which is a latent force.

Is that as much as to say that the idea of *individual identity* alone is sufficient?

No, we must add to it that of *social similarity,* as we shall see, and it is only in combining these two notions that we can find the plausible solution of the problem. In order for me to judge an individual to be responsible for a criminal action committed a year, ten years ago, is it enough for me to believe that he is the identical author of this action? No, for though I might have brought the same judgment of identity to bear in the case of a murder committed on a European by a savage of a newly discovered isle, yet I would not have the same feeling of moral indignation and of virtuous hatred as a similar act carried out by one European on another, or by one islander on another, would inspire within me. Therefore one indispensable condition for the arousing of the feeling of moral and penal responsibility is that the perpetrator and the victim of a deed should be and should feel themselves to be more or less fellow-countrymen from a social standpoint, that they should present a sufficient number of resemblances, of social, that is to say, of imitative origin. This condition is not fulfilled when the incriminating act emanates from someone who is insane, or from an epileptic at the moment he is seized with a paroxysm, or even from one addicted to alcoholism in certain cases. This sort of people, at the very moment when they have acted, have not belonged to the society of which they are reputed to be members. But when the two conditions pointed out above are met with and are together developed to a high degree, the feeling of responsibility bursts forth with remarkable strength. Among every people, such as the ancient Egyptians, the Romans, the Chinese, the English, wherever, on the one hand, the assimilation of individuals to one another, or the homogeneity of society, is well developed, and where, on the other hand, faith in the identity of the person is pushed even to the dogma of the immortal soul, one can see that fellow-citizens in their mutual relations feel that they have a grave responsibility as far as their faults and their obligations are concerned. In China, for example, in spite of what has been said as to the want of integrity of this nation, "the guilty man," Simon tells us, "is *convinced* before being sentenced. I have seen," he adds, "Chinese convicts themselves hold out their legs for the irons which were to be placed upon them." More than this, the law of the Central Empire in certain cases authorizes the substitution by one for another to undergo the penalty of death. So that we find old scoundrels who, being the shame of their family, are willing to serve as substitutes on the scaffold in order that they may rehabilitate themselves in the eyes of their relations. Nothing can better picture for us the family spirit in the Far East than this characteristic; but at the same time, "all this assumes a conception of justice [in the dealings with one another of the Chinese] carried to an extreme of power."

Freedom and Responsibility*

Although the considerations which are about to follow are of interest primarily to the ethicist, it may nevertheless be worthwhile after these descriptions and arguments to return to the freedom of the for-itself and to try to understand what the fact of this freedom represents for human destiny.

The essential consequence of our earlier remarks is that man being condemned to be free carries the weight of the whole world on his shoulders; he is responsible for the world and for himself as a way of being. We are taking the word "responsibility" in its ordinary sense as "consciousness (of) being the incontestable author of an event or of an object." In this sense the responsibility of the for-itself is overwhelming since he is the one by whom it happens that *there is* a world; since he is also the one who makes himself be, then whatever may be the situation in which he finds himself, the for-itself must wholly assume this situation with its peculiar coefficient of adversity, even though it be insupportable. He must assume the situation with the proud consciousness of being the author of it, for the very worst disadvantages or the worst threats which can endanger my person have meaning only in and through my project; and it is on the ground of the engagement which I am that they appear. It is therefore senseless to think of complaining since nothing foreign has decided what we feel, what we live, or what we are.

Furthermore this absolute responsibility is not resignation; it is simply the logical requirement of the consequences of our freedom. What happens to me happens through me, and

I can neither affect myself with it nor revolt against it nor resign myself to it. Moreover everything which happens to me is *mine*. By this we must understand first of all that I am always equal to what happens to me qua man, for what happens to a man through other men and through himself can be only human. The most terrible situations of war, the worst tortures, do not create a nonhuman state of things; there is no nonhuman situation. It is only through fear, flight, and recourse to magical types of conduct that I shall decide on the nonhuman, but this decision is human, and I shall carry the entire responsibility for it. But in addition the situation is *mine* because it is the image of my free choice of myself, and everything which it presents to me is *mine* in that this represents me and symbolizes me. Is it not I who decide the coefficient of adversity in things and even their unpredictability by deciding myself?

Thus there are no *accidents* in a life; a community event which suddenly bursts forth and involves me in it does not come from the outside. If I am mobilized in a war, this war is *my* war; it is in my image and I deserve it. I deserve it first because I could always get out of it by suicide or desertion; these ultimate possibilities are those which must always be present for us when there is a question of envisaging a situation. For lack of getting out of it, I have *chosen* it. This can be due to inertia, to cowardice in the face of public opinion, or because I prefer certain other values to the value of refusal to join in the war (the good opinion of my relatives, the honor of my family, etc.). Anyway you look at it, it is a matter of a choice. This choice will be repeated later on again and again without a break until the end of the war. Therefore we must agree with the statement by J.

* Jean-Paul Sartre, *Being and Nothingness: An Essay on Phenomenological Ontology,* trans. Hazel E. Barnes (New York: Philosophical Library, 1956), pp. 553–56, reprinted by permission of the publishers.

Romains, "In war there are no innocent victims." If therefore I have preferred war to death or to dishonor, everything takes place as if I bore the entire responsibility for this war. Of course others have declared it, and one might be tempted perhaps to consider me as a simple accomplice. But this notion of complicity has only a juridical sense, and it does not hold here. For it depended on me that for me and by me this war should not exist, and I have decided that it does exist. There was no compulsion here, for the compulsion could have got no hold on a freedom. I did not have any excuse, for as we have said repeatedly in this book, the peculiar character of human-reality is that it is without excuse. Therefore it remains for me only to lay claim to this war.

But in addition the war is *mine* because by the sole fact that it arises in a situation which I cause to be and that I can discover it there only by engaging myself for or against it, I can no longer distinguish at present the choice which I make of myself from the choice which I make of the war. To live this war is to choose myself through it and to choose it through my choice of myself. There can be no question of considering it as "four years of vacation" or as a "reprieve," as a "recess," the essential part of my responsibilities being elsewhere in my married, family, or professional life. In this war which I have chosen I choose myself from day to day, and I make it mine by making myself. If it is going to be four empty years, then it is I who bear the responsibility for this.

Finally, as we pointed out earlier, each person is an absolute choice of self from the standpoint of a world of knowledge and of techniques which this choice both assumes and illumines; each person is an absolute upsurge at an absolute date and is perfectly unthinkable at another date. It is therefore a waste of time to ask what I should have been if this war had not broken out, for I have chosen myself as one of the possible meanings of the epoch which imperceptibly led to war. I am not distinct from this same epoch; I could not be transported to another epoch without contradiction. Thus *I am* this war which restricts and limits and makes comprehensible the period which preceded it. In this sense we may define more precisely the responsibility of the for-itself if to the earlier quoted statement,

"There are no innocent victims," we add the words, "We have the war we deserve." Thus, totally free, undistinguishable from the period for which I have chosen to be the meaning, as profoundly responsible for the war as if I had myself declared it, unable to live without integrating it in *my* situation, engaging myself in it wholly, and stamping it with my seal, I must be without remorse or regrets as I am without excuse; for from the instant of my upsurge into being, I carry the weight of the world by myself alone without anything or any person being able to lighten it.

Yet this responsibility is of a very particular type. Someone will say, "I did not ask to be born." This is a naïve way of throwing greater emphasis on our facticity. I am responsible for everything, in fact, except for my very responsibility, for I am not the foundation of my being. Therefore everything takes place as if I were compelled to be responsible. I am *abandone*d in the world, not in the sense that I might remain abandoned and passive in a hostile universe like a board floating on the water, but rather in the sense that I find myself suddenly alone and without help, engaged in a world for which I bear the whole responsibility without being able, whatever I do, to tear myself away from this responsibility for an instant. For I am responsible for my very desire of fleeing responsibilities. To make myself passive in the world, to refuse to act upon things and upon Others is still to choose myself, and suicide is one mode among others of being-in-the-world. Yet I find an absolute responsibility from the fact that my facticity (here the fact of my birth) is directly inapprehensible and even inconceivable, for this fact of my birth never appears as a brute fact but always across a projective reconstruction of my for-itself. I am ashamed of being born or I am astonished at it, or I rejoice over it, or in attempting to get rid of my life I affirm that I live and I assume this life is bad. Thus in a certain sense I *choose* being born. This choice itself is integrally affected with facticity since I am able not to choose, but this facticity in turn will appear only in so far as I surpass it toward my ends. Thus facticity is everywhere but inapprehensible; I never encounter anything except my responsibility. That is why I cannot ask, "*Why* was I born? or curse the day of my birth, or declare that I did not ask to be born, for these various attitudes toward my birth—i.e., toward the *fact* that I realize a presence in the world—are absolutely nothing else but ways of assuming this birth in full responsibility and of making it *mine.* Here again I encounter only myself and my projects so that finally my abandonment—i.e., my facticity—consists simply in the fact that I am condemned to be wholly responsible for myself. I am the being which *is* in such a way that in its being its being is in question. And this "is" of my being *is* as present as inapprehensible.

Under these conditions since every event in the world can be revealed to me only as an *opportunity* (an opportunity made use of, lacked, neglected, etc.), or better yet since everything which happens to us can be considered as a *chance* (i.e., can appear to us only as a way of realizing this being which is

in question in our being) and since others as transcendences-transcended are themselves only *opportunities* and *chances,* the responsibility of the for-itself extends to the entire world as a peopled-world. It is precisely thus that the for-itself apprehends itself in anguish; that is, as a being which is neither the foundation of its own being nor of the Other's being nor of the in-itselfs which form the world, but a being which is compelled to decide the meaning of being—within it and everywhere outside of it. The one who realizes in anguish his condition as *being* thrown into a responsibility which extends to his very abandonment has no longer either remorse or regret or excuse; he is no longer anything but a freedom which perfectly reveals itself and whose being resides in this very revelation. But as we pointed out in the beginning of this work, most of the time we flee anguish in bad faith.

CHAPTER II

THE WILL

The world is independent of my will—and anything's
being as I want it is a "grace of fate."

L. WITTGENSTEIN, *Tractatus Logico-Philosophicus*

And the problem arises: what is left over if I subtract
the fact that my arm goes up from the fact that I raise
my arm.

L. WITTGENSTEIN, *Philosophical Investigations*

If the knee is tapped, the leg normally flies out. If the surface of the eye is touched, the eyelid normally closes. The reflex movements of the leg and the eyelid may be contrasted with the movements of a doctor who tests reflexes by tapping knees. The reflex movements are involuntary; the doctor's movements are voluntary. Even strict determinists agree that there is some fundamental difference between voluntary and involuntary behavior. There is comparatively little agreement, however, on the definition of voluntary behavior.

Voluntary behavior is commonly defined in terms of "an act of will," "willing," "an effort of will," or "volitional activity." An act of will is what is left over if we subtract the fact that my arm goes up from the fact that I raise my arm. In some cases things *happen* to us, in other cases we *do* things; and what is present whenever we *do* things, and absent whenever things *happen* to us, is an act of will. Thus "an act" is commonly defined in legal literature as "an external manifestation of the will."

The readings in this chapter bear on the attempt to define voluntary behavior. Four problems in particular may be singled out.

First, what are the limits of the will? What do we imply when we say that a person has willed something? Can "to will" be identified with any of these concepts: to desire, to choose, to decide, to consent to, to attend to, to set oneself to, to be able to? If not, how is it related to each of these? For example, what must be true of my state of mind if I am to will something rather than simply desire it? Aristotle said that wish relates to the end, choice to the means. Is his statement relevant to the will?

Second, if it is true that the act of will involves a relationship of some kind, what are the elements that are related? Philosophers disagree at this point. James believes that the elements are on the one hand either a Self or the will, and on the other hand some mental state, an idea. Others claim that the second element is some non-mental state—a muscular motion, for example, or even an object apart from our body. When I raise my arm, James says, the willing consists in a relation between my Self and the *idea* "my arm going up"; the will terminates with the idea, and the actual movement of my arm is simply an "effect" of my willing. Others maintain that the Self is directly related to the arm, that the will terminates not with the idea but with the movement. What is it about willing that leads to these different views? How shall we go about adjudicating the differences?

Third, how are the will and what is willed related? Are they causally related? Or is there some "immediate non-causal bringing about"? Or is there perhaps some queer coincidence between mental and non-mental states? When I raise my arm, is my will causally related to my arm going up in the same way that my pushing a cart is related to its moving? If not, in what way does it differ? There has been a strong contemporary reaction against mechanistic portrayals of the relationship between the will and what is willed, on the ground that they are unintelligible. And yet what are we to put in their place?

Finally, it is evident from these readings that many regard acts of will as highly suspect domiciliaries of that region called the mind, and "acts of will" as a concept hardly suited to elucidate the mysteries of voluntary behavior. If we cannot adequately delimit voluntary behavior with this concept, is there perhaps some other way of doing so? The most provocative suggestion to appear in recent years is Wittgenstein's: "Voluntary movement is marked by the absence of surprise." Schopenhauer perhaps makes the same point when he writes: "Will is the knowledge *a priori* of the body, and the body is the knowledge *a posteriori* of the will." In later chapters we consider further concepts such as "knowledge without observation" and "mistakes in performance" which are essentially connected with the Wittgensteinian analysis of voluntary behavior.

Of the Will*

(*In Five Articles*)

We next consider the will. Under this head there are five points of inquiry: (1) Whether the will desires something of necessity? (2) Whether it desires everything of necessity? (3) Whether it is a higher power than the intellect? (4) Whether the will moves the intellect? (5) Whether the will is divided into irascible and concupiscible?

* St. Thomas Aquinas, *The Summa Theologica of St. Thomas Aquinas* (London: Burns, Oates & Washbourne Ltd., 1920), IV, Question LXXXII, 135–46, reprinted by permission of Burns & Oates Ltd., London, and Benziger Brothers, Inc., N.Y.

FIRST ARTICLE

Whether the Will Desires Something of Necessity?

We proceed thus to the First Article:

Objection 1. It would seem that the will desires nothing of necessity. For Augustine says (*De Civ. Dei* v. 10) that if anything is necessary, it is not voluntary. But whatever the will desires is voluntary. Therefore nothing that the will desires is desired of necessity.

Obj. 2. Further, the rational powers, according to the Philosopher (*Metaph.* viii. 2), extend to opposite things. But the will is a rational power, because, as he says (*De Anima* iii. 9), *the will is in the reason.* Therefore the will extends to opposite things, and therefore it is determined to nothing of necessity.

Obj. 3. Further, by the will we are masters of our own actions. But we are not masters of that which is of necessity. Therefore the act of the will cannot be necessitated.

On the contrary, Augustine says (*De Trin.* xiii. 4) that *all desire happiness with one will.* Now if this were not necessary, but contingent, there would at least be a few exceptions. Therefore the will desires something of necessity.

I answer that, The word *necessity* is employed in many ways. For that which must be is necessary. Now that a thing must be may belong to it by an intrinsic principle— either material, as when we say that everything composed of contraries is of necessity corruptible, or formal, as when we say that it is necessary for the three angles of a triangle to be equal to two right angles. And this is *natural* and *absolute necessity.* In another way, that a thing must be, belongs to it by reason of something extrinsic, which is either the end or the agent. On the part of the end, as when without it the end is not to be attained or so well attained : for instance, food is said to be necessary for life, and a horse is necessary for a journey. This is called *necessity of end,* and sometimes also *utility.* On the part of the agent, a thing must be, when someone is forced by some agent, so that he is not able to do the contrary. This is called *necessity of coercion.*

Now this necessity of coercion is altogether repugnant to the will. For we call that violent which is against the inclination of a thing. But the very movement of the will is an inclination to something. Therefore, as a thing is called natural because it is according to the inclination of nature, so a thing is called voluntary because it is according to the inclination of the will. Therefore, just as it is impossible for a thing to be at the same time violent and natural, so it is impossible for a thing to be absolutely coerced or violent, and voluntary.

But necessity of end is not repugnant to the will, when the end cannot be attained except in one way : thus from the will to cross the sea, arises in the will the necessity to wish for a ship.

In like manner neither is natural necessity repugnant to the will. Indeed, more than this, for as the intellect of necessity adheres to the first principles, the will must of necessity adhere to the last end, which is happiness : since the end is in practical matters what the principle is in speculative matters. For what befits a thing naturally and immovably must be the root and principle of all else appertaining thereto, and every movement arises from something immovable.

Reply Obj. 1. The words of Augustine are to be understood of the necessity of coercion. But natural necessity *does not take away the liberty of the will,* as he says himself (*ibid.*).

Reply Obj. 2. The will, so far as it desires a thing naturally, corresponds rather to the intellect as regards natural principles than to the reason, which extends to opposite things. Wherefore in this respect it is rather an intellectual than a rational power.

Reply Obj. 3. We are masters of our own actions by reason of our being able to choose this or that. But choice regards not the end, but *the means to the end,* as the Philosopher says (*Ethic.* iii. 9). Wherefore the desire of the ultimate end does not regard those actions of which we are masters.

SECOND ARTICLE

Whether the Will Desires of Necessity, Whatever It Desires?

We proceed thus to the Second Article:

Objection 1. It would seem that the will desires all things of necessity, whatever it desires. For Dionysius says (*Div. Nom.* iv.) that *evil is outside the scope of the will.* Therefore the will tends of necessity to the good which is proposed to it.

Obj. 2. Further, the object of the will is compared to the will as the mover to the thing movable. But the movement of the movable necessarily follows the mover. Therefore it seems that the will's object moves it of necessity.

Obj. 3. Further, as the thing apprehended by sense is the object of the sensitive appetite, so the thing apprehended by the intellect is the object of the intellectual appetite, which is called the will. But what is apprehended by the sense moves the sensitive appetite of necessity : for Augustine says (*Gen. ad lit.* ix. 14) that *animals are moved by things seen.*

Therefore it seems that whatever is apprehended by the intellect moves the will of necessity.

On the contrary, Augustine says (*Retract.* i. 9) that *it is the will by which we sin and live well,* and so the will extends to opposite things. Therefore it does not desire of necessity all things whatsoever it desires.

I answer that, The will does not desire of necessity whatsoever it desires. In order to make this evident we must observe that as the intellect naturally and of necessity adheres to the first principles, so the will adheres to the last end, as we have said already (A. 1). Now there are some things intelligible which have not a necessary connection with the first principles; such as contingent propositions, the denial of which does not involve a denial of the first principles. And to such the intellect does not assent of necessity. But there are some propositions which have a necessary connection with the first principles: such as demonstrable conclusions, a denial of which involves a denial of the first principles. And to these the intellect assents of necessity, when once it is aware of the necessary connection of these conclusions with the principles; but it does not assent of necessity until through the demonstration it recognizes the necessity of such connection. It is the same with the will. For there are certain individual goods which have not a necessary connection with happiness, because without them a man can be happy: and to such the will does not adhere of necessity. But there are some things which have a necessary connection with happiness, by means of which things man adheres to God, in Whom alone true happiness consists. Nevertheless, until through the certitude of the Divine Vision the necessity of such connection be shown, the will does not adhere to God of necessity, nor to those things which are of God. But the will of the man who sees God in His Essence of necessity adheres to God, just as now we desire of necessity to be happy. It is therefore clear that the will does not desire of necessity whatever it desires.

Reply Obj. 1. The will can tend to nothing except under the aspect of good. But because good is of many kinds, for this reason the will is not of necessity determined to one.

Reply Obj. 2. The mover, then, of necessity causes movement in the thing movable, when the power of the mover exceeds the thing movable, so that its entire capacity is subject to the mover. But as the capacity of the will regards the universal and perfect good, its capacity is not subjected to any individual good. And therefore it is not of necessity moved by it.

Reply Obj. 3. The sensitive power does not compare different things with each other, as reason does: but it simply apprehends some one thing. Therefore, according to that one thing, it moves the sensitive appetite in a determinate way. But the reason is a power that compares several things together: therefore from several things the intellectual appetite—that is, the will—may be moved; but not of necessity from one thing.

THIRD ARTICLE

Whether the Will Is a Higher Power than the Intellect?

We proceed thus to the Third Article:

Objection 1. It would seem that the will is a higher power than the intellect. For the object of the will is good and the end. But the end is the first and highest cause. Therefore the will is the first and highest power.

Obj. 2. Further, in the order of natural things we observe a progress from imperfect things to perfect. And this also appears in the powers of the soul: for sense precedes the intellect, which is more noble. Now the act of the will, in the natural order, follows the act of the intellect. Therefore the will is a more noble and perfect power than the intellect.

Obj. 3. Further, habits are proportioned to their powers, as perfections to what they make perfect. But the habit which perfects the will—namely, charity—is more noble than the habits which perfect the intellect: for it is written (I Cor. xiii. 2): *If I should know all mysteries, and if I should have all faith, and have not charity, I am nothing.* Therefore the will is a higher power than the intellect.

On the contrary, The Philosopher holds the intellect to be the highest power of the soul (*Ethic.* x. 7).

I answer that, The superiority of one thing over another can be considered in two ways: *absolutely* and *relatively.* Now a thing is considered to be such absolutely which is considered such in itself: but relatively as it is such with regard to something else. If therefore the intellect and will be considered with regard to themselves, then the intelllect is the higher power. And this is clear if we compare their respective objects to one another. For the object of the intellect is more simple and more absolute than the object of the will; since the object of the intellect is the very idea of appetible good; and the appetible good, the idea of which is in the intellect, is the object of the will. Now the more simple and the more abstract a thing is, the nobler and higher it is in itself; and therefore the object of the intellect is higher than the object of the will. Therefore, since the proper nature of a power is in its order to its object, it follows that the intellect in itself and absolutely is higher and nobler than the will. But relatively and by comparison with something else, we find that the will is sometimes higher than the intellect, from the fact that the object of the will occurs in something higher than that in which occurs the object of the intellect. Thus, for instance, I might say that hearing is relatively nobler than sight, inasmuch as something in which there is sound is nobler than something in which there is color, though color is nobler and simpler than sound. For, as we have said above (Q. XVI., A. 1; Q. XXVII., A. 4), the action of the intellect consists in this—that the idea of the thing understood is in the one who understands; while the act of the will consists in this—that the will is inclined to the thing itself as existing in itself. And therefore the Philosopher says in *Metaph.* vi. (Did. v. 2) that *good and evil,* which are objects of the will, *are in things,* but *truth and error,* which are objects of the intellect, *are in the mind.* When, therefore, the thing in which there is good is nobler than the soul itself, in which is the idea understood; by comparison with such a thing, the will is higher than the intellect. But when the thing which is good is less noble than the soul, then even in comparison with that thing the intellect is higher than the will. Wherefore the love of God is better than the knowledge of God; but, on the contrary, the knowledge of corporeal things is better than the love thereof. Absolutely, however, the intellect is nobler than the will.

Reply Obj. 1. The aspect of causality is perceived by comparing one thing to another, and in such a comparison the idea of good is found to be nobler: but truth signifies something more absolute, and extends to the idea

of good itself: wherefore even good is something true. But, again, truth is something good: forasmuch as the intellect is a thing, and truth its end. And among other ends this is the most excellent: as also is the intellect among the other powers.

Reply Obj. 2. What precedes in order of generation and time is less perfect: for in one and the same thing potentiality precedes act, and imperfection precedes perfection. But what precedes absolutely and in the order of nature is more perfect: for thus act precedes potentiality. And in this way the intellect precedes the will, as the motive power precedes the thing movable, and as the active precedes the passive; for good which is understood moves the will.

Reply Obj. 3. The reason is verified of the will as compared with what is above the soul. For charity is the virtue by which we love God.

FOURTH ARTICLE

Whether the Will Moves the Intellect?

We proceed thus to the Fourth Article:

Objection 1. It would seem that the will does not move the intellect. For what moves excels and precedes what is moved, because what moves is an agent, and *the agent is nobler than the patient,* as Augustine says (*Gen. ad lit.* xii. 16), and the Philosopher (*De Anima* iii. 5). But the intellect excels and precedes the will, as we have said above (A. 3). Therefore the will does not move the intellect.

Obj. 2. Further, what moves is not moved by what is moved, except perhaps accidentally. But the intellect moves the will, because the good apprehended by the intellect moves without being moved; whereas the appetite moves and is moved. Therefore the intellect is not moved by the will.

Obj. 3. Further, we can will nothing but what we understand. If, therefore, in order to understand, the will moves by willing to understand, that act of the will must be preceded by another act of the intellect, and this act of the intellect by another act of the will, and so on indefinitely, which is impossible. Therefore the will does not move the intellect.

On the contrary, Damascene says (*De Fid. Orth.* ii. 26): *It is in our power to learn an art or not, as we list.* But a thing is in our power by the will, and we learn art by the intellect. Therefore the will moves the intellect.

I answer that, A thing is said to move in two ways: First, as an end; for instance, when we say that the end moves the agent. In this way the intellect moves the will, because the good understood is the object of the will, and moves it as an end. Secondly, a thing is said to move as an agent, as what alters moves what is altered, and what impels moves what is impelled. In this way the will moves the intellect, and all the powers of the soul, as Anselm says (Eadmer, *De Similitudinibus*). The reason is, because wherever we have order among a number of active powers, that power which regards the universal end moves the powers which regard particular ends. And we may observe this both in nature and in things politic. For the heaven, which aims at the universal preservation of things subject to generation and corruption, moves all inferior bodies, each of which aims at the preservation of its own species or of the individual. The king also, who aims at the common good of the whole kingdom, by his rule moves all the governors of cities, each of whom rules over his own particular city. Now the object of the will is good and the end in general, and each power is directed to some suitable good proper to it, as sight is directed to the perception of color, and the intellect to the knowledge of truth. Therefore the will as an agent moves all the powers of the soul to their respective acts, except the natural powers of the vegetative part, which are not subject to our will.

Reply Obj. 1. The intellect may be considered in two ways: as apprehensive of universal being and truth, and as a thing and a particular power having a determinate act. In like manner also the will may be considered in two ways: according to the common nature of its object—that is to say, as appetitive of universal good—and as a determinate power of the soul having a determinate act. If, therefore, the intellect and will be compared with one another according to the universality of their respective objects, then, as we have said above (A. 3), the intellect is simply higher and nobler than the will. If, however, we take the intellect as regards the common nature of its object and the will as a determinate power, then again the intellect is higher and nobler than the will, because under the notion of being and truth is contained both the will

itself, and its act, and its object. Wherefore the intellect understands the will, and its act, and its object, just as it understands other species of things, as stone or wood, which are contained in the common notion of being and truth. But if we consider the will as regards the common nature of its object, which is good, and the intellect as a thing and a special power; then the intellect itself, and its act, and its object, which is truth, each of which is some species of good, are contained under the common notion of good. And in this way the will is higher than the intellect, and can move it. From this we can easily understand why these powers include one another in their acts, because the intellect understands that the will wills, and the will wills the intellect to understand. In the same way good is contained in truth, inasmuch as it is an understood truth, and truth is good, inasmuch as it is a desired good.

Reply Obj. 2. The intellect moves the will in one sense, and the will moves the intellect in another, as we have said above.

Reply Obj. 3. There is no need to go on indefinitely, but we must stop at the intellect as preceding all the rest. For every movement of the will must be preceded by apprehension, whereas every apprehension is not preceded by an act of the will; but the principle of counseling and understanding is an intellectual principle higher than our intellect—namely, God—as also Aristotle says (*Eth. Eudemic.* vii. 14), and in this way he explains that there is no need to proceed indefinitely.

Whether We Should Distinguish Irascible and Concupiscible Parts in the Superior Appetite?

We proceed thus to the Fifth Article:

Objection 1. It would seem that we ought to distinguish irascible and concupiscible parts in the superior appetite, which is the will. For the concupiscible power is so called from *concupiscere* (*to desire*), and the irascible part from *irasci* (*to be angry*). But there is a concupiscence which cannot belong to the sensitive appetite, but only to the intellectual, which is the will; as the concupiscence of wisdom, of which it is said (Wisd. vi. 21): *The concupiscence of wisdom bringeth to the eternal kingdom.* There is also a certain anger which cannot belong to the sensitive appetite, but only to the intellectual; as when our anger is directed against vice. Wherefore Jerome commenting on Matt. xiii. 33 warns us *to have the hatred of vice in the irascible part.* Therefore we should distinguish irascible and concupiscible parts in the intellectual soul as well as in the sensitive.

Obj. 2. Further, as is commonly said, charity is in the concupiscible, and hope in the irascible part. But they cannot be in the sensitive appetite, because their objects are not sensible, but intellectual. Therefore we must assign an irascible and a concupiscible power to the intellectual part.

Obj. 3. Further, it is said (*De Spiritu et Anima*) that *the soul has these powers*—namely, the irascible, concupiscible, and rational—*before it is united to the body.* But no power of the sensitive part belongs to the soul alone, but to the soul and body united, as we have said above (Q. LXXVIII., A.A. 5, 8). Therefore the irascible and concupiscible powers are in the will, which is the intellectual appetite.

On the contrary, Gregory of Nyssa (Nemesius, *De Nat. Hom.*) says *that the irrational* part of the soul is divided into the desiderative and irascible, and Damascene says the same (*De Fid. Orth.* ii, 12). And the Philosopher says (*De Anima* iii. 9) *that the will is in the reason, while in the irrational part of the soul are concupiscence and anger,* or *desire and animus.*

I answer that, The irascible and concupiscible are not parts of the intellectual appetite, which is called the will. Because, as was said above (Q. LIX., A. 4; Q. LXXIX., A. 7), a power which is directed to an object according to some common notion is not differentiated by special differences which are contained under that common notion. For instance, because sight regards the visible thing under the common notion of something colored, the visual power is not multiplied according to the different kinds of color: but if there were a power regarding white as white, and not as something colored, it would be distinct from a power regarding black as black.

Now the sensitive appetite does not consider the common notion of good, because neither do the senses apprehend the universal. And therefore the parts of the sensitive appetite are differentiated by the different notions of particular good: for the concupiscible regards as proper to it the notion of good, as something pleasant to the senses and suitable to nature: whereas the irascible regards the notion of good as something that wards off and repels what is hurtful. But the will regards good according to the common notion of good, and therefore in the will, which is the intellectual appetite, there is no differentiation of appetitive powers, so that there be in the intellectual appetite an irascible power distinct from a concupiscible power: just as neither on the part of the intellect are the apprehensive powers multiplied, although they are on the part of the senses.

Reply Obj. 1. Love, concupiscence, and the like can be understood in two ways. Sometimes they are taken as passions—arising, that is, with a certain commotion of the soul. And thus they are commonly understood, and in this sense they are only in the sensitive appetite. They may, however, be taken in another way, as far as they are simple affections without passion or commotion of the soul, and thus they are acts of the will. And in this sense, too, they are attributed to the angels and to God. But if taken in this sense, they do not belong to different powers, but only to one power, which is called the will.

Reply Obj. 2. The will itself may be said to be irascible, as far as it wills to repel evil, not from any sudden movement of a passion, but from a judgment of the reason. And in the same way the will may be said to be concupiscible on account of its desire for good. And thus in the irascible and concupiscible are charity and hope—that is, in the will as ordered to such acts. And in this way, too, we may understand the words quoted (*De Spiritu et Anima*); that the irascible and concupiscible powers are in the soul before it is united to the body (as long as we understand priority of nature, and not of time), although there is no need to have faith in what that book says. Whence the answer to the third objection is clear.

The Idea of Power*

1. The mind being every day informed, by the senses, of the alteration of those simple ideas it observes in things without, and taking notice how one comes to an end, and ceases to be, and another begins to exist which was not before; reflecting also on what passes within himself, and observing a constant change of its ideas, sometimes by the determination of its own choice; and concluding from what it has so constantly observed to have been, that the like changes will for the future be made in the same things by like agents, and by the like ways; considers in one thing the possibility of having any of its simple ideas changed, and in another the possibility of making that change: and so comes by that idea which we call power. Thus we say, fire has a power to melt gold, i.e., to destroy the consistency of its insensible parts, and consequently its hardness, and make it fluid; and gold has a power to be melted: that the sun has a power to blanch wax, and wax a power to be blanched by the sun, whereby the yellowness is destroyed, and whiteness made to exist in its room. In which, and the like cases, the power we consider is in reference to the change of perceivable ideas: for we cannot observe any alteration to be made in, or operation upon, any thing, but by the observable change of its sensible ideas; nor conceive any alteration to be made, but by conceiving a change of some of its ideas.

2. *Power active and passive.* Power thus considered is twofold; viz., as able to make, or able to receive, any change: the one may be called "active," and the other "passive," power. . . .

. . .

4. *The clearest idea of active power had from spirit.* We are abundantly furnished with the idea of passive power, by almost all sorts of sensible things. In most of them we cannot avoid observing their sensible qualities, nay, their very substances, to be in a continual flux: and therefore with reason we look on them as liable still to the same change. Nor have we of active power (which is the more proper signification of the word "power") fewer instances; since, whatever

change is observed, the mind must collect a power somewhere, able to make that change, as well as a possibility in the thing itself to receive it. But yet, if we will consider it attentively, bodies, by our senses, do not afford us so clear and distinct an idea of active power, as we have from reflection on the operations of our minds. For, all power relating to action, and there being but two sorts of action whereof we have any idea, viz., thinking and motion, let us consider whence we have the clearest ideas of the powers which produce these actions. (1) Of thinking, body affords us no idea at all: it is only from reflection that we have that. (2) Neither have we from body any idea of the beginning of motion. A body at rest affords us no idea of any active power to move; and when it is set in motion itself, that motion is rather a passion than an action in it. For when the ball obeys the stroke of a billiard-stick, it is not any action of the ball, but bare passion: also when by impulse it sets another ball in motion that lay in its way, it only communicates the motion it had received from another, and loses in itself so much as the other received; which gives us but a very obscure idea of an active power moving in body, whilst we observe it only to transfer but not produce any motion. For it is but a very obscure idea of power, which reaches not the production of the action, but the continuation of the passion. For so is motion, in a body impelled by another: The continuation of the alteration made in it from rest to motion being little more than an action, than the continuation of the alteration of its figure by the same blow is an action. The idea of the beginning of motion we have only from reflection on what passes in ourselves, where we find by experience, that, barely by willing it, barely by a thought of the mind, we can move the parts of our bodies which were before at rest. So that it seems to me, we have, from the observation of the operation of bodies by our senses, but a very imperfect, obscure, idea of active power, since they afford us not any idea in themselves of the power to begin any action, either motion or thought. But if from the impulse bodies are observed to make one upon another, anyone thinks he has a clear idea of power, it serves as well to my purpose, sensation being one of those ways whereby the mind comes by its

* John Locke, *An Essay Concerning Human Understanding* (London: George Routledge and Sons Ltd. [n.d.]), pp. 162–77.

ideas: only I thought it worth while to consider here by the way, whether the mind doth not receive its idea of active power clearer from reflection on its own operations, than it doth from any external sensation.

5. *Will and understanding two powers.* This at least I think evident, that we find in ourselves a power to begin or forbear, continue or end, several actions of our minds and motions of our bodies, barely by a thought or preference of the mind ordering, or, as it were, commanding the doing or not doing such or such a particular action. This power which the mind has thus to order the consideration of any idea, or the forbearing to consider it, or to prefer the motion of any part of the body to its rest, and vice versa, in any particular instance, is that which we call "the will." The actual exercise of that power, by directing any particular action or its forbearance, is that which we call "volition" or "willing." The forbearance of that action consequent to such order or command of the mind, is called "voluntary"; and whatsoever action is performed without such a thought of the mind, is called "involuntary." . . .

6. *Faculties.* These powers of the mind, viz., of perceiving and of preferring, are usually called by another name: and the ordinary way of speaking, is that the understanding and will are two faculties of the mind; a word proper enough, if it be used, as all words should be, so as not to breed any confusion in men's thoughts by being supposed (as I suspect it has been) to stand for some real beings in the soul, that performed those actions of understanding and volition. For when we say, the will is the commanding and superior faculty of the soul; that it is or is not free; that it determines the inferior faculties; that it follows the dictates of the understanding, etc.; though these and the like expressions, by those that carefully attend to their own ideas, and conduct their thoughts more by the evidence of things than the sound of words, may be understood in a clear and distinct sense: yet I suspect, I say, that this way of speaking of faculties has misled many into a confused notion of so many distinct agents in us, which had their several provinces and authorities, and did command, obey, and perform several actions, as so many distinct beings; which has been no small occasion of wrangling, obscurity, and uncertainty in questions relating to them.

7. *Whence the ideas of liberty and necessity.* Everyone, I think, finds in himself a power to begin or forbear, continue or put an end to, several actions in himself. From the consideration of the extent of this power of the mind over the actions of the man, which everyone finds in himself, arise the ideas of liberty and necessity.

8. *Liberty, what.* All the actions that we have any idea of, reducing themselves, as has been said, to these two, viz., thinking and motion, so far as a man has a power to think or not to think, to move or not to move, according to the preference or direction of his own mind, so far is a man free. Wherever any performance or forbearance are not equally in a man's power, wherever doing or not doing will not equally follow upon the preference of his mind directing it, there he is not free, though perhaps the action may be voluntary. So that the idea of liberty is the idea of a power in any agent to do or forbear any particular action, according to the determination or thought of the mind, whereby either of them is preferred to the other; where either of them is not in the power of the agent, to be produced by him according to his volition, there he is not at liberty, that agent is under necessity. So that liberty cannot be where there is no thought, no volition, no will; but there may be thought, there may be will, there may be volition, where there is no liberty. A little consideration of an obvious instance or two may make this clear.

9. *Supposes the understanding and will.* A tennis-ball, whether in motion by the stroke of a racket, or lying still at rest, is not by anyone taken to be a free agent. If we inquire into the reason, we shall find it is, because we conceive not a tennis-ball to think, and consequently not to have any volition, or preference of motion to rest, or vice versa; and therefore has not liberty, is not a free agent; but all its both motion and rest come under our idea of necessary, and are so called. Likewise a man falling into the water (a bridge breaking under him) has not herein liberty, is not a free agent. For though he has volition, though he prefers his not falling to falling; yet the forbearance of that motion not being in his power; the stop or cessation of that motion follows not upon his volition; and therefore therein he is not free. So a man striking himself or his friend, by a convulsive motion of his arm, which it is not in his

power, by volition or the direction of his mind, to stop or forbear, nobody thinks he has, in this, liberty; everyone pities him, as acting by necessity and restraint.

10. *Belongs not to volition.* Again: Suppose a man be carried, whilst fast asleep, into a room, where is a person he longs to see and speak with, and be there locked fast in, beyond his power to get out; he awakes, and is glad to find himself in so desirable company, which he stays willingly in, i.e., prefers his stay to going away. I ask, is not this stay voluntary? I think nobody will doubt it; and yet, being locked fast in, it is evident he is not at liberty not to stay, he has not freedom to be gone. So that liberty is not an idea belonging to volition, or preferring; but to the person having the power of doing, or forbearing to do, according as the mind shall choose or direct. Our idea of liberty reaches as far as that power, and no farther. For wherever restraint comes to check that power, or compulsion takes away that indifferency of ability on either side to act, or to forbear acting, there liberty, and our notion of it, presently ceases.

11. *Voluntary opposed to involuntary, not to necessary.* We have instances enough, and often more than enough, in our own bodies. A man's heart beats, and the blood circulates, which is not in his power by any thought or volition to stop; and therefore, in respect of these motions, where rest depends not on his choice, nor would follow the determination of his mind, if it should prefer it, he is not a free agent. Convulsive motions agitate his legs, so that, though he wills it never so much, he cannot by any power of his mind stop their motion (as in that odd disease called *chorea sancti Viti*), but he is perpetually dancing: he is not at liberty in this action, but under as much necessity of moving as a stone that falls or a tennis-ball struck with a racket. On the other side, a palsy or the stocks hinder his legs from obeying the determination of his mind, if it would thereby transfer his body to another place. In all these there is want of freedom, though the sitting still even of a paralytic, whilst he prefers it to a removal, is truly voluntary. Voluntary, then, is not opposed to necessary, but to involuntary. For a man may prefer what he can do, to what he cannot do; the state he is in, to its absence or change, though necessity has made it in itself unalterable.

12. *Liberty, what.* As it is in the motions of the body, so it is in the thoughts of our minds: where any one is such, that we have power to take it up, or lay it by, according to the preference of the mind, there we are at liberty. A waking man, being under the necessity of having some ideas constantly in his mind, is not at liberty to think, or not to think, no more than he is at liberty, whether his body shall touch any other or no: but whether he will remove his contemplation from one idea to another, is many times in his choice; and then he is, in respect of his ideas, as much at liberty as he is in respect of bodies he rests on: he can at pleasure remove himself from one to another. But yet some ideas to the mind, like some motions to the body, are such as in certain circumstances it cannot avoid, nor obtain their absence by the utmost effort it can use. A man on the rack is not at liberty to lay by the idea of pain, and divert himself with other contemplations: and sometimes a boisterous passion hurries our thoughts, as a hurricane does our bodies, without leaving us the liberty of thinking on other things, which we would rather choose. But as soon as the mind regains the power to stop or continue, begin or forbear any of these motions of the body without, or thoughts within, according as it thinks fit to prefer either to the other, we then consider the man as a free agent again.

13. *Necessity, what.* Wherever thought is wholly wanting, or the power to act or forbear according to the direction of thought, there necessity takes place. This, in an agent capable of volition, when the beginning or continuation of any action is contrary to that preference of his mind, is called "compulsion"; when the hindering or stopping any action is contrary to this volition, it is called "restraint." Agents that have no thought, no volition at all, are in everything necessary agents.

14. *Liberty belongs not to the will.* If this be so (as I imagine it is), I leave it to be considered, whether it may not help to put an end to that long-agitated, and I think unreasonable, because unintelligible question, viz., Whether man's will be free or no? For, if I mistake not, it follows, from what I have said, that the question itself is altogether improper; and it is as insignificant to ask whether man's will be free, as to ask whether his sleep be swift, or his virtue square: liberty being as little applicable to the will, as swiftness of

motion is to sleep, or squareness to virtue. Everyone would laugh at the absurdity of such a question as either of these; because it is obvious that the modifications of motion belong not to sleep, nor the difference of figure to virtue: and when anyone well considers it, I think he will as plainly perceive, that liberty, which is but a power, belongs only to agents, and cannot be an attribute or modification of the will, which is also but a power.

15. *Volition.* Such is the difficulty of explaining and giving clear notions of internal actions by sounds, that I must here warn my reader that "ordering, directing, choosing, preferring," etc., which I have made use of, will not distinctly enough express volition, unless he will reflect on what he himself does when he wills. For example: "Preferring," which seems perhaps best to express the act of volition, does it not precisely. For though a man would prefer flying to walking, yet who can say he ever wills it? Volition, it is plain, is an act of the mind knowingly exerting that dominion it takes itself to have over any part of the man, by employing it in or withholding it from any particular action. And what is the will, but the faculty to do this? And is that faculty anything more in effect than a power—the power of the mind to determine its thought to the producing, continuing, or stopping any action, as far as it depends on us? For, can it be denied, that whatever agent has a power to think on its own actions, and to prefer their doing or omission either to other, has that faculty called "will"? Will then is nothing but such a power. Liberty, on the other side, is the power a man has to do or forbear doing any particular action, according as its doing or forbearance has the actual preference in the mind; which is the same thing as to say, according as he himself wills it.

16. *Powers belong to agents.* It is plain then that the will is nothing but one power or ability, and freedom another power or ability: so that to ask whether the will has freedom, is to ask whether one power has another power, one ability another ability? a question at first sight too grossly absurd to make a dispute, or need an answer. For who is it that sees not, that powers belong only to agents, and are attributes only of substances, and not of powers themselves? So that this way of putting the question, viz., Whether the will be free? is in effect to ask, Whether the will be a substance, an agent? or at least to suppose it, since freedom can properly be attributed to nothing else. If freedom can with any propriety of speech be applied to power, it may be attributed to the power that is in a man to produce or forbear producing motions in parts of his body, by choice or preference; which is that which denominates him free, and is freedom itself. But if anyone should ask whether freedom were free, he would be suspected not to understand well what he said; and he would be thought to deserve Midas's ears, who, knowing that "rich" was a denomination from the possession of riches, should demand whether riches themselves were rich.

17. However the name "faculty" which men have given to this power called the "will," and whereby they have been led into a way of talking of the will as acting, may, by an appropriation that disguises its true sense, serve a little to palliate the absurdity; yet the will, in truth, signifies nothing but a power or ability to prefer or choose; and when the will, under the name of a "faculty," is considered as it is, barely as an ability to do something, the absurdity in saying it is free or not free, will easily discover itself. For if it be reasonable to suppose and talk of faculties as distinct beings that can act (as we do when we say, "The will orders," and "The will is free"), it is fit that we should make a speaking faculty, and a walking faculty, and a dancing faculty, by which those actions are produced, which are but several modes of motion; as well as we make the will and understanding to be faculties by which the actions of choosing and perceiving are produced, which are but several modes of thinking; and we may as properly say, that it is the singing faculty sings, and the dancing faculty dances, as that the will chooses, or that the understanding conceives; or, as is usual, that the will directs the understanding, or the understanding obeys or obeys not the will: it being altogether as proper and intelligible to say, that the power of speaking directs the power of singing, or the power of singing obeys or disobeys the power of speaking.

18. This way of talking, nevertheless, has prevailed, and, as I guess, produced great confusion. For, these being all different powers in the mind or in the man to do several actions, he exerts them as he thinks fit: but the

power to do one action is not operated on by the power of doing another action. For the power of thinking operates not on the power of choosing, nor the power of choosing on the power of thinking; no more than the power of dancing operates on the power of singing, or the power of singing on the power of dancing: as anyone who reflects on it will easily perceive: and yet this is it which we say when we thus speak, that the will operates on the understanding, or the understanding on the will.

19. I grant that this or that actual thought may be the occasion of volition, or exercising the power a man has to choose; or the actual choice of the mind, the cause of actual thinking on this or that thing; as the actual singing of such a tune may be the occasion of dancing such a dance; and the actual dancing of such a dance, the occasion of singing such a tune. But in all these it is not one power that operates on another; but it is the mind that operates and exerts these powers; it is the man that does the action, it is the agent that has power, or is able to do. For powers are relations, not agents: and that which has the power or not the power to operate, is that alone which is or is not free, and not the power itself: for freedom, or not freedom, can belong to nothing but what has or has not a power to act.

20. *Liberty belongs not to the will.* The attributing to faculties that which belonged not to them, has given occasion to this way of talking; but the introducing into discourses concerning the mind, with the name of faculties, a notion of their operating, has, I suppose, as little advanced our knowledge in that part of ourselves, as the great use and mention of the like invention of faculties in the operations of the body has helped us in the knowledge of physics. Not that I deny there are faculties, both in the body and mind: they both of them have their powers of operating, else neither the one nor the other could operate. For nothing can operate that is not able to operate; and that is not able to operate that has no power to operate. Nor do I deny that those words, and the like, are to have their place in the common use of languages that have made them current. It looks like too much affectation wholly to lay them by; and philosophy itself, though it likes not a gaudy dress, yet when it appears in public, must have so much complacency as to be clothed

in the ordinary fashion and language of the country, so far as it can consist with truth and perspicuity. But the fault has been that faculties have been spoken of and represented as so many distinct agents. For it being asked, what it was that digested the meat in our stomachs? it was a ready, and very satisfactory answer, to say, that it was the digestive faculty. "What was it that made anything come out of the body?" The expulsive faculty. "What moved?" The motive faculty: and so in the mind, the intellectual faculty, or the understanding, understood; and the elective faculty, or the will, willed or commanded: which is, in short, to say that the ability to digest, digested; and the ability to move, moved; and the ability to understand, understood. For "faculty, ability, and power," I think, are but different names of the same things: which ways of speaking, when put into more intelligible words, will, I think, amount to thus much; that digestion is performed by something that is able to digest; motion, by something able to move; and understanding, by something able to understand. And in truth it would be very strange, if it should be otherwise; as strange as it would be for a man to be free without being able to be free.

21. *But to the agent or man.* To return, then, to the inquiry about liberty, I think the question is not proper, whether the will be free, but whether a man be free. Thus, I think,

(1) That so far as anyone can, by the direction or choice of his mind preferring the existence of any action to the nonexistence of that action, and vice versa, make it to exist or not exist, so far he is free. For if I can by a thought directing the motion of my finger make it move when it was at rest, or vice versa, it is evident that, in respect of that, I am free; and if I can, by a like thought of my mind preferring one to the other, produce either words or silence, I am at liberty to speak or hold my peace: and as far as this power reaches, of acting or not acting, by the determination of his own thought preferring either, so far is a man free. For how can we think anyone freer than to have the power to do what he will? And so far as anyone can, by preferring any action to its not being, or rest to any action, produce that action or rest, so far can he do what he will. For such a preferring of action to its absence, is the willing of it; and we can scarce tell

how to imagine any being freer than to be able to do what he wills. So that, in respect of actions within the reach of such a power in him, a man seems as free as it is possible for freedom to make him.

22. *In respect of willing a man is not free.* But the inquisitive mind of man, willing to shift off from himself, as far as he can, all thoughts of guilt, though it be by putting himself into a worse state than that of fatal necessity, is not content with this: freedom, unless it reaches farther than this, will not serve the turn: and it passes for a good plea, that a man is not free at all, if he be not as free to will as he is to act what he wills. Concerning a man's liberty, there yet therefore is raised this farther question, whether a man be free to will? which, I think, is what is meant, when it is disputed whether the will be free. And as to that I imagine,

23. (2) That willing or volition being an action, and freedom consisting in a power of acting or not acting, a man, in respect of willing or the act of volition, when any action in his power is once proposed to this thoughts, as presently to be done, cannot be free. The reason whereof is very manifest: for it being unavoidable that the action depending on his will should exist or not exist, and its existence or not existence following perfectly the determination and preference of his will, he cannot avoid willing the existence or not existence of that action; it is absolutely necessary that he will the one or the other, i.e., prefer the one to the other; since one of them must necessarily follow; and that which does follow, follows by the choice and determination of his mind; that is, by his willing it; for if he did not will it, it would not be. So that, in respect of the act of willing, a man in such a case is not free: liberty consisting in a power to act or not to act, which, in regard of volition, a man upon such a proposal has not. For it is unavoidably necessary to prefer the doing or forbearance of an action in a man's power, which is once so proposed to his thoughts; a man must necessarily will the one or the other of them: upon which preference or volition, the action or its forbearance certainly follows, and is truly voluntary. But the act of volition, or preferring one of the two, being that which he cannot avoid, a man, in respect of that act of willing, is under a necessity, and so cannot be free; unless necessity and freedom can con-

sist together, and a man can be free and bound at once.

24. This, then, is evident, that, in all proposals of present action, a man is not at liberty to will or not to will, because he cannot forbear willing; liberty consisting in a power to act, or to forbear acting, and in that only. For a man that sits still is said yet to be at liberty, because he can walk if he wills it. But if a man sitting still has not a power to remove himself, he is not at liberty; so likewise a man falling down a precipice, though in motion, is not at liberty, because he cannot stop that motion if he would. This being so, it is plain that a man that is walking, to whom it is proposed to give off walking, is not at liberty whether he will determine himself to walk or give off walking, or no: he must necessarily prefer one or the other of them, walking or not walking; and so it is in regard of all other actions in our power so proposed, which are the far greater number. For, considering the vast number of voluntary actions that succeed one another every moment that we are awake in the course of our lives, there are but few of them that are thought on or proposed to the will, till the time they are to be done: and in all such actions, as I have shown, the mind, in respect of willing, has not a power to act or not to act, wherein consists liberty. The mind in that case has not a power to forbear willing; it cannot avoid some determination concerning them. Let the consideration be as short, the thought as quick, as it will, it either leaves the man in the state he was before thinking, or changes it; continues the action, or puts an end to it. Whereby it is manifest, that it orders and directs one in preference to or with neglect of the other, and thereby either the continuation or change becomes unavoidably voluntary.

25. *The will determined by something without it.* Since, then, it is plain that in most cases a man is not at liberty whether he will *will* or no; the next thing demanded is, whether a man be at liberty to will which of the two he pleases, motion or rest? This question carries the absurdity of it so manifestly in itself, that one might thereby sufficiently be convinced that liberty concerns not the will. For to ask, whether a man be at liberty to will either motion or rest, speaking or silence, which he pleases? is to ask, whether a man can will what he wills, or be pleased with

what he is pleased with? a question which, I think, needs no answer : and they who can make a question of it, must suppose one will to determine the acts of another, and another to determine that; and so on *in infinitum.*

26. To avoid these and the like absurdities, nothing can be of greater use than to establish in our minds determined ideas of the things under consideration. If the ideas of liberty and volition were well fixed in our understandings, and carried along with us in our minds, as they ought, through all the questions that are raised about them, I suppose a great part of the difficulties that perplex men's thoughts and entangle their understandings would be much easier resolved; and we should perceive where the confused signification of terms, or where the nature of the thing, caused the obscurity.

27. *Freedom.* First, then, it is carefully to be remembered, that freedom consists in the dependence of the existence or not existence of any action upon our volition of it, and not in the dependence of any action, or its contrary, on our preference. A man standing on a cliff is at liberty to leap twenty yards downward into the sea, not because he has a power to do the contrary action, which is to leap twenty yards upwards, for that he cannot do; but he is therefore free, because he has a power to leap or not to leap. But if a greater force than his either holds him fast, or tumbles him down, he is no longer free in that case: because the doing or forbearance of that particular action is no longer in his power. He that is a close prisoner in a room twenty feet square, being at the north side of his chamber, is at liberty to walk twenty feet southward, because he can walk or not walk it: but is not at the same time at liberty to do the contrary; i.e., to walk twenty feet northward.

In this, then, consists freedom, viz., in our being able to act, or not to act, according as we shall choose or will.

28. *Volition what.* Secondly. We must remember that volition, or willing, is an act of the mind directing its thought to the production of any action, and thereby exerting its power to produce it. To avoid multiplying of words, I would crave leave here, under the word "action," to comprehend the forbearance, too, of any action proposed; sitting still, or holding one's peace, when walking or speaking are proposed, though mere forbearances,

requiring as much the determination of the will, and being often as weighty in their consequences, as the contrary actions, may, on that consideration, well enough pass for actions too: but this I say that I may not be mistaken, if for brevity's sake I speak thus.

29. *What determines the will.* Thirdly. The will being nothing but a power in the mind to direct the operative faculties of a man to motion or rest, as far as they depend on such direction; to the question, "What is it determines the will?" the true and proper answer is, The mind. For that which determines the general power of directing to this or that particular direction, is nothing but the agent itself exercising the power it has that particular way. If this answer satisfies not, it is plain the meaning of the question, "What determines the will?" is this, "What moves the mind in every particular instance to determine its general power of directing to this or that particular motion or rest?" And to this I answer, The motive for continuing in the same state or action is only the present satisfaction in it; the motive to change is always some uneasiness; nothing setting us upon the change of state, or upon any new action, but some uneasiness. This is the great motive that works on the mind to put it upon action, which for shortness' sake we will call "determining of the will"; which I shall more at large explain.

30. *Will and desire must not be confounded.* But, in the way to it, it will be necessary to premise, that though I have above endeavored to express the act of volition by "choosing, preferring," and the like terms, that signify desire as well as volition, for want of other words to mark that act of the mind whose proper name is "willing" or "volition"; yet it being a very simple act, whosoever desires to understand what it is, will better find it by reflecting on his own mind, and observing what it does when it wills, than by any variety of articulate sounds whatsoever. This caution of being careful not to be misled by expressions that do not enough keep up the difference between the will and several acts of the mind that are quite distinct from it, I think the more necessary, because I find the will often confounded with several of the affections, especially desire; and one put for the other, and that by men who would not willingly be thought not to have had very distinct notions of things, and not to have

writ very clearly about them. This, I imagine, has been no small occasion of obscurity and mistake in this matter, and therefore is as much as may be to be avoided; for he that shall turn his thoughts inward upon what passes in his mind when he wills, shall see that the will or power of volition is conversant about nothing but that particular determination of the mind whereby, barely by a thought, the mind endeavors to give rise, continuation, or stop to any action which it takes to be in its power. This, well considered, plainly shows that the will is perfectly distinguished from desire, which in the very same action may have a quite contrary tendency from that which our will sets us upon. A man, whom I cannot deny, may oblige me to use persuasions to another, which, at the same time I am speaking, I may wish may not prevail on him. In this case, it is plain the will and desire run counter. I will the action that tends one way, whilst my desire tends another, and that the direct contrary. A man who, by a violent fit of the gout in his limbs, finds a doziness in his head or a want of appetite in his stomach removed, desires to be eased too of the pain of his feet or hands (for wherever there is pain there is a desire to be rid of it), though yet, whilst he apprehends that the removal of the pain may translate the noxious humor to a more vital part, his will is never determined to any one action that may serve to remove this pain. Whence it is evident that desiring and willing are two distinct acts of the mind, and consequently that the will, which is but the power of volition, is much more distinct from desire.

31. *Uneasiness determines the will.* To return, then, to the inquiry, "What is it that determines the will in regard to our actions?" And that upon second thoughts I am apt to imagine, is not, as is generally supposed, the greater good in view, but some (and, for the most part, the most pressing) uneasiness a man is at present under. This is that which successively determines the will, and sets us upon those actions we perform. This uneasiness we may call, as it is, "desire"; which is an uneasiness of the mind for want of some absent good. All pain of the body, of what sort soever, and disquiet of the mind, is uneasiness; and with this is always joined desire equal to the pain or uneasiness felt, and is scarce distinguishable from it. For, desire being nothing but an uneasiness in the want of an absent good, in reference to any pain felt, ease is that absent good; and till that ease be attained, we may call it desire, nobody feeling pain that he wishes not to be eased of with a desire equal to that pain, and inseparable from it. Besides this desire of ease from pain, there is another of absent positive good; and here also the desire and uneasiness are equal. As much as we desire any absent good, so much are we in pain for it. But here all absent good does not, according to the greatness it has, or is acknowledged to have, cause pain equal to that greatness; as all pain causes desire equal to itself: because the absence of good is not always a pain, as the presence of pain is. And therefore absent good may be looked on and considered without desire. But so much as there is anywhere of desire, so much there is of uneasiness.

32. *Desire is uneasiness.* That desire is a state of uneasiness, everyone who reflects on himself will quickly find. Who is there that has not felt in desire what the wise man says of hope (which is not much different from it), that it being deferred makes the heart sick? and that still proportionable to the greatness of the desire, which sometimes raises the uneasiness to that pitch that it makes people cry out, "Give me children," give me the thing desired, "or I die"? Life itself, and all its enjoyments, is a burden cannot be borne under the lasting and unremoved pressure of such an uneasiness.

33. *The uneasiness of desire determines the will.* Good and evil, present and absent, it is true, work upon the mind; but that which immediately determines the will, from time to time, to every voluntary action, is the uneasiness of desire, fixed on some absent good, either negative, as indolency to one in pain, or positive, as enjoyment of pleasure. That it is this uneasiness that determines the will to the successive voluntary actions whereof the greatest part of our lives is made up, and by which we are conducted through different courses to different ends, I shall endeavor to show both from experience and the reason of the thing.

Of the Idea of Necessary Connection*

PART I

The great advantage of the mathematical sciences above the moral consists in this, that the ideas of the former, being sensible, are always clear and determinate, the smallest distinction between them is immediately perceptible, and the same terms are still expressive of the same ideas without ambiguity or variation. An oval is never mistaken for a circle, nor a hyperbola for an ellipsis. The isosceles and scalenum are distinguished by boundaries more exact than vice and virtue, right and wrong. If any term be defined in geometry, the mind readily, of itself, substitutes on all occasions the definition for the term defined, or, even when no definition is employed, the object itself may be presented to the senses and by that means be steadily and clearly apprehended. But the finer sentiments of the mind, the operations of the understanding, the various agitations of the passions, though really in themselves distinct, easily escape us when surveyed by reflection, nor is it in our power to recall the original object as often as we have occasion to contemplate it. Ambiguity, by this means, is gradually introduced into our reasonings: similar objects are readily taken to be the same, and the conclusion becomes at last very wide of the premises.

One may safely, however, affirm that if we consider these sciences in a proper light, their advantages and disadvantages nearly compensate each other and reduce both of them to a state of equality. If the mind, with greater facility, retains the ideas of geometry clear and determinate, it must carry on a much longer and more intricate chain of reasoning and compare ideas much wider of each other in order to reach the abstruser truths of that science. And if moral ideas are apt, without extreme care, to fall into obscurity and confusion, the inferences are always much shorter in these disquisitions, and the intermediate steps which lead to the conclusion much fewer than in the sciences which treat of quantity and number. In reality, there is scarcely a proposition in Euclid so simple as not to consist of more parts than are to be found in

any moral reasoning which runs not into chimera and conceit. Where we trace the principles of the human mind through a few steps, we may be very well satisfied with our progress, considering how soon nature throws a bar to all our inquiries concerning causes and reduces us to an acknowledgment of our ignorance. The chief obstacle, therefore, to our improvement in the moral or metaphysical sciences is the obscurity of the ideas and ambiguity of the terms. The principal difficulty in the mathematics is the length of inferences and compass of thought requisite to the forming of any conclusion. And, perhaps, our progress in natural philosophy is chiefly retarded by the want of proper experiments and phenomena, which are often discovered by chance and cannot always be found when requisite, even by the most diligent and prudent inquiry. As moral philosophy seems hitherto to have received less improvement than either geometry or physics, we may conclude that if there be any difference in this respect among these sciences, the difficulties which obstruct the progress of the former require superior care and capacity to be surmounted.

There are no ideas which occur in metaphysics more obscure and uncertain than those of "power," "force," "energy," or "necessary connection," of which it is every moment necessary for us to treat in all our disquisitions. We shall, therefore, endeavor in this Section to fix, if possible, the precise meaning of these terms and thereby remove some part of that obscurity which is so much complained of in this species of philosophy.

It seems a proposition which will not admit of much dispute that all our ideas are nothing but copies of our impressions, or, in other words, that it is impossible for us to *think* of anything which we have not antecedently *felt,* either by our external or internal senses. I have endeavored to explain and prove this proposition, and have expressed my hopes that by a proper application of it men may reach a greater clearness and precision in philosophical reasonings than what they have hitherto been able to attain. Complex ideas may, perhaps, be well known by definition, which is nothing but an enumeration of those parts or simple ideas that compose them. But when we have pushed up definitions to the

* David Hume, *Enquiry Concerning the Human Understanding*, 2d ed. (Oxford: Clarendon Press, 1902), pp. 60–77.

most simple ideas and find still some ambiguity and obscurity, what resources are we then possessed of? By what invention can we throw light upon these ideas and render them altogether precise and determinate to our intellectual view? Produce the impressions or original sentiments from which the ideas are copied. These impressions are all strong and sensible. They admit not of ambiguity. They are not only placed in a full light themselves, but may throw light on their correspondent ideas, which lie in obscurity. And by this means we may perhaps obtain a new microscope or species of optics by which, in the moral sciences, the most minute and most simple ideas may be so enlarged as to fall readily under our apprehension and be equally known with the grossest and most sensible ideas that can be the object of our inquiry.

To be fully acquainted, therefore, with the idea of power or necessary connection, let us examine its impression and, in order to find the impression with greater certainty, let us search for it in all the sources from which it may possibly be derived.

When we look about us toward external objects and consider the operation of causes, we are never able, in a single instance, to discover any power or necessary connection, any quality which binds the effect to the cause and renders the one an infallible consequence of the other. We only find that the one does actually in fact follow the other. The impulse of one billiard ball is attended with motion in the second. This is the whole that appears to the *outward* senses. The mind feels no sentiment or *inward* impression from this succession of objects; consequently, there is not, in any single particular instance of cause and effect, anything which can suggest the idea of power or necessary connection.

From the first appearance of an object we never can conjecture what effect will result from it. But were the power or energy of any cause discoverable by the mind, we could foresee the effect, even without experience, and might, at first, pronounce with certainty concerning it by the mere dint of thought and reasoning.

In reality, there is no part of matter that does ever, by its sensible qualities, discover any power or energy, or give us ground to imagine that it could produce anything, or be followed by any other object, which we could denominate its effect. Solidity, extension, mo-

tion—these qualities are all complete in themselves and never point out any other event which may result from them. The scenes of the universe are continually shifting, and one object follows another in an uninterrupted succession; but the power or force which actuates the whole machine is entirely concealed from us and never discovers itself in any of the sensible qualities of body. We know that, in fact, heat is a constant attendant of flame; but what is the connection between them we have no room so much as to conjecture or imagine. It is impossible, therefore, that the idea of power can be derived from the contemplation of bodies in single instances of their operation, because no bodies ever discover any power which can be the original of this idea.[1]

Since, therefore, external objects as they appear to the senses give us no idea of power or necessary connection by their operation in particular instances, let us see whether this idea be derived from reflection on the operations of our own minds and be copied from any internal impression. It may be said that we are every moment conscious of internal power while we feel that, by the simple command of our will, we can move the organs of our body or direct the faculties of our mind. An act of volition produces motion in our limbs or raises a new idea in our imagination. This influence of the will we know by consciousness. Hence we acquire the idea of power or energy, and are certain that we ourselves and all other intelligent beings are possessed of power. This idea, then, is an idea of reflection since it arises from reflecting on the operations of our own mind and on the command which is exercised by will both over the organs of the body and faculties of the soul.

We shall proceed to examine this pretension and, first, with regard to the influence of volition over the organs of the body. This influence, we may observe, is a fact which, like all other natural events, can be known only by experience, and can never be foreseen from any apparent energy or power in the

---

[1] Mr. Locke, in his chapter of Power, says that, finding from experience that there are several new productions in matter, and concluding that there must somewhere be a power capable of producing them, we arrive at last by this reasoning at the idea of power. But no reasoning can ever give us a new, original, simple idea, as this philosopher himself confesses. This, therefore, can never be the origin of that idea.

cause which connects it with the effect and renders the one an infallible consequence of the other. The motion of our body follows upon the command of our will. Of this we are every moment conscious. But the means by which this is effected, the energy by which the will performs so extraordinary an operation—of this we are so far from being immediately conscious that it must forever escape our most diligent inquiry.

For, *first,* is there any principle in all nature more mysterious than the union of soul with body, by which a supposed spiritual substance acquires such an influence over a material one that the most refined thought is able to actuate the grossest matter? Were we empowered by a secret wish to remove mountains or control the planets in their orbit, this extensive authority would not be more extraordinary, nor more beyond our comprehension. But if, by consciousness, we perceived any power or energy in the will, we must know this power; we must know its connection with the effect; we must know the secret union of soul and body, and the nature of both these substances by which the one is able to operate in so many instances upon the other.

Secondly, we are not able to move all the organs of the body with a like authority, though we cannot assign any reason, besides experience, for so remarkable a difference between one and the other. Why has the will an influence over the tongue and fingers, not over the heart or liver? This question would never embarrass us were we conscious of a power in the former case, not in the latter. We should then perceive, independent of experience, why the authority of the will over the organs of the body is circumscribed within such particular limits. Being in that case fully acquainted with the power or force by which it operates, we should also know why its influence reaches precisely to such boundaries, and no further.

A man suddenly struck with a palsy in the leg or arm, or who had newly lost those members, frequently endeavors, at first, to move them and employ them in their usual offices. Here he is as much conscious of power to command such limbs as a man in perfect health is conscious of power to actuate any member which remains in its natural state and condition. But consciousness never deceives. Consequently, neither in the one

case nor in the other are we ever conscious of any power. We learn the influence of our will from experience alone. And experience only teaches us how one event constantly follows another, without instructing us in the secret connection which binds them together and renders them inseparable.

Thirdly, we learn from anatomy that the immediate object of power in voluntary motion is not the member itself which is moved, but certain muscles and nerves and animal spirits, and, perhaps, something still more minute and more unknown, through which the motion is successively propagated ere it reach the member itself whose motion is the immediate object of volition. Can there be a more certain proof that the power by which this whole operation is performed, so far from being directly and fully known by an inward sentiment or consciousness, is to the last degree mysterious and unintelligible? Here the mind wills a certain event; immediately another event, unknown to ourselves and totally different from the one intended, is produced. This event produces another, equally unknown, till, at last, through a long succession the desired event is produced. But if the original power were felt, it must be known; were it known, its effect must also be known, since all power is relative to its effect. And, vice versa, if the effect be not known, the power cannot be known nor felt. How indeed can we be conscious of a power to move our limbs when we have no such power, but only that to move certain animal spirits which, though they produce at last the motion of our limbs, yet operate in such a manner as is wholly beyond our comprehension?

We may therefore conclude from the whole, I hope, without any temerity, though with assurance, that our idea of power is not copied from any sentiment or consciousness of power within ourselves when we give rise to animal motion or apply our limbs to their proper use and office. That their motion follows the command of the will is a matter of common experience, like other natural events; but the power or energy by which this is effected, like that in other natural events, is unknown and inconceivable.[2]

[2] It may be pretended, that the resistance which we meet with in bodies, obliging us frequently to exert our force and call up all our power, this gives us the idea of force and power. It is this *nisus* or strong endeavor of which we are conscious, that is the original impression from which this idea is copied. But,

Shall we then assert that we are conscious of a power or energy in our own minds when, by an act or command of our will, we raise up a new idea, fix the mind to the contemplation of it, turn it on all sides, and at last dismiss it for some other idea when we think that we have surveyed it with sufficient accuracy? I believe the same arguments will prove that even this command of the will gives us no real idea of force or energy.

First, it must be allowed that when we know a power, we know that very circumstance in the cause by which it is enabled to produce the effect, for these are supposed to be synonymous. We must, therefore, know both the cause and effect and the relation between them. But do we pretend to be acquainted with the nature of the human soul and the nature of an idea, or the aptitude of the one to produce the other? This is a real creation, a production of something out of nothing, which implies a power so great that it may seem, at first sight, beyond the reach of any being less than infinite. At least it must be owned that such a power is not felt, nor known, nor even conceivable by the mind. We only feel the event, namely, the existence of an idea consequent to a command of the will; but the manner in which this operation is performed, the power by which it is produced, is entirely beyond our comprehension.

Secondly, the command of the mind over itself is limited, as well as its command over the body; and these limits are not known by reason or any acquaintance with the nature of cause and effect, but only by experience and observation, as in all other natural events and in the operation of external objects. Our authority over our sentiments and passions is much weaker than that over our ideas; and even the latter authority is circumscribed within very narrow boundaries. Will anyone

pretend to assign the ultimate reason of these boundaries, or show why the power is deficient in one case, not in another?

Thirdly, this self-command is very different at different times. A man in health possesses more of it than one languishing with sickness. We are more master of our thoughts in the morning than in the evening; fasting, than after a full meal. Can we give any reason for these variations except experience? Where then is the power of which we pretend to be conscious? Is there not here, either in a spiritual or material substance, or both, some secret mechanism or structure of parts upon which the effect depends, and which, being entirely unknown to us, renders the power or energy of the will equally unknown and incomprehensible?

Volition is surely an act of the mind with which we are sufficiently acquainted. Reflect upon it. Consider it on all sides. Do you find anything in it like this creative power by which it raises from nothing a new idea and, with a kind of *fiat,* imitates the omnipotence of its Maker, if I may be allowed so to speak, who called forth into existence all the various scenes of nature? So far from being conscious of this energy in the will, it requires as certain experience as that of which we are possessed to convince us that such extraordinary effects do ever result from a simple act of volition.

· · ·

PART II

But to hasten to a conclusion of this argument, which is already drawn out to too great a length: We have sought in vain for an idea of power or necessary connection in all the sources from which we would suppose it to be derived. It appears that in single instances of the operation of bodies we never can, by our utmost scrutiny, discover anything but one event following another, without being able to comprehend any force or power by which the cause operates or any connection between it and its supposed effect. The same difficulty occurs in contemplating the operations of mind on body, where we observe the motion of the latter to follow upon the volition of the former, but are not able to observe or conceive the tie which binds together the motion and volition, or the energy, by which the mind produces this effect. The authority of the will over its own faculties and ideas

---

first, we attribute power to a vast number of objects where we never can suppose this resistance or exertion of force to take place to the Supreme Being, who never meets with any resistance; to the mind in its command over its ideas and limbs, in common thinking and motion, where the effect follows immediately upon the will, without any exertion or summoning up of force; to inanimate matter, which is not capable of this sentiment. *Secondly,* this sentiment of an endeavor to overcome resistance has no known connection with any event: What follows it we know by experience, but could not know it *a priori.* It must, however, be confessed that the animal *nisus* which we experience, though it can afford no accurate precise idea of power, enters very much into that vulgar, inaccurate idea which is formed of it.

is not a whit more comprehensible, so that, upon the whole, there appears not, throughout all nature, any one instance of connection which is conceivable by us. All events seem entirely loose and separate. One event follows another, but we never can observe any tie between them. They seem *conjoined,* but never *connected.* But as we can have no idea of anything which never appeared to our outward sense or inward sentiment, the necessary conclusion *seems* to be that we have no idea of connection or power at all, and that these words are absolutely without any meaning when employed either in philosophical reasonings or common life.

But there still remains one method of avoiding this conclusion, and one source which we have not yet examined. When any natural object or event is presented, it is impossible for us, by any sagacity or penetration, to discover, or even conjecture, without experience, what event will result from it, or to carry our foresight beyond that object which is immediately present to the memory and senses. Even after one instance or experiment where we have observed a particular event to follow upon another, we are not entitled to form a general rule or foretell what will happen in like cases, it being justly esteemed an unpardonable temerity to judge of the whole course of nature from one single experiment, however accurate or certain. But when one particular species of events has always, in all instances, been conjoined with another, we make no longer any scruple of foretelling one upon the appearance of the other, and of employing that reasoning which can alone assure us of any matter of fact or existence. We then call the one object "cause," the other "effect." We suppose that there is some connection between them, some power in the one by which it infallibly produces the other and operates with the greatest certainty and strongest necessity.

It appears, then, that this idea of a necessary connection among events arises from a number of similar instances which occur, of the constant conjunction of these events; nor can that idea ever be suggested by any one of these instances surveyed in all possible lights and positions. But there is nothing in a number of instances, different from every single instance, which is supposed to be exactly similar, except only that after a repetition of similar instances the mind is carried by habit, upon the appearance of one event, to expect its usual attendant and to believe that it will exist. This connection, therefore, which we *feel* in the mind, this customary transition of the imagination from one object to its usual attendant, is the sentiment or impression from which we form the idea of power or necessary connection. Nothing further is in the case. Contemplate the subjects on all sides, you will never find any other origin of that idea. This is the sole difference between one instance, from which we can never receive the idea of connection, and a number of similar instances by which it is suggested. The first time a man saw the communication of motion by impulse, as by the shock of two billiard balls, he could not pronounce that the one event was *connected,* but only that it was *conjoined* with the other. After he has observed several instances of this nature, he then pronounces them to be *connected.* What alteration has happened to give rise to this new idea of *connection?* Nothing but that he now *feels* these events to be *connected* in his imagination, and can readily foretell the existence of one from the appearance of the other. When we say, therefore, that one object is connected with another, we mean only that they have acquired a connection in our thoughts and gave rise to this inference by which they become proofs of each other's existence—a conclusion which is somewhat extraordinary, but which seems founded on sufficient evidence. Nor will its evidence be weakened by any general diffidence of the understanding or skeptical suspicion concerning every conclusion which is new and extraordinary. No conclusions can be more agreeable to skepticism than such as make discoveries concerning the weakness and narrow limits of human reason and capacity.

And what stronger instance can be produced of the surprising ignorance and weakness of the understanding than the present? For surely, if there be any relation among objects which it imports us to know perfectly, it is that of cause and effect. On this are founded all our reasonings concerning matter of fact or existence. By means of it alone we attain any assurance concerning objects which are removed from the present testimony of our memory and senses. The only immediate utility of all sciences is to teach us how to control and regulate future events by their causes. Our thoughts and inquiries are, therefore, every moment employed about this relation; yet so imperfect are the ideas which we form concerning it that it is impossible to give any just definition of cause, except what is drawn from something extraneous and foreign to it. Similar objects are always conjoined with similar. Of this we have experience. Suitably to this experience, therefore, we may define a cause to be *an object followed by another, and where all the objects, similar to the first, are followed by objects similar to the second.* Or, in other words, *where, if the first object had not been, the second never had existed.* The appearance of a cause always conveys the mind, by a customary transition, to the idea of the effect. Of this also we have experience. We may, therefore, suitably to this experience, form another definition of cause and call it *an object followed by another, and whose appearance always conveys the thought to that other.* But though both these definitions be drawn from circumstances foreign to the cause, we cannot remedy this inconvenience or attain any more perfect definition which may point out that circumstance in the cause which gives it a connection with its effect. We have no idea of this connection, nor even any distinct notion what it is we desire to know when we endeavor at a conception of it. We say, for instance, that the vibration of this string is the cause of this particular sound. But what do we mean by that affirmation? We either mean *that this vibration is followed by this sound, and that all similar vibrations have been followed by similar sounds; or, that this vibration is followed by this sound, and that, upon the appearance of one, the mind anticipates the senses and forms immediately an idea of the other.* We may consider the relation of cause and effect in either of these two lights; but beyond these we have no idea of it.[3]

[3] According to these explications and definitions, the idea of *power* is relative as much as that of *cause*; and both have a reference to an effect, or some other event constantly conjoined with the former. When we consider the unknown circumstance of an object by which the degree or quantity of its effect is fixed and determined, we call that its power. And accordingly, it is allowed by all philosophers that the effect is the measure of the power. But if they had any idea of power as it is in itself, why could they not measure it in itself? The dispute, whether the force of a body in motion be as its velocity, or the square of its velocity; this dispute, I say, need not be decided by comparing its effects in equal or unequal times, but by a direct mensuration and comparison.

As to the frequent use of the words "force," "power," "energy," etc., which everywhere occur in common conversation as well as in philosophy, that is no proof that we are acquainted, in any instance, with the connecting principle between cause and effect, or can account ultimately for the production of one thing by another. These words, as commonly used, have very loose meanings annexed to them, and their ideas are very uncertain and confused. No animal can put external bodies in motion without the sentiment of a *nisus* or endeavor; and every animal has a sentiment or feeling from the stroke or blow of an external object that is in motion. These sensations, which are merely animal, and from which we can a *priori* draw no inference, we are apt to transfer to inanimate objects, and to suppose that they have some such feelings whenever they transfer or receive motion. With regard to energies, which are exerted without our annexing to them any idea of communicated motion, we consider only the constant experienced conjunction of the events; and as we *feel* a customary connection between the ideas, we transfer that feeling to the objects, as nothing is more usual than to apply to external bodies every internal sensation which they occasion.

The Objectification of the Will*

... Thus we see already that we can never arrive at the real nature of things from without. However much we investigate, we can never reach anything but images and names. We are like a man who goes round a castle seeking in vain for an entrance, and sometimes sketching the façades. And yet this is the method that has been followed by all philosophers before me.

* Arthur Schopenhauer, *The World as Will and Idea,* trans. R. B. Haldane and J. Kemp (London: Routledge & Kegan Paul Ltd., 1883) 3 Vols., I, 128–33; II, 405–8, reprinted by permission of the publishers. Footnotes are omitted.

§ 18. In fact, the meaning for which we seek of that world which is present to us only as our idea, or the transition from the world as mere idea of the knowing subject to whatever it may be besides this, would never be found if the investigator himself were nothing more than the pure knowing subject (a winged cherub without a body). But he is himself rooted in that world; he finds himself in it as an *individual,* that is to say, his knowledge, which is the necessary supporter of the whole world as idea, is yet always given through the medium of a body, whose affections are, as we have shown, the starting-point for the understanding in the perception of that world. His body is, for the pure knowing subject, an idea like every other idea, an object among objects. Its movements and actions are so far known to him in precisely the same way as the changes of all other perceived objects, and would be just as strange and incomprehensible to him if their meaning were not explained for him in an entirely different way. Otherwise he would see his actions follow upon given motives with the constancy of a law of nature, just as the changes of other objects follow upon causes, stimuli, or motives. But he would not understand the influence of the motives any more than the connection between every other effect which he sees and its cause. He would then call the inner nature of these manifestations and actions of his body which he did not understand a force, a quality, or a character, as he pleased, but he would have no further insight into it. But all this is not the case; indeed the answer to the riddle is given to the subject of knowledge who appears as an individual, and the answer is *will*. This and this alone gives him the key to his own existence, reveals to him the significance, shows him the inner mechanism of his being, of his action, of his movements. The body is given in two entirely different ways to the subject of knowledge, who becomes an individual only through his identity with it. It is given as an idea in intelligent perception, as an object among objects and subject to the laws of objects. And it is also given in quite a different way as that which is immediately known to everyone, and is signified by the word *will*. Every true act of his will is also at once and without exception a movement of his body. The act of will and the movement of the body are not two different things objectively known, which the bond of causality unites; they do not stand in the relation of cause and effect; they are one and the same, but they are given in entirely different ways— immediately, and again in perception for the understanding. The action of the body is nothing but the act of the will objectified, i.e., passed into perception. It will appear later that this is true of every movement of the body, not merely those which follow upon motives, but also involuntary movements which follow upon mere stimuli, and, indeed, that the whole body is nothing but objectified

will, i.e., will become idea. All this will be proved and made quite clear in the course of this work. In one respect, therefore, I shall call the body the *objectivity of will*; as in the previous book, and in the essay on the principle of sufficient reason, in accordance with the one-sided point of view intentionally adopted there (that of the idea), I called it *the immediate object*. Thus in a certain sense we may also say that will is the knowledge *a priori* of the body, and the body is the knowledge *a posteriori* of the will. Resolutions of the will which relate to the future are merely deliberations of the reason about what we shall will at a particular time, not real acts of will. Only the carrying out of the resolve stamps it as will, for till then it is never more than an intention that may be changed, and that exists only in the reason *in abstracto*. It is only in reflection that to will and to act are different; in reality they are one. Every true, genuine, immediate act of will is also, at once and immediately, a visible act of the body. And corresponding to this, every impression upon the body is also, on the other hand, at once and immediately an impression upon the will. As such it is called pain when it is opposed to the will; gratification or pleasure when it is in accordance with it. The degrees of both are widely different. It is quite wrong, however, to call pain and pleasure ideas, for they are by no means ideas, but immediate affections of the will in its manifestation, the body; compulsory, instantaneous willing or not-willing of the impression which the body sustains. There are only a few impressions of the body which do not touch the will and it is through these alone that the body is an immediate object of knowledge, for, as perceived by the understanding, it is already an indirect object like all others. These impressions are, therefore, to be treated directly as mere ideas, and excepted from what has been said. The impressions we refer to are the affections of the purely objective senses of sight, hearing, and touch, though only so far as these organs are affected in the way which is specially peculiar to their specific nature. This affection of them is so excessively weak an excitement of the heightened and specifically modified sensibility of these parts that it does not affect the will, but only furnishes the understanding with the data out of which the perception arises, undisturbed by any excitement of the will. But every stronger or different kind of affection of these organs of sense is painful, that is to say, against the will, and thus they also belong to its objectivity. Weakness of the nerves shows itself in this, that the impressions which have only such a degree of strength as would usually be sufficient to make them data for the understanding reach the higher degree at which they influence the will, that is to say, give pain or pleasure, though more often pain, which is, however, to some extent deadened and inarticulate, so that not only particular tones and strong light are painful to us, but there ensues a generally unhealthy and hypochondriacal disposition which is not distinctly understood. The identity of the body and the will shows itself further, among other ways, in the circumstance that every vehement and excessive movement of the will, i.e., every emotion, agitates the body and its inner constitution directly, and disturbs the course of its vital functions. . . .

Lastly, the knowledge which I have of my will, though it is immediate, cannot be separated from that which I have of my body. I know my will, not as a whole, not as a unity, not completely, according to its nature, but I know it only in its particular acts, and therefore in time, which is the form of the phenomenal aspect of my body, as of every object. Therefore the body is a condition of the knowledge of my will. Thus, I cannot really imagine this will apart from my body. . . . So far as I know my will specially as object, I know it as body.

. . .

. . . We can turn the expression of this truth in different ways and say: My body and my will are one; or, What as an idea of perception I call my body, I call my will, so far as I am conscious of it in an entirely different way which cannot be compared to any other; or My body is the *objectivity* of my will; or, My body considered apart from the fact that it is my idea is still my will, and so forth.

. . .

Kant's chief result may in substance be thus concisely stated: "All conceptions which have not at their foundation a perception in space and time (sensuous intuition), that is to say then, which have not been drawn from such a perception, are absolutely empty, i.e., give no knowledge. But since now perception can afford us only *phenomena,* not things in them-selves, we have also absolutely no knowledge of things-in-themselves." I grant this of everything, with the single exception of the knowledge which each of us has of his own *willing* : this is neither a perception (for all perception is spatial) nor is it empty; rather it is more real than any other. Further, it is not *a priori,* like merely formal knowledge, but entirely *a posteriori*; hence also we cannot anticipate it in the particular case, but are hereby often convicted of error concerning ourselves. In fact, our *willing* is the one opportunity which we have of understanding from within any event which exhibits itself without, consequently the one thing which is known to us *immediately,* and not, like all the rest, merely given in the idea. Here, then, lies the datum which alone is able to become the key to everything else, or, as I have said, the single narrow door to the truth. Accordingly we must learn to understand nature from ourselves, not conversely ourselves from nature. What is known to us immediately must give us the explanation of what we only know indirectly, not conversely. Do we perhaps understand the rolling of a ball when it has received an impulse more thoroughly than our movement when we feel a motive? Many imagine so, but I say it is the reverse. Yet we shall attain to the knowledge that what is essential in both the occurrences just mentioned is identical; although identical in the same way as the lowest audible note of harmony is the same as the note of the same name ten octaves higher.

Meanwhile it should be carefully observed, and I have always kept it in mind, that even the inward experience which we have of our own will by no means affords us an exhaustive and adequate knowledge of the thing-in-itself. This would be the case if it were entirely an immediate experience; but it is effected in this way: the will, with and by means of the corporization, provides itself with an intellect (for the sake of its relations to the external world), and through this now knows itself as will in self-consciousness (the necessary counterpart of the external world); this knowledge therefore of the thing-in-itself is not fully adequate. First of all, it is bound to the form of the idea, it is apprehension, and as such falls asunder into subject and object. For even in self-consciousness the I is not absolutely simple, but consists of a knower—the intellect—and a known—the will. The former is not known, and the latter does not know, though both unite in the consciousness of an I. But just on this account that I is not thoroughly *intimate* with itself, as it were transparent, but is opaque, and therefore remains a riddle to itself, thus even in inner knowledge there also exists a difference between the true being of its object and the apprehension of it in the knowing subject. Yet inner knowledge is free from two forms which belong to outer knowledge, the form of *space* and the form of *causality,* which is the means of effecting all sense-perception. On the other hand, there still remains the form of *time,* and that of being known and knowing in general. Accordingly in this inner knowledge the thing-in-itself has indeed in great measure thrown off its veil, but still does not yet appear quite naked. In consequence of the form of time which still adheres to it, everyone knows his will only in its successive *acts,* and not as a whole, in and for itself: therefore no one knows his character *a priori,* but only learns it through experience and always incompletely. But yet the aprehension, in which we know the affections and acts of our own will, is far more immediate than any other. It is the point at which the thing-in-itself most directly enters the phenomenon and is most closely examined by the knowing subject; therefore the event thus intimately known is alone fitted to become the interpreter of all others.

For in every emergence of an act of will from the obscure depths of our inner being into the knowing consciousness a direct transition occurs of the thing-in-itself, which lies outside time, into the phenomenal world. Accordingly, the act of will is indeed only the closest and most distinct *manifestation* of the thing-in-itself; yet it follows from this that if all other manifestations or phenomena could be known by us as directly and inwardly, we would be obliged to assert them to be that which the will is in us. Thus in this sense I teach that the inner nature of everything is

will, and I call will the thing-in-itself. Kant's doctrine of the unknowableness of the thing-in-itself is hereby modified to this extent, that the thing-in-itself is only not absolutely and from the very foundation knowable, that yet by far the most immediate of its phenomena, which by this immediately is *toto genere* distinguished from all the rest, represents it for us; and accordingly we have to refer the whole world of phenomena to that one in which the thing-in-itself appears in the very thinnest of veils, and only still remains phenomenon in so far as my intellect, which alone is capable of knowledge, remains ever distinguished from me as the willing subject, and moreover does not even in *inner* perfection put off the form of knowledge of *time.*

Accordingly, even after this last and furthest step, the question may still be raised, what that will, which exhibits itself in the world and as the world, ultimately and absolutely is in itself? i.e., what it is, regarded altogether apart from the fact that it exhibits itself as will, or in general *appears,* i.e., in general is *known.* This question can never be answered: because, as we have said, becoming known is itself the contradictory of being in itself, and everything that is known is as such only phenomenal. But the possibility of this question shows that the thing-in-itself, which we know most directly in the will, may have, entirely outside all possible phenomenal appearance, ways of existing, determinations, qualities, which are absolutely unknowable and incomprehensible to us, and which remain as the nature of the thing-in-itself, when, as is explained in the fourth book, it has voluntarily abrogated itself as *will,* and has therefore retired altogether from the phenomenon, and for our knowledge, i.e., as regards the world of phenomena, has passed into empty nothingness. If the will were simply and absolutely the thing-in-itself this nothing would also be *absolute,* instead of which it expressly presents itself to us there as only *relative.*

Will*

Desire, wish, will, are states of mind which everyone knows, and which no definition can

* William James, *The Principles of Psychology* (London: Macmillan and Co., 1902), Vol. II, pp. 468–93, 518–28, 560–69, reprinted by permission of Holt, Rinehart and Winston, Inc., New York. Footnotes are renumbered.

make plainer. We desire to feel, to have, to do, all sorts of things which at the moment are not felt, had, or done. If with the desire there goes a sense that attainment is not possible, we simply *wish*; but if we believe that the end is in our power, we *will* that the desired feeling, having, or doing shall be real; and real it presently becomes, either immediately upon the willing or after certain preliminaries have been fulfilled.

The only ends which follow *immediately* upon our willing seem to be movements of our own bodies. Whatever *feelings* and *havings* we may will to get, come in as results of preliminary movements which we make for the purpose. This fact is too familiar to need illustration, so that we may start with the proposition that the only *direct* outward effects of our will are bodily movements. The mechanism of production of these voluntary movements is what befalls us to study now. The subject involves a good many separate points which it is difficult to arrange in any continuous logical order. I will treat of them successively in the mere order of convenience; trusting that at the end the reader will gain a clear and connected view.

The movements we have studied hitherto have been automatic and reflex, and (on the first occasion of their performance, at any rate) unforeseen by the agent. The movements to the study of which we now address ourselves, being desired and intended beforehand, are of course done with full prevision of what they are to be. It follows from this that *voluntary movements must be secondary, not primary functions of our organism.* This is the first point to understand in the psychology of Volition. Reflex, instinctive, and emotional movements are all primary performances. The nerve-centers are so organized that certain stimuli pull the trigger of certain explosive parts; and a creature going through one of these explosions for the first time undergoes an entirely novel experience. . . . Of course if such a reaction has many times occurred we learn what to expect of ourselves, and can then foresee our conduct, even though it remain as involuntary and uncontrollable as it was before. But if, in voluntary action properly so-called, the act must be foreseen, it follows that no creature not endowed with divinatory power can perform an act voluntarily for the first time. Well, we are no more endowed with prophetic vision of what movements lie in our power, than we are endowed with prophetic vision of what sensations we are capable of receiving. As we must wait for the sensations to be given us, so we must wait for the movements to be

performed involuntarily,[1] before we can frame ideas of what either of these things are. We learn all our possibilities by the way of experience. When a particular movement, having once occurred in a random, reflex, or involuntary way, has left an image of itself in the memory, then the movement can be desired again, proposed as an end, and deliberately willed. But it is impossible to see how it could be willed before.

A supply of ideas of the various movements that are possible left in the memory by experiences of their involuntary performance is thus the first prerequisite of the voluntary life.

Now the same movement involuntarily performed may leave many different kinds of ideas of itself in the memory. If performed by another person, we of course *see* it, or we *feel* it if the moving part strikes another part of our own body. Similarly we have an auditory image of its effects if it produces sounds, as for example when it is one of the movements made in vocalization, or in playing on a musical instrument. All these *remote* effects of the movement, as we may call them, are also produced by movements which we ourselves perform; and they leave innumerable ideas in our mind by which we distinguish each movement from the rest. It *looks* distinct; it *feels* distinct to some distant part of the body which it strikes; or it *sounds* distinct. These remote effects would then, rigorously speaking, suffice to furnish the mind with the supply of ideas required.

But in addition to these impressions upon remote organs of sense, we have, whenever we perform a movement ourselves, another set of impressions, those, namely, which come up from the parts that are actually moved. These *kinesthetic* impressions . . . are so many *resident* effects of the motion. Not only are our muscles supplied with afferent as well as with efferent nerves, but the tendons, the ligaments, the articular surfaces, and the skin about the joints are all sensitive, and, being stretched and squeezed in ways characteristic of each particular movement, give us as many distinctive feelings as there are movements possible to perform.

It is by these resident impressions that we are made conscious of *passive movements*— movements communicated to our limbs by

---

[1] I am abstracting at present for simplicity's sake, and so as to keep to the elements of the matter, from the learning of acts by seeing others do them.

others. If you lie with closed eyes, and another person noiselessly places your arm or leg in any arbitrarily chosen attitude, you receive an accurate feeling of what attitude it is, and can immediately reproduce it yourself in the arm or leg of the opposite side. Similarly a man waked suddenly from sleep in the dark is aware of how he finds himself lying. At least this is what happens when the nervous apparatus is normal. But in cases of disease we sometimes find that the resident impressions do not normally excite the centers, and that then the sense of attitude is lost. . . .

When the feelings of passive movement as well as all the other feelings of a limb are lost, we get such results as are given in the following account by Professor A. Strümpell of his wonderful anesthetic boy, whose only sources of feeling were the right eye and left ear:

Passive movements could be imprinted on all the extremities to the greatest extent, without attracting the patient's notice. Only in violent forced hyperextension of the joints, especially of the knees, there arose a dull vague feeling of strain, but this was seldom precisely localized. We have often, after bandaging the eyes of the patient, carried him about the room, laid him on a table, given to his arms and legs the most fantastic and apparently the most inconvenient attitudes, without his having a suspicion of it. The expression of astonishment in his face, when all at once the removal of the handkerchief revealed his situation, is indescribable in words. Only when his head was made to hang away down he immediately spoke of dizziness, but could not assign its ground. Later he sometimes inferred from the sounds connected with the manipulation that something special was being done with him. . . . He had no feelings of muscular fatigue. If, with his eyes shut, we told him to raise his arm and to keep it up, he did so without trouble. After one or two minutes, however, the arm began to tremble and sink without his being aware of it. He asserted still his ability to keep it up. . . . Passively holding still his fingers did not affect him. He thought constantly that he opened and shut his hand, whereas it was really fixed.

. . .

All these cases, whether spontaneous or experimental, show the absolute need of *guiding sensations* of some kind for the successful carrying out of a concatenated series of movements. It is, in fact, easy to see that, just as where the chain of movements is automatic, each later movement of the chain has to be discharged by the impression which the next earlier one makes in being executed, so also, where the chain is voluntary, we need to know at each movement just *where we are in it,* if we are to will intelligently what the next link shall be. A man with no feeling of his movements might lead off never so well, and yet be sure to get lost soon and go astray. But patients like those described, who get no kinesthetic impressions, can still be guided by the sense of sight. Thus Strümpell says of his boy:

One could always observe how his eye was directed first to the object held before him, then to his own arm; and how it never ceased to follow the latter during its entire movement. All his voluntary movements took place under the unremitting lead of the eye, which as an indispensable guide, was never untrue to its functions.

. . .

This is perhaps all that need be said about the existence of passive sensations of movement and their indispensableness for our voluntary activity. We may consequently set it down as certain that, *whether or no there be anything else in the mind at the moment when we consciously will a certain act, a mental conception made up of memory-images of these sensations, defining which special act it is, must be there.*

Now *is there anything else in the mind when we will to do an act?* We must proceed in this chapter from the simpler to the more complicated cases. My first thesis accordingly is, that *there need be nothing else,* and that *in perfectly simple voluntary acts there is nothing else, in the mind but the kinesthetic idea, thus defined, of what the act is to be.*

. . .

If the ideas by which we discriminate between one movement and another, at the instant of deciding in our mind which one we shall perform, are always of sensorial origin, then the question arises, "Of which sensorial order need they be?" It will be remembered that we distinguished two orders of kinesthetic impression, the *remote* ones, made by the movement on the eye or ear or distant skin, etc., and the *resident* ones, made on the moving parts themselves, muscles, joints, etc. Now do resident images, exclusively, form what I have called the mental cue, or will remote ones equally suffice?

There can be no doubt whatever that the mental cue may be either an image of the resident or of the remote kind. Although, at the outset of our learning a movement, it would seem that the resident feelings must come strongly before consciousness . . . , later this need not be the case. The rule, in fact, would seem to be that they tend to lapse more and more from consciousness, and that the more practiced we become in a movement, the more "remote" do the ideas become which form its mental cue. What we are *interested* in is what sticks in our consciousness; everything else we get rid of as quickly as we can. Our resident feelings of movement have no substantive interest for us at all, as a rule. What interests us are the ends which the movement is to attain. Such an end is generally an outer impression on the eye or ear, or sometimes on the skin, nose, or palate. Now let the idea of the end associate itself definitely with the right motor innervation, and the thought of the innervation's *resident* effects will become as great an encumbrance as we formerly concluded that the feeling of the innervation itself would be. The mind does not need it; the end alone is enough.

The idea of the end, then, tends more and more to make itself all-sufficient. Or, at any rate, if the kinesthetic ideas are called up at all, they are so swamped in the vivid kinesthetic feelings by which they are immediately overtaken that we have no time to be aware of their separate existence. As I write, I have no anticipation, as a thing distinct from my sensation, of either the look or the digital feel of the letters which flow from my pen. The words chime on my mental *ear,* as it were, before I write them, but not on my mental eye or hand. This comes from the rapidity with which often-repeated movements follow on their mental cue. An end consented to as soon as conceived innervates directly the center of the first movement of the chain which leads to its accomplishment, and then the whole chain rattles off *quasi*-reflexly . . .

The reader will certainly recognize this to be true in all fluent and unhesitating voluntary acts. The only special fiat there is at the outset of the performance. A man says to himself, "I must change my shirt," and involuntarily he has taken off his coat, and his fingers are at work in their accustomed manner on his waistcoat-buttons, etc.; or we say, "I must go downstairs," and ere we know

it we have risen, walked, and turned the handle of the door—all through the idea of an end coupled with a series of guiding sensations which successively arise. It would seem indeed that we fail of accuracy and certainty in our attainment of the end whenever we are preoccupied with much ideal consciousness of the means. We walk a beam the better the less we think of the position of our feet upon it. We pitch or catch, we shoot or chop the better the less tactile and muscular (the less resident), and the more exclusively optical (the more remote) our consciousness is. Keep your *eye* on the place aimed at, and your hand will fetch it; think of your hand, and you will very likely miss your aim.

. . .

I trust that I have now made clear what that "idea of a movement" is which must precede it in order that it be voluntary. It is not the thought of the innervation which the movement requires. It is the anticipation of the movement's sensible effects, resident or remote, and sometimes very remote indeed. Such anticipations, to say the least, determine *what* our movements shall be. I have spoken all along as if they also might determine *that* they shall be. This, no doubt, has disconcerted many readers, for it certainly seems as if a special fiat, or consent, to the movement were required in addition to the mere conception of it, in many cases of volition; and this fiat I have altogether left out of my account. This leads us to the next point in the psychology of the Will.

IDEO-MOTOR ACTION

The question is this: *Is the bare idea of a movement's sensible effects its sufficient mental cue, or must there be an additional mental antecedent, in the shape of a fiat, decision, consent, volitional mandate, or other synonymous phenomenon of consciousness, before the movement can follow?*

I answer: Sometimes the bare idea is sufficient, but sometimes an additional conscious element, in the shape of a fiat, mandate, or express consent, has to intervene and precede the movement. The cases without a fiat constitute the more fundamental, because the more simple, variety. The others involve a special complication, which must be fully discussed at the proper time. For the present let us turn to *ideo-motor action,* as it has been termed, or the sequence of movement upon the mere thought of it, as the type of the process of volition.

Wherever movement follows *unhesitatingly and immediately* the notion of it in the mind, we have ideo-motor action. We are then aware of nothing between the conception and the execution. All sort of neuromuscular processes come between, of course, but we know absolutely nothing of them. We think the act, and it is done; and that is all that introspection tells us of the matter. . . . Whilst talking I become conscious of a pin on the floor, or of some dust on my sleeve. Without interrupting the conversation I brush away the dust or pick up the pin. I make no express resolve, but the mere perception of the object and the fleeting notion of the act seem of themselves to bring the latter about. Similarly, I sit at table after dinner and find myself from time to time taking nuts or raisins out of the dish and eating them. My dinner properly is over, and in the heat of the conversation I am hardly aware of what I do, but the perception of the fruit and the fleeting notion that I may eat it seem fatally to bring the act about. There is certainly no express fiat here; any more than there is in all those habitual goings and comings and rearrangements of ourselves which fill every hour of the day, and which incoming sensations instigate so immediately that it is often difficult to decide whether not to call them reflex rather than voluntary acts. . . .

In all this the determining condition of the unhesitating and resistless sequence of the act seems to be *the absence of any conflicting notion in the mind*. Either there is nothing else at all in the mind, or what is there does not conflict. The hypnotic subject realizes the former condition. Ask him what he is thinking about, and ten to one he will reply "nothing." The consequence is that he both believes everything he is told, and performs every act that is suggested. The suggestion may be a vocal command, or it may be the performance before him of the movement required. Hypnotic subjects in certain conditions repeat whatever they hear you say, and imitate whatever they see you do. . . .

We know what it is to get out of bed on a freezing morning in a room without a fire, and how the very vital principle within us protests against the ordeal. Probably most persons have lain on certain mornings for an hour at a time unable to brace themselves to the resolve. We think how late we shall be, how the duties of the day will suffer; we say, "I *must* get up, this is ignominious," etc.; but still the warm couch feels too delicious, the cold outside too cruel, and resolution faints away and postpones itself again and again just as it seemed on the verge of bursting the resistance and passing over into the decisive act. Now how do we *ever* get up under such circumstances? If I may generalize from my own experience, we more often than not get up without any struggle or decision at all. We suddenly find that we *have* got up. A fortunate lapse of consciousness occurs; we forget both the warmth and the cold; we fall into some revery connected with the day's life, in the course of which the idea flashes across us, "Hollo! I must lie here no longer" —an idea which at that lucky instant awakens no contradictory or paralyzing suggestions, and consequently produces immediately its appropriate motor effects. It was our acute consciousness of both the warmth and the cold during the period of struggle, which paralyzed our activity then and kept our idea of rising in the condition of *wish* and not of *will*. The moment these inhibitory ideas ceased, the original idea exerted its effects.

This case seems to me to contain in miniature form the data for an entire psychology of volition. It was in fact through mediating on the phenomenon in my own person that I first became convinced of the truth of the doctrine which these pages present, and which I need here illustrate by no farther examples. The reason why that doctrine is not a self-evident truth is that we have so many ideas which *do not* result in action. But it will be seen that in every such case, without exception, that is because other ideas simultaneously present rob them of their impulsive power. But even here, and when a movement is inhibited from *completely* taking place by contrary ideas, it will *incipiently* take place. To quote Lotze once more:

The spectator accompanies the throwing of a billiard-ball, or the thrust of the swordsman, with slight movements of his arm; the untaught narrator tells his story with many gesticulations; the reader while absorbed in the perusal of a battle-scene feels a slight tension runs through his muscular system, keeping time as it were with the actions he is reading of. These results become the more marked the more we are absorbed in thinking of the movements which suggest them; they grow fainter exactly in proportion as a complex consciousness, under the dominion of a crowd of other representations, withstands the passing over of mental contemplation into outward action.

. . .

We may then lay it down for certain that *every representation of a movement awakens in some degree the actual movement which is its object; and awakens it in a maximum degree whenever it is not kept from so doing by an antagonistic representation present simultaneously to the mind.*

The express fiat, or act of mental consent to the movement, comes in when the neutralization of the antagonistic and inhibitory idea is required. But that there is no express fiat needed when the conditions are simple, the reader ought now to be convinced. Lest, however, he should still share the common prejudice that voluntary action without "exertion of will power" is Hamlet with the prince's part left out, I will make a few further remarks. The first point to start from in understanding voluntary action, and the possible occurrence of it with no fiat or express resolve, is the fact that consciousness is *in its very nature impulsive.*[2] We do not have a sensation or a thought and then have to *add* something dynamic to it to get a movement. Every pulse of feeling which we have is the correlate of some neural activity that is already on its way to instigate a movement. Our sensations and thoughts are but cross-sections, as it were, of currents whose essential consequence is motion, and which no sooner run in at one nerve than they run out again at another. The popular notion that mere consciousness as such is not essentially a forerunner of activity, that the latter must

result from some superadded "will force," is a very natural inference from those special cases in which we think of an act for an indefinite length of time without the action taking place. These cases, however, are not the norm; they are cases of inhibition by antagonistic thoughts. When the blocking is released we feel as if an inward spring were let loose, and this is the additional impulse or *fiat* upon which the act effectively succeeds. We shall study anon the blocking and its release. Our higher thought is full of it. But where there is no blocking, there is naturally no hiatus between the thought-process and the motor discharge. *Movement is the natural immediate effect of feeling, irrespective of what the quality of the feeling may be. It is so in reflex action, it is so in emotional expression, it is so in the voluntary life.* Ideo-motor action is thus no paradox, to be softened or explained away. It obeys the type of all conscious action, and from it one must start to explain action in which a special fiat is involved.

It may be remarked in passing, that the inhibition of a movement no more involves an express effort or command than its execution does. Either of them *may* require it. But in all simple and ordinary cases, just as the bare presence of one idea prompts a movement, so the bare presence of another idea will prevent its taking place. Try to feel as if you were crooking your finger, whilst keeping it straight. In a minute it will fairly tingle with the imaginary change of position; yet it will not sensibly move, because *its not really moving* is also a part of what you have in mind. Drop *this* idea, think of the movement purely and simply, with all brakes off; and, presto! it takes place with no effort at all.

A waking man's behavior is thus at all times the resultant of two opposing neural forces. With unimaginable fineness some currents among the cells and fibers of his brain are playing on his motor nerves, whilst other currents, as unimaginably fine, are playing on the first currents, damming or helping them, altering their direction or their speed. The upshot of it all is, that whilst the currents must always end by being drained off through *some* motor nerves, they are drained off sometimes through one set and sometimes through another; and sometimes they keep each other in equilibrium so long that a superficial ob-

---

[2] I abstract here from the fact that a certain *intensity* of the consciousness is required for its impulsiveness to be effective in a complete degree. There is an inertia in the motor processes as in all other natural things. In certain individuals, and at certain times (disease, fatigue), the inertia is unusually great, and we may then have ideas of action which produce no visible act, but discharge themselves into merely nascent dispositions to activity or into emotional expression. The inertia of the motor parts here plays the same role as is elsewhere played by antagonistic ideas. We shall consider this restrictive inertia later on, it obviously introduces no essential alteration into the law which the text lays down.

server may think they are not drained off at all. Such an observer must remember, however, that from the physiological point of view a gesture, an expression of the brow, or an expulsion of the breath is a movement as much as an act of locomotion is. A king's breath slays as well as an assassin's blow; and the outpouring of those currents which the magic imponderable streaming of our ideas accompanies need not always be of an explosive or otherwise physically conspicuous kind.

· · ·

WILL IS A RELATION BETWEEN THE MIND
AND ITS "IDEAS"

In closing in, therefore, after all these preliminaries, upon the more *intimate* nature of the volitional process, we find ourselves driven more and more exclusively to consider the conditions which make ideas prevail in the mind. With the prevalence, once there as a fact, of the motive idea the *psychology* of volition properly stops. The movements which ensue are exclusively physiological phenomena, following according to physiological laws upon the neura events to which the idea corresponds. The *willing* terminates with the prevalence of the idea; and whether the act then follows or not is a matter quite immaterial, so far as the willing itself goes. I will to write, and the act follows. I will to sneeze, and it does not. I will that the distant table slide over the floor toward me; it also does not. My willing representation can no more instigate my sneezing-center than it can instigate the table to activity. But in both cases it is as true and good willing as it was when I willed it to write.[3] In a word, volition is a psychic or moral fact pure and simple, and is absolutely completed when the stable state of

[3] This sentence is written from the author's own consciousness. But many persons say that where they disbelieve in the effects ensuing, as in the case of the table, they cannot will it. They "cannot exert a volition that a table should move." This personal difference may be partly verbal. Different people may attach different connotations to the word "will." But I incline to think that we differ psychologically as well. When one knows that he has no power, one's desire of a thing is called a *wish* and not a will. The sense of impotence inhibits the volition. Only by abstracting from the thought of the impossibility am I able to imagine strongly the table sliding over the floor, to make the bodily "effort" which I do, and to will it to come toward me. It may be that some people are unable to perform this abstraction, and that the image of the table stationary on the floor inhibits the contradictory image of its moving, which is the object to be willed.

the idea is there. The supervention of motive is a supernumerary phenomenon depending on executive ganglia whose function lies outside the mind.

In St. Vitus' dance, in locomotor ataxy, the representation of a movement and the consent to it take place normally. But the inferior executive centers are deranged, and although the ideas discharge them, they do not discharge them so as to reproduce the precise sensations anticipated. In aphasia the patient has an image of certain words which he wishes to utter, but when he opens his mouth he hears himself making quite unintended sounds. This may fill him with rage and despair—which passions only show how intact his will remains. Paralysis only goes a step farther. The associated mechanism is not only deranged but altogether broken through. The volition occurs, but the hand remains as still as the table. The paralytic is made aware of this by the absence of the expected change in his afferent sensations. He tries harder, i.e., he mentally frames the sensation of muscular "effort," with consent that it shall occur. It does so: he frowns, he heaves his chest, he clinches his other fist, but the palsied arm lies passive as before.[4]

We thus find that *we reach the heart of our inquiry into volition when we ask by what process it is that the thought of any given object comes to prevail stably in the mind.* Where thoughts prevail without effort, we have sufficiently studied in the several chapters on sensation, association, and attention the laws of their advent before consciousness and of their stay. We will not go over that ground again, for we know that interest and association are the words, let their worth be what it may, on which our explanations must perforce rely. Where, on the other hand, the prevalence of the thought is accompanied by the phenomenon of effort, the case is much less clear. Already in the chapter on attention we postponed the final consideration of voluntary attention with effort to a later place. We have now brought things to a point at which we see that attention with effort is all that any case of volition implies. *The essential*

[4] A normal palsy occurs during sleep. We will all sorts of motions in our dreams, but seldom perform any of them. In nightmare we become conscious of the nonperformance, and make a muscular "effort." This seems then to occur in a restricted way, limiting itself to the occlusion of the glottis and producing the respiratory anxiety which wakes us up.

achievement of the will, in short, when it is most "voluntary," is to ATTEND *to a difficult object and hold it fast before the mind.* The so-doing *is* the *fiat*; and it is a mere physiological incident that when the object is thus attended to, immediate motor consequences should ensue. A *resolve,* whose contemplated motor consequences are not to ensue until some possibly far distant future conditions shall have been fulfilled, involves all the psychic elements of a motor fiat except the word *"now"*; and it is the same with many of our purely theoretic beliefs. We saw in effect in the appropriate chapter, how in the last resort belief means only a peculiar sort of occupancy of the mind, and relation to the self felt in the thing believed; and we know in the case of many beliefs how constant an effort of the attention is required to keep them in this situation and protect them from displacement by contradictory ideas.[5]

Effort of attention is thus the essential phenomenon of will.[6] Every reader must know by his own experience that this is so, for every

[5] Both resolves and beliefs have of course immediate motor consequences of a quasi-emotional sort, changes of breathing, of attitude, internal speech movements, etc.; but these movements are not the *objects* resolved on or believed. The movements in common volition are the objects willed.

[6] This *volitional* effort pure and simple must be carefully distinguished from the *muscular* effort with which it is usually confounded. The latter consists of all those peripheral feelings to which a muscular "exertion" may give rise. These feelings, whenever they are massive and the body is not "fresh," are rather disagreeable, especially when accompanied by stopped breath, congested head, bruised skin of fingers, toes, or shoulders, and strained joints. And it is only *as thus disagreeable* that the mind must make its *volitional* effort in stably representing their reality and consequently bringing it about. That they happen to be made real by muscular activity is a purely accidental circumstance. A soldier standing still to be fired at expects disagreeable sensations from his muscular passivity. The action of his will, in sustaining the expectation, is identical with that required for a painful muscular effort. What is hard for both is *facing an idea as real.*
Where much muscular effort is not needed or where the "freshness" is very great, the volitional effort is not required to sustain the idea of movement, which comes then and stays in virtue of association's simpler laws. More commonly, however, muscular effort involves volitional effort as well. Exhausted with fatigue and wet and watching, the sailor on a wreck throws himself down to rest. But hardly are his limbs fairly relaxed, when the order "To the pumps!" again sounds in his ears. Shall he, can he, obey it? Is it not better just to let his aching body lie, and let the ship go down if she will? So he lies on, till, with a desperate heave of the will, at last he staggers to his legs, and to his task again. Again, there are instances where the fiat demands great volitional effort though the muscular exertion be insignificant, e.g., the getting out of bed and bathing one's self on a cold morning.

reader must have felt some fiery passion's grasp. What constitutes the difficulty for a man laboring under an unwise passion of acting as if the passion were unwise? Certainly there is no physical difficulty. It is as easy physically to avoid a fight as to begin one, to pocket one's money as to squander it on one's cupidities, to walk away from as toward a coquette's door. The difficulty is mental; it is that of getting the idea of the wise action to stay before our mind at all. When any strong emotional state whatever is upon us the tendency is for no images but such as are congruous with it to come up. If others by chance offer themselves, they are instantly smothered and crowded out. If we be joyous, we cannot keep thinking of those uncertainties and risks of failure which abound upon our path; if lugubrious, we cannot think of new triumphs, travels, loves, and joys; nor if vengeful, of our oppressor's community of nature with ourselves. The cooling advice which we get from others when the fever-fit is on us is the most jarring and exasperating thing in life. Reply we cannot, so we get angry; for by a sort of self-preserving instinct which our passion has, it feels that these chill objects, if they once but gain a lodgment, will work and work until they have frozen the very vital spark from out of all our mood and brought our airy castles in ruin to the ground. Such is the inevitable effect of reasonable ideas over others—*if they can once get a quiet hearing*; and passion's cue accordingly is always and everywhere to prevent their still small voice from being heard at all. "Let me not think of that! Don't speak to me of that!" This is the sudden cry of all those who in a passion perceive some sobering considerations about to check them in mid-career. "*Hæc tibi erit janua leti,*" we feel. There is something so icy in this cold-water bath, something which seems so hostile to the movement of our life, so purely negative, in Reason, when she lays her corpse-like finger on our heart and says, "Halt! give up! leave off! go back! sit down!" that it is no wonder that to most men the steadying influence seems, for the time being, a very minister of death.

The strong-willed man, however, is the man who hears the still small voice unflinchingly, and who, when the death-bringing consideration comes, looks at its face, consents to its presence, clings to it, affirms it, and holds it fast, in spite of the host of exciting mental images which rise in revolt against it and would expel it from the mind. Sustained in this way by a resolute effort of attention, the difficult object ere long begins to call up its own congerers [*sic*] and associates and ends by changing the disposition of the man's consciousness altogether. And with his consciousness, his action changes, for the new object, once stably in possession of the field of his thoughts, infallibly produces its own motor effects. The difficulty lies in the gaining possession of that field. Though the spontaneous drift of thought is all the other way, the attention must be kept strained on that one object until at last it *grows,* so as to maintain itself before the mind with ease. This strain of the attention is the fundamental act of will. And the will's work is in most cases practically ended when the bare presence to our thought of the naturally unwelcome object has been secured. For the mysterious tie between the thought and the motor centers next comes into play, and, in a way which we cannot even guess at, the obedience of the bodily organs follows as a matter of course.

In all this one sees how the immediate point of application of the volitional effort lies exclusively in the mental world. The whole drama is a mental drama. The whole difficulty is a mental difficulty, a difficulty with an object of our thought. If I may use the word *idea* without suggesting associationist or Herbartian fables, I will say that it is an idea to which our will applies itself, an idea which if we let it go would slip away, but which we will not let go. Consent to the idea's undivided presence, this is effort's sole achievement. Its only function is to get this feeling of consent into the mind. And for this there is but one way. The idea to be consented to must be kept from flickering and going out. It must be held steadily before the mind until it *fills* the mind. Such filling of the mind by an idea, with its congruous associates, *is* consent to the idea and to the fact which the idea represents. If the idea be that, or include that, of a bodily movement of our own, then we call the consent thus laboriously gained a motor volition. For Nature here "backs" us instantaneously and follows up our inward willingness by outward changes on her own part. She does this in no other instance. Pity she should not have been more generous, nor made a world whose other parts were as immediately subject to our will!

. . . In describing the "reasonable type" of decision, it was said that it usually came when the right conception of the case was found. Where, however, the right conception is an anti-impulsive one, the whole intellectual ingenuity of the man usually goes to work to crowd it out of sight, and to find names for the emergency, by the help of which the dispositions of the moment may sound sanctified, and sloth or passion may reign unchecked. How many excuses does the drunkard find when each new temptation comes! It is a new brand of liquor which the interests of intellectual culture in such matters oblige him to test; moreover it is poured out and it is sin to waste it; or others are drinking and it would be churlishness to refuse; or it is but to enable him to sleep, or just to get through this job of work; or it isn't drinking, it is because he feels so cold; or it is Christmas day; or it is a means of stimulating him to make a more powerful resolution in favor of abstinence than any he has hitherto made; or it is just this once, and once doesn't count, etc., etc., *ad libitum*—it is, in fact, anything you like except *being a drunkard. That* is the conception that will not stay before the poor soul's attention. But if he once gets able to pick out that way of conceiving, from all the other possible ways of conceiving the various opportunities which occur, if through thick and thin he holds to it that this is being a drunkard and is nothing else, he is not likely to remain one long. The effort by which he succeeds in keeping the right *name* unwaveringly present to his mind proves to be his saving moral act.

Everywhere then the function of the effort is the same: to keep affirming and adopting a thought which, if left to itself, would slip away. It may be cold and flat when the spontaneous mental drift is toward excitement, or great and arduous when the spontaneous drift is toward repose. In the one case the effort has to inhibit an explosive, in the other to arouse an obstructed will. The exhausted sailor on a wreck has a will which is obstructed. One of his ideas is that of his sore hands, of the nameless exhaustion of his whole frame which the act of further pumping involves, and of the deliciousness of sinking into sleep. The other is that of the hungry sea engulfing him. "Rather the aching toil!" he says; and it becomes reality then, in spite of the inhibiting influence of the relatively luxurious sensations which he gets from lying still. But exactly similar in form would be his consent to lie and sleep. Often it is the thought of sleep and what leads to it which is the hard one to keep before the mind. If a patient afflicted with insomnia can only control the whirling chase of his thoughts so far as to think of *nothing at all* (which can be done), or so far as to imagine one letter after another of a verse of scripture or poetry spelt slowly and monotonously out, it is almost certain that here, too, specific bodily effects will follow, and that sleep will come. The trouble is to keep the mind upon a train of objects naturally so insipid. *To sustain a representation, to think,* is, in short, the only moral act, for the impulsive and the obstructed, for sane and lunatics alike. Most maniacs know their thoughts to be crazy, but find them too pressing to be withstood. Compared with them the sane truths are so deadly sober, so cadaverous, that the lunatic cannot bear to look them in the face and say, "Let these alone be my reality!"

. . .

To sum it all up in a word, *the terminus of the psychological process in volition, the point to which the will is directly applied, is always an idea.* There are at all times *some* ideas from which we shy away like frightened horses the moment we get a glimpse of their forbidding profile upon the threshold of our thought. *The only resistance which our will can possibly experience is the resistance which such an idea offers to being attended to at all.* To attend to it is the volitional act, and the only inward volitional act which we ever perform.

I have put the thing in this ultra-simple way because I want more than anything else to emphasize the fact that volition is primarily a relation, not between our Self and extra-mental matter (as many philosophers still maintain), but between our Self and our own states of mind. But when, a short while ago, I spoke of the filling of the mind with an idea as being equivalent to consent to the idea's object, I said something which the reader doubtless questioned at the time, and which certainly now demands some qualification ere we pass beyond.

It is unqualifiedly true that if any thought *do* fill the mind exclusively, such filling is consent. The thought, for that time at any rate, carries the man and his will with it. But it is not true that the thought *need* fill the mind exclusively for consent to be there; for we often consent to things whilst thinking of other things, even of hostile things . . . The effort to *attend* is therefore only a part of what the word "will" covers; it covers also the effort to *consent* to something to which our attention is not quite complete. Often, when an object has gained our attention exclusively, and its motor results are just on the point of setting in, it seems as if the sense of their imminent irrevocability were enough of itself to start up the inhibitory ideas and to make us pause. Then we need a new stroke of effort to break down the sudden hesitation which seizes upon us, and to persevere. So that although attention is the first and fundamental thing in volition, *express consent to the reality of what is attended to* is often an additional and quite distinct phenomenon involved.

The reader's own consciousness tells him of course just what these words of mine denote. And I freely confess that I am impotent to carry the analysis of the matter any farther, or to explain in other terms of what this consent consists. It seems a subjective experience *sui generis,* which we can designate but not define. We stand here exactly where we did in the case of belief. When an idea *stings* us in a certain way, makes as it were a certain electric connection with our self, we believe that it *is* a reality. When it stings us in another way, makes another connection with our Self, we say, *let it be* a reality. To the word "is" and to the words "let it be" there correspond peculiar attitudes of consciousness which it is vain to seek to explain. The indicative and the imperative moods are as much ultimate categories of thinking as they are of grammar. The "quality of reality" which these moods attach to things is not like other qualities. It is a relation to our life. It means *our* adoption of the things, *our* caring for them, *our* standing by them. This at least is what it practically means for us; what it may mean beyond that we do not know. And the transition from merely considering an object as possible, to deciding or willing it to be real; the change from the fluctuating to the stable personal attitude concerning it; from the "don't care" state of mind to that in which "we mean business," is one of the most familiar things in life. We can partly enumerate its conditions; and we can partly trace its consequences, especially the momentous one that when the mental object is a move-

ment of our own body, it realizes itself outwardly when the mental change in question has occurred. But the change itself as a subjective phenomenon is something which we can translate into no simpler terms.

Acting, Willing, Desiring*

The question "What is acting or doing something?" seems at first unreal, i.e., a question to which we already know the answer. For it looks as though everyone knows what doing something is and would be ready to offer instances. No one, for instance, would hesitate to say to another "You ought to go to bed," on the ground that neither he nor the other knows the kind of thing meant by "going to bed." Yet, when we consider instances that would be offered, we do not find it easy to state the common character which we think they had which led us to call them actions.

If, as a preliminary, we look for help to the psychologists, from whom we naturally expect to get it, we find we fail. We find plenty of talk about reflex actions, ideo-motor actions, instinctive actions, and so on, but no discussion of what actions are. Instead, they seem to take for granted that our actions are physical processes taking place within our body, which they certainly are not.

We should at first say that to do something is to originate or to bring into existence, i.e., really, to cause, some not yet existing state either of ourselves or of someone else, or, again, of some body. But, for clearness' sake, we should go on to distinguish those actions in doing which we originated some new state directly from those in which we did this only indirectly, i.e., by originating directly some other state, by originating which we indirectly originated the final state. As instances of the former we might give moving or turning our head, and as instances of the latter, curing our toothache by swallowing aspirin, and killing another by pressing a switch which exploded a charge underneath him. If challenged, however, we should have to allow that even in instances of the former kind we

did not originate directly what the instances suggest that we did, since what we did originate directly must have been some new state or states of our nerve cells, of the nature of which we are ignorant. We should, however, insist that in doing any action we must have originated *something* directly, since otherwise we could not originate anything indirectly.

The view that to act is to originate something was maintained by Cook Wilson in a paper on *Means and End*. In the course of this paper he also maintained (1) that an action required the desire to do it, and (2) that it is important to avoid the mistake of thinking that the origination of something X is the willing of X, apparently on the ground that if it were, X would exist as soon as we willed it, and yet it usually does not. He also appeared to hold that the origination of X, though not identical with willing the origination, required it, so that when I originated a movement of my hand, this required as an antecedent my willing this origination, and this willing in turn required the desiring to originate the movement.

According to Cook Wilson, then, in considering an action we have to distinguish three things: first, the action itself, the originating something; second, the required willing to originate this; and third, the required desire to originate this. And according to him what we will and what we desire are the same, viz., the action.

Professor Macmurray, in a Symposium[1] on "What is action?," takes substantially the same view of what an action is. He says: "An action is not the concomitance of an intention in the mind and an occurrence in the physical world: it is the *producing* of the occurrence by the Self, the *making* of a change in the external world, the *doing* of a deed. No

* H. A. Prichard, *Moral Obligation* (Oxford: Clarendon Press, 1949), pp. 187–98, reprinted by permission of the publishers. Footnotes are renumbered.

[1] Aristotelian Society, Supplementary Volume XVII (1938).

process which terminates in the mind, such as forming an intention, deciding to act, or willing, is either an action or a component of action." But he goes on to add: "In certain circumstances such a mental event or process may be followed *necessarily* by action."

Now, so far as I can see, this account of what an action is, though plausible and having as a truth underlying it that usually in acting we do cause something, is not tenable.

Unquestionably the thing meant by "an action" is an activity. This is so whether we speak of a man's action in moving his hand, or of a body's action such as that of the heart in pumping the blood, or that of one electron in repelling another. But though we think that some man in moving his hand, or that the sun in attracting the earth, causes a certain movement, we do not think that the man's or the sun's activity *is* or *consists in* causing the movement. And if we ask ourselves: "Is there such an activity as originating or causing a change in something else?," we have to answer that there is not. To say this, of course, is not to say that there is no such thing as causing something, but only to say that though the causing a change may require an activity, it is not itself an activity. If we then ask: "What is the kind of activity required when one body causes another to move?," we have to answer that we do not know, and that when we speak of a force of attraction or of repulsion we are only expressing our knowledge that there is some activity at work, while being ignorant of what the kind of activity is. In the case, however, of a man, i.e., really, of a man's mind, the matter is different. When, e.g., we think of ourselves as having moved our hand, we are thinking of ourselves as having performed an activity of a certain kind, and, it almost goes without saying, a *mental* activity of a certain kind, an activity of whose nature we were dimly aware in doing the action and of which we can become more clearly aware by reflecting on it. And that we are aware of its special nature is shown by our unhesitatingly distinguishing it from other special mental activities such as thinking, wondering, and imagining. If we ask "What is the word used for this special kind of activity?," the answer, it seems, has to be "willing." (I now think I was mistaken in suggesting that the phrase in use for it is "setting oneself to cause.") We also have to admit that while we know the general char-

acter of that to which we refer when we use the word "willing," this character is *sui generis* and so incapable of being defined, i.e., of having its nature expressed in terms of the nature of other things. Even Hume virtually admits this when he says: "By the *will*, I mean nothing but *the internal impression we feel and are conscious of, when we knowingly give rise to any new motion of our body or new perception of our mind*,"[2] and then goes on to add that the impression is impossible to define. Though, however, the activity of willing is indefinable, we can distinguish it from a number of things which it is not. Thus obviously, as Locke insisted, willing is different from desiring, and again, willing is not, as some psychologists would have it, a species of something called conation of which desiring is another species. There is no such genus. Again, it is not, as Green in one passage[3] implies, a species of desiring which is desiring in another sense than that ordinary sense in which we are said to desire while hesitating to act.

In addition, plainly, willing is not resolving, nor attending to a difficult object, as James holds, nor for that matter attending to anything, nor, again, consenting to the reality of what is attended to, as James also maintains, nor, indeed, consenting to anything, nor, once more, identifying ourself with some object of desire, as Green asserts in another passage.[4]

Consequently, there seems to be no resisting the conclusion that where we think of ourselves or of another as having done a certain action, the kind of activity of which we are thinking is that of willing (though we should have to add that we are thinking of our particular act of will as having been the doing of the action in question, only because we think it caused a certain change), and that when we refer to some instance of this activity, such as our having moved our finger or given some friend a headache, we refer to it thus not because we think it was, or consisted in, the causing our finger to move or our friend's head to ache, but because we think it had a certain change of state as an effect.

If, as it seems we must, we accept this conclusion, that to act is really to will something,

[2] Hume, *Treatise* (Selby-Bigge, p. 399).
[3] *Prolegomena*, §§ 140–42.
[4] *Prolegomena*, § 146.

we then become faced by the question : "What sort of thing is it that we will?"

Those who, like Cook Wilson, distinguish between acting and willing, answer that what we will is an action, which, according to him is the originating some change. Thus Green says: "To will an event" (i.e., presumably some change) "as distinguished from an act is a contradiction." And by this he seems to mean that, for instance, in the case which he takes of our paying a debt, what we will is the paying of our debt and not our creditor's coming into possession of what we owe him. Again, James and Stout, though they do not consider the question, show by their instances that they take for granted that what we will is an action. Thus James says: "I will to write, and the act follows. I will to sneeze and it does not."[5] And Stout illustrates a volition by a man's willing to produce an explosion by applying a lighted match to gunpowder.[6] But, unfortunately, James speaks of what he has referred to as, the act of writing which I will, as certain physiological movements, and similarly Stout speaks of, the production of an explosion which I will, as certain bodily movements. And, of course, the bodily movements to which they are referring are not actions, though they may be the effects of actions. Plainly, then, both are only doing lip-service to the idea that what we will is an action. And James, at least, drops doing even this. For immediately after making the statement just quoted, viz., "I will to write, and the act follows. I will to sneeze, and it does not," he adds: "I will that the distant table slide over the floor toward me; it also does not." Yet no one would say that the sliding of the table, as distinct from my sliding it, was an action.

In this connection it is well for clearness' sake to bear two things in mind. The first is that some transitive verbs used for particular actions are also used intransitively. Thus one not only speaks of turning one's head but also says that one's head turned. And the second is that, while the phrase "turning one's head" stands for an action and so for an activity of one's mind, yet when I say "my head turned" I am speaking simply of a movement of my head which is a change of place and not an action. The difference is made clear

by considering what is plainly a mistake made by Professor Macmurray. He says that the term "action" is ambiguous. He says: "It may refer either to what is done or to the doing of it. It may mean either 'doing' or 'deed.' When we talk of 'an action' we are normally referring to what is done. . . . To act is to effect a change in the external world. The deed is the change so effected." And he emphasizes what he considers the ambiguity in order to indicate that it is doings and not deeds that he is considering. Obviously, however, there is no ambiguity whatever. When I move my hand, the movement of my hand, though an effect of my action, is not itself an action, and no one who considered the matter would say it was, any more than he would say that the death of Caesar, as distinct from his murder, was an action or even part of an action.

This difference between, e.g., my moving my hand and a movement of my hand, is one which James and Stout seem to ignore, as becomes obvious when James speaks of the sliding of a table as, like writing, an action. We find the same thing, too, in Locke. For though, e.g., he says that "we find by experience, that, barely by willing it, we can move the parts of our bodies,"[7] yet in contrasting a human with a physical action he implies that what we will is a movement of our body. Probably, if pressed, he would have said that, strictly speaking, what we will is a movement and so not an action. In addition, James and Stout seem to treat the distinction between an act of willing, or, as they prefer to call it, a volition, and what is willed, as if it were the same as the distinction between an act of willing and its effect, although they are totally different.

It should be clear from what I have just said that those who hold that what we will is an action must, to be successful, mean by an action something which really is an action. They may, of course, maintain that what we will is a physical process, such as a movement of my hand, but if they do they are really denying that what we will is an action.

It should also now be clear that if we face the question "What sort of thing do we will?," we have only two answers to consider: (1) that it is some change of state of some thing or person; and (2) that it is an action. If,

[5] James, *Psychology*, II, 560.
[6] Stout, *Manual of Psychology*, IV, 641.

[7] Locke, *Essay*, Vol. II, § 4, p. 21.

however, we are forced to conclude, as we have been, that doing something is an act of willing, we seem forced to exclude the second answer, simply on the ground that if it were true, then whenever we think of ourselves as having done some action, we must be thinking of ourselves as having willed some action, i.e., as having willed the willing of some change X; and to think this seems impossible. By the very nature of willing, it seems, what we will must be something other than willing, so that to will the willing of a change X must be an impossibility. And if we even try to deny this, we find ourselves forced to admit that the willing of X, which (we are contending) is what we will, must in turn really be the willing the willing of something else, and so on, and thus become involved in an infinite regress. It is true that Cook Wilson, in a long unpublished discussion, tried to vindicate the analogous idea that in certain limiting cases, viz., those in which the desire moving us is not the desire of some change but the desire to cause it ourselves, as happens in playing golf or patience, what we originate is identical with our origination of something. But he never seems to me to succeed in meeting the objection that this identity must be impossible. Similarly, it seems to me, it is impossible for there to be a case in which the willing the willing of X is identical with willing X.

We are thus left with the conclusion that where we think we have done some action, e.g., have raised our arm or written a word, what we willed was some change, e.g., some movement of our arm or some movement of ink to a certain place on a piece of paper in front of us. But we have to bear in mind that the change which we willed may not have been the same as the change we think we effected. Thus, where I willed some movement of my second finger, I may at least afterward think that the change I effected was a movement of my first finger, and, only too often, where I willed the existence of a certain word on a piece of paper, I afterward find that what I caused was a different word. Again, in two cases of the act we call trying to thread a needle, what I willed may have been the same, though the changes I afterward think I effected were very different, being in the one case the thread's going through the needle and in the other its passing well outside it.

Suppose now that it be allowed that so far

I have been right. Then the following admissions must be made:

1. An action, i.e., a human action, instead of being the originating or causing of some change, is an activity of willing some change, this usually causing some change, and in some cases a physical change, its doing or not doing this depending on the physical conditions of which the agent is largely ignorant.

2. Sometimes, however, we have performed such an activity without, at any rate so far as we know, having caused any physical change. This has happened when, e.g., we willed a movement of our hand, at a time when it was either paralyzed or numb with cold, whether we knew this or not. No doubt in such cases our activity would not ordinarily be called an action, but it is of the same sort as what we ordinarily call and think of as an action.

3. There is no reason to limit the change which it is possible to will to a movement of some part of our body, since, as James says in effect, we can just as much will the sliding of a table toward us as a movement of our hand toward our head. Indeed, we may, in fact, will this in order to convince ourselves or someone else that by doing so we shall not cause the table to slide. And it looks as though we sometimes will such things in ordinary life, as when in watching a football match we want some player's speed to increase, and will it to increase.

4. Where we have willed some movement of our body and think we have caused it, we cannot have directly caused it. For what we directly caused, if anything, must have been some change in our brain.

5. Where we think that by willing some change we effected some change in the physical world, we are implying the idea that in doing so, we are butting into, or interfering with, the physical system, just as we think of an approaching comet as effecting a breach in the order of the solar system, so long as we do not regard the comet as part of the system. This idea is, of course, inconsistent with our belief in the uniformity of nature unless we include in nature minds as well as bodies; and in any case it is inconsistent with our belief in the conservation of energy. But so long as we think, as we do, that at any rate on some occasions we really effect something in the physical world, we must admit this. And if we knew that such effecting was impossible, we should give up acting.

We have now to face another question, viz., "Does acting require a desire, and if it does, the desire of what?"

It is at least very difficult to avoid Aristotle's conclusion that acting requires a desire, if only for the reason he gives, viz., that διάνοια αὐτὴ οὐθὲν κινεῖ. It seems that, as Locke maintained, if we never desired something we should never do anything. But what is the desire required?

Here only one or other of two answers seems possible, viz., (1) that it is a desire of the change X which we will, and (2) that it is a desire of the willing of X. And when we try, we do not find it easy to decide between them. For on the one hand, the desire required seems to have to be the desire of X, on the ground that, if we are to will X, we must desire X. And on the other hand, it seems that it must be the desire to will X, since unless we *desired* to will X we could not will X. Indeed, just for this reason Plato seems to have gone too far in the *Gorgias* when he maintained that in acting we never desire to do what we do, but only that for the sake of which we do it. For, if acting is willing, it seems that the desire required must be a desire of the willing, even though the desire be a dependent desire, i.e., a desire depending on the desire of something else for its own sake, viz., that for the sake of which we do the action. And Plato's mistake seems to have been that of restricting desiring to desiring something for its own sake.

The two answers are, of course, radically different. For if the desire required is the desire of X, the thing desired and the thing willed will be the same, as indeed Green implies that they are when he maintains that willing is desiring in a special sense of "desiring." But if so, while the willing of X will require what for want of a better term we seem to have to call the thought of X, as being something involved in the desire of X, it will not require either the desire of the willing of X or, for that reason, even the thought of willing X. On the other hand, if the desire required is the desire to will X, the thing desired and the thing willed will necessarily be different, and while the willing of X will require the desire of willing X and so also the thought of willing X, it will not *require* the desire of X, though it will require the thought of X, as being something involved in the thought of willing X. It should, however,

be noted that in the case of the latter alternative, the desire of X may in some cases be required indirectly as a condition of our desiring the willing of X.

To repeat here for clearness' sake what is central—if the desire required is the desire of X, the willing of X will not require either the desire of the willing of X or even the thought of willing X, while, if the desire required is the desire of willing X, the willing of X will not require the desire of X, though it will require the thought of X.

On consideration, however, we have to reject the idea that the desire required is the desire of X, on three grounds. First, if it were true, we should always will any change which we desired to happen, such as the sliding of the table, whether or not we thought that if we were to will it to happen we should thereby cause it to happen; and obviously we do not. Second, we occasionally will a change to happen without any desire for it to happen. This must occur, e.g., if a man ever does an act moved solely by the desire for revenge, willing, say, the movement of a switch which he is confident will result in the death of another, not from any desire for his death but solely from the desire to cause it by willing the movement. And even if there are no acts animated solely by the desire for revenge, there are certainly actions approximating to this. At all events, in the case of playing a game the desire at work must be not the desire of some change but the desire to cause it. A putter at golf, e.g., has no desire for the ball to fall into the hole; he only desires to cause it to fall in. This contention is, I think, not met by maintaining, as Cook Wilson in fact does, that the player desires the falling into the hole as caused by his action, and so desires the falling as part of, or an element in, his action. Its falling is neither a part of, nor an element in, his action; at best it is only an effect of it. And the player could only be said to desire the falling if, as he does not, he desired it to happen irrespectively of what would cause it to happen. And in this connection it may be added that if the desire required were the desire of X, it would be impossible to do any act as one which we think would or might fulfill some obligation, since *ex hypothesi* the desire required will be a desire for a change X and not a desire to *will* a change X. Then, third, there is a consideration which comes to

light if we consider more closely what it is
that we will in certain cases, and more especially in those in which we describe an action
as one of trying to do so and so. Suppose,
e.g., I have done what we describe as having
tried to jump a ditch, and so imply that beforehand I was doubtful of success. Obviously
I did not will a movement of my body which
I was sure would land me, say, two clear yards
on the other side, since if I had thought of
willing this I should have realized that willing
this would not result in my getting across. I
willed that movement the willing of which,
if I were to will it, I thought the most likely
of all the willings of movements in my power
to result in my landing on the farther bank.
And in this connection it seems worth noting
that what we call trying to do something is
as much doing something as what we ordinarily call doing something, although the word
"trying" suggests that it is not. It is the willing a change described in the way in which I
have just described what I willed in trying
to jump a ditch.

It therefore seems that the desire required
must be the desire of the willing of a certain
change X. Yet this conclusion is exposed to
two objections. The first is that if it were
true, it would be impossible to will something
X for the first time. For in this context we
mean by a desire to will X a desire we can
only have in consequence of thinking that if
we were to will X, our doing so would be
likely to cause something else, and ultimately
something which we desire for its own sake.
But we cannot desire to will something X,
unless we at least have a conjecture that if
we were to will X, our willing X might cause
some change which we desire for its own sake.
And this conjecture requires the thought that
on some previous occasion we have willed X
and thence concluded from what we think
followed this willing of X that it may have
caused something else Y. Yet *ex hypothesi*
we cannot have willed X on this previous
occasion from the desire to will X, since then
we had no idea of what willing X might cause.
James expresses what is really this objection,
though in a misleading way, when he says:
"If, in voluntary action properly so-called"
(i.e., in what is really an action), "the act
must be foreseen, it follows that no creature
not endowed with divinatory power can perform an act voluntarily for the first time."[8]

⁸ James, *Psychology*, II, 487.

The statement as it stands is, of course, absurd, because no one before acting *knows* what
his act will be, or even that he will act. But
it can be taken as an inaccurate way of expressing the thought that an act of will
requires an idea of something which we may
cause if we perform the act.

To this objection I have to confess that I
cannot see an answer. Yet I think that there
must be an answer, since, however it has come
about, for us as we are now an act of will does
seem to require the desire of it, and so some
idea of something which it might effect. I
need hardly add that it is no answer to maintain that the desire immediately required by
willing something X is in some cases the
desire of X, and in others the desire of willing X.

The second objection is one which seems to
me, though insidious, an objection which can
be met. It can be stated thus: "It is all very
well to say that the desire immediately presupposed by willing X is the desire to will X.
But to say this is not enough. For we often
desire to will X, and yet do not, as when we
hesitate to get out of bed or out of a warm
bath, and when this is so, obviously something
else is required, and this something can only
be the willing to will X, so that after all there
must be such a thing as willing to will." But
to this the reply seems clear. Though it is
possible to desire to desire, as when I desire
to desire the welfare of my country more than
I do, it is impossible to will to will, for the
reason already given. And where we hesitate
to will X, what is required is not the willing
to will X but either a certain increase in our
desire to will X or a decrease in our aversion
to doing so. Certainly, too, we often act on
this idea, hoping, e.g., that by making ourselves think of the coldness of our breakfast
if we stay in bed we shall reach a state of
desire in which we shall will certain movements of our body. And sometimes we succeed, and when we do, we sometimes, as James
puts it, suddenly find that we have got up, the
explanation of our surprise apparently being
that we, having been absorbed in the process
of trying to stimulate our desire to get up,
have not reflected on our state of desire and
so have not noticed its increase.

There is also to be noticed in this connection
a mistake into which we are apt to fall which
leads us to think that there must be such a
thing as willing to will. We of course frequently want certain changes to happen and

also want to will certain changes. But we are apt not to notice that the objects of these desires differ in respect of the conditions of their realization, and in consequence to carry the account of the process of deliberation described by Aristotle one step too far—as Aristotle did not. According to him, when we want the happening of something Z which is not an action of ours and which we think we cannot cause directly, we often look for something else Y from the happening of which the happening of Z would result, and then if necessary for something else X from the happening of which Y would result, until we come to think of something A from the happening of which X, Y, and Z would in turn result, and which we also think it in our power to cause by a certain act α. And when we have found A the process stops. We, however, are apt to carry the process one step farther, and apply to the act α, i.e., the willing of something β, the willing of which we think likely to cause A, the same process that we applied to Z, Y, X, and A, thus treating the willing of β as if it were not the willing of something (which it is), but a change which some act of willing might cause. As a result of doing this we ask "From what act of willing would the willing of β result?," and the answer has to be "The willing the willing of β." But the very question is mistaken, because the willing of β is not a change like Z, Y, X, and A. The only proper question at this stage must be not "From what *willing* would the willing of β result?" but "From what *something* would the willing of β result?" And the proper answer must be: "From a certain increase in our desire to will β."

Willing and Intending*

611. "Willing too is merely an experience," one would like to say (the "will" too only "idea"). It comes when it comes, and I cannot bring it about.

Not bring it about?—like *what*? What can I bring about, then? What am I comparing willing with when I say this?

612. I should not say of the movement of my arm, for example: it comes when it comes, etc. And this is the region in which we say significantly that a thing doesn't simply happen to us, but that we *do* it. "I don't need to wait for my arm to go up—I can raise it." And here I am making a contrast between the movement of my arm and, say, the fact that the violent thudding of my heart will subside.

613. In the sense in which I can ever bring anything about (such as stomach-ache through over-eating), I can also bring about an act of willing. In this sense I bring about the act of willing to swim by jumping into the water. Doubtless I was trying to say: "I can't will willing; that is, it makes no sense to speak of willing willing. "Willing" is not the name of an action; and so not the name of any voluntary action either. And my use of a wrong expression came from our wanting to

think of willing as an immediate noncausal bringing-about. A misleading analogy lies at the root of this idea; the causal nexus seems to be established by a mechanism connecting two parts of a machine. The connection may be broken if the mechanism is disturbed. (We think only of the disturbances to which a mechanism is normally subject, not, say, of cogwheels suddenly going soft, or passing through one another, and so on.)

614. When I raise my arm "voluntarily" I do not use any instrument to bring the movement about. My wish is not such an instrument either.

615. "Willing, if it is not to be a sort of wishing, must be the action itself. It cannot be allowed to stop anywhere short of the action." If it is the action, then it is so in the ordinary sense of the word; so it is speaking, writing, walking, lifting a thing, imagining something. But it is also trying, attempting, making an effort—to speak, to write, to lift a thing, to imagine something, etc.

616. When I raise my arm, I have *not* wished it might go up. The voluntary action excludes this wish. It is indeed possible to say: "I hope I shall draw the circle faultlessly." And that is to express a wish that one's hand should move in such-and-such a way.

617. If we cross our fingers in a certain

* Ludwig Wittgenstein, *Philosophical Investigations*, trans. G. E. M. Anscombe (Oxford: Basil Blackwell, 1953), pp. 159e–67e, 185e–86e, by permission of the publisher.

special way we are sometimes unable to move a particular finger when someone tells us to do so, if he only *points* to the finger—merely shows it to the eye. If on the other hand he touches it, we can move it. One would like to describe this experience as follows: we are unable to *will* to move the finger. The case is quite different from that in which we are not able to move the finger because someone is, say, holding it. One now feels inclined to describe the former case by saying: one can't find any point of application for the will till the finger is touched. Only when one feels the finger can the will know where it is to catch hold. But this kind of expression is misleading. One would like to say: "How am I to know where I am to catch hold with the will, if feeling does not show the place?" But then how is it known to what point I am to direct the will when the feeling is there?

That in this case the finger is as it were paralyzed until we feel a touch on it is shown by experience; it could not have been seen *a priori*.

618. One imagines the willing subject here as something without any mass (without any inertia); as a motor which has no inertia in itself to overcome. And so is only a mover, not a moved. That is: One can say "I will, but my body does not obey me"—but not: "My will does not obey me." (Augustine.)

But in the sense in which I cannot fail to will, I cannot try to will either.

619. And one might say: "I can always will only inasmuch as I can never try to will."

620. *Doing* itself seems not to have any volume of experience. It seems like an extensionless point, the point of a needle. This point seems to be the real agent. And the phenomenal happenings only to be consequences of this acting. "I *do* . . ." seems to have a definite sense, separate from all experience.

621. Let us not forget this: when "I raise my arm," my arm goes up. And the problem arises: what is left over if I subtract the fact that my arm goes up from the fact that I raise my arm?

(Are the kinesthetic sensations my willing?)

622. When I raise my arm I do not usually *try* to raise it.

623. "At all costs I will get to that house." But if there is no difficulty about it, *can* I try at all costs to get to the house?

624. In the laboratory, when subjected to an electric current, for example, someone says with his eyes shut, "I am moving my arm up and down"—though his arm is not moving. "So," we say, "he has the special feeling of making that movement."—Move your arm to and fro with your eyes shut. And now try, while you do so, to tell yourself that your arm is staying still and that you are only having certain queer feelings in your muscles and joints!

625. "How do you know that you have raised your arm?" "I feel it." So what you recognize is the feeling? And are you certain that you recognize it right? You are certain that you have raised your arm; isn't this the criterion, the measure, of the recognition?

626. "When I touch this object with a stick I have the sensation of touching in the tip of the stick, not in the hand that holds it." When someone says, "The pain isn't here in my hand, but in my wrist," this has the consequence that the doctor examines the wrist. But what difference does it make if I say that I feel the hardness of the object in the tip of the stick or in my hand? Does what I say mean "It is as if I had nerve-endings in the tip of the stick?" *In what sense* is it like that?— Well, I am at any rate inclined to say "I feel the hardness, etc., in the tip of the stick." What goes with this is that when I touch the object I look not at my hand but at the tip of the stick; that I describe what I feel by saying "I feel something hard and round there" — not "I feel a pressure against the tips of my thumb, middle finger, and index finger." If, for example, someone asks me, "What are you now feeling in the fingers that hold the probe?" I might reply: "I don't know—I feel something hard and rough *over there*."

627. Examine the following description of a voluntary action: "I form the decision to pull the bell at 5 o'clock, and when it strikes 5, my arm makes this movement."—Is that the correct description, and not *this* one: ". . . and when it strikes 5, I raise my arm"?—One would like to supplement the first description: "and see! my arm goes up when it strikes 5." And this "and see!" is precisely what doesn't belong here. I do *not* say, "See, my arm is going up!" when I raise it.

628. So one might say: voluntary movement is marked by the absence of surprise. And now I do not mean you to ask, "But *why* isn't one surprised here?"

629. When people talk about the possibility of foreknowledge of the future they always forget the fact of the prediction of one's own voluntary movements.

630. Examine these two language-games:

(a) Someone gives someone else the order to make particular movements with his arm, or to assume particular bodily positions (gymnastics instructor and pupil). And here is a variation of this language-game: the pupil gives himself orders and then carries them out.

(b) Someone observes certain regular processes—for example, the reactions of different metals to acids—and thereupon makes predictions about the reactions that will occur in certain particular cases.

There is an evident kinship between these two language-games, and also a fundamental difference. In both one might call the spoken words "predictions." But compare the training which leads to the first technique with the training for the second one.

631. "I am going to take two powders now, and in half-an-hour I shall be sick."—It explains nothing to say that in the first case I am the agent, in the second merely the observer. Or that in the first case I see the causal connection from inside, in the second from outside. And much else the same.

Nor is it to the point to say that a prediction of the first kind is no more infallible than one of the second kind.

It was not on the ground of observations of my behavior that I said I was going to take two powders. The antecedents of this proposition were different. I mean the thoughts, actions, and so on, which led up to it. And it can only mislead you to say: "The only essential presupposition of your utterance was just your decision."

632. I do not want to say that in the case of the expression of intention "I am going to take two powders" the prediction is a cause—and its fulfillment the effect. (Perhaps a physiological investigation could determine this.) So much, however, is true: we can often predict a man's actions from his expression of a decision. An important language-game.

633. "You were interrupted a while ago; do you still know what you were going to say?"—If I do know now, and say it, does that mean that I had already thought it before and only not said it? No. Unless you take the certainty with which I continue the inter-rupted sentence as a criterion of the thought's already having been completed at that time. But, of course, the situation and the thoughts which I had contained all sorts of things to help the continuation of the sentence.

634. When I continue the interrupted sentence and say that *this* was how I had been going to continue it, this is like following out a line of thought from brief notes.

Then don't I *interpret* the notes? Was only one continuation possible in these circumstances? Of course not. But I did not *choose* between interpretations. I *remembered* that I was going to say this.

635. "I was going to say . . ."—You remember various details. But not even all of them together show your intention. It is as if a snapshot of a scene had been taken, but only a few scattered details of it were to be seen: here a hand, there a bit of a face, or a hat—the rest is dark. And now it is as if we knew quite certainly what the whole picture represented. As if I could read the darkness.

636. These "details" are not irrelevant in the sense in which other circumstances which I can remember equally well are irrelevant. But if I tell someone, "For a moment I was going to say . . . ," he does not learn those details from this, nor need he guess them. He need not know, for instance, that I had already opened my mouth to speak. But he *can* "fill out the picture" in this way. (And this capacity is part of understanding what I tell him.)

637. "I know exactly what I was going to say!" And yet I did not say it.—And yet I don't read it off from some other process which took place then and which I remember.

Nor am I *interpreting* that situation and its antecedents. For I don't consider them and don't judge them.

638. How does it come about that in spite of this I am inclined to see an interpretation in saying "For a moment I was going to deceive him"?

"How can you be certain that for the space of a moment you were going to deceive him? Weren't your actions and thoughts much too rudimentary?"

For can't the evidence be too scanty? Yes, when one follows it up it seems extraordinarily scanty; but isn't this because one is taking no account of the history of this evidence? Certain antecedents were necessary for me to have had a momentary intention of pretending to someone else that I was unwell.

If someone says "For a moment . . . ," is he really only describing a momentary process?

But not even the whole story was my evidence for saying "For a moment . . . "

639. One would like to say that an opinion *develops*. But there is a mistake in this too.

640. "This thought ties on to thoughts which I have had before."—How does it do so? Through a *feeling* of such a tie? But how can a feeling really tie thoughts together?—The word "feeling" is very misleading here. But it is sometimes possible to say with certainty: "This thought is connected with those earlier thoughts," and yet be unable to show the connection. Perhaps that comes later.

641. "My intention was no less certain as it was than it would have been if I had said, 'Now I'll deceive him.' "—But if you had said the words, would you necessarily have meant them quite seriously? (Thus the most explicit expression of intention is by itself insufficient evidence of intention.)

642. "At that moment I hated him."—What happened here? Didn't it consist in thoughts, feelings, and actions? And if I were to rehearse that moment to myself I should assume a particular expression, think of certain happenings, breathe in a particular way, arouse certain feelings in myself. I might think up a conversation, a whole scene in which that hatred flared up. And I might play this scene through with feelings approximating to those of a real occasion. That I have actually experienced something of the sort will naturally help me to do so.

643. If I now become ashamed of this incident, I am ashamed of the whole thing: of the words, of the poisonous tone, etc.

644. "I am not ashamed of what I did then, but of the intention which I had."—And didn't what I did *include* the intention? What justifies the shame? The whole history of the incident.

645. "For a moment I meant to . . ." That is, I had a particular feeling, an inner experience; and I remember it.—And now remember *quite precisely*! Then the "inner experience" of intending seems to vanish again. Instead one remembers thoughts, feelings, movements, and also connections with earlier situations.

It is as if one had altered the adjustment of a microscope. One did not see before what is now in focus.

646. "Well, that only shows that you have adjusted your microscope wrong. You were supposed to look at a particular section of the culture, and you are seeing a different one."

There is something right about that. But suppose that (with a particular adjustment of the lenses) I did remember a *single* sensation; how have I the right to say that it is what I call the "intention"? It might be that (for example) a particular tickle accompanied every one of my intentions.

647. What is the natural expression of an intention?—Look at a cat when it stalks a bird; or a beast when it wants to escape.

(Connection with propositions about sensations.)

648. "I no longer remember the words I used, but I remember my intention precisely; I meant my words to quiet him." What does my memory *show* me; what does it bring before my mind? Suppose it did nothing but suggest those words to me!—and perhaps others which fill out the picture still more exactly. ("I don't remember my words any more, but I certainly remember their spirit.")

649. "So if a man has not learned a language, is he unable to have certain memories?" Of course; he cannot have verbal memories, verbal wishes or fears, and so on. And memories, etc., in language, are not mere threadbare representations of the *real* experiences; for is what is linguistic not an experience?

650. We say a dog is afraid his master will beat him; but not, he is afraid his master will beat him tomorrow. Why not?

651. "I remember that I should have been glad then to stay still longer."—What picture of this wish came before my mind? None at all. What I see in my memory allows no conclusion as to my feelings. And yet I remember quite clearly that they were there.

652. "He measured him with a hostile glance and said . . ." The reader of the narrative understands this; he has no doubt in his mind. Now you say: "Very well, he supplies the meaning, he guesses it."—Generally speaking: no. Generally speaking he supplies nothing, guesses nothing.—But it is also possible that the hostile glance and the words later prove to have been pretense, or that the reader is kept in doubt whether they are so

or not, and so that he really does guess at a possible interpretation. — But then the main thing he guesses at is a context. He says to himself for example: The two men who are here so hostile to one another are in reality friends, etc., etc.

("If you want to understand a sentence, you have to imagine the psychical significance, the states of mind involved.")

653. Imagine this case: I tell someone that I walked a certain route, going by a map which I had prepared beforehand. Thereupon I show him the map, and it consists of lines on a piece of paper; but I cannot explain how these lines are the map of my movements, I cannot tell him any rule for interpreting the map. Yet I did follow the drawing with all the characteristic tokens of reading a map. I might call such a drawing a "private" map; or the phenomenon that I have described "following a private map." (But this expression would, of course, be very easy to misunderstand.)

Could I now say: "I read off my having then meant to do such-and-such, as if from a map, although there is no map"? But that means nothing but: *I am now inclined to say,* "I read the intention of acting thus in certain states of mind which I remember."

654. Our mistake is to look for an explanation where we ought to look at what happens as a "proto-phenomenon." That is, where we ought to have said: *this language-game is played.*

655. The question is not one of explaining a language-game by means of our experiences, but of noting a language-game.

656. What is the purpose of telling someone that a time ago I had such-and-such a wish?— Look on the language-game as the *primary* thing. And look on the feelings, etc., as you look on a way of regarding the language-game, as interpretation.

It might be asked: how did human beings ever come to make the verbal utterances which we call reports of past wishes or past intentions?

657. Let us imagine these utterances always taking this form: "I said to myself: 'if only I could stay longer!'" The purpose of such a statement might be to acquaint someone with my reactions. (Compare the grammar of *meinen* and *vouloir dire.*)

658. Suppose we expressed the fact that a man had an intention by saying "He as it were

said to himself 'I will . . .'"—That is the picture. And now I want to know: how does one employ the expression "as it were to say something to oneself"? For it does not mean to say something to oneself.

659. Why do I want to tell him about an intention too, as well as telling him what I did?—Not because the intention was also something which was going on at that time. But because I want to tell him something about *myself,* which goes beyond what happened at that time.

I reveal to him something of myself when I tell him what I was going to do. Not, however, on grounds of self-observation, but by way of a response (it might also be called an intuition).

. . .

"My kinesthetic sensations advise me of the movements and position of my limbs."

I let my index finger make an easy pendulum movement of small amplitude. I either hardly feel it, or don't feel it at all. Perhaps a little in the tip of the finger, as a slight tension. (Not at all in the joint.) And this sensation advises me of the movement?—for I can describe the movement exactly.

"But after all, you must feel it, otherwise you wouldn't know (without looking) how your finger was moving." But "knowing" it only means: being able to describe it.—I may be able to tell the direction from which a sound comes only because it affects one ear more strongly than the other, but I don't feel this in my ears; yet it has its effect: I *know* the direction from which the sound comes; for instance, I look in that direction.

It is the same with the idea that it must be some feature of our pain that advises us of the whereabouts of the pain in the body, and some feature of our memory image that tells us the time to which it belongs.

A sensation *can* advise us of the movement or position of a limb. (For example, if you do not know, as a normal person does, whether your arm is stretched out, you might find out by a piercing pain in the elbow.)—In the same way the character of a pain can tell us where the injury is. (And the yellowness of a photograph how old it is.)

What is the criterion for my learning the shape and color of an object from a sense-impression?

What sense-impression? Well, *this* one; I use words or a picture to describe it.

And now: what do you feel when your fingers are in this position?—"How is one to define a feeling? It is something special and indefinable." But it must be possible to teach the use of the words!

What I am looking for is the grammatical difference.

Let us leave the kinesthetic feeling out for the moment.—I want to describe a feeling to someone, and I tell him "Do *this,* and then you'll get it," and I hold my arm or my head in a particular position. Now is this a description of a feeling? and when shall I say that he has understood what feeling I meant? —He will have to give a *further* description

of the feeling afterward. And what kind of description must it be?

I say "Do *this,* and you'll get it." Can't there be a doubt here? Mustn't there be one, if it is a feeling that is meant?

This looks *so; this* tastes *so; this* feels *so.* "This" and "so" must be differently explained.

Our interest in a "feeling" is of a quite *particular* kind. It includes, for instance, the "degree of the feeling," its "place," and the extent to which one feeling can be submerged by another. (When a movement is very painful, so that the pain submerges every other slight sensation in the same place, does this make it uncertain whether you have really made this movement? Could it lead you to find out by looking?)

The Will*

I. FOREWORD

Most of the mental-conduct concepts whose logical behavior we examine in this book, are familiar and everyday concepts. We all know how to apply them and we understand other people when they apply them. What is in dispute is not how to apply them, but how to classify them, or in what categories to put them.

The concept of volition is in a different case. We do not know in daily life how to use it, for we do not use it in daily life and do not, consequently, learn by practice how to apply it, and how not to misapply it. It is an artificial concept. We have to study certain specialist theories in order to find out how it is to be manipulated. It does not, of course, follow from its being a technical concept that it is an illegitimate or useless concept. "Ionization" and "off-side" are technical concepts, but both are legitimate and useful. "Phlogiston" and "animal spirts" were technical concepts, though they have now no utility.

I hope to show that the concept of volition belongs to the latter tribe.

II. THE MYTH OF VOLITIONS

It has for a long time been taken for an indisputable axiom that the Mind is in some

* Gilbert Ryle, *The Concept of Mind* (London: Hutchinson's University Library, 1949), pp. 62–69, reprinted with the permission of the author and The Hutchinson Group, London.

important sense tripartite, that is, that there are just three ultimate classes of mental processes. The Mind or Soul, we are often told, has three parts, namely, Thought, Feeling, and Will; or, more solemnly, the Mind or Soul functions in three irreducibly different modes, the Cognitive mode, the Emotional mode, and the Conative mode. This traditional dogma is not only not self-evident, it is such a welter of confusions and false inferences that it is best to give up any attempts to refashion it. It should be treated at one of the curios of theory.

The main object of this chapter is not, however, to discuss the whole trinitarian theory of mind but to discuss, and discuss destructively, one of its ingredients. I hope to refute the doctrine that there exists a Faculty, immaterial Organ, or Ministry, corresponding to the theory's description of the "Will," and, accordingly, that there occur processes, or operations, corresponding to what it describes as "volitions." I must however make it clear from the start that this refutation will not invalidate the distinctions which we all quite properly draw between voluntary and involuntary actions and between strong-willed and weak-willed persons. It will, on the contrary, make clearer what is meant by "voluntary" and "involuntary," by "strong-willed" and "weak-willed," by emancipating these ideas from bondage to an absurd hypothesis.

Volitions have been postulated as special

acts, or operations, "in the mind," by means of which a mind gets its ideas translated into facts. I think of some state of affairs which I wish to come into existence in the physical world, but, as my thinking and wishing are unexecutive, they require the mediation of a further executive mental process. So I perform a volition which somehow puts my muscles into action. Only when a bodily movement has issued from such a volition can I merit praise or blame for what my hand or tongue has done.

It will be clear why I reject this story. It is just an inevitable extension of the myth of the ghost in the machine. It assumes that there are mental states and processes enjoying one sort of existence, and bodily states and processes enjoying another. An occurrence on the one stage is never numerically identical with an occurrence on the other. So, to say that a person pulled the trigger intentionally is to express at least a conjunctive proposition, asserting the occurrence of one act on the physical stage and other on the mental stage; and, according to most versions of the myth, it is to express a causal proposition, asserting that the bodily act of pulling the trigger was the effect of a mental act of willing to pull the trigger.

According to the theory, the workings of the body are motions of matter in space. The causes of these motions must then be *either* other motions of matter in space *or*, in the privileged case of human beings, thrusts of another kind. In some way which must forever remain a mystery, mental thrusts, which are not movements of matter in space, can cause muscles to contract. To describe a man as intentionally pulling the trigger is to state that such a mental thrust did cause the contraction of the muscles of his finger. So the language of "volitions" is the language of the para-mechanical theory of the mind. If a theorist speaks without qualms of "volitions," or "acts of will," no further evidence is needed to show that he swallows whole the dogma that a mind is a secondary field of special causes. It can be predicted that he will correspondingly speak of bodily actions as "expressions" of mental processes. He is likely also to speak glibly of "experiences," a plural noun commonly used to denote the postulated nonphysical episodes which constitute the shadow-drama on the ghostly boards of the mental stage.

The first objection to the doctrine that overt actions, to which we ascribe intelligence-predicates, are results of counterpart hidden operations of willing is this. Despite the fact that theorists have, since the Stoics and Saint Augustine, recommended us to describe our conduct in this way, no one, save to endorse the theory, ever describes his own conduct, or that of his acquaintances, in the recommended idioms. No one ever says such things as that at 10 A.M. he was occupied in willing this or that, or that he performed five quick and easy volitions and two slow and difficult volitions between midday and lunch-time. An accused person may admit or deny that he did something, or that he did it on purpose, but he never admits or denies having willed. Nor do the judge and jury require to be satisfied by evidence, which in the nature of the case could never be adduced, that a volition preceded the pulling of the trigger. Novelists describe the actions, remarks, gestures, and grimaces, the daydreams, deliberations, qualms, and embarrassments of their characters; but they never mention their volitions. They would not know what to say about them.

By what sorts of predicates should they be described? Can they be sudden or gradual, strong or weak, difficult or easy, enjoyable or disagreeable? Can they be accelerated, decelerated, interrupted, or suspended? Can people be efficient or inefficient at them? Can we take lessons in executing them? Are they fatiguing or distracting? Can I do two or seven of them synchronously? Can I remember executing them? Can I execute them, while thinking of other things, or while dreaming? Can they become habitual? Can I forget how to do them? Can I mistakenly believe that I have executed one, when I have not, or that I have not executed one, when I have? At which moment was the boy going through a volition to take the high dive? When he set foot on the ladder? When he took his first deep breath? When he counted off "One, two, three—Go," but did not go? Very, very shortly before he sprang? What would his own answer be to those questions?

Champions of the doctrine maintain, of course, that the enactment of volitions is asserted by implication, whenever an overt act is described as intentional, voluntary, culpable, or meritorious; they assert too that any person is not merely able but bound to know that he is willing when he is doing so, since volitions are defined as a species of conscious process. So if ordinary men and women fail to mention their volitions in their descriptions of their own behavior, this must be due to their being untrained in the dictions appropriate to the description of their inner, as distinct from their overt, behavior. However, when a champion of the doctrine is himself asked how long ago he executed his last volition, or how many acts of will be executes in, say, reciting "Little Miss Muffet" backward, he is apt to confess to finding difficulties in giving the answer, though these difficulties should not, according to his own theory, exist.

If ordinary men never report the occurrence of these acts, for all that, according to the theory, they should be encountered vastly more frequently than headaches, or feelings of boredom; if ordinary vocabulary has no nonacademic names for them; if we do not know how to settle simple questions about their frequency, duration, or strength, then it is fair to conclude that their existence is not asserted on empirical grounds. The fact that Plato and Aristotle never mentioned them in their frequent and elaborate discussions of the nature of the soul and the springs of conduct is due not to any perverse neglect by them of notorious ingredients of daily life but to the historical circumstance that they were not acquainted with a special hypothesis the acceptance of which rests not on the discovery, but on the postulation, of these ghostly thrusts.

The second objection is this. It is admitted that one person can never witness the volitions of another; he can only infer from an observed overt action to the volition from which it resulted, and then only if he has any good reason to believe that the overt action was a voluntary action, and not a reflex or habitual action, or one resulting from some external cause. It follows that no judge, schoolmaster, or parent ever knows that the actions which he judges merit praise or blame; for he cannot do better than guess that the action was willed. Even a confession by the agent, if such confessions were ever made, that he had executed a volition before his hand did the deed would not settle the question. The pronouncement of the confession is only another overt muscular action. The curious conclusion results that though volitions were called in to explain our appraisals of actions,

this explanation is just what they fail to provide. If we had no other antecedent grounds for applying appraisal-concepts to the actions of others, we should have no reasons at all for inferring from those actions to the volitions alleged to give rise to them.

Nor could it be maintained that the agent himself can know that any overt action of his own is the effect of a given volition. Supposing, what is not the case, that he could know for certain, either from the alleged direct deliverances of consciousness, or from the alleged direct findings of introspection, that he had executed an act of will to pull the trigger just before he pulled it, this would not prove that the pulling was the effect of that willing. The connection between volitions and movements is allowed to be mysterious, so, for all he knows, his volition may have had some other movement as its effect and the pulling of the trigger may have had some other event for its cause.

Thirdly, it would be improper to burke the point that the connection between volition and movement is admitted to be a mystery. It is a mystery not of the unsolved but soluble type, like the problem of the cause of cancer, but of quite another type. The episodes supposed to constitute the careers of minds are assumed to have one sort of existence, while those constituting the careers of bodies have another sort; and no bridge-status is allowed. Transactions between minds and bodies involve links where no links can be. That there should be any causal transactions between minds and matter conflicts with one part; that there should be none conflicts with another part of the theory. Minds, as the whole legend describes them, are what must exist if there is to be a causal explanation of the intelligent behavior of human bodies; and minds, as the legend describes them, live on a floor of existence defined as being outside the causal system to which bodies belong.

Fourthly, although the prime function of volitions, the task for the performance of which they were postulated, is to originate bodily movements, the argument, such as it is, for their existence entails that some mental happenings also must result from acts of will. Volitions were postulated to be that which makes actions voluntary, resolute, meritorious, and wicked. But predicates of these sorts are ascribed not only to bodily movements but also to operations which, according to the theory, are mental and not physical operations. A thinker may ratiocinate resolutely, or imagine wickedly; he may try to compose a limerick and he may meritoriously concentrate on his algebra. Some mental processes then can, according to the theory, issue from volitions. So what of volitions themselves? Are they voluntary or involuntary acts of mind? Clearly either answer leads to absurdities. If I cannot help willing to pull the trigger, it would be absurd to describe my pulling it as "voluntary." But if my volition to pull the trigger is voluntary, in the sense assumed by the theory, then it must issue from a prior volition and that from another ad infinitum. It has been suggested, to avoid this difficulty, that volitions cannot be described as either voluntary or involuntary. "Volition" is a term of the wrong type to accept either predicate. If so, it would seem to follow that it is also of the wrong type to accept such predicates as "virtuous" and "wicked," "good" and "bad," a conclusion which might embarrass those moralists who use volitions as the sheet-anchor of their systems.

In short, then, the doctrine of volitions is a causal hypothesis, adopted because it was wrongly supposed that the question, "What makes a bodily movement voluntary?" was a causal question. This supposition is, in fact, only a special twist of the general supposition that the question, "How are mental-conduct concepts applicable to human behavior?" is a question about the causation of that behavior.

Champions of the doctrine should have noticed the simple fact that they and all other sensible persons knew how to decide questions about the voluntariness and involuntariness of actions and about the resoluteness and irresoluteness of agents before they had ever heard of the hypothesis of the occult inner thrusts of actions. They might then have realized that they were not elucidating the criteria already in efficient use, but, tacitly assuming their validity, were trying to correlate them with hypothetical occurrences of a para-mechanical pattern. Yet this correlation could, on the one hand, never be scientifically established, since the thrusts postulated were screened from scientific observation; and, on the other hand, it would be of no practical or theoretical use, since it would not assist our appraisals of actions, depending as it would on the presupposed validity of those appraisals.

Nor would it elucidate the logic of those appraisal-concepts, the intelligent employment of which antedated the invention of this causal hypothesis.

Before we bid farewell to the doctrine of volitions, it is expedient to consider certain quite familiar and authentic processes with which volitions are sometimes wrongly identified.

People are frequently in doubt what to do; having considered alternative courses of action, they then, sometimes, select or choose one of these courses. This process of opting for one of a set of alternative courses of action is sometimes said to be what is signified by "volition." But this identification will not do, for most voluntary actions do not issue out of conditions of indecision and are not therefore results of settlements of indecisions. Moreover it is notorious that a person may choose to do something but fail, from weakness of will, to do it; or he may fail to do it because some circumstance arises after the choice is made, preventing the execution of the act chosen. But the theory could not allow that volitions ever fail to result in action, else further executive operations would have to be postulated to account for the fact that sometimes voluntary actions are performed. And finally the process of deliberating between alternatives and opting for one of them is itself subject to appraisal-predicates. But if, for example, an act of choosing is describable as voluntary, then, on this suggested showing, it would have in its turn to be the result of a prior choice to choose, and that from a choice to choose to choose. . . .

The same objections forbid the identification with volitions of such other familiar processes as that of resolving or making up our minds to do something and that of nerving or bracing ourselves to do something. I may resolve to get out of bed or go to the dentist, and I may, clenching my fists and gritting my teeth, brace myself to do so, but I may still backslide. If the action is not done, then, according to the doctrine, the volition to do it is also unexecuted. Again, the operations of resolving and nerving ourselves are themselves members of the class of creditable or discreditable actions, so they cannot constitute the peculiar ingredient which, according to the doctrine, is the common condition of any performance being creditable or discreditable.

Willing*

There is a difference between my arm rising and my raising my arm, between my muscles moving and my moving my muscles—in short, between a bodily movement or happening and an action. In this paper I examine one attempt to make out the nature of this difference.

Consider the following. Whenever I raise my arm (deliberately, let us say) I bring to pass certain muscle movements: I make these happen. Hence I raise my arm by moving (contracting and expanding) certain muscles of my arm. This, then, is how I raise my arm. This of course is a bad argument. We cannot identify what one does with what one makes happen. When I flex the biceps brachii of my arm many things are brought to pass, made to happen. Nerve impulses are transmitted to the muscles, neural circuits in the brain are opened and closed, protein molecules in the brain are set into oscillation, and many more things of which I have not the faintest intimation. But let us consider the conclusion on its own merits. Certainly I can contract certain muscles at will. If someone points to the biceps brachii of my arm and asks me to flex it, this I can easily do. So it is tempting to say that when I raise my arm, I do so by moving certain muscles *just as* when I signal, I do so by raising my arm.

But how do I move certain muscles? There is a difference between my biceps becoming flexed and *my* flexing my biceps, just as there is a difference between my arm getting raised and my raising my arm. The flexing of my biceps may occur through no doing of mine (someone might raise my arm and in doing so cause my biceps to be flexed), just as my arm getting raised may be something that happens to me through the action of another person who raises my arm and not through anything I do. And what can the difference be between the occurrence of a muscle movement in my arm and my moving that muscle, except that in the latter case it is by doing something that I bring the muscle movement to pass? In short, if it is sensible to say that I raise my arm by moving certain muscles, it is equally sensible to hold that I move those muscles by doing something that brings those muscle movements to pass. And what can this latter doing be that has these muscle movements as effect?

Consider the biceps brachii of my arm. Someone points to it and says, "Flex it!" What must I do in order to comply? Must I say to myself, "Move, muscle, move"? If I do this, nothing will happen. Does nothing happen because I do not mean it? Then how do I mean it? "Meaning what I say"—is this something I do when I say whatever it is that I do say? And how do I do that? Shall we say that I shall mean it only when I *want* my muscle to move? But if I want my biceps to move and stare at it again nothing will happen; I must do something about my want, that is, get what it is that I want. Is it necessary that I set myself—to use H. A. Prichard's expression—to move my biceps?[1] But if "setting myself" means getting ready, putting myself in a state of readiness, again nothing will happen. And if "setting myself to do" means trying to do or exerting myself to do, then I need do nothing of the sort. I do not try to raise my arm unless, for example, it is held down—I simply raise it; and I do not try to flex my biceps unless there is some obstacle to be overcome or some chance of failure.

What then is the difference between my muscles being contracted and my contracting my muscles? A familiar doctrine is that in the latter case I will my muscles to move; in the former case there are causes other than the act of volition. So I move my muscles by performing an act of volition which in turn produces a muscle movement.

Grant for a moment that an event labeled "an act of volition" produces a muscle movement; there is a difference surely between the occurrence of such an event and my producing it. We saw that there is a difference between the occurrence of a muscle movement and my moving that muscle; hence it was that the supposition of acts of volition was invoked. But equally there would seem to be a difference between the occurrence of an act of volition and my performing such an act. Who can say that volitions may occur through no doing of the subject and in consequence of interior

* A. I. Melden, "Willing," *The Philosophical Review*, LXIX (October 1960), 475–84, reprinted with the permission of the author and *The Philosophical Review*.

[1] Cf. the essay "Duty and Ignorance of Fact" in *Moral Obligation* (Oxford, 1949).

mental events deep within the hidden recesses of the self? If so, willing the muscle movement is not enough; one must will the willing of the muscle movement, and so on ad infinitum. Here someone may retort impatiently: "When I will a muscle movement, *I* will it and that is the end of the matter; there is no other doing by virtue of which this act of volition gets done—I simply will the movement." But even if this reply were correct it would not serve to explain what an action is, as distinguished from a mere happening. It explains the "action" of raising the arm in terms of an internal action of willing, and hence all it does at best is to change the locus of action. Indeed it invites the view argued by Prichard that, strictly speaking and contrary to the notion conveyed by our ordinary ways of speaking, one does not raise one's arm at all: all one does or can do is will and by means of this action produce various effects such as the rising on one's arm. In any case if willing is some sort of doing which one performs not by means of any other doing—one wills and that is the end of the matter—why not say the same with respect to the muscle movement itself, or the tensing of one's biceps? One simply tenses it and there is no doing by virtue of which the tensing gets done. But the troubles involved in the supposition that there are interior acts of willing go even deeper than this; the doctrine, familiar though it may be, is a mare's nest of confusions.

How shall we describe the alleged action of willing? Surely a description of this action independently of the consequence alleged for it—the production of a muscle movement— must be forthcoming. Let us call the act of willing A; then A produces B (a muscle movement, this being taken to be a causal sequence. Now in general if A causes B, a description of A other than that it has the causal property of producing B must be forthcoming; otherwise "A causes B" degenerates into "the thing that produces B produces B." But what description of the act of volition can be offered? If something causes me to jump in fright, jerk my arm, or move my head, "What caused you to . . . ?" is intelligible and answerable. It is no good saying, "That which caused me to do it," for this is no answer but a bit of rudeness or a feeble attempt at humor. How then shall one describe the act of willing?

It is at this point that the resort to indefinables appears attractive.[2] Willing is *sui generis*, indefinable, a bit of mental self-exertion in which we engage, an activity not capable of further description but different from the wonderings, thinkings, supposings, expectings, picturings, and so forth, that comprise our mental activities. Yet the appeal to indefinables is a desperate defense that purchases immunity from further attack only at the expense of unintelligibility. If all that can be said about the alleged act of volition by virtue of which a muscle movement is produced is that it is the sort of thing that produces a muscle movement, there is every uncertainty that anyone has understood what is meant by "the act of volition." And if an attempt to rescue this doctrine is made by appealing to something with which, it is alleged, each of us is intimately familiar and hence will have no difficulty in recognizing—the act of volition that produces the muscle movement—the retort must surely by "*What* do I recognize when I recognize an act of volition?" Unless I can recognize this act by having some description in mind that applies to such acts and only to these, it is at best a simple begging of the question to insist that all of us really understand what is being referred to; in fact, it is an implied charge of dishonesty directed at those who refuse to give their assent. And in philosophy, when good manners alone stand in the way of the open parade of charges of this sort, there is something seriously amiss in one's thinking.

But the difficulty in this talk about acts of volition is not merely that some account of acts of volition in general is needed, failing which we can only conclude that the expression "act of volition" can play no role in our discourse, it is equally serious in other respects as well. Let us grant that there is some peculiar mental activity of willing the causal consequence of which is that certain muscles are contracted and others relaxed as we perform our diverse bodily movements, and let us now ask first of all how it is that we are able to learn how to perform these bodily movements. Surely the act of volition involved in the production of one muscle movement must be distinguished from the act

[2] Indeed, this is the move made by Prichard in the essay "Acting, Willing, Desiring," written in 1945 and published posthumously in *Moral Obligation* (Oxford, 1949). This essay is worth careful reading; in it Prichard abandons his earlier accounts of "willing" as setting oneself to do.

of volition involved in the production of any other. There will then be different acts of volition, v_1, v_2, v_3, and so forth, which respectively, move muscles m_1, m_2, m_3, and so forth. If $v_1 \rightarrow m_1$, $v_2 \rightarrow m_2$, $v_3 \rightarrow m_3$, and so forth, represent causal relations, then just as m_1, m_2, m_3 are distinguishable, so v_1, v_2, v_3 will needs be different in kind. And if I am to learn how to produce m_1 by performing the act of volition v_1, I must not only recognize the difference between v_1 and other acts of volition that have other effects; I must also recognize the causal relation holding between v_1 and m_1. Now this would seem to imply at least two things: (1) It must be possible to offer a set of characterizations of these acts of volition each different from the other, corresponding to the set of characterizations that can be given, surely, for the muscle movements m_1, m_2, m_3, m_4, and so forth. (2) I can learn only from experience that m_1 is produced by v_1, m_2 by v_2, m_3 by v_3, and so on. Hence, unless I suppose myself to have been endowed with superhuman prescience, I cannot have been surprised or astonished the first time I performed the act of volition v_1 to discover that muscle movement m_1 occurred, and antecedently I should have no reason for ruling out the possibility that m_2 would not occur; I should have no reason, for example, to suppose that when I performed the act of volition by which in fact my biceps became flexed, my right leg would not have been raised.

Consider the first of these consequences. Now I can certainly distinguish between muscle movements m_1 and m_2, say, the biceps of my right arm from that of my left arm. But how shall I distinguish between the acts of volition v_1 and v_2 by which these distinct muscle movements are produced? If I produce these muscle movements by performing these acts of volition, this at any rate is something I learn to do, an ability I come to acquire. But if I can learn to do this, I must be able to distinguish between the volitions v_1 and v_2. Surely it must be possible to describe the difference. And if this cannot be done, learning to produce m_1 by producing v_1 and learning to produce m_2 by producing v_2 is impossible. How then shall we describe v_1 as distinguished from v_2? Shall we say that not only are volitions in general indefinable, but that the difference between v_1 and v_2 is also something indefinable? At least, however, the difference must be recognizable. Is it that our vocabulary is inadequate? Then let us introduce words that will enable us to mark the distinction. And now that the words have been introduced, explain how they are to be employed! Is it that we can only *point*: v_1 is *this* thing, the one that one finds one performs when m_1 is produced, v_2 is *that* thing, the one that one finds that one performs when m_2 is produced? But this will do the trick only if I already know what sorts of things to look for and only if it is at least possible for me to go on and describe the difference between v_1 and v_2 independently of the considerations that v_1 produces m_1 and v_2 produces m_2. By pointing one can succeed in explaining the meaning of a term or expression, but only if by doing so one can help fill in a gap or supply the links missing in some initial background understanding we have of that term or expression. But here we do not know where to look or what to find. No background understanding is present; we are told that there are certain things—call them "acts of volition"—that they are indefinable, and that nothing more can be said about them at all in explaining how this expression "act of volition" is to be employed. Against this background, how can pointing serve to provide any explanation at all of the difference between act of volition$_1$ (call it mental-muscle-doing$_1$) and act of volition$_2$ (mental-muscle-doing$_2$)? To say at this point that the difference itself is indefinable is, surely, to carry philosophical pretension beyond all limits of credulity.

As far as I know, philosophers are quite unwilling to pile indefinables upon indefinables in this fulsome manner. Prichard for one, despite his characteristic resort to indefinables, is admirable for an equally characteristic subtlety that leads him to reject such simpleminded answers even though, as he himself recognizes, he must accept a conclusion that is open to objections he cannot meet. Consider the second of the two consequences of the doctrine of acts of volition. That v_1 produces m_1 rather than m_2 is a causal fact; but if so, I should have no reason to suppose, when I first performed the act of volition v_1 that m_1 rather than m_2 would follow; for on this view the statement that, for example, I move the biceps brachii of my right arm by performing the act of volition v_1, rather than the biceps brachii of my left arm or the biceps femoris of my right leg, is justified only on the basis of inductive evidence. Now Prichard holds that an act of volition involves a desire to will whatever it is that one wills, and hence some idea of what the volition is likely to produce. This, however, is impossible on the present view since on the first occasions on which I performed v_1 and thereby produced m_1, v_1 would require the thought that I would be doing something that would produce m_1 and by hypothesis I should have no reason to expect what, if anything, v_1 would produce. Prichard is therefore led to the conclusion that an "act of will requires an idea of something which we may cause if we perform the act," a conclusion—indeed a difficulty—he is unable to avoid.[3]

Prichard's predicament involves a matter of central importance which can be stated quite independently of his insistence that if one is to perform an act of volition, one must be moved by a desire to perform that act of volition. The important issue raised by Prichard is whether or not it is intelligible to speak of an act of volition where the very notion of such an act does not involve a reference to the relevant bodily event. Let the act of volition issue in a muscle movement, then, as Prichard himself recognizes, the act must be the willing of that muscle movement; otherwise we should have only inductive grounds for supposing the act to issue in that particular muscle movement. Accordingly we are faced with the following dilemma: If in thinking of v_1 (some particular act of volition) we are of necessity to think of it as the willing of m_1 (some particular muscle movement), then v_1 cannot be any occurrence, mental or physiological, which is causally related to m_1, since the very notion of a causal sequence logically implies that cause and effect are intelligible without any logically internal relation of the one to the other. If, on the other hand, we think of v_1 and m_1 as causally related in the way in which we think of the relation between the movements of muscles and the raising of one's arm, then we must conclude that when first we perform v_1 we should be taken completely by surprise to find that m_1 does in fact ensue. If to avoid this later consequence we maintain that the thought of the muscle movement enters into the very character of the act of volition (as Prichard puts it, "the *thinking*

enters into the character of the *willing*"[4]), no description of the act of volition can be given that does not involve an account of the muscle movement, and hence we must abandon the idea that the act of volition v_1 is a cause that produces m_1, the muscle movement. Prichard's predicament is that his conclusion that "an act of will requires an idea of something which we may cause if we perform the act" is nothing less than self-contradictory.

This then is the logical incoherence involved in the doctrine of acts of volition. Acts of volition are alleged to be direct causes of certain bodily phenomena (whether these be brain occurrences, as Prichard supposed them to be, or muscle movements, as we have been assuming for the sake of argument, is of no matter) just as the latter are causes of the raising of one's arm. For, it is alleged, just as we raise our arms by moving our muscles, so we move our muscles by willing them to move. But no account of the alleged volitions is intelligible that does not involve a reference to the relevant bodily phenomena. And no interior cause, mental or physiological, can have this logical feature of acts of volition. Let the interior event which we call "the act of volition" be mental or physical (which it is will make no difference at all), it must be logically distinct from the alleged effect: this surely is one lesson we can derive from a reading of Hume's discussion of causation. Yet nothing can be an act of volition that is not logically connected with that which is willed; the act of willing is intelligble only as the act of willing whatever it is that is willed. In short, there could not be such an interior event like an act of volition since (here one is reminded of Wittgenstein's famous remark about meaning) nothing of that sort could have the required logical consequences.

Let me review the course of the argument. The doctrine of acts of volition was introduced, it will be remembered, in order to elucidate the distinction between one's arm rising and one's raising one's arm. The former need involve no doing or action performed by the agent; the latter surely does. But instead of rejecting the question "How does one raise one's arm?" by a "One just does" retort, the reply we considered was "One raises one's arm by moving certain muscles." Here the same question arises again: how can one dis-

[3] *Moral Obligation,* pp. 196–97. See also his second thoughts about his earlier notion of "setting oneself" in the footnotes to his earlier essay, "Duty and Ignorance of Fact," which appear in the same volume (p. 38).

[4] *Ibid.,* p. 38.

tinguished between "moving certain muscles" and "certain muscles getting moved"? The latter need involve no action on my part at all. And if it makes sense to ask, "How does one raise one's arm?" surely it makes sense to ask, "How does one move certain muscles?" Hence the doing required in order to preserve the distinction between "moving certain muscles" and "certain muscles getting moved" must be a doing other than the doing described as "moving certain muscles." At this point the philosophical doctrine of acts of volition—willings performed by an agent—appears attractive. By willing we move certain muscles; by moving certain muscles we raise our arm. But the acts of volition in question are the ill-begotten offspring of the mating of two quite incompatible ideas: the supposition that such acts are causes, and the requirement that the volitions in question be the willings of the muscle movements. As causes, willings are events on a par with other events including muscle and other bodily movements, with respect to which the inevitable question must arise once more: "How does one perform such an action?" since after all there is the distinction to be preserved between "performing a willing" and "a willing occurring." But if to avoid the threatened regress of "willing a willing" and "willing the willing of a willing," and so on, one rejects the question and questions the intelligibility of such locutions as "willing a willing," the willing in question can only be understood as "the willing of a muscle movement." If so, the willing in question cannot be a cause of the muscle movement, since the reference to the muscle movement is involved in the very description of the willing. In that case to say

that one moves certain muscles by willing them to move is not to give any causal account at all. But if this is so, what can it mean to say that one wills a muscle movement—since the willing in question cannot possibly be any interior occurrence in which one engages? If it is intelligible at all it means simply that one moves a muscle. In that case, the alleged elucidation of the statement that one moves certain muscles (in raising one's arm) by willing them to move degenerates into something that is no elucidation at all, namely, that one moves certain muscles by moving them. And if this is so, to say that one wills the movement of certain muscles is not to answer the question "How does one move those muscles?"; it is in fact to reject it. If this is the outcome, why not refuse to plunge into the morass and reject the initial question "How does one raise one's arm?" by saying "One just does"? If, on the other hand, "willing a muscle movement" does not mean "moving a muscle," what on earth can it possibly mean? Surely it is an understatement to say that the philosophical talk about acts of volition involves a mare's nest of confusions!

It is not my contention that the doctrine of volitions is designed to answer only those questions I have raised so far. It is of course true that frequently this doctrine is also invoked in order to give some account of the difference between action that is voluntary and action that is not. Nor do I deny that there is any legitimacy in our familiar use of such locutions as "acting willingly," "doing something of one's own will," "acting willfully," and so on. But these are matters to be examined in their own right and at the proper time.

CHAPTER III

ACT

What is action? What is inaction? Even the wise are
puzzled by these questions.

Bhagavad-Gita

"An act is essential for criminal and civil liability." Some consider this
principle a cornerstone of our liberties. But is it clear what this principle
means? And, to be slightly bolder, is there such a principle?

It may mean that a person cannot be held liable in our law for his thoughts
alone. Often this is expressed by saying "an *overt* act is essential. . . ." But
sometimes the principle means, not this, but rather, "a *voluntary* act is
essential. . . ." There is "no act" if one causes injury by involuntary movement. Suppose, then, we say, less elliptically, that "a voluntary and overt act
is essential. . . ." But is this so? If the principle is interpreted in this way,
how can it accommodate omissions?

The "voluntary" requirement can be applied to omissions without any
difficulty. If a paralytic stroke prevents a man from complying with the law
so that he omits to do what is legally required, he is not held liable. The defense may be that there was "no act," i.e., that the defendant was not a voluntary agent. The more troublesome concept is "overt." When a person is
held liable for an omission, is liability imposed for his thoughts alone? Surely
it is not. The person is liable, not for planning or intending an omission, but
for the omission itself; not for scheming to avoid the draft, but for failing to
register. If, then, the requirement of an overt act simply prevents imposing
liability "for thoughts alone," omissions satisfy that requirement. Thus, a
person who says, "an act is essential . . ." may mean to include omissions
within the meaning of "act."[1]

These are, of course, only some of the problems of interpretation and
scope raised by this principle. A person who by some involuntary movement
injures another may be held liable if he had reason to believe that he would
make such a movement. How does the principle cover such cases? How are
crimes of possession to be treated? In cases of vicarious liability is there always an act? If there is, whose act must it be?

---

[1] Various modifications of the principle are required when "act" is given different meanings. If
it is identified, as often it is in legal literature, with "a voluntary *bodily movement*," the legal principle
must be amended to read, "An act or (voluntary) omission is essential. . . ." Finally, if the Model
Penal Code definition of act as "a bodily movement" is adopted, the principle must be phrased in this
way: "A voluntary act or voluntary omission is essential. . . ."

In a casebook on criminal law the authors pose this question after our first selection in this chapter, the case of *Fain v. Commonwealth* : "Is an act essential to criminality because it is deemed impolitic to make a state of mind criminal or because states of mind can be known only through verbal or non-verbal behavior?"[2] A perplexing question, since the facts of *Fain* raise the issue of "voluntary act," whereas the question makes sense only if "act" is interpreted as "overt act." Why do we require that an act be both voluntary and overt? Do we seek to avoid different harmful consequences by these different requirements, or do they constitute a double defense against the same harmful consequences?

The definition of an act as "a voluntary bodily movement," favored in legal theory since John Austin, generates two separate groups of problems: those requiring attempts to define "voluntary" and those connected with the restriction of "act" to bodily movements.

How define "voluntary"? Some theorists postulate "a positive mental state": a voluntary act is "an external manifestation of the will." Some prefer a hypothetical definition: voluntary behavior is behavior which would have been otherwise if the agent had willed or chosen it to be otherwise. Others argue that the concept can be elucidated only in terms of conditions which would defeat an act's being voluntary. Still others believe that a voluntary act must be defined in terms of "a rule" or "set of practices" or "convention"; Melden, for example, seeks to clarify the concept of action by appealing to the analogy of a chess game with its various types of rules. Finally, there are those who defend the view that the concept is indefinable.

Why are acts limited by philosophers and legal theorists to bodily movements or, alternatively and apparently without serious change in meaning for most theorists, to muscular contractions or muscular movements? There are at least two, and possibly three, different paths that have been taken to reach this particular resting-place so distant from our ordinary way of talking. First, Austin's attempt at definition reflects a commitment to the will. He believes that what we *do* (our act) is limited to what we can will; since we can will only movements of our body, it follows that acts are willed bodily movements. Here is a metaphysical view that is in no apparent way influenced by the practical requirements that may be paramount in defining "act" for purposes of some code of laws.

Cook, by contrast, defined an act as "a willed muscular contraction" without any help from metaphysics. Cook believed in a "strict and scientific use" of terms, in analytic neatness, and in practical utility. He envisaged certain practical difficulties if all "consequences" of an act were included within the meaning of "act." One question that concerned him was this: Should we ever be able to draw the line and say "This is not X's act" if we once went beyond X's bodily movements?

Is it any more than coincidence that Austin and Cook held the same views on the nature of an act? Finally, why are acts restricted to bodily movements

---

[2] Jerome Michael and Herbert Wechsler, *Criminal Law and Its Administration* (New York: The Foundation Press, 1940), p. 35.

in the Restatement of the Law of Torts and in the Model Penal Code? The difficulties that Cook foresaw may have had their influence. It is possible, however, that another consideration played a role as well. The definition of "act" is principally relevant in these documents to the defense of "no voluntary act." Typical cases in which such a defense is raised are cases of involuntary *bodily movements*. Thus, the draftsmen of these documents may have thought that "act" need only be defined in terms of such movements.

Since it is obviously one thing to criticize a metaphysical position and quite another to criticize a definition introduced for some limited purpose, we must first determine precisely what is being done in any given instance. The readings which follow divide nicely into those where the theorist asks and puzzles over the question "What is an act?" and those where he asks "What shall we label an act?" and puzzles over the consequences of defining it one way rather another.

*Fain v. Commonwealth**

JUDGE COFER delivered the opinion of the court.

The appellant was indicted and tried for the murder of Henry Smith, a porter at the Veranda Hotel at Nicholasville. He was found guilty of manslaughter, and sentenced to confinement in the penitentiary for two years. From that judgment he prosecutes this appeal.

The prisoner and his friend George Welch went to the Veranda Hotel after dark on an evening in February. The weather was cold, and there was snow upon the ground. They sat down in the public room and went to sleep. In a short time Welch awoke, and, finding the deceased in the barber's shop, in the next room, called for a bed for himself and the prisoner, to pay for which he handed the deceased a bill. Welch attempted to awaken the prisoner by shaking him, but failed. He then told the deceased to wake him up. The deceased shook him for some time, and failing to wake him, said he believed he was dead. Welch said no, he is not: wake him up. The deceased shook him harder and harder until the prisoner looked up and asked what he wanted. The deceased said he wanted him to go to bed. The prisoner said he would not, and told the deceased to go away and let him alone. The deceased said it was getting late, and he wanted to close the house, and still

* 78 Ky. 183, 39 Am. Rep. 213 (1879).

holding the prisoner by the coat, the latter either raised or was lifted up, and, as he arose, he threw his hand to his side as if to draw a weapon. A bystander said to him, don't shoot; but without noticing or giving any sign that he heard what was said, he drew a pistol and fired. The deceased instantly grappled him to prevent him from shooting again, but a second shot was fired almost immediately, and a third soon followed. After the third shot was fired the prisoner was thrown down and held by the deceased. The prisoner, while being held on the floor, hallooed *hoo-wee* very loud two or three times, and called for Welch. He asked the deceased to let him get up; but the deceased said, "If I do, you will shoot me again." The prisoner said he would not, and the deceased released his hold and allowed him to get up. Upon getting up the prisoner went out of the room with his pistol in his hand. His manner was that of a frightened man. He said to a witness, "Take my pistol and defend me," said he had shot someone, but did not know who it was, and upon being told who it was, expressed sorrow for what he had done.

It did not appear that the prisoner knew or had ever seen the deceased before. There was not the slightest evidence of a motive on his part to injure the deceased, nor does there appear to have been anything in what the deceased did or the manner of doing it which, the facts being understood, was calculated to excite anger, much less a desire to kill him. At that time the prisoner was about thirty-three years of age, and he introduced evidence to show that he had been a man of good character and of peaceable and orderly habits.

He also offered to prove that he had been a sleepwalker from his infancy; that he had to be watched to prevent injury to himself; that he was put to sleep in a lower room, near that of his parents, and a servant-man was required to sleep in the room to watch him; that frequently, when aroused from sleep, he seemed frightened, and attempted violence as if resisting an assault, and for some minutes seemed unconscious of what he did or what went on around him; that sometimes, when partly asleep, he resisted the servant who slept in the room with him, as if he supposed the servant was assaulting him.

He also offered to prove by medical experts that persons asleep sometimes act as if awake; that they walk, talk, answer questions, and do many other things, and yet are unconscious of what they do; that with many persons there is a period between sleeping and walking in which they are unconscious, though they seem to be awake; that loss of sleep, and other causes which produce nervous depression or mental anxiety, may produce such a state of unconsciousness between sleep and waking; and that for some days previous his children had been afflicted with a dangerous disease, and he had, in consequence, lost much sleep.

He likewise offered to prove that his life had been threatened by a person living near where he had been on business during the day, and that he had on that morning borrowed the pistol with which he shot the deceased, and had stated at the time that he was required to go near to where the person lived who had threatened him, and he wanted the pistol to defend himself in case he was attacked.

The court rejected all this proffered evidence, and the prisoner excepted.

All the modern medico-legal writers to whose writings we have had access, recognize a species of mental unsoundness connected with sleep, which they commonly treat under the general head of Somnambulism. . . .

The writings of medical and medicolegal authors contain accounts of many well-authenticated cases in which homicides have been committed while the perpetrator was either asleep or just being aroused from sleep . . .

These authorities, corroborated as they are by common observation, are sufficient to prove that it is possible for one, either in sleep or between sleeping and waking, to commit homicide, either unconsciously or under the influence of hallucination or illusion resulting from an abnormal condition of the physical system. . . .

But we are not under the necessity of relying wholly upon writers on medical jurisprudence as authority upon this point. It is one of the fundamental principles of the criminal law that there can be no criminality in the absence of criminal intention; and when we ascertain from medical experts or otherwise that there is such a thing in nature as somnolentia and somnambulism, the task of the jurist is ended, so far as relates to the right of one accused of crime to offer evidence conducing to prove that he committed the act imputed to him as a crime while in a paroxysm of somnolentia or somnambulism. In criminal trials, the jury must try every pertinent question of fact the evidence conduces to prove. When evidence is offered, the sole question for the court is, will it conduce to prove any fact material in the case? and if the law gives an affirmative response, the evidence must be admitted. If, as claimed, the appellant was unconscious when he fired the first shot, it cannot be imputed to him as a crime. Nor is he guilty if partially conscious, if, upon being partially awakened, and finding the deceased had hold of him and was shaking him, he imagined he was being attacked, and believed himself in danger of losing his life or of sustaining great bodily injury at the hands of his assailant, he shot in good faith, believing it necessary to preserve his life or his person from great harm. In such circumstances, it does not matter whether he had reasonable grounds for his belief or not. He had been asleep, and could know nothing of the surrounding circumstances. In his condition he may have supposed he was assailed for a deadly purpose, and if he did, he is not to be punished because his half-awakened consciousness deceived him as to the real facts, any more than if, being awake, the deceased had presented a pistol to his head with the apparent intention to shoot him, when in fact he was only jesting, or if the supposed pistol, though sufficiently resembling a deadly weapon to be readily mistaken for one, was but an inoffensive toy.

The evidence conducing to prove that the appellant's children had been sick, and that he had recently lost considerable sleep, should have been admitted as conducing to show that, at the moment of being aroused, he may have been unconscious, or partly so, and, therefore, unable readily to understand the real circumstances of his situation.

The physicians introduced would have proved, as the appellant avowed, that loss of sleep and mental anxiety each has a tendency to develop a predisposition to somnolentia, or sleep drunkenness, as it is otherwise called, and in this they would but corroborate the opinions of medical jurists.

We are also of the opinion that the offered evidence in regard to the alleged threats against the prisoner should have been admitted.

The central position of the defense was that the prisoner fired the fatal shots while partially or wholly unconscious, under the false impression that he was being assaulted by the deceased.

His effort was to show that he was subject to a peculiar affection which made him imagine, when suddenly aroused from sleep, that he was being assaulted by the person arousing him, and that under that impression he was accustomed to make unconsciously violent resistance; that at such times he mistook the mere creatures of his imagination for real facts and circumstances.

If he had been threatened, it was natural, or at least not unnatural, especially while near the person who had threatened him, that the threat should make such an impression on his mind as would contribute to develop with more than ordinary force the predisposition to imagine himself assaulted and to make resistance, and particularly so when, on being aroused, he found himself in the hands of a stranger, by whom he was being persistently and violently shaken.

We do not see any legitimate bearing the fact that he borrowed the pistol could have upon any of the issues in the case, and what he said was not admissible to prove that he had been threatened.

As the case must go back for a new trial, and it is, in some of its features, one of first impression, we will, at the risk of being prolix,

consider the law applicable to it somewhat in detail.

There are several phases in which the case presents itself, all of which should be submitted to the jury.

1. If the prisoner, when he shot the deceased, was unconscious, or so nearly so that he did not comprehend his own situation and the circumstances surrounding him, or that he supposed he was being assailed, and that he was merely resisting an attempt to take his life or do him great bodily injury, he should be acquitted—in one case, because he was not legally responsible for any act done while in that condition, and in the other, because he is excusable on the ground of self-defense; for although it is clear that he was not in danger, and had no reasonable grounds to believe he was, yet if, through derangement of his perceptive faculties, it appeared to him that he was in danger, he is as free from punishable guilt as if the facts had been as he supposed them to be.

2. If he was so far unconscious when he fired the first shot, or the first and second, that he supposed he was defending himself against a dangerous assault, and regained consciousness before he fired the second or third shot, the question of guilt or innocence will depend upon whether he then believed in good faith that he was in danger of losing his life or of sustaining great bodily injury.

It was not necessary, under the circumstances, that he should have reasonable grounds to believe he was in danger. In the view we are now taking of the case we are supposing he was unconscious or partly so when he fired the first shot. If so, when he regained consciousness and found himself seized and held by a stranger who was struggling to overpower him, it would be unreasonable to expect him to wait until he could discover the purpose or apparent purpose of his antagonist, as it might have appeared to those who, in the full possession of their faculties and senses, had witnessed the whole affair.

But if he fired after he became conscious, and did not at the time in good faith believe he was in danger of loss of life or great personal injury, he is guilty of either murder or manslaughter,—murder if he was actuated by malice, manslaughter if he acted without malice.

3. Although he may have been so far con-

scious when he fired the first shot as to understand what he was doing, yet, if he did not understand the purpose of his assailant, and believed he was attempting to inflict on him great personal injury, he should be acquitted, for, as already remarked, if, in consequence of a derangement of his perceptive faculties, or from being suddenly aroused from sleep and finding the deceased holding and shaking him, he believed he was in great danger of losing his life or suffering great personal injury, although there was in fact no danger, and, those who had witnessed the affair, had no reason to apprehend danger, he is no more guilty than if there had been actual danger. Such a case admits of no other test than the good faith of the prisoner, to be judged of by the jury.

4. If the prisoner was conscious of what he was himself doing, and that the purpose of the deceased was merely to wake him up, and the prisoner shot him simply because he did so, he is guilty of either murder or manslaughter:

murder if the shooting was malicious, manslaughter if without malice.

If the prisoner is and has been afflicted in the manner claimed, and knew, as he no doubt did, his propensity to do acts of violence when aroused from sleep, he was guilty of a grave breach of social duty in going to sleep in the public room of a hotel with a deadly weapon on his person, and merits, for that reckless disregard of the safety of others, some degree of punishment, but we know of no law under which he can be punished. Our law only punishes for overt acts done by responsible moral agents. If the prisoner was unconscious when he killed the deceased, he cannot be punished for that act, and as the mere fact that he had the weapon on his person and went to sleep with it there did not do injury to anyone, he cannot be punished for that. . . .

For the errors indicated, the judgment is reversed, and the cause is remanded for a new trial upon principles not inconsistent with this opinion.

Definition of Act*

The word "act" is used throughout the Restatement of this Subject to denote an external manifestation of the actor's will and does not include any of its results even the most direct, immediate, and intended.

Comment

a. *Necessity of volition.* There cannot be an act without volition. Therefore, a contraction of a person's muscles which is purely a reaction to some outside force, such as a knee jerk or the blinking of the eyelids in defense against an approaching missile, or the convulsive movements of an epileptic, are not acts of that person. So too, movements of the body during sleep when the will is in abeyance are not acts. Since some outward manifestation of the defendant's will is necessary to the existence of an act which can subject him to liability, it is not enough to subject a defendant to liability that a third person has utilized a part of his body as an instrument

to carry out his own intention to cause harm to the plaintiff. In such case, as in the case of the knee jerk, the actor is the third person who has used the defendant's body as an instrument to accomplish some purpose of his own or who has struck the defendant's leg so as to have caused the knee jerk.

b. *Freedom of actor's will.* It is not necessary that the actor's will, if it in fact manifests itself by some muscular contraction, including those which are necessary to the speaking of words, should operate freely and without pressure from outside circumstances. Indeed, the fact that the pressure is irresistible, in the sense that it is one which reasonable men cannot be expected to resist, does not prevent its manifestation from being an act, although it may make the act excusable. A muscular reaction is always an act unless it is a purely reflexive reaction in which the mind and will have no share. Thus, if A, finding himself about to fall, stretches his hand out to seize some object, whether a fellow human being or a mere inanimate object, to save himself from falling, the stretching out of his hand and the grasping of the object is an act in the sense in which that word has hitherto been used, since the defendant's mind has grasped the situation and has dictated a muscular contraction which his rapidly formed judgment leads him to believe to be helpful to prevent his fall. While the decision is formed instantaneously, nonetheless the movement of the hand is a response to the will exerted by a mind which has already determined upon a distinct course of action. The exigency in which the defendant is placed, the necessity for a rapid decision, the fact that the decision corresponds to a universal tendency of mankind, may be enough to relieve the defendant from liability, but it is not enough to prevent his grasping of the object from being his act.

c. *Act and its consequences.* The word "act" includes only the external manifestation of the actor's will. It does not include any of the effects of such manifestation no matter how direct, immediate, and intended. Thus, if the actor, having pointed a pistol at another, pulls the trigger, the act is the pulling of the trigger and not the impingement of the bullet upon the other's person. So too, the actor intentionally strikes another, the act is only the movement of the actor's hand and not the contact with the other's body immediately established thereby.

Model Penal Code*

Section 1.14. Definitions

In this Code unless a different meaning plainly is required : . . .

(2) "act" or "action" means a bodily movement whether voluntary or involuntary;

(3) "voluntary" has the meaning specified in Section 2.01;

(4) "omission" means a failure to act;

(5) "conduct" means an action or omission and its accompanying state of mind, or where relevant, a series of acts and omissions . . .

ARTICLE II.
GENERAL PRINCIPLES OF LIABILITY

Section 2.01. Requirement of Voluntary Act; Omission as Basis of Liability; Possession as an Act

(1) A person is not guilty of an offense unless his liability is based on conduct which includes a voluntary act or the omission to perform an act which it was physically possible to perform.

(2) The following are not voluntary acts within the meaning of this section:

(a) a reflex or convulsion;

(b) a bodily movement during unconsciousness [coma?] or sleep;

(c) conduct during hypnosis or resulting from hypnotic suggestion;

(d) a bodily movement that otherwise is not a product of the effort or determination of the actor, either conscious or habitual.

(3) Liability for the commission of an offense may not be based on an omission unaccompanied by action unless :

(a) the omission is expressly made sufficient by the law defining the offense; or

(b) a duty to perform the omitted act is otherwise imposed by law.

(4) Possession is an act, within the meaning of this section, if the possessor knowingly procured or received the thing possessed or was aware of his control for a sufficient period to have been able to terminate his possession.

·   ·   ·

COMMENTS TO ARTICLE II.
GENERAL PRINCIPLES OF LIABILITY

Section 2.01. Requirement of Voluntary Act; Omission as Basis of Liability; Possession as an Act

1. Paragraph (1) requires that criminal liability be based on conduct and that the conduct which gives rise to liability include a voluntary act or the omission to perform an act which it was physically possible to have performed. This is not, of course, to say that these conditions are enough for the establishment of liability but only that they are essential elements when liability obtains.

That penal sanctions cannot be employed with justice unless these requirements are satisfied seems wholly clear. The law cannot hope to deter involuntary movement or to stimulate action that cannot physically be performed; the sense of personal security would be short-lived in a society where such movement or inactivity could lead to formal social condemnation of the sort that a conviction necessarily entails. People whose involuntary movements threaten harm to others may present a public health or safety problem, calling for therapy or even for custodial commitment; they do not present a problem of correction.

These are axioms under the present law, though dealt with only indirectly by our penal legislation in the states where legislation touches the subject at all. See, e.g., *California Penal Code* § 20: "In every crime or public offense there must exist a union, or joint operation of act and intent, or criminal negligence"; *ibid.* § 26: "All persons are capable of committing crimes except . . . persons who committed the act charged without being conscious thereof" and "persons who committed the act or made the omission charged through misfortune or by accident, when it appears that there was no evil design, intention or culpable negligence." . . .

2. It will be noted that the formulation does not state that liability must be based on the voluntary act or the omission *simpliciter,* but rather upon conduct which *includes* such action or omission. The distinction has some analytical importance. If the driver of an automobile loses consciousness with the result that he runs over a pedestrian, none of the movements or omissions that accompany or follow this loss of consciousness may in themselves give rise to liability. But a prior voluntary act, such as the act of driving, or a prior omission, such as failing to stop as he felt illness approaching, may, under given circumstances, be regarded as sufficiently negligent for liability to be imposed. In that event, however, liability is based on the entire course of conduct, including the specific conduct that resulted in the injury. It is enough, in short, that the conduct included action or omission that satisfied the requirements of paragraph (1), and the further requirements for the establishment of culpability, as to which see Section 2.02. . . .

(3) Paragraph (2) defines "voluntary" partially and indirectly by describing movements that are excluded from the meaning of the term.

Any definition must exclude a reflex or convulsion. The case of unconsciousness is equally clear when unconsciousness implies collapse, or coma, as perhaps it does in ordinary usage of the term. There are, however, states of physical activity where self-awarenes is grossly impaired or even absent, as in epileptic fugue, amnesia, extreme confusion and equivalent conditions. . . .

The case of hypnotic suggestion also seems to warrant explicit treatment. Hypnosis differs from both sleep and fugue but it is characterized by such dependence of the subject on the hypnotist, that it does not seem politic to treat conduct resulting from hypnotic suggestions as voluntary, despite the state of consciousness involved. . . .

Paragraph 2(d) formulates a residual category of involuntary movements, describing them as those that "otherwise are not a product of the effort or determination of the actor, either conscious or habitual." The formulation seeks to express the main content of the idea of an "external manifestation of the actor's will" (*Restatement of Torts,* § 2), without putting the matter as a definition of the will. The formulation would, of course, cover the classic case where the actor is moved by force, as distinguished from threat; such motion never has been viewed as action of the victim. (See, e.g., *Hale, Pleas of the Crown,* I, 434.) In other respects it is designed to have only the marginal meaning of the Torts Restatement definition of an act. The difficult cases are dealt with specifically in paragraphs (b) and (c).

It should be added that the application of these provisions to cases of self-induced intoxication or narcosis presents a special problem which will be dealt with in detail in Section 2.08.

4. Paragraph (3) states the conventional position with respect to omission unaccompanied by action as a basis of liability. Unless the omission is expressly made sufficient by the law defining the offense, a duty to perform the omitted act must have been otherwise imposed by law for the omission to have the same standing as a voluntary act for purposes of liability. It should, of course, suffice, as the courts now hold, that the duty arises under some branch of the civil law. If it does, this minimal requirement is satisfied, though whether the omission constitutes an offense depends as well on many other factors.

It is arguable that affirmative duties to act should be enlarged in scope, especially when action is required to prevent bodily injury. This is a problem to be faced, however, in the definition of particular offenses, not in this section of the Code.

5. Crimes of possession constitute an important category of offenses. But possession is neither a bodily movement nor an omission. The application of paragraph (1) to such situations must, therefore, be made clear. Paragraph (4) provides, accordingly, that possession is an act within the meaning of the section, if the possessor knowingly procured or received the thing possessed or was aware of his control thereof for a sufficient period to have been able to terminate his possession. The "thing possessed" refers, of course, to the physical object, not to its specific quality or properties; that aspect of the problem pertains rather to the problem of *mens rea,* with which later sections deal. . . .

Of Human Actions in General*

1. The business of government is to promote the happiness of the society, by punishing and rewarding. That part of its business which consists in punishing is more particularly the subject of penal law. In proportion as an act tends to disturb that happiness, in proportion as the tendency of it is pernicious, will be the demand it creates for punishment. What happiness consists of we have already seen: enjoyment of pleasures, security from pains.

2. The general tendency of an act is more or less pernicious, according to the sum total of its consequences: that is, according to the difference between the sum of such as are good, and the sum of such as are evil.

3. It is to be observed, that here, as well as henceforward, wherever consequences are spoken of, such only are meant as are *material*. Of the consequences of any act, the multitude and variety must needs be infinite; but such of them only as are material are worth regarding. Now among the consequences of an act, be they what they may, such only, by one who views them in the capacity of a legislator, can be said to be material, as either consist of pain or pleasure, or have an influence in the production of pain or pleasure.

4. It is also to be observed, that into the account of the consequences of the act, are to be taken not such only as might have ensued, were intention out of the question, but such also as depend upon the connection there may be between these first-mentioned consequences and the intention. The connection there is between the intention and certain consequences is, as we shall see hereafter, a means of producing other consequences. In this lies the difference between rational agency and irrational.

5. Now the intention, with regard to the consequences of an act, will depend upon two things: (1) The state of the will or intention, with respect to the act itself. And (2) The state of the understanding, or perceptive faculties, with regard to the circumstances which it is, or may appear to be, accompanied with. Now with respect to these circumstances, the perceptive faculty is susceptible of three states: consciousness, unconsciousness, and false consciousness. Consciousness, when the party believes precisely those circumstances, and no others, to subsist, which really do subsist: unconsciousness, when he fails of perceiving certain circumstances to subsist, which, however, do subsist: false consciousness, when he believes or imagines certain circumstances to subsist, which in truth do not subsist.

6. In every transaction, therefore, which is examined with a view to punishment, there are four articles to be considered: (1) The *act* itself, which is done. (2) The *circumstances* in which it is done. (3) The *intentionality* that may have accompanied it. (4) The *consciousness,* unconsciousness, or false consciousness, that may have accompanied it. . . .

7. There are also two other articles on which the general tendency of an act depends: and on that, as well as on other accounts, the demand which it creates for punishment. These are (1) the particular *motive* or motives which gave birth to it. (2) The general *disposition* which it indicates. . . .

* Jeremy Bentham, *An Introduction to the Principles of Morals and Legislation* (Oxford: Basil Blackwell, 1948), pp. 189–99.

8. Acts may be distinguished in several ways, for several purposes.

They may be distinguished, in the first place, into *positive* and *negative*. By positive are meant such as consist in motion or exertion: by negative, such as consist in keeping at rest; that is, in forbearing to move or exert one's self in such and such circumstances. Thus, to strike is a positive act: not to strike on a certain occasion, a negative one. Positive acts are styled also acts of commission; negative, acts of omission or forbearance.[1]

9. Such acts, again, as are negative, may either be *absolutely* so, or *relatively*: absolutely, when they import the negation of all positive agency whatsoever; for instance, not to strike at all: relatively, when they import the negation of such or such a particular mode of agency; for instance, not to strike such a person or such a thing, or in such a direction.

10. It is to be observed, that the nature of the act, whether positive or negative, is not to be determined immediately by the form of the discourse made use of to express it. An act which is positive in its nature may be characterized by a negative expression: thus, not to be at rest, is as much as to say to move. So also an act, which is negative in its nature, may be characterized by a positive expression: thus, to forbear or omit to bring food to a person in certain circumstances, is signified by the single and positive term to *starve*.

11. In the second place, acts may be distinguished into *external* and *internal*. By external, are meant corporal acts; acts of the body:

[1] The distinction between positive and negative acts runs through the whole system of offenses, and sometimes makes a material difference with regard to their consequences. To reconcile us the better to the extensive, and, as it may appear on some occasions, the inconsistent signification here given to the word *act,* it may be considered: That in many cases, where no exterior or overt act is exercised, the state which the mind is in at the time when the supposed act is said to happen is as truly and directly the result of the will, as any exterior act, how plain and conspicuous soever. The not revealing a conspiracy, for instance, may be as perfectly the act of the will, as the joining in it. In the next place, that even though the mind should never have had the incident in question in contemplation (insomuch that the event of its not happening should not have been so much as obliquely intentional) still the state of the person's mind was in at the time when, if he *had* so willed, the incident might have happened, as in many cases productive of as material consequences; and not only as likely, but as fit to call for the interposition of other agents, as the opposite one. Thus, when a tax is imposed, your not paying it is an act which at any rate must be punished in a certain manner, whether you happened to think of paying it or not.

by internal, mental acts; acts of the mind. Thus, to strike is an external or exterior act: to intend to strike, an internal or interior one.

12. Acts of *discourse* are a sort of mixture of the two external acts, which are no ways material, nor attended with any consequences, any farther than as they serve to express the existence of internal ones. To speak to another to strike, to write to him to strike, to make signs to him to strike, are all so many acts of discourse.

13. Third, acts that are external may be distinguished into *transitive* and *intransitive*. Acts may be called transitive, when the motion is communicated from the person of the agent to some foreign body: that is, to such a foreign body on which the effects of it are considered as being *material*; as where a man runs against you, or throws water in your face. Acts may be called intransitive, when the motion is communicated to no other body, on which the effects of it are regarded as material, than some part of the same person in whom it originated: as where a man runs, or washes himself.

14. An act of the transitive kind may be said to be in its *commencement,* or in the *first* stage of its progress, while the motion is confined to the person of the agent, and has not yet been communicated to any foreign body, on which the effects of it can be material. It may be said to be in its *termination,* or to be in the last stage of its progress, as soon as the motion or impulse has been communicated to some such foreign body. It may be said to be in the *middle* or intermediate stage or stages of its progress, while the motion, having passed from the person of the agent, has not yet been communicated to any such foreign body. Thus, as soon as a man has lifted up his hand to strike, the act he performs in striking you is in its commencement: as soon as his hand has reached you, it is in its termination. If the act be the motion of a body which is separated from the person of the agent before it reaches the object, it may be said, during that interval, to be in its intermediate progress, or in *gradu mediativo*: as in the case where man throws a stone or fires a bullet at you.

15. An act of the *in*transitive kind may be said to be in its commencement, when the motion or impulse is as yet confined to the member or organ in which it originated; and has not yet been communicated to any mem-

ber or organ that is distinguishable from the former. It may said to be in its termination, as soon as it has been applied to any other part of the same person. Thus, where a man poisons himself, while he is lifting up the poison to his mouth, the act is in its commencement: as soon as it has reached his lips, it is in its termination.

16. In the third place, acts may be distinguished into *transient* and *continued*. Thus, to strike is a transient act: to lean, a continued one. To buy, a transient act: to keep in one's possession, a continued one.

17. In strictness of speech there is a difference between a *continued* act and a *repetition* of acts. It is a repetition of acts, when there are intervals filled up by acts of different natures: a continued act, when there are no such intervals. Thus, to lean, is one continued act: to keep striking, a repetition of acts.

18. There is a difference, again, between a *repetition* of acts, and a *habit* or *practice*. The term repetition of acts may be employed, let the acts in question be separated by ever such short intervals, and let the sum total of them occupy ever so short a space of time. The term habit is not employed but when the acts in question are supposed to be separated by long-continued intervals, and the sum total of them to occupy a considerable space of time. It is not (for instance) the drinking ever so many times, nor ever so much at a time, in the course of the same sitting, that will constitute a habit of drunkenness: it is necessary that such sittings themselves be frequently repeated. Every habit is a repetition of acts; or, to speak more strictly, when a man has frequently repeated such and such acts after considerable intervals, he is said to have persevered in or contracted a habit: but every repetition of acts is not a habit.

19. Fourth, acts may be distinguished into *indivisible* and *divisible*. Indivisible acts are merely imaginary: they may be easily conceived, but can never be known to be exemplified. Such as are divisible may be so, with regard either to matter or to motion. An act indivisible with regard to matter, is the motion or rest of one single atom of matter. An act indivisible with regard to motion, is the motion of any body, from one single atom of space to the next to it.

Fifth, acts may be distinguished into *simple* and *complex*: simple, such as the act of striking, the act of leaning, or the act of drinking, above instanced: complex, consisting each of a multitude of simple acts, which, though numerous and heterogeneous, derive a sort of unity from the relation they bear to some common design or end; such as the act of giving a dinner, the act of maintaining a child, the act of exhibiting a triumph, the act of bearing arms, the act of holding a court, and so forth.

20. It has been every now and then made a question, what it is in such a case that constitutes *one* act: where one act has ended, and another act has begun: whether what has happened has been one act or many. These questions, it is now evident, may frequently be answered, with equal propriety, in opposite ways: and if there be any occasion on which they can be answered only in one way, the answer will depend upon the nature of the occasion, and the purpose for which the question is proposed. A man is wounded in two fingers at one stroke—Is it one wound or several? A man is beaten at 12 o'clock, and again at 8 minutes after 12—Is it one beating or several? You beat one man, and instantly in the same breath you beat another—Is this one beating or several? In any of these cases it may be *one,* perhaps, as to some purposes, and *several* as to others. These examples are given, that men may be aware of the ambiguity of language: and neither harass themselves with unsolvable doubts, nor one another with interminable disputes.

21. So much with regard to acts considered in themselves: we come now to speak of the *circumstances* with which they may have been accompanied. These must necessarily be taken into the account before anything can be determined relative to the consequences. What the consequences of an act may be upon the whole can never otherwise be ascertained: it can never be known whether it is beneficial, or indifferent, or mischievous. In some circumstances even to kill a man may be a beneficial act: in others, to set food before him may be a pernicious one.

22. Now the circumstances of an act are what? Any objects whatsoever. Take any act whatsoever, there is nothing in the nature of things that excludes any imaginable object from being a circumstance to it. Any given object may be a circumstance to it. Any given object may be a circumstance to any other.

23. We have already had occasion to make mention for a moment of the *consequences* of

an act: these were distinguished into material and immaterial. In like manner may the circumstances of it be distinguished. Now *materiality* is a relative term: applied to the consequences of an act, it bore relation to pain and pleasure; applied to the circumstances, it bears relation to the consequences. A circumstance may be said to be material, when it bears a visible relation in point of causality to the consequences: immaterial, when it bears no such visible relation.

24. The consequences of an act are events. A circumstance may be related to an event in point of causality in any one of four ways: (1) In the way of causation or production. (2) In the way of derivation. (3) In the way of collateral connection. (4) In the way of conjunct influence. It may be said to be related to the event in the way of causation, when it is of the number of those that contribute to the production of such event: in the way of derivation, when it is of the number of the events to the production of which that in question has been contributory: in the way of collateral connection, where the circumstance in question, and the event in question, without being either of them instrumental in the production of the other, are related, each of them, to some common object, which has been concerned in the production of them both: in the way of conjunct influence, when, whether related in any other way or not, they have both of them concurred in the production of some common consequence.

25. An example may be of use. In the year 1628, Villiers, Duke of Buckingham, favorite and minister of Charles I of England, received a wound and died. The man who gave it him was one Felton, who, exasperated at the mal-administration of which that minister was accused, went down from London to Portsmouth, where Buckingham happened then to be, made his way into his anti-chamber, and finding him busily engaged in conversation with a number of people round him, got close to him, drew a knife, and stabbed him. In the effort, the assassin's hat fell off, which was found soon after, and, upon searching him, the bloody knife. In the crown of the hat were found scraps of papers, with sentences expressive of the purpose he was come upon. Here then, suppose the event in question is the wound received by Buckingham: Felton's drawing out his knife, his making his way into the chamber, his going down to Ports-

mouth, his conceiving an indignation at the idea of Buckingham's administration, that administration itself, Charles' appointing such a minister, and so on, higher and higher without end, are so many circumstances, related to the event of Buckingham's receiving the wound, in the way of causation or production: the bloodiness of the knife, a circumstance related to the same event in the way of derivation: the finding of the hat upon the ground, the finding the sentences in the hat, and the writing them, so many circumstances related to it in the way of collateral connection: and the situation and conversation of the people about Buckingham, were circumstances related to the circumstances of Felton's making his way into the room, going down to Portsmouth, and so forth, in the way of conjunct influence; inasmuch as they contributed in common to the event of Buckingham's receiving the wound, by preventing him from putting himself upon his guard upon the first appearance of the intruder.

26. These several relations do not all of them attach upon an event with equal certainty. In the first place, it is plain, indeed, that every event must have some circumstance or other, and in truth, an indefinite multitude of circumstances, related to it in the way of production: it must of course have a still greater multitude of circumstances related to it in the way of collateral connection. But it does not appear necessary that every event should have circumstances related to it in the way of derivation: nor therefore that it should have any related to it in the way of conjunct influence. But of the circumstances of all kinds which actually do attach upon an event, it is only a very small number that can be discovered by the utmost exertion of the human faculties: it is a still smaller number that ever actually do attract our notice: when occasion happens, more or fewer of them will be discovered by a man in proportion to the strength, partly of his intellectual powers, partly of his inclination. It appears therefore that the multitude and description of such of the circumstances belonging to an act, as may appear to be material, will be determined by two considerations: (1) By the nature of things themselves. (2) By the strength or weakness of the faculties of those who happen to consider them.

27. Thus much it seemed necessary to premise in general concerning acts, and their cir-

cumstances, previously to the consideration of the particular sorts of acts with their particular circumstances, with which we shall have to do in the body of the work. An act of some sort or other is necessarily included in the notion of every offense. Together with this act, under the notion of the same offense, are included certain circumstances: which circumstances enter into the essence of the offense, contribute by their conjunct influence to the production of its consequences, and in conjunction with the act are brought into view by the name by which it stands distinguished. These we shall have occasion to distinguish hereafter by the name of *criminative* circumstances. Other circumstances again entering into combination with the act and the former set of circumstances are productive of still farther consequences. These additional consequences, if they are of the beneficial kind, bestow, according to the value they bear in that capacity, upon the circumstances to which they owe their birth the appellation of *exculpative* or *extenuative* circumstances: if of the mischievous kind, they bestow on them the appellation of *aggravative* circumstances. Of all these different sets of circumstances, the criminative are connected with the conse-

quences of the original offense, in the way of production; with the act, and with one another, in the way of conjunct influence: the consequences of the original offense with them, and with the act, respectively, in the way of derivation: the consequences of the modified offense, with the criminative, exculpative, and extenuative circumstances, respectively, in the way also of derivation: these different sets of circumstances, with the consequences of the modified act or offense, in the way of production: and with one another (in respect of the consequences of the modified act or offense) in the way of conjunct influence. Lastly, whatever circumstances can be seen to be connected with the consequences of the offense, whether directly in the way of derivation, or obliquely in the way of collateral affinity (to wit, in virtue of its being connected, in the way of derivation, with some of the circumstances with which they stand connected in the same manner) bear a *material* relation to the offense in the way of evidence, they may accordingly be styled *evidentiary* circumstances, and may become of use, by being held forth upon occasion as so many proofs, indications, or evidences of its having been committed.

Act*

Every legal duty— whether it be relative or absolute or whether it be *obligatio* or *officium* is a duty to do (or forbear from) an outward act or acts, and flows from the Command (signified expressly or tacitly) of the person or body which is *sovereign* in some given society.

To fulfill the duty which the command imposes is *just* or *right*. That is to say, the party does the act, or the party observes the forbearance, which is *jussum* or *directum* by the author of the command.

To omit (or forbear from) the act which the command enjoins, or to do the act which the command prohibits, is a wrong or *injury*: A term denoting (when taken in its largest signification) every act, forbearance, or omission, which amounts to disobedience of a Law (or of disobedience of any other command)

emanating directly or circuitously from a Monarch or Sovereign Number. . . .

A party lying under a duty, or upon whom a duty is incumbent, is liable to evil or inconvenience (to be inflicted by sovereign authority) in case he disobey the Command by which the duty is imposed. This conditional evil is the *Sanction* which enforces the duty, or the duty is *sanctioned* by this conditional evil: And the party bound or obliged *is* bound or obliged, because he is obnoxious to this evil, in case he disobey the command. That bond, *vinculum,* or *ligamen,* which is of the essence of *duty,* is, simply or merely, liability or *obnoxiousness* to a *Sanction.*

Now it follows from these considerations that, before I can complete the analysis of legal *right* and *duty,* I must advert to the nature or essentials of legal Injuries or Wrongs, and of legal or political Sanctions. As Person, Thing, Act, and Forbearance are inseparably connected with the terms "Right"

* John Austin, *Lectures on Jurisprudence* (London: John Murray, 1873), I, 421–29, 433. Footnotes are omitted.

and "Duty," so are Injury and Sanction imported by the same expressions.

But before we can determine the import of "Injury" and "Sanction" (or can distinguish the compulsion or restraint, which is implied in Duty or Obligation, from that compulsion or restraint which is merely physical) we must try to settle the meaning of the following perplexing terms: namely, Will, Motive, Intention, and Negligence. . . .

Accordingly, I shall now endeavor to state or suggest the significations of "Motive" and "Will." In other words, I shall attempt to distinguish desires, as *determining* to acts or forbearances, from those remarkable desires which are named *volitions,* and by which we are not *determined* to acts or forbearances, although they are the immediate antecedents of such bodily movements as are styled (strictly and properly) human *acts or actions.*

Nor is this incidental excursion into the Philosophy of Mind a wanton digression from the path which is marked out by my subject.

For (first) the party who lies under a duty is bound or obliged by a *sanction.* This conditional evil determines or inclines his *will* to the act or forbearance enjoined. In other language, he wishes to avoid the evil impending from the Law, although he may be averse from the fulfillment of the duty which the Law imposes upon him.

Consequently, if we would know precisely the import of "Duty," we must endeavor to clear the expressions "Motive" and "Will" from the Obscurity with which they have been covered by philosophical and popular jargon.

Secondly, the *objects* of duties are acts and forbearances. But every act, and every forbearance from an act, is the consequence of a volition, or of a determination of the will. Consequently, if we would know precisely the meaning of act and forbearance, and, therefore, the meaning of duty or obligation, we must try to know the meaning of the term "Will."

Thirdly, some injuries are *intentional.* Others are consequences of *negligence* (in the large signification of the term). Consequently, if we would know the nature of injuries or wrongs, and of various important differences by which they are distinguished, we must try to determine the meanings of "Intention" and "Negligence."

It is absolutely necessary that the import

of the last-mentioned expressions should be settled with an approach to precision. For *both* of them run, in a continued vein, through the doctrine of injuries or wrongs; and of the rights and obligations which are begotten by injuries or wrongs. And *one* of them (namely, "Intention"), meets us at *every* step, in *every* department of Jurisprudence.

But, in order that we may settle the import of the term "Intention," we must settle the import of the term "Will." For, although an intention is not a volition, the facts are inseparably connected. And, since "Negligence" implies the *absence* of a *due* volition and intention, it is manifest that the explanation of that expression supposes the explanation of these.

Accordingly, I will now attempt to analyze the expressions "Will" and "Motive."

Certain parts of the human body obey the *will.* Changing the expression, certain parts of our bodies move in certain ways so soon as we *will* that they should. Or, changing the expression again, we have the *power* of moving, in certain ways, certain parts of our bodies.

Now these expressions, and others of the same import, merely signify this:

Certain movements of our bodies follow invariably and *immediately* our wishes or desires for those *same* movements: Provided, that is, that the bodily organ be sane, and the desired movement be not prevented by an outward obstacle or hindrance. If my arm be free from disease, and from chains or other hindrances, my arm rises, so soon as I wish that it should. But if my arm be palsied, or fastened down to my side, my arm will not move, although I desire to move it.

These antecedent wishes and these consequent movements, are human *volitions* and *acts* (strictly and properly so called). They are the only objects to which those terms will strictly and properly apply.

But, besides the antecedent desire (which I style a *volition*), and the consequent movement (which I style an *act*), it is commonly supposed that there is a certain "*Will*" which is the cause or author of both. The desire is commonly called an act of the *will*; or is supposed to be an effect of a *power or faculty of willing,* supposed to reside in the man.

That this same "*will*" is just nothing at all, has been proved (in my opinion) beyond controversy by the late Dr. Brown: Who has also expelled from the region of entities those fancied beings called *"powers,"* of which this imaginary *"will"* is one. Many preceding writers had stated or suggested generally the true nature of the relation between cause and effect. They had shown that a *cause* is nothing but a given event invariably or usually *preceding* another given event; that an *effect* is nothing but a given event invariably or usually *following* another given event; and that the *power* of *producing* the effect which is ascribed to the cause, is merely an abridged (and, therefore, an obscure) expression for the customary antecedence and sequence of the two events. But the author in question, in his analysis of that relation, considered the subject from numerous aspects equally new and important. And he was (I believe) the first who understood what we would be at, when we talk about the *Will,* and the *power or faculty of willing.*

All that I am able to discover when I *will* a movement of my body amounts to this: I *wish* the movement. The movement *immediately* follows my wish of the movement. And when I conceive the *wish,* I expect that the movement wished *will* immediately follow it. Any one may convince himself that this is the whole of the case, by carefully observing what passes in himself, when he *wills* to move any of the bodily organs, which are said to obey the *will,* or the *power* or *faculty* of willing. . . .

The wishes which are immediately followed by the bodily movements wished are the only wishes *immediately followed by their objects.* Or (changing the expression) they are the only wishes which *consummate themselves:* The only wishes which attain their *ends* without the intervention of *means.*

In every other instance of wish or desire, the object of the wish is attained (in case it be attained) through a *mean;* and (generally speaking) through a *series* of means: Each of the means being (in its turn) the object of a distinct wish; and each of them being wished (in its turn) as a step to that object which is the end at which we aim.

For example, if I wish that my arm should rise, the desired movement of my arm immediately follows my wish. There is nothing to which I resort, nothing which I wish, as a mean or instrument wherewith to attain my purpose. But if I wish to lift the book which

is now lying before me, I wish certain movements of by bodily organs, and I employ these as a mean or instrument for the accomplishment of my ultimate end.

Again: If I wish to look at a book lying beyond my reach, I resort to certain movements of my bodily organs, coupled with an additional something which I employ as a *further* instrument. For instance, I grasp and raise the book now lying before me; and *with* the book which I grasp and raise, I get the book which I wish to look at, but which lies on a part of the table beyond the reach of my arm.

It will be admitted by all (on the bare statement) that the dominion of the will is limited or restricted to *some* of our bodily organs: that is to say, that there are only *certain parts* of our bodily frames which change their actual states for different states *as* (and so *soon* as) we wish or desire that they should. Numberless movements of my arms and legs immediately follow my desires of those same movements. But the motion of my heart would not be immediately affected by a wish I might happen to conceive that it should stop or quicken.

That the dominion of the will extends not to the mind may appear (at first sight) somewhat disputable. It has, however, been *proved* by the writers to whom I have referred. Nor, indeed, was the proof difficult, so soon as a definite meaning had been attached to the term *will.* Here (as in most cases) the confusion arose from the indefiniteness of the language by which the subjects of the inquiry were denoted.

If volitions be nothing but wishes immediately followed by their objects, it is manifest that the mind is not obedient to the will. In other words, it will not change its *actual* for *different* states or conditions *as* (and so *soon* as) it is wished or desired that it should. Try to recall an absent thought, or to banish a present thought, and you will find that your desire is not immediately followed by the attainment of its object. It is, indeed, manifest that the attempt would imply an absurdity. Unless the thought desired be present to the mind *already,* there is no determinate object at which the desire aims, and which it can attain *immediately,* or without the intervention of a mean. And to desire the absence of a thought actually present to the mind is to *conceive* the thought of which the absence is desired, and (by consequence) to perpetuate its presence.

Changes in the state of the mind, or in the state of the ideas and desires, are not to be attained immediately by desiring those changes, but through long and complex series of intervening means, beginning with desires which *really* are *volitions*.

Our desires of those bodily movements which immediately follow our desires of them are therefore the only objects which can be styled *volitions*; or (if you like the expression better) which can be styled acts of the will. For that is merely to affirm, "that they are the only desires which are followed by their objects *immediately,* or without the intervention of means." They are distinguished from other desires by the name of *volitions,* on account of this, their essential or characteristic property.

And as these are the only *volitions*; so are the bodily movements, by which they are immediately followed, the only *acts* or *actions* (properly so called). It will be admitted on the mere statement, that the only objects which can be called acts are consequences of Volitions. A voluntary movement of my body, or a movement which follows a volition, is an *act*. The *in*voluntary movements which are the consequences of certain diseases are *not* acts. But as the bodily movements which immediately follow volitions are the only *ends* of volition, it follows that those bodily movements are the only objects to which the term "acts" can be applied with perfect precision and propriety.

The only difficulty with which the subject is beset, arises from the concise or abridged manner in which (generally speaking) we express the objects of our discourse.

Most of the names which seem to be names of acts, are names of acts, *coupled with certain of their consequences.* For example, If I kill you with a gun or pistol, I *shoot* you: And the long train of incidents which are denoted by that brief expression are considered (or spoken of) as if they constituted an *act,* perpetrated by me. In truth, the only parts of the train which are my act or acts are the muscular motions by which I raise the weapon; point it at your head or body, and pull the trigger. These I *will*. The contact of the flint and steel; the ignition of the powder, the flight of the ball toward your body, the wound and subsequent death, with the numberless incidents included in these, are consequences of the act which I *will*. I *will* not those consequences, although I may *intend* them.

Nor is this ambiguity confined to the names by which our *actions* are denoted. It extends to the term "will"; to the term "volitions"; and to the term "acts of the will." In the case which I have just stated, I should be said to *will* the whole train of incidents; although I should only *will* certain muscular motions, and should *intend* those consequences which constitute the rest of the train. But the further explanation of these and other ambiguities must be reserved for the explanation of the term "intention."

The desires of those bodily movements which immediately follow our desires of them are imputed (as I have said) to an imaginary being, which is styled the *Will*. They are called *acts of the will*. And this imaginary being is said to be *determined* to action, by *Motives*.

All which (translated into intelligible language) merely means this: I wish a certain object. That object is not attainable *immediately,* by the wish or desire itself. But it is attainable by means of bodily movements which will immediately follow my desire of them. For the purpose of attaining that which I cannot attain by a wish, I wish the movements which will immediately follow my wish, and *through* which I expect to attain the object which is the end of my desires (as in the foregoing instance of the book).

A motive, then, is a wish causing or preceding a volition: A wish for a something not to be attained by wishing it, but which the party believes he shall probably or certainly attain, by *means* of those wishes which are styled acts of the will.

In a certain sense, motives may precede motives as well as acts of the will. For the desired object which is said to determine the will may itself be desired as a mean to an ulterior purpose. In which case, the desire of the object which is the ultimate end prompts the desire which immediately precedes the volition. . . .

That the will should have attracted great attention is not wonderful. For by means of the bodily movements which are the objects of volitions, the business of our lives is carried on. That the will should have been thought to contain something extremely mysterious, is equally natural. For volitions (as we have seen) are the only desires which consummate themselves: the only desires which attain their objects without the intervention of means.

. . .

. . . I must pause a moment for the purpose of correcting a mistake which I made in a former Lecture.

In that Lecture, I distinguished acts into acts *internal,* and acts *external.* Meaning by acts *internal,* volitions or determinations of the will: and meaning by acts *external,* the bodily movements which are the appropriate *objects* of volitions.

I am convinced, on reflection, that the terms are needless, and tend to darken their subjects. The term "volitions," or the term "determinations of the will," sufficiently denotes the objects to which I applied the term *"internal* acts": And it is utterly absurd (unless we are talking in metaphor) to apply such terms as "act" and "movement" to *mental* phenomena. I, therefore, repudiate the term *"internal* acts"; and, with that term, the superfluous distinction in question. I hastily borrowed the distinction from the works of Mr. Bentham: A writer, whom I much revere, and whom I am prone to follow, though I will not receive his dogmas with blind and servile submission. Imposters exact from their disciples "prostration of the understanding," because their doctrines will not endure examination. A man of Mr. Bentham's genius may provoke inquiry; and may rest satisfied with the ample and genuine admiration which his writings will infallibly extort from scrutinizing and impartial judges. . . .

Acts*

. . . The general conditions of penal liability are indicated with sufficient accuracy in the legal maxim. *Actus non facit reum, nisi mens sit rea*—the act alone does not amount to guilt; it must be accompanied by a guilty mind. That is to say, there are two conditions to be fulfilled before penal responsibility can rightly be imposed. The one is the doing of some *act* by the person to be held liable. A man is to be accounted responsible only for what he himself does, not for what other persons do, or for events independent of human activity altogether. The other is the *mens rea* or guilty mind with which the act is done. It is not enough that a man has done some act which on account of its mischievous results the law prohibits; before the law can justly punish the act, an inquiry must be made into the mental attitude of the doer. For although the act may have been objectively wrongful, the mind and will of the doer may have been innocent.

We shall see later that the *mens rea* or guilty mind includes two, and only two, distinct mental attitudes of the doer toward the deed. These are intention and recklessness. Generally speaking, a man is penally respon-

sible only for those wrongful acts which he does either willfully or recklessly. Then and only then is the *actus* accompanied by the *mens rea.* Apart from *mens rea* in the strict sense, there is the form of fault known as inadvertent negligence, which sometimes attracts penal liability. Where neither *mens rea* nor inadvertent negligence is present, punishment is generally unjustifiable. Hence inevitable accident or mistake—the absence both of wrongful intention or recklessness and of culpable negligence—is in the general a sufficient ground of exemption from penal responsibility. . . .

§131. "Acts"

The term act is one of ambiguous import, being used in various senses of different degrees of generality. When it is said, however, that an act is one of the essential conditions of liability, we use the term in the widest sense of which it is capable. We mean by it any event which is subject to the control of the human will. Such a definition is, indeed, not ultimate, but it is sufficient for the purpose of the law. As to the nature of the will and of the control exercised by it, it is not for lawyers to dispute, this being a problem of psychology or physiology, not of jurisprudence.

* John Salmond, *Jurisprudence,* 11th ed. by Williams (London: Sweet & Maxwell Ltd., 1957), pp. 398–402, reprinted by permission of the publishers and the copyright owners. Footnotes are omitted.

(1) *Positive and negative acts.* Of acts as so defined there are various species. In the first place, they are either positive or negative, either acts of commission or acts of omission. A wrongdoer either does that which he ought not to do, or leaves undone that which he ought to do. The term act is often used in a narrow sense to include merely positive acts, and is then opposed to omissions or forbearances instead of including them. This restriction, however, is inconvenient. Adopting the generic sense, we can easily distinguish the two species as positive and negative; but if we restrict the term to acts of commission, we leaves ourselves without a name for the genus, and are compelled to resort to an enumeration of the species.

(2) *Internal and external acts.* In the second place, acts are either internal or external. The former are acts of the mind, while the latter are acts of the body. In each case the act may be either positive or negative, lying either in bodily activity or passivity, or in mental activity or passivity. To think is an internal act: to speak is an external act. To work out an arithmetical problem in one's head is an act of the mind; to work it out on paper is an act of the body. Every external act involves an internal act which is related to it; but the converse is not true, for there are many acts of the mind which never realize themselves in acts of the body. The term act is very commonly restricted to external acts, but this is inconvenient for the reason already given in respect of the distinction between positive and negative acts.

(3) *Intentional and unintentional acts.* Acts are further distinguishable as being either intentional or unintentional. The nature of intention is a matter to which particular attenton will be devoted later, and it is sufficient to say here that an act is intended or intentional when it is the outcome of a determination of the actor's will directed to that end. In other words, it is intentional when it was foreseen and desired by the doer, and this foresight and desire realized themselves in the act through the operation of the will. It is unintentional, on the other hand, when, and in so far as, it is not the result of any determination of the will toward what actually takes place as the desired issue.

In both cases the act may be either internal or external, positive or negative. The term omission, while often used in a wide sense to include all negative acts, is also used in a narrower signification to include merely unintentional negative acts. It is then opposed to a forbearance, which is an intentional negative act. If I fail to keep an appointment through forgetfulness, my act is unintentional and negative; that is to say, an omission. But if I remember the appointment, and resolve not to keep it, my act is intentional and negative; that is to say, a forbearance.

The term act is very commonly restricted to intentional act, but this restriction is inadmissible in law. Intention is not a necessary condition of legal liability, and therefore cannot be an essential element in those acts which produce such liability. An act is an event subject to the control of the will; but it is not essential that this control should be actually exercised; there need be no actual determination of the will, for it is enough that such control or determination is possible. If the control of the will is actually exercised, the act is intentional; if the will is dormant, the act is unintentional; but in each case, by virtue of the existence of the power of control, the event is equally an act. The movements of a man's limbs are acts; those of his heart are not. Not to move his arms is an act; not to move his ears is not. To meditate is an act; to dream is not. It is the power possessed by me of determining the issue otherwise which makes any event *my* act, and is the ground of my responsibility for it.

Every act is made up of three distinct factors or constituent parts. These are (1) its *origin* in some mental or bodily activity or passivity of the doer, (2) its *circumstances,* and (3) its *consequences.* Let us suppose that in practicing with a rifle I shoot some person by accident. The material elements of my act are the following: its origin or primary stage, namely a series of muscular contractions, by which the rifle is raised and the trigger pulled; secondly, the circumstances, the chief of which are the facts that the rifle is loaded and in working order, and that the person killed is in the line of fire; thirdly, the consequences, the chief of which are the fall of the trigger, the explosion of the powder, the discharge of the bullet, its passage through the body of the man killed, and his death. A similar analysis will apply to all acts for which a man is legally responsible. Whatever act the law prohibits as being wrongful is so prohibited in respect of its origin, its circumstances and its consequences. For unless it has its origin in some mental or physical activity or passivity of the defendant, it is not his act at all; and apart from its circumstances and results it cannot, in general, be legally wrongful. All acts are, in respect of their origin, indifferent. No bodily motion is in itself illegal. To crook one's finger may be a crime, if the finger is in contact with the trigger of a loaded pistol; but in itself it is not a matter which the law is in any way concerned to take notice of.

Circumstances and consequences are of two kinds, according as they are relevant or irrelevant to the question of liability. Out of the infinite array of circumstances and the endless chain of consequences the law selects some few as material. They and they alone are constituent parts of the wrongful act. All the others are irrelevant and without legal significance. They have no bearing or influence on the guilt of the doer. It is for the law, at its own good pleasure, to select and define the relevant and material facts in each particular species of wrong. In theft the hour of the day is irrelevant; in burglary it is material.

An act has no *natural* boundaries, any more than an event or a place has. Its limits must be artificially defined for the purpose in hand for the time being. It is for the law to determine, in each particular case, what circumstances and what consequences shall be counted within the compass of the act with which it is concerned. To ask what act a man has done is like asking in what place he lives.

By some writers the term act is limited to that part of the act which we have distinguished as its origin. According to this opinion the only acts, properly so called, are movements of the body. "An act," it has been said, "is always a voluntary muscular contraction and nothing else." That is to say, the circumstances and consequences of an act are not part of it, but are wholly external to it. This limitation, however, seems no less inadmissible in law than contrary to the common usage of speech. We habitually include all material and relevant circumstances and consequences under the name of the act. The act of the murderer is the shooting or poisoning of his victim, not merely the muscular contractions by which this result is effected. To trespass on another man's land is a wrongful act; but the act includes the circumstance that the land belongs to another man, no less than the bodily movements by which the trespasser enters upon it.

It may be suggested that although an act must be taken to include some of its consequences, it does not include all of them, but only those which are direct or immediate. Any such distinction, however, between direct and indirect, proximate and remote, consequences is nothing more than an indeterminate difference of degree. The distinction between an act and its consequences, between doing a thing and causing a thing, is a merely verbal one, a matter of convenience of speech. There is no firm line between the act of killing a man and the act of doing something which results (however remotely) in his death.

Act*

. . . It is a common saying that every crime may be looked at as composed of two elements: (1) an *act* and (2) the *intention, or state of mind* with which the act is done. In connection with the latter the question most commonly asked is, "Did or did not the one who did the act *intend* to bring about the results which actually took place? Was that his *intention?*" However simple and clear such statements and questions may appear to be at first sight, a moment's reflection reveals

that the two terms, *act* and *intention,* are by no means free from ambiguity. One writer or judge will use them in one sense, another in a different sense; indeed, the same writer will not always be consistent in his usage. We must, therefore, begin by noting the various possible meanings which each of these terms may have—meanings more or less sanctioned by current modes of expression in the legal world. When this has been done, we may perhaps be in a position to give to each of these words some one particular meaning which will be the most useful for the purposes of the present discussion.

* Walter Wheeler Cook, "Act, Intention and Motive," *Yale Law Journal,* XXVI (1917), 645–51, reprinted with the permission of the Yale Law Journal.

First then of the term *act*: no word is more commonly used by judges and writers upon law, as a rule apparently without much thought of any possible ambiguity. Legal literature is full of phrases such as "the criminal act," "an act of homicide," "an act of trespass," etc., etc. Let us analyze one of these phrases. Take, for example, "an act of homicide." Suppose A murders B by shooting him with a pistol. What is "the act"? The usual answer would probably be, "the act of killing B." Even a brief consideration shows us that we have here a complex rather than a simple thing; that if we are to use words in an accurate, scientific manner we must recognize that the term *act* is here used so as to include more than one thing. Apparently it covers (1) what may be called the act (or series of acts) in a narrow sense of the word, i.e., a muscular movement (or movements) willed by the actor; (2) some reference to the surrounding circumstances; (3) the consequences or results of the movement (or movements). It seems obvious that if we are to make any careful analysis, we must distinguish between these three things; to do so, we need to have separate names for them. Perhaps we cannot do better than to restrict the word *act* to the narrower sense above suggested, i.e., so that it means simply a *muscular movement that is willed*. If we do this, we can say that in considering criminal liability we have to consider (1) the act (or acts); (2) the concomitant circumstances; (3) the consequences; (4) the actor's state of mind at the time he acts with reference to these circumstances and consequences. In the concrete case which we are considering, in this narrower sense of the word the *acts* of A consist of a series of muscular movements willed by A. The *concomitant circumstances* include, for example, the fact that B was within range of the pistol; that the pistol was loaded, etc., etc. The *consequences* of A's acts are of course very numerous; some are, for example, the pistol is raised and turned in B's direction; the trigger is pulled back; the hammer falls; the powder is ignited and explodes; the bullet is expelled from the pistol, goes through the air toward B, strikes the surface of B's body and penetrates the same; as a result B's body undergoes physical changes which result in death. Strictly and scientifically, all these things and many others are not parts of A's *act* but merely the *consequences* of the same.

This use of the term *act* in this narrow sense is sanctioned by many of the most eminent writers on jurisprudence. . . .

. . .

Mr. Justice Oliver Wendell Holmes expresses his agreement with this view in the following characteristically terse passage:

An act is always a voluntary muscular contraction, and nothing else. The chain of physical sequences which it sets in motion or directs to the plaintiff's harm is no part of it, and very generally a long train of such sequences intervenes.[1]

Often, however, as some of the phrases quoted above show, the term *act* is used more loosely, and may be regarded as a more or less convenient shorthand expression to describe not only the act in this narrow sense but also some portion of the accompanying circumstances as well as of the consequences. . . .

. . .

It is believed by the present writer that in a careful analysis of legal responsibility the less wide meaning given to *act* . . . is preferable to this looser usage. The suggestion of Salmond that so to limit the word is to run counter to accepted usage seems incorrect, except in so far as that is involved in all attempts to limit to one meaning a word which in popular speech has more than one.

The difficulties involved in the broader use of the term are shown by the following passage from Salmond . . . :

It may be suggested that although an act must be taken to include some of its consequences, it does not include all of them, but only those which are direct or immediate. Any such distinction, however, between direct and indirect, proximate and remote, consequences is nothing more than an indeterminate difference of degree, and cannot be made the basis of any logical definition. The distinction between an act and its consequences, between doing a thing and causing a thing, is a merely verbal one; it is a matter of convenience of speech, and not the product of any scientific analysis of the conception involved. There is no logical distinction between the act of killing a man and the act of doing something which results (however remotely) in his death.[2]

This leads us into this difficulty: the death of the victim is not the last consequence of

---

[1] *The Common Law*, p. 91.
[2] John Salmond, *Jurisprudence* (4th ed.), pp. 326–27.

the act; an infinite series of more remote consequences follows. As a further result, for example, the victim's family was starved to death because of nonsupport, etc., etc. Are all these "logically" parts of "the act" as thus defined? Is it really intended to include under *act* all the consequences, however remote, of a voluntary muscular movement? If so, all that can be said is that even popular language does not go so far, and there seems to be no utility in so extending the meaning of the word. Indeed, the difficulties into which we fall if we use *act* in this wider sense could not be more clearly illustrated than by the passage just quoted. "The distinction between an act and its consequences . . . is a merely verbal one," says the learned author, adding in explanation: "There is no logical distinction between the *act of killing a man* and the act of doing something which results (how-

ever remotely) in his death." This is quite true if we use *act* to include consequences, but not if we use it in the narrow and more accurate sense of a muscular movement that is willed. The distinction between that and its consequences in the outer world is not "merely verbal" but a very important one in fact.

To be sure, when no strict and accurate analysis is involved there is perhaps no very serious objection to the rather loose usage current among both laymen and lawyers and it has a certain convenience as a shorthand method of expression. The moment, however, that we leave the field of loose discussion and enter that of careful analysis, we need terms that express distinctions which clearly do exist and must be taken account of. For this reason in the present discussion the term *act* will be used, unless otherwise indicated, to signify *a muscular movement that is willed.*

The Criminal Act*

1. THE NECESSITY FOR AN ACT

The chief problems in the general part of criminal law pertain to the requirement of a criminal state of mind, *mens rea*; but these cannot be adequately discussed without a preliminary exploration of the nature of an *actus reus*. Although much of the discussion in this first chapter will be concerned with terminology, acceptance of a satisfactory terminology is of the first importance for securing workable rules.

That crime requires an act is invariably true if the proposition be read as meaning that a private thought is not sufficient to found responsibility. Shakespeare's lines express sound legal doctrine.

His act did not o'ertake his bad intent;
And must be buried but as an intent
That perish'd by the way: thoughts are no subjects,
Intents but merely thoughts.

"So long as an act rests in bare intention," said Lord Mansfield, "it is not punishable by our laws,"[1] and this is so even though the intention be abundantly proved by the confession of the accused.

It is worth pausing to inquire into the reason for this rule. A reason commonly given is the supposed impossibility of proving a mental state. "A tribunal," said Blackstone, "cannot punish for what it cannot know."[2] So also Brian, C. J.: "The thought of man is not triable, for the devil himself knoweth not the thought of man."[3] But Brian was speaking of an intent not declared in words or conduct, and on another occasion he recognized that intent can be inferred from acts. Similarly, it can be inferred from a confession. Hence it is not true to say that intent cannot be tried. Better reasons for the rule would be (1) the difficulty of distinguishing between daydream and fixed intention in the absence of behavior tending toward the crime intended, and (2) the undesirability of spreading the criminal law so wide as to cover a mental state that the accused might be too irresolute even to begin to translate into action. There can hardly be anyone who has never thought evil. When a desire is inhibited it may find expression into fantasy; but it would be absurd to condemn this natural psychological mechanism as illegal.

Some propositions relating to the criminal

* Glanville L. Williams, *Criminal Law: The General Part* (London: Stevens & Sons Ltd., 1953), pp. 1–25, reprinted with the permission of the author and the publishers. Footnotes have been renumbered.
[1] Scofield (1784) Cald. 402.

[2] *Comm.* iv 21.
[3] Y.B. (1477) P. 17 E.4 2a pl.2.

act are well settled and may be briefly dismissed.

Although thoughts are free, the uttering of them is another matter. Speaking or writing is an act, and is capable of being treason, sedition, conspiracy, or incitement; indeed, almost any crime can be committed by mere words, for it may be committed by the accused ordering an innocent agent (e.g., a child under eight) to do the act. But to constitute a criminal act there must be (as said already) something more than a mere mental resolution. Apparent, but not real, exceptions to this proposition are treason and conspiracy. It is treason to compass the King's death, but the law requires an overt act manifesting the intention; and this act must be something more than a confession of the intention. It must be an act intended to further the intention; perhaps, too, it must actually do so. As Clark observes:

Except in cases of admitted gross injustice and tyranny, such as the monstrous judgment related by Hale as delivered under Edward IV, and the later trials of Peachum and Sydney the overt act required by statute has usually been not merely matter evidencing intention, but a step, however slight, towards performance.[4]

Conspiracy, too, must be manifested in conduct, even though such conduct is only the uttering of words of agreement. Thus, the words must be in furtherance or (at least) intended furtherance of the crime; mere words of confession are not enough.

In crimes requiring *mens rea* as well as *actus reus* the physical act must be contemporaneous with the guilty mind; it is not enough that a mentally innocent act is subsequently followed by *mens rea*. Nor does a subsequent intent amount to a crime without another act (or culpable omission) in which it becomes manifested. These propositions are well known in connection with the law of larceny, and are of general validity.

A person may be guilty as a secondary party to a crime in respect of an act done before the crime itself: e.g., an accessory before the fact in respect of his previous act of counseling.

2. OMISSIONS

In some instances an omission will create criminal responsibility without any positive act. The prohibition of omissions presents greater legislative problems than the prohibition of positive acts. The underlying philosophy was well stated by Macaulay.

It is, indeed, most highly desirable that men should not merely abstain from doing harm to their neighbours, but should render active services to their neighbours. In general, however, the penal law must content itself with keeping men from doing positive harm, and must leave to public opinion, and to the teachers of morality and religion, the office of furnishing men with motives for doing positive good. It is evident that to attempt to punish men by law for not rendering to others all the service which it is their duty to render to others would be preposterous. We must grant impunity to the vast majority of those omissions which a benevolent morality would pronounce reprehensible, and must content ourselves with punishing such omissions only when they are distinguished from the rest by some circumstance which marks them out as peculiarly fit objects of penal legislation.[5]

The legal duty to act, therefore, is a circumscribed one; and it must be positively laid down by the law. It is possible for the law to provide that whoever does so-and-so shall be punishable; but it is not possible for the law to provide that whoever omits to do so-and-so shall be punishable, because in many cases that would make almost everyone punishable. If a child is neglected, it is not only his father who omits to look after him; everyone else omits to look after him also. In law, as in morals, the concept of culpable omission presupposes a duty to act; and a rule penalizing an omission must state to whom this duty belongs.

When we speak of an omission we mean something that the accused could have done if he had been minded to do so and had prepared himself in time, or at least something that another in his place could have done. Absolute impossibility is a defense. . . . The single exception to this proposition in English law will be noticed presently (§4).

It follows from the principle stated by Macaulay that the criminal law does not impose a duty upon someone to act to prevent a consequence whenever it imposes a duty not to bring about the consequence. The law relating to omissions is not coextensive with the law relating to acts. It is largely coextensive in manslaughter and murder, but here the

[4] Edwin C. Clark, *Analysis of Criminal Liability* (Cambridge: Cambridge University Press, 1880), pp. 15–16.

[5] Lord Macaulay, *Works,* ed. by Lady Trevelyan, VII (London: Longmans, Green and Co., 1866), 497 ("Notes on the Indian Penal Code, 1837").

event of death leads the law to look upon the omission with special severity. Most crimes, particularly those at common law, are defined to need a positive act; but a tendency is discernible to extend the law to omissions. For example, assault and battery require a positive act, and cannot be committed by a bare omission. Yet it may be that an innominate misdemeanor has been developed which supplements the law of assault and battery in respect of omissions, and makes the duty to prevent harm short of death coextensive with the duty to prevent death. This is so, at least, in respect of the neglect of helpless persons. Again, an intentional omission to disclose information is not deceit; yet a statement may be false and deceitful not only because of what is stated but also because of what is concealed, omitted or implied.

. . .

In some cases entry upon performance of an undertaking creates a duty to complete.

If a surgeon from benevolence cuts the umbilical cord of a new-born child he cannot stop there and watch the patient bleed to death. It would be murder wilfully to allow death to come to pass in that way.[6]

In a Massachusetts case the interesting question arose whether arson could be committed by an omission. An appeal court upheld a direction to the jury that if, when a fire had accidentally started on the defendant's premises, he deliberately refrained from extinguishing it in order that the whole building might be destroyed and he could claim the insurance money, he was guilty of arson, just as much as if he had started the fire.[7] Although the decision accords with common sense it may be questioned whether it does not represent a judicial extension of the law. Perhaps a parallel is an English case relating to cruelty to animals, in which it was held that a duty to relieve suffering could arise from the fact that the suffering was originally caused, albeit without fault, by the accused's acts. Another extension of the duty to act was perhaps suggested under the Highway Act, 1835, s. 72, which makes it an offense to cause damage to the highway. The defendant's lorry caught fire, and he did all he could to put it out. It was held that he could not

be convicted in the absence of a "willful act or omission." This may mean that although the fire was not willfully caused, there would be responsibility on the basis of causation if the defendant willfully omitted to minimize the damage. In somewhat the same way a surveyor of highways who placed stones on a road for the purpose of repair but did not light them at night was adjudged guilty of willfully "obstructing" the highway, though if he had lighted them it would not have been an obstruction. Another illustration may be drawn from the law of abduction. If a young girl comes to a man without any persuasion, he does not become guilty of abduction by not returning her to her father; but if she came in consequence of his persuasion, though he no longer wishes to have her at the time when she comes, he becomes guilty of the crime by not returning her.

. . .

3. POSSESSION

Is unlawful possession a sufficient act to engage criminal responsibility? It has been decided that an indictment charging a person with having something in his possession (e.g., coining tools or counterfeit silver or obscene prints) for a criminal purpose does not charge an act, and so is bad at common law; but a charge of procuring a thing does charge an act, and such procuring may be evidenced by possession. A statute may make the bare possession criminal, but even in this event the accused must presumably be guilty either of an act of procuring or of a conscious retention of possession—an omission in breach of a duty to surrender up or destroy.

. . .

4. CRIMES WITHOUT ANY PERSONAL ACT OR OMISSION

Since the law almost always requires an act or omission to constitute a crime, one might be forgiven for supposing that such act or omission must be that of the party charged with the crime. Often this is so, but not invariably. A person may be vicariously or strictly responsible for the act or omission of another. Instances are when a grocer's assistant, without his authority, makes a false representation as to the goods sold . . . and when a publican's servant in his absence permits gaming, etc., on the premises. The master can be convicted although his only act was in put-

[6] Holmes, *The Common Law*, p. 278.
[7] *Commonwealth v. Cali* (1923), 247 Mass. 20, 141 N.E. 510.

ting the servant in charge of the establishment. . . . If the "act" rule is an expression of moral principle, such instances of responsibility for the culpable conduct of another must be admitted to be unethical.

In one isolated case criminal responsibility has been imposed without any act, culpable omission, or even culpable mental state, on the part of anyone. This was *Larsonneur* (1933),[8] where the facts were as follows: A Frenchwoman came to England with permission. Being required by the authorities to depart, she complied by going to the Irish Free State. Not being desired there either, she was arrested and handed back in custody to the English police. The latter prosecuted her under Article 18 (1) (b) of the Aliens Order, 1920, for being an alien who was "found" in the United Kingdom without permission. Now it was of course true that the defendant had been "found" in the United Kingdom, in one sense of the word—she was found in a police cell. The Court of Criminal Appeal accordingly pronounced the offense to have been committed, and confirmed a sentence of three days' imprisonment with a recommendation for deportation. The defendant had been guilty of no act, nor (in any usual sense of the word) of an omission. It seems regrettable that the word "found" in the Order was interpreted to include "found by the police in their own custody."

5. THE MENTAL ELEMENT IN AN ACT

The law might define an act to mean any bodily movement, but in practice it does not do this. The classic definition of an act for legal purposes is that of Holmes (following Austin) : it is a muscular contraction that results from an operation of the will. The important point about his definition is that it splices part of the mental element of crime onto the physical element. The mental requirement for an act rules out not only reflexes like yawning but also cases where the bodily movement is compelled by immediate force, and even sleep-walking. The last is a difficult case, because the conduct of a sleepwalker may be purposive (though not recollected on waking), and may be regarded as expressing unconscious desire. However, unconscious desire is not sufficient either for an act or for *mens rea* (§12).

Conduct while sleep-walking is not an act

even though the accused contemporaneously has a dream corresponding more or less to what he is doing. Thus, suppose that a mother dreams that her daughter is being seduced by a soldier; she gets up in her sleep, takes an axe, and kills her daughter, probably thinking that she is killing the supposed soldier. Here, according to the dream facts, the mother is killing a human being in circumstances that do not, even if true, constitute in themselves a defense. Nevertheless the mother is not guilty of murder, for dream "knowledge" is not knowledge for legal purposes. The case is not one of insanity (sleep-walking being at most a neurosis), and the *McNaghten* rules are inapplicable. . . .

There is no English authority on whether conduct under hypnotic influence (including post-hypnotic suggestion) may be regarded as the same in law as sleep-walking. It seems that French and German law treat it as an instance of absence of *mens rea*. The argument is that hypnotic suggestion creates a very great compulsion to perform the act. "The suggested actions appear to execute themselves, and the subject feels rather like a helpless spectator who does not initiate or even ratify them."[9] But there are difficulties. Hypnosis is not a state of unconsciousness. "While it is going on it is a coherent conscious experience capable of being clearly remembered afterwards. The subject's behaviour when he has his eyes open and is talking and moving about may be outwardly indistinguishable from his usual wide-awake state."[10] It is, therefore, doubtful whether a relevant distinction can be made between hypnotic suggestion and insane impulse, the law being that the latter does not exclude the possibility of an "act." Moreover, although the scientific evidence is not absolutely conclusive, the weight of opinion favors the view that a hypnotized person cannot be forced to perform acts that are repugnant to him. If this is true, the most that the hypnotist can do in the direction of criminal activity is to remove an inhibition and cause the subject to commit a crime to which he is already inclined. On the whole, the preferable view would seem to be that the hypnotized subject performs an act and is legally responsible, his condition going only to the question of punishment.

[8] 97 J.P. 206 (C.C.A.).

[9] Robert W. White, *The Abnormal Personality*, 2d ed. (Ronald, 1956), p. 203.
[10] *Ibid.*, p. 202.

The definition of an act in this regard is governed largely by policy. A drunkard who, in his partly insensate condition, does some injury is deemed to perform an act, though in fact his condition may be very like that of the sleep-walker. Drunkenness is a self-induced condition; sleep-walking is not. On the other hand, an injury done in a drunken sleep receives the same exemption as any other injury during sleep. A lunatic is deemed to perform an act even where he is acting as an automaton, though he will be exempted from criminal responsibility. . . .

When there is consciousness, a party is capable of "acting" even though he is subject to an incontrollable impulse. . . . An act presupposes will, but not "free" will.

The requirement of an act with its element of will is not so important a restriction upon criminal responsibility as may at first appear. The requirement does not in itself involve that the harmful consequence should be intended. Whether the consequence must be intended pertains to the doctrine of *mens rea,* not to the doctrine of the act. If a robber fires at the person robbed and kills him, when he intended only to wound, there is an act, and the robber will be guilty of murder, although the consequence was not intended. Another reason for the comparative unimportance of the "act" doctrine is that when an act seems at first sight to be lacking it is sometimes possible for the court to look critically back through the accused's past until a culpable act is discovered. Stephen, for example, who discussed the example of the robber, suggested that if the robber's gun had gone off by accident he would not be guilty of murder because there would be no act; but the opposite has now been decided, and the reason evidently is that the required act is not the act of pressing the trigger (which, in this instance, is absent) but the act of presenting the gun, which is construed as an act of violence in pursuance of a felony of violence. Again, a sleep-walker who kills another person with a revolver is not for that reason alone guilty of homicide; but if, knowing himself to be given to sleep-walking, he had gone to sleep with the loaded revolver by his side, the putting it there would be an act that might well be sufficiently negligent to make him guilty of manslaughter. Finally, a positive act is not always needed, because there may be responsibility for an omission.

At the present day the exemption from responsibility, such as it is, given by the "act" doctrine could, in respect of the requirement of will, just as well be put on the ground of absence of *mens rea.* The importance of saying that there is no act is said to relate to crimes of strict responsibility (e.g., under the Food and Drugs Act), for these do not need *mens rea,* while they do generally need an act. But it is hard to imagine a practical case: selling is not a reflex, and grocers and dairymen are unlikely to be given to sleep-walking during business hours. To classify absence of will as absence of an act makes the legal distinction between act and state of mind a jagged one, and sometimes it may lead to error in reasoning. In *Harrison-Owen* (1951),[11] the defendant was found in a dwelling-house at night and gave the explanation that he must have entered in a state of automatism. On his trial for burglary, when this explanation was raised as a defense, the judge directed counsel to put to the accused a number of previous convictions for burglary. It was well settled that evidence of previous similar acts was admissible when the defense was lack of *mens rea.* But the Court of Criminal Appeal determined that the rule did not apply where, as here, the defense was that there was no voluntary act; the previous convictions should not have been put, and the conviction of the accused was quashed. With respect, the decision seems to be wrong, for the distinction between lack of *mens rea* and absence of the mental element in an act is only one of legal arrangement, not one of substance.

Apart from its questionable logic the decision is inexpedient, for previous convictions are of great probative force in displacing a defense of automatism, and the defense may be difficult to rebut in any other way. It is possible for a man to enter another's house in a dream-state resulting from temporary mental disorder, such as epilepsy or hysterical fugue, and such an entry is neither burglary nor housebreaking. To prevent abuse of this defense, it is necessary to allow the prosecution to put in evidence every fact tending to show that the alleged automatism is a fake.

The application of the idea of voluntariness to an omission is troublesome. If the defendant has directed his mind to the question

---

[11] (1951)2 All E.R. 726, W.N. 483, 115 J.P. 545 (C.C.A.).

whether to act or not, and has decided not to act, one may speak of his omission as an intentional one; and it is even possible to speak of an omission as intentional when the defendant is merely aware of the fact that he is not acting. . . . In some crimes, however, like manslaughter, a mere negligent omission is punished, as when a man thinks he has acted properly but in fact has not acted. Here it is difficult to find an "act" in any meaning of the term; the culprit is punished not because of any wrongful act or of any mental state that he possesses, but because he has not done the act or had the mental state that he ought to have done or had. It is assumed that the culprit could have done or had it if he had been more conscientious in directing his mind to his legal duties. For the purpose of exposition, whatever the ultimate theory may be, it is convenient to treat a negligent omission as a type of act.

6. OTHER ELEMENTS OF AN ACT; THE *actus reus*

Hitherto an act has been taken as a willed movement; but this does not reach the full meaning of the word. "An act," says the Clown in *Hamlet*, "hath three branches; it is, to act, to do, and to perform." The end of this sentence is as disappointing to the lawyer as the beginning was promising. An "act" in criminal law has indeed three branches, but they are as follows:

(a) A willed movement (or omission).

(b) Certain surrounding circumstances (including past facts).

(c) Certain consequences.

To take a simple illustration, we commonly speak of the act of shooting, but shooting is much more than muscular contraction. It involves the fact that the finger is on the trigger of a gun (concomitant circumstance), and the consequence that a bullet leaves the gun. The act of killing a man by shooting involves the further consequence that the bullet enters the victim's body and kills him.

Some writers (such as Holmes) desire to restrict the term "act" to the voluntary muscular contraction in (a); others (such as Salmond) include (b) and (c). It is hardly necessary for a writer on criminal law to attempt to settle this question of desirable usage, because he can make use of the technical term *actus reus* (or its civilian alternative, *corpus delicti*) to express exactly what he means. To this we now turn.

It is not enough to create criminal responsibility that there are *mens rea* and an act: the *actus* must be *reus*. In other words, the act must be one that (assuming the requisite mental element) is proscribed by the law. If I carry off my own umbrella thinking that I am stealing somebody else's, there are the *mens rea* of larceny and an act, but not the *actus reus* of larceny. (Whether, in this illustration, there is the *actus reus* of attempted larceny is another question, which will be considered in its place.) . . .

Criminal law is generally concerned to repress conduct hurtful to society, and (putting inchoate crime on one side) the same muscular contraction may be or not be punishable according as it has or has not the given hurtful consequence. Thus: D shoots at P, misses him and kills a rabbit. This is not murder. There is an act, namely of shooting. But the *actus reus* of murder requires a harmful result in addition to the act of shooting; it requires the killing of a human being. This result is not present in the illustration.

Examples of crimes requiring a result against the social welfare are homicide and obtaining by false pretenses. Examples of crimes that are made punishable by reason of their mischievous tendencies, irrespective of harmful result, are forgery, perjury, and inchoate crimes. Thus harm may or may not be part of the *actus reus*. Where harm is required, it must be caused by the physical act (or omission), and the causal connection must not be too remote in law.

Again, the specification of a crime requires various circumstances to accompany the physical act. In perjury the accused must have been sworn as a witness, and in bigamy he must already be married; in treason he must be a British subject or otherwise owe allegiance; in receiving stolen goods the goods must already be stolen, and in burglary the physical act must take place at night. The circumstance may even be a negative fact, such as the absence of consent in larceny and rape, and the absence of relationship of husband and wife in rape.

Even in common speech an act involves more than Holmes's muscular contraction: it includes certain circumstances and consequences. When we use the technical term *actus reus*, we include all the external circumstances and consequences specified in the rule of law as constituting the forbidden situation. It will be observed that *reus* does not signify that the act in itself creates criminal responsibility, for that neglects the requirement of *mens rea*. *Reus* must be taken as simply a technical way of indicating that the situation specified in the *actus reus* is one that, given any necessary mental element, is forbidden by law. In other words, *actus reus* means the whole definition of the crime with the exception of the mental element—and it even includes a mental element in so far as that is contained in the definition of an act. This meaning of *actus reus* follows inevitably from the proposition that all the constituents of a crime are either *actus reus* or *mens rea*.

The point is so important in constructing a satisfactory terminology, and is so frequently misunderstood, that it may be well to invoke approved authors in support. Salmond says:

Circumstances and consequences are of two kinds, according as they are relevant or irrelevant to the question of liability. Out of the infinite array of circumstances and the endless chain of consequences the law selects some few as material. They and they alone are constituent parts of the wrongful act. All the others are irrelevant and without legal significance. . . . It is for the law . . . to select and define the relevant and material facts in each particular species of wrong. In theft the hour of the day is irrelevant; in burglary it is material.[12]

The outcome of this view is that the same physical movement may constitute different "acts" for the purpose of different crimes. This is well put by Terry.

A bodily movement may be followed by a series of consequences and it is possible to take any one of these as the definitional consequence to be included in and definitional of the act in the wider sense. . . . Thus we may speak of the act of firing a pistol, the act of shooting a man, and the act of killing him, three distinguishable acts, which, however, all include the same bodily movements, but are distinguished by different definitional consequences being referred to.[13]

It will be seen in discussing the subject of *mens rea* that the courts have sometimes tried to distinguish between the physical act and its surrounding circumstances, holding that while knowledge is requisite in respect of the former, it is not always requisite in respect of the latter. These attempts have not been

happy, because it is not possible to draw a satisfactory line between the physical act and its environment. One cannot formulate a test for the ingredients of an act, except the test of what is required by law for the external situation of a crime. Writers have often pointed out that there is generally no harm in a man's crooking his right forefinger, unless it is (for example) around the trigger of a loaded gun which is pointing at someone. The muscular contraction, regarded as an *actus reus,* cannot be separated from its circumstances. When the specification of a crime includes a number of circumstances, all of these are essential to the crime and all must be regarded as part of the *actus reus*. It will be shown later that any narrower view is undesirable because it creates great uncertainty and also because it leads straight to haphazard strict responsibility in crime, enabling different judges to pick and choose in different ways between the elements of a crime for the purpose of the requirement of *mens rea*. The view that *actus reus* means *all* the external ingredients of the crime is not only the simplest and clearest but the one that gives the most satisfactory results.

A further step may now be taken. *Actus reus* includes, in the terminology here suggested, not merely the whole objective situation that has to be proved by the prosecution, but also the absence of any ground of justification or excuse, whether such justification or excuse be stated in any statute creating the crime or implied by the courts in accordance with general principles. The *actus reus* of murder, for instance, includes not only D's killing of P, but also the fact that P is under the king's peace, that P has not been sentenced to be hanged by D, that the killing is within English territorial jurisdiction (or that D is a British subject), and so on, even though the evidential or persuasive burden of proof in respect of these matters may rest on the accused. In brief, *actus reus* includes negative as well as positive elements, and it is not affected by questions of burden of proof. . . .

This, it is true, makes *actus reus* mean something different from an act in the layman's sense of the word. In the above example D's act would popularly be said to be merely the killing of another human being P. It is not believed that "act" in this sense is a particularly useful technical term, because, as pointed out already, there is no certainty as to its

[12] *Jurisprudence,* 10th ed., p. 369.
[13] "Duties, Rights and Wrongs" (1924), *A.B.A.J.,* p. 123.

limit. A layman would be puzzled if he were asked whether P's "act" was in killing a specific person P, or in killing a human being, or in killing a mammal; he would not see the point of the question. Legally the question is important in circumstances of mistake, and the answer to it is that D's act is killing a human being. . . . This is the legally relevant feature; hence (1) if D mistakes P's identity, thinking him another person, the act is still intentional (as to a human being), while (2) if he thinks P is a pig his act is not intentional (as to a human being). In the same way, (3) if D being the public executioner mistakenly thinks that P is a condemned criminal, D's act is not intentional in any relevant way. It is intentional in one respect, just as the act in (2) was intentional as to killing a mammal; but it is not intentional as a complete *actus reus,* which is all that matters in law.

Having said so much in favor of a wide definition of *actus reus,* one very limited concession may now be made. It is possible to argue that some elements in the specification of a crime are occasionally not part of the *actus reus.* There are some rather curious offenses of "being found" in certain predicaments, where the fact of being found may be said to be a condition of the offense though not part of it. Even if this is so, it is altogether exceptional. For example, the general rule that only a British subject can be guilty of treason in respect of an act done abroad may seem at first sight to state a condition of responsibility as opposed to an ingredient of the *actus reus;* but the first impression would be wrong. It is true that the traitor is not punished for being a British subject; but he is punished for the violation of a duty of allegiance that (as a general rule in respect of acts committed abroad) is coextensive with British nationality. The fact that he is a British subject proves his duty of allegiance and is, in this sense, part of his guilt. The future discussion will ignore the possible existence of conditions of responsibility that are not part of legal guilt, because they raise no problem in the law of *mens rea.*

The foregoing remarks relate to terminology, and, since terminology is a matter on which it is difficult to secure agreement, the point of substance may now be restated briefly in different language. If a narrow definition is preferred for *actus reus,* the concept for which that expression is here employed may instead be denoted by the phrase "external situation." Thus the proposition that there must generally be *mens rea* as to the *actus reus* becomes, in this language, the proposition that there must generally be *mens rea* as to the external situation specified by law for the crime. That, it is submitted, is the legal principle, in whatever words it may be expressed.

7. *Mens rea* AS AFFECTING *actus reus*

In an endeavor to keep the concepts of *actus reus* and *mens rea* distinct, *actus reus* has here been defined as the whole situation forbidden by law with the exception of the mental element (but including so much of the mental element as is contained in the definition of an act). This definition rather supposes that the situation forbidden by law is something distinct from the mental element. Sometimes this is not true. The act constituting a crime may in some circumstances be objectively innocent, and take its criminal coloring entirely from the intent with which it is done. This is so in attempt, where the act of the accused, though sufficiently proximate to the intended crime, has not gone far enough to be mischievous. Although innocent apart from the intent, such an act is an *actus reus* in legal theory, because it is the act constituting crime of attempt . . . It must be confessed that in this application the term *actus reus* is somewhat misleading.

On principle, what is true for attempt should be true for inchoate treason. Yet in an American case an American citizen who joined a corps of American troops thinking they were British was adjudged not guilty of treason, his act being innocent. Surely he should have been convicted of compassing, for in an inchoate crime it is no defense that the overt act was objectively innocent.

Conspiracy falls into place under the same rule. Bad motive may make an agreement criminal when good motive does not: the agreement, which is the *actus reus,* is the same in each case, and the only difference is in the state of mind. Here again the crime is an inchoate one.

It is submitted that this situation is found only in inchoate crimes, that is to say, in crimes where some ulterior crime is intended by the actor. An ordinary crime cannot be constituted by *mens rea,* where the act is objectively innocent. The point was expressed by Macaulay in language of pellucid clarity.

When an act is of such a description that it would be better that it should not be done, it is quite proper to look at the motives and intentions of the doer, for the purpose of deciding whether he shall be punished or not. But when an act which is really useful to society, an act of a sort which it is desirable to encourage, has been done, it is absurd to inquire into the motives of the doer, for the purpose of punishing him if it shall appear that his motives were bad.

If A kills Z, it is proper to inquire whether the killing was malicious; for killing is prima facie a bad act. But if A saves Z's life, no tribunal inquires whether A did so from good feeling, or from malice to some person who was bound to pay Z an annuity; for it is better that human life should be saved from malice than not at all.[14]

This may sound so obvious as hardly to be worth the statement; yet there is authority tending to the contrary view, at least to the extent of saying that intent is a factor in adjudging a defense of justification or excuse. In *Dadson* (1850)[15] the question arose in this way. D arrested P for cutting and stealing wood; in itself P's act was a summary offense, but P had twice been convicted of the offense before, and therefore his act on this occasion was a felony. D did not know that P had previously been convicted. It was held by the Court for Crown Cases Reserved that D was rightly convicted for shooting at P in order to prevent his escape, because the arrest was unlawful in the absence of knowledge by D of the facts that made it lawful. In other words, it is not enough, in arresting a felon, that he is actually a felon, if the arrester does not know (or thinks he knows) the facts that make the other a felon in law.

The judgment in the case is laconically reported and its soundness is contestable. The consequence is hard for an officer who relies upon "second sight" in effecting an arrest: that such an officer should commit a wrong if he arrests the wrong man is intelligible, but not if he arrests the right man. In America, where the same rule is applied, it has resulted in the exclusion of evidence obtained in consequence of the illegal arrest. Thus, if a constable by intuition suspects a man of illegally carrying a revolver (an offense for which he has power to arrest), and if he arrests the man on that ground and finds him in possession of the revolver, no evidence can be given on a subsequent charge against the person arrested that the revolver was found in his possession. Such a rule is scarcely fair to the police or socially expedient.

The point of interest here is that the rule seems hard to reconcile with the requirement of an *actus reus*. In *Dadson* the arrester had *mens rea,* for he intended to arrest the other and on the facts as he knew them the arrest was unlawful. But common sense would suggest that objectively the arrest was lawful, because there was no *actus reus*.

To make the point clearer, suppose a converse case, where D is a policeman who arrests P reasonably thinking that he is a felon, when in fact he is not a felon. D is not guilty of a crime in effecting the arrest because he has no *mens rea* . . . but he has committed the *actus reus* of battery or false imprisonment. There is an *actus reus* because P is in fact not a felon. What saves D from conviction is something in his mind, namely, his belief that P committed a felony; were it not for that he would be convicted.

Now in *Dadson,* where P was a felon, D had no need to rely on a defense of lack of *mens rea* (nor could he have done so); but on principle he should have had the defense that his conduct was not interdicted by law. It is true that, in attempt, *mens rea* may make *reus* an *actus* that otherwise would not be so; but it seems to occasion needless difficulty to admit the same doctrine in completed crimes.

If *Dadson* is right, the conclusion is (and it is a conclusion drawn and approved by an American writer on the subject)[16] that "if a sheriff who had no knowledge of any sentence of death having been pronounced should take the life of his prisoner for some unlawful purpose of his own, it would be no answer to a murder charge that there existed, unknown to him, a mandate for him to execute that man on that very day." This is surely untenable. If the execution were carried out according to the forms of law, there would be no *actus reus,* and the sheriff's ignorance or motive could not in itself make him guilty of a crime. There is no *actus reus* because "the accident has turned up in his favour." The law desires the criminal to be executed in a certain way, and it is not for the law to complain if

---

[14] *Works*, VII, 552.
[15] 2 Den. 35, 169 E.R. 407.

[16] Perkins in (1946) 36 J.Cr.L. & Cr. at 409.

he is executed in that very way. Suppose that the sheriff (or his deputy the under-sheriff) were charged with dereliction of duty in not hanging the man in the manner provided by law: surely his answer would be that he had done so. Suppose that the sheriff knew of the death sentence and was glad to execute it because he wanted revenge: his motive would clearly not make him guilty of murder. It is the same if coupled with this motive there is lack of knowledge of the sentence.

If the sheriff in the illustration were adjudged guilty one would have to go further and say that a British soldier who kills an enemy in action, believing himself to be killing his own drill-sergeant, is guilty of murder. This is surely preposterous.

It is submitted that the decision in *Dadson* is wrong. The law desires felons to be arrested. In the old days it used to be said that even private persons not merely have the power but are under a duty to arrest. If the arrest of felons is something that the law desires to bring about, it would seem to follow that neither the bad motive nor the ignorance of the arrester can turn the arrest of the felon into an *actus reus*. The law governs conduct, not purity of intention.

The Concept of an Omission*

"An omission," wrote Stroud, "is not like an act, a real event, but is merely an artificial conception consisting of the negation of a particular act."[1] By this is presumably meant than an act is sensible to feeling and to sight, while an omission is not observable by the senses but is only a significance legally attributed to passivity. Bishop, too, perhaps had this in mind when he wrote: "A neglect is not properly an act, yet in a sense it is. It is a departure from the order of things established by law. It is a checking of action; or it is like the case of a man who stands still while the company to which he is attached moves along, when we say, he leaves the company."[2]

These statments are valuable in pointing to the essential nature of an omission, but they suffer from a failure to specify the exact sense in which they use the idea of an act. "Act" must be defined before an omission can be distinguished; and no agreed juristic concept of an act exists. Austin defined an act as a motion of the body consequent upon a determination of the will, but this approach implies a concept of volitions which has now been sufficiently exploded by Professor Ryle. Holmes regarded an act as a "voluntary muscular contraction," which might be more acceptable, if "voluntary" is suitably defined. For the purposes of the criminal law, neither definition is very helpful. The criminal law never prohibits mere muscular contractions. It is not yet an offense to twitch. What the criminal law prohibits is muscular contractions in certain circumstances and, perhaps, productive of certain consequences. The act of homicide in any particular instance must include the accompanying circumstance of the victim's existence and the consequence of the victim's death. The only fruitful concept of an act for the criminal law must synthesize the defendant's physical movements with external accompanying circumstances and, sometimes, with certain consequences.

And so with omissions. The definition of the specific offense must again single out physical movement in accompanying circumstances and, possibly, with certain consequences. It is not quite accurate to say, as Stroud did, that an omission is not, like an act, a "real event." The legal notion of omission, like that of an act, involves tangible happenings. Of course, in offenses which are purely those of commission, such as rape, the criminal act occurs when the general scheme of conduct projected by the statutory language is realized in the particular by the physical movements of the defendant in appropriate circumstances. In offenses purely of omission, such as misprision of treason, the criminal occurrence is the failure of the defendant in appropriate circumstances to make concrete the general pattern of conduct prescribed by the legal norm. The defendant may be acting constantly, but the legal significance is attributed to the absence of particular action realizing the legal pattern.

There is a third possibility: the offense which in its legislative expression seems pro-

---

* Graham Hughes, "Criminal Omissions," *Yale Law Journal*, LXVII (1958), 597–600, reprinted with the permission of the Yale Law Journal. Footnotes have been renumbered.
[1] Stroud, *Mens Rea*, 4 (1914).
[2] 1 Bishop, *Criminal Law*, § 433 (5th ed. 1872).

hibitive only, but which, by a process of judicial interpretation, has come to be regarded as capable of perpetration by omission. An example is homicide in a jurisdiction which refers only to the act of killing, as in New York, but where the courts have shown willingness to apply liability to one who causes death through neglect. No term of art in Anglo-American criminal law describes the liability for such an offense incurred through a failure to act. The French neatly call it "délit de commission par omission."[3]

The nature of certain offenses may make classification difficult. Examples might be drawn from the offenses of practicing certain callings without a license. Does the offense lie in practicing—commission—or in failing to obtain a license? The question is clearly absurd for neither practicing nor failing to get a license is in isolation criminal. The offense is practicing without a license and is committed by embarking on one course of conduct without first doing something else. It therefore contains elements of commission and omission. What the prosecution must show to obtain a conviction will constitute an effective test: here, both facts—practicing and no license—are necessary. The burden of showing a license may be on the defendant, but the essential character of the absence of a license as an ingredient of guilt is not thereby destroyed. The act receives a criminal color from a prior omission. The defendant could have escaped the penal provision either by obtaining a license or by not practicing the calling. It is clearly the most tedious kind of verbal dispute to argue about the proper description of his offense in terms of action or omission. It is sufficient to notice that it contains elements of both natures.

Possibly, of course, the lawmaker may have a choice of pursuing his chosen policy by creating either an offense of commission or one of omission. But only rarely can identical results be achieved. Thus, householders might be required to set out garbage in specified receptacles between the hours of 9:00 P.M. and 7:00 A.M., or the setting out of garbage between 7:00 A.M. and 9:00 P.M. might be prohibited. But clearly, the alternative formulations lead to different results. The first would seem to be a sanitary measure designed to insure the collection and disposal of garbage,

the second rather to show concern for the defacement of streets in the daytime. To prohibit from killing is very different from commanding the preservation of life.

Classification of Omissions

The criminal law may impose a duty to act under a variety of circumstances. The duty to embark upon physical activity only arises when the particular surroundings envisaged by the notional pattern of conduct occur. Here may be found a useful way of classifying offenses of omission. The following categories are suggested.

In rare instances, a duty is geared by an event entirely unconnected with the activity of the defendant. In this category are the duty to aid anyone in peril, to be found in some European systems, the duty to report treasonable activities and the duty to register for military service. Such duties are imposed on the citizen solely by operation of law and because of his general participation in community life. Second, the duty may be imposed by virtue of a status relationship between individuals, as the duty of the husband to protect his wife or the parent to care for his child. Here, an element of voluntary assumption of the burden by the individual is apparent in his entrance into the relationship or his, possibly intentional, fathering of children. The status need not be domestic: the duty of the master, recognized by common law, to care for his servant or the captain of a ship to care for the crew might be included. As a third category, the duty may be imposed as a result of the defendant's exercise of a privilege to practice a calling or engage in a business or trade. Fourth, the duty may stem from the individual's decision to participate in some permitted sphere of public activity, such as the duty of those who have incomes to file tax returns or of those who drive automobiles to carry certain equipment. In this field, certain special duties may be imposed by the impingement of external events on the citizen in his chosen sphere of activity. The accident in which the motorist is involved, though none of his making, may place him under a duty to report to the authorities or to render aid to the injured.[4]

---

[3] Albaret-Montpeyroux, *L'Inaction en Droit Pénal* (1944), p. 85.

[4] The duty may arise from the defendant's participating in illegal activity, as with the duty imposed on felons in some communities to register with the authorities. This is a complex example, as here the duty rests upon three prior occurrences: embarking on criminal conduct by defendant; conviction by a court for felony; and defendant's finding himself in the locality which imposes the duty to register. . . .

These third and fourth categories include the great bulk of offenses of omission, and they reflect the contemporary policy of approving the imposition of duties on those who elect certain activities. Last is the duty to discharge properly burdens which one has undertaken by contract or even gratuitously, where their neglect might and does lead to death. This category includes liability for homicide through negligent or reckless inactivity. Possibly, the proposition is true in other crimes as well. If X is requested by Y to copy Y's will and deliberately omits a provision, thus altering the effect of the will, he may well be guilty of forgery.

This classification is probably neither exhaustive nor exclusive, but it does indicate the sphere in which most present offenses of omission are found and the policy which underlies their creation. To state that policy briefly, in the immense complexity and interdependency of modern life, those who elect to pursue certain activities or callings must, for the welfare of their fellow citizens, submit to a host of regulations, some of which will naturally and properly impose positive duties to act. That regulation through imposition of positive duties should be increasing is not surprising. Whether the traditional processes of the criminal law are always the most suitable means of insuring the observance of such regulation is more debatable.

Freedom: The First Condition of Action*

It is strange that philosophers have been able to argue endlessly about determinism and free will, to cite examples in favor of one or the other thesis without ever attempting first to make explicit the structures contained in the very idea of *action*. The concept of an act contains, in fact, numerous subordinate notions which we shall have to organize and arrange in a hierarchy: to act is to modify the *shape* of the world; it is to arrange means in view of an end; it is to produce an organized instrumental complex such that by a series of concatenations and connections the modification effected on one of the links causes modifications throughout the whole series and finally produces an anticipated result. But this is not what is important for us here. We should observe first that an action is on principle *intentional*. The careless smoker who has through negligence caused the explosion of a powder magazine has not *acted*. On the other hand the worker who is charged with dynamiting a quarry and who obeys the given orders has acted when he has produced the expected explosion; he knew what he was doing or, if you prefer, he intentionally realized a conscious project.

This does not mean, of course, that one must foresee all the consequences of his act. The

* Jean-Paul Sartre, *Being and Nothingness: An Essay on Phenomenological Ontology*, trans. Hazel E. Barnes (New York: Philosophical Library, 1956), pp. 433–38, 476–81, reprinted by permission of the publisher. Footnotes are omitted.

emperor Constantine, when he established himself at Byzantium, did not foresee that he would create a center of Greek culture and language, the appearance of which would ultimately provoke a schism in the Christian Church and which would contribute to weakening the Roman Empire. Yet he performed an act just in so far as he realized his project of creating a new residence for emperors in the Orient. Equating the result with the intention is here sufficient for us to be able to speak of action. But if this is the case, we establish that the action necessarily implies as its condition the recognition of a "desideratum"; that is, of an objective lack or again of a *négatité*. The intention of providing a rival for Rome can come to Constantine only through the apprehension of an objective lack; Rome lacks a counterweight; to this still profoundly pagan city ought to be opposed a Christian city which at the moment *is missing*. Creating Constantinople is understood as an *act* only if first the conception of a new city has preceded the action itself or at least if this conception serves as an organizing theme for all later steps. But this conception cannot be the pure representation of the city as *possible*. It apprehends the city in its essential characteristic, which is to be a *desirable* and not yet realized possible.

This means that from the moment of the first conception of the act, consciousness has been able to withdraw itself from the full world of which it is consciousness and to leave the level of being in order frankly to approach that of non-being. Consciousness, in so far as it is considered exclusively in its being, is perpetually referred from being to being and cannot find in being any motive for revealing non-being. The imperial system with Rome as its capital functions positively and in a certain real way which can be easily discovered. Will someone say that the taxes are collected badly, that Rome is not secure from invasions, that it does not have the geographical location which is suitable for the capital of a Mediterranean empire which is threatened by barbarians, that its corrupt morals make the spread of the Christian religion difficult? How can anyone fail to see that all these considerations are *negative*; that is, that they aim at what is not, not at what is. To say that sixty per cent of the anticipated taxes have been collected can pass, if need be for a positive appreciation of the situation *such as it is*. To say that they are *badly* collected is to consider the situation across a situation which is posited as an absolute end but which precisely *is not*. To say that the corrupt morals at Rome hinder the spread of Christianity is not to consider this diffusion for what it is; that is, for a propagation at a rate which the reports of the clergy can enable us to determine. It is to posit the diffusion in itself as insufficient; that is, as suffering from a secret nothingness. But it appears as such only if it is surpassed toward a limiting-situation posited *a priori* as a value (for example, toward a certain rate of religious conversions, toward a certain mass morality). This limiting-situation cannot be conceived in terms of the simple consideration of the real state of things; for the most beautiful girl in the world can offer only what she *has,* and in the same way the most miserable situation can by itself be designated only as it *is* without any reference to an ideal nothingness.

In so far as man is immersed in the historical situation, he does not even succeed in conceiving of the failures and lacks in a political organization or determined economy; this is not, as is stupidly said, because he "is accustomed to it," but because he apprehends it in its plenitude of being and because he cannot even imagine that he can exist in it otherwise. For it is necessary here to reverse common opinion and, on the basis of what it is not, to acknowledge the harshness of a sit-

uation or the sufferings which it imposes, both of which are motives for conceiving of another state of affairs in which things would be better for everybody. It is on the day that we can conceive of a different state of affairs that a new light falls on our troubles and our suffering and that we *decide* these are unbearable. A worker in 1830 is capable of revolting if his salary is lowered, for he easily conceives of a situation in which his wretched standard of living would be not as low as the one which is about to be imposed on him. But he does not represent his sufferings to himself as unbearable; he adapts himself to them not through resignation but because he lacks the education and reflection necessary for him to conceive of a social state in which these sufferings do not exist. Consequently *he does not act*. Masters of Lyon following a riot, the workers at Croix-Rousse do not know what to do with their victory; they return home bewildered, and the regular army has no trouble in overcoming them. Their misfortunes do not appear to them "habitual" but rather *natural*; they *are,* that is all, and they constitute the worker's condition. They are not detached; they are not seen in the clear light of day, and consequently they are integrated by the worker with his being. He suffers without considering his suffering and without conferring value upon it. To suffer and to *be* are one and the same for him. His suffering is the pure affective tenor of his non-positional consciousness, but he does not *contemplate* it. Therefore this suffering cannot be in itself a *motive* for his acts. Quite the contrary, it is after he has formed the project of changing the situation that it will appear intolerable to him. This means that he will have had to give himself room, to withdraw in relation to it, and will have to have effected a double nihilation: on the one hand, he must posit an ideal state of affairs as a pure *present* nothingness; on the other hand, he must posit the actual situation as nothingness in relation to this state of affairs. He will have to conceive of a happiness attached to his class as a pure possible—that is, presently as a certain nothingness—and on the other hand, he will return to the present situation in order to illuminate it in the light of this nothingness and in order to nihilate it in turn by declaring: "I *am not* happy."

Two important consequences result. (1) No factual state whatever it may be (the political and economic structure of society, the psychological "state," etc.) is capable by itself of motivating any act whatsoever. For an act is a projection of the for-itself toward what is not, and what is can in no way determine by itself what is not. (2) No factual state can determine consciousness to apprehend it as a *négatité* or as a lack. Better yet no factual state can determine consciousness to define it and to circumscribe it since, as we have seen, Spinoza's statement, "Omnis determinatio est negatio," remains profoundly true. Now every action has for its express condition not only the discovery of a state of affairs as "lacking in . . ."—i.e., as a *négatité*—but also, and before all else, the constitution of the state of things under consideration into an isolated system. There *is* a factual state—satisfying or not—only by means of the nihilating power of the for-itself. But this power of nihilation cannot be limited to realizing a simple *withdrawal* in relation to the world. In fact in so far as consciousness is "invested" by being, in so far as it simply suffers what is, it must be included in being. It is the organized form — worker-finding-his-suffering-natural — which must be surmounted and denied in order for it to be able to form the object of a revealing contemplation. This means evidently that it is by a pure wrenching away from himself and the world that the worker can posit his suffering as unbearable suffering and consequently can *make of it the motive* for his revolutionary action. This implies for consciousness the permanent possibility of effecting a rupture with its own past, of wrenching itself away from its past so as to be able to consider it in the light of a non-being and so as to be able to confer on it the meaning which it *has* in terms of the project of a meaning which it *does not have*. Under no circumstances can the past in any way by itself produce *an act*; that is, the positing of an end which turns back upon itself so as to illuminate it. This is what Hegel caught sight of when he wrote that "the mind is the negative," although he seems not to have remembered this when he came to presenting his own theory of action and of freedom. In fact as soon as one attributes to consciousness this negative power with respect to the world and itself, as soon as the nihilation forms an integral part of the *positing* of an end, we must recognize that the indispensable and funda-

mental condition of all action is the freedom of the acting being.

Thus at the outset we can see what is lacking in those tedious discussions between determinists and the proponents of free will. The latter are concerned to find cases of decision for which there exists no prior cause, or deliberations concerning two opposed acts which are equally possible and possess causes (and motives) of exactly the same weight. To which the determinists may easily reply that there is no action without a *cause* and that the most insignificant gesture (raising the right hand rather than the left hand, etc.) refers to causes and motives which confer its meaning upon it. Indeed the case could not be otherwise since every action must be *intentional*; each action must, in fact, have an end, and the end in turn is referred to a cause. Such indeed is the unity of the three temporal ekstases;[1] the end or temporalization of my future implies a cause (or motive); that is, it points toward my past, and the present is the upsurge of the act. To speak of an act without a cause is to speak of an act which would lack the intentional structure of every act; and the proponents of free will by searching for it on the level of the act which is in the process of being performed can only end up by rendering the act absurd. But the determinists in turn are weighting the scale by stopping their investigation with the mere designation of the cause and motive. The essential question in fact lies beyond the complex organization "cause-intention-act-end"; indeed we ought to ask how a cause (or motive) can be constituted as such.

Now we have just seen that if there is no act without a cause, this is not in the sense that we can say that there is no phenomenon without a cause. In order to be a *cause,* the *cause* must be *experienced* as such. Of course this does not mean that it is to be thematically conceived and made explicit as in the case of deliberation. But at the very least it means

---

[1] The translator provides this definition of "ekstasis": Used in the original Greek sense of "standing out from." The For-itself is separated from its Self in three successive ekstases: (1) Temporality. The For-itself nihilates the In-itself (to which in one sense it still belongs) in the three dimensions of past, present, and future (the three temporal ekstases). (2) Reflection. The For-itself tries to adopt an external point of view on itself. (3) Being-for-others. The For-itself discovers that it has a Self for-the-Other, a Self which it is, but which it can never know or get hold of. (Editor's note.)

that the for-itself must confer on it its value as cause or motive. And, as we have seen, this constitution of the cause as such cannot refer to another real and positive existence; that is, to a prior cause. For otherwise the very nature of the act as engaged intentionally in non-being would disappear. The motive is understood only by the end; that is, by the nonexistent. It is therefore in itself a *négatité*. If I accept a niggardly salary it is doubtless because of fear; and fear is a motive. But it is *fear of dying from starvation*; that is, this fear has meaning only outside itself in an end ideally posited; which is the preservation of a life which I apprehend as "in danger." And this fear is understood in turn only in relation to the *value which I* implicitly give to this life; that is, it is referred to that hierarchal system of ideal objects which are values. Thus the motive makes itself understood as what it is by means of the ensemble of beings which "are not," by ideal existences, and by the future. Just as the future turns back upon the present and the past in order to elucidate them, so it is the ensemble of my projects which turns back in order to confer upon the *motive* its structure as a motive. It is only because I escape the in-itself by nihilating myself toward my possibilities that this in-itself can take on value as cause or motive. Causes and motives have meaning only inside a projected ensemble which is precisely an ensemble of nonexistents. And this ensemble is ultimately myself as transcendence; it is Me in so far as I have to be myself outside of myself.

If we recall the principle which we established earlier—namely, that it is the apprehension of a revolution as possible which gives to the workman's suffering its value as a motive—we must thereby conclude that it is by fleeing a situation toward our possibility of changing it that we organize this situation into complexes of causes and motives. The nihilation by which we achieve a withdrawal in relation to the situation is the same as the ekstasis by which we project ourselves toward a modification of this situation. The result is that it is in fact impossible to find an act without a motive but that this does not mean that we must conclude that the motive is an integral part of the act. For as the resolute project toward a change is not distinct from the act, the motive, the act, and the end are all

constituted in a single upsurge. Each of these three structures claims the two others as its meaning. But the organized totality of the three is no longer explained by any particular structure, and its upsurge as the pure temporalizing nihilation of the in-itself is one with freedom. It is the act which decides its ends and its motives, and the act is the expression of freedom. . . .

. . .

At the end of this long discussion, it seems that we have succeeded in making a little more precise our ontological understanding of freedom. It will be well at present to gather together and summarize the various results obtained.

(1) A first glance at human reality informs us that for it being is reduced to doing. The psychologists of the nineteenth century who pointed out the "motor" structures of drives, of the attention, of perception, etc., were right. But motion itself is an act. Thus we find no *given* in human reality in the sense that temperament, character, passions, principles of reason, would be acquired or innate *data* would exist in the manner of things. The empirical consideration of the human being shows him as an organized unity of conduct patterns or of "behaviors." To be ambitious, cowardly, or irritable is simply to conduct oneself in this or that matter in this or that circumstance. The Behaviorists were right in considering that the sole positive psychological study ought to be of conduct in strictly defined situations. Just as the work of Janet and the Gestalt School have put us in a position to discover types of emotional conduct, so we ought to speak of types of perceptive conduct since perception is never conceived outside an attitude with respect to the world. Even the disinterested attitude of the scientist, as Heidegger has shown, is the assumption of a disinterested position with regard to the object and consequently one conduct among others. Thus human reality does not exist first in order to act later; but for human reality, to be is to act, and to cease to act is to cease to be.

(2) But if human reality is action, this means evidently that its determination to action is itself action. If we reject this principle, and if we admit that human reality can be determined to action by a prior state of

the world or of itself, this amounts to putting a *given* at the beginning of the series. Then these acts disappear as acts in order to give place to a series of *movements*. Thus the notion of conduct is itself destroyed with Janet and with the Behaviorists. The existence of the act implies its autonomy.

(3) Furthermore, if the act is not pure motion, it must be defined by an *intention*. No matter how this intention is considered, it can be only a surpassing of the given toward a result to be obtained. This given, in fact, since it is pure presence, cannot get out of itself. Precisely because it is, it is fully and solely what it is. Therefore it cannot provide the reason for a phenomenon which derives all its meaning from a result to be attained; that is, from a nonexistent. When the psychologists, for example, view the drive as a factual state, they do not see that they are removing from it all its character as an *appetite* (*ad-petitio*). In fact, if the sexual drive can be differentiated from the desire to sleep, for example, this can be only by means of its end, and this end does not exist. Psychologists ought to have asked what could be the ontological structure of a phenomenon such that it makes known to itself what it is by means of something which does not yet exist. The intention, which is the fundamental structure of human-reality, can in no case be explained by a given, not even if it is presented as an emanation from a given. But if one wishes to interpret the intention by its end, care must be taken not to confer on this end an existence as a *given*. In fact if we could admit that the end is given prior to the result to be attained, it would then be necessary to concede to this end a sort of being-in-itself at the heart of its nothingness and an attractive virtue of a truly magical type. Moreover we should not succeed any better in understanding the connection between a given human reality and a given end than in understanding the connection between consciousness-substance and reality-substance in the realists' arguments. If the drive or the act is to be interpreted by its end, this is because the intention has for its structure *positing* its end outside itself. Thus the intention makes itself be by choosing the end which makes it known.

(4) Since the intention is choice of the end and since the world reveals itself across our conduct, it is the intentional choice of the end which reveals the world, and the world is revealed as this or that (in this or that order) according to the end chosen. The end, illuminating the world, is a state of the world to be obtained and not yet existing. The intention is a thetic consciousness *of* the end. But it can be so only by making itself a non-thetic consciousness of its own possibility. Thus my *end* can be a good meal if I am hungry. But this meal which beyond the dusty road on which I am traveling is projected as the *meaning* of this road (it goes *toward* a hotel where the table is set, where the dishes are prepared, where I am expected, etc.) can be apprehended only correlatively with my non-thetic project toward my own possibility of eating this meal. Thus by a double but unitary upsurge the intention illuminates the world in terms of an end not yet existing and is itself defined by the choice of its possible. My end is a certain objective state of the world, my possible is a certain structure of my subjectivity; the one is revealed to the thetic consciousness, the other flows back over the non-thetic consciousness in order to characterize it.

(5) If the given cannot explain the intention, it is necessary that the intention by its very upsurge realize a rupture with the given, whatever this may be. Such must be the case, for otherwise we should have a present plenitude succeeding in continuity a present plenitude, and we could not prefigure the future. Moreover, this rupture is necessary for the *appreciation* of the given. The given, in fact, could never be a *cause* for an action if it were not appreciated. But this appreciation can be realized only by a withdrawal in relation to the given, a putting of the given into parentheses, which exactly supposes a break in continuity. In addition, the appreciation if it is not to be gratuitous, must be effected in the light of something. And this something which serves to appreciate the given can only be the end. Thus the intention by a single unitary upsurge posits the end, chooses itself, and appreciates the given in terms of the end. Under these conditions the given is appreciated in terms of something which does not yet exist; it is in the light of non-being that being-in-itself is illuminated. There results a double nihilating coloration of the given; on the one hand, it is nihilated in the rupture that makes it lose all efficacy over the intention; on the other hand, it undergoes a new nihilation due to the fact that efficacy is re-

turned to it in terms of a nothingness appreciation. Since human reality is act, it can be conceived only as being at its core a rupture with the given. It is the being which causes *there to be* a given by breaking with it and illuminating it in the light of the not-yet-existing.

(6) The necessity on the part of the given to appear only within the compass of a nihilation which reveals it is actually the same as the *internal negation* which we described in Part Two. It would be vain to imagine that consciousness can exist without a given; in that case it would be consciousness (of) itself as consciousness of nothing—that is, absolute nothingness. But if consciousness exists in terms of the given, this does not mean that the given conditions consciousness; consciousness is a pure and simple negation of the given, and it exists as the disengagement from a certain existing given and as an engagement toward a certain not yet existing end. But in addition this internal negation can be only the fact of a being which is in perpetual withdrawal in relation to itself. If this being were not its own negation, it would be what it is—i.e., a pure and simple given. Due to this fact it would have no connection with any other *datum* since the given is by nature only what it is. Thus any possibility of the appearance of a world would be excluded. In order not to be a given, the for-itself must perpetually constitute itself as in withdrawal in relation to itself; that is, it must leave itself behind it as a *datum* which it already no longer is. This characteristic of the for-itself implies that it is the being which finds *no help, no pillar of support* in what it was. But on the other hand, the for-itself is free and can cause there to be a world because the for-itself is *the being which has to be what it was in the light of what it will be.* Therefore the freedom of the for-itself appears as its *being.* But since this freedom is neither a given nor a property, it can be only by choosing itself. The freedom of the for-itself is always *engaged*; there is no question here of a freedom which could be undetermined and which would pre-exist its choice. We shall never apprehend ourselves except as a choice in the making. But freedom is simply the fact that this choice is always unconditioned.

(7) Such a choice made without base of support and dictating its own causes to itself can very well appear *absurd,* and in fact it is

absurd. This is because freedom is a *choice* of its being but not the *foundation* of its being. We shall return to this relation between freedom and facticity in the course of this chapter. For the moment it will suffice us to say that human-reality can choose itself as it intends but is not able to choose itself. It cannot even refuse to be; suicide, in fact, is a choice and affirmation—of being. By this being which is *given* to it, human reality participates in the universal contingency of being and thereby in what we may call absurdity. This choice is absurd, not because it is without reason but because there has never been any possibility of not choosing oneself. Whatever the choice may be, it is founded and reapprehended by being, for it is choice which *is.* But what must be noted here is that this choice is not absurd in the sense in which in a rational universe a phenomenon might arise which would not be bound to others by any *reasons.* It is absurd, in this sense—that the choice is that by which all foundations and all reasons come into being, that by which the very notion of the absurd receives a meaning. It is absurd as being beyond all reasons. Thus freedom is not pure and simple contingency in so far as it turns back toward its being in order to illuminate its being in the light of its end. It is the perpetual escape from contingency; it is the interiorization, the nihilation, and the subjectivizing of contingency, which thus modified passes wholly into the gratuity of the choice.

(8) The free project is fundamental, for it is my being. Neither ambition nor the passion to be loved nor the inferiority complex can be considered as fundamental projects. On the contrary, they of necessity must be understood in terms of a primary project which is recognized as the project which can no longer be interpreted in terms of any other and which is total. A special phenomenological method will be necessary in order to make this initial project explicit. This is what we shall call existential psychoanalysis. We shall speak of this in the next chapter. For the present we can say that the fundamental project which I am is a project concerning not my relations with this or that particular object in the world, but my total being-in-the-world; since the world itself is revealed only in the light of an end, this project posits for its end a certain type of relation to being which the for-itself wills to adopt. This project is not

instantaneous, for it cannot be "in" time. Neither is it nontemporal in order to "give time to itself" afterward. That is why we reject Kant's "choice of intelligible character." The structure of the choice necessarily implies that it be a choice in the world. A choice which would be a choice *in terms of nothing,* a choice *against nothing* would be a choice of nothing and would be annihilated as choice. There is only one phenomenal choice, provided that we understand that the phenomenon is here the absolute. But in its very upsurge, the choice is temporalized since it causes a future to come to illuminate the present and to constitute it as a present by giving the meaning of *pastness* to the in-itself "data." However we need not understand by this that the fundamental project is coextensive with the entire "life" of the for-itself. Since freedom is a being-without-support and without-a-springboard, the project in order to be must be constantly renewed. I choose myself perpetually and can never be merely by virtue of having-been-chosen; otherwise I should fall into the pure and simple existence of the in-itself. The necessity of perpetually choosing myself is one with the pursued-pursuit which I am. But precisely because here we are dealing with a *choice,* this choice as it is made indicates in general other choices as possibles. The possibility of these other choices is neither made explicit nor posited, but it is lived in the feeling of unjustifiability; and it is this which is expressed by the fact of the *absurdity* of my choice and consequently of my being. Thus my freedom eats away my freedom. Since I am free, I project my total possible, but I thereby posit that I am free and that I can always nihilate this first project and make it past.

Thus at the moment at which the for-itself thinks to apprehend itself and make known to itself by a projected nothingness what it *is,* it escapes itself; for it thereby posits that it can be other than it is. It will be enough for it to make explicit its unjustifiability in order to cause the *instant* to arise; that is, the appearance of a new project on the collapse of the former. Nevertheless this upsurge of the new project has for its express condition the nihilation of the former, and hence the for-itself cannot confer on itself a new existence. As soon as it rejects the project which has lapsed into the past, it has to be this project in the form of the "was": this means that this lapsed project belongs hence-

forth to the for-itself's situation. No law of being can assign an *a priori* number to the different projects which I am. The existence of the for-itself in fact conditions its essence. But it is necessary to consult each man's history in order to get from it a particular idea with regard to each individual for-itself. Our particular projects, aimed at the realization in the world of a particular end, are united in the global project which we are. But precisely because we are wholly choice and act, these partial projects are not determined by the global project. They must themselves be choices; and a certain margin of contingency, of unpredictability, and of the absurd is allowed to each of them although each project as it is projected is the specification of the global project on the occasion of particular elements in the situation and so is always understood in relation to the totality of my being-in-the-world.

With these few observations we think that we have described the freedom of the for-itself in its original existence. But it will have been observed that this freedom requires a given, not as its condition but for other sound reasons. First, freedom is conceived only as the nihilation of a given (5); and to the extent that it is an internal negation and a consciousness, it participates (6) in the necessity which prescribes that consciousness be consciousness of something. In addition freedom is the freedom of choosing but not the freedom of not choosing. Not to choose is, in fact, to choose not to choose. The result is that the choice is the foundation of being-chosen but not the foundation of choosing. Hence the absurdity (7) of freedom. There again we are referred to a given which is none other than the very facticity of the for-itself. Finally the global project while illuminating the world in its totality can be made specific on the occasion of this or that element of the situation and consequently of the contingency of the world. All these remarks therefore refer us to a difficult problem: that of the relation of freedom to facticity. Moreover we shall inevitably meet other concrete objections. Can I choose to be tall if I am short? To have two arms if I have only one? etc. These depend on the "limitations" which my factual situation would impose on my free choice of myself. It will be well therefore to examine the other aspect of freedom, its "reverse side": its relation to facticity.

Ascription of Responsibility*

There are in our ordinary language sentences whose primary function is not to describe things, events, or persons or anything else, nor to express or kindle feelings or emotions, but to do such things as claim rights ("This is mine"), recognize rights when claimed by others ("Very well, this is yours"), ascribe rights whether claimed or not ("This is his"), transfer rights ("This is now yours"), and also to admit or ascribe or make accusations of responsibility ("I did it," "He did it," "You did it"). My main purpose in this article is to suggest that the philosophical analysis of the concept of a human action has been inadequate and confusing, at least in part because sentences of the form "He did it" have been traditionally regarded as primarily descriptive whereas their principal function is what I venture to call *ascriptive,* being quite literally to ascribe responsibility for actions much as the principal function of sentences of the form "This is his" is to ascribe rights in property. Now ascriptive sentences and the other kinds of sentence quoted above, though they may form only a small part of our ordinary language, resemble in some important respects the formal statements of claim, the indictments, the admissions, the judgments, and the verdicts which constitute so large and so important a part of the language of lawyers; and the logical peculiarities which distinguish these kinds of sentences from descriptive sentences, or rather from the theoretical model of descriptive sentences with which philosophers often work, can best be grasped by considering certain characteristics of legal concepts, as these appear in the practice and procedure of the law rather than in the theoretical discussions of legal concepts by jurists who are apt to be influenced by philosophical theories. . . .

As everyone knows, the decisive stage in the proceedings of an English law court is normally a *judgment* given by the court to the effect that certain facts (Smith put arsenic in his wife's coffee and as a result she died) are true and that certain legal consequences (Smith is guilty of murder) are attached to those facts. Such a judgment is therefore a compound or blend of facts and law; and, of course, the claims and the indictments upon which law courts adjudicate are also blends of facts and law, though claims, indictments, and judgments are different from each other. Now there are several characteristics of the legal element in these compounds or blends which conspire to make the way in which facts support or fail to support legal conclusions, or refute or fail to refute them, unlike certain standard models of how one kind of statement supports or refutes another upon which philosophers are apt to concentrate attention. This is not apparent at once: for when the judge decides that on the facts which he has found there is a contract for sale between A and B, or that B, a publican, is guilty of the offense of supplying liquor to a constable on duty, or that B is liable for trespass because of what his horse has done on his neighbor's land, *it looks* from the terminology as if the law must consist of a set, if not a system, of legal concepts such as "contract," "the offense of supplying liquor to a constable on duty," "trespass," invented and defined by the legislature or some other "source," and as if the function of the judge was simply to say "Yes" or "No" to the question: "Do the facts come within the scope of the formula defining the necessary and sufficient conditions of 'contract,' 'trespass,' or 'the offense of supplying liquor to a constable on duty'?"

But this is for many reasons a disastrous oversimplification and indeed distortion, because there are characteristics of legal concepts which make it often absurd to use in connection with them the language of necessary and sufficient conditions. One important characteristic which I do not discuss in detail is no doubt vaguely familiar to most people. In England, the judge is not supplied with explicitly formulated general criteria defining "contract," or "trespass"; instead he has to decide by reference to past cases or precedents whether on the facts before him a contract has been made or a trespass committed; and in doing this he has a wide freedom, in judging whether the present case is sufficiently near to a past precedent, and also in determining what the past precedent in fact amounts to, or, as lawyers say, in identifying the *ratio decidendi* of past cases. This imports to legal concepts a vagueness of character very loosely

---

* H. L. A. Hart, "Ascription of Responsibility and Rights," *Proceedings of the Aristotelian Society,* New Series, XLIX (1949), 171–75, 179–81, 187–94, reprinted by permission of the author and The Aristotelian Society, London. Footnotes are omitted.

controlled by judicial traditions of interpretation, and it has the consequence that usually the request for a definition of a legal concept— "What is a trespass?" "What is a contract?" —cannot be answered by the provision of a verbal rule for the translation of a legal expression into other terms or one specifying a set of necessary and sufficient conditions. *Something* can be done in the way of providing an outline, in the form of a general statement of the effect of past cases, and that is how the student starts to learn the law. But beyond a point, answers to the questions "What is trespass?," "What is contract?," if they are not to mislead, must take the form of references to the leading cases on the subject, coupled with the use of the word "etcetera."

But there is another characteristic of legal concepts, of more importance for my present purpose, which makes the word "unless" as indispensable as the word "etcetera" in any explanation or definition of them; and the necessity for this can be seen by examining the distinctive ways in which legal utterances can be challenged. For the accusations or claims upon which law courts adjudicate can usually be challenged or opposed in two ways. First, by a denial of the facts upon which they are based (technically called a traverse or joinder of issue) and secondly by something quite different, namely, a plea that although all the circumstances on which a claim could succeed are present, yet in the particular case, the claim or accusation should not succeed because other circumstances are present which bring the case under some recognized head of exception, the effect of which is either to defeat the claim or accusation altogether, or to "reduce" it so that only a weaker claim can be sustained. Thus a plea of "provocation" in murder cases, if successful, "reduces" what would otherwise be murder to manslaughter; and so in a case of contract a defense that the defendant has been deceived by a material fraudulent misrepresentation made by the plaintiff entitles the defendant in certain cases to say that the contract is not valid as claimed, nor "void," but "voidable" at his option. In consequence, it is usually not possible to define a legal concept such as "trespass" or "contract" by specifying the necessary and sufficient conditions for its application. For any set of conditions may be adequate in some cases but not in others, and such concepts can only be explained with the aid of a list of exceptions or negative examples showing where the concept may not be applied or may only be applied in a weakened form.

This can be illustrated in detail from the law of contract. When the student has learned that in English law there are positive conditions required for the existence of a valid contract, i.e., at least two *parties,* an *offer* by one, *acceptance* by the other, a *memorandum* in writing in some cases and *consideration,* his understanding of the legal concept of a contract is still incomplete and remains so even if he has learned the lawyers' technique for the interpretation of the technical but still vague terms, "offer," "acceptance," "memorandum," "consideration." For these conditions, although necessary, are not always sufficient and he has still to learn what can *defeat* a claim that there is a valid contract, even though all these conditions are satisfied. That is, the student has still to learn what can follow on the word "unless," which should accompany the statement of these conditions. This characteristic of legal concepts is one for which no word exists in ordinary English. The words "conditional" and "negative" have the wrong implications, but the law has a word which with some hesitation I borrow and extend: this is the word *"defeasible,"* used of a legal interest in property which is subject to termination or *"defeat"* in a number of different contingencies but remains intact if no such contingencies mature. In this sense, then, contract is a defeasible concept.

. . .

The principal field where jurists have, I think, created difficulties for themselves (in part under the influence of the traditional philosophical analysis of action) by ignoring the essentially defeasible character of the concepts they seek to clarify is the Criminal Law. There is a well-known maxim, *"actus non est reus nisi mens sit rea,"* which has tempted jurists (and less often judges) to offer a general theory of "the mental element" in crime (*mens rea*) of a type which is logically inappropriate just because the concepts involved are defeasible and are distorted by this form of definition. For in the case of crime, as in contract, it is possible to compile a list of the defenses or exceptions with which different criminal charges may with differing effect be met, and to show that attempts to define in general terms "the mental conditions" of liability, like the general theory of contract suggested in the last paragraph, are only not misleading if their positive and general terms are treated merely as a restatement or summary of the fact that various heterogeneous defenses or exceptions are admitted. It is true that in crime the position is more complicated than in contract, since fewer defenses apply to all crimes (there being notable differences between crimes created by statute and common-law crimes), and for some crimes proof of a specific intention is required. Further it is necessary in the case of crime to speak of defenses *or exceptions* because in some cases, e.g., murder, the onus of proof may be on the Prosecution to provide evidence that circumstances are not present which would, if present, defeat the accusation. Yet, nonetheless, what is meant by the mental element in criminal liability (*mens rea*) is only to be understood by considering certain defenses or exceptions, such as Mistake of Fact, Accident, Coercion, Duress, Provocation, Insanity, Infancy, most of which have come to be admitted in most crimes, and in some cases exclude liability altogether, and in others merely "reduce" it. The fact that these are admitted as defenses or exceptions constitutes the cash value of the maxim *"actus non est reus nisi mens sit rea."* But in pursuit of the will-o'-the-wisp of a general formula, legal theorists have sought to impose a spurious unity (as judges occasionally protest) upon these heterogeneous defenses and exceptions, suggesting that they are admitted as merely evidence of the absence of some single element ("intention") or, in more recent theory, two elements ("foresight" and "voluntariness") universally required as necessary conditions of criminal responsibility. And this is misleading because what the theorist misrepresents as evidence negativing the presence of necessary mental elements are, in fact, multiple criteria or grounds defeating the allegation of responsibility. But it is easy to succumb to the illusion that an accurate and satisfying "definition" can be formulated with the aid of notions like "voluntariness" because the logical character of words like "voluntary" is anomalous and ill-understood. They are treated in such definitions as words having positive force, yet, as can be seen from Aristotle's discussion in Book III of the *Nicomachean Ethics,* the word "voluntary" in fact

serves to exclude a heterogeneous range of cases such as physical compulsion, coercion by threats, accidents, mistakes, etc., and not to designate a mental element or state; nor does "involuntary" signify the absence of this mental element or state. And so in a murder case it is a defense that the accused pulled the trigger reasonably but mistakenly believing that the gun was unloaded; or that there was an accident because the bullet unexpectedly bounced off a tree; or that the accused was insane (within the legal definition of insanity) or an infant; and it is a partial defense reducing the charge from murder to manslaughter that the accused fired the shot in the heat of the moment when he discovered his wife in adultery with the victim. It is, of course, *possible* to represent the admission of these different defenses or exceptions as showing that there is a single mental element ("voluntariness") or two elements ("voluntariness" and "foresight") required as necessary mental conditions (*mens rea*) of full criminal liability. But in order to determine what "foresight" and "voluntariness" are and how their presence and absence are established it is necessary to refer back to the various defenses; and then these general words assume merely the status of convenient but sometimes misleading summaries expressing the absence of all the various conditions referring to the agents' knowledge or will which eliminate or reduce responsibility.

. . .

. . . I now wish to defend the similar but perhaps more controversial thesis that the concept of a human action is an ascriptive and a defeasible one, and that many philosophical difficulties come from ignoring this and searching for its necessary and sufficient conditions. The sentences "I did it," "you did it," "he did it" are, I suggest, primarily utterances with which we *confess* or *admit* liability, make accusations, or *ascribe* responsibility; and the sense in which our actions are ours is very much like that in which property is ours, though the connection is not necessarily a *vinculum juris,* a responsibility under positive law. Of course, like the utterances already examined, connected with the nondescriptive concept of property, the verb "to do" and generally speaking the verbs of action have an important descriptive use, especially in the present and future senses, their ascriptive use being mainly in the past tense, where the verb is often both timeless and genuinely refers to the past as distinguished from the present. Indeed, the descriptive use of verbs of action is so important as to obscure even more in their case than in the case of "this is yours," "this is his," etc., the nondescriptive use, but the logical character of the verbs of action is, I think, betrayed by the many features which sentences containing these verbs, in the past tense, have in common with sentences in the present tense using the possessive pronouns ("this is his," etc.), and so with judicial decisions by which legal consequences are attached to facts.

I can best bring out my point by contrasting it with what I think is the mistaken, but traditional philosophical analysis of the concept of an action. "What distinguishes the physical movement of a human body from a human action?" is a famous question in philosophy. The old-fashioned answer was that the distinction lies in the occurrence before or simultaneously with the physical movement of a mental event related (it was hoped) to the physical movement as its psychological cause, which event we call "having the intention" or "setting ourselves" or "willing" or "desiring" to do the act in question. The modern answer is that to say that X performed an action is to assert a categorical proposition about the movement of his body, *and* a general hypothetical proposition or propositions to the effect that X would have responded in various ways to various stimuli, or that his body would not have moved as it did or some physical consequence would have been avoided, had he chosen differently, etc. Both these answers seem to me to be wrong or at least inadequate in many different ways, but both make the common error of supposing that an adequate analysis can be given of the concept of a human action in any combination of descriptive sentences, categorical or hypothetical, or any sentences concerned wholly with a single individual. To see this, compare with the traditional question about action the question "What is the difference between a piece of earth and a piece of property?" Property is not a descriptive concept and the difference between "this is a piece of earth" or "Smith is holding a piece of earth" on the one hand, and "this is someone's property" and "Smith owns a piece of property" on the other cannot be explained without reference to the non-

descriptive utterances by means of which laws are promulgated and decisions made, or at the very least without reference to those by which rights are recognized. Nor, I suggest, can the difference between "His body moved in violent contact with another's" and "He did it" (e.g., "He hit her") be explained without reference to the nondescriptive use of sentences by which liabilities or responsibility are ascribed. What is fundamentally wrong in both the old and the new version of the traditional analysis of action as a combination of physical and psychological events or a combination of categorical and hypothetical descriptive sentences, is its mistake in identifying the meaning of a nondescriptive utterance ascribing responsibility in stronger or weaker form, with the factual circumstances which support or are good reasons for the ascription. In other words, though of course not all the rules in accordance with which, in our society, we ascribe responsibility are reflected in our legal code nor vice versa, yet our concept of an action, like our concept of property, is a social concept and logically dependent on accepted rules of conduct. It is fundamentally not descriptive, but ascriptive in character; and it is a defeasible concept to be defined through exceptions and not by a set of necessary and sufficient conditions whether physical or psychological. This contention is supported by the following considerations:

First, when we say after observing the physical movements of a living person in conjunction with another, "Smith hit her," or "Smith did it" in answer to the question "Who hit her?" or "Who did it?" we surely do not treat this answer as a combined assertion that a physical movement of Smith's body took place, and that some inferred mental event occurred in Smith's mind (he set himself or intended to hit her); for we would be adding something to this answer if we made any such reference to psychological occurrences. Nor do we treat this answer as a combination of categorical or hypothetical sentences descriptive of a physical movement and of Smith's disposition or what would have happened had he chosen differently. On the contrary, saying "He hit her" in these circumstances is, like saying "That is his," a blend. It is an ascription of liability justified by the facts; for the observed physical movements of Smith's body are the circumstances which, in the absence of some defense, support, or are good reasons for the ascriptive sentence "He did it." But, of course, "He did it" differs from "That is his" for we are ascribing responsibility not rights.

Secondly, the sentence "Smith hit her" can be challenged in the manner characteristic of defeasible legal utterances in two distinct ways. Smith or someone else can make a flat denial of the relevant statement of the physical facts, "No, it was Jones, not Smith." Alternatively (but since we are not in a law court, not also cumulatively), any of a vast array of defenses can be pleaded by Smith or his friends which, though they do not destroy the charge altogether, soften it, or, as lawyers say, "reduce" it.

Thus, to "He did it" ("He hit her") it may be pleaded:

1. "Accidentally" (she got in his way while he was hammering in a nail).

2. "Inadvertently" (in the course of hammering in a nail, not looking at what he was doing).

3. "By mistake for someone else" (he thought she was Mary, who had hit him).

4. "In self-defense" (she was about to hit him with a hammer).

5. "Under great provocation" (she had just thrown the ink over him).

6. "But he was forced to by a bully" (Jones said he would thrash him).

7. "But he is mad, poor man."

Thirdly. It is, of course, possible to take the heroic line and say that all these defenses are just so many signs of the absence in each case of a common psychological element, "intention," "voluntariness," "consciousness," required in a "full" definition of an action, i.e., as one of its necessary and sufficient conditions, and that the concept is an ordinary descriptive concept after all. But to this, many objections can be made. These positive-looking words "intention," etc., if put forward as necessary conditions of all action only succeed in posing as this if in fact they are a comprehensive and misleadingly positive-sounding reference to the absence of one or more of the defenses, and are thus only understandable when interpreted in the light of the defenses, and not vice versa. Again, when we are ascribing an action to a person, the question whether a psychological "event" occurred does not come up in this suggested positive form at all, but

in the form of an inquiry as to whether any of these extenuating defenses cover the case. Further, when a more specific description of the alleged common mental element is given, it usually turns out to be something quite special, and characteristic only of a special kind of action, and by no means an essential element in all actions. This is plainly true of Professor H. A. Prichard's "setting ourselves," which well describes some grim occurrences in our lives, but is surely not an essential ingredient in all cases where we recognize an action.

Fourthly. The older psychological criterion affords no explanation of the line we draw between what we still call an action though accidental and other cases. If I aim at a post and the wind carries my bullet so that it hits a man, I am said to have shot him accidentally, but if I aim at a post, and the bullet then ricochets off and hits a man, this would not be said to be my action at all. But in neither case have I intended, set myself to do, or wished what occurred.

Fifthly. The modern formula according to which to say that an action is voluntary is to say that the agent could have avoided it if he had chosen differently either ignores the heterogeneous character of our criteria qualifying "He did it" when we use words like "accidentally," "by mistake," "under coercion," etc., or only avoids this by leaving the meaning of the protasis "If he had chosen differently" intolerably vague. Yet our actual criteria for qualifying "He did it," though multiple and heterogeneous, are capable of being stated with some precision. Thus, if the suggested general formula is used to explain our refusal to say "He did it" without qualification when a man's hand is forcibly moved by another, it is misleading to use the same formula in the very different cases of accident, mistake, coercion by threats, or provocation. For in the first case the statement "the agent could not have acted differently if he had chosen" is true in the sense that he had no control over his body and his decision was or would have been ineffective; whereas in, e.g., the case of accident the sense in which the statement is true (if at all) is that though having full control of his body the agent did not foresee the physical consequences of its movements. And, of course, our qualification of "He did it" in cases of coercion by threats or provocation (which have to be taken into account in any analysis of our usage of verbs of action) can only be comprehended under the suggested general formula if the protasis is used in still different senses so that its comfortable generality in the end evaporates; for there will be as many different senses as there are different types of defenses, or qualifications of "He did it." Some seek to avoid this conclusion by saying that in cases where we qualify "He did it," e.g., in a case of accident, there are, in fact, two elements of which one is *the genuine* action (firing the gun) and the other are its effects (the man being hit), and that our common usage whereby we say in such cases "He shot him accidentally" is inaccurate or loose. "Strictly," it is urged, we should say "He fired the gun" (action in the strict sense) and "the bullet hit the man." But this line of thought, as well as supposing that we can say what a "genuine" action is independently of our actual usage of verbs of action, breeds familiar but unwelcome paradoxes. If cases of accident must be analyzed into a genuine action *plus* unintended effects, then, equally, normal action must be analyzed into a genuine action *plus* intended effects. Firing the gun must be analyzed on this view into pulling the trigger *plus* . . . and pulling the trigger into cocking the finger *plus* . . . So that in the end the only "genuine actions" (if any) will be the minimal movements we can make with our body where nothing "can" go wrong. These paradoxes are results of the insistence that "action" is a descriptive concept definable through a set of necessary and sufficient conditions.

Sixthly. When we ascribe as private individuals rights or liabilities, we are not in the position of a judge whose decision is authoritative and final, but who is required only to deal with the claims and defenses actually presented to him. In private life, decisions are not final, and the individual is not relieved, as the judge often is, from the effort of inquiring what defenses might be pleaded. If, therefore, on the strength of merely the physical facts which we observe we judge "Smith hit her" and do not qualify our judgment, it can be wrong or defective in a way in which the judge's decision cannot be. For if, on investigating the facts, it appears that we should have said "Smith hit her accidentally," our first judgment has to be qualified. But it is important to notice that it is not withdrawn as a false statement of fact or as a false inference that some essential mental event necessary for the truth of the sentence "He did it" had occurred. Our ascription of responsibility is no longer justified in the light of the new circumstances of which we have notice. So we must judge again: not *describe* again.

Finally, I wish to say, out of what lawyers call abundant caution, that there are two theses I have not maintained. I have maintained no form of behaviorism, for although it often is correct to say "He did it" on the strength only of the observed physical movements of another, "He did it" never, in my view, merely describes those movements. Secondly, I wish to distinguish from my own thesis, often now maintained as a solution or dissolution of the problem of free will, that to say that an action is voluntary *means* merely that moral blame would tend to discourage the agent blamed from repeating it, and moral praise would encourage him to do so. This seems to me to confuse the question of what we mean by saying that a man has done an action with the question of why we bother to assign responsibility for actions to people in the way we do. Certainly, there is a connection between the two questions, that is, between theories of punishment and reward and attempts to elucidate the criteria we do in fact employ in assigning responsibility for actions. No doubt we have come to employ the criteria we do employ because, among other things, in the long run, and on the whole not for the wretched individual in the dock but for "society," assigning responsibility in the way we do assign it tends to check crime and encourage virtue; and the social historian may be able to show that our criteria slowly alter with experience of the reformative or deterrent results obtained by applying them. But this is only one of the things which applying these criteria does for us. And this is only one of the factors which lead us to retain or modify them. Habit, or conservatism, the need for certainty, and the need for some system of apportioning the loss arising from conduct, are other factors, and though, of course, it is open to us to regret the intrusion of "nonutilitarian" factors, it yet seems to me vital to distinguish the question of the history and the pragmatic value and, in one sense, the morality of the distinctions we draw, from the question what these distinctions are.

Action*

We speak not only of the actions of infants, wild beasts, and lunatics but also of the actions of normal human beings in walking, talking, working, and playing. Yet we recognize an important difference between these two groups of cases. Infants, wild beasts, and lunatics may behave in ways that are fortunate or unfortunate to themselves and to others, but nothing done by such individuals is subject to moral criticism of any sort. Moral terms like "right" and "wrong" are appropriately applied only to the actions of normal and relatively mature human beings. In this paper I shall reserve the term "action" for the cases in which what an individual does can be in principle and in the appropriate circumstances the subject of moral review. This restricted usage of the term will enable us to avoid circumlocutions in addressing ourselves to the topic to be discussed: the relation between bodily movements and actions in the present restricted sense. When I perform an action, there is some bodily movement that occurs, but not every bodily movement counts as an action—not even those of normal adult human beings—since there are reflex movements, the activities of those who walk in their sleep, and the behavior of those under hypnosis. Hence it appears as though an action were a bodily movement of a special sort and that we need only specify the distinctive features of bodily movements that count as actions in order to elucidate the concept of an action. We are inclined, accordingly, to look for certain psychological factors in order to mark off bodily movements that count as actions from all those that do not. I shall argue that the familiar programs of analysis suggested by this approach rest upon fundamental misconceptions concerning the logical features of the concept of an action, and I shall then go on to indicate in outline at least the manner in which the concept of an action is related to that of a bodily movement.

I

It is difficult to resist the temptation to offer a simple summary formula in explanation of the concept of action, and, frequently, one of the first moves made in this direction

* A. I. Melden, "Action," *The Philosophical Review*, LXV (1956), 523–41, reprinted with the permission of the author and *The Philosophical Review.* Footnotes are omitted.

is the suggestion that an action is a voluntary bodily movement. This, however, is to forget Aristotle's important reminder that the term "voluntary" does not help, since it is applied to a wide variety of bodily movements and serves only as a blanket term covering far too many different sorts of things. Indeed, Aristotle regards the term "voluntary" as much too wide, since voluntary behavior is encountered in animals and small children who are exempt from moral criticism. And surely Aristotle is correct in rejecting the view that an action is a bodily movement that is chosen or deliberated, for "choice" and "deliberation" do not apply to spur-of-the-moment actions which we call "voluntary" and for which an agent is held responsible. When, for example, the traffic light turns red as I approach in my automobile, I do not in general deliberate and then choose to release the accelerator and apply the brakes. Indeed, most of the actions we perform are done without deliberation or choice. In most cases habits, desires, and impulses prevail—we act as we do as a matter of course, straight off, without reflection or pondering of any kind. But Aristotle's own elucidation of the term "voluntary" is wholly unilluminating; and the view which he seems to hold of the nature of action is less than satisfactory. Behavior is voluntary, he tells us, if "the moving principle is in a man himself." What he means by a moving principle he does not say, and so far the formula adds nothing to the various examples he cites and would mean nothing apart from them. But since Aristotle recognizes that infants and animals who are not responsible for what they do engage in voluntary behavior, even an adequate account of the concept "voluntary" will need to be supplemented by a further condition. As I understand his doctrine, this condition is that there be rational choice; but since not all actions are deliberated and chosen, e.g., spur-of-the-moment or impulsive acts, rational choice is introduced in connection with the formation of the states of character from which such impulsive actions are alleged to spring. We are responsible for impulsive actions since we are responsible for the states of character from which they spring; and we are responsible for such states even though we are not now masters of them, because rational choice was exercised in the actions which led to their formation. Hence an action would seem to be a case of behavior which is voluntary and in which, either in cause or in actual occurrence, there is rational choice.

But not even this will do, if we reflect upon the simple case in which, on the spur of the moment, one stops one's automobile when the traffic light turns red. The attempt to read deliberation and choice into the many cases of which this is only one instance by reference to some earlier choice to obey the relevant law whenever any occasion arises to which it applies is as fanciful as the attempt to discover some original covenant into which each of us has entered before engaging in our normal political dealings or some omnibus choice in favor of morality prior to the acquisition of the moral habits we exhibit in our normal moral affairs. When we do decide to learn to drive an automobile, we do not in general decide, in addition, to obey the traffic laws. For most of us, at any rate, there is no option in favor of such obedience—to learn to drive an automobile is to learn to operate the conveyance as we see it operated in the normal sort of way by stopping at the red light, starting at the green light, and so on. Until such practices have been acquired, there is a failure to operate the automobile with the requisite skill. We can of course imagine cases in which people do learn to drive cars in happy isolation from all traffic regulations, and we can imagine people whose first desire is to operate the controls of a car and who, on learning that there are laws governing its operation in traffic, then decide that they will observe the law; but for most of us, at any rate, it would be far more correct to say that the decision to obey the laws occurs only after we have learned how to obey by repeated practice, and only in those occasional situations in which it is burdensome to obey and on considering briefly whether we should, we then decide after all to do so. There are, therefore, actions in which either in cause or in actual performance no rational choice is involved.

It is the enormous variety of cases that defeats any attempt to provide a summary account of the nature of action in terms of bodily and psychological factors. Some of my actions are deliberate. I weigh alternatives and choose. Some of my actions are done with a motive but without deliberation and choice. When I slam the brakes on as the car ahead of mine suddenly stops, I do so with a motive —in order to avoid a collision—but without the choice I exercise when I consider quickly whether or not to run through the light that has just changed to red and thus risk a traffic fine. Some things I do without any motive. I pass the salt to my dinner companion not in order to please him or with any other motive or purpose in mind, but because I am polite. I act out of politeness rather than for the sake of politeness. Some things I do simply because I want to, or on the spur of the moment and for no reason at all. If we consider the mental processes attending the relevant bodily movements, we find an enormous variation in what transpires. The cases range from those in which nothing that seems at all relevant happens except the occurrence of the bodily movement—one responds to the situation in which one finds oneself almost automatically, guided as it were by habit and the whole accumulation of past experience—to the cases in which force of mind, great effort, or internal struggles are involved as habit is resisted or passions and temptations conquered (the sorts of cases by reference to which meaning can be given to Plato's expression "the spirited element" and Prichard's term "setting oneself"). The characteristic philosophic vice of generalizing from special cases is involved in the familiar summary explanation of the concept of action in terms of various psychological factors or processes. Perhaps the most frequent instance is the explanation given in terms of motives, in which the preoccupation with the textbook examples of actions performed with ends in view leads the philosopher to ignore the very many sorts of actions in which no end in view is present at all.

There are still other formulae that need to be considered. Shall we say that bodily behavior is a case of action if it is free from compulsion? But animals and infants may move their limbs without compulsion. Indeed, there are internal compulsions that disqualify bodily movements as actions. Further, "compusion" is as unilluminating as "voluntary." One is compelled by one's conscience (e.g., Luther's "Here I stand and can do no other"), but shall we say that there can be no conscientious action? One is compelled by hunger, but in different ways: the starving man reaches desperately for food, the hungry man steals a loaf of bread, and the man without any livelihood and faced with the prospect of hunger steals in order to avoid it—in all such cases one is compelled, but not in the same sense of the term. We need not multiply cases—what in one sense is compulsion is freedom from compulsion in another. The present formula is as unhelpful as Aristotle's "internal moving principle"; what is common to the great variety of cases that count as action is the verbal formula, and this, apart from a specification of the wide spectrum of cases falling under it, is wholly unilluminating.

When difficulties appear in the attempt to provide an analysis of an apparently categorical statement, the suggestion is often made that contrary-to-fact conditionals will do the trick. So in the present case it may be suggested that an item of bodily behavior is an instance of an action if the agent could have done otherwise, or if the agent could have done otherwise if he had chosen, or even if the agent could have done otherwise if he had chosen and he could have chosen. Here, again, the crucial phrase "could have done" provides us with only the semblance of an explanation. Consider the many different kinds of cases of which it would be true to say that a person could not have done otherwise. The man was insane, subject to compulsive desire, strong temptation, social pressure; or he was misinformed, responding through habit, unthinking, or even bound by conscience. What in one sense a person could have done, in another he could not. So too with "could have chosen." A person could not have chosen to ignore his conscience, but it is correct to say even of those in whom conscience prevails that in some sense they could have chosen to do other than what conscience demanded.

Finally I shall consider another and even more desperate measure. It might be thought that the problem of dealing with the great variety of cases falling under the term "action" could be disposed of in the following way: Instead of taking a simple statement about a physical movement and conjoining with it some psychological statement about a motive, choice, or so on, we might construct a disjunction, each disjunct of which is itself a conjunction of two statements, one reporting bodily movement, the other some psychological factor. Such a proposal would indeed meet the requirement that our account of an action must fit the wide variety of cases; it would fail nonetheless. Suppose one of the disjuncts

to contain a statement about the presence of a motive, then any physical movement in respect of which the agent has a motive will count as a moral action. Are we, however, to deny that animals, children, and even those occasional men who are not responsible for their conduct and who are, therefore, not blamed but hospitalized or otherwise confined have motives for their conduct? Consider, too, the fact that an action may be one done impulsively, on the spur of the moment, without reflection, choice, or motive. As far as the psychological phenomena are concerned, there need be nothing to distinguish such actions from those for which no responsibility is incurred by the agent. It is for this reason that the proposed disjunction is unsatisfactory—it will fit the wide variety of cases called "action" only by failing to distinguish such cases from those clearly excluded by the term. This is not to say that it would be impossible in principle to discover a disjunctive formula that would fit all those cases we call "action" and no others. It is perhaps possible that some elaborate disjunctive statement in terms of gross physical movements, the actions of synapses, or even the presence of peculiar feelings could be contrived which would fit action and only action. But such an elaboration, even if it were successful, would be perfectly futile; for it would provide us with a true statement of the conditions present at the time any action occurred, not with an elucidation of the concept.

These are the results with which we are faced: (1) Any formula that fits the wide variety of actions turns out on inspection to be useless because the key term must be employed in a variety of ways. For the bodily movements that count as actions constitute a very complex range or family of cases, not a single group with its characteristic borderline fringe. (2) The attempt to distinguish bodily movements that do, from those that do not, count as actions in terms of occurrent psychological processes is doomed to failure. What passes through my mind as I now act may be anything or nothing; it may be that all that happens is that without anything relevant passing through my mind, I just act.

II

If one considered the question "What is a chess move?" it is easy to see that each of the kinds of answers considered and rejected in the preceding section will not do at all. It may be, when I move my chess piece during a game, that all that happens is that my fingers push a piece from one square to another. As long as we confine our attention to bodily and psychological processes, there may be nothing to distinguish a chess move from the mere change of position of chessmen resulting from an infant's random movements. And, clearly, the appeals to absence of compulsion (but consider the many sorts of moves called "forced"), to "could have beens," "would have beens," and even to the use of elaborate disjunctive functions, such as we considered in the preceding section, would be greeted with amusement. Nevertheless, to make a move in a game of chess is after all to engage in a bodily movement of some sort, so whatever else one is doing in saying that a move was made, is one not saying that a certain bodily movement took place? And, similarly, in the case of other actions, is it not a part of what one is saying, in saying that an action has taken place, that certain relevant movements of fingers, arms or legs, and so on, have occurred? Plausible as this may be, it is in my opinion mistaken.

1. If there were such a so-called descriptive component, then in order that I might know what I was doing in any given case, I would need to know what bodily movements took place, and this I could know only by observing my own movements. But if someone asks me, "Do you know what you have done?" the affirmative answer I give is in no way predicated upon any observation I may have made of my bodily movements. If my answer is in error (I gave the clerk a five, instead of a one, dollar bill), the error is not one of observation. When I do something and know what I am doing, it is not that I observe myself in action, and if I were to watch my arms, legs, and so on as I performed many of the familiar actions in which I engage, I would very likely fumble. But even when I take care in what I do, it is not that I observe my bodily movements and guide them as I would my child's movements as she learns to write, ride a bicycle, or skate. If someone were to say to me reproachfully, "You did not watch what you were doing" as I drove my car, he would not be reproaching me for failing to observe my bodily movements, nor would he be urging me to watch them if he were to say, "Watch what you are doing!"

2. Consider third-person statements. Unless A had engaged in a bodily movement of some sort, he could not have done what he did, and unless I had used my eyes in observing what had gone on, I could not have described his action as I did. But from this it does not follow that in describing A's action I am describing his bodily movements. For there are descriptions and descriptions, the physiologist's descriptions of muscle movements, my descriptions of the movements of arms and legs, and our familiar descriptions of actions—passing the salt hastily, paying one's bill distastefully, and so forth. To say that John paid his bill distastefully is not to say two things, one of which is that his body moved in a certain way, any more than to say the latter is to assert in part at least that such-and-such muscles were brought into operation. And because the latter must be true if his arms and legs moved as they did, it simply does not follow that in offering my description of the bodily movement, I am, among other things, offering a physiological description of what took place. But there is just as much reason for saying this as for saying that a third-person action statement is a blend of diverse things, one of which is a descriptive component about the occurrence of a bodily movement.

The truth is that in saying as we do that A paid his bill, performed the castling maneuver, or passed the salt to his companion, we are in no way interested in the minutiae of bodily movements that may have taken place, just as one interested in the movements of arms, legs, and fingers, e.g., a dancer, may be sublimely ignorant of the physiological and biochemical changes that take place. Consider the example of the chess move. One who knows no chess may see only the movements of arms and fingers as odd-shaped objects are moved about on a checkered surface; one who knows the game may see a given offensive or defensive move taking place. The former simply does not know what takes place during the game, and the latter, far from offering a description that overlaps the former's curious description of what takes place, is saying something radically different in character.

3. But suppose a statement describing an action were a blend of diverse items, one being a description of a bodily movement. How must this "descriptive component" be supplemented in order that we may be provided with

the force of a statement about an action? It will be apparent that the attempt to provide a supplement by means of another "descriptive" statement, to the effect that the movement is voluntary, chosen, and so forth, must lead to one of two consequences. Either the crucial term (e.g., "voluntary," "chosen," "motivated") is much too restrictive or it is too broad, or if no change in the application of the term "action" is to ensue, a shift must be made in the use of the crucial term (e.g., voluntary) and all of the puzzles about action reappear once more in connection with this new usage. If, however, the supplementation is to be made by means of disguised contrary-to-fact conditionals, the same dilemma faces us in a new guise. It will not do to say, for example, that an action which took place is a certain kind of bodily movement that could have been other than what it was in the sense in which any physical occurrence could have been other than what it was, or in the sense appropriate to the familiar remark that a conscientious agent could not have acted otherwise. The sense of "could have been" required for the present purpose is just that sense involved in saying that the bodily movement counts as an action; but this does not help us.

It should not surprise us in view of these results to encounter even more drastic proposals. It has been agreed that the concept of an action is "fundamentally nondescriptive," and among those to whom this proposal seems only to generate new paradoxes, it would not be unreasonable to expect to find representatives of the indefinability thesis. It would be dangerous to generalize, but the appearance of this familiar triad of theories is due to a familiar mistake—the failure to attend to the relevant context in which expressions have a use. The pattern of thought is as follows: "Actions are happenings. Statements describing actions are true or false. What happens is always some bodily movement and need be nothing more than this. Hence, whatever else a statement about an action may do, it describes such a movement." The underlying mistake is that what occurs when an action is performed can be understood independently of its context and hence need only be a bodily movement. How this is so I want to illustrate by reference to the analogous problem of the nature of a chess move.

III

Consider the relatively artificial situation in which a chess move is made. Here there is an obvious change of context from the ordinary situation in which conduct occurs. There is little temptation to define a chess move in terms of bodily and psychological phenomena or to argue that the concept is "nondescriptive" or "indefinable." The concept is obviously social in character, logically connected with the concept of rules. How does this connection with the notion of rules enable us to distinguish between the random movements of an infant pushing chess pieces about on a checkered board and the chess moves of players? I want to argue that this distinction is intelligible only by reference to the notion of *following* or *observing* the given rules.

Central to the concept of a rule is the idea of obeying or following it. The notion of disobeying is dependent upon the more fundamental idea of obeying. Infants who push chess pieces about on a chessboard do not disobey or violate the rules of chess—they do not play chess at all. A chess player may violate the rule only after he has learned to obey. Without obedience there can be no disobedience, just as without the telling of the truth there can be no lying. Further, a rule is no mere statement which we can understand independently of the practice that is the obeying or the following of the rule. To understand the rule is to understand the kind of thing that would be obeying it, and it is only because we have followed or obeyed rules that any statement of a new rule, one we have not so far learned to follow, is intelligible. Again, to follow or obey a rule is not to repeat to oneself what the rule requires, reflect upon the situation in which one finds oneself in order to determine that it is one to which the rule applies, and then decide to obey it. Such an account, if it were true, would only serve to create a doubt that the person in question had learned the rule, for at best it could only describe the learner's fumbling, hesitating procedure. Once we have learned the rules, we do not interpret the rule to apply to the given situation and follow this with a decision to obey—we simply obey. And if in any given situation we choose to disobey, such choice is only parasitic upon the general practice in which no choice is exercised at all. Finally, obeying a rule is not something that can occur only once. I do not mean that there may not be such a thing as a new rule which is such that only one occasion arises to which it applies and such that after it has been obeyed only once it is then set aside. If such a case should ever arise, it would happen only because one had already learned what rules were in other situations and in learning these rules had engaged in the practice of obeying them. The point is that to obey a rule is to acquire a custom, habit, practice, and if only one instance suffices, this is owing to the derivative function of habits established with respect to other rules. Again, this is not to say that every instance of acting from habit or custom is a case of obeying a rule. "This is our practice," "this is what we do," need only express the things we do *as a rule,* in general, and through social habit, not the things we do in *following a rule.* Nevertheless, the familiar cases of obeying a rule are the cases in which the agent has acquired a habit, practice, custom—that way of thinking and doing that characterizes the man who knows his way about in situations by following the relevant rules. We need, therefore, to distinguish between the case in which what someone does *accords* with the rule and the case in which someone *follows* the rule. A child may push a piece called "the knight" from one square on a chessboard to another in such a way that what it does accords with the rule governing the piece, but in reporting this fact we need only observe the single item of behavior of the child. In saying of a child that it followed the rule, much more is at stake, namely, the question whether the child has learned the rules of the game (including the one concerning the knight) and in doing so has acquired the specific way of thinking and doing which is the playing of chess.

To attempt to understand a move in a game of chess in terms of bodily and psychological processes occurring at the time the agent makes his move is to leave out what is essential to the move—the fact that what transpires in the way of such occurrent processes is a case of following the rules. Similarly, to attempt to understand the concept of a chess player in terms of occurrent psychological processes, the order of percepts, or some presumed psychical substance is once more to ignore that feature of the agent that consists in the fact that he has learned by repeated doings and hence has acquired the practice of acting as he does. In both cases the circumstances in which the bodily and psychological processes occur are crucial; for what makes the bodily movement a case of a move is the fact that movement of the piece on the board is a case of following a rule, and what makes the agent a chess player is that he has acquired that custom or practice—that way of thinking and doing—that characterizes those who follow the rules of chess. Chess player and chess move are thus correlative notions, and neither can be understood in terms of processes, bodily or psychological, viewed in isolation from the rules that have been learned and the characteristic ways of thinking and doing thereby achieved. Hence it is not that a piece has been pushed from one square to another that constitutes a chess move but that the bodily movement is that of an agent who, during the course of a game, exhibits the characteristic practice in thinking and doing that he has acquired. For someone who does not know what it is to make a move in a game, no report of what transpires at the times the moves were made would make any sense at all, and, observe as he would, such a being would have *no* idea of what was going on. For someone who knew no chess but did know what it was to follow the rules of *some* game, the reports of such activities would be understood only in the most fragmentary way; he might know that a game was being played but would not know what was going on. It is only because we ourselves have acquired that practice of following the rules of chess—the characteristic custom of doing things on a chessboard in a way that we understand because we share it with others who play chess—that the reports of a game are understood by us and recognized as true or false. The significance of the utterances we employ in reporting the activities on a chessboard is thus dependent upon the fact that we share with those involved in these activities the practices, in Wittgenstein's felicitous phrase, the form of life, of those who follow certain rules in the social transaction that is the playing of a game of chess.

Without this practice of obeying the rules, what we see is merely bodily movement. With it, we see this movement as a chess move, for we treat the physical movement made as a move in the play that takes place, and in our doing so, the physical movement that occurs takes on a wholly new aspect. It is because we supply this practical context of acquired skill that we can understand the descriptive accounts of those who report to us the progress of a game; without it such accounts are unintelligible.

All this may be granted; but it will be objected that a chess move is only one very special kind of action. We act in all sorts of ways, even in sweeping the chessmen off the board, thus bringing the play to an abrupt end. With this I should certainly agree, but the case of the chess move is nonetheless important, for the very artificiality of the example may serve to remind us of what is too easily forgotten in the case of other types of action, namely, the crucial importance of the practical context of common or shared practices involved in following rules, applying criteria, observing principles, acting on policies, and so on. Actions do constitute a whole family of cases, but in various respects this practical context is essential to an understanding of the distinction between a bodily movement and an action.

IV

Consider some of the things we commonly do; we purchase food, drive automobiles, play, work, help and hinder our fellows. In all such activities, we have learned by imitating or following the instructions of others in obeying rules, employing criteria, following policies in the practices in which we engage. Thus in purchasing food our selection is guided by criteria for excellence, ripeness, and so on, and in paying for the items selected, our behavior is guided by various criteria and rules governing the use of currency. We act in such instances without reflection precisely because we have acquired the requisite skills. Or consider the enormously complex set of practices acquired by those driving their automobiles through traffic, responding to a variety of cues—the condition of the road surface, the sound of the motor, the presence of pedestrians and vehicles blocking the way, the signals of other motorists, the road signs, the traffic lights, and the instructions of the traffic police. In this complex set of practices we may recognize the observance of rules, the application of criteria, the response to instructions, the following of policies of safe, economical, or efficient driving, and so on. These practices are supplemented by other complicating and even supervening practices. One may drive an automobile in order to make up

one's mind whether to purchase it or in order to test it, and throughout one will be guided in general in one's thinking and doing by the observance of moral rules and principles. It is not that there are practices and practices, each independent of the other, so that at one time one is driving an automobile, at another making a purchase, at another responding to the moral requirements of the situation. It is rather that we have a blending of the practices we have acquired, in the activities in which we engage, where various practices are themselves affected by the general practice of observing moral rules and principles. It is this ability to carry out a complex and organized set of practices in which throughout the agent is guided without reflection by moral rules that marks the achievement of responsibility. Even in the relatively artificial case of a chess move, what takes place when the move is made has to be understood in terms of the practice of observing not only the rules of chess but also those of good conduct and good manners, for these are involved in the agent's way of thinking and doing.

It is equally important to bear in mind the enormous difference between the permissive rules of chess and the prescriptive and justifying rules of morality, between the justification of the rules of traffic and the justification of the rules of morality, between the inevitable conflicts of rules (and the resulting exceptions) in the field of morality and the occasional predicament that may arise when the ill-formed rules of a game are discovered to be in conflict. Understanding a moral rule does involve understanding the kind of cases which may be excepted, but there cannot be any exception to the rules governing the movement of the knight in chess. These differences are so important that it is misleading to speak of the term "rule" as univocal.

One more comment on important differences: If I do not play chess, I shall not understand what a chess player does as his fingers push a piece from one square to another, but if I do not drive a car, it does not follow that I am incapable of knowing what someone at the wheel is doing when I see his arm pulling at the handbrake. Here we need to recall the reference made earlier to the derivative effects of the mastery of rules in order to see that this difference, important as it is, is no objection to the general contention. For the practices we share with others need not coincide precisely, indeed they cannot if there is to be diversity in the activities of individuals, but there must be enough similarity between the practices involved in different activities in order to allow for an understanding of one kind of activity which derives from the practice involved in another. Where there is no such similarity, as in the case of a bushman who has never seen or heard of machines of any sort, there is no understanding of what is being done, no matter how carefully attention is paid by such individuals to the bodily movements of agents when they engage, respectively, in games of chess or in the driving of automobiles.

It is impossible within the limits of this paper to guard against all of the misunderstandings to which the analogy I wish to draw between chess moves and other actions may give rise. Briefly, I am maintaining that just as in the case of the concept of a chess move, so in the case of the concept of any action in the context of practices in which rules are obeyed, criteria employed, policies are observed—a way of thinking and doing—is essential to the understanding of the difference between such bodily movements and actions. Just as this way of thinking and doing marks in the one case the chess player, so it marks in the other the responsible agent, one who has acquired a complex of practices, among others the practice of observing moral rules and principles. The concepts "action" and "moral agent" or "person" are thus correlative. Because we share so largely in our ways of thinking and doing, because in particular we are guided by moral rules and principles, we treat each other's bodily movements as actions, items of behavior for which the agent is responsible. Just as we supply a background of skills in understanding the bodily behavior of those engaged in playing chess, so we supply a complex background of skills in which rules are obeyed, criteria are employed, policies are observed, and so on, in understanding each other's behavior as action. This practical context—our common form of life—is crucial to our understanding. Without it we notice only bodily movements, and with it we see actions as we observe each other's behavior. Without it we employ the cool language of those who like coroners and physiologists are concerned to describe and explain bodily movements and effects, and with it we are enabled to participate in the use of discourse by which we impute responsibility to individuals when we treat them as persons or moral agents and their bodily movements as actions.

But this, it will be objected, is in effect to succumb to the philosophic vice of generalizing from very special cases—those actions performed in the social arena for which agents may be praised or blamed, such as cheating or dealing honestly in making purchases and driving with care or with unconcern for the safety of others. The very language employed for such conduct implies that the individuals referred to or treated are responsible moral agents and subject to praise or blame for what they do. But there are other cases of action, surely, with respect to which a specifically moral way of thinking and doing, the practice of observing moral rules, seems altogether out of bounds, so that the alleged correlativity of the terms "moral agent" and "person" is only evidence of unrestrained generalization from very special cases. My concluding remarks are directed at this objection.

In order to understand the concept of an action, we need to see how sentences in which typical action verbs are employed are used. Admittedly there is no single use. Some sentences are employed in praising or blaming (e.g., "*He* did it" uttered accusingly or "He *did* it" uttered exultingly with a view to determining whether blame is appropriate but where no blaming may actually occur as in the hearings held in courts or during legislative fact-finding inquiries). Again, we may speak of actions where no verdict is anticipated, moral or legal. If my wife relates to me the various things she saw my neighbor doing, she might do so with a view to supporting the low opinion in which she holds him, but, equally, she may do so in order to make conversation or because she knows me to have a friendly interest in my neighbor's activities. And in giving me this information or in describing to me how he behaved, is she not speaking of just the sort of thing for which in appropriate circumstances any neighbor *can* be praised or blamed, action in the present sense of the term? For consider the remarks appropriate to such employments by my wife of sentences about the activities of my neighbor: "What on earth is he up to?" "I hope he will not leave the hole there; children may fall into it and hurt themselves," and so on. In reporting or describing as she does the actions of my neighbor, my wife does *not* employ the neutral language of those concerned to relate or describe bodily movements. It is rather to treat the bodily movements that did occur as behavior of a responsible agent, to impute to him not only the practices of those who have learned by imitation, following instructions, and so forth the ways in which tools are employed and activities of various sorts conducted but also the general practice of attending to the interests and well-being of others. If we consider the remarks appropriate to such employments of action sentences and contrast them with those appropriate to the behavior of lunatics, infants, and wild animals, it becomes clear that such normal uses of action sentences risk defeat on two quite distinct grounds : First, on learning that the individual engaged in the observed bodily movements is not responsible or morally competent and second, on learning that the alleged bodily movements did not occur (e.g., it was really someone else). For normal use of action sentences, we ascribe responsibility to the individuals in question by treating the bodily behavior as action, and this we do by viewing it against the background of a set of practices, among others the practice of observing moral rules and principles. In short, we impute to the individual our common moral form of life.

There are cases, of course, in which sentences are employed in describing the behavior of our fellows and in which there is no ascription of responsibility. I have already mentioned the language of coroners and physiologists, in which a position of neutrality is taken with respect to the responsibility of the individual. But in what sorts of cases of an admittedly responsible agent would the question of common practices including that of observing moral rules be irrelevant? Would it be a case in which the individual raises his arm? But in that case we must not describe what the individual does as signaling, saluting, leading others in physical exercise drill, and so on. For those descriptions at once bring us within the social arena in which common forms of life have been achieved and by reference to which action statements can be understood and bodily movements treated as actions. No, we shall even have to deny that in raising his arm the individual was even pretending to engage in these activities, exercising, following the instructions of his physician, and so on. We shall have to rest content with the statement that he was simply raising his arm and never mind any further queries. But in that case, when the individual raises his arm what happens is that a bodily movement, not an action, occurs.

CHAPTER IV

INTENTION AND MOTIVE

> . . . as an adult who is master of himself foresees
> with mysterious accuracy the outward adjustment
> which will follow his inward effort, that adjustment
> may be said to be intended.
>
> HOLMES, *The Common Law*

Austin observed that intention "meets us at *every* step, in *every* department of Jurisprudence." It does, but in a number of different ways. First, it
is frequently necessary to determine whether or not a person has *acted intentionally*. If a person has acted unintentionally, he may be excused or
charged with a less serious offense. Second, a person's *present intention to
do a future act* may be legally relevant. This is sometimes so, for example,
in cases of conspiracy and attempt. In such cases the relevant fact is not what
a person intentionally does but what he intends to do in the future. Third, the
intention with which a person acts may often have legal significance. When
intentionally striking another or breaking into the house of another, for example, a person often, though not always, has some intention *in* so acting.
This intention may have as its object some future act of his, but it need not.
Its object might be quite different, as when the intention with which we act
is to arouse fear in another. In some contexts, lawyers refer, perhaps misleadingly, to this intention as "specific intent." Finally, a person sometimes
intends that another person shall perform some act. Some theorists challenge
whether this is conceptually possible. We talk as if it were when we discuss
coercion or duress.

There are other ways intention may become legally relevant. For example, we are often concerned with what a person *meant* or *intended* by
using certain words or gestures or sentences. The meaning, we say, is not
clear. There is a potential problem of this kind in every communication that
has legal significance. The four applications of the concept that I have listed—
if indeed they are applications of the same concept—are, however, of special
relevance to our inquiry.

Legal theorists traditionally attempt to elucidate the concept of intention
in terms of two other concepts: *desire for*, or *expectation of*, certain foreseen
consequences. There has always been disagreement over which of the two is
essentially related to intention. Some theorists take the line that intention is

a kind of "active" desire. Whether or not a person *expects* a certain consequence to follow from his act is irrelevant. If he desires the consequence to
follow from his act, he intends the consequence. If it in fact follows, it is intentional. One can, then, intend a consequence however improbable it is
believed to be. And so, to take a popular case, if one shoots at a person who
is a great distance away, desiring (wishing?) to kill that person but believing
success highly improbable, in this view one intends to kill the person. Further,
if one should succeed, one has done so intentionally. Consider another example. You flip a coin and desire (wish?) that it should turn up "heads."
In this view you intend that it so turn up, and if it does, you have intentionally
"flipped heads." Such an analysis of intention leads to the conceptual oddity
that one may intentionally do something and be unaware that one has done it.

Theorists who adopt this view of intention introduce a distinction between desiring something "as a means" and desiring something "as an end"
to meet the following objection. When I am coerced into handing over my
wallet by some thief, without doubt I do so intentionally but it is strange to
say that I desire to do so. The objection is countered by the claim that I
desire to hand over the wallet as a means to some end that I desire; it is therefore an intentional act. Or consider another popular example. Suppose that
X tosses a bomb into a crowded carriage, desiring to kill his enemy who is
in the carriage but expecting to kill everyone else in the carriage as well. Has
he intended to kill everyone in the carriage? Yes, some answer, for they claim
that he desired to kill those other than his enemy as a means to the death of
his enemy. Others prefer the view that the intent in such cases is "transferred" or "constructive": although X did not in fact intend everyone's death,
it is desirable to proceed as if he had.

Another approach rejects this analysis. What is essential is an *expectation* that a consequence will follow one's act; desire is irrelevant. There is
some disagreement over what constitutes expectation. Austin's view is that
to expect a consequence one need only believe it to be probable. Others require the belief that the consequence is substantially certain to follow. It
is clear that advocates of both the expectation and desire analyses will reach
similar conclusions on the carriage case. Their conclusions in the long-shot
and coin-flipping cases will, however, differ. If a person does not expect to
kill another, as in the long-shot case, he does not intend to kill. And since
there is no more reason to expect heads to turn up than tails, one cannot
intentionally flip heads.

Legal definitions of intention are frequently legislative rather than analytical. Particular legal policies influence legal theorists and judges and the
definitions they provide often do not correspond with the ordinary meaning
outside the law. A notorious example of this is intentional trespass in the
law of torts. It is possible to commit such a trespass even though one is
unaware of crossing the property line of another. And it is quite irrelevant,
of course, that one does not desire or expect to trespass.

Philosophers, not pressed to define the concept for legal purposes, have
provided analyses which differ from those offered by legal theorists. Some,

for example, believe that the concept "knowledge without observation," which we first encountered in Wittgenstein, is essential for the elucidation of an intentional act. In their view flipping heads on a coin normally cannot be an intentional act, for we normally have no knowledge without observation of doing so. I may intentionally flip a coin, but believing as I do that the probability is one-half that heads will turn up, I cannot intentionally flip heads. But there are problems raised by this criterion. If intentional acts are those known without observation, can we speak of an "intentional killing"? Indeed, if we accept this criterion are the consequences of an act ever intentional? Does the man who sends poisoned whiskey to his whiskey-loving enemy through the mail intentionally poison his enemy in the event the whiskey is drunk? What is it, in this view, that I can intend? Can I only intend those things which, should they come about, I can know without observation? If so, can I ever intend that *another* person act? Is a more appropriate concept here "trying to get him" to act? If I try to do something, is intending to do it ruled out? And are there things that I can neither intend nor try to do? Given just one chance, can I try to flip heads?

Theorists who reject an analysis in terms of desire, because we can achieve what we desire without success being intentional, may also take exception to elucidating intention in terms of expectation. For example, as I type these words I expect, having the knowledge I do, that I shall be making noises with the typewriter, that I shall be getting fatigued, that my fingers will feel a certain way, etc. But do I normally intend these things when I type? Suppose we are surrounded at night by hostile Indians who are unaware of our precise location. Suddenly you observe a rattlesnake coiled to strike me. You know that your firing the gun will alert the Indians, but fearful that certain and painful death awaits me if you do not kill the snake, you fire. Have you intended to alert them?

Philosophers have handled such cases in different ways. Hart and Hampshire claim that a person's intentional act is the one that he would specify in response to the question "What are you doing?" If honest, I should now reply to this question, "I'm typing." Anscombe believes that intention is essentially related to the concept of motive. The intentional act is one for which there was a motive. When I type I normally have a motive for typing and not for making a noise. You do not have a motive for alerting the Indians but you do for firing the gun.

But what are motives? Are they a kind of "mental thrust" that pushes us into action? Or is Ryle's view correct that a motive does not imply such queer mental happenings, but rather a generalization such as "The person always or very often acts in this way under like circumstances"? If motives are analyzed in this way, how shall we distinguish an explanation in terms of a motive from one in terms of a character trait? Is there not a difference between saying "He did it out of curiosity" and "He did it because he is a curious person"?

The view of many legal theorists is that motives are a species of intention. Others argue that there are various kinds of motives; some are intentions, others are not. For example, Anscombe claims that an intention *in* doing something is a "forward-looking motive." But a motive like gratitude or pity, which does not imply any intention *in* doing something, she terms "backward-looking." Among other things, the readings in this chapter should stimulate further investigation of a relatively neglected philosophical area, namely, the kinds of logically distinct explanations of conduct.

We also consider another philosophically neglected concept—omissions. When is an omission intentional? An act is intentional in our law whether or not a person is aware of a legal prohibition. Shall we say that an omission is intentional whether or not a person is aware of the legal requirement to act? What ought to be the rule here? When we say that we have tried to do something or intended to do something by omitting to do something, what is implied? Does one who stands by and watches another drown whom he might have saved, intend for that person to drown? Are his motives relevant? Is there some conceptual difference between allowing something to happen and omitting something?

Another problem considered in these readings is the relevance of motives and intentions to moral and legal responsibility. If it is true that the law largely disregards the motive that a person has in acting, why is this so? Should it be so? Do moral judgments of a person ever involve consideration of intentions? Are motives alone relevant?

The Talmud*

MISHNAH. If one extinguishes the lamp because he is afraid of gentiles, robbers, or an evil spirit, or for the sake of an invalid, that he should sleep, he is not culpable. If because he would spare the lamp, the oil, or the wick, he is culpable. R. Jose exempts him in all cases, except of the wick, because he makes charcoal.

* Reprinted from *The Babylonian Talmud* (London: The Soncino Press, 1938), Shabbath 29b p. 131.

Lang v. Lang, 3 W.L.R. 762 (1954)*

. . . At this point, and before proceeding with any summary of the facts, their Lordships think it desirable to make certain general observations about the law (a) of desertion; (b) of so called "constructive desertion." Both in England and Australia, to establish desertion two things must be proved: first, certain outward and visible conduct—the "factum" of desertion; secondly, the "animus deserendi"—the intention underlying this conduct to bring the matrimonial union to an end.

* Suit for divorce on grounds of constructive desertion.

In ordinary desertion the factum is simple: it is the act of the absconding party in leaving the matrimonial home. The contest in such a case will be almost entirely as to the "animus." Was the intention of the party leaving the home to break it up for good, or something short of, or different from that?

Since 1860 in England, and for a long time in Australia, it has been recognized that the party truly guilty of disrupting the home is not necessarily or in all cases the party who first leaves it. The party who stays behind (their Lordships will assume this to be the husband) may be by reason of conduct on his part making it unbearable for a wife with reasonable self-respect, or powers of endurance, to stay with him, so that he is the party really responsible for the breakdown of the marriage. He has deserted her by expelling her: by driving her out. In such a case the factum is the course of conduct pursued by the husband—something which may be far more complicated than the mere act of leaving the matrimonial home. It is not every course of conduct by the husband causing the wife to leave which is a sufficient factum. A husband's irritating habits may so get on the wife's nerves that she leaves as a direct consequence of them, but she would not be justified in doing so. Such irritating idiosyncrasies are part of the lottery in which every spouse engages on marrying, and taking the partner of the marriage "for better, for worse." The course of conduct—the "factum" —must be grave and convincing.

In the present case there is not the slightest question that the "factum" is sufficient. The facts are not in dispute. There are in effect concurrent findings that the husband grossly ill-used and insulted his wife over a period of five years and gave her ample justification for leaving him.

The whole and sole question is whether the wife has proved the necessary animus or intent on the part of the husband. How should that animus be ascertained? In particular, (1) is it enough for her to show a course of conduct on the part of the husband which in the eyes of a reasonable man would, by making her life insufferable, be calculated to drive the wife out, the husband's actual intention being immaterial on the footing that every man is presumed to intend the natural and probable consequences of his acts? Or (2) should the objective criterion of the reasonable man's reactions be rejected on the footing that the real question is, did this particular husband (who may not have been reasonable) know that his conduct, if persisted in, would in all human probability result in the wife's departure— it being remembered that it is possible (human nature being what it is) for such knowledge on the husband's part to coexist with a desire that she should stay, since people often desire a thing but deliberately act in a way which makes that desire unrealizable. Or again (3), should inferences, which would naturally be drawn be wholly disregarded and an intention which would naturally be drawn from the husband's conduct negatived provided there is proved to exist, de facto, on his part a genuine desire (however illogical or impossible it may be to square such a desire with his conduct) that the matrimonial union should continue? On this view the husband's desire to maintain the home is conclusive whatever his conduct. All three of these views have found expression in the decided cases.

Their Lordships have thought it convenient to state in very general outline the legal issues involved before citing any authorities or concluding their summary of the facts. To this last task they now revert. The material facts are conveniently summarized in the judgment of the Supreme Court of Victoria by Lowe, J.:

But I take up the story in some detail from the respondent's return from the Middle East in 1942. He had been on active service, and that was the time of his return. In a conversation with his son—and the substance of it was repeated to others—he said that thenceforward he was going to be master; and when the son asked him whether that meant that he was going to knock his mother about he said that was the only thing she understood. From this time on, I find a series of constant disturbances and acts of violence on his part. There were slaps and punches which he administered to the petitioner on the face and the body. He struck her on occasions with a ruler and with a cane and with a slipper and did this in the undignified way, on occasion, of placing her across his knee and administering punishment in that way. There were bruises put upon her body by these means and the bruises on occasions were seen by other people. He twisted her arms behind her back and so caused her pain, and on occasion he so held the twisted arms in a position that continued for nearly an hour, and when the police arrived, on the summons of one of the children, he was still holding his wife's arms in that position. On two occasions at least he dragged her by the hair into the bathroom and held her under the cold shower. He abused her and constantly called her a bitch, and there were nightly disturbances created by him, destroying his wife's rest. Now that is a series of incidents and a course of conduct which persisted over several years. She told him on a number of occasions that if he continued that conduct she would have to leave as that conduct was affecting her health. And on one occasion she did leave, and left for some little time. I shall deal with that more particularly, but on another occasion she left and walked the street for the night so that she might not stop in the house.

She separated from him on two occasions, viz., in 1943 and in July, 1948, before they finally parted. On the first occasion she remained away for about two months and was induced to return by promises of amendment, which were however promptly and continuously thereafter violated. On some date in July, 1948, he treated her with such violence that, not for the first time, the police had to be invoked. She then asked him to leave, and he did: returning however on August 11. On August 13 occurred the culminating incident which caused her finally to leave him. The husband professed to have taken advice from a psychiatric friend as to how he could improve his relations with his wife, and to have been advised to try "Caveman stuff."

It is a little surprising that this suggestion was treated by the husband as a new departure: "Caveman stuff" is not an unfair description for the treatment he had been applying to his wife for years past and which had twice caused her to leave him. . . . She finally left and filed her petition, ignoring a number of letters which he wrote begging her to return but not expressing any intention to treat her differently if she did. Her patience was not unnaturally exhausted, and even if he had expressed penitential sentiments it would not have been unreasonable for the wife to doubt their sincerity.

In the present case the existence of conduct by the husband being of sufficient gravity to constitute the necessary *factum*, the question is what he intended, or must be taken to have intended, while so conducting himself. Did he intend to bring the matrimonial relations to an end? Let it be supposed that a husband intentionally persists in conduct which the hypothetical reasonable man would think calculated to cause the wife to leave him; is he necessarily guilty of constructive desertion, notwithstanding that he genuinely desires the marriage to survive? If so, evidence of his consistently expressed desire that the wife should stay with him is irrelevant and inadmissible. The formula, if satisfied, creates an irrebuttable presumption.

In other words, if a man deliberately makes his wife's life unbearable according to an objective standard, i.e., the reasonable man's reactions, is he conclusively presumed to intend to drive her out—the presumption that a man intends the natural and probable consequences of his acts being treated as irrebuttable?

(The Court proceeds to review the law in Australia and England.)

Prima facie, a man who treats his wife with gross brutality may be presumed to intend the consequences of his acts. Such an inference may indeed be rebutted, but if the only evidence is of continuous cruelty and no rebutting evidence is given, the natural and almost inevitable inference is that the husband intended to drive out the wife. The court is at least entitled and, indeed, driven to such an inference unless convincing evidence to the contrary is adduced. In their Lordships' opinion this is the proper approach to the problem, and it must therefore be determined whether the natural inference has been rebutted in this present case.

The fact that the question at issue involves a consideration of the effect of the actions of one person upon another adds to the complexities of the case. But apart from this, the distinction between intention and desire has to be borne in mind. A man may wish one thing and intend another—"Video meliora proboue, Deteriora sequo"—and, indeed, as the High Court have pointed out, a man's intention does not necessarily always remain constant but fluctuates from time to time. Nevertheless, some general principle must be sought and adopted.

But before the question of rebutting evidence is reached it has first to be determined what is the exact connotation of the word "intention" as used in the relevant cases.

In *Bain v. Bain*[1] the High Court visualizes the problem which may arise where the husband appears to be actuated by "intents" which conflict with, or contradict, each other. The answer given is in substance that in such a conjuncture the dominant intention must be ascertained and looked to. . . .

Their Lordships . . . venture to question whether as a matter of strict terminology a man can be said to entertain conflicting "intentions." A man may well have incompatible desires. He may have an intention which conflicts with a desire: i.e., he may will one thing, and wish another, as when he renounces some cherished article of diet in the interest of health. But "intention" necessarily connotes an element of volition: desire does not. Desires and wishes can exist without any element contributed by the will. What, then, is the legal result where an intention to bring about a particular result (be it proved directly or by inference from conduct) coexists with a

[1] (1923) 33 C.L.R. 317.

desire that that result should not ensue? That is the substantial point raised by this appeal. The issue may be put more concretely. What legal inference is to be drawn where the whole of a husband's conduct is such that reasonable men would know—that the particular husband must know—that in all human probability it will result in the departure of the wife from the matrimonial home? Apart from rebutting evidence this, in their Lordships' opinion, is sufficient proof of an intention to disrupt the home: but suppose, further, a husband's hope is that in some way his actions will not produce these natural consequences, that the wife will stay and that the home will not be disrupted. Where a man's own actions are concerned and not their effect on another, the answer is easy. If he desires to resist temptation but yields to it his intention is evidenced by his acts. His better self is, it may be, overborne, yet in the end his intention is to yield. Where, however, the effect of his actions upon other people is concerned and there is no certainty but only a high degree of probability as to what the result will be, is a court to say that if he did entertain an unjustified hope that his wife would stay, the intention normally to be inferred from his acts is rebutted, and is the correct conclusion

that he did not intend to drive her out? In their Lordships' opinion no such conclusion is justified. If the husband knows the probable result of his acts and persists in them, in spite of warning that the wife will be compelled to leave the home, and indeed, as in the present case, has expressed an intention of continuing his conduct and never indicated any intention of amendment, that is enough however passionately he may desire or request that she should remain. His intention is to act as he did, whatever the consequences, though he may hope and desire that they will not produce their probable effect.

To say that it is not enough unless he knows that separation must inevitably result from his actions is to ask too much. Men's actions and judgments are not founded upon certainty—in most cases certainty is unascertainable—but on probabilities. No doubt a high degree of probability is required, but no more.

With these considerations in mind, can it be said that the appellant has rebutted the natural inference, which would be drawn from his acts if no countervailing testimony was given? In their Lordships' opinion no sufficient ground has been given for rejecting the finding of the High Court. . . .

Model Penal Code*

Section 2.02. General Requirements of Culpability

(1) Minimum requirements of culpability. Except as provided in Section 2.05, a person is not guilty of an offense unless he acted purposely, knowingly, recklessly, or negligently, as the law may require, with respect to each material element of the offense.

(2) Kinds of culpability defined.

    (a) *Purposely.*

    A person acts purposely with respect to a material element of an offense when:

        (1) if the element involves the nature of his conduct or a result thereof, it is his conscious object to engage in

conduct of that nature or to cause such a result; and

        (2) if the element involves the attendant circumstances, he knows of the existence of such circumstances.

    (b) *Knowingly.*

    A person acts knowingly with respect to a material element of an offense when:

        (1) if the element involves the nature of his conduct or the attendant circumstances, he knows that his conduct is of that nature or he knows of the existence of such circumstances; and

        (2) if the element involves a result of his conduct, he knows that his conduct will necessarily cause such a result.

    . . .

* Copyright 1956. Reprinted with the permission of The American Law Institute from *Model Penal Code* (Philadelphia: The American Law Institute, 1956), Tentative Draft No. 4, Art. 2, § 2.02, pp. 12–15, 123–25.

(6) Requirement of purpose satisfied if purpose is conditional.

When a particular purpose is an element of an offense, the element is established although such purpose is conditional, unless the condition negatives the harm or evil sought to be prevented by the law defining the offense.

(7) Requirement of knowledge satisfied by knowledge of substantial probability.

When knowledge of the existence of a particular fact is an element of an offense, such knowledge is established if a person is aware of a substantial probability of its existence, unless he actually believes that it does not exist.

(8) Requirement of willfulness satisfied by acting knowingly.

A requirement that an offense be committed willfully is satisfied if a person acts knowingly with respect to the material elements of the offense, unless a purpose to impose further requirements plainly appears.

(9) Knowledge of illegality not an element of offenses.

Knowledge that conduct constitutes an offense or of the existence, meaning, or application of the law determining the elements of an offense is not an element of such offense, unless the definition of the offense or the Code plainly so provides.

(10) Culpability as determinant of grade of offense.

When the grade or degree of an offense depends on whether the offense is committed purposely, knowingly, recklessly, or negligently, its grade or degree shall be the lowest for which the determinative kind of culpability is established with respect to any material element of the offense.

. . .

COMMENTS

Section 2.02. General Requirements of Culpability

This section attempts the extremely difficult task of articulating the general *mens rea* requirements for the establishment of liability.

1. The approach is based upon the view that clear analysis requires that the question of the kind of culpability required to establish the commission of an offense be faced separately with respect to each material element of the crime; and that, as indicated in section 1.14, the concept of "material element" include the facts that negative defenses on the merits as well as the facts included in the definition of the crime.

The reason for this treatment is best stated by suggesting an example. Given a charge of murder, the prosecution normally must prove intent to kill (or at least to cause serious bodily injury) to establish the required culpability with respect to that element of the crime that involves the result of the defendant's conduct. But if self-defense is claimed as a defense, it is enough to show that the defendant's belief in the necessity of his conduct to save himself did not rest upon reasonable grounds. As to the first element, in short, purpose or knowledge is required; as to the second negligence appears to be sufficient. Failure to face the question separately with respect to each of these ingredients of the offense results in obvious confusion.

A second illustration is afforded by the law of rape. A purpose to effect the sexual relation is most certainly required. But other circumstances also are essential to establish the commission of the crime. The victim must not have been married to the defendant and her consent to sexual relations would, of course, preclude the crime. Must the defendant's purpose have encompassed the facts that he was not the husband of the victim and that she opposed his will? These are certainly entirely different questions. Recklessness, for example, on these points may be sufficient although purpose is required with respect to the sexual result which is an element of the offense.

Under the draft, therefore, the problem of the kind of culpability that is required for conviction must be faced separately with respect to each material element of the offense, although the answer may in many cases be the same with respect to each such element.

2. The draft acknowledges four different kinds of culpability: purpose, knowledge, recklessness, and negligence. It also recognizes that the material elements of offenses vary in that they may involve (1) the nature of the forbidden conduct or (2) the attendant circumstances or (3) the result of conduct. With respect to each of these three types of elements, the draft attempts to define each of the kinds of culpability that may arise. The resulting distinctions are, we think, both nec-

essary and sufficient for the general purposes of penal legislation.

The purpose of articulating these distinctions in detail is, of course, to promote the clarity of definitions of specific crimes and to dispel the obscurity with which the culpability requirement is often treated when such concepts as "general criminal intent," *"mens rea,"* "presumed intent," "malice," "willfulness," "scienter" and the like must be employed. . . .

3. In defining the kinds of culpability, a narrow distinction is drawn between acting purposely and knowingly, one of the elements of ambiguity in legal usage of "intent." . . . Knowledge that the requisite external circumstances exist is a common element in both conceptions. But action is not purposive with respect to the nature or the result of the actor's conduct unless it was his conscious object to perform an action of that nature or to

cause such a result. The distinction is no doubt inconsequential for most purposes of liability; acting knowingly is ordinarily sufficient. But there are areas where the discrimination is required and is made under existing law, using the awkward concept of "specific intent." This is true in treason, for example, in so far as a purpose to aid the enemy is an ingredient of the offense (see Haupt v. United States, 330 U.S. 631, 641 [1947]) and in attempts and conspiracy, where a true purpose to effect the criminal result is requisite for liability. See, e.g., Dennis v. United States, 341 U.S. 494, 499–500 (1951); Hartzel v. United States, 322 U.S. 680 (1944).

The distinction also has utility in differentiating among grades of an offense for purposes of sentence, e.g., in the case of homicide.

Intention and Sin*

PROLOGUE

In the study of morals we deal with the defects or qualities of the mind which dispose us to bad or good actions. Defects and qualities are not only mental, but also physical. There is bodily weakness; there is also the endurance which we call strength. There is sluggishness or speed; blindness or sight. When we now speak of defects, therefore, we presuppose defects of the mind, so as to distinguish them from the physical ones. The defects of the mind are opposed to the qualities; injustice to justice; cowardice to constancy; intemperance to temperance.

CHAPTER I

The Defect of Mind Bearing upon Conduct

Certain defects or merits of mind have no connection with morals. They do not make human life a matter of praise or blame. Such are dull wits or quick insight; a good or a bad memory; ignorance or knowledge. Each of these features is found in good and bad alike. They have nothing to do with the system of morals, nor with making life base or honorable. To exclude these we safeguarded

* *Abailard's Ethics,* trans. J. Ramsay McCallum (Oxford: Basil Blackwell, 1935), pp. 15–24, 28–34, 46–47, reprinted by permission of the translator and the publishers. Footnotes are omitted.

above the phrase "defects of mind" by adding "which dispose to bad actions," that is, those defects which incline the will to what least of all either should be done or should be left undone.

CHAPTER II

How Does Sin Differ from a Disposition to Evil?

Defect of this mental kind is not the same thing as sin. Sin, too, is not the same as a bad action. For example, to be irascible, that is, prone or easily roused to the agitation of anger is a defect and moves the mind to unpleasantly impetuous and irrational action. This defect, however, is in the mind so that the mind is liable to wrath, even when it is not actually roused to it. Similarly, lameness, by reason of which a man is said to be lame, is in the man himself even when he does not walk and reveal his lameness. For the defect is there though action be lacking. So, also, nature or constitution renders many liable to luxury. Yet they do not sin because they are like this, but from this very fact they have the material of a struggle whereby they may, in the virtue of temperance, triumph over themselves and win the crown. As Solomon says: "Better a patient than a strong man; and the Lord of his soul than he that taketh a city" (Prov. xvi, 32). For religion does not think it degrading to be beaten by man; but it is degrading to be beaten by one's lower self. The former defeat has been the fate of good men. But, in the latter, we fall below ourselves. The Apostle commends victory of this sort: "No one shall be crowned who has not truly striven" (2 Tim. ii, 5). This striving, I repeat, means standing less against men than against myself, so that defects may not lure me into base consent. Though men cease to oppose us, our defects do not cease. The fight with them is the more dangerous because of its repetition. And as it is the more difficult, so victory is the more glorious. Men, however much they prevail over us, do not force baseness upon us, unless by their practice of vice they turn us also to it and overcome us through our own wretched consent. They may dominate our body; but while our mind is free, there is no danger to true freedom. We run no risk of base servitude. Subservience to vice, not to man, is degradation. It is the overlordship of defects and not physical serfdom which debases the soul.

CHAPTER III

Definition of "Defect" and of Sin

Defect, then, is that whereby we are disposed to sin. We are, that is, inclined to consent to what we ought not to do, or to leave undone what we ought to do. Consent of this kind we rightly call sin. Here is the reproach of the soul meriting damnation or being declared guilty by God. What is that consent but to despise God and to violate his laws? God cannot be set at enmity by injury, but by contempt. He is the highest power, and is not diminished by any injury, but He avenges contempt of Himself. Our sin, therefore, is contempt of the Creator. To sin is to despise the Creator; that is, not to do for Him what we believe we should do for Him, or, not to renounce what we think should be renounced on His behalf. We have defined sin negatively by saying that it means not doing or not renouncing what we ought to do or renounce. Clearly, then, we have shown that sin has no reality. It exists rather in *not being* than in *being*. Similarly we could define shadows by saying: The absence of light where light usually is.

Perhaps you object that sin is the desire or will to do an evil deed, and that this will

or desire condemns us before God in the same way as the will to do a good deed justifies us. There is as much quality, you suggest, in the good will as there is sin in the evil will; and it is no less "in being" in the latter than in the former. By willing to do what we believe to be pleasing to God we please Him. Equally, by willing to do what we believe to be displeasing to God, we displease Him and seem either to violate or despise His nature.

But diligent attention will show that we must think far otherwise of this point. We frequently err; and from no evil will at all. Indeed, the evil will itself, when restrained, though it may not be quenched, procures the palm-wreath for those who resist it. It provides, not merely the materials for combat, but also the crown of glory. It should be spoken of rather as a certain inevitable weakness than as sin. Take, for example, the case of an innocent servant whose harsh master is moved with fury against him. He pursues the servant, drawing his sword with intent to kill him. For a while the servant flies and avoids death as best he can. At last, forced all unwillingly to it, he kills his master so as not to be killed by him. Let anyone say what sort of evil will there was in this deed. His will was only to flee from death and preserve his own life. Was this an evil will? You reply: "I do not think this was an evil will. But the will that he had to kill the master who was pursuing him was evil." Your answer would be admirable and acute if you could show that the servant really willed what you say that he did. But, as I insisted, he was unwillingly forced to his deed. He protracted his master's life as long as he could, knowing that danger also threatened his own life from such a crime. How, then, was a deed done voluntarily by which he incurred danger to his own life?

Your reply may be that the action was voluntary because the man's will was to escape death even though it may not have been to kill his master. This charge might easily be preferred against him. I do not rebut it. Nevertheless, as has been said, that will by which he sought to evade death, as you urge, and not to kill his master, cannot at all be condemned as bad. He did, however, fail by consenting, though driven to it through fear of death, to an unjust murder which he ought rather to have endured than committed. Of his own will, I mean, he took the sword. It was not handed to him by authority. The Truth saith: "Everyone that taketh the sword shall perish by the sword" (Matt. xxvi, 52). By his rashness he risked the death and damnation of his soul. The servant's wish, then, was not to kill his master, but to avoid death. Because he *consented,* however, as he should not have done, to murder, this wrongful consent preceding the crime was sin.

Someone may interpose: "But you cannot conclude that he wished to kill his master because, in order to escape death, he was willing to kill his master. I might say to a man: I am willing for you to have my cape so that you may give me five shillings. Or, I am glad for you to have it at this price. But I do not hand it over because I desire you to have possession of it." No, and if a man in prison desired under duress, to put his son there in his place that he might secure his own ransom, should we therefore admit that he wished to send his son to prison?

It was only with many a tear and groan that he consented to such a course.

The fact is that this kind of will, existing with much internal regret, is not, if I may so say, *will,* but a passive submission of mind. It is so because the man wills one thing on account of another. He puts up with *this* because he really desires *that.* A patient is said to submit to cautery or lancet that he may obtain health.

·   ·   ·

Sin, therefore, is sometimes committed without an evil will. Thus sin cannot be defined as "will." True, you will say, when we sin under constraint, but not when we sin willingly, for instance, when we will to do something which we know ought not to be done by us. There the evil will and sin seem to be the same thing. For example, a man sees a woman; his concupiscence is aroused; his mind is enticed by fleshly lust and stirred to base desire. This wish, this lascivious longing, what else can it be, you say, than sin?

I reply: What if that wish may be bridled by the power of temperance? What if its nature is never to be entirely extinguished but to persist in struggle and not fully fail even in defeat? For where is the battle if the antagonist is away? Whence the great reward without grave endurance? When the

fight is over, nothing remains but to reap the reward. Here we strive in contest in order elsewhere to obtain as victors a crown. Now, for a contest, an opponent is needed who will resist, not one who simply submits. This opponent is our evil will over which we triumph when we subjugate it to the divine will. But we do not entirely destroy it. For we needs must ever expect to encounter our enemy. What achievement before God is it if we undergo nothing contrary to our own will, but merely practice what we please? Who will be grateful to us if in what we say we do for him we merely satisfy our own fancy?

You will say, what merit have we with God in acting willingly or unwillingly? Certainly none: I reply. He weighs the intention rather than the deed in his recompense. Nor does the deed, whether it proceed from a good or an evil will, add anything to the merit, as we shall show shortly. But when we set His will before our own so as to follow His and not ours, our merit with God is magnified, in accordance with that perfect word of Truth: "I came not to do mine own will, but the will of Him that sent me" (John vi, 38). . . . .

When the Scripture says: "Go not after your own desires" (Eccles. xviii, 30), and: "Turn from your own will" (*ibid.*), it instructs us not to fulfill our desires. Yet it does not say that we are to be wholly without them. It is vicious to give in to our desires; but not to have any desires at all is impossible for our weak nature.

The sin, then, consists not in desiring a woman, but in consent to the desire, and not the wish for whoredom, but the consent to the wish is damnation.

Let us see how our conclusions about sexual intemperance apply to theft. A man crosses another's garden. At the sight of the delectable fruit his desire is aroused. He does not, however, give way to desire so as to take anything by theft or rapine, although his mind was moved to strong inclination by the thought of the delight of eating. Where there is desire, there, without doubt, will exists. The man desires the eating of that fruit wherein he doubts not that there will be delight. The weakness of nature in this man is compelled to desire the fruit which, without the master's permission, he has no right to take. He conquers the desire, but does not extinguish it. Since, however, he is not enticed into consent, he does not descend to sin.

What, then, of your objection? It should be clear from such instances, that the wish or desire itself of doing what is not seemly is never to be called sin, but rather, as we said, the consent is sin. We consent to what is not seemly when we do not draw ourselves back from such a deed, and are prepared, should opportunity offer, to perform it completely. Whoever is discovered in this intention, though his guilt has yet to be completed in deed, is already guilty before God in so far as he strives with all his might to sin, and accomplishes within himself, as the blessed Augustine reminds us, as much as if he were actually taken in the act.

. . .

We come, then, to this conclusion, that no one who sets out to assert that all fleshly desire is sin may say that the sin itself is increased by the doing of it. For this would mean extending the consent of the soul into the exercise of the action. In short, one would be stained not only by consent to baseness, but also by the mire of the deed, as if what happens externally in the body could possibly soil the soul. Sin is not, therefore, increased by the doing of an action: and nothing mars the soul except what is of its own nature, namely, consent. This we affirmed was alone sin, preceding action in will, or subsequent to the performance of action. Although we wish for, or do, what is unseemly, we do not therefore sin. For such deeds not uncommonly occur without there being any sin. On the other hand, there may be consent without the external effects, as we have indicated. There was wish without consent in the case of the man who was attracted by a woman whom he caught sight of, or who was tempted by his neighbor's fruit, but who was not enticed into consent. There was evil consent without evil desire in the servant who unwillingly killed his master.

Certain acts which ought not to be done often are done, and without any sin, when, for instance, they are committed under force or ignorance. No one, I think, ignores this fact. A woman under constraint of violence, lies with another's husband. A man, taken by some trick, sleeps with one whom he supposed to be his wife, or kills a man, in the belief that he himself has the right to be both judge and executioner. Thus to desire the wife of another or actually to lie with her is not sin. But to consent to that desire or to that action is sin. This consent to covetousness the law calls covetousness in saying: "Thou shalt not covet" (Deut. v, 21). Yet that which we cannot avoid ought not to be forbidden, nor that wherein, as we said, we do not sin. But we should be cautioned about the consent to covetousness. So, too, the saying of the Lord must be understood: "Whosoever shall look upon a woman to desire her" (Matt. v, 28). That is, whosoever shall so look upon her as to slip into consent to covetousness, "has already committed adultery with her in his heart" (Matt. v, 28), even though he may not have committed adultery in deed. He is guilty of sin, though there be no sequel to his intention.

Careful account will reveal that wherever actions are restricted by some precept or prohibition, these refer rather to will and consent than to the deeds themselves. Otherwise nothing relative to a person's moral merit could be included under a precept. Indeed, actions are so much the less worth prescribing as they are less in our power to do. At the same time, many things we are forbidden to do for which there exists in our will both the inclination and the consent.

The Lord God says: "Thou shalt not kill. Thou shalt not bear false witness" (Deut. v, 17, 20). If we accept these cautions as being only about actions, as the words suggest, then guilt is not forbidden, but simply the activity of guilt. For we have seen that actions may be carried out without sin, as that it is not sin to kill a man or to lie with another's wife. And even the man who desires to bear false testimony, and is willing to utter it, so long as he is silent for some reason and does not speak, is innocent before the law, that is, if the prohibition in this matter be accepted literally of the action. It is not said that we should not *wish* to give false witness, or that we should not *consent* in bearing it, but simply that we should not bear false witness.

Similarly, when the law forbids us to marry or have intercourse with our sisters, if this prohibition relates to deed rather than to intention, no one can keep the commandment, for a sister unless we recognize her, is just a woman. If a man, then, marries his sister in error, is he a transgressor for doing what the law forbade? He is not, you will reply, because, in acting ignorantly in what he did, he did not consent to a transgression. Thus a transgressor is not one who *does* what is prohibited. He is one who *consents* to what is prohibited. The prohibition is, therefore, not about action, but about consent. It is as though in saying: "Do not do this or that," we meant: "Do not consent to do this or that," or, "Do not wittingly do this." . . .

Whether you actually give alms to a needy person, or charity makes you ready to give, makes no difference to the merit of the deed. The will may be there when the opportunity is not. Nor does it rest entirely with you to deal with every case of need which you encounter. Actions which are right and actions which are far from right are done by good and bad men alike. The intention alone separates the two classes of men.

• • •

God considers not the action, but the spirit of the action. It is the intention, not the deed wherein the merit or praise of the doer consists. Often, indeed, the same action is done from different motives: for justice sake by one man, for an evil reason by another. Two men, for instance, hang a guilty person. The one does it out of zeal for justice; the other in resentment for an earlier enmity. The action of hanging is the same. Both men do what is good and what justice demands. Yet the diversity of their intentions causes the same deed to be done from different motives, in the one case good, in the other bad.

• • •

Briefly to summarize the above argument: Four things were postulated which must be carefully distinguished from one another.
1. Imperfection of soul, making us liable to sin.
2. Sin itself, which we decided is consent to evil or contempt of God.
3. The will or desire of evil.
4. The evil deed.

• • •

CHAPTER XI
The Good Action Springs from the Good Intention

We call the intention good which is right in itself, but the action is good, not because it contains within it some good, but because it issues from a good intention. The same act may be done by the same man at different times. According to the diversity of his intention, however, this act may be at one time good, at another bad. So goodness and badness vary. Compare the proposition: "Socrates sits." One conceives this statement either truly or falsely according as Socrates actually does sit, or stands. This alteration in truth and falsity, Aristotle affirms, comes about not from any change in the circumstances which compose the true or false situation, but because the subject-matter of the statement (that is, Socrates) moves in itself, I mean changes from sitting to standing or vice versa.

Intentions and Motives*

1. So much with regard to the two first of the articles upon which the evil tendency of an action may depend: viz., the act itself, and the general assemblage of the circumstances with which it may have been accompanied. We come now to consider the ways in which the particular circumstance of intention may be concerned in it.
2. First, then, the intention or will may

* Jeremy Bentham, *An Introduction to the Principles of Morals and Legislation* (Oxford: Basil Blackwell, 1948), pp. 200–21. Footnotes have been renumbered.

regard either of two objects: (1) The act itself: or (2) Its consequences. Of these objects, that which the intention regards may be styled *intentional*. If it regards the act, then the act may be said to be intentional:[1] if

[1] On this occasion the words *voluntary* and *involuntary* are commonly employed. These however, I purposely abstain from, on account of the extreme ambiguity of their signification. By a voluntary act is meant sometimes, any act, in the performance of which the will has had any concern at all; in this sense it is synonymous to *intentional*: sometimes such acts only, in the production of which the will has been determined by motives not of a painful nature; in this sense it is synonymous to uncon-

the consequences, so then also may the consequences. If it regards both the act and consequences, the whole action may be said to be intentional. Whichever of those articles is not the object of the intention, may of course be said to be *unintentional*.

3. The act may very easily be intentional without the consequences; and often is so. Thus, you may intend to touch a man without intending to hurt him: and yet, as the consequences turn out, you may chance to hurt him.

4. The consequences of an act may also be intentional, without the act's being intentional throughout; that is, without its being intentional in every stage of it: but this is not so frequent a case as the former. You intend to hurt a man, suppose, by running against him, and pushing him down: and you run toward him accordingly: but a second man coming in on a sudden between you and the first man, before you can stop yourself, you run against the second man, and by him push down the first.

5. But the consequences of an act cannot be intentional, without the act's being itself intentional in at least the first stage. If the act be not intentional in the first stage, it is no act of yours: there is accordingly no intention on your part to produce the consequences: that is to say, the individual consequences. All there can have been on your part is a distant intention to produce other consequences, of the same nature, by some act of yours, at a future time: or else, without any intention, a bare *wish* to see such event take place. The second man, suppose, runs of his own accord against the first, and pushes him down. You had intentions of doing a thing of the same nature: viz., To run against him, and push him down yourself; but you had done nothing in pursuance of those intentions: the individual consequences therefore of the act, which the second man performed

in pushing down the first, cannot be said to have been on your part intentional.[2]

6. Second. A consequence, when it is intentional, may either be *directly* so, or only *obliquely*. It may be said to be directly or lineally intentional, when the prospect of producing it constituted one of the links in the chain of causes by which the person was determined to do the act. It may be said to be obliquely or collaterally intentional, when, although the consequence was in contemplation, and appeared likely to ensue in case of the act's being performed, yet the prospect of producing such consequence did not constitute a link in the aforesaid chain.

7. Third. An incident, which is directly intentional, may either be *ultimately* so, or only *mediately*. It may be said to be ultimately intentional, when it stands last of all exterior events in the aforesaid chain of motives; insomuch that the prospect of the production of such incident, could there be a certainty of its taking place, would be sufficient to determine the will, without the prospect of its producing any other. It may be said to be mediately intentional, and no more, when there is some other incident, the prospect of producing which forms a subsequent link in the same chain: insomuch that the prospect of producing the former would not have operated as a motive, but for the tendency which it seemed to have toward the production of the latter.

8. Fourth. When an incident is directly intentional, it may either be *exclusively* so, or *inexclusively*. It may be said to be exclusively intentional, when no other but that very individual incident would have answered the purpose, insomuch that no other incident had any share in determining the will to the act in question. It may be said to have been inex-

---

strained, or *uncoerced*: sometimes such acts only, in the production of which the will has been determined by motives which, whether of the pleasurable or painful kind, occurred to a man himself, without being suggested by anybody else; in this sense it is synonymous to *spontaneous*. The sense of the word involuntary does not correspond completely to that of the word voluntary. Involuntary is used in opposition to intentional; and to unconstrained: but not to spontaneous. It might be of use to confine the signification of the words voluntary and involuntary to one single and very narrow case, which will be mentioned in the next note.

[2] To render the analysis here given of the possible states of the mind in point of intentionality absolutely complete, it must be pushed to such a farther degree of minuteness, as to some eyes will be apt to appear trifling. On this account it seemed advisable to discard what follows from the text to a place where anyone who thinks proper may pass by it. An act of the body, when of a positive kind, is a motion: now in motion there are always three articles to be considered: 1. The quantity of matter that moves: 2. The direction in which it moves: and 3. The velocity with which it moves. Correspondent to these three articles, are so many modes of intentionality, with regard to an act, considered as being only in its first stage. To be completely unintentional, it must be unintentional with respect to every one of these three particulars. This is the case with those acts which alone are properly termed *involuntary*: acts, in the performance of which the will has no sort of share: such as the contraction of the heart and arteries. . . .

clusively intentional, when there was some other incident, the prospect of which was acting upon the will at the same time.

9. Fifth. When an incident is inexclusively intentional, it may be either *con*junctively so, *dis*junctively, or *indiscriminately*. It may be said to be conjunctively intentional with regard to such other incident, when the intention is to produce both: disjunctively, when the intention is to produce either the one or the other indifferently, but not both: indiscriminately, when the intention is indifferently to produce either the one or the other, or both, as it may happen.

10. Sixth. When two incidents are disjunctively intentional, they may be so with or without *preference*. They may be said to be so with preference, when the intention is, that one of them in particular should happen rather than the other: without preference, when the intention is equally fulfilled, whichever of them happens.[3]

11. One example will make all this clear. William II, king of England, being out on a stag-hunting, received from Sir Walter Tyrrel a wound, of which he died. Let us take this case, and diversify it with a variety of suppositions, correspondent to the distinctions just laid down.

  1. First then, Tyrrel did not so much as entertain a thought of the king's death: or, if he did, looked upon it as an event of which there was no danger. In either of these cases the incident of his killing the king was altogether unintentional.

  2. He saw a stag running that way, and he saw the king riding that way at the same time: what he aimed at was to kill the stag: he did not wish to kill the king: at the same time he saw that if he shot, it was as likely he should kill the king as the stag: yet for all that he shot, and killed the king accordingly. In this case the incident of his killing the king was intentional, but obliquely so.

  3. He killed the king on account of the hatred he bore him, and for no other reason than the pleasure of destroying him. In this case the accident of the king's death was not only directly but ultimately intentional.

  4. He killed the king, intending fully so to do; not for any hatred he bore him, but for the sake of plundering him when dead. In this case the incident of the king's death was directly intentional, but not ultimately: it was mediately intentional.

  5. He intended neither more nor less than to kill the king. He had no other aim nor wish. In this case it was exclusively as well as directly intentional: exclusively, to wit, with regard to every other material incident.

  6. Sir Walter shot the king in the right leg, as he was plucking a thorn out of it with his left hand. His intention was, by shooting the arrow into his leg through his hand, to cripple him in both those limbs at the same time. In this case, the incident of the king's being shot in the leg was intentional: and that conjunctively with another which did not happen; viz., his being shot in the hand.

  7. The intention of Tyrrel was to shoot the king either in the hand or in the leg, but not in both; and rather in the hand than in the leg. In this case the intention of shooting in the hand was disjunctively concurrent, with regard to the other incident, and that with preference.

  8. His intention was to shoot the king either in the leg or the hand, whichever might happen: but not in both. In this case the intention was inexclusive, but disjunctively so: yet that, however, without preference.

  9. His intention was to shoot the king either in the leg or the hand, or in both, as it might happen. In this case the intention was indiscriminately concurrent, with respect to the two incidents.

. . .

12. It is to be observed that an act may be unintentional in any stage or stages of it, though intentional in the preceding: and, on the other hand, it may be intentional in any stage or stages of it, and yet unintentional in the succeeding. But whether it be intentional

---

[3] There is a difference between the case where an incident is altogether unintentional, and that in which, it being disjunctively intentional with reference to another, the preference is in favor of that other. In the first case, it is not the intention of the party that the incident in question should happen at all: in the latter case, the intention is rather that the other should happen, but if that cannot be, then that this in question should happen rather than that neither should, and that both, at any rate, should not happen.

All these are distinctions to be attended to in the use of the particle *or*: a particle of very ambiguous import, and of great importance in legislation.

or no in any preceding stage is immaterial, with respect to the consequences, so it be unintentional in the last. The only point, with respect to which it is material, is the proof. The more stages the act is unintentional in, the more apparent it will commonly be that it was unintentional with respect to the last. If a man, intending to strike you on the cheek, strikes you in the eye, and puts it out, it will probably be difficult for him to prove that it was not his intention to strike you in the eye. It will probably be easier, if his intention was really not to strike you, or even not to strike at all.

13. It is frequent to hear men speak of a good intention, of a bad intention; of the goodness and badness of a man's intention: a circumstance on which great stress is generally laid. It is indeed of no small importance, when properly understood: but the import of it is to the last degree ambiguous and obscure. Strictly speaking, nothing can be said to be good or bad, but either in itself; which is the case only with pain or pleasure: or on account of its effects; which is the case only with things that are the causes or preventatives of pain and pleasure. But in a figurative and less proper way of speech, a thing may also be styled good or bad, in consideration of its cause. Now the effects of an intention to do such or such an act, are the same objects which we have been speaking of under the appellation of its *consequences*: and the causes of intention are called *motives*. A man's intention then on any occasion may be styled good or bad with reference either to the consequences of the act, or with reference to his motives. If it be deemed good or bad in any sense, it must be either because it is deemed to be productive of good or of bad consequences, or because it is deemed to originate from a good or from a bad motive. But the goodness or badness of the consequences depend upon the circumstances. Now the circumstances are no objects of the intention. A man intends the act: and by his intention produces the act: but as to the circumstances, he does not intend them: he does not, inasmuch as they are circumstances of it, produce them. If by accident there be a few which he has been instrumental in producing, it has been by former intentions, directed to former acts, productive of those circumstances as the consequences: at the time in question he takes them as he finds them. Acts, with

their consequences, are objects of the will as well as of the understanding: circumstances, as such, are objects of the understanding only. All he can do with these, as such, is to know or not to know them: in other words, to be conscious of them, or not conscious. To the title of Consciousness belongs what is to be said of the goodness or badness of a man's intention, as resulting from the consequences of the act: and to the head of Motives, which is to be said of his intention, as resulting from the motive.

CHAPTER IX
Of Consciousness

1. So far with regard to the ways in which the will or intention may be concerned in the production of any incident: we come now to consider the part which the understanding or perceptive faculty may have borne, with relation to such incident.

2. A certain act has been done, and that intentionally: that act was attended with certain circumstances: upon these circumstances depended certain of its consequences; and amongst the rest, all those which were of a nature purely physical. Now then, take any one of these circumstances, it is plain that a man, at the time of doing the act from whence such consequences ensued, may have been either conscious, with respect to this circumstance, or unconscious. In other words, he may either have been aware of the circumstance, or not aware: it may either have been present to his mind, or not present. In the first case, the act may be said to have been an *advised act,* with respect to that circumstance: in the other case, an *unadvised* one.

3. There are two points with regard to which an act may have been advised or unadvised: (1) The *existence* of the circumstance itself. (2) The *materiality* of it.

4. It is manifest, that with reference to the time of the act, such circumstance may have been either *present, past, or future.*

5. An act which is unadvised is either *heedless,* or not heedless. It is termed heedless when the case is thought to be such that a person of ordinary prudence, if prompted by an ordinary share of benevolence, would have been likely to have bestowed such and so much attention and reflection upon the material circumstances as would have effectually disposed him to prevent the mischievous incident from

taking place: not heedless, when the case is not thought to be such as above mentioned.

6. Again. Whether a man did or did not suppose the existence or materiality of a given circumstance, it may be that he *did* suppose the existence and materiality of some circumstance, which either did not exist, or which, though existing, was not material. In such case the act may be said to be *mis-advised,* with respect to such imagined circumstance: and it may be said that there has been an erroneous supposition, or a *mis-supposal* in the case.

7. Now a circumstance, the existence of which is thus erroneously supposed, may be material either (1) In the way of prevention: or (2) In that of compensation. It may be said to be material in the way of prevention when its effect or tendency, had it existed, would have been to prevent the obnoxious consequences: in the way of compensation, when that effect or tendency would have been to produce other consequences, the beneficialness of which would have outweighed the mischievousness of the others.

8. It is manifest that, with reference to the time of the act, such imaginary circumstance may in either case have been supposed either to be *present, past, or future.*

9. To return to the example exhibited in the preceding chapter.

10. Tyrrel intended to shoot in the direction in which he shot; but he did not know that the king was riding so near that way. In this case the act he performed in shooting, the act of shooting, was unadvised, with respect to the existence of the circumstance of the king's being so near riding that way.

11. He knew that the king was riding that way: but at the distance at which the king was, he knew not of the probability there was that the arrow would reach him. In this case the act was unadvised, with respect to the *materiality* of the circumstance.

12. Somebody had dipped the arrow in poison, without Tyrrel's knowing it. In this case the act was unadvised, with respect to the existence of a *past* circumstance.

13. At the very instant that Tyrrel drew the bow, the king, being screened from his view by the foliage of some bushes, was riding furiously, in such manner

as to meet the arrow in a direct line: which circumstance was also more than Tyrrel knew of. In this case the act was unadvised, with respect to the existence of a *present* circumstance.

14. The king, being at a distance from court, could get nobody to dress his wound till the next day; of which circumstance Tyrrel was not aware. In this case the act was unadvised with respect to what was then a *future* circumstance.

15. Tyrrel knew of the king's being riding that way, of his being so near, and so forth; but being deceived by the foliage of the bushes, he thought he saw a bank between the spot from which he shot, and that to which the king was riding. In this case the act was *mis-advised,* proceeding on the *mis-supposal* of a *preventive* circumstance.

16. Tyrrel knew that everything was as above, nor was he deceived by the supposition of any preventive circumstance. But he believed the king to be an usurper: and supposed he was coming up to attack a person whom Tyrrel believed to be the rightful king, and who was riding by Tyrrel's side. In this case the act was also mis-advised, but proceeded on the mis-supposal of a *compensative* circumstance.

10. Let us observe the connection there is between intentionality and consciousness. When the act itself is intentional, and with respect to the existence of all the circumstances *advised,* as also with respect to the materiality of those circumstances, in relation to a given consequence, and there is no mis-supposal with regard to any preventive circumstance, that consequence must also be intentional: in other words, advisedness, with respect to the circumstances, if clear from the mis-supposal of any preventive circumstance, extends the intentionality from the act to the consequences. Those consequences may be either directly intentional, or only obliquely so: but at any rate they cannot but be intentional.

11. To go on with the example. If Tyrrel intended to shoot in the direction in which the king was riding up, and knew that the king was coming to meet the arrow, and knew the probability there was of his being shot in that same part in which he was shot, or in another

as dangerous, and with that same degree of force, and so forth, and was not misled by the erroneous supposition of a circumstance by which the shot would have been prevented from taking place, or any such other preventive circumstance, it is plain he could not but have intended the king's death. Perhaps he did not positively wish it; but for all that, in a certain sense he intended it.

12. What heedlessness is in the case of an unadvised act, rashness is in the case of a misadvised one. A misadvised act then may be either rash or not rash. It may be termed rash, when the case is thought to be such that a person of ordinary prudence, if prompted by an ordinary share of benevolence, would have employed such and so much attention and reflection to the imagined circumstance, as, by discovering to him the nonexistence, improbability, or immateriality of it, would have effectually disposed him to prevent the mischievous incident from taking place.

13. In ordinary discourse, when a man does an act of which the consequences prove mischievous, it is a common thing to speak of him as having acted with a good intention or with a bad intention, of his intention's being a good one or a bad one. The epithets good and bad are all this while applied, we see, to the intention: but the application of them is most commonly governed by a supposition formed with regard to the nature of the motive. The act, though eventually it prove mischievous, is said to be done with a good intention, when it is supposed to issue from a motive which is looked upon as a good motive: with a bad intention, when it is supposed to be the result of motive which is looked upon as a bad motive. But the nature of the consequences intended, and the nature of the motive which gave birth to the intention, are objects which, though intimately connected, are perfectly distinguishable. The intention might therefore with perfect propriety be styled a good one, whatever were the motive. It might be styled a good one, when not only the consequences of the act *prove* mischievous, but the motive which gave birth to it *was* what is called a bad one. To warrant the speaking of the intention as being a good one, it is sufficient if the consequences of the act, had they proved what to the agent they seemed likely to be, *would* have been of a beneficial

nature. And in the same manner the intention may be bad, when not only the consequences of the act prove beneficial, but the motive which gave birth to it was a good one.

14. Now, when a man has a mind to speak of your *intention* as being good or bad, with reference to the consequences, if he speaks of it at all he must use the word intention, for there is no other. But if a man means to speak of the *motive* from which your intention originated, as being a good or a bad one, he is certainly not obliged to use the word intention: it is at least as well to use the word motive. By the supposition he means the motive; and very likely he may *not* mean the intention. For what is true of the one is very often not true of the other. The motive may be good when the intention is bad: the intention may be good when the motive is bad: whether they are both good or both bad, or the one good and the other bad, makes, as we shall see hereafter, a very essential difference with regard to the consequences. It is therefore much better, when motive is meant, never to say intention.

15. An example will make this clear. Out of malice a man prosecutes you for a crime of which he believes you to be guilty, but of which in fact you are not guilty. Here the *consequences* of his conduct are mischievous: for they are mischievous to you at any rate, in virtue of the shame and anxiety which you are made to suffer while the prosecution is depending: to which is to be added, in case of your being convicted, the evil of the punishment. To you therefore they are mischievous; nor is there anyone to whom they are beneficial. The man's *motive* was also what is called a bad one: for malice will be allowed by everybody to be a bad motive. However, the *consequences* of his conduct, had they proved such as he believed them likely to be, would have been good: for in them would have been included the punishment of a criminal, which is a benefit to all who are exposed to suffer by a crime of the like nature. The *intention* therefore, in this case, though not in a common way of speaking the motive, might be styled a *good* one. But of motives more particularly in the next chapter.

16. In the same sense the intention, whether it be positively good or no, so long as it is not bad, may be termed innocent. Accordingly, let the consequences have proved mischievous,

and let the motive have been what it will, the intention may be termed innocent in either of two cases: (1) In the case of *unadvisedness* with respect to any of the circumstances on which the mischievousness of the consequences depended: (2) In the case of *misadvisedness* with respect to any circumstance, which, had it been what it appeared to be, would have served either to prevent or to outweigh the mischief.

. . .

18. The above-mentioned definitions and distinctions are far from being mere matters of speculation. They are capable of the most extensive and constant application, as well to moral discourse as to legislative practice. Upon the degree and bias of a man's intention, upon the absence or presence of consciousness or mis-supposal, depend a great part of the good and bad, more especially of the bad consequences of an act; and on this, as well as other grounds, a great part of the demand for punishment. The presence of intention with regard to such or such a consequence, and of consciousness with regard to such or such a circumstance, of the act will form so many criminative circumstances, or essential ingredients in the composition of this or that offense: applied to other circumstances, consciousness will form a ground of aggravation, annexable to the like offense. In almost all cases, the absence of intention with regard to certain consequences, and the absence of consciousness, or the presence of mis-supposal, with regard to certain circumstances, will constitute so many grounds of extenuation.

CHAPTER X

Of Motives

1. It is an acknowledged truth, that every kind of act whatever, and consequently every kind of offense, is apt to assume a different character, and be attended with different effects, according to the nature of the *motive* which gives birth to it. This makes it requisite to take a view of the several motives by which human conduct is liable to be influenced.

2. By a motive, in the most extensive sense in which the word is ever used with reference to a thinking being, is meant anything that can contribute to give birth to, or even to prevent, any kind of action. Now the action of a thinking being is the act either of the body, or only of the mind: and an act of the mind is an act either of the intellectual faculty, or of the will. Acts of the intellectual faculty will sometimes rest in the understanding merely, without exerting any influence in the production of any acts of the will. Motives which are not of a nature to influence any other acts than those may be styled purely *speculative* motives, or motives resting in speculation. But as to these acts, neither do they exercise any influence over external acts, or over their consequences, nor consequently over any pain or any pleasure that may be in the number of such consequences. Now it is only on account of their tendency to produce either pain or pleasure, that any acts can be material. With acts, therefore, that rest purely in the understanding, we have not here any concern: nor therefore with any object, if any such there be, which, in the character of a motive, can have no influence on any other acts than those.

3. The motives with which alone we have any concern are such as are of a nature to act upon the will. By a motive then, in this sense of the word, is to be understood any thing whatsoever, which, by influencing the will of a sensitive being, is supposed to serve as a means of determining him to act, or voluntarily to forbear to act, upon any occasion. Motives of this sort, in contradistinction to the former, may be styled *practical* motives, or motives applying to practice.

4. Owing to the poverty and unsettled state of language, the word *motive* is employed indiscriminately to denote two kinds of objects, which, for the better understanding of the subject, it is necessary should be distinguished. On some occasions it is employed to denote any of those really existing incidents from whence the act in question is supposed to take its rise. The sense it bears on these occasions may be styled its literal or *unfigurative* sense. On other occasions it is employed to denote a certain fictitious entity, a passion, an affection of the mind, an ideal being which upon the happening of any such incident is considered as operating upon the mind, and prompting it to take that course toward which it is impelled by the influence of such incident. Motives of this class are Avarice, Indolence, Benevolence, and so forth; as we shall see more particularly farther on. This latter may be styled the *figurative* sense of the term *motive*.

5. As to the real incidents to which the name of motive is also given, these too are of two very different kinds. They may be either (1) The *internal* perception of any individual lot of pleasure or pain, the expectation of which is looked upon as calculated to determine you to act in such or such a manner; as the pleasure of acquiring such a sum of money, the pain of exerting yourself on such an occasion, and so forth: or (2) Any *external* event, the happening whereof is regarded as having a tendency to bring about the perception of such pleasure or such pain; for instance, the coming up of a lottery ticket, by which the possession of the money devolves to you; or the breaking out of a fire in the house you are in, which makes it necessary for you to quit it. The former kind of motives may be termed interior, or internal: the latter exterior, or external.

6. Two other senses of the term *motive* need also to be distinguished. Motive refers necessarily to action. It is a pleasure, pain, or other event, that prompts to action. Motive then, in one sense of the word, must be previous to such event. But, for a man to be governed by any motive, he must in every case look beyond that event which is called his action; he must look to the consequences of it: and it is only in this way that the idea of pleasure, of pain, or of any other event, can give birth to it. He must look, therefore, in every case, to some event posterior to the act in contemplation: an event which as yet exists not, but stands only in prospect. Now, as it is in all cases difficult, and in most cases unnecessary, to distinguish between objects so intimately connected, as the posterior possible object which is thus looked forward to, and the present existing object or event which takes place upon a man's looking forward to the other, they are both of them spoken of under the same appellation, *motive*. To distinguish them, the one first mentioned may be termed a motive in *prospect,* the other a motive in *esse*: and under each of these denominations will come as well exterior as internal motives. A fire breaks out in your neighbor's house: you are under apprehension of its extending to your own: you are apprehensive, that if you stay in it, you will be burnt: you accordingly run out of it. This then is the act: the others are all motives to it. The event of the fire's breaking out in your neighbor's house is an external motive, and that in

esse: the idea or belief of the probability of the fire's extending to your own house, that of your being burnt if you continue, and the pain you feel at the thought of such a catastrophe, are all so many internal events, but still in *esse*: the event of the fire's actually extending to your own house, and that of your being actually burnt by it, external motives in prospect: the pain you would feel at seeing your house a burning, and the pain you would feel while you yourself were burning, internal motives in prospect: which events, according as the matter turns out, may come to be in *esse*: but then, of course, they will cease to act as motives.

7. Of all these motives, which stand nearest to the act, to the production of which they all contribute, is that internal motive in *esse* which consists in the expectation of the internal motive in prospect: the pain or uneasiness you feel at the thoughts of being burnt.[4] All other motives are more or less remote: the motives in prospect, in proportion as the period at which they are expected to happen is more distant from the period at which the act takes place, and consequently later in point of time: the motives in *esse,* in proportion as they also are more distant from that period, and consequently earlier in point of time.

8. It has already been observed that with motives of which the influence terminates altogether in the understanding, we have nothing here to do. If then, amongst objects that are spoken of as motives with reference to the understanding, there be any which concern us here, it is only in as far as such objects may, through the medium of the understanding, exercise an influence over the will. It is in this way, and in this way only, that any objects, in virtue of any tendency they may have to influence the sentiment of belief, may in a practical sense act in the character of motives. Any objects, by tending to induce a belief concerning the existence, actual, or probable, of a practical motive; that is, concerning the probability of a motive in prospect, or the

---

[4] Whether it be the expectation of being burnt, or the pain that accompanies that expectation, that is the immediate internal motive spoken of, may be difficult to determine. It may even be questioned, perhaps, whether they are distinct entities. Both questions, however, seem to be mere questions of words, and the solution of them altogether immaterial. Even the other kinds of motives, though for some purposes they demand a separate consideration, are, however, so intimately allied, that it will often be scarce practicable, and not always material, to avoid confounding them, as they have always hitherto been confounded.

existence of a motive in *esse*; may exercise an influence on the will, and rank with those other motives that have been placed under the name of practical. The pointing out of motives such as these is what we frequently mean when we talk of giving reasons. Your neighbor's house is on fire as before. I observe to you that at the lower part of your neighbor's house is some woodwork, which joins on to yours; that the flames have caught this woodwork, and so forth; which I do in order to dispose you to believe as I believe, that if you stay in your house much longer you will be burnt. In doing this, then, I suggest motives to your understanding; which motives by the tendency they have to give birth to or strengthen a pain, which operates upon you in the character of an internal motive in *esse,* join their force, and act as motives upon the will.

§2. No motives either constantly good or constantly bad

9. In all this chain of motives, the principal or original link seems to be the last internal motive in prospect: it is to this that all the other motives in prospect owe their materiality: and the immediately acting motive its existence. This motive in prospect, we see, is always some pleasure, or some pain; some pleasure, which the act in question is expected to be a means of continuing or producing: some pain which it is expected to be a means of discontinuing or preventing. A motive is substantially nothing more than pleasure or pain, operating in a certain manner.

10. Now, pleasure is in *itself* a good: nay, even setting aside immunity from pain, the only good: pain is in itself an evil; and, indeed, without exception, the only evil; or else the words good and evil have no meaning. And this is alike true of every sort of pain, and of every sort of pleasure. It follows, therefore, immediately and incontestably, that *there is no such thing as any sort of motive that is in itself a bad one.*[5]

11. It is common, however, to speak of

[5] Let a man's motive be ill-will; call it even malice, envy, cruelty; it is still a kind of pleasure that is his motive: the pleasure he takes at the thought of the pain which he sees, or expects to see, his adversary undergo. Now even this wretched pleasure, taken by itself, is good: it may be faint; it may be short; it must at any rate be impure; yet while it lasts, and before any bad consequences arrive, it is as good as any other that is not more intense. . . .

actions as proceeding from *good* or *bad* motives: in which case the motives meant are such as are internal. The expression is far from being an accurate one; and as it is apt to occur in the consideration of almost every kind of offense, it will be requisite to settle the precise meaning of it, and observe how far it quadrates with the truth of things.

12. With respect to goodness and badness, as it is with everything else that is not itself either pain or pleasure, so is it with motives. If they are good or bad, it is only on account of their effects: good, on account of their tendency to produce pleasure, or avert pain: bad, on account of their tendency to produce pain, or avert pleasure. Now the case is that from one and the same motive, and from every kind of motive, may proceed actions that are good, others that are bad, and others that are indifferent. This we shall proceed to show with respect to all the different kinds of motives, as determined by the various kinds of pleasures and pains.

13. Such an analysis, useful as it is, will be found to be a matter of no small difficulty; owing, in great measure, to a certain perversity of structure which prevails more or less throughout all languages. To speak of motives, as of anything else, one must call them by their names. But the misfortune is that it is rare to meet with a motive of which the name expresses that and nothing more. Commonly along with the very name of the motive is tacitly involved a proposition imputing to it a certain quality; a quality which, in many cases, will appear to include that very goodness or badness, concerning which we are here inquiring whether, properly speaking, it be or be not imputable to motives. To use the common phrase, in most cases, the name of the motive is a word which is employed either only in a good sense, or else only in a *bad sense.* Now, when a word is spoken of as being used in a good sense, all that is necessarily meant is this: that, in conjunction with the idea of the object it is put to signify, it conveys an idea of *approbation*: that is, of a pleasure or satisfaction, entertained by the person who employs the term at the thoughts of such object. In like manner, when a word is spoken of as being used in a bad sense, all that is necessarily meant is this: that, in conjunction with the idea of the object it is put to signify, it conveys an idea of *disapprobation*: that is, of a displeasure entertained by

the person who employs the term at the thoughts of such object. Now the circumstance on which such approbation is grounded will, as naturally as any other, be the opinion of the *goodness* of the object in question, as above explained : such, at least it must be, upon the principle of utility : so, on the other hand, the circumstance on which any such disapprobation is grounded will as naturally as any other be the opinion of the badness of the object : such, at least, it must be, in as far as the principle of utility is taken for the standard.

Now there are certain motives which, unless in a few particular cases, have scarcely any other name to be expressed by but such a word as is used only in a good sense. This is the case, for example, with the motives of piety and honor. The consequence of this is that if, in speaking of such a motive, a man should have occasion to apply the epithet bad to any actions which he mentions as apt to result from it, he must appear to be guilty of a contradiction in terms. But the names of motives which have scarcely any other name to be expressed by, but such a word as is used only in a bad sense, are many more. This is the case, for example, with the motives of lust and avarice. And accordingly, if in speaking of any such motive, a man should have

occasion to apply the epithets good or indifferent to any actions which he mentions as apt to result from it, he must here also appear to be guilty of a similar contradiction.

This perverse association of ideas cannot, it is evident, but throw great difficulties in the way of the inquiry now before us. Confining himself to the language most in use, a man can scarce avoid running, in appearance, into perpetual contradiction. His propositions will appear, on the one hand, repugnant to truth ; and on the other hand, adverse to utility. As paradoxes, they will excite contempt : as mischievous paradoxes, indignation. For the truths he labors to convey, however important, and however salutary, his reader is never the better : and he himself is much the worse. To obviate this inconvenience, completely, he has but this one unpleasant remedy ; to lay aside the old phraseology and invent a new one. Happy the man whose language is ductile enough to permit him this resource. To palliate the inconvenience, where that method of obviating it is impracticable, he has nothing left for it but to enter into a long discussion, to state the whole matter at large, to confess that for the sake of promoting the purposes, he has violated the established laws of language, and to throw himself upon the mercy of his readers.

Intention*

The bodily movements which immediately follow our desires of them are *acts* (properly so called).

But every act is followed by consequences ; and is also attended by *concomitants,* which are styled its *circumstances.*

To desire the *act* is to *will* it. To *expect* any of its *consequences* is to *intend* those consequences.

The act itself is *intended* as well as *willed.* For every volition is accomplished by an expectation or belief that the bodily movement wished will immediately follow the wish.

A consequence of the act is never *willed.* For none but acts themselves are the appropriate objects of volitions. Nor is it always *intended.* For the party who wills the act,

may not expect the consequence. If a consequence of the act be *desired,* it is probably *intended.* But (as I shall show immediately) an *intended* consequence is not always desired. Intentions, therefore, regard *acts* : or they regard the *consequence of acts.*

When I will an act, I expect or intend the *act* which is the appropriate object of the volition. And when I will an act, I may expect, contemplate, or intend some given event, as a certain or contingent *consequence* of the act which I will.

Hence (no doubt) the frequent confusion of Will and Intention. Feeling *that will implies intention* (or that the appropriate objects of volitions are intended as well as willed) numerous writers upon Jurisprudence (and Mr. Bentham amongst the number) employ "will" and "intention" as synonymous or

* John Austin, *Lectures on Jurisprudence* (London: John Murray, 1873), I, 433–37, 449–54.

equivalent terms. They forget *that intention does not imply will*; or that the appropriate objects of certain intentions are not the appropriate objects of volitions. The agent may not intend a consequence of his act. In other words, when the agent wills the act, he may not contemplate that given event as a certain or contingent consequence of the act which he wills.

For example:

My yard or garden is divided from a road by a high paling. I am shooting with a pistol at a mark chalked upon this paling. A passenger then on the road, but whom the fence intercepts from my sight, is wounded by one of the shots. For the shot pierces the paling; passes to the road; and hits the passenger.

Now, when I aim at the mark, and pull the trigger, I may not *intend* to hurt the passenger. I may not contemplate the hurt of a passenger as a contingent consequence of the act. For though the hurt of a passenger *be* a probable consequence, I may not think of it, or advert to it, *as* a consequence. Or, though I may advert to it as a possible consequence, I may think that the fence will intercept the shot, and prevent it from passing to the road. Or the road may be one which is seldom traveled, and I may think the presence of a stranger at that place and time extremely improbable.

On any of these suppositions, I am clear of *intending* the harm: Though (as I shall show hereafter) I may be guilty of *heedlessness* or *rashness*. Before *intention* can be defined exactly, the import of those terms must be taken into consideration.

Where the agent *intends* a consequence of the act, he may wish the consequence, or he may *not* wish it.

And, if he *wish* the consequence, he may wish it as an *end,* or he may wish it as a *mean* to an end.

I will illustrate these three suppositions by adducing examples. But before I exemplify these three suppositions, I will endeavor to explain what I mean, when I say "that a consequence of an act may be wished as an *end.*"

Strictly speaking, no external consequence of any act is desired as an *end.*

The end or ultimate purpose of every volition and act is a feeling or sentiment: is pleasure, direct or positive; or is the pleasure which arises *in*directly from the removal or prevention of pain. But where the pleasure, which (in strictness) is the end of the act, can only be attained through a *given* external consequence, that external consequence is inseparable from the end; and is styled (with sufficient precision) the end of the act and the volition. For example, If you shoot me to death because you hate me mortally, my death is a necessary condition to the attainment of your end. The end of the act is to allay the deadly antipathy. But the end can only be attained through my death. And my death (which is an intended consequence of the act) may, therefore, be styled the *end* of the act and the volition.

I stated in my last Lecture that the bodily movements which are the appropriate objects of volitions are not desired as *ends.*

But that is true of every outward object which is the object of a desire. This, therefore, will not distinguish volitions from other desires.

Nor can it be said, that the appropriate objects of volitions are desired as means to ends external, or to remote ends. In most cases they are. But in some they are not. Namely, dancing, etc., for nothing but the present pleasure.

The true test is that they are the only desires immediately followed by their appropriate or direct objects.

Where an intended consequence is wished as an *end* or a *mean,* motive and intention concur. In other words, The consequence intended is also wished; and the wish of that consequence suggests the volition.

I will now exemplify these three varieties of intention at which I have pointed already.

The varieties are the following:

First. The agent may *intend* a consequence; and that consequence may be the *end* of his act.

Secondly. He may *intend* a consequence; but he may desire that consequence as a *mean* to an end.

Thirdly. He may *intend* the consequence, without desiring it.

As examples of these three varieties, I will adduce three cases of intentional killing.

You hate me mortally: And, in order that you may appease that painful and importunate feeling, you shoot me dead.

Now here you *intend* my death: And (taking the word *"end"* in the meaning which I have just explained) my death is the *end* of the act, and of the volition which precedes the act. Nothing but that consequence would accomplish the purpose, which (speaking with metaphysical precision) is the end of the act and the volition. Nothing but that consequence would allay the painful sentiment of which you purpose ridding yourself when you shoot me. Nothing but that consequence would appease your hate, or satisfy your malice.

Again:

You shoot me, that you may take my purse. I refuse to deliver my purse when you demand it. I defend my purse to the best of my ability. And, in order that you may remove the obstacle which my resistance opposes to your purpose, you pull out a pistol and shoot me dead.

Now here you *intend* my death, and you also *desire* my death. But you desire it as a *mean,* and not as an *end.* Your desire of my death is not the ultimate *motive* suggesting the volition and the act. Your ultimate motive is your desire of my purse. And if I would deliver my purse, you would not shoot me.

Lastly:

You shoot at Sempronius or Styles, at Titius or Nokes, desiring and intending to kill him. The death of Styles is the *end* of your volition and act. Your desire of his death is the *ultimate motive* to the volition. You contemplate his death, as the probable consequence of the act.

But when you shoot at Styles, *I* am talking with him, and am standing close by him. And, from the position in which I stand with regard to the person you aim at, you think it not unlikely that you may kill *me* in your attempt to kill *him.* You fire, and kill me accordingly. Now here you *intend* my death, without *desiring* it. The *end* of the volition and act is the death of Styles. *My* death is neither desired as an *end,* nor is it desired as a *mean*: *My* death *subserves not* your end: you are not a bit the nearer to the death of Styles by killing *me.* But since you contemplate my death as a probable consequence of your act, you *intend* my death although you *desire* it not.

It follows from the nature of Volitions, that *forbearances from acts* are not *willed,* but *intended.*

To *will* is to wish or desire one of those bodily movements which immediately follow our desires of them. These movements are the only *acts,* properly so called. Consequently, "To will a forbearance" (or "to will the absence or negation of an act") is a flat contradiction in terms.

When I forbear from an act, I *will.* But I will an act *other* than that from which I forbear or abstain: And knowing that the act which I will excludes the act forborne, I *intend* the forbearance. In other words, I contemplate the forbearance as a *consequence* of the act which I will; or, rather, as a necessary *condition* to the act which I will. For if I willed the act from which I forbear, I should not will (at this time) the act which I presently will.

For example, It is my duty to come hither at seven o'clock. But, instead of coming hither at seven o'clock, I go to the Playhouse at that hour, conscious that I ought to come hither.

Now, in this case, my absence from the room is *intentional.* I know that my coming hither is inconsistent with my going thither: that, if my legs brought me to the University, they would not carry me to the Playhouse.

If I *forgot* that I ought to come hither, my absence would not be *intentional,* but the effect of *negligence.*

• • •

The intentions which I considered in my last Lecture are coupled with present volitions, and with present acts.

The party wishes or wills certain of the bodily movements which immediately follow our desires of them. He expects or believes, at the moment of the volition, that the bodily movements which he wills will certainly and immediately follow it: and he also expects or believes, at the moment of the volition, that some given event or events will certainly or probably follow those bodily movements.

In other words, he presently *wills* some given act; intending the act (as the consequence of the volition) and intending some further event (as the consequence of the volition and the act).

But a *present* intention to do a *future* act is coupled neither with the performance of the act, nor with a present will to do it. The present intention is not coupled with the present performance of the act. For the intention, though present, regards the future. Nor is it coupled with the present *will* to *do* the act intended. For to *will* an act is to *do* the act, provided that the bodily organ, which is the instrument of the volition and the act, be in a sound or healthy state.

Consequently, to do an act with a present intention is widely different from a present intention to do a future act. In the first case, the act is willed and done. In the second case, it is neither willed nor done, although it is intended.

A present intention to do a future act may (I think) be resolved into the following elements.

First, The party *desires* a given object, either as an end, or as a mean to an end.

Secondly, He *believes* that the object is attainable through acts of his own: Or (speaking more properly) he believes that acts of his own would give him a chance of attaining it.

Thirdly, He *presently* believes that he shall do acts *in future,* for the purpose of attaining the object.

A *belief* "that the desired object is attainable through acts of our own" and "that we shall do acts thereafter for the purpose of attaining it" are necessary constituents of the complex notion which is styled "a present intention to do a future act."

If these be absent, we simply desire the object.

Unless I believe that the object be attainable through acts of my own, I cannot presently believe that I shall do acts hereafter for the purpose of attaining the object. I cannot believe that I shall try to attain an object, knowing that my efforts to attain it are utterly ineffectual.

Intention supposes that the object is attainable through conduct of our own. Or (as it is commonly said) that the attainment of the object depends upon our will. And though I believe that the object be attainable through acts of my own, I *simply desire* or *barely wish* the object, unless I *presently* believe that I shall do acts *hereafter* for the purpose of attaining it.

For example, if I wish for a watch hanging in a watchmaker's window, but without believing that I shall try to take it from the owner, I am perfectly clear of *intending* to steal the watch, although I am guilty of *coveting* my neighbor's goods (provided that the wish recur frequently).

The belief "that the desired object is attainable through acts of our own" is necessarily implied in the belief "that we shall do acts hereafter for the purpose of attaining it."

Consequently, a present intention to do a future act may be defined to be: "A present *desire* of an object (either as an end or a mean), coupled with a present *belief* that we shall do acts hereafter for the purpose of attaining the object."

It may also be distinguished briefly from a present volition and intention in the following manner:

In the latter case, we presently will, and presently act, *expecting* a given consequence. In the former case, we neither presently will nor presently act, but we *presently* expect or believe that we *shall* will *hereafter.*

When we *will* a present act, intending a given consequence, it is frequently said "that we *will* the consequence as well as the act." And when we intend a future act, it is frequently said "that we *will* the act *now,* although we postpone the execution to a future time." In either case, will is confounded with intention.

When we intend a future act, it is also commonly said "that we resolve or determine to do it"; or "that we make up our minds to do it." Frequently, too, a verbal distinction is taken between a strong and a weak intention; that is to say, between a strong or a weak belief that we shall do the act in future. Where the belief is strong, we are more apt to say "that we *intend* the act." Where the belief is weak, we are more apt to say "that we *believe* we shall do it."

Such being the forms of langue, it is somewhat difficult to admit, at first hearing, "that a present *intention* to do a future act is nothing but a present *belief* that we shall do an act in future." But that nothing but this really passes in the mind any man may convince himself by examining the state of his mind when he intends a future act.

When we speak of *willing* a future act, we are not speaking of our intention to do the future act, but of our wish for the object which we believe may be attained through the act. Or, rather, our wish for the object, and our intention of resorting to the mean, are blended and confounded. And as every volition is a desire, and is also coupled with an intention, the compound of desire and intention is naturally styled a volition, although it is impossible (from the nature of the case) that we *can* will an act of which we defer the execution.

When we say "that we have resolved or determined on an act," or "that we have made up our minds to do an act," we merely mean this : "that we have examined the object of the desire, and have considered the means of attaining it, and that, since we think the object worthy of pursuit, we believe we shall resort to the means which will give us a chance of getting it."

Here also, the desire of the object is confounded with the *belief* which properly constitutes the intention. Every genuine volition being a desire, and every genuine volition being coupled with an intention, we naturally extend the terms which are proper to *volitions* to every desire which is combined with an intention.

It is clear that such expressions as "determining," "resolving," "making up one's mind," can only apply in strictness to "volitions" : that is to say, to those desires which are instantly followed by their objects, and by which it may be said that we are *concluded,* from the moment at which we conceive them. He who wills necessarily acts as he wills, and cannot will (with effect) that he will retract or recall the volition. He has "determined" : he has "resolved" : He has "made up his mind." He is *concluded* by his own volition. He cannot *un*-will that which he has willed.

But when such expressions as "resolving" and "determining" are applied to a present intention to do a future act, they simply denote that we desire the object *intensely,* and that we believe (with corresponding confidence) we shall resort to means of attaining it.

And this perfectly accords with common apprehension, although it may sound (at first hearing) as if it were a paradox. For, every *intention* (or every so-styled *will*), which regards the future, is *ambulatory* or *revocable.* That is to say, the present *desire* of the object may cease hereafter ; and the present *belief* that we shall resort to the means of attaining it will, of course, cease with the wish for it. We cannot *believe* that we shall try to get that, for which we *know* that we care not.

It is clear that we may presently intend a future forbearance as well as a future *act.*

We may either desire an object inconsistent with the act to be forborne, *or* we may positively dislike the probable consequences of the act. In the first case, we may presently believe that we shall forbear from the act hereafter, in order that we may attain the object which we wish or desire. In the latter case, we may presently believe that we shall forbear from the act hereafter, in order that we may avoid the consequences from which we are averse.

[*Every* present *forbearance* from a given act is not preceded or accompanied by a present *volition* to do another act.

[It may be preceded or accompanied by mere inaction ; e.g., I may lie perfectly still, *intending* not to rise.

[But, still, it is generally true that every present forbearance *is* preceded or accompanied by a volition. In our waking hours, our lives are a series (nearly unbroken) of volitions and acts. And, when we forbear, we commonly do a something inconsistent with the act forborne, and which we are conscious is inconsistent with it.]

Where a forbearance is preceded or accompanied by inaction, the desire leading to the forbearance is not to be compared to a volition. The forbearance is not like the act, the direct and appropriate object of the wish.

All that can be said (in general) of intentions to *act* in future, may be applied (with slight modifications) to intentions to *forbear* in the future. I confine myself to intentions to *act* in future, in order that my expressions may be less complex, and, by consequence, more intelligible.

When we intend a future act, we also intend certain of its consequences. In other words, we believe that certain consequences will follow that future act, which we presently believe we shall hereafter will. This is necessarily implied in every intention of the sort. For our present wish or desire of some probable consequence of the act is our reason for believing *presently* that we shall do the act *in future.*

But we may also intend or expect that the act may be followed by consequences, which we do not desire, or from which we are averse. For example ; I may intend to shoot at and kill you, so soon as I can find an opportunity. But knowing that you are always accompanied by friends or companions, I believe that I may kill or wound one of these in my intended attempt to kill you.

Here, the object which I wish or desire is

your death. I *intend* the act, or I believe that I *shall* will it, because I desire your death. But I also believe that the act will be followed by a consequence from which I am averse—by a consequence which is not the *ground* of my present intention, although I intend *in spite of it.* I intend a future act. I intend a consequence which I desire. And I also intend a consequence from which I am averse.

The execution of every intention to do a future act, is necessarily postponed to a future time.

Every intention to do a future act is also revocable or ambulatory. That is to say, before the intention be carried into execution, the desire which is the ground of the intention may cease or be extinguished, or, although it continue, may be outweighed by inconsistent desires.

But though the execution of the intention be always contingent, the intention itself may be certain or uncertain. I may regard the intended act as one which I shall certainly will; or I may regard it as one which I shall will on the happening of a given contingency. In either case, I may either intend a precise and definite act, or I may merely intend some act for the purpose of attaining my object.

For example; I may intend to kill you by *shooting,* at a given *place* and *time.* Or (though I intend to kill you) I may neither have determined the *mode* by which I shall attain my object, nor the *time* or *place* for executing the murderous design. In cases of the first class, the intention, design, or purpose, is settled, determinate, or matured. In cases of the latter class, it is unsettled, indeterminate, or undigested.

Psychological Hedonism*

... The truth is that there is an ambiguity in the word Pleasure. ... By Pleasure we commonly mean an agreeable sensation not necessarily connected with desire or volition, as it may arise from external causes without having been foreseen or desired at all. But when we speak of a man doing something at his own "pleasure," or as he "pleases," we signify the mere fact of choice or preference; the mere determination of the will in a certain direction. Now, if by "pleasant" we mean that which influences choice, exercises a certain attractive force on the will, it is not a psychological truth, but a tautological assertion, to say that we desire what is pleasant—or even that we desire a thing in proportion as it appears pleasant. But if we take "pleasure" to mean "agreeable sensation," it then becomes a really debatable question whether our active impulses are always consciously directed toward the attainment of agreeable (or the avoidance of disagreeable) sensations as their end. ...

... Butler, as is well known, distinguishes self-love, or the impulse toward our own pleasure, from "particular movements toward particular external objects—honor, power, the

harm or good of another"; the actions proceeding from which are "no otherwise interested than as every action of every creature must from the nature of the case be; for no one can act but from a desire, or choice, or preference of his own." Such particular passions or appetites are, he goes on to say, *"necessarily presupposed by the very idea* of an interested pursuit; since the very idea of interest or happiness consists in this, that an appetite or affection enjoys its object." We could not pursue pleasure at all, unless we had desires for something else than pleasure; for pleasure consists in the satisfaction of just these "disinterested" impulses.

Butler has clearly over-stated his case; for many pleasures, such as those of sight, hearing, and smell, together with many emotional pleasures, occur to us without any relation to previous desires, and it is quite *conceivable* that our appetitive consciousness might consist entirely of impulses toward such pleasures as these. But as a matter of fact, it seems to me that throughout the whole scale of our impulses, sensual, emotional, and intellectual alike, we can distinguish desires of which the object, what we are consciously moved to realize, is something other than our own pleasure.

We may take an illustration of this from

* Henry Sidgwick, *The Methods of Ethics* (London: Macmillan and Co., 1877), pp. 37–46. Footnotes have been renumbered.

the impulses commonly placed lowest in the scale. Hunger, so far as I can observe, is a direct impulse to eat food. Its indulgence is no doubt commonly attended with an agreeable feeling of more or less intensity: but it cannot, I think, be strictly said that this agreeable feeling is the object of hunger, and that it is the representation of this pleasure which stimulates the will of the hungry man. Of course hunger is frequently and naturally accompanied with anticipation of the pleasure of eating: but careful introspection seems to show that the two are by no means inseparable: and that even when they occur together the pleasure is the object not of the primary appetite, but of a secondary desire which is to be distinguished from the former.

Indeed it is so obvious that hunger is something different from the desire for pleasure that some writers have regarded its volitional stimulus (and that of appetite generally) as a case of aversion from pain. This, however, seems to me a distinct mistake in psychological classification, though one very natural and easily explained. Hunger, and we may say desire generally, is a state of consciousness so far similar to pain that in both we feel a stimulus prompting us to pass from the present state into a different one. But in pain the impulse is to get out of the present state and pass into some other state which is only negatively represented as different from the present: whereas in desire proper we are indifferent to the present consciousness, and the impulse is toward the realization of some future end positively conceived. The desire itself seems to be a state of excitement which becomes pleasurable or painful according to the nature of its concomitant circumstances, and is often not definitely either the one or the other. When it is, for any reason, balked of its effect in causing action, it is generally painful in some degree, and so a secondary aversion to the state of desire is generated, which blends itself with the desire and may easily be confounded with it. But here we may distinguish the two impulses by observing the different kinds of conduct to which they occasionally prompt: for the aversion to the pain of ungratified desire, though it may act as an additional stimulus toward the gratification of the desire, may also (and often does) prompt us to get rid of the pain by suppressing the desire. We may observe also that desire, even when it has become a pain or uneasiness, is

often but very slightly painful: so that the mere aversion to it as pain is but a small part of the total volitional stimulus of which we are conscious.

When, however, the desire is having its natural effect in causing the actions which tend to the attainment of its object, it seems to be commonly a more or less pleasurable consciousness: even when this attainment is still remote. Or at least the consciousness of eager activity, in which this desire is an essential element, is highly pleasurable: and in fact such pleasures, which we may call generally the pleasures of Pursuit, constitute a considerable item in the total enjoyment of life. Indeed it is almost a commonplace to say that they are more important than the pleasures of Attainment: and in many cases it is the prospect of the former rather than of the latter that induces us to engage in the pursuit. In such cases it is peculiarly easy to distinguish the desire of the object pursued from a desire of the pleasure of attaining it: as in fact attainment is not originally represented in the mind as a source of pleasure, but only becomes pleasant in prospect because the pursuit itself stimulates a desire for what is pursued. Take, for example, a favorite amusement of rich Englishmen. What is the motive that impels a man to fox-hunting? It is not the pleasure of catching the fox. Nobody, before entering on the chase, represents to himself the killing of the fox as a source of gratification, apart from the eagerness produced by pursuit. What the fox-hunter deliberately and before the chase desires is, not the capture of the fox, but the pleasure of pursuing it; only of this pleasure a temporary vehement desire to catch the fox is an essential condition. This desire, which does not exist at first, is stimulated to considerable intensity by the pursuit itself: and in proportion as it is thus stimulated both the mere pursuit becomes pleasurable, and the capture, which was originally indifferent, comes to afford a keen enjoyment.[1]

The same phenomenon is exhibited in the case of more intellectual kinds of pursuit, where the objects sought are more abstract. It often happens that a man, feeling his life languid and devoid of interests, begins to

---

[1] To avoid misapprehension, it may be well to observe that I am not trying to give a complete analysis of the whole enjoyment of hunting, but only to define accurately a single (but the most characteristic) element of it.

occupy himself in the pursuit of some end, for the sake not of the end but of the occupation. At first, very likely, the occupation is irksome: but soon, as he foresaw, he begins to "take an interest" in the end at which he is aiming: so that his pursuit becoming eager becomes also a source of agreeable sensations. Here, again, it is no doubt true that in proportion as his desire for the end becomes strong, the attainment of it becomes pleasant in prospect: but it would be inverting cause and effect to say that it is this prospective pleasure that he desires.

When we compare these pleasures with those previously discussed, another important observation suggests itself. In the former case, though we could distinguish appetite, as it appears in consciousness, from the desire of the pleasure attending the satisfaction of appetite, there appeared to be no incompatibility between the two. The fact that the gourmand is dominated by the desire of the pleasures of eating in no way impedes the development in him of the appetite which is a necessary condition of these pleasures. But when we turn to the pleasures of the chase, we seem to perceive this incompatibility to a certain extent. In all forms of pursuit a certain enthusiasm is necessary to obtain full enjoyment. A man who maintains throughout an epicurean mood, fixing his aim on his own pleasure, does not catch the full spirit of the chase; his eagerness never gets just the sharpness of edge which imparts to the pleasure its highest zest and flavor. Here comes into view what we might call the fundamental paradox of Hedonism, that the impulse toward pleasure, if too predominant, defeats its own aim. This effect is not visible, or at any rate is scarcely visible, in the case of passive sensual pleasures. But of our active enjoyments generally, whether the activities on which they attend are classed as "bodily" or as "intellectual" (as well as of many emotional pleasures), it may certainly be said that we cannot attain them, at least in their best form, so long as we concentrate our aim on them. Nor is it only that the exercise of our faculties is insufficiently stimulated by the mere desire of the pleasure attending it, and requires the presence of other more objective, "extra-regarding," impulses, in order to be fully developed: we may go further and say that these other impulses must be temporarily predominant and absorbing, if the exercise and its attendant gratification are to attain their full height. Many middle-aged Englishmen would maintain the doctrine that business is more agreeable than amusement; but they would hardly find it so, if they transacted the business with a perpetual conscious aim at the attendant pleasure. Similarly, the pleasures of thought and study can only be really enjoyed by those who have an ardor of curiosity which carries the mind temporarily away from self and its sensations. In all kinds of Art, again, the exercise of the creative faculty is attended by intense and exquisite pleasures: but in order to get them, one must forget them: the desire of the artist is always said to be concentrated and fixed upon the realization of his ideal of beauty.

The important case of the benevolent affections is at first sight somewhat more doubtful. On the one hand it is of course true, that when those whom we love are pleased or pained, we ourselves feel sympathetic pleasure and pain: and further, that the flow of love or kindly feeling is itself highly pleasurable. So that it is at least plausible to interpret the benevolent impulse as aiming ultimately at the attainment of one or both of these two kinds of pleasures, or at the averting of sympathetic pain. But we may observe, first, that the impulse to beneficent action produced in us by sympathy is often so much out of proportion to any actual consciousness of sympathetic pleasure and pain in ourselves that it would be paradoxical to regard this latter as its object. Often indeed we cannot but feel that a tale of actual suffering arouses in us an excitement on the whole more pleasurable than painful, like the excitement of witnessing a tragedy; and yet at the same time stirs in us an impulse to relieve it, even when the process of relieving is painful and laborious and involves various sacrifices of our own pleasures. Again, we may often free ourselves from sympathetic pain most easily by merely turning our thoughts from the external suffering that causes it: and we sometimes feel an egoistic impulse to do this, which we can then distinguish clearly from the properly sympathetic impulse prompting us to relieve the original suffering. And finally, the much-commended pleasures of benevolence seem to require, in order to be felt in any considerable degree, the pre-existence of a desire to do good to others for their sakes and not for our own. As Hutcheson explains, we may *cultivate* benevolent affection for the sake of the pleasures attending it (just as the gourmand cultivates appetite), but we cannot produce it at will, however strong may be our desire of these pleasures: and when it exists, even though it may owe its origin to a purely egoistic impulse, it is still essentially a desire to do good to others for their sake and not for our own.

It cannot perhaps be said that the self-abandonment and self-forgetfulness, which seemed an essential condition of the full development of the other elevated impulses before noticed, characterize benevolent affection normally and permanently; as love seems naturally to involve a desire for reciprocated love, strong in proportion to the intensity of the emotion; and thus the consciousness of self and of one's own pleasures and pains seems often heightened by the very intensity of the affection that binds one to others. Still we may at least say that this self-suppression and absorption of consciousness in the thought of other human beings and their happiness is observable as a frequent incident of all strong affections: and it is said that persons who love strongly often feel a sense of antagonism between the egoistic and altruistic elements of their desire, and an impulse to suppress the former, which sometimes exhibits itself in acts of fantastic and extravagant self-sacrifice.

If then reflection on our moral consciousness seems to show that "the pleasure of virtue is one which can only be obtained on the express condition of its not being the object sought,"[2] we need not distrust this result of observation on account of the abnormal nature of the phenomenon. We have merely another illustration of a psychological law, which, as we have seen, is exemplified throughout the whole range of our desires. It is not (as Kant seems to hold) that the *natural* determination of the Will is by motives of pleasure and pain, but that when our action is truly *rational,* a higher law of causation comes into play. Rather (as Butler maintains) in the promptings of Sense no less than in those of Intellect or Reason we find the phenomenon of strictly disinterested impulse: base and trivial external ends may be sought without ulterior aim, as well as the sublime and ideal: and there are many pleasures of the merely animal life which can only be obtained on condition of not being directly sought, no less than the satisfactions of a good conscience.

[2] Lecky, *History of European Morals,* Introduction.

§ 3. So far I have been concerned to insist on the felt incompatibility of "self-regarding" and "extra-regarding" impulses only as a means of proving their essential distinctness. I do not wish to overstate this incompatibility: I believe that most commonly it is only momentary, and that our greatest happiness—if that be our deliberate aim—is generally attained by means of a sort of alternating rhythm of the two impulses in consciousness. A man's predominant desire is, I think, most commonly not a conscious impulse toward pleasure; but where there is strong desire in any direction, there is commonly keen susceptibility to the corresponding pleasures; and the most devoted enthusiast is sustained in his work by the recurrent consciousness of such pleasures. But it is important to point out that the familiar and obvious instances of conflict between self-love and some extra-regarding impulse are not paradoxes and illusions to be explained away, but phenomena which the analysis of our consciousness in its normal state, when there is no such conflict, would lead us to expect. If we are continually acting from impulses whose immediate objects are something other than our own happiness, it is quite natural that we should occasionally yield to such impulses when they prompt us to an uncompensated sacrifice of pleasure. Thus a man of weak self-control, after fasting too long, may easily indulge his appetite for food to an extent which he knows to be unwholesome: and that not because the pleasure of eating appears to him, even in the moment of indulgence, at all worthy of consideration in comparison with the injury to health: but merely because he feels an impulse to eat food, too powerful to be resisted. Thus, again, men have sacrificed all the enjoyments of life, and even life itself, to obtain posthumous fame: not from any illusory belief that they would be somehow capable of deriving pleasure from it, but from a direct desire of the future admiration of others, and a preference of it to their own pleasure. And so, again, when the sacrifice is made for some ideal end, as Truth, or Freedom, or Religion: it is or may be a real sacrifice of the individual's happiness, and not merely the preference of one highly refined pleasure (or of the absence of one special pain) to all the other elements of happiness. No doubt this preference is possible: a man may feel that the high and severe delight of serving his ideal is a "pearl of great price" outweighing in value all other pleasures. But he may also feel that the sacrifice will not repay *him,* and yet determine that it shall be made.

So far, then, from our conscious active impulses being always directed toward the production of agreeable sensations in ourselves, it would seem that we find everywhere in consciousness extra-regarding impulses, directed toward something that is not pleasure; and, in fact, that a most important part of our pleasure depends upon the existence of such impulses: while on the other hand they are in many cases so far incompatible with the desire of our own pleasure that the two kinds of impulse do not easily coexist in the same moment of consciousness; and more occasionally (but by no means rarely) the two come into irreconcilable conflict, and prompt to opposite courses of action. And this incompatibility (though it is important to notice it in other instances) is no doubt specially prominent in the case of the impulse toward the end which competes in ethical controversy with pleasure; the love of virtue for its own sake, or desire to do what is right as such.

§ 4. The psychological observations on which my argument is based will not perhaps be directly controverted, at least to such an extent as to involve my main conclusion: but there are two lines of reasoning by which it has been attempted to weaken the force of this conclusion without directly denying it. In the first place, it is urged that Pleasure, though not the only conscious aim of human action, is yet always the result to which it is unconsciously directed. The proposition would be difficult to disprove: since no one denies that pleasure in some degree normally accompanies the attainment of a desired end: and when once we go beyond the testimony of consciousness there seems to be no clear method of determining which among the consequences of any action is the end at which it is aimed. For the same reason, however, the proposition is at any rate equally difficult to prove. But I should go further, and maintain that if we seriously set ourselves to consider human action on its unconscious side, we can only conceive it as a combination of movements of the parts of a material organism: and that if we try to ascertain what the "end" in any case of such movements is, it is natural to conclude that it is some material result, some organic condition conducive to the preservation either of the individual organism or of the race to which it belongs. In fact, the doctrine that pleasure (or the absence of pain) is the end of all human action can neither be supported by the results of introspection, nor by the results of external observation and inference: it rather seems to be reached by an arbitrary and illegitimate combination of the two.

But again, it is sometimes said that whatever be the case with our present adult consciousness, our original impulses were all directed toward pleasure, and that any impulses otherwise directed are derived from these by "association of ideas." I have seen no evidence tending to prove this: so far as we can observe the consciousness of children, the two elements, extra-regarding impulse and desire for pleasure, seem to coexist in the same manner as they do in mature life. In so far as there is any difference, it seems to be in the opposite direction; as the actions of children being more instinctive and less reflective are more prompted by extra-regarding impulse, and less by conscious aim at pleasure. No doubt the two kinds of impulse, as we trace them back to more rudimentary phases of consciousness, gradually become indistinguishable: but this obviously does not justify us in identifying with either of the two the more indefinite impulse out of which both have been developed.

But even supposing it were found that our earliest appetites were all merely appetites for pleasure, it would have little bearing on the present question. What I am concerned to maintain is that men do not *now* normally desire pleasure alone, but to an important extent other things also: some in particular having impulses toward virtue, which may and do conflict with their conscious desire for their own pleasure. To say in answer to this that all men *once* desired pleasure is, from an ethical point of view, irrelevant: except on the assumption that there is an original type of man's appetitive nature, to which, as such, it is right or best for him to conform. But probably no Hedonist would expressly maintain this; though such an assumption, no doubt, is frequently made by writers of the Intuitional school.

Motives, Deliberation, and Choice*

There is doubtless some sense in saying that every conscious act has an incentive or motive. But this sense is as truistic as that of the not dissimilar saying that every event has a cause. Neither statement throws any light on any particular occurrence. It is at most a maxim which advises us to search for some other fact with which the one in question may be correlated. Those who attempt to defend the necessity of existing economic institutions as manifestations of human nature convert this suggestion of a concrete inquiry into a generalized truth and hence into a definitive falsity. They take the saying to mean that nobody would do anything, or at least anything of use to others, without a prospect of some tangible reward. And beneath this false proposition there is another assumption still more monstrous, namely, that man exists naturally in a state of rest so that he requires some external force to set him into action.

The idea of a thing intrinsically wholly inert in the sense of absolutely passive is expelled from physics and has taken refuge in the psychology of current economics. In truth man acts anyway, he can't help acting. In every fundamental sense it is false that a man requires a motive to make him do something. To a healthy man inaction is the greatest of woes. Anyone who observes children knows that while periods of rest are natural, laziness is an acquired vice—or virtue. While a man is awake he will do something, if only to build castles in the air. If we like the form of words we may say that a man eats only because he is "moved" by hunger. The statement is nevertheless mere tautology. For what does hunger mean except that one of the things which man does naturally, instinctively, is to search for food—that his activity naturally turns that way? Hunger primarily names an act or active process not a motive to an act. It is an act if we take it grossly, like a babe's blind hunt for the mother's breast; it is an activity if we take it minutely as a chemico-physiological occurrence.

The whole concept of motives is in truth extra-psychological. It is an outcome of the attempt of men to influence human action, first that of others, then of a man to influence

* John Dewey, *Human Nature and Conduct* (New York: The Modern Library, 1930), pp. 118–22, 190–93, reprinted by permission of Holt, Rinehart and Winston, Inc., New York.

his own behavior. No sensible person thinks of attributing the acts of an animal or an idiot to a motive. We call a biting dog ugly, but we don't look for his motive in biting. If however we were able to direct the dog's action by inducing him to reflect upon his acts, we should at once become interested in the dog's motives for acting as he does, and should endeavor to get him interested in the same subject. It is absurd to ask what induces a man to activity generally speaking. He is an active being and that is all there is to be said on that score. But when we want to get him to act in this specific way rather than in that, when we want to direct his activity, that is to say, in a specified channel, then the question of motive is pertinent. A motive is then that element in the total complex of a man's activity which, if it can be sufficiently stimulated, will result in an act having specified consequences. And part of the process of intensifying (or reducing) certain elements in the total activity and thus regulating actual consequence is to impute these elements to a person as his actuating motives.

A child naturally grabs food. But he does it in our presence. His manner is socially displeasing and we attribute to his act, up to this time wholly innocent, the motive of greed or selfishness. Greediness simply means the quality of his act as socially observed and disapproved. But by attributing it to him as his motive for acting in the disapproved way, we induce him to refrain. We analyze his total act and call his attention to an obnoxious element in its outcome. A child with equal spontaneity, or thoughtlessness, gives way to others. We point out to him with approval that he acted considerately, generously. And this quality of action when noted and encouraged becomes a reinforcing stimulus of that factor which will induce similar acts in the future. An element in an act viewed as a tendency to produce such and such consequences is a motive. A motive does not exist prior to an act and produce it. It is an act *plus* a judgment upon some element of it, the judgment being made in the light of the consequences of the act.

At first, as was said, others characterize an act with favorable or condign qualities which they impute to an agent's character. They react in this fashion in order to encourage him in future acts of the same sort, or in order to dissuade him—in short to build or destroy a habit. This characterization is part of the technique of influencing the development of character and conduct. It is a refinement of the ordinary reactions of praise and blame. After a time and to some extent, a person teaches himself to think of the results of acting in this way or that before he acts. He recalls that if he acts this way or that some observer, real or imaginary, will attribute to him noble or mean disposition, virtuous or vicious motive. Thus he learns to influence his own conduct. An inchoate activity taken in this forward-looking reference to results, especially results of approbation and condemnation, constitutes a motive. Instead then of saying that a man requires a motive in order to induce him to act, we should say that when a man is going to act he needs to know *what* he is going to do—what the quality of his act is in terms of consequences to follow. In order to act properly he needs to view his act as others view it; namely, as a manifestation of a character or will which is good or bad according as it is bent upon specific things which are desirable or obnoxious. There is no call to furnish a man with incentives to activity in general. But there is every need to induce him to guide his own action by an intelligent perception of its results. For in the long run this is the most effective way of influencing activity to take this desirable direction rather than that objectionable one.

A motive in short is simply an impulse viewed as a constituent in a habit, a factor in a disposition. In general its meaning is simple. But in fact motives are as numerous as are original impulsive activities multiplied by the diversified consequences they produce as they operate under diverse conditions.

. . .

. . . Deliberation is a dramatic rehearsal (in imagination) of various competing possible lines of action. It starts from the blocking of efficient overt action, due to that conflict of prior habit and newly released impulse . . . . Then each habit, each impulse, involved in the temporary suspense of overt action takes its turn in being tried out. Deliberation is an experiment in finding out what the various lines of possible action are really like. It is an experiment in making various

combinations of selected elements of habits and impulses, to see what the resultant action would be like if it were entered upon. But the trial is in imagination, not in overt fact. The experiment is carried on by tentative rehearsals in thought which do not affect physical facts outside the body. Thought runs ahead and foresees outcomes, and thereby avoids having to await the instruction of actual failure and disaster. An act overtly tried out is irrevocable, its consequences cannot be blotted out. An act tried out in imagination is not final or fatal. It is retrievable.

Each conflicting habit and impulse takes its turn in projecting itself upon the screen of imagination. It unrolls a picture of its future history, of the career it would have if it were given head. Although overt exhibition is checked by the pressure of contrary propulsive tendencies, this very inhibition gives habit a chance at manifestation in thought. Deliberation means precisely that activity is disintegrated, and that its various elements hold one another up. While none has force enough to become the center of a re-directed activity, or to dominate a course of action, each has enough power to check others from exercising mastery. Activity does not cease in order to give way to reflection; activity is turned from execution into intra-organic channels, resulting in dramatic rehearsal.

If activity were directly exhibited it would result in certain experiences, contacts with the environment. It would succeed by making environing objects, things and persons, copartners in its forward movement; or else it would run against obstacles and be troubled, possibly defeated. These experiences of contact with objects and their qualities give meaning, character, to an otherwise fluid, unconscious activity. We find out what seeing means by the objects which are seen. They constitute the significance of visual activity which would otherwise remain a blank. "Pure" activity is for consciousness pure emptiness. It acquires a content or filling of meanings only in static termini, what it comes to rest in, or in the obstacles which check its onward movement and deflect it. As has been remarked, the object is that which objects.

There is no difference in this respect between a visible course of conduct and one proposed in deliberation. We have no direct consciousness of what we purpose to do. We can judge its nature, assign its meaning, only by following it into the situations whither it leads, noting the objects against which it runs and seeing how they rebuff or unexpectedly encourage it. In imagination as in fact we know a road only by what we see as we travel on it. Moreover the objects which prick out the course of a proposed act until we can see its design also serve to direct eventual overt activity. Every object hit upon as the habit traverses its imaginary path has a direct effect upon existing activities. It reinforces, inhibits, redirects habits already working or stirs up others which had not previously actively entered in. In thought as well as in overt action, the objects experienced in following out a course of action attract, repel, satisfy, annoy, promote, and retard. Thus deliberation proceeds. To say that at last it ceases is to say that choice, decision, takes place.

What then is choice? Simply hitting in imagination upon an object which furnishes an adequate stimulus to the recovery of overt action. Choice is made as soon as some habit, or some combination of elements of habits and impulse, finds a way fully open. Then energy is released. The mind is made up, composed, unified. As long as deliberation pictures shoals or rocks or troublesome gales as marking the route of a contemplated voyage,

deliberation goes on. But when the various factors in action fit harmoniously together, when imagination finds no annoying hindrance, when there is a picture of open seas, filled sails, and favoring winds, the voyage is definitely entered upon. This decisive direction of action constitutes choice. It is a great error to suppose that we have no preferences until there is a choice. We are always biased beings, tending in one direction rather than another. The occasion of deliberation is an *excess* of preferences, not natural apathy or an absence of likings. We want things that are incompatible with one another; therefore we have to make a choice of what we *really* want, of the course of action, that is, which most fully releases activities. Choice is not the emergence of preference out of indifference. It is the emergence of a unified preference out of competing preferences. Biases that had held one another in check now, temporarily at least, reinforce one another, and constitute a unified attitude. The moment arrives when imagination pictures an objective consequence of action which supplies an adequate stimulus and releases definitive action. All deliberation is a search for a *way* to act, not for a final terminus. Its office is to facilitate stimulation.

Causes and Motives*

Did we not say indeed that passion is the *motive* of the act—or again that the passional act is that which has passion for its motive? And does not the will appear as the decision which follows deliberation concerning causes and motives? What then is a cause? What is a motive?

Generally by cause we mean the *reason* for the act; that is, the ensemble of rational considerations which justify it. If the government decides on a conversion of Government bonds, it will give the causes for its act: the lessening of the national debt, the rehabilitation of the Treasury. Similarly it is by *causes* that historians are accustomed to explain the acts of ministers or monarchs; they will seek

the *causes* for a declaration of war: the occasion is propitious, the attacked country is disorganized because of internal troubles; it is time to put an end to an economic conflict which is in danger of lasting interminably. If Clovis is converted to Catholicism, then inasmuch as so many barbarian kings are Arians, it is because Clovis sees an opportunity of getting into the good graces of the episcopate which is all powerful in Gaul. And so on. One will note here that the cause is characterized as an objective appreciation of the situation. The cause of Clovis' conversion is the political and religious state of Gaul; it is the relative strengths of the episcopate, the great landowners, and the common people. What motivates the conversion of the bonds is the state of the national debt. Nevertheless this objective appreciation can be made only in the light of a presupposed end and within

* Jean-Paul Sartre, *Being and Nothingness: An Essay on Phenomenological Ontology*, trans. Hazel E. Barnes (New York: Philosophical Library, 1956), pp. 445–51, reprinted by permission of the publishers. Footnotes are omitted.

the limits of a project of the for-itself toward this end. In order for the power of the episcopate to be revealed to Clovis as the cause of his conversion (that is, in order for him to be able to envisage the objective consequences which this conversion could have) it is necessary first for him to posit as an end the conquest of Gaul. If we suppose that Clovis has other ends, he can find in the situation of the Church causes for his becoming Arian or for remaining pagan. It is even possible that in the consideration of the Church he can even find no cause for acting in any way at all; he will then discover nothing in relation to this subject; he will leave the situation of the episcopate in the state of "unrevealed," in a total obscurity. We shall therefore use the term *cause* for the objective appreciation of a determined situation as this situation is revealed in the light of a certain end as being able to serve as the means for attaining this end.

The motive, on the contrary, is generally considered as a subjective fact. It is the ensemble of the desires, emotions, and passions which urges me to accomplish a certain act. The historian looks for motives and takes them into account only as a last resort when the causes are not sufficient to explain the act under consideration. Ferdinand Lot, for example, after having shown that the reasons which are ordinarily given for the conversion of Constantine are insufficient or erroneous, writes: "Since it is established that Constantine had everything to lose and apparently nothing to gain by embracing Christianity, there is only one conclusion possible—that he yielded to a sudden impulse, pathological or divine as you prefer." Lot is here abandoning the explanation by causes, which seems to him unenlightening, and prefers to it an explanation by motives. The explanation must then be sought in the psychic state—even in the "mental" state—of this historical agent. It follows naturally that the event becomes wholly contingent since another individual with other passions and other desires would have acted differently. In contrast to the historian the psychologist will by preference look for motives; usually he supposes, in fact, that they are "contained in" the state of consciousness which has provoked the action. The ideal rational act would therefore be the one for which the motives would be practically nil and which would be uniquely inspired by an objective appreciation of the situation. The irrational or passionate act will be characterized by the reverse proportion.

It remains for us to explain the relation between causes and motives in the everyday case in which they exist side by side. For example, I can join the Socialist party because I judge that this party serves the interests of justice and of humanity or because I believe that it will become the principal historical force in the years which will follow my joining; these are causes. And at the same time I can have motives: a feeling of pity or charity for certain classes of the oppressed, a feeling of shame at being on the "good side of the barricade," as Gide says, or again an inferiority complex, a desire to shock my relatives, etc. What can be meant by the statement that I have joined the Socialist party for these causes *and* these motives? Evidently we are dealing with two radically distinct layers of meaning. How are we to compare them? How are we to determine the part played by each of them in the decision under consideration? This difficulty, which certainly is the greatest of those raised by the current distinction between causes and motives, has never been resolved; few people indeed have so much as caught a glimpse of it. Actually under a different name it amounts to positing the existence of a conflict between the will and the passions. But if the classic theory is discovered to be incapable of assigning to cause and motive their proper influence in the simple instance when they join together to produce a single decision, it will be wholly impossible for it to explain or even to conceive of a conflict between causes and motives, a conflict in which each group would urge its individual decision. Therefore we must start over again from the beginning.

To be sure, the cause is objective; it is the state of contemporary things as it is revealed to a consciousness. It is *objective* that the Roman plebs and aristocracy were corrupted by the time of Constantine or that the Catholic Church is ready to favor a monarch who at the time of Clovis will help it triumph over Arianism. Nevertheless this state of affairs can be revealed only to a for-itself since in general the for-itself is the being by which "there is" a world. Better yet, it can be revealed only to a for-itself which chooses itself in this or that particular way—that is, to a for-itself which has made its own individuality. The for-itself must of necessity have projected itself in this or that way in order to discover the instrumental implications of instrumental-things. Objectively the knife is an instrument made of a blade and a handle. I can grasp it objectively as an instrument to slice with, to cut with. But lacking a hammer, I can just as well grasp the knife as an instrument to hammer with. I can make use of its handle to pound in a nail, and this apprehension is no less *objective*. When Clovis appreciates the aid which the Church can furnish him, it is not certain that a group of prelates or even one particular priest has made any overtures to him, or even that any member of the clergy has clearly thought of an alliance with a Catholic monarch. The only strictly objective facts, those which any for-itself whatsoever can establish, are the great power of the Church over the people of Gaul and the anxiety of the Church with regard to Arian heresy. In order for these established facts to be organized into a cause for conversion, it is necessary to isolate them from the ensemble—and thereby to nihilate them—and it is necessary to transcend them toward a particular potentiality: the Church's potentiality objectively apprehended by Clovis will be to give its support to a converted king. But this potentiality can be revealed only if the situation is surpassed toward a state of things which does not yet exist—in short, toward a nothingness. In a word the world gives counsel only if one questions it, and one can question it only for a well-determined end.

Therefore the cause, far from determining the action, appears only in and through the project of an action. It is in and through the project of imposing his rule on all of Gaul that the state of the Western Church appears objectively to Clovis as a cause for his conversion. In other words the consciousness which carves out the cause in the ensemble of the world has already its own structure; it has given its own ends to itself, it has projected itself toward its possibles, and it has its own manner of hanging on to its possibilities: this peculiar manner of holding to its possibles is here affectivity. This internal organization which consciousness has given to itself in the form of non-positional self-consciousness is strictly correlative with the carving out of causes in the world. Now if one reflects on the matter, one must recognize that

the internal structure of the for-itself by which it effects in the world the upsurge of causes for acting is an "irrational" fact in the historical sense of the term. Indeed we can easily understand rationally the technical usefulness of the conversion of Clovis under the hypothesis by which he would have projected the conquest of Gaul. But we cannot do the same with regard to his project of conquest. It is not "self-explanatory." Ought it to be interpreted as a result of Clovis' *ambition*? But precisely what is the ambition if not the purpose of conquering? How could Clovis' ambition be distinguished from the precise project of conquering Gaul? Therefore it would be useless to conceive of this original project of conquest as "incited" by a pre-existing motive which would be ambition. It is indeed true that the ambition is a motive since it is wholly subjectivity. But as it is not distinct from the project of conquering, we shall say that this first project of his possibilities in the light of which Clovis discovers a cause for being converted is precisely the *motive*. Then all is made clear and we can conceive of the relations of these three terms: causes, motives, ends. We are dealing here with a particular case of being-in-the-world: just as it is the upsurge of the for-itself which causes there to be a world, so here it is the very being of the for-itself—in so far as this being is a pure project toward an end—which causes there to be a certain objective structure of the world, one which deserves the name of cause in the light of this end. The for-itself is therefore the consciousness *of* this cause. But this positional consciousness *of* the cause is on principle a non-thetic consciousness of itself as a project toward an end. In this sense it is a motive; that is, it experiences itself non-thetically as a project, more or less keen, more or less passionate, toward an end at the very moment at which it is constituted as a revealing consciousness of the organization of the world into causes.

Thus cause and motive are correlative, exactly as the non-thetic self-consciousness is the ontological correlate of the thetic consciousness *of* the object. Just as the consciousness of something is self-consciousness, so the motive is nothing other than the apprehension of the cause in so far as this apprehension is self-consciousness. But it follows obviously that the cause, the motive, and the end are the three indissoluble terms of the thrust of a free and living consciousness which projects itself toward its possibilities and makes itself defined by these possibilities.

How does it happen then that the motive appears to the psychologist as the affective content of a fact of consciousness as this content determines another fact of consciousness or a decision? It is because the motive, which is nothing other than a non-thetic self-consciousness, slips into the past with this same consciousness and along with it ceases to be living. As soon as a consciousness is made-past, it is what I have to be in the form of the "was." Consequently when I turn my back toward my consciousness of yesterday, it preserves its intentional significance and its meaning as subjectivity, but, as we have seen, it is fixed: it is outside like a thing, since the past is in-itself. The motive becomes then that *of which* there is consciousness. It can appear to me in the form of "empirical knowledge"; as we saw earlier, the dead past haunts the present in the aspect of a *practical knowing*. It can also happen that I turn back toward it so as to make it explicit and formulate it while guiding myself by the knowledge which it is for me in the present. In this case it is an object of consciousness; it is this very consciousness *of which I am conscious*. It appears therefore—like my memories in general—simultaneously as *mine* and as transcendent. Ordinarily we are surrounded by these motives which "no longer enter," for we not only have to decide concretely to accomplish this or that act but also to accomplish actions which we decided upon the day before or to pursue enterprises in which we are engaged. In a general way consciousness at whatever moment it is grasped is apprehended as engaged and this very apprehension implies a practical knowing of the motives of the engagement or even a thematic and positional explanation of these causes. It is obvious that the apprehension of the motive refers at once to the cause, its correlate, since the motive, even when made-past and fixed in in-itself, at least maintains as its meaning the fact that it has been a consciousness of a cause; i.e., the discovery of an objective structure of the world. But as the motive is *in-itself* and as the cause is objective, they are presented as a dyad without ontological distinction; we have seen, indeed, that our past is lost in the midst of the world. That is why we put them on the same level and why we

are able to speak of the causes *and* of the motives of an action as if they could enter into conflict or both concur in determined proportion in a decision.

Yet if the motive is transcendent, if it is only the irremediable being which we have to be in the mode of the "was," if like all our past it is separated from us by a breadth of nothingness, then it can act only if it is *recovered*; in itself it is without force. It is therefore by the very thrust of the engaged consciousness that a value and a weight will be conferred on motives and on prior causes. What they have been does not depend on consciousness, but consciousness has the duty of maintaining them in their existence in the past. I have willed this or that: here is what remains irremediable and which even constitutes my essence, since my essence is what I have been. But the meaning held for me by this desire, this fear, these objective considerations of the world when presently I project myself toward my futures—this must be decided by me alone. I determine them precisely and only by the very act by which I project myself toward my ends. The recovery of former motives—or the rejection or new appreciation of them—is not distinct from the project by which I assign new ends to myself and by which in the light of these ends I apprehend myself as discovering a supporting cause in the world. Past motives, past causes, present motives and causes, future ends, all are organized in an indissoluble unity by the very upsurge of a freedom which is beyond causes, motives, and ends.

The result is that a voluntary deliberation is always a deception. How can I evaluate causes and motives on which I myself confer their value before all deliberation and by the very choice which I make of myself? The illusion here stems from the fact that we endeavor to take causes and motives for entirely transcendent things which I balance in my hands like weights and which possess a weight as a permanent property. Yet on the other hand we try to view them as contents of consciousness, and this is self-contradictory. Actually causes and motives have only the weight which my project—i.e., the free production of the end and of the known act to be realized—confers upon them. When I deliberate, the chips are down. And if I am brought to the point of deliberating, this is simply because it is a part of my original project to realize motives by means of *deliberation* rather than by some other form of discovery (by passion, for example, or simply by action, which reveals to me the organized ensemble of causes and of ends as my language informs me of my thought). There is therefore a choice of deliberation as a procedure which will make known to me what I project and consequently what I am. And *the choice* of deliberation is organized with the ensemble motives-causes and end by free spontaneity. When the will intervenes, the decision is taken, and it has no other value than that of making the announcement.

Motives*

I. FOREWORD

In this chapter I discuss certain of the concepts of emotion and feeling.

This scrutiny is necessary because adherents of the dogma of the ghost in the machine can adduce in support of it the consent of most philosophers and psychologists to the view that emotions are internal or private experiences. Emotions are described as turbulences in the stream of consciousness, the owner of which cannot help directly registering them; to external witnesses they are, in consequence, necessarily occult. They are occurrences which take place not in the public, physical world but in your or my secret, mental world.

I shall argue that the word "emotion" is used to designate at least three or four different kinds of things, which I shall call "inclinations" (or "motives"), "moods," "agitations" (or "commotions") and "feelings." Inclinations and moods, including agitations, are not occurrences and do not therefore take place either publicly or privately. They are propensities, not acts or states. They are, however, propensities of different kinds, and their differences are important. Feelings, on the other hand, are occurrences, but the place that mention of them should take in descriptions of human behavior is very different from that which the standard theories accord to it. Moods or frames of mind are, unlike motives, but like maladies and states of the weather, temporary conditions which in a certain way *collect* occurrences, but they are not themselves extra occurrences.

II. FEELINGS VERSUS INCLINATIONS

By "feelings" I refer to the sorts of things which people often describe as thrills, twinges,

pangs, throbs, wrenches, itches, prickings, chills, glows, loads, qualms, hankerings, curdlings, sinkings, tensions, gnawings, and shocks. Ordinarily, when people report the occurrence of a feeling, they do so in a phrase like "a throb of compassion," "a shock of surprise," or a "a thrill of anticipation."

It is an important linguistic fact that these names for specific feelings, such as "itch," "qualm," and "pang," are also used as names of specific bodily sensations. If someone says that he has just felt a twinge, it is proper to ask whether it was a twinge of remorse or of rheumatism, though the word "twinge" is not necessarily being used in quite the same sense in the alternative contexts.

There are further respects in which the ways in which we speak of, say, qualms of apprehension are analogous to the ways in which we speak of, say, qualms of sea-sickness. We are ready to characterize either as acute or faint, sudden or lingering, intermittent or steady. A man may wince from a pricking of his conscience or from a pricking in his finger. Moreover, we are in some cases ready to locate, say, the sinking feeling of despair in the pit of the stomach or the tense feeling of anger in the muscles of the jaw and fist. Other feelings which we are not prepared to locate in any particular part of the body, like glows of pride, seem to pervade the whole body in much the same way as do glows of warmth.

James boldly identified feelings with bodily sensations, but for our purposes it is enough to show that we talk of feelings very much as we talk of bodily sensations, though it is possible that there is a tinge of metaphor in our talk of the former which is absent from our talk of the latter.

On the other hand, it is necessary to do justice to the crucial fact that we do report feelings in such idioms as "qualms of appre-

* Gilbert Ryle, *The Concept of Mind* (London: Hutchinson's University Library, 1949), pp. 83–93, 110–15, reprinted with the permission of the author and The Hutchinson Group, London.

hension" and "glows of pride"; we do, that is, distinguish a glow of pride from a glow of warmth, and I shall have to try to bring out the force of such distinctions. I hope to show that though it is quite proper to describe someone as feeling a throb of compassion, his compassion is not to be equated with a throb or a series of throbs, any more than his fatigue is his gasps; so no disillusioning consequences would follow from acknowledging that throbs, twinges, and other feelings are bodily sensations.

In one sense, then, of "emotion" the feelings are emotions. But there is quite another sense of "emotion" in which theorists classify as emotions the motives by which people's higher-level behavior is explained. When a man is described as vain, considerate, avaricious, patriotic, or indolent, an explanation is being given of why he conducts his actions, daydreams, and thoughts in the way he does, and, according to the standard terminology, vanity, kindliness, avarice, patriotism, and laziness rank as species of emotion; they come thence to be spoken of as feelings.

But there is a great verbal muddle here, associated with a great logical muddle. To begin with, when someone is described as a vain or indolent man, the words "vain" and "indolent" are used to signify more or less lasting traits in his character. In this use he might be said to have been vain since childhood, or indolent during his entire half-holiday. His vanity and indolence are dispositional properties, which could be unpacked in such expressions as "Whenever situations of certain sorts have arisen, he has always or usually tried to make himself prominent" or "Whenever he was faced by an option between doing something difficult and not doing it, he shirked doing the difficult thing." Sentences beginning with "Whenever" are not singular occurrence reports. Motive words used in this way signify tendencies or propensities and therefore cannot signify the occurrence of feelings. They are elliptical expressions of general hypothetical propositions of a certain sort, and cannot be construed as expressing categorical narratives of episodes.

It will however be objected that, besides this dispositional use of motive words, there must also be a corresponding active use of them. For a man to be punctual in the dispositional sense of the adjective, he must tend to be punctual on particular occasions; and

the sense in which he is said to be punctual for a particular rendezvous is not the dispositional but the active sense of "punctual." "He tends to be at his rendezvous on time" expresses a general hypothetical proposition, the truth of which requires that there should also be corresponding true categorical propositions of the pattern "he was at today's rendezvous in good time." So, it will be argued, for a man to be a vain or indolent man there must be particular exercises of vanity and indolence occurring at particular moments, and these will be actual emotions or feelings.

This argument certainly establishes something, but it does not establish the point desired. While it is true that to describe a man as vain is to say that he is subject to a specific tendency, it is not true that the particular exercises of this tendency consist in his registering particular thrills or twinges. On the contrary, on hearing that a man is vain we expect him, in the first instance, to behave in certain ways, namely to talk a lot about himself, to cleave to the society of the eminent, to reject criticisms, to seek the footlights, and to disengage himself from conversations about the merits of others. We expect him also to indulge in roseate daydreams about his own successes, to avoid recalling past failures, and to plan for his own advancement. To be vain is to tend to act in these and innumerable other kindred ways. Certainly we also expect the vain man to feel certain pangs and flutters in certain situations; we expect him to have an acute sinking feeling when an eminent person forgets his name, and to feel buoyant of heart and light of toe on hearing of the misfortunes of his rivals. But feelings of pique and buoyancy are not more directly indicative of vanity than are public acts of boasting or private acts of daydreaming. Indeed they are less directly indicative, for reasons which will shortly appear.

Some theorists will object that to speak of an act of boasting as one of the direct exercises of vanity is to leave out the cardinal factor in the situation. When we explain why a man boasts by saying that it is because he is vain, we are forgetting that a disposition is not an event and so cannot be a cause. The cause of his boasting must be an event antecedent to his beginning to boast. He must be moved to boast by some actual "impulse," namely an impulse of vanity. So the immediate or direct actualizations of vanity are particular vanity impulses, and these are feelings. The vain man is a man who tends to register particular feelings of vanity; these cause or impel him to boast, or perhaps to will to boast, and to do all the other things which we say are done from vanity.

It should be noticed that this argument takes it for granted that to explain an act as done from a certain motive, in this case from vanity, is to give a causal explanation. This means that it assumes that a mind, in this case the boaster's mind, is a field of special causes; that is why a vanity feeling has been called in to be the inner cause of the overt boasting. I shall shortly argue that to explain an act as done from a certain motive is not analogous to saying that the glass broke because a stone hit it, but to the quite different type of statement that the glass broke, when the stone hit it, because the glass was brittle. Just as there are no other momentary actualizations of brittleness than, for example, flying into fragments when struck, so no other momentary actualizations of chronic vanity need to be postulated than such things as boasting, daydreaming about triumphs, and avoiding conversations about the merits of others.

But before expanding this argument I want to show how intrinsically unplausible the view is that, on each occasion that a vain man behaves vaingloriously, he experiences a particular palpitation or pricking of vanity. To put it quite dogmatically, the vain man never feels vain. Certainly, when thwarted, he feels acute dudgeon and when unexpectedly successful, he feels buoyant. But there is no special thrill or pang which we call a "feeling of vanity." Indeed, if there were such a recognizable specific feeling, and the vain man was constantly experiencing it, he would be the first instead of the last person to recognize how vain he was.

Take another example. A man is interested in Symbolic Logic. He regularly reads books and articles on the subject, discusses it, works out problems in it, and neglects lectures on other subjects. According to the view which is here contested, he must therefore constantly experience impulses of a peculiar kind, namely, feelings of interest in Symbolic Logic, and if his interest is very strong these feelings must be very acute and very frequent. He must therefore be able to tell us whether these feelings are sudden, like twinges, or lasting, like aches; whether they succeed one another several times a minute or only a few times an hour; and whether he feels them in the small of his back or in his forehead. But clearly his only reply to such specific questions would be that he catches himself experiencing no particular throbs or qualms while he is attending to his hobby. He may report a feeling of vexation, when his studies are interrupted, and the feeling of a load off his chest, when distractions are removed; but there are no peculiar feelings of interest in Symbolic Logic for him to report. While undisturbedly pursuing his hobby, he feels no perturbations at all.

Suppose, however, that there were such feelings cropping up, maybe, about every two or twenty minutes. We should still expect to find him discussing and studying the subject in the intervals between these occurrences, and we should correctly say that he was still discussing and studying the subject from interest in it. This point by itself establishes the conclusion that to do something from a motive is compatible with being free from any particular feelings while doing it.

Of course, the standard theories of motives do not speak so crudely of qualms, pangs, or flutters. They speak more sedately of desires, impulses, or promptings. Now there are feelings of wanting, namely, those we call "hankerings," "cravings," and "itchings." So let us put our question in this way. Is being interested in Symbolic Logic equivalent to being liable or prone to feel certain special hankerings, gnawings, or cravings? And does working at Symbolic Logic from interest in it involve feeling one such itching before each bit of the work is begun? If the affirmative answer is given, then there can be no answer to the question "From what motive does the student work at the subject in the intervals between the itchings?" And if to say that his interest was strong meant that the supposed feelings were frequent and acute, the absurd consequences would follow that the more strongly a man was interested in a subject the more his attention would be distracted from it. To call a feeling or sensation "acute" is to say that it is difficult not to attend to it, and to attend to a feeling is not the same thing as to attend to a problem in Symbolic Logic.

We must reject, then, the conclusion of the argument which tried to prove that motive words are the names of feelings or else of tendencies to have feelings. But what was wrong with the argument for this conclusion?

There are at least two quite different senses in which an occurrence is said to be "explained"; and there are correspondingly at least two quite different senses in which we ask "why" it occurred and two quite different senses in which we say that it happened "because" so and so was the case. The first sense is the causal sense. To ask why the glass broke is to ask what caused it to break, and we explain, in this sense, the fracture of the glass when we report that a stone hit it. The "because" clause in the explanation reports an event, namely, the event which stood to the fracture of the glass as cause to effect.

But very frequently we look for and get explanations of occurrences in another sense of "explanation." We ask why the glass shivered when struck by the stone and we get the answer that it was because the glass was brittle. Now "brittle" is a dispositional adjective; that is to say, to describe the glass as brittle is to assert a general hypothetical proposition about the glass. So when we say that the glass broke when struck because it was brittle, the "because" clause does not report a happening or a cause; it states a law-like proposition. People commonly say of explanations of this second kind that they give the "reason" for the glass breaking when struck.

How does the law-like general hypothetical proposition work? It says, roughly, that the glass, if sharply struck or twisted, etc., *would* not dissolve or stretch or evaporate but fly into fragments. The matter of fact that the glass did at a particular moment fly into fragments, when struck by a particular stone, is explained, in this sense of "explain," when the first happening, namely the impact of the stone, satisfies the protasis of the general hypothetical proposition, and when the second happening, namely, the fragmentation of the glass, satisfies its apodosis.

This can now be applied to the explanation of actions as issuing from specified motives. When we ask "Why did someone act in a certain way?" this question might, so far as its language goes, either be an inquiry into the cause of his acting in that way, or be an inquiry into the character of the agent which accounts for his having acted in that way on that occasion. I suggest, what I shall now try to prove, that explanations by motives are

explanations of the second type and not of the first type. It is perhaps more than a merely linguistic fact that a man who reports the motive from which something is done is, in common parlance, said to be giving the "reason" for the action. It should be also noticed that there are lots of different kinds of such explanations of human actions. A twitch may be explained by a reflex, the filling of a pipe by an inveterate habit; the answering of a letter by a motive. Some of the differences between reflexes, habits, and motives will have to be described at a later stage.

The present issue is this. The statement "he boasted from vanity" ought, on one view, to be construed as saying that "he boasted and the cause of his boasting was the occurrence in him of a particular feeling or impulse of vanity." On the other view, it is to be construed as saying, "he boasted on meeting the stranger and his doing so satisfies the law-like proposition that whenever he finds a chance of securing the admiration and envy of others, he does whatever he thinks will produce this admiration and envy."

My first argument in favor of the second way of construing such statements is that no one could ever know or even, usually, reasonably conjecture that the cause of someone else's overt action was the occurrence in him of a feeling. Even if the agent reported, what people never do report, that he had experienced a vanity itch just before he boasted, this would be very weak evidence that the itch caused the action, since for all we know, the cause was any one of a thousand other synchronous happenings. On this view the imputation of motives would be incapable of any direct testing and no reasonable person would put any reliance on any such imputation. It would be like water-divining in places where well-sinking was forbidden.

In fact, however, we do discover the motives of other people. The process of discovering them is not immune from error, but nor are the errors incorrigible. It is or is like an inductive process, which results in the establishment of law-like propositions and the applications of them as the "reasons" for particular actions. What is established in each case is or includes a general hypothetical proposition of a certain sort. The imputation of a motive for a particular action is not a causal inference to an unwitnessed event but the subsumption of an episode proposition under a law-like proposition. It is therefore analogous to the explanation of reactions and actions by reflexes and habits, or to the explanation of the fracture of the glass by reference to its brittleness.

The way in which a person discovers his own long-term motives is the same as the way in which he discovers those of others. The quantity and quality of the information accessible to him differ in the two inquiries, but its items are in general of the same sort. He has, it is true, a fund of recollections of his own past deeds, thoughts, fancies, and feelings; and he can perform the experiments of fancying himself confronted by tasks and opportunities which have not actually occurred. He can thus base his appreciations of his own lasting inclinations on data which he lacks for his appreciations of the inclinations of others. On the other side, his appreciations of his own inclinations are unlikely to be unbiased and he is not in a favorable position to compare his own actions and reactions with those of others. In general we think that an impartial and discerning spectator is a better judge of a person's prevailing motives, as well as of his habits, abilities, and weaknesses, than is that person himself, a view which is directly contrary to the theory which holds that an agent possesses a Privileged Access to the so-called springs of his own actions and is, because of that access, able and bound to discover, without inference or research, from what motives he tends to act and from what motive he acted on a particular occasion.

We shall see later on . . . that a person who does or undergoes something, heeding what he is doing or undergoing, can, commonly, answer questions about the incident without inference or research. But what gives him those ready-made answers can and often does give his companions also those same ready-made answers. He does not have to be a detective, but nor do they.

Another argument supports this thesis. A person replying to an interrogation might say that he was delving into a ditch in order to find the larvae of a certain species of insect; that he was looking for these larvae in order to find out on what fauna or flora they were parasitic; that he was trying to find out on what they were parasitic in order to test a certain ecological hypothesis; and that he

wanted to test this hypothesis in order to test a certain hypothesis about Natural Selection. At each stage he declares his motive or reason for pursuing certain investigations. And each successive reason that he gives is of a higher level of generality than its predecessor. He is subsuming one interest under another, somewhat as more special laws are subsumed under more general laws. He is not recording a chronological series of earlier and earlier stages, though of course he could do this if asked the quite different questions What first aroused your interest in this problem? and in that?

In the case of every action, taken by itself, for which it is natural to ask "From what motive was it done?" it is always possible that it was not done from a motive but from force of habit. Whatever I do or say, it is always conceivable, though nearly always false, that I did it, or said it, in complete absence of mind. The performance of an action from a motive is different from its performance out of habit; but the sorts of things which belong to the one class also belong to the other. Now to say that an action was done from force of habit is patently to say that a specific disposition explains the action. No one, I trust, thinks that "habit" is the name of a peculiar internal event or class of events. To ask whether an action was done from force of habit or from kindliness of heart is therefore to ask which of two specified dispositions is the explanation of the action.

Finally, we should consider by what tests we should try to decide a dispute about the motive from which a person had done something; did he, for example, throw up a well-paid post for a relatively humble Government job from patriotism or from a desire to be exempt from military service? We begin, perhaps, by asking him; but on this sort of matter his avowals, to us or to himself, would very likely not be frank. We next try, not necessarily unsuccessfully, to settle the dispute by considering whether his words, actions, embarrassments, etc., on this and other occasions square with the hypothesis that he is physically timorous and averse from regimentation, or whether they square with the hypothesis that he is relatively indifferent to money and would sacrifice anything to help win the war. We try, that is, to settle by induction the relevant traits in his character.

In applying, then, the results of our induction to his particular decision, i.e., in explaining why he came to it, we do not press him to recall the itches, pangs, and throbs that he registered in making it; nor, probably, do we trouble to infer to their occurrence. And there is a special reason for not paying much heed to the feelings had by a person whose motives are under investigation, namely that we know that lively and frequent feelings are felt by sentimentalists whose positive actions show quite clearly that their patriotism, e.g., is a self-indulgent make-believe. Their hearts duly sink when they hear that their country's plight is desperate, but their appetites are unaffected and the routines of their lives are unmodified. Their bosoms swell at a march-past, but they avoid marching themselves. They are rather like theatregoers and novel readers, who also feel genuine pangs, glows, flutters, and twinges of despair, indignation, exhilaration, and disgust, with the difference that the theatregoers and novel readers realize that they are making-believe.

To say, then, that a certain motive is a trait in someone's character is to say that he is inclined to do certain sorts of things, make certain sorts of plans, indulge in certain sorts of daydreams, and also, of course, in certain situations to feel certain sorts of feelings. To say that he did something from that motive is to say that this action, done in its particular circumstances, was just the sort of thing that that was an inclination to do. It is to say "he *would* do that."

. . .

VII. THE CRITERIA OF MOTIVES

So far it has been argued that to explain an action as done from a certain motive is not to correlate it with an occult cause, but to subsume it under a propensity or behavior-trend. But this is not enough. To explain an action as due to habit, or as due to an instinct, or a reflex, squares with this formula, yet we distinguish actions done, say, from vanity or affection from those done automatically in one of these other ways. I shall restrict myself to trying to indicate some of the criteria by which we would ordinarily decide that an agent had done something not from force of habit but from a specified motive. But it must not be supposed that the two classes are demarcated from one another as an equatorial

day from an equatorial night. They shade into one another as an English day shades into an English night. Kindliness shades into politeness through the twilight of etiquette. The drill of a keen soldier is not quite like the drill of a merely docile soldier.

When we say that someone acts in a certain way from sheer force of habit, part of what we have in mind is this, that in similar circumstances he always acts in just this way; that he acts in this way whether or not he is attending to what he is doing; that he is not exercising care or trying to correct or improve his performance; and that he may, after the act is over, be quite unaware that he has done it. Such actions are often given the metaphorical title "automatic." Automatic habits are often deliberately inculcated by sheer drill, and only by some counter-drill is a formed habit eradicated.

But when we say that someone acts in a certain way from ambition or sense of justice, we mean by implication to deny that the action was merely automatic. In particular we imply that the agent was in some way thinking or heeding what he was doing, and would not have acted in that way if he had not been thinking what he was doing. But the precise force of this expression "thinking what he was doing" is somewhat elusive. I certainly can run upstairs two stairs at a time from force of habit and at the same time notice that I am doing so and even consider how the act is done. I can be a spectator of my habitual and of my reflex actions and even a diagnostician of them, without these actions ceasing to be automatic. Notoriously such attention sometimes upsets the automatism.

Conversely, actions done from motives can still be naïve, in the sense that the agent has not coupled, and perhaps cannot couple, his action with a secondary operation of telling himself or the company what he is doing, or why he is doing it. Indeed even when a person does pass internal or spoken comments upon his current action, this second operation of commenting is ordinarily itself naïve. He cannot also be commenting on his commentaries *ad infinitum*. The sense in which a person is thinking what he is doing, when his action is to be classed not as automatic but as done from a motive, is that he is acting more or less carefully, critically, consistently, and purposefully, adverbs which do not signify the prior or concomitant occurrence of extra operations of resolving, planning, or cogitating, but only that the action taken is itself done not absent-mindedly but in a certain positive frame of mind. The description of this frame of mind need not mention any episodes other than this act itself, though it is not exhausted in that mention.

In short, the class of actions done from motives coincides with the class of actions describable as more or less intelligent. Any act done from a motive can be appraised as relatively sagacious or stupid, and vice versa. Actions done from sheer force of habit are not characterized as sensible or silly, though of course the agent may show sense or silliness in forming, or in not eradicating, the habit.

But this brings up a further point. Two actions done from the same motive may exhibit different degrees of competence, and two similar actions exhibiting the same degree of competence may be done from different motives. To be fond of rowing does not entail being accomplished or effective at it, and, of two people equally effective at it, one may be rowing for the sport and the other for the sake of health or glory. That is, the abilities with which things are done are personal characteristics of a different kind from the motives or inclinations which are the reasons why they are done; and we distinguish acts done from force of habit from nonautomatic actions by the fact that the latter are exercises of both at once. Things done quite absent-mindedly are done neither with methods nor for reasons, though they may be efficacious and they may have complex procedures.

In ascribing a specific motive to a person we are describing the sorts of things that he tends to try to do or bring about, while in ascribing to him a specific competence we are describing the methods and the effectiveness of the methods by which he conducts these attempts. It is the distinction between aims and techniques. The more common idiom of "ends and means" is often misleading. If a man makes a sarcastic joke, his performance cannot be split up into steps and landings, yet the judgment that it was made from hatred is still distinguishable from the judgment that it was made with ingenuity.

Aristotle realized that in talking about motives we are talking about dispositions of a certain sort, a sort different from compe-

tences; he realized too that any motive, unlike any competence, is a propensity of which it makes sense to say that in a given man in a given walk of life this motive is too strong, too weak, or neither too strong, nor too weak. He seems to suggest that in appraising the moral, as distinct from the technical, merits and demerits of actions we are commenting on the excessive, proper, or inadequate strength of the inclinations of which they are the exercises. Now we are not concerned here with ethical questions, or with questions about the nature of ethical questions. What is relevant to our inquiry is the fact, recognized by Aristotle as cardinal, that the relative strengths of inclinations are alterable. Changes of environment, companionship, health and age, external criticisms, and examples can all modify the balance of power between the inclinations which constitute one side of a person's character. But so can his own concern about this balance modify it. A person may find that he is too fond of gossip, or not attentive enough to other people's comfort, and he may, though he need not, develop a second-order inclination to strengthen some of his weak, and weaken some of his strong propensities. He may become not merely academically critical, but executively corrective of his own character. Of course, his new second-order motive for schooling his first-order motives may still be a prudential or economic one. An ambitious hotel-proprietor might drill himself in equability, considerateness, and probity solely from the desire to increase his income; and his techniques of self-regimentation might be more effective than those employed by a person whose ideal was loftier. In the case, however, of the hotel-proprietor there would be one inclination the relative strength of which *vis-à-vis* the others had been left uncriticized and unregulated, namely, his desire to get rich. This motive might be, though it need not be, too strong in him. If so, we might call him "shrewd," but we should not yet call him "wise." To generalize this point, a part of what is meant by saying of any inclination that it is too strong in a given agent is that the agent tends to act from that inclination even when he is also inclined to weaken that inclination by deliberately acting differently. He is a slave of nicotine, or of allegiance to a political party, if he can never bring himself to take enough of the serious steps by which alone the strength of these motives could be reduced, even though he has some second-order inclination to reduce it. What is here being described is part of what is ordinarily called "self-control," and when what is ordinarily miscalled an "impulse" is irresistible and therefore uncontrollable, it is a tautology to say that it is too strong.

VIII. THE REASONS AND CAUSES OF ACTIONS

I have argued that to explain an action as done from a specified motive or inclination is not to describe the action as the effect of a specified cause. Motives are not happenings and are not therefore of the right type to be causes. The expansion of a motive-expression is a law-like sentence and not a report of an event.

But the general fact that a person is disposed to act in such and such ways in such and such circumstances does not by itself account for his doing a particular thing at a particular moment; any more than the fact the the glass was brittle accounts for its fracture at 10 P.M. As the impact of the stone at 10 P.M. caused the glass to break, so some antecedent of an action causes or occasions the agent to perform it when and where he does so. For example, a man passes his neighbor the salt from politeness; but his politeness is merely his inclination to pass the salt when it is wanted, as well as to perform a thousand other courtesies of the same general kind. So besides the question "for what reason did he pass the salt?" there is the quite different question "what made him pass the salt at that moment to that neighbor?" This question is probably answered by "he heard his neighbor ask for it," or "he noticed his neighbor's eye wandering over the table," or something of the sort.

We are perfectly familiar with the sorts of happenings which induce or occasion people to do things. If we were not, we could not get them to do what we wish, and the ordinary dealings between people could not exist. Customers could not purchase, officers could not command, friends could not converse, or children play, unless they knew how to get other people and themselves to do things at particular junctures.

The object of mentioning these important trivialities is twofold; first, to show that an action's having a cause does not conflict with its having a motive, but is already prescribed for in the protasis of the hypothetical proposition which states the motive; and second, to show that, so far from our wanting to hear of occult or ghostly causes of actions, we already know just what sorts of familiar and usually public happenings are the things which get people to act in particular ways at particular times.

If the doctrine of the ghost in the machine were true, not only would people be absolute mysteries to one another, they would also be absolutely intractable. In fact they are relatively tractable and relatively easy to understand.

IX. CONCLUSION

There are two quite different senses of "emotions," in which we explain people's behavior by reference to emotions. In the first sense we are referring to the motives or inclinations from which more or less intelligent actions are done. In the second sense we are referring to moods, including the agitations or perturbations of which some aimless movements are signs. In neither of these senses are we asserting or implying that the overt behavior is the effect of a felt turbulence in the agent's stream of consciousness. In a third sense of "emotion," pangs and twinges are feelings or emotions, but they are not, save *per accidens,* things by reference to which we explain behavior. They are things for which diagnoses are required, not things required for the diagnoses of behavior. Impulses, described as feelings which impel actions, are para-mechanical myths. This does not mean that people never act on the impulse of the moment, but only that we should not swallow the traditional stories about the occult antecedents of either deliberate or impulsive actions.

Consequently, though the description of the higher-level behavior of people certainly requires mention of emotions in the first two senses, this mention does not entail inferences to occult inner states or processes. The discovery by me of your motives and moods is not analogous to uncheckable water-divining; it is partly analogous to my inductions to your habits, instincts, and reflexes, partly to my inferences to your maladies and your tipsiness. But, in favorable circumstances, I find out your inclinations and your moods more directly than this. I hear and understand your conversational avowals, your interjections, and your tones of voice; I see and understand your gestures and facial expressions. I say "understand" in no metaphorical sense, for even interjections, tones of voice, gestures, and grimaces are modes of communication. We learn to produce them, not indeed from schooling, but from imitation. We know how to sham by putting them on and we know, in some degree, how to avoid giving ourselves away by assuming masks. It is not only their vocabularies that make foreigners difficult to understand. My discovery of my own motives and moods is not different in kind, though I am ill-placed to see my own grimaces and gestures, or to hear my own tones of voice. Motives and moods are not the sorts of things which could be among the direct intimations of consciousness, or among the objects of introspection, as these factitious forms of Privileged Access are ordinarily described. They are not "experiences," any more than habits or maladies are "experiences."

Intention*

What distinguishes actions which are intentional from those which are not? The answer that suggests itself is that they are the actions to which a certain sense of the question "Why?" is given application; the sense is defined as that in which the answer, *if positive,* gives a reason for acting. But this hardly gets us any further, because the questions "What is the relevant sense of the question 'Why?'" and "What is meant by 'reason for acting?'" are one and the same.

To see the difficulties here, consider the question "Why did you knock the cup off the table?" answered by "I thought I saw a face at the window and it made me jump." Now we cannot say that since the answer mentions something previous to the action, this will be a cause as opposed to a reason; for if you ask "Why did you kill him?" the answer "he killed my father" is surely a reason rather than a cause, but what it mentions is previous to the action. It is true that we don't ordinarily think of a case like giving a sudden start when we speak of a *reason for acting.* "Giving a sudden start," someone might say, "is not *acting* in the sense suggested by the expression 'reason for acting.'" Hence, though indeed we readily say, e.g., "What was the reason for your starting so violently?" this is totally unlike "What is your reason for excluding so-and-so from your will?" or "What is your reason for sending for a taxi?" But what *is* the difference? Why is giving a start or gasp not an "action," while sending

for a taxi or crossing the road is one? The answer cannot be "Because an answer to the question 'why?' may give a reason in the latter cases," for the answer may "give a reason" in the former cases too; and we cannot say "Ah, but not a *reason for acting*"; we should be going round in circles. We need to find the difference between the two kinds of "reason" without talking about "acting"; and if we do, perhaps we shall discover what is meant by "acting" when it is said with this special emphasis.

It will hardly be enlightening to say "in the case of the sudden start the 'reason' is a *cause*"; the topic of causality is in a state of too great confusion; all we know is that this is one of the places where we do use the word "cause." But we also know that this is rather a strange case of causality; the subject is able to give a cause of a thought or feeling or bodily movement in the same kind of way as he is able to state the place of his pain or the position of his limbs. Such statements are not based on observation.

Nor can we say: "Well, the 'reason' for a movement is a cause, and not a reason in the sense of 'reason for acting,' when the movement is involuntary; it is a reason as opposed to a cause, when the movement is voluntary and intentional." This is partly because in any case the object of the whole enquiry is really to delineate such concepts as the voluntary and the intentional, and partly because one can also give a "reason" which is only a "cause" for what is voluntary and intentional. E.g., "Why are you walking up and down like that?" — "It's that military band; it excites me." Or "What made you

* G. E. M. Anscombe, "Intention," *Aristotelian Society Proceedings,* LVII (1956–57), pp. 321–32, reprinted with the permission of the author and The Aristotelian Society, London.

sign the document at last?" — "The thought: 'It is my duty' kept hammering always in my mind until I said to myself 'I can do no other,' and so signed."

Now we can see that the cases where this difficulty arises are just those where the cause itself, *qua* cause (or perhaps one should rather say the causation itself), is in the class of things known without observation.

I will call the type of cause in question a *"mental cause."* Mental causes are possible, not only for actions ("The martial music excites me, that is why I walk up and down") but also for feelings and even thoughts. In considering actions, it is important to distinguish between mental causes and motives; in considering feelings, such as fear or anger, it is important to distinguish between mental causes and objects of feeling. To see this, consider the following cases:

A child saw a bit of red stuff on a turn in a stairway and asked what it was. He thought his nurse told him it was a bit of Satan and felt dreadful fear of it. (No doubt she said it was a bit of satin.) What he was frightened of was the bit of stuff; the cause of his fright was his nurse's remark. The object of fear may be the cause of fear, but, as Wittgenstein[1] remarks, is not *as such* the cause of fear. (A hideous face appearing at the window would of course be both cause and object, and hence the two are easily confused.) Or again, you may be angry *at* someone's action, when what makes you angry is some reminder of it, or someone's telling you of it.

This sort of cause of a feeling or reaction may be reported by the person himself, as well as recognized by someone else, even when it is not the same as the object. Note that this sort of causality or sense of "causality" is so far from accommodating itself to Hume's explanations that people who believe that Hume pretty well dealt with the topic of causality would entirely leave it out of their calculations; if their attention were drawn to it they might insist that the word "cause" was inappropriate or was quite equivocal. Or conceivably they might try to give a Humeian account of the matter as far as concerned the outside observer's recognition of the cause; but hardly for the patient's.

Now one might think that when the ques-

tion "Why?" is answered by giving the intention with which a person acts — a case of which I will here simply characterize by saying that it mentions something future — this is also a case of a mental cause. For couldn't it be recast in the form: "Because I wanted . . ." or "Out of a desire that . . ."? If a feeling of desire for an apple affects me and I get up and go to a cupboard where I think there are some, I might answer the question what led to this action by mentioning the desire as having made me . . . etc. But it is not in all cases that "I did so and so in order to . . ." can be backed up by "I *felt* a desire that . . ." I may, e.g., simply hear a knock on the door and go downstairs to open it without experiencing any such desire. Or suppose I feel an upsurge of spite against someone and destroy a message he has received so that he shall miss an appointment. If I describe this by saying "I wanted to make him miss that appointment," this does not necessarily mean that I had the thought "If I do this, he will . . ." and that it affected me with a desire of bringing that about which led up to my action. This may have happened, but need not. It could be that all that happened was this: I read the message, had the thought "That unspeakable man!" with feelings of hatred, tore the message up, and laughed. Then if the question "Why did you do that?" is put by someone who makes it clear that he wants me to mention the mental causes—i.e., what went on in my mind and issued in the action—I should perhaps give this account; but normally the reply would be no such thing. That particular enquiry is not very often made. Nor do I wish to say that it always has an answer in cases where it can be made. One might shrug or say "I don't know that there was an definite history of the kind you mean," or "It merely occurred to me . . . "

A "mental cause," of course, need not be a mental event, i.e., a thought or feeling or image; it might be a knock on the door. But if it is not a mental event, it must be something perceived by the person affected—e.g., the knock on the door must be heard—so if in this sense anyone wishes to say it is always a mental event, I have no objection. A mental cause is what someone would describe if he were asked the specific question: what produced this action or thought or feeling in you? i.e., what did you see or hear or feel, or what ideas or images cropped up in your

[1] *Philosophical Investigations*, § 476.

mind, and led up to it? I have isolated this notion of a mental cause because there *is* such a thing as this question with this sort of answer, and because I want to distinguish it from the ordinary senses of "motive" and "intention," rather than because it is in itself of very great importance; for I believe that it is of very little. But it is important to have a clear idea of it, partly because *a* very natural conception of "motive" is that it is what *moves* (the very word suggests that)—glossed as "what *causes*" a man's actions, etc. And "what causes" them is perhaps then thought of as an event that brings the effect about—though *how*—i.e., whether it should be thought of as a kind of pushing in another medium, or in some other way—is of course completely obscure.

In philosophy a distinction has sometimes been drawn between "motives" and "intentions in acting" as referring to quite different things. A man's intention is *what* he aims at or chooses; his motive is what determines the aim or choice; and I suppose that "determines" must here be another word for "causes."

Popularly, "motive" and "intention" are not treated as so distinct in meaning. E.g., we hear of "the motive of gain"; some philosophers have wanted to say that such an expression must be elliptical; gain must be the *intention,* and *desire of gain* the motive. Asked for a motive, a man might say "I wanted to . . ." which would please such philosophers; or "I did it in order to . . ." which would not; and yet the meaning of the two phrases is here identical. When a man's motives are called good, this may be in no way distinct from calling his intentions good—e.g., "he only wanted to make peace among his relations."

Nevertheless there is even popularly a distinction between the meaning of "motive" and the meaning of "intention." E.g., if a man kills someone, he may be said to have done it out of love and pity, or to have done it out of hatred; these might indeed be cast in the forms "to release him from this awful suffering," or "to get rid of the swine"; but though these are forms of expression suggesting objectives, they are perhaps expressive of the spirit in which the man killed rather than descriptive of the end to which the killing was a means—a future state of affairs to be produced by the killing. And this shows us

part of the distinction that there is between the popular senses of motive and intention. We should say: popularly, "motive for an action" has a rather wider and more diverse application than "intention with which the action was done."

When a man says what his motive was, speaking popularly, and in a sense in which "motive" is not interchangeable with "intention," he is not giving a "mental cause" in the sense that I have given to that phrase. The fact that the mental causes were such-and-such may indeed help to make his claim intelligible. And further, though he may say that his motive was this or that one straight off and without lying—i.e., without saying what he knows or even half knows to be untrue—yet a consideration of various things, which may include the mental causes, might possibly lead both him and other people to judge that his declaration of his own motive was false. But it appears to me that the mental causes are seldom more than a very trivial item among the things that it would be reasonable to consider. As for the importance of considering the motives of an action, as opposed to considering the intention, I am very glad not to be writing either ethics or literary criticism, to which this question belongs.

Motives may explain actions to us; but that is not to say that they "determine," in the sense of causing, actions. We do say, "His love of truth caused him to . . ." and similar things, and no doubt such expressions help us to think that a motive must be what produces or brings about a choice. But this means rather "He did this in that he loved the truth"; it interprets his action.

Someone who sees the confusions involved in radically distinguishing between motives and intentions and in defining motives, so distinct, as the determinants of choice, may easily be inclined to deny both that there is any such thing as mental causality, and that "motive" means anything but intention. But both of these inclinations are mistaken. We shall create confusion if we do not notice (*a*) that phenomena deserving the name of mental causality exist, for we can make the question "Why?" into a request for the sort of answer that I considered under that head; (*b*) that mental causality is not restricted to choices or voluntary or intentional actions but is of wider application; it is restricted to the wider field of things the agent knows about *not* as an observer, so that it includes some involuntary actions; (*c*) that motives are not mental causes; and (*d*) that there is application for "motive" other than the applications of "the intention with which a man acts."

Revenge and gratitude are motives; if I kill a man as an act of revenge I may say I do it in order to be revenged, or that revenge is my object; but revenge is not some further thing obtained by killing him, it is rather that killing him is revenge. Asked why I killed him, I reply "Because he killed my brother." We might compare this answer, which describes a concrete past event, to the answer describing a concrete future state of affairs which we sometimes get in statements of objectives. It is the same with gratitude, and remorse, and pity for something specific. These motives differ from, say, love or curiosity or despair in just this way: something that *has happened* (or is at present happening) is given as the ground of an action or abstention that is good or bad for the person (it may be oneself, as with remorse) at whom it is aimed. And if we wanted to explain, e.g., revenge, we should say it was harming someone because he had done one some harm; we should not need to add some description of the feelings prompting the action or of the thoughts that had gone with it. Whereas saying that someone does something out of, say, friendship cannot be explained in any such way. I will call revenge and gratitude and remorse and pity backward-looking motives, and contrast them with motive-in-general.

Motive-in-general is a very difficult topic which I do not want to discuss at any length. Consider the statement that one motive for my signing a petition was admiration for its promoter, X. Asked "Why did you sign it?" I might well say "Well, for one thing, X, who is promoting it, did . . ." and describe what he did in an admiring way. I might add "Of course, I know that is not a ground for signing it, but I am sure it was one of the things that most influenced me"—which need *not* mean: "I thought explicitly of this before signing." I say "Consider this" really with a view to saying "let us not consider it here." It is too complicated. The account of motive popularized by Professor Ryle does not appear satisfactory. He recommends construing "he boasted from vanity" as saying "he boasted . . . and his doing so satisfies the law-like proposition that whenever he finds a chance of securing the admiration and envy of others, he does whatever he thinks will produce this admiration and envy."[2] This passage is rather curious and roundabout in its way of putting what it seems to say, but I can't understand it unless it implies that a man could not be said to have boasted from vanity unless he always behaved vainly, or at least very often did so. But this does not seem to be true.

To give a motive (of the sort I have labeled "motive-in-general," as opposed to backward-looking motives and intentions) is to say something like "See the action in this light." To explain one's own actions by an account indicating a motive is to put them in a certain light. This sort of explanation is often elicited by the question "Why?" The question whether the light in which one so puts one's action is a true light is a notoriously difficult one.

The motives admiration, curiosity, spite, friendship, fear, love of truth, despair, and a host of others are either of this extremely complicated kind, or are forward-looking or mixed. I call a motive forward-looking if it is an intention. For example, to say that someone did something for fear of . . . often comes to the same as saying he did so lest . . . or in order that . . . should not happen.

Leaving, then, the topic of motive-in-general or "interpretative" motive, let us return to backward-looking motives. Why is it that in revenge and gratitude, pity and remorse, the past event (or present situation) is a reason for acting, not just a mental cause?

Now the most striking thing about these four is the way in which good and evil are involved in them. E.g., if I am grateful to someone, it is because he has done me some good, or at least I think he has, and I cannot show gratitude by something that I intend to harm him. In remorse, I hate some good things for myself; I could not express remorse *by* getting myself plenty of enjoyments, or *for* something that I did not find bad. If I do something out of revenge which is in fact advantageous rather than harmful to my enemy, my action, in its description of being advantageous to him, is involuntary.

These facts are the clue to our present problem. If an action has to be thought of by the

2 *The Concept of Mind*, p. 89.

agent as doing good or harm of some sort, and the thing in the past as good or bad, in order for the thing in the past to be the reason for the action, then this reason shows not a mental cause but a motive. This will come out in the agent's elaborations on his answer to the question "Why?"

It might seem that this is not the most important point, but that the important point is that a *proposed* action can be questioned and the answer be a mention of something past. "I am going to kill him."—"Why?"—"He killed my father." But do we yet know what a proposal to act is; other than a prediction which the predictor justifies, if he does justify it, by mentioning a reason for acting? and the meaning of the expression "reason for acting" is precisely what we are at present trying to elucidate. Might one not predict mental causes and their effects? Or even their effects after the causes have occurred? E.g., "This is going to make me angry." Here it may be worth while to remark that it is a mistake to think one cannot choose whether to act from a motive. Plato saying to a slave "I should beat you if I were not angry" would be a case. Or a man might have a policy of never making remarks about a certain person because he could not speak about that man unenviously or unadmiringly.

We have now distinguished between a backward-looking motive and a mental cause, and found that here at any rate what the agent reports in answer to the question "Why?" is a reason-for-acting if, in treating it as a reason, he conceives it as something good or bad, and his own action as doing good or harm. If you could, e.g., show that either the action for which he has revenged himself, or that in which he has revenged himself, was quite harmless or beneficial, he ceases to offer a reason, except prefaced by "I thought." If it is a proposed revenge, he either gives it up or changes his reasons. No such discovery would affect an assertion of mental causality. Whether in general good and harm play an essential part in the concept of intention is something it still remains to find out. So far good and harm have only been introduced as making a clear difference between a backward-looking motive and a mental cause. When the question "Why?" about a present action is answered by description of a future state of affairs, this is already distinguished

from a mental cause just by being future. Here there does not so far seem to be any need to characterize intention as being essentially of good or of harm.

Now, however, let us consider this case:

> Why did you do it?
> Because he told me to.

Is this a cause or a reason? It appears to depend very much on what the action was or what the circumstances were. And we should often refuse to make any distinction at all between something's being a reason and its being a cause of the kind in question; for that was explained as what one is after if one asks the agent what led up to and issued in an action, but being given a reason and accepting it might be such a thing. And how would one distinguish between cause and reason in such a case as having hung one's hat on a peg because one's host said "Hang up your hat on that peg"? Nor, I think, would it be correct to say that this is a reason and not a mental cause because of the understanding of the words that went into obeying the suggestion. Here one would be attempting a contrast between this case and, say, turning round at hearing someone say Boo! But this case would not in fact be decisively on one side or the other; forced to say whether the noise was a reason or a cause, one would probably decide by how sudden one's reaction was. Further, there is no question of understanding a sentence in the following case: "Why did you waggle your two fore-fingers by your temples?"—"Because *he* was doing it"; but this is not particularly different from hanging one's hat up because one's host said "Hang your hat up." Roughly speaking, if one were forced to go on with the distinction, the more the action is described as a mere response, the more inclined one would be to the word "cause"; while the more it is described as a response to something as having a *significance* that is dwelt on by the agent, or as a response surrounded with thoughts and questions, the more inclined one would be to use the word "reason." But in very many cases the distinction would have no point.

This, however, does not mean that it never has a point. The cases on which we first grounded the distinction might be called "full-blown": that is to say, the case of, e.g., revenge on the one hand, and of the thing that made me jump and knock a cup off a table on the other. Roughly speaking, it establishes something as a reason to object to it, not as when one says "Noises should not make you jump like that: hadn't you better see a doctor?" but in such a way as to link it up with motives and intentions. "You did it because he told you to? But why do what he says?" Answers like "he has done a lot for me";

"he is my father"; "it would have been the worse for me if I hadn't" give the original answer a place among reasons. Thus the full-blown cases are the right ones to consider in order to see the distinction between reason and cause. But it is worth noticing that what is so commonly said, that reason and cause are everywhere sharply distinct notions, is not true.

Decision, Intention, and Certainty*

There is a kind of certainty about human actions, wants, likes, and dislikes, which is different from the kind of certainty about these subjects that is based upon empirical evidence: it is a kind of certainty, or knowledge, to which the notion of evidence is irrelevant. And it is different again from the kind of knowledge that is knowing how to do something, that is, the knowledge that is a skill or competence.

In each of the following pairs of sentences knowledge of this peculiar kind is mentioned: (1) "I am not sure which of these I like best." "I know which I like." (2) "He does not know what he wants." "I now know what I want." (3) "I think I will do it, but I am not sure." "I know now what I will do" (where an entirely voluntary action is envisaged). The kind of knowledge referred to in each of these sentences, as they are normally used, would be dissociated from any possible appeal to evidence. This is the most important, but not the only, respect in which there is an analogy between the pairs of sentences (1), (2), and (3). There is also an analogy in the grammatical form of these sentences. But in this article we are concerned with only one case of the kind of certainty or knowledge that cannot be associated with any appeal to evidence: namely, case (3), a man's knowledge of his own present and future voluntary actions. Our thesis is that there is a necessary connection between certainty of this kind, and upon this topic, and deciding to do something, and also that there is a necessary connection between certainty of this kind

and intending to do something, and doing it intentionally.

The necessary connection between certainty about future voluntary action and decision emerges in the following entailments: (1) "I have decided to do this" entails "I am certain that I will do this, unless I am in some way prevented." (2) "I am certain that I will do this" (where the action referred to is entirely voluntary) entails "I have decided to do this." (3) "I do not know what I will do in such-and-such a contingency" (where the possible actions are envisaged as entirely voluntary and as a matter of my own choice) entails "I have not decided what I will do in such-and-such a contingency." (4) "I have not decided what I will do in such-and-such a contingency" entails "I am uncertain what I will do in such-and-such a contingency." (5) "He has not yet decided what he will do" entails "He does not yet know what he will do." (6) "He does not yet know what he will do" entails "He has not yet decided what he will do." (7) "He is wondering what to do" entails "He is uncertain what he will do." (8) "He has made up his mind what he will do" entails "There is no doubt in his mind about what he will do."

If a man is in the position of still having to decide between two or more courses of action open to him, then he must be uncertain what he will do. His uncertainty might in principle be terminated in two very different ways: either, after considering the evidence of his own behavior and reactions in similar situations in the past, he may become certain in his own mind that he will in fact do so-and-so, or at least try to do it, when the time comes: this would be certainty based upon empirical evidence, and his announce-

* Stuart Hampshire and H. L. A. Hart, "Decision, Intention, and Certainty," *Mind,* LXVII (January 1958), 1–12, reprinted with the permission of the authors and the editor, Gilbert Ryle.

ment of it would, for this reason, count as a *prediction,* and not as a decision: or, after reflection on the *reasons* for acting in one way rather than another, he may become certain (make up his mind) what he will do, or at least try to do: in this case his announcement will count as an announcement of his *decision,* and not as a prediction. If a man does claim to be able to predict with certainty his own future actions, basing his prediction on induction, then he is implying that the actions in question will be in some sense, or to some degree, involuntary, the effect of causes outside his own control. If action in the situation envisaged were entirely voluntary, then it must be up to him to decide what he will do. If it is up to him to decide what he is going to do, then he must still be uncertain what he will do until he has made a decision or until his intentions are formed. While he is making the decision, and while he is reviewing reasons for acting in one way rather than another, he must be in a state of uncertainty about what he is going to do. The certainty comes at the moment of decision, and indeed constitutes the decision, when the certainty is arrived at in this way, as a result of considering reasons, and not as a result of considering evidence.

Many, if not most, voluntary and deliberate actions are not preceded by any datable event which could be called a moment of decision. An action is often performed, voluntarily and deliberately, without the agent's having stopped to wonder whether he would perform it or not, and without his having rehearsed in his mind the reasons for and against performing it. It might still be true that, if he had been asked what he was going to do, he would have been able to answer with complete confidence. He knew what he would do, and he might even be said to have decided to do it, although he had never considered alternatives. But the word "decision," as opposed to the word "intention," is more naturally associated with conditions in which the agent has asked himself the question "Shall I do it or shall I not?"—thereby showing his uncertainty about what he is going to do, an uncertainty of the kind which constitutes indecision. When he has made his decision, that is, when, after considering reasons, all uncertainty about what he is going to do has been removed from his mind, he will be said to intend to do whatever he has decided to do,

until either he falls into uncertainty again, as a result of further reasons suggesting themselves, or until he definitely changes his mind.

As there are degrees of knowledge, ranging from complete certainty to complete uncertainty, so there are degrees of decision. "Will you accept the appointment?" "I think I will, but I am not sure." In English the word "intend" often has a suggestion of the tentative and of the not entirely certain; good intentions may come to nothing. But "decide" has a ring of finality. If I say that I had decided to do action X, but admit that I did not in fact do it, or even try to do it, then I strictly imply either that I later changed my mind, or that I was somehow prevented, or that I altogether lost control of myself. It may be objected that "deciding" and "changing my mind" represent an act, something that I *do,* and that therefore deciding cannot be adequately characterized as simply becoming certain about one's own future voluntary action after considering reasons, and not considering evidence. One may be inclined to say that the certainty is the consequence or outcome of the decision, and must be distinguished from the decision itself. But what is the force of saying that to decide to do something is to perform an act? This category-word, in this as in other contexts, is entirely unclear. Certainly one can say: "You ought to decide, to make up your mind." Or one can give a blunt order: "Make up your mind." The possibility of using the imperative, or the quasi-imperative form, of the verb might be taken as a sufficient condition of saying that the verb represents an act. There is also the idiom: "I cannot make up my mind: I am quite unable to decide between these two courses of action." It looks therefore as if there is something which I cannot *do,* and it is not the actions themselves, but rather the preliminary action of deciding between them. But these idioms are often misleading. Often the order to decide is an order to do one or other of the actions, no matter which, and often it is an order to announce a decision. But even when the imperative, or quasi-imperative form cannot be attached to another verb—as it cannot in the phrases "Never hesitate" or "Always decide what you are going to do in advance"—it is still an imperative which has a parallel use with the cognitive verbs. One may intelligibly be told not to believe information of a certain kind, or one may be told that one ought not to believe it. One may even be told that one ought not to doubt some matter of fact, and that one ought to accept it as something which is certainly true. Doubt and certainty about an action are not in this respect essentially different from doubt and certainty about a statement; the one is as little, or as much, an act as the other.

II

If there are two possible kinds of certainty about one's own future actions—inductive certainty, and certainty based upon reasons, which is decision—it is evidently possible that they may on occasion come into conflict with each other. This is one part of the problem of free will. Suppose a man to have been offered an appointment: he is undecided, and expresses his state of indecision in the appropriate form —"I am uncertain whether to do it or not." In this state of indecision, and therefore of uncertainty, he asks himself the question "Shall I do it or shall I not?" reviewing reasons for and against, with a view to ending the uncertainty, that is, to deciding. If he has confronted choices exactly like this one on many occasions in the past, and if he has always passed through a phase of indecision and then refused, he may acknowledge to himself that this is good evidence that he will in fact ultimately refuse the appointment on this occasion: he may confess to having a feeling or premonition that he will ultimately refuse, while saying that he has still not decided. But the evidence of his past behavior, or of the behavior of people like him, or even the evidence of a well-tested psychological law, cannot by itself convince him that he will in fact refuse, *if* he still maintains that his refusal or acceptance is a matter for his own decision. If he is convinced by empirical evidence alone that he will certainly refuse, then he must have been convinced by this evidence that it is not in his power not to refuse, and that, in spite of appearances, the outcome will not be determined by his decision. And there certainly are occasions when a man may in this way adopt a spectator's attitude to his own conduct, convinced by experience, or perhaps even by scientific knowledge, that the appearance of free decision is delusive and that, when it comes to the moment of action, he will certainly act in a certain way. If he *admits* that this is his conviction, it would be senseless for him to claim that he was making any decision in the matter; nothing would count as a decision to do that which he is certain on other grounds that he will in any case do, and nothing would count as a decision to do that which he is certain that he will not do. A man may decide to *try* to achieve a result which he thinks, on the basis of evidence, that he will almost certainly fail to achieve; but then there must be some action or actions, which constitute the attempt, and which he is certain that he will perform, and certain not on empirical evidence.

There may be mixed, confused situations in which a man drifts into a course of action, fatalistically certain on the evidence of his own past, that this is the course of action that he will in fact follow, while at the same time not denying that his own conduct in this sphere could be changed by his own decisions. He half decides to continue as before, and half feels himself to be passive in the matter, his certainty about his future action being based on a mixture of the evidence of his past behavior together with reasons for not making the effort to change. The psychology of human decision can be very complicated. But the fact that there are these mixed cases does not invalidate the general distinction between the certainty about one's own future action that is based upon evidence and induction, and the certainty that is based upon reasons.

This kind of certainty, or knowledge, about our own future actions will help to illuminate the concept of intention also.

Intention

Usually a person engaged in doing something knows, and is able to specify, what action he is doing, and often, though not always, a persons knows, and is able to specify, some action which he will later try to do. Yet in neither of these cases is the agent's knowledge of his own present or future action normally derived from observation nor is it a conclusion from evidence. Other people are often able to say what action someone is doing or is going to do, when they know this either from observation of his movements or as a conclusion from evidence available to them. They make use of criteria or evidence in determining what he is doing or going to do; but the agent himself does not. The segregation of this form of knowledge which the agent has of his own present or future actions, and the identification of corresponding uses of expressions such as "not knowing what one is doing," "being certain or uncertain," "being mistaken," is an essential element in the elucidation of the concept of intention. We shall consider the dependence upon this form of knowledge (practical knowledge) of certain distinct but related applications of the notion of intention.

There are two principal ways in which intention is connected with action. First, when a person has done something, e.g., struck another person, the question of whether he did it intentionally or unintentionally may arise, and this is equivalent, except in certain trivial respects, to the question whether he intended, or did not intend, to do what he has in fact done. Secondly, the question may arise as to whether a person intends, or does not intend, to do some action in the future; and a similar question may arise about his past intention to do some action, even if he did not in fact do it.

These two applications of the notion of intention do not of course exhaust the notion. Besides them there is the special application of intention in cases where it has close connection with the notions of meaning and reference. What did he intend by those words? To whom did he intend to refer by that name? There is also the use of intention in conjunction with the actions of other people: we may intend other people to do certain things or even to have certain experiences. "I intended you to take that book," "I intended him to suffer." Although there are these and other applications of the concept of intention, the first two are of special relevance to the present subject.

Acting intentionally. We must first consider the type of context required if the question whether a person has done something intentionally or not is to have any point. In any ordinary narrative describing ordinary actions done in normal circumstances, it would be pointless to say that a person did these things intentionally; for normally there is fulfilled presumption that if a person does something, he does it intentionally. This is a feature of the whole conceptual scheme involved in our description of persons in terms of actions. If I am telling you simply what someone did, e.g., took off his hat or sat down, it would normally be redundant, and hence misleading, though not false, to say that he

sat down intentionally. The primary point of saying that someone acted intentionally is to rebut a *prima facie* suggestion that he was in some way ignorant of, or mistaken about, some element involved in this action. Usually the suggestion arises from the fact that what he has done is abnormal or wrong in some way or that it is something which ordinary people would not do except unintentionally. Part of the force of "He did it intentionally" is just to rule out the suggestion that he did it unintentionally, where "unintentionally" means that the agent did what he did through some accident or by mistake. This suggests that the whole meaning of "intentionally" simply lies in its negation of accident or mistake, and that once these two ideas are elucidated, as they easily can be, the analysis of the notion of intentionally doing something is within our grasp. On this view the analysis will simply be (1) a description of the appropriate context for the use of the expression "intentionally" as rebutting accident or mistake, and (2) the elucidation of the ideas of accident and mistake. But this would only be the first step toward the analysis of the notion of intentionally doing something; for the assertion that someone has done something intentionally, or that he intended to do what he has done, is not merely the equivalent of the assertion that he did not do it unintentionally, or that he did not do it accidentally or by mistake. Accident and mistake are certainly incompatible with the agent's doing what he did intentionally; but the assertion that someone did what he did intentionally does not merely exclude these cases of unintentional action. This may be seen from the following example. A man fires and shoots another: if asked what he was doing, and if he was prepared to give an honest answer, he would identify his action as shooting at someone. But in a perfectly ordinary sense of "know," he would know that shooting at someone involved making the loud noise which in fact the shot had made. In such a case it is clear that he did not make the noise by mistake or by accident; it is therefore clear that he did not make it unintentionally. But on these facts it would be misleading to say he intentionally made the noise, or that he intended to make the noise; for this would suggest that this is what the agent would say that he was doing, if asked. Always the expression "He intended to do it" means more than, though it also includes, "He did not do it unintentionally."

If an action is to be intentional, or to be what the agent intended to do, two different kinds of requirement must be satisfied. First, the agent must have ordinary empirical knowledge of certain features of his environment and of the nature and characteristics of certain things affected by his movements. Precisely what knowledge of this sort he must have will depend upon precisely what action is ascribed to him. If, for example, he is said intentionally to have shot at a bird, he must know in the ordinary sense of "know," that what he has in his hands is a gun, and that there is a bird in the line of fire. He must also have certain types of general knowledge, for example of the consequences of pulling the trigger of a loaded gun. Without such knowledge as this, his action in shooting the bird would be accidental or done by mistake, and hence would be ranked as unintentional. Second, and more important, if his action is intentional (what he intended to do), the agent must know what he was doing in some sense which would differentiate his shooting at the bird from other nonaccidental actions performed at the same time, such as making the cartridge explode. This is the action which he himself would specify, if he were prepared to give an honest reply to the question "What are you doing?"

The special kind of knowledge involved in intentional action may emerge from a comparison of the agent's own declaration or description of what he is doing ("I am shooting at X") and statements made about his action by others ("He is shooting at X"). The latter statements are generally made on the strength of observation of the agent's movements; and these movements provide logically sufficient grounds for such statements ("He is shooting at X"), though they do not exhaust the meaning of the statement, which is liable to qualification, though not withdrawal, if it later appears that certain abnormalities were present in the situation. In the case of statements made by others, the question "How do you know that he is shooting at X?" is one which could be properly answered by referring to his observed movements. But the agent does not himself use these, or any other criteria, in declaring what he is doing; there is a corresponding pointlessness in the question, "How do you know you are shooting at X?" or

"What grounds have you for saying that you were shooting at X?" The suggestion that before answering the question "What are you doing?" we first look and see how our body is disposed is absurd. The ascription to ourselves of some action (the declaration of what we are currently doing) is not a report of our bodily movements nor a conclusion from the observation of movements. Perhaps the absurdity is most evident in the case of speech action; if someone to whom we are talking asks us what we are saying, we do not have to listen or recall the sound of our own words before answering, and our answer is not a report of those sounds nor a conclusion from evidence provided by them.

Secondly, a knowledge of the position or movements of our own body would not be sufficient to enable us to answer the question "What are you doing?" In the relevant sense of knowing what we are doing, it is perfectly possible that we should recognize, and be able to describe, such features of the situation as that a knife is in our hands, and yet we may have forgotten what we were engaged in doing. Except in abnormal cases, memory returns and we may then say that we were sharpening a pencil. This illustrates the irrelevance of prior observation by the agent of his bodily movements to his declarations of what he is currently engaged in doing.

Thirdly, there is a sense in which our own declarations about our current actions may be mistaken. We may say that we are sharpening a pencil when in fact, owing to inadvertence, we were cutting away at a pen. In these cases the natural comment would be, not that the agent's statement was false (though there would also be occasions for that comment), but that he was doing something unintentionally or by mistake. But it is important to notice that, whereas statements made by others concerning a person's action characteristically leave open the question whether he has done what he has done unintentionally, it is a distinguishing feature of the agent's own statement about his actions that an answer of the form "I am doing this but I am not doing it intentionally" would be absurd. It would be the virtual equivalent of "I am doing this but I do not know what I am doing."

The normal ability of an agent to say what he is doing without prior observation suggests two explanations, both of which, though tempting, are mistaken. It may seem that the agent's ability to specify what he is doing in this way is explained by the fact that, prior to acting, he must always have considered and decided what to do; in saying what he is actually doing he is simply recalling the previous decision. The objections to this are, first, that very frequently we know what we are doing, and so are doing it intentionally, although this has never been preceded by any stage of prior deliberation or doubt. I may just break off drawing in order to sharpen a pencil without prior deliberation, and yet I can still answer correctly the question "What are you doing?" without first observing my own movements. And, even where there has been prior deliberation and decision, the question "What are you doing?" is answered without recall of this earlier stage.

The second explanation, suggested by certain passages in Wittgenstein's *Philosophical Investigations,* is that, since the agent in declaring what he is doing makes no use of any criteria, and in particular does not use the criteria upon which other persons rely, the agent's own declaration should be treated, not as a statement, but as a "signal," to be assimilated to the behavior-criteria which are the basis of third-person statements about his actions. But this explanation, though it may serve to correct some mistakes (notably that the agent's own statements about his actions are made on the basis of observation), surely distorts the facts and is open to now familiar objections. The agent's own statements about his actions may be true or false; we contrast an agent's *telling us what he is doing* with other forms of words which he might use and which might be our evidence that he is doing some action. His statement about his own action stands in recognizable logical relations with statements made by other persons. If the agent says, "I am shooting a bird," and a third party says, "He is not shooting a bird," these statements are contradictories. If the third party says, "He is shooting a bird," and the agent says, "I am shooting a bird," the latter statement confirms the first. These relationships would be impossible if first-person statements were to be treated as signals, and therefore as having a different meaning from third-person statements about action. Only a doctrinaire identification of the meaning of the statement with the means of its verification

entails this result. Action is a concept which, like many concepts involving reference to states of consciousness (I expect, he expects; I believe, he believes), exhibits this asymmetry between first-person and third-person statements.

Intention to do a future act. In those cases where the agent announces his intention to do an action in the future, there is a similar need to distinguish a belief which the agent may have formed as to the course of his future actions as a result of observation, or as a conclusion from evidence, from a belief which he has formed independently of observation or evidence; for the second is essentially involved in this application of the notion of intention.

It is clear that a person's announcement of his intention to do some action in the future is not a prediction that he will do this action, although others may base their predictions upon such announcements by the agent. That such statements are not predictions is evident from the fact that if the agent does not act as he says that he intends to act, this exposes him, not to the criticism that what he said was false, or that he was mistaken, but to the charge that he has changed his mind. He may be accused, if he does not do what he says that he intends to do, of having lied about his intentions. But it is possible for him to exculpate himself from this charge by convincing others that he had changed his mind.

The obviously mistaken analysis of announcements of intention to do an act in the future must be distinguished from an analysis of such an announcement as a statement by the agent of his present belief as to his future action. On this view, "I intend to do X" will at least entail, "I believe that I shall do X." Certainly this needs qualification: for it is plain that "I intend to do X" is compatible with "I believe I shall do X unless prevented or unless I fail by reason of circumstances outside my control." The statement "I intend to do X" is also compatible with "I believe I shall do X unless a change of circumstances leads me to change my mind," though there is at least a suggestion that if the agent thus leaves open the possibility of a change of mind, he does not yet really intend to do the future action. If we take these qualifications into account, the minimum force of "I intend to do X" is "I believe that I will try to do X." Hence it would be a contradiction to say, "I intend to do X though I do not believe I will even try to do X when an opportunity arises." But again the salient characteristic of this form of belief is that it is not a conclusion from evidence, and that it is neither proper to ask, nor necessary to answer, the question: "Why do you believe that you will try to do X?" The contrast with ordinary professions of belief is plain.

The contrast between first- and third-person statements is instructive. An observer who says "He intends to do X" makes his statement on the basis of observation or evidence, and he could be asked to support his statement by evidence, which may range from remote circumstantial evidence to a report of X's statement of his own future intentions. On the other hand, the third person who says that X intends to do a future action is committed to the statement that X believes that he will at least try to do X if the occasion arises. He has evidence that X does so believe, but it would be absurd to suggest that X himself has evidence that he does so believe or has evidence in favor of the truth of his belief.

In many cases the agent will have formed the intention to do a future action as a result of considering alternatives and deciding between them, and perhaps the characteristics of intentions to do a future act best emerge from a study of such cases. But not all intention is formed as a result of prior decision. I intend to go home after writing this essay, but I have never decided to do this. If we consider those intentions which emerge as a result of deliberation and decision, we can trace certain parallels with the formation of theoretical certainty about the future, as well as the major contrast we have noticed with regard to the independence of evidence. In deliberation we consider whether to do, or not to do, something, and we oscillate between these alternatives: we attend to reasons for or against the proposed action, and we attribute more or less weight to these reasons: we then decide what to do. In the theoretical case we consider whether something is or is not be the case, and we attend to the evidence in favor of one or other alternative: we find the evidence in favor of one alternative convincing and then decide that it is or is not be the case. In both cases we could substitute for the expression "decision" expressions such as "being certain" or "making up our mind." But neither the deliberative process concerning future action nor its theoretical counterpart need issue in decision. We may remain undecided, on the one hand whether to do something or not, and on the other hand whether something is the case or not. We may be unable to decide, and may give up both the practical or theoretical problem as too difficult, leaving others to tell us what to do or what is to be the case.

The characteristic termination of the practical inquiry is the settled frame of mind when we are no longer undecided what to do. We have made up our mind and are both certain what to do and certain what we will try to do. In describing this termination of deliberation, we cannot separate the temporal reference to the future from the solution of the practical question. We have decided what to do, and that we shall at least try to do it. We cannot have this form of confident belief about our future voluntary action without this form of practical certainty about what to do.

Mens Rea and Personal Guilt*

To facilitate following the course of this discussion, an outline of a pertinent means-end situation may be suggestive. The most common of human experiences is the direction of conduct toward the attainment of goals. Such

*Jerome Hall, General Principles of Criminal Law, 2d ed. (Indianapolis: The Bobbs-Merrill Co., 1960), pp. 76–77, 92–100, reprinted with the permission of the author and the publishers. Footnotes are omitted.

conduct involves (a) an end sought; (b) deliberate functioning to reach that end, which manifests the intentionality of the conduct; and (c) the reasons or grounds for the end-seeking, i.e., its motivation. The ethical distinction relevant to such action is that between "good" and "right," and their opposites. This distinction is very old; it is probably the most important one in ethics and, as will appear, it is fundamental in penal liability. If we examine a person's conduct with a view to assessing its moral significance, we can distinguish these two basic components, e.g., a man who gives property to an orphan asylum does right, but if he did that because he hated his heirs, his motive was bad. On the other hand, a motive may be good, although the act done is wrong, e.g., Jean Valjean. Finally, a good motive may coincide with a right act—which, of course, represents the ideal.

It must be emphasized that the distinction between goodness (or badness) of motive and the rightness (or wrongness) of what is done does not imply an actual bifurcation in the relevant conduct. Every act that is morally significant is motivated as well as intentional. We are, in fact, concerned with a unified process, a course of action which always, at every step and at each moment, involves both motive and intentionality. This is true even though it may also be true that motive precedes intention. If we do not recognize this or if we lose sight of it, we are apt to relegate motive to a prior and concluded area or, for some other reason, we are apt to concentrate on one of the essential components of action. In sum, the above distinction is analytical. It implies the necessity of viewing morally significant conduct from two perspectives, i.e., with reference to the goodness or badness of the motive and the rightness ("fitness") or wrongness of what was done.

. . .

In sum, motive in penal law is distinguished from intention (*mens rea*) and from the scientific sense of "cause." The former distinction is clarified if ulterior intention is ascribed to an objective or end, while motive retains its personal subjective meaning as a ground or reason of action. . . . That an action was motivated excludes accident and negligence and implies intention. An intention is thus descriptive of a mode of conduct that is contrasted with accident and inadvertent movement. A motive answers the question why, neither in terms of causation nor in those of a further ulterior objective, but in terms that give a reason which is the subject of an ethical appraisal. For when we ask questions about a person's motives, we are asking for data relevant to evaluation of his character or at least of the morality of a particular act. Given a motive, a relevant intention can be inferred. But the converse does not apply; i.e., one may be positive that certain conduct was intentional without knowing any motive for it. All of this conforms to the preponderant ethical-legal meaning of motive and to its exclusion from the scope of *mens rea*.

"MENS REA" AND PERSONAL GUILT

Moral culpability, i.e., personal guilt, includes both *mens rea* and motivation. For example, D kills T; all agree that what he did is morally wrong. But the appraisal of D's moral culpability must also take account of his motive: was D acting from cupidity, knowing he was named the chief beneficiary of T's will? Or was the motive his love for his sick wife, who needed an operation? Just as we cannot pass an adequate moral judgment if we know only what harm has been committed but not the motive for committing it, so, too, we cannot properly estimate conduct solely on the basis of its motivation—we need to know also what was done. It is necessary to unite these judgments in a single evaluation to determine the moral culpability of the actor.

Difficult problems concern harms perpetrated from laudable motives, e.g., theft of food for a hungry family, actions inspired by religious convictions, certain cases of euthanasia, some political crimes, and the like. The relevant moral judgment implied in the penal law is absolute: no matter how good the actor's motive, since he voluntarily (*mens rea*) committed a penal harm he is to some degree morally culpable—"sufficiently" so to warrant at least control under probation. The legal restriction of the *substantive* law to that aspect of the actor's guilt has not been understood by criminologists and psychiatrists who assert that the law is not interested in an offender's motives; but it also raises serious questions for lawyers.

Even if it is granted that a point is reached in some cases where no harm was committed, nay, that a benefit was conferred, e.g., in the assassination of a brutal tyrant, such marginal cases cannot be made the sound basis for incorporating motive as an essential element in the definition of crimes. Instead, it should be recognized that the preservation of the objective meaning of the principle of *mens rea* as well as of the attendant principle of legality has its price. For it is impossible to forbid any class of harms without including rare marginal instances where a maximum of good motivation combines with the minimum of the proscribed harm, or even no harm at all, so that the final estimate is that the value protected by the rule was not impaired in that instance. When cases involving this type of problem recur, e.g., infanticide by mothers shortly after birth, which were formerly within the definition of murder, it is possible to construct a new crime by defining a separate class in terms which accord with the objective meaning of *mens rea* and harm, i.e., in terms which do not refer to motivation. The exercise of official discretion even to the point of foregoing prosecution or suspending sentence, e.g., as regards a Jean Valjean, is the "safety valve" which preserves the principles of *mens rea* and legality in the vast majority of cases. What needs emphasis is that there is an extremely important difference between the preservation of the legality and ethical significance of the principle of *mens rea* by allocating questions of motivation to administration and the depreciation of both penal law and its ethical significance by making the relevant rules vague, if motive is made material.

Despite the doubts raised by marginal cases, the logic of the substantive law excludes the possibility that there can ever be a violation of a penal law that is not a legal harm. The parallel ethical rationale implies equally that there can never be such action that is not immoral. Legal liability in the marginal cases does not therefore imply that the penal law is amoral, that it seeks mere outward conformity. It implies that it is based on an objective ethics, expressed in the principle of *mens rea* and, accordingly, that conscience may err. The premise is that the morality of a sound body of penal law is objective in the sense that it may be validly opposed to individual opinion. In extreme cases of impaired conscience, the M'Naghten Rules exclude liability; and in many others, where the motives were good, mitigation makes its greatest appeal.

Holmes emphasized the fact that penal law disregards the defendant's ethical insensitivity and lack of education; and we shall later discuss his theory. It may be noted here that in view of the simple valuations expressed in penal law, these factors should not be exaggerated—it does not require a college educa-

tion or extraordinary sensitivity to understand that it is wrong to kill, rape, or rob. Recent anthropological studies stressing universal values regarding homicide, treason, incest, theft, and so on, are also relevant. At the same time, one who defends the objective morality of the modern principle of *mens rea* must postulate a sound, spontaneously constructed penal law, the product of experience and inquiry functioning freely over many centuries; and this premise encounters difficulty in some parts of every actual legal system.

There are cases which trouble those who are concerned that actual guilt be the essential condition of penal liability. Sometimes organic disabilities are evident and there are other impairments which are not fully recognized in current legal rules, e.g., regarding addiction to alcohol and narcotics. Cultural differences sometimes engender attitudes which strongly oppose those represented in the penal law. For example, in certain Latin-American countries the sexual mores of the dominant minority are imposed by penal law upon the Indian population which for centuries approved the conduct that the code condemns as a serious crime. A neighborhood group of delinquents who respect each other's possessions and may be courageous and self-sacrificing think it is quite proper, perhaps praiseworthy, to take property from the automobiles of the "rich." So, too, occasional visitors from other countries find in some important respects a different criminal code. There are Mormons in the United States who believe they are obeying a divine injunction as well as an onerous social obligation when they contract multiple marriages. There are other religious minorities, e.g., Jehovah's Witnesses and Christian Scientists, who also encounter difficulty with prevalent opinion and penal law. There are conscientious objectors and political rebels. And, finally, we must recall the ethically insensitive, thoughtless persons, Shaw's "sick consciences," sometimes members of criminal or juvenile gangs, who often do not share the values of the majority. In sum, there are undoubtedly many cases of violence, theft, bigamy, political subversion, and so on, where the offenders acted in accordance with their conscience.

With reference to some of these offenders, it is pertinent to observe that penal law has an educational function to perform. But if it be granted that some of these offenders are not only well motivated but also enlightened, what can be done in their behalf that is compatible with the preservation of legality? Occasionally, a court takes cognizance of the standards of the community from which the defendant comes, as did an English court in *Wilson v. Inyang*; but while this can always be done in fixing the sentence, its recognition as a defense in substantive law would raise serious difficulties. A radical solution of the problem of justice in such cases might suggest the abandonment of the entire penal law. If that is excluded, there is no escape from the alternative that a functioning legal order must cleave to the objective meaning of the principle of *mens rea* (the constant premise being a sound, freely constructed penal law); and this undoubtedly falls far short of perfect justice. Mitigation is, of course, very much in order in such cases, but full exculpation would not only contradict the values of penal law, it would also undermine the foundation of a legal order. This is the difficult problem which confronts officials who wish to preserve legality and also dispense justice. The tensions are insistent and they sometimes lead to the enactment of provisions which are at odds with the principle of legality.

This is the tendency of provisions to the effect that if a negligent or an ignorant harm-doer "could" have acted with due care or "could" have known he was at fault, the conditions of just punishment are satisfied. In support of these provisions it is urged that they apply the test of actual fault, i.e., they exculpate if the defendant lacked such competence. But this is a very dubious claim, and it may well be the case that, instead of achieving that result, the actual effect is the imposition of a verbally disguised objective liability, aggravated by the concomitant depreciation of legality. If the requirement is competence to know the law, the ethical force of such provisions is illusory. For example, if sitting on a park bench is punishable by ten years' imprisonment, can it be successfully maintained that the fact that an offender could have discovered that there was such a law justifies the punishment or indeed any liability? With reference to Muslims, Mormons, Christian Scientists, Jehovah's Witnesses, and political and other rebels, what is pertinent is not that they could have known the law but

that they espouse a different code of morals. So, too, it does not seem persuasive to argue that they "could" have known what was ethically right.

"Capacity," as that is determined by officials interpreting such vague provisions as that noted above, probably means the competence to form correct valuations, which are assumed to be those represented in the penal code. If that assumption is sound, it is only the intrusion of substantive incompatibility when sanctions are imposed because an offender "could" have known, and so on, or when there is exculpation on the ground that, though normal, he "could not" have known, etc. What is compatible with objectively moral penal law is the enforcement of it, mitigated by discretion and the occasional use of the "safety valve" to effect complete exculpation. The fact that this must be the over-all conclusion does not exclude the most enlightened individualization that is compatible with legality, e.g., the definition of crimes to reflect objective differences such as first offenders and habitual ones, a wide choice of sanctions, and the humane administration of penal-correctional institutions.

The need to exclude motive from the scope of *mens rea* may be further seen in the consequences of a contrary rule. Suppose it were enacted that criminal conduct required proof not only of the intentional or reckless doing of a forbidden act but also of a bad motive. The result would be that the judge and jury would hear evidence about *why* the defendant did the act; and they would be required to find not only what his motives actually were but also to evaluate them. Now, although motives are not always the dark unknowables they are sometimes believed to be, it is also true that it is often very difficult and sometimes impossible to discover them—a criminal sometimes refuses to talk and nothing may be known about him. Even in the usual run of less-difficult cases, a detailed case-history of the defendant's past life may be needed if reliable knowledge of his motivation is to be discovered. In some cases, a very long time would be required to complete the investigation; in others the results would be quite negative—the true motivation is sometimes concealed from the actor himself who rationalizes his conduct in terms of what he mistakenly believes his motives were. But suppose that in a majority of the cases the motives could be established with reasonable assurance. The equally difficult task remains — to evaluate them. In doing this, the actor's own estimate could hardly be accepted even if he had undoubtedly followed his conscience—unless one is prepared to hold that every fanatic has *carte blanche* to wreak whatever harm he wishes to inflict. Moreover, if a court could exculpate because it found that the harmdoer's motives were good, it would also be empowered to refuse exculpation because it thought his motives bad. These are among the reasons for excluding motive from the definition of *mens rea* and holding it not essential in criminal conduct.

Intention in the Criminal Law*

9. Nature of the requirement of *mens rea*

There is no need here to go into the remote history of *mens rea*; suffice it to say that the requirement of a guilty state of mind (at least for the more serious crimes) had been developed by the time of Coke, which is as far back as the modern lawyer needs to go. "If one shoot at any wild fowl upon a tree, and the arrow killeth any reasonable creature afar off, without any evil intent in him, this is *per infortunium.*"[1]

It may be said that any theory of criminal punishment leads to a requirement of some kind of *mens rea*. The deterrent theory is workable only if the culprit has knowledge of the legal sanction, and if a man does not foresee the consequence of his act he cannot appreciate that punishment lies in store for him if he does it. The retributive theory presupposes moral guilt; incapacitation supposes social danger; and the reformative aim is out of place if the offender's sense of values is not warped.

However, the requirement as we have it in the law does not harmonize perfectly with any of these theories. It does not quite fit the deterrent theory, because a man may have *mens rea* although he is ignorant of the law. On the deterrent theory, ignorance of the law should be a defense; yet it is not. Again, the requirement does not quite conform to the retributive theory, because the *mens rea* of English law does not necessarily connote an intention to engage in moral wrongdoing. A crime may be committed from the best of motives and yet

remain a crime. (In this respect the phrase *mens rea* is somewhat misleading.) There are similar difficulties with incapacitation and reform.

What, then, does legal *mens rea* mean? It refers to the mental element necessary for the particular crime, and this mental element may be either *intention* to do the act or bring about the consequences or (in some crimes) *recklessness* as to that consequence.[2] These two concepts hold the key to the understanding of a large part of criminal law. Some crimes require intention and nothing else will do, but most can be committed either intentionally or recklessly. Some crimes require particular kinds of intention or knowledge.

Outside the class of crimes requiring *mens rea* there are some that do not require any particular state of mind but do require negligence. Negligence in law is not necessarily a state of mind; and thus these crimes are best regarded as not requiring *mens rea*. However, negligence is a kind of legal fault, and in that respect they are akin to crimes requiring *mens rea*.

Yet other crimes do not even require negligence. They are crimes of strict or vicarious responsibility, and, like crimes of negligence, they constitute exceptions to the adage *Actus non facit nisi mens sit rea.*

---

* Glanville L. Williams, *Criminal Law: The General Part* (London: Stevens & Sons Ltd., 1953), pp. 28–45, 77–81, reprinted with the permission of the author and the publishers. Footnotes have been renumbered.

[1] Co. *Inst.* iii 56.

[2] H. L. A. Hart in (1949) 49 *Proc. Arist. Soc.* at 179–80, tries to overthrow the general theory of *mens rea,* saying that it is only to be understood by considering certain defenses or exceptions, such as mistake of fact, accident, duress, infancy; he admits, however, the existence of some crimes in which proof of specific intention is required. The question may be largely verbal, but my preference is for the converse position, that the meaning of the so-called defenses of mistake and accident can only be understood by considering the general theory of *mens rea.* In reality mistake and accident are not defenses but modes of denying the case for the Crown.

10. The concept of responsibility and a radical proposal

For children and persons of unsound mind the question of technical conviction for crime has lost much of its importance, because they can frequently be treated in much the same way whether they are found guilty of an offense or not. An approved school, for example, contains juveniles who are "in need of care or protection" as well as offenders, and Broadmoor contains lunatic criminals as well as persons acquitted of crime on the ground of insanity. As penal treatment becomes more directed to the cure of the offender, it approximates more to the nonpenal treatment of those who are found to be in need of it. The resulting tendency is to erase the line between legal responsibility and nonresponsibility, or at least to confine its importance chiefly to matters of procedure.

Some writers on penology would have us carry this to the conclusion that the notion of legal responsibility should be altogether abandoned. For most crimes the notion of responsibility involves proof that the accused has committed the criminal act with the requisite state of mind. Accordingly, the abandonment of the concept of responsibility would involve an abandonment of one or other of these elements, or both, as conditions precedent to the compulsory treatment of sane adults. (1) If the requirement of *mens rea* were abandoned, a person who committed a criminal act could be dealt with by the courts though he lacked what has hitherto been regarded as the necessary *mens rea*: for instance, when he has made a silly mistake, he could be subjected to compulsory education to prevent him making the same mistake in future. But such education would usually be unnecessary; even a foolish person does not usually make the same serious mistake twice; he is more likely to make a variety of mistakes. Our legal system has found ways of modifying the requirement of *mens rea* where necessary without abandoning the concept of responsibility: a man may be convicted of crime in some instances where he has merely been negligent, judged by an objective standard, or even (a more dubious development) where he has been without fault. Thus if any particular kind of inadvertent harmful act is thought to require compulsory re-education of the offender, it can be done within the framework of the existing concepts.

(2) If the requirement of a criminal act were given up, people could be treated by the criminal courts not only if they did or attempted a criminal act but also if they made remote preparation for it or even if they showed dangerous tendencies. Most lawyers would resist at least the last part of this proposal because it would lead to an abandonment of constitutional safeguards. It is not consistent with the principles of a free society that a sane adult should be subject to be legally interfered with merely because he thinks dangerous thoughts or from his utterances appears to have tendencies. . . .

It is now proposed to analyze the kinds of fault in the abstract, and to consider how far they are required in various crimes. . . .

11. Intention as desire of consequence

The definition of intention is not an investigation into psychological facts: it is (as definition always is) a question of verbal usage and convenience. In the present study I shall adopt the definition advanced by certain writers on jurisprudence because I believe it to be satisfactory and to represent the basis of the legal use. How far particular decisions diverge from it will be considered in the proper place.

Subject to what is to be said in the next two articles, and in Chapter 5,[3] intention may be defined as a state of mind consisting of desire that certain consequences shall follow from the party's physical act or omission. Other words used to express the same idea are "intent," "will," "wantonness," "volition," "purpose," "aim," "design," and "deliberation," with their derivatives; also "means to." A dyslogistic synonym much favored in criminal law is "willfulness." . . .

It may be observed that every physical movement involved in an act requires by definition an exercise of the will . . . , and is therefore desired and intended. However, to say that a given act is "intentional" in the abstract is misleading; for, as said above, "act" commonly includes certain consequences, and it is intentional only as regards consequences that are foreseen and desired. If any consequence comes about that was not desired,

[3] In Chapter 5, Professor Williams states: "The principle is that where a circumstance is not known to the actor, his act is not intentional as to that circumstance." [Editor's note.]

the act is not intentional as to that consequence.

For instance, a motorist presses the accelerator of his car. He wishes to go faster, and his act is then intentional as to going faster. But if it should happen that through going faster he hits a pedestrian, it obviously cannot be deduced that his act is intentional as to this consequence. It is so only if he desired to hit the pedestrian. Otherwise his act is unintentional or accidental as to the impact. Thus the same physical act may be both intentional and unintentional according to the result that is spoken of. It might be better, in view of the ambiguity of "act," if in every case we attributed the notion of intention to the consequence rather than to the act, asserting that the consequence is intended or unintended according as it is desired or not desired.

A consequence may, of course, be desired not as an end in itself but as a means to the satisfaction of another desire. Extreme cases sometimes make this use of the concept of intention somewhat forced. Thus one (non-legal) writer remarks that "to class as suicide the altruistic self-sacrifice of people like Captain Oates, who gave his life while on a polar expedition, in order that his comrades might be able to make their stock of rations last until relief came, would be as uncharitable as it would be untrue."[4] For legal purposes, however, it is better to class such an act as suicide, while admitting the fullest moral—and perhaps legal — justification for it. It would throw legal terminology into confusion to assert that an act done from a good motive is not done intentionally.

A consequence may also be desired although it is not expected as probable. D takes a "long shot" at P; the consequence of hitting P is intended even though not thought likely. On the other hand the mere fact that a consequence is expected as probable does not make it an intended consequence, unless it was desired. . . .

The difference between intention and desire in this respect is merely that there may be a passive desire, not related to actual or proposed conduct, which we would not call intention. If D desires P's death but has not decided to take any step to bring it about we should not say that D intends P's death. Intention is that species of desire on the part of a person that is coupled with his own actual or proposed conduct to achieve satisfaction. . . .

12. Unconscious motivations

The discovery of unconscious motivations raises a difficult legal question on the definition of intention. Probably unconscious intention is to be ignored for legal purposes (1) because it is difficult to prove satisfactorily, (2) because we have little knowledge of how far the threat of a sanction can influence the unconscious. The most that the law can demand is that socially undesirable wishes should be repressed; it cannot make the individual responsible for intention if the repressed urge manifests itself in some neurotic symptom which is also of an undesirable nature. Thus: a soldier wishes to escape from the danger of battle, but out of a sense of duty he represses this striving, which becomes unconscious but manifests itself in a neurotic symptom such as paralysis, fainting, or a hysterical fugue. The result may be that initially desired—that he escape danger; and it is "purposive from the point of view of the patient's personality"; but it is not brought about by conscious intention; it is concealed from awareness; and it is therefore regarded as involuntary.

A similar state of dissociation seems to account for the manifestations of some "psychic mediums." The medium may be genuinely unable to remember in his normal condition what he said in his trance, and may believe that he speaks in truth as the mouthpiece of a departed spirit.

Henderson and Gillespie[5] relate that a feeble-minded girl of 15 was sent into domestic service by her psychopathic mother. After a few weeks she was sent home because she had broken so much china, which she said she could not help. When interviewed she said that she picked up things and let them fall, being surprised when she heard the crash, for she had not known even that she had the article in her hand. She went on naïvely to say that she had disliked domestic service intensely and that she had wished very much to get home. The authors comment: "Such frank purposive dissociations are possible only in persons of low intelligence and education, and

---

[4] John C. Goodwin, *Insanity and the Criminal* (New York: George H. Doran Co., 1923), p. 212.

[5] *Textbook of Psychiatry*, David Anderson and R. D. Gillespie (London: Oxford University Press, 1950), 7th ed., p. 195.

with a very defective 'health-conscience.' They probably account also for a proportion of so-called 'kleptomaniacs.' "

Again, it is said that dreams frequently express unconscious thoughts and volitions that temporarily become conscious; but a man is not criminally responsible for what he does in a dream. . . . This would be so even if the dream happened to coincide with a conscious desire. D wishes that his wife were dead and considers the possibility of strangling her. One night he dreams that he is carrying out his plan, and actually strangles her in his sleep. This, assuming the facts to be established, is not murder. The *mens rea* of a dream is not a *mens rea* for which a man is punishable; it is only the waking consciousness that involves criminal culpability.

The field of the unconscious is irrelevant to responsibility where it pertains merely to motives, for even conscious motives are ruled out. . . . To illustrate, a man may steal because of an early antagonism to his father, since repressed, which unconsciously leads him to do something of which his father would disapprove. The stealing is deliberate; it is only the motive that belongs to the unconscious. The analysis of neurotic motives is, of course, important in the realm of treatment.

13. Intention also includes foresight of certainty

There is one situation where a consequence is deemed to be intended though it is not desired. This is where it is foreseen as substantially certain. To take a somewhat highly-colored illustration, suppose that D, an eccentric and amoral surgeon, wishes to remove P's heart completely from P's body in order to experiment upon it. D does not desire P's death (being perfectly content that P shall go on living if he can do so without his heart), but recognizes that in fact his death is inevitable from the operation to be performed. Such a case would clearly be murder, and this without resort to any of the forms of constructive malice. Again, on an indictment for burning a mill with intent to injure the possessors it is enough to prove the intentional burning, for in such a case the accused "necessarily intends that which must be the consequence of the act." . . .

It may be objected that certainty is a mat-

ter of degree. In a philosophical view, nothing is certain; so-called certainty is merely high probability. Consider the following case, which came before a British court in Eritrea. The two accused had agreed with pilgrims to take them to Mecca by sea in a dhow, but had marooned them on a rocky island inhabited only by voracious land-crabs. Eighteen of the pilgrims died; four were rescued by the chance visit of a vessel. The two miscreants were sentenced for murder.[6] It may be said that here, even if the accused were indifferent whether the pilgrims lived or not, the conviction for murder was right because there was a "moral certainty" of death. Yet it was not complete certainty, and in fact four pilgrims had the good fortune to survive.

This difficulty, though serious, is by no means fatal. We do in fact speak of certainty in ordinary life; and for the purpose of the present rule it means such a high degree of probability that common sense would pronounce it certain. Mere philosophical doubt, or the intervention of an extraordinary chance, is to be ignored. . . .

A few cases may appear to be against this extended view of intention. In *Ahlers*,[7] a German consul helped his compatriots to return to Germany after the outbreak of war in 1914. It was held by the Court of Criminal Appeal that he could not be convicted of treason if he did not intend to aid the King's enemies but intended only to do his duty as consul. The decision, though an admirable example of judicial balance in wartime, is almost certainly wrong in law, so far as the decision of a court ever can be pronounced wrong when it has not been overruled. It seems impossible to reconcile with the later decision of the same court in *Kupfer*,[8] where a charge of paying money for the benefit of the enemy was sustained although the accused made the payments with the intention of benefiting himself. It seems obvious that in both cases the defendant must have foreseen that the enemy would be benefited by what he did, and, if so, even a good motive could not expunge his legal guilt.

Another case to be considered is *Steane* (1947).[9] The defendant was charged under a

---

[6] *The Times,* July 5, 1951.
[7] [1915] 1 K.B. 616 (C.C.A.), criticized by Kenny in 31 *L.Q.R.* 229.
[8] [1915] 2 K.B. 321 (C.C.A.).
[9] [1947] K.B. 997 (C.C.A.).

defense regulation (now repealed) with doing an act likely to assist the enemy with intent to assist the enemy. He had broadcast for Germany during the war, but only under the pressure of threats, and being "beaten up," and in order to save his wife and children (who were in Germany) from a concentration camp. The Court of Criminal Appeal held that the jury were entitled on this evidence to find that the accused did not intend to assist the enemy. There was no discussion of the question whether foresight that the broadcasting was bound to assist the enemy was equivalent in law to an intent to assist the enemy, and the decision is therefore not authoritative on it. It may be submitted that a more satisfactory way of deciding the case would have been to say that the accused did in law intend to assist the enemy, but that duress was a defense.

This may perhaps be seen by supposing that Steane's defense was that he had not intended to assist the enemy but had intended only to earn a packet of cigarettes. Clearly such a defense would not have availed him. The real difference between one who aids the enemy in order to escape blows and one who aids the enemy in order to earn favors is not that the second acts intentionally and the first not, but that the first acts under duress and the second not.

Another example may show the superiority of the "duress" approach to this type of problem. A man is charged with revealing state secrets to the enemy, and the result of his revelation has been to endanger the lives of many thousands of his fellow-subjects. On the principles of duress, which can be held to allow a balancing of evils, a judge will be inclined to say that no fear for his own safety can justify the accused in what he did. . . . Yet if the decision in Steane is applied, the fact that the accused was motivated by fear is enough to show that he had no criminal intent.

A more difficult problem was raised in a Ceylon case.[10] The Ceylon Penal Code makes it a criminal trespass to enter or remain on another's property with intent to annoy him. D refused to vacate rooms belonging to the Government which he and his forebears had occupied for seventy years, and he was thereupon convicted of trespass. The magistrate found that his intention was to cause annoy-

[10] *Sinnasamy Selvanayagam* [1951] A.C. 83 (P.C.).

ance to the Government superintendent, since that would be the natural consequence of his action. In allowing an appeal, the Privy Council said: "Even if the appellant did anticipate that [the superintendent] would be annoyed, it is perfectly clear from his evidence that his dominant intention was to remain on the estate where he and his family had lived for generations and not to find himself homeless. Entry upon land, made under a *bona fide* claim of right, however ill-founded in law that claim may be, does not become criminal merely because a foreseen consequence of the entry is annoyance to the occupant." It seems that the true reason why the appeal was allowed was that the appellant had a claim of right; if he had known that he had no legal right to remain on the premises, he might, it seems, have been convicted. His knowledge of the certainty of causing annoyance might then have been regarded as equivalent to intention.

That this is so can be seen from taking a hypothetical case not involving a claim of right. Suppose that a scientist surreptitiously administers an emetic to his assistant, for the purpose of a scientific experiment. Assuming that the emetic is a noxious thing, could the scientist be convicted of maliciously administering a noxious thing with intent to annoy? The question is whether he could defend himself by saying that his dominant intention was the advancement of science, though he realized that his assistant would inevitably be annoyed by what he did. It seems that the courts would say that on such facts, where there is no claim of right, there is in law an intention to annoy.

There may be exceptions to the rule that foresight of certainty is tantamount to intention. For example, where the defendant acted with the object of provoking another to break the peace, he may himself be guilty of a crime; but where the defendant's conduct is lawful, the mere fact that he knows that it will cause others to behave illegally does not, it seems, make him responsible for a crime of intention. (He may, however, be guilty of a crime not requiring an intention to provoke a breach of the peace, such as insulting behavior or obstructing the police.) . . .

Mere foresight of probability does not amount to intention. . . . Such foresight is part of the concept of recklessness.

14. Intentional omissions; willful neglect

There is some practical difficulty in classifying omissions as intentional or negligent. In considering whether conduct is intentional, it is unnecessary to ascertain whether the party knew of the rule of law, and whether (if he knew of it) he was adverting to it at the time in question. . . . Suppose, then, that a chemist, not knowing, or forgetting, that a particular substance is a statutory poison, sells it without complying with the Poisons Act. Is his omission to comply with the Act intentional or negligent? The ordinary man would call it negligent, but in view of the rule just stated (as to knowledge of the law) it would seem to be intentional. He intentionally sells the drug without formality, which is the *actus reus* of the offense.

This analysis seems to leave little room for negligent omissions, unless the party has made a negligent mistake, or unless he has negligently allowed himself to become unconscious (e.g., asleep). However, even if an omission is legally intentional, the consequence of the omission may not be intended.

It would seem that the practical test of intention in omission is as follows. If the defendant had been asked at any time while the omission was continuing: "Are you doing so-and-so?" (which the statute makes it his duty to do) would the true answer based on the facts as he knows them be: "I am not"? If so, the omission is intentional. In effect this makes intentional omission equivalent to conscious omission. Intention is, however, displaced by mistake, where the accused thinks that he is doing the required act.

The foregoing test assumes that intention is required to exist at the moment of the legal omission, but there must be some qualification upon this. If the accused, knowing that it will be his duty to act in five minutes' time, allows himself to go to sleep, without intending to wake up to perform his duty, the omission is clearly intentional, although there is no mental state at the time when the omission takes place. Yet it cannot be said that every omission during sleep is an intentional omission. The only way of drawing the line is to say that an omission is intentional if the accused, when he fell asleep, realized what his duty was, and that he was disabling himself from performing it. To this extent a knowledge of the law is a requisite of *mens rea*.

An intentional omission is frequently expressed in law by the phrase "willful neglect." This is not a contradiction in terms, because although "neglect" may sometimes mean negligence, in this context it refers merely to an omission. Thus a parent who willfully neglects his child is a parent who willfully omits to look after it.

15. Intention and motive

The word "motive" has two related meanings. (1) It sometimes refers to the emotion prompting an act, e.g., "D killed P, his wife's lover, from a motive of jealousy." (2) It sometimes means a kind of intention, e.g., "D killed P with the motive (intention, desire) of stopping him from paying attentions to D's wife."

In the second sense, which is the one in which the term is used in criminal law, motive is ulterior intention—the intention with which an intentional act is done (or, more clearly, the intention with which an intentional consequence is brought about). Intention, when distinguished from motive, relates to the means, motive to the end; yet the end may be the means to another end, and the word "intention" is appropriate to such medial end. Much of what men do involves a chain of intention (D pulls the trigger of his revolver in order to make the bullet enter P's body in order to kill P in order to get him out of the way, etc.), and each intention is a motive for that preceding it. In criminal law, it is generally convenient to use the term "intention" with reference to intention as to the constituents of the *actus reus,* and the term "motive" with reference to the intention with which the *actus reus* was done.

The definition of some crimes involves an intention to commit another crime. This is so, for example, with attempt and burglary. If D tries to take aim at P with his revolver, with intent to pull the trigger and kill P, he is guilty of an attempt to murder. The *actus reus* of the attempt is the struggling to take aim at P, though behind this there lies in intention the *actus reus* of another crime— murdering P. The *mens rea* of the attempt is the intention, in the first place, to take aim at P, and, in the second place, to pull the trigger in order to kill P. This second intention may in one use of language be said to be a motive; but in criminal law it is more convenient to refer to it simply as intention. Similarly in burglary, the *actus reus* is breaking and entering a dwelling-house by night; but it is an essential of the crime that there should be an intent to commit also a second *actus reus,* namely a felony inside the house. The intent to commit this second *actus reus* is conveniently called intention rather than motive, because it would be confusing to use the same word "motive" both for the burglar's intention to commit larceny in the house and for his intention to use the proceeds of the larceny to provide for his paralytic daughter. The former is an intrinsic part of the crime; the latter is legally irrelevant except as reducing punishment in the discretion of the court. In short, whenever an intention to commit another crime is involved in the definition of a crime, it is generally referred to as intention and not as motive. It is commonly called by lawyers a "specific intent."

The same usage is adopted where the intent required for the crime is to bring about some result that in itself is not necessarily criminal. Forgery, for example, requires an intent to defraud or deceive; but fraud and deception are not in themselves necessarily criminal. The intent is referred to by lawyers as a "specific intent" rather than as a motive. The adjective "specific" seems to be somewhat pointless, for the intent is no more specific than any other intent required in criminal law. The most it can mean is that the intent is specifically referred to in the indictment. There is no substantive difference between an intent specifically mentioned and one implied in the name of the crime.

If the foregoing definition of motive is accepted, it becomes tautologous to say that motive is irrelevant to legal responsibility. For as soon as the word "motive" is uttered, it is impliedly asserted to be irrelevant to responsibility.

In two exceptional instances lawyers use the term "motive" in defining a crime. The term is used in connection with libel, where bad motive (otherwise called express malice) defeats a defense of fair comment or qualified privilege. There is no reason for making this verbal distinction between specific intent in forgery and bad motive in libel, save that the latter covers a wider range of motives than the former. Similarly the term "motive" is used in the crime of conspiracy. If the law

were to be codified it would be convenient to avoid the term "motive" in these two contexts and to use instead "[ulterior] intent." The latter expression could also replace "specific intent." "Motive" could then be reserved for that kind of ulterior intent that is irrelevant to the definition of the crime.

As a principle of legislation, it may be suggested that wherever possible a criminal statute should be drafted so as to require a wicked or dishonest intention. Such a requirement tends to bring the law into consonance with popular feeling.

An act may be done with two or more intents, or, to use alternative language, from a mixed motive. If both intents were unlawful, the culprit may be charged with either of them, and there is no necessity to inquire which was the principal and which the subordinate intent. If one intent is lawful and the other is unlawful, the general rule is again that he may be charged with the unlawful intent. This is, however, modified in conspiracy cases, for there one must sometimes seek the dominant intent. The decisions in *Ahlers* and *Steane* have already been considered. . . .

16. Crimes requiring intention

Hitherto the discussion has centered chiefly on the jurisprudential analysis of intention. This would not be important if there were not some crimes that demand intention as an element. Attempt, conspiracy, rape, and treason are crimes that can be committed intentionally and (generally) in no other way. Similarly, crimes involving a "specific intent" require intention as to a given consequence, not merely recklessness. A burglar must intend to commit a felony in the house, not merely be reckless as to it. A thief must in general intend to deprive the owner permanently of his property, not merely be reckless as to such deprivation. It is possible to commit murder without intending the death, as where the death follows from great bodily harm caused intentionally. But what is in fact an assault with intent to do great bodily harm cannot be charged as an assault with intent to murder. There must be the actual intent to kill. Again, a person cannot be a principal in the second degree to a crime requiring a specific intent unless he knew of the intent of the principal in the first degree. . . .

When it is said that given crimes need intention, what is referred to is an intention as to consequence, which is what is under consideration in this chapter. Some of these crimes are satisfied with recklessness as to an accompanying circumstance. Thus burglary, though a crime exclusively of intention in respect of the felony to be committed in the house, is also a crime of recklessness (perhaps even strict responsibility) in respect of the time and place. . . . Similarly, treason is perhaps a crime of recklessness in respect of allegiance. . . . This subject of the mental element in relation to accompanying circumstances is to be considered at length in Chapter 5.

. . .

27. The supposed presumption of intention

It is often said that a man is presumed to intend the natural consequences of his acts. This maxim, though many judges have been fond of it, contains a serious threat to any rational theory of intention. It is not true in fact that a man necessarily intends the natural consequences of his acts; and it is not true in law that he is compellingly presumed to do so. The maxim will here be discussed as a supposed rule of substantive law, leaving it for later treatment as a supposed rebuttable presumption.

Juries have sometimes been directed in terms of the maxim, and appellate pronouncements have been founded on it, as though there is a legal equivalence between a natural consequence and an intended consequence.[11] Now the expression "natural" in law must mean probable; otherwise "natural" would be meaningless, for "everything that happens, happens in the order of nature and is therefore 'natural.'" Hence the maxim is tantamount to saying that a consequence is intended though it is not desired, or even foreseen as possible or probable, provided that it was probable in fact—i.e., a reasonable man would have foreseen it as probable. If this view were accepted the results would be to destroy the subjective definition of intention and to efface

the line between intention and negligence. When a defendant is held guilty of causing damage by negligence, this is because a reasonable man would have foreseen the damage. Now if a reasonable man would have foreseen it, it must be the probable consequence of the defendant's conduct. If it is the probable consequence of his conduct, the defendant, according to the maxim, is presumed to have intended it. Thus, all these cases of negligent conduct are turned into cases of intentional conduct. Such a mangling of the concept of intention cannot be admitted.

The maxim could be stretched to impose responsibility for fictitious intention even where there is no negligence. Literally it would mean that a surgeon who performed a risky operation in an otherwise hopeless case would on the failure of the operation (if without negligence it accelerated the patient's death) be guilty of murder.

In reality the maxim is not used to give these results. Many instances can be put where a probable consequence has not been held to be an intended consequence. For example, the fact that an act is likely to obstruct a coroner in holding an inquest is not sufficient to convict of intentional obstruction. In *Ahlers* (1915), the court regarded it as possible that the accused did not intend to assist the King's enemies though that was the result—and from the outset the probable result—of what he did. His conviction was quashed for lack of a proper direction to the jury. There was a like decision in *Steane,* and in other cases that have already been mentioned. . . .

The maxim is sometimes taken as expressing a psychological theory. It is said that one cannot delve into the mind but must judge a man on his outward acts. This is a half-truth. It is platitudinous to say that intent must frequently be gathered from conduct on the basis of a supposed uniformity of human nature. But (1) the accused's conduct at the time is not the only evidence of his intention : there are also confessions, denials, demeanor in the witness-box, and circumstantial evidence. (2) The fact that an ordinary person would have foreseen the consequence is not conclusive that the accused foresaw it, much less that he desired it. Circumstances may negative the inference, as where, for instance, the accused was drunk . . . , or insane, or a child. To quote Bowen, L. J., in a civil case:

---

[11] See, e.g., *per* Lord Simon, L.C., in *Crofter Hand Woven Harris Tweed Co. v. Veitch* [1942] A.C. at 44: "In some branches of the law, 'intention' may be understood to cover results which may reasonably flow from what is deliberately done, on the principle that a man is to be treated as intending the reasonable consequences of his acts." Trying to avoid this ambiguity, Lord Simon had to make quite an involved statement of what should have been a simple proposition.

So far from saying that you cannot look into a man's mind, you must look into it, if you are going to find fraud against him; and unless you think you see what must have been in his mind, you cannot find him guilty of fraud.[12]

(3) Even where intent is inferred from acts, this does not mean that responsibility for intention is based upon noncompliance with an external standard. As Holdsworth remarked, "so to argue is to confuse the evidence for a proposition with the proposition proved by that evidence."[13] A tribunal may make mistakes in telling the mind's construction, but that risk is present with all circumstantial evidence.

Some years ago the maxim might have seemed to derive support from the behaviorist movement in psychology; but it is significant that that movement is now dead.

Many cases that repeat the maxim do not rest upon it: the maxim is merely pressed into service to reach results that can stand on their own legs. Thus, it has been used to include consequences foreseen as certain within the concept of intention; to create responsibility for recklessness in some (but not all) crimes, and in particular to reach the modern meaning of malice; to extend intention to cover general intention and transferred intention (transferred malice); to extend malice aforethought in murder to include cases where the accused intended to do great bodily harm short of death; to extend intention to cover mistake of the victim's identity; to express the fact that an act may be intended as to means as well as

ends; to support the rule that an intent to defraud is not inconsistent with an intent to make good the loss; to reduce to a fiction the allegation of malice in libel; to rule out evidence of good motive in obscenity; and as a technical argument for supporting a particular indictment, or unnecessary make-weight when the crime does not need intention. In none of these cases did the maxim have a harmful effect, for the decision was supportable on other grounds. On the other hand, it does seem to have resulted in sedition being treated in some cases as a crime of negligence. . . . On principle and according to other authorities this is wrong: sedition as a common-law offense requires *mens rea*. As Cave, J., said:

In order to make out the offence of speaking seditious words, there must be a criminal intent upon the part of the accused, they must be words spoken with a seditious intent; and although it is a good working rule, to say that a man must be taken to intend the natural consequences of his acts, yet, if it is shown from other circumstances, that he did not actually intend them, I do not see how you can ask a jury to act upon what has then become a legal fiction.[14]

It is now generally agreed, in conformity with this opinion, that the maxim does not represent a fixed principle of law, and that there is no equiparation between probability and intent. . . . Recently Denning, L. J., said: "There is no 'must' about it; it is only 'may.' The presumption of intention is not a proposition of law but a proposition of ordinary good sense."[15]

[12] *Angus v. Clifford* [1891] 2 Ch. at 471 (C.A.).
[13] *History of English Law*, iii, 375.

[14] *Burns* (1886), 16 Cox at 364.
[15] *Hosegood v. Hosegood* [1950] 1 T.L.R. 735, [1950] W.N. 218 (C.A.).

Omissions and *Mens Rea**

Mens rea, which creaked through the criminal courts for centuries, has recently been dug up, scrubbed, repainted, and paraded for the admiration of criminal lawyers. The old mumblings about "guilty mind" have been replaced by the ice-cutting concepts of intention and recklessness. And with offenses of commission these new tools on the whole work very

nicely. In an offense of commission, the mind of the actor is almost always to some extent addressed to the prohibited conduct, even though he may be unaware of the legal prohibition. In these offenses, *mens rea* can quite usefully be generalized as an intention to bring about the prohibited consequences or, at the least, recklessness with regard to such consequences. With omissions, the great difficulty is that the mind of the offender may not be addressed at all to the enjoined conduct, if he is unaware of the duty to act. One may

* Graham Hughes, "Criminal Omissions," *Yale Law Journal*, LXVII (1958), 600–607, reprinted with the permission of the Yale Law Journal. Footnotes have been renumbered.

not know that it is prohibited to place garbage cans on the sidewalk between 9:00 A.M. and 7:00 P.M., but one can hardly place such a can on the sidewalk without knowing that he is doing it. Rare cases of somnambulism or insanity occur, but here the traditional approach is to deny liability on the ground that the accused cannot be said to have performed any voluntary act. This approach is clearly of no use with omissions, where the accused does not have to perform any act to incur liability. What of the offender who violates a regulation requiring garbage to be put out in suitable receptacles at certain times? If he was quite unaware of the existence of the rule, in what sense can he be said to have been addressing his mind at all to the conduct required of him by law? This is the difficulty which plagues the analysis of omissions in terms of the conventional concepts of *mens rea*.

Let us consider the case of the pharmacist who is under a duty to register the sale of all poisonous substances listed in a statutory catalogue. If he does not register such a sale, there are many possible explanations. A few may be suggested:

(1) He knows of the statutory rule and knows that the substance he is selling is a poison within the meaning of the law but decides not to register the sale.

(2) He has no knowledge of the existence of the rule and has never kept a poison book.

(3) He knows of the rule and does keep a poison book, but he does not know that the substance he is selling has been recently added to the list of poisons within the meaning of the act.

(4) He is mistaken about the chemical nature of the substance and thinks it is not a poison within the meaning of the act when in fact it is.

(5) He is undecided whether the substance comes within the meaning of the act but neglects to resolve this doubt by consulting the act.

(6) He is undecided about the chemical nature of the substance but neglects to resolve this doubt by further research and risks a sale without making an entry in the poison book.

In an offense of commission, a solution might be reached by applying concepts of intention, recklessness, and perhaps negligence to the conduct prohibited. But with omissions, with the pharmacist, for example, the approach is senseless until an inquiry has been made into the state of his mind about the duty to act, for until this knowledge is established, in no sense can he be said to address his mind to the conduct enjoined.

Of the possible explanations of the pharmacist's omission, examples two, three, and five raise the question of the offender's ignorance of the existence of the legal duty to act. In example two, he is quite ignorant of the existence of the duty. In example three, he knows of the general existence of such a duty but is ignorant that it has recently been extended to cover the substance with which he is dealing; and in example five, he is doubtful about the extent of the duty and neglects research.

In these circumstances, his liability should depend upon the culpability of his ignorance which, in turn, should depend on the answer to several questions. What steps are taken by governmental agencies to bring the existence of such duties and changes in their scope to the notice of pharmacists? What likelihood is there that by the nature of their activities pharmacists should have knowledge of the existence of the duty? What special circumstances can the defendant show which might take him out of the normal expectation of knowledge in a pharmacist? Clearly, the pharmacist's state of mind in example five should be no defense. There, he had a suspicion of the applicability of the duty and elected to make no further investigation. This might be called a reckless ignorance, a reckless refusal to consult easily available information when a suspicion of duty to act had arisen. In example two, it is difficult to imagine how a defendant engaged in the trade of pharmacist could allege that complete lack of knowledge is not culpable. The opportunities for acquiring this information must be so manifold that the prosecution's burden of proof in showing culpable ignorance would be easily discharged. Example three is the really interesting one, in that the defendant's lack of knowledge is conceivably not culpable. Perhaps, the official authority concerned neglected to inform the trade immediately of its new regulation. No way may have been available to the pharmacist to acquire the information, short of legal research.

The imposition of strict liability in such a situation is futile and distressing. It can serve no purpose of deterrence, it protects the public in no way at all and it contributes nothing to the strict enforcement of regulations. The maxim, "ignorance of the law is no excuse," ought to have no application in the field of criminal omissions, for the mind of the offender has no relationship to the prescribed conduct if he has no knowledge of the relevant regulation. The strictest liability that makes any sense is a liability for culpable ignorance. We may say with some plausibility that the defendant ought to be punished even though he did not know that he was supposed to do something, if he ought to have known that he should have done something. But to find him liable whether he knew of the duty or not, and whether he ought to have known of it or not, is to impose more than a strict liability. It is a liability for a complete absence of relevant conduct. Such liability is indefensible even by the weak and compromised arguments which are conventionally used to justify strict liability in cases of commission.

The application of *mens rea* ideas to criminal omissions cannot, of course, end with an investigation of the accused's knowledge or ignorance of the duty to act. If knowledge or culpable ignorance of the law is found, a conventional discussion, as with crimes of commission, of the accused's mental state becomes necessary with respect to the physical circumstances under which the duty arose.[1] The pharmacist in examples four and six does not have certain knowledge that the substance is chemically, not legally, within the scope of the law. He knows the law but does not know that his present situation brings him within its compass. Clearly, liability ought to be recognized for recklessness, as in example six; and in the field of public welfare offenses, a liability for negligence ought perhaps to be admitted. For nonculpable ignorance, it is submitted that there should be no liability.

The conventional analyses of *mens rea* in omissions suffer either from a complete neglect of the aspect of ignorance of the law or a tendency to confuse the two separate issues of ignorance of the duty and ignorance

of the circumstances which triggered the duty. So, Dr. Glanville Williams, in his admirable work on criminal law, treats this topic in a brief and unsatisfactory way:

There is some practical difficulty in classifying omissions as intentional or negligent. In considering whether conduct is intentional it is unnecessary to ascertain whether the party knew of the rule of law, and whether (if he knew of it) he was adverting to it at the time in question. Suppose, then, that a chemist, not knowing, or forgetting, that a particular substance is a statutory poison, sells it without complying with the Poisons Act. Is his omission to comply with the Act intentional or negligent? The ordinary man would call it negligent, but in view of the rule just stated (as to knowledge of the law) it would seem to be intentional. He intentionally sells the drug without formality which is the *actus reus* of the offense.[2]

Dr. Williams continues:

It would seem that the practical test of intention in omission is as follows. If the defendant had been asked at any time while the omission was continuing: "Are you doing so-and-so?" (which the statute makes it his duty to do), would the true answer based on the facts as he knows them be: "I am not"? If so, the omission is intentional. In effect this makes intentional omission equivalent to conscious omission. Intention is, however displaced by mistake, where the accused thinks that he is doing the required act.[3]

This is a very strange view of intention. If I am eating an orange in a chair at home and someone asks me "Are you climbing Mount Everest?" I will reply "No," but it would not seem very sensible to interpret this as meaning that at the moment I was eating the orange I was intending not to be climbing Mount Everest. When a legal concept strays so ludicrously far from common understanding, the suspicion that something is wrong is justified. Dr. Williams goes on:

The foregoing test assumes that intention is required to exist at the moment of the legal omission, but there must be some qualification upon this. If the accused, knowing that it will be his duty to act in five minutes' time, allows himself to go to sleep, without intending to wake up to perform his duty, the omission is clearly intentional, although there is no mental state at the time when the omission takes place. Yet it cannot be said that every omission during sleep is an intentional omission. The only way of drawing the line is to say that the omission is intentional if the accused, when he fell asleep, realized what

---

[1] See Westrup v. Commonwealth, 123 Ky. 95, 101, 93 S.W. 646, 648 (1906): "One cannot be said in any manner to neglect or refuse to perform a duty unless he has knowledge of the condition of things which require performance at his hands." This statement should be qualified by the remarks of the Louisiana court in State v. Irvine, 126 La. 434, 446, 52 So. 567, 572 (1910), that one is not "exculpated by his ignorance" if "he was charged with the special duty of being informed."

[2] Williams, *Criminal Law* (1953), p. 40.
[3] *Ibid.*

his duty was and that he was disabling himself from performing it. To this extent a knowledge of the law is a requisite of *mens rea*.[4]

So, starting with a declaration that knowledge of the law is irrelevant to intention, the learned author is later driven to admit that cases may exist in which it is not sensible to speak of intention without taking into account knowledge of the duty to act. But one may ask why he confines his reservation to the hypothetical case of the sleeper who does not awaken. In Dr. Williams's analysis, the chemist who sells a poison not knowing that it is covered by the statute is guilty of an intentional omission, while the man who falls asleep, not knowing that he will be under a duty to act in five minutes' time, is not. This analysis is misleading. The chemist's omission, in Dr. Williams's analysis, is intentional not because he has knowledge of the duty—he hasn't—but because he has knowledge of the activity — selling the substance — which causes the duty to be imposed. The sleeper, too, has no knowledge of the law. Accordingly, Dr. Williams's implication must be that knowledge of the activity which gears the duty is sufficient to make the omission intentional. If so, it is by no means certain that a man who falls asleep not knowing that it will be his duty to act in five minutes is not guilty of an intentional omission. For, although he does not know of the duty to act, he may know that an event will occur in five minutes, and that event may be the circumstance which causes the duty to be imposed. Why then should his ignorance of the duty be relevant on Dr. Williams's analysis? His position is no different from the chemist's before investigation of his knowledge of the imminence of the event. To make his analysis consistent, Dr. Williams should have maintained that the sleeper's intention will depend not on his knowledge of an approaching duty to act when he fell asleep but on his knowledge, when he fell asleep, of an approaching circumstance which, unknown to him, imposes a duty to act. Dr. Williams is thus led into an inconsistency by failing to take up a central position on ignorance of the law in crimes of omission.[5]

But these difficulties are more apparent than real. They are a revelation of the unfortunate tendency which besets men generally and jurists in particular to construct generalizations from individual instances and then to suppress or avoid the fresh instance which defies the generalization. The concept of *mens rea* and its subconcepts, intention and recklessness, were constructed as generalizations of the instances of liability for offenses of commission. They cannot be fluently applied to offenses of omission, and it is a mistake to attempt to do so. The real concern should not be with the circumstances in which an omission may properly be described as intentional but with those circumstances in which an omission is excusable or ought to be excusable.

Professor H. L. A. Hart has argued that many legal concepts are only understandable through a recognition of their "defeasible" character.[6] By this, he means that many legal concepts are attempts to state in an affirmative generalization a collection of negative conditions which must be present to invoke the appropriate rule. So a contract will be binding unless there is undue influence, unless there is fraud or unless there is fundamental mistake. But we attempt to summarize these conditions which may defeat a contract by an affirmative statement that consent must be free and full. So in the criminal law, an act will be criminal unless the accused was insane, acted under mistake of fact or, perhaps, was coerced. We tend to forget the reality

---

[4] *Ibid.*
[5] Though the language is rather obscure, Stroud, *Mens Rea* (1914), p. 5, while avoiding the question of ignorance of law, seems more consistent in analysis: "An omission may be due to passivity, or to acts inconsistent with the act omitted. Cases of the former kind, which are few and almost negligible, may be called passive omissions. Cases where an omission is due to inconsistent action are frequent in occurrence, and are divisible into two classes, according as the inconsistent acts committed are prior to or coincident with the omission. In the former case the omission is nothing more or less than a consequence of the acts preceding it. This distinction is of importance in the consideration of any question as to whether an omission is intended or not. If the omission be entirely attributable to present inconsistent action, or to mere passivity, intention consists of advertence alone, the omission being intentional if the person adverts to the act omitted and does some other act in lieu thereof, or remains passive. If, however, as would usually be the case, the omission be due to prior inconsistent action, the omission being merely a consequence of what has already been done, intention consists of advertence coupled with expectation, as in the case of any other consequence of an act done." But in most cases, the person would probably not advert to the act omitted, unless he had a knowledge of the duty to act.
[6] Hart, "The Ascription of Responsibility and Rights," 49 *Proceedings of the Aristotelian Society* (n.s.) (1948–49), p. 171.

of this set of exemptive circumstances and impose upon them what Professor Hart calls a "spurious unity" by stating generally that the accused's act must be "voluntary," or that it must be "intentional" or "reckless." "In order," Professor Hart writes, "to determine what 'foresight' and 'voluntariness' are and how their presence and absence are established it is necessary to refer back to the various defenses and then these general words assume merely the status of convenient but sometimes misleading, summaries, expressing the absence of all the various conditions referring to the agent's knowledge or will which eliminate or reduce responsibility."[7]

This thesis of Hart's is supported by the reflection, too rarely made explicit in works on criminal law, that the burden of proving *mens rea* is very infrequently a real burden on the prosecution. In practice, the individual burden is usually on the defense to come forward with some evidence which takes the accused out of the normal field of liability. And the main inquiry should thus always be into the circumstances the law will permit the accused to raise successfully as a defense and, of course, into the circumstances he should be allowed to raise.

Again, a modern writer in the areas of phi-losophy and psychology, Professor Ryle, has convincingly demonstrated that voluntariness is not a state of mind or a mental operation but a concept of action in certain circumstances :[8]

In their most ordinary employment "voluntary" and "involuntary" are used, with a few minor elasticities, as adjectives applying to actions which ought not to be done. We discuss whether someone's action was voluntary or not only when the action seems to have been his fault. He is accused of making a noise and the guilt is his, if the action was voluntary, like laughing; he has successfully excused himself if he satisfies us that it was involuntary, like a sneeze.[9]

Ryle goes on to submit that the decision whether an act was voluntary in fact rests on whether the actor had the competence to do the right thing and whether any external coercion prevented him from doing it. This is a thesis of particular interest for the approach to omissions in the criminal law. If we can reject the mesmerizing impact of the affirmative concepts of *mens rea* and begin to approach the defendant's position by considering exactly what he alleges by way of excuse, most of the difficulties will disappear.

[7] *Id.* at 181.

[8] Ryle, *The Concept of Mind* (Barnes & Noble, 1949), pp. 62–74.
[9] *Id.* at 69.

CHAPTER V

NEGLIGENCE, RECKLESSNESS, AND STRICT LIABILITY

> If a man strikes a free man in an affray and in-
> flicts a wound on him, that man may swear "Surely I
> did not strike him wittingly," and he shall pay the sur-
> geon.
>
> *Code of Hammurabi*

> Reason demands that a loss shall lie where it falls, un-
> less some good purpose is to be served by changing its
> incidence; and in general the only purpose so served is
> that of punishment for wrongful intent or negligence.
> There is no more reason why I should insure other per-
> sons against the harmful results of my own activities,
> in the absence of any *mens rea* on my part, than why
> I should insure them against the inevitable accidents
> which result to them from the forces of nature indepen-
> dent of human actions altogether.
>
> SALMOND, *Jurisprudence*

If human beings were constructed in some fundamentally different way, they might not injure one another. As it is, of course, they do, and one function of law—principally the law of torts—is to distribute the cost of such injuries in accord with certain principles. The traditional view is that our law has done so, at least until quite recently, in accord with some notion of individual responsibility or fault. This means that if one person injures an-other, but is not at fault, he is not held liable. The loss lies where it has fallen. If both persons are at fault and the fault of each contributes to the injury one suffers, the loss also lies where it has fallen. But if an innocent person is injured by one who is at fault, the law shifts the loss from the injured in-nocent person to the wrongdoer, provided, of course, that certain other re-quirements are satisfied.

Traditionally, then, at least three principles related to fault govern dis-tribution of costs in the law of torts: (1) a person without fault is not held liable, (2) a person at fault is not allowed recovery if his fault contributed to his injury, (3) a person at fault is held liable provided other legal require-ments are satisfied.

The arguments that have been offered for these principles differ. The first principle, "no liability without fault," is justified on at least two grounds:

that it is unfair to shift the cost of some injury from one innocent person to another, and that shifting losses to innocent persons will discourage admittedly acceptable and often quite desirable activity. The second principle is frequently justified by citing the maxim, "One ought not to profit from one's own wrong." It is also argued that unless this principle is applied, there are insuperable difficulties in apportioning damages. The third principle is justified on grounds of justice and social expediency. In shifting the loss to the person who is at fault, we not only compensate the innocent but also deter others from behaving in socially undesirable ways.

Negligence constitutes a special kind of fault. There are two popular theories on the nature of negligence—the mental and conduct theories. Mental theories divide into those that claim negligence is some mental shortcoming not necessarily involving unreasonable conduct and those that claim that it is unreasonable conduct occasioned by a particular kind of mental shortcoming. The mental concepts cited by advocates of this view are inattentiveness, indifference, and inadvertence. Edgerton rejects these thories on grounds that they do not represent the law either as it is or as it ought to be. He argues, however, that while no particular mental shortcoming is present in all cases of negligent conduct, "to say that an act is negligent is to say that it would not have been done by the possessor of a normal mind functioning normally." How would Edgerton determine whether or not a person has "a normal mind functioning normally"? He must have in mind some standard such that failing to meet it is always indicative of a mental shortcoming. This leads to the next important matter in connection with negligence.

In the law of torts the conduct of a person charged with negligence is put alongside a standard. If the conduct falls below that standard, it is negligent. In our law the standard employed is that of "the reasonable and prudent man." The question asked is, "Did the man act as a reasonable and prudent man would have acted in his circumstances?" If so, he is not negligent; if not, he is. This standard is often described as "objective"; i.e., the "reasonable and prudent man" is cloaked with attributes that need not correspond to those of the particular party charged with negligence. As Seavey's essay shows, this description is misleading. Some attributes of the particular party charged with negligence will be taken into account by the law while others will be disregarded. For example, a short man will be held to the standard of conduct of a reasonable man of his height. A man, however, who is "short" on intelligence is required to behave not as one would reasonably behave given his limited intelligence, but as the reasonable man behaves who has, presumably, average intelligence. Why is this so? Is it fair, as both Holmes and Seavey maintained, to visit upon the fool the consequences of his folly? Why is it fair to make him liable but not the blind man? If the fool does his best, it is legally irrelevant; if the blind man does what a reasonable blind man would do, he is excused.

Is not 'fault" being used, then, in an attenuated sense in these principles? It is customary to say that where an idiot or insane person is held liable for damages, moral fault or personal moral shortcoming is absent, but that in most cases of negligence it is not. It is assumed that moral fault *is* involved when a reasonable man lapses from reasonable conduct. But is negligence *ever* indicative of some personal moral shortcoming? What conditions must obtain if one is morally at fault? Are these conditions present in cases of negligent conduct? If moral fault is clearly irrelevant in some cases and possibly not present in any case of negligent conduct, how well do the fault principles reflect basic moral attitudes?

Salmond argued that the aim of the law of torts was to prevent men from harming one another. Principles governing the distribution of costs are designed, in his view, to accomplish this aim. Some theorists today reject this idea. They claim, first, that fault principles do not now dominate and never have dominated the law (witness vicarious and strict liability), and, second, that fault ought not to be the factor which governs the distributions of costs. Harper and James have long been in the forefront of those who argue that justice and social expediency may demand shifting costs in cases in which no one is at fault. They argue that whereas nothing is gained from merely shifting a burden of equal weight from one innocent person to another, something may be gained by widely distributing costs. Indeed, some theorists would be prepared to argue for the desirability in some cases of placing the burden upon innocent persons rather than on wrongdoers if the former are in a better position to distribute or bear costs. There are today a number of rationales for shifting costs in accord with principles other than those of fault. In some cases the argument may be that those who derive benefits from an activity occasioning accidents should be prepared to assume the costs of such accidents, and not just those unfortunate souls upon whom they immediately fall. In some tort cases there may be no benefit involved and yet in terms of opportunity for convenient cost distribution it may be thought desirable to shift the costs to innocent persons.

Why is it that those who strongly advocate extending strict liability in the law of torts are equally strongly opposed to its introduction into the law of crimes? What is it about the criminal law that makes such liability improper and to some would make improper the employment of objective standards in cases of criminal negligence and recklessness? Wasserstrom finds that arguments against strict liability in the criminal law do not withstand critical examination. Can a general argument be made against strict liability in the criminal law, or may it be that in some areas such liability is defensible?

*Commonwealth v. Welansky**

LUMMUS, Justice. On November 28, 1942, and for about nine years before that day, a

* Supreme Judicial Court of Massachusetts, 1944. 55 N.E.2d 902. 316 Mass. 383. Footnotes are omitted.

corporation named New Cocoanut Grove, Inc., maintained and operated a "night club" in Boston, having an entrance at 17 Piedmont Street, for the furnishing to the public for compensation of food, drink, and entertainment, consisting of orchestra and band music, singing and dancing. It employed about eighty persons. The corporation, its officers and employees, and its business, were completely dominated by the defendant Barnett Welansky, who is called in this opinion simply the defendant, since his codefendants were acquitted by the jury. He owned, and held in his own name or in the names of others, all the capital stock. He leased some of the land on which the corporate business was carried on, and owned the rest, although title was held for him by his sister. He was entitled to, and took, all the profits. Internally, the corporation was operated without regard to corporate forms, as though the business were that of the defendant as an individual. It was not shown that responsibility for the number or condition of safety exits had been delegated by the defendant to any employee or other person.

The defendant was accustomed to spend his evenings at the night club, inspecting the premises and superintending the business. On November 16, 1942, he became suddenly ill, and was carried to a hospital, where he was in bed for three weeks and remained until discharged on December 11, 1942. During his stay at the hospital, although employees visited him there, he did not concern himself with the night club, because as he testified, he "knew it would be all right" and that "the same system . . . [he] had would continue" during his absence. There is no evidence of any act, omission, or condition at the night club on November 28, 1942 (apart from the lighting of a match hereinafter described), that was not within the usual and regular practice during the time before the defendant was taken ill when he was at the night club nearly every evening. While the defendant was at the hospital, his brother James Welansky and an employee named Jacob Goldfine, who were made co-defendants, assumed some of the defendant's duties at the night club, but made no change in methods. Under these circumstances the defendant was not entitled to a verdict of not guilty on the ground that any acts or omissions on the evening of November 28, 1942, were the transitory and unauthorized acts or omissions of servants or other persons, for which the defendant could not be held criminally responsible. . . .

The physical arrangement of the night club on November 28, 1942, as well as on November 16, 1942, when the defendant last had personal knowledge of it, was as follows. The total area of the first or street floor was nine thousand seven hundred sixty-three square feet. Entering the night club through a single revolving door at 17 Piedmont Street, one found himself in a foyer or hall having an area of six hundred six square feet. From the foyer there was access to small rooms used as toilets, to a powder room and a telephone room, to a small room for the checking of clothing, and to another room with a vestibule about five feet by six feet in size adjoining it, both of which were used as an office in the daytime and for the checking of clothing in the evening. In the front corner of the foyer, to the left, beyond the office, was a passageway leading to a stairway about four feet wide, with fifteen risers. That stairway led down to the Melody Lounge in the basement, which was the only room in the basement open to the public. There were to be found a bar, tables, and chairs.

The extreme dimensions of the Melody Lounge were about thirty-six feet by fifty-five feet, and its area was one thousand eight hundred ninety-five square feet. It was separated from a narrow corridor leading to the kitchen (which was located under the main dining room) by a wooden partition. In that partition was a wooden door, two feet and two inches wide, which could have been found to be unmarked. Passing from the Melody Lounge through that door, and thus entering the narrow corridor, one could turn to the left and go to a door which swung inward and could be opened only to a width of eighteen inches, at the top of three steps. That door was barred by a wooden bar that had to be lifted off before the door could be opened at all. On opening that door, one could pass into an outdoor alley about three and one-half feet wide. That alley led to a yard, from which egress could be had through in-swinging doors into another passageway and thence to Shawmut Street.

If, instead, one passing from the Melody Lounge into the narrow corridor should turn to the right, he might pass, as employees were accustomed to do, through a door two and one-half feet wide swinging into the corridor from the kitchen. Once in the kitchen, he could traverse that room with all its equipment to the other end of it near Shawmut Street, and then go upstairs and through swinging doors into a corner of the main dining room.

It is evident that in an emergency escape from the Melody Lounge by either of these courses would be difficult for a patron not thoroughly familiar with parts of the premises not ordinarily open to him.

Returning to the foyer, and standing as though one had just entered it by the revolving door, to the right, in the front of the building on Piedmont Street, was a room called the Caricature Bar, with an area of one thousand three hundred ninety-nine square feet, containing two bars, stools, and chairs. Toward Shawmut Street, and separated from the Caricature Bar by a railing, was the main dining room, with an area of three thousand seven hundred sixty-five square feet. The foyer opened into both the Caricature Bar and the main dining room. In the main dining room was a dance floor with an area of six hundred sixty square feet, and behind it, in the direction of Broadway, was a stage with an area of four hundred thirty-six square feet.

From the Caricature Bar and from the main dining room one could pass into a corridor near the stage, about four feet wide, up some steps and through a passageway about seven feet wide into the new Cocktail Lounge, which was first opened on November 17, 1942, and which had an area of seven hundred eighty-one square feet. There one found a bar, stools, tables, and seats, and also a check room and toilets. In the farther corner of the Cocktail Lounge was a door three feet wide, swinging inward, through which one could enter a small vestibule from which he could go through a pair of doors to Broadway at 59 Broadway.

That pair of doors, and the revolving door at 17 Piedmont Street, were the only entrances and exits intended for the ordinary use of patrons. Besides these doors, and the exit through the wooden partition from the Melody Lounge, already described, there were five possible emergency exits from the night club, all on the first or street floor. These will now be listed and described.

(1) A door, opening outward to Piedmont Street, two and one-half feet wide, at the head of the stairway leading to and from the basement Melody Lounge. That door apparently was not visible from the greater part of the foyer, for it was in a passageway that ran from one end of the foyer past the office to the stairway. That door was marked "Exit" by an electric sign. It was equipped with a "panic" or "crash" bar, intended to unbolt and open the door upon pressure from within the building. But on the evidence it could have been found that the device just mentioned was regularly made ineffective by having the door locked by a separate lock operated by a key that was kept in a desk in the office. . . .

(2) A door two and one-third feet wide leading from the foyer, near the revolving door, into the small vestibule adjoining the office, already described. From that vestibule another similar door, swinging inward, gave egress to Piedmont Street, near the revolving door. The door to Piedmont Street could not be opened fully, because of a wall shelf. And that door was commonly barred in the evening, as it was on November 28, 1942, by a removable board with clothing hooks on it, and by clothing, for in the evening the office and vestibule were used for checking clothing.

(3) A door, opening outward, from the middle of the wall of the main dining room to Shawmut Street, and marked "Exit" by an electric sign. The opening was about three and two-thirds feet wide. The defendant testified that this was the principal exit provided for emergencies. From the sides of the opening hung double doors, equipped with "panic" bars intended to unbolt and open the doors upon pressure from within. But on the evening of November 28, 1942, one of the two doors did not open upon pressure, and had to be hammered with a table before it would open. Besides the "panic" doors were hidden from the view of diners by a pair of "Venetian" wooden doors, swinging inward, and fastened by a hook, which had to be opened before one could operate the "panic" doors. In addition, dining tables were regularly placed near the Venetian doors, one of them within two feet, and these had to be moved away in order to get access to the doors. That condition prevailed on the evening of November 28, 1942.

(4) The service door, two and one-half feet wide, swinging inward, leading to Shawmut Street at 8 Shawmut Street. This door was near the stage, at the foot of a stairway

leading to dressing rooms on the second floor, and was in a part of the premises to which patrons were not admitted and which they could not see. This door was known to employees, but doubtless not to patrons. It was kept locked by direction of the defendant, and the key was kept in a desk in the office.

(5) The door, two and three-fourths feet wide, swinging inward, leading from a corridor into which patrons had no occasion to go, to Shawmut Street at 6 Shawmut Street. No patron was likely to know of this door. It was kept locked by direction of the defendant, but he ordered the key placed in the lock at seven every evening.

We now come to the story of the fire. A little after ten o'clock on the evening of Saturday, November 28, 1942, the night club was well filled with a crowd of patrons. It was during the busiest season of the year. An important football game in the afternoon had attracted many visitors to Boston. Witnesses were rightly permitted to testify that the dance floor had from eighty to one hundred persons on it, and that it was "very crowded." . . . Witnesses were rightly permitted to give their estimates, derived from their observations, of the number of patrons in various parts of the night club. Upon the evidence it could have been found that at that time there were from two hundred fifty to four hundred persons in the Melody Lounge, from four hundred to five hundred in the main dining room and the Caricature Bar, and two hundred fifty in the Cocktail Lounge. Yet it could have been found that the crowd was no larger than it had been on other Saturday evenings before the defendant was taken ill, and that there had been larger crowds at earlier times. There were about seventy tables in the dining room, each seating from two to eight persons. There was testimony that all but two were taken. Many persons were standing in various rooms. The defendant testified that the reasonable capacity of the night club, exclusive of the new Cocktail Lounge, was six hundred fifty patrons. He never saw the new Cocktail Lounge with the furniture installed, but it was planned to accommodate from one hundred to one hundred twenty-five patrons.

A bartender in the Melody Lounge noticed that an electric light bulb which was in or near the cocoanut husks of an artificial palm tree in the corner had been turned off and

that the corner was dark. He directed a sixteen-year-old bar boy who was waiting on customers at the tables to cause the bulb to be lighted. A soldier sitting with other persons near the light told the bar boy to leave it unlighted. But the bar boy got a stool, lighted a match in order to see the bulb, turned the bulb in its socket, and thus lighted it. The bar boy blew the match out, and started to walk away. Apparently the flame of the match had ignited the palm tree and that had speedily ignited the low cloth ceiling near it, for both flamed up almost instantly. The fire spread with great rapidity across the upper part of the room, causing much heat. The crowd in the Melody Lounge rushed up the stairs, but the fire preceded them. People got on fire while on the stairway. The fire spread with great speed across the foyer and into the Caricature Bar and the main dining room, and thence into the Cocktail Lounge. Soon after the fire started the lights in the night club went out. The smoke had a peculiar odor. The crowd were panic stricken, and rushed and pushed in every direction through the night club, screaming, and overturning tables and chairs in their attempts to escape.

The door at the head of the Melody Lounge stairway was not opened until firemen broke it down from outside with an axe and found it locked by a key lock, so that the panic bar could not operate. Two dead bodies were found close to it, and a pile of bodies about seven feet from it. The door in the vestibule of the office did not become open, and was barred by the clothing rack. The revolving door soon jammed, but was burst out by the pressure of the crowd. The head waiter and another waiter tried to get open the panic doors from the main dining room to Shawmut Street, and succeeded after some difficulty. The other two doors to Shawmut Street were locked, and were opened by force from outside by firemen and others. Some patrons escaped through them, but many dead bodies were piled up inside them. A considerable number of patrons escaped through the Broadway door, but many died just inside that door. Some employees, and a great number of patrons, died in the fire. Others were taken out of the building with fatal burns and injuries from smoke, and died within a few days. . . .

The defendant, his brother James Welansky, and Jacob Goldfine, were indicted for manslaughter in sixteen counts of an indictment numbered 413, each count for causing the death of a person described as "Jane Doe," "John Doe," or the like. The first six counts were quashed, leaving the last ten counts. . . .

Each of the counts numbered from 7 to 12, inclusive, as amended alleged in substance that the New Cocoanut Grove, Inc., a corporation, did for a period of time prior to and including November 28, 1942, maintain and operate a night club, to which it invited members of the general public; that it was under a legal duty to its invitees to use reasonable care to keep its premises safe for their use; that the three persons indicted were authorized by the corporation to maintain, control, operate, construct, alter, supervise, and manage its premises in its behalf; that said three persons accepted the responsibility for such acts, and were therefore under a duty to its invitees to use such reasonable care; that in reckless disregard of such duty to one (naming the victim) who was lawfully upon said premises pursuant to such invitation to the general public, and of the probable harmful consequences to him of their failure to perform said duty, they and each of them did "wilfully, wantonly, and recklessly neglect and fail to fulfil their said legal duty and obligation to the said" victim, by reason whereof he on November 28, 1942, received a mortal injury, as a result of which on that day he died.

Each of the thirteenth and fourteenth counts is in shorter form, and alleges in substance that the three persons indicted and each of them on November 28, 1942, did "maintain, manage, operate, and supervise certain premises," describing them, "and solicited and invited the patronage of the public to the said premises"; that at the aforesaid time and place the named victim was lawfully upon the aforesaid premises as a customer on the said invitation, and that the three persons indicted and each of them did "assault and beat" the said victim, and by said assault and beating did kill him "by wilfully, wantonly, and recklessly maintaining, managing, operating, and supervising the said premises." . . .

Another indictment numbered 414 in sixteen counts was returned against the same three persons. The first six counts were quashed, and a verdict of not guilty was directed upon the sixteenth count. That left nine counts, numbered 7 to 15, inclusive. . . .

The defendant was found guilty upon counts 7 to 16, inclusive, of indictment 413 and upon counts 7 to 15, inclusive, of indictment 414. He was sentenced to imprisonment in the State prison upon each count for a term of not less than twelve years and not more than fifteen years, the first day of said term to be in solitary confinement and the residue at hard labor . . . , the sentences to run concurrently. . . .

The Commonwealth disclaimed any contention that the defendant intentionally killed or injured the persons named in the indictments as victims. It based its case on involuntary manslaughter through wanton or reckless conduct. The judge instructed the jury correctly with respect to the nature of such conduct.

Usually wanton or reckless conduct consists of an affirmative act, like driving an automobile or discharging a firearm, in disregard of probable harmful consequences to another. But where as in the present case there is a duty of care for the safety of business visitors invited to premises which the defendant controls, wanton or reckless conduct may consist of intentional failure to take such care in disregard of the probable harmful consequences to them or of their right to care. . . .

To define wanton or reckless conduct so as to distinguish it clearly from negligence and gross negligence is not easy. . . . Sometimes the word "willful" is prefaced to the words "wanton" and "reckless" in expressing the concept. That only blurs it. Willful means intentional. In the phrase "willful, wanton, or reckless conduct," if "willful" modifies "conduct" it introduces something different from wanton or reckless conduct, even though the legal result is the same. Willfully causing harm is a wrong, but a different wrong from wantonly or recklessly causing harm. If "willful" modifies "wanton or reckless conduct" its use is accurate. What must be intended is the conduct, not the resulting harm. . . . The words "wanton" and "reckless" are practically synonymous in this connection, although the word "wanton" may contain a suggestion of arrogance or insolence or heartlessness that is lacking in the word "reckless." But intentional conduct to which either word applies is followed by the same legal consequences as though both words applied.

The standard of wanton or reckless conduct is at once subjective and objective, as has been recognized ever since Commonwealth v. Pierce, 138 Mass. 165, 52 Am. Rep. 264. Knowing facts that would cause a reasonable man to know the danger is equivalent to knowing the danger. . . . The judge charged the jury correctly when he said, "To constitute wanton or reckless conduct, as distinguished from mere negligence, grave danger to others must have been apparent and the defendant must have chosen to run the risk rather than alter his conduct so as to avoid the act or omission which caused the harm. If the grave danger was in fact realized by the defendant, his subsequent voluntary act or omission which caused the harm amounts to wanton or reckless conduct, no matter whether the ordinary man would have realized the gravity of the danger or not. But even if a particular defendant is so stupid [or] so heedless . . . that in fact he did not realize the grave danger, he cannot escape the imputation of wanton or reckless conduct in his dangerous act or omission, if an ordinary normal man under the same circumstances would have realized the gravity of the danger. A man may be reckless within the meaning of the law although he himself thought he was careful."

The essence of wanton or reckless conduct is intentional conduct, by way either of commission or of omission where there is a duty to act, which conduct involves a high degree of likelihood that substantial harm will result to another. . . . Wanton or reckless conduct amounts to what has been variously described as indifference to or disregard of probable consequences to that other. . . . But we are not prepared to give unqualified approval to a further statement found in some of our reported decisions, for example in Query v. Howe, 273 Mass. 92, 96, 172 N.E. 887, that to constitute wanton or reckless conduct, disregard of the rights of another must be as

complete or utter as though such rights did not exist. If taken literally, that statement would permit a trifling regard for the rights of another to exonerate a defendant from the criminal consequences of flagrant wrongdoing.

The words "wanton" and "reckless" are thus not merely rhetorical or vituperative expressions used instead of negligent or grossly negligent. They express a difference in the degree of risk and in the voluntary taking of risk so marked, as compared with negligence, as to amount substantially and in the eyes of the law to a difference in kind. . . . For many years this court has been careful to preserve the distinction between negligence and gross negligence, on the one hand, and wanton or reckless conduct on the other. . . . In pleadings as well as in statutes the rule is that "negligence and willful and wanton conduct are so different in kind that words properly descriptive of the one commonly exclude the other." . . .

Notwithstanding language used commonly in earlier cases, and occasionally in later ones, it is now clear in this Commonwealth that at common law conduct does not become criminal until it passes the borders of negligence and gross negligence and enters into the domain of wanton or reckless conduct. There is in Massachusetts at common law no such thing as "criminal negligence." . . .

Wanton or reckless conduct is the legal equivalent of intentional conduct. . . . If by wanton or reckless conduct bodily injury is caused to another, the person guilty of such conduct is guilty of assault and battery. . . . And since manslaughter is simply a battery that causes death . . . , if death results he is guilty of manslaughter. . . .

To convict the defendant of manslaughter, the Commonwealth was not required to prove that he caused the fire by some wanton or reckless conduct. Fire in a place of public resort is an ever present danger. It was enough to prove that death resulted from his wanton or reckless disregard of the safety of patrons in the event of fire from any cause. . . .

Model Penal Code*

Section 2.02. General Requirements of Culpability

(c) *Recklessly*

A person acts recklessly with respect to a material element of an offense when he consciously disregards a substantial and unjustifiable risk that the material element exists or will result from his conduct. The risk must be of such a nature and degree that, considering the nature and purpose of the actor's conduct and the circumstances known to him, its disregard involves culpability of high degree. [Alternative: its disregard involves a gross deviation from proper standards of conduct.]

(d) *Negligently*

A person acts negligently with respect to a material element of an offense when he should be aware of a substantial and unjustifiable risk that the material element exists or will result from his conduct. The risk must be of such a nature and degree that the actor's failure to perceive it, considering the nature and purpose of his conduct, the circumstances known to him and the care that would be exercised by a reasonable person in his situation, involves substantial culpability. [Alternative: considering the nature and purpose of his conduct and the circumstances known to him, involves a substantial deviation from the standard of care that would be exercised by a reasonable man in his situation.]

. . .

A broader discrimination is perceived between acting either purposely or knowingly and acting recklessly. As we use the term, recklessness involves conscious risk creation. It resembles acting knowingly in that a state of awareness is involved but the awareness is of risk, that is, of probability rather than certainty; the matter is contingent from the actor's point of view. Whether the risk relates to the nature of the actor's conduct or to the existence of the requisite attendant circumstances or to the result that may ensue is immaterial; the concept is the same. The

* Copyright 1956. Reprinted with permission of The American Law Institute from *Model Penal Code* (Philadelphia: The American Law Institute, 1956), Tentative Draft No. 4, Art. 2, § 2.02, pp. 13, 125–27.

draft requires, however, that the risk thus consciously disregarded by the actor be "substantial" and "unjustifiable"; even substantial risks may be created without recklessness when the actor seeks to serve a proper purpose, as when a surgeon performs an operation which he knows is very likely to be fatal but reasonably thinks the patient has no other, safer chance. Accordingly, to aid the ultimate determination, the draft points expressly to the factors to be weighed in judgment: the nature and degree of the risk disregarded by the actor, the nature and purpose of his conduct, and the circumstances known to him in acting.

Some principle must be articulated, however, to indicate what final judgment is demanded after everything is weighed. There is no way to state this value-judgment that does not beg the question in the last analysis; the point is that the jury must evaluate the conduct and determine whether it should be condemned. The draft, therefore, proposes that this difficulty be accepted frankly and the jury asked if the defendant's conduct involved "culpability of high degree." The alternative suggested asks if it "involves a gross deviation from proper standards of conduct." This formulation is designed to avoid the difficulty inherent in defining culpability in terms of culpability, but the accomplishment seems hardly more than verbal; it does not really avoid the tautology or beg the question less. It may, however, be a better way to put the issue to a jury, especially as some of the conduct to which the section must apply may not involve great moral culpability, even when the defendant acted purposely or knowingly, as in the violation of some minor regulatory measure.

The fourth kind of culpability is negligence. It is distinguished from acting purposely, knowingly, or recklessly in that it does not involve a state of awareness. It is the case where the actor creates inadvertently a risk of which he ought to be aware, considering its nature and degree, the nature and the purpose of his conduct, and the care that would be exercised by a reasonable person in his situation. Again, however, it is quite impossible to avoid tautological articulation of the final question. The tribunal must evaluate the actor's failure of perception and determine whether, under all the circumstances, it was serious enough to be condemned. Whether that finding is verbalized as "substantial culpability," as the draft proposes or as "substantial deviation from the standard of care that would be exercised by a reasonable man under the circumstances," as the alternative would put it, presents the same problem here as in the case of recklessness. The jury must find fault and find it was substantial; that is all that either formulation says or, we believe, that can be said in legislative terms.

A further point merits attention: the draft invites consideration of the "care that would be exercised by a reasonable person in his [i.e., the actor's] situation." There is an inevitable ambiguity in "situation." If the actor were blind or if he had just suffered a blow or experienced a heart attack, these would certainly be facts to be considered, as they would be under present law. But the heredity, intelligence, or temperament of the actor would not now be held material in judging negligence; and could not be without depriving the criterion of all its objectivity. . . .

Of the four kinds of culpability defined, there is, of course, least to be said for treating negligence as a sufficient basis for imposing criminal liability. Since the actor is inad-

vertent by hypothesis, it has been argued that the "threat of punishment for negligence must pass him by, because he does not realize that it is addressed to him." . . . So, too, it has been urged that education or corrective treatment, not punishment, is the proper social method for dealing with persons with inadequate awareness, since what is implied is not a moral defect. . . . We think, however, that this is to oversimplify the issue. Knowledge that conviction and sentence, not to speak of punishment, may follow conduct that inadvertently creates improper risk supplies men with an additional motive to take care before acting, to use their faculties, and draw on their experience in gauging the potentialities of contemplated conduct. To some extent, at least, this motive may promote awareness and thus be effective as a measure of control. Certainly legislators act on this assumption in a host of situations and it seems to us dogmatic to assert that they are wholly wrong. Accordingly, we think that negligence, as here defined, cannot be wholly rejected as a ground of culpability which may suffice for purposes of penal law, though we agree that it should not be generally deemed sufficient in the definition of specific crimes, and that it often will be right to differentiate such conduct for the purposes of sentence. The content of the concept must, therefore, be treated at this stage.

Negligence, Heedlessness, and Rashness*

The states of mind which are styled "Negligence" and "Heedlessness" are precisely alike. In either case the party is inadvertent. In the first case, he does *not* an act which he was bound to do, because he adverts not to it. In the second case he *does* an act from which he was bound to forbear, because he adverts not to certain of its probable consequences. Absence of a thought, which one's duty would naturally suggest, is the main ingredient in each of the complex notions which are styled "negligence" and "heedlessness."

The party who is guilty of Temerity or Rashness, like the party who is guilty of heedlessness, does an act, and breaks a positive duty. But the party who is guilty of heedless-

ness, thinks not of the probable mischief. The party who is guilty of rashness *thinks* of the probable mischief; but, in consequence of a missupposition begotten by insufficient advertence, he assumes that the mischief will not ensue in the given instance or case. Such (I think) is the meaning invariably attached to the expressions, "Rashness," "Temerity," "Foolhardiness," and the like. The radical idea denoted is always this. The party runs a risk of which he is conscious; but he thinks (for a reason which he examines insufficiently) that the mischief will probably be averted in the given instance.

I will again illustrate my meaning, by recurring to the example to which I have just alluded.

When I fire at the mark chalked upon the fence, it occurs to my mind that a shot may

* John Austin, *Lectures on Jurisprudence* (London: John Murray, 1873), I, 440–44. Footnotes are omitted.

pierce the fence, and may chance to hit a passenger. But without examining carefully the ground of my conclusion, I conclude that the fence is sufficiently thick to prevent a shot from passing to the road. Or, without giving myself the trouble to look into the road, I assume that a passenger is not there, because the road is seldom passed. In either case, my confidence is *rash*; and, through my *rashness* or *temerity,* I am the author of the mischief. My assumption is founded upon evidence which the event shows to be worthless, and of which I should discover the worthlessness if I scrutinized it as I ought.

By the Roman Lawyers, Rashness, Heedlessness, or Negligence is, in certain cases, considered equivalent to "Dolus": that is to say, to intention. "Dolo comparatur." "Vix est ut a certo nocendi *proposito* discerni possit." Changing the expression, they suppose that rashness, heedlessness, or negligence can hardly be distinguished, in certain cases, from intention.

Now this (it appears to me) is a mistake. Intention (it seems to me) is a *precise* state of the mind, and cannot coalesce or commingle with a different state of the mind. "To intend" is to believe that a given act will follow a given volition, or that a given consequence will follow a given act. The chance of the sequence may be rated higher or lower; but the party *conceives* the future event, and believes that there *is* a chance of its following his volition or act. Intention, therefore, is a state of consciousness.

But negligence and heedlessness suppose *un*consciousness. In the first case, the party does *not* think of a given act. In the second case, the party does *not* think of a given consequence.

Now a state of mind between consciousness and unconsciousness—between intention on the one side and negligence or heedlessness on the other—seems to be impossible. The party thinks, or the party does *not* think, of the act or consequence. If he think of it, he *intends.* If he do not think of it, he is *negligent* or *heedless.* To say that a negligence or heedlessness may run into intention is to say that a thought may be *absent* from the mind, and yet (after a fashion) *present* to the mind.

Nor is it possible to conceive that supposed mongrel or monster, which is *neither* temerity *nor* intention, but partakes of both: A state

of mind lying on the confines of each, without belonging precisely to the territory of either.

The party who is guilty of Rashness *thinks* of a given consequence: but, by reason of a missupposition arising from insufficient advertence, he concludes that the given consequence will *not* follow the act in the given instance. Now if he surmise (though never so hastily and faintly) that his missupposition is unfounded, he *intends* the consequence. For he *thinks* of that consequence; he believes that his missupposition *may* be a missupposition; and he, therefore, believes that the consequence *may* follow his act.

I will again revert to the example which I have already cited repeatedly.

When I fire at the mark chalked upon the fence, it occurs to my mind that the shot may pierce the fence, and may chance to hit a passenger. But I assume that the fence is sufficiently thick to intercept a pistol-shot. Or, without going to the road in order that I may be sure of the fact, I assume that a passenger cannot be there *because* the road is seldom passed.

Now if my missupposition be absolutely confident and sincere, I am guilty of rashness only.

But, instead of assuming confidently that the fence will intercept the ball, or that no passenger is then on the road, I may surmise that the assumption upon which I act is not altogether just. I think that a passenger may chance to be there, though I think the presence of a passenger somewhat improbable. Or, though I judge the fence a stout and thick *paling,* I tacitly admit that a brick wall would intercept a pistol-shot more certainly. Consequently, I *intend* the hurt of the passenger who is actually hit and wounded. I think of the mischief, when I will the act; I believe that my missupposition *may* be a missupposition; and I, therefore, believe there is a *chance* that the mischief to which I advert may follow my volition.

The proposition of the Roman Lawyers is, therefore, false.

The mistake (I have no doubt) arose from a confusion of ideas which is not unfrequent: from the confusion of *probandum* and *probans* of the *subject* of an inquiry into a matter of fact—with the *evidence.*

The state of a man's mind can only be

known by others through his acts: through his own declarations, or through other conduct of his own. Consequently, it must often be difficult to determine whether a party *intended,* or whether he was merely negligent, heedless, or rash. The acts to which we must resort as evidence of the state of his mind, may be *ambiguous*: insomuch that they lead us to one conclusion as naturally as to the other. Judging from his conduct, the man may have *intended,* or he may have been negligent, heedless, or rash. Either hypothesis would fit the appearances which are open to our observation.

But the difficulty which belongs to the *evidence* is transferred to the *subject of the inquiry.* Because we are unable to determine *what* was the state of his mind, we fancy that the state of his mind was itself *indeterminate*: that it lay between the confines of consciousness and unconsciousness, without belonging exactly to either. We forget that these are antagonist notions, incapable of blending.

When it was said by the Roman Lawyers "that Negligence, Heedlessness, or Rashness, is equivalent, in certain cases, to *Dolus* or Intention," their meaning (I believe) was this:

Judging from the conduct of the party, it is impossible to determine whether he *intended,* or whether he was negligent, heedless, or rash. And, such being the case, it shall be *presumed* that he *intended,* and his liability shall be adjusted accordingly, *provided that the question arise in a civil action.* If the question had arisen in the course of a criminal proceeding, then the presumption would have gone in favor of the party, and not against him.

Such (I think) is the meaning which floated before their minds: Although we must infer (if we take their expressions literally) that they believed in the possibility of a state of mind lying between consciousness and unconsciousness.

If I attempted to explain the matter fully, I should enter upon certain distinctions between civil and criminal liability, and upon the nature of *proesumptiones juris* or legal presumptions.

It is, therefore, clear to me, that Intention is always separated from Negligence, Heedlessness, or Rashness, by a precise line of demarcation. The state of the party's mind is always *determined,* although it may be difficult (judging from his conduct) to ascertain the state of his mind.

Before I quit this subject, I may observe that *hasty* intention is frequently styled *rashness.* For instance, an intentional manslaughter is often styled *rash,* because the act is not premeditated, or has not been preceded by deliberate intention. Before we can distinguish hasty from deliberate intention, we must determine the nature of intention *as it regards future acts.* But it is easy to see that sudden or hasty intention is utterly different from rashness. When the act is done, the party contemplates the consequence, although he has not *premeditated* the consequence or the act.

To resume:

It is manifest that Negligence, Heedlessness, and Rashness, are closely allied. *Want* of the *advertence* which one's duty would naturally suggest is the fundamental or radical idea in each of the complex notions. But though they are closely allied, or are modes of the same notion, they are broadly distinguished by differences.

In cases of Negligence, the party performs not an act to which he is obliged. He breaks a positive duty.

In cases of Heedlessness or Rashness, the party does an act from which he is bound to forbear. He breaks a negative duty.

In cases of Negligence, he adverts not to the act, which it is his duty to do.

In cases of Heedlessness, he adverts not to *consequences* of the act which he does.

In cases of Rashness, he adverts to those consequences of the act; but, by reason of some assumption *which he examines insufficiently,* he concludes that those consequences will not follow the act in the instance before him.

And, since the notions are so closely allied, they are (as might be expected) often confounded. Heedlessness is frequently denoted by the term "negligence"; and the same term has even been extended to rashness or temerity. But the three states of mind are nevertheless distinct; and, in respect of differences between their consequences, should be distinguished.

Negligence*

Negligence is often defined as consisting of a breach of duty. That is wrong. The duty in such a case can be defined only as a duty to use care, i.e., not to act negligently; and to define the duty so, and then to define negligence as consisting of a breach of the duty, is to define in a circle. The misconception has arisen from a failure to distinguish between a negligent wrong, which, like all wrongs, involves a breach of duty, and the negligence itself, which is one element in the wrong. It is true that negligence which in the particular case is not a breach of any legal duty is of no legal importance; but that does not touch the question of its nature as negligence. There are many cases where the law does not require care, where therefore negligence is not legally wrong; but it is none the less negligence. We must have a conception of negligence as it is in itself, independent of the conception of duty, in order that we may use it as a *praecognoscendum* in the definition of various duties. The subject of this article is the nature of negligence, not duties to use care. . . .

Negligence is conduct which involves an unreasonably great risk of causing damage. Due care is conduct which does not involve such a risk.

Negligence is conduct, not a state of mind. It is most often caused by carelessness or heedlessness; the actor does not advert properly to the consequences that may follow his conduct, and therefore fails to realize that his conduct is unreasonably dangerous. But it may be due to other states of mind. Thus the actor may recognize the fact that his conduct is dangerous, but may not care whether he does the injury or not; or, though he would prefer not to do harm, yet for some reason of his own he may choose to take a risk which he understands to be unreasonably great. This state of mind is recklessness, which is one kind of willfulness, and negligent conduct due to recklessness is often called willful negligence. Some courts have denied that there is any such thing as willful negligence. But that is because they have failed to distinguish between negligence, which is outward conduct, and carelessness, which is a state of mind.

Negligent conduct may also be due to a mere error of judgment, where the actor gives due consideration to his conduct and its possible consequences, and mistakenly makes up his mind that the conduct does not involve any unreasonably great risk. He is not therefore excused, if his conduct is in fact unreasonably dangerous. As will be explained later, he must judge and decide as a reasonable and prudent man would; so that if he is not in fact such a man, he may decide wrongly and be guilty of legal negligence though he acted as well as he knew how to. The rule that mere error in judgment is not negligence has a different meaning, which will be explained further on. Whatever the state of mind be that leads to negligent conduct, the state of mind, which is the cause, must be distinguished from the actual negligence, which is its effect. Conversely, if in a given case the actor does nothing that involves an unreasonably great risk, his conduct is not negligent, it amounts legally to due care, however careless or reckless he may be in his mind. Just as a man can do wrong though his state of mind is not blameworthy, so he can do right though his state of mind is blameworthy.

Negligent conduct may consist in acts or omissions, in doing unreasonably dangerous acts or in omitting to take such precautions as reasonableness requires against danger. As will be explained below there is generally no duty to take such precautions. But the failure to take them is nevertheless negligent. It has often been laid down that negligence is doing what a reasonable and prudent man would not have done or not doing what such a man would have done. It has indeed been said that negligence always consists in omission. This arises from confusion between negligence and carelessness. Carelessness does consist in an omission to take thought about the consequences of one's conduct; and it is that omission which has been mistaken for negligence in the legal sense.

To make conduct negligent the risk involved in it must be unreasonably great; some injurious consequences of it must be not only possible or in a sense probable, but unreasonably probable. It is quite impossible in the business of life to avoid taking risks of injury to one's self or others, and the law does not

* Henry T. Terry, "Negligence," *Harvard Law Review*, XXIX (1915), 40–50, reprinted by permission of the publishers. Copyright 1915 by The Harvard Law Review Association. Footnotes are omitted.

forbid doing so; what it requires is that the risk be not unreasonably great. The essence of negligence is unreasonableness; due care is simply reasonable conduct. There is no mathematical rule of percentage of probabilities to be followed here. A risk is not necessarily unreasonable because the harmful consequence is more likely than not to follow the conduct, nor reasonable because the chances are against that. A very large risk may be reasonable in some circumstances, and a small risk unreasonable in other circumstances. When due care consists in taking precautions against harm, only reasonable precautions need be taken, not every conceivable or possible precaution. And precautions need not be taken against every conceivable or foreseeable danger, but only against probable dangers. The books are full of cases where persons have been held not negligent for not guarding against a certain harmful event, on the ground that they need not reasonably have expected it to happen.

Sometimes a person is under a duty to insure safety, absolutely to prevent the happening of certain damage. Such duties, which may be called peremptory duties, lie entirely outside of the law of negligence. However, the failure to perform the duty is often called negligence, or it is said that in such a case negligence is conclusively presumed, as has been said, for instance, where the keeper of a savage dog has failed to prevent it from biting someone. But that is a mere misconception, or at best a useless and misleading fiction.

The reasonableness of a given risk may depend upon the following five factors:

(1) The magnitude of the risk. A risk is more likely to be unreasonable the greater it is.

(2) The value or importance of that which is exposed to the risk, which is the object that the law desires to protect, and may be called the principal object. The reasonableness of a risk means its reasonableness with respect to the principal object.

(3) A person who takes a risk of injuring the principal object usually does so because he has some reason of his own for such conduct, is pursuing some object of his own. This may be called the collateral object. In some cases, at least, the value or importance of the collateral object is properly to be considered in

deciding upon the reasonableness of the risk.

(4) The probability that the collateral object will be attained by the conduct which involves risk to the principal; the utility of the risk.

(5) The probability that the collateral object would not have been attained without taking the risk; the necessity of the risk. The following case will serve as an illustration.

The plantiff's intestate, seeing a child on a railroad track just in front of a rapidly approaching train, went upon the track to save him. He did save him, but was himself killed by the train. The jury were allowed to find that he had not been guilty of contributory negligence. The question was of course whether he had exposed himself to an unreasonably great risk. Here the above-mentioned elements of reasonableness were as follows:

(1) The magnitude of the risk was the probability that he would be killed or hurt. That was very great.

(2) The principal object was his own life, which was very valuable.

(3) The collateral object was the child's life, which was also very valuable.

(4) The utility of the risk was the probability that he could save the child. That must have been fairly great, since he in fact succeeded. Had there been no fair chance of saving the child, the conduct would have been unreasonable and negligent.

(5) The necessity of the risk was the probability that the child would not have saved himself by getting off of the track in time.

Here, although the magnitude of the risk was very great and the principal object very valuable, yet the value of the collateral object and the great utility and necessity of the risk counterbalanced those considerations, and made the risk reasonable. The same risk would have been unreasonable had the creature on the track been a kitten, because the value of the collateral object would have been small. There is no general rule that human life may not be put at risk in order to save property; but since life is more valuable than property, such a risk has often been held unreasonable in particular cases, which has given rise to *dicta* to the effect that it is always so. But in the circumstances of other cases a risk of that sort has been held reasonable.

Sometimes the collateral object, and therefore the utility and necessity of the risk, which relate to that object only, cannot be considered at all in deciding upon the reasonableness of the risk. There are certain objects which the law designs to protect, which may be called legal objects, and others which it does not attempt to protect, which may be called personal objects. Thus the law protects human life and bodily safety, the safety of property, and various other valuable objects. To some extent it protects pecuniary condition, i.e., the avoidance of pecuniary loss is generally, but, as the decisions now stand, not always, a legal object. A person has rights of life, bodily security, property, and pecuniary condition, and other rights in various objects or conditions of fact. But generally, subject to some exceptions which are not important here, the law does not protect the state of a person's mind or feelings. There is no general right of mental security, as there is of bodily security, which can be violated by a person's being subjected to disagreeable or painful mental experiences, such as fright, anxiety, mortification, or discomfort.

. . .

Conduct which is not directed to any object, which is aimless, is per se unrational. When, however, in a particular case the collateral object cannot be considered, it must not be assumed that the risk was taken wantonly and for no object. The question will then be whether, considering how people generally act and the ordinary exigencies of life, it will generally be reasonable to act in that way, can a general rule be laid down that that sort of conduct is generally reasonable or unreasonable; e.g., is it generally reasonable to get off of a fast-moving railroad train because it does not stop at one's station? However, the fact that no reason is shown for doing a dangerous act may be evidence that it was unreasonable and negligent.

The test of reasonableness is what would be the conduct or judgment of what may be called a standard man in the situation of the person whose conduct is in question.

A standard man does not mean an ideal or perfect man, but an ordinary member of the community. He is usually spoken of as an ordinarily reasonable, careful, and prudent man. That definition is not exactly correct, because in certain cases other qualities than reasonableness, carefulness, or prudence, e.g., courage, may be important; but it will do for

our present purpose. It is because the jury is supposed to consist of standard men, and therefore to know of their own knowledge how such a man would act in a given situation, that questions of reasonableness and negligence are usually left to the jury.

Every man, whether he is a standard man or not, is required to act as a standard man would. If by chance he is not such a man, he may, as has been said, make a mistake and act so as to be guilty of legal negligence, though he has used all such care and forethought as he was capable of. In the case of contributory negligence there is an exception to this rule in the case of abnormal persons, such as children and persons of unsound mind. They are not required to act like a standard man, but only to use such judgment as they are capable of. But as to negligence which is not merely contributory, as to negligent wrongs against others, the standard-man test applies to their conduct also. Women are not abnormal persons, except perhaps in respect to courage.

Anything that a standard man would do is reasonable. If there are several different courses which he might take, any one of them is reasonable, even though one would be more reasonable than another. All that the law requires of a man is reasonable conduct, not the most reasonable nor even the more reasonable. Also even a standard man, being human and therefore fallible, may err in his judgment. Conduct which in fact causes injury, if due to an error of judgment which a standard man might make, is not negligent. This is the meaning of the statement above mentioned, that mere error of judgment is not negligence. But this must be distinguished from an error which a standard man would not make.

The situation of the actor is subjective, not objective. It consists of such facts as are known to him. It would plainly be absurd and unjust to require a person to regulate his conduct with reference to facts of which he was ignorant. When, however, a person knows that he is ignorant of essential facts, it may be unreasonable for him to act at all. But in some circumstances a person may be charged with knowledge which in fact he has not, and be held to accountability as if he had it. When a person is under a duty to take precautions against a possible danger, there is usually an ancillary duty to use care to find out what precautions are needed; and for the purpose of the principal duty he is charged with all knowledge which he would have got by properly performing the ancillary duty.

The jury in deciding whether certain conduct involved an unreasonably great risk are deemed to be acquainted with the teachings of common experience, and evidence to prove that is not necessary nor admissible. It has been thought that the actor himself must be deemed to have the same knowledge, and should be held negligent, if he does something that the common experience of mankind shows to be unreasonably dangerous. It is believed that the cases of the jury and the actor are not parallel, and that as to the latter there is only a prima facie presumption that he has such knowledge, which he may, if he can, rebut by evidence of his ignorance. Thus if a man should try to open a can which he knew to contain nitroglycerine with a chisel and hammer, and an explosion should result, if the question were of his negligence in doing so, in the present state of our knowledge the jury could find without any evidence being adduced that his act was in fact very dangerous. It would no doubt be presumed that the actor knew it; but it is believed that he would be allowed to prove in his defense that he was actually ignorant of the properties of that substance. Of course, if he thought that the can contained not nitroglycerine but con-

densed milk, that belief of his would be a part of his situation, and no question would arise as to the teachings of experience about nitroglycerine.

. . .

The reasonableness or unreasonableness of conduct is an inference from data. The data consist of the conduct in question and the facts of the actor's situation. The existence of the data is a question of fact. When the data are disputed, the question of negligence must go to the jury, with proper instructions from the court if necessary. The data being given, the inference of reasonableness or unreasonableness, of due care or negligence, is in its nature one of fact, the data furnishing the minor premise and the major premise being drawn from common experience, whereas in a true inference of law the major premise is a rule of law. Therefore the question is regularly for the jury. But in a perfectly clear case, where it is plain that only one reasonable inference is possible, the court will decide it as law. If no reasonable inference is possible, the court must decide the question against the party who has the burden of proof, usually the party who asserts that the other was negligent, and must not permit the jury to make a decision which would rest upon a mere guess and not upon reasonable inference.

The Relation of Mental States to Negligence*

According to Melville M. Bigelow, "It should be made clear at the outset that negligence is a state of mind; a fact obscured by the circumstance that stated external standards are applied to the proof of it."[1] According to Henry T. Terry, "Negligence is conduct, not a state of mind."[2] The second view is perhaps the more orthodox;[3] but the opinion that negligence is, or involves, a particular mental state is by no means peculiar to

* Henry W. Edgerton, "Negligence, Inadvertence, and Indifference; The Relation of Mental States to Negligence," *Harvard Law Review*, XXXIX (1926), 849–59, 865–69, reprinted by permission of the publishers. Copyright 1926 by The Harvard Law Review Association. Footnotes have been renumbered.
[1] Bigelow, *Torts*, 8th ed., 19.
[2] Henry T. Terry, "Negligence," 29 *Harv. L. Rev.* 40.
[3] *Cf.* Holmes, *The Common Law*, p. 110; Pollock, *Torts*, 12 ed., pp. 443–44; Beven, *Negligence*, 3 ed., p. 16.

Professor Bigelow. It has a considerable currency and it is strongly entrenched in legal phraseology.

THE MENTAL THEORY

The question (1) whether negligence consists of (or requires) an indifferent state of mind or dangerous conduct, is not the same as the question (2) whether the measure of negligence, the standard to which one must conform, is fixed by the individual capacities of the actor or by the capacities of a normal or standard person; though the words subjective and objective are applicable in connection with each question. About the second question, as a general proposition and apart from specific difficulties of application, there seems to be little or no dispute; the measure or standard is objective, external. But the general agreement on the second question does not foreclose the first. There is no logical obstacle to taking the subjective or mental view of the first along with the objective or external view of the second. That is, one may conceive that although the actor is required to conform to the standard of a normal man and not to any personal standard of his own, yet the *respect in which* he must conform is mental and not physical; that he is required, not to act as safely, but to attend as closely or feel as anxiously, as a normal man would in the same circumstances; that negligence is a mental phenomenon, or that it is conduct produced or accompanied by a particular mental phenomenon.

This mental view takes a variety of forms. Sir John Salmond elaborated it in an extreme form, and adhered to it in successive editions of his works on Torts and Jurisprudence. Negligence, he said, "consists in a certain mental attitude of the defendant toward the consequences of his act. . . . He is guilty of negligence . . . when he does not desire the consequences, and does not act in order to produce them, but is nevertheless indifferent or careless whether they happen or not, and therefore does not refrain from the act notwithstanding the risk that they may happen."[4] "Negligence . . . essentially consists in the *mental attitude of undue indifference with respect to one's conduct and its consequences.* . . . Negligence, as so defined, is rightly treated as a form of *mens rea,* standing side by side with wrongful intention as a formal ground of responsibility."[5] Professor Chapin, in his book on Torts, takes a milder view; not that negligence is, but that it necessarily involves, a particular mental fact. "Negligence . . . presupposes culpable inadvertence."[6] . . .

THE CONDUCT THEORY

I submit that all this is erroneous. Negligence neither is nor involves ("presupposes") either indifference, or inadvertence, or any other mental characteristic, quality, state, or process. Negligence is unreasonably dangerous conduct—i.e., conduct abnormally likely to cause harm. Freedom from negligence (commonly called "due care") does not require care, or any other mental phenomenon, but requires only that one's conduct be reason-

ably safe—as little likely to cause harm as the conduct of a normal person would be.

But when it is said that negligence is conduct, what is meant by conduct? Acts are "exertions of the will manifested in the external world." An act, then, is a physical motion plus a mental process. It may well be asked, can reasonableness or unreasonableness always be attributed to the motion independently of the process? The motions involved in starting a car, reasonable in one who is reasonably ignorant of a defect in the car, may be negligent in one who knows of the defect. So much an advocate of the conduct theory must admit. Its opponents, on the other hand, would admit that no mental state can be a ground of liability without an act. . . .

Is the question whether negligence is conduct or a state of mind a "matter of indifference"? "Is the practical result . . . the same"? It is, in the sense and to the extent that theories about negligence do not decide cases; that courts and juries really decide on the basis of an intuitive feeling that a defendant ought, or ought not, to be held. This is partly true, but it is not wholly true. If, as many courts and writers say, negligence involves or "presupposes" indifference or inadvertence, this means that "that anxious consideration of consequences which is called care" precludes negligence. If, as some eminent authors say, negligence *is* "a mental attitude of undue indifference," this means not only that anxious consideration precludes negligence, but also that indifference conclusively proves negligence. On the other hand, the proposition that negligence is conduct means that there is negligence if there are unreasonably dangerous motions, and not otherwise; consequently, that no particular mental shortcoming proves negligence or is necessary to negligence, and no particular mental attainment precludes negligence. Non-negligent conduct, and consequent freedom from liability, may coexist with a mental state that is dangerous, as involving inadvertence, lack of normal anxiety to avoid harm, or any other unsafe mental fact; negligent conduct, and consequent liability, may coexist with normal and proper advertence and anxiety.

When one's intent is in issue, he may and often does testify regarding it. "In only one jurisdiction has any clear sanction been given to a rule that parties or other persons are disqualified to testify to their own intent or

---

[4] Salmond, *Torts,* 6th ed., 21.
[5] Salmond, *Jurisprudence,* 7th ed., 410.
[6] Chapin, *Torts,* 499.

motive. In all others where the question has been raised there is a general repudiation of that notion in all its aspects."[7] Dean Wigmore cites a multitude of cases in which such testimony has been held admissible. If negligence means indifference and is therefore, as Salmond says, "a form of *mens rea*, standing side by side with wrongful intention as a formal ground of responsibility"—and equally if negligence "presupposes" indifference—we should expect to find another multitude of cases in which the actor's testimony to his anxiety (or indifference) has been admitted. Similarly, if negligence involves inadvertence, there should be many cases in which the actor's testimony to his advertence has been admitted. As negligence cases are commoner than cases involving wrongful intention, there should be even more instances of testimony to anxiety or advertence than of testimony to intention. But so far as appears, such testimony is practically never even offered. . . .

Again, a belief that a given act is not likely to cause damage seems to negative both the indifference which is sometimes, and the inadvertence which is more often, said to be the essence of negligence. If, therefore, inadvertence or indifference were really the issue in a negligence case, the actor's belief concerning the probability of his course causing harm would be highly material. It is held to be immaterial.

Though one need not actually use or have any particular mental characteristic in order to be free from negligence, one must *act as if he had* (as safely as if he had) a normal complement of *all* mental characteristics which would be useful in avoiding harm in the particular circumstances. Though no particular mental shortcoming is necessary to negligence, any mental shortcoming may result in negligence. If the actor's motions are less safe than those of a person with a normal mental equipment would be, they are unreasonably dangerous, and therefore negligent, no matter what particular mental shortcoming it is that produces the risk and the harm. Negligence may be due—for example—to a lack of common knowledge, memory, observation, imagination, foresight, intelligence, judgment, quickness of reaction, deliberation, coolness, self-control, determination, courage, or altruism. Few negligence cases show clearly—because it is immaterial—what mental shortcoming produced the negligent act in question. But in some cases it is quite apparent that it was not indifference or inadvertence but ignorance, stupidity, bad judgment, timidity, excitability, or forgetfulness.

The individual's actual mental characteristics and qualities, capacities, and habits, reactions and processes, are not, then, among the "circumstances" which the law considers in determining whether his conduct was, under the circumstances, reasonably safe. He must behave as well (as safely) as if he were in all mental respects normal, though he may be in some respect subnormal; he need behave no better, though he may be in some respect super-normal. In fact, the broad proposition that no merely mental fact about the (sane) individual is material, would seem to require only one substantial qualification; his special knowledge is highly material. Knowledge or suspicion that a glass contains poison makes conduct negligent which would be innocent in one who reasonably believed it to contain water. But knowledge, though obviously a mental fact, is one of a peculiar sort. All normal persons acquire, not only normally but inevitably, many items of special knowledge. If one has a normal memory and uses it normally, his conduct will reflect his acquisitions. Accordingly, the requirement that one who has useful special knowledge should use it, does not conflict with the principle that mental normality, and only that, is demanded. As knowledge results from experience, it would even be possible in most cases to twist the requirement into an objective form by disregarding the knowledge and treating the experience (in consequence of which the actor "knew or ought to have known") as the pertinent circumstance. And there are practical reasons quite as clear as the theoretical ones for treating special knowledge differently from other mental facts. The question whether one knew the glass contained poison commonly is or has been capable of a more definite and positive answer than the question whether his capacity for reasoning or observation (for example) was above normal. If some such capacities have become or are becoming as measurable as knowledge, the law has not had time to reflect the fact. Moreover, failures to use special knowledge are more frequently, and in general more seriously, hurtful than failures to use special intelligence and the like. If one acts like a man of merely normal mental capacities, he may do very little harm, but if one refuses to use his special knowledge, he will do a vast amount of harm. A failure to use special knowledge is, therefore, not only more obvious and more irritating but more to be discouraged in the interest of the general security, than a failure to use special mental gifts.

While negligence does not involve always the same mental shortcoming, it probably always involves *some* mental shortcoming. If a person of no temporary or permanent shortcoming either of desire or of capacity might make certain motions, by the same token "the ordinary prudent man, acting prudently" might do so, and it is not negligent to do so. Accordingly, to say that an act is negligent is to say that it would not have been done by the possessor of a normal mind functioning normally. But, though some mental shortcoming or other, of desire or capacity, must be present or a negligent act would not occur, to prove the shortcoming does not prove the plaintiff's case and is no part of the plaintiff's case. If A is a good lawyer, he must have studied law; but proving the study does not conclusively prove the skill, and the skill may be proved without proving the study. Just so, if A has acted negligently, he must have fallen below normal in some mental respect; but proving his mental shortcoming does not prove the negligence, and the negligence may be proved without proving the mental shortcoming.

Though negligence is conduct, and mental facts neither establish nor rebut it, there is, then, this modicum of truth in the propositions that negligence is or involves inadvertence or indifference, and that "negligence in the one sense is necessarily accompanied by negligence in the other also." When there is negligent conduct, there has been a shortcoming in some mental respect; and when a shortcoming in any mental respect leads to dangerous conduct, it leads to negligent conduct.

. . .

JUSTIFICATION OF THE CONDUCT
THEORY

One objection to making negligence turn on state of mind instead of conduct is that states of mind are much more difficult to prove. The difficult question whether conduct is reasonably safe is simple and easy compared to the question whether the actor's attention is reasonably focused or his feelings are reasonably anxious. Either test involves, in its application, the comparison of particular facts with a standard that is nebulous; but in the case of the mental test the particular facts also are nebulous (viz., the actor's mental and emotional state), while in the case of the physical test the particular facts are relatively clear (viz., the actor's movements).

So far as any mental test leads in practice to different results from the conduct test, the results are bad. It is conduct, not a state of mind, that causes harm. Is it not as unreasonable to make negligence turn on a state of mind as on a state of body? If one's conduct is abnormally dangerous and causes harm, one does not escape liability by virtue of his good health and strong muscles; should he escape it by virtue of his close attention or his earnest contemporaneous regret? The mental excellence and the physical alike may prevent him from causing harm another time; but this time they did not prevent him from causing it, and causing it by dangerous conduct. Yet either the theory that negligence is, or the much commoner theory that it necessarily involves or "presupposes," a particular mental condition would protect the attentive and anxious man from liability for his dangerous conduct. On the other hand, suppose P, who has only one leg, walks in the street and is injured by D's negligence. It appears that a two-legged man could not have escaped injury. Clearly P can recover; either his walking as he did was not negligent, or it was negligence which had nothing to do with causing the injury. No one would argue that he ought to suffer because his defect, though it did him no harm on this occasion, may some time do him harm. Suppose P, instead of lacking a leg, lacks normal attentiveness or normal anxiety to avoid injury, but makes just those motions which a man normally attentive and anxious would make. Is he to be denied recovery because his defect, though it had nothing whatever to do with causing his injury, may cause him injury at another time? This is precisely the result of the theory that negligence *is* inadvertence or indifference (though not necessarily of the theory that it "presupposes" it, since under the latter theory dangerous conduct as well as an inadvertent state of mind might be required). And so if it is the defendant whose negligence is in question. No one would contend that if an automobile driver acts like a two-legged man—does all that such a man would do to prevent an accident—he should be liable because he is one-legged. Would it not be equally absurd to make a driver who acts like a man normally attentive and anxious to avoid harm liable because he does not feel so?

By imposing liability for the consequences of dangerous conduct, and of dangerous conduct only, the law of negligence discourages such conduct, and thereby protects the general security, with a minimum of interference with individual freedom of action. The mental theory in either of its chief forms—that negligence is, or that it necessarily involves, inadvertence or indifference—would leave the general security unprotected against that vast amount of dangerous and harmful conduct which results not from inadvertence or indifference but from deficiencies in knowledge, memory, observation, imagination, foresight, intelligence, judgment, quickness of reaction, deliberation, coolness, self-control, determination, courage, or the like. This is the great vice of the theory. As Mr. Justice Holmes has said, "when men live in society, a certain average of conduct, a sacrifice of individual peculiarities going beyond a certain point, is necessary to the general welfare. If, for instance, a man is born hasty and awkward, is always having accidents and hurting himself or his neighbors, no doubt his congenital defects will be allowed for in the courts of Heaven, but his slips are no less troublesome to his neighbors than if they sprang from guilty neglect. His neighbors accordingly require him, at his proper peril, to come up to their standard, and the courts which they establish decline to take his personal equation into account."[8] Dean Pound has put as the "jural postulate of civilized society," which underlies our doctrine of negligence, that "men must be able to assume that their fellow men, when they act affirmatively, will do so with due care, that is, with the care which the ordinary understanding and moral sense of the community exacts, with respect to consequences that may reasonably be anticipated."[9] The context makes it clear that the word "care" is here used in its technical sense, with no intention of giving aid and comfort to the enemies of the conduct theory. In terms of conduct: Men must be able to assume that when their fellow men act affirmatively, their action will be reasonably safe, that is, will create no greater risk or harm than the ordinary understanding and moral sense of the community permits.

Besides leaving the community without protection against the dangerous acts of attentive and anxious persons, the theory that negligence *is* a particular mental condition would tend at the same time to impose a needless and hurtful restraint on the nondangerous activity of relatively inadvertent and indifferent persons. The liability which it would impose is liability for a coincidence; the coincidence between relative indifference (or inadvertence) in the actor, and conduct which whether dangerous or safe happens to result in harm. It is true that indifference and inadvertence *tend* to result in dangerous and harmful acts, and that to impose liability upon the indifferent and inadvertent whenever their acts, though reasonably safe, happen to result in harm, would tend to eliminate indifference and inadvertence, and so to prevent dangerous acts and resulting harm on other occasions; but the argument would be quite as strong for imposing liability upon the indifferent bystander, as upon the indifferent actor whose *conduct* in the particular case, though it happened to result in harm, was no more dangerous than an attentive and anxious actor's would have been. It is as true of the bystander as of the actor that his shortcoming may cause harm on other occasions; it is as true of the actor as of the bystander that his shortcoming has caused no harm on this occasion. The relation of the shortcoming of each of the harm is one of pure coincidence. Penalizing the bystander for the coincidence would discourage, along with indifference, only bystanding; penalizing the actor for it would discourage, along with indifference, safe and reasonable activity.

The theory that negligence is or involves a state of mind is an outgrowth of the artificial use of words like "care," "reasonable," and "prudent"; of the proposition that negligence involves "fault," and of a supposed analogy between negligent and intentional harms; all aspects, more or less, of the nineteenth-century attempt to Romanize the common law by making all liability rest, not simply and directly upon the social advantage of discouraging certain conduct and compensating certain harms, but upon a guilty mind or will. . . .

[8] Holmes, *The Common Law*, p. 108.
[9] Pound, *Introduction to the Philosophy of Law*, pp. 169, 170.

Negligence—Subjective or Objective?*

This paper is primarily an attempt to ascertain how far the conduct of one charged with negligence is tested in the light of his individual qualities and how far his peculiar qualities are ignored, and incidentally to deal with certain terms which are in customary use. Since, in such cases, some personal attributes are considered by the courts and others are not, it first becomes necessary to classify them tentatively. Following classical terminology, we may divide human qualities into three divisions, physical, mental, and what are here described as moral.

The physical qualities include, of course, such obvious ones as the use of the senses, strength, height. This is on the assumption of the existence of a mind and will which direct a bodily mechanism. It would seem to follow that the nervous, or nonsentient qualities would fall within the physical group. Thus where A is struck on the kneecap as a result of which his foot flies up, the courts would not describe the resulting movement as his "act." But this is not essentially different from any "nervous" shock which prevents the body from obeying the mind. Assuming that acts are the result of a will directing the body, the nervous system would be part of the body which the mind controls. Therefore to the extent that the nervous system does not respond to the will, such a cause of an event is physical rather than mental. Thus the difference in "reaction time" between two individuals is, in large measure at least, a physical difference.

The second group of qualities—the mental —may be divided into two other groups, labeled for convenience, knowledge and intelligence. Describing knowledge as being the consciousness of the existence of a fact, it implies advertence, or the focusing of the mind upon a fact. To acquire knowledge, a number of more or less diverse functions must be used. There must be sense impressions, either prior or present; there must be coordination with other sense impressions, since all knowledge is arrived at by comparison. To make possible the coordination, there must be the quality called memory. Using knowledge in what is perhaps a more usual sense as including all that to which the mind would advert upon the ordinary stimulus, another function is called into being, the power of advertence. This is obviously different from memory since it varies, as does memory, in different individuals. Thus one person may retain a considerable store of information, but, being "absent-minded," has difficulty in adverting to it; while another may easily advert to what he knows although permanently retaining little. The *second* kind of mental quality, labeled intelligence, may be divided into two kinds of capacities, that of coordination and that of coordinating quickly. That the two are different is indicated by the fact that some people have great reasoning powers, but require considerable time for the solution of even simple problems, while others have a low intellectual ceiling which, however, they attain rapidly.

The qualities described here as the group of moral qualities may also be divided into two kinds. The *first* is the personification of a process which is described as the will. Whether it exists, and if it does what it is, is not clear. It is enough that it is assumed to be the director of our movements. It directs both acts and thoughts, the body and the mind. Either mind or body may act independently of the will, or against its orders, as where eyelids fall "instinctively" or against the will as where one thinks of disagreeable and uninstructive incidents while forgetting what he desires to remember. The *second* of the moral qualities may be described as the ability to evaluate interests; or, to put it in accord with the classical statement, the ability to distinguish right from wrong. Again it seems useless to attempt to philosophize concerning the nature of right or wrong. It is worthwhile here to point out only that while these are spoken of in terms of absolutes, it is obvious that they have reference only to standards created by someone and that, like adjectives, they are relatives. Thus one fact may exist without reference to other facts, but conduct cannot be either right or wrong without other conduct with which to compare it, or without reference to consequences. There must be reference to some pre-conceived standard of

* Warren A. Seavey, "Negligence—Subjective or Objective?" *Harvard Law Review*, XLI (1927), 1–28, reprinted by permission of the publishers. Copyright 1927 by The Harvard Law Review Association. Footnotes are omitted.

comparison, as to which the conduct described falls above or below.

SUBJECTIVE-OBJECTIVE

Before proceeding to inquire as to which of the human qualities of an actor are pertinent in judging his conduct in negligence actions, it would perhaps be well to do what may be done to indicate that we cannot decide on the simple basis that negligence is objective or subjective, or depends or does not depend upon fault—at least until we know what is meant by each term.

It may be assumed that the term "subjective standard" connotes that one's conduct is judged with reference alone to his qualities; that with an "objective standard," legal consequences follow without regard to them. As used, however, these phrases mean only that we permit consideration of more (subjective) or less (objective) of the qualities of the person whose conduct is judged.

That we cannot judge accurately on the basis of what another is, seems obvious since we may judge only from what we observe and we are aware that we may observe but little and know still less concerning the other. Further, in attempting to classify his conduct as right or wrong, we necessarily carry into our judgment an indefinite amount of our mental equipment, including our own standards and our own will. If we say that a person "did not do the best he could have done," we are assuming both that he had the same standards of conduct as those which we have created for ourselves out of our own environment, subject to allowances which we may guess at because of his different experiences, and that he had some element of will, estimated with reference to our own, which he disregarded.

That the law has never attempted anywhere a purely subjective test is at once apparent. If we speak of legal fault, we mean only that the actor's conduct has departed from the standards of the community because the actor is different from others in one of two respects. He may differ from the community in his ideas of the relative values of different interests, or may fall below the community standard in the exercise of his will. The law does not consider, in the absence of a mental disease, whether one is capable of distinguishing what the community calls right from what it calls wrong; nor does it consider whether one is able to resist protecting his own interests at the expense of another's. Thus "fault" becomes a failure to exercise the will or the improper exercise of it with reference to a standard will and a standard valuation of desirables and undesirables. There is no subjective legal fault.

On the other hand, we do not now judge an actor without reference to his motives and qualities. Liability does not follow from the fact that A's arm struck B. Even in trespass to land, where there is a prima facie cause of action from the fact of entry, the beliefs and purpose of the one entering may create a defense. Physical distinctions are important in trespass to the person, as where a weak or lame man may use means in self-defense barred to the strong or the swift. Even in contracts, now the stronghold of objectivism, we may consider, within limits, mental elements, as where there is a mutual error, or where one knows that the other is mistaken.

It would seem impossible, therefore, to use in their literal sense the terms objective and subjective. Furthermore, the meaning of either term is not necessarily the same in different branches of law. Probably this is not necessary; it would be sufficient to have the words consistently applied in torts. And if it were true that in all cases where the actor does not intend a result which is injurious, the courts refuse to consider his physical capacities, and his mental content or qualities, it would be sufficiently accurate to say that there is an objective test for negligent conduct. As will be pointed out later, the courts have not done this, but while asking the triers of fact to apply an external test as to some elements, as to others they have permitted consideration of the actor's qualities. It would not seem possible, therefore, to say more than that, as to some elements, an objective test is used, meaning by this that some external standard is set up with which, as to such elements, the actor's conduct is compared.

RISK-DANGER

These words are discussed here, because when used in connection with negligence there is often the connotation that there is a dangerous act or a risky act, independent of any human consciousness and occurring "objectively" in a purely physical world. Thus, if we say that negligence is conduct involving undue risk of injury to others, we tend to think of the physical event, without considering that what creates the risk must be the anticipation by someone that harm may follow. Thus we may say that it is dangerous to shoot in a place in which people are accustomed to be. But of course, it is or is not capable of harm depending upon whether in fact someone is or is not there. In determining whether or not it was dangerous, we immediately go back to the position of the actor. If we assume that he knew everyone in town had left and no strangers had come in, we would not say his act was risky. If he did not know, we would say it was, although the physical facts would, of course, be the same. In either event it was impossible that he should hurt someone since there was no one to hurt. But it is equally true that there is no possibility of his hitting a person who is present unless a combination of other factors exists. The gun must be aimed so that, considering wind and relative location, a bullet might reach him; the powder must be capable of explosion; the firing pin must make contact with the cap. Unless all essential factors exist, the other cannot get hurt. If they all do exist, he is sure to get hurt. In either case there is no possibility of the other event happening, assuming the existence or non-existence of the factors. The "risk" then is due only to lack of knowledge as to whether all necessary factors are or are not present. But risk is equally dependent upon knowledge. There can be no "risk" without advertence to the result risked. Assume a savage or a child plays with dynamite. It does not explode and a subsequent examination by an expert determines that it could not have exploded owing, say, to dampness. But had one, knowing that it was dynamite, been standing by, he would have said it was a dangerous act. The fact that the substance could not explode, as subsequently determined, would not prevent the act from being, to him, dangerous. To the savage with no knowledge of dynamite or its qualities there was no danger. The danger or risk was purely subjective to the observer, created by his knowledge of the qualities of dynamite and his lack of knowledge of the qualities of this particular lot.

Risk, then, would seem to include the advertence of someone to the possibility that an event may occur. It would seem to exclude a certainty of belief that it will occur. Thus we can be said to have no risk of death; the risk is only as to time, place, and manner. In either case, to find risk, we must take the standpoint of some person who has imperfect knowledge, since if one were omniscient there would be certainty and hence no risk. We cannot, therefore, adopt the standpoint of a supposed observer who knows all the facts; we may not even adopt the standpoint of a supposed observer who has standardized information in regard to the existence of events, since as to the happening of particular events there can be no standardized knowledge. What has been done is to create a fictitious entity, the standard man, endowing him with the knowledge of the actor, and, in some cases, further knowledge. To the extent that further knowledge is added, so that the actor is held for what he "ought to know," but does not, risk is standardized. In a sense it is objective; but only in the sense that it has reference to a person in the position of the actor with such differences in knowledge and qualities from those of the actor as may be required to make him the "man of average prudence."

UNDUE-UNREASONABLE

Assuming that risk has been found, that is, that the standard man averts to the possibility of an injurious event happening because of the actor's conduct, the actor is not liable unless the risk is undue. What constitutes the "undueness" is not within the limits of this paper. It must be pointed out, however, that if we find that risk exists only in the consciousness of some person (whom we have found to be the man of ordinary prudence), the same person must determine whether or not the risk is undue. In doing this, he must consider the mathematical chance of injury, on the assumed hypothesis of known and unknown factors, the seriousness of the injury anticipated, the value of the interest subjected to injury, the value of the actor's interest being protected by his conduct, the chance of protecting his interests by other means, and all the other relevant factors. In this computation there are involved two distinct kinds of problems. The first is purely mathematical, namely the ascertainment of the degree of likelihood that certain events will or will not occur. As to this, the result would be the same under any system of law; it is achieved by purely intellectual processes. The complete answer can be obtained, however, only by solving the other type of problem, that is, the comparative values of the conflicting interests of the actor and the one whose interests are threatened. This evaluation calls for the so-called moral qualities. To the extent that the solution of these problems involves standardized elements or, phrasing it differently, to the extent that the actor's conduct is determined with reference to the community valuations, we may say that an objective test applies.

THE MAN OF ORDINARY PRUDENCE

The foregoing may serve as an apology for the introduction of this old friend and to indicate that we cannot well get along without him. Ordinarily fictions keep us at least one step from the truth and conceal the operation of the legal machine. But the invention of a mythical person with whose conduct we may compare the actor's conduct seems not only to be necessary but also not subject to the usual criticisms. The substitution of phrases which make his introduction unnecessary, like "unreasonable conduct," or "subjecting the plaintiff to undue risk," are excellent shorthand expressions which, however, conceal the fact which is perhaps the basis of the whole liability, namely, that we are dealing with conduct only from the standpoint of some person at the place and time of injury. Using hindsight, the conduct is most unreasonable, since it caused the plaintiff to suffer a loss which, by hypothesis, the defendant could not intentionally cause without liability. The personification of a standard person helps us realize that the actor's conduct is to be compared with that of a human being with all of the human failings. It is true that it would perhaps be as easy to say that the actor is not to be charged unless he was guilty of "fault," with the assumption that he has certain standardized qualities. But it is even more difficult to imagine the actor with different qualities than he has (which would have to be done unless a purely subjective test is used) than it is to imagine an entirely new personality in the actor's place with certain described qualities.

The difficult question is to describe the qualities with which to endow our standard of comparison. Sometimes he is described as a man of prudence, or a man of average prudence, or one of ordinary prudence and intelligence. Sometimes he is placed in the position of the actor; at times it is stated that he has the knowledge or means of knowledge of the actor. Alderson's famous phrase makes him a reasonable man guided by those considerations which ordinarily regulate the conduct of human affairs. Brett visualizes the "man of ordinary sense using ordinary care and skill." Some of these statements are more complete than others. Most of them are intended to convey identical ideas. It is obvious that in such brief statements we cannot find more than a hint as to what qualities are given to him. "Prudence" has a selfish connotation, obviously not intended here, except in the case of contributory negligence. "Care" avoids this but obviously avoids reference to a possibility of error as to valuation of interests. "Sense" refers only to intellectual elements. "Skill," as will be indicated later, probably combines too many elements for us to require the actor to have standardized skill in all situations. These objections are probably captious since it is obvious that whatever short expression is used cannot contain a consideration of all the qualities which go to make up the fictitious personality with whose conduct we compare the actor's, in ascertaining whether he acted reasonably or unreasonably. It is of great importance, however, to ascertain what the qualities are.

MORAL QUALITIES

That a purely objective standard applies to the moral qualities is beyond question. The standard man evaluates interests in accordance with the valuation placed upon them by the community sentiment crystallized into law. Not only, therefore, is the actor not excused if he knowingly places values different from those fixed by the community, but he is not excused although he believes, without personal moral fault, that his values are the same as those of the community. One who unintentionally kills a sacred elephant in saving human life might, in some countries, find that a very remote chance of killing the elephant caused his conduct to become unreasonable. Furthermore, the fact that the actor's variation from the normal would, by the community, be regarded as morally praiseworthy, does not protect him if it causes additional burdens to be placed upon another. Thus if a train endangers the life of a person under such circumstances that an attempt at rescue might reasonably be expected, if the actor, arriving too late to act without overwhelming risk to himself, "heroically" attempts the rescue and is injured, his injury is not actionable, and, if there has been no negligence on the part of the railroad, he would be liable for any damage to it caused by his act. Excessive altruism is as much a departure from the standard morality as excessive selfishness, although in practice it is seldom actionable.

That our standard man has also the standard will is equally clear. The law is not concerned whether the actor has less than normal control over his volitions. Even in criminal law, where, if anywhere, we might expect most nearly to approximate a subjective standard, the lack of power of resistance to "temptation" (except possibly where due to a mental disease) is not considered. On the other hand, it would seem that the actor is not charged with any excess of power of control over his will. If, from what is known of him, there is an indication that he normally has a will above the standard in its powers of resistance to illicit temptations, liability does not follow because he fails to use it. We may say, then, that as to both the moral elements—the will and the evaluation of interests—the personality of the actor is disregarded and our mythical man is completely standardized. That he should be so standardized seems desirable. At least it is in conformity to all other branches of the law. The rule that failure to know the law is not an excuse for doing an unlawful act is a very effective method of coercing people to become acquainted with the community ideals. To permit one who knows but does not accede to the community valuation of interests to have an individual standard would at once destroy the law. To permit one to set up his own defective will as a defense would obviously be to encourage disregard for others' rights. The likelihood that a civil action will follow antisocial conduct is, to some extent at least, a deterrent, and it does not shock our sense of justice to impose liability upon moral defectives.

INTELLIGENCE

That the law adopts an objective standard in regard to intelligence seems reasonably clear. The word has found its way into some of the definitions of the standard man, and "prudence" connotes it, since the prudent man cannot be a fool. That the actor is held to a standard in this is also indicated by the approval which has been given the famous statement in *Vaughan v. Menlove* that "it is not enough that the defendant did the best he knew how."

This quality includes the ability to estimate the effect of conduct in the light of existing factors. A jaywalker in a crowded city may have as lively an appreciation of the value of his life as others have, but he may be unconscious of the risk owing to the lack of coordination. It is less clear than in the case of the moral factors why an objective standard should be set; we do not customarily, upon reflection, ascribe fault to a fool, as we do to those who differ from us in their estimate of social values. There is, however, an element of coercion in an objective standard of intelligence since the general tendency is to restrain action by those of subnormal mentality or, at least, to induce them to use greater efforts to prevent harm to others. Nor is it unfair that the consequences of his folly should be visited upon the fool.

There are some doubts as to the extent of the rule. Is it material that an actor has superior intelligence so that he can more easily estimate the risk from known factors than could the average person? As will be indicated, his liability is affected by his superior knowledge and skill, and in any given case his intelligence is so interwoven with them that it is difficult to extricate the separate quality. I hazard a guess that because of its close connection with them the actor is required to use what intelligence he has.

The other doubt is in regard to the time factor in intelligence, although in expressing a doubt perhaps I am going too far since I have found nothing to indicate that the courts differentiate the ability to understand from the time it takes in understanding. It is true that an experienced or skilled man suddenly confronted with the necessity for instant action would be treated differently from one who is inexperienced; but that is explainable upon a difference in knowledge or physical ability. I would again hazard a guess that as to this there is a minimum but no maximum standard. Finally, there may be a doubt as

to the situation where one, without his volition, is subjected to immediate and great
peril. Here I suspect the individual qualities
may sometimes be of importance.

In physical characteristics, the standard
man appears to be identical with the actor.
Unless we are to have a completely objective
standard and eliminate all connotation of fault
even in a popular sense, we cannot require
that a person, in order to escape liability for
negligence, shall do that which another might
do but which it is physically impossible for
him to do. Thus, if an injury can be avoided
by a jump of ten feet, it is clear that it is a
relevant question whether the actor is a jump-
er or a one-legged man. So where one is blind,
unless we would drive blind men from all
contacts with others, we cannot require him
to act as though he could see. A blind or
otherwise physically incapacitated person is
sometimes classified with groups of those
mentally incompetent, like children or the insane. But there is a considerable difference
in that we have placed demented and immature persons in distinct categories while the
law has not attempted any grouping of physical defects. Assuming for the present that,
for tort purposes, there is a separate group of
insane persons, the law does not consider mental defectiveness until it has reached an extreme stage. With physical characteristics,
however, there is no classification; a stiff knee
would be considered equally with a missing
leg, and rheumatism which prevents quick
action equally with paralysis which denies any
action. As there would seem to be no minimum standard, equally there is no maximum.
A hardy, strong, tall man may enter upon a
course of action which would be foolhardy
upon the part of the average person. There
are no "imputed" physical characteristics.
The existence of the specific qualities is
sometimes spoken of as one of the conditions
in which the standard man finds himself. It
does no particular harm to deal with them in
this manner, but they are not part of the
group of facts external to him. They are as
subjective as the condition of the mind, differing only in the fact that many of them are
more easily observable or demonstrable.

The doubt is as to what are to be con-

sidered as physical characteristics. If the suggestion previously made is followed, that they
include all nonsentient qualities, we undoubtedly get to the edge of the decisions and perhaps beyond. In extreme cases there is no
difficulty. Thus, if, owing to a nervous defect, a person is completely prostrated so that
his ensuing movements have no elements of
volition, it is clear that the question as to
whether an average person would be so prostrated is immaterial in determining his liability for harm caused by the prostration. But,
in most cases, the person of little nervous resistance is not entirely deprived of volition
and hence the question is complicated with
that of whether he has a standard will. Assume, for instance, a person of normal power
of will and appreciation of the interests of
others, but who is so affected by the sight of
blood that he can act only with great difficulty. If his abnormality is sufficiently great
to be recognizable, it should be considered.
He is similar to one who stammers and, because of this cannot speak. The same is true
in regard to reaction time, a factor which,
though not generally considered until recently,
has been known and made use of by astrono-
mers for many years. This is something which
may be discovered with almost mathematical
exactness; it is as purely physical as strength
or the sense of touch. It is in fact considered
in every case where it is deemed relevant that
the actor is old and hence cannot move rapidly.

Of the same nature as agility, which combines reaction time with the flexibility of the
nerves and muscles, is clumsiness. Mr. Justice
Holmes, adopting the objective theory to its
fullest extent, has said that clumsiness is a
misfortune for which the possessor must pay
if it causes injury to another. It may be described as the absence of skill without reference to knowledge or intellect. The matter of
skill will be discussed later, but it is worth
while pointing out here that an excess of clumsiness is not always unreasonable conduct. It
may be due entirely to lack of nerve response.
Thus a partially paralyzed man is clumsy because he cannot control his movements. So
is one benumbed by cold, and obviously the
numbness would always be considered. I
assume, however, that Mr. Justice Holmes
would not include such cases of obvious defects ordinarily caused by external events.

He has reference to persons whose clumsiness cannot be ascribed to any particular cause but who do not generally control their movements as well as others. The boy who is constantly knocking over small objects, the person who is continually tripping, the dinner guest who usually succeeds in dropping his fork, come within his statement. In fact, such conduct is very apt to be caused by a lack in one of the moral qualities. Attention is more difficult with some; with others there is less desire to observe the welfare of others. Clumsiness beyond the normal induced in this manner is of course no excuse. On the other hand, there may be clumsiness similar to that of the benumbed man, as in the shaking hand of age or the faltering steps of infancy. To the extent that this can be differentiated from a defect due to lack of the moral or intellectual qualities, the actor should be held liable only for his own standard. The only difficulty is one of proof and this is becoming increasingly less difficult. It is to be noted that if the actor is less clumsy than the average, or if he is one having a better than usual nervous system or a speedier reaction time, he should be judged on the basis of his own qualities. It should be noted also that the person with physical defects may be, and often is, negligent not because he fails to act reasonably at the time of the accident, but because, being aware of his limitations, he has entered a situation in which one of his sort ought not to go. Thus the clumsy person, knowing himself to be such, has a different problem than one who is not clumsy since one of the factors is different in every situation. The result of this and the duty of self-knowledge will be discussed later.

BELIEF-KNOWLEDGE

Describing knowledge as belief in the existence of a fact, belief is the mental element which if coincident with truth creates knowledge. Belief is also used in another sense. I not only believe in certain existing facts but I may also believe or have no doubt but that certain events will occur. When I so believe, I am said to intend the event if at the time of doing an act I believe that the act will be one of the factors in producing the event.

When belief is used in this sense, the belief of the actor that his conduct will result in harm to another's interest must always be considered, since if he has such belief he is liable, unless his invasion of the other's interests is privileged, irrespective of whether it is antecedently probable that his conduct will cause the other injury. It is only where he does not have such belief (and of course where he had no desire to do the injury) that we are in the field of negligence. On the other hand, the fact that our standard man would believe that the event would be a certain consequence of the defendant's conduct, does not prevent the actor's conduct from being negligent, although in such cases the jury would tend to find him guilty of a willful and not a negligent tort.

Our present inquiry is not, however, with belief as used in this sense but with belief as to existing facts. How far has knowledge or belief been standardized? How far does the advertence of the actor differ from that of the fictitious person whose conduct we use as a standard of comparison? In other words, is liability created by conduct, which, upon the facts adverted to by the actor, is reasonable, but which would be unreasonable if the actor had adverted to facts which would be known to our standard man?

It is clear from the cases that there is no standard of knowledge as to the existence of the physical facts surrounding any situation. This must be so since everyone has varying experiences and can know but a small part of all the events known to others. As has been pointed out, lack of advertence to an event may be due to: (1) lack of physical sensation; or (2) lack of coordination at the time of a sensation; or (3) lack of memory; or (4) lack of power of advertence. Of these the first is ordinarily the result of purely physical (including nervous) conditions. One fails to see a particular event, because one is not present, because some intervening object prevents sight, or because the optic nerve is injured. On the other hand, lack of advertence may be due, not to lack of physical sensation alone, but to lack of "mind focus." Thus, there may be an impression on the retina and we may assume that there is some impression on the brain cells, but there may be no conscious mental reaction. The unthinking but not the thoughtful mind may be affected. One thus failing to see cannot be held liable on the basis of having seen that which never came within his thinking mind; he has never had knowledge. If he is liable it must be because, owing to lack of some standardized quality, the actor has failed to acquire the knowledge. This duty of advertence will be dealt with later.

In addition to advertence to a physical object, there must also be knowledge of its qualities in order to have knowledge in a real sense. Thus A sees a pile of small grains, which to him represent specks of sand. To B they are grains of powder. Both persons have identical sense impressions; both could equally well describe all outward characteristics; but the vital knowledge of the qualities of the grains is denied to A because he is lacking the other mental elements. This may be due to the fact that he has never seen nor heard of powder before. His lack of original knowledge may be due to outside circumstance or to a physical defect—as where he is blind and deaf. In either event, he should not be affected by the fact that others know of powder and its qualities. That this is true ordinarily is clear. There is no standard of knowledge of isolated events. Assuming this, there should be no standard of knowledge based upon a common community experience. Thus, a hermit hearing, without explanation, a radio for the first time, or a savage, suddenly dropped from his native swamps into the streets of New York, cannot be judged except with reference to what he knows. It is true that there is an inference that all persons in the community have had a common experience and because of this know certain matters of "common knowledge," this inference being often sufficient to create a presumption against a defendant. It is also true that others may assume that everyone knows what is a matter of common knowledge and may base their actions upon the assumption, so that a citizen of New York would not be guilty of negligence if he acts toward the savage as he would toward others, unless the ignorance of the savage was observable. Furthermore, those who have exercised choice in arriving at a particular place— as at New York from Lapland—are ordinarily made conscious of change of conditions such that, if they were to exercise the standardized faculties, they would realize the duty to refrain from acting until more information had been acquired. It may be also that certain rules, as that to "look and listen," have become so crystallized in particular jurisdictions, that

the courts would ignore the individual factors.

Assuming there has been a physical sensation of an event, there must be an exercise of the mind to make it effective. This is coordination, partly an intellectual process, partly a memory process, since it depends upon a continuance of prior sense impressions and a comparison between them and the present sensations. Memory seems to be a purely mechanical process existing independently of the will, although undoubtedly will is a powerful factor in originating memory by causing the original image to be deeply impressed. But, after the creation of the original impression the will has little to do with memory, except as it may deepen impressions by adverting to the event.

Not only do we forget much that we will to remember, but we remember many things we would like to forget. Thus the mental processes connected with memory approximate the purely physical processes. In view of this it would seem that liability should not be based upon a standardized memory. Thus assume that while driving through a town to which he does not intend to return, A sees an obstruction in the road. Three nights later, he runs into the obstruction in the dark. Assume also that a man of average memory would remember the obstruction but that within a short time after passing the obstruction, A has so far forgotten that even the strongest stimulus and effort of the will could not cause it to be focused on his consciousness. Is there any reason for dealing with A as if he had remembered? If he had come over another road or if the obstruction had been obscured at the time of passing, he would not be charged. Assuming that it was on the left-hand side of the outgoing road, he had no duty to see it originally. Nor can we say that he ever had a duty to keep it in his consciousness, when he had no reason to believe that it would again be useful information. His lack of memory would operate no differently from lack of eyesight. If he had no reason to will to remember, he should not be liable if against or without his will the obstruction passed from his power of recollection.

The same result could be reached even where the present lack of knowledge is due to a prior lack of any of the intellectual or moral qualities, assuming that in each case the only connection between the injury and the lack of knowledge is that the event causing the injury would not have happened had the knowledge existed in the actor.

Suppose the manager of a plant manufacturing explosives completely fails to perform his duties of management, intentionally violating his duties to all around him. As a result he does not know that a certain substance is explosive or that it is packed in tins of a certain color. His lack of knowledge causes him to throw a tin out of a window. For the resulting injury he is, of course, liable. But would he be liable for an injury caused by him years later while doing an act which to a person without knowledge of explosives would seem innocent of danger? There is nothing to connect his past transgression with the later injury. His early misconduct was a violation of a standard fixed for conduct in dealing with known explosives at that time and place; he committed a breach of duty to those who might reasonably be expected to be injured as a result of it. But when he ceased to deal with explosives, going from the position rendering necessary knowledge in regard to them, he returned to the obligations of one with no special knowledge. Were this otherwise and were persons charged with knowledge of all that which they would have acquired with reasonable effort or average mentality, one who attends a medical college only to find at the end that he has been too lazy or stupid to become a physician, would go through life burdened with a liability based upon the knowledge of the average physician. If it is said that one is charged with knowledge of that which the standard person in the actor's position would know, or that the actor is charged with a knowledge of that which he should know, the statement cannot have reference to knowledge which the actor might have acquired by the exercise of ordinary mentality or diligence, except in cases where the failure to acquire the knowledge involves not only a breach of duty to someone, but a breach of duty connected in some way with the present event more than by the fact that the injury would not have occurred had the duty been performed.

In creating liability in part from the fact that the actor should have known facts, the law does not, and should not, go beyond the time when the actor had in mind, or would have had in mind if he had exercised standard moral and intellectual qualities, that his failure to acquire knowledge might result in injury to the plaintiff or someone in a general category in which we may place the plaintiff. If, however, the actor fails at that time, that is, at a time when he might expect that injury may result from his failure to acquire or retain knowledge, he may be liable for such failure.

Thus assume that a master of a vessel in putting out from a small harbor is conscious that he should examine the wharves and contours of the land in order to prevent possible injury to the wharves if he should have to put back in a storm, as seems not unlikely. He does not do so. The return is made in a storm under conditions which would make it reasonable for a stranger to the harbor to enter it, in spite of a perceptible chance of injury to property, and without liability for ensuing damage. The actor does harm to property which he would not have done had he made use of the opportunity he had previously. It is at least arguable that the actor would be liable in this case, not because of his lack of knowledge of the way to enter without harm to others, but because, by defects in qualities which are treated by the law objectively, he failed to acquire the knowledge at a time when it seemed substantially likely that injury of the sort which occurred might result if he should fail in getting the information.

If this is correct, failures to advert to a particular danger at the time of accident may be placed upon the same ground. Thus in the cases given, if the actor once knew but subsequently forgot, his liability would be based upon the answer to the question as to whether or not at the time he forgot he should have anticipated that forgetting the fact might be a cause of injury and whether the forgetting was due to a failure in his "objective" qualities. Thus assume in the above ship case, that the actor examined the harbor, but subsequently forgot. If the forgetfulness was the result of an outside force, as if in the interim he had suffered an injury, there would be no liability based upon his prior knowledge. On the other hand if, having a normal memory, he forgot owing to lack of exercise of the will, his forgetfulness would be no excuse. But suppose his forgetfulness was due to the fact that he had an abnormally poor memory, or that he was abnormally absent-minded.

This suggests a further possible basis for liability—one I suspect which explains not only cases within this group but also cases dealing with those who are physically defective. This principle is that it is negligent for one to enter into a course of conduct when he knows or should know that because of his individual qualities he either should not enter upon the undertaking at all or should do so only by making special provision to guard against results expectable from his defects.

Where there is an obvious physical defect, the reasoning and the cases are clear. A blind man is sometimes said to have to use a higher degree of care than one who can see. Without argument as to whether there may be degrees of care, it is obvious that blind men take different precautions than those taken by men who can see and that conduct which would be careful in one who can see is negligent in one who cannot. But this is not alone because he is blind; it is as much because he knows he is blind. Thus assume that immediately after the actor's hand becomes paralyzed, suddenly and without his knowledge, he relies upon its normal functioning and because it will not respond, another person is injured. We would not call him negligent. Just as in the case of external facts, the actor's conduct is to be judged not from the facts as they are but from the facts as they reasonably appear to him. Therefore, the actor cannot be required to take other than the ordinary precautions unless he has some reason to believe that he is defective. One whose bad eyesight causes him to injure another can certainly be treated no more harshly than one whose bad brakes cause injury to another. In the latter case it is clear the actor is not liable unless he had reason to know that the brakes were bad. Ordinarily one has had an opportunity for discovering his defects since they come gradually and if he makes the observations which one of normal mentality would make he would discover them so that, if it is a defect which might be a cause of harm to others, he is charged with a duty to know and, knowing, to act with reference to them. Even in Pennsylvania a blind man is not negligent if he "fails to look" at a railroad crossing; if he is negligent it is because he fails to do some other act required of men knowing themselves blind. Where the actor does not know himself to be blind, as where he suddenly becomes blind on a dark night, he would be neglectful in failing to will to look, but of course this failure would have no legal consequences since it could not have affected his conduct or the result.

The same basis of liability exists in many other situations. Thus one who enters upon a course of conduct as to the details of which he has no information, or one who enters a strange country would realize, if having standard intellectual and moral qualities, that because of his unfamiliarity he must either not act at all or act more cautiously than one with greater knowledge. So one without knowledge of medicine who, except in a so-called emergency, administers medicines, is responsible for injury caused, not for his failure to know about them, but because he has entered upon an undertaking in which, were he normally intelligent and considerate of others, he would know that he should not act. This is, I take it, the "gross ignorance" for which it is said one may be even criminally liable. So again the awkward man, were he to exercise the standard qualities would, by observation, discover that certain actions of his bring disastrous results. He would ordinarily, therefore, be charged with a knowledge of his awkwardness which he must take into consideration in ordering his movements. So with a person having slow reaction time or other defect of the nerves. It is not present knowledge and present action which alone cause an actor to be liable, but past failures, which at the time were under such conditions that the actor might then have anticipated that someone would be hurt because of a subsequent reliance upon nonexistent or imperfect functions.

The same reasoning applies not only to the acquisition of knowledge, but also to forgetfulness. Assume that A is absent-minded, likely because of this to forget where he is while walking in the street. He should not be charged with negligence at the time if it is mechanical forgetfulness, not due to any defect of the will to remember. Thus, if one were to receive a blow on the head which causes him to walk into crowded traffic without realization of his position, he would not be considered neglectful. But one can scarcely grow up with one's self without learning of memory ability under different conditions. In moments of advertence to any abnormal defect in memory, provision must be made to guard against its consequences. The same applies to sleep. If one is overcome while driving, we may say that there is a duty to keep awake. Ordinarily there is, because as one feels drowsiness overtaking him, the man of average mental powers will realize that it may become complete. But if it comes on unaware, as where one is suddenly overcome by odorless fumes from his own vehicle, there would be no liability for injury caused. Normally, of course, lack of advertence to previously known facts is due to a defect, not of the memory per se, but of the moral factors. Thus if, while driving, the actor talks with a passenger and "forgets" to watch the street, his conduct is due to lack of normal regard for the safety of others. It may be worth while to point out that it is often of importance to determine the particular act or "fact" which constitutes the negligence, as where the doctrine of "the last clear chance" prevails.

SKILL

In many cases, liability may be predicated upon a "holding out" and this entirely aside from contractual liability. Perhaps this may be best discussed in connection with "skill," a composite, including knowledge, intelligence, and the physical qualities. Since of these qualities only intelligence has been standardized, it is clear that there is, generally speaking, no standard skillful man. It is equally clear, however, that if one undertakes work requiring a minimum of skill, there is ordinarily liability for failures due to falling below the standard. This is obvious where there is a contractual relationship, as between master and servant. The resulting liability in tort may be based either upon the fact that one enters upon an undertaking when he knows or should know that his conduct may cause injury to another or because he has represented to others that he has the requisite ability. In the servant case, if he injures other servants, his liability may be based upon the first ground; if he injures his employer's property, it may be based upon the second. The new and unskillful driver who runs into a window is liable because he ought to know his unskillfulness will cause damage; if he runs into another car, the driver of which relies upon the fact that the actor will act nor-

mally, his liability may be placed upon both grounds. So if one invites a guest to ride, not disclosing an entire ignorance of driving, even in jurisdictions in which the gratuitous host is dealt with subjectively, it would seem that there has been a representation of some minimum amount of skill. On the other hand, if he reveals his lack of skill, the guest should not recover, even aside from any doctrine of assumption of risk or contributory negligence.

Eliminating these suggested reasons for liability, there would seem to be no standard skill, any more than there is standard eyesight. No one is born with skill; everyone acquires it gradually. There must always be beginners. All those who now drive cars have had to learn. All we can expect of them is that in learning they shall do so with the least possible risk to third persons. The new driver in a crowded street is doubtless ordinarily negligent. But assume that he drives on the most remote streets and employs the usual safeguards of beginners but, owing to some unforeseen event, as a neighborhood fire, he suddenly finds himself in the midst of a crowd. His conduct should not be judged by that of the ordinarily skilled operator. He differs from the physically defective only in one respect. The blind or deaf man must use the streets if he is to have a decent life; it becomes reasonable for him, therefore, in the light of his necessities, to do that which, but for them, would be negligent. The unskilled driver, however, is not permitted to go into traffic ordinarily because his interests in driving are not sufficiently great. They may become so however—as if Paul Revere, being injured, could find only an unskilled horseman to carry on the message. So one who has no knowledge of medicine may in an "emergency" dispense. But an emergency is only a situation in which the hazards of mistaken choice are more obvious and where the choice must be made quickly. The emergency cases represent a general principle.

CONCLUSION

Reviewing the whole matter briefly, it would appear that there is no standardized man; that there is only in part an objective test; that there is no such thing as reasonable or unreasonable conduct except as viewed with reference to certain qualities of the actor

—his physical attributes, his intellectual powers, probably, if superior, his knowledge, and the knowledge he would have acquired had he exercised standard moral and at least average mental qualities at the time of action or at some connected time. It is quite true that negligence does not depend upon moral fault; it is equally true that it does not depend upon fault even in a legal sense. It is not true, however, that there can be an objectively negligent act, unless we create for "objective" a special meaning to be used only in negligence.

Whether it would be better to determine liability without reference to the qualities of the actor is a different question. Liability for conduct follows, usually belatedly, popular conceptions of justice. In primitive law it was "just" that vengeance should be visited upon the cause of the harm; in the age of economic expansion and individualism, it was "just" that the burden of loss should be shifted only where the cause of the harm was a knave or a fool. With a mechanistic philosophy as to human motives and a socialistic viewpoint as to the function of the state, we may return to the original result of liability for all injurious conduct, or conceivably have an absence of liability for any conduct, with the burden of loss shifted either to groups of persons or to the entire community. The lawyer cannot determine that our rules of liability for negligence are either just or unjust, unless he has first discovered what the community desires (which determines justice for the time and place), and whether the rules are adapted to satisfying those desires (which I assume to be the end of law).

Recklessness*

19. Recklessness as foresight of consequence

Negligence is of two kinds, being either advertent negligence (commonly called recklessness) or inadvertent negligence. In recklessness there is foresight in the possible consequence of conduct, whereas in inadvertent negligence there is no such foresight. For many, if not most, legal purposes recklessness is classed with intention. It is like intention in that the consequence is foreseen, but the difference is that whereas in intention the consequence is desired, or is foreseen as a certainty, in recklessness it is foreseen as possible or probable but not desired.

Convenience requires a narrow use of the term "negligence" to signify inadvertent negligence unless the context precludes this meaning. Recklessness can thus be contrasted with negligence, though in a more general sense both are species of the same genus.

If the defendant foresaw the probability of the consequence he is regarded as reckless, even though he fervently desired and hoped for the exact opposite of the consequence, and even though he did his best (short of abandoning his main project) to avoid it. Judges in speaking of recklessness frequently insert words to the effect that the defendant "did not care whether he caused damage or not,"[1] but the better view is that this is irrelevant. Recklessness is any determination to pursue conduct with knowledge of the risks involved though without a desire that they should eventuate.

In order to convict of recklessness one must come to the conclusion that the accused foresaw the result, not merely that he should have foreseen it. Proof of foresight may be difficult. Intention is sometimes readily shown, for when a man sets himself a certain end, his behavior is generally different from what it would have been if he had not done so. Recklessness is another matter, for awareness may be a mere passing realization, instantly dismissed, which leaves no effect on conduct. Also, a man is capable of self-deception: he may decide that an unpleasant result is not likely because he does not want it to be likely.

In practice a tribunal is forced to draw inferences on the supposition that the defendant is of normal mentality; and this may in practice let in the objective criterion. To illustrate: if a man throws a stone at another

* Glanville L. Williams, *Criminal Law: The General Part* (London: Stevens & Sons Ltd., 1953), pp. 49–59, reprinted with the permission of the author and the publishers.

[1] E.g., *Welch* (1875) 1 Q.B.D. 23; *Derry v. Peek* (1889) 14 App. Cas. at 350.

during a general disorderly fight, and the stone breaks a window, the jury may refuse to find that he foresaw that the window might be broken; but if there were no fight going on and he threw a stone at another who was standing immediately in front of the window, they may conclude that he must have contemplated (that is, did contemplate) the possibility of the window being broken. The inference may be erroneous, but it is the best that human justice can do. However great the risk of error, the fact remains that the inquiry is into the mental state; and the court should always be alert to any indication that the particular defendant did not have normal foresight.

This then, is "subjective" recklessness; and this is the meaning in which the term is employed in the present book. Unfortunately the term is sometimes used also in an "objective" sense, meaning gross negligence (whether advertent or inadvertent). Even inadvertent negligence, if sufficiently flagrant, is occasionally termed recklessness.[2]

The confusion that this is capable of introducing may be illustrated by *Ackroyd v. Barett* (1894).[3] In that case it was held to be no assault for a cyclist to ride "in a furious and reckless manner" and so hit a pedestrian. On the face of it this ruling seems to deny that an assault can be committed recklessly; but it is capable of being interpreted otherwise. The word "reckless" in the case stated may have been intended to bear the meaning "with gross inadvertent negligence," and if so the judgment does not deny that an assault can be committed with recklessness in the sense of foresight of consequence. If the cyclist had foreseen the probability of hitting the pedestrian in front of him and yet gone on with his speed unchecked, that might possibly have been counted sufficient *mens rea* for assault . . . . It is, however, very hard to prove foresight in a case of this type.

. . .

The use of recklessness in the objective sense is undesirable, for if it is wished to refer to inadvertent negligence, whether gross or otherwise, there is no reason why the latter word should not be used. "Recklessness," in its ordinary sense connotes a state of mind,

and it is better to keep the word to this meaning.

Although in the normal case of recklessness (as that term will here be used) the consequence must be foreseen, it seems that a person may be convicted of recklessness although it cannot be demonstrated that the consequence was foreseen, provided it can be inferred that he would still have acted as he did even if he had foreseen the consequence. Thus: D stabs at P meaning to wound him, and in fact cuts P's clothes. It seems that D could be convicted of maliciously (i.e., recklessly) cutting P's clothes, although he testifies (and is believed in his assertion) that he did not think of P's clothes at the time of the stabbing. For it is humanly certain that a person who is prepared to stab another would not be deterred from doing so by the reflection that he may injure the victim's clothes; consequently, even if D had thought of it, he would still have acted as he did. . . .

20. Recklessness involves negligence

Even the kind of fault here called subjective recklessness has an objective aspect. This remark is not so paradoxical as it sounds, and some illustrations may make the meaning clearer. A surgeon who tries to save life is not guilty of legal recklessness, although he foresees the possibility of death resulting from the operation. The operation, being reasonable, is not negligent. This example shows that deliberately taking a chance is not necessarily negligent. It is the same with the running of trains. The responsible officers of a railway company (or transport authority) know that by causing trains to run at sixty or eighty miles an hour there is some risk of causing injury to passengers—more risk than if all trains were run at slower speeds. Knowing this risk, they may decide to incur it. If recklessness is defined merely as foresight of possible consequence, their conduct is reckless. Nevertheless it is not negligent—not even negligent in the law of tort. On the whole the hazard is too small to be taken into account by a reasonable man, particularly when balanced against the public advantage of fast trains. As a community we prefer speed to safety to a certain extent. There is therefore no recklessness for legal purposes. Recklessness is a branch of the law of negligence; it is that kind of negligence where there is foresight of consequences. The

[2] E.g., *Restatement,* Torts, Negligence, § 500.
[3] 11 T.L.R. 115.

concept is therefore a double-barreled one, being in part subjective and in part objective. It is subjective in that one must look into the mind of the accused in order to determine whether he foresaw the consequence. If the answer is in the affirmative, that is the end of the subjective part of the inquiry and the beginning of the objective part. One must ask whether in the circumstances a reasonable man having such foresight would have proceeded with his conduct notwithstanding the risk. Only if this second question, too, is answered in the affirmative is there subjective recklessness for legal purposes.

If the first requirement is negatived one may still proceed to ask the second question, but the result can then only be to establish inadvertent negligence.

Since recklessness is a kind of negligence, it presupposes a duty to take care. If a landowner sets a steel rabbit trap hoping that a trespasser will catch his foot in it, and the trespasser does so, the landowner is presumably guilty of maliciously inflicting grievous bodily harm. But if he set the trap in order to catch rabbits, realizing that a trespasser might be injured, it may be held that he is not guilty of acting "maliciously" toward the trespasser (that word including the notion of recklessness), because, although he advertently took the risk, he was under no duty of care toward trespassers whose presence was not actually known. The latter is the traditional view; but it is possible that the courts may come to extend the very narrow duty that has hitherto been imposed toward trespassers.

21. The degree of probability of the consequence

Consequences may range in every degree from the remote and unexpected, through the reasonably possible, the likely or probable, to the inevitable.

It has been shown that if the consequence is foreseen as morally certain it is taken to be intended. Recklessness occurs where the consequence is foreseen not as morally or substantially certain but only as "probable" or "likely,"[4] or perhaps merely "possible."

On a determinist philosophy, the consequences of every act are physically certain; it is only knowledge of the consequences that is uncertain. For legal purposes such terms as possibility, probability, and likelihood are to be construed as referring to this imperfect knowledge. A result is possible if it is reasonably conceivable; it is probable or likely if there is a somewhat high chance of its occurring, though how high this chance must be has not been authoritatively defined.

In many cases the matter does not admit of mathematical calculation; but some may be imagined in which it does. Suppose that D possesses a number of pistols; he knows that all are unloaded save one, but does not know which one is loaded. He selects one at random and fires it at P, in order to obtain the excitement of putting P in peril. Here, the smaller the number of unloaded pistols, the greater is the probability that the pistol selected is the loaded one. Superficially one might think that the law ought to declare how many unloaded pistols to the single loaded one make a killing merely "possible" and how many make it "probable" or "likely." The authorities furnish no guidance on this, and do not indicate whether foresight of possibility is enough to constitute recklessness. According to the Criminal Law Commissioners of 1833 it does. After putting the illustration of the pistols just given, they expressed the opinion that a killing with the loaded pistol is to be regarded as a killing with foresight of the probable consequence, however many unloaded pistols were with it when the choice was made. "The probability of a fatal result would be diminished as the number from which the selection was made was increased, but still there would be a willful risking of life attended with a fatal result, and as it seems a total absence of any intelligible principle of distinction for penal purposes."[5] "Probable" here means what is usually called "possible."

The opinion of the Commissioners may be accepted, for a person is not generally at liberty to bring another causelessly even within slight danger of death. However, this does not mean that foresight as bare possibility is in every case tantamount to recklessness. The

---

[4] In ordinary usage "likely" is a weaker term than "probable." If a coin is spun it cannot be said to be probable that it will come down tails, but it might be said to be quite likely that it will do so (not, of course,

more likely than that it will come down heads). "Likely" thus seems to be a strong possible and a weak probable.

[5] 7th Rep. (1843), *Parl. Pap.*, xix, 28.

illustration is comparatively easy to deal with because it is supposed that the pulling of the trigger is without social purpose; but the difficulty of the situation would become apparent if there were some social advantage in the conduct. Thus, everyone who drives a car knows that a possible consequence is that he will kill a pedestrian, but a killing is not for that reason reckless. The important difference between the two situations is that driving cars has social utility and is regarded as generally reasonable and as justifying the taking of some risks. The difference is not in the degree of danger, for it may be statistically less dangerous to select one pistol from a million (one only being loaded) and aim it at a man than to drive from London to Edinburgh.

To put another illustration, a field surgeon having to perform an urgent operation may know that one out of his four scalpels is unsterilized, without knowing which; and he may then have to weigh the risk of not performing the operation immediately against the risk of picking the unsterilized scalpel, and the risk that if he picks it this scalpel may aggravate the patient's condition. The only rule that can be stated is that a risk may be run for reasonable cause; and whether the cause is reasonable may depend upon the magnitude of the risk undertaken, i.e., the degree of probability of damage and the extent of the damage if it occurs.

A very slight social advantage in the conduct in question may be sufficient to shift the inquiry from one of possibility to one of probability. Thus: a music-hall performer doing a "William Tell" act fires at a cigarette in his assistant's mouth, and he finds that on the average he can perform the act without harm 2,000 times for every occasion that he punctures his assistant's cheek. If he is prosecuted for a particular mishap, and the question of recklessness arises, it seems that the exhibition of skill would be regarded as a sufficient value to justify an inquiry into the degree of probability of harm.[6]

The conclusion is that knowledge of bare possibility is sufficient to convict of recklessness if the conduct has no social utility, but

that the slightest social utility of the conduct will introduce an inquiry into the degree of probability of harm and a balancing of this hazard against its social utility. If this is the law, it would be useless to define probability in mathematical terms, because the degree of probability that is to constitute recklessness must vary in each instance with the magnitude of the harm foreseen and the degree of utility of the conduct.

A few words may perhaps be added on the nature of probability. According to Russell, two different concepts may be meant by this word.

On the one hand, there is mathematical probability: if a class has n members, and m of them have a certain characteristic, the mathematical probability that an unspecified number of this class will have the characteristic in question is m/n. On the other hand, there is a wider and vaguer concept, which I call "degree of credibility," which is the amount of credence that it is rational to assign to a more or less uncertain proposition.[7]

Russell gives as an example of degree of credibility the proposition: "Probably Zoroaster existed." The suggestion may perhaps be made that degree of credibility is mathematical probability where the wider class is imagined. Thus, if I assert that there is a three-to-one chance that Zoroaster existed, what I mean is that given, say, a hundred persons whose historicity is doubtful, the evidence being comparable with that for Zoroaster, the judgment that they existed would in my opinion be right in seventy-five of the cases.

A statement of probability (at least in relation to macroscopic phenomena) always supposes inadequate knowledge. This is true even for mathematical probability. Thus when we say that the chance of a coin coming down heads is half, we refer to the particular case merely as an instance. If we could consider it in all its particularity, we should, in theory, be able to predict the fall.

It is possible to make a statement of mathematical probability even in relation to an event that has happened, if the outcome is not known. For one of full knowledge, the event is determined uniquely, but for one of imperfect knowledge it still belongs to the realm

---

[6] A further question would arise on this problem, whether one must take account of the performer's determination to perform his act many thousands of times. The risk of hitting the assistant on any one occasion is small, but the risk of hitting him during a lifetime of performances is great.

[7] Bertrand Russell, *Human Knowledge: Its Scope and Limits* (New York: Simon and Schuster, 1948), p. 11.

of probability. "Thus when we speak of the probability of a definite event having some characteristic, we must always specify the data relative to which the probability is to be estimated."[8]

A statement of probability must therefore be taken in relation to the actual or supposed knowledge of the person making the statement at the time in question. However, according to Russell, probability is not entirely subjective. Even degree of credibility, he says, is objective in the sense that it is the degree of credence that a *rational* man will give. This follows from Russell's own definition of "degree of credibility"; but there is another concept, called by Ramsey "partial belief," which is entirely subjective.[9] It is this subjective probability that is important for the theory of legal recklessness, while Russell's "degree of credibility" is used only in assessing inadvertent negligence. The probability of an event rests upon knowledge or experience, and for recklessness, which involves a subjective state, one must take the actual knowledge and experience of the accused. Suppose that a man adverts to the question whether a given result is likely to follow from his conduct, and decides that the chance is too remote to be practically considered. If he is wrong in his estimate of the chances, he may be held guilty of inadvertent negligence, but is not guilty of recklessness, provided that the value of his conduct is sufficiently great to justify the risk as the risk seems to him.

Thus the extent of probability of damage is a subjective question, dependent on the foresight of the accused; yet the social desirability of the risky conduct, and the question whether it balances the foreseen danger, are objective questions to be judged by the standard of the reasonable man.

An illustration may show how this works in the common case of negligent driving. Every motorist knows that driving a car (whether negligently or not) may cause harm; but knowledge of this bare possibility does not turn negligent driving into reckless driving, because driving a car is part of the legitimate business of life. What is required is not knowledge of the possibility but knowledge of the probability in the particular circum-

stances. If the driver knows the probability of harm from the manner in which he is driving he is guilty of reckless driving under section 11 (1) of the Road Traffic Act, 1930. If, though the subjective element is lacking, he is grossly negligent, it seems that he is guilty of dangerous driving under the same subsection . . . . If his negligence is less, he is guilty of driving without due care and attention under section 12.

Similarly, knowledge of the possibility of harm resulting from sport or physical exercise is not sufficient to constitute recklessness. There must be knowledge of such a degree of possibility as to be accounted probability.

There is perhaps no case where knowledge of the barest possibility of harm is enough to constitute recklessness, except that already considered where the accused acts from practically no other motive than to bring the prosecutor into risk of harm. In any other circumstances the accused is entitled, from the point of view of the law of recklessness, to live his life as he wishes, and is responsible only where the harm was foreseen as probable.

It follows that the distinction between inadvertent and advertent negligence is not so sharp as the names imply. If a man foresees the possibility of causing damage, but dismisses the possibility as being too remote for consideration, and if in fact there was a *probability* of damage (which would have been foreseen by a reasonable man), he may be held guilty of inadvertent negligence; but he is not guilty of advertent negligence, because he did not foresee the degree of possibility that a reasonable man would have foreseen. In order, therefore, to determine whether a particular instance of negligence is inadvertent or advertent, it is not strictly correct to ask whether the defendant foresaw the possibility of harm; one must ask what degree of possibility he foresaw.

This analysis of subjective recklessness is of some importance in the crime of manslaughter. It is commonly said that involuntary manslaughter requires gross negligence; but against this it has been suggested by some that gross negligence is simply a synonym for recklessness (i.e., subjective recklessness). The suggestion seems to be that by reading gross negligence as a synonym for recklessness we are absolved from the necessity of inquiring into the "grossness" of the negli-

[8] *Ibid.*, p. 370.
[9] F. P. Ramsey, *The Foundations of Mathematics* (London, 1931), pp. 156ff.

gence. It is submitted that such an assumption would be false. Even if it be true to say that gross negligence means exclusively recklessness, not inadvertent negligence, this does not dispense with the necessity of the negligence being gross. To revert to our railway directors, it is not now regarded as negligence per se to schedule trains at eighty miles an hour. Suppose, however, that the railway authority decided experimentally to run passenger trains at some very much greater speed, it seems that at some speed—say 200 miles an hour—the court might (on evidence as to present technical attainment) say that the risk was unreasonable and that the running of trains at that speed was civil negligence, because on balance, it would not have been done by a reasonable man. At some still greater speed—say 250 miles an hour—it might be regarded as even criminal negligence. Yet at each of these speeds—80, 200, and 250 miles an hour—there was foresight of danger and

so, in one sense of the term, recklessness. It seems clear that the recklessness of which the law of manslaughter speaks is recklessness of a grossly negligent kind.

22. Crimes requiring intention or recklessness

It is a general, though not a universal, principle that recklessness is classed with intention for legal purposes. The thing that usually matters is not desire of consequence but merely foresight of consequence, which is the factor common to intention and recklessness. It is this foresight of consequence that, it is submitted, constitutes *mens rea*.[10] Consequently every crime requiring *mens rea*, if it does not positively require intention, requires either intention or recklessness. . . .

[10] This is a somewhat simplified statement, for both intention and recklessness involve a certain knowledge of surrounding circumstances as well as foresight of consequence. (Professor Williams discusses this matter in Chapter 5 of his work.)

Accidents, Fault, and Social Insurance*

. . . We have seen above the sort of studies that have recently been made concerning the causes of accidents, and the findings concerning accident proneness. It will be well at this time to examine some of the possible implications of these studies and their conclusions for the fault principle of liability. This of course should be done in the light of the possible objectives which a rational system of accident liability should serve. These, we have noted, are: (1) the moral objective; (2) compensation of accident victims; (3) prevention of accidents and promotion of safety; (4) avoidance of undue collateral disadvantages such as the overburdening of desirable activity. Possible implications of the recent studies for the fault principle will be treated under these heads.

1. *The moral objective.* The fault principle is sought to be justified in part by the inherent fairness of imposing liability on him who has been guilty of some personal moral shortcoming (here generally negligence) and of

shielding from liability the man who has been free from blame. This is a kind of moral objective—an attempt to equate legal liability to the culpability of the individual participants in the accident. Of course, the legal standard of conduct is largely external and does not take into account the actor's personal equation with the result that legal fault does not entirely coincide with moral fault. But apologists of the present system justify it on the ground that by and large the two do coincide. The tendency of the recent studies, however, has been to cut down the importance of personal moral shortcoming as a factor in causing accidents and to do so in many cases where the "layman's common sense" would find something to blame. To be sure, personal fault is not entirely ruled out, but the scope of personal blameworthiness has been very drastically narrowed. This means either one of two things. If liability continues to be broadly imposed for substandard conduct the system will be ever harder to justify on any notion of its general correspondence with personal blame. If, on the other hand, the fault principle is carried to its logical conclusion (so that liability is imposed only where there is personal blame) liability will

* Fowler V. Harper and Fleming James, Jr., *The Law of Torts* (Boston: Little, Brown and Company, 1956), 3 vols., II, 752–64, 771–77, reprinted by permission of the publishers. Footnotes have been renumbered.

become more and more restricted and the cost of more and more accidents will be thrown on the victims. What has been said does not at all necessarily lead to the conclusion that accident law should abandon a moral objective. It does show that the existing system as presently administered largely lacks the moral justification which is often claimed for it. But the conclusion to be drawn from this showing is not that the fault basis should be perpetuated without regard to morals, but rather that other and broader moral considerations call for an entirely different system of liability (namely a wise distribution of accident losses over society, without regard to fault, as under workmen's compensation laws). . . .

2. *Compensation of accident victims.* The present system recognizes this too as one of its objectives and awards compensatory damages whenever that may be done without offending its premises as to morality, as by making a blameless man pay damages, or as to expediency, as by unduly inhibiting desirable conduct. But we have just seen how the recent studies have narrowed the sphere of culpability and how this would cause a great restriction of liability if many accident-prone but morally blameless people are not to be held liable. This would mean, in turn, that a greatly increased number of victims would go uncompensated. The recent studies thus emphasize sharply the essential conflict between refining the fault principle and compensating accident victims. Of course, as we shall see, the existing rules are now and could continue to be administered so as to *conceal* this dilemma, e.g., by the use of an external standard of conduct for defendants; but this goes a long way toward an abandonment of the moral justification of the fault principle.

That does not, of course, end the matter, for even if personal culpability should be disregarded altogether, the present system could perhaps be justified on the ground of expediency. The claims of the injured innocent are meritorious and will be satisfied where the injury is caused by *unreasonably dangerous* conduct, for such conduct, by hypothesis, involves danger out of proportion to its social worth. But the exaction of compensation from one whose conduct is *not unreasonably dangerous* would impose an undue burden on desirable, affirmative activity which would be out of proportion to the benefit conferred on

victims. The line which separates these two kinds of conduct, then, is the expedient one to draw between liability and nonliability for injury, since it combines a considerable incentive toward safety and a minimum of interference with desirable enterprise. In view of this possible contention, let us see what implications the recent studies have for the argument from expediency.

3. *The deterrence of conduct which causes accidents.* The fault principle is sought to be justified in part on the ground that it does not burden all affirmative activity but only that which is unreasonably dangerous thereby combining a considerable incentive toward safety with a minimum of interference with desirable enterprises. Now it is clear that the results of the recent studies will themselves tend to promote safety and reduce accidents under *any* system of liability. The question is whether the tendency to do so will be greater if the fault principle is retained, or if the principle of strict liability is substituted for it. We believe that the tendency would be stronger under a system of strict liability.

In the first place the recent studies emphasize the extent to which large units (such as transportation companies, the government, insurance companies, and the like) are in a strategic position to reduce accidents; and conversely, they emphasize the relatively insignificant part which the individual's conscious free choice or will plays in causing or preventing many types of accidents. This is shown in several ways. For one thing the studies themselves have been undertaken or pushed by such large units. Then, their results have been put into practical operation by large enterprises or groups and to a considerable extent this is inevitable because the tests and findings have maximum validity when applied on a broad statistical basis. On the other hand the individual is often unaware of the fact he is accident-prone, or of the factors which lead to his accident proneness, or of the kind of training or treatment or precaution that his case requires. Indeed, as we have seen, the individual may be quite helpless to prevent some of his own accident-producing behavior (such as that which is compulsive), so that it would be altogether idle to expect the fear of paying damages to deter it.

Secondly, a system of absolute liability tends to increase the pressure toward accident prevention on large groups and enterprises, where we have seen it will do the most good, rather than on the individual, where it will do relatively little good. This is so for three reasons: (a) large units are involved in many accidents and appear often as defendants, rarely as claimants; (b) even where the accident is caused by an individual while acting for himself, in his aspect as potential defendant he is increasingly becoming covered by liability insurance, so that the pressure of increased liability is put in the first instance on the insurance company; (c) the abolition of the defense of contributory negligence—which usually accompanies a shift to absolute liability—clearly adds a further incentive to safety on the part of perennial defendants, and if there is a corresponding loss of incentive (which is not at all clear) it is on the part of the individuals who are potential accident victims.

Since the large business or governmental unit is in a far better position to reduce accidents than is the isolated individual, and since absolute liability puts added pressure to reduce accidents on the large unit, it follows that absolute liability will be a greater spur to safety than a system of less strict liability. "If the law requires a perfect score in result, the actor is more likely to strive for that than if the law requires only the ordinary precautions to be taken."[1] Available facts substantiate theory rather dramatically. Not only were the recent studies themselves undertaken by large units, but they were in the main undertaken because of the increased liability put upon such units by workmen's compensation acts. Moreover, the drop in the industrial fatality rate since the passage of those acts has been truly remarkable—it was cut in half between the two wars.

4. *Avoidance of undue collateral disadvantages such as the overburdening of desirable activity.* Perhaps the heaviest artillery which the proponents of the fault principle can muster is the contention that any stricter rule of liability will discourage affirmative activity and unduly fetter desirable enterprise. If this were true, it would constitute a pragmatic objection to a scheme of absolute liability which would certainly deserve serious consid-

eration. But like so many appeals to practical common sense this one probably rests on no solid foundation of fact but simply on a bald assertion of plausible error. If a system of absolute liability involves fixed limitations on the amount to be recovered, as in the case of workmen's compensation, it may actually cost little or no more than a system where liability is for negligence as determined by a jury without limitation on the amount. In any event there is small reason to claim that the advent of workmen's compensation has had any effect in checking the phenomenal advances in applied science and industry which have taken place since that time. On the contrary, there is good reason to believe that any pressure which the stricter liability has exerted has spurred the businessman's ingenuity to find new devices and new ways of doing things which have at the same time cut down accidents and also increased productive efficiency. The coupling of these results will not be merely sporadic and accidental. Aside from any question of civil liability, accidents are costly to employers and disrupt production, and on the whole the cost of devices and techniques for avoiding them will be more than offset by the elimination of this waste and disruption. The recent studies show that the type of behavior which produces accidents is often inefficient behavior from the point of view of production, even where it does not actually succeed in bringing about an accident; and they illustrate how effective efforts toward safety may serve the end of productivity as well. More broadly they illustrate how the fear of greater accident liability tends not to discourage but actually to foster the most useful kind of productive activity.

. . .

. . . Beginning with workmen's compensation in 1910 and getting great impetus from the depression of the 1930's, social insurance legislation has grown apace in America. Such legislation is based on a faith that the general welfare is best served by protecting individuals from the consequences of pecuniary loss through such vicissitudes of life as accident, old age, sickness, and unemployment. The chief pecuniary losses are destruction of earning power and the expenses of medical care and cure and rehabilitation. Under these schemes, such losses are met (or partly met) without regard to questions of personal fault

---

[1] Seavey, "Speculations as to 'Respondent Superior,'" in Harv. Legal Essays, pp. 433, 447 (1934) . . .

in causing them and are distributed over a wide segment of society. So much all this legislation has in common, but beyond this there are differences. The broadest possible scheme would largely disregard the source of loss and distribute its cost either by general taxation or by tax contributions levied at a flat rate upon a very large group (e.g., all employers). The philosophy of workmen's compensation, on the other hand, is that losses should be allocated to the enterprise that creates the hazards that cause the losses, and ultimately distributed among those who consume its products. Under such a system there is room for private insurance, and most of our states permit it to be handled that way. Still a third type of scheme seeks to distribute its costs among its beneficiaries, much as voluntary accident or health insurance does. And these variant notions are often found in combination. The trend in England has been toward the more socialized type of contributory system, that in this country toward the more individualized type, at least in fields which lend themselves to such treatment, e.g., workmen's compensation and unemployment compensation.

§ 13.2. *Comparison with fault principle.* Where this principle finds expression in a system which puts initial liability on the individual members of a group engaged in a risk-creating enterprise, it suggests similarities to the older liability for trespass. In both there is strict liability without regard to fault. Jeremiah Smith called workmen's compensation acts "a distinct reversion to earlier conceptions that he who causes harm, however innocently, is, as its author, bound to make it good."[2] On the other hand social insurance certainly rejects the limitations of the fault principle and it has for that reason been condemned as "offending the sense of justice."[3] The truth is that social insurance, even in its typically American individualized form, is a fundamentally different thing from either trespass or negligence. Formerly tort liability under either principle was looked on as shifting a loss that had already occurred from one individual to another—generally from the person who suffered it to the person who caused it.

It is against the background of this way of

looking at things that nearly all of our conventional reasoning about the objectives of tort law has developed and that nearly all of our conclusions have been drawn and our rules formulated. But society has no interest in the mere shifting of a loss between individuals just for the sake of shifting it. The loss, by hypothesis, has already happened. A has been killed, or his leg broken or his automobile smashed up. If the only question is whether B shall be made to pay for this loss, any good that may come to society from having compensation made to one of its members is exactly offset by the harm caused by taking that amount away from another of its members. In that view of the problem there had to be some additional reason for a defendant to compensate a plaintiff for his injury before society would compel compensation. As we have seen, these reasons might be (1) a feeling of what is fair or just; (2) a desire to discourage dangerous conduct, or of course a combination of both. Now the trespass principle probably represents a fairly primitive sense of fairness, and the negligence principle embodies the morality of individualism and laissez faire. But in each case matters of fairness or deterrence were all considered on the assumption that plaintiff and defendant were alone involved and that what happened between them was the real issue—that tort liability was paid for out of the defendant's own pocketbook. This focused attention on the moral quality of the conduct of the individual participants in the accident. As the earlier, mechanical imputation of blame to any injurious activity gave way, the result came to be the general principle of no liability without fault as we know it today.

There is however an altogether different approach to tort law. Human failures in a machine age cause a large and fairly regular—though probably reducible—toll of life, limb, and property. The most important aspect of these failures is not their moral quality; frequently they involve little or nothing in the way of personal moral shortcoming. The really important problems they pose are, rather, those of accident prevention and concern for the welfare of the victims. According to the view we are discussing, the problem of decreasing the accident toll can best be solved through the pressure of safety regulations with penal and licensing sanctions, and of self-interest in avoiding the host of nonlegal dis-

---

[2] Sequel to Workmen's Compensation Acts, 27 Harv. L. Rev. 235, 246 (1914).
[3] Holmes, *The Common Law* (1881), p. 96.

advantages that flow from accidents. But when this is all done, human losses remain. It is the principal job of tort law today to deal with these losses. They fall initially on people who as a class can ill afford them, and this fact brings great hardship upon the victims themselves and causes unfortunate repercussions to society as a whole. The best and most efficient way to deal with accident loss, therefore, is to assure accident victims of substantial compensation, and to distribute the losses involved over society as a whole or some very large segment of it. Such a basis for administering losses is what we have called social insurance.

This at once brings in an important new element. For while no social good may come from the mere shifting of a loss, society does benefit from the wide and regular distribution of losses, taken alone. The administration of losses in this way may entirely change evaluations of what is fair. If a certain type of loss is the more or less inevitable by-product of a desirable but dangerous form of activity it may well be just to distribute such losses among all the beneficiaries of the activity though it would be unjust to visit them severally upon those individuals who had happened to be the faultless instruments causing them.

Another difference between social insurance and older notions of liability concerns the assurance of compensation wherever there is liability. This is an integral part of the newer concept; formerly it was considered quite outside the scope of tort law.

To sum up: a scheme of social insurance involves (1) liability without fault (within the field of its operation), (2) an assurance that the amount of compensation theoretically due under the system will in fact be paid, and (3) a wide, regular and equitable distribution of losses under the system.

. . .

§ 13.5. *Effect of liability insurance on accident prevention.* There is another way in which the fact of widely held insurance may have affected the practical operation of tort law. One of the traditional objectives of tort law has been to deter unreasonably dangerous conduct and to promote the taking of reasonable precautions. If an individual actor must pay for the cost of his carelessness out of his own pocket, the way in which this works is pretty plain to be seen. But how does insurance affect this? In what types of situations, if any, does it dilute the deterrent effect of liability upon the individual? Does this dilution tend to foster irresponsibility, or are there countervailing forces brought into play which promote accident prevention—perhaps even more than the fear of individual liability would do? In this inquiry one thing should be kept constantly in mind. Accident prevention is not the only aim of tort law, and tort liability is not the only incentive to accident prevention. If anything leads to more adequate care of injured people and their dependents, it may be justified on that ground alone. Those aspects of tort law in operation which lead to the compensation and wide distribution of losses should be judged favorably, and extended, unless they actually bring about an increase in the accident rate. What then are the factors in the present situation which make for care or for carelessness?

In the first place it is obvious that fear of legal liability is not the only thing that spurs a man on to be careful. There are many situations, for instance, where one's negligence is likely to bring physical injury upon himself, as well as upon others. This is true of some of the commonest cases, such as driving an automobile, where the individual takes an active part in the situation at the time it is dangerous. In other types of situations, to be sure, a man's negligent conduct carries no real threat of bodily harm to himself either because of the nature of the case or because the man is acting through an agent. And, of course, a corporation cannot suffer this kind of injury. Even where the fear of personal bodily harm is absent, however, there are incentives to care. Accidents disrupt the normal processes of individual or business life. They often destroy valuable property. They are apt to cost money in collateral ways, quite apart from any question of possible damages. They may create bad public relations, or bad labor relations. Sometimes they threaten injury to a member of the family, or to a productive employee. And sometimes they involve the threat of criminal liability. Then, too, the simply humanitarian impulses furnish at least some people with a motive to take precautions for the safety of others. Another thing should be noted. In situations of employment, agency, and the like, there are usually two sets of incentives at work: for the employer, those last mentioned; for the employee, the risk of personal injury and also the fear of discipline for a job badly done.

The factors referred to above operate quite independently of liability for civil damages. But the fear of such damages may afford some additional incentive to be careful, and the next questions are whether liability insurance appreciably dilutes this effect and whether it promotes or detracts from safety in other ways. The direct evidence on the first point is worth little. No doubt the protection given by insurance makes some individuals callous and every now and then a man will admit as much in his own case. But no one has measured how widespread such a reaction is. There are, however, certain facts which can be known and which shed considerable light on the net effect which the institution of liability insurance has on the matter of accident prevention. They are as follows:

(1) Insurance has made direct contributions to the work of accident prevention. The wide combination of risks has brought together large aggregations of capital. This has put the insurance companies in a strategic position effectively to carry out programs to promote safety. . . . Some such companies and organizations have very extensive technical and engineering staffs which devote all their time in well-directed and expert efforts along this line. This is the sort of service that only the largest industrial concerns could perform at all effectively if they had to do it for themselves. It includes analysis of past accidents generally, and of specific current accidents, to determine whether they disclose defects in supervision, equipment, or in the habits or states of mind of workers. It also includes inspection of equipment and survey of operations to discover in advance defects, practices, personal factors, and the like, which are dangerous, and the working out of devices, rules, and arrangements which will minimize the danger. In some lines of insurance, the amount of money spent on accident prevention exceeds the amount paid for losses.

The insurance companies and organizations have also cooperated actively with other groups engaged in safety promotion, and have contributed materially to the education of the general public along this line.

(2) Insurance companies can and do adjust their rates and select their risks so as to furnish an incentive toward safety. Over-all rates in any field reflect over-all losses. And the latter are, of course, very much affected by the accident rate (among other factors). Probably there is a rather vague general realization of this relationship and it may afford some slight motive to be careful, but the effect of any individual's conduct on the general rate structure is so little that the motive can hardly be strong.

There are several ways, however, in which rating practices have rewarded or penalized individual assureds for their own safety records. Large risks are being increasingly written on an experience basis so that the rate for each more or less reflects the loss experience encountered on that risk itself. And before the war there was in wide use one form or another of a safe-driver reward plan for individual automobile owners. These have been pretty generally abandoned, largely it seems because of the administrative difficulties they entailed. But in this and other fields, companies do exert an influence for safety by rejecting risks which have had bad experience or accepting them only at higher premiums.

(3) Great strides toward safety have been made in many fields where insurance is widely held. This is notably true in the case of elevators, boilers, and machinery. Here, as one writer puts it, "the [insurance] rates have long been based largely upon the cost of accident prevention. The result of that work is a degree of safety little short of phenomenal."[4] And industrial accidents generally have sharply declined in the course of a generation. During the first World War there were in this country some 36,000 industrial fatalities a year. During the last war, although output was stepped up as never before, annual industrial deaths were held to about 17,000. In the field of aviation, some of the pioneer safety work has been claimed by insurance companies.

Automobile accidents, on the other hand, continue to occur at an alarming rate. Probably here, in the case of the individual car owner at any rate, the insurance companies have less effective leverage to implement their safety campaigns than in the case of larger risks where many operations are under the

---

[4] Sawyer, Retooling Casualty Insurance, 45 Best's Ins. News, No. 9, p. 37 (Fire & Cas. ed. 1945).

control of a single insured whose premiums vary with his loss experience. On the other hand, motor accident statistics contain no indication that the presence of insurance makes accident rates go up. Indeed, accident records are better on the whole in states where there is a relatively high proportion of insured owners.

The foregoing facts point to the following inferences: (1) in many fields the practical operation of liability insurance has been definitely to promote safety rather than foster carelessness, (2) in fields such as automobile and personal liability insurance the insurance companies have less effective means at their disposal to promote safety and their success in doing so is less readily demonstrable. On the other hand, there is no significant evidence to show that insurance protection leads to increased carelessness. And the insurance companies are engaging in these fields too in

efforts to promote safety which in the long run will probably have material effect. All in all, therefore, it is safe to conclude that the benefits of social insurance which come even under the present law through the operation of liability insurance are not offset by any encouragement of irresponsibility. On the contrary, there has probably been some concomitant net gain in accident prevention. Moreover, there is no reason to expect any threat to safety from further extensions of the insurance principle in the field of accidents. It is clear that the liability-without-fault aspect of social insurance (if considered alone) will be a greater incentive to safety on the part of potential defendants than a system of liability for negligence only. In this connection it should be noted that the recent studies of safety were spurred to a considerable extent by the absolute liability provisions of workmen's compensation laws.

Strict Liability in the Criminal Law*

The proliferation of so-called "strict liability" offenses in the criminal law has occasioned the vociferous, continued, and almost unanimous criticism of analysts and philosophers of the law.[1] The imposition of severe criminal sanctions[2] in the absence of any requisite mental element has been held by many to be incompatible with the basic requirements of our Anglo-American, and, indeed, any civilized jurisprudence.

The Model Penal Code, for example, announces that its provisions for culpability make a "frontal attack" upon the notion of strict, or absolute, liability.[3] Francis B. Sayre, in his classic article on "Public Welfare Offenses," contends that since the real menace

to society is the intentional commission of undesirable acts, evil intent must remain an element of the criminal law. "To inflict substantial punishment upon one who is morally entirely innocent, who caused injury through reasonable mistake or pure accident, would so outrage the feelings of the community as to nullify its own enforcement."[4] And Jerome Hall, perhaps the most active and insistent critic of such offenses, has consistently denounced the notion of strict liability as anathema to the coherent development of a rational criminal law: "It is impossible to defend strict liability in terms of or by reference to the only criteria that are available to evaluate the influence of legal controls on human behavior. What then remains but the myth that through devious, unknown ways some good results from strict liability in 'penal' law?"[5]

Without attempting to demonstrate that strict liability offenses are inherently or instrumentally desirable, one can question the force of the arguments which have been of-

---

* Richard A. Wasserstrom, "Strict Liability in the Criminal Law," *Stanford Law Review*, XII (1960), 730–45, reprinted by permission of the Stanford Law Review. Footnotes have been renumbered.

[1] The history of those strict liability offenses which are of legislative origin is of quite recent date. One of the first cases in which a statute was interpreted as imposing strict criminal liability was Regina v. Woodrow, 15 M. & W. 404, 153 Eng. Rep. 907 (1846). For an exhaustive account of the early history of these statutory offenses see Sayre, "Public Welfare Offenses," 33 *Colum. L. Rev.* 55, 56–66 (1933).

[2] "Severe criminal sanctions" refer to imprisonment as opposed to the mere imposition of a fine.

[3] Model Penal Code § 2.05, comment (Tent. Draft No. 4, 1955).

[4] Sayre, *supra* note 1, at 56.

[5] Hall, *General Principles of Criminal Law* (1947), pp. 304–5. See also Williams, *Criminal Law* (1953), §§ 70–76; Hart, "The Aims of Criminal Law," 23 *Law & Contemp. Prob.*, pp. 401, 422–25 (1958).

fered against them. It is not evident, for example, that strict liability statutes cannot have a deterrent effect greater than that of ordinary criminal statutes. Nor, is it clear that all strict liability statutes can most fruitfully be discussed and evaluated as members of a single class of criminality. The notion of "fault" is sufficiently ambiguous, perhaps, so as to obscure the sense or senses in which these statutes do impose liability "without fault." And finally, the similarities between strict liability and criminal negligence are such that it seems difficult to attack the former without at the same time calling the latter into comparable question. Issues of this kind are, then, the explicit subjects for examination here.

THE CONCEPT OF STRICT CRIMINAL LIABILITY

Neither the arguments against the imposition of strict criminal liability nor the justifications for such imposition can be evaluated intelligently until the meaning of the phrase "strict criminal liability" has been clarified. One possible approach—and the one selected here as appropriate for the scope of this analysis—is that of ostensive definition. That is to say, a small, but representative, sample of the kinds of offenses which are usually characterized as strict liability offenses can be described briefly so as to make the common characteristics of this class relatively obvious upon inspection.

At the outset, it is essential that strict liability offenses not be confused with Sayre's "public welfare" offenses, i.e., those which he defines as essentially regulative in function and punishable by fine rather than imprisonment.[6] This inquiry is concerned with those offenses which cannot be distinguished from other criminal conduct by virtue of the fact that the punishment involved is consistently less than imprisonment.[7] Thus, the cases here selected as exemplary of strict criminal liability are all cases in which the prescribed sentences are surely not minimal in degree or merely regulative in function.

The landmark case in American jurisprudence is undoubtedly *United States v. Balint*.[8] The defendant was indicted under a statute which made it unlawful to sell narcotics without a written order. The defendant claimed that the indictment was insufficient because it failed to allege that he had known that the drugs sold were narcotics. The United States Supreme Court held that his conviction did not deny due process.

Another classic example is *State v. Lindberg*.[9] The statute in question provided that "every director and officer of any bank . . . who shall borrow . . . any of its funds in an excessive amount . . . shall . . . be guilty of a felony."[10] The defendant contended that he had borrowed the money in question only after he had been assured by another official of the bank that the money had come from a bank other than his own. But the court held that the reasonableness of the defendant's mistake was not a defense.

The final case, *Regina v. Prince*,[11] is famous in both English and American jurisprudence. Prince was indicted under a statute which made it a misdemeanor to "unlawfully take . . . any unmarried Girl, being under the Age of Sixteen Years, out of the Possession and against the Will of her Father or Mother . . . ."[12] One of the defenses which Prince sought to interpose rested upon the reasonableness of his belief that the girl in question was over sixteen years old. The majority of the court interpreted the statute to make the reasonableness of a belief as to the girl's age irrelevant, and found Prince guilty.

Assuming these cases to be representative,[13] strict liability offenses might be tentatively described (although not defined) as those in which the sole question put to the jury is whether the jury believes the defendant to have committed the act proscribed by the statute.[14] If it finds that he did the act, then it is obliged to bring in a verdict of guilty.[15]

---

[6] Sayre, *supra* note 1, at 83.
[7] If the offenses were always punishable by something less than imprisonment then it would surely be relevant to ask in what sense they were penal in anything but name. This appears in part to be Hall's criticism of Sayre's article. See Hall, *op. cit. supra* note 5, at 279.

[8] 258 U.S. 250 (1922).
[9] 125 Wash. 51, 215 Pac. 41 (1923).
[10] Wash. Comp. Stat. § 3259 (Remington 1922).
[11] 13 Cox Crim. Cas. 138 (1875).
[12] Offenses Against the Person Act, 1861, 24 & 25 Vict., c. 100, § 55.
[13] Exhaustive enumerations of leading strict liability cases can be found in Sayre, "Public Welfare Offenses," 33 *Colum. L. Rev.* 55 (1933).
[14] Jackson, "Absolute Prohibition in Statutory Offences," 6 *Camb. L.J.* 83, 88 (1938).
[15] There is, of course, a sense in which the notion of having "committed an act" is far from unambiguous. Depending upon how "act" is defined, it

Whether this characterization of the above three cases is either precise or very helpful is a question which must await further discussion below. For the present, however, it is perhaps sufficient to observe that whatever it is that the concept of *mens rea* is thought to designate, it is this which needs not be shown to be predicable of the defendant.[16]

THE JUSTIFICATION OF STRICT
LIABILITY

Before attempting to assess the arguments for and against the notion of strict criminal liability, it should be made clear that the author agrees with most of the critics in not finding many of the usual justifications of strict liability at all persuasive. The fact, for example, that slight penalties are usually imposed, or that *mens rea* would be peculiarly unsusceptible of proof in these cases, does not, either singly or in combination, justify the presence of these offenses in the criminal law. But to reject these and comparable arguments is not necessarily to prove that plausible justifications cannot be located. In fact, it is precisely when the "stronger" arguments of the opponents of strict liability are considered in detail that the case against strict liability is found to be less one-sided than the critics so unanimously suppose.

Critics of strict criminal liability usually argue that the punishment of persons in accordance with the minimum requirements of strict liability (1) is inconsistent with any or all of the commonly avowed aims of the criminal law; and (2) runs counter to the accepted standards of criminal culpability which prevail in the community. They assert that the imposition of criminal sanctions in a case in which—conceivably—the defendant acted both reasonably and with no intention to produce the proscribed events cannot be justified by an appeal to the deterrent, the rehabilitative,

or the incarcerative functions of punishment.[17] And, in fact, they assert the practical effect of strict liability offenses is simply to create that anomalous situation in which persons not morally blamed by the community are nevertheless branded criminal.[18] Although the two lines of criticism are intimately related, for purposes of discussion they will be treated somewhat separately.

The notion that strict liability statutes can be defended as efficacious deterrents has been consistently rejected. It has been proposed, for example, that strict liability offenses cannot be a deterrent simply because they do not proscribe the kind of activity which is obviously incompatible with the moral standards of the community. Thus Gerhard Mueller argues that the substance of common-law *mens rea* is the "awareness of evil, *the sense of doing something which one ought not. . . ."*[19] Since all common-law crimes involved the commission of some act which was known by all the members of the community to be morally wrong, there was, he suggests, no problem in finding the presence of *mens rea* in cases of common-law criminal acts. Such, he insists, is not true of strict liability offenses. They do not punish those activities which a person would know to be wrong independently of the existence of a particular statute. Thus strict liability statutes are to be condemned because they necessarily imply that a person might be punished even though he could not have appealed to that one certain indicia of criminality—the moral laws of the community —to decide whether he was doing something which would violate the law.

If I understand Mr. Mueller's argument

---

[17] One author has suggested that the question of whether a crime has been committed ought to be determined solely by deciding whether the defendant committed the specific act proscribed by the statute. The actor's mental state would be relevant to the separate question of the actor's punishment. Levitt, "Extent and Function of the Doctrine of Mens Rea," 17 *Ill. L. Rev.* 578 (1923). This bifurcation is unobjectionable in so far as it recognizes that one of the factors to be considered in the sentencing of an individual is his mental state at the time of the crime. The author seems to imply that in the absence of a finding of the requisite mental element it would be proper for the court not to punish the defendant at all. This, too, is perhaps in itself unobjectionable. The question remains then whether it makes any sense to speak of this defendant as having committed a crime.

[18] Hall, *General Principles of Criminal Law* pp. 302–3 (1947); Williams, *Criminal Law* § 76, at 269 (1953); Sayre, "Public Welfare Offenses," 33 *Colum. L. Rev.* 55, 56 (1933).

[19] Mueller, *op. cit. supra* note 16, at 1060.

---

may or may not be true that the sole question is whether the defendant committed the act. The fact that the defendant was sleepwalking or insane at the time might be treated as bearing upon the issue of whether the "act" was committed. There is an obvious sense in which even this determination requires some inquiry into the defendant's state of mind.

[16] This would be true whether *mens rea* is interpreted as requiring only that the person "intend" to do the act, or as requiring that the person intend to do something which is morally wrong. The latter interpretation is advanced in Mueller, "On Common Law Mens Rea," 42 *Minn. L. Rev.* 1043 (1958).

correctly, then it clearly proves too much to be of any special significance as a criticism of strict liability offenses. The argument rests upon the obviously sound premise that a person cannot be deterred if he does not know or have reason to believe that his intended action will violate the law. And if this theory about common-law *mens rea* is correct, it only demonstrates that everyone either knew or should have known that certain kinds of activity would be legally punishable. These two points, however, at best imply that ignorance of the law ought—on deterrent grounds—to be always admitted as a complete defense to any criminal prosecution founded upon a statute which does not incorporate an express moral rule or practice into the criminal law.[20] Concomitantly, if a person knew of the existence and import of a statute of this kind, it seems wholly irrelevant to distinguish strict liability statutes from those requiring some greater "mental element." It is just as possible to know that one might be violating a strict liability statute as it is to know that one might be violating some other kind of criminal statute. Thus, unless special reasons exist for believing that strict liability offenses are not effective deterrents, Mr. Mueller's argument leaves them undifferentiated from many other statutory crimes which do not incorporate the moral law of the community.[21]

Just such special reasons for rejecting the deterrent quality of strict liability offenses are offered by Jerome Hall, among others. He rejects the argument that a *strict* liability statute is a more efficacious deterrent than an ordinary criminal statute for at least two reasons: (a) it is not plausible to suppose that the "strictness" of the liability renders it more

of a deterrent than the liability of ordinary criminal statutes; and (b) persons are not, as a matter of fact, deterred by those penalties usually imposed for the violation of a strict liability offense.[22]

The first of these objections is, it is submitted, inconclusive. For there seem to be at least two respects in which strict liability statutes might have a greater deterrent effect than "usual" criminal statutes. In the first place, it should be noted that Hall's first proposition is just as apt to be false as to be true. That is to say, it might be the case that a person engaged in a certain kind of activity would be more careful precisely because he knew that this kind of activity was governed by a strict liability statute. It is at least plausible to suppose that the knowledge that certain criminal sanctions will be imposed if certain consequences ensue might induce a person to engage in that activity with much greater caution than would be the case if some lesser standard prevailed.

In the second place (and this calls Hall's second premise into question as well), it seems reasonable to believe that the presence of strict liability offenses might have the added effect of keeping a relatively large class of persons from engaging in certain kinds of activity.[23] A person who did not regard himself as capable of conducting an enterprise in such a way so as not to produce the deleterious consequences proscribed by the statute might well refuse to engage in that activity at all. Of course, if the penalties for violation of the statute are minimal—if payment of fines is treated merely as a license to continue in operation—then unscrupulous persons will not be deterred by the imposition of this sanction. But this does not imply that unscrupulous persons would be quite so willing to engage in these activities if the penalties for violation

---

[20] Mueller cites the recent case of Lambert v. California, 355 U.S. 225 (1957) as implicitly attacking all strict liability statutes on this ground. Such a reading of the case seems plainly incorrect. At *most*, the reasoning of the Court can be construed as suggesting that strict liability statutes of which the defendant neither had nor ought to have had notice might violate due process. More plausibly, the Court struck down the conviction in *Lambert* because the statute there reached a very general kind of activity which the defendant could not reasonably have supposed to be regulated by statute at all: namely, the mere fact that the defendant came into a city and failed to register with the sheriff as an ex-convict. Surely, it is reading too much into the opinion to find a disposition on the part of the Court to group all strict liability statutes in this class.

[21] It is assumed throughout the remainder of this Article that knowledge of the relevant strict liability statutes is possessed or is readily capable of being possessed by those subject to the statutes.

[22] "There is, first, the opinion of highly qualified experts that the present rules are regarded by unscrupulous persons merely 'as a license fee for doing an illegitimate business.'" Hall, *op. cit. supra* note 18, at 301.

[23] Glanville Williams concedes both of these points. Williams, *op. cit. supra* note 18, § 73, at 258. But he argues in part that this kind of deterrent places an "undesirable restraint on proper activities." *Ibid.* Yet, to a considerable extent, this only succeeds in raising the precise point at issue; namely, whether the restraint which is imposed upon activity is undesirable. The legislature might believe that for certain kinds of activity, at least, the restraint was less undesirable than the production of those consequences proscribed by the statute.

were appreciably more severe. In effect, Hall's second argument, if it proves anything, shows only that stronger penalties are needed if strict liability statutes are to be effective.

If the above analysis of the possible deterrent effect of strict liability offenses is plausible, then one of the results of their continued existence and enforcement might very well be that few if any persons would be willing to engage in certain kinds of conduct. The presence of statutes such as that in the *Lindberg* case might have the effect of inducing persons not to engage in banking as an occupation since the risks, one might suppose, are just too great to be compensated by the possible rewards. More plausibly, such a statute might merely have the effect of discouraging bankers from borrowing money—or possibly only from borrowing money from banks. But these effects, too, might conceivably make banking a less attractive occupation, although they would probably not cause the disappearance of banking as an institution in society. However, if we assume the strongest of all results—that a statute of this kind would lead to the disappearance of the institution involved —what conclusions are to be drawn?

The case of socially undesirable activity is easy. If the operation of the felony murder rule has the effect of inducing persons to refuse to commit felonies, there are surely few if any persons who would object to this consequence.[24] Where socially beneficial activities, such as banking and drug distribution,[25] are concerned, the case is more troublesome. If it is further assumed that at least some of the strict liability statutes in these areas have been rigidly enforced, it is also to be noted that these institutions have not disappeared from the society. One possible conclusion to be drawn is that these strict liability offenses have been deemed to impose a not unreasonable risk. The fact that banking is still con-

sidered an extremely attractive endeavor (despite the possibility of a prison sentence for borrowing money from one's own bank) might be interpreted as evidence that people believe they can be successful bankers without violating this or a comparable strict liability statute. They believe, in other words, that they can operate with sufficient care so as not to violate the statute. Admittedly, the evidence in support of this thesis is not particularly persuasive. Perhaps most people who have gone into banking never even knew of the existence of the statute. Perhaps there is no such statute in most jurisdictions. Perhaps they knew of the statute but believed it would never attach to their conduct. And perhaps they took the statute into account incorrectly and should have been deterred by the statute. In part, the difficulty stems from the fact that there is so little empirical evidence available. It is suggested only that the above interpretation of the extant evidence is just as plausible as are the contrary inferences so often drawn.

The fact that strict liability statutes might cause the disappearance of socially desirable undertakings raises, in a specific context, one important feature of the kind of justification which might be offered for these statutes. If it is conceded that strict liability statutes have an additional deterrent effect, then a fairly plausible utilitarian argument can be made for their perpetuation.

To the extent to which the function of the criminal law is conceived to be that of regulating various kinds of conduct, it becomes relevant to ask whether this particular way of regulating conduct leads to more desirable results than possible alternative procedures. The problem is not peculiar to strict liability statutes but is endemic to the legal system as a whole. Consider, for instance, one such justification of the present jury system. In order to prevent the conviction of persons who did not in fact commit the crimes of which they are accused, it is required that a unanimous jury of twelve persons find, among other things, that they believe the accused did the act in question. Perhaps if the concern were solely with guaranteeing that no innocent man be convicted, a twenty- or thirty-man jury in which unanimous consent was required for conviction would do a better job. But such is not the sole concern of the criminal law ; there is also the need to prevent too many guilty

---

[24] Nor do there appear to be any very serious undesirable societal consequences in discouraging persons from having intercourse with females who may be around the age of sixteen. See Regina v. Prince, 13 Cox Crim. Cas. 138 (1875).

[25] See the more recent federal case, United States v. Dotterweich, 320 U.S. 277 (1943), where the defendant, president of a drug company, was indicted and convicted under the Federal Food, Drug, and Cosmetic Act, 52 Stat. 1040 (1938), 21 U.S.C. §§ 301–92 (1958) for shipping misbranded and adulterated drugs in interstate commerce. There was no showing that Dotterweich personally was either negligently or intentionally engaged in the proscribed conduct. It was sufficient that he was the president of the company.

persons from going free. Here, a twelve-man jury is doubtless more effective than a thirty-man jury. Requiring unanimous vote for acquittal would be a still more efficacious means of insuring that every guilty man be convicted. The decision to have a twelve-man jury which must be unanimous for conviction can be justified, in other words, as an attempt to devise an adjudicatory procedure (perhaps it is unsuccessful) which will yield a greater quantity of desirable results than would any of the alternatives.

Precisely the same kind of analysis can be made of strict liability offenses. One of the ways to prevent the occurrence of certain kinds of consequences is to enact strict liability offenses, since, *ex hypothesi,* these will be an added deterrent. One of the deleterious consequences of strict liability offenses is the possibility that certain socially desirable institutions will be weakened or will disappear. The problem is twofold: first, one must decide whether the additional deterrent effect of the strict liability statutes will markedly reduce the occurrence of those events which the statute seeks quite properly to prevent. And second, one must decide whether this additional reduction in undesirable occurrences is more beneficial to society than the possible deleterious effects upon otherwise desirable activities such as banking or drug distribution. For even if it be conceded that strict liability offenses may have the additionally undesirable effect of holding as criminal some persons who would not on other grounds be so regarded, strict liability could be supported on the theory that the need to prevent certain kinds of occurrences is sufficiently great so as to override the undesirable effect of punishing those who might in some other sense be "innocent."

I do not urge that either or both of these arguments for strict liability offenses are either irrefutable or even particularly convincing. But I do submit that this is a perfectly plausible kind of argument which cannot be met simply by insisting either that strict liability is an inherently unintelligible concept or that the legislative judgment of the desirability of strict criminal liability is necessarily irrational.[26] It is one thing to

attack particular legislative evaluations on the grounds that they have misconstrued either the beneficial effects of strict liability or its attendant deleterious consequences, but it is quite another thing to attack the possible rationality of any such comparative determination.[27]

As was observed earlier, the second of the two major kinds of criticism directed against strict criminal liability is that punishment of persons in accordance with the minimal requirements of strict liability—the punishment of persons in the absence of *mens rea*—is irreconcilable with those fundamental, long extant standards of criminal culpability which prevail in the community. As usually propounded the thesis is a complex one; it is also considerably more ambiguous than many of its proponents appear to have noted. One possible, although less interesting, implication concerns the notion of criminal culpability. The claim is made that the imposition of strict liability is inconsistent with the concept of criminal culpability—criminal culpability being defined to mean "requiring *mens rea.*" But unless the argument is to be vacuous it must be demonstrated that independent reasons exist for selecting just this definition which precludes strict liability offenses from the class of actions to which the criminal sanctions are to attach.

A more troublesome and related question is whether the proposition is presented as a *descriptive* or *prescriptive* assertion. It is not clear whether the imposition of strict liability is thought to be incompatible with the accepted values of society or whether the prevalence

---

[26] In this connection, it has been suggested that there is little evidence that legislatures consciously intend criminal statutes to be strict liability statutes. The most exhaustive examination of this issue is in a recent study conducted by the *Wisconsin Law Review.* 1956 *Wis. L. Rev.* 625. And while it seems clear that there is little affirmative evidence on this score, what evidence is available seems to indicate that at times the legislature has consciously intended the statute to be a strict criminal liability statute. *Cf. id.* at 644. Additionally, Glanville Williams argues that Parliament seems to have intended to retain strict liability in the statute interpreted by the court in the *Prince* case. See Williams, *op. cit. supra* note 18, § 73, at 259–60.

[27] *Cf.* Note, 74 *L.Q. Rev.* 321, 343 (1958). "It must always be remembered that the primary purpose of the criminal law is to prevent the commission of certain acts which it regards as being against the public interest and not to punish or to reform a wrongdoer. It may, therefore, be necessary to provide for strict liability when this is the only practical way to guard against the commission of the harmful act."

While I do not feel committed to the view that the primary function of the criminal law is that of the prevention of certain acts, the writer of the Note seems correct in suggesting that if an essentially utilitarian view of the criminal law is adopted, then the justification of many strict liability offenses becomes increasingly plausible.

of strict liability is inconsistent with what ought to be accepted values.

As an empirical assertion the protest against strict liability on the grounds that it contravenes public sentiment is, again, at best an open hypothesis. Those who seek to substantiate its correctness turn to the fact that minimal penalties are often imposed. They construe this as indicative of the felt revulsion against the concept of strict criminal liability. That judges and juries often refuse to impose those sanctions which would be imposed in the comparable cases involving the presence of *mens rea* is taken as additional evidence of community antipathy.

The evidence is, however, no less (and probably no more) persuasive on the other side. The fact that most strict liability offenses are creatures of statute has already been alluded to. While few persons would seriously wish to maintain that the legislature is either omniscient or a wholly adequate reflection of general or popular sentiment, the fact that so many legislatures have felt such apparently little compunction over enacting such statutes is surely indicative of the presence of a comparable community conviction. Strict liability offenses, as the critics so persistently note, are not mere sports, mere sporadic legislative oversights or anomalies. They are, again as the critics note, increasing in both number and scope. It may very well be the case that strict liability offenses ought to be condemned by the community; it is much more doubtful that they are presently held in such contumely.

"MENTAL" REQUIREMENTS, STRICT LIABILITY, AND NEGLIGENCE

The arguments against strict liability offenses which remain to be examined go to what is conceived to be the very heart of a strict liability offense; namely, the imposition of criminal sanctions in the absence of any *fault* on the part of the actor.

Since that liability [strict liability] is meaningful only in its complete exclusion of fault, it is patently inconsistent to assert, e.g., that a businessman is honest, exercises care and skill; and also, if a misbranded or adulterated package of food somehow, unknown to anyone, is shipped from his establishment, that he should be punished or coercively educated to increase his efficiency.[28]

The actor has, *ex hypothesi,* lacked precisely those mental attributes upon which fault is properly predicated—indeed, proof of his state of mind is irrelevant. Thus, the argument concludes, the vicious character of convictions founded upon strict liability is revealed. Intelligent understanding and evaluation of this objection must await, however, the clarification of several critically ambiguous notions. In particular, the ways in which a strict liability offense may fail to take the defendant's state of mind into account are far from clearly delineated. More seriously, still, there seem to be a variety of alternative meanings of "fault" which should be explored and discriminated.

That certain offers of proof concerning the defendant's state of mind might not be irrelevant even in the case of a putative violation is apparent. Quite apart from the ambiguous meaning of the word "act,"[29] there are several other questions about the defendant's mental state which might be permitted in a strict liability prosecution. For example, suppose the defendant in the *Lindberg* case were to offer to prove that he had never intended to become a director or officer of the bank and that he reasonably believed that he was merely becoming an employee. Is it clear that this offer would be rejected as irrelevant? Or, suppose the offer of proof was that the defendant had never intended to borrow any money and reasonably believed that he was receiving a bonus. Would this statement be excluded? Thus, it can be argued that if strict liability statutes are to be characterized as "strict" because of their failure to permit inquiry as to the defendant's state of mind, this description is too broad. More appropriately, each criminal statute must be examined to determine in what respects it is "strict."

The ambiguity in the notion of "fault" can be illustrated by a hypothetical situation. Consider a statute which reads: "If a bank director borrows money in excess of [a certain amount] from the bank of which he is a director, then the directors of any other bank shall be punishable by not more than ten years in the state prison." Suppose that there is no connection between the various banks in the jurisdiction, that a director of bank *A* had borrowed money in excess of the statutory amount from his own bank, and that a director

---

[28] Hall, *op. cit. supra* note 18, at 304.

[29] See note 15 *supra*.

of bank *B*, a wholly unrelated bank, was accused and convicted. This, it is submitted, would be a case of "stricter" liability. The example is surely chimerical; the point is not. It serves to illustrate the way in which ordinary strict liability statutes do require "fault."

If the notion of fault requires that there be some sort of causal relationship between the accused and the act in question, it is arguable that the *Lindberg* case takes account of such a relationship. The defendant in the *Lindberg* case by virtue of his position *qua* officer of the bank had considerable control over the affairs of that bank. And he had even greater control over his own borrowing activities. If the element of control is sufficient to permit some kind of a causal inference as to events occurring within that control, then a finding of fault in this sense does not seem arbitrary in the same manner in which a finding of fault in the hypothetical clearly would be.

Admittedly, there is a second, more restricted sense of "fault" which was clearly not present in the *Lindberg* case. This would require that the actor intended to have the particular act—borrowing money *from his own bank*—occur. And yet, there was a conscious intent to engage in just that activity—banking—which the defendant knew or should have known to be subject to criminal sanctions if certain consequences ensued. And there was a still clearer intent to do the more specific act—borrow money—which the defendant knew or should have known to be subject to criminal sanctions under certain specified circumstances. Strict liability offenses can be interpreted as legislative judgments that persons who intentionally engage in certain activities and occupy some peculiar or distinctive position of control are to be held accountable for the occurrence of certain consequences.

It is entirely possible that such a characterization of fault might still be regarded as unsatisfactory.[30] The mere fact that there was control over the general activity may be insufficient to justify a finding of fault in every case in which certain results ensue. The kind of fault which must be present before criminal sanctions ought to be imposed, so the argument might continue, is one which is predicated upon some affirmative state of mind with respect to the particular act or consequence.

[30] Hall, *op. cit. supra* note 18, at 304, clearly regards such a definition as unsatisfactory.

There may be good reasons why this more restrictive concept of fault ought to be insisted upon in the criminal law. Indeed, I think such reasons exist and are persuasive. Furthermore, "deontological" arguments, which rest upon analysis of what ought to be entailed by concepts of justice, criminal guilt, and culpability might support the more restrictive definition. Arguments of this nature will not be challenged here, for to a considerable extent this article is written in the hope that others will feel the need to articulate these contentions more precisely. However, there remains one final thesis which must be questioned. That is, that a person who accepts this more restrictive notion of fault can consistently believe that negligent acts ought to be punished by the criminal law.[31]

If the objection to the concept of strict liability is that the defendant's state of mind is irrelevant, then a comparable objection seems to lie against offenses founded upon criminal negligence. For the jury in a criminal negligence prosecution asks only whether the activity of the defendant violated some standard of care which a reasonable member of the community would not have violated.[32] To the extent that strict liability statutes can be interpreted as legislative judgments that conduct which produces or permits certain consequences is unreasonable, strict criminal liability is similar to a jury determination that conduct in a particular case was unreasonable.

There are, of course, important differences between the two kinds of offenses. Precisely because strict liability statutes require an antecedent judgment of per se unreasonableness,

[31] The "Model Penal Code," §§ 2.02, 2.05 (Tent. Draft No. 4, 1955), appears to take this approach.
[32] I find highly unpersuasive, attempts to treat negligence as in fact requiring *mens rea*. It has been argued that "in the case of negligence . . . the law operates with an objective standard which, based upon experience, closely approximates that under which the defendant must have operated in fact. In my opinion, therefore, we are here confronted with the use of a schematic and crude way of establishing the *mens rea*, but one which nevertheless evidences the law's concern for the mental attitude of the defendant." Mueller, *supra* note 16, at 1063–64.
If Mueller is suggesting merely that when certain kinds of consequences occur in certain kinds of situations it is reasonable to infer that the defendant in fact had a certain state of mind, then I find nothing objectionable about his claim. But, of course, *mutatis mutandis*, the same can be said for many strict liability offenses. If, on the other hand, he is suggesting that negligence in fact requires the jury to make a determination as to the presence or absence of the defendant's *mens rea*, then I do not understand in what sense this is accurate.

they necessarily require a more general classification of the kind of activity which is to be regulated. They tend, and perhaps inherently so, to neglect many features which ought to be taken into account before such a judgment is forthcoming. Criminal negligence, on the other hand, demands an essentially *a posteriori* judgment as to the conduct in the particular case. As such, it surely provides more opportunity for the jury to consider just those factors which are most significant in determining whether the standard of care was observed.

In spite of these important distinctions, in so far as strict liability statutes are condemned because they fail to require a mental element, negligence as a category of criminality ought to be likewise criticized. There may be independent reasons for urging the retention or rejection of the category of criminal negligence—just as there may be such reasons for accepting or disallowing strict liability offenses. But the way in which the two kinds of criminal liability are similar must be kept in mind whenever they are evaluated.

CONCLUSION

It is readily conceded that many strict liability statutes do not perform any very meaningful or desirable social function. It is admitted, too, that legislatures may have been both negligent and unwise in their selection of strict criminal liability as the means by which to achieve certain ends. But until the issues raised in the preceding discussion have been considered more carefully and precisely, it will *not* be immediately evident that all strict liability statutes are inherently vicious and irrational legislative or judicial blunders.

CHAPTER VI

CAUSATION

> The word "cause" is so inextricably bound up with
> misleading associations as to make its complete exclu-
> sion from the philosophical vocabulary desirable.
>
> BERTRAND RUSSELL, *On the Notion of Cause*

When it is clear that there has been both harm and wrongdoing, the law must frequently decide whether or not the harm is attributable to the wrongdoing. Two principles traditionally guide us in making this determination: (*a*) the wrongdoing must be the *cause* of the harm, and (*b*) the wrongdoing must be the *proximate cause* of the harm. A ship captain negligently omits to have his lifeboats in the required position. A passenger falls overboard and sinks immediately without any trace. Though wrongful, the captain's conduct is not a cause of the harm, for had he complied with his duty the outcome would have been the same. He is not held liable because his wrongdoing was not the cause of the harm. Owing to your negligence a fire breaks out in your house. An unusually strong wind fans the flames; neighborhood houses catch fire; soon there is a conflagration of major proportions. Most lawyers would claim that your negligent conduct was a cause but not a proximate cause of all the damage.

Two major questions are considered in these readings: first, what is the meaning of "cause" and "proximate cause"; and second, what justifies the particular legal principles used in attributing harm to wrongdoing.

The following points must be kept in mind when we consider the relation between harm and wrongdoing. First, a person may be legally responsible in the absence of damage or harm. For example, neither tortious trespass nor criminal attempt requires proof of actual damage or harm. Second, a person may be legally responsible although his conduct is not causally responsible for the harm that has occurred. Thus, in cases of vicarious and strict liability it is not necessary to establish that the person held responsible is causally related to the harm. He may be related, but he need not be. For example, a few moments after X sells his business to Y, an employee negligently injures a customer. Y is legally but not causally responsible for the harm. Suppose the law allows recovery in the absence of any fault if soil from one person's land moves onto and damages another person's land. A landowner may be liable even though he could not have prevented the damage. Again, he is legally but not causally responsible.

Third, a person's conduct may cause harm, but for a variety of reasons the law may not hold him legally responsible. In some cases the person's conduct is simply not wrongful. Thus, an involuntary movement may cause harm, but one is not normally held liable for such harm. In some cases a person's conduct may be voluntary and the cause of harm, but the interest harmed may not be the one that the law protects. The unhappiness, for example, that follows a broken engagement is not a compensable harm. There are still other situations in which a person may have a defense such as contributory negligence and so avoid liability although his wrongdoing is causally related to harm. And there are cases such as *Palsgraf* in which admitted wrongdoing may be causally related to harm but the harm is not legally attributable to the wrongdoing. These different situations make clear that causal responsibility does not entail legal responsibility.

Fourth, it is sometimes essential to determine whether or not some non-human agency such as a machine or a natural occurrence has caused harm. Insurance contracts often involve such matters. Finally, the law is not always preoccupied with harm; it is sometimes necessary to determine whether or not some *benefit* has been caused. For example, if X injures Y and because of the injury Y receives some benefit from Z, the benefit may reduce the amount of Y's recovery against X.

The meaning of "cause" in the law and in everyday life is not univocal. Hart and Honoré in their book on causation[1] point out three different senses of cause which are relevant to the law. First, cause may refer to a contingency which produces some change exemplifying a general connection between events. For example, "the doctor caused the patient's leg to fly out by tapping his knee." Second, one person may cause or make another person do something: "He made me hand over the money by threatening harm to my children." (This differs from the first kind of cause in that the person made to act has a motive for acting.) Finally, by forgetting to lock your door at night you may provide a thief with an otherwise unavailable opportunity for stealing. Providing other persons with an opportunity to do things is often treated in causal terms by the law: "The book was stolen as a result of your leaving the door open." These different senses of cause should be compared with those uncovered in Collingwood's analysis.

There are interesting conceptual problems raised by omissions. Can omissions cause harm? Some theorists have argued that an omission is "nothing" and nothing cannot be a cause of anything. This position is ridiculed by some theorists, but may there be some explanation for it in some cases? X makes no effort to save a drowning person. Has he therefore caused the drowning? Surely not, and yet the train switchman may, by omitting to pull the switch, cause the train wreck. Why the difference? Is it simply that there is a duty in the one case and not in the other? This, however, seems relevant not to causation but to moral or legal responsibility.

How do we determine in the law whether some contingency, say human

[1] *Causation in the Law* (Oxford: Clarendon Press, 1959).

conduct, is a cause of harm? If the harm would not have happened "but for" the conduct, it is said that the conduct is a cause of the harm. Lawyers realize that there are problems with this simple and popular solution. First, suppose that there are two or more independent wrongdoers, each of whom alone would have caused harm. X is simultaneously shot in the head by Y and Z. Either bullet would have killed him. Who has caused his death? In what way must the "but for" test be supplemented to take care of such cases? Second, suppose that a beach house, momentarily about to topple into the sea because of the pounding of the waves, is destroyed by fire owing to the defendant's negligence. Can we say that the house would not have been destroyed but for the negligence of the defendant? Who should bear the burden in such cases? Consider, too, the following unusual situation. X pushes Y off a building to certain death below. As Y is falling Z shoots and kills him. Can the test be applied without injustice in such cases? Is there an essential difference between the two cases? Third, suppose that X, who is violating the law by hunting out of season, accidentally but without fault shoots Y. Is not his wrongdoing the cause of the harm? Had he not been hunting, would the accident have taken place? Must the test be supplemented for such cases? Is such a case more appropriately treated in terms of "absence of proximate cause"?

Are there any principles by which we determine what is the cause and what are mere conditions? For Mill mere conditions are those factors which are already known; the cause is the unknown factor. Collingwood argues that the cause is the condition which we can control. Hart and Honoré believe that the principles which guide judgments in everyday life influence legal thinking on this question. In their opinion the contrasts between normal and abnormal occurrences and between voluntary and nonvoluntary conduct are crucial in determining the cause. Still others, principally lawyers, argue that the singling out of the cause is a policy decision. There are an infinite number of necessary conditions for any occurrence, and the one singled out as the cause is simply that condition upon which it is most desirable to exert public pressure. Might it be that Mill, Collingwood, Hart, and Honoré pick out elements all of which are relevant in determining cause in some cases but none of which is common to all cases?

In the law when we settle the question of so-called "cause in fact," we often must go on to consider the question of proximate cause. Many lawyers claim that a finding of proximate cause is simply a "policy decision" disguised as a factual discovery, that the term has been used in so many ways that it no longer has a personality of its own, and that it should be expunged from the legal vocabulary. Hart and Honoré argue, on the other hand, that while policy plays its role in determining "proximate cause," common-sense principles provide the framework within which legal decisions are made. In assessing these different viewpoints, various situations have to be considered.

The *Palsgraf* type of case nicely raises the issue of remoteness. Given some harm and some wrongdoing causally related to that harm, what limits should be set to the burden a wrongdoer should bear? If an innocent person is injured, should not the wrongdoer bear the cost rather than the innocent person? But should not the liability reflect in some way the nature of the wrongdoing? Should not the scope of one's duty be governed by the scope of foreseeable risk?

Some cases induce lawyers to talk in metaphorical language of "extraneous cause" and of "causal chains being cut." Consider several such cases. X strikes Y with intent to kill, but only dislocates Y's jaw. The ambulance carrying Y to the hospital is struck by lightning and Y is killed. Has X caused Y's death? Now suppose that X strikes Y without intent to kill. Owing, however, to Y's hemophilia, which is unknown to his assailant, Y bleeds to death from the wound. The legal consequences in these two cases are different. Should they be?

Finally, suppose that a person's wrongful conduct is followed by the wrongful conduct of another such that the harm produced would not have resulted but for the behavior of each. X shoots Y with intent to kill. Y is not mortally wounded but anesthesia is negligently administered to him in the hospital and he dies. Has X caused his death? Should X be held responsible for his death? Should it make a difference if the wound is a mortal one?

These are not, of course, the only kinds of cases in which judges have spoken in terms of proximate cause. These few situations, however, should make it quite clear that there are philosophical questions connected with causation other than those popularized by philosophers preoccupied with Hume's treatment of causation.

Palsgraf v. Long Island Railroad Company, 248 N.Y. 339, 162 N.E. 99 (1928).

CARDOZO, Ch. J. Plaintiff was standing on a platform of defendant's railroad after buying a ticket to go to Rockaway Beach. A train stopped at the station, bound for another place. Two men ran forward to catch it. One of the men reached the platform of the car without mishap, though the train was already moving. The other man, carrying a package, jumped aboard the car, but seemed unsteady as if about to fall. A guard on the car, who had held the door open, reached forward to help him in, and another guard on the platform pushed him from behind. In this act, the package was dislodged, and fell upon the rails. It was a package of small size, about fifteen inches long, and was covered by a newspaper. In fact it contained fireworks, but there was nothing in its appearance to give notice of its contents. The fireworks when they fell exploded. The shock of the explosion threw down some scales at the other end of the platform, many feet away. The scales struck the plaintiff, causing injuries for which she sues.

The conduct of the defendant's guard, if a wrong in its relation to the holder of the package, was not a wrong in its relation to the plaintiff, standing far away. Relatively to her it was not negligence at all. Nothing in the situation gave notice that the falling package had in it the potency of peril to persons thus removed. Negligence is not actionable unless it involves the invasion of a legally protected interest, the violation of a right. "Proof of negligence in the air, so to speak, will not do" (Pollock, *Torts,* 11th ed., p. 455; *Martin* v. *Herzog,* 228 N.Y. 164, 170; cf. Salmond, *Torts,* 6th ed., p. 24). "Negligence is the absence of care, according to the circumstances" (Willes, J., in *Vaughan* v. *Taff Vale Ry. Co.,* 5 H. & N. 679, 688 . . .). The plaintiff as she stood upon the platform of the station might claim to be protected against intentional invasion of her bodily security.

Such invasion is not charged. She might claim to be protected against unintentional invasion by conduct involving in the thought of reasonable men an unreasonable hazard that such invasion would ensue. These, from the point of view of the law, were the bounds of her immunity, with perhaps some rare exceptions, survivals for the most part of ancient forms of liability, where conduct is held to be at the peril of the actor (*Sullivan* v. *Dunham,* 161 N.Y. 290). If no hazard was apparent to the eye of ordinary vigilance, an act innocent and harmless, at least to outward seeming, with reference to her, did not take to itself the quality of a tort because it happened to be a wrong, though apparently not one involving the risk of bodily insecurity, with reference to someone else. "In every instance, before negligence can be predicated of a given act, back of the act must be sought and found a duty to the individual complaining, the observance of which would have averted or avoided the injury" (McSherry, C. J., in *W. Va. Central R. Co.* v. *State,* 96 Md. 652, 666 . . .). The plaintiff sues in her own right for a wrong personal to her, and not as the vicarious beneficiary of a breach of duty to another.

A different conclusion will involve us, and swiftly too, in a maze of contradictions. A guard stumbles over a package which has been left upon a platform. It seems to be a bundle of newspapers. It turns out to be a can of dynamite. To the eye of ordinary vigilance, the bundle is abandoned waste, which may be kicked or trod on with impunity. Is a passenger at the other end of the platform protected by the law against the unsuspected hazard concealed beneath the waste? If not, is the result to be any different, so far as the distant passenger is concerned, when the guard stumbles over a valise which a truckman or a porter has left upon the walk? The passenger far away, if the victim of a wrong at all, has a cause of action, not derivative, but original and primary. His claim to be protected against invasion of his bodily security is neither greater nor less because the act resulting in the invasion is a wrong to another far removed. In this case, the rights that are said to have been violated, the interests said to have been invaded, are not even of the same order. The man was not injured in his person nor even put in danger. The purpose of the act, as well as its effect, was

to make his person safe. If there was a wrong to him at all, which may very well be doubted, it was a wrong to a property interest only, the safety of his package. Out of this wrong to property, which threatened injury to nothing else, there has passed, we are told, to the plaintiff by derivation or succession a right of action for the invasion of an interest of another order, the right to bodily security. The diversity of interests emphasizes the futility of the effort to build the plaintiff's right upon the basis of a wrong to someone else. The gain is one of emphasis, for a like result would follow if the interests were the same. Even then, the orbit of the danger as disclosed to the eye of reasonable vigilance would be the orbit of the duty. One who jostles one's neighbor in a crowd does not invade the rights of others standing at the outer fringe when the unintended contact casts a bomb upon the ground. The wrongdoer as to them is the man who carries the bomb, not the one who explodes it without suspicion of the danger. Life will have to be made over, and human nature transformed, before prevision so extravagant can be accepted as the norm of conduct, the customary standard to which behavior must conform.

The argument for the plaintiff is built upon the shifting meanings of such words as "wrong" and "wrongful," and shares their instability. What the plaintiff must show is "a wrong" to herself, i.e., a violation of her own right, and not merely a wrong to someone else, nor conduct "wrongful" because unsocial, but not "a wrong" to anyone. We are told that one who drives at reckless speed through a crowded city street is guilty of a negligent act and, therefore, of a wrongful one irrespective of the consequences. Negligent the act is, and wrongful in the sense that it is unsocial, but wrongful and unsocial in relation to other travelers, only because the eye of vigilance perceives the risk of damage. If the same act were to be committed on a speedway or a race course, it would lose its wrongful quality. The risk reasonably to be perceived defines the duty to be obeyed, and risk imports relation; it is risk to another or to others within the range of apprehension. . . . This does not mean, of course, that one who launches a destructive force is always relieved of liability if the force, though known to be destructive, pursues an unexpected path. "It was not necessary that the defendant should have had notice of the particular method in which an accident would occur, if the possibility of an accident was clear to the ordinarily prudent eye" (*Munsey* v. *Webb,* 231 U.S. 150, 156; *Condran* v. *Park & Tilford,* 213 N.Y. 341, 345; *Robert* v. *U.S.E.F. Corp.,* 240 N.Y. 474, 477). Some acts, such as shooting, are so imminently dangerous to anyone who may come within reach of the missile, however unexpectedly, as to impose a duty of prevision not far from that of an insurer. Even today, and much oftener in earlier stages of the law, one acts sometimes at one's peril. . . . Under this head, it may be, fall certain cases of what is known as transferred intent, an act willfully dangerous to A resulting by misadventure in injury to B. . . . These cases aside, wrong is defined in terms of the natural or probable, at least when unintentional (*Parrot* v. *Wells-Fargo Co. (The Nitro-Glycerine Case),* 15 Wall. (U.S.) 524). The range of reasonable apprehension is at times a question for the court, and at times, if varying inferences are possible, a question for the jury. Here, by concession, there was nothing in the situation to suggest to the most cautious mind that the parcel wrapped in newspaper would spread wreckage through the station. If the guard had thrown it down knowingly and willfully, he would not have threatened the plaintiff's safety, so far as appearances could warn him. His conduct would not have involved, even then, an unreasonable probability of invasion of her bodily security. Liability can be no greater where the act is inadvertent.

Negligence, like risk, is thus a term of relation. Negligence in the abstract, apart from things related, is surely not a tort, if indeed it is understandable at all. . . . Negligence is not a tort unless it results in the commission of a wrong, and the commission of a wrong imports the violation of a right, in this case, we are told, the right to be protected against interference with one's bodily security. But bodily security is protected, not against all forms of interference or aggression, but only against some. One who seeks redress at law does not make out a cause of action by showing without more that there has been damage to his person. If the harm was not willful, he must show that the act as to him had possibilities of danger so many and apparent as to entitle him to be protected against the doing of it though the harm was

unintended. Affront to personality is still the keynote of the wrong. Confirmation of this view will be found in the history and development of the action on the case. Negligence as a basis of civil liability was unknown to medieval law (8 Holdsworth, *History of English Law,* p. 449; Street, *Foundations of Legal Liability,* vol. 1, pp. 189, 190). For damage to the person, the sole remedy was trespass, and trespass did not lie in the absence of aggression, and that direct and personal (Holdsworth, *op. cit.,* p. 453; Street, *op. cit.,* vol. 3, pp. 258, 260, vol. 1, pp. 71, 74). Liability for other damage, as where a servant without orders from the master does or omits something to the damage of another, is a plant of later growth (Holdsworth, *op. cit.,* pp. 450, 457; Wigmore, *Responsibility for Tortious Acts,* vol. 3, *Essays in Anglo-American Legal History,* pp. 520, 523, 526, 533). When it emerged out of the legal soil, it was thought of as a variant of trespass, an offshoot of the parent stock. This appears in the form of action, which was known as trespass on the case (Holdsworth, *op. cit.,* p. 449; cf. *Scott* v. *Shepard,* 2 Wm. Black, 892; Green, *Rationale of Proximate Cause,* p. 19). The victim does not sue derivatively, or by right of subrogation, to vindicate an interest invaded in the person of another. Thus to view his cause of action is to ignore the fundamental difference between tort and crime (Holland, *Jurisprudence,* 12th ed., p. 328). He sues for breach of a duty owing to himself.

The law of causation, remote or proximate, is thus foreign to the case before us. The question of liability is always anterior to the question of the measure of the consequences that go with liability. If there is no tort to be redressed, there is no occasion to consider what damage might be recovered if there were a finding of a tort. We may assume, without deciding, that negligence, not at large or in the abstract, but in relation to the plaintiff, would entail liability for any and all consequences, however novel or extraordinary (*Bird* v. *St. Paul F. & M. Ins. Co.,* 224, N.Y. 47, 54; *Ehrgott* v. *Mayer,* etc., of N.Y., 96 N.Y. 264; *Smith* v. *London & S.W. Ry. Co.,* L.R. 6 C.P. 14; 1 Beven, *Negligence,* p. 106; Street, op. cit. vol. 1, p. 90; Green, *Rationale of Proximate Cause,* pp. 88, 118; cf. *Matter of Polemis,* L.R. 1921, 3 K.B. 560; 44 *Law Quarterly Review,* 142). There is room for argument that a distinction is to be drawn according to the diversity of interests invaded by the act, as where conduct negligent in that it threatens an insignificant invasion of an interest in property results in an unforeseeable invasion of an interest of another order, as, e.g., one of bodily security. Perhaps other distinctions may be necessary. We do not go into the question now. The consequences to be followed must first be rooted in a wrong.

The judgment of the Appellate Division and that of the Trial Term should be reversed, and the complaint dismissed, with costs in all courts.

ANDREWS, J. (dissenting). Assisting a passenger to board a train, the defendant's servant negligently knocked a package from his arms. It fell between the platform and the cars. Of its contents the servant knew and could know nothing. A violent explosion followed. The concussion broke some scales standing a considerable distance away. In falling they injured the plaintiff, an intending passenger.

Upon these facts may she recover the damages she has suffered in an action brought against the master? The result we shall reach depends upon our theory as to the nature of negligence. Is it a relative concept—the breach of some duty owing to a particular person or to particular persons? Or where there is an act which unreasonably threatens the safety of others, is the doer liable for all its proximate consequences, even where they result in injury to one who would generally be thought to be outside the radius of danger? This is not a mere dispute as to words. We might not believe that to the average mind the dropping of the bundle would seem to involve the probability of harm to the plaintiff standing many feet away whatever might be the case as to the owner or to one so near as to be likely to be struck by its fall. If, however, we adopt the second hypothesis we have to inquire only as to the relation between cause and effect. We deal in terms of proximate cause, not of negligence.

Negligence may be defined roughly as an act or omission which unreasonably does or may affect the rights of others, or which unreasonably fails to protect oneself from the dangers resulting from such acts. Here I confine myself to the first branch of the definition. Nor do I comment on the word "unreasonable." For present purposes it sufficiently describes that average of conduct that society requires of its members.

There must be both the act or the omission, and the right. It is the act itself, not the intent of the actor, that is important. (*Hover* v. *Barkhoof*, 44 N.Y. 113; *Metz* v. *Connecticut Co.*, 217 N.Y. 475.) In criminal law both the intent and the result are to be considered. Intent again is material in tort actions, where punitive damages are sought, dependent on actual malice—not on merely reckless conduct. But here neither insanity nor infancy lessens responsibility. (*Williams* v. *Hays*, 143 N.Y. 442.)

As has been said, except in cases of contributory negligence, there must be rights which are or may be affected. Often though injury has occurred, no rights of him who suffers have been touched. A licensee or trespasser upon my land has no claim to affirmative care on my part that the land be made safe. (*Meiers* v. *Koch Brewery*, 229 N.Y. 10.) Where a railroad is required to fence its tracks against cattle, no man's rights are injured should he wander upon the road because such fence is absent. (*Di Caprio* v. *N.Y.C.R.R.*, 231 N.Y. 94.) An unborn child may not demand immunity from personal harm. (*Drobner* v. *Peters*, 232 N.Y. 220.)

But we are told that "there is no negligence unless there is in the particular case a legal duty to take care, and this duty must be one which is owed to the plaintiff himself and not merely to others." (Salmond, *Torts*, 6th ed., p. 24.) This, I think too narrow a conception. Where there is the unreasonable act, and some right that may be affected there is negligence whether damage does or does not result. That is immaterial. Should we drive down Broadway at a reckless speed, we are negligent whether we strike an approaching car or miss it by an inch. The act itself is wrongful. It is a wrong not only to those who happen to be within the radius of danger but to all who might have been there—a wrong to the public at large. Such is the language of the street. Such the language of the courts when speaking of contributory negligence. Such again and again their language in speaking of the duty of some defendant and discussing proximate cause in cases where such a discussion is wholly irrelevant on any other theory. (*Perry* v. *Rochester Line Co.*, 219 N.Y. 60.) As was said by Mr. Justice Holmes many years ago, "the measure of the defendant's duty in determining whether a wrong has been committed is one thing, the measure of liability when a wrong has been committed is another." (*Spade* v. *Lynn & Boston R.R. Co.,* 172 Mass. 488.) Due care is a duty imposed on each one of us to protect society from unnecessary danger, not to protect A, B, or C alone.

It may well be that there is no such thing as negligence in the abstract. "Proof of negligence in the air, so to speak, will not do." In an empty world negligence would not exist. It does involve a relationship between man and his fellows. But not merely a relationship between man and those whom he might reasonably expect his act would injure. Rather, a relationship between him and those whom he does in fact injure. If his act has a tendency to harm someone, it harms him a mile away as surely as it does those on the scene. We now permit children to recover for the negligent killing of the father. It was never prevented on the theory that no duty was owing to them. A husband may be compensated for the loss of his wife's services. To say that the wrongdoer was negligent as to the husband as well as to the wife is merely an attempt to fit facts to theory. An insurance company paying a fire loss recovers its payment of the negligent incendiary. We speak of subrogation—of suing in the right of the insured. Behind the cloud of words is the fact they hide, that the act, wrongful as to the insured, has also injured the company. Even if it be true that the fault of father, wife, or insured will prevent recovery, it is because we consider the original negligence not the proximate cause of the injury. . . .

In the well-known *Polemis Case* (1921, 3 K.B. 560), Scrutton, L. J., said that the dropping of a plank was negligent for it might injure "workman or cargo or ship." Because of either possibility the owner of the vessel was to be made good for his loss. The act being wrongful, the doer was liable for its proximate results. Criticized and explained as this statement may have been, I think it states the law as it should be and as it is. . . .

The proposition is this. Everyone owes to the world at large the duty of refraining from those acts that may unreasonably threaten the safety of others. Such an act occurs. Not only is he wronged to whom harm might reasonably be expected to result, but he also who is in fact injured, even if he be outside what would generally be thought the danger zone. There needs be duty due the one complaining but this is not a duty to a particular individual because as to him harm might be expected. Harm to someone being the natural result of the act, not only that one alone, but all those in fact injured may complain. We have never, I think, held otherwise. Indeed in the *Di Caprio* case we said that a breach of a general ordinance defining the degree of care to be exercised in one's calling is evidence of negligence as to everyone. We did not limit this statement to those who might be expected to be exposed to danger. Unreasonable risk being taken, its consequences are not confined to those who might probably be hurt.

If this be so, we do not have a plaintiff suing by "derivation or succession." Her action is original and primary. Her claim is for a breach of duty to herself—not that she is subrogated to any right of action of the owner of the parcel or of a passenger standing at the scene of the explosion.

The right to recover damages rests on additional considerations. The plaintiff's rights must be injured, and this injury must be caused by the negligence. We build a dam, but are negligent as to its foundations. Breaking, it injures property down stream. We are not liable if all this happened because of some reason other than the insecure foundation. But when injuries do result from our unlawful act we are liable for the consequences. It does not matter that they are unusual, unexpected, unforeseen, and unforeseeable. But there is one limitation. The damages must be so connected with the negligence that the latter may be said to be the proximate cause of the former.

These two words have never been given an inclusive definition. What is a cause in a legal sense, still more, what is a proximate cause, depend in each case upon many considerations, as does the existence of negligence itself. Any philosophical doctrine of causation does not help us. A boy throws a stone into a pond. The ripples spread. The water level rises. The history of that pond is altered to all eternity. It will be altered by other causes also. Yet it will be forever the resultant of all causes combined. Each one will have an influence. How great only omniscience can say. You may speak of a chain, or if you please, a net. An analogy is of little aid. Each cause brings about future events. Without each the future would not be the same. Each is proximate in the sense it is essential. But that is not what we mean by the word. Nor on the other hand do we mean sole cause. There is no such thing.

Should analogy be thought helpful, however, I prefer that of a stream. The spring, starting on its journey, is joined by tributary after tributary. The river, reaching the ocean, comes from a hundred sources. No man may say whence any drop of water is derived. Yet for a time distinction may be possible. Into the clear creek, brown swamp water flows from the left. Later, from the right comes water stained by its clay bed. The three may remain for a space, sharply divided. But at last, inevitably no trace of separation remains. They are so commingled that all distinction is lost.

As we have said, we cannot trace the effect of an act to the end, if end there is. Again, however, we may trace it part of the way. A murder at Serajevo may be the necessary antecedent to an assassination in London twenty years hence. An overturned lantern may burn all Chicago. We may follow the fire from the shed to the last building. We rightly say the fire started by the lantern caused its destruction.

A cause, but not the proximate cause. What we do mean by the word "proximate" is that because of convenience, of public policy, of a rough sense of justice, the law arbitrarily declines to trace a series of events beyond a certain point. This is not logic. It is practical politics. Take our rule as to fires. Sparks from my burning haystack set on fire my house and my neighbor's. I may recover from a negligent railroad. He may not. Yet the wrongful act as directly harmed the one as the other. We may regret that the line was drawn just where it was, but drawn somewhere it had to be. We said the act of the railroad was not the proximate cause of our neighbor's fire. Cause it surely was. The words we used were simply indicative of our notions of public policy. Other courts think differently. But somewhere they reach the point where they cannot say the stream comes from any one source.

Take the illustration given in an unpublished manuscript by a distinguished and helpful writer on the law of torts. A chauffeur negligently collides with another car which is filled with dynamite, although he could not know it. An explosion follows. A, walking on the sidewalk nearby, is killed. B, sitting in a window of a building opposite, is cut by flying glass. C, likewise sitting in a window a block away, is similarly injured. And a further illustration. A nursemaid, ten blocks away, startled by the noise, involuntarily drops a baby from her arms to the walk. We are told that C may not recover while A may. As to B it is a question for court or jury. We will all agree that the baby might not. Because, we are again told, the chauffeur had no reason to believe his conduct involved any risk of injuring either C or the baby. As to them he was not negligent.

But the chauffeur, being negligent in risking the collision, his belief that the scope of the harm he might do would be limited is immaterial. His act unreasonably jeopardized the safety of anyone who might be affected by it. C's injury and that of the baby were directly traceable to the collision. Without that, the injury would not have happened. C had the right to sit in his office, secure from such dangers. The baby was entitled to use the sidewalk with reasonable safety.

The true theory is, it seems to me, that the injury to C, if in truth he is to be denied recovery, and the injury to the baby is that their several injuries were not the proximate result of the negligence. And here not what the chauffeur had reason to believe would be the result of his conduct, but what the prudent would foresee, may have a bearing. May have some bearing, for the problem of proximate cause is not to be solved by any one consideration.

It is all a question of expediency. There are no fixed rules to govern our judgment. There are simply matters of which we may take account. We have in a somewhat different connection spoken of "the stream of events." We have asked whether that stream was deflected—whether it was forced into new and unexpected channels. (*Donnelly* v. *Piercy Contracting Co.,* 222 N.Y. 210.) This is rather rhetoric than law. There is in truth little to guide us other than common sense.

There are some hints that may help us. The proximate cause, involved as it may be with many other causes, must be, at the least, something without which the event would not happen. The court must ask itself whether there was a natural and continuous sequence between cause and effect. Was the one a substantial factor in producing the other? Was there a direct connection between them, without too many intervening causes? Is the effect of cause on result not too attenuated? Is the cause likely, in the usual judgment of mankind, to produce the result? Or by the exercise of prudent foresight could the result be foreseen? Is the result too remote from the cause, and here we consider remoteness in time and space. . . . Clearly we must so consider, for the greater the distance either in time or space, the more surely do other causes intervene to effect the result. When a lantern is overturned the firing of a shed is a fairly direct consequence. Many things contribute to the spread of the conflagration—the force of the wind, the direction and width of streets, the character of intervening structures, other factors. We draw an uncertain and wavering line, but draw it we must as best we can.

Once again, it is all a question of fair judgment, always keeping in mind the fact that we endeavor to make a rule in each case that will be practical and in keeping with the general understanding of mankind.

Here another question must be answered. In the case supposed it is said, and said correctly, that the chauffeur is liable for the direct effect of the explosion although he had no reason to suppose it would follow a collision. "The fact that the injury occurred in a different manner than that which might have been expected does not prevent the chauffeur's negligence from being in law the cause of the injury." But the natural results of a negligent act the results which a prudent man would or should foresee—do have a bearing upon the decision as to proximate cause. We have said so repeatedly. What should be foreseen? No human foresight would suggest that a collision itself might injure one a block away. On the contrary, given an explosion, such a possibility might be reasonably expected. I think the direct connection, the foresight of which the courts speak, assumes prevision of the explosion, for the immediate results of which, at least, the chauffeur is responsible.

It may be said this is unjust. Why? In fairness he should make good every injury flowing from his negligence. Not because of tenderness toward him we say he need not answer for all that follows his wrong. We look back

to the catastrophe, the fire kindled by the spark, or the explosion. We trace the consequences—not indefinitely, but to a certain point. And to aid us in fixing that point we ask what might ordinarily be expected to follow the fire or the explosion.

This last suggestion is the factor which must determine the case before us. The act upon which defendant's liability rests is knocking an apparently harmless package onto the platform. The act was negligent. For its proximate consequences the defendant is liable. If its contents were broken, to the owner; if it fell upon and crushed a passenger's foot, then to him. If it exploded and injured one in the immediate vicinity, to him also as to A in the illustration. Mrs. Palsgraf was standing some distance away. How far cannot be told from the record—apparently twenty-five or thirty feet. Perhaps less. Except for the explosion, she would not have been injured. We are told by the appellant in his brief "it cannot be denied that the explosion was the direct cause of the plaintiff's injuries." So it was a substantial factor in producing the result—there was here a natural and continuous sequence—direct connection. The only intervening cause was that instead of blowing her to the ground the concussion smashed the weighing machine which in turn fell upon her. There was no remoteness in time, little in space. And surely, given such an explosion as here, it needed no great foresight to predict that the natural result would be to injure one on the platform at no greater distance from its scene than was the plaintiff. Just how no one might be able to predict. Whether by flying fragments, by broken glass, by wreckage of machines or structures no one could say. But injury in some form was most probable.

Under these circumstances I cannot say as a matter of law that the plaintiff's injuries were not the proximate result of the negligence. That is all we have before us. The court refused to so charge. No request was made to submit the matter to the jury as a question of fact, even would that have been proper upon the record before us.

The judgment appealed from should be affirmed, with costs.

POUND, LEHMAN and KELLOGG, JJ., concur with CARDOZO, Ch. J.; ANDREWS, J., dissents in opinion in which CRANE and O'BRIEN, JJ., concur.

Judgment reversed, etc.

Causality in Everyday Life and in Recent Science*

I

There is an old rule, formulated long ago in scholastic philosophy, that warns us against confusing the "post hoc" and the "propter hoc." This means that from the fact that an event E happened after another event C we must not infer that E happened "because of" C. In other words, the rule maintains that the meaning of the proposition "E follows C" is entirely different from the meaning of the proposition "E is the effect of the cause C." But what *is* the difference between the two meanings? This question, it seems to me, is the philosophical problem of Causality.

I call it philosophical, because it is a question of meaning only, not of truth. It deals with the signification of the word "propter" or "because of"; we have to know what these words signify in order to understand the mere meaning of the principle of causality; the question whether this principle (if we can discover any meaning in it) is true or false would be a scientific problem, i.e., it could be decided only by observation and experience.

Our rule seems to presuppose that we are already acquainted with the signification of the words *post* and *propter,* for if we were not, there would be no possibility of ever applying the rule to any particular case. At best it would yield us an information of an entirely negative nature: it would tell us that the causal relation is *not* merely the relation of temporal succession, but something more; yet it would not give the slightest hint as to the positive essence of the causal relation.

Now there is no doubt that we do apply the rule continually and that it is a perfectly good and sound rule which people ought to follow even much more frequently than they do. If we take a certain medicine and get well after it, it would be very rash to assert that the medicine was the *cause* of our getting well. Or if we try to discover the causes of the depression, we know we are looking for much more than merely for events which *preceded* the depression. It is evident, therefore, that we actually are in possession of some kind of criterion which enables us to

distinguish between events that merely follow each other and events that cause each other; for we do make this distinction every day, and we make it with a sufficient accuracy to have nearly all our behavior guided by it.

We simply have to observe how this distinction is actually made in order to find out the meaning of the concept of causality as it is used in our daily experience. This simple proceeding will surely not be difficult, and yet it is the general method—and I am convinced the only method—of philosophy: it discovers the meaning of propositions by finding out just how they are verified, i.e., how their truth or falsity is tested.

This is what I propose to do with propositions in which the concept of causality is used. I shall certainly not propose any "theory of causality"; I believe there can be no such thing. There are no theories and hypotheses in philosophy; hypotheses are the material out of which the sciences are constructed, and I believe that philosophy is something different from the sciences.

How, then, do we verify the statement that the taking of some medicine was not only the antecedent but also the *cause* of the recovery of the patient?

At a first glance there seem to be two different ways of such a verification (remember, we do not ask how it *should* be done, but how it is really done in practice):

1. We try the medicine many times and perhaps on many different patients. If we find that in every single case a person suffering from a particular complaint is cured, we shall say: the recovery after the use of the medicine was not a mere *chance*, but was *caused* by it. In other words: if the event E *always* occurs after the event C has occurred before, if C never occurs without being followed by E, then we do not hesitate to call C the cause and E the effect. It is important to notice that we do this whether we are able to "explain" the cure or not; there are cases in which we just know that a medicine is good without knowing how it works.

This is a fact; and I should like to express it, as it has often been expressed by thinkers of the positivist school, by saying that the difference between a mere temporal sequence and a causal sequence is the regularity, the

* Moritz Schlick, *University of California Publications in Philosophy,* XV (1932), 99–125, by permission of the publisher, University of California Press, Berkeley. Footnotes are omitted.

uniformity of the latter. If C is *regularly* followed by E, then C is the cause of E; if E only "happens" to follow C now and then, the sequence is called a mere chance. And since (as we just saw) the observation of the regularity was, in this case, the *only* thing that was done, it was necessarily the *only* reason for speaking of cause and effect, it was the *sufficient* reason. The word cause, as used in everyday life, implies *nothing but* regularity of sequence, because *nothing else* is used to verify the propositions in which it occurs.

I am sure the reader must feel very much disappointed to have me repeat these old "positivistic" statements which have been discussed and, some believe, refuted so many times. I appeal to his patience and hope he will presently see the import of these remarks for the higher aspects of the problem of causality as they are presented by recent science.

Metaphysicians will, of course, find fault with our representation of the facts. Although they will admit, I think, that in the above example the verification consisted entirely in the observation of uniformity and nothing else, they will probably maintain that even the most unprejudiced observer never thinks that the regularity of sequence constitutes the whole of causality, but regards it only as a sign or as the consequence of something else, of some "real connection" or some peculiar "intimacy" between cause and effect, or by whatever name he may call the unobservable "tie" which he believes to be present in causation.

I do not deny that this may be so, but I answer: we are not concerned with what any observer thinks or says; our investigation of meaning is concerned only with what he *does* and can show us. Speaking, thinking, believing, implies interpretation; we must not discuss interpretations or the results of philosophical analysis, we have to do with verification only, which is always an act or an activity. With regard to meaning we have to be pragmatists, whatever we may be with regard to the conception of truth. If the existence of that mysterious "tie" is verified *only* by the observation of regular sequence, then this regularity will be all the meaning the word "tie" actually has, and no thinking, believing, or speaking can add anything to it.

Perhaps the best known objection against the identification of causality and regularity is the remark that nothing is more regular

than the succession of day and night, and yet we do not call the one the cause of the other. But this is simply accounted for by the fact that "day" and "night" are really not names for "events" at all in the sense in which this word is used in science. And as soon as we analyze day and night into the series of natural events for which these names stand, we find that the sequence of those events must be regarded as a very good example of "causal connection."

The real difficulties involved in the notion of uniformity are of a different nature and much more serious. We said that E was called the effect of a cause C, if in many cases it was observed to follow C each time without exception. Should we not ask: *how many* times? A physician who has tried a medicine in six cases and has seen the patient get better six times may feel pretty confident that his remedy was the cause of the recovery of his patients (provided, of course, that in his former experience they did not get well without the medicine), but undoubtedly it is possible that in all future cases the remedy will fail to have the desired result; and then we shall say: those first six times were nothing but a chance, the word "chance" meaning simply the negation of causality. If instead of six times the experiment were repeated successfully a hundred times, surely everybody would believe in the beneficial effect of the medicine; nevertheless it must be admitted that the future may bring exceptions and destroy the regularity. A hundred will be considered better than six, but evidently *no* number will be considered absolutely satisfactory; for if in one single case only C were not followed by E, one would feel no longer justified to call C the cause of E, and for all we know such a crucial case might always occur in the future.

So this is the state of affairs: the proposition "C is the cause of E" seemed to mean nothing but "C is always followed by E"; but this latter proposition can unfortunately never be verified on account of the unfortunate "always" it contains. Verification would be possible only if a finite number is substituted for "always," but no finite number is satisfactory, because it does not exclude the possibility of exceptions.

This difficulty has been pointed out about as many times as the problem of induction has been discussed, and the conclusion has usually been that causality cannot be explained as meaning uniformity, but that it must mean simply something else. Perhaps so. But we must insist: it *can* mean something else only if there is a way of verifying causal judgments different from the one we have described. What shall we do if no such way is discovered?

We can do nothing but stick to the facts with absolute frankness. Since the meaning of a proposition lies entirely in its verification, it will have meaning only *in so far* as it is verified. And if the verification is never considered complete and final, if we never declare a certain C to be the cause of a certain E without reserving the right of revocation (and this, it is important to notice, not on account of any incorrect observation or similar "mistake"), then we shall have to admit that we simply have no clear concept of causality. Where there is no definite verification, there can be no definite meaning. The function of the word "cause" will be vague. A sentence containing this word may serve a very good purpose in the practice of everyday life as well as of science, but it will have no theoretical meaning.

There is a very curious way in which the difficulty hidden in the word "always" is sometimes apparently overcome. It consists in saying: if it cannot be verified that E *always* follows C, it can also never be falsified, for the cases in which it does not seem to be the case can be explained as mere appearances, and so our belief in the causal relation between C and E can never be proved to be false. A physician, for instance, who has had complete success with a cure in ninety-nine cases but finds it to fail in the hundredth case, will by no means give up his belief that his treatment has been the "cause" of the ninety-nine recoveries, but will explain that in the negative case there must have been a circumstance which intervened and prevented the effect. And we shall very likely accept this explanation as very natural, just as we would not blame a medicine for not making a patient well, if five minutes after taking it he were killed by an automobile accident. Theoretically, and in a very crude symbolism, we might say that in the negative case the cause is not any more C at all, but C + C', where C' is the intervening circumstance, and C + C' does *not* have the effect E, which C alone would

have had. This statement must, of course, be capable of being verified by really observing C'; if we were to admit unobservable C's we could consider *any* event to be the cause of any other event by merely assuming the existence of convenient C's, and then surely our judgments about causal relations would lose all meaning. There are certain philosophers, those who advocate the doctrine of "conventionalism," who believe that this is really the nature of all our causal judgments; in their opinion all these judgments—which would include all laws of nature—have no real meaning, they do not say anything about the world, but only indicate the way in which we select, or even arbitrarily invent, events in order to make them fit into a preconceived scheme, which we have decided to use as our most convenient means of describing nature. . . .

We must note here that the interpretation of negative cases by means of disturbing influences—intervening C's—does *not* offer any criterion of causality other than uniformity of sequence; on the contrary, it saves causality only by substituting a hidden regularity for an apparent irregularity.

The regularity may at first be hidden, but it must be discoverable, if we are not to fall into the snares of conventionalism; that is, we must be able to find a C' such that C and C' together will always be followed by an E' which is different from E. And if there should be cases in which C + C' is not followed by an E', we have to find a new event C", and so on. Evidently it would be a great advantage and would help to elucidate special cases of causality, if there were a way of making sure that no further C's could possibly intervene. There would be no hope of doing this, if *any* event in the world could eventually play the rôle of the C' for which we are looking. But if these events were restricted in a certain way so that it would be possible to examine *all* of them, then we would know that no other disturbing element could come into question, and verification would become more satisfactory.

Now it has usually been assumed by science that the possible causes were indeed very definitely restricted. In looking for the cause of a given event E, it was thought that we could exclude all events happening *long before* E, and all events happening *at a great distance* from E (events occurring *after* E had, of course, been already ruled out by pre-scientific thinking). Assuming these conditions in their most rigorous and consistent form, one arrived at the idea that no event could be regarded as the proper cause of E unless it occurred in the immediate spatial and temporal vicinity of E.

So the causal relation between two events C and E was thought to imply their contiguity in space and time. Action-at-a-distance (temporal as well as spatial distance) was considered impossible. If this were so, one would have to look for the causes of any event only in its immediate neighborhood, there would indeed be no time and no room for any other event to interfere. It is irrelevant that this view was supported by *a priori* arguments such as "an event can act only at the place where it occurs, and nowhere else"; nevertheless such arguments show that one believed one could *understand* the causal relation better if there was contiguity; if cause and effect were separated from each other, their relation appeared to be more mysterious. This brings us to the consideration of the second way in which the existence of a causal relation seems to be established (the first one being observation of uniformity of sequence).

2. Supposing there were a case in which we believed we really and completely "understood" the working of a certain treatment or medicine in the human body: in such a case we should not have to wait for any repetition of the sequence treatment-recovery in order to assert a causal relation between these two events; we could assert it even before it occurred a single time, because our "understanding" of this particular causation would imply our conviction that the first event would entail the second one, or, as it is often put, C would *necessarily* be followed by E. If a surgeon amputates a man's leg, he will know beforehand that the man will be one-legged afterward. Nobody thinks that we must wait for a long series of experiences in order to know that amputation results in the loss of a limb. We feel we "understand" the whole process and therefore know its result without having experienced it.

So there seems to be a second way of verifying a causal judgment independent of observation of regularity: it consists in simply pointing to the "understanding" of the particular causal relation. And those who believe

in this second way will immediately add that it is the only real way, the only legitimate method, and that our first criterion—uniformity of occurrence—was nothing but an untrustworthy system, which might be good enough for an empiristic scientist, but could never satisfy the philosopher.

But let us examine what exactly is meant by "understanding" as the word is used here.

It is usually supposed to be a matter of "pure reason." Now, the only sense I can find for this term is the purely logical, which would mean the same as the purely deductive, the merely analytical. And there is indeed a purely logical element in the case we have just been examining. That amputation of a leg causes a man to be one-legged is an identical inference; it is, like all logical inferences, a mere tautology. But it is easy to see, unfortunately, that this has nothing to do with causation. The causal connection is hidden in the word "amputation." We usually believe we understand this connection, because we think we comprehend the process, say, of a saw cutting through a bone: the hard particles of the steel are in immediate contact with the soft particles of the bone, and the latter somehow must give way to the former. Here again we have contiguity in space and time, which appears to flatter our imagination, but apart from that we have again nothing but a sequence of events which we have often observed to happen in a similar way and which we therefore expect to happen again. For aught we know we might some day come across a bone that would resist any saw and that no human power would be able to cut in two.

So we see that, at least in our example, we were led to think we understood or comprehended the causal nexus: partly by a misinterpretation of the way in which logical inference entered into our thought, and partly by analyzing the causal process into a spatial and temporal continuity of events. This means that our second criterion is really only a hidden application of the first one; it is not different, and consequently not any better.

The examination of any other example leads to the same result. What, for instance, is the difference between a case in which we *understand* that a certain medicine must have a certain effect, and another case in which we just know by experience that it does have that effect? It is evidently this: in the second case we observe only two events, the application of the drug and, after a reasonable lapse of time, the recovery of the patient; in the first case we know how the gap between cause and effect is filled by an unbroken chain of events which are contiguous in space and time. The drug, e.g., is injected into the veins, we know it comes into immediate contact with the blood particles, we know that these will then undergo a certain chemical change, they will travel through the body, they will come into contact with a certain organ, this organ will be changed in a particular way, and so on. In this way we infer that in the end the patient *must* be healed, *if* all the other events follow each other in the way we have assumed. And how do we know that they do follow each other so? All we know is that in former experiences in the laboratory this has always been the regular course of things.

From all this we must draw the negative conclusion that it is impossible—at least in so far as the judgments of everyday life and of qualitative science are concerned—to find any meaning for the word causation, except that it implies regularity of sequence. And this is rather vague, because there is no rule as to how many instances have to be observed in order to justify our speaking of regularity.

But the two chief things we can learn from the foregoing considerations seem to me to be these:

1. The "understanding" of a causal relation is not a process of logical reasoning; what is called causal necessity is absolutely different from logical necessity (which is nothing but identity). But at the same time we see why former philosophers so frequently made the mistake of confusing the two and believing that the effect could be logically inferred from the cause. . . .

2. We learn that the causal relation between two separate events is actually explained or understood when we can conceive the two as being connected by a chain of intermediate events. If some of these are still separated, we have to look for new events between them, and so on, until all the gaps are filled out and the chain has become perfectly continuous in space and time. But evidently *we can go no further,* and it would be nonsense to expect more of us. If we look for the causal link that links two events together, we cannot find anything but another

event (or perhaps several). Whatever can be observed and shown in the causal chain will be the links, but it would be nonsense to look for the linkage.

This shows that we are perfectly right when we think of cause and effect as connected by a causal chain, but that we are perfectly wrong when we think that this chain could consist of anything but events, that it could be a kind of mysterious tie called "causality." The conception of such a "tie," which is really not a concept but a mere word, is due to a faulty process of thinking that is very common in the history of philosophy: the continuation of a thought beyond its logical limit; we transcend the region in which a word makes sense and necessarily find ourselves in the region of nonsense. After the scientist has successfully filled up all the gaps in his causal chains by continually interpolating new events, the philosopher wants to go on with this pleasant game after all the gaps are filled. So he invents a kind of glue and assures us that in reality it is only his glue that holds the events together at all. But we can never find the glue; there is no room for it, as the world is already completely filled by events which leave no chinks between them. Even in our times there are some philosophers who say that we directly experience causation, e.g., in the act of volition, or even in the feeling of muscular effort. But whatever such feelings of willing or of effort may be, they are certainly events in the world; they can be glued to other events, but they cannot be the glue.

All this has of course been seen very clearly by Hume when he said that it was impossible to discover any "impression" for the idea of causal nexus. Only we can express this even more strongly by saying that we are already committing a kind of nonsense when we try to *look* for such an impression. At this point we find complete agreement between Hume and Kant. Kant applauded Hume for seeing that when we speak of causation we cannot possibly mean a sort of tie which connects the events or establishes a kind of intimacy between them, and he conceived causality as something entirely different, namely as a Principle of Order. He believed that the human mind imposed a certain order on the events of its experience, and that causality was one of the principles according to which this was done. And according to him, the human mind did this because it could not help doing it; the Principle was simply part of its metaphysical nature.

Although we must of course reject the latter part of Kant's view, we can most heartily consent to his opinion that if causality is anything at all it can be nothing but a Principle of Order.

II

It is the object of science to discover Order in the world. This is done by finding and formulating Laws of Nature. So there must be a relationship between causality and the laws of nature, and it is easy to see what it is. The principle of causality seems to assert that every definite cause will have a definite effect, and a law of nature tells us, what will be the particular event that belongs to a given cause as its effect. So the principle of causality itself is not a law but can be regarded as the statement that all events in nature are subject to laws. And this must not be interpreted as if a law of nature were something imposed upon reality, compelling nature to behave in a certain way, just as a civic law would force a certain behavior upon the citizens. Laws of nature do not *prescribe* a certain order *to* the world, but simply *describe* the order *of* the world; they do not command what must happen, but simply formulate what does happen. The "necessity" which we attribute to them must not be misunderstood as a kind of compulsion (this term would imply the possibility of "obedience" and "disobedience"), but it means only that there is *no exception* to the laws, that they hold in *all* cases.

From what I said a moment ago we might expect all laws of nature to have the form: "the cause so-and-so has the effect so-and-so"; but if we look at the actual formulations in science, we do not find a single law of this form, wherever the expression is perfectly precise, as is the case in theoretical physics. What we do find there is always a mathematical equation. The vague notions of cause and effect have been replaced by the more precise concept of mathematical function. Cause and effect are both names for events, and one of the reasons why it seems impossible to use them with the necessary scientific precision lies in the fact that it is impossible to *isolate* events. If I drop my pencil on the table, this

would be considered as one event in everyday language; but think of the innumerable facts it involves: the motions of all the molecules of my fingers, of the table, of the surrounding air! It would be hopeless to give a complete description of such an "event," and still more impossible to find its complete *cause*; we know that, for instance, the position of the moon would somehow enter into the cause, as the presence of the moon contributes to the gravitational field in which the pencil is falling.

So science does not speak of causes and effects, but of functional relations between measurable quantities; it starts with measurement of quantities rather than with description of occurrences. And it seems to be the essence of every law of nature that it states the way in which the values of some quantities measured at certain places and times depend on the values of some other quantities measured at certain other places and times.

This introduction of mathematical functions is an enormous advantage, but we must not believe that all our difficulties in interpreting causality can be overcome by simply abandoning the use of the terms cause and effect.

In the first place it must be remembered that the scientific conception of nature as a system of functional relations is a sort of idealized scheme which acquires physical meaning only by being applied or attached to reality; it is referred to reality only by observation, of course; and every observation is an observation of an event (such as the change of color of a liquid in a chemical experiment or the motion of the mercury in a thermometer), which will be regarded as isolated and as causally connected with other events (e.g., certain manipulations of the observer). In this way the old concepts which have been eliminated from the system of science seem to reappear when we examine the actual experiences on which science is based. It is true that a careful analysis would show that this is not a very serious predicament in itself, and it is also true that the difficulties connected with the isolation of events can be minimized by careful experimental arrangements; but the recent development of physics has shown that there is a definite limit to this isolation, and the consequences of this fact *are* serious.

In the second place, we must not rejoice too much in the replacement of the concept of causality by the concept of law, before we are quite sure that we know exactly what we mean by the word *law*. Is it really a satisfactory explanation to say (as we did a little while ago) that a law of nature is a function between measured quantities? I think it is not sufficient. In order to show this let us consider a special form of law which corresponds to the ideas of classical physics (but our arguments would remain true in a more general case).

Let us suppose that there is no "action-at-a-distance," so that the occurrence of any event at a given point of space and at a given time would depend only on what happened immediately before and in the immediate vicinity of that point. The laws describing such a kind of dependence would be expressed by differential equations. Now consider a physical system within a closed surface, the happenings in which were completely governed by these laws: then it seemed possible for classical physics to give a perfectly precise expression of the Principle of Causality for such a system. It used to be given by the following statement: "The state of the system (i.e., the totality of the events within our surface) at any time t is completely determined by its state at some other time t_0 and by all the events which happen *on* the closed boundary during the whole time-interval $t - t_0$." (If *nothing* were happening at the boundary—i.e., if we had a completely isolated system—or if there were no boundary—which would be the case if our system were the whole universe, as Laplace considered it in his famous formula—then the same statement could be made more simple by saying that the state of the system at *any* particular time determines its states at *all* other times.) This is, of course, a formulation of determinism.

We must analyze very carefully what can be meant by this statement. The clue must evidently be found in the word "determine," which is used here. The word indicates a certain relation between two states of the system: one which determines and one which is determined. This is, of course, nothing but our *causal* relation, and we see that the word determination has taken the place of the word causation. This does not seem to be a great advantage; but let us see how the scientist uses the word determination—then we shall find out what he *means* by it. When he says that the state E at the time t is determined

by the state C at the time t_0, he means that his differential equations (his Laws) enable him to *calculate* E, if C and the boundary conditions are known to him. Determination therefore means Possibility of Calculation, *and nothing else*.

It does *not* mean that C in some magic way *produces* E. And yet we can now understand how the idea of production comes in and what justification can be given for it. "To produce" literally means to bring forth; and in a very definite sense the calculation does "bring out" if not E, at least the complete description of E, i.e., the values of all the physical quantities which are characteristic of E. From the logical point of view a mathematical computation is a process of analysis which can bring out only what is already contained in the presuppositions; and in fact, the description of the initial state C (and of the boundary conditions) together with the Laws do logically contain the description of all the succeeding states E, in the same sense in which all the terms of a series may be said to be contained in the law of the series together with its first term.

Here again it might seem as if the causal relation were in some way reduced to a sort of logical inherence of the effect in the cause, and as if a logical interpretation of "production" were found; but a moment's thought shows the futility of such an interpretation. For calculation can only show what will occur *if* certain laws are valid, but it can never show that they *are* valid. In other words: the logical equivalence does not hold between cause and effect, or in fact between anything in reality, but it holds only between the two propositions: (1) State C has been observed and certain states E will follow; and (2) State C has been observed and certain laws L are valid. The meaning of these two propositions is identical (if the proper substitutions are made for E and L), and the calculation is nothing but the analytic method of transforming one into the other. Mathematical analysis teaches us how to express a sequence of events by means of a Law, *if* there is a certain order in nature; the principle of causality asserts that there *is* order in nature. These are two entirely different and independent things. Logical necessity and "production" belong to calculus, causality belongs to real nature.

We see again that laws of nature must not be thought of as supernatural powers forcing nature into a certain behavior and thereby "producing" the effects of given causes, but simply as abbreviated expressions of the order in which events do follow each other.

. . .

We now return to our analysis of the concept of determination. We found it to mean "possibility of calculation"; and from what we have seen thus far it seems that possibility of calculation implied nothing but the existence of some mathematical functions which connect the values of the quantities that describe different states of a physical system at different times. But here we strike a serious difficulty. It is this: whatever the succeeding states of a physical system may be—after we have observed them it is *always* possible to find functions connecting them in such a way that if one of those states is given, all the rest of them can be computed by means of those functions. The mathematician assures us that he has no difficulty in constructing analytical functions which with any desired degree of approximation will represent any succeeding states of the system, however chaotic it may be. This proves that we cannot identify Law with functional relations; for if *any* sequence of events can be described by functions, then the possibility of such a description cannot be used to distinguish an orderly or causal sequence from a chaotic or non-causal one. The principle of causality would always be true: whatever happened, it would be a mere tautology which says nothing about nature.

We conclude that "possibility of calculation" cannot simply mean possibility of description by functions; something more is needed. It is usually thought that what is needed is some kind of specification of the functions, so that laws of nature must be defined by functions possessing some special property.

The first property which presents itself here is *simplicity*. Many writers hold that the difference between a causal chain of events and a noncausal one is this, that the former can be described by simple function, the latter only by complicated ones. I do not doubt for a moment that all the laws we know, and probably even all the laws we shall ever know, do comply with this criterion, which I usually call the aesthetic criterion, because simplicity

seems to be an aesthetic rather than a scientific concept. Nevertheless, it is entirely unsatisfactory from the logical point of view, and this for two reasons. The first one is that we cannot give a strict definition that will enable us to distinguish between simple and complicated functions; I suppose the latter ones are those that can be handled successfully only by a very skillful mathematician—but evidently no such definition could have the necessary objectivity and clarity. The second reason is that we can easily imagine circumstances in which nobody would refuse to regard even the most complicated function as a perfectly good law of nature. This would be the case if all the predictions made by the complicated formula were found to be true, and no simpler function of equal efficiency could be discovered. For these reasons the logician must dismiss the criterion of simplicity as inadequate.

Another criterion of causality that might be chosen consists in postulating that the functional relations describing the flow of events must not contain the space and time coordinates in an explicit form. This sounds rather technical, but it is nothing but the mathematical formulation of the principle: Same cause, same effect. It means that if under certain circumstances at a particular place and time a certain sequence of events is observed, then a similar sequence of events will be observed if similar circumstances occur at some other place and some other time. This postulate has been adopted by such a great authority as Maxwell, and it may perhaps be regarded as a special form of the simplicity principle, as the absence of explicit space and time values could be considered as a particular kind of simplicity of the functions. The postulate is fulfilled if space and time enter only as the independent variables of differential equations, and this is true in our present-day physics.

Now again I certainly expect that all laws of nature will actually conform to Maxwell's criterion just as well as to the general criterion of simplicity (if they did not, it would mean that we should have to change our views concerning the nature of space and time considerably)—none the less it remains theoretically possible that a future physics might have to introduce formulae which contain space and time in an explicit form, so that the same cause would never have the same effect, but the effect would also depend, in a definite way, e.g., on the date, and would be different tomorrow, or next month, or next year.

However improbable this may seem to be—the philosopher has to take into account all possibilities, no matter how remote they are; he must never tie himself down to the particular state of science at this time, which is always only one of many possible states; his realm is the field of possibilities, because it is the realm of all meaningful propositions. In our case he must ask himself: would we regard the universe as noncausal or chaotic, if it did not conform to Maxwell's criterion? And the answer is: by no means! If we knew formulae which we could use just as successfully for the description of that strange universe as we use our present scientific formulae to describe the actual world, we should have to say that both worlds were completely orderly. This brings us to the essential point, at last: we have to see how the formulae are actually *used*.

Instead of inventing definitions of *law*, which always prove more or less artificial, we must direct our attention to the way in which the scientist really tests a formula in each particular case and tries to verify whether or not it represents the law for which he is looking. He first constructs a function by connecting all the observed data, and he will certainly try to construct it so that it obeys Maxwell's criterion as well as that of simplicity—but he is not content with this. His success in finding a function of this nature is not a sufficient, and not even a necessary, reason for him to be convinced that the law is found. He will proceed to apply it to *new* data, which have not been used for the construction of his formula. If observation shows that the function fits the new data he will triumph and believe that it expresses the real law. He will *believe* it; he will never be absolutely sure, because new data may come up in the future which will not fit into the formula. But, of course, his faith will grow with the number of verifications. The mathematician can always construct an analytic formula that will cover all the observed data, but he can never guarantee that it will also fit future data which he does not know yet and which nature will furnish after having been asked to do so by the skillful experiments and observations of the scientist.

Now at last we know what is meant by the "possibility of calculation" which we found to

be the essence of causality or "determination." It does not mean possibility of finding a function with particular mathematical properties, but it means possibility of *applying* a function with *any* properties to such data (or "events" or "states of a physical system") as have not been used for its construction. The technical term for this procedure is "extrapolation," and so we can now say that in science causality stands for possibility of extrapolation. From the way in which we introduce the term "possibility" it is clear that it implies correspondence with observation or (which is saying the same thing) with reality: when we say that it is possible to extrapolate from a physical formula we mean that the extrapolated values will correspond to the values which are really observed. This process of computing values which are confirmed by future experience is usually called *prediction*, and so we may say quite simply: a Law is a formula which allows us to make true predictions.

The criterion of causality is successful prediction. That is all we can say. It is not much more than what we said in the beginning, after analyzing causality in everyday life, where we ended by speaking of regularity of sequences. Regularity of occurrence in the ordinary sense is just a particular case in which the method of prediction is especially easy to grasp. Our former difficulty in understanding causality was that we were unable to say when a causal judgment should be considered definitely verified, and therefore could give no definite meaning to it. This difficulty has not been overcome by our analysis of scientific law. Even in science there is no way of ever establishing a law as absolutely valid and thereby proving the existence of causation in any particular case. We can never be sure that *all* predictions from a law will come true. Although in practice a small number of successful predictions will suffice to cause a very strong belief in a law, and sometimes even one single verification will be regarded as sufficient: from the strictly logical point of view all our formulae will always remain hypotheses, theoretically it will always remain possible to say that the verifications were just "chance."

There is no room to discuss the logical consequences of this situation and we must turn to the most recent development of science in order to see whether it agrees with the results of our analysis. Does it support the view that the *only* criterion, and therefore the only meaning, of causality is successful prediction?

It is gratifying to state that the recent discussions of causality in connection with the quantum theory afford a very striking confirmation of our view. As is well known, the quantum theory in its present form asserts that a strictly deterministic description of nature is impossible; in other words, that physics has to abandon the Principle of Causality.

What does physics mean when it thus denies causality? In order to find this out we need only examine the specific reasons which are given for this denial.

If causality were defined by simplicity of mathematical functions, as was done by the aesthetic criterion, then its denial would mean that it is impossible to describe nature by simple functions. Does science assert this? Does it despair of causality because the formulae it has to use are too complicated? Certainly not! Therefore its rejection of determinism is not guided by the aesthetic criterion.

If causality were essentially defined by Maxwell's criterion, i.e., by the principle that the describing functions must not contain space and time coordinates in an explicit form (which, as we saw it, is equivalent to the rule "same cause, same effect"), then denial of determinism would mean: it is impossible to describe nature by equations in which space and time do not occur explicitly. And is this the great revelation made by the quantum theory? By no means! Therefore violation of Maxwell's criterion is not the reason why determinism is rejected.

What *is* the real reason? None other but that it is found impossible to *predict* phenomena with perfect accuracy. Within certain well-defined limits it is impossible to construct functions that can be used for extrapolation. This is the essential consequence of Heisenberg's famous Uncertainty Principle, and it proves that the physicist in his actual proceeding has adopted just that view of causality which we have been advocating.

It is true that the formulation given by most physicists seems to be a little different. They usually insist on the impossibility, not of prediction of future states, but of complete description of the present state of a physical system. But an easy analysis shows that this must be interpreted as involving incapacity of

extrapolation. For the sake of simplicity we may assume that a description of a system would be complete if it included the positions of all the electric particles composing the system at the present moment, and the velocities of all these particles at the same moment. But what is "velocity"? What does it mean in actual experience when we assert that a certain particle moves with a certain velocity? It means nothing but that the particle which at one moment has been observed at a definite particular place will, after a definite short interval of time, be observed at another definite place. Thus assigning a certain velocity to a particle at a given moment means predicting its position at a given future moment. Theoretically, the Principle of Indeterminacy does not make it impossible to observe two succeeding positions of a particle in a short interval of time and assign to it a velocity equal to the ratio of the distance and the time interval, but in this way we have described only the *past* behavior of the particle—or, I should rather say, its *observed* behavior. As soon as we try to use this value of velocity for an extrapolation in order to get a future position of the particle, the Uncertainty Principle steps in to tell us that our attempt is in vain; our value of velocity is no good for such a prediction, our own observation will have changed the velocity in an unknown way, therefore the particle will probably not be found in the predicted place, and there is no possibility of knowing where it could be found.

In this way the concept of velocity is connected with prediction, and only because there is no predictability here, does the ordinary procedure of science (which is implied by the words Law and Causation) become inapplicable.

Perhaps it is not unnecessary to remind the reader that these consequences of the Uncertainty Principle become practically serious only when we are concerned with very small particles whose position we try to describe with unlimited accuracy. If we are content to determine the position with a certain approximation, we shall be able to predict future positions with a probability the exact amount of which is stated by Heisenberg's formula. And if we have to do with larger particles, such as molecules for instance, not to speak of rifle bullets or billiard balls, the approximation and the probability reach such enormous amounts that the certainty of our predictions becomes incomparably greater than the accuracy of our most perfect observations.

This is very fortunate from the practical point of view, for it means that for all ordinary purposes of science and everyday life the deterministic attitude not only remains justified but is the only one compatible with our knowledge of nature. If it were otherwise, if Planck's constant h, which in a way measures the uncertainty of our predictions, were more than 10 times greater than it actually is, then the Principle of Indeterminacy would make our lives very difficult, because hardly anything could ever be planned ahead. If human beings could exist at all in a world of so much disorder, they would have to give up many pursuits, such as medicine, engineering, and they would have to give up morality. For there can be no morals without responsibility, and there could be no responsibility if human actions were simply random events in the world. (Lack of determination means pure chance, randomness; the alternative "either determination or chance" is a logical one, there is no escape from it, no third possibility.) A serious amount of indeterminism would be nothing to rejoice about, it would mean fatal disorder. Such considerations make us wonder why metaphysicians so often thought it necessary to defend indeterminism for ethical or religious reasons; they have been misled by a strange confusion concerning the terms necessity and law, freedom and determinism. But we are not concerned with this here.

The situation is a little different in the case of those philosophical writers and philosophizing scientists who have derived great satisfaction from the recent development of science because the indeterminism to which it leads is a *physical* indeterminism. They rejoice in the incomplete determination of nature by physical laws because it seems to leave room for Mind in the universe. If there are little gaps in physical causation, why should they not be filled by the activity of mental factors, such as thoughts or feelings, which would in this way have some influence on the course of events?

If this view were logically sound it would mean that the happenings in the physical world which modern physics leaves partly indetermined could be made deterministic again by the introduction of mental events (either partly, if only some of the gaps were supposed to be filled, or wholly, if mental factors were believed to be at work everywhere). Reduced to sober scientific language this would mean that the psychologist could make exact predictions in cases where the physicist must fail; if, e.g., the laws of physics could not tell him where a certain electron was going, he would still be able to predict the future position of this electron by consulting certain psychological laws.

I admit that there might be some intellectual satisfaction in this restoration, or partial restoration, of determinism; but I fail to see why the metaphysician should welcome it as satisfying his deepest desires. It is only through some secret additions and misinterpretations that this view could seem so valuable to him. But in reality I am convinced that the whole view is logically unsound. To regard physical and mental events as two different entities which between themselves determine the course of the universe in the described manner seems to me to be a particularly shallow and crude attempt to deal with the so-called Psychophysical Problem, and to rest on a very naïve and uncritical use of the terms "physical" and "mental." A view that succeeds in finding a place for Mind in the universe only with the utmost difficulty and only after physics has discovered the principle of indeterminacy—such a view, I am sure, must be based on an analysis of the term "mind" which is fundamentally wrong. The true analysis of the terms "physical" and "mental" (with which we are not concerned here) will show that they cannot be used in this dualistic way without severe violation of the rules of philosophical grammar, and that the understanding of the real meaning of these terms has nothing to do with any particular theory of physics and is quite independent of any present doctrines and of the progress of science.

No metaphysical conclusion can be drawn from the discoveries of recent science—as indeed such conclusions cannot be drawn from *anything*. Science, as the pursuit of truth, can and must stimulate philosophy, as the pursuit of meaning, but one of these can never be the explanation of the other.

We found that recent science confirmed the view that causality must be understood as meaning "possibility of extrapolation," because we found that this was exactly the sense in which the word is used in quantum physics. But, of course, our view and our analysis in no way presuppose the truth of the present state of quantum physics. If future science should abandon the principle of indeterminacy and should return to a deterministic interpretation of nature, our result would not be affected. For determinism could be restored only by showing that the laws of nature did not set any finite limit to the accuracy of our predictions. This would mean that we should have no more reason definitely to lose confidence in the applicability of our extrapolations, and it would presuppose just that view of causality which I have been trying to explain here.

On the So-Called Idea of Causation*

The argument of this paper may be summarized as follows. Causal propositions (propositions of the type "*x* causes *y*") are ambiguous. Such a proposition may have any one of three meanings (possibly more; but three is enough for this paper). The ambiguity, however, is of a rather odd kind. Sense I, which is historically the original sense, is presupposed by the others, and remains strictly speaking the one and only "proper" sense. When we assert propositions containing the word cause in senses II and III, we are "saying" one thing and "meaning" another; we are describing certain things as if they were things of a kind which we do not actually believe them to be. This always has an element of danger in it: the danger of inadvertently beginning to "mean" what one had only intended to "say," i.e., of thinking that things are what we describe them as if they were. This danger is much worse when our "metaphors" get "mixed." This is what has happened with the so-called "idea of causation" from the time of Kant onward. It is a confusion of certain characteristics belonging to sense II with certain others belonging to sense III. Nothing can be done, therefore, toward clearing up our minds about causation, by merely analyzing the idea as it stands and detailing the various elements it contains; for these elements are mutually contradictory. We must carry the process further, by segregating the elements under different heads, and distinguishing these as different "senses" of the word. But even this is not enough. A further step in the process is needed: namely, a critical discussion of each "sense" taken singly. When this is done it will be found that the best way of avoiding confusion will be to restrict our use of the word cause to occasions on which it is used in its "proper" sense, No. I; that on the occasions on which we use it in sense II we should be wise to use instead the terminology of means and ends; and that when we use it in sense III we should do better to speak of "laws" and their "instances."

I

In the first sense of the word cause, that which is caused is the free and deliberate act of a conscious and responsible agent, and "causing" him to do it means affording him a motive for doing it. For "causing," we may substitute "making," "inducing," "persuading," "urging," "forcing," "compelling," according to differences in the kind of motive in question.

This is at the present time a current and familiar sense of the word (together with its cognates, correlatives, and equivalents) in English, and of the corresponding words in other modern languages; also of *causa* in ancient Latin and αἴτιον in ancient Greek. A headline in a newspaper in 1936 ran "Mr. Baldwin's speech causes adjournment of House." This did not mean that Mr. Baldwin's speech compelled the Speaker to adjourn the House whether or no that event conformed with his own ideas and intentions; it meant that on hearing Mr. Baldwin's speech the Speaker freely made up his mind to adjourn. In the same sense we say that a solicitor's letter causes a man to pay a debt, or that bad weather causes him to return from an expedition.

. . .

A cause in this sense consists of two elements, a *causa quod* or efficient cause and a

* R. G. Collingwood, "On the So-Called Idea of Causation," *Proceedings of the Aristotelian Society*, XXXVIII (1938), 85–108, reprinted by permission of The Aristotelian Society, London. Footnotes have been renumbered.

causa ut or final cause. The *causa quod* is a situation, or state of things existing; the *causa ut* is a purpose, or state of things to be brought about. Neither of these could be a cause if the other were absent. A man who tells his stockbroker to sell a certain holding may be caused to act thus by a rumor about the financial position of that company; but this rumor would not cause him to sell out unless he wanted to avoid being involved in the affairs of an unsound business. And *per contra,* a man's wish to avoid falling over a precipice would not cause him to stop walking in a certain direction if he knew there was no precipice in that direction.

The *causa quod* is not a situation or state of things as such, it is a situation or state of things known or believed by the agent in question to exist. If a prospective litigant briefs a certain barrister because of his exceptional ability, the cause of his doing so is not this ability simply as such, it is this ability as something known to the litigant or believed in by him.

The *causa ut* is not a desire or wish as such, it is an intention. A man is "caused" to act in a certain way not by wanting to act in that way (for it is possible to want so to act without so acting) but by meaning to act in that way. There may be cases where mere desire leads to action without the intermediate phase of intention; but such action is not deliberate.

Causes of this kind may come into operation through the act of a second conscious and responsible agent, in so far as he (1) informs or persuades the first that a certain state of things exists, as when a man's solicitor informs or persuades him of a certain barrister's exceptional ability; or (2) exhorts or otherwise persuades the first to form a certain intention. This second agent is said to "cause" the first to do a certain act, or to "make him do it."

The act so caused, however, is still an act; it could not be done (and therefore could not be caused) unless the agent did it of his own free will. If A causes B to do an act β, β is B's act and not A's; B is a free agent in doing it, and is responsible for it. If β is a murder, which A persuaded B to commit by pointing out certain facts or urging certain expediencies, B is the murderer. There is no contradiction between the proposition that the act β was caused by A, and the proposition

that B was a free agent in respect of β, and is thus responsible for it. On the contrary, the first proposition implies the second.

Nevertheless, in this case A is said to "share the responsibility" for the act β. This does not imply that a responsibility is a divisible thing, which would be absurd; an absurdity into which people do no doubt fall, e.g., when they speak of collective guarantees. It means that whereas B is responsible for the act β, A is responsible for his own act, α, viz., the act of pointing out certain facts to B or urging upon him certain expediencies, whereby he induces him to commit the act β. When a child, accused of a misdeed, rounds on its accuser saying, "you made me do it," he is not excusing himself, he is implicating his accuser as an accessory. This is what Adam was doing when he said "the woman whom thou gavest me, she gave me of the tree and I did eat."

A man is said to act "on his own responsibility" or "on his sole responsibility" when (1) his knowledge or belief about the situation is not dependent on information or persuasion from anyone else, and (2) his intentions or purposes are similarly independent. In this case (the case in which a man is ordinarily said to exhibit "initiative") his action is not uncaused. It still has both a *causa quod* and a *causa ut*. But because he has done for himself, unaided, the double work of envisaging the situation and forming the intention, which in the alternative case another man (who is therefore said to cause his action) has done for him, he can now be said to *cause* his own action as well as to *do* it. If he invariably acted in that way, the total complex of his activities could be called self-causing (*causa sui*); an expression which simply refers to an absence of persuasion or inducement on the part of another, and has been unintelligently denounced as nonsensical only because people will not ask themselves what they mean by the word cause.

II

In sense II, no less than in sense I, the word cause expresses an idea relative to human action; but the action in this case is an action intended to control, not other human beings, but things in "nature," or "physical" things. In this sense, the "cause" of an event in nature is the handle, so to speak, by which we can manipulate it. If we want to produce or to prevent such a thing, and cannot produce or prevent it immediately (as we can produce or prevent certain movements of our own bodies), we set about looking for its "cause." The question "what is the cause of an event y?" means in this case "how can we produce or prevent y at will?"

This sense of the word may be defined as follows. *A cause is an event or state of things which it is in our power to produce or prevent, and by producing or preventing which we can produce or prevent that whose cause it is said to be.* When I speak of "producing" something, I refer to such occasions as when, e.g., one turns a switch and thus produces the state of things described by the proposition "the switch is now at the ON position." By preventing something I mean producing something incompatible with it, e.g., turning the switch to the OFF position.

This is an extremely common sense in modern everyday usage. The cause of a bruise is the kick which a man received on his ankle; the cause of malaria is the bite of a mosquito; the cause of a boat's sinking is her being overloaded; the cause of books going mouldy is their being kept in a damp room; the cause of a person's sweating is that he has taken aspirin; the cause of a furnace going out in the night is that the draught door was insufficiently open; the cause of seedlings dying is that nobody watered them; and so forth.

The search for causes in sense II is "natural science" in that sense of the phrase in which natural science is what Aristotle calls a "practical science," valued not for its truth pure and simple but for its utility, for the "power over nature" which it gives us: Baconian science, where "knowledge is power" and where "nature is conquered by obeying her." The field of a "practical science" is the contingent, or in Aristotle's terminology "what admits of being otherwise." The switch, for example, is on, but it admits of being off; i.e., I find by experiment that I am able to turn it to the OFF position. To discover that things are contingent is to discover that we can produce and prevent them.

A conspicuous example of practical natural science is medicine. A great deal of time and money is now being spent on "cancer research," whose purpose is "to discover the cause of cancer." If we knew the cause of it, we should be able to prevent or cure it;

that is the aim of all this work. But why should it be assumed that knowing the cause of cancer would enable us to produce or prevent it? Suppose someone claimed to have discovered the cause of cancer, but added that his discovery though genuine would not in practice be of any use because the cause he had discovered was not a thing that could be produced or prevented at will. Such a person would be universally ridiculed and despised. No one would admit that he had done what he claimed to do. It would be pointed out that he did not know what the word cause (in the context of medicine, be it understood) meant. For in such a context a proposition of the form "x causes y" implies the proposition "x is something that can be produced or prevented at will" as part of the definition of "cause."

. . .

A "cause" in sense II never means something which is able by itself to produce the "effect." When in this sense we say that x causes y, we are never talking about x by itself. We are always talking about x in combination with other things which we do not specify; these being called *conditiones sine quibus non*. For example, damp will not cause books to go mouldy unless there are mould-spores about.

The relation between the cause and these "conditions," as I shall call them, has often been misunderstood, for example, by Mill. Mill defines the cause of an event as its invariable antecedent (a definition applicable to sense III, not to sense II). If so, the event should follow given the cause and nothing else. If certain conditions are necessary, over and above the cause, in order that the event should follow (which is true of sense II not of sense III), then surely the *true* cause is not what we have just called the cause but this *plus* the said conditions. Mill concludes that the true cause is the sum of a set of conditions, and that what people ordinarily call the cause is one of these, arbitrarily selected and, by a mere misuse of language, dignified with a name that properly belongs only to the whole set.

Closer inspection would have shown Mill that this "selection" is by no means arbitrary. It is made according to a definite principle. If my car "conks out" on a hill and I wonder what the cause is, I shall not consider my problem solved by a passer-by who tells me that the top of a hill is further away from the earth's center than its bottom, and that consequently more power is needed to take a car uphill than to take her along the level. All this is quite true; what the passer-by has described is one of the conditions which, together, form the "true cause" of my car's stopping; and as he has "arbitrarily selected" one of these and called it the cause, he has done just what Mill says we always do. But now suppose an A.A. man comes along, opens the bonnet, holds up a loose high-tension lead, and says "look here, sir, you're running on three cylinders." My problem is now solved. I know the cause of the stoppage. It is *the* cause, just because it has not been "arbitrarily selected"; it has been correctly identified as the thing that I can put right, after which the car will go properly. If had I been a person who could flatten out hills by stamping on them, the passer-by would have been right to call my attention to the hill as the cause of the stoppage; not because the hill is a hill, but because I can flatten it out.

The cause is not "arbitrarily selected," it is identified according to a principle which is in fact the definition of the term cause in sense II. It is not, properly speaking, "selected" at all; for selection implies that the person selecting has before him a finite number of things from among which he takes his choice. But this does not happen. In the first place, the conditions of any given event are quite possibly infinite in number, so that no one *could* thus marshal them for selection even if he tried. In the second place, no one ever tries to enumerate them completely. Why should he? If I find that I can get a result by certain means, I may be pretty sure that I should not be getting it unless a great many conditions were fulfilled; but so long as I get it I do not mind what these conditions are. If owing to a change in one of them I fail to get it, I still do not want to know what they *all* are; I only want to know what the one is that has changed.

From this a principle follows which I shall call " the relativity of causes." Suppose that the conditions of an event *y* include three things, α, β, γ; and suppose that there are three persons, A, B, C, of whom A is able to produce or prevent α and only α; B is able to produce or prevent β and only β; and C is able to produce or prevent γ and only γ. Then

if each of them asks "what was the cause of *y*?" each will have to give a different answer. For A, α is the cause; for B, β; and for C, γ. The principle may be stated by saying that *for any given person, the cause of a given thing is that one of its conditions which he is able to produce or prevent.* For example, a car skids while cornering at a certain point, turns turtle, and bursts into flame. From the car-driver's point of view, the cause of the accident was cornering too fast, and the lesson is that one must drive more carefully. From the county surveyor's point of view, the cause was a defective road-surface, and the lesson is that one must make skid-proof roads. From the motor-manufacturer's point of view, the cause was defective design, and the lesson is that one must place the center of gravity lower.

If one of these three parties "threw the blame" for the accident on one of the others, if for example the surveyor said "it is the business of drivers to prevent accidents of that sort; it isn't mine," we all know that nothing would be done, by him at any rate, toward preventing them; that is to say, his "knowledge" of their cause would be a "knowledge" that did not result in power. But since a cause in this sense of the word is by definition something whose knowledge *is* power, this means that his so-called knowledge is not knowledge at all. The proposition in which he states it is in fact a nonsense proposition: "the cause of *y* from my point of view, i.e., that one of its conditions which I am able to produce or prevent, is something which somebody else is able to produce or prevent, but I am not." Hence the futility of blaming other people in respect of events in which we and they are together involved. Everyone knows that such blame is futile; but without such analysis of the idea of cause as I am here giving, it is not easy to see why it should be.

A further corollary of the same principle is that, for a person who is not able to produce or prevent any of its conditions, a given event has no cause at all, and any statement he makes about it will be a nonsense statement. Thus, the managing director of a large insurance company once told me that his wide experience of motor accidents had convinced him that the cause of all accidents was people driving too fast. This of course was a nonsense statement; but one could expect nothing better from a man whose practical concern with these affairs was limited to their after-effects. In sense II of the word cause, only a person who is practically concerned with a certain kind of event can form an opinion about its cause. For a mere spectator there are no causes. When Hume tried to show how the mere act of spectation could in time generate the idea of a cause, where "cause" meant the cause of empirical science, he was trying to explain how something happens which in fact does not happen.

If sciences are constructed consisting of causal propositions in sense II of the word cause, they will of course be in essence codifications of the various ways in which the people who construct them can bend nature to their purposes, and of the means by which in each case this can be done. Their constituent propositions will be (*a*) experimental (*b*) general.

(*a*) In calling them experimental I mean that their assertion will depend on "experiment." No amount of "observation" will serve to establish such a proposition; for any such proposition is a declaration of our ability to produce or prevent a certain state of things by the use of certain means, and no one knows what he can do, or how he can do it, until he tries. Nevertheless, he may by "observing" and "thinking" form the opinion that he can *probably* do a given thing that resembles one he has done in the past.

(*b*) Because the proposition "*x* causes *y*" is a constituent part of a practical science, it is essentially something that can be "applied" to cases arising in practice; that is to say, the terms *x* and *y* are not individuals but universals, and the proposition itself, rightly understood, reads "any instance of *x* is a thing whose production or prevention is means, respectively, of producing or preventing some instance of *y*." It would be nonsense, in this sense of the word cause, to inquire after the cause of any individual thing as such. It is a peculiarity of sense II, that every causal proposition is a "general proposition" or "propositional function." In sense I, every causal proposition is an "individual proposition," which cannot be read in the above form. In sense III, causal propositions might equally well be either individual or general.

If the above analysis of the cause-effect relation (in sense II) into a means-end relation is correct, why do people describe this means-end relation in cause-effect terminology? People do not choose words at random, they choose them because they think them appropriate. If they apply cause-effect terminology to things whose relation is really that of means and end, the reason must be that they want to apply to those things some idea which is conveyed by the cause-effect terminology and not by the means-end terminology. What is this idea? The answer, I think, is not doubtful. The cause-effect terminology conveys an idea not only of one thing's leading to another, but of one thing's forcing another to happen or exist; an idea of power or compulsion or constraint.

From what impression, as Hume pertinently asks, is this idea derived? I answer, from impressions received in our social life, in the practical relations of man to man; specifically, from the impression of "compelling" or "causing" some other man to do something when, by argument or command or threat or the like, we place him in a situation in which he can only carry out his intentions by doing that thing; and conversely, from the impression of being compelled or caused to do something.

Why, then, did people think it appropriate to apply this idea, thus derived, to the case of actions in which we achieve our ends by means, not of other human beings, but of things in nature? In order to answer this question we must remember that sense II of the word cause is especially a Greek sense, and in modern times especially associated with the revival of Greek ideas in the earlier Renaissance thinkers; and that both the Greeks and the earlier Renaissance thinkers held quite seriously an animistic theory of nature. They thought of what we call the material or physical world as a living organism or complex of living organisms, each with its own sensations and desires and intentions and thoughts. In Plato's *Timaeus,* and in the Renaissance Platonists whose part in the formation of modern science was so decisive, the constant use of language with animistic implications is neither an accident nor a metaphor; these expressions are meant to be taken literally and to imply what they seem to imply, namely, that the way in which men use what we nowadays call inorganic nature as means to our ends is not in principle different from the way in which we use other men. We use other men by assuming them to be free agents with wills of their own, and influencing them in such a way that they shall decide to do what is in conformity with our plans. This is "causing" them so to act, in the first and original sense of that word. If "inorganic nature" is alive in much the same way as human beings, we must use it according to the same principles; and therefore we can apply to this use of it the same word "cause" in the same sense, viz., as implying

(1) That there are certain ways in which natural things behave if left to themselves;

(2) That man, being more powerful than they, is able to thwart their inclination to behave in these ways, and by the exercise of his superior magic to make them behave, not as they like, but as he likes.

And if anybody is so truthful as to admit that, in our experimental science, we do constantly use language which taken literally implies all this, but argues that it is "mere metaphor" and never meant to be taken literally, I reply: then express yourself literally; and you will find that all this language about causation disappears, and that you are left with a vocabulary in which all that is said is that we find certain means useful to certain ends.

III

Sense III of the word cause represents an attempt to apply it not to "practical science" but to "theoretical science." I shall first explain the characteristics which would belong to this sense if the attempt were successful, and then consider certain difficulties which in the long run prove fatal to it.

(1) In the contingent world to which sense II belongs, a cause is contingent (*a*) in its existence, as depending for its existence on human volition, (*b*) in its operation, as depending for the production of its effect on *conditiones sine quibus non*. In the necessary world to which sense III belongs, a cause is necessary (*a*) in its existence, as existing whether or no human beings want it to exist, (*b*) in its operation, as producing its effect no matter what else exists or does not exist. There are no *conditiones sine quibus non*. The cause leads to its effect by itself, or "unconditionally"; in other words the relation between cause and effect is a one-one relation. There can be no relativity of causes, and no diversity of effects due to fulfilment or non-fulfilment of conditions.

I propose to distinguish the one-many and many-one[1] character of the cause-effect relation in sense II from its one-one character in sense III by calling these senses *loose* and *tight*, respectively. A loose cause requires some third thing extraneous both to itself and to its effect to bind the two together; a tight cause is one whose connection with its effect is independent of such adventitious aids.

In order to illustrate the implications of sense III, I will refer to the contradiction between the traditional denial of *actio in distans* (which, I suppose, would hold as against action across a lapse of time, no less than across a distance in space) and the assumption, commonly made nowadays, that a cause precedes its effect in time. I shall argue that *actio in distans* is perfectly intelligible in sense II, but nonsense in sense III.

If I set fire to the end of a time-fuse, and five minutes later the charge at its other end explodes, there is a "causal" connection between the first and second events, and a time-interval of five minutes between them. But this interval is occupied by the burning of the fuse at a determinate rate of feet per minute; and this process is a *conditio sine qua non* of the causal efficacy ascribed to the first event. That is to say, the connection between the lighting of the fuse and the detonation of the charge is "causal" in the loose sense, not the tight one. If in the proposition "*x* causes the explosion" we wish to use the word cause in the tight sense, *x* must include any such *conditio sine qua non*. That is, it must include the burning of the whole fuse; not its burning until "just before" that process reaches the detonator, for then there would still be an interval to be bridged, but its burning until the detonator is reached. Only then is the cause in sense III complete; and when it is complete it produces its effect, not afterward (however soon afterward) but then. Cause in sense III is simultaneous with effect.

Similarly, it is coincident with its effect in space. The cause of the explosion is where the explosion is. For suppose *x* causes *y*, and suppose that *x* is in a position p_1 and *y* in a position p_2, the distance from p_1 to p_2 being δ. If "cause" is used in sense II, δ may be any distance, so long as it is bridged by a

---

[1] One-many, because a cause in sense II leads to its effect only when the *conditiones sine quibus non* are fulfilled. Many-one, because of the relativity of causes.

series of events which are *conditiones sine quibus non* of *x* causing *y*. But if "cause" is used in sense III, δ must equal zero. For if it did not, p_2 would be any position on the surface of a sphere whose center was p_1 and whose radius would be δ; so the relation between p_1 and p_2 would be a one-many relation. But the relation between *x* and *y*, where *x* causes *y* in sense III, is a one-one relation. Therefore where δ does not equal zero, *x* cannot cause *y* in sense III.

The denial of *actio in distans,* spatial or temporal, where the "agent" is a cause in sense III, is therefore logically involved in the definition of sense III.

(2) The main difficulty about sense III is to explain what is meant by saying that a cause "produces" or "necessitates" its effect. When similar language is used of senses I and II we know what it means: in sense I it means that *x* affords somebody a motive for doing *y*, in sense II that *x* is somebody's means of bringing *y* about. But what (since it cannot mean either of these) does it mean in sense III?

There are two well-known answers to this question, which may be called the rationalist and empiricist answers respectively.

(i) The rationalist answer runs: "necessitation means implication." A cause, on this view, is a "ground" and its relation to its effect is the relation of ground to consequent, a logical relation. When someone says that *x* necessitates *y* he means on this view that *x* implies *y*, and is claiming the same kind of insight into *y* which one has (for example) into the length of one side of a triangle given the lengths of the other two sides and the included angle. Whatever view one takes as to the nature of implication, one must admit that in such a case the length of the third side can be ascertained without measuring it and even without seeing it, e.g., when it lies on the other side of a hill. The implication theory, therefore, implies that "if the cause is given the effect follows," not only in the sense that if the cause exists the effect actually follows, but that if the cause is thought the effect follows logically. That is to say, anyone who wishes to discover the effect of a given thing *x* can discover the answer by simply thinking out the logical implications of *x*. Nothing in the nature of observation or experiment is needed.

This is in itself a tenable position in the sense that, if anyone wants to construct a system of science in which the search for causes means a search for grounds, there is nothing to prevent him from trying. This was in fact what Descartes tried to do. His projected "universal science" was to be a system of grounds and consequents. And if, as is sometimes said, modern physics represents a return in some degree to the Cartesian project, it would seem that the attempt is being made once more. But the rationalist theory of causation, however valuable it may be as the manifesto of a particular scientific enterprise, cannot be regarded as an "analysis" of the causal propositions asserted by existing science. If it were accepted, these propositions would have to be abandoned as untrue. For no one thinks that they can be established by sheer "thinking," that is, by finding the so-called effects to be logically implied in the so-called causes; it is just because this is impossible that the questions, what causes a given effect, and what effect a given cause produces, have to be answered by observation and experiment. Hence the result of establishing a science of the Cartesian type would be, not an analysis of propositions of the type "*x* causes *y*" into propositions of the type "*x* implies *y*," but the disuse of causal propositions in that kind of science and the use of implicational propositions instead; while in the sciences of observation and experiment causal propositions not analyzable into implicational propositions would still be used; the meaning of "necessity" in these causal propositions being still doubtful.

This situation would not be really illuminated by alleging that the sciences in which causal propositions occur are "backward" or "immature sciences." Such a statement would imply that the idea of causation is a half-baked idea which when properly thought out will turn into the different idea of implication. This I take to be the Hegelian theory of the dialectic of concepts, and if anyone wishes to maintain it, I do not want to prevent him; but I must observe that it does not excuse him from answering the question what the half-baked idea is *"an sich,"* that is, before its expected transformation has happened.

(ii) I turn to the empiricist answer: "necessitation means observed uniformity of conjunction." Like the former answer, this one cannot be taken literally; for no one, I think, will pretend that the proposition "*x* necessitates y" means *merely* "all the observed x's have been observed to be conjoined with y's," and does not also imply "x's observed in the future will also be conjoined with y's." In fact the question (so urgent for, e.g., Hume and Mill) how we proceed from the mere experience of conjunction to the assertion of causal connection resolves itself into the question how we pass from the first of these two propositions to the second; so that the proposition "all the observed x's have been observed to be conjoined with y's" is not what we mean by saying "x necessitates y," but is only the empirical evidence on the strength of which we assert the very different proposition "x necessitates y." Thus, if anyone says "necessitation means observed uniformity of conjunction," it must be supposed either that he is talking without thinking; or that he is carelessly expressing what, expressed more accurately, would run "necessitation is something we assert on the strength of observed uniformity of conjunction," without telling us what he thinks necessitation to be; or, thirdly, that he is expressing still more carelessly what should run "in order to assert a necessitation we must pass from the first of the above propositions to the second; now I cannot see how this is possible; therefore we ought never to assert necessitations, but on the occasions when we do assert them we ought to be asserting something quite different, namely, observed conjunction."

(iii) A third answer to our question has been given by Mr. Russell, in a paper[2] of very great importance, to which I shall have to refer again; but I want here and now to express my great admiration for it and my great indebtedness to it. He says "*necessary* is a predicate of a propositional function meaning that it is true for all possible values of its argument or arguments." This I will call the "functional" answer. In so far as it amounts to saying that causation in sense III implies a one-one relation between cause and effect, I entirely agree. But I find myself, very reluctantly, unable to accept all of what I take Mr. Russell to mean.

(α) How, on the functional theory, could anyone ever know a causal proposition to be true, or even know that the facts in his possession tended to justify a belief in it? Only,

I submit, if there is a relation of implication between x and y. For "all *possible* values" of x may be an infinite number; and, even if they are not, it may not be practicable to examine them individually. If a, b, c are the sides of any triangle, we know that $a + b - c$ will always be a positive quantity, because that is implied in the definition of a triangle. Thus the functional theory presupposes the rationalistic or implicational theory, which I have already given reasons for rejecting.

(β) I do not know whether Mr. Russell's statement quoted above was intended to mean "*necessity* is, etc., and never anything else." But if so, I deny it. Necessity has a second meaning, as when on receiving Mr. Hannay's demand for a paper last summer I said "I can't get out of it this time," i.e., "I am necessitated or compelled to read a paper on this occasion." If I say "it is necessary for me to read a paper," the word necessary is not a predicate of a propositional function; it refers to a case of causation in sense I, and means that Mr. Hannay has compelled me so to act. This second sense of necessity, in which it refers to compulsion, is (I shall try to show) the sense which is involved not only in sense I and sense II of the word cause but in sense III also.

(γ) The functional theory would imply that there can be no necessitation and therefore no causation of the individual. Anything that happened only once, like the origin of life on the earth (assuming that all organisms are derived from one original organism and that life exists nowhere else), would be "contingent," not in the sense of being capable of alteration by human interference, but in the sense of being a causeless event in nature. No doubt, it would be impossible on Hume's theory of knowledge, and also on Mill's, to discover the cause of an event *sui generis*; but it seems to be generally agreed nowadays that every event has a cause, even though we cannot discover what its cause is; and if a theory is put forward to the effect that an event *sui generis* has no cause, it may or may not be metaphysically true, but it certainly cannot be a true account of "our idea" of causation; for it contradicts that idea.

(3) Most people think that when we use the word causation in sense III we mean to express it by something different from logical implication, and something more than uniformity of conjunction, whether observed

[2] "On the Notion of Cause." *Proc. Arist. Soc.* (1912), and reprinted in the volume *Mysticism and Logic* (London: Barnes and Noble, 1954).

only, or observed in the past and also expected in the future; and that this "something different" and "something more" is in the nature of compulsion. I think that this view is correct.

We have now to ask the same question which we asked when we found the same idea present in sense II; and we shall have to answer it in the same way. From what impression is this idea derived? It seems to be quite clear that it is derived from our experience of occasions on which we have compelled others to act in certain ways by placing them in situations (or calling their attention to the fact that they are in situations) of such a kind that only by so acting can they realize the intentions we know or rightly assume them to entertain: and conversely, occasions in which we have ourselves been thus compelled. Compulsion is an idea derived from our social experience, and applied in what is called a "metaphorical" way not only to our relations with things in nature (sense II of the word cause) but also to the relations which these things have among themselves (sense III). Causal propositions in sense III are descriptions of natural events in anthropomorphic terms.

The reason why we are in the habit of using these anthropomorphic terms is, of course, that they are traditional. Inquiry into the history of the tradition shows that it grew up in connection with the same animistic theory of nature to which I referred in discussing sense II of the word cause, but that in this case the predominant factor was a theology of neo-Platonic inspiration.

If a man can be said to "cause" certain events in nature by adopting certain means to bringing them about, and if God is conceived anthropomorphically as having faculties like those of the human mind but greatly magnified, it will follow that God also will be regarded as bringing about certain things in nature by the adoption of certain means. Now comes a step in the argument which, if we tried to reconstruct it without historical knowledge, we should probably reconstruct quite wrongly. If x is a thing in nature produced by God as a means of producing y, we might fancy x to be a purely passive instrument in God's hand, having no power of its own, but "inert," as Berkeley in the true spirit of post-Galilean physics insists that matter must be. And in that case God alone would

possess that compulsive force which is expressed by the word cause; that word would not be given as a name to x, and God would be the "sole cause." Actually, God is for medieval thinkers not the "sole cause" but the "first cause." This does not mean the first term in a series of efficient causes (a barbarous misinterpretation of the phrase), but a cause of a peculiar kind, as distinct from "secondary causes." The *Liber de Causis,* a neo-Platonic Arabic work of the ninth century, whose influence on medieval cosmology was at this point decisive, lays it down that God in creating certain instruments for the realization of certain ends confers upon these instruments a power in certain ways like his own, though inferior to it. Thus endowed with a kind of minor and derivative godhead, these instruments accordingly acquire the character of causes, and constitute that division of nature which, according to John the Scot, "both is created and creates." Their causality is thus a special kind of causality existing wholly within nature, whereby one thing in nature produces or necessitates another thing in nature. The words "produces" and "necessitates" are here used literally and deliberately to convey a sense of volition and compulsion; for the anthropomorphic account of natural things is taken as literally true; the activity of these secondary causes is a scaled-down version of God's and God's is a scaled-up version of man's.

This was the atmosphere in which our modern conception of nature took shape, and in which the categories appertaining to that conception were worked out. For in the 16th and 17th centuries, when the animistic conception of nature was replaced among scientists and philosophers by a mechanical one, the word cause was not a novelty; it was a long-established term, and its meaning was rooted in these neo-Platonic notions.

Thus, when we come to Newton, and read the *Scholium* appended to his first eight definitions, we find him using as a matter of course a whole vocabulary which, taken literally, ascribes to "causes" in nature a kind of power which properly belongs to one human being inducing another to act as he wishes him to act. Newton assumes that a cause is something capable of "impressing some force" upon that in which its effect is produced. For example, if what is produced is a movement of a certain body, Newton says that such movement "is neither generated nor altered, but by some force impressed upon the body moved." Here, and throughout his treatment of the subject, it is perfectly clear that for him the idea of causation is the idea of force, compulsion, constraint, exercised by something powerful over another thing which if not under this constraint would behave differently; this hypothetical different behavior being called by contrast "free" behavior. This constraint of one thing in nature by another is simply the secondary causation of medieval cosmology. Taken *au pied de la lettre*, Newton is implying that a billiard-ball struck by another and set in motion would have liked to be left in peace; it is reluctant to move, and this reluctance, which is called inertia, has to be overcome by an effort on the part of the ball that strikes it. This effort costs the striker something, namely, part of its own momentum, which it pays over to the sluggard ball as an inducement to move. I am not suggesting that this reduction of physics to social psychology is the doctrine Newton set out to teach; all I say is that he expounded it, no doubt as a metaphor beneath which the truths of physics are concealed.

It is worth while to notice that in Newton there is no law of universal causation. He not only does not assert that every event must have a cause, he explicitly denies it; and this in two ways. (i) In the case of a body moving freely (even though its motion be what he calls "true" motion as distinct from relative motion), there is uncaused motion; for caused means constrained, and free means unconstrained. If a body moves freely from p_1 to p_2 and thence to p_3, the "event" which is its moving from p_2 to p_3 is in no sense caused by the preceding "event" of its moving from p_1 to p_2; for it is not caused at all. Newton's doctrine is that any movement which happens according to the laws of motion is an uncaused event; the laws of motion are in fact the laws of free or causeless motion. (ii) He asserts that there is such a thing as relative motion; but, as he puts it, "relative motion may be generated or altered without any force impressed upon the body." If, therefore, it were possible to show, either that all motion is "free," that is to say, takes place according to laws having the same logical character as the Newtonian laws of motion; or that all motion is "relative"; then on Newton's own

principles it would follow that no motion is caused, and the cat would be out of the bag. It would have become plain that there is *no* truth concealed beneath the animistic metaphor; and that "the idea of causation" is simply a relic of animism foisted upon a science to which it is irrelevant.

This, I take it, is what modern physics has done. Developing the Newtonian doctrine in the simplest and most logical way, it has eliminated the notion of cause altogether. In place of that notion, we get a new and highly complex development of the Newtonian "laws of motion." Of the two Newtonian classes of events, (a) those that happen according to law and (b) those that happen as the effects of causes, class (a) has expanded to such an extent as to swallow up (b). At the same time, the survival of the term cause in certain sciences other than physics, such as medicine, is not a symptom of their "backwardness," because in them the word cause is not used in the same sense. They are practical sciences, aiming at results, and they accordingly use the word cause in sense II. Doubtless, the use of the word in that sense carries with it a flavor of magic; but this is not disliked by, e.g., the medical profession. A dose of superstition may serve its purpose.

IV

The situation in post-Newtonian philosophy has been very different. Kant, whose gigantic effort at a synthesis of all existing philosophies here overreached itself, swept into one bag the Baconian tradition, with its insistence on causes in sense II, the Cartesian identification of causes (in sense III) with grounds, the Leibnitzian law of sufficient reason, and the Humean conception of the cause as an event prior in time to its effect; and, unhappily neglecting the one thing in Newton which modern physics has found most valuable, namely, the doctrine that what happens according to a law does not need a cause, produced as the result a doctrine which has oppressed mankind ever since: the doctrine that (a) *every event has a cause;* (b) *the cause of every event is a prior event;* and (c) *this is known to us not from experience but a priori.*

(a) What could be meant by saying that every event has a cause? It would plainly be nonsense if "cause" were used in sense I. In sense II it would mean "there is nothing in nature that man is not able" (or, if we allow for looseness of expression, "may not hope to become able") "to produce or prevent at will," which is hardly what Kant intended, though a Bacon might have played with the idea in a rash moment. "Cause" must be used in sense III. But what warrant can there be for Kant's statement? I can only suppose that he was assuming the identity of cause with ground (though he accepted Hume's disproof of that identification) and accordingly thought that (*a*) was a mere restatement of the Law of Sufficient Reason.

(*b*) The cause of an event can be a prior event (see III, 1) only when cause is used in sense II. If, in the proposition "*x* causes *y*," "causes" means "logically necessitates," *x* cannot be an event happening before *y*. An event may have implications, but its implications cannot be subsequent events. The birth of a second son logically necessitates the first son's becoming a brother; these two events happen simultaneously; not successively, however close together. Thus the only assumption that can justify Kant's first assertion is an assumption that is incompatible with his second. Assertion (*a*) is in fact a relic of his Leibnitzian upbringing, (*b*) is a lesson from his later empiricist teachers. The combination of the two is an unsuccessful attempt at philosophical syncretism, marred by the fact

(which Kant has failed to observe) that in the two component propositions the word "cause" is used in different senses. Their combination is therefore, to put it plainly, nonsense; a hybrid concept, deserving the description once given to the mule, as a creature having "neither pride of ancestry nor hope of posterity."

Mill, unlike most of his philosophical critics and disciples, showed a certain understanding of the situation in which science had been left by Newton when he tried to reject sense III and get back to sense II; rejecting the notion of a cause "which is not only followed by, but actually *produces* the effect" in favor of "such a notion of cause as can be gained from experience." Consistently with this, he does away with the one-one relation of cause to effect, and insists on a real plurality of causes—a scandal to his critics, who have commonly assumed that the only possible sense of the word cause is sense III. But when he defines causation as "invariability of succession," he goes back unaware from loose causation to tight causation, for "invariability" implies the impossibility of variation, i.e., the necessity of the conjunction. If he is using it loosely for uniformity in cases hitherto observed, his advocacy of sense II becomes consistent. And in any case, Mill's pages on the subject stand out from those of almost all other writers as exceptionally clear-headed as to the sense in which the word cause is used.

Legal Cause*

§ 20.1. *Introductory.* Negligence is not a ground of liability unless it causes injury or damage to some interest which the law recognizes and protects. Moreover, it does not make a defendant liable for any injury or damage that is not a consequence of the negligence. The establishment of the requisite causal connection is therefore an element of a plaintiff's cause of action for negligence, to be pleaded and proven by him. And where a cause of action exists, the question of causal connection will determine the scope of liability

* Fowler V. Harper and Fleming James, Jr., "Legal Cause," in *The Law of Torts,* 3 Volumes (Boston: Little, Brown and Co., 1956), II, 1108–11, 1121–28, 1132–60, reprinted by permission of the publisher. Footnotes have been renumbered.

—the extent of the injury or damage for which defendant will have to pay. The question then naturally arises what is the kind of causal connection or relationship that the law requires to be proven. Obviously the legal test includes a requirement that the wrongful conduct must be a *cause in fact* of the harm; but if this stood alone the scope of liability would be vast indeed, for "the causes of causes [are] infinite" — "the fatal trespass done by Eve was cause of all our woe." But the law has not stopped there—it has developed further restrictions and limitations. The concept this development has produced is generally called "proximate" or "legal" cause. To be sure this concept is only one of the devices used to limit the fact and the extent of liability for negligence. In the progress of negligence law, however, the concept of proximate cause has been greatly overworked to limit or control both the liability of defendant and the effect of contributory negligence because of many considerations which can be treated in a more meaningful and significant way in connection with other issues, such as that of duty, standard of conduct and the like. . . .

TOPIC A. CAUSE IN FACT

§ 20.2. *Causal relation or cause in fact.* Through all the diverse theories of proximate cause runs a common thread; all agree that defendant's wrongful conduct must be a cause in fact of plaintiff's injury before there is liability. This notion is not a metaphysical one but an ordinary, matter-of-fact inquiry into the existence or nonexistence of a causal relation as laymen would view it. Clearly this is not a quest for a *sole* cause. Probably it cannot be said of any event that it has a single causal antecedent; usually there are many. For the purpose of the present inquiry it is enough that defendant's negligence be *a* cause in fact of the harm.

A rough working test of this relation, valid for most cases and enjoying wide currency, is the "but for" or *sine qua non* test: defendant's negligence is a cause in fact of an injury where the injury would not have occurred *but for* defendant's negligent conduct. It is probably safe to say that wherever this test is met, the cause in fact relation does exist. But the test is not universally valid as a test of exclusion of causes in fact. There is one situation where it will not work. If two independent causes concur to produce a result which either of them alone would have produced, each is a cause in fact of that result though it would have happened without *either* cause (but not if *both* causes were absent). Thus if two fires from separate sources combine as they reach plaintiff's property, and consume it, each is a cause though it be assumed or shown that the property would have been consumed as completely by either fire alone.

So far as the *substantive* law of torts goes, the cause in fact aspect of the requirement of legal cause gives little trouble, and it has been called a simple one. Yet there are problems here which often beset the trial court and practitioner and prove fatal to many a case. The most serious of these problems is that of sufficiency of proof where the ascertainable facts are meager, or where they present complicated questions of science, medicine, engineering, or the like. Another—usually less serious—problem is in finding appropriate language for the charge.

. . .

§ 20.3. *Multiple causes in fact.* It was pointed out at the beginning of the last section that no injury proceeds from a single cause. But by law if *no injury* would have occurred to plaintiff *but for* defendant's conduct, then defendant is liable—if at all—for the whole injury. This is true regardless of its position in the string of acts leading to the injury even though one or more of the other causes contributing to the result also involved wrongdoing on the part of other persons. In that case the others may also be liable but the law attempts no apportionment of damages among such tort-feasors, though a plaintiff is entitled only to a single satisfaction of his claim. So if two negligently driven cars collide and the collision injures a third person, both drivers are liable for his injury; or if A negligently leaves an obstruction in the highway and B negligently drives into it so that injury to C ensues, A and B are both liable to C.

A more serious question arises where defendant's negligence and another cause for which defendant is not responsible would each have caused the *whole* injury even in the absence of other cause. Where both causes involve the wrongful acts of legally responsible human beings there is virtual unanimity among courts in holding both (or either) liable for the whole injury just as in the situations described in the last paragraphs. A leading case is *Corey v. Havener*,[1] in which the two defendants on motorcycles passed plaintiff's horse, one on either side, and so frightened it by their speed, noise, and smoke that the horse ran away and injured plaintiff. Plaintiff had recovery against both defendants in spite of the obvious probability that either motorcycle alone would have produced the result and the fact that each was sued separately (the actions were tried together).

The authorities are divided, however, in the

[1] 182 Mass. 250, 65 N.E. 69 (1902).

case where the other cause (which would alone have produced the injury) is a natural force or the innocent act of another.[2] The case for denying liability here has been well put by Edgerton. He concedes that defendant's act stands in the same logical relation to the result "whether the other is a wrongdoer, an innocent person, or a thunderstorm." "But," he continues, "our sense of justice demands the imposition of liability when the harm should not have happened but for the wrongful act of human beings, while it does not make the same demand when the harm would have been produced by an innocent person or a natural force, if there had been no wrongful human action."[3] The opposing view, which appears to be of greater merit, rejects this reasoning and holds the wrongdoer in the case put. In terms of the fault principle the argument for the majority position is that after all defendant has committed a wrong and this has been in fact *a* cause of the injury; further, such negligent conduct will be more effectively deterred by imposing liability than by giving the wrongdoer a windfall in cases where an all-sufficient innocent cause happens to concur with his wrong in producing harm. If the objective of compensating accident victims be stressed, the scale is tipped heavily in favor of liability, however evenly balanced the opposing arguments in terms of fault.

So far we have been dealing with cases where the harm is not even theoretically apportionable, either because none of it would have happened but for defendant's negligence or because there would be no feasible way, even in the light of omniscience, to attribute any identifiable part of it to defendant's act rather than another cause, as in the case of the two fires which unite to burn property which either alone would have consumed. But there are many situations in which each of several causes (without the concurrence of any of the others) produces *some* (but not *all* the) harm. In such a case it may be hard or even impossible on the facts practically available to tell just how much of the harm each of these causes brought about, but at least in *theory* (i.e., to the eye of omniscience) they are capable of separation. Where this is the case, each of the defendants responsible for these causes may still be liable for the whole injury. This will be so where they acted in concert or in the course of a joint enterprise so that each is responsible vicariously for the acts of the others. The notion of action in concert involves the intentional aiding or abetting of a wrong, the "coming [together] to do an unlawful act," as where several ruffians set upon a man and beat him, each inflicting separate wounds. This concept has limited application to the field of accidental injuries. Joint enterprise is more appropriate to this field but this concept is rarely invoked except in connection with contributory negligence.

Even where defendants are not all liable for the whole injury, there are some situations where one is liable for the whole but the other is not. Where, for instance, A's act injures plaintiff and also foreseeably exposes him to further injury by B, A is liable for the whole harm, but B only for that part of it which he inflicted. This would be the case if one driver negligently ran down a pedestrian and, as he was lying there, another driver ran over him, breaking his leg. Another situation where this notion is commonly applied is that where, after defendant negligently injures plaintiff, a doctor's treatment of the injury negligently makes it worse. The defendant is liable for the whole injury including the aggravation although the doctor would of course be liable only for the aggravation his malpractice caused. Another case in which one defendant will be liable for all the injury is that in which he is vicariously responsible for the conduct of the others acting with him, and each inflicts some injury.

Except in the situations described in the last two paragraphs, the prevailing rule is that where each of several defendants causes only *part* of defendant's injury, so that the parts would be capable of separation if all the facts were known, then each is liable only to the extent of that part. Thus where two dogs run together and kill sheep, each of the separate owners of the dogs is liable only for the sheep his dog killed. If each of several riparian

---

[2] E.g., two fires, one negligently set by the defendant and the other the product of nature (lightning), combine and are blown across the plaintiff's property, burning his house. Or, a boy loses his balance and is falling to his death (or to serious injury) on rocks below when he is caught upon the defendant's wires, with respect to which the defendant is negligent toward him, and electrocuted. Or, a house so undermined by the pounding of the sea that it would topple at the next high tide is negligently destroyed by defendant's fire hours before high tide occurs. See Peaslee, "Multiple Causation and Damage," 47 *Harv. L. Rev.* (1934), pp. 1127, 1135.

[3] Edgerton, "Legal Cause," 72 *U. Pa. L. Rev.* (1924), pp. 211, 345, 346, 347 . . . .

owners pollutes a stream somewhat, he is liable only for the damage resulting from his own contribution to the pollution (unless of course it can be said that none of the damage would have resulted but for his contribution, in which case he would probably be liable for it all).

Where each of several independent actors has inflicted successive injuries, each actor's liability is limited again to his own contribution to the injury (except, as we have seen, the original actor will be liable for the later injuries if they arise from a risk the likelihood of which made his conduct negligent). A like result is reached when the same defendant by two successive acts causes separate injuries, and the defendant is not liable for the first but for the second act. Thus where a trolley runs down a careless pedestrian and the motorman injures him again through negligence in trying to extricate him from his position of danger, the company will be liable for the second but not for the first injury. And an employer who exposed his workman to the danger of silicosis over a period of time extending back beyond the statute of limitations will be liable for the aggravation of the disease caused by the exposure within the statutory period.

At the time of their injuries accident victims are in all sorts of diverse conditions, physically, mentally, financially, and in many other ways. And these pre-existing conditions may have the greatest bearing on the extent of the injury actually suffered by any particular plaintiff in a given case. Thus the same slight blow in the abdomen might cause only fleeting discomfort to a man but a miscarriage to a pregnant woman. Or a slight touch, scarcely noticed by the recipient, might be so aggravated by the presence of latent disease at the point of impact as to cause the loss of the use of a limb. These situations too involve concurring causes just as do the situations we have been discussing before in this section. And the cases will be seen to fall into the same patterns. Thus defendant's act may be a cause in fact of the whole injury (as in the case of the miscarriage or the diabetic's leg), and where it is not even theoretically divisible defendant will be liable for the whole of it. But defendant's act may only aggravate an illness or injury which would have caused some harm anyway, or accelerate a loss—death, for instance—which would have taken place any-

way. And in such a case defendant's liability extends only to the amount of harm which he in fact caused.

.   .   .

TOPIC B. PROXIMATE CAUSE

§ 20.4. *In general.* We have seen how some reasonable showing of cause in fact is always a requisite of liability. But such showing may not suffice for liability. There may still be problems under the fault system and there would be even under other systems of compensation. Workmen's compensation schemes, for instance, limit recovery to accidents which are regarded as incidental to the employment, and this limitation poses questions which go beyond the mere inquiry whether a given accident was the cause in fact of a specific injury, or whether this causal relation was a substantial one. Schemes to compensate victims of traffic accidents would need an analogous limitation, and so on. Our present system is not designed along any such functional lines but has traditionally focused attention on the defendant's individual fault, and the limitations on his liability bear the mark of the fault formula as we shall see.

It should be noted at this point that many courts and legal writers have stressed the fact that policy considerations underlie the doctrine of proximate cause. Of course they do, but the policies actually involved often fail to get explicit treatment. One consideration which is common to all cases under any system is the practical need to draw the line somewhere so that liability will not crush those on whom it is put. Even under comprehensive social insurance for all vicissitudes to the body there would have to be limits on the kinds of injuries to be compensated (many kinds like worry, loss of enjoyment, prestige, etc., probably would not be), and on the amount of compensation. Under any system of more limited scope, liability is placed on individuals, groups, enterprises, and the like, rather than upon the whole of society, and there will have to be further limitations to protect these groups or individuals from being saddled with more than their fair share of the social cost of accident. Under an individualistic fault system these limitations will be geared to fault and will reflect the policy of making the extent of liability reflect the degree of fault or the factors which make conduct blameworthy. As the fact of insurance and loss distribution increasingly permeates our system and the importance of individual blameworthiness wanes, the limitations (of proximate cause, or duty, etc.) may be expected to take on more and more the character of limitations measured by what is felt to be normally incidental to the kind of activity or enterprise which is footing the bill (e.g., motoring, railroad transportation, the manufacture of canned foods, the owning and management of apartments, etc.).

Another policy consideration which pervades all the cases is the need to work out rules which are feasible to administer, and yield a workable degree of certainty.

. . .

We now turn to examine the considerations by which our law limits liability for negligent conduct even where a cause in fact relation exists. It is Dean Green's view that *all* limitations on liability other than those imposed by the cause in fact requirement should be administered as part of some issue other than cause.[4] But while this simple and helpful analysis has gained *partial* acceptance by *some* courts (and the American Law Institute),[5] this acceptance has been far from complete, and the present treatment would itself be incomplete if it failed to take account of the many theories and lines of reasoning which have had some currency in the decisions.

§ 20.5. *The test of foreseeability.* From the very beginning the notion of foreseeability has been intertwined with the development of liability for negligence. And the limitations imposed by this notion have frequently been stated in terms of proximity of cause or consequence. Thus in summing up the earlier law, Holdsworth points out that in an action on the case there must be damage, but it might be an indirect consequence of the wrong, and the courts were familiarized with the concept of negligence by the need of determining whether the damage complained of "could be said to be a sufficiently proximate consequence of the defendant's act to entail liability," a question which in turn came to be resolved

"by asking whether any ordinary prudent man would have foreseen that damage would probably result from his act."[6] Pollock, whose work on torts is still one of the leading British authorities on the subject, through all his life insisted that the extent of liability for negligence was measured by what was foreseeable at the time of the act or omission complained of.[7] This view, however, was never accepted by all hands as a universal solvent, and two leading English cases dramatically showed that liability would often be extended to entirely unforeseeable consequences.[8] These cases and the writings of leading commentators led to a wide acceptance of the view expressed thus by Beven: "The defendant's view of the possibilities of his act is very material to determine whether his act is negligent or not; it is utterly immaterial to limit liability when once negligence has been established."[9] But this view also failed of acceptance as a universal solvent, and many courts and writers continued to bring "foreseeability" into their discussions of proximate cause. The matter cannot be left, therefore, by embracing the appealing (apparent) simplicity of either of these extreme views. Foreseeability does play a large part in limiting the extent of liability. "Attempts to escape from the significance of foresight in the field of legal remote-

---

[4] Green, *Rationale of Proximate Cause* (1927), discussion of cases, pp. 77–121 and 144–68 (both inclusive). For further exposition, see Green, "Are There Dependable Rules of Causation?" 77 *U. Pa. L. Rev.* (1929), p. 601, and Green, "Proximate Cause in Texas Negligence Law," 28 *Texas L. Rev.* (1950), pp. 471, 621, 755.

[5] 2 *Restatement of Torts* §§ 281, 430. . . .

[6] 8 Holdsworth, *A History of English Law*, 2d ed. (1937), p. 450. Later on Holdsworth says, "If we are basing liability on a negligent act, and if negligence consists in the failure to foresee results which ought reasonably to be foreseen, it would seem that the negligent person ought only to be made liable to the extent to which he ought to have foreseen those results." *Id.* at p. 463.

[7] Pollock, *Torts* 8, 14th ed. (1939), p. 24. According to Pollock, "the accepted test of liability for negligence in the first instance is . . . also the proper measure of liability for the consequences of proved or admitted default." The test is whether the damage is "such as the defendant could reasonably be expected to anticipate." . . .

[8] In re Polemis & Furness, Withy & Co., [1921] 3 K.B. 560 (plank negligently knocked into ship's hold caused spark at instant of impact which ignited flammable vapor present in the hold and ultimately resulted in the total destruction of the ship by fire); *Smith v. London & S.W. Ry.*, L.R. 5 C.P. 98, L.R. 6 C.P. 14 (1870) (after defendant's engine passed, fire, originating in or near dried cut-grass which defendant had negligently left along right of way, spread through a hedge bordering right of way, then two hundred yards across an adjoining stubble field, across a road, and burnt plaintiff's cottage). Goodhart, "Restatement of the Law of Torts," 83 *U. Pa. L. Rev.*, pp. 968, 994 n.106 (1935), has argued that the consequences in the Polemis case were foreseeable. . . .

[9] Beven, *Negligence in Law*, 3d ed. (1908), p. 89 n.2. . . .

ness are attempts to escape from our culture."[10] Notions about what should be foreseen, in other words, are very much interwoven with our feelings about fair and just limits to legal responsibility, though it is not clear they will always coincide. On the other hand there may be liability for unforeseeable consequences. The problem calls for further discussion which may for convenience be broken down into more or less distinct considerations:

(1) Foreseeability of damage is altogether irrelevant in determining the existence of the cause in fact relationship. Acts or omissions constantly help to bring about consequences which no man will be held to foresee. It follows that under an analysis like Dean Green's, foreseeability has no place in the issue of proximate cause. But it does not follow that such an analysis would exclude all consideration for foreseeability in determining the limits of liability, as we shall see.

(2) It is well-nigh universally conceded that unreasonable likelihood of harm (however tenuous or fictitious that concept may be) is the gist of liability for negligence. This in itself, of course, is *some* limitation on liability for acts and omissions that turn out to be injurious. Just *how much* of a limitation it is depends upon how one views the scope of the duty to use care. Courts and writers have from time to time taken the position that if defendants should anticipate that certain conduct is fraught with unreasonable probability of *some* harm to *somebody,* then the duty to refrain from that conduct is owed to anyone who may in fact be hurt by it. As we have seen, this was the view taken in the dissenting opinion of Judge Andrews in *Palsgraf v. Long Island Railroad Co.* If such a notion is accepted, it would open up very wide possibilities indeed as to the extent of liability unless the court or jury were to consider some limiting factor (such as the source and range of harm reasonably to be anticipated from the act) in connection with the cause issue. Thus Judge Andrews would consider the likelihood that the cause "in the usual judgment of mankind" would produce the result—whether "by the exercise of prudent foresight the result [could] be foreseen"—as a factor in determining proximate cause.

The view currently prevailing in this coun-

[10] Morris, "Proximate Cause in Minnesota," 34 *Minn. L. Rev.* (1950), pp. 185, 197 . . . .

try, however, does limit the scope of the duty to do or refrain from doing a given act to (1) those persons or interests that are likely to be endangered by the act or omission, and (2) harm (to such person or interest) from a risk the likelihood of which made the act or omission negligent. Thus the careless pushing of a prospective train passenger was not negligence to Mrs. Palsgraf who stood many feet outside the range of probable effects of such conduct. And carelessness in giving a gun to a young child is not negligence with respect to injury caused by dropping the gun on plaintiff's foot, since the risk of the child's dropping a fairly heavy object was not (we assume) so fraught with the chance of injury as to make the entrustment unreasonable. It is obvious that under such an analysis of the duty problem, foreseeability is distinctly a factor which puts a considerable limitation on the extent of liability, even though it should be held to play no part whatever in determining the issue of proximate cause. It is also clear that if this analysis of the duty problem is accepted, no good, but only confusion, can result from repeating the same inquiries as to foreseeability under the cause issue as were asked and answered (or should have been) under the duty issue. Where, however, the duty problem is analyzed in the older, less limited way, or is not clearly analyzed at all, courts tend strongly to impose pretty much the same limitations (i.e., those imposed by the narrower concept of duty) by importing into the issue of proximate cause a requirement of probability or foreseeeability.

Very much the same result is occasionally produced by an insistence that the causal relation be shown to exist between *that aspect of defendant's conduct which is wrongful* and the injury. Under this approach the court asks whether the same injury would have been caused if defendant's conduct had been careful (or not violative of statute) but in all other respects had been the same as it actually was. If a speeding automobile strikes a child, could the event have been avoided by a driver who was proceeding at a reasonable speed? If not, then the requisite causal connection does not exist. Now this is in essence the same as an inquiry into whether the accident resulted from the hazard (namely, lack of control) which made it negligent to drive too fast, and so fell within the scope of the duty not to speed. And it is submitted that the inquiry in the latter form is more meaningful and more likely to focus attention on the real problem involved at least in terms of the fault principle (e.g., Why should one not speed? What are the peculiar risks of speeding? etc.). Moreover it is confusing to think hypothetically and hard to frame with precision the terms of a condition contrary to fact.

Much of what has been said about the scope of common-law duties is applicable also to duties imposed by statutes. Here, however, the emphasis is upon the statutory purpose in determining the interests protected by the duty and the evils sought to be prevented by legislative proscription of conduct, rather than upon what a reasonable person in defendant's place would foresee.[11] Because the statutory purpose doctrine was probably clearly and expressly articulated at an earlier time than its counterpart, the limitation on the scope of common-law duties, there has been perhaps slightly less urge to obfuscate the former inquiry by pursuing it in terms of proximate cause, but this is done all too often even today. Thus where plaintiff's playmate pushed him under a middle car of defendant's train which was passing at a speed in violation of a local ordinance, the court admitted that the defendant was guilty of negligence *per se* but found that the "intervening, independent, sole, proximate cause" of the injury was the other boy's push.[12] And where defendant has parked his unlocked car on the street, with the key in the ignition switch in violation of an ordinance, and the car is stolen by a person who, while driving it, causes some damage, the owner has been held not liable on the ground that the proximate cause of the injury was the action of the thief and not the negligence of the owner.[13]

(3) There is one kind of problem to which Pollock's test limiting proximate consequences to those which are foreseeable will yield a different answer from that given by the great weight of authority in this country and England. There are cases where defendant has been negligent toward plaintiff or his prop-

erty (even under the restrictive view of the scope of duty) and where injury has come through the very hazard that made the conduct negligent, but where because the stage is set for it the *extent* of the injury passes all bounds of reasonable anticipation. A milkman, for instance, negligently leaves a bottle with a chipped lip, and this scratches a housewife's hand as she takes it in. All this is easily within the range of foresight. This particular housewife, however, has a blood condition so that what to most women would be a trivial scratch leads to blood poisoning and death.[14] Or a careless stevedore drops a plank from hoisting tackle into the hold of a vessel. This might well have damaged a member of the crew, or the ship, or cargo, but the plank happens to ignite a spark which in turn ignites petrol vapor in the hold and leads to total destruction of the ship and cargo.[15] In these and like cases of what well may be called direct consequences, the courts generally hold defendant liable for the full extent of the injury without regard to foreseeability.

This result has been attacked as one quite inconsistent with the prevailing limitation on the scope of duty to interests and hazards which are foreseeable. "[If] we once reject the idea that an act has a general quality of wrongfulness where different persons are concerned, it would seem to follow logically that we must also reject the idea that an act has a general quality of wrongfulness where different consequences are concerned."[16] But the criticism stems from too much insistence on mechanical consistency. There is no reason to apply the restrictive foreseeability test to all problems just because it is applied to some. There are strong reasons, both within the framework of fault and to secure more effective compensation, for holding a wrongdoer liable for all injuries he causes innocent men, and rejecting the foreseeability limitation altogether.[17] Counter considerations have pre-

---

[11] See Morris, "Duty, Negligence, and Causation," 101 *U. Pa. L. Rev.* (1952), pp. 189, 203 (complaining that "the judicially invented statutory purpose doctrine can produce highly restrictive and somewhat irrational limitations on civil liability").

[12] *Lineberry v. North Carolina Ry. Co.*, 187 N.C. 786, 123 S.E. 1 (1924). . . .

[13] See, e.g., *Wannebo v. Gates,* 227 Minn. 194, 34 N.W. 2d 695 (1948). . . .

[14] *Koehler v. Waukesha Milk Co.*, 190 Wis. 52, 208 N.W. 901 (1926).

[15] In re Polemis & Furness, Withy & Co., [1921] 3 K.B. 560. . . .

[16] Goodhart, "The Unforeseeable Consequences of a Negligent Act," 39 *Yale L.J.* (1930), pp. 449, 465.

[17] In terms of fault it may be contended that any foreseeability limitation would deprive an *innocent* victim of recovery for some damages caused in fact by a wrongdoer. And obviously such a limitation shuts off compensation for some of the damages actually suffered. Both of these consequences are unfortunate and must be counted as *costs* of a foreseeability rule. In those fields of accident law where liability tends in practice to *distribute* (rather than

vailed to limit the risks of negligent conduct as to persons (or interests) and types of hazard. Why should not that much of a concession to one group of competing considerations be thought enough? The choice is between emphasizing, on the one hand, the limited and inconsequential nature of the fault, and, on the other, the very wide and serious nature of the damage that calls for compensation. Is it not one of the judicial functions to make a practical compromise where policies conflict? At any rate here the line is drawn in fact and any deviation from it is not likely to be in the direction of ruling out unforeseeable consequences of the kind being discussed. It should be noted that what is said under the present head applies only where pre-existing conditions and causes have already laid the train for the surprisingly great extent of the damage which defendant's act sets off.

(4) It has been urged, with considerable force, that foreseeability should not limit the class of those who may recover for injuries *directly* caused by defendant's negligence. Such a rule would give an "unforeseeable plaintiff" a remedy for *direct* results of negligence on much the same basis as that suggested above to justify the foreseeable plaintiff's recovery for injuries unforeseeable in extent. There is judicial language broad enough to support such a rule, but the actual decisions virtually all deal with plaintiffs whose dangers were readily foreseeable, unless an artificially narrow view of foresight is invoked.

(5) Where there are forces intervening between defendant's act and plaintiff's injury courts generally tend to invoke the test of foreseeability. To the eye of philosophy the distinction between intervening and pre-existing causes or conditions is tenuous if it exists at all. The philosophic determinist would see no essential distinction between the gasoline vapor already in the hold of the good ship *Thrasyvoulos* before the ill-starred stevedore dropped the plank, and the hurricane or flood that arose *after* defendant's negligence left plaintiff's property vulnerably exposed to such a hazard, or for that matter the malpractice of the surgeon which caused gangrene to set in in plaintiff's wound. To the determinist the

stage for all these things was irrevocably set long before any time that matters in this discussion. Of course the law generally—certainly the law of fault—does not accept any such philosophy.[18] But even those who reject determinism can see that a wind or storm or flood was often inevitably in the making before defendant's negligence took place, though it appeared on the immediate scene thereafter. Yet even such considerations are generally too refined for the law's roughhewn tests. By and large, external forces will be regarded as intervening if they appear on the scene after defendant had acted, unless perhaps their pending inevitability at the time of defendant's negligent act or omission is made crystal clear.[19] And when a new force (for which defendant is not responsible) "intervenes" in this crude sense to bring about a result that defendant's negligence would not otherwise have produced, defendant is generally held for that result only where the intervening force was foreseeable. As many cases put it, a new and unforeseeable force breaks the causal chain. A better analysis is to regard the intervening force as a risk or hazard and to ask whether its foreseeability was such as to make defendant's act negligent with regard to it. It is better, in other words, to inquire whether defendant's duty extends to such a risk as the intervening force, because the question in this form focuses attention on a more significant and less fictitious problem than that of cause. But the result is likely to be the same. As we have seen, there is probably some modern trend toward greater use of the duty analysis but this is perhaps more observable when the new force intervenes between defendant's act and any injury at all to plaintiff than when the new force aggravates the extent of injuries concededly caused by defendant's negligence, though as a theoretical matter it might be pretty hard to defend such a distinction.

Where voluntary acts of responsible human beings intervene between defendant's conduct

---

merely to *shift*) losses, the refusal to afford compensation for actual damage is even more unfortunate. . . .

[18] "The lawyer cannot afford to adventure himself with philosophers in the logical and metaphysical controversies that beset the idea of cause." Pollock, *Torts*, 11th ed. (1920), p. 36.
[19] The definition offered by McLaughlin, "Proximate Cause," 39 *Harv. L. Rev.* (1925), pp. 149, 159, is clear and comprehensive: "An intervening force is a force which is neither operating in the defendant's presence, nor at the place where the defendant's act takes effect at the time of the defendant's act, but comes into effective operation at or before the time of the damage." . . .

and plaintiff's injury, the problem of foreseeability is the same and courts generally are guided by the same test. If the likelihood of the intervening act was one of the hazards that made defendant's conduct negligent—that is, if it was sufficiently foreseeable to have this effect—then defendant will generally be liable for the consequences; otherwise he will generally not be, provided, of course, that the intervening force is a cause of the injury. Here, however, when voluntary acts of *legally responsible persons* are concerned, other factors besides foreseeability sometimes come into the picture as we shall see.

So far as scope of duty (or, as some courts put it, the relation of proximate cause) is concerned, it should make no difference whether the intervening actor is negligent or intentional or criminal. Even criminal conduct by others is often reasonably to be anticipated. After all, if I leave a borrowed car on the streets of New York or Chicago with doors unlocked and key in ignition, I am negligent (at least toward the owner) because of the very likelihood of theft. And if I lend a car to one known by me to be habitually careless, I am negligent precisely because of the likelihood of his negligent operation of my car. Again the importance of the factor of foreseeability is not altered if the intervening act is that of plaintiff himself, nor is it if that act is a negligent one. When I lent my car to the careless driver, one of the risks that made me negligent was surely the chance that he might hurt himself. If he is barred from recovery for such hurt, it is because of his contributory fault, not for want of a causal connection or because he is beyond the scope of my duty. One other point should be noted here. There are cases where defendant's wrong would not have caused plaintiff's injury if some third person had taken intervening precautions which he was legally bound to take. In such a case it might be said that the third person's negligent omission intervened between defendant's wrong and the injury. Where that is the case, foreseeability is less likely to be used as a test of exclusion of the original defendant's liability than where an affirmative act intervenes.

(6) Foreseeability does not mean that the precise hazard or the exact consequences which were encountered should have been foreseen. Upon this all are agreed, whether they regard foreseeability as relevant only to the duty issue, or to questions of proximate cause as well. "[W]hen it is found that a man ought to have foreseen in a general way consequences of a certain kind, it will not avail him to say that he could not foresee the precise course or the full extent of the consequences, being of that kind, which in fact happened."[20] In *Hill v. Winsor*,[21] the defendants, while operating their tug in a negligent manner, bumped the fender of a bridge on which plaintiff was at work, causing the braces between certain piles to fall so that the piles sprang together, catching plaintiff between them to his injury. The accident was a most unusual one in the manner of its occurrence, yet the plaintiff was obviously put in danger by the tug's negligence, and the risk of his being struck by the tug itself or injured somehow by the blow of the vessel against the structure on which he was working were among the risks that made the operation of the tug negligent. So defendant was held though probably no one could have anticipated the actual train of events. The hazard, in other words, was not defined narrowly as a risk that the piles would spring together when a blow caused the braces between them to fall. On the other hand, the risk or hazard to be perceived and guarded against cannot be defined too vaguely, or the present restriction would lose all meaning and every defendant whose acts were a cause in fact would be liable.

The example of the speeding car striking the child will illustrate this. If the rule against excessive speed be viewed as simply designed to prevent automobile accidents or the striking of pedestrians, collision will be seen to have arisen out of the breach of duty if a reasonable speed would not have brought the car to the point of collision when the child was there. Yet if the child darted out from behind a tree on a lonely road immediately in front of defendant's automobile so that the accident would have been unavoidable *then* even if defendant had been proceeding at a reasonable rate, most courts will not hold him. The hazards peculiar to speed are those involved in diminished control of the vehicle.

The inquiry then into the nature of the risks or hazards, the foreseeability of which

---

[20] Pollock, "Liability for Consequences," 38 *L.Q. Rev.* (1922), pp. 165, 167. 2 *Restatement of Torts*, § 435, is in agreement. . . .
[21] 118 Mass. 251 (1875).

makes conduct negligent, must be neither too refined nor too coarse. It is a matter of judgment in drawing the line. It is often not enough to ask whether the rule of conduct violated is one to prevent traumatic bodily injury, or the like; the nature of the hazards peculiar to the proscribed conduct must be sought. But these must not be described in too specific and detailed a way—it is enough that their general nature be indicated, and this will vary from situation to situation. While it is negligent to speed on an ordinary highway because of the risk of bringing about injury through diminished control, it might be negligent to drive a car in some places crowded with pedestrians at any speed or under any practicable degree of control because of the likelihood of striking someone in any manner at all. The inquiry is but an aspect of that made under the issue of negligence (which includes the sub-issues of standard of conduct, scope of duty, and breach): was defendant's conduct negligent in the light of all the risks to be foreseen by the eye of prudence under the circumstances? For that reason it is futile and confusing to repeat the inquiry under the heading of cause.

(7) Foreseeability is to be determined in the light of what a reasonable man would have foreseen and is not limited to what defendant did in fact foresee, though it includes that.

(8) Foreseeability is not a term of precision, and there will not be anything like uniformity in judgments of what is reasonably "within the risk" foreseeably created by defendant's negligence. The decision—whether made by court or jury—will often depend upon which circumstances in the case are selected for emphasis. "It all depends upon what factors in the evidence a court is willing to isolate and emphasize for the purpose of making this decision, which process in turn depends pretty much on what outcome the court wishes to achieve or thinks to be politic. This factor in the judgment process, in turn, is not usually a matter of conscious choice but may be a function of the judge's accumulated experience in and observations of the world he lives in."[22] It may also depend on what formula is chosen. In many cases, from the point of view of one in the actor's shoes at the time of the act or omission complained

of, neither the exact chain of consequences nor their precise nature and extent were probably to be actually anticipated. But in these same cases if it is asked whether such occurrences and consequences would have seemed extraordinary and out of the range of probability if they had then been called to the actor's attention, they will often appear to be more foreseeable. The formula chosen by the *Restatement* in its sections on proximate cause, with its emphasis on what seems "extraordinary" in the light of hindsight, seems to abandon the foreseeability test.[23] But careful analysis shows that it does not. "When we have hindsight nothing is extraordinary, for we can see each step following inevitably on the other; when, after an event, we say, 'What a highly extraordinary result,' we mean that a person before the event could not have expected it."[24] The proposed test probably does, however, amount to an invitation to take a broad view toward what is foreseeable. The same is probably true of the use of the word "normal" (rather than foreseeable, or probable) as the opposite of extraordinary. It is too bad that this formula was not used in defining the negligence issue where such considerations more appropriately belong.

(9) The limitations of liability to consequences foreseeably "within the risk" (with the exceptions noted above) is probably well enough adapted to an accident law in transition from one based on fault to one affording compensation without regard to fault. This is so partly because it is vague and imprecise enough to allow courts and juries a good deal of elasticity in responding to trends which are only half articulated, without putting too much strain on the logical framework. This elasticity also accommodates the fact that the range of foreseeability may grow with increase of knowledge about human behavior and about the propensities of animate and inanimate things (including machines, atoms, and microbes). But beyond all this, if the importance of fault continues to wane, the test will lend itself readily to becoming a rational one under the new dispensation—the inquiry whether the consequence is within the risk incident to the particular act or omission which is claimed to be negligent may gradually be transformed

[22] Gregory, "Proximate Cause in Negligence—A Retreat from 'Rationalization,'" 6 *U. Chi. L. Rev.* (1938), pp. 36, 50. . . .

[23] 2 *Restatement of Torts,* § 433(b) and Comment *e.* . . . .

[24] Goodhart, "The Restatement of the Law of Torts, II," 83 *U. Pa. L. Rev.* (1935), pp. 968, 994.

into the question whether it is within a risk incident to the enterprise or activity which is to be charged for compensating it.

§ 20.6. *Other proposed tests.* There is a variety of other tests of the defendant's liability, which have had more or less currency and which find occasional favor today. Some of these are more, and others less, restrictive than the prevailing modified foreseeability or risk test. Still others would substitute a formula which, after inviting inquiry along one or more false scents, comes down in the last analysis to nothing more than the foreseeability test.

(1) Courts have infrequently confined liability within arbitrary limits of time or space, restricting it far more than would a test in terms of foreseeability or risk. Thus the New York courts, and formerly those of Pennsylvania, limit liability for the spread of a fire to harm done to property on the first premises to which the fire has spread (i.e., premises adjacent to the defendant's, wherein the fire started, except where the fire has leapt an intervening roadway or a vacant lot, nothing on which was ignited). This rule has been quite properly rejected in every other jurisdiction.

(2) Going to the other extreme, so far as predictability is concerned, Edgerton has proposed that an "average sense of justice" be the yardstick and that a "justly attachable cause" be deemed a proximate cause.[25] A just decision is one which is "socially advantageous"—which balances "competing individual and social interests," favoring those which are most important. Each decision serves the double function of achieving a just balance of interests in the particular case and, where liability is imposed, of discouraging unsocial conduct of a similar nature in the future. In each of its functions this test is open to criticism. Insofar as it is intended to have a deterrent effect it is, like all other tests similarly purposed, based on a misconception, for most torts are unintentional or are committed in disregard or ignorance of legal consequences. The test is hardly more helpful in reaching decisions in individual cases. A sense of justice is of course essential in any decision-making process, for liability should never be imposed unfairly. But in most cases there is serious dispute as to the justice of any given result. In such cases it may be helpful to have this underlying consideration articulated, but it should not be expected that a mere statement of the goal will assure its attainment.[26] Justice, as a goal, is too abstract to be self-applying and self-evident in particular cases. The process of adapting and translating the abstract goal to particular situations may take one or two forms. On one hand, all hope may be abandoned of categorizing or systematizing human experience. Edgerton appears to prefer this solution for he would shun fixed rules and formulae and would instead permit the jury to consider any circumstances thought to be pertinent to impose liability upon "justly attachable" causes on grounds of fairness and social advantage. On the other hand, the quest may be pursued for more or less definite rules, adapted from decisions in fairly discernible groups of cases with similar fact situations. An advantage of the latter treatment is to be found in the greater predictability of decision it affords.

(3) Though it may be undesirable to entrust the jury with almost complete discretion in imposing liability, a single rule or formula which attempts to reduce all the cases to a simple pattern may not be any more desirable. For example, the division of antecedent forces into *conditions* (which merely made possible the harm, and for which there is no liability) and *causes* (upon which liability will be imposed) is of deceptive simplicity and certainty. It may be convenient for a commentator to be able to group those cases in which no liability was imposed under the heading of "condition," and to say that the courts have found the defendant's conduct to be a "cause" in all cases in which that defendant was held liable. But as an aid in *reaching* decisions in particular cases the dichotomy is worse than useless. It can only be related to actual fact situations if all active forces are denominated "causes" and all passive situations attributable to the defendant are classed as "conditions." But even if a valid, definitive distinction between active and passive antecedents could be made in every case, it would often not indicate the proper decision of the proximate cause question. The distinction between cause and condition is only determinative in a concrete case when modified by exceptions in terms of the

[25] Edgerton, "Legal Cause," 72 *U. Pa. L. Rev.* (1924), pp. 210, 343.

[26] Edgerton's fear is that the ultimate goal, justice, is being lost sight of in the maze of rigid rules of causation. His effort to restore proper perspective makes justice the only standard by which to judge. His test is thus little better than a question with regard to its ability to assure an answer, for it forecloses from all consideration the use of established intermediate reasoning aids and standards.

class of risks to be anticipated or the foresee-ability of intervention of an injuring force—and since, as we have seen, such "exceptions" in themselves constitute an adequate test, it would seem far better to omit altogether any dependence upon the "cause-condition" formula. Most jurisdictions do not even mention it, and many others expressly repudiate it.

(4) Considerably wider acceptance has been achieved by a formula which differentiates the "direct" from the "indirect" consequences of an act. Liability is imposed for all consequences which follow, without the intervention of new external forces, in unbroken natural sequence from the original act. At first glance this test presents merely a problem of semantics, for its most essential ingredient is an acceptable definition of a "new, external, intervening force." But though sufficiently generalized definitions are frequently proposed, the test does not become a workable one unless the court or jury is willing to refuse to go beyond a certain point in looking for new active forces. Therefore, until such time as a court indicates the preciseness and thoroughness with which it intends to search for such forces this test must produce a high degree of uncertainty of decisions.

Even the most enthusiastic adherents to the direct-indirect test would not press it to its logically symmetrical extreme by excusing from liability *all* defendants whose acts only indirectly caused the plaintiff's injuries. But what they fail to realize is that not even all direct causes are "proximate," for there may be no liability even for the direct consequences of an act if the defendant was not under a duty to protect the plaintiff from the type of hazard encountered.

In spite of its shortcomings, however, the distinction between direct and indirect causes has some importance in determining the extent to which foreseeability limits liability for the consequences of a negligent act.

(5) Another restrictive test, emphasizing chiefly the chronology of intervening human acts, holds only the *last wrongdoer* liable for an injury produced by the combined effect of successive acts of wrongdoing. This rule may have stemmed in part from a notion (which once had some currency) that the law fulfilled its function if it offered *one* legally liable defendant to a plaintiff, so that it was superfluous and in some peculiar way uneconomical to

offer more. The rule may also be traceable to the reluctance of courts to admit that subsequent unlawful action may be expectable or that earlier wrongdoers should be responsible for such action. At any rate, whatever the reason, the last wrongdoer rule has been used infrequently and capriciously to limit liability throughout the history of negligence law.

The sporadic instances of such use have probably been confined to a few situations where the law, for reasons of real or supposed policy, has disfavored a type of claim or defense which it nevertheless allows. Thus recovery has been denied in a suit against a municipality for a highway defect if the accident was also contributed to by the wrongful act of a third person. . . . In nearly all states the doctrine of last clear chance, a variant of the last wrongdoer rule, is employed as a limitation on the disfavored defense of plaintiff's contributory negligence. Occasionally, the defense of contributory negligence itself has been called merely an application of the last wrongdoer rule. And a harsh, indefensible doctrine has recently been fashioned by a few courts to exonerate an illegally parked vehicle from liability, even to innocent victims, wherever the moving driver saw the parked vehicle in time to avoid hitting it. The principle has also been used outside of the field of negligence as, e.g., to limit liability of defendants in disfavored actions for defamation.

The last wrongdoer rule is subject to criticism wherever it is invoked. It reflects no vital modern policy, but only earlier mechanistic notions. And it is irreconcilable with large bodies of existing case law. The last wrongdoer is not always held liable for damage which ensues; on the other hand, a wrongdoer who is not closest in point of time to the plaintiff's injury is often held liable. At best the last wrongdoer test yields a "correct" result only by chance.

(6) Jeremiah Smith suggested that liability be limited to those cases in which the defendant's tort was "a substantial factor in producing the damage complained of."[27] This "test" for limiting liability attracted no following in the courts, and only scant attention from commentators, until the *Restatement of Torts* adopted it in 1934.[28] Since that time its popu-

[27] Smith, "Legal Cause in Actions of Tort," 25 *Harv. L. Rev.* (1912), pp. 103, 303, 309.
[28] 2 *Restatement of Torts*, §§ 431, 433, 435, and text, *infra*, at notes 41 et seq.

larity has greatly increased and today more than a dozen states at least pay lip service to it.

The distinction between substantial factors and others may perhaps be significant and useful in practically fixing the limits of the cause in fact relation between defendant's wrong and plaintiff's damage. But as Smith and originally the *Restatement* presented the test, it appeared to go further than this and to be, in effect, a test of *proximate* cause. Thus the *Restatement* provides that negligence is a legal cause of harm if it is a substantial factor in bringing that harm about, and if there is no rule of law which relieves the actor from liability because of the way the harm was brought about. The next section, 432, declares in effect that conduct cannot be a substantial factor in producing harm *unless* it is a cause in fact of the harm. Then Section 433 proceeds to list factors which may be important in determining whether negligence is a substantial factor in causing harm, and among these factors was originally put the curious foreseeability-of-hindsight test discussed above. But, as we have seen, foreseeability has no place at all in solving the cause in fact problem. Rather it represents a limitation which would relieve a defendant, for reasons of policy, from liability for harm which he in fact caused. The Institute has recognized this, and, in 1948, Section 433 was amended to delete the foreseeability-of-hindsight clause.[29] The amendment is wise. "Substantial factor" as a test of *proximate cause* is no more helpful than proximate cause itself. If defendant's wrong is a substantial cause in fact of plaintiff's harm, recovery should not be denied because of any further consideration of cause. To be sure, recovery may be prevented by other kinds of considerations such as limitations on the scope of duty. But the term "substantial factor" is no more appropriate to describe these considerations than is any of the other cause formulas treated above.

[29] *Restatement of Torts* (1948 Supp.), p. 733. As the new added comment makes clear, the substantial factor formula is applicable only to the cause in fact question. "It is completely faulty analysis" and "is confusing the question of policy with the question of fact" to use the criterion of foreseeability (the "highly extraordinary" formula) in determining such a question. . . .

Causation in the Law*

I. INTRODUCTION

"Modern cases have substituted the test of responsibility or fault for that of causation."[1] "Instead of asking three questions I should have thought that in many cases it would be simpler and better to ask the one question; is the consequence within the risk?" and again "Is the consequence to be regarded as fairly within the risk created by the negligence?"[2] No one who has attempted to find and state principles behind the legal use of causal terminology can fail to sympathize with the wish to substitute plain definable issues for the baffling question whether a defendant's act or omission was the "efficient" or "predominant" or "proximate" or "direct" cause of the plaintiff's injury, or whether a causal "chain" has been broken by an "unforeseen" cause. But even in the English law of negligence, as the tentative language of the second quotation suggests, a substitution of "fault" for causation is not yet a *fait accompli*; and it is of course arguable that if the notions of "fault," "within the risk," "reasonable foresight" were used as a test of remoteness of damage as well as of liability, they would soon begin to lose their apparent attractive simplicity. In any case where liability in tort is strict and *a fortiori* in the many important branches of the law where liability is not based on any act of a defendant, a general elimination of the notion of causation would be an absurdity, however attractive it may seem in cases of negligence and possibly in certain branches of the criminal law. Thus it is obvious that where courts have to determine such questions as whether some harm or loss was

* H. L. A. Hart and A. M. Honoré, "Causation in the Law," *Law Quarterly Review*, LXXII (1956), Pt. I., 58–90, reprinted with the permission of the authors and the publishers, Stevens & Sons Ltd., London. Footnotes have been renumbered. The most comprehensive treatment to date of the topic of causation is the author's *Causation in the Law* (Oxford: Clarendon Press, 1959).

[1] A. L. Goodhart, "Notes of an Address on Special Problems of the Law of Torts," p. 11, reprinted in (1955) 71 *L.Q.R.* 402 at p. 413.

[2] *Per* Denning, L.J., *Roe v. Minister of Health* [1954] 2 Q.B. 66, 86. The three questions are "duty," "causation," and "remoteness."

"caused by the discharge of any missile by the enemy," or "attributable" to war service, or "occurred owing to the presence of a vehicle on a road," or "occurred as a direct result of action taken by the enemy," or to adjudicate on claims under policies of insurance that some loss or damage was the consequence of some specified contingency, causal questions cannot be simply bypassed; they must be answered even though they involve the use of perplexing distinctions like those between mere "conditions" and "causes" and the determination of what is or is not an "extraneous" or "superseding" cause. In all such cases notions of fault or foresight are irrelevant. "It does not matter what the man who discharged the missile might reasonably have expected to occur or what the War Department who accepted the man for service might reasonably have expected to happen. The award of a pension depends on causation and causation alone."[3]

Of course many writers have urged that whenever the courts are by the form of the relevant legal rules driven to use causal language in deciding cases, all they do and can do is to select as the cause one of an infinite number of necessary conditions without which ("but for" which) the loss or damage in question would not have occurred. And it is urged that such a selection of one necessary condition can only represent a preference for one result rather than another, since there is no factual distinction to be drawn between the necessary conditions of an event all of which are, factually speaking, equivalent. As early as 1874 this view was put forcibly by N. St. J. Green: "Where a court says the damage is remote, it does not follow naturally, it is not proximate, all they mean and can mean is that they think that in all circumstances the plaintiff should not recover."[4] The advocacy

and illustration of this view by many able writers has certainly shown that considerations of what may be broadly termed policy inevitably enter into the judicial determination of causal questions. Yet the view that the distinction between causes and mere conditions is wholly without objective or factual warrant is really an exaggeration, and obscures as much as it reveals of the issues which courts decide in causal terminology and of the manner in which these are decided.

Most of the persuasive force of this view is drawn not from clear evidence that causal terms are in fact used by courts merely as a means of presenting a decision reached on other grounds, but from the assumption, which is now in some danger of freezing into a juristic dogma, that no objective or factual distinction can be drawn between the necessary conditions of an event, and that all alike have, so far as the facts go, equal title to be treated as its cause. But this assumption needs careful scrutiny: for though the doctrine of the equivalence of conditions may in its time have served as a warning against certain metaphysical absurdities, in its juristic formulation it misrepresents the scientist's use of the notion of causation (so far as he does use it) and has obscured for lawyers the very commonsense notion of causation which the courts, in common-law jurisdictions at least, profess to apply to the cases before them.

In the constant reference made by the courts to the common-sense principles of causation there are in fact two connected paradoxes worth considering. The first is that though the courts insist that their investigations of causal questions are "practical inquiries" not "scientific inquests,"[5] that "the cause of an event is to be decided on common-sense principles,"[6] and that questions of causation are pure questions of fact which, if they are to be answered by a judge, must yet be answered by him as an ordinary man,[7] such remarks

[3] Per Denning, L.J., in *Minister of Pensions v. Chennell* [1947] K.B. 250, pp. 253–54.
[4] IV *American Law Review*, p. 200. This is the view taken (*inter alios*) by Glanville Williams (*Joint Torts and Contributory Negligence*, p. 239), by Fleming James and Perry (1951) 60 *Yale L.J.* 761, and by Esmein (Planiol-Ripert, 2d ed., VI, 73). It is to be found expressed in two different forms: (1) that the questions of causal connection which courts decide are not purely questions of fact but a blend of fact and policy, for they include both the genuine question of fact whether the alleged cause was a *sine qua non* of the loss and also a non-factual question masquerading under such names as proximate or legal cause; (2) that the question of causation is purely a question of fact, but that decisions do not turn simply on causation but on a combination of causation and responsibility. . . . Common to both these formulations

is the thesis that the only factual part of causal questions is whether or not the alleged cause was a *sine qua non* of what has occurred.
[5] *Weld-Blundell v. Stephens* [1920] A.C. 956, 986, *per* Lord Sumner.
[6] *Boiler Inspector and Insurance Company of Canada v. Sherwin Williams Company of Canada Ltd.* [1951] A.C. 319, 339.
[7] *Hogan v. Bentinck Collieries* [1949] 1 All E.R. 588; *Leyland Shipping Co. v. Norwich Union Fire Insurance Society* [1918] A.C. 350, 363, *per* Lord Dunedin: "I think the case turns on a pure question of fact to be determined by common-sense principles. What is the cause of the loss?"

have never been accompanied by an attempt to explain what are the common-sense principles of causation or how the notion of cause is used in ordinary practical inquiries. Yet the fact that the notion of cause used by the law is a common-sense notion surely does not mean that it stands for something so simple that any elucidation of it is unnecessary, or that it is a merely intuitive notion which cannot be further elucidated. Common sense is not a matter of inexplicable or arbitrary assertions and the notion of cause which it employs, though flexible and complex, is governed by statable principles even though the ordinary man who uses the notion may not, without assistance, be able to make them explicit. The plain man may have quite adequate mastery of concepts such as cause within the field of its day-to-day use, but this may coincide with a great need for clarification of the principles involved in its use; and this need may become acute when, as in the law, the notion has to be applied to circumstances vastly more complex and more subtly differentiated than those of everyday life.

The second paradox is this: side by side with the court's insistence that the notion of cause which the law applies is a common-sense notion, judges use a host of recurrent metaphors when causal questions arise which rarely appear in the vocabulary of the ordinary man and which are as baffling as the philosophical or psychological distinctions which they are designed to replace. Perhaps "conduit pipes," "transmission gears," "networks" have gone forever, but besides the inexpugnable "chain" of causation and its "snapping" or "interruption," references are still made to causes as being so "powerful"[8] as to supersede other causes, or so powerful as to "reduce" other causes to part of the circumstances,[9] or to causes as being *functus officio*,[10] or to circumstances being "part of the background in front of which the subsequent event has taken place."[11] Of course metaphors are not in themselves objectionable even in the law; the objection to these particular metaphors is that they do not function (as good ones do) as a convenient or illuminating or

striking substitute for a literal expression of well-understood facts or distinctions, but are used in contexts where distinctions are felt to be of importance but no clear or literal expression of them is forthcoming. Most of this class of causal metaphors are used in the effort to distinguish what, among a set of total conditions, is to be treated as the cause of an occurrence from the mere conditions. But the need to draw this distinction is not a peculiarity of the legal use of causal concepts. It is drawn in everyday life by the ordinary man, the moralist, and the historian. And it is possible, though the matter is indeed complex, to give some literal description of the principal ways in which it is drawn. A man picks up a box of matches, deliberately strikes a match, and kindles a fire. In ordinary life when we say that his action was the cause of the resulting fire and distinguish this both from the oxygen in the air and the manufacturer's action in making the match (though in *some* sense all three conditions are equally necessary), we make use of certain principles for distinguishing causes from conditions which are at the root of the legal distinction between proximate and remote cause and the associated metaphors.

There are of course many reasons why an effort should be made to free the law from an unnecessary dependence on metaphorical modes of expression. But in the case of the particular group of metaphors that have clustered around the notion of cause there is a special need to do this, for they keep alive a confused conception of cause as something which, like a moving thing or human being, may possess more or less power and exert more or less influence. This conception of cause has in the past provoked needless puzzles for the law: if a cause is analogous to the force of a moving thing, how can a mere omission or a failure to act be a cause or interrupt a chain of causation? How can a static condition be a cause? On the whole in England the courts have overcome these particular difficulties. But it is true that the whole notion of an intervening or supervening cause is still darkened by analogies with a thing which is active or moves.

We propose therefore in the first of these two articles to give some account of this common-sense principle of causation according to which the courts say causal questions must be decided, and in the second article to show

[8] *Minister of Pensions v. Chennell* [1947] K. B. 250, 256.
[9] *Ibid.*, p. 256.
[10] *Davies v. Swan Motor Company* [1949] 2 K.B. 291, p. 318.
[11] *Norris v. William Moss & Son, Ltd.* [1954] 1 W.L.R. 346, 351, *per* Vaisey, J.

how literal description of the crucial distinctions inherent in the common-sense notion can be used to clarify the discussion of problems of superseding cause. But it is important to appreciate the limits which any such enterprise must have. It would be absurd to claim that the principles latent in the common-sense notion of causation provide conclusive answers to the complex causal questions which the courts have to face: it is not in this simple sense that courts "have to decide such questions according to common-sense principles." In legal contexts complexities arise and distinctions have to be drawn which often make a simple application of the principles commonly used in daily life impossible. Hence ordinary common-sense principles serve rather as an organizing framework for answers to the complex legal questions of causation which the courts have to decide: they mark certain distinctions requiring attention in all causal reasoning over practical affairs, but they will often leave a choice to be made between logically open alternatives and a line to be drawn in many matters of degree. Within this organizing framework, but not in place of it, appeal to considerations of "policy" will be inescapable and intelligible. It is worth noticing that in this respect the use of common-sense principles of causation in the law is similar to its use of other highly general notions such as those of temporal or spatial location. It would be correct to say for the law that the question of where or when something happened was a question to be decided according to common-sense principles; yet it would be absurd to pretend that common-sense principles, subtle and flexible though they are, in accordance with which events are spatially or temporally located, would be adequate to answer the type of question that may perplex the lawyer. In ordinary life the questions "where is X?" or "where did X happen?" demand answers (as they arise: if we ask where a given chess piece is, any of the answers "at K3," "on the board," "in my room," "in Oxford" may be appropriate in different contexts). This relativity to context is part of the common-sense notions of spatial location, and if we appreciate it, we may understand better certain questions which arise in the law about the place of events. But of course common-sense principles could not yield an answer to the type of question concerning the place where a contract was made which arises in the conflict of laws; in ordinary life, we do not have to locate the making of contracts with an eye to the distinction between the place where the offeree spoke (over the telephone) words of acceptance and the place where the offeror heard them. For similar reasons common-sense principles would provide no answer to the question where one man killed another, when a distinction has to be drawn between the place where the trigger was pulled and the place where the victim was hit, which is so vital a distinction for the law when a jurisdictional border separates the two. Before an answer can be given to such questions as these, common-sense criteria have to be supplemented by legal principles and a decision made between alternatives which are necessarily left open by common-sense principles, though these define the limits within which such questions have to be answered.

It is above all important to remember that courts are sometimes compelled to answer questions of causation (and indeed of temporal and spatial location) which the ordinary man might refuse to answer; he might claim that the complexity or oddity of the facts was such that no answer could be given according to common-sense principles to causal questions in the form which the law demands. Thus in *The Matiana*[12] the court was *forced* to say whether the convoy commodore's order to proceed on a zig-zag course (a war-like operation) or the hidden reef struck after the ship had complied with the order (a marine peril) was *the* cause of the disaster. Faced with this question the ordinary man might well say "Neither was *the* cause" or "It depends on how you look at it" or that "Both these events were causes." It is plain therefore that in cases such as these (and in cases of contributory negligence under the old rules) the law may actually do violence to common-sense principles by insisting that something be identified as "the cause," where common sense would wish to speak of "a cause" or "concurrent causes." In other types of case (e.g., those of "superseding cause") common-sense principles may point toward a decision one way or another rather than determine it conclusively. Hence it is truer to say that the notion of cause applied in the law has its roots in the common-sense notion

12 [1921] A.C. 104.

than that it is identical with it; and the utility of the elucidation of common-sense principles lies, not in its capacity to provide answers to the difficult questions arising in the law, but in the extent to which it brings to light the precise issues which have to be faced in such questions, permits these issues to be formulated in literal terms, and exhibits the termini within which a field is open for judicial choice and discretion.

II. EXPLANATION AND RESPONSIBILITY: THE DISCOVERY OF CAUSES AND THE ATTRIBUTION OF CONSEQUENCES

Before we identify in detail common-sense principles of causation, it is important to distinguish two principal ways in which causal questions arise both for common sense and for the law, for though they share important features they are marked by differences specially relevant in legal contexts. In ordinary life and in the law we may be presented with some contingency (a railway accident or someone's sudden death) which we find puzzling: we do not know why or how it happened. In such cases to inquire for the cause of the contingency is to ask for an explanation which, when provided, makes what has happened intelligible, because it shows it to be, after all, something which exemplifies known general laws as to how things happen, though some considerable analysis of the facts of the situation and much further evidence beyond the initial information may be required before this causal explanation can be given. Thus an inquiry into the cause of a railway accident would bring to light previously unknown facts (that a rail was bent or the driver fainted), and when these are established the accident will be explained since the new fact that has been learned, in conjunction with what is already known, is sufficient to account for the accident; the existence of the bent rail, together with the facts relating to the weight and speed of the train, account for its running off the line. Very often in the courts, as a preliminary step to a final decision as to a defendant's liability for some loss or harm, causal inquiry is ultimately to determine questions of responsibility, at this stage the inquiry is in a sense theoretical, designed to explain.

Thus, to take examples from recent cases, where the question before the court was whether or not the defendant's breach of

building regulations in failing to provide certain protective boards was the cause of the plaintiff's injury, a preliminary question arose as to the precise manner in which the plaintiff was injured. He had been struck by a falling pipe, but this partial explanation left much to be explained, for there was no evidence to show how the pipe had fallen from the boards on which it had been placed. "The cause of its fall . . . is . . . a mystery." In the end the court drew the conclusion that it rolled in some way unexplained from the board on which it had been placed, and on this footing the accident was causally connected with the defendant's breach of the regulations in failing to provide a protective tail board.[13] Such preliminary causal inquiries designed to establish how or why something happened are often fraught with difficulty: sometimes the courts, in order to arrive at any conclusion, have to make use of presumptions, and sometimes a plaintiff may fail to discharge the onus of showing how his injuries happened. But, difficult though such inquiries are, it is not this type of causal question that creates the main perplexities over the use of causation in the law. These perplexities arise even where it is perfectly clear how or why some loss or harm happened, but the courts have still to determine whether such loss or harm can be attributed to the defendant's wrongful act (or some other type of contingency designated by the relevant rules of law) as its consequence. This type of question we shall, for clarity's sake, call a question of attribution as opposed to explanation. The contrast between these two types of causal inquiry may be crudely presented thus: in cases where we seek a cause as an explanation, our starting point is some known loss or harm (the putative effect), and we try to find some contingency connected with it by known general laws which explain its occurrence; the movement of thought is roughly from the known to the previously unknown earlier or contemporaneous event. But when questions of attribution are in issue, we are given *ab initio* two starting points as the termini of our inquiry: these are some wrongful act (or other contingency defined by law) and (usually) some loss or harm, and the problem is to determine whether the loss or harm is so connected with the wrongful act that it is its consequence. In simple cases

[13] *Hughes v. McGoff and Vickers, Ltd.* [1955] 1 W.L.R. 416.

the answer may be obvious. The defendant dropped a lighted cigarette into the wastepaper basket and the house burned down. Here the wrongful act, together with the other normal conditions present, was sufficient to produce the fire and we should confidently attribute the damage to the wrongful act as its consequence. If challenged to say why we regarded the damage as the consequence *propter hoc* and not merely *post hoc,* we would appeal to well-known generalizations which show that what was done, in conjunction with the normal circumstances present, was sufficient to account for the fire. In such cases the difference between explanatory causal inquiries and attributive inquiries is not very striking; if asked to explain how the loss occurred, we might equally well cite the dropping of the cigarette. The distinctive character of attributive inquiries emerges only when these are difficult; instead of the simple cases just cited, suppose that the cigarette thrown into the wastepaper basket was on the point of flickering out when a third party put some highly inflammable material into the basket. Here there is no puzzle as to how the loss occurred but a question has arisen whether the loss is to be attributed to the defendant's negligent act or the third party's; this is a problem compared with the simple case, because there is now present among the conditions required to account for the fire a factor (the third party's act) which has some of the characteristics by which common sense distinguishes causes from mere conditions, whereas in the simple case no such further factor was present. The general form of such problems is whether or not a given loss can be attributed to a given wrongful act, having regard to the presence of some special third factor : they are often stated in the form "Was the third factor a superseding cause?" Did it "break the causal chain?" Another form of attributive inquiry is whether a given third factor though neither a "superseding" cause nor a "mere condition" of loss is a cause or a concurrent cause along with some other factor.

When questions of attribution have to be answered by the courts it is often necessary to embark on discussions of a type which would not normally arise when we are searching for the cause of some contingency in order to explain how it occurred. In doubtful cases of attribution the degree to which some third

factor possesses one or more of the characteristics by which causes are distinguished from mere conditions may have to be assessed. Such questions, as we later show, largely turn on the extent to which in different situations a human action is voluntary or suffers from any of those defects which (by ordinary common-sense criteria) render it not wholly voluntary; or they turn upon the extent to which a conjunction of events is abnormal or normal. Such questions in law as in daily life are often borderline questions, for the central notions involved are flexible and in some contexts vague. They are not therefore questions which it would be useful to classify as *ordinary* questions of fact and, of course, decisions on "remoteness" are often reviewed by appellate tribunals. . . . On the other hand, in cases where the attribution of a consequence to a defendant's act is in issue just because the law sets here the termini of the inquiry, certain types of question which arise when we are searching for the cause as the explanation of some contingency will not arise.

Hence two sorts of causal inquiries have their place in the law and it is important to grasp the distinction between these two types of inquiry, for if it is not understood in its place, an *exaggerated* distinction is apt to be drawn between a factual scientific use of the concept of cause, which allegedly makes no distinction between causes and mere conditions, and on the other hand a legal use (legal causation) which makes this distinction but without any factual or objective warrant for it. In fact the distinction between causes and mere conditions is not a peculiarity of the legal uses of causal notions: it enters both into those factual inquiries of everyday life where we seek for the cause of some contingency in order to explain how it occurred, and into those inquiries in which we ask, can a given loss be attributed to a given action as its consequence in view of some third factor which looks like a cause? We make the distinction between causes and conditions whenever, for example, we select the bent rail as the cause of a railway accident and relegate the weight and speed of the train to the status of mere conditions. Distinctions made on similar lines enter, though at a different point, into questions of attribution when we have to decide whether some loss may be attributed to some specified act as its consequence, or whether the presence of some third factor among the set of conditions accounting for the loss prevents this attribution because it has, in some greater or less degree, those characteristics by which causes may be distinguished from conditions. And the same distinctions enter into those questions of attribution which are answered by saying that a given contingency is a cause along with something else.

III. PARTICULAR CAUSAL STATEMENTS AND CAUSAL GENERALIZATIONS

(a) *Particular Causal Statements*

If we are to elicit the common-sense principle of causation, it is important to bear in mind a sufficient range of different examples, for nothing is so misleading here as an over-concentration on a single sort of example. Here then is a selection of ordinary examples which will serve to make the initial point that for common sense, as for the law, causes are not restricted to what may ordinarily be called events. A cause may be an action, an event, a state, a failure to act, the nonoccurrence of an event and the nonoccurrence of a condition, and we shall use the neutral word "contingency" to cover all these different types of causes. "The cause of the fire was the dropping of a lighted cigarette into the wastepaper basket." "The cause of the workman's injury was the fall of the lead pipe." "The cause of the accident was the icy state of the road." "The cause of the accident was the signalman's failure to pull the signal." "The cause of the famine in India was the lack of rain." "The cause of the famine in India was the failure of the government to build up adequate reserves." All of the above examples are statements that a particular contingency caused some other contingency, and it is most important to distinguish from such particular causal statements general causal statements; these are general statements often dignified with the title of causal laws, and they assert, not that some particular event caused another, but that some kind of action, omission, condition, or event is the cause of another. These generalizations may either be part of a common stock of knowledge, and if so may be roughly formulated generalizations like "swallowing arsenic causes death," "drought causes famine," "striking a match causes it to burst into flame"; or they may be stricter generalizations incorporating scientific knowledge. "Heating a gas causes an increase of pressure

upon the sides of its container," "contact with the flame of nitrate of soda causes dinitrophenol to explode."

Much philosophical discussion has of course been concerned with the nature of those generalizations which are ranked as causal generalizations or causal laws and in particular with the question whether any statements of observed regularities in nature have this status. We do not propose to discuss this question here for it is not the source of the lawyer's perplexities about causation; but it is vital to remember, if we are to understand the character of particular causal statements (which *are* the source of those perplexities), that every particular causal statement implies one or more generalizations in the sense that its truth depends (*inter alia*) on their truth. This dependence of particular causal statements on the truth of generalizations may be overlooked because of the familiarity of many simple causal laws. When we say that A's blow caused B's injuries we may hardly realize that we are applying here, to a particular case, generalizations about mechanical and physiological processes in nature; only when someone challenges the causal connection asserted here as distinct from the truth of the separate statements which are involved (i.e., that A hit B and that B's leg is broken) are the implied generalizations brought into the open to show that B's broken leg was a case of *propter hoc* and not *post hoc*. The notion of a causal connection between two events, as distinct from their mere sequence in time, depends on the truth of such generalizations. Indeed even the humbler assertion that one event is a necessary condition or *sine qua non* of another (e.g., that a fire would not have happened had oxygen not been in the air or certain combustible material had not been in a certain place) depends on the truth of generalizations; if we did not know that fires never occur without oxygen or unless certain types of material are combustible we should never be able to identify a *sine qua non* on a particular occasion.

The courts are of course usually concerned with particular causal statements as part of the process of establishing the civil or criminal liability of a particular defendant or accused person, and the precise form in which the statements are expressed may depend on the precise language of the rule of law or instrument under which liability arises. The range of different expressions includes the following: "X was the cause of Y," "X caused Y," "Y was caused by X," "Y was the result of X," "Y was the consequence of X," "Y is attributable to X," "Y arose from X," "Y was due to X." For some purposes it will be important to draw distinctions between these various types of causal locution; obviously "X was *a* cause of Y" will differ in important respects from "X was *the* cause of Y"; nonetheless there are certain general principles which we believe apply to them all and constitute vital elements in both the lawyer's and the layman's use of the concept of causation.

(b) Jointly Sufficient Conditions

It is perhaps a theoretical scientific ideal that the general propositions by which particular causal statements must be supported should be general statements to which there are no exceptions, and that every apparent exception is to be explained by saying that the causal law has not been stated with sufficient precision. But the particular causal statements of everyday life, though they too require to be supported, if challenged, by general laws showing that this must happen in nature, fall short of this scientific ideal. The observed regularities need not be without exceptions; it is enough that they preponderate. So we can say that A's throwing his lighted cigarette into the wastepaper basket caused the fire and was not merely followed by it, even though we cannot support this with general laws showing that this must happen in *every* such case. But we may be very easily misled in thinking about causation by the apparently elliptical form in which we normally assert the general causal generalizations known to us. We speak as if a *single* occurrence of one kind were known regularly to precede or follow another, and this hides the fact that we are never able to identify just one occurrence (immersion of iron in water, dropping a lighted cigarette into the wastepaper basket) and say that this is always followed by some occurrence of a given kind (rusting, outbreak of fire). Instead, our causal generalizations in fact inform us that an occurrence of a given kind regularly follows upon *a complex set of conditions*: many other conditions besides the one we designate as the cause must also exist if the effect is to follow. The icy condition of the roads will not lead to acci-

dents unless certain other conditions are satisfied: the vehicles moving over them must be of a certain weight, construction, and move at a certain minimum speed; dropping of a lighted cigarette into a wastepaper basket will lead to fire only in conjunction with certain other positive and negative conditions, viz., oxygen in the air, the presence of combustible material, absence of moisture above a certain minimum, etc.

So "*the* cause" is one condition selected from a complex set of conditions which, according to known generalizations, are together sufficient to produce the consequence. Each member of this complex set of conditions is required to complete the set (the oxygen in the air is therefore as necessary as the dropping of the cigarette), and if we were to state fully the causal laws known to us without the usual ellipsis, they would always appear as asserting that a given complex *set* of conditions is uniformly followed by an occurrence of a given kind.[14] Now, in these articles we shall refer to this complex set of conditions not as necessary conditions but as a *jointly sufficient set* for the following reason. It is part of the common-sense notion of a cause (and it remains true of the application of cause in legal contexts) that for any given kind of occurrence there may be more than one complex set of conditions jointly sufficient to produce occurrences of that kind. In ordinary life and in the law we treat, e.g., the death of a human being as an effect sometimes of poisoning (plus other conditions), sometimes of shooting (plus other conditions), sometimes of starvation (plus other conditions); similarly for common sense, heat may be the effect of friction, chemical change or percussion (in each case together with other conditions). This being so, we can only say of any one such complex set of conditions that it is *sufficient,* according to our general laws, to produce the effect, not that it is *necessary,* according to these laws, though, as we shall show in discussing the ambiguous notion of a *sine qua non* or "necessary condition," there is a sense of necessary condition in which a member of such a jointly sufficient set of con-

---

[14] Even this fuller formulation is in a sense elliptical, for the complete formulation of *all* the conditions required for the production of an effect remains an unattainable ideal. Even the scientist can only isolate sets of sufficient conditions which are uniformly followed by a specified consequence in a wide range of varying circumstances not in "all possible" circumstances.

ditions may be properly referred to as "necessary."

It is next important to notice that the jointly sufficient set of conditions may include negative conditions as well as positive ones, and very often even the particular one of the set which common sense selects as the cause or a cause may be a negative condition. "The failure of the signalman to pull the signal was the cause of the accident," "The drought was the cause of the famine." This is only mysterious or puzzling if we allow ourselves to be influenced by the metaphors that have grown round the notion of cause and misconceive a cause as something always strictly analogous to physical movement. It is, however, true that in specifying the jointly sufficient set of conditions of some occurrence we do not usually mention negative conditions unless we have some special reason to comment on the exceptional absence of some condition which is normally present. Thus in the cigarette case we would not naturally include in our statement of a set of jointly sufficient conditions the negative condition that some known counteracting cause (e.g., a heavy shower of rain penetrating the building) was absent. It would be otiose to do this since it is generally understood that any cause may be counteracted and we have therefore no need to refer to the absence of some counteracting cause unless this is exceptional.

IV. CAUSE AND CONDITIONS

Within the jointly sufficient set of conditions of an occurrence, common sense often obstinately marks a distinction between one or more which are selected as the cause or causes and the remaining conditions in the set which are classified as the mere conditions or the circumstances in which the cause "operates," although, as we have seen, all the conditions in the set are in fact equally required if the effect is to follow. This distinction is built into the very structure of our ordinary thought about practical affairs and could not be abandoned without extreme paradox, such as that involved in saying that the manufacturer's production of the match with which a fire is kindled or the oxygen in the air has an equal title with the deliberate action of kindling the fire to be called the cause of the fire. But the central question before us is whether any intelligible principles control the distinction so obstinately marked by

common sense between mere conditions and causes, or whether we must say that this is arbitrary and without factual basis. Is it true that only reasons of "policy" or the wish to punish behavior of which we disapprove, or some confused metaphysical notion that certain events have greater causal "potency" than others, can account for a distinction so firmly embedded in common sense?

Professor Glanville Williams[15] says "Modern philosophers and scientists refuse to differentiate between causes or between 'a cause' and the accompanying causal 'conditions,'" and cites Professor Ayer in support.[16] But all that modern philosophers have in fact denied is a confused philosophical misrepresentation of the common-sense distinction. This has taken the form of asserting that one of a set of jointly sufficient conditions has greater "potency," "power," or "force" than the rest. In fact the common-sense distinction is quite independent of this metaphysical theory, which draws any plausibility it has from the misleading conception of a cause as analogous to a moving body or more or less powerful force. The line between cause and mere condition is in fact drawn by common sense on principles which vary in a subtle and complex way, both with the type of causal question in issue and the circumstances in which causal questions arise. Any general account of these principles is therefore always in danger of oversimplifying them: perhaps the only general observation of value is that in distinguishing between causes and conditions two contrasts are of prime importance. These are the contrasts between what is abnormal and what is normal in relation to any given subject-matter and between a free deliberate human action and all other conditions. The simple notions in these pairs of contrasts lie at the root of most of the legal metaphors we have noticed and must be used in any literal discussion of the facts which they obscure. We shall now consider separately how these pairs of contrasts serve to distinguish causes from mere conditions in explanatory and attributive inquiries.

(a) Explanatory Inquiries

(1) In the sciences, causes may be sought to explain what usually or normally happens: the processes of continuous growth, the tides,

[15] *Joint Torts and Contributory Negligence*, p. 240.
[16] *Foundations of Empirical Knowledge*, p. 181.

planetary motions, increase in the pressure of gases, senile decay. But in ordinary life, as in the law, a causal explanation is most often prompted by the occurrence of something unusual: we ask for the causes of accidents, catastrophes, deviations from the normal or accepted course of events. It is an important feature of causal inquiries that from the outset it is always assumed that a considerable number of circumstances are present which, though they may be in fact necessary conditions of some loss or harm or accident, etc., are known to be normal conditions also present on occasions when no disaster occurs. Thus anyone who asks what is the cause of a railway accident would assume until corrected that the train was moving at a normal speed, carrying a normal weight, that the driver stopped and started, accelerated and slowed down at normal times. To mention these normal conditions would obviously provide no explanation of the disaster, for they are also present when no disaster occurs; whereas the mention of the bent rail does provide an explanation. Accordingly, though all the conditions mentioned are equally necessary, the bent rail is the cause and the others are mere conditions. It is the bent rail we say which "made the difference" between disaster and normal functioning.

(2) What is normal and what is abnormal will of course be relevant to the context of any given inquiry, and it is important to grasp this relativity to context so that we shall not surrender prematurely to the temptation to say that the distinction between causes and mere conditions is arbitrary or subjective or merely the expression of a preference for a given result. In most cases it would of course be eccentric to cite the presence of oxygen as the cause of the fire, necessary condition though it is of fire. What makes it eccentric is partly that it is the accompaniment of *every* fire and in ordinary life, as in the law, we want to know, not the cause of fire whenever it breaks out, but of some particular fire which has broken out where fire usually does not. But a citation of the presence of oxygen as the cause of the fire would be eccentric also because, like the usual speed of a train in the accident case, it is part of the normal conditions. On the other hand it is easy to imagine cases where the exclusion of oxygen would be normal, i.e., when some laboratory experiment or delicate manufacturing process depended on its exclusion for safety from fire

and hence for success, and in such cases it would be correct to identify the abnormal presence of oxygen as the cause of a fire. The conception of what, in relation to any given subject-matter, rank as normal conditions will very often depend on the practical purposes that may lie behind the search for a causal explanation and also upon many other factors. An Indian peasant may say correctly that the cause of the famine was the drought; the World Food Commission, with experience of what is done by many countries, may say that the government's failure to build up reserves was the cause of the famine. The victim of a motor accident may say the cause of the accident was the failure of the driver to slow down on passing an awkward corner; a traffic authority, with a wider experience of the habits of motorists, not only at this spot but elsewhere, may treat the motorist's conduct as normal and the awkward corner as the abnormal deviation from normal road conditions. Collingwood drew from such examples of the relativity of the distinction between cause and conditions the moral that what is selected as the cause is always something that may be controlled or operated by human agency in order to produce a desired result. And this pragmatic approach has been developed by some jurists. But the identification of the cause as what is alterable by human agencies makes too close a connection between the identification of causes and the practical purposes behind causal inquiries. Sometimes the connection is not there at all, for we may ask what is the cause of the explosion of a star. And even where the connection is present it is indirect, merely controlling what, in a given context, is to be treated as normal conditions for a given class of case.

(3) Though what is treated as normal represents in many ways our practical interests and our attitude to nature, it would be wrong to identify as the normal and so always as part of the mere conditions of events the ordinary course of nature unaffected by human intervention. This is an oversimplification, because what is taken as normal for the purpose of the distinction between cause and mere conditions is very often an artifact of human habit, custom, or convention. This is so because men have discovered that nature is not only sometimes harmful if we intervene but is also sometimes harmful unless we intervene, and have developed customs, procedures,

and routines to counteract such harm. These have become a second "nature" and so a second "norm." The effect of drought is regularly neutralized by governmental precautions in conserving water or food; disease is neutralized by inoculation; rain by the use of umbrellas. When such man-made normal conditions are established, deviation from them will be regarded as exceptional and so rank as the cause of harm. It is obvious that in such cases what is selected as the cause from the total set of conditions will often be an omission which coincides with what is reprehensible by established standards of behavior. But this does not justify the conclusion that it is so selected merely because it is reprehensible.

(4) It is natural but mistaken to think of the mere conditions of an event as always existing contemporaneously with what is identified as the cause of that event: perhaps this is due to the natural metaphors of a "background" or a "medium" for the "operation" of causes which we use when we refer to mere conditions. But it is vital to appreciate that what are contrasted with the cause as mere conditions always include some events or conditions subsequent in time to the cause. Conditions are *mere* conditions, as distinct from causes, because they are normal and not because they are contemporaneous with the cause. Thus if X lights a fire in the open and shortly after a normal gentle breeze gets up and the fire spreads to Y's property, X's action is the cause of the harm, though without the subsequent breeze no harm would have occurred; the bare fact that the breeze was subsequent to X's action (and also causally independent of it) does not destroy its status as a mere condition or make it a "superseding" cause. To achieve the latter status a subsequent occurrence must at least have some characteristic by which common sense usually distinguishes causes from mere conditions.

(5) So far we have considered cases where the search for causal explanation terminates in the identification of some abnormal physical event as the cause. But of course in many cases a human action or omission may be found in such inquiries to be the cause. The cause of the railway accident may be the signalman's failure to pull the signal, and the cause of someone's death may be the malicious administration of poison. Explanation of this kind provides in its turn an explanation of abnormal physical conditions, and has for

common sense a finality which is often lacking where the explanation stops short with the production of some abnormal physical condition or event. We feel that it is not enough to be told that a man died from the presence of unusual quantities of arsenic in his body, and we press on for the more satisfying explanation in terms of human agency. At the common-sense level, once we have reached this point, we have reached an explanation with a special finality and usually do not press further for a causal explanation of a deliberate human action. This is not of course to say that scientific inquiries into the psychological or other causes of human behavior are absurd or that determinism as a theory is mistaken; but it is to insist that in the common-sense notion of causation a deliberate human action has a special status as a cause and is not regarded in its turn as something which is caused.

(b) *Attributive Inquiries*

In attributive inquiries we no longer ask the open question "What is the cause of this loss or harm?" but the circumscribed question "Given this wrongful act (or other designated event) and given this loss or harm, is the latter the consequence of the former?" and our purpose in asking this question is not to understand what has happened but to determine responsibility. Though there is much that is common to both types of causal inquiry, there are also differences affecting the manner in which and the point at which the distinction between cause and mere conditions is drawn. It is of course true that we have less nonlegal material on which to draw to elucidate the use of this distinction in attributive inquiries for, while the exigencies of daily life have imposed upon us a constant need to discover the causes of disasters and the causes that counteract them, there is no similar pressure outside the law to determine with great precision what range or type of loss or harm is attributable to our own or other persons' behavior as its consequence. There is no precise system of rewards, punishments, or compensation to be administered by common sense. Accordingly here common-sense principles are less precise: yet they exist and are the rudimentary counterparts of the legal terminology of "proximate," "remote," and "superseding" causes, and it is in terms of these rudimentary distinctions that the metaphors of "flowing directly," "part of the background," "part of the history," etc., can obtain a literal translation.

Common to the explanatory and attributive inquiries is the important fact that, in relation to any given subject-matter, normal conditions are prima facie ranked as the mere conditions and distinguished from the cause or a cause of contingencies. To both types of inquiry there apply the points already developed concerning the relativity of what is normal to the subject-matter in hand, the possibility that what is normal may be either what usually happens or what is normally done by human beings, and the important fact that mere conditions will always include normal contingencies which are subsequent in time to the cause. The principal differences between the two sorts of inquiry are twofold. First, the need to make the distinction between causes and mere conditions arises at a different point, for we draw it in determining whether some third factor prevents the attribution of a given harm to a given action or contingency as its consequence. Secondly, though in drawing the distinction between causes and conditions here we use as our main criteria the notion of a free human action and also that of an abnormal occurrence, the relative importance of these two criteria is different. To illustrate these points we may use again our previous simple example:

(i) A man throws his lighted cigarette into a wastepaper basket; there is a fire which destroys the house. The attributive question is "Is this loss the consequence of A's action?" Here prima facie A's action has completed a set of conditions sufficient to lead to fire, and at this simple level the only doubt is the possibility that, in spite of the prima facie appearances, the fire may merely have succeeded A's action in point of time and had no causal connection with it. To settle this simple question, further investigation of the facts may be required to show that the events between A's action and the destruction of the house did indeed exemplify causal laws concerning the start and spread of fires. These laws we should apply in order to dispose of the suggestion that A's cigarette had in fact harmlessly flickered out and that the fire was caused by some quite independent occurrence such as a short circuit. But it is important to see that what makes the case so simple, once we have disposed of this suggestion, is that, though A's action alone could not be sufficient to lead to fire, the other elements required to complete a sufficient set of conditions are all normal events, even though some, like the continued presence of oxygen in the air or the movement of air currents, are subsequent to A's action and independent of it. The attribution of the loss to A's action is, in this case, simple because there is no human intervention and nothing out of the ordinary besides A's action. There is accordingly nothing to prevent us saying that the loss is the consequence of A's action.

(ii) Our case would lose its primitive simplicity if an examination of the facts showed that A's action and the other normal conditions present would not have led to fire unless conjoined with some other human agent's action (or in suitable cases omission). Suppose just as A's cigarette is flickering out in the wastepaper basket B deliberately puts in some highly inflammable material. Here common sense and the law would say that the loss was the consequence of B's action, not of A's: of course the fire did not merely succeed A's action in point of time; the "but for" test would reveal it (and also the oxygen, the manufacture of the cigarette and the growth of its tobacco) as a necessary condition or *sine qua non*. But we cease to treat A's action as the cause of the fire because it is now one of the circumstances which B's deliberate free action is now conceived as exploiting. B is not a victim of his circumstances; he is a free agent able to choose between alternative developments of the situation. The claim that in singling out B's action here as the cause or superseding cause of the fire we are merely giving expression to our wish to punish or hold liable an agent of whose actions we disapprove scarcely bears examination. We may or may not wish to punish B or hold him liable, and if we do, he is punished or made liable because he has caused the disaster and not vice versa. We should still say that B has caused the loss even if we thoroughly approved of his action as we would if A were a clerk in Hitler's headquarters during the war and B a British agent, or if we were quite indifferent, as we might be, if A and B were both members of a gang of thieves and the house were the thieves' den.

The special status accorded to a deliberate

human action is in fact a generally pervasive feature of the common-sense conception of causation and is not a mere derivative of "policy" or the wish to punish one person rather than another. In explanatory inquiries causal explanations in terms of deliberate human agency have as we said a *finality* which explanations in other terms often lack; in attributive inquiries a deliberate human action interacting with any other sort of contingency is regarded as the paradigm case of a cause, and, whatever the metaphysics of the matter may be, such a human action is never regarded as itself *caused* or as an *effect*, though not every deliberate human action is regarded as a "superseding" cause. Two corollaries of this special status accorded to deliberate human action are important. When we do speak of a human action as caused, this is with the strong implication that the agent acted in one or more of those many different circumstances which are treated as inconsistent with his action being fully voluntary: we imply if we speak of an action as "caused" that the agent acted under coercion or domination, or that he had lost self-control, or was submitted to some special stress or emergency, or was mistaken or misled, or forced to act in some way even though the compulsion was only a moral one. "What caused you to swerve?" If we ask this of a motorist we assume that his answer will explain his action by reference to such circumstances as that he was forced to swerve to avoid an oncoming car; or that his wheel skidded on a greasy patch, or he had a sudden blackout, etc. If it turns out that there were no such special circumstances, the natural conclusion would be that nothing *caused* him to swerve: he just deliberately did so. English law fairly consistently reproduces this tendency of common sense only to speak of a human action as caused where it is in some recognized way not fully voluntary: examples are to be found in those cases where it is necessary to determine whether or not one agent has caused another to act in a certain way. Here a firm line is drawn between one person providing the opportunity for another's deliberate action and one person causing another to act.

The second corollary of the special importance accorded by common-sense principles of causation to a deliberate human action is that a factor indicating that a human action is defective or less than fully voluntary (by the common-sense criteria already mentioned) prevents such an action ranking as a "superseding cause" in attributive contexts. Common sense usually assimilates human actions which are defective in this way and also deliberate actions done as part of a normal or customary routine to natural conditions upon or in which causes work (and hence as mere conditions) for the purpose of determining whether some loss is the consequence of some other human action. Most of the curiously phrased legal questions whether a cause has or has not "spent its force," "become part of the history," "ceased to operate," or "has been reduced to the level of a condition" are in fact often concerned with whether or not some human action subsequent in time to some suggested cause of a disaster is sufficiently free from those defects to be ranked as fully voluntary and so as a "new" or "intervening" cause. If X leaves his car unlighted in a dark street and Y, seeing it, deliberately casts himself upon it, this is one clear case where both law and common sense treat the second act as the cause of the injury, and the first as creating only the circumstances in which Y acted. At the other extreme is another clear case where X throws a lighted squib at Y, and Y in a panic flings it away with the result that someone else is injured. Between these extremes there are many gradations where decisions will be difficult and will be rightly guided by considerations of policy. But the difficulty of making and understanding these decisions may be diminished if literal descriptions can be given of the factors that establish the clear cases and so count (though sometimes in legal contexts not conclusively) in favor of a decision one way or another in the disputable area between.

(iii) While the metaphor of "superseding" cause is explicable by reference to the notion of deliberate human action, the metaphor of an "extraneous" cause is explicable by reference to the distinct common-sense notion of a *coincidence*. A hits B intending to kill him; B suffers only minor injuries but faints; at that moment a huge tree crashes to the ground where B has fallen. B is killed, though but for A's blow would have been out of range of the tree. Here both for common sense and for the law A has caused B's minor injuries but not his death. For common sense the fall of the tree at that moment is a coincidence; for the law it is an "extraneous" cause. The metaphor "extraneous" is in fact here dangerously misleading, as an analysis of the notion of a coincidence will show; for it calls to mind a contingency that is merely subsequent to and causally independent of some other given contingency, and, of course, the fall of the tree in relation to A's blow has both these features. But these two features are never enough to constitute a coincidence or "an extraneous cause": for (as we have insisted perhaps *ad nauseam*) in every case where A is the cause of B there will always be some factors both subsequent in time and causally independent of A which are ranked as mere conditions and not extraneous causes. Thus a normal change in the direction of the wind or movement of air currents after A has kindled a fire near B's trees are subsequent to A's action and causally independent of it; yet they do not constitute "extraneous causes" though they are among the necessary conditions of the spread of the flames to B's trees: A certainly in such a case has caused B's loss. In fact the criteria for a coincidence and hence for an "extraneous" cause are threefold. First, there must be a conjunction of events which, as a conjunction, is abnormal or exceptional even though, as in the case of the falling tree, neither member of the conjunction (a man falling to the ground beneath a tree, an old tree crashing) need be of a rare or abnormal kind. Secondly, the abnormal conjunction must not be something which is designed or contrived by human agency. If A knew that the tree was about to fall and hit B, intending that he should fall to the ground within its range and be hit by it, A has caused B's death if his plan succeeds. The common-sense principle that a contrived conjunction cannot be a coincidence is the analogue of the legal principle that an intended consequence cannot be too remote. Thirdly, in order that we should speak of a coincidence, it is necessary though not sufficient that two members of the conjunction should be causally independent of each other and have no common cause: If B's fall had caused by impact the fall of the tree, its fall would not be an "extraneous" cause so as to prevent us saying that A's blow had caused B's death.

This last refinement on the falling-tree theme raises a point of some importance. We have seen that a contingency among the necessary conditions of some loss will not rank as an "extraneous cause" of that loss *merely* because it is subsequent in time and causally independent of some earlier necessary condition suggested as the cause of that loss. But can an abnormal condition existing at the time of an agent's action constitute an extraneous cause (if it has all the other features mentioned above) so as to "sever" the causal connection between the agent's action and the loss? Common sense does seem to distinguish between such *contemporaneous* abnormal conditions and *subsequent* events: suppose A innocently gives B a tap on the head of a normally quite harmless character but because B is then suffering from a highly abnormal condition of the arteries the tap has as we say "fatal results." Here surely A has caused B's death (killed B) though unintentionally. The general principle seems to be that, *at least* in cases where a human agent initiates some change, an abnormal condition existing at the time of his action, unlike subsequent abnormal events, will be ranked as a mere condition not as an "extraneous" cause for the purpose of tracing out causal connections according to physical, physiological or other scientific laws.

The points assembled in this section only sketch the outline of the logic of the common-sense use of causal notions, but they will serve perhaps to show that the doctrine of the equivalence of conditions would grossly misrepresent that use. It also of course misrepresents the application in any empirical discipline (e.g., history or medicine) of causal notions to particular cases. There is in fact no actual "scientific" or "factual" sense of cause in which all the necessary conditions of an event are equally entitled to be called its cause. The familiar legal distinctions of "proximate" and "remote" cause, etc., are deeply entrenched in common-sense principles. But since they are applied in the law to circumstances more complex than those envisaged by common sense, the elucidation of these principles cannot serve as a code to resolve legal difficulties but only to prize away from the facts the metaphors that obscure them and to render the issues clear.

V. NECESSARY CONDITION OR SINE QUA NON

In delineating those features of the common-sense conception of causation which are of particular importance in legal contexts, we have stressed the fundamental importance of the notion of a sufficient condition and especially of a set of conditions jointly sufficient for the occurrence of some contingency. We have advisedly not made use of the notion of a *necessary* condition or *sine qua non*, though most juristic writers treat these as at least the starting point of any analysis. In our view, in spite of the apparent attractive simplicity of the "but for" test, the elucidation of causality in terms of a necessary condition is unsatisfactory for two main reasons. First, the notion of a necessary condition is ambiguous, since it covers many different factual situations, and secondly, unless supplemented by the more fundamental causal notion of a set of jointly sufficient conditions, its application may yield absurd results in certain types of case.

It is important to distinguish some of the very many different senses in which one contingency may be a necessary condition of another and the corresponding many senses in which it can be said that some contingency would not have happened "but for" another.

1. If we consider the simple case where a man's action in throwing a lighted cigarette into a wastepaper basket would be treated both by common sense and by the law as the cause of the fire, it is plain that here both the man's action and the oxygen in the air are required to complete a complex set of conditions which we know are generally sufficient to produce the fire. Therefore both the oxygen in the air and the man's action are necessary just in the sense that each is a necessary element in this one complex set of conditions.

2. But the oxygen and the man's action, though alike in the above respect, differ in another important respect. It is the case that the presence of oxygen is known to be a necessary condition of fire in the sense that *no* fire can occur without it, but of course it is not true that no fire can occur unless a man drops a lighted cigarette into a wastepaper basket. Dropping a lighted cigarette is a member of one set of conditions sufficient for the production of fire, but at a common-sense level we believe that there are many other alternative sets of sufficient conditions for fire, though these share certain common features such as the presence of oxygen. If of course we have grounds for thinking, as we usually do, that on a given occasion only one of such sets of sufficient conditions for fire was present, then

every member of the set including the man's action would be a necessary condition of fire *on that occasion*; but the presence of oxygen is necessary on *all* occasions.

3. The difference between these two ways in which a condition may be a necessary condition of some contingency is concealed just by the fact that we normally do believe that on any given occasion only one set of sufficient conditions for the occurrence of a given contingency is present. But, at a common-sense level this normal assumption may break down; there is nothing to prevent two sets of sufficient conditions of a given contingency (e.g., a man's death) being present on a given occasion. Two men may simultaneously fire and lodge a bullet in their victim's brain, or may simultaneously approach escaping gas with a lighted candle. If what each does is sufficient, in conjunction with the other conditions, to bring about the disaster, it would be natural to treat each as having caused the disaster. But the identification of cause with a necessary condition would entail that neither action could be ranked even as *a* cause. This conclusion can be avoided only by supplementing the definition of cause in terms of necessary condition with a provision that a condition may rank as a cause either if it is a necessary condition or would have been necessary if no other conditions sufficient to produce the effect had been present. But if the doctrine has to be supplemented in this way it would seem better to abandon it in favor of an elucidation of causality in terms of sets of sufficient conditions.

4. A different reason for supplementing the notion of necessary condition with that of a set of sufficient conditions arises in cases of the following sort: A, in breach of contract, loads B's goods on the wrong ship. The ship and the goods are destroyed by marine risk, but so is the ship on which they would have been loaded according to the contract. Here most lawyers would say that A's breach of contract was not the cause of the loss and that he is not liable. But in what sense of necessary condition is it true that A's breach in loading the goods on the wrong ship was *not* a necessary condition of the loss? The facts are that in this case both compliance with the contract and its breach are known to be sufficient (given the other conditions in the case) to lead to the loss and that if the first of these two sufficient conditions had not taken place

the second would have: and it is only on this ground that we can say of the first that it was not a necessary condition.

5. The conception of necessary condition involved in the juristic statement of the doctrine of the equivalence of conditions does not include merely conditions related to the effect in the way in which both the presence of oxygen in the air and the man's action in dropping the cigarette was related to fire, but includes *any* condition, however remote in time (the manufacturer's action in making the match or the growth of the tree from which the wood to make it came) if it can be said "but for" this condition the effect would not have occurred. "Every event has a number of causes and each of these causes in turn has a number of causes so that . . . every event is the result of a cone of causation stretching back in time."[17] The paradox involved in extending the notion of cause to remote conditions of this sort arises from the following facts. Common sense would admit that both the oxygen in the air and the man's action in dropping the cigarette are causally relevant to the outbreak of fire although it would distinguish between these two, treating the second as the cause and the first as a mere condition, but would treat the manufacturer's action as causally irrelevant: the dropping of the cigarette and the oxygen are both members of a set of conditions which are sufficient to produce the fire without the concurrence of any contingency such as a voluntary human action or an abnormal event which would be classified by common sense as a cause. But the manufacturer's action has no such normal or general connection with dropping of a lighted cigarette and hence with the outbreak of fire: its only connection with a fire in any particular case is that it accounts for the existence of a match which itself would be ranked by common sense as a condition. An alternative statement of the same point is that the manufacturer's action in making the match is "severed" from the outbreak of fire by the intervention of the voluntary action of the man in using it to kindle the fire, and this accounts for the metaphor of interruption of a causal chain which the law has adopted. It is important to see that "the cone of causation" is not a reason for abandoning the distinction which common sense would draw

between the man's action in dropping the cigarette and the manufacturer's action in making it, because the theory upon which the cone of causation depends, that for every event that occurs there is an infinite series of events each of which is "a *cause*" of the last, is only plausible if the distinction between cause and conditions is abandoned: if we adhere with common sense to this distinction, "the cone of causation" does not develop. "The argument in the old fable in which the loss of a kingdom is traced back to an originating and ultimate cause in the loss of a single nail from a horse's shoe does not commend itself to me as adaptable to this case."[18] It is important to observe that it is only in a fable that we make use of "the cone of causation."

Moreover, there is a range of legal questions in which absurd results would be obtained unless we treat the notion of a set of sufficient conditions as relevant to the question of causation. Often in the law we have to determine whether some loss is the consequence of a wrongful action defined by law in a very complex manner and we may be presented with cases where only some of the characteristics which make the act wrongful are causally relevant to the production of some given loss in an actual case. There may be a causal connection between a defendant's act as defined in one way and the harm for which it is sought to hold him liable but not between that harm and his act as defined in the way which makes it in law harmful. As Fleming James and Perry say, "The causal relation must be shown to exist between *that aspect of a defendant's conduct which is wrongful* and the injury."[19] This may be illustrated from the simple and familiar conundrum set by a statute which forbids the driving of motor-vehicles on Sunday.

Thus D, driving in breach of the statute on Sunday but without negligence, injures P. Here most lawyers would agree that D's wrongful act is not the cause of P's injury: the natural comment of lawyer and layman alike would be that that aspect of the defendant's action which is wrongful ("the Sunday element") was causally irrelevant. But no simple application of the notion of necessary

[17] Glanville Williams, *op. cit.*, p. 233.

[18] *Norris v. William Moss & Sons, Ltd.* [1954] 1 W.L.R. 346, 351.
[19] 60 *Yale L.J.* 761, 789.

condition or the "but for" test unless supplemented by the notion of sufficient conditions will enable us to prove the causal irrelevance of the fact that D in this case drove on Sunday in breach of the statute. A crude application of the "but for" test might lead to the argument that if D had not driven on Sunday he would not have knocked this plaintiff down and that therefore the Sunday element was relevant. The fallacy here can only be exposed if we are allowed to argue that the effects with which we are legally concerned here (physical injury, not physical injury on Sunday) would have been produced by a set of conditions identical with those present in this particular case with the one exception that it was on some other day than Sunday. But to argue in this way is to make use of the concept of a set of sufficient conditions which we have insisted is at the heart of both the common-sense notion of cause and its legal application. Essentially the same point arose in *Thurogood v. van den Berghs & Jurgens Ltd. . . .*[20] Here too the wrongful act was defined in complex terms: in effect it was "setting in motion on the floor of a factory a fan without a guard." If, as most lawyers would agree, a workman who caught a chill in consequence of the draught from the fan cannot truly say that his chill was caused by the defendant's wrongful act, the reasoning required to show this to be so must take the form of an appeal to causal generalizations which would show the presence or absence of a guard (one feature of the defendant's action required to make it wrongful) was causally irrelevant to the production of the chill: this in its turn involves showing that a guarded fan constituted, together with the other conditions in the case, a sufficient set of conditions for the production of a chill. It is true that in some cases it will be possible to show that a condition was necessary for the production of some effect without an implicit appeal to the notion of a set of sufficient conditions: this will be the case where the condition in question is a common member of every set of conditions as oxygen is a member of every set of conditions of fire. But where it is important to show that some condition was *not* on a particular occasion a necessary condition, as in the cases under discussion, it is not

possible to dispense with this appeal to the more fundamental notion of a set of sufficient conditions.

Two distinct points of importance emerge from this examination of the notion of a necessary condition or *sine qua non*. The first point is that if we say that a cause is a necessary condition we shall have to make exceptions for the class of cases noticed above where two sets of conditions, each adequate to produce the harm or loss, are present on a single occasion. The second point is that even if we were to admit this as an exception to a general principle, we should still have to use the notion of a set of sufficient conditions in order to determine whether or not some factor was, on a given occasion, a necessary condition. These two points together suggest the advisability of making the notion of a set of sufficient conditions central in elucidating the notion of causation; we should then account for cases such as those noticed in (iv) above, by the simple principle that the law will not treat an agent's action in breach of a legal obligation as the cause of loss if compliance with the obligation would also constitute a set of conditions sufficient to produce the same loss.

VI. SUMMARY

1. The legal use of the concept of causation has, as the courts insist, its roots in common-sense principles, but these have been obscured by metaphorical expression of the leading distinctions made by common sense and require an elucidation in literal terms.

2. The doctrine of the equivalence of conditions (that all the necessary conditions of an event are equally entitled to be called the cause of that event) is false for common sense and any empirical discipline (e.g., history or medicine) which makes use of the notion of causation. The distinctions made by the law between causes and mere conditions, proximate, remote, and superseding causes, are extensions and refinements of common-sense distinctions, not peculiarities of the legal use of cause, though considerations of policy are involved in their application in legal contexts.

3. The central element in the common-sense notion of cause is not that of a necessary condition but that of a set of conditions jointly sufficient for the occurrence of some contin-

[20] [1951] 2 K.B. 537.

gency; within this jointly sufficient set of conditions common sense like the law distinguishes mere conditions from causes though all are equally necessary to complete the set.

4. The principal criteria for the distinction between cause and condition lie in the contrast between (*a*) a voluntary human action and other conditions, (*b*) an abnormal occurrence and normal conditions. The legal distinctions of *novus actus*, superseding cause and proximate cause may be defined in terms of these contrasts involved.

5. Causal questions arise in daily life as in the law in two main contexts:

(i) where an explanation is required to show how some contingency happened,

(ii) where, after an explanation has been provided or where none is needed, the question is whether some loss may be attributed to some act or other given contingency as its consequence in view of the presence of some third factor.

6. The notion of a necessary condition (*sine qua non*, material cause) is ambiguous and unless supplemented by the notion of a set of sufficient conditions, fails to provide an answer to many causal questions arising in the law.

CHAPTER VII

IGNORANCE AND MISTAKE

You shall hear. He whom I killed had sought to kill
me first. The law acquits me, innocent as ignorant,
of what I did.

Oedipus at Colonus

If you take another person's money in the belief that it is your own or
poison a man in the belief that you are serving him harmless sugar, you are
ignorant of certain facts; and if your ignorance is not attributable to your
negligence or recklessness, you are normally excused. "Ignorance or mistake of fact excuses" is a legal as well as a moral principle.

If, however, you gamble or engage in a certain business activity unaware
that the law prohibits what you are doing, even if you have done all that
reasonably could be done to acquire the relevant legal knowledge, your
ignorance does not excuse you. The principle "Ignorance of the law is no
excuse," while not so happily wedded to morality as the other, may have a
moral analogue. Aristotle, for example, claimed that ignorance of "the
universal," of what we should probably call "moral principle," does not
excuse. Does a person who believes that murder and dishonesty are morally
permissible thereby furnish himself with an excuse for murdering or telling
lies? If not, we shall want to consider whether the reasons for rejecting this
excuse are similar to the reasons for rejecting ignorance of law as an excuse.

It is not easy to fence in the subject of freedom and responsibility. This
becomes particularly evident with ignorance and mistake, where a sizable
literature on the theory of knowledge becomes relevant to our inquiry. Descartes is included, for he introduces the will—an old friend—into his discussion of error. In extending itself more widely than the understanding,
the will leads us into error. If we restrict our will to what is clearly and
distinctly before us, we avoid erroneous judgment. Is there, then, some act
of will involved in every judgment? Or is it rather a serious conceptual
confusion which leads to this connecting of judgment and will?

Hall's treatment of error illustrates the influence that contemporary philosophic theories of perception may have on legal theory. Has this influence
been entirely healthy? How well, for example, do erroneous sensa, "sense
impressions that do not fit the facts," account for cases of ignorance and
mistake in law? A person erroneously believes that a closed drawer contains
jewels; a person believes that a thief is behind a curtain, when in fact it is
his servant. What are the erroneous sensa in such cases?

Some philosophers insist that there is a difference between mistakes in judgment and mistakes in performance. Sometimes we *judge* something to be other than what it is. Our judgment is erroneous. Sometimes we *do* something other than what we intended doing. We have made a mistake in performance. Consider the following situation. You fire at and hit a bird that you think is a wild pigeon. Actually it is a homing pigeon. What description of this case is appropriate? Was there a mistake in judgment, a mistake in performance, or both? Is a slip of the tongue a clear case of saying something other than what one intended to say? Shall we say, then, that a slip is a mistake in performance? But it might be advisable to pause here and ask, in the manner of J. L. Austin, "Why, then, a 'slip' and not a 'mistake'?" Finally, when there is a slip of the tongue, does one fail to say what one means or not mean what one says? Was Alice hasty in her reply to the March Hare when she claimed that saying what you mean and meaning what you say are the same thing?

Very little philosophic or legal literature is devoted to justifying ignorance of fact as an excuse. Perhaps theorists have not wished to expose themselves to charges of demonstrating what is obvious. And yet, however obvious the justification may be, it is desirable to have it stated explicitly. *Reg. v. Prince* is proof that judges, at least, do not always apply the principle. And it will be recalled, too, that Aristotle has a class of actions done owing to ignorance in which the agent does not repent. He thought it important to distinguish such agents from an involuntary agent who does repent. What sorts of cases did Aristotle have in mind? Are they ones in which ignorance of fact does not excuse?

It is clear that morally praiseworthy and law-abiding persons may be punished on the principle that ignorance of the law is no excuse. Legal theorists are not insensitive to this possibility. Austin, Holmes, and Hall, while in agreement on the principle itself, differ in their justifications of it. Austin argues its practical necessity : courts would be involved in indeterminable inquiry if ignorance of the law excused. Holmes believes that any departure from this principle would encourage ignorance where the law's policy is to discourage it. Hall's position is perhaps the most interesting. He argues that to admit ignorance of the law as an excuse would be to contradict a postulate of the legal order which requires that the law be determined not by what private persons believe it to be but rather by what authoritative organs declare it to be. The drafters of the *Model Penal Code,* by contrast, make a significant move toward modifying a principle which in many of its applications deviates from our common moral convictions.

Finally, if we draw this distinction between ignorance of fact and ignorance of law, we should be prepared to say in particular cases whether fact or law is involved. X sets a trap for a trespasser, believing that he has the right to do so. Is this ignorance of fact or law if he does not have the right? X destroys certain goods in the belief that he is their legal owner. His belief is erroneous. Is he ignorant of fact or law?

Reg. v. Prince, 2 C.C.R. 154 (1875)

Case stated by Denman, J.

At the assizes for Surrey, held at Kingston-upon-Thames, on the 24th of March last, Henry Prince was tried upon the charge of having unlawfully taken one Annie Phillips, an unmarried girl, being under the age of sixteen years, out of the possession and against the will of her father. The indictment was framed under s. 55 of 24 & 25 Vict. c. 100.

He was found guilty.

All the facts necessary to support a conviction existed, unless the following facts constituted a defence. The girl Annie Phillips, though proved by her father to be fourteen years old on the 6th of April following, looked very much older than sixteen, and the jury found upon reasonable evidence that before the defendant took her away she had told him that she was eighteen, and that the defendant bona fide believed that statement, and that such belief was reasonable.

.   .   .

The following judgements were delivered:

BRETT, J. . . . The quesiton is, whether upon such proof and such findings of the jury, the prisoner ought or ought not, in point of law, to be pronounced guilty of the offence with which he was charged. He, in fact, did each and everything which is enumerated in the statute as constituting the offence to be punished, if what he did was done unlawfully within the meaning of the statute. If what he did was unlawful within the meaning of the statute, it seems impossible to say that he ought not to be convicted. If what he did was not unlawful within the meaning of the statute, it seems impossible to say that he ought to be convicted. The question, therefore, is, whether the findings of the jury, which are in favour of the prisoner, prevent what he is proved to have done from being unlawful within the meaning of the statute. It cannot, as it seems to me, properly be assumed that what he did was unlawful within the meaning of the statute, for that is the very question to be determined.

Now, on the other side, it is said that the prisoner is proved to have done every particular thing which is enumerated in the Act as constituting the offence to be punished, and that there is no legal justification for what he

did, and, therefore, that it must be held, as a matter of law, that what he did was unlawful within the meaning of the statute, and that the statute was therefore satisfied, and the crime completed. On the other side, it is urged that if the facts had been as the prisoner believed them to be, and as by the findings of the jury he might reasonably believe them to be, and was deceived into believing them to be, he would have been guilty of no criminal offence at all, and therefore he had no criminal intent at all, and therefore that what he did was not criminally unlawful within the meaning of the criminal statute under which he was indicted.

It has been said that even if the facts had been as the prisoner believed them to be he would still have been doing a wrongful act. The first point, therefore, to be considered would seem to be, what would have been the legal position of the prisoner, if the facts had been as he believed them to be, that is to say, what is the legal position of a man who without force takes a girl of more than sixteen years of age, but less than twenty-one years of age, out of the possession of her father and against his will. The statute of 4 & 5 Phil. & Mary, c. 8, has been said to recognise the legal right of a father to the possession of an unmarried daughter up to the age of sixteen. The statute 12 Car. 2, c. 24, seems to recognise the right of a father to such possession up to the age of twenty-one. Mr. Hargreave, in notes 12 and 15 to Co. Lit. 88, b, seems to deduce a right in the father to possession up to the age of twenty-one from those two statutes, and that such right is to be called in law a right jure naturae. If the father's right be infringed he may apply for a habeas corpus. When the child is produced in obedience to such writ, issued upon the application of a father, if the child be under twenty-one, the general rule is, that "if the child be of an age to exercise a choice, the court leaves it to elect where it will go; if it be not of that age, and a want of discretion would only expose it to dangers or seductions, the court must make an order for its being placed in the proper custody, and that undoubtedly is the custody of the father": Lord Denman, C.J., in *Rex. v. Glenhill*; but if the child be a female under sixteen, the court will order it to be handed over to the father, in the absence of certain objections to his custody, even though the child object to return to the father. If the child be between sixteen and twenty-one, and refuse to return to the father, the court, even though the child be a female, gives to the child the election as to the custody in which it will be. "Now the cases which have been decided on this subject shew that, although a father is entitled to the custody of his children till they attain the age of twenty-one, this court will not grant a habeas corpus to hand a child which is below that age over to its father, provided that it has attained an age of sufficient discretion to enable it to exercise a wise choice for its own interests. The whole question is, what is that age of discretion? We repudiate utterly, as most dangerous, the notion that any intellectual precocity in an individual female child can hasten the period which appears to have been fixed by statute for the arrival of the age of discretion; for that very precocity, if uncontrolled, might very probably lead her to irreparable injury. The legislature has given us a guide, which we may safely follow, in pointing out sixteen as the age up to which the father's right to the custody of his female child is to continue; and short of which such a child has no discretion to consent to leaving him": Cockburn, C.J., in *Reg. v. Howes*. But if a man take out of her father's possession without force and with her consent a daughter between sixteen and twenty-one, the father would seem to have no legal remedy for such taking. It may be that the father, if present at the taking, might resist such taking by necessary force, so that to an action for assault by the man he might plead a justification. But for a mere such taking without seduction, there is not action which the father could maintain. There never was a writ applicable to such a cause of action. . . . Neither can a man who with her consent, and without force, takes a daughter who is more than sixteen years old, but less than twenty-one, out of her father's possession or custody, be indicted for such taking. There never has been such an indictment. The statute 3 Hen. 7, c. 2, was enacted against "the taking of *any woman* so against her will unlawfully, that is to say, maid, widow, or wife, that such taking, &c., be felony." It was held in *Lady Fulwood's Case* that the indictment must further charge that the defendant carried away the woman *with*

intent to marry or defile her. . . . It follows from this review that if the facts had been as the prisoner, according to the findings of the jury, believed them to be, and had reasonable ground for believing them to be, he would have done no act which has ever been a criminal offence in England; he would have done no act in respect of which any civil action could have ever been maintained against him; he would have done no act for which, if done in the absence of the father, and done with the continuing consent of the girl, the father could have had any legal remedy.

We have then next to consider the terms of the statute, and what is the meaning in it of the word "unlawfully." "The usual system of framing criminal Acts has been to specify each and every act intended to be subjected to any punishment"; Criminal Law Consolidation Acts, by Greaves, Introduction, p. xxxvii.; and then in some way to declare whether the offence is to be considered as a felony or as a misdemeanor; and then to enact the punishment. It seems obvious that it is the prohibited acts which constitute the offence, and that the phraseology which indicates the class of the offence does not alter or affect the facts, or the necessary proof of those facts, which constitute the offence. There are several usual forms of criminal enactment: "If any one shall with such or such an intent do such and such acts, he shall be guilty of felony, or misdemeanor, as the case may be." Whether the offence is declared to be a felony or a misdemeanor depends upon the view of the legislature as to its heinousness. But the class in which it is placed does not alter the proof requisite to support a charge of being guilty of it. Under such a form of enactment there must be proof that the acts were done, and done with the specified intent. Other forms are: "If any one shall *feloniously* do such and such acts he shall be liable to penal servitude," &c., or "If any one shall *unlawfully* do such and such acts, he shall be liable to imprisonment, &c." The first of these forms makes the offence a felony by the use of the word "feloniously"; the second makes the offence a misdemeanor by the use of the word "unlawfully." The words are used to declare the class of the offence. But they denote also a part of that which constitutes the offence. They denote that which is equivalent to, though not the same as, the specific intent mentioned in the first form, to which allusion has been made. Besides denoting the class of the offence, they denote that something more must be proved than merely that the prisoner did the prohibited acts. They do not necessarily denote that evidence need, in the first instance, be given of more than that the prisoner did the prohibited acts; but they do denote that the jury must find, as matter of ultimate proof, more than that the prisoner did the prohibited acts. What is it that the jury must be satisfied is proved, beyond merely that the person did the prohibited acts? It is suggested that they must be satisfied that the prisoner did the acts with a criminal mind, that there was "mens rea." The true meaning of that phrase is to be discussed hereafter. If it be true that this must be proved, the only difference between the second forms and the first form of enactment is, that in the first the intent is specified, but in the second it is left generally as a criminal state of mind. As between the two second forms the evidence, either direct or inferential, to prove the criminal state of mind must be the same. The proof of the state of mind is not altered or affected by the class in which the offence is placed.

Another common form of enactment is, "If any person *knowingly, wilfully,* and *maliciously* do such or such acts he shall be guilty of felony," or, "if any person *knowingly* and *wilfully* do such and such acts, he shall be guilty of misdemeanor," or "if any person *knowingly, wilfully,* and *feloniously,* do such or such acts, he shall be liable, &c." or "if any person *knowingly* and *unlawfully* do such and such acts, he shall be liable, &c." The same explanation is to be given of all these forms as between each other as before. They are mere differences in form. And though they be all, or several of them be, in one consolidating statute, they are not to be construed by contrast. "If any question should arise in which any comparison may be instituted between different sections of any one or several of these Acts, it must be carefully borne in mind in what manner these Acts were framed. None of them was rewritten; on the contrary, each contains enactments taken from different Acts passed at different times and with different views, and frequently varying from each other in phraseology; and, for the reasons stated in the introduction, these enactments for the most part stand in these Acts with little or no variation in their phraseology, and consequently their differences in that respect will be found generally to remain in these Acts. It follows, therefore, from hence, that any argument as to a difference in the intention of the legislature which may be drawn from a difference in the terms of one clause from those in another will be entitled to no weight in the construction of such clauses; for that argument can only apply with force where an Act is framed from beginning to end with one and the same view, and with the intention of making it thoroughly consistent throughout": Greaves on Criminal Law Consolidation Acts, p. 3. I have said that as between each other the same explanation is to be given of these latter forms of enactment as of the former mentioned in this judgement. But as between these latter and the former forms, there is the introduction in the latter of such words as "knowingly," "wilfully," "maliciously." "Wilfully" is more generally applied when the prohibited acts are in their natural consequences not necessarily or very probably noxious to the public interest, or to individuals; so that an evil mind is not the natural inference or consequence to be drawn from the doing of the acts. The presence of the words requires somewhat more evidence on the part of the prosecution to make out a prima facie case, than evidence that the prisoner did the prohibited acts. So as to the word "maliciously," it is usual where the prohibited acts may or may not be such as in themselves import prima facie a malicious mind. In the same way the word "knowingly" is used, where the noxious character of the prohibited acts depends upon a knowledge in the prisoner of their noxious effect, other than the mere knowledge that he is doing the acts. The presence of the word calls for more evidence on the part of the prosecution. But the absence of the word does not prevent the prisoner from proving to the satisfaction of the jury that the *mens rea,* to be prima facie inferred from his doing the prohibited acts, did not in fact exist. In *Rex v. Marsh* the measure of the effect of the presence in the enactment of the word "knowingly" is explained. The information and conviction were against a carrier for having game in his possession contrary to the statute 5 Anne, c. 14, which declares "that any carrier having game in his possession is guilty of an offense unless it be sent by a qualified person." The only evidence given was, that the defendant was a carrier, and that he had game in his waggon on the road. It was objected, that there was no evidence that the defendant knew of the presence of the game, or that the person who sent it was not a qualified person. The judges held that there was sufficient prima facie evidence, and that it was not rebutted by the defendant by sufficient proof on his part of the ignorance suggested on his behalf. The judgements clearly import, that if the defendant could have satisfied the jury of his ignorance, it would have been a defence, though the word "knowingly' was not in the statute. In other words, that its presence or absence in the statute only alters the burden of proof. "Then, as to knowledge, the clause itself says nothing about it. If that had been introduced, evidence to establish knowledge must have been given on the part of the prosecutor; but under this enactment the party charged must shew a degree of ignorance sufficient to excuse him. Here there was prima facie evidence that the game was in his possession as carrier. Then it lay on the defendant to rebut that evidence": Bayley, J. "The game was found in his waggon employed in the course of his business as a carrier. That raises a presumption prima facie that he knew it, and that is not rebutted by the evidence given on the part of the defendant": Littledale, J.

From these considerations of the forms of criminal enactments, it would seem that the ultimate proof necessary to authorize a conviction is not altered by the presence or absence of the word "knowingly," though by its presence or absence the burden of proof is altered; and it would seem that there must be proof to satisfy a jury ultimately that there was a criminal mind, or *mens rea,* in every offence really charged as a crime. In some enactments, or common law maxims of crime, and therefore in the indictments charging the committal of those crimes, the name of the crime imports that a *mens rea* must be proved, as in murder, burglary, &c. In some the *mens rea* is contained in the specific enactments as to the intent which is made a part of the crime. In some the word "feloniously" is used, and in such cases it has never been doubted but that a felonious mind must ultimately be found by the jury. In enactments in a similar form, but in which the prohibited acts are to be classed as a misdemeanor, the word "unlawfully" is used instead of the word "feloniously." What reason is there why, in like manner, a criminal mind, or *mens rea,* must not ultimately be found by the jury in order to justify a conviction, the distinction always being observed, that in some cases the proof of the committal of the acts may prima facie, either by reason of their own nature, or by reason of the form of the statute, import the proof of the *mens rea?* But even in those cases it is open to the prisoner to rebut the prima facie evidence, so that if, in the end, the jury are satisfied that there was no criminal mind, or *mens rea,* there cannot be a conviction in England for that which is by the law considered to be a crime.

There are enactments which by their form seems to constitute the prohibited acts into crimes, and yet by virtue of which enactments the defendants charged with the committal of the prohibited acts have been convicted in the absence of the knowledge or intention supposed necessary to constitute a *mens rea.* Such are the cases of trespass in pursuit of game, or of piracy of literary or dramatic works, or of the statutes passed to protect the revenue. But the decisions have been based upon the judicial declaration that the enactments do not constitute the prohibited acts into crime, or offences against the Crown, but only prohibit them for the purpose of protecting the individual interest of individual persons, or of the revenue. Thus, in *Lee v. Simpson,* in an action for penalties for the representation of a dramatic piece, it was held that it was not necessary to shew that the defendant knowingly invaded the plantiff's right. But the reason of the decision given by Wilde, C. J., is: "The object of the legislature was to protect authors against the piratical invasion of their rights. In the sense of having committed an offense against the Act, of having done a thing that is prohibited, the defendant is an offender. But the plaintiff's rights do not depend upon the innocence or guilt of the defendant." So the decision in *Morden v. Porter* seems to be made to turn upon the view that the statute was passed in order to protect the individual property of the landlord in game reserved to him by his lease against that which is made a statutory trespass against him, although his land is in the occupation of his tenant. There are other cases in which the ground of decision is that specific evidence of knowledge or intention need not be given, because the nature of the prohibited acts is such that, if done, they must draw with them the inference that they were done with the criminal mind or intent which is a part of every crime. Such is the case of the possession and distribution of obscene books. If a man possesses them, and distributes them, it is a necessary inference that he must have intended that their first effect must be that which is prohibited by statute, and that he cannot protect himself by shewing that his ultimate object or secondary intent was not immoral. . . . This and similar decisions go rather to shew what is *mens rea,* than to shew whether there can or cannot be conviction for crime proper without *mens rea.*

As to the last question, it has become very necessary to examine the authorities. In Blackstone's Commentaries, by Stephen, 2nd ed., vol. lv., book 6, Of Crimes, p. 98: "And as a vicious will without a vicious act is no civil crime, so, on the other hand, an unwarrantable act without a vicious will is no crime at all. So that, to constitute a crime against human laws, there must be first a vicious will, and secondly an unlawful act consequent upon such vicious will. Now there are three cases in which the will does not join with the act: 1. Where there is a defect of understanding, &c.; 2. Where there is understanding and will sufficient residing in the party, but not called forth and exerted at the time of the action done, which is the case of all offences committed by chance or ignorance. Here the will sits neuter, and neither concurs with the act nor disagrees to it." And at page 105: "Ignorance or mistake is another defect of will, when a man, intending to do a lawful act, does that which is unlawful; for here, the deed and the will acting separately, there is not that conjunction between them which is necessary to form a criminal act. But this must be an ignorance or mistake in fact, and not an error in point of law. As if a man, intending to kill a thief or housebreaker in his own house, by mistake kills one of his family, this is no criminal action; but if a man thinks he has a right to kill a person excommunicated or outlawed wherever he meets him, and does so, this is wilful murder." In *Fowler v. Padget* the jury

found that they thought the intent of the plaintiff in going to London was laudable; that he had no intent to defraud or delay his creditors, but that delay did actually happen to some creditors. Lord Kenyon said: "Bankruptcy is considered as a crime, and the bankrupt in the old laws is called an offender; but it is a principle of natural justice and of our laws that *actus non facit reum nisi mens sit rea.* The intent and the act must both concur to constitute the crime." And again: "I would adopt any construction of the statute that the words will bear, in order to avoid such monstrous consequences as would manifestly ensue from the construction contended for."

. . .

In *Reg. v. Hibbert* the prisoner was indicted under the section now in question. The girl, who lived with her father and mother, left her home in company with another girl to go to a Sunday school. The prisoner met the two girls and induced them to go to Manchester. At Manchester he took them to a public house and there seduced the girl in question, who was under sixteen. The prisoner made no inquiry and did not know who the girl was, or whether she had a father or mother living or not, but he had no reason to, and did not believe that she was a girl of the town. The jury found the prisoner guilty, and Lush, J., reserved the case. In the Court of Criminal Appeal, Bovill, C.J., Channell and Pigott, BB., Byles and Lush, JJ., quashed the conviction. Bovill, C.J.: "In the present case there is no statement of any finding of fact that the prisoner knew, or had reason to believe, that the girl was under the lawful care or charge of her father or mother, or any other person. In the absence of any finding of fact on this point the conviction cannot be supported." This case was founded on *Reg. v. Green,* before Martin, B. The girl was under fourteen, and lived with her father, a fisherman, at Southend. The prisoners saw her in the street by herself and induced her to go with them. They took her to a lonely house, and there Green had criminal intercourse with her. Martin B., directed an acquittal: "There must, he said, be a taking out of the possession of the father. Here the prisoners picked up the girl in the street, and for anything that appeared, they might not have known the girl had a father. The girl was not taken out of the possession of any one. The prisoners had, no doubt, done a very immoral act, but the question was whether they had committed an illegal act. The criminal law ought not to be strained to meet a case which did not come within it. The act of the prisoners was scandalous, but it was not any legal offence."

In each of these cases the girl was surely in the legal possession of her father. The fact of her being in the street at the time could not possible prevent her from being in the legal possession of her father. Everything, therefore, prohibited was done by the prisoner in fact. But in each case the ignorance of facts was held to prevent the case from being the crime to be punished.

In *Reg. v. Tinckler,* in a case under this section, Cockburn, C.J., charged the jury thus: "It was clear the prisoner had no right to act as he had done in taking the child out of Mrs. Barnes's custody. But inasmuch as no improper motive was suggested on the part of the prosecution, it might very well be concluded that the prisoner wished the child to live with him, and that he meant to discharge the promise which he alleged to have made to her father, and that he did not suppose he was breaking the law when he took the child away. This being a criminal prosecution, if the jury should take this view of the case, and be of opinion that the prisoner honestly believed that he had a right to the custody of a child, then, although the prisoner was not legally justified, he would be entitled to an acquittal." The jury found the prisoner not guilty.

·   ·   ·

In the cases of *Reg. v. Robins* and *Reg. v. Olifier* there was hardly such evidence as was given in this case, as to the prisoner being deceived as to the age of the girl, and having reasonable ground to believe the deception, and there certainly were no findings by the jury equivalent to the findings in this case.

In *Reg. v. Forbes and Webb,* although the policeman was in plain clothes, the prisoners certainly had strong ground to suspect, if not to believe, that he was a policemen; for the case states that they repeatedly called out to rescue the boy and pitch into the constable.

Upon all the cases I think it is proved that there can be no conviction for crime in England in the absence of a criminal mind or *mens rea.*

Then comes the question, what is the true meaning of the phrase. I do not doubt that it exists where the prisoner knowingly does acts which would constitute a crime if the result were as he anticipated, but in which the result may not improbably end by bringing the offence within a more serious class of crime. As if a man strikes with a dangerous weapon, with intent to do grievous bodily harm, and kills, the result makes the crime murder. The prisoner has run the risk. So, if a prisoner do the prohibited acts, without caring to consider what the truth is as to facts—as if a prisoner were to abduct a girl under sixteen without caring to consider whether she was in truth under sixteen—he runs the risk. So if he without abduction defiles a girl who is in fact under ten years old, with a belief that she is between ten and twelve. If the facts were as he believed he would be committing the lesser crime. Then he runs the risk of his crime resulting in the greater crime. It is clear that ignorance of the law does not excuse. It seems to me to follow that the maxim as to *mens rea* applied whenever the facts which are present to the prisoner's mind, and which he has reasonable ground to believe, and does believe to be the facts, would, if true, make his acts no criminal offence at all.

It may be true to say that the meaning of the word "unlawfully" is, that the prohibited acts be done without justification or excuse; I, of course, agree that if there be a legal justification there can be no crime; but I come to the conclusion that a mistake of facts, on reasonable grounds, to the extent that if the facts were as believed the acts of the prisoner would make him guilty of no criminal offence at all, is an excuse, and that such excuse is implied in every criminal charge and every criminal enactment in England. I agree with Lord Kenyon that "such is our law," and with Cockburn, C.J., that "such is the foundation of all criminal procedure."

The following judgment (in which Cockburn, C.J., Mellor, Lush, Quain, Denman, Archbald, Field, and Lindley, JJ., and Pollock, B., concurred) was delivered by

BLACKBURN, J. In this case we must take it as found by the jury that the prisoner took an unmarried girl out of the possession and against the will of her father, and that the girl was in fact under the age of sixteen, but that the prisoner bona fide, and on reasonable grounds, believed that she was above sixteen, viz., eighteen, years old. No question arises as to what constitutes a taking out of the possession of her father; nor as to what circumstances might justify such taking as not being unlawful; nor as to how far an honest though mistaken belief that such circumstances as would justify the taking existed, might form an excuse; for as the case is reserved, we must take it as proved that the girl was in the possession of her father, and that he took her, knowing that he trespassed on the father's rights, and had no colour of excuse for so doing.

. . .

The argument in favour of the prisoner must therefore entirely proceed on the ground that, in general, a guilty mind is an essential ingredient in a crime, and that where a statute creates a crime, the intention of the legislature should be presumed to be to include "knowingly" in the definition of the crime, and the statute should be read as if that word were inserted, unless the contrary intention appears. We need not inquire at present whether the canon of construction goes quite so far as above stated, for we are of opinion that the intention of the legislature sufficiently appears to have been to punish the abduction, unless the girl, in fact, was of such an age as to make her consent an excuse, irrespective of whether he know her to be too young to give an effectual consent, and to fix that age at sixteen. The section in question is one of a series of enactments, beginning with s. 48, and ending with s. 55, forming a code for the protection of women, and the guardians of young women. These enactments are taken with scarcely any alteration from the repealed statute, 9 Geo. 4, c. 31, which had collected them into a code from a variety of old statutes all repealed by it.

Sect. 50 enacts, that whosoever shall "unlawfully and carnally know and abuse any girl under the age of ten years," shall be guilty of felony. Sect. 51, whoever shall "unlawfully and carnally know and abuse any girl being above the age of ten years, and under the age of twelve years," shall be guilty of a misdemeanor.

It seems impossible to suppose that the intention of the legislature in those two sections could have been to make the crime depend upon the knowledge of the prisoner of the girl's actual age. It would produce the monstrous result that a man who had carnal connection with a girl, in reality not quite ten years old, but whom he on reasonable grounds believed to be a little more than ten, was to escape altogether. He could not, in that view of the statute, be convicted of the felony, for he did not know her to be under ten. He could not be convicted of the misdemeanor, because she was in fact not above the age of ten. It seems to us that the intention of the legislature was to punish those who had connection with young girls, though with their consent, unless the girl was in fact old enough to give a valid consent. The man who has connection with a child, relying on her consent, does it at his peril, if she is below the statutable age.

The 55th section, on which the present case arises, used precisely the same words as those in ss. 50 and 51, and must be construed in the same way, and, if we refer to the repealed statute 4 & 5 Phil. & Mary, c. 8, from the 3rd section of which the words in the section in question are taken, with very little alteration, it strengthened the inference that such was the intention of the legislature.

The preamble states, as the mischief aimed at, that female children, heiresses, and others having expectations, were, unawares of their friends, brought to contract marriages of disparagement, "to the great heaviness of their friends"; and then, to remedy this, enacts, by the 1st section, that it shall not be lawful for anyone to take an unmarried girl, being under sixteen, out of the custody of the father, or the person to whom he, either by will or by act in his lifetime, gives the custody, unless it be bona fide done by or for the master or mistress of such child, or the guardian in chivalry, or in socage of such child. This recognizes a legal right to the possession of the child, depending on the real age of the child, and not on what appears. And the object of the legislature, being, as it appears by the preamble it was, to protect this legal right to the possession, would be baffled, if it was an excuse that the person guilty of the taking thought the child above sixteen. The words "unlawfully take," as used in the 3rd section of 4 and 5 Phil. & Mary, c. 8, means without the authority of the master or mistress, or guardian, mentioned in the immediately preceding section.

There is not much authority on the subject, but it is all in favour of this view. . . .

. . .

The following judgement (in which Kelly, C.B., Cleasby, Pollock, and Amphlett, BB., and Grove, Quain, and Denman, JJ., concurred) was delivered by

BRAMWELL, B. The question in this case depends on the construction of the statute under which the prisoner is indicted. That enacts that "whosoever shall unlawfully take any unmarried girl under the age of sixteen out of the possession and against the will of her father or mother, or any other person having the lawful care or charge of her, shall be guilty of a misdemeanor." Now the word "unlawfully" means "not lawfully," "otherwise than lawfully," "without lawful cause," such as would exist, for instance, on a taking by a police officer on a charge of felony, or a taking by a father of his child from his school. The statute, therefore, may be read thus: "Whosoever shall take, &c., without lawful cause." Now the prisoner had no such cause, and consequently, except in so far as it helps the construction of the statute, the word "unlawfully" may in the present case be left out, and then the question is, has the prisoner taken an unmarried girl under the age of sixteen out of the possession of and against the will of her father? In fact, he has; but it is said not within the meaning of the statute, and that that must be read as though the word "knowingly," or some equivalent word, was in; and the reason given is, that as a rule the *mens rea is* necessary to make any act a crime or offence, and that if the facts necessary to constitute an offence are not known to the alleged offender, there can be no *mens rea*. I have used the word "knowingly"; but it will, perhaps, be said that here the prisoner not only did not do the act knowingly, but knew, as he would have said, or believed, that the fact was otherwise than such as would have made his act a crime; that here the prisoner did not say to himself, "I do not know how the fact is, whether she is under sixteen or not, and will take the chance," but acted on the reasonable belief that she was over sixteen; and that if he had done what he did, knowing or believing neither way, but hazarding it, there would be a *mens rea,* there is not one when, as he believes, he knows that she is over sixteen.

It is impossible to suppose that, to bring the case within the statute, a person taking a girl out of her father's possession against his will is guilty of no offence unless he knows she is under sixteen; that he would not be guilty if the jury were of opinion that he knew neither one way nor the other. Let it be, then, that the question is whether he is guilty where he knows, as he thinks, that she is over sixteen. This introduces the necessity for reading the statute with some strange words introduced; as thus: "Whosoever shall take any unmarried girl, being under the age of sixteen, and not believing her to be over the age of sixteen, out of the possession," &c. Those words are not there, and the question is, whether we are bound to construe the statute as though they were, on account of the rule that the *mens rea* is necessary to make an act a crime. I am of opinion that we are not, nor as though the word "knowingly" was there, and for the following reasons: The act forbidden is wrong in itself, if without lawful cause; I do not say illegal, but wrong. I have not lost sight of this, that though the statute probably aims at seduction for carnal purposes, the taking may be by a female with a good motive. Nevertheless, though there may be such cases, which are not immoral in one sense, I say that the act forbidden is wrong.

Let us remember what is the case supposed by the statute. It supposes that there is a *girl*—it does not say a woman, but a girl— something between a child and a woman; it supposes she is in the *possession* of her father or mother, or other persons having lawful *care or charge* of her; and it supposes there is a *taking,* and that that taking is *against the will* of the person in whose possession she is. It is, then, a *taking* of a *girl,* in the *possession* of some one, *against his will.* I say that done without lawful cause is wrong, and that the legislature meant it should be at the risk of the taker whether or no she was under sixteen. I do not say that taking a woman of fifty from her brother's or even father's house is wrong. She is at an age when she has a right to choose for herself; she is not a *girl,* nor of such tender age that she can be said to be in the *possession* of or under the *care or charge* of anyone. I am asked where I draw the line; I answer at when the female is no longer a *girl* in anyone's possession.

But what the statute contemplates, and what

I say is wrong, is the taking of a female of such tender years that she is properly called a *girl,* can be said to be in another's *possession,* and in that other's *care or charge.* No argument is necessary to prove this; it is enough to state the case. The legislature has enacted that if anyone does this wrong act, he does it at the risk of her turning out to be under sixteen. This opinion gives full scope to the doctrine of the *mens rea.* If the taker believed that he had the father's consent, though wrongly, he would have no *mens rea;* so if he did not know she was in anyone's possession, nor in the care or charge of anyone. In those cases he would not know he was doing the *act* forbidden by the statute—an act which, if he knew she was in possession and in care or charge of anyone, he would know was a crime or not, according as she was under sixteen or not. He would not know he was doing an act wrong in itself, whatever was his intention, if done without lawful cause.

In addition to these considerations, one may add that the statute does use the word "unlawfully," and does not use the words "knowingly" or "not believing to the contrary." If the question was whether his act was unlawful, there would be no difficulty, as it clearly was not lawful.

This view of the section, to my mind, is much strengthened by a reference to other sections of the same statute. Sect. 50 makes it a felony to unlawfully and carnally know a girl under the age of ten. Sect. 51 enacts when she is above ten and under twelve to unlawfully and carnally know her is a misdemeanor. Can it be supposed that in the former case a person indicted might claim to be acquitted on the ground that he believed the girl was over ten though under twelve, and so that he had only committed a misdemeanor; or that he believed her over twelve, and so had committed no offence at all; or that in a case under s. 51 he could claim to be acquitted, because he believed her over twelve. In both cases the act is intrinsically wrong; for the statute says if "unlawfully" done. The act done with a *mens rea* is unlawfully and carnally knowing the girl, and the man doing that act does it at the risk of the child being under the statutory age. It would be mischievous to hold otherwise. So s. 56, by which, whoever shall take away any child under fourteen with intent to deprive parent or guardian of the possession of the child, or with intent to steal any article upon such child, shall be guilty of felony. Could a prisoner say, "I did take away the child to steal its clothes, but I believed it to be over fourteen?" If not, then neither could he say, "I did take the child with intent to deprive the parent of its possession, but I believed it over fourteen." Because if words to that effect cannot be introduced into the statute where the intent is to steal the clothes, neither can they where the intent is to take the child out of the possession of the parent. But if those words cannot be introduced in s. 56, why can they be in s. 55?

The same principle applies in other cases. A man was held liable for assaulting a police officer in the execution of his duty, though he did not know he was a police officer. Why? because the act was wrong in itself. So, also, in the case of burglary, could a person charged claim an acquittal on the ground that he believed it was past six when he entered, or in housebreaking, that he did not know the place broken into was a house? Take, also, the case of libel, published when the publisher thought the occasion privileged, or that he had a defence under Lord Campbell's Act, but was wrong; he could not be entitled to be acquitted because there was no *mens rea.* Why? because the act of publishing written defamation is wrong where there is no lawful cause.

As to the case of the marine stores, it was held properly that there was no *mens rea,* where the person charged with the possession of naval stores with the Admiralty mark, did not know the stores he had bore the mark: *Reg. v. Sleep;* because there is nothing prima facie wrong or immoral in having naval stores unless they are so marked. But suppose his servant had told him that there was a mark, and he had said he would chance whether or not it was the Admiralty mark? So in the case of the carrier with game in his possession; unless he knew he had it, there would be nothing done or permitted by him, no intentional act or omission. So of the vitriol senders; there there was nothing wrong in sending such packages as were sent unless they contained vitriol.

Further, there have been four decisions on this statute in favour of the construction I contend for. I say it is a question of construction of this particular statute in doubt, bringing thereto the common law doctrine of *mens rea* being a necessary ingredient of the crime. It seems to me impossible to say that where a person takes a girl out of her father's possession, not knowing whether she is or is not under sixteen, that he is not guilty; and equally impossible when he believes, but erroneously, that she is old enough for him to do a wrong act with safety. I think the conviction should be affirmed.

DENMAN. J. I agree in the judgement of my Brothers Bramwell and Blackburn, and I wish what I add to be understood as supplementary to them. The defendant was indicted under the 24 & 25 Vict. c. 100, s. 55, which enacts that "whosoever shall *unlawfully* take, or cause to be taken, any unmarried girl, being under the age of sixteen years, out of the possession and against the wish of her father or mother, or of any other person *having the lawful care or charge of her,* shall be guilty of a misdemeanor."

I cannot hold that the word "unlawfully" is an immaterial word in an indictment framed upon this clause. I think that it must be taken to have a meaning, and an important meaning, and to be capable of being either supported or negatived by evidence upon the trial : see *Reg. v. Turner: Reg. v. Ryan.*

In the present case the jury found that the defendant had done everything required to bring himself within the clause as a misdemeanant, unless the fact that he bona fide and reasonably believed the girl taken by him to be eighteen years old constituted a defence. That is, in other words, unless such bona fide and reasonable belief prevented them from saying that the defendant in what he did acted "unlawfully" within the meaning of the clause. The question, therefore, is whether, upon this finding of the jury, the defendant did unlawfully do the things which they found him to have done.

The solution of this question depends upon the meaning of the word "unlawfully" in s. 55. If it means "with a knowledge or belief that every single thing mentioned in the section existed at the moment of the taking," undoubtedly the defendant would be entitled to an acquittal, because he did not believe that a girl under sixteen was being taken by him at all. If it only means "without lawful excuse" or justification, then a further question arises, viz., whether the defendant had any lawful

excuse or justification for doing all the acts mentioned in the clause as constituting the offence, by reason, merely, that he bona fide and reasonably believed the girl to be older than the age limited by the clause. Bearing in mind the previous enactments relating to the abduction of girls under sixteen, 4 & 5 Phil. & Mary, c. 8, s. 2, and the general course of the decisions upon those enactments, and upon the present statute, and looking at the mischief intended to be guarded against, it appears to me reasonably clear that the word "unlawfully," in the true sense in which it was used, is fully satisfied by holding that it is equivalent to the words "without lawful excuse," using those words as equivalent to "without such an excuse as being proved would be a complete legal justification for the act, even where all the facts constituting the offence exist."

Cases may be easily suggested where such a defence might be made out, as, for instance, if it were proved that he had the authority of a Court of competent jurisdiction, or of some legal warrant, or that he acted to prevent some illegal violence not justified by the relation of parent and child, or school-mistress, or other custodian, and requiring forcible interference by ways of protection.

In the present case the jury find that the defendant believed the girl to be eighteen years of age; even if she had been of that age, she would have been in the lawful care and charge of her father, as her guardian by nature : see Co. Litt. 88, b, n. 12, 19th ed., recognized in *Reg. v. Howes.* Her father had a right to her personal custody up to the age of twenty-one, and to appoint a guardian by deed or will, whose right to her personal custody would have extended up to the same age. The belief that she was eighteen would be no justification to the defendant for taking her out of his possession, and against his will. By taking her, even with her own consent, he must at least have been guilty of aiding and abetting her in doing an unlawful act, viz., in escaping against the will of her natural guardian from his lawful care and charge. This, in my opinion, leaves him wholly without lawful excuse or justification for the act he did, even though he believed that the girl was eighteen, and therefore unable to allege that what he has done was not unlawfully done, within the meaning of the clause. In other words, having knowingly done a wrongful act, viz., in taking the girl away from the lawful possession of her father against his will, and in violation of his rights as guardian by nature, he cannot be heard to say that he thought the girl was of an age beyond that limited by the statute for the offence charged against him. He had wrongfully done the very thing contemplated by the legislature: He had wrongfully and knowingly violated the father's rights against the father's will. And he cannot set up a legal defence by merely proving that he thought he was committing a different kind of wrong from that which in fact he was committing.

Conviction affirmed.

Concerning Ignorance of Law and Fact*

I. PAULUS, ON THE EDICT, BOOK XLIV

Ignorance is either of fact or of law.

(1) For where anyone is not aware that he to the possession of whose property he is entitled is dead, time does not run against him. Where, indeed, he is aware that his relative is dead, but he does not know that his estate belongs to him on account of his being the next of kin, or, where he is aware that he has been appointed an heir, but does not know that the Praetor grants the possession of the property of a deceased person to those who have been appointed his heirs; time will run against him because he is mistaken with respect to the law. The same rule applies where the brother of the deceased thinks that his mother has the preference.

(2) If anyone does not know that he is related to the deceased, sometimes he is mistaken concerning the law, and sometimes with reference to the fact; for if he is aware that he is free, and who his parents were, but does not know that he is entitled to the rights of relationship, he is mistaken as to the law. Where anyone who is a foundling does not know who his parents are, and serves another as a slave, thinking that he himself is a slave, he is mistaken rather as to the fact than as to the law.

(3) Moreover, where anyone knows that another is entitled to the possession of the property of an estate, but does not know that the time during which he should have taken possession of the same has elapsed, he is mistaken as to the fact. The same rule applies where he thinks that he has obtained possession of the property. Where, however, he knows that he has not claimed the estate, and that he has allowed the time to elapse, but is ignorant that he is entitled to the possession of the property on the ground of succession, time will run against him because he is mistaken with respect to the law.

(4) We hold the same where a man is appointed heir to an entire estate, but does not think that he has a right to demand possession of the same before the will is opened; but if he is ignorant that there is a will, he will be mistaken with reference to the fact.

II. NERATIUS, PARCHMENTS, BOOK V

Error in law should not, in every instance, be considered to correspond with ignorance of the fact; since the law can, and should be definitely settled, but the interpretation of the fact very frequently deceives even the wisest men.

III. POMPONIUS, ON SABINUS, BOOK III

There is a great deal of difference whether anyone is not informed regarding the case and acts of another, or whether he is ignorant of the law which affects himself.

(1) Cassius states that Sabinus holds that it should be understood that ignorance, in this instance, does not refer to a person of abandoned character, or to one who, through negligence, thinks himself secure.

. . .

V. TERENTIUS CLEMENS, ON THE LEX
JULIA ET PAPIA, BOOK II

It seems to be most unjust that knowledge should injure another rather than its pos-

* Reprinted from *The Digests or Pandects,* Bk. XXII, Title VI, *The Civil Law* trans. S. P. Scott (Cincinnati: The Central Trust Co., 1932), V. 237–40, by permission of the copyright owners, The Jefferson Medical College of Philadelphia, and John M. Rankin, trustee for the Estate of Samuel P. Scott.

sessor, or that the ignorance of one person should profit another.

VI. ULPIANUS, ON THE LEX JULIA ET PAPIA, BOOK XVIII

Neither gross ignorance of the facts should be tolerated, nor scrupulous inquiry be exacted, but such knowledge should be demanded that neither excessive negligence, too great unconcern, nor the inquisitiveness that characterizes informers may be exhibited.

VII. PAPINIANUS, QUESTIONS, BOOK XIX

Ignorance of the law is not advantageous to those who desire to acquire it, but it does not injure those who demand their rights.

VIII. THE SAME, DEFINITIONS, BOOK I

An error of fact does not, indeed, prejudice the rights of men where they seek to obtain property, or to avoid losing it; and ignorance of the law is no advantage, even to women, when they attempt to acquire it. A mistake in law, however, does not injure any person in an attempt to avoid the loss of property.

IX. PAULUS, ON IGNORANCE OF LAW AND FACT

The ordinary rule is, that ignorance of law injures anyone, but ignorance of fact does not. Therefore, let us examine to what instances this rule is applicable, for it may be stated, in the first place, that minors under twenty-five years of age are permitted to be ignorant of the law; and this also is held with respect to women in certain cases, on account of the weakness of the sex; hence, so long as no crime has been committed, but only ignorance of the law is involved, their rights are not prejudiced.

On the same principle, if a minor under the age of twenty-five lends money to a son under his father's control, relief is granted him, just as if he had not lent the money to a son subject to paternal authority.

(1) Where a son under paternal control, who is a soldier, is appointed heir by a comrade-in-arms, and does not know that he can enter upon the estate without the permission of his father, he can ignore the law in accordance with the Imperial Constitution; and therefore the time prescribed for the acceptance of the estate does not run against him.

(2) Ignorance of the fact, however, does not injure anyone unless he should be guilty of gross negligence; for example, what if everyone in the town knew what he alone does not? Labeo very properly says that neither the knowledge of the most inquisitive, or the most negligent man, should be understood to be meant, but that of him who can obtain it by diligent inquiry.

(3) Labeo, however, thinks that ignorance of the law ought not to be considered excusable unless the party should not have access to a magistrate, or is not intelligent enough to easily ascertain that ignorance of the law is a detriment to him, which is very rarely the case.

(4) Where anyone does not know that the vendor is the owner of the property sold, more attention should be paid to the transaction itself than to the opinion of the purchaser; and therefore, although he may believe that he bought the property from someone who was not its owner, still, if it is delivered to him by the owner, it will belong to him.

(5) Where a party who is ignorant of the law does not avail himself of the *Lex Falcidia,* a Rescript of the Divine Pius says that his rights will be prejudiced. Moreover, the Emperors Severus and Antoninus stated the following in a Rescript, namely: "Where, in discharging a trust, money is paid which is not due, it cannot be recovered, unless it was paid by mistake. Wherefore, the heirs of Cargilianus, when they paid over money left by will for the purpose of building an aqueduct for the Republic of Cirta, not only did not require the bonds which are usually executed to compel the repayment by municipalities of any excess which they might receive above what was permitted by the *Lex Falcidia;* but they even stipulated that the said sum of money should not be applied to any other purpose, and knowingly and deliberately suffered the said money to be used for the construction of the aqueduct, hence they had no right to demand that anything should be returned to them by the Republic of Cirta, on the ground that they paid more than was due; since there would be injustice on both sides, for the money to be recovered which had been given for the purpose of building an aqueduct, and for the Republic to be compelled to pay out of the funds belonging to it for a work which entirely represented the glory derived from the liberality of another.

"If, however, the heirs thought that the

claim for the recovery of said money was well founded, for the reason that they failed, through lack of information, to profit by the provisions of the *Lex Falcidia,* they should know that ignorance of fact would be of advantage to them, but ignorance of law would not; and that relief is granted, not to fools, but to those who are honestly mistaken with reference to the facts." Although municipalities are mentioned in this Rescript, still the same rule should be observed with reference to all kinds of persons. And while, in the case stated, mention is made of money left for the purpose of constructing an aqueduct, in this instance alone it must be held that an action for its recovery will not lie, for the beginning of this constitution is of general application, as it shows that if, through mistake, the trust was not discharged, any money paid which is not due cannot be recovered.

Moreover, that section is also of general application which sets forth that parties are not entitled to recover who, through ignorance of the law, did not avail themselves of the benefit of the *Lex Falcidia;* and, according to this, it can be stated that if money which was left in trust and had been paid, had not been left for some specified purpose, even though it had not been expended but remained in the hands of the person to whom it was paid, an action to recover it will not lie.

X. PAPINIANUS, OPINIONS, BOOK VI

Youths who have not arrived at puberty and act without the authority of their guardians are not considered to know anything.

Model Penal Code*

Section 2.04. Ignorance or Mistake as a Defense.

(1) Ignorance or mistake as to a matter of fact or law is a defense if:

(a) the ignorance or mistake negatives the purpose, knowledge, belief, recklessness, or negligence required to establish a material element of the offense; or

(b) the law provides that the state of mind established by such ignorance or mistake constitutes a defense.

(2) When ignorance or mistake affords a defense to the offense charged but the defendant would be guilty of another (and included) offense had the situation been as he supposed it was, he may be convicted of that other offense.

(Alternative (1): "he may be convicted of an attempt to commit that other offense.")

(Alternative (2): "he may be convicted of the offense charged but shall be sentenced only as may be authorized if the situation had been as he supposed.")

(3) A reasonable belief that conduct does not legally constitute an offense is a defense to a prosecution for that offense based upon such conduct, when:

(a) the statute or other enactment defining the offense is not known to the actor and has not been published or otherwise reasonably made available to him prior to the conduct alleged; or

(b) he acts in reasonable reliance upon an official statement of the law, afterward determined to be invalid or erroneous, contained in (i) a statute or other enactment; (ii) a judicial decision, opinion or judgment; (iii) an administrative order or grant of permission; or (iv) an official interpretation of the public officer or body charged by law with responsibility for the interpretation, administration or enforcement of the law defining the offense.

(4) A defense arising under paragraph (3) of this section constitutes an affirmative defense which the defendant is required to prove by a preponderance of evidence. The reasonableness of the belief claimed to constitute the defense shall be determined as a question of law by the Court.

. . .

Comment. Section 2.04.
Ignorance or mistake as a defense.

1. Paragraph (1) states the conventional position under which the significance of ignorance or mistake on the part of the defendant is determined by the mental state required for

* Copyright 1956. Reprinted with the permission of The American Law Institute from *Model Penal Code* (Philadelphia: The American Law Institute, 1956), Tentative Draft No. 4, Art. 2, Sec. 2.04, pp. 17–18, 135–38.

the commission of the offense involved. The ignorance or mistake is a defense when it negatives the existence of such an essential state of mind or establishes a state of mind which constitutes a defense under a rule of law establishing defenses. In other words, ignorance or mistake has only evidential import; it is significant whenever it is logically relevant and it may be relevant to negate the required mode of culpability or to establish a special defense.

. . .

To put the matter in this way is not, of course, to say anything that would not otherwise be true, even if no provision on the subject should be made. As Glanville Williams summarized the matter, the rule relating to mistake "is not a new rule; and the law could be stated equally well without reference to mistake . . . It is impossible to assert that a crime requiring intention or recklessness can be committed although the accused labored under a mistake that negatived the requisite intention or recklessness. Such an assertion carries its own refutation." (*Criminal Law*, p. 137.) This obvious point is, however, sometimes overlooked in general formulations purporting to require that mistake be reasonable if it is to exculpate, without regard to the mode of culpability required to commit the crime. Article 16 of the Louisiana Code, for example, provides: "Unless there is a provision to the contrary in the definition of a crime, *reasonable* ignorance of fact or mistake of fact which precludes the presence of any mental element required in that crime is a defense to any prosecution for that crime." This is unexceptionable in the case of an offense which can be committed negligently. What justification can there be, however, for requiring that ignorance or mistake be reasonable if the crime or the element of the crime involved requires acting purposely or knowingly for its commission? The fact seems to be that formulations of this kind are drawn from the law of homicide, where negligence suffices for liability; and that they are not and they cannot be applied with generality to crimes in which the ignorance or mistake is relevant to the existence of an essential element of purpose or of knowledge.

. . .

2. Paragraph (2) is addressed to a limited problem that may produce distortion in the application of a Code. Burglary of a dwelling house may, for example, reasonably be treated as an offense of greater gravity than burglary of a store; and it is not unreasonable to require knowledge that the structure is a dwelling or at least recklessness that such may be the case. If we conceive of a defendant who had every ground to think it was a store, although it actually was a dwelling, it may not be right to hold him for the graver crime. The doctrine that when one intends a lesser crime he may be convicted of a graver offense committed inadvertently leads to anomalous results if it is generally applied in the penal law; and while the principle obtains to some extent in homicide, its generality has rightly been denied. . . .

If the defendant in the circumstances supposed is exculpated of the graver crime, it seems clear, however, that he should not be acquitted. One possibility, and the Reporter recommends this treatment, is to hold that he is guilty of the lesser crime which on his own assumptions he committed—even though his assumptions were quite wrong and even though one of the objective elements of the lesser offense (the store) cannot, by hypothesis, be proved. An alternative, which is analytically more appropriate though practically it may well be less acceptable, is to convict him only of attempting to commit the lesser offense. A second alternative, proposed in the Advisory Committee, is to authorize conviction of the graver crime but limit sentence to that authorized for the offense which the defendant would have committed had the situation been as he believed.

There is, however, an important problem of procedure as to how far the suggested principle may be applied. No difficulty is presented when the lesser offense is an included crime, conviction of which is permitted generally on the indictment or information filed. The issue may arise, however, when one offense is not included in the other. The defendant, for example, may be charged with knowingly possessing narcotics. If his defense is that he thought the package found in his possession contained a different kind of contraband, is it procedurally necessary that he be acquitted if his defense is believed? Some members of the Council of the Institute consider that it is, upon the ground that the offense which the defendant thought he was committing is not included in the accusation made. The Reporter thinks that the procedural requirement should be susceptible of relaxation in this special situation; the defendant needs no notice of the charge when he avows his effort to commit another crime to escape conviction of the crime that has been charged. But if the Institute considers the procedural objection valid, the section can be limited to cases where an included offense is involved and still have some substantial value.

3. Paragraph (3) is designed to provide a limited affirmative defense based on a reasonable belief on the part of a defendant that the law is such that his conduct does not constitute an offense, i.e., a limited exception to the general position of article 2.02(9) that knowledge of illegality is not an element of an offense.

All the categories dealt with in the formulation involve situations where the act charged is consistent with entire law-abidingness of the actor, where the possibility of collusion is minimal, and a judicial determination of the reasonableness of the belief in legality should not present substantial difficulty. It is difficult, therefore, to see how any purpose can be served by a conviction. It should be added that in the area of *mala prohibita,* where the defense would normally apply, the case that is appropriate for penal sanctions is that of deliberate evasion or defiance; when less than this is involved, lesser sanctions should suffice. For this typically is a situation where a *single* violation works no major public or private injury; it is persistent violation that must be brought to book. And obviously the defense afforded by this section would normally be available to a defendant only once; after a warning he can hardly have a reasonable basis for belief in the legality of his behavior.

Ignorance of Law*

In order that an obligation may be effectual (or, in other words, in order that the sanction may operate as a motive to fulfillment), two conditions must concur. First, it is necessary that the party should know the law, by which the *Obligation* is imposed, and to which the *Sanction* is annexed. Secondly, it is necessary that he should actually know (or, by due attention or advertence, *might* actually know), that the given act, or the given forbearance or omission, would *violate* the law, or amount to a *breach* of the obligation. Unless these conditions concur, it is impossible that the sanction should operate upon his desires. Or (changing the expression) the given act, or the given forbearance or omission, cannot be imputed to an unlawful intention, or to any of those modes of unlawful inadvertence which are styled negligence, heedlessness, or rashness.

Accordingly, inevitable ignorance or error in respect to matter of fact is considered, in every system, as a ground of exemption.

With regard to ignorance or error in respect to the state of the law, the provisions of different systems appear to differ considerably; although they all concur in assuming

* John Austin, *Lectures on Jurisprudence* (London: John Murray, 1873), I, 496–501. Footnotes are omitted.

generally that it shall not be a ground of exemption. "*Regula* est, juris ignorantiam cuique nocere," is the language of the Pandects. And *per* Manwood, as reported by Plowden, "It is to be presumed that no subject of this realm is misconusant of the Law whereby he is governed. Ignorance of the Law excuseth none."

I have no doubt that this rule is expedient, or, rather, is absolutely necessary. But the reasons assigned for the rule, which I have happened to meet with, are not satisfactory.

The reason given in the Pandects is this: "In omni parte, error *in jure* non eodem loco quo *facti* ignorantia haberi debetit, quum jus *finitum* et possit esse et debeat: facti interpretatio plerumque etiam prudentissimos fallat."

Which reasoning may be expressed thus:

"Ignorance or error with regard to matter of fact is often inevitable: that is to say, no attention or advertence could prevent it. But ignorance or error with regard to the state of the law is never inevitable. For the law is definite and knowable, or might or ought to be so. Consequently, ignorance or error with regard to the law is no ground for exemption. If the conduct of the party be imputable to ignorance of law, it is not imputable *directly* to unlawful intention or inadvertence. But as the ignorance to which it is imputable is the consequence of unlawful inadvertence, his conduct, in the last result, is caused by his negligence."

The reasoning involves the small mistake of confounding "is" with "might be" and "ought to be." That law *might* be knowable by all who are bound to obey it, or that law *ought* to be knowable by all who are bound to obey it—*"finitum" et possit esse et debeat"*—is, I incline to think, true. That any actual system *is* so knowable, or that any actual system has ever been so knowable, is so notoriously and ridiculously false that I shall not occupy your time with proof of the contrary.

Blackstone produces the same *pretiosa ratio,* flavored with a spice of that circular argumentation wherein he delights. "A mistake (says he) in point of Law, which every person of discretion, not only *may,* but is bound and presumed to know, is in criminal cases no sort of defense."

Now to affirm "that every person *may* know the law" is to affirm the thing which is not. And to say "that his ignorance should not excuse him *because* he is *bound* to know" is simply to assign the rule as a reason for itself. Being bound to know the law, he cannot effectually allege his ignorance of the law as a ground of exemption from the law. But *why* is he bound to know the law? or *why* is it presumed, *juris et de jure,* that he knew the law?

The only *sufficient* reason for the rule in question, seems to be this: that if ignorance of law were admitted as a ground of exemption, the Courts would be involved in questions which it were scarcely possible to solve, and which would render the administration of justice next to impracticable. If ignorance of law were admitted as a ground of exemption, ignorance of law would always be alleged by the party, and the Court, in every case, would be bound to decide the point.

But, in order that the Court might decide the point, it were incumbent upon the Court to examine the following questions of fact: First, was the party ignorant of the law at the time of the alleged wrong? Secondly, assuming that he was ignorant of the law at the time of the wrong alleged, was his ignorance of the law *inevitable* ignorance, or had he been previously placed in such a position that he might have known the law, if he had duly tried?

It is manifest that the latter question is not less material than the former. If he might have known the law in case he had duly tried, the reasoning which I have produced from the Pandects would apply to his case. That is to say, Inasmuch as the conduct in question were *directly* imputable to his ignorance, it were not imputable *directly* to unlawful intention or inadvertence. But, inasmuch as his ignorance of the law were imputable to unlawful inadvertence, the conduct in question were imputable, in the last result, to his *negligence.*

Now either of these questions were next to insoluble. Whether the party was *really* ignorant of the law, and was *so* ignorant of the law that he had no *surmise* of its provisions, could scarcely be determined by any evidence accessible to others. And for the purpose of determining the *cause* of his ignorance (its *reality* being ascertained), it were incumbent upon the tribunal to unravel his previous history, and to search his whole life for the elements of a just solution.

The reason for the rule in question would, therefore, seem to be this: It not unfrequently happens that the party is ignorant of the law, and that his ignorance of the law is inevitable. But if ignorance of law were a ground of exemption, the administration of justice would be arrested. For, in almost every case, ignorance of law would be alleged. And, for the purpose of determining the *reality* and ascertaining the *cause* of the ignorance, the Court were compelled to enter upon questions of fact, insoluble and interminable.

That the party shall be presumed *peremptorily* conusant of the law, or (changing the shape of the expression) that his ignorance shall not exempt him, seems to be a rule so necessary, that law would become ineffectual if it were not applied by the Courts generally. And if due pains were taken to promulge the law, and to clear it of needless complexity, the presumption would accord with the truth in the vast majority of instances. The party (generally speaking) *would* actually *know* the law. Or the party, at least, might so *surmise* its provisions, that he could shape his conduct safely. The reasoning in the Pandects would then be just. The law would be in *fact* as *"finitum"* and knowable, as *"possit esse, et debeat."*

The admission of ignorance of *fact* as a ground of exemption is not attended with those inconveniences which would seem to be the reason for rejecting ignorance of *law* as a valid excuse. Whether the ignorance really existed, and whether it was imputable or not to the inadvertence of the party, is a question which may be solved by looking at the circumstances of the case. The inquiry is limited to a given incident, and to the circumstances attending that incident, and is, therefore, not interminable.

I have said that the provisions of different systems seem to differ considerably with regard to the principle which I am now considering.

In our own law, "ignorantia juris non excusat" seems to obtain without exception. I am not aware of a single instance in which ignorance of law (considered *per se*) exempts or discharges the party, civilly or criminally. In the case of infancy, and in certain other cases to which I shall advert directly, the presumed incapacity of the party to know the law would seem to be *one* of the grounds upon which the exemption rests. But his presumed incapacity to know the law is only *one* of those grounds. His exemption rests *generally* upon his *general* incapacity (real or presumed) to judge sanely of law or fact.

From an opinion thrown out by Lord Eldon, in the case of *Stockley v. Stockley,* I am inclined to think (at the first blush) that a party would be relieved, in certain instances, from a contract into which he had entered in ignorance of law. But, admitting the justness of Lord Eldon's conclusion, the agreement (I conceive) would be void, not because the party was ignorant of the law, but because there is no consideration to support the promise.

According to the Roman Law, there are certain classes of persons, "quibus permissum est jus ignorare." They are exempt from liability (at least for certain purposes), not by reason of their general imbecility, but because

it is presumed that their capacity is not adequate to a knowledge of the law. Such are women, soldiers, and persons who have not reached the age of twenty-five. Here, ignorance of law (as a specific ground for exemption) is only admissible in favor of persons who belong to certain classes.

And this (I apprehend) shows distinctly, that the exclusion of *ignorantia juris,* as a ground of exemption, is deducible from the reason which I have already assigned. In ordinary cases, the admission of *ignorantia juris* as a ground of exemption would lead to interminable inquiry. But, in these excepted cases, it is *presumed* from the *sex,* or from the *age,* or from the *profession* of the party that the party was ignorant of the law, and that the ignorance was inevitable. The inquiry into the matter of fact is limited to a given point: namely, the sex, age, or profession of the party who insists upon the exemption. That obvious fact being ascertained, the legal presumption or inference is drawn by the tribunal without further investigation.

Whether the legal presumption ought to obtain, or whether in most cases it do not conflict with the truth, is a distinct question. What I advance is this: that in ordinary cases, the inquiry were impracticable, because the facts upon which the solution depends are not to be ascertained.

In these excepted cases the inquiry is practicable, because it is predetermined by a general rule, that certain facts which *may* be ascertained shall be received by the Courts as evidence of the facts in question. There is a *presumptio juris et de jure,* and evidence is not admissible to rebut it. Nor would the case be materially altered, assuming that the presumption may be rebutted. For the counter evidence must necessarily consist of a specific fact or facts. The large and vague inquiry is shut out by the legal presumption.

Ignorance of Law*

Ignorance of the law is no excuse for breaking it. This substantive principle is sometimes put in the form of a rule of evidence, that everyone is presumed to know the law. It has accordingly been defended by Austin

* O. W. Holmes, Jr., *The Common Law* (Boston: Little, Brown and Company, 1923), pp. 47–48.

and others, on the ground of difficulty of proof. If justice requires the fact to be ascertained, the difficulty of doing so is no ground for refusing to try. But everyone must feel that ignorance of the law could never be admitted as an excuse, even if the fact could be proved by sight and hearing in every case. Furthermore, now that parties can testify, it may be doubted whether a man's knowledge of the law is any harder to investigate than many questions which are gone into. The difficulty, such as it is, would be met by throwing the burden of proving ignorance on the lawbreaker.

The principle cannot be explained by saying that we are not only commanded to abstain from certain acts, but also to find out that we are commanded. For if there were such a second command, it is very clear that the guilt of failing to obey it would bear no proportion to that of disobeying the principal command if known, yet the failure to know would receive the same punishment as the failure to obey the principal law.

The true explanation of the rule is the same as that which accounts for the law's indifference to a man's particular temperament, faculties, and so forth. Public policy sacrifices the individual to the general good. It is desirable that the burden of all should be equal, but it is still more desirable to put an end to robbery and murder. It is no doubt true that there are many cases in which the criminal could not have known that he was breaking the law, but to admit the excuse at all would be to encourage ignorance where the lawmaker has determined to make men know and obey, and justice to the individual is rightly outweighed by the larger interests on the other side of the scales.

Mutual and Unilateral Mistake in Contract*

Statements are exceedingly common, both in texts and in court opinions, that relief will not be given on the ground of mistake unless the mistake is "mutual." Such a broad generalization is misleading and untrue. Seldom is it accompanied by either definition or analysis. A study of thousands of cases is not necessary to convince us that to err is human, both in the sense of having mistaken ideas and in the sense of performing acts that are evil or unwise. But such a study will show that human mistakes are of great variety in kind with a great variety of causes, that they have a great variety of results, and that the juristic effects vary as the combinations of factors vary.

Cases do not always submit readily to be classified with either "mutual mistake" or "unilateral mistake." And even when they do submit, the solution does not mechanically follow in accordance with a separate set of rules for each class. Very often relief has been and will be granted where the mistake is unilateral. And relief is not necessarily granted, even though the mistake is mutual. It depends very materially upon the form of relief sought. Reformation is often refused on the ground that the mistake was not "mutual," when the correct reason is that the parties never agreed upon any terms other

than those in the erroneous writing. In such cases the appropriate remedy is rescission or cancellation, unless there is sufficient basis for an estoppel.

As we have seen in other connections, the term "mutuality" has an appeal that must not be overlooked, even though it has blinded us at times to facts and reality. The idea behind the term is of importance; but it is not one that lends itself easily to the statement of broad principles and just working rules. Statements are very numerous to the effect that the mistake of only one of the parties to a contract is not a ground for relief either at law or in equity. Such a statement can be accepted only in case the party seeking relief proves no more than that his action was induced by his erroneous thought. The statement will seldom be found in cases in which relief is granted; in the cases refusing relief and making the statement as a reason for so doing, the court has always considered and weighed the additional factors that accompanied the mistake.

Let us consider, first, mistakes made in the process of making a contract. Sometimes one party is mistaken as to the identity of the other, clearly a case in which the other party would not be laboring under the same mistake; but if that other party knows or has reason to know of the mistake, seldom if ever can he hold the first party to the agreement. The rights of innocent purchasers and other

---

* Arthur L. Corbin, *Contracts* (St. Paul: West Publishing Co., 1951), III, § 608, pp. 669–78, reprinted by permission of the publisher. Footnotes are omitted.

third parties will depend upon a variety of factors.

In the famous case of the ships named Peerless, neither party made a mistake in expression; each one correctly described the ship that he meant to describe. The mistake that each one made was in believing that the other party intended to describe the same ship that he himself described. Here they were "mutually" mistaken, which means that both were mistaken. Were these "mutual" mistakes identical? Not quite, although they had common elements. Both parties believed that there was only one ship named Peerless sailing from Bombay, when in fact there were two; both believed that there was agreement in meaning, when in fact there was not. But in believing that the other party meant the same ship as himself, they were making closely similar but not identical mistakes. Here, it is not the fact of mutuality that is decisive; rather it is the fact that neither one made a negligent mistake and caused harm thereby.

When one party, in expressing his assent, so negligently chooses his words that the other reasonably gives them a meaning different from the one intended, a valid contract is often held to have been made, in spite of the fact that, as in the Peerless case, both parties are making a mistake. Just as in that case, both parties believe that there is agreement in meaning, that the other party means the same as himself. Just as in that case, the parties are "mutually" mistaken, though their mental errors are not quite identical. In spite of this "mutuality," there is a contract, due to the negligence of the one and the reasonableness of the other.

Next, consider the case of a scrivener's error in reducing an oral agreement to written form. The two parties are in exact agreement; but when they sign the writing they both mistakenly believe that the writing accords with their oral expressions. If one of them reads the document more carefully than the other, he may sign making no mistake himself, but he is aware that the other is mistaken. In either case, the result is the same in most respects. The antecedent oral agreement is still enforceable; the mistaken document is not.

Consider, thirdly, a mistake made before either party has made an offer. A contractor puts certain figures on paper, makes an erroneous addition, and then sends in his written bid offering to erect a building for the sum indicated in that addition. The offeree accepts the bid; and a formal contract is forthwith executed. In the making of this contract, no mistake of any kind is made by either party. The bidder knows the amount of his bid and the writing is correct; he means exactly what the writing says. This he has been caused to say, and to mean, by an antecedent arithmetical error. Such an error can scarcely be described as other than negligent; and if it leads to a material change of position by the party who accepts the bid, there is a valid and enforceable contract. But if the mistake is discovered and notice thereof promptly given before any such change of position, there are numerous cases holding that the contract may be avoided.

In cases of this sort and of other "unilateral" mistakes, it is often said that there is no contract because there was no "meeting of the minds." Probably the statement is made in an effort to make a just decision seem to square with the notion that relief cannot be given unless the mistake is "mutual," or unless it can be shown that there is "no contract." There are, indeed, mistakes that make a bargain void. There are some that prevent a "meeting of the minds." But there are others that make a bargain voidable only, at the option of one of the parties; they make it thus voidable even though there was a real "meeting of the minds." The law of mistake as it actually works, as it is demonstrated in decisions, is not capable of being reduced to any broad single doctrine.

If the mistake of one party to a written instrument is in thinking that it contains a larger promise by the other party than in fact it does, and the other party has no reason to know of this mistake, of course the mistaken party cannot hold the other to the large promise that he did not make, by getting reformation or otherwise. In such a case, the court may say that there can be no relief unless the mistake was "mutual," or that a party is "conclusively presumed to know its contents." But when a mistaken party asks for rescission and restoration of the *status quo,* he is asking for a remedy that is very different from enforcement against the other party of a contract that the mistaken party thought was made but was not.

Frequently, the existence of a factor as to which a mistake is made is of material importance to only one of the contracting parties; and he is the only one who is likely to seek relief or who will be given it if he does. In such a case, it is practically immaterial whether the mistake was made by both parties or by one only. What the court needs to know before giving a remedy is whether the mistake substantially affects the party seeking relief, whether the other party can be put *in statu quo,* how the granting of relief will affect third parties, and whether the petitioner's conduct has created an estoppel. The fact that the defendant also made the same mistake may add nothing to the determination of the issue.

In these cases the fact that the defendant did not make the same mistake may aid the plaintiff's case, the defendant's conduct being regarded as fraudulent or in bad faith.

In the case of a unilateral contract of donation, its words are to be interpreted for the purpose of giving effect to the actual intention of the single promisor. If in the drafting or execution of such a contract the promisor labored under a mistake that causes the legal effect produced to be materially different from that intended by him, he has a right to correction of the instrument. The fact that the mistake is unilateral does not prevent relief. The same is true of other donative acts, such as the change of beneficiary of an insurance policy by the insured. If such a change was made under a mistake that leads to a result different from that intended by the insured, the change will be modified in equity at the suit of the original beneficiary or other party in interest so as to carry out the actual intention of the insured.

The distinction between "mutual" mistake and "unilateral" mistake has some importance. In the matter of the remedy to be granted, it may be a decisive factor. But we must not begin with any broad generalizations based upon this distinction. We must not say that relief will be denied unless the mistake is "mutual"; or that a "unilateral" mistake does not affect the validity of a contract. Every attempt at a generalization or stated rule must take into account a variety of factors and must be limited to some particular combination of them.

The American Law Institute states the law to be that a contract is not made voidable by a unilateral mistake, however material it may be to the interests of the mistaken party.

Without doubt, this has been the prevailing form of statement, along with the even more common form that mistake is not operative unless it is mutual. It is supported by some decisions and by many dicta; but the decisions that are inconsistent with it are too numerous and too appealing to the sense of justice to be disregarded.

Cases are very numerous in which conveyances have been canceled and contracts rescinded because of a material mistake made by one of the parties as to the contents or the legal operation of the deed of conveyance or other instrument. In these cases the fact that the mistake was not "mutual" did not prevent relief "in equity." The effect of this is that, under our presently existing systems of law and procedure, the mistake in question would be good ground for rescission or cancellation and would be a good defense in an action for specific performance or for damages. It need no longer be described as an "equitable defense," although it would have been otherwise a century ago in an action for damages in a court that regarded itself as a "court of law."

It must be borne in mind, however, that the circumstances accompanying the mistake must always be considered, just as they were considered by the former courts of Chancery. It has never been asserted, and it is not being asserted here, that a party ever makes out a sufficient case for relief, either affirmative or defensive, by merely proving that he was caused to execute a deed or to make a promise by the fact that he had a mistaken thought. Many of the pertinent factors have been listed in the first section of this chapter. No one of them can be said to be absolutely necessary for the granting of relief; the combination of factors existing in the specific case must be considered. Here are two of the more important factors: Did the other party participate either intentionally or innocently in causing the mistake? Is it still possible to restore the other party to his original position?

In United States Plywood Corp. v. Hudson Lbr. Co., 113 F. Supp. 529 (D.C.N.Y., 1953) appeal dismissed, C.A., 210 F.2d 462, a dispute arose as to the meaning and application of a definition of "logging costs" contained in the written contract, two different methods of computation being asserted. One party asked for rescission on the ground of mistake. This was denied because of delay and change of position. The court said that asking rescission meant that the mistake must have been unilateral, because if it was bilateral the only remedy would be reformation. This statement is not justified by the facts. If the parties understood the words of the definition in different senses, they were both mistaken as to the fact of agreement. Nevertheless, reformation should be denied if the understanding of one party was reasonable and that of the other party was not. But the reasons given for denying rescission would still be good.

Ignorance and Mistake*

The meaning of "factual error," as defined in the criminal law, represents a common sense version of the philosopher's definition: "All error consists in taking for real what is mere appearance."[1] For example, a person looks at a far-off object and believes he sees a man; later, on closer approach, he decides it is a tree. The first opinion is then recognized as error. But the object may not actually be a tree; perhaps it is a dead stump or a bit of sculpture. Indeed, on examining it the next morning by aid of daylight and a clear head, our actor decides that he was mistaken in both judgments the night before. In this view he will be supported by all normal persons who, viewing the object under "adequate" conditions, agree: "It is a tree stump"; moreover, they would not concede the possibility of the slightest error in this opinion. Thus, an opinion (judgment or belief) is erroneous by reference to another opinion which corresponds to the facts. In sum, "error" implies:

1. That facts exist;
2. That sense *impressions* of facts, "sensa," are different from the facts;
3. That the sensa fit (correspond to, are congruent with) or do not fit the facts;
4. That erroneous sensa (those that do not fit the facts) are for a time accepted as true, i.e., they are believed to be congruent with the facts; and
5. That this is later recognized as erroneous, i.e., certain opinions become error when they are subjected to a broader experience,

especially when relatively adequate conditions of correct perception obtain.

All mistakes of fact can be reduced to the above elements which are frequently directly applicable to the cases. There is, e.g., a mistake in identity in believing that a pocket or drawer contains things, that a person is being attacked, that a dangerous weapon is in an assailant's hand, and so on. But while every case of mistake of fact can be stated in terms of the above criteria, it is also true that many such mistakes involve much more than perception. For example, in situations relevant to libel, perjury, or bigamy, the defendant may never have sensed the phenomena which he erroneously interpreted. Someone may have told him that X served a term in the penitentiary for forgery; he may have heard X's employer discharge him, and read in the newspaper that forged checks had been found in the possession of a certain employee of that firm; or someone may have informed a woman that he had learned "on good authority" of the death of her husband. Thus, mistakes of fact often result not only from faulty perception but also from erroneous higher types of cognitive experience, e.g., the ideas already in the interpreter's mind, including his bias. In the case of an inventor who makes certain mistakes of fact, these ideas may include invalid theories of physics.

To understand the rationale of *ignorantia facti excusat*, it is necessary to recognize and take account of the relevant ethical principle, namely, moral obligation is determined not by the actual facts but by the actor's opinion regarding them. It is determined by the actor's error concerning a situation, not by the actual situation. This is implicit in the decisions, and occasionally it has been rather definitely expressed. For example, the driver of an

* Jerome Hall, *General Principles of Criminal Law,* 2d ed. (Indianapolis: The Bobbs-Merrill Co., Inc., 1960), pp. 361–67, 375–78, 382–90, 392–94, 402–8, reprinted with the permission of the author and the publisher.
[1] G. F. Stout, "Error," in *Studies in Philosophy and Psychology* (London: Macmillan Co., 1930), p. 271.

automobile who turned a corner very quickly, although he thought he would probably meet a car coming from the opposite direction, would certainly be culpable despite the fact that there was actually no car there. Again, it is often impossible to know the facts or to know that any act of ours will improve a situation. If the actual facts determined our duties, we would sometimes be under a moral obligation without knowing it, perhaps without being able to discover it. Accordingly, apart from questions of previous incapacitation, the morality of an act is determined by reference to the actor's opinion of the facts, including his erroneous beliefs. . . .

Illustrative Cases

That the above ethical principle has long been expressed in the criminal law is apparent from an early seventeenth-century case.[2] The defendant was awakened in the night by strange noises in his house; thinking he was attacking a burglar, he ran his sword through a cabinet where the intruder was hiding and killed a friend of his servant, present by the latter's invitation. This was held not to be manslaughter, "for he did it ignorantly without intention of hurt to the said Frances."[3] Perhaps the most frequent situation in the cases and certainly the least doubted instance of the recognized defense of mistake of fact concerns apparently necessary self-defense. Here the courts hold "it is not necessary . . . that defendant should have been actually in danger of death or great bodily harm at the time he fired the fatal shot, or that retreat would have really increased his peril, in order for him to have been justified in shooting deceased."[4] So, too, if the mistake stimulates an attack, perpetrated in apparently necessary self-defense, the harm is privileged. The doctrine has expanded far beyond such primary interests as those involved in the above cases. A railroad conductor "is justified in forcibly ejecting him [a passenger] from the car, because he, the conductor, honestly believes that the passenger has not paid his fare, but persistently refuses so to do."[5] The defense was

also allowed where the defendant voted before he was twenty-one, believing he was of age;[6] in charges of uttering a forged instrument;[7] in larceny, where the defendant was mistaken as to the denomination of the bill handed him[8] . . . Thus, in a very large number of cases, the criminal law seems to be in complete accord with purely ethical appraisal of action in mistake of fact.

In the above cases the mistake of fact excluded any *mens rea*. This raises a question concerning harms which would not have been committed except for a mistake, but where the actor's intention was nonetheless criminal, e.g., a mistake in the identity of the intended victim of an assault. One who inflicted a mortal wound on an intimate friend, whom he mistook for a person who had attacked him earlier in the evening, could derive no advantage from his error. There is an ambiguity in the court's assertion that "he intended to kill the man at whom the knife was directed";[9] but it is clear, in any event, that such a mistake is not legally significant since the defendant intended to kill or seriously injure a human being. Thus, the doctrine must be qualified as follows: mistake of fact is a defense if, because of the mistake, *mens rea* is lacking. This qualification is quite consistent with the ethical principle represented in *ignorantia facti excusat*.

Restrictions:
(a) Reasonableness of the Error

But Anglo-American criminal law restricts the scope of *ignorantia facti* in ways which constitute serious limitations and, sometimes, a complete repudiation of the underlying policy. These restrictions concern (a) the requirement that the mistake be a "reasonable" one (the civilian expression is that the ignorance be "invincible") and (b) certain sexual offenses, bigamy and other types of strict liability.

An actual mistake of fact is not sufficient. "The apprehension of danger must be bona fide and reasonable."[10] Not the defendant's erroneous perception of the facts, but the facts

---

[2] Levett's Case (K.B. 1638), Cro. Car. 538, 79 Eng. Rep. 1064.
[3] *Ibid.* Cf. ". . . if this be ignorance of fact it excuses. . . ." The Mirror of Justices 137 (Seld. Soc'y ed., 1893).
[4] Williams v. State, 18 Ala. App. 473, 93 S. 57, 58 (1922).
[5] State v. McDonald, 7 Mo. App. 510 (1879).

[6] Gordon v. State, 52 Ala. 308 (1875).
[7] United States v. Carll, 105 U.S. 611, 26 L. Ed. 1135 (1882).
[8] Regina v. Hehir, (1895) 2 Ir. R. 709.
[9] McGehee v. State, 42 Miss. 747 (1885).
[10] Hill v. State, 194 Ala. 11, 23, 69 S. 941, 946 (1915), 2 A.L.R. 509, 518 (1915).

"as they reasonably appeared to him" determine whether he is criminally liable.[11] . . .

The plain consequence of this application of objective liability to *ignorantia facti* is that persons who commit harms solely because they are mistaken regarding the material facts are nonetheless criminally liable despite the complete lack of criminal intent. Moreover, a person who has acted "unreasonably" seems occasionally to have been held just as culpable as he would have been if he had actually intended to commit the harm; and we shall see that this is often done in convictions of bigamy and sexual offenses. There are surprisingly few reports of homicide cases which specifically discuss this question, but the indicated holding is that a killing by the defendant in the unreasonable mistake that his life was in danger is manslaughter.

. . .

Mention must be made, finally, of a type of factual ignorance which is not usually discussed in relation to *ignorantia facti,* namely, ignorance of elementary science, e.g., regarding sickness, medicine, and the use of physicians. The defendants in these cases are sometimes very stupid persons, unaware of the gravity of a child's illness and the availability of physicians.[12] In other cases the defendants are members of religious sects which believe, e.g., that the devout cannot be harmed even by the bite of a rattlesnake[13] or that it is sinful to use medicine. There are surprisingly few reports of such cases, apparently because prosecutors are reluctant to initiate proceedings and, when they do, juries are apt to acquit. But there have been a number of convictions, and the relevant holdings imply that ignorance of ordinary factual knowledge, possessed by every "normal" adult in the community except such eccentrics as these defendants, is no defense. Although mitigation is undoubtedly frequent, it is assumed that the ignorance was "unreasonable," and the conduct is held criminal. Such decisions raise difficult questions regarding the application of objective *mens rea* and the quality of legal justice.

IGNORANTIA JURIS NEMINEM EXCUSAT

Fact and Law

In current discussions of criminal law theory, it is sometime argued that *ignorantia juris neminem excusat* is an archaism that should be discarded. This doctrine seems to hold morally innocent persons criminally liable, and to do so in reliance upon an obvious fiction—that everyone is presumed to know the law. But if the meaning of *ignorantia juris* differs greatly from that of *ignorantia facti,* their respective functions should also be very different. The first step toward the solution of this problem is to elucidate the terms that distinguish the two doctrines.

Certain differences between fact and law are easily recognized. Law is expressed in distinctive propositions, whereas facts are qualities or events occurring at definite places and times. Facts are particulars directly sensed in perception and introspection. Legal rules are generalizations; they are not sensed, but are understood in the process of cognition.[14] Law and fact are, of course, closely interrelated—law is "about" facts, it gives distinctive meaning to facts. For example, that A kills B is a fact; that this is murder is signified by certain legal propositions. When practical questions must be decided, what is "fact" and what is "law" differ in various contexts, e.g., if the purpose is to determine the respective functions of judge and jury or if a question of foreign law is in issue.

Although the terms of the doctrines concerning *ignorantia* indicate that it is important to make the above distinctions, it will be seen later that the crucial difference is not between fact and law, but between what is and what is not morally significant. Indeed, we have already seen that fact is subordinated to a mistaken belief about fact, i.e., to what is relevant to morality. Again, the distinction of property and other nonpenal law from penal law and treating the former as "fact,"

---

[11] Nalley v. State, 28 Tex. Ct. App. 387, 391, 13 S.W. 670, 671 (1890).

[12] Stehr v. State, 92 Neb. 755, 139 N.W. 676 (1913).

[13] Kirk v. Commonwealth, 186 Va. 839, 44 S.E. 2d 409 (1947).

[14] It is important to distinguish this meaning of "law" from its equally important sociological meaning, where it denotes a type of social fact, i.e., it is viewed as an external "thing" which influences behavior. This would fit the following definition of "fact": "No one doubts that there are coercive factors in general experience which certainly determine action, and also in some degree determine thought and will, though to an extent which is disputable. These existences, science, like common sense, calls facts." F. Barry, *The Scientific Habit of Thought* (New York: Columbia University Press, 1928), p. 93. . . .

to be discussed later in relation to property crimes and bigamy, will also be seen to support the hypothesis that the two doctrines move in different directions because they function differently in relation to the moral significance of criminal law. But we must first relate the distinctions drawn above regarding law and fact to *ignorantia*.

"Ignorantia"

Of the various sources of difficulty encountered in analysis of *ignorantia juris,* the most serious one concerns the meaning of *"ignorantia."* Since that term suggests a negative condition, i.e., the absence of "knowledge," analysis of this problem must deal with the latter term. It may be inferred from the distinctions drawn above between fact and law, that perception is a primitive form of knowledge, and that knowledge of law, the cognition of legal propositions, is much more complex. More important is that perception of facts is relatively certain; given external objects, all normal persons who perceive them under "adequate" conditions arrive at uniform judgments, and errors are attributed to excitement, negligence, poor conditions of observation, intoxication, and the like. But with reference to knowledge of law, there can never be such certainty as that. Although it is true that one is sometimes just as certain that a particular situation is within a rule as he is that he sees an external object, much more is required to determine the meaning of the rule. To do that one must take account of the vagueness of legal rules at their periphery, the unavoidable attribute of all propositions that refer to facts. Hence, no one can say with certainty that a rule of law means precisely thus and so.

These differences regarding knowledge of law and knowledge of fact indicate that *ignorantia facti* is an apt expression because "mistake" implies the possibility of certitude, but that *ignorantia juris* is not apt. In any case, whatever view of the two kinds of knowledge or *ignorantia* is preferred, the relatively much greater difficulty of knowing the law suggests that the two doctrines may implement very different policies. This preliminary insight into the nature of legal knowledge provides a perspective from which to gauge the significance of various theories of *ignorantia juris.*

. . .

A defensible theory of *ignorantia juris* must, it is suggested, find its origin in the central fact noted above, namely, that the meaning of the rules of substantive penal law is unavoidably vague, the degree of vagueness increasing as one proceeds from the core of the rules to their periphery. It is therefore possible to disagree indefinitely regarding the meaning of these words. But in adjudication, such indefinite disputation is barred because that is opposed to the character and requirements of a legal order, as is implied in the principle of legality. Accordingly, a basic axiom of legal semantics is that legal rules do or do not include certain behavior; and the linguistic problem must be definitely solved one way or the other, on that premise. These characteristics of legal adjudication imply a degree of necessary reliance upon authority. The debate must end and the court must decide one way or the other within a reasonable time. The various needs are met by prescribing a rational procedure and acceptance of the decisions of the "competent" officials as authoritative. Such official declaration of the meaning of a law is what the law is, however circuitously that is determined.

Now comes a defendant who truthfully pleads that he did not know that his conduct was criminal, implying that he thought it was legal. This may be because he did not know that any relevant legal prohibition existed (ignorance) or, if he did know any potentially relevant rule, that he decided it did not include his intended situation or conduct (mistake). In either case, such defenses always imply that the defendant thought he was acting legally. If that plea were valid, the consequence would be: whenever a defendant in a criminal case thought the law was thus and so, he is to be treated as though the law were thus and so, i.e., *the law actually is thus and so.* But such a doctrine would contradict the essential requisites of a legal system, the implications of the principle of legality.

This is apparent when we examine some necessary elements of a legal order, signified by the principle of legality, in greater detail. These are:

(1) that rules of law express objective meanings;

(2) that certain persons (the authorized "competent" officials) shall, after a prescribed procedure, declare what those meanings are.

They shall say, e.g., that situations A, B, C but not X, Y, Z are included within certain rules; and

(3) that these, and only these, interpretations are binding, i.e., only these meanings of the rules are the law.

To permit an individual to plead successfully that he had a different opinion or interpretation of the law would contradict the above postulates of a legal order. For there is a basic incompatibility between asserting that the law is what certain officials declare it to be after a prescribed analysis, and asserting, also, that those officials *must* declare it to be, i.e., that the law is, what defendants or their lawyers believed it to be. A legal order implies the rejection of such contradiction. It opposes objectivity to subjectivity, judicial process to individual opinion, official to lay, and authoritative to nonauthoritative declarations of what the law is. This is the rationale of *ignorantia juris neminem excusat.*

This rationale can also be expressed in terms of the ethical policy of *ignorantia juris neminem excusat,* namely, that the criminal law represents certain moral principles; to recognize ignorance or mistake of the law as a defense would contradict those values.[15]

Reference to the criminal cases where a defense of ignorance was pleaded supports this insight. A plea of ignorance or mistake of law is rarely encountered in prosecutions for serious crimes; it is raised almost solely in relation to minor offenses. Thus no sane defendant has pleaded ignorance that the law forbids killing a human being or forced intercourse or taking another's property or burning another person's house. In such cases, which include the common-law felonies and the more serious misdemeanors, instead of asserting that knowledge of law is presumed, it would be much more to the point to assert that knowledge of law (equally, ignorance or mistake of law) is wholly irrelevant. But many have and do plead ignorance of laws requiring them to supply certain reports or

forbidding the manufacture or sale of intoxicating liquor, the possession of gambling appliances, conducting a lottery, betting on horse races, keeping a saloon open on election day, and the like. In the relatively few cases of major crimes where ignorance of law was pleaded, no challenge was raised concerning the validity of the moral principle generally implied, but it was claimed that the situation in which the defendant acted was "exceptional." Thus, in a murder case, the defendant sought to justify his action on the ground that his victim was a willful trespasser;[16] in another homicide, on the ground that he was protecting his sister from one who was attempting to drug her to facilitate her rape.[17] There are kidnapping cases, defended by police officers, where suspected offenders were held *incommunicado* under a claim that the penal law permitted such conduct.[18] But none of the above defendants alleged that he was ignorant that the criminal law forbade murder or kidnapping. This problem is closely related to the valuation of harms in the criminal law, expressed in the principle of *mens rea.*

It is pertinent to recall here that the criminal law represents an objective ethics which must sometimes oppose individual convictions of right. Accordingly, it will not permit a defendant to plead, in effect, that although he knew what the facts were, his moral judgment was different from that represented in the penal law. The only defensible method is to apply the established ethical judgments of the community; and the only relatively certain data evidencing them are the penal laws.

They may not validly be contrasted with individual ethics because the individual participates in the determination and development of the community's ethics, hence, in that sense these are, also, his ethics. The process of legislation, viewed broadly to include discussion by the electorate, provides additional assurance that the legal valuations are soundly established. Thus, as regards the homicide of a willful trespasser or of a spouse's paramour in adultery, it is clear that the defendant, though he may have acted in accordance with honest conviction, was mistaken in his moral judgment. Indeed, his action and judgment

---

[15] The same considerations do not apply to *ignorantia facti* because: (a) Such a mistake is particular, i.e., it concerns a unique experience which in no way opposes the meaning of rules of law. These meanings are generalizations; they can be and are fitted to mistakes of fact, while, as seen, a plea of mistake of law challenges the meaning of the rules. (b) Behavior in ignorance of the facts is "involuntary"; it is not immoral while at least action violative of a major criminal law is immoral regardless of ignorance of the law.

[16] Weston v. Commonwealth, 111 Pa. 251, 2 A. 191 (1886).

[17] People v. Cook, 39 Mich. 236 (1878).

[18] People v. Weiss, 276 N.Y. 384, 12 N.E. 2d 514 (1938).

were undoubtedly influenced by his emotional disturbance; hence the probability is that he would, himself, take another view of his action if he considered the situation calmly. While a person who acts in accordance with his honest convictions is certainly not as culpable as one who commits a harm knowing it is wrong, it is also true that conscience sometimes leads one astray. Penal liability based on *mens rea* implies the objective wrongness of the harms proscribed—regardless of motive or conviction.

This is also required to preserve the principle of legality. As is widely believed, the principle of legality functions as a limitation on the authority of officials and, thus, as a major protection of the individual. This aspect of the "rule of law" has been emphasized in political and legal literature on the subject. But, as a necessary corollary, the shield has its other side—certain conduct definitely *does* fall within the rules and is punishable. This often predominates in the popular view as the primary function of the criminal law—to locate and take control of certain harm-doers. These functions of the criminal law are interrelated and inseparable; neither can be modified without affecting the other. If a crime were defined in vague terms (e.g., by including bad motives) it would be easier to bring harm-doers and "anti-social" persons within its scope and under the State's control; but the protection of individuals, now assured by precise case-law implementation of legality, would also suffer proportionately. A sharply defined concept definitely excludes everything except the class it definitely includes; but if the concept is confused by setting up incompatible criteria, its vitality to carry out both functions becomes weakened. The survival of the principle of legality requires the preservation of the definiteness of the rules, which must not be dissolved by the incompatible recognition of the opinions of litigants and lawyers as authoritative.

There are, thus, two aspects of the rationale of *ignorantia juris neminem excusat.* The doctrine is an essential postulate of a legal order, a phase of the "rule of law." And, second, legality cannot be separated from morality in a sound system of penal law. In such a system, at least the penal law of the major crimes represents both the formal criteria of legality and sound values. It follows that the two

theories discussed above, (1) that the principle of legality implies the doctrine of *ignorantia juris,* and (2) that the doctrine is necessary to the maintenance of the objective morality of the community, can be combined in a single rationale—the legally expressed values may not be ignored or contradicted. Thus, the direction of reform of the doctrine is also indicated, e.g., to take account of ignorance or mistake of property laws, other technical rules and certain petty penal laws. This will be discussed later.

With reference to the position presented above, it is possible, of course, to challenge the underlying premise—the desirability of having a legal system. Some may prefer decision by individuals who exercise completely unfettered power; and occasionally cases arise regarding which almost everyone wishes a decision could be rendered without restriction by existing laws. But this issue need not be discussed here. For present purposes it is necessary to assume the existence of a legal system and the consequent implications of the principle of legality. The validity of the above theory of *ignorantia juris neminem excusat* must be tested by criteria which are relevant to that basic premise.

Application of the Rationale of Ignorantia Juris

In light of the above discussion we may consider certain problems raised in the literature and case-law on *ignorantia juris.* Two proposed exceptions to *ignorantia juris neminem excusat*—mistake based on the "advice of counsel" and the "indefiniteness" of a law—may be disposed of briefly. The above analysis reveals the reason for the uniform holding that the advice of counsel regarding the meaning of a criminal law is not a defense. It is not that the lawyer may be incompetent or corrupt, but that lawyers are not law-declaring officials; it is not their function to interpret law authoritatively. Suppose that an opinion was obtained from the most distinguished lawyers, that the subject was not complicated, that numerous precedents were found, and that the law was clear and simple —in short, a situation where knowledge of law was easy to acquire. A person acts upon such advice, then a prosecution is instituted. His plea of ignorance would nonetheless be invalid because the court before whom the case is tried cannot substitute the opinion of counsel for its own "knowledge."[19]

This leads to a major conclusion previously suggested, namely, that "knowledge" of law (and thus ignorance or mistake of it) has not only the usual meaning discussed above but also a meaning that is distinctive and decisive as regards the doctrine of *ignorantia juris*. "Knowledge" of the law in this context means *coincidence with the subsequent interpretation of the authorized law-declaring official*. If there is coincidence, the defendant knew the law and his action is legal. If there is not coincidence, it can avail nothing that the defendant thought his conduct was legal. This is the special meaning of *ignorantia*, which distinguishes it from the ordinary meaning of ignorance, expressed, e.g., in *ignorantia facti*.

The above analysis also indicates the invalidity of the other proposal, that indefiniteness in the meaning of a penal law should provide an exception to the doctrine of *ignorantia juris*. This problem is presently dealt with in terms of strict construction and "due process." If a criminal statute is ambiguous, its meaning is rendered "sufficiently" precise by excluding the disadvantageous sense of the words. And if a penal statute is vague, it is unconstitutional.[20] The survival of a rule, after being subjected to the tests of strict construction and due process, is an authoritative finding that it is sufficiently definite to constitute law. Accordingly, the defendant cannot be permitted to raise the question of indefiniteness again under a plea of ignorance of the law and avoid liability by that procedure.

But there are certain large areas of criminal law which are presently assumed to be within the scope of *ignorantia juris* although, actually, the doctrine is not relevant to them. If this can be shown, the presently wide range of the doctrine will be substantially narrowed and its meaning should become proportionately clearer. One of the most important of these situations concerns the effect of changes in the validity of a statute or regulation. For example, a statute forbidding the sale of intoxicants is held unconstitutional; then, this decision is overruled and the statute is held constitutional. The courts usually state that they are required to deal with *ignorantia juris* in cases involving, e.g., the sale of intoxicants after the first decision and prior to the second, the validating, one. They say this is an "exception" justified on the ground that it is "manifestly unfair" to hold the defendant to a greater knowledge of the law than that possessed by the State's Supreme Court. But when an individual's conduct conforms to the decisions of the highest court, the claim that he acted "in ignorance of the law" is almost fantastic. It is submitted that the above situation does not call for application of an exceptional rule because neither ignorance nor mistake of law is involved.

This is evident if the traditional theory of the unbroken validity of the statute in question is repudiated so far as penal law is concerned. The above situation would then be interpreted, in effect, as: enactment, repeal by judicial decision, and "re-enactment" by the later decision.[21] The traditional theory should not apply to criminal law because the policy prohibiting *ex post facto* enactment excludes the dependence of penal liability upon any subsequent law-making, such as a decision reversing a previous one that held a statute unconstitutional. The traditional theory implies that the law covers all possible situations and that it is certain in meaning. At the opposite extreme is the skepticism which asserts that the law is only what the judges in each particular case say it is—nothing more. Neither theory is persuasive. Law does pre-exist, but not in the degree of specificity required for all subsequent adjudications. It pre-exists "sufficiently" to bar arbitrariness and to limit the scope of judicial legislation, but judicial decision plays an essential role in its development. Without adding details, it may be concluded that when a court (certainly the highest court) holds the law to be thus and so, that is what the law is from that date on. Thus the correct *ratio* of the decisions dealing with the above type of situation is not that the defendant

---

[19] To allow such a defense would make "the opinion of the attorney paramount to the law." People v. McCalla, 63 Cal. App. 783, 795, 220 P. 436, 441 (1923). So, too, in Needham v. State, 32 P. 2d 92, 93 (Okla. 1934), and Hopkins v. State, 193 Md. 489, 69 A. 2d 456 (1949).

[20] Lanzetta v. New Jersey, 306 U.S. 451, 83 L. Ed. 888, 59 S. Ct. 618 (1939); United States v. Cohen Grocery Co., 255 U.S. 81, 89, 65 L. Ed. 516, 41 S. Ct. 298 (1921).

[21] This, however, does not explain how a void statute can be revived by the later decision. It is preferable, therefore, to speak of the unconstitutional statute as unenforceable rather than void.

acted in ignorance of the law, that it is unfair to require him to know the law when the Supreme Court was ignorant of it, etc. It is, on the contrary, that the defendant is not criminally liable because the law at the time he acted was what the Supreme Court declared it to be; in short, his conduct conformed to the law.

. . .

Knowledge of Illegality Included in Mens Rea

This problem arises chiefly in relation to larceny, embezzlement, malicious destruction of property, willful trespasses, and other similar offenses where the defendant did not know that another person's legal rights were being violated. The uniform exculpation of the defendants in these cases does not represent an exception to *ignorantia juris neminem excusat*. It is not because the defendants were ignorant of the law that they are not criminals, but because, being ignorant of certain law, they lacked the required *mens rea*. Can these cases be distinguished from criminal homicide and other crimes where ignorance of the illegality of the conduct is not relevant to the *mens rea*?

In the above cases, the defendants were mistaken regarding the law of property, hence their exculpation would obviously not involve any exception to *ignorantia juris neminem excusat* if that doctrine, when employed in penal law, were interpreted to exclude property law. But no insight or elucidation is provided regarding the above problem by asserting that property crimes require a specific intent.

If we compare (1) a situation where the defendant shoots a trespasser, thinking he has a legal right to do so, and (2) the typical property case, where the defendant takes a chattel, thinking he has a legal right to its possession, we note that both situations involve private and criminal law. In (1) the defendant's ignorance of the law is not a defense to a criminal charge, whereas in (2) it is. The reason is not merely that the mistake in (2) concerns property law but rather that in (1) we have facts that are directly characterized as criminal, i.e., there is a penal law that proscribes shooting a trespasser whereas in (2) we do not have such facts. In (1) no private law exists which can place any interpretation on the facts that would alter their

meaning for penal law; in (2) no meaning can be ascribed to the facts that is relevant to the penal law until the defendant's opinion regarding the right of possession is determined. But this is little more than recognizing, somewhat more clearly, perhaps, that in some crimes an opinion regarding certain private law qualifies the criminal significance of the conduct. Such opinions function as facts, and such ignorance or mistake falls within the meaning and purpose of *ignorantia facti*. But is there an underlying reason for this?

It was suggested above that it is not the distinction between private and penal law or even the factual quality of the error regarding the former, but the moral significance of the respective norms, and consequently of the defendant's conduct, that is decisive. Accordingly, *"juris"* should not be restricted to criminal law nor should a plea of ignorance of all nonpenal law be allowed. For example, parts of torts and family law, like the law defining the major crimes, also reflect simple moral values. The plea of lack of *mens rea*, resulting from ignorance of the above property law, is not inconsistent with the ethical principle that it is wrong to steal another's chattel. That value is not contradicted if the actor thinks he has a right to its possession. On the other hand, a defendant's plea of ignorance of the criminal law, e.g., in killing a trespasser, would contradict the ethics of the criminal law. This conclusion regarding ignorance of certain private law is consistent with *ignorantia facti excusat*. For there, too, the defendant does not challenge the moral norms represented in the criminal law. It may be noted, finally, that "knowledge" of certain private law is given its ordinary meaning, similar to "knowledge of fact" and that, so far as penal law is concerned, the principle of legality is compatible with the recognition, as a defense, of certain mistakes of law, indicated above.

. . .

PETTY OFFENSES

One result of the above discussion is to narrow the scope of *ignorantia juris neminem excusat* considerably since many situations presently treated as both within the meaning of, and also "exceptions" to, that doctrine were shown to be irrelevant to it. The correct *ratio decidendi* of the cases dealing with those situations is either that the requisite *mens rea* included knowledge that the act was illegal (larceny, bigamy) or that the act conformed to the law declared by the authorized officials. *Ignorantia juris*, as thus restricted, was defended in terms of its rationale—a fusion of the principle of legality and the ethics of criminal law. We shall now consider the implications of this theory of *ignorantia juris* with reference to the reform of that doctrine in relation to certain petty offenses.

In an ideal system, ancient laws, no longer useful, would be discarded by a rule of desuetude. The legislature would never enact laws favoring special interests; like Plato's ideal legislator, it would be influenced only by reason and science. And all normal persons would be sufficiently sensitive and informed to recognize even very minor offenses as immoral. In such circumstances, it could be said with complete persuasiveness that any person who intentionally or recklessly did anything forbidden by the criminal law, however small the penalty, acted immorally and merited penal liability.

But actual systems of penal law fall short of such perfection. In the absence of any principle of desuetude, there are instances of prosecutors' digging into ancient books to exhume and enforce long-forgotten statutes. As regards some minor offenses, newly created ones, and those regulating certain businesses, there is frequently a gap between public opinion and the policy of the enactment, between mores and morality. These segments of existing criminal law raise serious questions concerning the reform of *ignorantia juris neminem excusat*.

The principle of *mens rea* requires the voluntary commission of a harm forbidden by penal law. Accordingly, if there was conduct expressing a *mens rea* and the relevant penal law had been promulgated, the ethical conditions of modern penal liability are satisfied.[22]

But as regards certain criminal offenses, indicated immediately above, *the knowledge that the relevant conduct is legally forbidden is an essential element of its immorality*. This is quite different from the judicial distinction between *mala in se* and *mala prohibita*. For, on the one hand, it does not imply that the former (i.e., major offenses) are immoral "apart from positive law"; nor, as regards the latter, does it imply that an act becomes immoral because it is legally forbidden. How could the mere prohibition under sanction of force effect such a change? The distinction that should be made, it is submitted, is that some acts are immoral regardless of the actor's ignorance of their being legally forbidden (e.g., the felonies and principal misdemeanors), whereas other acts are immoral *only* because the actor knows they are legally forbidden. If that judicial construction were abandoned, then, instead of saying that because an act is *malum prohibitum* it is unnecessary to find any criminal intent, the rule would be that, since the only rational basis for finding a criminal intent in these cases is knowledge that the act is legally forbidden, a finding of such knowledge is essential. As was suggested above, ignorance of penal law, of itself, i.e., of sheer positivist illegality, presents no general ground for exculpation. But as regards certain petty offenses, where normal conscience (moral attitudes) and understanding cannot be relied upon to avoid the forbidden conduct, knowledge of the law is essential to culpability; hence the doctrine of *ignorantia juris* should not be applied there. This has recently been recognized to a limited but potentially very significant extent by the United States Supreme Court in *Lambert*.[23]

Since the questions requiring determination, in order to demark the exact area within which ignorance of the law is a defense, are beyond the province of the judicial function, the need for legislation is clear. A likely area would include recent misdemeanors punishable only by small fines, various ordinances and technical regulations of administrative boards. Here actual knowledge of the illegality should be required. It seems necessary to retain the presumption that there was such knowledge, allowing the defendant to introduce evidence tending to prove his ignorance or mistake of the law, but placing the final burden of prov-

---

[22] Opportunity to examine and study the laws is implied in democratic theory which would not be satisfied if conflicts were adjudicated according to laws inaccessible to public inquiry. In addition, promulgation is a condition of valid determination of the law, i.e., the ground of adjudication must be public to permit criticism and appraisal. But these do not imply that knowledge of law is essential to the just imposition of criminal liability. The principle of legality functions primarily as a limitation on official conduct, not as a determinant of culpability. It rests on the wide ethical considerations that concern the legitimacy of a government. . . .

[23] Lambert v. California, 355 U.S. 225, 2 L. Ed., 2d 228, 78 S. Ct. 240 (1957). . . .

ing *mens rea,* in the above sense, upon the State.

The above general direction to be taken in reform of *ignorantia juris* seems defensible, but certain difficult questions need to be considered somewhat further. If we examine the petty offenses more closely, we find that there are different types of them. First, as noted, there are archaic, long-forgotten offenses—the curiosities of the statute-books and, also, other obviously unsound enactments; and second, there are new, technical and regulative offenses, e.g., that it is criminal to drive an uninsured automobile, that land must be used in conformity with the purpose of a local authority, that it is criminal to sell eggs except on a prescribed grading system,[24] that minimum wages determined by certain classifications must be paid to certain employees,[25] that one who undertakes the care of a foster child for reward must give notice to the local welfare authorities, and so on. But third, some petty offenses, e.g., insults, minor assaults and others are neither new nor technical; instead, they are well known and many of them are of the same type of harm as major crimes, only less serious. And fourth, there are petty offenses which are not intuitively recognized as immoral,[26] but if the forbidden harm is considered, the correct evaluation will be made. As will appear, this category raises difficult questions.

Reform is also complicated by the fact that to some degree there is an unavoidable clash between the principles of criminal law and historical accretions. For example, if criminal theory is based upon principles defining "harm" partly in terms of morality, the first class lies outside its range. So, too, if *mens rea* is defined in terms of objective morality, the law cannot admit, nor is it the judge's function to allow, nullification of any law on the ground that it is unsound. Reform can, of course, override such theoretical considerations and, on practical grounds, warrant the

restriction of the doctrine of *ignorantia juris.*

In addition to a classification of petty offenses, perhaps along the lines of the criteria suggested above, there are other important questions to be decided with regard to reform of the doctrine. For example, should every kind of ignorance of the law defining the designated petty offenses be a defense or should only "invincible" ignorance be thus recognized? Should the prosecution be required to prove not only that the ignorance was vincible but also that it was the result of recklessness? And, still within the specified area of petty offenses, should mistake of the relevant penal law be distinguished and treated differently from ignorance of it?

A person who is ignorant of a law or regulation may have been on the high seas when it was adopted or he may have been in a hospital or so distraught with serious troubles that he failed to read the newspaper or a bulletin of his Association, giving the pertinent information. These may be instances where definite use can be made of "invincible ignorance" consistently with the test of recklessness. Or, the defendant may be very inexperienced in the operation of his new business or merely stupid, but not to the point of legally recognized incompetence. On the other hand, the defendant may have received the necessary publication or other information but was indifferent to it or positively set against acquiring knowledge of the pertinent rules. Except for the last, the recklessly ignorant, there is no *mens rea* in the above cases. As has been urged with reference to negligence, education, not punishment, is indicated wherever ignorance is not the result of a voluntary indifference to the acquisition of the relevant legal knowledge. Such pleas of ignorance of the law do not contradict the principle of legality.

Mistake of law, however, raises more difficult problems. The mistaken person is in a more meritorious position than the recklessly ignorant one, since he has made an effort, perhaps to the extent of consulting a lawyer, to discover what his duty is under the criminal law. That certainly recommends mitigation; indeed, if knowledge of the illegality is the only ground for inferring a *mens rea,* there should be complete exculpation. This would seem to apply rather clearly to the first two classes of petty offenses noted above. On

---

[24] Witte, *A Break for the Citizen,* 9 State Government 73 (1936).

[25] Borderland Const. Co. v. State, 49 Ariz. 523, 68 P. 2d 207 (1937).

[26] E.g., carrying a pistol in public: Crain v. State, 69 Tex. Cr. R. 55, 153 S.W. 155 (1913). Travel interstate with intent to avoid testifying in a criminal case: Hemans v. United States, 163 F. 2d 228 (6th Cir. 1947). Tapping the wife's telephone wire: United States v. Gris, 247 F. 2d 860, 864 (2d Cir. 1957).

the other hand, the plea of mistake implies that the penal law in question was actually brought to the defendant's attention, that he examined the relevant words in the code, statute, or decisions. This places the defendant in a much less favorable position than that of the invincibly ignorant person. For error implies acquaintance and opportunity to form a correct opinion and that might support a charge of recklessness.

But this estimate may be deemed too refined for everyday decision and an exaggeration of the sensitivity of normal conscience regarding the policy of petty offenses. It may be urged that all that is pertinent is analysis of the meaning of certain words and a lawyer's definite opinion of the scope of those words. As a practical matter, probably most persons would agree with Salmond, "That he who breaks the law of the land disregards at the same time the principles of justice and honesty is in many instances far from the truth. In a complex legal system a man requires other guidance than that of common sense and a good conscience."[27] The difficulty, however, so far as *ignorantia juris* is concerned, is that the defendant and his lawyer, in effect, are setting their interpretation of the words defining a penal law against that of the authorized officials. From a theoretical viewpoint, this is precisely what a legal order cannot consistently admit. From that viewpoint, i.e., with reference to the principles of legality and *mens rea* (in its objective meaning), and on the assumption that only social

[27] Salmond, *Jurisprudence* (10th ed., 1947), p. 408.

harms are proscribed, mistake of penal law cannot be recognized as a defense.

Thus, the solution of this problem seems to be caught between two fires. On the one hand, a defendant's interpretation of the law cannot prevail over official declarations of it. On the other hand, where mistakes of non-penal law directly exclude *mens rea*, e.g., larceny, bigamy, etc., such mistakes are admitted as a defense. But penal law, presumably, is composed of moral norms, hence even the pettiest of penal laws, by definition, proscribes a social harm binding on normal conscience. And theory also recalls the objective meaning of *mens rea* and the judicial duty to assume that all penal laws are sound. But the voice of practical sense replies that, in fact, the accepted "penal" law contains many petty proscriptions of conduct which are not recognized by normal persons as having moral significance, and that when social harm becomes so diluted that it cannot be thus recognized, it is time in the sphere of positive criminal law to do justice in light of the facts.

This is the kind of problem where authority should step in to resolve the issues; and, as was suggested above, the proper authority is the legislature. Such practical resolution of a difficult problem should be respected in a branch of law that must represent thoughtful public attitudes. Legal systems survive and prosper despite the incompatibility of some of their rules, indeed, because they are able to tolerate such antinomies. How much of such incompatibility a legal system can and should tolerate is a question regarding which there are probably many opinions.

Error*

. . . Turning now specially to my own case and considering the nature of my errors—for they alone argue imperfection in me—I observe that they depend on two concurrent causes: on my faculty of cognition, and my faculty of choice or free will; that is, on the intellect and at the same time on the will.

* René Descartes, *Meditations on First Philosophy*, trans. Elizabeth Anscombe and Peter Thomas Geach in *Descartes: Philosophical Writings* (Edinburgh: Thomas Nelson and Sons, 1954), pp. 95–98, 100, reprinted by permission of the publishers. Footnotes are omitted.

By the mere intellect I do no more than perceive the ideas that are matter for judgment; and precisely so regarded, the intellect contains, properly speaking, no error. There may be innumerable things of which I have no idea; but this is not properly to be called a privation, but merely a negative lack, of the ideas. I can bring forward no reason to show that God ought to have given me a greater power of knowledge than he did; however skilled I understand an artisan to be, I do not think he ought to have put into every one of his works all the perfections he is able to put into any.

Again, I cannot complain that I received from God a restricted or imperfect will or freedom; for I am aware of no bounds upon its scope. Indeed, the following seems to me very remarkable. Nothing else in me is so perfect or so great but that I understand the possibility of something still more perfect, still greater. For instance, if I consider the faculty of understanding, I discern at once that in me it is very slight and greatly restricted. I thereupon form the idea of a far greater faculty; indeed, of the greatest possible, an infinite one; and I perceive, from the mere fact that I can form the idea of this, that it belongs to the nature of God. Similarly, if I examine my faculty of memory, or imagination, or any other, I find none that I do not see to be slight and circumscribed in me, but immeasurable in God. It is only will, or freedom of choice, that I experience in myself in such a degree that I do not grasp the idea of any greater; so that it is in this regard above all, I take it, that I bear the image and likeness of God. For although God's will is incomparably greater than mine, both by reason of the knowledge and power that accompany it and make it more firm and efficacious, and by reason of its object—of its greater scope— yet it does not seem to be greater when considered precisely as will. Will consists simply in the fact that we are able alike to do and not to do a given thing (that is, can either assert or deny, either seek or shun); or rather, simply in the fact that our impulse toward what the intellect presents to us as worthy of assertion or denial, as a thing to be sought or shunned, is such that we feel ourselves not to be determined by any external force. There is no need for me to be impelled both ways in order to be free; on the contrary, the more I am inclined one way—either because I clearly understand it under the aspect of truth and goodness, or because God has so disposed my inmost consciousness (*intima cogitationis meae*)—the more freely do I choose that way. Divine grace and natural knowledge certainly do not diminish liberty; they rather increase and strengthen it. Indeed, the indifference that I am aware of when there is no reason urging me one way rather than the other, is the lowest grade of liberty; it argues no perfection of free will, but only some defect or absence of knowledge; if I always saw clearly what is good and true, I should never deliberate as to what I ought to judge or choose; and thus, although entirely free, I could never be indifferent.

From this I see that the cause of my errors is not the power of willing that I have from God, considered in itself; for that is most ample, and perfect of its kind; nor yet is it the power of understanding; for there is no doubt that whatever I understand, since my understanding it comes from God, I understand correctly, and cannot possibly be deceived about. Whence then do my errors originate? Surely, just from this: my will extends more widely than my understanding, and yet I do not restrain it within the same bounds, but apply it to what I do not understand. Since it is here indifferent, it easily turns aside from truth and goodness; and so I fall into both error and sin.

For instance, during these last few days I have been considering whether anything in the world exists, and have observed that, from the very fact that I am examining the question, it necessarily follows that I do exist. I could not but judge to be true what I understood so clearly; not because I was compelled to do so by any external cause, but because the great illumination of my understanding was followed by a great inclination of the will; and my belief was the more free and spontaneous for my not being indifferent in the matter. But at this moment I am not merely knowing that I exist, in so far as I am a conscious being; there occurs to me also an idea of a corporeal nature; and it so happens that I am doubtful whether the consciousness (*natura cognitans*) that is in me—or rather, that is myself—is different from this corporeal nature, or whether both are the same thing; and, let us suppose, so far there is no convincing reason that occurs to my mind in favor of either view. Surely just on this account I am indifferent whether I assert or deny either, or even abstain from judgment on the matter altogether.

This indifference, moreover, extends not only to things that the understanding knows absolutely nothing about, but in general to everything that the understanding does not know clearly enough at the time when the will deliberates. However much I may be drawn one way by probable conjectures, the mere knowledge that they are only conjectures and not certain and indubitable reasons, is enough to incline my assent the other way. I have had proof enough of this in the last few days; all the things in whose truth I had previously had the greatest possible belief, I now supposed to be quite false, simply because I had observed the possibility of having some sort of doubt about them.

Now when I do not perceive clearly and distinctly enough what the truth is, it is clear that if I abstain from judgment I do right and am not deceived. But if I assert or deny, I am using my free will wrongly; if the side I take is falsehood, then clearly I shall be in error; if I embrace the other side, I shall by chance fall upon the truth, but nevertheless this decision will be blameworthy; for it is obvious by the light of nature that perception by the understanding should always come before the determination of the will. There is inherent in this wrong use of free will the privation in which the nature (*forma*) of erorr consists; this privation, I say, is inherent in the actual operation in so far as it proceeds from me; not in the faculty I received

from God, nor even in the operation, in so far as it depends on him.

· · ·

. . . I think today's meditation has been of no small service, since I have been investigating the cause of error and falsehood. And surely no other cause is possible than the one I have explained. For whenever I restrain my will in making decisions, so that its range is confined to what the understanding shows it clearly and distinctly, I just cannot go wrong. For every clear and distinct perception is something; so it cannot come from nothingness, but must have God for its author; God, I say, the supremely Perfect, who it is absurd should be deceitful; therefore, it is indubitably true. Thus today I have learned, not only what to avoid, so as not to be deceived, but also what to do, so as to attain the truth; I shall certainly attain it if only I take enough notice of all that I perfectly understand, and distinguish this from everything else, which I apprehend more obscurely and confusedly. For the future I will take good care of this.

Duty and Ignorance of Fact*

The question which I propose to consider is essentially dull and tiresome; it worries us little, if at all, in practical life; and it is apt to be ignored or, at least, only casually treated by those whose business is theory. Nevertheless, at any rate for theory, it is important.

As it first presents itself the question is: "If a man has an obligation, i.e., a duty, to do some action, does the obligation depend on certain characteristics of the situation in which he is, or on certain characteristics of his thought about the situation?" The question is vague because of the vagueness of the term "thought," but at the outset this does not matter. Consideration of it, however, will force us to consider another question, viz.: "Can an obligation really be an obligation to do some *action,* and, if not, what should be substituted for the term 'action'?" And, should a substitute prove necessary, the main ques-

tion will have to be modified accordingly.

To appreciate the importance, and even the meaning, of the question, we have first to see how it arises.

We have all from time to time thought that we ought, and again that we ought not, to do certain actions. And, if we were asked to give a general account of these actions, we should be inclined to say that, though not all of one sort, yet they all fall under one or other of a limited number of kinds of action which are set out in current moral rules, i.e., current general statements each stating that a man ought or ought not to do an action of a certain kind. Further, at any rate until certain difficulties have occurred to us, we think these rules true. We think, for instance, that a man ought to speak the truth, to carry out the orders of his government, not to steal, and not to hurt the feelings of another. And this is not surprising, since these rules are simply the result of an attempt to formulate those various general characteristics of the particular acts we have thought duties, which have led us to think them duties.

Elucidation, however, is needed of the gen-

* H. A. Prichard, "Duty and Ignorance of Fact," in *Moral Obligation* (Oxford: Clarendon Press, 1949), pp. 18–39, reprinted by permission of the publishers. Footnotes are omitted. The notes found at the end of the article were added at a later date by the author to his original text of 1932.

eral character of the meaning of a moral rule, and therefore also of the thought which it is used to express.

It is, no doubt, not easy to say what we mean by "an action" or by "doing something." Yet we have in the end to allow that we mean by it originating, causing, or bringing about the existence of something, viz., some new state of an existing thing or substance, or, more shortly, causing a change of state of some existing thing. This is shown by the meaning of our phrases for various particular actions. For by "moving our hand" we mean causing a change of place of our hand; by "posting a letter" we mean bringing about that a letter is in a pillar-box; and so on. We may be tempted to go farther, and say that we mean by "an action" the *conscious* origination of something, i.e., the originating something knowing that we are doing so. But this will not do; for no one, for instance, thinks himself to be denying that he has hurt a man's feelings when he says that he did not know that he was hurting them and, indeed, thought he was not. Correspondingly, we mean by "doing an action of a certain kind" bringing about something of a certain kind, viz., a state of a certain kind, of a thing of a certain kind. Consequently the meaning of a moral rule can be stated in the form: "A man ought, or ought not, to bring about a thing of a certain kind." Thus by "A man ought to honor his parents" we mean: "A man ought to bring about in his parents the knowledge that he holds them in honor."

But this is not all. We ordinarily think that in doing certain actions we bring about the things which we do directly, while in doing certain others we do so indirectly, i.e., by indirectly bringing about other things which in turn cause them. Thus we think that in moving our head we bring about a change of place of our head directly, whereas in giving a friend the family news we bring about his receipt of the news indirectly, i.e., by bringing about directly certain other changes which in turn cause it. No doubt on reflection we may find it difficult to defend the thought that, e.g., in moving our head we directly cause our head to change its place; and we may be reduced to thinking that, in moving our head, what we bring about directly is some new state of certain cells of our brain of which we are wholly unaware in doing the action. But such a reflection does not conflict with

our thought that we bring about certain things indirectly. Nor does it lead us to deny the distinction between bringing something about directly and bringing something about indirectly, since, so long as we think that we bring about certain things indirectly, we inevitably imply that there are certain things which we bring about directly, even if we do not know what they are. It is as impossible for all bringing about to be indirect as for all knowledge to be indirect. And, if we now turn to the phrase for the act of a certain kind referred to in some moral rule, we find that in every case it stands for bringing about something of a certain kind indirectly. We mean, for instance, by "honoring a parent" causing a parent to find himself held in honor by causing something else to cause it; we mean by "speaking the truth" causing another to know our thought by causing certain sounds which cause him to have this knowledge; and so on. We can therefore say generally that the meaning of a moral rule has the form: "A man ought, or ought not, to bring about a thing of a certain kind indirectly."

To bring about something indirectly is, however, to bring it about in a less strict sense than that of bringing it about directly. For, where we bring about something by causing something to cause it, the result is not wholly due to us. And, where we bring about something X indirectly, what we bring about in the strict sense is the thing which causes X. Correspondingly, we use the term "action" both in a strict sense in which it means bringing about something directly, and also in a looser sense in which it means bringing about something whether directly or indirectly. And where, e.g., some action of ours is referred to as giving some relation the family news, we must allow that our action in the strict sense is some such act as transferring certain ink to certain places on a piece of paper; and in support of this admission we might point out that, in the strict sense of "action," our action must cease with the cessation of our activity. We have, therefore, to allow that if a moral rule is stated in terms of "doing something" and of "bringing about something" in the strict sense, its meaning will be of the form: "A man ought to do such an act or acts, i.e., bring about such a thing or things, as will cause a thing of the kind A to assume a state of the kind X."

Further, in stating some moral rule, we are

plainly in two respects speaking elliptically. Thus, in asserting that a man ought to support his indigent parents, we clearly do not mean that a man ought at *any* time to support his indigent parents. We are thinking, and expect to be understood as asserting, that the duty exists only when two conditions are satisfied. The first is, of course, that the man has parents who are indigent and willing to receive the means of support; and the second is that he is able to support them. For we never think that an action can be a man's duty unless he is able to do it. But since to support parents is to bring about something indirectly, the realization of the second condition involves the existence of a certain combination of things capable of having certain changes of state effected in them, such that, on the one hand, the man can produce the changes directly, and also such that, on the other hand, if these changes are produced, they will result in the parents' having the means of support. In asserting a moral rule, however, we take for granted that a man has permanently the capacity of bringing about certain things directly, and therefore we think of the realization of the second condition as consisting simply in the fact that the situation in which the man is is such that some one, or some group, of the things which he can bring about directly would, if produced, effect his parents' possession of the means of subsistence. Consequently, to generalize, we can say that any moral rule, when modified to express fully the thought which it is used to express, will be of the following form: "When the situation in which a man is contains a thing of the kind A capable of having a state of the kind X effected in it, and when also it is such that some state or combination of states Y which the man can bring about directly would, if brought about, cause a state of the kind X in A, the man ought to bring about that state or combination of states."

Again, once the thought is expressed in this form, it becomes obvious that, in having the thought, we are implying that when a man has an obligation to do some act in the strict sense, corresponding to the rule, what renders him bound to do the action is the special character of the situation in which he is, in the two respects just indicated, this being what gives rise to the fact that, if he were to do the action, he would indirectly be causing a state of the kind in question. Plainly,

therefore, if we were to put forward a particular set of rules as exhaustive, we should be implying that the question whether we are bound to do some particular action, in the strict sense, will turn on whether the existing situation contains any of the various pairs of conditions which would bring the act under one or other of the rules. Clearly also, even if we did not think such rules as we could offer exhaustive, we should still think that the question could only be settled in the same kind of way, although we could not settle it.

Now when we reflect on this general idea or thought underlying our assertion of a set of moral rules, viz., that where we have an obligation to do some action in the strict sense, it depends on certain characteristics of the situation, we find it in two related respects very attractive. For, first, being the thought that any obligation depends solely on certain characteristics of the situation, it is on its negative side the thought that the obligation is wholly independent of our knowledge and thought about the situation. And we welcome this negative side, since we do not like to think that the question whether some action is a duty turns not on the nature of the situation but on that of our attitude toward it in respect of knowledge and thought. Moreover, the thought seems implied in much of our procedure in actual life. For frequently when in doubt, as we often are, whether some action in the narrow sense is a duty, our doubt seems to arise from doubt about the actual facts. Thus when I see someone who shows symptoms of having fainted and it occurs to me that, if I shouted, I might revive him, I may doubt whether I am bound to shout; and, when I do, my doubt sometimes seems to arise partly from doubt whether he has really fainted, and partly from doubt whether shouting would revive him. And if I try to resolve my doubt about the duty by resolving my doubt about the facts, I at least seem to be implying that the question whether I am bound to shout turns on what the facts really are. Second, the thought implies that if some action is a duty, it would bring about some state referred to in a moral rule, such as the recovery of a sick man, and would not be merely an act which we think would be likely to do so; and we welcome this implication because we should like to think that, if we have done some duty, we have achieved some change to which a moral rule refers, e.g., that we have helped a man out of trouble, and not merely done something which we thought would do this but which possibly has in fact damaged a man who was in no trouble at all.

Yet there is no denying that if we try to defend this thought we become involved in very awkward consequences. There are various admissions which we shall have to make which we thoroughly dislike when we come to reflect on them.

The most awkward of these emerges as soon as we ask: "How am I to *know* that some moral rule is applicable to me here and now?" The rule being of the form recently stated, the question becomes: "How am I to *know* that the situation satisfies the two conditions necessary for the application of the rule, viz., first, that it contains a particular thing of the kind *A* capable of having a state of the kind *X* effected in it, and, second, that it is such that some act or acts which I can do would cause this *A* to assume a state of the kind *X*?" And as regards the first condition, we shall have to admit that the situation may often satisfy it, without my knowing, or even being able to discover, that it does so. We may perhaps insist that sometimes I know that there is someone to whom I have made a promise, or again that I have parents who are in difficulties; but we cannot deny that sometimes I am uncertain whether there is someone to whom I have made a promise, or whether my parents are in difficulties, or again whether a man whom I meet is ill, at any rate with an illness which anything I can do would be likely to diminish. And we shall have to allow that in most of these latter cases I have no means of resolving my doubt. We shall therefore have to admit that for this reason alone I may often have a duty without knowing, or even being able to discover, that I have. Again, as regards the second condition, there are, undeniably, absolutely no occasions on which, where some particular state *Y* which I can bring about directly would cause an effect of the kind *X*, I either *know*, or can even come to *know*, that it would, although of course I may have a strong opinion about the matter. For plainly I never either do or can *know* that any particular action which I can do in the narrow sense would have a certain effect. Thus, unquestionably, I neither do nor can know that giving a man a certain drug would cause his recovery; and if in fact I give him the drug, and afterward find that he has recovered, even then I cannot *know* that I have cured him, though I may think it very likely. Again, I never *know* that by uttering certain sounds I shall cause a man to know what I think; and I know that however much I may try to speak the truth, I may fail. Consideration, then, of the second condition forces us to admit that there is absolutely no occasion on which a moral rule applies to me on which I can know that I have the duty in question. In fact, reflection on these conditions compels us to admit that no moral rule can express knowledge, and that, to express knowledge, we must substitute a hypothetical statement in which we replace the word "when" of a moral rule by "if." To express knowledge, its form will have to be: "*If* the situation in which a man is contains a thing of the kind *A* capable of having a state of the kind *X* produced in it, and *if* also it be such that one of the things which he can bring about directly will, if he brings it about, cause *A* to assume such a state, then he ought to bring about that thing." The need of this substitution is obvious, since for the reasons given an individual is sometimes uncertain whether the first, and always uncertain whether the second, condition is realized. Indeed, on this view that an obligation, if there be one, depends on certain features of the situation, we are driven to the extreme conclusion that, although we may have duties, we cannot know but can only believe that we have; and therefore we are even rendered uncertain whether we, or anyone else, has ever had, or will ever have, a duty.

Here we may note the answer which this view requires us to give to a question which is often raised. Obviously at different times opposite views have been taken of the rightness or wrongness of certain kinds of action, in consequence of different views concerning matters of fact. Thus while some men must in the past have been sincerely convinced that it was a duty to torture heretics, most men are now equally convinced that a man ought not to do so; and the explanation obviously lies in a difference of opinion about the effects of torture. And the question is often asked: "Where there is such a difference of view concerning the rightness or wrongness of a certain kind of action, which party is right?" To this question, on the view we are considering, the answer can only be: "We do not know; no one knows; and no one ever will know. Even those, e.g., who considered it a duty to torture heretics may have been right."

That we can never know that we have a duty is not, however, the only conclusion to which we are driven on this view. There are others related to it. One is that, though we may have duties, we can never, strictly speaking, do a duty, if we have one, *because* it is a duty, i.e., really in consequence of *knowing* it to be a duty. And the reason is, of course, simply that we can never have the knowledge. At best, if we have a duty, we may do it because we think without question, or else believe, or again think it possible, that the act is a duty. Another conclusion is that some past act of mine may have been a duty although in doing it I believed that the act was one which I ought not to do. Thus my shouting on seeing a man may have been in fact a duty, because he was faint and shouting would revive him, and yet I may have shouted to satisfy a grudge, believing that he was asleep and that my shouting would disturb him. A third is that I may do some act which is in fact a duty, although in doing it I do not even suspect that it will have the effect which renders it a duty. This would happen, e.g., if I shouted simply to attract the attention of the passers-by and without noticing the man's condition at all. Similar conclusions, too, have to be drawn with regard to acts of the kinds which we think we ought not to do.

These conclusions being all unwelcome, we naturally want to discover what modification of the form of a moral rule would enable us to escape them, and then to consider how we fare if we accept it. Now what the conclusions all followed from was the thought underlying the assertion of a set of moral rules, that if some particular action is a duty, the obligation depends on certain facts of the situation. And to this thought there is only one alternative, viz., the thought that the obligation depends on our being in a certain attitude of mind toward the situation in respect of knowledge, thought, or opinion. This thought can be described as the subjective view of the basis of an obligation, not in the sense that no acts are really right or really wrong, but in the sense of the view that the ground of an obligation lies in some state of the man's own mind. And in contrast the opposed view can be designated the objective view.

The question, therefore, at once arises: "What have we to represent this state or attitude as being, if we are to render this alternative view at least plausible?" The most obvious suggestion is, of course, to represent it as our thinking certain things likely or probable, and to represent the alternative view as being that if, e.g., I am bound to shout, it is because I think it likely that the man in front of me has fainted and that, if he has fainted shouting would cure him, i.e., have his revival as an effect. But, when we come to consider this view, we find that we do not like it either.

It seems to have, no doubt, at least one definite advantage over the view which it is to replace. It seems not to preclude us from thinking that it is possible to *discover* our duties, since, when we think something likely, we either know, or at least by reflecting can discover, that we do. The question whether I am thinking something likely is no more one about which I can be mistaken than is the question whether I have a certain pain. Consequently, also, the view does not preclude us from thinking that it is sometimes possible for us to do some action, knowing that we ought to do it. For the same reason it saves us from having to allow that we are, and must always remain, uncertain whether we have or shall ever have a duty.

On the other hand, it of course inevitably implies that any obligation I may have depends not on the fact that the action would have a certain character, if I were to do it—that of producing a certain effect—but on my thinking it likely that it would. It implies, e.g., that where I am bound to shout, my obligation depends not on the fact that if I were to shout I should be reviving a man who has fainted, but on my thinking it likely that I should. And a paradox involved comes to light if we imagine ourselves omniscient beings, who in consequence knew the circumstances. For if we were such beings, the analogous view would be that, if we were bound to shout, what would render us bound to shout would not be the fact that shouting would cure the man, but our knowing that it would; and it would therefore imply that this knowledge, so far from being the knowledge of the ground of the obligation, was itself the ground of the obligation, and that our knowledge of the ground of the obligation consisted in our knowing that we knew that shouting would cure the man.

Again, to defend the view, we shall have to modify it at least to the extent of maintaining that if, for instance, I am bound to shout, what renders me so bound is not simply my thinking it likely but my thinking it at least in a certain degree likely that shouting would cure the man. For no one would maintain that I am bound to shout if I think the likelihood remote beyond a certain degree. But then we are faced by the question: "What degree is necessary?" And we have to answer that we can formulate it only within certain limits which differ in different cases according to the degree of benefit to the other man which I think likely to accrue from my shouting. We shall, therefore, also have to allow that I shall not always be able to discover whether I ought to shout, since there will be border-line cases in which I shall be unable to discover whether the degree to which I think the act likely to confer a certain benefit is sufficient to render it a duty. And therefore we shall have to allow that even on this view I may have a duty without being able to discover that I have it.

Again, the view, at any rate unless further modified, implies not only that in similar circumstances it may be one man's duty but not another's to do some action, owing to some difference in their thought about the facts, but also that the same thing is true of a single individual at different moments. For I may at first think it just, but only just, possible that shouting would cure a man, and then on further consideration think that there is a very good chance that it will; and, if so, while at first I shall not be bound to shout, afterward I shall. And, again, the converse may happen.

Also, we have to distinguish from "thinking likely" what for lack of a better phrase we may call "thinking without question." For on seeing a man who has fainted, instead of thinking it likely, I may from lack of reflection think without question that shouting would cure him, not being uncertain that it would, and therefore not "thinking it likely," but at the same time not being certain. And on the view in question, unless it be modified, we shall have to hold that when this happens I am not bound to shout, in spite of thinking

without question that shouting would cure him, since I am not thinking it likely.

It will, however, probably occur to us that these last two difficulties can be met by a further modification. This is to maintain (1) that I am bound to shout only if I think it likely that shouting would effect a cure, *after* having considered the circumstances fully, i.e., after having considered as fully as I can whether he is ill and whether shouting would cure him if he is, and so having obtained the best opinion I can about the circumstances, and (2) that whenever I have not done this I am bound to do something else, viz., to consider the circumstances fully.

This modification, it must be allowed, does remove the difficulties. Nevertheless, the idea that, where we have not done so, we ought to consider the circumstances fully, is itself not free from difficulty. This becomes obvious as soon as we ask: "*Why,* for instance, when it first strikes me that shouting might cure the man, am I bound to consider fully whether it would?" For the answer which we are first inclined to give is: "Because, if I were to consider the matter fully, I might come to think shouting in a certain degree likely to cure him, and, if I did, I should then be bound to shout." And yet this answer cannot be right. For plainly the duty of doing one action cannot possibly depend on the possibility of the duty of doing another, the duty of doing which cannot arise unless the former action has actually been done. Moreover, if the answer were right, I could always escape a duty to shout merely by abstaining from considering the circumstances, and yet no one thinks this possible. The truth is that our having a duty to consider the circumstances cannot be based on the possibility of our having a future duty of another kind if we were to consider them. Rather, to vindicate such a duty, we must represent the two so-called duties as, respectively, an element and a possible element in a *single* duty, viz., to consider the circumstances, and then *if,* but only if, as a result, we reach a certain opinion, to do a certain future action. And if we do this we can explain the need of this complicated and partially hypothetical phrase for what is, after all, a single duty by the fact that the duty is one of the full nature of which we are at the time inevitably ignorant owing to our ignorance of the facts.

Again, if the view is to correspond with what we ordinarily think, still further modifications may seem necessary for various reasons, of which one is that we ordinarily think, for instance, that before it can be a duty for me to shout I must also have considered what is likely to be the effect of shouting on anyone else who may be within range.

But, in order to consider the main issue, we need not inquire what, if any, further modifications are needed. For, even if they are needed, the fundamental issue will remain the same, viz.: "If I have an obligation, does it depend on the existence of certain facts of the situation or on my having certain thoughts about certain facts of the situation?"

Here it may be noted that the issue is not avoided by those who would deny the truth of any set of moral rules on the ground that, if we think them true, we are involved in the absurdity of admitting that we may at any moment have conflicting duties, i.e., two or more duties only one of which we can carry out. For, in order to avoid this admission, they have to maintain that where some action is a duty it is because it would possess some such character as that of producing something good in a greater degree than any other of the acts which the man is able to do. And, in maintaining this, they will be faced with the same question in a slightly different form, viz.: "Does the obligation depend on the fact that the action would possess this character in a greater degree than any other, or does it depend on the fact that the man, after full consideration, thinks it likely that it would?"

The issue, then, being as stated, the first thing to do appears to consist in ascertaining which of the alternative views better corresponds with the thought of our ordinary life.

There are two ways in which this thought appears to imply the objective view. First, we frequently think without question both that the situation contains something in a certain state, and also that some action which we could do would produce a change in it of a certain kind, and then think without question that we ought to do the action. Thus, when we do not reflect, we frequently think without question that a man whom we meet has some malady and that giving him some drug would relieve it, and, where we do, we think without question that we ought to give the drug. And here we seem to imply that what

renders us bound to do the act is just the fact that the situation is of a certain sort, together with the fact that the act would have a certain effect in that situation. Secondly, we often seek to change the mind of someone else about a duty by trying to convince him that he is mistaken about the facts; and, in doing so, we seem to imply that the question whether he has the duty depends on the nature of the facts. Thus, where A thinks he ought to vote for X rather than Y, B may try to convince A that he ought to vote for Y by arguing that X and Y will, if elected, act otherwise than as A expects. Again, we may argue with a friend that he ought to send his child to school M rather than school N, which he considers the better, on the ground that M is really the better. And if someone were to maintain that he ought to torture a certain heretic, as the only way of saving his soul, we should presumably try to convince him that he was mistaken by convincing him that torture would not have this effect.

On the other hand, at any rate a large portion of our ordinary thought is in direct conflict with the objective view. Consider, e.g., our attitude to the question: "Ought we to stop, or at least slow down, in a car, before entering a main road?" If the objective view be right, (1) there will be a duty to slow down only if in fact there is traffic; (2) we shall be entitled only to think it likely—in varying degrees on different occasions—that we are bound to slow down; and (3) if afterward we find no traffic, we ought to conclude that our opinion that we were bound to slow down was mistaken. Yet, provided that after consideration we think that there is even a small chance of traffic, we, in fact, think that there is definitely a duty to slow down, and that the subsequent discovery that there was no traffic would not prove us mistaken. Again, imagine that we are watching a car approaching along a road which we know forks, and of which one fork has, we know, just suffered a landslide, and that we have no idea which road the driver is intending to take, or whether he knows about the landslide. The objective view would require us to think that there is a duty to stop the car only if it is going to destruction, so that, if we are anxious to do what we ought, we can only insure ourselves against the possibility of failure to do what we ought by stopping the car, knowing that, after all, we may be doing something we are not bound to do. Yet plainly we in fact think without any doubt whatever that we are bound to stop the car, unless we have reason for being quite confident that the car is about to take the safe fork. Again, no nurse thinks that she is bound to light a fire in her patient's room only if in fact there will be a frost next morning. She thinks she is bound to do so, unless she thinks there is practically no chance of a frost. Indeed, the objective view is in direct conflict with all the numerous cases in which we think without question that we ought to do something which we are thinking of as of the nature of *an insurance* in the interest of someone else.

Moreover, the extent to which our ordinary thought involves the subjective view is usually obscured for us by our tendency to think that the terms "likely" and "probable" refer to facts in nature. For we are apt, for instance, to express our thought that someone has probably fainted, and that shouting would probably revive him, by the statements "He has probably fainted" and "Shouting would probably revive him." We are then apt to think that these statements state the existence of certain facts in nature called probabilities, in the spirit which leads some physicists to regard electron-waves as waves of probability; and we are then apt to think that an obligation to shout arises from these probabilities. It needs, however, but little reflection to realize that there are no such things as probabilities in nature. There cannot, e.g., be such a thing as the probability that someone has fainted, since either he has fainted or he has not. No doubt it is extremely difficult to formulate the precise nature of the fact which we express, for instance, by the statement: "X has probably fainted." But at least we must allow that, whatever its precise nature may be, the fact must consist in our mind's being in a certain state or condition. And, once this is realized, it becomes obvious that most of our ordinary thought involves the subjective view.

Again, even when we try to change someone else's mind about a duty, we do not really imply the objective view. This is shown by our thinking that when our attempt to change his opinion about the facts is over, then, whether we have or have not succeeded, the question whether he is bound to do the action will turn on the nature of *his opinion* about the facts. Thus we think that, provided the

would-be torturer remained, in spite of all we have said, in a very high degree confident that torturing, and torturing only, would save the heretic, he would be bound to inflict the torture. No doubt we also think that we should take steps to prevent him; but here there is no inconsistency. And, in fact, we not infrequently think ourselves bound to do some action which will prevent someone else doing something which he is bound to do. Indeed, if this were not so, few would fight conscientiously for their country.

Undoubtedly, then, the subjective view better corresponds with our ordinary thought. Yet, as should now be obvious, it is exposed to various difficulties. Of these the chief are two. The first is that on this view knowledge of the existence of borderline cases precludes us from thinking that we can always discover our duties. Still in this respect it is more satisfactory than the objective view, since the latter implies that we can never discover a duty. The second and more fundamental difficulty is that it represents the duty of doing some action as depending not on the fact that the action would have a certain character if we were to do it, but on our thinking it likely that it would. And to maintain this seems impossible.

We thus seem to have reached an impasse. For both the alternative views lead to fundamental difficulties, and yet there is no third course.

Before, however, we consider the matter further, we ought to consider a difficulty which is common to both views, and which, if it proves well founded, will force us to modify both.

In considering the problem, we have throughout been taking for granted that an obligation is necessarily an obligation to do some *action,* and, strictly speaking, an action in the strict sense. But we ought at least to ask ourselves whether this assumption, obvious though it seems, is true.

Unquestionably an obligation must be an obligation to perform some *activity.* An obligation can be an obligation only to be active, and not to be *affected,* in a particular way. And to say that an obligation is always an obligation to do some *action,* in the strict sense, e.g., to move my arms, is really to say that the activity which an obligation is an obligation to perform consists in *doing* something, as distinct from an activity of some other kind, such as thinking or imagining. But, as was said earlier, by "doing something" in the strict sense, we mean bringing about something directly, i.e., bringing about something in the strict sense. Therefore to assert that an obligation is an obligation to do something is really to assert that the activity of the kind which an obligation is an obligation to perform consists in bringing about something. And in making this assertion we are implying that there is a special *kind* of activity, and indeed a special kind of *mental* activity, for which the proper phrase is "bringing about something." For if we thought that what we call "bringing about *X*" really consists in performing an activity of some other kind of which *X* will be an effect, we should have to allow that what we call the obligation to bring about *X* is really the obligation to perform some particular activity of this other kind of which *X* would be an effect, and that, therefore, an obligation, so far from being an obligation to do something, is always an obligation to perform an activity of this other kind. In asserting, then, that an obligation is an obligation to *do* something, we are implying that there is a special kind of activity consisting in doing something, i.e., bringing about something.*

On reflection, however, we become forced to admit that, though on certain occasions we do bring certain things about, yet there is no kind of activity consisting in bringing about something. We can realize this in the following way. It will, of course, be allowed that where we think of some past action of ours as one in which we indirectly brought about some particular thing, as where we think of ourselves as having cured someone's illness, we think it fair to ask: "*How* did we do the action?" We take the question to have the intelligible meaning: "What was that by the direct production of which we indirectly produced what we did?"; and we can give some sort of answer. But we can also ask a question verbally similar, where we think of some past action as one in which we directly brought about something. Where, e.g., I think of myself as having moved my hand, I can ask: "*How* did I move it?" In such a case, of course, the question cannot be of the same kind, because *ex hypothesi* I am not thinking

* Notes embodying the author's second thoughts on this paragraph and subsequent paragraphs will be found on p. 388.

of the action as one in which I caused some particular thing by causing something else, and so I cannot be asking: "By directly causing what, did I cause what I did?" The legitimate question is: "What was the activity by performing which I caused my hand to move?" and an answer would be "Willing the existence of the movement." And in so answering I should be implying that what I called moving my hand really consisted in setting myself to move it, and that I referred to this activity as moving my hand because I thought that this activity had a change of place of my hand as an effect. Again, in another case my answer might be: "By setting myself to move my other hand," the case being one in which I set myself to move one hand and in fact moved the other. And here also I should be implying that what I called "moving my hand" really consisted in a particular activity of another sort of which the change of place of my hand was an effect. The general moral can be stated thus: In no case whatever, where we think of ourselves as having brought about something directly, do we think that our activity was that of bringing about that something. On the contrary, we think of the activity as having been of another sort, and mean, by saying that we brought about directly what we did, that this activity of another sort had the change in question as a direct effect.

The same conclusion can be reached by considering what we really mean by saying "I can do so and so," when we use "do" in the strict sense. It may first be noticed that if in ordinary life we are asked whether we can do some action in the strict sense, we cannot always give a definite answer. No doubt if we were asked: "Can we make a noise identical in pitch with the highest C of the piano?" we should unhesitatingly answer "No"; and if we were asked: "Can we make a loud noise?" we should unhesitatingly answer "Yes." But if we were asked: "Can we make a noise similar in pitch to the middle C of the piano?" we should have to answer "I don't know," though we might possibly add "But I *think* I can." It may next be noticed that even where we unhesitatingly answer "Yes" we are, if pressed, inclined to hedge to the extent of saying: "Well, at least I can do the action, e.g., should *if* I choose." Such a statement, however, as we see when we reflect, is very odd. It cannot be meant literally, and can at best be only an idiom. For while it is sense to say: "If I choose to make a loud noise, I shall in fact make it," it cannot be sense to say: "If I choose to make it, I *can* make it." And no one would maintain that our *ability* to do something, as distinct from our *doing* it, can depend on our choosing to do it. Indeed, the statement really presupposes the thought that I *can* choose to make a loud noise, and is in fact only a brachylogical way of saying: "Since I can choose to make a loud noise, and since choosing to make it would in fact have a loud noise as an effect, I can make it." At the same time "choose" cannot be an accurate phrase for what we mean, since "choose" means choose between alternatives, and in fact we have no alternatives in mind. "Will," the verb corresponding to "volition," might perhaps be suggested as the proper substitute; but the term would be merely artificial. What seems wanted is one or other of the two phrases which have already been used, viz., "setting myself to," or "exerting myself to," so that "choosing to make a loud noise" becomes "setting or exerting myself to make a loud noise." And, if this is right, what is in our minds when we say "I can make a loud noise" is not the thought that there is a special kind of activity of which I am capable consisting in bringing about a loud noise, but rather the thought that a special kind of activity of which I am capable, consisting in setting myself to bring about a loud noise, would have a loud noise as an effect.

Two conclusions are at once obvious. (1) The first is that the true answer to any question of the form "Can I do so and so?" must be "I don't know." This is, of course, clear in certain cases. Plainly we never *know* that if we were to set ourselves to thread a needle, we should thread it; or that if we were to set ourselves to draw a line through a point on a piece of paper, we should succeed. But in the last resort this is the only answer ever possible, since we never *know* that we have not become paralyzed. Even in the case of moving our arms or making a noise we do not *know* that, if we were to set ourselves to do it, we should do anything, though, of course, we may think it very likely both that we should do something, and also that we should move our arms, or make a noise, in particular. (2) The second conclusion is that whatever we are setting ourselves to do, we never in so setting ourselves *know* that we shall be doing what we are setting ourselves to do, bringing about what we are setting ourselves to bring about, or indeed that we are doing anything at all. In other words, it follows that where we are setting ourselves to do something, we never *know* what we shall be doing, and at best can only find out afterwards what we have done. And for this reason alone we cannot sustain the view to which reference was made earlier that "doing something" means not simply bringing about something, but bringing about something knowing that we are doing so. For, apart from other objections, if it did, we in using the phrase should be implying that there is a special kind of activity consisting in bringing about something, of the special nature of which we are aware in performing the activity; and we do not think this. At the same time, the view has an underlying element of truth; for though bringing about something is *not*, setting ourselves to bring about something *is*, a special kind of activity of the special nature of which we are aware in performing it; and therefore the idea underlying the view is sound, though misapplied.

As regards an obligation, the moral is obvious. It is simply that, contrary to the implication of ordinary language and of moral rules in particular, an obligation must be an obligation, not to *do* something, but to perform an activity of a totally different kind, that of setting or exerting ourselves to do something, i.e., to bring something about.

It may be objected that, if an obligation were an obligation to perform a mental activity of a special kind other than that of bringing something about, the nature of that activity would have to be describable by itself, and not solely by reference to something else, as it is implied to be if we describe it as setting ourselves to bring something about. But to this two replies can be given. The first is that we find no difficulty in allowing the appropriateness of this procedure in analogous cases. Thus we have no difficulty in allowing the existence of such a kind of thing as desire, although we are perfectly aware that to desire is necessarily to desire something, e.g., the eating of an apple or the prosperity of our country, so that no desire can be described simply in terms of a certain state of mind. Again, we readily allow that there is such a thing as a state of wondering, or, again, of being angry, although we are quite aware that to wonder is to wonder, for instance, whether rain is coming, and to be angry is to be angry with someone for what he has done. The second reply is simply that if we try to describe the nature of the activity which we perform when we think we are bringing about something, without reference to bringing about something, we find that we totally fail.

If, however, we allow, as we now must, that an obligation must be an obligation not to do something but to set ourselves to do something, we have to modify accordingly not only the original question but also both the alternative views of the basis of the obligation.

The effect, however, as regards the relation between the alternatives is simply to intensify their difference. For, given the modification, on either view an obligation will be obligation not to bring about something directly but to set ourselves to do so. And if there be an obligation to set ourselves to bring about some particular thing Y directly, then, on the objective view, the obligation will depend on an additional fact the existence of which we shall be unable to discover, viz., that setting ourselves to bring about Y would bring it about directly, while on the subjective view it will depend in part on an additional thinking something likely, viz., our thinking that setting ourselves to bring about Y would be likely to bring it about.

The question therefore arises whether this modification renders it any easier to decide between the alternatives. And the answer appears to be that in one respect it does. For once it has become common ground that the kind of activity which an obligation is an obligation to perform is one which may bring about nothing at all, viz., setting ourselves to bring about something, we are less inclined to think that, for there to be an obligation to perform some particular activity, it must have a certain indirect effect. To this extent the modification diminishes the force of the objective view without in any way impairing that of its rival. Yet undoubtedly it does nothing to remove what is, after all, the outstanding difficulty of the subjective view—a difficulty compared with which the others are only difficulties of detail, i.e., difficulties concerning its precise nature. This difficulty of the view in its original form lies in its representing the obligation to do some action as depending not on the fact that the action would have a certain character, if we were to do it, but on our thinking it likely

that it would. This dependence seems impossible. For an obligation to do some action seems to be a character of the action; and therefore, it would seem, it must depend on the fact that the action would have a certain characteristic, if it were done, and not on our thinking it likely that it would. And if here we substitute for "do some action" "set ourselves to do some action," there is a difficulty of precisely the same kind.

It is, however, worth considering whether, after all, this difficulty is insuperable, and whether it may not simply arise from a mistake. We are apt to think of an obligation to do some action as if it were, like its goodness or badness, a sort of quality or character of the action. Just as we think that when we say of some action which we could do that it would be good, or, again, bad, we are stating that, in a wide sense of the term "character," it would have a certain character, so we are apt to think that when we say of it that we are bound, or bound not, to do it, we are stating that it would have a certain character, for which the proper term would be "ought-to-be-doneness" or "ought-not-to-be-doneness." And this tendency is fostered by our habit of using the terms "right" and "wrong" as equivalents for "ought" and "ought not." For when we express our thought that we ought, or ought not, to do some action by saying that the act would be right, or wrong, our language inevitably implies that the obligation or disobligation is a certain character which the act would have if we were to do it, a character for which the only existing words are "rightness" in the one case and "wrongness" in the other. And when we think this, we inevitably go on to think that the obligation or disobligation must depend on some character which the act would have. But, as we recognize when we reflect, there are no such characteristics of an action as ought-to-be-doneness and ought-not-to-be-doneness. This is obvious; for, since the existence of an obligation to do some action cannot possibly depend on actual performance of the action, the obligation cannot itself be a property which the action would have, if it were done. What does exist is the fact that you, or that I, ought, or ought not, to do a certain action, or rather to set ourselves to do a certain action. And when we make an assertion containing the term "ought" or "ought not," that to which we are attributing a certain character is not a certain activity but a certain man. If our being bound to set ourselves to do some action were a character which the activity would have, its existence would, no doubt, have to depend on the fact that the activity would have a certain character, and it could not depend on our thinking that it would. Yet since, in fact, it is a character of ourselves, there is nothing to prevent its existence depending on our having certain thoughts about the situation and, therefore, about the nature of the activity in respect of its effects. Indeed, for this reason, its existence must depend on some fact about ourselves. And while the truth could not be expressed by saying: "*My setting myself to do so-and-so* would *be* right, because *I think* that it would have a certain effect"—a statement which would be as vicious in principle as the statement "*Doing so-and-so* would *be* right because *I think* it would be right"—there is nothing to prevent its being expressible in the form "*I* ought to set myself to do so-and-so, because I think that it would have a certain effect." We are therefore now in a position to say that the fundamental difficulty presented by the subjective view is simply the result of a mistake.

This being so, there remains only one thing to do. This is to consider, in some instance where we have considered the circumstances as fully as we can, whether we ought to perform some particular activity, and then ask: "Does the answer to this question turn on the nature of our *thought* about the situation, and therefore about the effect of the activity, or on the nature of the *situation* and therefore on that of the effect of the activity?" This must be our remaining task, once general difficulties have been cleared away. For there is no way of discovering whether some general doctrine is true except by discovering the general fact to which the problem relates; and there is no way of discovering some general fact except by apprehending particular instances of it. And here there is little that need be said. For we have only to carry out this procedure to find not that we are *inclined to think*, or even that we are of the opinion that, but that we are *certain*, i.e., *know*, that the answer turns not on the nature of the situation but on that of our thought about it. This certainty is attainable most readily if the instance taken is similar to those already considered in which our doubts about the nature of the situation are considerable. But it is attainable in any instance, provided that we really face the question.

We therefore cannot but allow that the subjective view is true, in spite of what at first seems its paradoxical character and that, therefore, in order to defend any moral rule whatever, we must first modify its form accordingly.

Pp. 384–85. The argument appears fallacious. For to say that an obligation is an obligation to do *some action* is consistent with holding that it is an obligation, e.g., to perform a particular activity of a certain sort which will have a certain particular effect. And we are only implying that there is a kind of activity which in certain cases has effects.

The concluding part seems to contain two mistakes:

(1) P. 385. It looks as though "willing X" at any rate as used technically is a synonym for what I have called "setting ourselves to bring about X." This, however, does not affect the general argument. But the other mistake does;

(2) Pp. 386–88. The difficulty put up for consideration is that the obligation to do some action must depend on some character that the action would have, and not on our thinking that it would have some character. And it is said to remain if we substitute for "some action" (i.e., bringing about X) "setting ourselves to do some action" (i.e., willing the existence of X). And it is resolved by denying that "duty" is a property of an *action* as distinct from a person.

This resolution, except indirectly, does not affect the difficulty—which is that if we ought, e.g., to will something X, it must be in virtue of a character which willing X would have and not in virtue of our thinking it would have it.

The proper resolution is to point out that if "willing X" be substituted for "bringing about X," then our thinking X likely to effect something else Y does enter into the character of the *activity* to which the "ought" refers. For to will X, thinking it likely to produce Y, is one willing, and to will X, thinking it unlikely to produce Y, or to will X, not thinking of Y at all, is another. In other words, the *thinking* enters into the character of the *willing*.

P. 386, para. 2. The moral should be that if an obligation is to *do* some particular action, i.e., to will a change the willing of which would cause a certain change, we can never know that we ought to do a certain action.

P. 386, para. 2, sentence beginning "And for this reason." Fallacious, because this reason can't prevent our meaning this by "doing something," but only shows that if we mean this by "doing something" we are mistaken in thinking there is such a thing.

In the next sentence the "if it did" statement is untrue.

Erroneously Carried-Out Actions*

I have here formed two groups of cases; all these cases in which the faulty effect seems to be the essential element—that is, the deviation from the intention—I denote as erroneously carried-out actions or defaults; the others, in which the entire action appears rather inexpedient, I call "symptomatic and chance actions." Again, no distinct line of demarcation can be formed; indeed, we are forced to conclude that all divisions used in this treatise are of only descriptive significance and contradict the inner unity of the sphere of manifestation. . . .

In former years, when I made more calls at the homes of patients than I do at present, it often happened, when I stood before a door where I should have knocked or rung the bell, that I would pull the key of my own house from my pocket, only to replace it, quite abashed. When I investigated in what patients' homes this occurred, I had to admit that the faulty action—taking out my key instead of ringing the bell—signified paying a certain tribute to the house where the error occurred. It was equivalent to the thought "Here I feel at home," as it happened only where I possessed the patient's regard. (Naturally, I never rang my own doorbell.)

The default was therefore a symbolic representation of a definite thought which was not accepted consciously as serious; for in reality, the psychiatrist is well aware that the patient seeks him only so long as he expects to be benefited by him, and that his own excessively warm interest for his patient is evinced only as a means of psychic treatment.

. . .

For many years, a reflex hammer and a tuning fork lay side by side on my desk. One day, I hurried off at the close of my office hours, as I wished to catch a certain train, and, despite broad daylight, put the tuning fork in my coat pocket in place of the reflex hammer. My attention was called to the mistake through the weight of the object drawing down my pocket. Anyone accustomed to reflect on such slight occurrences would, with-

out hesitation, explain the faulty action by the hurry of the moment, and excuse it. In spite of that, I preferred to ask myself why I took the tuning fork instead of the hammer. The haste could just as well have been a motive for carrying out the action properly in order not to waste time over the correction.

"Who last grasped the tuning fork?" was the question which immediately flashed through my mind. It happened that only a few days ago, an idiotic child, whose attention to sensory impressions I was testing, had been so fascinated by the tuning fork that I found it difficult to tear it away from him. Could it mean, therefore, that I was an idiot? To be sure, so it would seem, as the next thought which associated itself with the hammer was *chamer* (Hebrew for "ass").

But what was the meaning of this abusive language? We must here inquire into the situation. I hurried to a consultation to see a patient who, according to the anamnesis which I received by letter, had fallen from a balcony some months before, and since then, had been unable to walk. The physician who invited me wrote that he was still unable to say whether he was dealing with a spinal injury or traumatic neurosis—hysteria. That was what I was to decide. This could therefore be a reminder to be particularly careful in this delicate differential diagnosis. As it is, my colleagues think that hysteria is diagnosed far too carelessly where more serious matters are concerned. But the abuse is not yet justified. Yes, the next association *was* that the small railroad station is the same place, in which, some years previous, I saw a young man who, after a certain emotional experience, could not walk properly. At that time, I diagnosed his malady as hysteria, and later put him under psychic treatment; but it afterward turned out that my diagnosis was neither incorrect nor correct. A large number of the patient's symptoms were hysterical, and they promptly disappeared in the course of treatment. But back of these, there was a visible remnant that could not be reached by therapy, and could be referred only to a multiple sclerosis. Those who saw the patient after me had no difficulty recognizing the organic affection. I could scarcely have acted or judged differently; still, the impression was that of a serious mistake; the promise of a cure

* Sigmund Freud, *Psychopathology of Everyday Life* from *The Basic Writings of Sigmund Freud*, trans. and ed. by Dr. A. A. Brill, Copyright 1938 by Random House, Inc. Reprinted by permission of the Brill Trust.

which I had given him could naturally not be kept.

The mistake in grasping the tuning fork instead of the hammer could therefore be translated into the following words: "You fool, you ass, get yourself together this time, and be careful not to diagnose again a case of hysteria where there is an incurable disease, as you did in this place years ago in the case of that poor man!" And fortunately for this little analysis, even if unfortunately for my mood, this same man, now showing a very spastic gait, had been to my office a few days before, one day after the examination of the idiotic child.

We observe that this time it is the voice of self-criticism which makes itself perceptible through the mistake in grasping. The erroneously carried-out action is specially suited to express self-reproach. The present mistake attempts to represent the mistake which was committed elsewhere.

. . .

In latter years, since I have been collecting such observations, it has happened several times that I have shattered and broken objects of some value, but the examination of these cases convinced me that it was never the result of accident or of my unintentional awkwardness. Thus, one morning while in my bathrobe and straw slippers, I followed a sudden impulse as I passed a room, and hurled a slipper from my foot against the wall so that it brought down a beautiful little marble Venus from its bracket. As it fell to pieces, I recited quite unmoved the following verse from Busch:

"Ach! Die Venus ist perdü—
Klickerdoms!—von Medici!"

This crazy action and my calmness at the sight of the damage are explained in the then-existing situation. We had a very sick person in the family, of whose recovery I had personally despaired. That morning, I had been informed that there was a great improvement; I know that I had said to myself, "After all she will live." My attack of destructive madness served therefore as the expression of a grateful feeling toward fate, and afforded me the opportunity of performing an "act of sacrifice," just as if I had vowed, "If she gets well, I will give this or that as a sacrifice." That I chose the Venus of Medici as this sac-

rifice was only gallant homage to the convalescent. But even today, it is still incomprehensible to me that I decided so quickly, aimed so accurately and struck no other object in close proximity.

. . .

The effects which result from mistakes of normal persons are, as a rule, of a most harmless nature. Just for this reason, it would be particularly interesting to find out whether mistakes of considerable importance, which could be followed by serious results, as, for example, those of physicians or druggists, fall within the range of our point of view.

As I am seldom in a position to deal with active medical matters, I can only report one mistake from my own experience. I treated a very old woman, whom I visited twice daily for several years. My medical activities were limited to two acts, which I performed during my morning visits: I dropped a few drops of an eye lotion into her eyes and gave her a hypodermic injection of morphine. I prepared regularly two bottles—a blue one, containing the eye lotion, and a white one, containing the morphine solution. While performing these duties, my thoughts were mostly occupied with something else, for they had been repeated so often that the attention acted as if free. One morning, I noticed that the automaton worked wrong; I had put the dropper into the white instead of into the blue bottle, and had dropped into the eyes the morphine instead of the lotion. I was greatly frightened, but then calmed myself through the reflection that a few drops of a *two per cent* solution of morphine would not likely do any harm even if left in the conjunctival sac. The cause of the fright manifestly belonged elsewhere.

In attempting to analyze the slight mistake, I first thought of the phrase, "to seize the old woman by mistake," which pointed out the short way to the solution. I had been impressed by a dream which a young man had told me the previous evening, the contents of which could be explained only on the basis of sexual intercourse with his own mother. The strangeness of the fact that the Oedipus legend takes no offense at the age of Queen Jocasta seemed to me to agree with the assumption that in being in love with one's mother, we never deal with the present personality, but with her youthful memory picture carried over from our childhood. Such incongruities always show themselves where one phantasy fluctuating between two periods is made conscious, and is then bound to one definite period.

Deep in thoughts of this kind, I came to my patient over ninety; I must have been well on the way to grasp the universal character of the Oedipus fable as the correlation of the fate which the oracle pronounces, for I made a blunder in reference to or on the old woman. Here, again, the mistake was harmless; of the two possible errors, taking the morphine solution for the eye, or the eye solution for the injection, I chose the one by far the least harmful. The question still remains open whether in mistakes in handling things which may cause serious harm, we can assume an unconscious intention as in the cases here discussed.

. . .

As the general result of the preceding separate discussion, we must put down the following principle: *Certain inadequacies of our psychic functions—whose common character will soon be more definitely determined—and certain performances which are apparently unintentional prove to be well motivated when subjected to psychoanalytic investigation, and are determined through the consciousness of unknown motives.*

In order to belong to the class of phenomena which can thus be explained, a faulty psychic action must satisfy the following conditions:

(a) It must not exceed a certain measure, which is firmly established through our estimation, and is designated by the expression "within normal limits."

(b) It must evince the character of the momentary and temporary disturbance. The same action must have been previously performed more correctly or we must always rely on ourselves to perform it more correctly; if we are corrected by others, we must immediately recognize the truth of the correction and the incorrectness of our psychic action.

(c) If we at all perceive a faulty action, we must not perceive in ourselves any motivation of the same, but must attempt to explain it through "inattention" or attribute it to an "accident."

CHAPTER VIII

LEGAL INSANITY

We are all mad.

ANON.

Legal insanity in the criminal law may be relevant to four different questions: (*a*) whether a person is legally responsible, (*b*) whether a person is triable, (*c*) whether a person may be sentenced, (*d*) whether a person is punishable. A person is not criminally responsible for acts performed while legally insane. A person sane at the time he commits a crime will not be tried while insane. A person who is convicted will not be sentenced if insane. And a person who becomes insane after conviction and sentencing will not be punished while insane.

New scientific theories have not in any significant way affected age-old defenses such as infancy, involuntary act, duress, and ignorance of fact. Many argue that they clearly do affect the defense of insanity. Changing conceptions of the human mind suggest to some a new test of insanity. It is understandable that most of the legal literature is devoted to discussion of what this test should be.

Several interrelated questions are considered in these readings. There is first the philosophical question: What is insanity? Schopenhauer describes insanity in terms of a defect in memory. What is especially appealing about his essay is that it forces us to consider how intimately tied to our concept of responsibility is our concept of a person. Can we say what it is to be a person without introducing that mysterious concept whose essence has so eluded philosophers—memory?

Next, what constitutes a psychosis for psychiatrists, and how are different psychoses related to criminal behavior? MacNiven's essay treats these topics and provides source material for a comparison of psychiatric and legal treatments of psychosis. It is not until we have before us the variety of psychotic behavior that we can fully appreciate the difficulties in framing a legal test of insanity.

Third, should there be a test formulated for legal insanity, and if so, what should that test be? The M'Naghten Rules provide the test which has been followed, with rare exception, in Anglo-American law. There have been vigorous assaults made upon these Rules, and here and there a courageous court leaves the M'Naghten camp and develops rules of its own. Inevitably these are in turn criticized. The chief objection to the M'Naghten Rules is that they incorporate an antiquated nineteenth-century intellectualistic psychology. There are those who argue that the Rules need only be supplemented by an "irresistible impulse" rule. Others argue that more is needed, that there are psychotics who should be excused and who are not under the influence of such impulses. Still others claim that no rule can be formulated, and that in each case the trier of fact should decide whether mental disease should absolve the defendant of responsibility.

As with the other defenses, we shall want to make explicit our reasons for believing it wrong to punish persons who are insane. Is it that insane persons cannot be deterred? Is it that we value choice in our society and believe that there must be at least a strong overriding social good involved if a person is to be punished who has acted without choice? But are there not psychotics who choose to do what they do? A mother, suffering from severe melancholia, may choose to kill her child after much deliberation. What grounds are there for excusing such a person? If she cannot help doing what she does, what analysis is to be offered of her incapacity? It seems clearly to be of a different order from that of an epileptic in a seizure.

An extreme view which we must consider is that all crime is a form of pathological behavior calling for treatment rather than punishment. Some argue that recent scientific advances in psychology require substituting a conception of social disease for crime, and medicine for law. Hall's essay is a sustained attack on such proposals.

The Nature of Madness*

A clear and complete insight into the nature of madness, a correct and distinct conception of what constitutes the difference between the sane and the insane, has, as far as I know, not as yet been found. Neither reason nor understanding can be denied to madmen, for they talk and understand, and often draw very accurate conclusions; they also, as a rule, perceive what is present quite correctly, and apprehend the connection between cause and effect. Visions, like the phantasies of delirium, are no ordinary symptom of madness: delirium falsifies perception, madness the thoughts. For the most part, madmen do not err in the knowledge of what is immediately *present*; their raving always relates to what is *absent* and *past,* and only through these to their connection with what is present. Therefore it seems to me that their malady specially concerns the memory; not indeed that memory fails them entirely, for

many of them know a great deal by heart, and sometimes recognize persons whom they have not seen for a long time; but rather that the thread of memory is broken, the continuity of its connection destroyed, and no uniformly connected recollection of the past is possible. Particular scenes of the past are known correctly, just like the particular present; but there are gaps in their recollection which they fill up with fictions, and these are either always the same, in which case they become fixed ideas, and the madness that results is called monomania or melancholy; or they are always different, momentary fancies, and then it is called folly, *fatuitas.* This is why it is so difficult to find out their former life from lunatics when they enter an asylum. The true and the false are always mixed up in their memory. Although the immediate present is correctly known, it becomes falsified through its fictitious connection with an imaginary past; they therefore regard themselves and others as identical with persons who exist only in their imaginary past; they

* Arthur Schopenhauer, *The World as Will and Idea,* trans. R. B. Haldane and J. Kemp (London: Routledge & Kegan Paul Ltd., 1883), 3 vols., I, 248–51, reprinted by permission of the publishers.

do not recognize some of their acquaintances at all, and thus while they perceive correctly what is actually present, they have only false conceptions of its relations to what is absent. If the madness reaches a high degree, there is complete absence of memory, so that the madman is quite incapable of any reference to what is absent or past, and is only determined by the caprice of the moment in connection with the fictions which, in his mind, fill the past. In such a case, we are never for a moment safe from violence or murder, unless we constantly make the madman aware of the presence of superior force. The knowledge of the madman has this in common with that of the brute, both are confined to the present. What distinguishes them is that the brute has really no idea of the past as such, though the past acts upon it through the medium of custom, so that, for example, the dog recognizes its former master even after years, that is to say, it receives the wonted impression at the sight of him; but of the time that has passed since it saw him it has no recollection. The madman, on the other hand, always carries about in his reason an abstract past, but it is a false past, which exists only for him, and that either constantly, or only for the moment. The influence of this false past prevents the use of the true knowledge of the present which the brute is able to make. The fact that violent mental suffering or unexpected and terrible calamities should often produce madness, I explain in the following manner. All such suffering is as an actual event confined to the present. It is thus merely transitory, and is consequently never excessively heavy; it only becomes unendurably great when it is lasting pain; but as such it exists only in thought, and therefore lies in the *memory*. If now such a sorrow, such painful knowledge or reflection, is so bitter that it becomes altogether unbearable, and the individual is prostrated under it, then, terrified Nature seizes upon *madness* as the last resource of life; the mind so fearfully tortured at once destroys the thread of its memory, fills up the gaps with fictions, and thus seeks refuge in madness from the mental suffering that exceeds its strength, just as we cut off a mortified limb and replace it with a wooden one.

The distracted Ajax, King Lear, and Ophelia may be taken as examples; for the creations of true genius, to which alone we can refer here, as universally known, are equal in truth to real persons; besides, in this case, frequent actual experience shows the same thing. A faint analogy of this kind of transition from pain to madness is to be found in the way in which all of us often seek, as it were mechanically, to drive away a painful thought that suddenly occurs to us by some loud exclamation or quick movement—to turn ourselves from it, to distract our minds by force.

We see, from what has been said, that the madman has a true knowledge of what is actually present, and also of certain particulars of the past, but that he mistakes the connection, the relations, and therefore falls into error and talks nonsense. Now this is exactly the point at which he comes into contact with the man of genius; for he also leaves out of sight the knowledge of the connection of things, since he neglects that knowledge of relations which conforms to the principle of sufficient reason, in order to see in things only their Ideas, and to seek to comprehend their true nature, which manifests itself to perception, and in regard to which *one thing* represents its whole species, in which way, as Goethe says, one case is valid for a thousand. The particular object of his contemplation, or the present which is perceived by him with extraordinary vividness, appear in so strong a light that the other links of the chain to which they belong are at once thrown into the shade, and this gives rise to phenomena which have long been recognized as resembling those of madness. That which in particular given things exists only incompletely and weakened by modifications, is raised by the man of genius, through his way contemplating it, to the Idea of the thing, to completeness: he therefore sees everywhere extremes, and therefore his own action tends to extremes; he cannot hit the mean, he lacks soberness, and the result is what we have said. He knows the Ideas completely but not the individuals. Therefore it has been said that a poet may know mankind deeply and thoroughly, and may yet have a very imperfect knowledge of men. He is easily deceived, and is a tool in the hands of the crafty.

The Rules in M'Naghten's Case (1843), 10 Cl. and F. 200 at p. 209

(Q.I.) "What is the law respecting alleged crimes committed by persons afflicted with insane delusion in respect of one or more particular subjects or persons: as for instance, where, at the time of the commission of the alleged crime, the accused knew he was acting contrary to law, but did the act complained of with a view, under the influence of insane delusion, of redressing or revenging some supposed grievance or injury, or of producing some supposed public benefit?"

(A.I.) "Assuming that your lordships' inquiries are confined to those persons who labor under such partial delusions only, and are not in other respects insane, we are of opinion that notwithstanding the accused did the act complained of with a view, under the influence of insane delusion, of redressing or avenging some supposed grievance or injury, or of producing some public benefit, he is nevertheless punishable, according to the nature of the crime committed, if he knew at the time of committing such crime that he was acting contrary to law, by which expression we understand your lordships to mean the law of the land."

(Q.II.) "What are the proper questions to be submitted to the jury where a person alleged to be afflicted with insane delusion respecting one or more particular subjects or persons is charged with the commission of a crime (murder, for example), and insanity is set up as a defence?"

(Q.III.) "In what terms ought the question to be left to the jury as to the prisoner's state of mind at the time when the act was committed?"

(A.II and A.III.) "As these two questions appear to us to be more conveniently answered together, we submit our opinion to be that the jury ought to be told in all cases that every man is presumed to be sane, and to possess a sufficient degree of reason to be responsible for his crimes, until the contrary be proved to their satisfaction; and that to establish a defence on the ground of insanity it must be clearly proved that, at the time of committing the act, the accused was labouring under such a defect of reason, from disease of the mind, as not to know the nature and quality of the act he was doing, or, if he did know it, that he did not know he was doing what was wrong. The mode of putting the latter part of the question to the jury on these occasions has generally been whether the accused at the time of doing the act knew the difference between right and wrong: which mode, though rarely, if ever, leading to any mistake with the jury, is not, as we conceive, so accurate when put generally and in the abstract as when put with reference to the party's knowledge of right and wrong, in respect to the very act with which he is charged. If the question were to be put as to the knowledge of the accused solely and exclusively with reference to the law of the land, it might tend to confound the jury, by inducing them to believe that an actual knowledge of the law of the land was essential in order to lead to conviction: whereas, the law is administered upon the principle that everyone must be taken conclusively to know it, without proof that he does know it. If the accused was conscious that the act was one that he ought not to do, and if that act was at the same time contrary to the law of the land, he is punishable; and the usual course, therefore, has been to leave the question to the jury, whether the accused had a sufficient degree of reason to know that he was doing an act that was wrong; and this course we think is correct, accompanied with such observations and explanations as the circumstances of each particular case may require."

(Q.IV.) "If a person under an insane delusion as to existing facts commits an offence in consequence thereof, is he thereby excused?"

(A.IV.) "The answer must, of course, depend on the nature of the delusion; but making the same assumption as we did before, namely, that he labors under such partial delusion only, and is not in other respects insane, we think he must be considered in the same situation as to responsibility as if the facts with respect to which the delusion exists were real. For example, if under the influence of his delusion he supposes another man to be in the act of attempting to take away his life, and he kills that man, as he supposes in self-defence, he would be exempt from punishment. If his delusion was that the deceased had inflicted a serious injury to his character and fortune, and he killed him in revenge for such supposed injury, he would be liable to punishment."

Psychoses and Criminal Responsibility*

The psychoses are those forms of mental illness in which the most profound disturbance of the personality occurs. The degree of disturbance varies within wide limits, and is dependent upon the type of psychosis and its degree of severity.

The personality changes which characterize the more severe psychotic illnesses result in changes in the patient's behavior, which affect his relations with his external environment, and it is this disturbed relationship between the patient and external reality which is the chief distinguishing feature between well-marked psychotic illness and the milder forms of mental illness, the neuroses and the psychoses, in which the patient's relations with his environment are only very slightly disturbed.

The symptoms of psychotic disorders do not differ qualitatively from the symptoms occurring in the minor forms of mental illness, the neuroses. Indeed, one can go further and say that psychotic symptoms are, in many instances, a distortion and exaggeration of mental processes which occur in the so-called normal mind.

The psychoses may be divided into two groups; one group comprising these conditions in which up till now no definite physical causative factor has been found: and the other comprising types of illness in which the mental symptoms arise from physical causes.

A typical example of the first group is the Manic-depressive psychosis, and General Paralysis of the Insane is an example of the second.

Our knowledge of the causation of the first group, the so-called functional psychoses, is still incomplete, and this lack of knowledge of specific causative factors makes it impossible to base a classification of the functional psychoses on a basis of etiology. The classification used is therefore still mainly based on symptomatology.

The types of mental illness we are discussing do not occur as clear-cut entities. The conditions are usually not present in pure cul-

ture, for in many cases, the clinical features are not typical of one particular type, but show characteristics of several different reaction forms. This is not surprising if we accept the view that an attack of mental illness represents an attempt by the patient to deal with psychic difficulties, and that the means used in meeting these difficulties will depend upon the pattern of the patient's mind, and that this pattern may enable the patient to make use of various mental mechanisms, some characteristic of one clinical entity, some of another.

Thus, a case in which the general picture suggests a diagnosis of manic-depressive psychosis may present schizophrenic features, and a condition which appears to be predominantly schizophrenic may have symptoms which are suggestive of the manic-depressive psychosis.

It is this lack of specificity in the symptomatology of mental disease that affords a partial explanation of the divergence of opinions sometimes expressed by medical men in evidence in court. The fact that one psychiatrist expresses the opinion that the patient is suffering from one form of mental disease, and his colleague uses a different diagnostic label, does not signify that one of them is in error. It is quite probable that as far as their essential understanding of the case is concerned, they are in agreement. It is only their terminology that is different.

The question of a specific diagnosis is seldom of importance in medico-legal cases, although there are certain instances in which the points at issue may depend upon an exact diagnosis, as, for instance, where a person has committed a criminal act in what appears to be a state of altered consciousness, and it is essential to decide whether he is an epileptic.

THE MANIC-DEPRESSIVE PSYCHOSIS

This is one of the commonest forms of mental illness. The condition varies greatly in its intensity. In some cases the symptoms are so mild that the condition is not recognized as a mental illness, and many mild attacks of this psychosis masquerade under such terms as "nervous breakdown" and "neurasthenia."

In its typical form, this psychosis is characterized by attacks of depression with inac-

---

* Angus Macniven, "Psychoses and Criminal Responsibility," *Mental Abnormality and Crime*, ed. by Radzinowicz and Turner (London: Macmillan and Co., Ltd., 1944), pp. 8–23, 26–32, 46–54, 57–58, 66–68, 70, reprinted by permission of the publisher and the Institute of Criminology, University of Cambridge.

tivity, or by attacks of mental exaltation with overactivity. To the former condition, the term "depression" or "melancholia" is applied: the latter condition is described as "mania." In the interval between the attacks, the patient seems to be in a normal state of mind though obsessional symptoms are sometimes present. The type of cycle which occurs varies in each individual patient: sometimes only attacks of depression occurring, sometimes only attacks of mania. In other cases attacks of mania alternate with attacks of depression.

The exact cause of the condition is unknown, but the most important etiological factor is hereditary predisposition which is present in eighty per cent of cases. An attack may be precipitated in a predisposed individual by any mental or physical strain. Common precipitating factors are: bereavement, financial loss, or any other form of domestic or business worry.

Melancholia. The symptoms of this condition are mental depression and retardation of mental and bodily activity. The patient's clarity of mind is preserved. The memory is not affected, and the intellectual functions are unimpaired. In mild cases the social behavior is not usually affected, and even in severe states of depression the patient may appear superficially a normal person.

A typical case of melancholia presents a characteristic appearance. The patient looks older than his years. His expression is one of dejection and despair. He moves slowly and with extreme effort. His conversation is slowed. He expresses himself as shortly as possible, sometimes in monosyllables. His emotional state is one of extreme misery. The feelings of guilt and inferiority are rarely absent, even in mild cases. In well-marked depression, these occupy the forefront of the clinical picture, and the patient then expresses the delusions of sin and unworthiness, which are such characteristic symptoms of this type of mental illness. He asserts that he has committed grievous sins, that he has brought ruin upon himself and his family, and that he merits the most drastic punishments for his misdeeds. He cannot entertain any hope of his recovery; indeed, he usually resents any suggestion that he will recover. He regards his illness as a just punishment upon him for his sins. His present state, he believes, is only a trivial misfortune to the dreadful punishment he will endure in the future.

Suicidal thoughts and impulses are usually present, even in mild cases, and are invariably present in the more serious forms of the illness, and unless suitable precautions are taken, the patient will attempt to take his own life.

In states of extreme depression, there may be almost complete arrest of the patient's normal activities. He may be mute. He is unable to do anything for himself and he requires to be fed and looked after like a child.

Mania. This condition is in many ways the antithesis of melancholia. The mood of depression is replaced by one of elation, and this is accompanied by extreme overactivity. The condition varies greatly in intensity. In its mildest form, termed hypomania, there is a feeling of increased well-being, with a greatly increased interest in external affairs. The patient has the feeling of increased self-importance, he is overconfident, and he has an exalted idea of his own capabilities. He is overtalkative, interfering, domineering, and sometimes aggressive. His judgment is warped by his elated emotional state, so that his conduct is apt to be embarrassing and indiscreet.

In a fully developed maniacal state, the patient shows extreme overactivity. He is rarely still, but the direction of his activities is constantly changing so that very little is accomplished. He talks with extreme rapidity, and sometimes the stream of thought is so rapid that his conversation seems disjointed and almost incoherent. A close study of it, however, will show that there is some association between each of the ideas expressed.

His mood is one of extreme elation which is shown by joyous singing, loud laughter, joking, punning, and rhyming. The mood is very changeable, and a happy amiable state quickly gives place to one of anger in which the patient becomes threatening, aggressive, and destructive. Except in states of extreme excitement, the mind is not confused. The patient is acutely aware of his surroundings, and his intellectual processes are quick and active. The general excitement and the inability to concentrate, however, prevents any constructive thought or activity.

The manic-depressive psychosis is a benign form of mental illness. In both mania and melancholia, recovery invariably occurs in young persons. There is, however, a tendency for attacks to recur throughout life, and as the patient gets older, the attacks tend to last longer, and recovery is less complete. When recovery does occur, it is usually complete, and the patient's working efficiency and his social adaptability are not in any way impaired. Even when complete recovery does not occur, the illness does not lead to the dementia which is a characteristic symptom of the chronic phase of other forms of mental illness. The average duration of the individual attacks varies from three to twelve months. Many cases last eighteen months or two years, and recovery has been known to occur in melancholia after several years.

A variety of infringements of the law, varying in gravity from simple breach of the peace to murder, may occur as symptoms of the manic-depressive psychoses. In fully developed cases of mania, violence and destructiveness are common symptoms, but the patient's aberration is so obvious that in most cases he is placed under supervision before he can do serious harm, so that it is rare for a maniacal patient to commit a serious criminal offense, although offenses of a minor character are very common.

In hypomania the position is different, and the illness may be present for a considerable time before it is detected. The exaltation of mood, the overconfidence, and the lack of self criticism—which are characteristic symptoms of hypomania—often lead to irregularities of conduct, such as wild extravagances, overindulgence in alcohol, practical joking, sexual offenses (usually not of a very serious type), and sometimes insulting and aggressive behavior, occasionally accompanied by violence. The fact that the patient's clarity of mind is preserved, that his behavior may only represent an exaggeration of his normal character traits, often results in the true nature of his condition being unrecognized, so that there is a risk that when a contravention of the law occurs, his offense is not regarded as a symptom of a psychotic illness, but as a manifestation of moral depravity or maliciousness.

· · ·

Alcoholic excess is not an uncommon symptom of the manic-depressive psychoses, particularly of mania, and this leads to a further loss of self-control and a blunting of the finer moral sentiments.

In the states of intense excitement which characterize acute mania, the patient may commit a serious assault on anyone who attempts to interfere with him, but, as a rule, he is easily distracted from his purpose, and his violence is often ill-directed, so that serious harm rarely occurs.

In melancholia, on the other hand, although generally speaking the patient's conduct is socially correct, very serious offenses are not infrequent. Melancholia is probably the most common cause of suicide and attempted suicide. Even in those cases where alcoholism seems to be the immediate cause of the suicidal attempt, it is probably the manic-depressive factor in the patient's personality that is the fundamental cause of his suicidal tendencies.

The methods of self-destruction selected by the patient depend partly upon chance, and are partly the result of unconscious motives which determine the choice of method. That unconscious motivation does play a part in the method selected, is suggested by the fact that frequently the patient chooses a painful method, when one causing very much less suffering is available.

A suicidal attempt may be an impulsive act, or it may be the result of deliberate planning.

The desire to commit suicide is always dormant in the mind of the melancholic, although the thought of suicide may not always be present in his consciousness. Frequently the attempt is precipitated by some trivial exacerbation of his worries, or by some petty frustration.

· · ·

A murder, or attempted murder, of persons who the patient believes are involved with him in the disasters which he believes he has brought upon himself, is a fairly common occurrence in melancholia.

A man in a state of depression, believing that he is financially ruined and that his family will end in the workhouse, attempts, by their destruction, to save them from misery and disgrace.

A woman believing that she has infected her children with some incurable disease or that they are to share the torture and punishment which she believes is in store for herself, may feel that it is her duty to destroy them.

· · ·

As a rule, when a person suffering from melancholia commits violence upon someone else, the conscious motive is an altruistic one; as, for instance, when a father kills his family under the belief that the future holds nothing but misery and disaster for them.

. . .

Impulses of an aggressive character which the patient is unable to explain sometimes occur as symptoms of the obsessional neuroses, but in these cases, the impulses are very rarely acted upon.

. . .

SCHIZOPHRENIA

The term schizophrenia has now generally replaced the older term of dementia praecox.

According to Henderson and Gillespie: "Schizophrenia, in its typical form, consists in a slow, steady deterioration of the entire personality, usually showing itself at the period of adolescence. It involves principally the affective life, and expresses itself in disorders of feeling, conduct, and of thought, and in an increasing withdrawal of interest from the environment."

The cause of the condition is unknown. Hereditary predisposition is a factor in the causation, but in a considerable number of cases, evidence of hereditary predisposition is absent. Many theories have been put forward to explain the condition, but none of these have won universal acceptance. Degenerative changes in the brain have been described by some workers, but many psychiatrists believe that schizophrenia is not characterized by any specific pathological changes in the central nervous system.

The illness is a very serious one. In the majority of cases recovery does not occur, and many of the cases end in a state of profound dementia. The morbid process may, however, be arrested at any stage in its development, and there are a certain number of cases in which very complete remissions occur. A certain type of personality appears to be associated with this form of illness. In childhood many of these patients show evidence of maladaptation. They are shy, reticent, sensitive individuals who have difficulty in making social contacts. They are easily rebuffed, and their general attitude to life is lacking in healthy aggression. They tend to withdraw into themselves and seek the satisfaction, which their inability to participate in normal healthy activities deny them, in daydreams and fantasies. Others react by an attitude of detachment. Many are lacking in emotional

warmth. They are stilted and uneasy in their contacts with other people, or they adopt an attitude of cold cynicism to life.

In dealing with his internal conflicts, the schizophrenic makes use of a greater variety of unconscious defense mechanisms than any other type of mental illness, but the mechanisms are used erratically and lack systematization, so that a great variety of symptoms characterize the illness, and fragmentation of the personality occurs, so that the patient, in his conduct, seems to act under uncontrolled impulses.

Perhaps nothing is more characteristic of the schizophrenic's attitude to life and to himself than a state of vague dissatisfaction which nothing appears to relieve. One gets the impression that he is constantly seeking some goal which he never attains.

Episodes occur in which the mental mechanisms characteristic of other types of mental illness appear; for instance, states of depression with acute feelings of guilt suggest melancholia. In other cases the projection mechanisms characteristic of paranoia are prominent features in the clinical picture.

The illness is usually insidious in its onset. Sometimes it is unnoticed until attention is called to the patient's state by some abnormal act, such as attempted suicide, or an act of violence against other people. Although as a rule the illness is of slow development, at times the onset takes the form of a sudden acute episode. These acute states often occur when the patient is faced with some major decision involving his emotional life, such as, for instance, the death of a relative, a love affair, or an impending marriage.

The four varieties of the condition: the simple, the hebephrenic, the paranoid, and the katatonic are usually described. It is not always possible to allocate a case to one or other of these groups.

Simple Schizophrenia. Simple schizophrenia usually shows itself in early adolescence by an insidious change in the personality of the patient. A marked loss of interest in work and social activity is noticed. At school the patient may neglect his studies. He seems to lack concentration. He is dreamy and detached. He does not take part in games, and he has no friends. He becomes quiet and moody. He seems lacking in ambition. Later he shows an inability to assume responsibility. He may become negligent in his personal habits and careless in his work. There seems to be a general impoverishment of the mind which shows itself in a state of apathy, a lack of animation, and a certain childishness and simplicity.

The absence of the acute symptoms often makes it possible for the patient to remain at home, and sometimes he is able to earn his living, provided the work does not call for initiative and responsibility. Many of the simple schizophrenics, however, are shiftless and erratic. They are unable to remain in employment for any length of time. Some are easily influenced, they fall into bad habits, and drift into crime.

Acute episodes occur in the course of the illness, characterized by mental confusion, vague persecutory delusions, and hallucinations.

Hebephrenia. The hebephrenic type usually begins before the age of twenty. A shallow depression with feelings of guilt about sexual matters is often the first symptom that calls attention to the patient's condition. Hypochondriacal delusions of a fantastic character and ideas of persecution with hallucinations of hearing are often prominent symptoms.

The patient begins to show marked signs of mental deterioration in an early stage of the illness. His conversation becomes incoherent. He becomes profoundly apathetic, and his conduct is characterized by strange antics and impulsive acts. Usually the condition ends in a profound state of dementia.

Katatonia. The katatonic form shows a more distinct clinical entity than any of the other types of schizophrenia. The onset of the illness is often acute. After a state of depression with lack of interest and apathy, the patient sinks into a state of stupor in which all his activities are reduced to a minimum. He lies motionless for weeks or months, mute and inaccessible. He makes no effort to do anything for himself, and he may require to be fed and dressed, and cared for in every way.

This state of complete inactivity may suddenly change into one of wild excitement, in which the patient, in a state of frenzy, behaves in a wildly impulsive way. He may make a sudden assault upon his nurses, or he may attempt suicide, or mutilate himself in the most gross manner. He may express delusions of persecution or feelings of influence. He hears hallucinatory commands upon which

he acts. Delusions of a mystical and religious character are frequently expressed. The patient feels that he is under Divine guidance, and God manifests himself to him in visions and dreams.

After a time the excitement subsides and a period of remission may follow, or the patient may relapse once more into a state of stupor. Many of these cases end in a state of dementia.

Paranoid Forms. The paranoid form usually begins later in life than the types already described.

Delusional ideas form the prominent symptom in this type. These delusions may take any form. They may be persecutory or grandiose in character, but whatever form they assume, they are usually quite unsystematized and often extremely bizarre in character. Hallucinations usually occur and the patient's conduct is often completely dominated by his hallucinatory experiences. Paranoid schizophrenia is distinguished from the other paranoid reaction types of mental illness by the fantastic character of the delusions, the disharmony between the patient's mood, and the ideas he expresses, and by the marked deterioration in the personality which occurs.

Any type of antisocial conduct may occur as a symptom of schizophrenia. The alienation from the social environment, which is such a marked symptom in the illness, tends to make the patient careless of his social obligations and liable to satisfy his immediate desires without regard to the welfare of others or to his own safety. In the general emotional deterioration which occurs, the moral sentiments are disorganized and no longer restrain the instinctive impulses. The patient's thinking is illogical, and his actions lack adequate motives, and it is particularly characteristic of schizophrenic conduct that it appears inexplicable and unreasonable. The patient himself is often unable to suggest any reason for his actions. When pressed, he may say that "something made him do it." Not infrequently his explanation is that he acted under some mystical influence, or at the command of a hallucinatory voice. Under the belief that he is the Messiah, and that he must save the world by self-sacrifice, he attempts to take his life. As God, the supreme ruler of the Universe, he has power of life and death over all, and he does not hesitate to punish, or even kill, anyone who offends him or attempts to frustrate his designs. Unconscious conflicting feelings of love and hate toward parents and parental figures are prominent features in the psychopathology of schizophrenia, and may result in the patient making violent attacks upon one or other parent, or upon his sweetheart. Or, overwhelmed with unconscious guilt, he may inflict severe mutilations on himself. These mutilations sometimes take the form of an actual or symbolic castration, or the patient may actually take his own life. Wedding-day suicides are often of this type. The failure on the part of the patient to reconcile his love and hatred is probably the unconscious motive behind the sexual assaults which the schizophrenic patients sometimes commit.

Aggressive and self-punitive tendencies exist simultaneously in the patient's mind, so that his behavior is often contradictory and incongruous.

A schizophrenic patient in an institution, in a state of excitement, struck his physician, who was talking to him, a violent blow on the jaw. He did not press the attack, but appeared to wait for the physician to retaliate upon him. When the physician did not do so, the patient burst into tears, and in a state of extreme agitation, called upon the physician to "strike him in the belly."

Although, in some instances, a blind, unreasoning impulse seems responsible for the patient's criminal acts, there are many cases in which there is evidence of careful planning and premeditation, and very frequently the patient is able to give a clear account of what occurred, but even when the act shows evidence of deliberate planning, the impression created is that the author of it was an automaton and that he was motivated by impulses beyond his understanding and control.

Although crimes of violence occur as symptoms of schizophrenia, it must not be thought that criminal violence is a characteristic symptom of this type of mental illness. On the contrary, the majority of these patients are quiet, timid, and apathetic. They lack the initiative to assert themselves, and their strongest desire seems to be to cut themselves off from contact with the outside world.

When the schizophrenic transgresses the law, the offense is often a technical one, and arises, not from criminal intent, but from his inability to cope with life's problems and to fulfill his social obligations. The enfeeblement of his mental powers and his lack of good sense, makes him yield readily to temptation, and he is often a helpless tool in the hands of unscrupulous associates.

It must also be realized that while the majority of these cases end in dementia, in a considerable number, the illness is arrested, and in quite a number of these arrested cases, the personality is retained at a good level, and the patient is able to maintain ordinary social relationships.

In simple schizophrenia where the absence of gross conduct disorder allows the patient to remain under home conditions, he is liable to become a burden upon society unless he is adequately supervised. Unable to compete on equal terms with his fellows in the labor market, he drifts into the ranks of the permanently unemployed. He becomes a vagrant, a street pedlar, or a beggar. He may steal, not because he is inherently dishonest, but because it seems to him the easiest thing to do.

Often minor crimes are committed in this type of illness while the patient is under the influence of alcohol.

Sometimes the patient, preoccupied with his own thoughts and out of contact with his environment, commits a criminal offense almost without realizing what he is doing.

．　．　．

PARANOID REACTION TYPES

Of all the standard devices used by the mind to deal with internal conflict, the mechanism of projection, by which unacceptable impulses are attributed to external sources, is one of the most frequently employed. The use of this mechanism in psychotic illnesses, in which the relations between the individual and external reality are disturbed, gives rise to delusions.

Delusional formation occurs at one stage or another in most types of psychotic illness, but there is a group of psychoses in which the formation of delusions is the predominating symptom, and it is these that are grouped under the term paranoid reaction types. The older psychiatrists isolated certain syndromes within this group which they regarded as distinct clinical entities to which they gave special names, but at the present time, it is usual to include all the paranoid reaction types under two headings: paranoia and paraphrenia.

Paranoia is a chronic mental illness which

develops gradually over a long period. The delusions, which are a characteristic symptom, are well systematized. It is an essential characteristic of the illness that the memory and the intellectual processes are well preserved. Hallucinations do not occur, and the essential core of the personality is preserved.

The study of the personality of persons who develop this type of illness usually reveals trends which help to explain the development and the clinical features of the disease.

In many cases a study of the patient's life shows that his general attitude to others has been one of suspicion, and that he has always been ready to attribute enmity and hostility to those with whom he has been associated. Persons of this type often appear shy, timid and sensitive, but these outward characteristics often conceal an underlying feeling of self-importance and a desire to lead and to dominate. Sometimes one finds that the patient has an exaggerated idea of his own abilities, and that his failure, through incompetence, to realize his ambitions, appears to be the starting point of a delusional system, the purpose of which seems to be to explain and excuse his failure in life.

Not infrequently a painful experience over which the patient has brooded until its true significance has become completely distorted, appears to have been the focus around which his morbid thoughts have developed. Thus, a technical offense which leads to an appearance in the police court, may sometimes be the starting point of a system of persecutory delusions. A failure in an examination, or in business, may initiate, in a predisposed person, a searching ruminative state of mind which gradually develops into a chronic delusional state.

There are, however, certain cases in which a study of the personality of the patient fails to show any outstanding characteristics, and it is not always possible to find evidence of any incident or worry in which the patient's illness has originated.

While actual incidents in the patient's life may appear to be closely related to the development of the illness, these incidents only act as precipitating factors which activate the unconscious forces from which the illness springs and takes its character. Freud, on the basis of his psychoanalytic study of these cases, expressed the view that paranoia results from unconscious homosexual tendencies

which are repudiated by the individual and then projected in the form of a delusional system.

Glover expresses the Freudian view thus: "Paranoia, however, is almost always connected with strong unconscious homosexual interests, which are denied and then projected. There are a number of stages in the development of this defense against homosexuality, but the essence of the matter is contained in the formula of delusional denial—'I do not love him, he hates me.' The homosexual defense is, however, not just the denial of a potentially active adult system, but the rejection of a reinforced, but repressed, infantile phase of homosexual development."

Although paranoid types of personality are very common, paranoia, in its fully developed form, is not a type of illness commonly met with in psychiatric practice, and these cases are comparatively rare in mental hospitals. There must be many cases of well-developed paranoia which never come under medical observation. The patient's formal social behavior may show little disturbance, and this, combined with the preservation of his intellectual faculties, makes it possible for him, in many instances, to live a fairly normal life at home, or even to carry on his trade or profession for many years after his illness has developed.

Although many paranoiacs are querulous, suspicious, and aggressive, many maintain friendly relations with those with whom they are in contact, and even with persons whom they believe are taking part in their persecution.

The paranoiac patient in a mental hospital is often on very good terms with those around him. Although firmly convinced that his detention in the hospital is unjust and illegal, he is yet able to maintain friendly and even cordial relations with the physician who refuses to release him.

A professional man, who believes that for years he has been victimized by the medical profession, who, he says, "make use of him" without his permission and without giving him the remuneration to which his services entitle him, is on the most friendly terms with the nurses and physicians in the hospital in which he is a patient. At times he interviews the Medical Superintendent and demands his discharge. He makes it clear that he holds the superintendent responsible for the injustices to which he has to submit, but the physician's refusal to accede to the patient's request for discharge, does not deter the latter from carrying out very useful work in the hospital, at considerable inconvenience to himself.

The degree in which the patient's conduct shows a departure from the normal standards depends on the character of his delusions and the stage of development which his illness has reached.

In those cases which form the majority, the illness is of gradual development, and there is usually a prodromal period during which the patient is uncertain about the truth of the delusional ideas which are slowly taking form in his mind. He is alert and suspicious. He feels that his suspicions are well founded, but he is willing to agree that the incidents which have aroused them may be capable of an innocent interpretation.

During this stage of the illness the patient may show very little outward signs of abnormality. He does not usually express his half-formed delusions, because he realizes that they may not be believed. He may appear preoccupied, and perhaps worried, but he continues his work, and his social relations are not usually grossly disturbed. He may decide to apply tests, with the object of proving or disproving his suspicions, but as his conclusions are determined, not by experience, but by unconscious mental processes, the results of the tests always seem to confirm his suspicions. At times he is completely convinced of the truth of his delusions: at other times his ideas can be shaken for the time being by discussion and reasoning.

This ebb-and-flow process may last a long time, and even when the illness is fully developed, periods of acute mental tension during which the patient is entirely dominated by his delusions may alternate with periods in which the morbid ideas appear to be in abeyance. These remissions in the illness are rarely permanent. When conviction has replaced suspicion, the patient may be forced to act in accordance with his delusional ideas. What action he will take will depend upon the nature of the delusions and upon his general character. If he has the delusion that he is being poisoned, he may consult a doctor, or he may adopt precautionary measures to ensure that his food is not adulterated in any way. If he is acted upon by electricity, he may insulate his bed. If gases are pumped

into his room, he may try to make the room gasproof. If his persecutor is some person accessible to him, he may confront him and ask for an explanation, or he may complain to the police. If the police fail to take action, he writes to a still higher authority. If he is by nature aggressive, his first protest may be an attack upon his aggressor. If he is timid, he may decide to flee from his imaginary persecutors, or he may, in a state of despair, commit suicide.

In some cases, a state of acute mental tension, in which the patient's conduct is almost entirely motivated by his delusions, may continue for years, but in most cases, sooner or later the patient's mind affects a compromise between the demands of reality and those of his fantasies. The delusions remain, and they continue to influence his thinking and his conduct, but he adjusts himself to the situation as a normal person may do to any enforced interference with his normal mode of life. He begins to participate, to some extent, in normal activities, and he attains a state of resignation, and even at times contentment. This evolutionary process occurs in many paranoiacs after their admission to a mental hospital. At first they are indignant and resentful, and some are combative and aggressive, but gradually, in the course of months or years, they adapt themselves to the life of the institution, and often participate with enjoyment and even enthusiasm in its activities. When this stage is attained, the patient's conduct, except for certain eccentricities, shows little abnormality, within the limit of his circumscribed life.

There are, however, certain cases which take a long time to reach this stage of tranquility. For them, the whole world is hostile and menacing, and everyone is an active agent in their persecution. Everything they hear has a double meaning. Every action done by anyone in their presence is misinterpreted as an insult, or a symbolic assault. They are mocked and humiliated. Their characters are besmirched, and life for them is a continuous battle against tyranny and persecution.

The paranoiac's persecutors may be a single individual, but usually it is a body of persons. Sometimes it is the Jews, sometimes the Free Masons, the Medical Profession, the Catholic Church, or the Government. At times it may be an undefined body specified by the patient as "they."

Criminal offenses of the patient suffering from paranoiac states are usually the direct outcome of the patient's delusions. When we consider the relentless persecution to which the patient believes he is subjected, it is surprising that crimes of violence in these cases do not occur more freqently than they do. No doubt crimes against the person would be committed more frequently by paranoiacs were it not for the fact that, in many instances, the patient is naturally law abiding, so that he usually tries by constitutional means to obtain redress from his wrongs before he resorts to violence. The fact that the patient's personality is retained and that his moral sentiments are preserved also explains why criminal offenses only occur in a small proportion of cases of this type of illness.

In East's series of 66 cases of paranoiac patient's who committed crimes, 12 committed crimes against the person, 10 violence to property, and 6 were cases in which violence was threatened. Fifteen per cent committed acts of dishonesty, such as theft and office breaking. The remaining offenses included vagrancy, use of obscene language, libel, sending obscene matter by post, neglect of family, obstruction, and drunkenness.

East points out that no case of sexual offense occurred in this series, and he remarks that this is a point of interest in view of the fact that the delusions of these patients are often sexual in character.

Offenses against the person may arise from different motives. They may be the result of the patient's natural impulse to retaliate upon his persecutors and mete out to them the punishment he believes they deserve, or he may resort to crime from altruistic motives. He may believe he is benefiting his country or the world by killing a tyrant. He may commit his offense not out of ill will toward his victim, but because he has failed to obtain redress for his injuries by constitutional means, and at last he comes to the conclusion that by committing a crime which will lead to his arrest or trial, he will have an opportunity of ventilating his grievances in court. The offense may be premeditated and carefully planned, or it may arise out of the impulse of the moment.

A man who believes that his wife is unfaithful to him, enraged by her denials of his accusations, may strike her impulsively, or he may lie in wait for her paramour and kill him.

Offenses against property may be motivated by revenge, as when a deluded patient attempts to get his own back on his persecutor by throwing a stone through a window in his house, or they may be the result of the patient's efforts to relieve his trying situation. If he believes that the interference to which he is subjected comes from his neighbor's house, he may attempt to destroy the house, perhaps by setting fire to it in the hope that the interferences will cease when their source has been destroyed.

The patient's persistent efforts to get into personal touch with his persecutors or with the authorities may lead to minor offenses. He may try to force his way into the magistrate's room in order to place his case before the legal authorities. He may interrupt a royal procession in an attempt to obtain a hearing from an important personage. He may denounce his enemy in the street and so render himself liable to a charge of breach of the peace, or he may send letters containing defamatory statements or obscene matter through the post. Occasionally the patient comes into conflict with the law through a technical offense. He is so preoccupied with his delusional system that he neglects to comply with the law in some way or other.

. . .

EPILEPSY

Epilepsy is not a specific clinical entity but a group of diseases of which the common features are recurring convulsions or disturbances of consciousness. It is therefore preferable to speak of "the epilepsies" rather than of epilepsy and to reserve the term epilepsy for idiopathic epilepsy, a condition of obscure etiology for which so far no physical cause has been discovered. Although many theories have been put forward to account for the disease none has won universal acceptance and the cause of the condition is unknown. Idiopathic epilepsy usually shows itself in childhood or in adolescence, and although the symptoms may vary greatly in their intensity and in the extent to which they interfere with the life of the patient the condition is in most cases progressive and incurable. The recurring attacks which form the distinctive features of the disease assume two forms: the major attack or grand mal and the minor or petit mal attack.

In a typical major epileptic attack there is

a sudden and complete loss of consciousness, which is immediately followed by a tonic spasm of the entire skeletal musculature. Breathing is obstructed by the spasm of the throat muscles. The patient's face becomes cyanosed. This stage, which only lasts a few seconds, is followed by the clonic phase of the paroxysm in which violent jerking movements of the muscles occur. The convulsive movements continue for a few seconds and then cease. There follows a state of coma, in which the patient lies as if asleep. When consciousness is regained there is usually some degree of mental confusion. This may be so slight and of such short duration that almost immediately the fit is over the patient may be able to get up and continue whatever he was doing before the fit. States of automatism may follow the fit. These are of medico-legal importance, because in such states of altered consciousness the patient may commit criminal acts of which he has afterward no memory.

In the minor attack a convulsion does not occur, and the attack takes the form of a momentary disturbance of consciousness. There is a sudden pause in the patient's activities, his gaze becomes fixed, and his movements are arrested, so that if he is taking a meal the fork may stop on the way to his mouth. When the attack is over he may assume his previous actions as if nothing had happened, but in some instances normal consciousness is not completely attained, and the patient's relations with his environment may continue to be imperfect for a considerable period. During this period actions are performed of which the patient has no recollection after he has regained his normal state. In this automatic state he may perform a stereotyped action, such as the removal of his collar and tie, he may undress himself completely, or he may urinate in public. Violent attacks upon bystanders may be committed in these automatic states.

The frequency of the paroxysms in epilepsy varies greatly in the individual case. The fits may only occur at intervals of months or years, or several fits may occur in one day. Sometimes the fits follow each other in rapid succession without any interval between each fit. In such a state of status epilepticus the patient may die of exhaustion.

The mental symptoms associated with epilepsy may vary between a slight change in the personality and a state of profound de-

mentia. Epilepsy is associated with certain personality traits of a distinctive kind, which constitute the so-called epileptic character. This epileptic character may sometimes show itself before the fits begin. Sensitiveness and egocentricity are usually described as the salient features of the epileptic character and certainly in many cases these character traits are well marked. The epileptic is usually profoundly interested in himself. He is insatiable in his demand for notice and attention. He demands redress for trivial worries and inconveniences. He has an acute awareness of the shortcomings of others, but he is blind to the faults in his own character. He is childish and sentimental in his emotional attachments. His conversation is often sententious and stereotyped. He shows a childish anxiety to please those whom he likes and on whom he has come to rely to satisfy his demands, which are not infrequently unreasonable. He responds to praise, but he will not tolerate criticism. He is easily hurt and insulted, and if one is to maintain good relations with him, he must be constantly humored. Some epileptics, but by no means all, are untruthful, irritable, spiteful, and quarrelsome.

Epilepsy is not incompatible with continued mental vigor, but in many cases there is well-marked mental enfeeblement which takes the form of impairment of memory, inability to concentrate, and a general slowing up of mental activity. The speech is slow and monotonous, and the patient has sometimes difficulty in finding words with which to express himself.

East suggests that the role of epilepsy in the causation of crime has been exaggerated. He quotes a series of cases of 8,731 male prisoners, in which only 39, or .4 per cent, were considered to be general epileptics by the Prison Medical Officers under whose care they were. In the case of 760 female prisoners 5, or .6 per cent, were epileptics.

The crimes of the epileptics may be divided into two types, those which are carried out in a state of clear consciousness, and those committed in states of epileptic automatism. I doubt, however, whether it is possible to make a clear distinction between these two types in all cases, but there is no doubt that the offenses carried out in states of epileptic automatism have very special characteristics. They often take the form of a habitual act, or a caricature of a habitual act: when the patient regains normal consciousness he has no memory of what occurred in the state of automatism. The offense lacks adequate motive, and no attempt at concealment is made.

In a state of altered consciousness, such offenses as indecent behavior, breach of the peace, and crimes of violence varying in gravity from minor assault to rape or murder may be carried out.

Where there is a history of epilepsy and in cases where the offense has the characteristic features already described there is little difficulty in relating the crime to the disease, but epileptics, like other people, may commit offenses in states of clear consciousness, and in these cases there may have been a difference of opinion on the question of the accused's responsibility. In every case of epilepsy there is some mental disturbance which permeates the whole personality, and we cannot see how any act committed by an epileptic can be completely dissociated from his disease, and we would be inclined to regard an epileptic who commits a serious offense as insane and not responsible for his act.

.   .   .

There is no sharp dividing line between normal and abnormal mental functioning. In mental disease the essential stuff of the mind is not changed. Nothing new is added to it, and everything arises from material already there. The difference between normal and abnormal mental functioning is quantitative, not qualitative. The devices, or mental mechanism, which in mental disease operate to produce symptoms, are also used extensively by the normal mind. There is thus no fundamental difference in character between minor forms of mental illness in which the question of a person's sanity does not arise, and in the psychotic disorders where the affected person is frequently insane. Indeed, one can go further and say that the psychotic's symptoms, which make it possible for a person to be certified insane, are, in many instances, a distortion and exaggeration of mental processes which occur in the so-called normal mind. Nevertheless, the quantitative difference between mental functioning in the normal mind and mental functioning as it occurs in the person suffering from a psychotic illness is very great, and it is this difference which is responsible for the gross changes in the patient's personality and his conduct, which are charac-

teristic symptoms of the psychotic types of mental illness.

It is frequently a deviation from normal behavior which attracts attention to the existence of mental illness, but while the fact that a person has been accepted as normal by his friends and associates is strong presumptive evidence of the absence of gross mental disorder, such evidence is not a proof that the patient is of sound mind, for in many instances a person may continue to behave correctly in his social relations long after his mind has become severely disturbed; for instance, the delusions of the paranoiac may be present for months and years before their existence becomes apparent by a change in the patient's behavior.

In many instances the conduct of a mentally disordered person is modified by his nature, his education, and his ethical and social training. A man who is naturally aggressive will tend to show his aggressiveness in an exaggerated form when his mind becomes disordered. On the other hand, a person whose conduct is guided by a strict code of morals is less likely to commit antisocial acts under the influence of mental disorder than a person of lower moral standards. There are, however, many exceptions to this generalization, and conduct in psychotic illness depends a great deal upon the type of illness. In some types of illness one finds that there is a complete reversal of the patient's previous personality and his standards of conduct. *Even the mildest psychotic illness influences the total personality and exerts some influence upon the patient's thinking and his behavior.* The mind does not function, either in health or disease, in parts, but as a whole. Therefore, it follows that when a person suffering from a mental illness commits a criminal act, it is wrong to assume his conduct was uninfluenced by his illness, because the act, in itself, does not seem to be irrational, but appears to have been brought about by such motives as self-interest or revenge which often dictate the conduct of a normal person. On the other hand, there are few cases of mental disease, except cases of advanced dementia, in which the patient is so completely dominated by his symptoms that he is uninfluenced in his behavior by motives such as self-esteem, fear of consequences, social sentiments, and a sense of duty, which regulate the behavior of normal persons.

In considering the motives determining the conduct of an insane person who commits an offense, we cannot assess with accuracy the relative influence of abnormal and normal processes in the motivation of his conduct, and the only safe rule is to assume that his offense could not be entirely uninfluenced by his abnormal state of mind.

One of the distinguishing features of psychotic mental illness is that it frequently deprives the patient of the ability to modify his conduct to meet social situations. Yet, although many psychotic patients appear to be completely detached from their environment, one finds many cases, even of patients who are grossly disordered and whose conduct seems completely uncontrolled, in which the patient can respond as a normal person does to the demands of the particular situation in which he finds himself.

Thus, a woman who is suffering from mania behaves in a most extravagant way while in the ward with other patients. She is rarely at rest. Her conversation, which never stops, is rambling and disjointed. She is mischievous, and her conduct is a source of serious annoyance to everyone around her. While she is in the ward, nothing will restrain her disorderly behavior, but this same woman behaves with almost perfect propriety when her relatives take her for a drive, or when she is asked to appear before a class of students.

On the other hand, many patients who are comparatively orderly in their behavior in the sheltered atmosphere of an institution would behave in an embarrassing and even dangerous manner in ordinary social surroundings.

It would be quite erroneous, however, to attribute the alteration in the behavior of either type of patient to deliberate conscious intention. In each case the patient responds to a particular situation in a characteristic way by a process of unconscious adaptation. An insane person who might otherwise commit an offense might certainly refrain from doing so because a policeman is looking on, but he does so, not necessarily because he has deliberately considered the situation and has decided that if he commits the offense he will be arrested and punished. The fear of the consequence of his act may, in many cases, influence the conduct of an insane person, but it is just as likely that in refraining from

committing an offense, he has acted without reflection and deliberation. His behavior, like that of the patient I have mentioned, is an unconscious response to the situation existing at the time. In the absence of the policeman, he might commit the offense, but the presence of the policeman adds a new factor to the situation, and the person responds automatically to it.

It is not the application of restraint or the fear of punishment which determines the orderly behavior of patients in an institution who would behave in a disorderly manner in other circumstances, it is rather that the general atmosphere acts upon the patient without his conscious awareness, and influences his conduct. When greater demands are made upon his powers of social adaptability, as, for instance, in his own home, internal mental tension is increased and finds expression in disordered conduct and perhaps in antisocial acts.

. . .

A person's capacity to know that what he is doing is wrong, is a mental process—a process which cannot exist apart from his mind. Therefore, the validity of an opinion on the ability of a person to know wrong depends upon whether the opinion is based on a true conception of mind, and its characteristics in health and in disease. If the conception of the mind upon which the opinion is based is erroneous, it is at least highly improbable that the opinion will have any validity.

Now, our knowledge of the mind and of mental disease is very imperfect. Much is unknown, and indeed, from the very nature of mind, it is doubtful whether complete knowledge of it and its working is possible, but while we cannot formulate accurate and precise laws about mental processes, we can say, in the light of modern knowledge, that the mind is not as it was conceived to be by the legislators responsible for the McNaghten rules. The mind upon whose capacity to know wrong a medical man is asked to express an opinion is not a real mind, but an artifact, an ingenious invention of the judges who made the rules.

If a motor engineer called as an expert witness in a case is asked his opinion about the behavior of a motor car in certain real or hypothetical circumstances, he would have every right to expect that the vehicle he is dealing with is a motor car as he knows it. He would find great difficulty in expressing an opinion if the judge insisted that the motor car with which the law is concerned is one which runs on rails and is yet able to move freely from one side of the street to the other, and one whose behavior is in no wise affected when its steering mechanism is out of action!

It is impossible for the doctor and the lawyer to reach agreement on the question of criminal responsibility while they approach the matter from a totally different standpoint, as they still do.

The law deals with an individual who is capable of clear-cut conceptions of right and wrong—an individual whose actions are guided by logic and reason, but this individual in whom reason reigns supreme is, in reality, an imaginary person. The real person with whom the physician has to deal when he comes to assess responsibility is only partially guided by reason in his conduct. His actions, like many of the actions of the normal person, spring from the unconscious mind which knows nothing of reason and logic, which is self-contradictory, and which is dominated by impulses which seek gratification, often regardless of the dictates of reality. The person whose mind functions according to the lawyer's psychology reminds one of Charles Lamb's Scotsman, of whom he says:

"His understanding is always at its meridian—you never see the first dawn, the early streaks. He has no falterings or self-suspicions: surmises, guesses, misgivings, half-intentions, semiconsciousnesses, partial illuminations, dim instincts, embryo conceptions, have no place in his brain or vocabulary. The twilight of dubiety never falls on him. Between the affirmative and the negative there is no borderline with him. He cannot compromise, or understand middle actions. There can be but right and wrong."

The real person with whom the physician has to deal is more like the youthful Gargantua, who we are told, "Sharpened his teeth with a top, washing his hands with his broth, and combed his head with a bowl. He would sit betwixt two stools, would cover himself with a wet sack and drink in eating his soup. He did eat his cake sometimes without bread, and bite in laughing, and laugh in biting, and hide himself in the water for fear of rain. He would strike out of the cold iron, would beat the dogs before the lion, put the plough before the ox, would beat the bushes without catching the birds, thought the moon was made of green cheese and that bladders were lanterns, and of his fist would make a mallet. He always looked a given horse in the mouth, leapt from the cock to the ass, and put one ripe between two green. By robbing Peter he paid Paul. He kept the moon from the wolves and hoped to catch larks if ever the Heavens should fall."

.   .   .

When can an act be said to have been carried out under an uncontrollable impulse? No doubt the answer to this question will depend upon whether it is based on the deterministic or the free-will theories of action.

The libertarian would no doubt say that an act which is carried out under an uncontrollable impulse is one which is not willed by the person who does it, but is, on the contrary, imposed upon him by some force which the will cannot resist.

To the determinist, however, on final analysis, an act carried out under an uncontrollable impulse is not very different from any other kind of act. To say that an act was carried out under an uncontrollable impulse to him means only that the act was carried out because no psychic or physical event occurred to prevent it, and this can be said of any act once it has been done, for in any action involving conflict, if the impulse or drive responsible for the act had not been irresistible, the act would not have been done.

Perhaps, however, by uncontrollable impulse is meant any impulse which could not be controlled except by the application of physical restraint. There are acts of this nature. An act carried out by a person in a state of acute mania in which the excitement amounts to frenzy or an act carried out in a state of delirium might well be termed an uncontrollable act, for in such states of profound mental disorder, the person affected acts blindly without appreciation of his surroundings and without apprehension of what he is doing. Similarly, the sudden meaningless acts of a schizophrenic patient may legitimately be regarded as uncontrollable acts, but such acts as these, when they are of a criminal character, already come within the McNaghten rules, for every mental expert would unhesitatingly say that the accused, in such cases, did not know the nature of the act or that it was wrong, and that he is therefore not responsible for it. It is not, however, such cases as I have mentioned that the Committee had in mind when they proposed the introduction of the rule of uncontrollable impulse. They suggest that the rule would be applicable to cases of mothers who are seized with the impulse to cut the throats or otherwise destroy their children to whom they are normally devoted.

Mothers who yield to impulses to murder their children usually do so because they are suffering from melancholia, and to introduce the doctrine of uncontrollable impulse in order to ensure that a melancholic woman who kills her child shall not be held responsible for her act, seems to us nonsensical, for in such cases the act lacks the essential character of a criminal act, because there is no intention on the part of the person committing it to do wrong. Moreover, it is open to argument whether a melancholic mother kills her child as a result of an uncontrollable impulse. If by uncontrollable impulse is meant an impulse which no power, short of physical force, can restrain, then it can be said, without hesitation, that this is not the kind of impulse which, in many instances, causes a melancholic to commit murder. The truth is that homicidal acts by melancholic patients frequently show evidence of premeditation and careful planning. Indeed, the act may appear to be more deliberate and more carefully executed than many criminal acts carried out by persons who are apparently free from mental disease. Moreover, there is every reason to believe that, in many cases, the melancholic's morbid impulses can be controlled by the same circumstances which act as inhibiting agents in the conduct of sane criminals. It must be very unusual for a melancholic patient to kill her child in the presence of a third person who would interfere and prevent her carrying out the act. If the melancholic is driven to murder her child by an uncontrollable impulse, presumably by the same reasoning, suicidal acts which occur frequently in cases of melancholia can be explained in the same way, but if this were true, every melancholic patient in a mental hospital known to have suicidal impulses would require mechanical restraint to prevent them committing the act. In practice we find that such a degree of restraint is very rarely necessary. Constant supervision is essential, and this alone is sufficient in almost every case to prevent the patient even attempt-

ing to commit suicide. Now whether the melancholic patient refrains from attempting suicide because she knows that the nurses in attendance upon her will interfere and frustrate her purpose, or whether the mere presence of the nurses brings about a change in the patient's mind, which for the time being abolishes or lessens the desire to commit suicide, one cannot say, but whichever way it happens, it seems that the patient has been able to resist the impulse.

If we believe that a free will governs the conduct, we are driven to the conclusion that the melancholic patient who refrains from committing suicide because of the presence of a nurse at the other end of the ward, has done so from the exercise of a free choice. If she is capable of free choice in this matter, then she cannot be dominated by an uncontrollable impulse. It might be suggested, however, that in these cases in which the melancholic patient refrains from suicide or homicide in the presence of a person who might restrain the attempt the impulse is not uncontrollable, and that it is only in cases where the patient does attempt the act that the impulse is uncontrollable. The carrying out of the act in these cases is the proof that the impulse was uncontrollable. But could not the same reasoning be applied to explain the criminal acts of a sane person, as, for instance, the housebreaker who waits until the policeman has disappeared round the corner before he breaks into the house? Could it not be said that the presence of the policeman enables the housebreaker to refrain from the act, but that when the policeman was out of sight the impulse to commit the act proved too strong and became uncontrollable? It may be argued, however, that the mental state of the housebreaker is entirely different from that of the melancholic woman in that in the one case the person is presumably free from mental illness, whereas in the other she is insane, and further, that the housebreaker has no desire to refrain from committing his act, whereas the melancholic patient is the victim of conflicting desires: one, impelling her to commit the act, and another working to restrain the morbid impulse.

It is probably true that, in most instances, the sane criminal is not troubled by scruples of conscience. No restraining impulse enters his consciousness, and it is also probably true that the melancholic patient feels that her desire to commit suicide or to murder her children is something foreign to herself: something imposed upon her.

It is doubtful whether these distinctions between the behavior of the insane offender and the sane criminal exist in all cases, but if we assume, for the sake of argument, that they do, the conclusion to which we are driven is that while the sane offender's conduct is rational (it is very doubtful whether it is in actuality) the melancholic patient's conduct is not. In the one case, the act is the product, or appears to be the product, of a sound mind, and in the other, it is a product of an unsound mind, and this is the only absolute distinction we can make between the act in the one case and in the other.

. . .

If we could make an absolute distinction between mental health and mental disease, and if we could say that every criminal act committed by a person suffering from mental disease has a characteristic, or characteristics, which are absent in every criminal act committed by a person who is free from mental disease, then we would be able to make a rule regarding responsibility which would be capable of universal application. We cannot, however, make such a perfect rule, and any rule that we make can only be capable of limited application. The McNaghten rules are very imperfect, but perhaps their merit lies in their very imperfection, for if a rule is so nearly perfect that it is capable of being applied in the majority of cases, the tendency will be to apply it rigorously to all cases, and this will result in an injustice in those cases in which the rule is inapplicable; whereas if the rule is recognized to be a bad rule, there will be no hesitation in discarding it in those cases which do not come within its scope. The tendency will be for each case to be dealt with on its merits, and when we are dealing with such an imponderable subject as human behavior, this is perhaps the safest course to adopt.

We agree with those who suggest that the only logical solution to the problem of criminal responsibility is to abolish the legal concept of responsibility and to regard everyone, whether sane or insane, who commits an offense as responsible, but not necessarily punishable, but this question leads to a consideration of matters which are outside the scope of the present discussion.

Legal Insanity*

(III) CONCLUSIONS
Preliminary

278. We make one fundamental assumption, which we should hardly have thought it necessary to state explicitly if it had not lately been questioned in some quarters. It has for centuries been recognized that if a person was, at the time of his unlawful act, mentally so disordered that it would be unreasonable to impute guilt to him, he ought not to be held liable to conviction and punishment under the criminal law. Views have changed and opinions have differed, as they differ now, about the standards to be applied in deciding whether an individual should be exempted from criminal responsibility for this reason; but the principle has been accepted without question. Recently, however, the suggestion has sometimes been made that the insane murderer should be punished equally with the sane, or that, although he ought not to be executed as a punishment, he should be painlessly exterminated as a measure of social hygiene. The argument is in each case the same—that his continued existence will be of no benefit to himself, and that he will be not only a useless burden, but also a potential danger to the community, since there is always a risk that he may escape and commit another crime. Such doctrines have been preached and practiced in National-Socialist Germany, but they are repugnant to the moral traditions of Western civilization and we are confident that they would be unhesitatingly rejected by the great majority of the population of this country. We assume the continuance of the ancient and humane principle that has long formed part of our common law.

279. For us, therefore, there are two essential questions—Do the M'Naghten Rules provide a just and reasonable standard by which

* Reprinted from *Royal Commission on Capital Punishment 1949–53 Report* (London: Her Majesty's Stationery Office, 1953), pp. 98–105, 107–16, by permission of the Controller of Her Britannic Majesty's Stationery Office.

to assess whether the mental state of an accused person was at the time of the crime so abnormal that he ought to be held irresponsible and exempted from punishment? And, if not, what change in the law, whether by amendment or by abrogation of the Rules, would be practicable and desirable? We shall approach these questions in a practical and empirical spirit, and we shall try to answer them without losing ourselves in the labyrinthine legal and philosophical arguments which have led to much barren controversy in the past.

The Nature of Criminal Responsibility

280. It has often been said that the question of criminal responsibility, although it is closely bound up with medical and ethical issues, is primarily a legal question. There is an important sense in which this is true. There is no *a priori* reason why every person suffering from any form of mental abnormality or disease, or from any particular kind of mental disease, should be treated by the law as not answerable for any criminal offense which he may commit, and be exempted from conviction and punishment. Mental abnormalities vary infinitely in their nature and intensity and in their effects on the character and conduct of those who suffer from them. Where a person suffering from a mental abnormality commits a crime, there must always be some likelihood that the abnormality has played some part in the causation of the crime; and, generally speaking, the graver the abnormality and the more serious the crime, the more probable it must be that there is a causal connection between them. But the closeness of this connection will be shown by the facts brought in evidence in individual cases and cannot be decided on the basis of any general medical principle. On the other hand, few persons, if any, would go so far as to suggest that anyone suffering from any mental abnormality, however slight, ought on that ground to be wholly exempted from responsibility under the criminal law. It therefore becomes necessary for the law to provide a method of determining what kind and degree of mental abnormality shall entitle offenders to be so exempted; and also to decide what account shall be taken of lesser degrees of mental abnormality, whether by way of mitigation of sentence or otherwise.

281. Yet, although in this sense the question of criminal responsibility may rightly be described as a question of law, there is another, and more important, sense in which this is at best a misleading half-truth. Discussion of this subject is often befogged through failure to distinguish clearly between the two questions "what is the law?" and "what ought the law to be?" The first is obviously a purely legal question; the second is obviously not. A just and adequate doctrine of criminal responsibility cannot be founded on legal principles alone. Responsibility is a moral question; and there is no issue on which it is more important that the criminal law should be in close accord with the moral standards of the community. There can be no pre-established harmony between the criteria of moral and of criminal responsibility, but they ought to be made to approximate as nearly as possible. The views of ordinary men and women about the moral accountability of the insane have been gradually modified by the development of medical science, and, if the law cannot be said to have always kept pace with them, it has followed them at a distance and has slowly adjusted itself to their changes. It is therefore proper and necessary to enquire from time to time whether the doctrine of criminal responsibility, as laid down by the common law and applied by the courts, takes due account of contemporary moral standards and of modern advances in medical knowledge about the effects of mental abnormality on personality and behavior.

282. This principle is no doubt easier to enunciate than to apply. The last hundred years have seen striking advances in scientific knowledge of insanity and mental abnormality; yet psychological medicine remains one of the youngest branches of science and it is often difficult to define the limits of recognized knowledge. There are many important questions on which psychiatrists of different schools are not agreed: there is no clear, precise, or universally accepted terminology; and there is not infrequently a marked conflict of views on individual cases. When we leave the domain of medicine and enter that of ethics or law, we find that there is no greater unanimity, and that psychiatrists express differing views about the kind and degree of mental abnormality which should entitle an offender to be absolved from responsibility for a criminal act.

283. These difficulties would be very grave, and perhaps insuperable, if responsibility were primarily a medical question. Even if it were on other grounds desirable to do so, it would, in the present state of medical knowledge, be out of the question to remove the issue of criminal responsibility from the courts and entrust its determination to a panel of medical experts, as has sometimes been suggested. In our view the question of responsibility is not primarily a question of medicine, any more than it is a question of law. It is essentially a moral question, with which the law is intimately concerned and to whose solution medicine can bring valuable aid, and it is one which is most appropriately decided by a jury of ordinary men and women, not by medical or legal experts.

284. Neither the law nor ethics can reasonably be expected to base itself on extreme and untried medical theories or to go beyond what appears to be the general consensus of moderate medical opinion. If the problem of criminal responsibility is approached from this point of view, it should not prove impossible to find a solution which will satisfactorily reconcile the requirements of justice with the moral feelings of the community at large.

285. As we have previously observed, mental abnormality varies widely in its intensity and in the extent to which it affects the behavior of the patient and his capacity to conduct himself like a normal person. It follows that the extent to which a mentally abnormal person should be considered less responsible for his actions than a normal person varies equally widely: there is an almost infinite range of degrees of responsibility. For practical purposes, however, the law must divide mentally abnormal offenders into a limited number of groups for the purpose of assessing criminal responsibility. In effect, the existing law of England takes cognizance of three such groups—those who are to be regarded as wholly irresponsible; those who are not regarded as wholly irresponsible and entirely exempted from conviction and punishment, but are nevertheless considered so much less responsible than a normal person as to justify some mitigation of punishment (by the exercise of the Prerogative of Mercy in capital cases, by the courts in others) ; and, lastly, those whose responsibility for their actions is so little affected that they can properly be dealt with in the same way as a normal person. But it must be recognized that the boundary between the first and the second group is not a clear-cut line of demarcation, and that the question whether an accused person should be regarded as wholly irresponsible is essentially a question of degree, which can be decided only by the exercise of a subjective, and to some extent arbitrary, judgment. There are not two all-inclusive classes—the black and the white, the responsible and the irresponsible—into one or other of which every offender must fall ; the question is rather whether the offender, as a result of insanity or mental abnormality, is so much less responsible than a normal person that it is just and right to treat him as wholly irresponsible. And if it appears that the crime was wholly or very largely caused by insanity, he ought to be treated as irresponsible ; for to punish a person for a crime caused by insanity would in effect be to punish him for his insanity; and this would not be in harmony with the moral feelings of the community.

286. The views expressed by medical witnesses differed in emphasis rather than in substance. The general conclusions we draw from their evidence are these. The question of criminal responsibility must be considered by the jury in each individual case on the basis of all the relevant evidence given by medical and other witnesses. It is not possible to define in medical terms any category of mental disease which should always, and without exception, exempt an offender from responsibility ; and there must always be doubtful and borderline cases, where it will be difficult to decide whether the accused ought to be held wholly irresponsible, either because it is difficult to diagnose his mental condition at the time of the offense or because it is difficult to judge how his mental condition affected his responsibility for his actions. Nevertheless, where a grave crime is committed by a person who is suffering from a psychosis and is so grossly disordered mentally that, in the opinion of experienced medical men, he could properly be certified as insane, the presumption that the crime was wholly or largely caused by the insanity is, in ordinary circumstances, overwhelmingly strong. It cannot indeed be maintained that if a person is certified, or certifiable, as insane, he should necessarily be held irresponsible in all cases, mainly because . . . certification is

sometimes determined by pragmatic considerations; it may be necessary to certify a patient whose mental disorder is comparatively slight in order to ensure that he should receive proper care and treatment. But cases will be extremely rare in which an accused person ought to be held criminally responsible when he is certifiable as insane and there is no reason to think that his condition was materially different at the time of the crime.

287. An equally strong presumption arises in relation to the grosser forms of mental deficiency (idiocy and imbecility) and to certain epileptic conditions. . . . It does not, we think, arise in relation to any forms of minor mental disorder. Where the accused is suffering from some lesser degree of abnormality, the evidence may sometimes be sufficient to show that he ought to be treated as irresponsible; usually, however, it will not justify such a conclusion, although his moral responsibility may often be diminished to such an extent as to justify mitigation of the extreme penalty.

288. Under the existing law, as we have seen, if a person charged with murder is alleged to be insane, three different tests of insanity are applied at different stages in the proceedings. The test applied by the jury to determine whether the accused should be found insane on arraignment is whether he is fit to plead, to understand the proceedings, and to instruct counsel. . . . The test applied by the jury in determining whether at the time of the offense he was insane so as not to be responsible for his actions and should therefore be found guilty but insane is that laid down by the M'Naghten Rules—whether he was laboring under such a defect of reason, from disease of the mind, that he did not know the nature and quality of his act or did not know that it was wrong. . . . The test applied by the Home Secretary in deciding whether he is precluded from allowing the prisoner to go to execution if convicted and sentenced to death is whether he is certifiable as insane. . . . Although there are reasons, as we have pointed out in paragraph 286, for which it would not be appropriate to assimilate the test applied by the jury to that later applied by the Home Secretary, and make criminal irresponsibility coextensive with certifiable insanity, we have no doubt that it would be desirable to approximate the two tests more closely than at present, and

it seems clear that, if this were done, it would obviate the passing of the death sentence in some of the cases in which it will not be carried out.

The Inadequacy of the M'Naghten Rules

289. It remains for us to consider whether amendment of the law is necessary in order to achieve this object. It may be suggested that, owing to the broadening interpretation of the M'Naghten Rules, few insane persons are in fact convicted of murder and sentenced to death, and that this tendency may be expected to continue and to develop still further. It may also be pointed out that . . . by no means all of the 48 persons who in the years 1900–1949 were convicted of murder and subsequently certified insane after a statutory medical inquiry had been convicted as a result of the operation of the M'Naghten Rules. It may therefore be argued that in practice few persons who ought to be found irresponsible are convicted of murder, and even fewer are so convicted owing to the application of the M'Naghten Rules, and that the mischief to be remedied is therefore too small to justify amendment of the law, which would certainly be difficult and controversial and which might make it too easy for offenders to escape just punishment.

290. We think that this argument is misconceived. The objections to retaining the M'Naghten Rules in their present form on the ground that in practice they rarely produce injustice were cogently stated by an American witness, Mr. Justice Frankfurter, in his evidence:

. . . The M'Naghten Rules were rules which the Judges, in response to questions by the House of Lords, formulated in the light of the then existing psychological knowledge. . . . I do not see why the rules of law should be arrested at the state of psychological knowledge of the time when they were formulated. . . . If you find rules that are, broadly speaking, discredited by those who have to administer them, which is, I think, the real situation, certainly with us—they are honored in the breach and not in the observance—then I think the law serves its best interests by trying to be more honest about it . . . I think that to have rules which cannot rationally be justified except by a process of interpretation which distorts and often practically nullifies them, and to say the corrective process comes by having the Governor of a State charged with the responsibility of deciding when the consequences of the rule should not be enforced, is not a desirable system . . . I am a great believer in being as candid as possible about my institutions. They are in large measure abandoned in practice, and therefore I think the M'Naghten Rules are in large measure shams. That is a strong word, but I think the M'Naghten Rules are very difficult for conscientious people and not difficult enough for people who say "We'll just juggle them" . . . I dare to believe that we ought not to rest content with the difficulty of finding an improvement in the M'Naghten Rules . . .

291. In our view the test of criminal responsibility contained in the M'Naghten Rules cannot be defended in the light of modern medical knowledge and modern penal views. It is well established that there are offenders who know what they are doing and know that it is wrong (whether "wrong" is taken to mean legally or morally wrong), but are nevertheless so gravely affected by mental disease that they ought not to be held responsible for their actions. It would be impossible to apply modern methods of care and treatment in mental hospitals, and at the same time to maintain order and discipline, if the great majority of the patients, even among the grossly insane, did not know what is forbidden by the rules and that, if they break them, they are liable to forfeit some privilege. Examination of a number of individual cases in which a verdict of guilty but insane was returned, and rightly returned, has convinced us that there are few indeed where the accused can truly be said not to have known that his act was wrong. We have been struck, for example, by the large number of cases where the offender was undoubtedly insane both at the time of the crime and afterward, but clearly showed, by his subsequent actions or by a remark made immediately after the crime (such as "I have killed her; shall I be hanged?"), that he knew what he was doing and that it was punishable by law.

292. This narrow scope of the Rules was long ago recognized by Lord Bramwell (although he regarded it as a merit) when he observed, in a famous phrase: "I think that, although the present law lays down such a definition of madness, that nobody is hardly ever really mad enough to be within it, yet it is a logical and good definition."[1] Lord Bramwell's view was that many insane persons may be influenced by the same motives and

considerations as the sane and that if a lunatic knew what he was doing and knew that it was wrong, and if he was so far amenable to threats that he would not have "yielded to his insanity if a policeman had been at his elbow," then, not only was there no reason why he should not be punished, but it was eminently desirable that he should be punished, so that persons whose power of self-control was weakened by mental disease might at any rate be restrained by the sanctions of the criminal law.

293. This view has long been abandoned, and, in most cases where the strict application of the M'Naghten Rules will require a verdict of "guilty" to be given against an insane person, this consequence is obviated by the common sense of juries and the readiness of judges to recognize that, when common sense says the verdict should be "guilty but insane" and the M'Naghten Rules say it should be "guilty," common sense must prevail. But the fact that usually a way is found of obviating the evil consequences liable to flow from the Rules is not a sufficient reason for retaining them. The evil consequences are not always obviated. Occasionally the Rules lead to a verdict of "guilty" and a sentence of death which might otherwise be avoided. Nor can we disregard the deplorable impression which the Rules make on the minds of persons interested in penal matters. The Rules bring the criminal law into disrepute and the doubts and anxieties they create in the minds of many critics are not removed by the consideration that the actual harm they do is much less than they are capable of doing.

294. Moreover the burden of "stretching" the M'Naghten Rules, so as to avoid the unfortunate results of their strict application, falls largely and unfairly on medical witnesses. If a doctor is prepared to infer from his diagnosis of the nature and degree of the prisoner's insanity that at the moment when he committed his act of violence he was probably unconscious that it was wrong, the court will often be ready to accept that inference, although there may be no other evidence to support it, and even when the prisoner's acts or words seem to belie it. It is unfair to the medical witness to place him in a position where he is aware that his evidence as to the nature and degree of the prisoner's mental disease and its effect on his responsibility may be treated as irrelevant unless he is prepared

---

[1] Minutes of Evidence of Select Committee on the Homicide Law Amendment Bill, 1874, Q. 186.

to hazard the opinion that at the crucial moment the prisoner was probably unaware of the wrongfulness of his act. We are aware that medical evidence is sometimes unsatisfactory and open to justified criticism, but we have little doubt that its defects are often in large measure due to the impossible position in which medical witnesses are placed by what is to them the manifest absurdity of the M'Naghten test, and that amendment of the law, by relieving them of this embarrassment, would do much to improve the quality of psychiatric evidence.

295. Finally, even if by a liberal and generous interpretation the M'Naghten Rules were in practice so applied as to exempt from criminal responsibility all those offenders who ought to be so exempted, they would still be open to the most serious objection. It is nearly fifty years since a medical man who had devoted much sober and careful study to this question wrote that, although judges, in trying a case that did not come within the original scope of the M'Naghten Rules, might sometimes direct juries in other terms, "the much more usual course is for the judge to adhere strictly to the terms of the answers, and then to stretch the plain meaning of the language of those answers, until the ordinary nonlegal user of the English language is aghast at the distortions and deformations and tortures to which the unfortunate words are subjected, and wonders whether it is worth while to have a language which can apparently be taken to mean anything the user pleases."[2] When the gap between the natural meaning of the law and the sense in which it is commonly applied has for so long been so wide, it is impossible to escape the conclusion that an amendment of the law, to bring it into closer conformity with the current practice, is long overdue.

296. For these reasons we are agreed that the time has come when the law ought to be amended. We have already described the two alternative remedies proposed by our witnesses. One is that the M'Naghten Rules should be extended, on the lines of the formula proposed by the British Medical Association, to cover cases where the accused "was laboring, as a result of disease of the mind, under . . . a disorder of emotion such

that, while appreciating the nature and quality of the act, and that it was wrong, he did not possess sufficient power to prevent himself from committing it." The other is that the Rules should be entirely abrogated and the jury be given express discretion to determine, on all the medical and other evidence, untrammeled by any rule of law, whether the accused was so insane (or mentally defective) as not, in the opinion of the jury, to be responsible for his actions.

297. Before examining these alternatives we must deal with the often repeated suggestion that if the present criterion of responsibility were enlarged, this would have dangerous repercussions in relation to other crimes, especially sexual crimes and crimes of violence against the person. In our view the probable effect of any such change on the general administration of the criminal law can easily be exaggerated. It is only in trials for murder that a defense of insanity is raised in a considerable proportion of cases and a verdict of guilty but insane frequently returned. In trials for other offenses the plea of insanity is seldom put forward. The explanation is no doubt the one usually given—that indefinite detention as a Broadmoor patient appears a preferable alternative only where the sentence on conviction is death, and that in other cases the accused prefers to run the risk of a fixed sentence of imprisonment, however long. We see no reason to suppose that this natural reluctance to court detention for an indeterminate period would be weakened by any change in the test of criminal responsibility or that, if the present test were relaxed, this would be likely to lead to an undesirable or unjustified increase in pleas of insanity or verdicts of guilty but insane in relation to offenses other than murder.

. . .

Should the M'Naghten Rules Be Revised?

308. The proposal to extend the M'Naghten Rules to cover those cases where a crime is committed as a result of insanity affecting not the reason or the intellect but the will or the emotions has much to commend it, and clearly merits the most careful consideration. This was the course proposed by the Atkin Committee, when they recommended that the Rules should be extended so as to include cases where the act was "committed under an impulse which the prisoner was by mental disease in substance deprived of any power

[2] C. Mercier, *Criminal Responsibility* (New York, 1905), p. 169.

to resist." To add such a limb to the formula which has been used in the courts for more than a hundred years would be a less radical change than to abrogate the Rules and leave the jury to decide the issue at large; and, other things being equal, a limited change is to be preferred to a more far-reaching one.

309. There can, moreover, be no doubt that if an adequate criterion of criminal responsibility could be devised, expressed in clear and simple nontechnical language, it would be a helpful guide to the jury. In many cases it may be very difficult to decide whether the accused was so gravely disordered mentally that he ought not to be held responsible for his actions. In capital cases a plea of insanity is often advanced on weak and inadequate grounds. Some medical evidence is obscure and may be imperfectly understood by the jury. There may be conflicting medical testimony, and the jury may have no standard by which to assess the relative value of the evidence given on either side. In such cases, if the test of responsibility is defined by law and the Judge is able to tell the jury that they may only return a verdict of guilty but insane if they find that the accused was, as a result of insanity, subject to certain specified incapacities of reason or will, the application of this yardstick may save them from being led astray and help them to arrive at a just conclusion.

310. The first question we have to consider is whether the M'Naghten Rules, as they stand, cover adequately those cases where insanity does result in a "defect of reason," or call for amendment in relation to cases of this kind as well as those where it results in disorder of the emotions or the will. It is beyond dispute that if, as a result of mental disease, a person does not know the nature and quality of the act—if, for example, he thinks that he is squeezing an orange when he is in fact strangling a human being—or if he does not know that the act is forbidden by law, he ought not to be held criminally responsible. The criterion is therefore sound so far as it goes. But it has for long been objected that it is too narrow. It has been pointed out, for example, that it does not cover the case of the lunatic who commits a crime, knowing that it is contrary to the laws of man, but believing that it is commanded by God. It has therefore been suggested that "wrong" should be interpreted to mean "morally wrong," as opposed to "punishable by law." This proposal does not however resolve the difficulty. If "morally wrong" is interpreted objectively to mean "wrong according to commonly accepted moral standards," it will not materially enlarge the present criterion; for a person who knows that a serious crime is forbidden by law will almost certainly also know that it is generally regarded as morally wrong. The alternative is to interpret "morally wrong" subjectively. The British Medical Association, for example, suggested that the existing test should be amended to provide that "wrong" should mean "not 'punishable by law' but morally wrong in the accused person's own opinion." We cannot regard this suggestion as satisfactory. The test would then become "whether the accused was laboring under a defect of reason such that he did not know that he was doing what was morally wrong in his own opinion." This somewhat confused formula would in effect substitute "did not think that it was wrong" for "did not know that it was wrong"; but if "defect of reason" is retained as a test of responsibility, it must be related to an objective standard. The substitution for "know" of a more subjective word, such as "appreciate," is open to similar objections. Our conclusion is that it is not practicable to enlarge the scope of the M'Naghten Rules by rewording the existing limbs, and that some other test must be added to those contained in the present formula if the Rules are to cover satisfactorily cases where a person knows what he is doing and that it is unlawful, but, as a result of insanity, does not regard it as morally wrong or falls so far short of understanding or appreciating how wrong it is that he ought to be regarded as irresponsible.

311. We recognize the difficulties of framing a precise formula which will not be open to objections, and we shall discuss them later in detail, but we must first consider the objections of a more general character that have been brought against any proposal to extend the M'Naghten Rules to cover cases where the accused knew what he was doing and that it was wrong, but, as a result of insanity, to borrow a phrase from common language, "he could not help doing it."

312. It is often suggested, and was suggested by some of our witnesses, that any such change in the law would lead to unjustified acquittals on the ground of insanity. We

believe that these apprehensions are largely without foundation. We should expect that the new formula would make it easier for medical witnesses to give a full and straightforward opinion on the mental condition of the accused, and that it would be reasonably interpreted by juries under wise guidance from the judges, who would emphasize that the jury must be satisfied not merely that the accused was unable to control himself (or to resist an impulse, or to prevent himself from committing the act) but that this inability was due to "insanity" or "disease of the mind." We see little reason to fear that it would be found too wide or would exempt persons suffering from lesser degrees of mental abnormality insufficient to excuse them. No doubt the question whether it was impossible, or only difficult, for the accused to control himself, or to prevent himself from committing the offense, would not always be easy for the medical witness to answer or for the jury to determine. But we agree with the British Medical Association that it would not in essence be more difficult than the question they have now to decide under the M'Naghten Rules. It is never possible, as the Association point out, "to provide scientific and conclusive proof of a complete lack of power to control conduct at the time when a crime was committed"; but the jury would have only to decide whether on a balance of probability the accused was unable to control himself, and we think that they should be capable of coming to a reasonable conclusion on this issue in the light of all the evidence.

313. Discussion of the merits of such proposals for enlarging the scope of the M'Naghten Rules to take account of the consensus of modern medical knowledge and opinion has been obscured by the long-standing controversy about the "irresistible impulse," and much of the evidence which we heard was colored by it. This is regrettable, not only because the concept of the "irresistible impulse" has been largely discredited as a result of past controversy, but because it is inherently inadequate and unsatisfactory. This is not because, as has often been suggested, it would be impossible for a jury to distinguish between an irresistible and a merely unresisted impulse. We do not think it would be impossible, though no doubt it might often be very difficult. Nor do we believe that recognition of the irresistible impulse would be

likely to lead to unjustifiable verdicts of insanity in cases of crimes prompted by anger or by normal or perverted sexual passion, provided that it was always made clear to the jury that they must be satisfied not only that there was an irresistible impulse but that the impulse was due to disease of the mind; and it must be remembered that no responsible person has ever proposed the recognition of irresistible impulse except in conjunction with insanity or mental disease. The general consensus of psychiatric opinion does not regard an aggressive psychopath or a sadist—and still less a person who is merely hot-tempered or sexually unrestrained—as suffering from insanity or mental disease; and though it might sometimes be possible to find medical witnesses prepared to express such views, their evidence would not be likely to find favor with a jury.

314. The real objection to the term "irresistible impulse" is that it is too narrow, and carries an unfortunate and misleading implication that, where a crime is committed as a result of emotional disorder due to insanity, it must have been suddenly and impulsively committed after a sharp internal conflict. In many cases, such as those of melancholia, this is not true at all. The sufferer from this disease experiences a change of mood which alters the whole of his existence. He may believe, for instance, that a future of such degradation and misery awaits both him and his family that death for all is a less dreadful alternative. Even the thought that the acts he contemplates are murder and suicide pales into insignificance in contrast with what he otherwise expects. The criminal act, in such circumstances, may be the reverse of impulsive. It may be coolly and carefully prepared; yet it is still the act of a madman. This is merely an illustration; similar states of mind are likely to lie behind the criminal act when murders are committed by persons suffering from schizophrenia or paranoid psychoses due to disease of the brain.

315. If, therefore, the M'Naghten Rules are to be extended by the addition of a third limb to meet the case of insanity affecting not the reason but the will, it is important that this should be formulated not merely in terms of inability to resist an impulse, but in wider terms, which will allow the court to take account of those cases where an insane person commits a crime after a long period of brooding and reflection or is gradually carried

toward it without any real attempt to resist this tendency.

316. In considering how this might best be done, we were attracted by the provisions of some of the Continental Penal Codes, and notably by the words of the Swiss Code, "incapable of appreciating the unlawful nature of his act or of acting in accordance with such appreciation." We think that this provision, reasonably interpreted, should enable the court to deal appropriately with any accused person who ought, as a result of any form of mental abnormality, whether permanent or transitory, to be regarded as not criminally responsible. But we have reluctantly been forced to the conclusion that, whatever the merits of such a definition, the concepts which it employs and the language in which it is expressed are rooted in a different system of law and could not satisfactorily be grafted on to rules whose purpose is to furnish an objective test for juries in this country.

317. The proposal of the British Medical Association . . . is that the M'Naghten Rules should be enlarged by adding to the existing tests the test whether the accused was laboring, as a result of disease of the mind, under "a disorder of emotion such that, while appreciating the nature and quality of the act, and that it was wrong, he did not possess sufficient power to prevent himself from committing it." No formula will be perfect or immune from criticism; but we think that some such words as these (though we should prefer to say more simply "was incapable of preventing himself") are as good as could be devised for enlarging the Rules so as to cover defect of will as well as of reason; and we therefore think it unnecessary to examine in detail the language of the numerous formulae which have been at different times propounded with the same object. We feel, however, that in the formula suggested by the Association the distinction drawn between "defect of reason" and "disorder of emotion," though it may have its place in the evidence of a medical witness or in a Judge's summing-up, is not suitable for inclusion in the formula itself. We think that the purport of the Association's formula would be adequately expressed more shortly in the following terms:

The jury must be satisfied that, at the time of committing the act, the accused, as a result of disease of the mind (or mental deficiency) (a) did not know the nature and quality of the act or (b) did not know that it was wrong or (c) was incapable of preventing himself from committing it.

318. Such an extension of the M'Naghten Rules would remove the most glaring defect of the present law, namely, that they enjoin a verdict of guilty unless certain conditions are fulfilled, and those conditions ignore one of the commonest causes of irresponsibility due to insanity. But would it remove this defect in a way that would prove in practice adequate? To examine this question it will be instructive to test the formula on the facts of a recent case of some notoriety—that of Ley ("the Chalkpit murder"), who coolly conceived and carried out an elaborate criminal plan over a period of time. There seems no doubt that he could not rightly be held responsible for his crime. The Lord Chief Justice, before whom he was tried, said in evidence before us, "I had no doubt the prisoner was insane; his whole conduct showed a typical case of paranoia." It is no less certain that he knew the nature and quality of his act and that it was wrong. If therefore he had pleaded insanity (which he refused to do), the jury would have been bound to find him guilty by the test of the M'Naghten Rules. Would decisions of this sort be avoided by adding the third question "was he incapable of preventing himself from committing it?"?

319. The answer depends on the interpretation put on the words "incapable of preventing himself." Ley, because of his insanity, lived in a twilight world of distorted values which resulted not so much in his being "incapable of preventing himself" from committing his crime, in the strict sense of those words, as in his being incapable of appreciating, as a sane man would, why he should try to prevent himself from committing it. It seems to us reasonable to argue that the words "incapable of preventing himself" should be construed so as to cover such states of mind; that they should be interpreted as meaning not merely that the accused was incapable of preventing himself if he had tried to do so, but that he was incapable of wishing or of trying to prevent himself, or incapable of realizing or attending to considerations which might have prevented him if he had been capable of realizing or attending to them. If each of Ley's acts is considered separately, it would be difficult to maintain that he could not have prevented himself from committing

them. Yet if his course of conduct is looked at as a whole, it might well be argued that, as a result of his insanity, he was incapable of preventing himself from conceiving the murderous scheme, incapable of judging it by other than an insane scale of ethical values, and, in that sense, incapable of preventing himself from carrying it out. If the addition to the M'Naghten Rules were construed in this way, it would serve its purpose well, and the Rules thus amended should cover most of the cases where a defense of insanity ought to be admitted. But they would fall very far short of the needs of the case if the courts felt bound to interpret the new rule narrowly, and it were held that a defense of insanity on the ground that the accused was incapable of preventing himself from committing the crime was bound to fail unless the jury were satisfied that he would not have refrained from committing it even if a policeman had been standing beside him. Such a construction would cover only acts committed in a state of semiconsciousness, automatism, or frenzy. In view of the rigidity with which the existing Rules are now sometimes construed, it is impossible to be sure that the broader interpretation would prevail, especially since, if the change were made by statute—as it would presumably have to be—judges might feel less free to apply them otherwise than strictly.

320. The question may well be asked whether, if the words we have suggested admit of so wide a difference of interpretation, it would not be better to remove doubt by wording the third limb in such a way as to make it clear that the wider interpretation is intended. We do not see how this could be done without destroying what is claimed to be the essential justification for the formulation of rules for the jury's guidance. That is that the jury must have simple, objective, factual questions to answer. "Did he know the nature and quality of his act?" and "Did he know that it was wrong?" are such questions. So is "Was he incapable of preventing himself?", however difficult it may be to answer. "Was he incapable of wishing or trying to prevent himself, or of realizing or attending to considerations which might have prevented him?" is not. For the Rules to formulate the question expressly in these wider terms would be tantamount to asking the jury to decide whether, on a balance of probabilities, the insanity of the accused was the effective cause

of his unlawful act. That would be no different from asking them whether he was so insane that he ought not to be regarded as responsible and abandoning the attempt to formulate rules for their guidance.

Should the M'Naghten Rules Be Abrogated?

321. This brings us to the alternative solution of dispensing with a legal formula altogether. The assumption which underlies the M'Naghten Rules, and would underlie any new criterion of criminal responsibility, is that, since insanity and irresponsibility cannot be taken as coextensive, some formula must be provided defining the relations between them. It is argued that, in the absence of some such formula, the jury have no objective standard by which to decide whether the degree of mental abnormality from which the accused suffers (whether it is insanity, mental deficiency, or some other mental disease) is such that he ought not to be held criminally responsible, and that this question cannot properly be left to their decision without some such guidance. It is therefore the function of the law to define the state or states of mind resulting from insanity which justify exemption from responsibility; and the function of the jury is limited to deciding a question of fact, namely, whether at the time of the offense the accused was in such a state of mind.

322. It seems clear from our evidence that this theory has largely broken down in practice. If the M'Naghten Rules were consistently applied, juries would be obliged to convict many persons who at the time of the offense were so insane that it would be wrong to hold them responsible. Sometimes they do, but usually such verdicts are not returned, because, unless the Judge charges them strictly in accordance with the M'Naghten Rules (and occasionally even when he does), juries exercise the discretion which the law in theory withholds from them. As stated in paragraph 293, when common sense says the verdict should be "guilty but insane" and the M'Naghten Rules say it should be "guilty," judges and juries usually recognize that common sense must prevail. And it is not only in cases where the M'Naghten criterion conflicts with common sense that it is apt to be disregarded. In many cases where a medical witness hazards the opinion that the accused

at the time of his act was not conscious that it was wrong, it is difficult to suppose that the ordinary juryman regards this point as crucial; there can be little doubt that he often addresses his mind to the essential question whether the accused was so insane that it would be unreasonable to hold him responsible for his actions. We have already referred . . . to the reply given by Lord Cooper, when he was asked whether it was not desirable to have some yardstick to guide the jury:

> I do not think so, for this reason. . . . However much you charge a jury as to the M'Naghten Rules or any other test, the question they would put to themselves when they retire is—"Is this man mad or is he not?"

We have little doubt that English juries often do the same.

323. The advantage of a new rule of law, widening the criterion laid down in the M'Naghten Rules, is that conflicts between the rule and common sense should be less frequent. But they could hardly be eliminated. Whatever the rule of law may say, and however broadly it may be interpreted, it can never be all-embracing and it must be expected that members of the jury will sometimes find that their common sense drives them to look behind the rule and to address their minds directly to the essential question of responsibility. For we are bound to recognize that it is not possible to define with any precision the state of mind which should exempt an insane person from responsibility. This opinion was emphatically expressed by Lord Blackburn as long ago as 1874.[3] He said:

> To that I can only say that on the question what amounts to insanity, that would prevent a person being punishable or not, I have read every definition which I ever could meet with, and never was satisfied with one of them, and have endeavoured in vain to make one satisfactory to myself; I verily believe that it is not in human power to do it. You must take it that in every individual case you must look at the circumstances and do the best you can to say whether it was the disease of the mind which was the cause of the crime, or the party's criminal will.

324. The gravamen of the charge against the M'Naghten Rules is that they are not in harmony with modern medical science, which, as we have seen, is reluctant to divide the mind into separate compartments—the intel-

[3] Minutes of Evidence of the Select Committee on the Homicide Law Amendment Bill, 1874, Q. 274.

lect, the emotions, and the will—but looks at it as a whole and considers that insanity distorts and impairs the action of the mind as a whole. The existing Rules, which so patently divorce the reason from other mental functions, are peculiarly open to this objection, and it would manifestly be lessened by the addition we have suggested. But the same argument applies, in varying degree, to any attempt to define responsibility in terms of impairment of any particular mental function whose sound operation is conceived to be a necessary element in criminal intent (*mens rea*). It is of course true that in an insane person the power to distinguish right from wrong, or the power of self-control, may be significantly impaired or even wholly lost, and in such a case it is right to hold a person not responsible. Yet these are abstractions from a single undivided reality—the disease of the mind as a whole. Such abstractions may often be harmless, and may sometimes serve a useful purpose, but they are all too likely to confuse the issue and to mislead those who seek to apply them. The symptoms of the disease can be classified; their effect on conduct can be described; but the state of mind itself remains indefinable. It is that state of mind to which Hamlet refers when he says "Hamlet does it not. . . . Who does it then? His madness." This indefinable state of mind has in different individuals different effects. To abstract particular mental faculties, and to lay it down that unless these particular faculties are destroyed or gravely impaired, an accused person, whatever the nature of his mental disease, must be held to be criminally responsible, is dangerous. Any rule based on such abstractions is liable to be fallible. It may be satisfactory when applied to some, perhaps to the majority, of the criminal cases which come before the courts, but it is likely that in others its application will lead to unjustifiable verdicts of "guilty."

325. On the other hand it may be said with truth that a criterion of criminal responsibility is not necessarily to be rejected because it is imperfect and cannot be guaranteed to cover every case which it ought to cover. All legal definitions necessarily involve an element of abstraction and approximation, which may make their application difficult in marginal cases and may reasonably exclude cases which ought to be included; this is inevitable, since it is precisely the function of the law to draw

clear lines for general guidance where there is no clear line in nature, and to deal with the difficulties and anomalies inherent in borderline cases by preserving a reasonable flexibility of interpretation. The rejoinder made to this argument is that, though it is valid generally, there are two reasons that make it inapplicable to the question of criminal responsibility. The first is that a criterion of criminal responsibility in relation to mental disease differs in this important respect from other legal definitions, that, if it is too narrow, it will result in the pronouncing of unjustifiable death sentences. The second is that (for reasons we shall consider more fully in the following paragraphs) a definition of the conditions of responsibility is unnecessary, and in practice only makes the issue more, rather than less, complicated and difficult for the jury.

326. In another sphere the law has already recognized that medical science can have no general definition which, when applied to all the varied types and manifestations of insanity, will enable a doctor to say "if as a result of mental disease the patient is in such or such a state of mind, he is so insane as to be irresponsible, and if he is not in such or such a state of mind, it can safely be inferred that, whatever his mental malady may be, he is not so insane as to be irresponsible for his actions." The lunacy law does not contain any definition of lunacy for the purpose of certification, or require that the magistrate, before making an order placing a lunatic under control, must find that he is in some specified state of mind. It is recognized that to lay down such a rule would be more likely to hinder than to help right decisions. The magistrate, after scrutinizing the medical certificates and making such enquiries as he may think advisable, is called on to exercise his discretion on each individual case, and to decide whether "the alleged lunatic is a lunatic and a proper person to be taken charge of and detained under care and treatment," or, where a petition is presented, whether a reception order "may properly be made."

327. To abrogate the Rules would mean abandoning the assumption that it is necessary to have a rule of law defining the relation of insanity to criminal responsibility; the jury would be left free to decide, in the light of all the evidence given in each particular case, whether the accused was by reason of mental disease (or mental deficiency) not responsible for his actions at the time of the act or omission charged. The objection most strongly urged to this course is that it would lay on the jury a difficult, indeed an impossible, task. It was said that it would require them to decide a purely medical issue beyond their capacity, and that they could not be expected to come to a sound conclusion on technical matters, of which they had no expert knowledge, and which they could not fully understand unless they were able to apply a simple test and the problem was presented to them in terms which they could appreciate and assess as ordinary men and women. We think that this objection is put too high: that it rests on a misapprehension about the nature of the issue and on too low an estimate of the capacity and common sense of juries, which in other contexts were highly praised by many witnesses. The issue, as we have pointed out, is not a purely medical one, but is essentially an ethical question, in which both medicine and the law are closely involved. Juries have shown themselves capable of deciding extremely complicated and technical issues without the aid of definitions or formulae, for example in some civil actions in respect of technical or professional negligence, and should not be incapable of deciding the issue of responsibility in cases of insanity or mental abnormality.

328. Indeed, such an addition to the existing Rules as "Was the accused at the time of the act incapable by reason of disease of the mind of preventing himself from committing it?", if interpreted in the broad way in which alone it would be useful (see paragraph 319), might not convey to members of a jury any better or clearer conception of the question they have to decide than the words "Was the accused at the time of his unlawful act insane to such a degree that he was not responsible for his actions?" It may sometimes be very difficult to decide whether the accused was insane to such a degree as not to be responsible for his actions, but in such cases it will usually be equally difficult to decide whether by reason of insanity he was "incapable of preventing himself from committing the act." The difficulties are due to the obscurity of the problem of insanity and to the limitations of present-day knowledge; and these inherent difficulties cannot be mitigated by any definition.

329. The most convincing answer to the objection that this would be too difficult a task for juries seems to us to be that they so often perform it already in cases where the application of the M'Naghten Rules would lead to a clearly wrong verdict. As Mr. Justice Frankfurter said:

I know the danger and the arguments against leaving too much discretion, but I submit with all due respect that at present the discretion is being exercised but not candidly. . . . I think probably the safest thing to do would be to do what they do in Scotland, because it is what it gets down to in the end anyhow.

If this were done, it would not be the first time in the history of English criminal law that juries, with the encouragement of judges, have found their own means of mitigating the harshness of a law that is no longer in accord with common sense or common humanity, and the law has been obliged to follow them at a distance.

330. We recognize that in capital cases pleas of insanity are often advanced on insufficient grounds; and it is important that proper measures should be taken to help the jury to come to right decisions in such cases. Witnesses have told us of the value of the M'Naghten Rules for this purpose. Because the M'Naghten definition is so narrow that it would exclude many good pleas of insanity if it were applied to them, it provides an easy and effective method of ensuring the failure of bad pleas; and it is suggested that some definition will always be essential for this purpose. This seems to us to be a highly questionable argument. If the Rules were abolished, there would of course be some risk of the jury's using their discretion wrongly in either direction, though we do not think it likely that they would send to Broadmoor scoundrels who ought to be convicted and punished. But the risk of human error is an inevitable risk which it is justifiable to take. It is a very different matter to guard against misguided leniency, by enshrining in the law a fallible definition, knowing that its fallibility may conduce to unwarranted sentences of death.

331. The strongest protection against pleas advanced on insufficient grounds is the common sense of juries; and one of the advantages claimed for dispensing with a definition, and placing on the jury express responsibility for deciding whether the accused can properly be held irresponsible, is that it would lessen any risk of jurors thinking that they have not to use their own judgment on this question, but must decide it in accordance with some legal definition.

332. It has been suggested that if there were no legal definition of criminal responsibility, the judges would find it necessary to devise one, or in particular cases to give directions to the jury as to the mental conditions which may exempt a person alleged to be insane from responsibility. But if the duty of deciding this question in the light of the facts of each case were placed squarely on the jury, the Judge, in summing up, would be free—as he was before 1843—to bring to their attention all such evidence as might tell for and against a decision that the accused was so insane as not to be responsible for his actions, and he might be helped rather than hindered by not being required to direct them that they must concentrate their attention on such points as are specified in a legal definition, to the exclusion or subordination of other points which may be of equal or greater importance for the right determination of the particular case before the court.

Conclusions

333. Our conclusions on this part of our Terms of Reference are as follows:

(i) (Mr. Fox-Andrews dissenting) that the test of responsibility laid down by the M'Naghten Rules is so defective that the law on the subject ought to be changed.

(ii) That an addition to the Rules on the lines suggested in paragraph 317 is the best that can be devised, consistently with their primary object, for improving them; and (Mr. Fox-Andrews dissenting) that it would be better to amend them in that way than to leave them as they are.

(iii) (Dame Florence Hancock, Mr. Macdonald and Mr. Radzinowicz dissenting) that a preferable amendment of the law would be to abrogate the Rules and to leave the jury to determine whether at the time of the act the accused was suffering from disease of the mind (or mental deficiency) to such a degree that he ought not to be held responsible.

(We shall also recommend . . . that, whether the M'Naghten Rules are retained, or amended, or abrogated, it should be made clear that mental deficiency no less than disease of the mind is a possible cause of irresponsibility.)

Model Penal Code*

ARTICLE 4. RESPONSIBIITY

Section 4.01. Mental Disease or Defect Excluding Responsibility

(1) A person is not responsible for criminal conduct if at the time of such conduct as a result of mental disease or defect he lacks substantial capacity either to appreciate the criminality of his conduct or to conform his conduct to the requirements of law.

(2) The terms "mental disease or defect" do not include an abnormality manifested only by repeated criminal or otherwise antisocial conduct.

Alternative formulations of paragraph (1)

(a) A person is not responsible for criminal conduct if at the time of such conduct as a result of mental disease or defect his capacity either to appreciate the criminality of his conduct or to conform his conduct to the requirements of law is so substantially impaired that he cannot justly be held responsible.

(b) A person is not responsible for criminal conduct if at the time of such conduct as a result of mental disease or defect he lacks substantial capacity to appreciate the criminality of his conduct or is in such state that the prospect of conviction and punishment cannot constitute a significant restraining influence upon him.

. . .

COMMENTS §4.01. ARTICLE 4.

RESPONSIBILITY

Section 4.01. Mental Disease or Defect Excluding Responsibility

The Problem of Defining the Criteria of Irresponsibility

1. No problem in the drafting of a penal code presents larger intrinsic difficulty than that of determining when individuals whose conduct would otherwise be criminal ought to be exculpated on the ground that they were suffering from mental disease or defect when they acted as they did. What is involved specifically is the drawing of a line between the use of public agencies and public force to condemn the offender by conviction, with resultant sanctions in which there is inescapably a punitive ingredient (however constructive we may attempt to make the process of cor-

rection) and modes of disposition in which that ingredient is absent, even though restraint may be involved. To put the matter differently, the problem is to discriminate between the cases where a punitive-correctional disposition is appropriate and those in which a medical-custodial disposition is the only kind the law should allow.

2. The traditional M'Naghten rule resolves the problem solely in regard to the capacity of the individual to know what he was doing and to know that it was wrong. Absent these minimal elements of rationality, condemnation and punishment are obviously both unjust and futile. They are unjust because the individual could not, by hypothesis, have employed reason to restrain the act; he did not and he could not know the facts essential to bring reason into play. On the same ground, they are futile. A madman who believes that he is squeezing lemons when he chokes his wife or thinks that homicide is the command of God is plainly beyond reach of the restraining influence of law; he needs restraint but condemnation is entirely meaningless and ineffective. Thus the attacks on the M'Naghten rule as an inept definition of insanity or as an arbitrary definition in terms of special symptoms are entirely misconceived. The *rationale* of the position is that these are cases in which reason can not operate and in which it is totally impossible for individuals to be deterred. Moreover, the category defined by the rule is so extreme that to the ordinary man the exculpation of the persons it encompasses bespeaks no weakness in the law. He does not identify such persons and himself; they are a world apart.

Jurisdictions in which the M'Naghten test has been expanded to include the case where mental disease produces an "irresistible impulse" proceed on the same *rationale*. They recognize, however, that cognitive factors are not the only ones that preclude inhibition; that even though cognition still obtains, mental disorder may produce a total incapacity for self-control. The same result is sometimes reached under M'Naghten proper, in the view, strongly put forth by Stephen, that "knowledge" requires more than the capacity to verbalize right answers to a question, it implies capacity to function in the light of knowledge. Stephen, *History of English Criminal Law*, Vol. 2, p. 171. . . . In modern psychiatric terms, the "fundamental difference between verbal or purely intellectual knowledge and the mysterious other kind of knowledge is familiar to every clinical psychiatrist; it is the difference between knowledge divorced from affect and knowledge so fused with affect that it becomes a human reality." Zilboorg, "Misconceptions of Legal Insanity," 9 *Am. J. Orthopsychiatry*, pp. 540, 552. . . .

3. The draft accepts the view that any effort to exclude the nondeterrables from strictly penal sanctions must take account of the impairment of volitional capacity no less than of impairment of cognition; and that this result should be achieved directly in the formulation of the test, rather than left to mitigation in the application of M'Naghten. It also accepts the criticism of the "irresistible impulse" formulation as inept in so far as it may be impliedly restricted to sudden, spontaneous acts as distinguished from insane propulsions that are accompanied by brooding or reflection. . . .

Both the main formulation recommended and alternative (a) deem the proper question on this branch of the inquiry to be whether the defendant was without capacity to conform his conduct to the requirements of law. . . .

Alternative (b) states the issue differently. Instead of asking whether the defendant had capacity to conform his conduct to the requirements of law, it asks whether, in consequence of mental disease or defect, the threat of punishment could not exercise a significant restraining influence upon him. To some extent, of course, these are the same inquiries. To the extent that they diverge, the latter asks a narrower and harder question, involving the assessment of capacity to respond to a single influence, the threat of punishment. Both Dr. Guttmacher and Dr. Overholser considered the assessment of responsiveness to this one influence too difficult for psychiatric judgment. Hence, though the issue framed by the alternative may well be thought to state the question that is most precisely relevant for legal purposes, the Reporter and the Council deemed the inquiry impolitic upon this ground. In so far as nondeterrability is the determination that is sought, it must be reached by probing general capacity to conform to the requirements of law. The validity of this conclusion is submitted, however, to the judgment of the Institute.

4. One further problem must be faced. In

addressing itself to impairment of the cognitive capacity, M'Naghten demands that impairment be complete: the actor must *not* know. So, too, the irresistible impulse criterion presupposes a complete impairment of capacity for self-control. The extremity of these conceptions is, we think, the point that poses largest difficulty to psychiatrists when called upon to aid in their administration. The schizophrenic, for example, is disoriented from reality; the disorientation is extreme; but it is rarely total. Most psychotics will respond to a command of someone in authority within the mental hospital; they thus have some capacity to conform to a norm. But this is very different from the question whether they have the capacity to conform to requirements that are not thus immediately symbolized by an attendant or policeman at the elbow. Nothing makes the inquiry into responsibility more unreal for the psychiatrist than limitation of the issue to some ultimate extreme of total incapacity, when clinical experience reveals only a graded scale with marks along the way. . . .

We think this difficulty can and must be met. The law must recognize that when there is no black and white it must content itself with different shades of gray. The draft, accordingly, does not demand *complete* impairment of capacity. It asks instead for *substantial* impairment. This is all, we think, that candid witnesses, called on to infer the nature of the situation at a time that they did not observe, can ever confidently say, even when they know that a disorder was extreme.

If substantial impairment of capacity is to suffice, there remains the question whether this alone should be the test or whether the criterion should state the principle that measures how substantial it must be. To identify the degree of impairment with precision is, of course, impossible both verbally and logically. The recommended formulation is content to rest upon the term "substantial" to support the weight of judgment; if capacity is greatly impaired, that presumably should be sufficient. Alternative (a) proposes to submit the issue squarely to the jury's sense of justice, asking expressly whether the capacity of the defendant "was so substantially impaired that he cannot justly be held responsible." Some members of the Council deemed it unwise to present questions of justice to the jury, preferring a submission that in form, at least, confines the inquiry to fact. The proponents of the alternative contend that since the jury normally will feel that it is only just to exculpate if the disorder was extreme, that otherwise conviction is demanded, it is safer to invoke the jury's sense of justice than to rest entirely on the single word "substantial," imputing no specific measure of degree. The issue is an important one and it is submitted for consideration by the Institute.

5. The draft rejects the formulation warmly supported by psychiatrists and recently adopted by the Court of Appeals for the District of Columbia in *Durham v. United States,* 214, F. 2d 862 (1954), namely, "that an accused is not criminally responsible if his unlawful act was the product of mental disease or defect." . . .

The difficulty with this formulation inheres in the ambiguity of "product." If interpreted to lead to irresponsibility unless the defendant would have engaged in the criminal conduct even if he had not suffered from the disease or defect, it is too broad: an answer that he would have done so can be given very rarely; this is intrinsic to the concept of the singleness of personality and unity of mental processes that psychiatry regards as fundamental. If interpreted to call for a standard of causality less relaxed than but-for cause, there are but two alternatives to be considered: (1) a mode of causality involving total incapacity or (2) a mode of causality which involves substantial incapacity. See Wechsler, "The Criteria of Criminal Responsibility," 22 *U. of Chi. L. Rev.* (1955), p. 367. But if either of these causal concepts is intended, the formulation ought to set it forth.

The draft also rejects the proposal of the majority of the recent Royal Commission on Capital Punishment, namely, "to leave to the jury to determine whether at the time of the act the accused was suffering from disease of the mind (or mental deficiency) to such a degree that he ought not to be held responsible." *Report* (1953), par. 333, p. 116. While we agree, as we have indicated, that mental disease or defect involves gradations of degree that should be recognized, we think the legal standard ought to focus on the *consequences* of disease or defect that have a bearing on the justice of conviction and of punishment. The Royal Commission proposal fails in this respect.

6. Paragraph (2) of section 4.01 is designed to exclude from the concept of "mental disease or defect" the case of so-called "psychopathic personality." The reason for the exclusion is that, as the Royal Commission put it, psychopathy "is a statistical abnormality; that is to say, the psychopath differs from a normal person only quantitatively or in degree, not qualitatively; and the diagnosis of psychopathic personality does not carry with it any explanation of the causes of the abnormality." While it may not be feasible to formulate a definition of "disease," there is much to be said for excluding a condition that is manifested only by the behavior phenomena that must, by hypothesis, be the result of disease for irresponsibility to be established. Although British psychiatrists have agreed, on the whole, that psychopathy should not be called "disease," there is considerable difference of opinion on the point in the United States. Yet it does not seem useful to contemplate the litigation of what is essentially a matter of terminology; nor is it right to have the legal result rest upon the resolution of a dispute of this kind.

Mental Disease*

If the defendant was insane at the time of the conduct in issue, the requisite *mens rea* was lacking and no crime was committed. Punishment presupposes normal competence and the relevant causing (authorship) of a proscribed harm; hence there can be no question of responsibility or punishment of insane persons. A psychotic harm-doer should, instead, be placed in a hospital.

The problem of mental disease and criminal responsibility has, therefore, the appearance of utter simplicity. It is merely a matter of finding out which harm-doers had a serious mental disease at the legally relevant time, and the experts in that kind of disease are psychiatrists. . . .

* Jerome Hall, *General Principles of Criminal Law,* 2d ed. (Indianapolis: The Bobbs-Merrill Company, Inc., 1960), pp. 449–71, 519–28, reprinted with the permission of the author and the publishers. Footnotes have been renumbered.

A disease is said to be an abnormal condition, and if one therefore seeks the meaning of "normal," i.e., the condition or standard by reference to which "disease" must be defined, one encounters the greatest diversity imaginable. Even in biology, where it might be thought that "health" referred to a definite standard, that conception of "normality" is a moot issue. Not only is there an enormous range in the relevant standards of different societies, but differences in vocation, social status and cultural factors also qualify the meaning of "physical health." This is further complicated by the divergence between "normality" as a standard and statistical "normality," referring to what is usual. The uncertainty of "disease" in biology is, however, restricted by the minimal norm of the functions required to survive.

But what is the norm by reference to which "mental disease" is to be determined? The criminal law answers this question in terms of ordinary rationality, especially as regards the valuation of serious personal harms. On the other hand, many psychiatrists believe that in their work they "cannot safely operate with ambiguous words and concepts, such as health and disease now are."[1]

The only point of relatively substantial agreement seems to be that it is possible and easy to recognize a mental disease which is a very great deviation from the ordinary standard of mental health in a particular culture. This implies that any intelligent person, given the facts, can recognize seriously disordered persons—the conclusion reached by a leading psychiatrist after careful study of the question. "I think," he said, "we [psychiatrists] know what the seriously ill person in a given culture is. That we do know. In this respect we agree, incidentally, with policemen, with the clerk in the drug store. Our crude diagnostic criteria are reasonably similar."[2] He finds that there are only "operational criteria" to guide psychiatrists in this regard, especially that seriously disordered persons create difficult social situations. There is an "urgency" to have them treated: "society responds to this

by legalizing removal of the seriously ill."[3] Thus, it is ordinary social judgment which determines who is psychotic, not any "medical science" that is even remotely like the knowledge used to determine that a person has tuberculosis or malaria.

This, however, does not prevent psychiatrists from having their individual, very definite ideas about "mental disease." Exactly what a psychiatrist has in mind when he uses that term in other than the above noted common meaning is one of the most difficult questions to answer. Some of them, e.g., say that all criminals are mentally diseased, while others say that only a small per cent of criminals are mentally diseased. An eminent psychiatrist has even suggested that normality is a mental disease[4] which, at least to an uninitiated reader, renders everything on the subject *bouleversé*. Thus, too, the psychiatrists on the staff of an excellent hospital, having previously agreed that psychopathy (sociopathy) was not a mental disease, changed their position and they now hold, and will testify, that it is a mental disease. The least effect of this uncertainty of expert views of "mental disease" is to dissolve the plain path leading to the apparently simple solution of an easy problem. Instead, we are plunged into the extremely complicated task of trying to establish the conditions of intelligible intercommunication among lawyers and psychiatrists.

In the course of pursuing that objective, one learns that much more than the vagueness of "mental disease" is involved. One learns, e.g., that approaches to the entire problem of crime and punishment differ vastly among psychiatrists and that there are many psychiatries, some of which are compatible with legal principles while others are diametrically opposed to them. This is the inevitable result of the fact that theories of mental disease are not restricted by psychiatrists to the cases recognizable by laymen, but are expanded by some of them to include almost every imaginable mental condition expressed in any "deviation." This, of course, involves the law of criminal responsibility and the entire structure of morality upon which that depends.

[1] Lewis, "Health as a Social Concept," 4 *Brit. J. Sociol.* (1953), p. 109. . . .
[2] F. C. Redlich, in *Interrelations Between the Social Environment and Psychiatric Disorders* (Milbank Mem. Fund, 1953), p. 120. See also, Redlich, "The Concept of Normality," 6 *Am. J. Psychotherapy* (1952), p. 551.

[3] Redlich, *id.* at p. 121.
[4] ". . . normality may be a form of madness which goes unrecognized because it happens to be a good adaptation to reality." Glover, "Medico-psychological Aspects of Normality," 23 *Brit. J. Psychol.* (1932), p. 165.

There is also a very insidious aspect of this expansion of "disease," resulting from the fact that persons who are found to have a "mental disease" on the basis of a psychiatrist's opinion can be incarcerated indefinitely. . . . Thus, on the one hand, the expansion of "mental disease" is made the basis of avoidance of criminal responsibility; while, on the other hand, a "mentally diseased" person may not only have his property taken from him, he may also be locked up indefinitely in a place called a "hospital" which, in fact, is sometimes a place of terror, more punitive than any penitentiary. This impelled a thoughtful student of the problem to suggest that ". . . any state of mind which our masters choose to call 'disease' can be treated as crime, and compulsorily cured."[5] It is, therefore, hardly self-evident that the grant of unfettered authority to psychiatrists to control the lives of human beings is more humane than control limited by the rule of law.

At the same time, in the writer's opinion, psychiatry has much to offer in the improvement of criminal law and its administration. The problem is to establish the basis on which a sound psychiatry, law, and legal science can cooperate. That this is not insuperable should be apparent if the question is viewed as essentially a problem of interdisciplinary knowledge. The principal barrier to such progress in forensic psychology is lack of understanding of the grounds on which psychiatry and law can meet. It is the purpose of this chapter to explore these grounds and then to reexamine the central questions concerning the law of criminal responsibility in the context of relevant psychiatric theories.

THE UNDERLYING ISSUES

The Conflict of Perspectives

The most important fact in the current polemics regarding psychiatry and criminal responsibility is the clash of elementary philosophical perspectives. Every science rests upon distinctive axioms or postulates that are accepted by the scientists as "given," while philosophers remain curious about them. Without describing the postulates of current psychiatry, we can perceive the general perspective that it, especially psychoanalysis,

draws from them. It purports to be rigorously scientific and therefore takes a determinist position. Its view of human nature is expressed in terms of drives and dispositions which, like mechanical forces, operate in accordance with universal laws of causation.

On the other hand, criminal law, while it is also a science in a wide sense of the term, is not a theoretical science whose sole concern is to understand and describe what goes on. It is, instead, a practical, normative science which, while it draws upon the empirical sciences, is also concerned to pass judgment on human conduct, entailing serious consequences for both individuals and the community. Its view of human nature asserts the reality of a "significant" degree of free choice, and that is incompatible with the thesis that the conduct of normal adults is merely a manifestation of imperious psychological necessity. Given the scientific purpose to understand conduct, determinism is a necessary, although by no means the only helpful, postulate. Given the additional purpose to evaluate conduct, some degree of autonomy is a necessary postulate.

Accordingly, there is no more validity in a scientific psychiatrist's criticism of the ethical perspective of the criminal law than there would be in a lawyer's criticism of the determinist perspective of theoretical science. It is not implied that psychiatrists have no business criticizing law; on the contrary, they have important contributions to offer. But whatever contribution they can and should make to criminal law will not result from the substitution of the perspective of empirical science for that of a normative one.

Unfortunately, this has often not been recognized. For example, a prominent psychiatrist denies the responsibility of any criminal since every crime is a "pathological phenomenon."[6] In explaining this position, it was said: " 'The phenomena of the will like other natural phenomena are subject to natural laws and are determined by antecedents; . . . responsibility, therefore, . . . does not exist scientifically in any case, sane or insane. . . . The scientific point of view presupposes an

[5] Lewis, "The Humanitarian Theory of Punishment," 6 *Res Judicatae* (1953), p. 229.

[6] Gregory Zilboorg, *Mind, Medicine, and Man* (New York: Harcourt, Brace, 1943), p. 282. Cf. "Man is predestined by anthropological, social, and physical causes to violate the law. . . ." Belbey, "Psychoanalysis and Crime," 4 *J. Crim. Psychopath.* (1943), pp. 639, 647.

irrevocable commitment to the concept of determinism in nature, as an article of faith.'" And he concluded: "The determinist can make no distinction between the killing of a human being through criminal violence or through toxines of a tubercle bacillus."[7] This represents the position of many psychiatrist-critics of criminal responsibility. In their view and terms, the instinctual drives, the pleasure-pain principle, the conflict between *id* and *superego,* repression and sublimation, etc., are conceived as operating in accordance with universal laws of causation.

The question thus raised concerns not only the substitution of a scientific for a normative perspective but also and beyond that, the utility of a rigorously scientific perspective in psychiatry. Many psychologists take a larger view of that discipline, one which takes account of the distinctive phenomena of decision-making, problem-solving, and evaluation; and this suggests that postulates other than that of physical science may also be fruitful in psychiatry. So, too, sociologists and other scholars present very different theories of human nature from that which dominates current scientific psychiatry. An increasingly large number of psychiatrists also express serious doubts regarding scientific psychiatry. They disagree especially with the Freudian disparagement of evaluation, e.g., Jung stresses the paramount importance of moral attitudes in a sound psychiatry.[8] Another critic writes that "Freud's causal interpretation of the analytic situation ... amounts to a denial of all personal autonomy in favor of the strictest possible determinism, that is to say, to a negation of life itself."[9]

Although Freud insisted on absolute adherence to the "scientific outlook on the world"[10] and expressed the "sharpest opposition" to the "illusion of psychic freedom,"[11] he realized that this postulate could not be employed rigorously even in diagnosis. "So

long," he wrote, "as we trace the development from its final stage backwards, the connection appears continuous. ... But if we proceed the reverse way, if we start from the premises inferred from the analysis and try to follow these up to the final result, then we no longer get the impression of an inevitable sequence of events which could not be otherwise determined. We notice at once that there might have been another result . . . ." This, however, presents the precise question of fact upon which decisions regarding legal responsibility turn, namely, the mental condition of the defendant prior to and at the time he committed the harm in issue.

Punishment

It is when they concern themselves with punishment that the psychiatrist-critics of the law disclose their philosophical predilections most definitely, making it abundantly clear that the issue is a clash of philosophies, not that of science versus common sense. The avowal of scientific indifference to responsibility and justice is forgotten, and the psychiatrist of this persuasion sallies forth as the most confident of positivists: The criminal law represents "vengeance [which] still functions but under a disguise, namely, the disguise of deterrence. . . ."[12] . . . "the time will come when stealing or murder will be thought of as a symptom, indicating the presence of a disease. . . ."[13] The corollary is that "all moral issues should be discharged from consideration . . . antisocial conduct should be considered as dispassionately as a broken leg. . . ."[14] Lombroso is hailed for his "epoch-making work," especially for his substitution of "social defense" for punishment.[15] "Dangerousness" must replace "the vague concept of the magnitude of the guilt"; it "alone should be the standard for the kind, and duration of the treatment."[16]

This view of punishment has been previously

[7] Brill, "Determinism in Psychiatry and Psychoanalysis," 95 *Am. J. Psychiatry* (1938), pp. 597, 600, 609, quoting Rosanoff.

[8] Jung gives as a specific reason for breaking with Freud his (Jung's) perception that "behind the confused deceptive intricacies of neurotic phantasies, there stands a *conflict,* which may be best described as a *moral* one." Carl G. Jung, *Analytical Psychology* (London: Baillière, Tindall, and Cox, 1916) trans. Long, p. 242.

[9] Otto Rank, *Beyond Psychology* (New York: Dover, 1941), p. 278.

[10] *Introductory Lectures on Psychoanalysis* (New York: Horace Liveright, 1920), p. 38.

[11] *Id.* at pp. 37–38.

[12] White, "The Need for Cooperation Between the Legal Profession and the Psychiatrist in Dealing with the Crime Problem," 7 *Am. J. Psychiatry* (1927), p. 502.

[13] Karl Menninger, "Medicolegal Proposals of the American Psychiatric Association," 19 *J. Cr. L. & Criminol.* (1928), p. 373.

[14] White, *supra* note 12 at p. 503.

[15] Overholser, "The Role of Psychiatry in the Administration of Criminal Justice," 93 *J.A.M.A.* (1925), pp. 830, 834.

[16] Brill, *supra* note 7 at pp. 609–10.

discussed;[17] and it need only be added, since the polemic rests upon the efficacy of treatment, that psychoanalysis has been conspicuously weak in therapy. Its position regarding the treatment of criminals is contradicted by many experts who have had experience in the administration of the criminal law. Of greater theoretical pertinence is the fact that from the viewpoint of an empirical science, punishment may be seen as emotional reaction, the vengeance of an angry group, a condition which must be included among the causal factors of behavior, and finally, as Alexander and other Freudians have emphasized,[18] as a vicarious experience which keeps a purely factual "sense of justice" in precarious equilibrium.

In the perspective of penal law, however, punishment must be interpreted consistently with a view of human nature that takes account of problem-solving and available empirical knowledge as well as of valuation. The key to this interpretation is the meaning of responsibility, which includes normal competence, authorship of a proscribed harm and accountability. In sum, punishment is a corollary of responsibility, based upon the concept of man as capable, within limits, of making free choices and putting them into effect. To do nothing to a normal adult who has killed or tortured someone or taken his property is the negation of responsibility in its social and legal significance. And a dogma that equates normal adults with helpless victims of disease is incompatible with respect for personality. On the other hand, since incarceration in a mental hospital not only entails the loss of freedom but is often extremely painful, the final result may be that punitive treatment is imposed without the benefit of, or control by, law.

The Rule of Law

The issues resulting from the conflict of philosophical perspectives, psychologies of human nature, and attitudes toward punishment must be resolved for practical as well as theoretical purposes. And the practical resolution involves another issue which also has far-ranging significance: the issue of the rule of law versus the unlimited power of officials over the lives and freedom of human beings.

We . . . confine this discussion to the instant question. The issue thus narrowed is usually stated as a conflict between the lawyer's interest in society and the doctor's concern for his patient—which can run to insistence upon complete individualization of therapy. As to this, it need only be recalled that the sovereignty of law protects even the worst type of convicted criminal from being coercively subjected to sanctions that are not prescribed by law. From a medical viewpoint, it may be absurd to release an offender at a fixed time that has no relation to his rehabilitation. But if no law fixes an upper limit, there is no protection for anyone.

The issue of the rule of law is involved in the criticism of the legal classification of defendants as either "sane" or "insane." This "black or white" business, say some psychiatrists, flies in the face of the known facts— the intermediate grays, the hardly perceptible differences forming an unbroken continuum between the ideal extremes. But a legal order, unlike the specific findings of unfettered experts, requires generalizations describing *classes* of persons, conduct, harms, and sanctions. Given such a class, it follows inexorably that any "item," e.g., a mental condition, falls within the class or it falls outside it, if only by a hair's breadth. The same holds equally for the classes of data defined in any science or discipline, and the difficulties encountered by psychiatrists in reaching agreement on a sound classification of the psychoses aptly illustrate the limitations that are inherent as well in legal systems. These limitations, as regards legal classification, could not be met by adding a class of the "partially responsible," for there would still be intermediates between the three classes. And so it would continue, no matter how many classes were provided.

Substantive penal law is constructed to determine the basic questions, who shall be subjected to the control of the state, and who shall remain free of that. The social interpretation of punishment qualifies the meaning of the relevant substantive classification—determines, that is, what kind of control shall be

---

[17] *Supra* chapter 9. E.g., in the above discussion, it was emphasized that treatment designed solely to reform is unjust if the innocent are not excluded, if it frees those who have committed major crimes or if it incarcerates for long periods those who have committed only petty transgressions. It also involves the untenable assumption that adequate empirical knowledge is available to rehabilitate or even to recognize with assurance those who can and those who cannot be reformed. . . .

[18] Franz Alexander and Hugo Staub, *The Criminal, the Judge, and the Public* (Chicago: Free Press, 1931), pp. 207–25.

exercised by the state. It assumes, therefore, that there are important differences between hospitals and prisons, even though the criminal law does not prevent wardens from using the services of psychiatrists or transferring sick inmates to hospitals or, for that matter, unfortunately, from converting hospitals into penitentiaries.

If some of the critics have ignored or misunderstood the function of legal classification and the relation of that to the rule of law, still their criticisms are not devoid of substance. It is a fact that among those who are sane and legally responsible there are appreciable degrees of mental impairment, and it is unjust to ignore that and impose uniform sentences. Within the rule of law there can and should be a substantial measure of individualization. For example, the definition of criminal conduct can be more directly guided by differences in types of offenders, social problems, and pertinent situations. Again, the disorganized mass of penal sanctions has long required thorough, systematic study. A more flexible but still legally controlled plan might be adopted, establishing sharply reduced prison terms, with added provisions for taking aggravating and mitigating circumstances into account in proper cases. Indeed, perhaps the entire initial sentencing function should be returned to the judge. The pre-sentence hearing, making use of evidence of impaired personality, motivation, and so on, could then be widely adopted. To such individualization of treatment within the rule of law, psychiatrists can make important contributions.

There is a further characteristic of the legal order that must be taken into account. The application of the principles of criminal law in a concrete situation is presently placed to a large extent in the hands of lay juries. Whether they should be replaced by experts as the triers of criminal responsibility is a separate question which will be examined shortly; but so long as we have juries performing that function, it is necessary to help the jurors understand what they are to do so that they may reach sound results. This necessitates, and is a principal function of, the "rule of law." While the law must adapt to a changing world and the increased knowledge of that world, the need for stability, certainty and predictability in the law must also be remembered.

THE EXPERT AND THE JURY

It is obvious that psychiatrists know far more about mental disease than do judges and jurors. Indeed, would anyone deny that if he were seeking knowledge about mental disease, he would consult psychiatrists rather than jurors, lawyers, and judges? Notwithstanding the obvious answer to this question, there are many reasons for not allocating the final authoritative fact-finding function to psychiatrists.

In the first place, a criminal trial, while it ought to use the best available knowledge, is not a scientific inquiry or an experiment in a clinic. For reasons which have long been persuasive, it is an adversarial investigation. The psychiatrists' work does not call upon them to decide whether their patients should or could have acted differently than they did, whether, i.e., they had the capacity to conform. But it is precisely this question which does make sense in everyday life; and it is the central issue in the trial. In many scientific inquiries a preponderance of the evidence suffices, and majority opinion among the élite prevails. In a criminal trial, because of the human values at stake, the jury must be convinced beyond any reasonable doubt, and they must be unanimous in their verdict. It is also rather widely believed that experts are prone to decide not on the evidence but "almost always on their own private opinion of the subject-matter."[19] Disagreement is frequent even among experts in well-established sciences. Disagreement among psychiatrists is to be expected; indeed, a lack of disagreement would raise doubts regarding their integrity or competence. Psychiatrists can defer their acceptance of any proffered theory or interpretation indefinitely and the thorough diagnosis of a single patient may take a year or longer; in a criminal trial definite decisions must be reached within a short time.

Moreover, the question of mental disease, viewed as a legal issue, cannot be separated from other legally material issues; hence, unless the entire body of relevant law were completely abandoned, it would still be necessary to have a jury or judge to interpret what the experts found and how that affected *mens rea* and the other issues. The criminal trial seeks

[19] J. F. Stephen, *General View of the Criminal Law of England* (London, 1863), p. 216.

to ascertain whether the accused had the normal competence to make a moral decision; many psychiatrists insist that they know nothing about this sort of question. There are also sound reasons of policy, implemented by constitutional guarantees, for the retention of trial by judge or jury; and a basic postulate in a democratic society is the avoidance of government by experts in crucial areas of law-making and adjudication.

Finally, it must also be recalled that "mental disease" is not disease in the ordinary sense, and that psychiatry cannot provide expert knowledge that a person's conduct is so far from normal as to be labeled "psychotic." In sum, the initial, apparently easy solution of the problem, i.e., simply to ask a "doctor" to diagnose a "disease," gives way, in the light of the various considerations discussed above, to the defensible conclusion that the prevailing methods of fact-finding are to be preferred.

THE STATUS OF PSYCHIATRY AMONG THE SCIENCES

We have previously discussed the scientific perspective of the psychiatry based upon a determinist cause-effect postulate (long regarded as outmoded among physicists). But a perspective is an approach; it is not a science. Nor is the "status" of a body of knowledge in the hierarchy of the sciences an arbitrary matter; there are definite criteria which determine that. Thus, it could easily be shown that psychiatry is far from being a science in a rigorous sense. A science, such as physics, has a highly systematized structure composed of empirically verified generalizations that express a covariation of variables and, most important, these empirical laws are logically interrelated, allowing deductive manipulation. Even judged by other, more lax criteria, e.g., of taxonomic sciences, psychiatry is not scientific.

Important advances have undoubtedly been made, but dissension among psychiatrists is more acute than anywhere else in psychology. . . .

Since there is better and worse psychiatry, who is to decide which is the best psychiatry as regards the soundest solution of the problems of criminal law? If many able experts, after much study, came to the above conclusions about current "scientific" psychiatry,

what is the lawyer, legislator, or judge expected to do? Is he to say that he understands psychiatry better than these expert critics, that they are mistaken in their appraisal of the present state of psychiatric knowledge? Is he to accept the claim of the psychiatrist-critics of criminal law, that their knowledge is scientific? Or is he to appraise the various theories from the viewpoint of common sense, experience, and compatibility with the psychology and ethics of the criminal law? It is submitted that the last is both valid and necessary in a democratic society.

Psychiatry is said to be superior to common-sense psychology, to have outmoded this living psychology of the thoughtful layman. This, however, apart from any comparison of specific point-by-point issues, ignores the respective perspectives and the diverse functions of the two types of psychology, i.e., the relevance of knowledge. Given the purpose to cure neurotic patients and, at the same time, construct a science, psychiatry provides relevant knowledge. By like token, given its perspective and purposes, common-sense psychology is both relevant and valid in daily life. It is not suggested that psychiatry is irrelevant to the problems of daily life. Psychiatry has already contributed very much to the common-sense psychology of intelligent laymen, and it is important in the trial of the insanity issue. But it has thus far largely been oriented to individual therapy and scientific theories, not to the type of competence and the social problems that are of particular concern in law. The present point concerns especially those elementary psychological truths that intelligent persons acquire regarding their daily decisions, appraisals, and actions. This psychology, while it may be enlightened, is not supplanted by, nor should it be supinely subordinated to, the "authoritative" tenets of a presumed scientific psychiatry. Perhaps the point can be further clarified by contrasting modern physics and common-sense perception. Physics is highly abstract and some of its findings, e.g., that matter is nonexistent or is reducible to energy, are both relevant to and significant for the high-level generalizations of physical theory. But that science does not exorcise tables and chairs from daily life or prove that the relevant common knowledge is outmoded. In the common-sense perspective, guns, broken heads, and dead bodies are very real and very meaningful. Neither physics nor psychiatry invalidates these truths.

It may be concluded that current psychiatry is far from having reached the scientific status of chemistry or biology. Neither in using expert witnesses nor in developing the legal formulas that govern the determination of socially harmful conduct should it be assumed that the psychology of modern penal law needs to give way to unassailable psychiatric authority based on relevant demonstrable truth. That psychiatry has much to offer to penal law is not disputed; but that knowledge must be carefully appraised, selected and fitted into the framework in which it can function usefully. The elements of this structure have been indicated in the above discussion: first, a view of human nature that recognizes a significant degree of free choice; second, corresponding legal principles that make punishment a corollary of responsibility; third, within this order of law, stable and workable classifications permitting consistency of treatment appropriately tempered to the needs of individual cases; fourth, effective application of these classifications through rules that can be understood and employed by the agencies of justice, the judge and the jury; and finally, a corresponding maximum use of empirical knowledge, including psychiatry that is compatible with the above requirements of the legal order.

. . .

AMENDMENT OF THE M'NAGHTEN RULES

If we set aside the philosophical implications of psychiatric science, especially regarding the ethics of criminal responsibility, and attend to what has impressed many thoughtful lawyers and psychiatrists, it is essentially this—that the M'Naghten Rules are intellectualistic, that they test only the rational function but leave untouched the volitional and the emotional facets of the personality. Unfortunately, as the above discussion shows, the issues run much deeper and are far more complicated than that, as is evident from the fact that all parties in the current polemics accept the psychological theory of the integration of the functions of personality. If that were the only issue involved, there would be no problem except that of formulating rules to implement this common viewpoint. There is, however, a very critical problem because certain psychiatrists are seeking not to implement the psychology of integration but to put an end to criminal responsibility and all that that implies. That is why they wish to terminate the test of rationality—the M'Naghten Rule—despite the fact that it stipulates an essential function of integrated personality.

It is a commonplace that a rule of law means what the courts say it means. And there is ample evidence that the vast majority of the courts take a very liberal view of the qualifications of experts, that the widest latitude is allowed psychiatrists in their testimony, and that, in effect, the M'Naghten Rules have in recent years been interpreted to include the volitional and affective aspects of the personality. Considerable testimony could be adduced in support of the opinion of experienced forensic psychiatrists that the M'Naghten Rules function very well, especially that they do not result in holding psychotic persons criminally responsible, although it is possible, of course, to find instances where trial courts have taken a restrictive view. In any event, it can hardly be expected that a rule, however formulated, will always be interpreted and applied in all courts in the best possible way.

There is a much more important point to be considered. Although it would be both interesting and important to have precise information regarding the actual functioning of the M'Naghten Rules, the fact that some courts or even that many courts interpreted them narrowly and unduly restricted the testimony of psychiatrists—assuming that this could be established—would not in the least signify that the M'Naghten Rules should be *abandoned*. Since it is agreed that such restrictive interpretation of the Rules is unwarranted, it is only necessary to give the word "know" in the Rules a wider definition so that it means the kind of knowing that is relevant, i.e., realization or appreciation of the wrongness of seriously harming a human being, as has been done by statute in Canada. The logic of reform is thus rigorously determined. There can be no question of abandoning the M'Naghten Rule of rationality but only of adding to it. As was suggested above, the word "know" in the M'Naghten Rules is the crux of the issue; and it is recognized by some critics of the Rules that a wide interpretation of that term would meet the current criticism.

In sum, a sound rule of criminal responsibility must (1) retain irrationality as a criterion of insanity; (2) be consistent with the theory of the integration of all the principal functions of personality; (3) be stated in terms that are understandable to laymen; and (4) facilitate psychiatric testimony. Accordingly, the following is suggested:

A crime is not committed by anyone who, because of a mental disease, is unable to understand what he is doing and to control his conduct at the time he commits a harm forbidden by criminal law. In deciding this question with reference to the criminal conduct with which a defendant is charged, the trier of the facts should decide (1) whether, because of mental disease, the defendant lacked the capacity to understand the nature and consequences of his conduct; and (2) whether, because of such disease, the defendant lacked the capacity to realize that it was morally wrong to commit the harm in question.

The proposed rule focuses attention upon the defendant's control of his conduct, thus taking full account of the volitional functions of personality. The emotional facet is not specified because that is significant and relevant in its effect on the volitional function or as evidence of irrationality, but the words "control his conduct" would make it easy for the expert witness to discuss the emotional result of dissociation and the like. The present allegedly restrictive word "know" gives way to the wider terms "understand" and "realize." These terms—the latter in association with the words "morally wrong"—should also facilitate interpretations that take account of the affective quality of personality. In short, the proposed rule, in conformity with the theory of integration, joins the rational and the volitional functions. Finally, it might be desirable, in instructing juries, to supplement the above rule by a longer statement, explaining in very simple terms the theory of the integration of the mental functions, preferably in relation to the facts in issue.

Since the capacity to make ordinary relevant valuations is retained in the proposed rule, it is necessary to consider the assertion that psychiatry cannot contribute to the adjudication of that issue. This assertion, it is submitted, is far from reflecting what is implied in psychiatric therapy. "Cure" implies a standard, as does the psychiatrist's painstaking effort to confront his patient with the truth about himself. Moreover, despite occasional assertions regarding the scientific rigor of psychiatry, clinical analysis consists largely of case-history and a reconstruction of the patient's experiences in terms of various theories. The essence of the principal method of diagnosis is the use of empathy, the sensitive re-living of the patient's experience. While the causal postulate and genetic explanation are employed, it is also widely recognized that such analysis would be both incomplete and inaccurate if the analyst did not attain considerable insight into the patient's scheme of values. This requires a vicarious experience of his moral conflicts and a diagnosis which, if it is meaningful, implies an ethical appraisal. The psychiatrist's purpose, as a physician, is to marshal the patient's potentialities to help him overcome his difficulties. Therapy looks to the future, and it assumes that at least some patients can assist their own recovery; and that, to a very large extent, requires them to cope with moral problems. Thus, it seems arbitrary to insist that psychiatrists can tell a jury nothing about the capacity of the defendant to appreciate the ordinary moral significance of his conduct.

Finally, insofar as it is true that some psychiatrists are not qualified to testify about such problems, it may be suggested that they have neglected the societal milieu in which mental disease occurs. . . . If more clinical psychiatrists could be persuaded to study the social environment in which mental diseases occur, they would be able to cooperate fully in the interpretation of the proposed rule, and they would also accelerate the development of forensic psychiatry. Fortunately, there are indications that many psychiatrists have recently been alerted to the pertinent issues, and they are giving increased attention to the social aspects of psychiatry, its interrelations with other disciplines, and the cogency of valuation in the study of human conduct.

The presently rudimentary character of forensic psychiatry is evident in the fact that it has hardly been noticed that the use of psychiatry in the administration of rules of law presents quite different problems than does the interrelation of psychiatry and an empirical legal discipline. The construction of interdisciplinary knowledge is also handicapped by the fact that psychiatry is based upon diverse conflicting theories and employs vague, strange words; and the day of a uniform terminology among psychiatrists, such as is found in biology, is remote. The difficulties in the way of constructing a forensic psychiatry are by no means due only to the limitations of psychiatry. They arise equally from the limitations of legal theory where it is necessary to clarify many fundamental problems, including, even, the difference between motive and *mens rea* and the exclusion of the former from the legal definition of criminal conduct.

One of the most difficult barriers to the progress of forensic psychiatry is the thesis advanced by judges and lawyers, and accepted by many psychiatrists, that criminal responsibility is a strictly legal question. In 1883, Stephen, e.g., wrote, "The question, 'What are the mental elements of responsibility?' is, and must be, a legal question."[20] And in 1923 Lord Atkin's Committee said, "much of the criticism directed from the Medical side at the M'Naghten Rules is based upon a misconception. It appears to assume that the rules contain a definition of insanity. . . ."[21] Since it is customary to emphasize the formal meaning of law, the inference is that lawyers are raising a "no trespassing" sign, that they are, in effect, saying, "insanity is a purely legal, technical matter which has nothing to do with psychiatry." But the plain fact is that psychiatry is very closely involved in the meaning of the legal tests of responsibility.

Stephen himself gave the clue to that when, after making the above quoted statement, he said, "the mental elements of responsibility . . . are knowledge that an act is wrong and power to abstain from doing it"[22]—in which statement not a single word is a legally technical one. Nonetheless, it is often asserted that the tests laid down in the M'Naghten Rules were not intended to, nor do they, specify any criteria of serious mental disease. Instead, it is said that mental disease is a psychiatric question, and that the legal question is, which mentally diseased harm-doers shall be held "insane," i.e., not legally responsible? But the facts of adjudication show that "psychosis" and "insanity" are far from being unrelated.

The definitions of "psychosis" that psychiatrists formulate in their classifications and for purposes of clinical work reflect their professional objectives. When a trial concerns the defendant's legal responsibility, certain questions are asked regarding "insanity," but they do not express peculiarly legal criteria or anything technical or arbitrary regarding the symptoms of serious mental disease. They specify characteristics of psychosis that are relevant to legally significant conduct. If those questions or tests had no foundations in fact, the testimony of psychiatrists would not be relevant to the issue of responsibility. But, of course, it is relevant; and the reason for its relevance is revealed in the application of the tests of responsibility. The facts of adjudication are that, given the case of a psychotic defendant, as determined by legally recognized methods, exculpation follows because a defensible, relevant meaning of "psychosis" is incapacity to understand the wrongness of one's extremely harmful conduct and to control oneself in that regard. Indeed, it is assumed or granted that the defendants excluded from responsibility by the M'Naghten Rules were psychotic. Does not this imply that the tests specify valid criteria of psychoses?

The triers of the facts do not first listen to the expert's testimony, decide that it signifies that the defendant was psychotic, and then later ask themselves, as an independent question, whether he was insane, knew what he was doing, and so on. On the contrary, not only are the experts asked to testify in direct relation to the terms of the tests, but every statement they make is also interpreted as telling the triers of the facts something about the accused's competence to understand and control his conduct. The inquiry proceeds upon the assumption that to have a psychosis means to be incompetent in the ways the tests designate. There is no requirement of science or language that there be only one correct or one scientific definition of "psychosis." A definition reflects a point of view and certain objectives, and all descriptive definitions, apart from an inevitable degree of vagueness, must find verification in the facts. In sum, the so-called "legal" definition of "insanity" is a *social* definition of "psychosis," relevant to the criteria of criminal responsibility. The notion has spread that "insanity" is a technical legal term because clinical psychiatrists have not been interested in the social aspects of psychiatry. Since the

[20] 2 Stephen, *A History of the Criminal Law of England* (1883), p. 183.
[21] Committee on Insanity and Crime, Report 6 (1923). So, too, Lord Hewart: "The law does not purport or presume to define insanity. That is a medical question." *Essays and Observations* (1930), p. 216. And see Wechsler, "The Criteria of Criminal Responsibility," 22 *U. Chi. L. Rev.* (1955), p. 373.
[22] 2 Stephen, *op. cit. supra* note 20.

definitions they use reflect their special clinical needs, they are bound to differ from the definitions of "psychosis" which they would propose if they studied the social incidence and meaning of mental disease.

In the present situation, the principal clue to a sound resolution of many issues concerning mental disease and criminal responsibility is that recognized by Stephen—the psychology of the integration of the functions of personality. This is the common ground upon which lawyers and psychiatrists can collaborate.

CHAPTER IX

FREE WILL

. . . only
The fool, fixed in his folly, may think
He can turn the wheel on which he turns.

T. S. ELIOT, *Murder in the Cathedral*

Man cannot be sometimes slave and sometimes free;
he is wholly and forever free or he is not free at all.

SARTRE, *Being and Nothingness*

Philosophers have a disconcerting habit of questioning familiar distinctions. No distinctions, for example, are more firmly embedded in our language than those of knowledge and belief, matter and mind. And yet, philosophers doubt whether we ever "really" know and whether matter "really" exists. It should come as no surprise, then, that some philosophers challenge the distinction between voluntary and involuntary conduct. These philosophers believe it is superficial to say that we are sometimes free and sometimes not. We are always free or we are never free.

The philosophers who deny free will, who claim that we are never "really" free, admit that choice is present in cases of voluntary conduct and absent in cases of involuntary conduct. But they argue that every choice is an event and every event is caused. What is caused is determined; and if something is determined, it cannot be other than it is. But then we are compelled to choose as we do and there is no free will. Voluntary and involuntary conduct are essentially alike. This line of argument raises at least three major questions.

There is, first, the problem of meaning. What is meant by terms such as "determinism," "free will," "cause," and "compel"? Some maintain that free will requires determinism, others that free will is incompatible with determinism. It is essential that we understand what these key terms mean before we attempt to evaluate these apparently conflicting claims. It is frequently claimed that desires cause choices and that these in turn cause us to act. Some advocates of free will, for example, claim that if a man's choice is the cause of what he does, the man is free. But in what sense of "cause" do desires cause choices and choices acts? Does "cause" mean in these cases what it means when we say that overeating causes indigestion? And in what sense of "cause" do causes compel us?

Second, is the controversy over free will one that may be resolved by collecting new information, or is it merely a dispute over words? Or is it similar to so many other philosophical disputes which are neither over facts nor over words?[1] Are psychoanalytic discoveries, for example, relevant to the philosophical controversy over free will? If the opponent of free will argues from the premise that every event has a cause, why should empirical material of any kind be relevant to his argument? Do not psychoanalytic materials simply suggest that the sphere of compelled behavior is wider than we had supposed?

Finally, of what relevance is the free will controversy to questions of responsibility? Some claim that determinism is necessary for responsibility. What is the point of holding a man responsible for an act if character does not determine what is done? Others argue that if choice is always determined, a man cannot help doing what he does and consequently moral guilt disappears. If punishment is nonetheless meted out, no one can suppose that it corresponds in any way to what a man "deserves." The helpless deserve sympathy and not punishment or blame.

Of Free Will*

We now inquire concerning free will. Under this head there are four points of inquiry: (1) Whether man has free will? (2) What is free will—a power, an act, or a habit? (3) If it is a power, is it appetitive or cognitive? (4) If it is appetitive, is it the same power as the will, or distinct?

FIRST ARTICLE
Whether Man Has Free Will?

We proceed thus to the First Article:

Objection 1. It would seem that man has not free will. For whoever has free will does what he wills. But man does not what he wills; for it is written (Rom. vii. 19): *For the good which I will I do not, but the evil which I will not, that I do.* Therefore man has not free will.

Obj. 2. Further, whoever has free will has in his power to will or not to will, to do or not to do. But this is not in man's power: for it is written (Rom. ix. 16): *It is not of him that willeth*—namely, to will—*nor of him that runneth*—namely, to run. Therefore man has not free will.

Obj. 3. Further, what is *free is cause of itself,* as the Philosopher says (*Metaph.* i. 2). Therefore what is moved by another is not

free. But God moves the will, for it is written (Prov. xxi. 1): *The heart of the king is in the hand of the Lord; whithersoever He will He shall turn it;* and (Phil. ii. 13): *It is God Who worketh in you both to will and to accomplish.* Therefore man has not free will.

Obj. 4. Further, whoever has free will is master of his own actions. But man is not master of his own actions: for it is written (Jer. x. 23): *The way of a man is not his: neither is it in a man to walk.* Therefore man has not free will.

Obj. 5. Further, the Philosopher says (*Ethic.* iii. 5): *According as each one is, such does the end seem to him.* But it is not in our power to be of one quality or another; for this comes to us from nature. Therefore it is natural to us to follow some particular end, and therefore we are not free in so doing.

On the contrary, It is written (Ecclus. xv. 14): *God made man from the beginning, and left him in the hand of his own counsel;* and the gloss adds: *That is of his free will.*

I answer that, Man has free will: otherwise counsels, exhortations, commands, prohibitions, rewards, and punishments would be in vain. In order to make this evident, we must observe that some things act without judg-

---

[1] On this topic see John Wisdom, *Other Minds* (Oxford: Basil Blackwell, 1952).

* St. Thomas Aquinas, "Of Free Will," The

Summa Theologica (London: Burns, Oates & Washbourne Ltd., 1920), IV, Question LXXXIII, 147–55, reprinted by permission of Burns & Oates Ltd., London, and Benziger Brothers, New York.

ment; as a stone moves downward; and in like manner all things which lack knowledge. And some act from judgment, but not a free judgment; as brute animals. For the sheep, seeing the wolf, judges it a thing to be shunned, from a natural and not a free judgment, because it judges, not from reason, but from natural instinct. And the same thing is to be said of any judgment of brute animals. But man acts from judgment, because by his apprehensive power he judges that something should be avoided or sought. But because this judgment, in the case of some particular act, is not from a natural instinct, but from some act of comparison in the reason, therefore he acts from free judgment and retains the power of being inclined to various things. For reason in contingent matters may follow opposite courses, as we see in dialectic syllogisms and rhetorical arguments. Now particular operations are contingent, and therefore in such matters the judgment of reason may follow opposite courses, and is not determinate to one. And forasmuch as man is rational is it necessary that man have a free will.

Reply Obj. 1. As we have said above(Q. LXXXI, A. 3, *ad 2*), the sensitive appetite, though it obeys the reason, yet in a given case can resist by desiring what the reason forbids. This is therefore the good which man does not when he wishes—namely, *not to desire against reason,* as Augustine says (*ibid.*).

Reply Obj. 2. Those words of the Apostle are not to be taken as though man does not wish or does not run of his free will, but because the free will is not sufficient thereto unless it be moved and helped by God.

Reply Obj. 3. Free will is the cause of its own movement, because by his free will man moves himself to act. But it does not of necessity belong to liberty that what is free should be the first cause of itself, as neither for one thing to be cause of another need it be the first cause. God, therefore, is the first cause, Who moves causes both natural and voluntary. And just as by moving natural causes He does not prevent their acts being natural, so by moving voluntary causes He does not deprive their actions of being voluntary: but rather is He the cause of this very thing in them; for He operates in each thing according to its own nature.

Reply Obj. 4. *Man's way* is said *not to be his* in the execution of his choice, wherein he may be impeded, whether he will or not. The

choice itself, however, is in us, but presupposes the help of God.

Reply Obj. 5. Quality in man is of two kinds: natural and adventitious. Now the natural quality may be in the intellectual part, or in the body and its powers. From the very fact, therefore, that man is such by virtue of a natural quality which is in the intellectual part, he naturally desires his last end, which is happiness. Which desire, indeed, is a natural desire, and is not subject to free will, as is clear from what we have said above (Q. LXXXII, AA. 1, 2). But on the part of the body and its powers man may be such by virtue of a natural quality, inasmuch as he is of such a temperament or disposition due to any impression whatever produced by corporeal causes, which cannot affect the intellectual part, since it is not the act of a corporeal organ. And such as a man is by virtue of a corporeal quality, such also does his end seem to him, because from such a disposition a man is inclined to choose or reject something. But these inclinations are subject to the judgment of reason, which the lower appetite obeys, as we have said (Q. LXXXI, A. 3). Wherefore this is in no way prejudicial to free will.

The adventitious qualities are habits and passions, by virtue of which a man is inclined to one thing rather than to another. And yet even these inclinations are subject to the judgment of reason. Such qualities, too, are subject to reason, as it is in our power either to acquire them, whether by causing them or disposing ourselves to them, or to reject them. And so there is nothing in this that is repugnant to free will.

SECOND ARTICLE

Whether Free Will Is a Power?

We proceed thus to the Second Article:

Objection 1. It would seem that free will is not a power. For free will is nothing but a free judgment. But judgment denominates an act, not a power. Therefore free will is not a power.

Obj. 2. Further, free will is defined as *the faculty of the will and reason.* But faculty denominates a facility of power, which is due to a habit. Therefore free will is a habit. Moreover Bernard says (*De Gratia et Lib., Arb.* 1, 2) that free will is *the soul's habit of disposing of itself.* Therefore it is not a power.

Obj. 3. Further, no natural power is forfeited through sin. But free will is forfeited through sin; for Augustine says that *man, by abusing free will, loses both it and himself.* Therefore free will is not a power.

On the contrary, Nothing but a power, seemingly, is the subject of a habit. But free will is the subject of grace, by the help of which it chooses what is good. Therefore free will is a power.

I answer that, Although free will[1] in its strict sense denotes an act, in the common manner of speaking we call free will, that which is the principle of the act by which man judges freely. Now in us the principle of an act is both power and habit; for we say that we know something both by knowledge and by the intellectual power. Therefore free will must be either a power or a habit, or a power with a habit. That it is neither a habit nor a power together with a habit can be clearly proved in two ways. First of all, because, if it is a habit, it must be a natural habit; for it is natural to man to have a free will. But there is no natural habit in us with respect to those things which come under free will: for we are naturally inclined to those things of which we have natural habits—for instance, to assent to first principles: while those things to which we are naturally inclined are not subject to free will, as we have said of the desire of happiness (Q. LXXXII, AA. 1, 2). Wherefore it is against the very notion of free will that it should be a natural habit. And that it should be a non-natural habit is against its nature. Therefore in no sense is it a habit.

Secondly, this is clear because habits are defined as that *by reason of which we are well- or ill-disposed with regard to actions and passions (Ethic.* ii. 5) ; for by temperance we are well-disposed as regards concupiscences, and by intemperance ill-disposed : and by knowledge we are well-disposed to the act of the intellect when we know the truth, and by the contrary habit ill-disposed. But the free will is indifferent to good or evil choice : wherefore it is impossible for free will to be a habit. Therefore it is a power.

Reply Obj. 1. It is not unusual for a power to be named from its act. And so from this act, which is a free judgment, is named the power which is the principle of this act. Otherwise, if free will denominated an act, it would not always remain in man.

Reply Obj. 2. Faculty sometimes denomi-

[1] Liberum arbitrium—i.e., free judgment.

nates a power ready for operation, and in this sense faculty is used in the definition of free will. But Bernard takes habit, not as divided against power, but as signifying a certain aptitude by which a man has some sort of relation to an act. And this may be both by a power and by a habit : for by a power man is, as it were, empowered to do the action, and by the habit he is apt to act well or ill.

Reply Obj. 3. Man is said to have lost free will by falling into sin, not as to natural liberty, which is freedom from coercion, but as regards freedom from fault and unhappiness. Of this we shall treat later in the treatise on Morals in the second part of this work (I.-II. Q. LXXXV, *seqq.*; Q. CIX.).

THIRD ARTICLE

Whether Free Will Is an Appetitive Power?

We proceed thus to the Third Article:

Objection 1. It would seem that free will is not an appetitive, but a cognitive power. For Damascene (*De Fid. Orth.* ii. 27) says that *free will straightway accompanies the rational nature.* But reason is a cognitive power. Therefore free will is a cognitive power.

Obj. 2. Further, free will is so called as though it were a free judgment. But to judge is an act of a cognitive power. Therefore free will is a cognitive power.

Obj. 3. Further, the principal function of the free will is to choose. But choice seems to belong to knowledge, because it implies a certain comparison of one thing to another, which belongs to the cognitive power. Therefore free will is a cognitive power.

On the contrary, The Philosopher says (*Ethic.* iii. 3) that choice is *the desire of those things which are in us.* But desire is an act of the appetitive power : therefore choice is also. But free will is that by which we choose. Therefore free will is an appetitive power.

I answer that, The proper act of free will is choice: for we say that we have a free will because we can take one thing while refusing another; and this is to choose. Therefore we must consider the nature of free will, by considering the nature of choice. Now two things concur in choice: one on the part of the cognitive power, the other on the part of the appetitive power. On the part of the cognitive power, counsel is required, by which we judge one thing to be preferred to another : and on the part of the appetitive power, it is required that the appetite should accept the judgment of counsel. Therefore Aristotle (*Ethic.* vi. 2) leaves it in doubt whether choice belongs principally to the appetitive or the cognitive power: since he says that choice is either *an appetitive intellect or an intellectual appetite.* But (*Ethic.* iii, *loc. cit.*) he inclines to its being an intellectual appetite when he describes choice as *a desire proceeding from counsel.* And the reason of this is because the proper object of choice is the means to the end: and this, as such, is in the nature of that good which is called useful: wherefore since good, as such, is the object of the appetite, it follows that choice is principally an act of the appetitive power. And thus free will is an appetitive power.

Reply Obj. 1. The appetitive powers accompany the apprehensive, and in this sense Damascene says that free will straightway accompanies the rational power.

Reply Obj. 2. Judgment, as it were, concludes and terminates counsel. Now counsel is terminated, first, by the judgment of reason; secondly, by the acceptation of the appetite: whence the Philosopher (*Ethic.* iii, *ibid.*) says that, *having formed a judgment by counsel, we desire in accordance with that counsel.* And in this sense choice itself is a judgment from which free will takes its name.

Reply Obj. 3. This comparison which is implied in the choice belongs to the preceding counsel, which is an act of reason. For though the appetite does not make comparisons, yet forasmuch as it is moved by the apprehensive power which does compare, it has some likeness of comparison by choosing one in preference to another.

FOURTH ARTICLE

Whether Free Will Is a Power Distinct from the Will?

We proceed thus to the Fourth Article:

Objection 1. It would seem that free will is a power distinct from the will. For Damascene says (*De Fid. Orth.* ii. 22) that Θέλησις is one thing and βούλησις another. But Θέλησις is the will, while βούλησις seems to be the free will, because βούλησις, according to him, is the will as concerning an object by way of comparison between two things. Therefore it seems that free will is a distinct power from the will.

Obj. 2. Further, powers are known by their acts. But choice, which is the act of free will, is distinct from the act of willing, because *the act of the will regards the end, whereas choice regards the means to the end* (*Ethic.* iii. 2). Therefore free will is a distinct power from the will.

Obj. 3. Further, the will is the intellectual appetite. But in the intellect there are two powers—the active and the passive. Therefore, also on the part of the intellectual appetite, there must be another power besides the will. And this, seemingly, can only be free will. Therefore free will is a distinct power from the will.

On the contrary, Damascene says (*De Fid. Orth.* iii. 14) free will is nothing else than the will.

I answer that, The appetitive powers must be proportionate to the apprehensive powers, as we have said above (Q. LXIV, A. 2). Now, as on the part of the intellectual apprehension we have intellect and reason, so on the part of the intellectual appetite we have will, and free will which is nothing else but the power of choice. And this is clear from their relations to their respective objects and acts. For the act of *understanding* implies the simple acceptation of something; whence we say that we understand first principles, which are known of themselves without any comparison. But to *reason,* properly speaking, is to come from one thing to the knowledge of another: wherefore, properly speaking, we reason about conclusions, which are known from the principles. In like manner on the part of the appetite to *will* implies the simple appetite for something: wherefore the will is said to regard the end, which is desired for itself. But to *choose* is to desire something for the sake of obtaining something else: wherefore, properly speaking, it regards the means to the end. Now, in matters of knowledge, the principles are related to the conclusion to which we assent on account of the principles: just as, in appetitive matters, the end is related to the means, which is desired on account of the end. Wherefore it is evident that as the intellect is to reason, so is the will to the power of choice, which is free will. But it has been shown above (Q. LXXIX, A. 8) that it belongs to the same power both to understand and to reason, even as it belongs to the same power to be at rest and to be in movement. Wherefore it belongs also to the same power to will and to choose: and on this account the will and the free will are not two powers, but one.

Reply Obj. 1. βούλησις is distinct from Θέλησις on account of a distinction, not of powers, but of acts.

Reply Obj. 2. Choice and will—that is, the act of willing—are different acts: yet they belong to the same power, as also to understand and to reason, as we have said.

Reply Obj. 3. The intellect is compared to the will as moving the will. And therefore there is no need to distinguish in the will an active and a passive will.

Of Liberty and Necessity*

PART I

It might reasonably be expected, in questions which have been canvassed and disputed with great eagerness since the first origin of science and philosophy, that the meaning of all the terms, at least, should have been agreed upon among the disputants, and our inquiries, in the course of two thousand years, been able to pass from words to the true and real subject of the controversy. For how easy may it seem to give exact definitions of the terms employed in reasoning, and make these definitions, not the mere sound of words, the object of future scrutiny and examination? But if we consider the matter more narrowly, we shall be apt to draw a quite opposite conclusion. From this circumstance alone, that a controversy has been long kept on foot and remains still undecided, we may presume that there is some ambiguity in the expression, and that the disputants affix different ideas to the terms employed in the controversy. For as the faculties of the mind are supposed to be naturally alike in every individual—otherwise nothing could be more fruitless than to reason or dispute together—it were impossible, if men affix the same ideas to their terms, that they could so long form different opinions of the same subject, especially when they communicate their views and each party turn themselves on all sides in search of arguments which may give them the victory over their antagonists. It is true, if men attempt the discussion of questions which lie entirely beyond the reach of human capacity, such as those concerning the origin of worlds or the economy of the intellectual system or region of spirits, they may long beat the air in their fruitless contests and never arrive at any determinate conclusion. But if the question regard any subject of common life and experience, nothing, one would think, could preserve the dispute so long undecided, but some ambiguous expressions which keep the antagonists still at a distance and hinder them from grappling with each other.

This has been the case in the long-disputed question concerning liberty and necessity, and to so remarkable a degree that, if I be not much mistaken, we shall find that all mankind, both learned and ignorant, have always been of the same opinion with regard to this subject, and that a few intelligible definitions would immediately have put an end to the whole controversy. I own that this dispute has been so much canvassed on all hands, and has led philosophers into such a labyrinth of obscure sophistry, that it is no wonder if a sensible reader indulge his ease so far as to turn a deaf ear to the proposal of such a question from which he can expect neither instruction nor entertainment. But the state of the argument here proposed may, perhaps, serve to renew his attention, as it has more novelty, promises at least some decision of the controversy, and will not much disturb his ease by any intricate or obscure reasoning.

I hope, therefore, to make it appear that all men have ever agreed in the doctrine both of necessity and of liberty, according to any reasonable sense which can be put on these terms, and that the whole controversy has hitherto turned merely upon words. We shall begin with examining the doctrine of necessity.

It is universally allowed that matter, in all its operations, is actuated by a necessary force, and that every natural effect is so precisely determined by the energy of its cause that no other effect, in such particular circumstances, could possibly have resulted from it. The degree and direction of every motion is, by the laws of nature, prescribed with such

* David Hume, "Of Liberty and Necessity," *Enquiry Concerning the Human Understanding* (Oxford: Clarendon Press, 1902), pp. 80–103.

exactness that a living creature may as soon arise from the shock of two bodies, as motion, in any other degree or direction than what is actually produced by it. Would we, therefore, form a just and precise idea of *necessity,* we must consider whence that idea arises when we apply it to the operation of bodies.

It seems evident that, if all the scenes of nature were continually shifted in such a manner that no two events bore any resemblance to each other, but every object was entirely new, without any similitude to whatever had been seen before, we should never, in that case, have attained the least idea of necessity or of a connection among these objects. We might say, upon such a supposition, that one object or event has followed another, not that one was produced by the other. The relation of cause and effect must be utterly unkown to mankind. Inference and reasoning concerning the operations of nature would, from that moment, be at an end; and the memory and senses remain the only canals by which the knowledge of any real existence could possibly have access to the mind. Our idea, therefore, of necessity and causation arises entirely from the uniformity observable in the operations of nature, where similar objects are constantly conjoined together, and the mind is determined by custom to infer the one from the appearance of the other. These two circumstances form the whole of that necessity which we ascribe to matter. Beyond the constant *conjunction* of similar objects and the consequent *inference* from one to the other, we have no notion of any necessity of connection.

If it appear, therefore, that all mankind have ever allowed, without any doubt or hesitation, that these two circumstances take place in the voluntary actions of men and in the operations of mind, it must follow that all mankind have ever agreed in the doctrine of necessity, and that they have hitherto disputed merely for not understanding each other.

As to the first circumstance, the constant and regular conjunction of similar events, we may possibly satisfy ourselves by the following considerations. It is universally acknowledged that there is a great uniformity among the actions of men, in all nations and ages, and that human nature remains still the same in its principles and operations. The same motives always produce the same actions; the same events follow from the same causes. Ambition, avarice, self-love, vanity, friendship, generosity, public spirit—these passions, mixed in various degrees and distributed through society, have been, from the beginning of the world, and still are, the source of all the actions and enterprises which have ever been observed among mankind. Would you know the sentiments, inclinations, and course of life of the Greeks and Romans? Study well the temper and actions of the French and English: you cannot be much mistaken in transferring to the former *most* of the observations which you have made with regard to the latter. Mankind are so much the same, in all times and places, that history informs us of nothing new or strange in this particular. Its chief use is only to discover the constant and universal principles of human nature by showing men in all varieties of circumstances and situations, and furnishing us with materials from which we may form our observations and become acquainted with the regular springs of human action and behavior. These records of wars, intrigues, factions, and revolutions are so many collections of experiments by which the politician or moral philosopher fixes the principles of his science, in the same manner as the physician or natural philosopher becomes acquainted with the nature of plants, minerals, and other external objects, by the experiments which he forms concerning them. Nor are the earth, water, and other elements examined by Aristotle and Hippocrates more like to those which at present lie under our observation than the men described by Polybius and Tacitus are to those who now govern the world.

Should a traveler, returning from a far country, bring us an account of men wholly different from any with whom we were ever acquainted, men who were entirely divested of avarice, ambition, or revenge, who knew no pleasure but friendship, generosity, and public spirit, we should immediately, from these circumstances, detect the falsehood and prove him a liar with the same certainty as if he had stuffed his narration with stories of centaurs and dragons, miracles and prodigies. And if we would explode any forgery in history, we cannot make use of a more convincing argument than to prove that the actions ascribed to any person are directly contrary to the course of nature, and that no human motives, in such circumstances, could ever induce him to such a conduct. The veracity of Quintus Curtius is as much to be suspected when he describes the supernatural courage of Alexander by which he was hurried on singly to attack multitudes, as when he describes his supernatural force and activity by which he was able to resist them. So readily and universally do we acknowledge a uniformity in human motives and actions as well as in the operations of body.

Hence, likewise, the benefit of that experience acquired by long life and a variety of business and company, in order to instruct us in the principles of human nature and regulate our future conduct as well as speculation. By means of this guide we mount up to the knowledge of men's inclinations and motives from their actions, expressions, and even gestures, and again descend to the interpretation of their actions from our knowledge of their motives and inclinations. The general observations, treasured up by a course of experience, give us the clue of human nature and teach us to unravel all its intricacies. Pretexts and appearances no longer deceive us. Public declarations pass for the specious coloring of a cause. And though virtue and honor be allowed their proper weight and authority, that perfect disinterestedness, so often pretended to, is never expected in multitudes and parties, seldom in their leaders, and scarcely even in individuals of any rank or station. But were there no uniformity in human actions, and were every experiment which we could form of this kind irregular and anomalous, it were impossible to collect any general observations concerning mankind, and no experience, however accurately digested by reflection, would ever serve to any purpose. Why is the aged husbandman more skillful in his calling than the young beginner, but because there is a certain uniformity in the operation of the sun, rain, and earth toward the production of vegetables, and experience teaches the old practitioner the rules by which this operation is governed and directed?

We must not, however, expect that this uniformity of human actions should be carried to such a length as that all men, in the same circumstances, will always act precisely in the same manner, without making any allowance for the diversity of characters, prejudices, and opinions. Such a uniformity, in every particular, is found in no part of nature. On the contrary, from observing the variety of conduct in different men we are enabled to form a greater variety of maxims which still suppose a degree of uniformity and regularity.

Are the manners of men different in different ages and countries? We learn thence the great force of custom and education, which mold the human mind from its infancy and form it into a fixed and established character. Is the behavior and conduct of the one sex very unlike that of the other? It is thence we become acquainted with the different characters which nature has impressed upon the sexes, and which she preserves with constancy and regularity. Are the actions of the same person much diversified in the different periods of his life from infancy to old age? This affords room for many general observations concerning the gradual change of our sentiments and inclinations, and the different maxims which prevail in the different ages of human creatures. Even the characters which are peculiar to each individual have a uniformity in their influence, otherwise our acquaintance with the persons, and our observations of their conduct, could never teach us their dispositions or serve to direct our behavior with regard to them.

I grant it possible to find some actions which seem to have no regular connection with any known motives and are exceptions to all the measures of conduct which have ever been established for the government of men. But if we could willingly know what judgment should be formed of such irregular and extraordinary actions, we may consider the sentiments commonly entertained with regard to those irregular events which appear in the course of nature and the operations of external objects. All causes are not conjoined to their usual effects with like uniformity. An artificer who handles only dead matter may be disappointed of his aim, as well as the politician who directs the conduct of sensible and intelligent agents.

The vulgar, who take things according to their first appearance, attribute the uncertainty of events to such an uncertainty in the causes as makes the latter often fail of their usual influence, though they meet with no impediment in their operation. But philosophers, observing that almost in every part of nature there is contained a vast variety of springs and principles which are hid by reason of their minuteness or remoteness, find that it is at least possible the contrariety of events may not proceed from any contingency in the cause but from the secret operation of contrary causes. This possibility is converted into certainty by further observation, when they remark that, upon an exact scrutiny, a contrariety of effects always betrays a contrariety of causes and proceeds from their mutual opposition. A peasant can give no better reason for the stopping of any clock or watch than to say that it does not commonly go right. But an artist easily perceives that the same force in the spring or pendulum has always the same influence on the wheels, but fails of its usual effect perhaps by reason of a grain of dust which puts a stop to the whole movement. From the observation of several parallel instances philosophers form a maxim that the connection between all causes and effects is equally necessary, and that its seeming uncertainty in some instances proceeds from the secret opposition of contrary causes.

Thus, for instance, in the human body, when the usual symptoms of health or sickness disappoint our expectation, when medicines operate not with their wonted powers, when irregular events follow from any particular cause, the philosopher and physician are not surprised at the matter, nor are ever tempted to deny, in general, the necessity and uniformity of those principles by which the animal economy is conducted. They know that a human body is a mighty complicated machine, that many secret powers lurk in it which are altogether beyond our comprehension, that to us it must often appear very uncertain in its operations, and that, therefore, the irregular events which outwardly discover themselves can be no proof that the laws of nature are not observed with the greatest regularity in its internal operations and government.

The philosopher, if he be consistent, must apply the same reasonings to the actions and volitions of intelligent agents. The most irregular and unexpected resolutions of men may frequently be accounted for by those who know every particular circumstance of their character and situation. A person of an obliging disposition gives a peevish answer; but he has the toothache, or has not dined. A stupid fellow discovers an uncommon alacrity in his carriage; but he has met with a sudden piece of good fortune. Or even when an action, as sometimes happens, cannot be particularly accounted for, either by the person himself or by others, we know, in general, that the char-

acters of men are to a certain degree inconstant and irregular. This is, in a manner, the constant character of human nature, though it be applicable, in a more particular manner, to some persons who have no fixed rule for their conduct, but proceed in a continual course of caprice and inconstancy. The internal principles and motives may operate in a uniform manner, notwithstanding these seeming irregularities—in the same manner as the winds, rains, clouds, and other variations of the weather are supposed to be governed by steady principles, though not easily discoverable by human sagacity and inquiry.

Thus it appears not only that the conjunction between motives and voluntary actions is as regular and uniform as that between the cause and effect in any part of nature, but also that this regular conjunction has been universally acknowledged among mankind and has never been the subject of dispute either in philosophy or common life. Now, as it is from past experience that we draw all inferences concerning the future, and as we conclude that objects will always be conjoined together which we find to have always been conjoined, it may seem superfluous to prove that this experienced uniformity in human actions is a source whence we draw *inferences* concerning them. But in order to throw the argument into a greater variety of lights, we shall also insist, though briefly, on this latter topic.

The mutual dependence of men is so great in all societies that scarce any human action is entirely complete in itself or is performed without some reference to the actions of others, which are requisite to make it answer fully the intention of the agent. The poorest artificer who labors alone expects at least the protection of the magistrate to insure him the enjoyment of the fruits of his labor. He also expects that when he carries his goods to market and offers them at a reasonable price, he shall find purchasers and shall be able, by the money he acquires, to engage others to supply him with those commodities which are requisite for his subsistence. In proportion as men extend their dealings and render their intercourse with others more complicated, they always comprehend in their schemes of life a greater variety of voluntary actions which they expect, from the proper motives, to cooperate with their own. In all these conclusions they take their measures from past experience, in the same manner as in their reasonings concerning external objects, and firmly believe that men, as well as all the elements, are to continue in their operations the same that they have ever found them. A manufacturer reckons upon the labor of his servants for the execution of any work as much as upon the tools which he employs, and would be equally surprised were his expectations disappointed. In short, this experimental inference and reasoning concerning the actions of others enters so much into human life that no man, while awake, is ever a moment without employing it. Have we not reason, therefore, to affirm that all mankind have always agreed in the doctrine of necessity, according to the foregoing definition and explication of it?

Nor have philosophers ever entertained a different opinion from the people in this particular. For, not to mention that almost every action of their life supposes that opinion, there are even few of the speculative parts of learning to which it is not essential. What would become of *history* had we not a dependence on the veracity of the historian according to the experience which we have had of mankind? How could *politics* be a science if laws and forms of government had not a uniform influence upon society? Where would be the foundation of *morals* if particular characters had no certain or determinate power to produce particular sentiments, and if these sentiments had no constant operation on actions? And with what pretense could we employ our *criticism* upon any poet or polite author if we could not pronounce the conduct and sentiments of his actors either natural or unnatural to such characters and in such circumstances? It seems almost impossible, therefore, to engage either in science or action of any kind without acknowledging the doctrine of necessity, and this *inference* from motives to voluntary action, from characters to conduct.

And, indeed, when we consider how aptly *natural* and *moral* evidence link together and form only one chain of argument, we shall make no scruple to allow that they are of the same nature and derived from the same principles. A prisoner who has neither money nor interest discovers the impossibility of his escape as well when he considers the obstinacy of the jailer as the walls and bars with which he is surrounded, and in all attempts for his freedom chooses rather to work upon the stone

and iron of the one than upon the inflexible nature of the other. The same prisoner, when conducted to the scaffold, foresees his death as certainly from the constancy and fidelity of his guards as from the operation of the ax or wheel. His mind runs along a certain train of ideas: the refusal of the soldiers to consent to his escape; the action of the executioner; the separation of the head and body; bleeding, convulsive motions, and death. Here is a connected chain of natural causes and voluntary actions, but the mind feels no difference between them in passing from one link to another, nor is less certain of the future event than if it were connected with the objects present to the memory or senses by a train of causes cemented together by what we are pleased to call a "physical" necessity. The same experienced union has the same effect on the mind, whether the united objects be motives, volition, and actions, or figure and motion. We may change the names of things, but their nature and their operation on the understanding never change.

Were a man whom I know to be honest and opulent, and with whom I lived in intimate friendship, to come into my house, where I am surrounded with my servants, I rest assured that he is not to stab me before he leaves it in order to rob me of my silver standish; and I no more suspect this event than the falling of the house itself, which is new and solidly built and founded. *But he may have been seized with a sudden and unknown frenzy.* So may a sudden earthquake arise, and shake and tumble my house about my ears. I shall, therefore, change the suppositions. I shall say that I know with certainty that he is not to put his hand into the fire and hold it there till it be consumed. And this event I think I can foretell with the same assurance as that, if he throw himself out of the window and meet with no obstruction, he will not remain a moment suspended in the air. No suspicion of an unknown frenzy can give the least possibility to the former event which is so contrary to all the known principles of human nature. A man who at noon leaves his purse full of gold on the pavement at Charing Cross may as well expect that it will fly away like a feather as that he will find it untouched an hour after. Above one-half of human reasonings contain inferences of a similar nature, attended with more or less degrees of certainty, proportioned to our experience of the usual conduct of mankind in such particular situations.

I have frequently considered what could possibly be the reason why all mankind, though they have ever, without hesitation, acknowledged the doctrine of necessity in their whole practice and reasoning, have yet discovered such a reluctance to acknowledge it in words, and have rather shown a propensity, in all ages, to profess the contrary opinion. The matter, I think, may be accounted for after the following manner. If we examine the operations of body and the production of effects from their causes, we shall find that all our faculties can never carry us further in our knowledge of this relation than barely to observe that particular objects are *constantly conjoined* together, and that the mind is carried, by a *customary transition,* from the appearance of the one to the belief of the other. But though this conclusion concerning human ignorance be the result of the strictest scrutiny of this subject, men still entertain a strong propensity to believe that they penetrate further into the powers of nature and perceive something like a necessary connection between the cause and the effect. When, again, they turn their reflections toward the operations of their own minds and *feel* no such connection of the motive and the action, they are thence apt to suppose that there is a difference between the effects which result from material force and those which arise from thought and intelligence. But being once convinced that we know nothing further of causation of any kind than merely the *constant conjunction* of objects and the consequent *inference* of the mind from one to another, and finding that these two circumstances are universally allowed to have place in voluntary actions, we may be more easily led to own the same necessity common to all causes. And though this reasoning may contradict the systems of many philosophers in ascribing necessity to the determinations of the will, we shall find, upon reflection, that they dissent from it in words only, not in their real sentiments. Necessity, according to the sense in which it is here taken, has never yet been rejected, nor can ever, I think, be rejected by any philosopher. It may only, perhaps, be pretended that the mind can perceive in the operations of matter some further connection between the cause and effect, and a connection that has not place in the voluntary actions of intelligent beings. Now, whether it be so or not can only appear upon examination, and it is incumbent on these philosophers to make good their assertion by defining or describing that necessity and pointing it out to us in the operations of material causes.

It would seem, indeed, that men begin at the wrong end of this question concerning liberty and necessity when they enter upon it by examining the faculties of the soul, the influence of the understanding, and the operations of the will. Let them first discuss a more simple question, namely, the question of body and brute unintelligent matter, and try whether they can there form any idea of causation and necessity, except that of a constant conjunction of objects and subsequent inference of the mind from one to another. If these circumstances form, in reality, the whole of that necessity which we conceive in matter, and if these circumstances be also universally acknowledged to take place in the operations of the mind, the dispute is at an end; at least, must be owned to be thenceforth merely verbal. But as long as we will rashly suppose that we have some further idea of necessity and causation in the operations of external objects, at the same time that we can find nothing further in the voluntary actions of the mind, there is no possibility of bringing the question to any determinate issue while we proceed upon so erroneous a supposition. The only method of undeceiving us is to mount up higher, to examine the narrow extent of science when applied to material causes, and to convince ourselves that all we know of them is the constant conjunction and inference above mentioned. We may, perhaps, find that it is with difficulty we are induced to fix such narrow limits to human understanding, but we can afterward find no difficulty when we come to apply this doctrine to the actions of the will. For as it is evident that these have a regular conjunction with motives and circumstances and character, and as we always draw inferences from one to the other, we must be obliged to acknowledge in words that necessity which we have already avowed in every deliberation of our lives and in every step of our conduct and behavior.[1]

But to proceed in this reconciling project

[1] The prevalence of the doctrine of liberty may be accounted for from another cause, viz., a false sensation, or seeming experience, which we have, or may have, of liberty or indifference in many of our actions. The necessity of any action, whether of matter or of

with regard to the question of liberty and necessity—the most contentious question of metaphysics, the most contentious science— it will not require many words to prove that all mankind have ever agreed in the doctrine of liberty as well as in that of necessity, and that the whole dispute, in this respect also, has been hitherto merely verbal. For what is meant by liberty when applied to voluntary actions? We cannot surely mean that actions have so little connection with motives, inclinations, and circumstances that one does not follow with a certain degree of uniformity from the other, and that one affords no inference by which we can conclude the existence of the other. For these are plain and acknowledged matters of fact. By liberty, then, we can only mean *a power of acting or not acting according to the determinations of the will;* that is, if we choose to remain at rest, we may; if we choose to move, we also may. Now this hypothetical liberty is universally allowed to belong to everyone who is not a prisoner and in chains. Here then is no subject of dispute.

Whatever definition we may give of liberty,

---

mind, is not, properly speaking, a quality in the agent but in any thinking or intelligent being who may consider the action; and it consists chiefly in the determination of his thoughts to infer the existence of that action from some preceding objects; as liberty, when opposed to necessity, is nothing but the want of that determination, and a certain looseness or indifference which we feel in passing, or not passing, from the idea of one object to that of any succeeding one. Now we may observe that though, in *reflecting* on human actions, we seldom feel such a looseness or indifference, but are commonly able to infer them with considerable certainty from their motives, and from the disposition of the agent; yet it frequently happens that, in *performing* the actions themselves, we are sensible of something like it; and as all resembling objects are readily taken for each other, this has been employed as a demonstrative and even intuitive proof of human liberty. We feel that our actions are subject to our will on most occasions, and imagine we feel that the will itself is subject to nothing, because, when by a denial of it we are provoked to try, we feel that it moves easily every way, and produces an image of itself (or a "velleity," as it is called in the schools), even on that side on which it did not settle. This image, or faint motion, we persuade ourselves, could at that time have been completed into the thing itself, because, should that be denied, we find upon a second trial that at present it can. We consider not that the fantastical desire of showing liberty is here the motive of our actions. And it seems certain that however we may imagine we feel a liberty within ourselves, a spectator can commonly infer our actions from our motives and character; and even where he cannot, he concludes in general that he might, were he perfectly acquainted with every circumstance of our situation and temper, and the most secret springs of our complexion and disposition. Now this is the very essence of necessity, according to the foregoing doctrine.

we should be careful to observe two requisite circumstances: *first,* that it be consistent with plain matter of fact; *secondly,* that it be consistent with itself. If we observe these circumstances and render our definition intelligible, I am persuaded that all mankind will be found of one opinion with regard to it.

It is universally allowed that nothing exists without a cause of its existence, and that chance, when strictly examined, is a mere negative word and means not any real power which has anywhere a being in nature. But it is pretended that some causes are necessary, some not necessary. Here then is the advantage of definitions. Let anyone *define* a cause without comprehending, as a part of the definition, a *necessary connection* with its effect, and let him show distinctly the origin of the idea expressed by the definition, and I shall readily give up the whole controversy. But if the foregoing explication of the matter be received, this must be absolutely impracticable. Had not objects a regular conjunction with each other, we should never have entertained any notion of cause and effect; and this regular conjunction produces that inference of the understanding which is the only connection that we can have any comprehension of. Whoever attempts a definition of cause exclusive of these circumstances will be obliged either to employ unintelligible terms or such as are synonymous to the term which he endeavors to define.[2] And if the definition above mentioned be admitted, liberty, when opposed to necessity, not to constraint, is the same thing with chance, which is universally allowed to have no existence.

PART II

There is no method of reasoning more common, and yet none more blamable, than in philosophical disputes to endeavor the refutation of any hypothesis by a pretense of its dangerous consequences to religion and morality. When any opinion leads to absurdity, it is certainly false; but it is not certain that

---

[2] Thus, if a cause be defined, *that which produces anything,* it is easy to observe that *producing* is synonymous to *causing.* In like manner, if a cause be defined, *that by which anything exists,* this is liable to the same objection. For what is meant by these words, "*by which*"? Had it been said that a cause is *that* after which *anything constantly exists,* we should have understood the terms. For this is, indeed, all we know of the matter. And this constancy forms the very essence of necessity, nor have we any other idea of it.

an opinion is false because it is of dangerous consequence. Such topics, therefore, ought entirely to be forborne as serving nothing to the discovery of truth, but only to make the person of an antagonist odious. This I observe in general, without pretending to draw any advantage from it. I frankly submit to an examination of this kind, and shall venture to affirm that the doctrines both of necessity and liberty, as above explained, are not only consistent with morality, but are absolutely essential to its support.

Necessity may be defined two ways, conformably to the two definitions of *cause* of which it makes an essential part. It consists either in the constant conjunction of like objects or in the inference of the understanding from one object to another. Now necessity, in both these senses (which, indeed, are at bottom the same), has universally, though tacitly, in the schools, in the pulpit, and in common life been allowed to belong to the will of man, and no one has ever pretended to deny that we can draw inferences concerning human actions, and that those inferences are founded on the experienced union of like actions, with like motives, inclinations, and circumstances. The only particular in which anyone can differ is that either perhaps he will refuse to give the name of necessity to this property of human actions—but as long as the meaning is understood I hope the word can do no harm—or that he will maintain it possible to discover something further in the operations of matter. But this, it must be acknowledged, can be of no consequence to morality or religion, whatever it may be to natural philosophy or metaphysics. We may here be mistaken in asserting that there is no idea of any other necessity or connection in the actions of the body, but surely we ascribe nothing to the actions of the mind but what everyone does and must readily allow of. We change no circumstance in the received orthodox system with regard to the will, but only in that with regard to material objects and causes. Nothing, therefore, can be more innocent at least than this doctrine.

All laws being founded on rewards and punishments, it is supposed, as a fundamental principle, that these motives have a regular and uniform influence on the mind and both produce the good and prevent the evil actions. We may give to this influence what name we please; but as it is usually conjoined with the action, it must be esteemed a *cause* and be looked upon as an instance of that necessity which we would here establish.

The only proper object of hatred or vengeance is a person or creature endowed with thought and consciousness; and when any criminal or injurious actions excite that passion, it is only by their relation to the person, or connection with him. Actions are, by their very nature, temporary and perishing; and where they proceed not from some *cause* in the character and disposition of the person who performed them, they can neither redound to his honor if good, nor infamy if evil. The actions themselves may be blamable; they may be contrary to all the rules of morality and religion; but the person is not answerable for them and, as they proceeded from nothing in him that is durable and constant and leave nothing of that nature behind them, it is impossible he can, upon their account, become the object of punishment or vengeance. According to the principle, therefore, which denies necessity and, consequently, causes, a man is as pure and untainted, after having committed the most horrid crime, as at the first moment of his birth, nor is his character anywise concerned in his actions, since they are not derived from it; and the wickedness of the one can never be used as a proof of the depravity of the other.

Men are not blamed for such actions as they perform ignorantly and casually, whatever may be the consequences. Why? But because the principles of these actions are only momentary and terminate in them alone. Men are less blamed for such actions as they perform hastily and unpremeditately than for such as proceed from deliberation. For what reason? But because a hasty temper, though a constant cause or principle in the mind, operates only by intervals and infects not the whole character. Again, repentance wipes off every crime if attended with a reformation of life and manners. How is this to be accounted for? But by asserting that actions render a person criminal merely as they are proofs of criminal principles in the mind; and when, by an alteration of these principles, they cease to be just proofs, they likewise cease to be criminal. But, except upon the doctrine of necessity, they never were just proofs, and consequently never were criminal.

It will be equally easy to prove, and from the same arguments, that *liberty*, according to that definition above mentioned, in which all men agree, is also essential to morality, and that no human actions, where it is wanting, are susceptible of any moral qualities or can be the objects of approbation or dislike. For as actions are objects of our moral sentiment so far only as they are indications of the internal character, passions, and affections, it is impossible that they can give rise either to praise or blame where they proceed not from these principles, but are derived altogether from external violence.

I pretend not to have obviated or removed all objections to this theory with regard to necessity and liberty. I can foresee other objections derived from topics which have not here been treated of. It may be said, for instance, that if voluntary actions be subjected to the same laws of necessity with the operations of matter, there is a continued chain of necessary causes, preordained and predetermined, reaching from the Original Cause of all to every single volition of every human creature. No contingency anywhere in the universe, no indifference, no liberty. While we act, we are at the same time acted upon. The ultimate Author of all our volitions is the Creator of the world, who first bestowed motion on this immense machine and placed all beings in that particular position whence every subsequent event, by an inevitable necessity, must result. Human actions, therefore, either can have no moral turpitude at all, as proceeding from so good a cause, or if they have any turpitude, they must involve our Creator in the same guilt, while he is acknowledged to be their ultimate cause and Author. For as a man who fired a mine is answerable for all the consequences, whether the train he employed be long or short, so, wherever a continued chain of necessary causes is fixed, that Being, either finite or infinite, who produces the first is likewise the author of all the rest and must both bear the blame and acquire the praise which belong to them. Our clear and unalterable ideas of morality establish this rule upon unquestionable reasons when we examine the consequences of any human action; and these reasons must still have greater force when applied to the volitions and intentions of a Being infinitely wise and powerful. Ignorance or impotence may be pleaded for so limited a creature as man, but those imperfections have no place in our Creator. He foresaw, he

ordained, he intended all those actions of men which we so rashly pronounce criminal. And we must, therefore, conclude either that they are not criminal or that the Deity, not man, is accountable for them. But as either of these positions is absurd and impious, it follows that the doctrine from which they are deduced cannot possibly be true, as being liable to all the same objections. An absurd consequence, if necessary, proves the original doctrine to be absurd in the same manner as criminal actions render criminal the original cause if the connection between them be necessary and inevitable.

This objection consists of two parts, which we shall examine separately:

First, that if human actions can be traced up, by a necessary chain, to the Deity, they can never be criminal, on acccount of the infinite perfection of that Being from whom they are derived, and who can intend nothing but what is altogether good and laudable. Or, *secondly,* if they be criminal, we must retract the attribute of perfection which we ascribe to the Deity and must acknowledge him to be the ultimate author of guilt and moral turpitude in all his creatures.

The answer to the first objection seems obvious and convincing. There are many philosophers who, after an exact scrutiny of the phenomena of nature, conclude that the WHOLE, considered as one system, is, in every period of its existence, ordered with perfect benevolence; and that the utmost possible happiness will, in the end, result to all created beings without any mixture of positive or absolute ill and misery. Every physical ill, say they, makes an essential part of this benevolent system, and could not possibly be removed, by even the Deity himself, considered as a wise agent, without giving entrance to greater ill or excluding greater good which will result from it. From this theory some philosophers, and the ancient Stoics among the rest, derived a topic of consolation under all afflictions, while they taught their pupils that those ills under which they labored were in reality goods to the universe, and that to an enlarged view which could comprehend the whole system of nature every event became an object of joy and exultation. But though this topic be specious and sublime, it was soon found in practice weak and ineffectual. You would surely more irritate than appease a man lying under the racking pains of the gout by preaching up to him the rectitude of those general laws which produced the malignant humors in his body and led them through the proper canals to the sinews and nerves, where they now excite such acute torments. These enlarged views may, for a moment, please the imagination of a speculative man who is placed in ease and security, but neither can they dwell with constancy on his mind, even though undisturbed by the emotions of pain or passion, much less can they maintain their ground when attacked by such powerful antagonists. The affections take a narrower and more natural survey of their object and, by an economy more suitable to the infirmity of human minds, regard alone the beings around us, and are actuated by such events as appear good or ill to the private system.

The case is the same with *moral* as with *physical* ill. It cannot reasonably be supposed that those remote considerations which are found of so little efficacy with regard to the one will have a more powerful influence with regard to the other. The mind of man is so formed by nature that, upon the appearance of certain characters, dispositions, and actions, it immediately feels the sentiment of approbation or blame; nor are there any emotions more essential to its frame and constitution. The characters which engage our approbation are chiefly such as contribute to the peace and security of human society, as the characters which excite blame are chiefly such as tend to public detriment and disturbance; whence it may reasonably be presumed that the moral sentiments arise, either mediately or immediately, from a reflection on these opposite interests. What though philosophical meditations establish a different opinion or conjecture that everything is right with regard to the whole, and that the qualities which disturb society are, in the main, as beneficial, and are as suitable to the primary intention of nature, as those which more directly promote its happiness and welfare? Are such remote and uncertain speculations able to counterbalance the sentiments which arise from the natural and immediate view of the objects? A man who is robbed of a considerable sum, does he find his vexation for the loss anywise diminished by these sublime reflections? Why, then, should his moral resentment against the crime be supposed incompatible with them? Or why should not the acknowledgment of a real distinction between vice and virtue be reconcilable to all speculative systems of philosophy, as well as that of a real distinction between personal beauty and deformity? Both these distinctions are founded in the natural sentiments of the human mind; and these sentiments are not to be controlled or altered by any philosophical theory or speculation whatsoever.

The *second* objection admits not of so easy and satisfactory an answer, nor is it possible to explain distinctly how the Deity can be the immediate cause of all the actions of men without being the author of sin and moral turpitude. These are mysteries which mere natural and unassisted reason is very unfit to handle; and whatever system she embraces, she must find herself involved in inextricable difficulties, and even contradictions, at every step which she takes with regard to such subjects. To reconcile the indifference and contingency of human actions with prescience or to defend absolute decrees, and yet free the Deity from being the author of sin, has been found hitherto to exceed all the power of philosophy. Happy, if she be thence sensible of her temerity, when she pries into these sublime mysteries, and, leaving a scene so full of obscurities and perplexities, return with suitable modesty to her true and proper province, the examination of common life, where she will find difficulties enough to employ her inquiries without launching into so boundless an ocean of doubt, uncertainty, and contradiction.

Indeterminacy and Indeterminism*

As regards the physical universe, then, I think we may remain unrepentant determin-

* Sir W. David Ross, *Foundations of Ethics* (Oxford: Clarendon Press, 1939), pp. 222–51, reprinted by permission of the publishers. Footnotes have been renumbered.

ists; must we be so as regards the universe of moral action? At the outset it must be said that we are much farther, in this region, from the possibility of empirical verification of the law of causation than in the region of physical action. When we conclude from the observation of two physical events that a greater force must have been at work to produce the one effect than to produce the other, we usually can verify by independent means the excess of the one force over the other. When we infer, because a man does the one and not the other of two acts, that he must have desired the one more than the other, we have no delicate instruments of measurement by which we can verify that one desire actually was stronger than the other. Sometimes we can do so by introspection, and then we are so far verifying the law of causation; but often it is only by observing what we proceed to *do* that we can know what we *desired* most. . . . We get no empirical verification of the law of causality, but nothing (in the mere fact mentioned) to lead us to doubt it. Those who are interested in the question of *a posteriori* reasons for determinism will find in Professor Broad's article a careful study of the facts which make such verification far less complete in the moral universe than it is in the physical.[1] But it is clear that the essential question is whether we have or have not *a priori* knowledge of the law of causality and of its application to moral action; and the empirical arguments on either side cut very little ice.

The strength of the *a priori* argument for determinism in ethics rests on the consideration that the law of causality does not present itself to our minds as one peculiar to physical events but as one applying to all events as such. An event which escaped its sway would be an event of which no explanation could be given. Suppose someone says that one is here taking one's notion of an event from physical events and applying it without reflection to mental events; my answer would have to be that I at least make no use of the conception of anything physical when I say every event must have a cause; by an event I mean *any* change, *anything* that takes place. And it is surely clear that even for a libertarian the line is drawn not between physical events and mental, but between one special class of mental events and all other events whether mental or physical. No one wants to exempt from the law of causation the occurrence of a sensation on the occasion of a physical stimulus; or the occurrence of an inference on the oc-

casion of the grasping of its premises. In the one case the event is thought to be completely determined by the physical stimulus plus the pre-existent nature and state of the body and of the mind; in the other by the occurrence of the grasping of the two premises in their connection. We certainly cannot choose what conclusion we shall draw from the premises; if we see their truth and notice their relevance to one another we cannot but see the truth which by the laws of logic follows from them. It is only acts where *choice* is involved that can with any plausibility be said to escape the law of causation. And while there might conceivably be some plausibility in making the law of causation apply to all physical and to no mental events, it is very unplausible to make it apply to all physical and some mental but not to other mental events.

The strength of the case for libertarianism, therefore, cannot be said to rest on any ontological ground upon which we could *expect* acts of choice to be free from the law of causation. It rests on two things alone—on the supposed intuition of freedom, and on the thought that morality involves freedom. These are the things at which we must look more closely. I may just say in passing that, if we could believe in occasional or even in universal indeterminacy in the physical world, that view, which is equivalent to a belief in blind chance, would furnish no support either for our intuition of freedom or for our awareness of duty.

In considering the intuition of freedom, we shall do well to consider separately the two questions of freedom to choose, or decide, or resolve, and of freedom to do what we have resolved upon. As regards choice, what is it that we really are aware of? We are aware that a certain kind of activity called choice or resolution takes place, which is different from any other activity—different, in particular, from desiring, and from desiring one thing more than another; and we are aware that it is we and not anything else that performs this activity. We are aware that desires are not like physical forces beating on a physical body from without, to which it is merely passive. They are occurrences happening in the very same being which chooses among them; and they are occurrences such that the mere occurrence of one stronger than all others does not *ipso facto* lead to corresponding action. We are aware that we often re-

[1] "Indeterminacy and Indeterminism," *Proceedings of the Aristotelian Society*, Supp. Vol. X (1931), pp. 146–49.

flect on them and come to see that a desire which as it originally presented itself was stronger than another, nevertheless harmonizes less well with the universe of our interests; and we are aware that when we come to see this, it becomes less strong, or some other becomes stronger, and that we then act on what was at first the weaker but is now the stronger desire, or follow the line of what was at first the greater but is now the lesser resistance. Can it be maintained that there is an intuition of freedom to which this account does not do justice? It seems to me that it cannot, and that reflection on the relations between opinion, desire, and choice shows that it cannot. Let us first take, as the simpler case, one in which the thought of duty does not occur, one in which we choose, for instance, between two courses promising different pleasant experiences to ourselves. The suggestion is that at one point in the nexus of events there comes a choice in which some element of the self operates quite freely, independent of the circumstances and also of the self's system of interests as they exist at the moment. Suppose (1) that the act of suspense, whereby we decline to act immediately on the strongest desire and instead subject the desires to reflection, has already taken place. It can hardly be maintained that then we can by an act of free choice (i.e., choice independent of the circumstances and of our system of interests) control the remolding which the desires undergo as they are brought into relation with our universe of interests. The existing universe of our interests determines that. Not that we are passive in this process; it is by the *activity* of thinking about the alternative courses of action that we come to desire one action more than the other. We are not a field on which desires as independent entities wage their battle. But the I which thinks and desires is the I which has been molded by its previous experiences and opinions and actions.

At the end of the process we are desiring one act more than the other. Can it be maintained, then, (2) that thereupon we are conscious of freedom nevertheless to do *either* of the two acts? Is it not clear that, in a case where the thought of duty does not come in, we inevitably do that which after reflection we most wish to do? And incidentally we may ask, "Would there be any moral value in a freedom to do, in such a case, what we

do not most wish to do?" It would be a freedom to act for no reason, and indeed against reason.

Can it be maintained (3) that, while the determinate self, with its universe of interests, determines what we do, *if* we perform the act of suspense, an indeterminate element in us performs the act of suspense? Is it not clear that we perform this act only if we think, for example, that the greater of two immediate pleasures may bring more pain in its train than the lesser of the two? And is it not clear again that we are not free either to think or not to think this, that whether we do or do not think it depends on the circumstances and on the determinate kind of being that we are when we compare the two pleasures? We cannot choose what opinion we shall form about the situation, and what we do think about it determines us to perform the act of suspense; or else fails to determine us to perform it, and then we do not perform it. Freedom to suspend or not to suspend action irrespective of any reason for doing either would, again, be a freedom not worth having. To sum up, then, we do not seem, on reflection, to be conscious either of a power of thinking what we please in the light of given evidence, or of a power of desiring what we please independently of our opinions, or of a power of doing what we do not most desire to do. Nor, if we had any of these powers, would it be of the slightest value. What would be the moral value of a power of forming opinions not based on the evidence, of desiring not in accordance with our opinion, or of acting to get what we do not desire?

"But," it might be said, "the situation is altered when we turn to cases in which the thought of duty occurs to us. Then, at least, we do not choose according to the strongest desire; we may choose to do our duty instead of what we desire." If one has done a conscientious act, and is then asked why one did it, the answer which first comes to one's lips is "because it was my duty"; and in this there is no mention of desire. Duty tends to be represented as something standing over against all objects of desire. But a little reflection shows that our answer was highly elliptical. It is clear that an act's being our duty is never the reason why we do it. For however much an act may be our duty we shall not be led on that account to do it, unless we *know* or *think* it to be our duty. And again, the thought that an act is our duty will lead us just as much to do it when it is not in fact our duty as when it is. Thus our answer "I did it because it was my duty" must be changed into the form "I did it because I knew it, or thought it (as the case may be), to be my duty." But even this is still elliptical. For it is a familiar fact that people often know or think an act to be their duty and yet do not do it. They will do it only if in addition to knowing or thinking it to be their duty they are impelled with a certain degree of intensity toward the doing of duty—with enough intensity to overcome the urge toward any of the alternative possible acts. Thus the fuller and truer answer would be, "I did the act because I knew, or thought, it to be my duty, and because I was more powerfully impelled, or attracted, toward it as being my duty than I was toward any alternative act." Now a question arises as to the nature of the impulsion. The simpler account would consist in saying that all impulsion is desire, and that therefore our answer may be put in the form, "I did the act because I knew, or thought, it to be my duty, and because I desired to do it, as being my duty, more than I desired to do any other act." And if this description is true, conscientious action would fall under the same description which we have seen to apply to actions in which the thought of duty does not occur; it would be action in accordance with the strongest desire present at the moment.

The alternative would be the view that what impels us to do our duty is not desire but a certain specific emotion which only the thought of duty arouses—the emotion which Kant calls *Achtung,* respect or reverence. Now I think it is clear that the thought of duty does arouse such a specific emotion. It arouses it in very varying degrees in different people, and in the same person at different times; and in some people the emotion is very weak. Not only do they habitually not do their duty, but they feel little or no shame or remorse at not having done it; while if the emotion in question had any considerable strength, this would at least lead to remorse after the act, even if it were not strong enough to overrule the desires that lead men to do the act. Still, in the ordinary man the clear recognition of duty undoubtedly arouses to some extent the emotion of respect. Kant represents the choice between doing and not doing our duty as resultant on a struggle between desire and respect, and resists strongly the suggestion that it is resultant on a struggle between desire and desire. But this seems to be due to his tendency to accept too readily the Hobbesian view that all desire is for the agent's pleasure. Since the motive in dutiful action is clearly not that, he infers that it is not desire at all. But it is now generally admitted that Hobbes was wrong; and if we recognize that there is a variety of desires for objects other than one's own pleasure, there seems to be no objection in principle to recognizing a desire to do one's duty; and certainly introspection seems to reveal such a desire. It seems to me, further, that the emotion of respect aroused by the thought that a certain act is one's duty produces, in proportion to its own strength, a desire to do that act, and that duty is done when and only when that desire is stronger than all those with which it has to contend.

But, it might be said, if action is described as following upon the strongest desire, is not resolution or choosing or deciding made completely nugatory? Would not the same act follow if the step called choosing were entirely omitted? The answer to this is in principle contained in what I have said previously. It is the nature of each single desire to be concentrated on a single feature in an imagined future, and if desire were left to itself we should act to get the most desired of these isolated features. But in fact every such desired feature involves, in the getting of it and as a result of the getting of it, many other features which are not desired. To get the single thing which at the moment we desire most of all things, we might involve ourselves in getting many things that will give us pain, or in doing actions to which we have a strong moral repugnance. In the deliberation which precedes choice we set ourselves, more or less thoroughly according to our character, to choose not between isolated objects of desire but between acts each of which is thought to involve a whole set of consequences, and it is one act with all its expected consequences that is chosen in preference to all others with all *their* expected consequences. The choice is thus determined not by the strength of the isolated desires as they were before the process of deliberation, but by the strength of the appeal which one act, with all that it is expected to involve, makes on us, as compared with the appeal which the alternatives make. Thus what is resolved on may be, and often is, very different from what would have been done if deliberation and choice had not intervened. What choice depends upon, and reveals, is not the strength of isolated desires but the trend of the whole character, of the whole system of more or less permanent desires, including of course the desire to do one's duty.

The nature of choice, and its importance, may, it seems to me, be brought out by contrasting the way in which we actually behave with two accounts of behavior which might suggest themselves as possible accounts. I assume that every desire must at any one moment be of a perfectly definite intensity, and that all desires must be comparable on a single scale of intensity, even though it must be admitted that we are quite incapable of distinguishing the intensities of two desires which are very much alike in intensity. Now it might be thought in the first place that action would be determined by the strongest single desire. That, however, is not what happens. I take a simple case. If I am attracted to act A by a desire, of intensity $3n$, to get a certain pleasure for myself, and to act B by a desire, of intensity $2n$, to give a certain pleasure to another person, and am attracted to act B also by a desire, of intensity $2n$, to give a certain pleasure to a third person, I shall actually do act B, though the strongest single desire that is affecting me is attracting me toward the other act. That is the truth that is vaguely expressed by saying that it is the universe of my desires that determines my action, and not the strongest single desire. But, on the other hand, it must not be supposed that all the desires that are present in me cooperate to determine my action, as the movement of a body is determined, in accordance with the parallelogram of forces, by all the forces that are acting on it. If that were so in human action, our action would be an attempt to get to some extent each and all of the many things we happen to be desiring; and it is clear that such action would be futile in the extreme. What happens, in persons of strong character, is something quite different; they make up their minds that certain of the things they want are incompatible with certain other things that they want more; and they then suppress the desires for the former, so far as concerns their becoming influences affecting their behavior. They cannot entirely suppress these desires; but they cause them to be, not motives modifying their action, but mere longings for certain objects, which remain even when these objects have been resolutely renounced. This, it seems to me, is the great difference between physical and mental causation, that in the latter there is no law of the composition of all the forces concerned, but some of the forces concerned are, by an act of choice, deprived of any effect on action.

If the line of thought I have tried to present is true, the libertarian belief in its complete form cannot be true. The libertarian belief is the belief that, the circumstances being what they are, and I being what I am, with that whole system of beliefs, desires, and dispositions which compose my nature, it is objectively possible for me here and now to do either of two or more acts. This is *not* possible, because whatever act I do, it must be because there is in me, as I am now, a stronger impulse to do that act than to do any other. Everyone would probably agree that this is so when neither of the two acts is being thought of as a duty. It would be agreed that then we must do the act, to do which we have the strongest desire, or rather the act to which the strongest mass of desire leads us. But it is equally true when one of the two acts *is* thought of as a duty, even if we take the view that what impels us to do an act of duty as such is not a desire but a specific emotion of respect or reverence. For even so we shall do the duty if and only if this emotion constitutes an impulse to do the act of duty, stronger than the impulse which moves us toward doing any other act. And if act A can only be done if I have a stronger impulse to do act A than to do act B, and if act B can only be done if I have a stronger impulse to do act B than to do act A, it cannot be the case that I can here and now equally do either act. It must follow from my nature and my present condition that I must do act A, or else that I must do act B.

Not only is it metaphysically impossible that I should be capable of doing either act indifferently, but if I could, the doing of either could have no moral value. It would have no value, because it would not be the result of any thought about the nature of the act, and of any consequent impulsion to do it. It would be an unintelligent and unmotived leap in the dark.

Nevertheless we all, when we are not philosophizing, tend to hold this opinion, and cannot altogether prevent ourselves from continuing to hold it even when we have come to think it incapable of being true. What then is the truth, if any, which underlies my belief that I can here and now, being what I am, yet do either of two or more acts?

This belief, in the form in which we ordinarily hold it, is the belief that I can cause any one of two or more changes in the state of affairs. In some cases the change we are thinking of is a change in the condition of one's own mind; but far more often a change of something in the physical world is at least part of the change we think we can cause. And such changes can only be caused by first causing a change in the state of one's own body. If I think, for instance, that I can here and now tell either the truth or a lie, there is involved in that the thought that I can cause either of two sets of movements of my vocal chords. And undoubtedly one main source of my sense of freedom to act in either of two ways is the conviction, well based on experience, that my soul or mind has the kind and degree of control over my body which will enable me, if I set myself to tell the truth, to produce certain movements of my vocal organs, and if I set myself to tell a lie, to produce certain other movements of them. This conviction is not, strictly speaking, knowledge; for since I last made the attempt, paralysis may have set in and deprived me of this power. But normally the chances are much against this having happened, and for practical purposes the conviction is justified and is almost as good as knowledge.

The existence of this power has of course sometimes been doubted. It has been thought that mind cannot act on body, and various forms of parallelism of mental and bodily events have been put forward in opposition to the belief in the action of mind on body. But, as several recent discussions of the question have brought out,[2] the theoretical arguments against action of mind on body are really very weak; and the argument for it from experience is very strong; and, to avoid a long digression into psychophysics, I am going to assume that common sense is justified in its belief that mind can act on body—provided of course that it is the body which belongs to the

mind. Now it seems clear that one great source of our belief in freedom is our conviction—a well-founded conviction, as I think—that there are in any set of circumstances more than one bodily change, any one of which the mind can and will produce if it sets itself to do so.

In saying that mind can produce changes in body, I do not mean merely that a certain change in our mental state is one of the conditions upon which there supervenes, and without which there would not supervene, a certain bodily change. What we naturally think is that, while there are certain static conditions, both of our body and of our mind, without which the bodily change would not take place, a mental act of self-exertion stands out from the background of these static conditions and is that which actually causes the bodily change to take place. To reduce causation to mere necessary sequence is to eviscerate it of a good deal of its natural meaning, and no cogent reason has ever been given for this evisceration.

When I say this, however, I ought to add that I have in the course of this discussion frequently used the word "causality" in another and wider sense which is also justified by common usage. When I have referred to the law of causality I have meant by this the principle that no change takes place in the absence of conditions upon which it necessarily follows; and in *this* conception of causality there is not necessarily involved the thought of one thing acting on and producing a change in another. And indeed in the causations which we have been mainly considering there is no question of one thing, i.e., one substance, acting on another. When one says that an act of will is caused by the previous desires and thoughts of the willer, there is no question of two substances being involved; for all that happens happens in or to one substance, the individual human being in question. One is then merely asserting a necessary connection between earlier and later events in the history of this individual. When, on the other hand, one says that a mind by an act of choice produces a change in its own body, one is, I believe, asserting something more than necessary connection; one is asserting the existence of activity and passivity. To avoid the ambiguity, one ought perhaps to use "determination" as the more general word to include both what is commonly called transeunt causation and

[2] See, for instance, the discussion in John Wisdom, *Problems of Mind and Matter* (Cambridge: Cambridge Univ. Press, 1934), pp. 65–102.

what is commonly called immanent causation, and should restrict the word "causation" to what is commonly called "transeunt causation," to the action of one substance on another, whether it be that of body on body, or that of body on mind, or that of mind on body, or (if this occurs) that of mind on mind.

The mind's power of controlling the body has great importance for the moral life. If it did not exist, our moral life, our range of moral activities, would be immensely impoverished. For if a man did not think that his mind can control his body, he would not set himself to make such movements as are involved in telling the truth, in paying his debts, in helping his neighbors, and the like; and if he discovered by experience that he cannot produce such results he would soon cease to set himself to produce them. His moral life would come to be restricted to setting himself to bring about changes in the state of his own character or of his own intellect. He would have a moral life of his own, but he would be cut off from the activities which make up by far the greater part of the moral life of most men.

Yet the question whether the mind can control the body is irrelevant to the question of the freedom of the will. For if we say that the mind can control the body, we are making a statement about the *effect* of an act of will, and are in fact saying that a certain causal nexus exists between acts of will and consequent bodily changes; while what Libertarianism maintains is not anything with regard to the *effects* of acts of will, but that acts of will are not themselves caused by the preexisting conditions. Suppose that a man had, without knowing it, lost the power of speech. He could still set himself, or make the effort, to tell the truth, or alternatively set himself to tell a lie. The activity of mind he would be exercising would be the same in the case in which the control over his vocal chords has ceased to exist, as it would be if he still had the control; and the activity of choosing between these two activities would be the same as if the control over the vocal chords still existed. Morally, both the act and the decision to act are just the same as they would be if the control over the body still existed. Thus control over the body, though it is a great part of what we usually think of when we assert our freedom to do this or to do that, is not the morally essential thing that is

being claimed. The essential thing that is being claimed is the power to set oneself to do this, or to set oneself to do that, i.e., to perform a mental activity which is just the same whether it is or is not followed by the appropriate bodily movement.

Is there any foundation for the belief that I am free to set myself to produce either of two or more bodily movements? If my previous argument is correct, the belief cannot itself be true. If my nature and condition and the circumstances are such and such, I shall set myself to produce one change; if they are different, I shall set myself to produce another. Yet, if it is not true that I can here and now set myself to produce either indifferently, it is true that in a certain sense I *could* set myself to produce either. For within the total range of my nature there are motives which in certain circumstances would lead me to make the one attempt; and other motives which in certain circumstances would lead me to make the other. Neither act seems to me impossible for me, because neither is clean outside the range of motives which I know to exist in myself. If I knew myself completely, I should know either that the one motive or set of motives is the stronger, in which case I shall set myself to do the one act, or that the other motive or set of motives is the stronger, in which case I shall set myself to do the other. But knowing that both motives are such as I am familiar with, and knowing further that both are present in my mind at the moment, and not knowing which is the stronger, or, if I happen to know which is the stronger now, not knowing which will have emerged as the stronger by the time when I act, the only reasonable belief for me to hold is that I am capable of doing either of the two acts.

Now if in the end I do the right act, then, if the defense of Determinism which I have put forward is sound, my doing the right act implies that, just before I did it, conditions which made it necessary for me to do it were present, and similarly my doing the wrong act, if I do *that,* implies that conditions which made it necessary to do that act were present. If the one act was objectively, in the precise circumstances, possible for me, the other was not; and if the other was possible, the first was not. Yet all the conditions which *ever* justify the assertion of possibility were present justifying the judgment that both acts were possible for me. For what are the conditions that justify the judgment that A may happen? A judgment of possibility may be of three kinds. It may be a judgment of the form "A may be the case here and now," or of the form "A may have happened in the past," or of the form "A may happen in the future." We need not trouble ourselves with any consideration of the first two types, for it is clearly the third that is relevant to the consideration of free will. Now the one essential condition needed to justify the judgment "A may happen" is that I do not know of any circumstance which makes the happening of A possible. If the general argument I have offered for Determinism is true, there is no such thing as possibility *in rerum natura*. If certain conditions are present, certain things will happen, and no alternative to them will happen; if certain other conditions are present, certain other things will happen, and no alternative to *them* will happen. Possibility is always related to a judger, and to say "so-and-so may happen" is just to say "I don't know that it won't." Now it often happens that I don't know that A will happen, and don't know that it won't. Then I am entitled to say that A may happen and may not happen. Now this is actually the position we are in with regard to the acts of any other person. We may have watched him in a hundred similar situations in the past and seen him always behave in one way, and we may therefore think it much more likely that he will behave in way A than in way B; but though the circumstances seem just alike to us, they may seem different to him; or his character may have improved since the last similar situation occurred to him, or it may have got worse; and it is the literal truth that we can neither say that he will do act A nor that he will do act B, but can only say that he may do either. And we are, in principle, in the same situation with regard to our own future acts, and even with regard to our acts in the immediate future. We can see that the situation is never *exactly* like any in which we have been in the past. It may be like in that our relation to one person who forms part of the situation is just like the relation in which we have stood to some person in the past, but it practically never happens that the whole set of people who enter into the situation is related to us just like the whole set of people who entered into previous situations we have been in, and

therefore we cannot infer that because we behaved in way A in the past we shall behave in way A now. Again, we may feel convinced that at the moment the motives inclining us to do act A are stronger than any inclining us to do any alternative act. But all motives or desires are subject to a constant alternating weakening and strengthening; we are perfectly familiar with the fact that a desire which at its inception is strong weakens as its novelty wears off. Then so long as *any* interval, however short, separates the present moment from that at which the act will be done, we do not *know* what the relative strength of the different motives will be when the latter moment arrives; and therefore do not *know* what we shall do, though we may of course think it highly probable that we shall do a certain act rather than any other.

Thus the logical precondition of my saying "I can either do my duty or fail to do it" is always present. But merely not knowing that A will not happen is not a sufficient *psychological* precondition of my judging that A may happen. I should be logically justified in saying, "Mr. Chamberlain may make Sir Stafford Cripps his next Minister of Labour." But I should not be likely to form this judgment unless I knew or thought, for instance, that Mr. Chamberlain had socialistic leanings; unless I knew or thought that there was something in Mr. Chamberlain's psychology which might lead to such an act. Such a psychological precondition of the judgment "I can either do my duty or not do it" is in fact present. For I know that the desire to do my duty is a desire that has a certain strength in me, and I also know that other desires which if followed would lead me not to do my duty have a certain strength in me, so that the possibility of my doing my duty is not (as we sometimes put the matter) a mere logical or abstract possibility, but a very real one, and the possibility of my not doing it is also such a possibility. Thus both the logical and the psychological condition of my making the judgment are present. Or, as we may also put it, it is not merely possible, but has an appreciable probability, that I shall do my duty, and it is not merely possible, but has an appreciable probability, that I shall not do it. Therefore the judgment "I may either do my duty or not do it" is fully justified.

The thought "I can do my duty" has also a further justification. The practical utility of a belief is never, indeed, a sufficient reason for holding that belief. If I did not on other grounds think that I can do my duty, the thought that I should be more likely to do my duty if I believed I could do it would not lead me to believe that I could; and if it did, the belief would be unjustifiable, since there would be no logical connection between the psychological cause of the belief and the belief itself. But if a belief is on other grounds justifiable, the fact that keeping the belief in our minds would have good results is a good reason for keeping the belief in our minds. Now I have tried to show that the belief that we can do our duty is on its own merits justified. I certainly do not know that I shall not do my duty, and I know that there is in me a motive, viz., sense of duty, which makes it appreciably probable that I shall do it. And the keeping of this belief before my mind will in fact make it more likely that I shall do my duty. Consider the effect of holding the opposite belief. Suppose I believed that I could not do my duty; then I should be thinking, in effect, this: "Though the act is the right one in the circumstances, and one which a better man ought to do, yet since I can't do it there is no use in my trying to do it." I should resign the struggle, and do the act which most appealed to me on other grounds. But if I keep before me the thought "that is the right thing to do, and I don't know of anything that makes it impossible for me to do it, and do know of something, viz., the sense of duty in me, which makes it appreciably probable that I shall do it," the wish to do my duty is kept alive and allowed to have its full weight in determining my action.

It is true that the thought "it is possible for me *not* to do my duty" is equally justified logically, and that this also is not a mere idle or abstract possibility, since I know there are motives in me inclining me to do something other than my duty. And it might at first sight seem that this thought would have as great a tendency to depress us and damp down our moral activity as the complementary thought "it is possible for me to do my duty" has to intensify our moral activity, and would simply neutralize the effect of the latter. This, however, is far from being the case. The joint thought "it is possible that I shall, and possible that I shall not, do my duty," which is the thought that the facts of the case justify, is precisely that which is most favorable to

the doing of our duty when the time comes. If we felt certain that we should do it, that would simply encourage us to take things too much for granted and to neglect the concentration on the thought of duty which alone will secure our doing it when the time comes. If we felt certain that we should *not* do it, that again would discourage us from paying any attention to the thought of duty. The recognition that we may either do or not do our duty is just that which is needed to induce us to keep our moral armor in the best possible repair.

I may illustrate this by a homely analogy. Of the candidates in an examination, those who are most likely to make the needed effort are neither those who feel sure that they will pass nor those who feel sure that they will fail, but those who know that they do not know whether they will pass or fail. And similarly the thought that it is possible that I shall do what is right and also possible that I shall do what is wrong is precisely that which is most conducive to my exercising that sort of control over my thoughts and desires which is in turn most conducive to my doing what is right, provided of course that a wish to do what is right is also present. This thought, then, is not only true, but one which it is very desirable to keep constantly before one's mind.

What, then, is the difference between the perfectly proper statement which I may make "it is possible that I may presently do this, and possible that I may presently do that," and the libertarian claim? Possibility is always compossibility. What I am saying when I make the above statement is that there are no existing conditions *known to me* with which my doing *A* is incompatible, and none with which my doing *B* is incompatible; and I probably should not make the statement unless I knew some important conditions to be actually present with which each action is compatible. What the libertarian says is that *all* the conditions, known and unknown, are compatible with my doing the one action, and also with my doing the other; and this cannot be true.

But the phrase "it is possible that I shall do what is right, and possible that I shall do what is wrong" does not do full justice to our actual thought when it takes its usual form "I can do what is right," though it expresses part of what that thought involves.

I could be content with that phrase only if I thought of myself as a mere spectator of the play of forces within my mind, as a looker-on at a game between fairly equal sides may say "this side may win, or that side may win." The fact that the spectator is also the agent makes the actual situation different. We say not merely "I may do right, and I may do wrong," but "I *can* do right, and I *can* do wrong." What exactly does this mean?

When I say "I can do this," which I will now use as a brachylogy for "I can perform this mental activity of self-exertion,"[3] I am not claiming that all the conditions necessary to my doing this are already present. If they were, I should be "doing this," whereas the claim "I can do this" is always made about something which one is at least not yet doing, and which perhaps one will never in fact do. If I say "I can do this," either I am not doing it, or at least I suppose I am not doing it, and if so, I cannot be supposing that *all* the conditions necessary to my doing it are already present. But I am claiming that some of those conditions are present, and present in me. I am in fact saying "certain of the conditions of my doing this are already present in me, and if certain conditions not yet present are added I shall actually do this." Now sometimes when I say "I can do this," I could specify certain external conditions which must be fulfilled if the power is to be translated into act. If I say "I can walk a mile in thirteen minutes," I should if I wanted to be more precise say "I can walk a mile in thirteen minutes if the road is not too uphill, if there is not too strong a wind against me, if I am not stopped on the way, if I am not too tired when I start," &c. But when "doing this" is not the effecting of a certain bodily movement or set of movements, as walking is, but is the purely mental activity of setting oneself to do a certain thing, such external conditions are irrelevant. Yet there must be *some* unfulfilled condition of my performing this activity of "setting myself"; else I should be doing it, and not merely saying "I can do it." The general formula must hold good, that "I can do this" is really a hypothetical proposition—"if a certain condition is added to conditions already present in me, I shall do so-and-so."

And it is easy to see what the additional condition must be. It consists of my wishing to do this. "I can do this" means "I have such a nature that if I want to perform the activity of setting myself to do this, I shall perform it"; and "I can refrain from doing this" means "I have such a nature that if I want to refrain from doing this, I shall refrain from doing it." Or, putting it briefly, "I can do this or that" means "I shall do this if I want, and I shall do that if I want"—"want" being here a brachylogy for "want predominantly." Now this claim is absolutely correct. For we have verified in experience over and over again two things, (1) that we have a faculty of setting ourselves to bring about changes, and (2) that this is exercised when we predominantly want to bring about these changes. Thus the claim which we instinctively make that we can perform either of two (or more) acts of setting ourselves to effect changes, seems to be absolutely correct, when we expand it to bring out what it really means. But what it points to is not the libertarian but the deterministic account; for we clearly imply that if the capacity of setting ourselves to effect changes has added to it a predominant wish to bring about a certain change, the setting oneself to bring it about will necessarily follow.

Suppose it is said that I am whittling away the claim of ordinary common sense, by adding the words "if I want." Suppose it is said that the claim is a claim to power not subject to this condition. If this were so, the claim would, I think, have to take one or other of two forms: (1) "I can do this whether I want or not." But does any one make this claim? Does any one really think that he could, for instance, set himself to do his duty if he did not wish to do his duty? Suppose that someone suggests that the motive of a dutiful act is not a wish but the emotion of respect or reverence which the thought of duty inspires, he will only be substituting a new condition for the condition "if I want" which I have suggested. He will be paraphrasing the phrase "I can do my duty" by the phrase "I shall do my duty if I am sufficiently under the influence of the motive of reverence." He cannot think that one who says "I can do my duty" is claiming that he can or will do it in the absence of this emotion as well as of desire.

(2) The second possible interpretation is "I

<hr>

[3] This alone is in question, since, as I have pointed out . . . , the mind's control over the body is not what is in question when we are discussing the freedom of the will.

have in me already all the necessary conditions of my doing the thing, except that of wanting to do it, and I can produce this condition." To this interpretation two fatal objections can be made. (*a*) We do not in the least think that we can produce wishes in ourselves by an act of choice, and (*b*) if this were the right analysis of the claim "I can do act *A*," then the right analysis of the statement "I can produce the condition of want" would be "I have in me already all the conditions of producing the condition of want, except the wish to produce this condition, and I can produce this wish." Thus the claim "I can do this" would involve the claim "I can produce the wish to do this"; that would imply "I can produce the wish to wish to do this"; and so *ad infinitum*—a regress which quite clearly is not involved in our simple claim "I can do this."

Thus both the attempts to remove the condition "if I want" fail, and our analysis of the claim "I can do this" remains good—that it means "I have in me a general capacity of setting myself to do things, and if I want to bring about change *A*, this capacity plus this desire will lead to my setting myself to produce change *A*." And if we thus interpret the claim "I can do act *A*," it is strictly true that I can do act *A* and that I can refrain from doing it. Thus the instinctive feeling that we can either do an act or refrain from doing it (or do some alternative act) is thoroughly justified. But it does not in turn justify the libertarian account. For it involves the assertion of the determined sequence of action on desire. As regards the origin of the desire it says nothing, but it certainly does not claim that desire is originated by an act of free choice, and in fact we never think of our desires as so originated, though we do think of our acts as so originated.

Thus what is claimed in the natural statement "I can either do act *A* or leave it undone" is that my doing or not doing act *A* depends entirely on myself. And this is in a sense true, because, while my effecting change *B* in my body, and indirectly change *C* in something beyond my body, depends on conditions in my body, and in that thing beyond my body, act *A*, being a purely mental activity of setting myself to effect changes *B* and *C*, cannot depend for its occurrence on the extent to which my body happens to be under the control of my mind.

Of course we are not claiming a complete nondependence of our acts of self-exertion on any conditions outside our mind. Most, at least, of our wants would never arise if they were not suggested to us by the perception of bodies outside us, and this is true even of the desire to do certain things as being our duty. For it is by the use of our bodily senses (though not by that alone) that we become aware of the existence of selves other than our own, and thus of duties to other selves. The independence that is claimed is the nondependence of our acts on any *immediately preceding* condition except the general capacity of setting ourselves to effect changes, and the wish to effect this or that change—both of which are conditions in our mind and nowhere else.

Thus a great deal of what is claimed in the claim to free will—not only the thought that either issue is still possible, but the thought that the issue will depend on us, our minds, our wishes, not our bodies, nor other minds or bodies, is absolutely true, as well as absolutely vital to the moral life. Again, the thought that the relative strength of our wishes is not already fixed once for all is both true and valuable. But it is a thought which a determinist can admit, as well as a libertarian. A determinist is not in the least bound to say that the effort after self-improvement is fruitless. He can admit quite freely that in a character that is bad on the whole there may yet be an element of desire for better things which, weak at first, may by the influence of example and of teaching, and of the effort after self-improvement which example and teaching may arouse, become the strongest element in the character.

The controversy between Libertarianism and Determinism is apt to present itself as one in which the metaphysical argument is in favor of Determinism and all the ethical arguments in favor of Libertarianism. This is far from being the case. It seems to me instructive to reflect, in this connection, on two features of the moral situation. The one is our reliance on the characters of other people, the reliance implied in the use of such words as "trustworthy." The other is our attitude when people surprise us by their behavior. The reliance which we place on the decent behavior of people whom we know and trust is so much evidence that we think that their actions, when they come to be done, are the result not of a will acting independently of their present character, but of the same continuing character which we have seen at work before. We are in no way detracting from the moral status of our friend if we say "I knew you could be trusted to do the right thing." "Know" is no doubt an exaggeration; for every heart has its secrets which no one knows, and the friends we know best may have their secret weakness which no former situation has revealed but which a new one will. But a confidence amounting almost to certainty is a tribute to our friend's moral worth, not a detraction from it; yet it is not compatible with the libertarian's view that any one may at any moment make a choice which is quite independent of his whole pre-existing character.

Again, if someone behaves, for better or for worse, in a way different from that which we had confidently expected, what is our reaction to this? We do not put down the unexpected act to the credit or discredit of an unmotivated choice. We always assume that there must have been, before the act, some existing but hitherto unknown trait of character which has now, perhaps for the first time, manifested itself in act. In our reaction to people's unexpected behavior, no less than in our expectation of their behavior, we betray the conviction that action is the result of continuing, even if constantly modified, character.

Another feature of our ordinary moral thought which really harmonizes better with the deterministic than with the libertarian account is the importance for good or evil which we attach to the formation of habits. We all think that if we repeatedly behave in a certain way we shall make it more likely that we shall go on behaving in that way, and more difficult for ourselves to behave otherwise. An attempt may be made to harmonize this with Libertarianism by saying that habits "incline without necessitating." But to describe them thus is to imply that a habit becomes *one* of the influences which operate on the will; and this is inconsistent with the thought of a transcendental will standing apart from the formed character and free to operate independently of it. The thought that habits incline without necessitating is in itself perfectly correct. It is simply one way of expressing the fact that a habitual tendency to behave in a certain way forms one element, and an important element, in the total character from which future action will spring, while yet there may coexist with it some other element which may prove stronger; some long unfulfilled but not extinguished longing after good which, brought to the surface by some feature of a new situation, may overcome a bad habit, or some lingering weakness which may lead us to yield to a new temptation though we have overcome many others. The thought of habits as inclining without necessitating, which is the true way of thinking of them, is also the most salutary, since it frees us from the despair which would overtake us if we thought of bad habits as completely necessitating, and from the carelessness that would come over us if we thought of them as leaving us as free to do well as we were before their formation.

I may add that the judgments which we make about the characters of other people (or about our own characters), in distinction from judgments about particular acts, imply the view that action is determined by character. For our judgments about character are mostly[4] based on observation of actions, and we are justified in drawing inferences from people's actions to their characters only if their actions flow from their characters. When we call a man a bad man we do not mean that he is a man who has done more bad acts than good (for that might be equally true of a reformed sinner), but that he still has substantially the same character which was evidenced by bad acts in the past and may be expected to be evidenced by more in the future. In fact Libertarianism is inconsistent with belief in the continuity of human character; but our actual moral judgments are evidence that we do believe in its continuity, though we think it a continuity that admits of modification for better or for worse.

I am far from contending that the whole of our ordinary thought about moral action is reconcilable with the doctrine of Determinism. But it is worth while to point out that it is by no means true that *all* the arguments drawn from the moral consciousness tell in favor of Libertarianism, and only the metaphysical argument tells in favor of Determinism.

If my line of argument is right, we must find the uniqueness of moral behavior not in

---

[4] Only mostly, because some judgments about character are based on observation of the expression on people's faces, their gestures, &c.

freedom from the general law of causation, but in the unique character of the activities which constitute such behavior—the activity of choosing or deciding, and the activity of setting oneself to do what one has decided to do, to which there is no analogy in the behavior of any physical thing; and in the further fact, to which there is nothing analogous in the behavior of a mere animal, that one of the thoughts under whose influence one can choose and set oneself to act is the thought of an action as right.

Besides the "intuition" of freedom, the other main reason which leads people to believe in the freedom of the will is the thought of responsibility for our acts, which is involved in the facts of remorse, blame, and punishment. These, it might seem, are unjustifiable and indeed unintelligible, unless we are really free to do either of two or more different acts. We must therefore set ourselves to examine the implications of these things. Professor Nicolai Hartmann[5] has argued that of these three phenomena, remorse is the one which is most clearly an evidence of free will. Blame and punishment, praise and reward, might, he argues, perhaps be explained as devices adopted for the encouragement of men to future good acts and their restraint from future bad acts, without involving a genuine imputation of freedom; but there can be no such utilitarian explanation of the free assignment by a man to himself of responsibility for his past acts, and of the accompanying remorse.

I think it possible that a society which had ceased to believe in the responsibility of individuals for their acts might retain praise and blame, reward and punishment, as utilitarian devices for the encouragement of virtue and the restraint of vice. But two comments may be made on this. In the first place, I think we should agree that the denial of responsibility is not the assumption on which we actually praise and blame, reward and punish. Our actual assumption is a belief in responsibility. And secondly, we should think it somewhat dishonest to continue to practice praise and blame, reward and punishment, if we had lost the belief in responsibility. We should be treating people as if they were responsible, when we had really ceased to believe that they were.

[5] *Ethics,* 3 Vols., translated by S. Coit (New York: Macmillan, 1932), III, 172–78.

I think, therefore, that we need not isolate remorse from praise and blame, reward and punishment, but should treat all alike as involving a belief in individual responsibility. The question we must now face is whether this belief is compatible with the Determinism which we have been led on other grounds to believe in, or whether it involves freedom of indifference. I may begin by pointing out that responsibility is always divided. Obviously responsibility for *results of action* can never be assigned to one person alone; there are always circumstances (and these will usually include acts by other people) which cooperate to produce the result, of whose complete cause one person's act is merely the most striking part. But it is also true that responsibility for *acts* is divided. It is never right to assign to one person the sole credit or the sole discredit for any of his acts. Other people by teaching and example, the writers of the books he has read, and so on, have all helped to mould his character into that form of which his action is the expression. But it is equally certain that the sole responsibility for any act can never be assigned to any person or persons *other* than the doer of the act. For acts spring from opinion and desire, and there is no possibility of forcibly implanting either an opinion or a desire in the mind of another. No opinion or desire will find a lodgment in his mind unless his mind accepts it, or rather responds to suggestion with a reaction which is all his own.

To recognize, then, that people and things other than the agent have been part causes of his act may be ground for mitigating the severity of our blame or the enthusiasm of our praise, but it is never in itself sufficient ground for withdrawing praise or blame from him altogether. Other people, and outside circumstances, have never been more than part causes of his act; the act is the reaction of his character to them, and his character is partly responsible.

.   .   .

. . . And, holding fast to Determinism, I am inclined to think that the only account we can give of responsibility is this: that bad acts can never be forced on any one in spite of his character; that action is the joint product of character and circumstances and is always therefore to some extent evidence of character; that praise and blame are not (though they serve this purpose also) mere utilitarian devices for the promotion of virtue and the restraint of vice, but are the appropriate reactions to action which is good or is bad in its nature just as much if it is the necessary consequence of its antecedents as it would be if the libertarian account were true; that in blaming bad actions we are also blaming and justifiably blaming the character from which they spring; and that in remorse we are being acutely aware that, whatever our outward circumstances may have been, we have ourselves been to blame for giving way to them where a person of better character would not have done so. I cannot pretend that this satisfies the whole of our natural thought about responsibility, but I think that in claiming more, in claiming that a moral agent can act independently of his character, we should be claiming a metaphysical impossibility.

A philosophical genius may some day arise who will succeed in reconciling our natural thought about freedom and responsibility with acceptance of the law of causality; but I must admit that no existing discussion seems to be very successful in doing so.

Free Will and Psychoanalysis*

O Thou, who didst with pitfall and with gin
Beset the Road I was to wander in,
 Thou wilt not with Predestined Evil round
Enmesh, and then impute my Fall to Sin!
　　—Edward FitzGerald, *The Rubaiyat of*
　　　　　　　　　　Omar Khayyám.

. . . It is extremely common for nonprofessional philosophers and iconoclasts to deny that human freedom exists, but at the same time to have no clear idea of what it is that they are denying to exist. The first thing that needs to be said about the free-will issue is that any meaningful term must have a meaningful opposite: if it is meaningful to assert that people are not free, it must be equally meaningful to assert that people *are* free, whether this latter assertion is in fact true or not. Whether it is true, of course, will depend on the meaning that is given the weasel-word "free." For example, if freedom is made dependent on indeterminism, it may well be that human freedom is nonexistent. But there seem to be no good grounds for asserting such a dependence, especially since lack of causation is the furthest thing from people's minds when they call an act free. Doubtless there are other senses that can be given to the word "free"—such as "able to do anything we want to do"—in which no human beings are free.

But the first essential point about which the denier of freedom must be clear is *what* it is that he is denying. If one knows what it is like for people not to be free, one must know what it *would* be like for them to *be* free.

Philosophers have advanced numerous senses of "free" in which countless acts performed by human beings can truly be called free acts. The most common conception of a free act is that according to which an act is free if and only if it is a *voluntary* act. But the word "voluntary" does not always carry the same meaning. Sometimes to call an act voluntary means that we can do the act *if* we choose to do it: in other words, that it is physically and psychologically possible for us to do it, so that the occurrence of the act follows upon the decision to do it. (One's decision to raise his arm is in fact followed by the actual raising of his arm, unless he is a paralytic; one's decision to pluck the moon from the sky is not followed by the actual event.) Sometimes a voluntary act is conceived (as by Moore[1]) as an act which would not have occurred if, just beforehand, the agent had chosen not to perform it. But these senses are different from the sense in which a voluntary act is an act resulting from *deliberation*, or perhaps merely from *choice*. For example, there are many acts which we could have avoided, if we had chosen to do so, but which we nevertheless did not *choose* to perform, much less *deliberate* about them. The act of raising one's leg in the process of taking

---

* John Hospers, "Meaning and Free Will," *Philosophy and Phenomenological Research*, X (1950), 313–30, reprinted with the permission of the author and *Philosophy and Phenomenological Research*. The selection appearing in this volume is taken from a revised version of "Meaning and Free Will" in Wilfrid Sellars and John Hospers, *Readings in Ethical Theory* (New York: Appleton, Century-Croft, Inc., 1952), pp. 560–75. Footnotes have been renumbered.

[1] G. E. Moore, *Ethics* (New York: Oxford University Press, 1947), pp. 15–16.

a step while out for a walk is one which a person could have avoided by choosing to, but which, after one has learned to walk, takes place automatically or semi-automatically through habit, and thus is not the result of choice. (One may have chosen to take the walk, but not to take this or that step while walking.) Such acts are free in Moore's sense but are not free in the sense of being deliberate. Moreover, there are classes of acts of the same general character which are not even covered by Moore's sense: sudden outbursts of feeling, in some cases at least, could not have been avoided by an immediately preceding volition, so that if these are to be included under the heading of voluntary acts, the proviso that the act could have been avoided by an immediately preceding volition must be amended to read "could have been avoided by a volition or series of volitions by the agent *at some time in the past*"—such as the adop-tion of a different set of habits in the agent's earlier and more formative years.

(Sometimes we call *persons*, rather than their acts, free. Stebbing, for example, declares that one should never call acts free, but only the doers of the acts.[2] But the two do not seem irreconcilable: can we not speak of a *person* as free *with respect to a certain act* (never just free in general) if that *act* is free—whatever we may then go on to mean by saying that an act is free? Any statement about a free act can then be translated into a statement about the doer of the act.)

Now, no matter in which of the above ways we may come to define "voluntary," there are still acts which are voluntary *but which we would be very unlikely to think of as free.* Thus, when a person submits to the command of an armed bandit, he may do so voluntarily in every one of the above senses: he may do so as a result of choice, even of deliberation, and he could have avoided doing it by willing not to—he could, instead, have refused and been shot. The man who reveals a state secret under torture does the same: he could have refused and endured more torture. Yet such acts, and persons in respect of such acts, are not generally called free. We say that they were performed *under compulsion*, and if an act is performed under compulsion we do not call it free. We say, "He wasn't free because

he was forced to do as he did," though of course his act was voluntary.

This much departure from the identification of free acts with voluntary acts almost everyone would admit. Sometimes, however, it would be added that this is all the departure that can be admitted. According to Schlick, for example,

Freedom means the opposite of compulsion; a man is *free* if he does not act under *compulsion*, and he is compelled or unfree when he is hindered from without in the realization of his natural desires. Hence he is unfree when he is locked up, or chained, or when someone forces him at the point of a gun to do what otherwise he would not do. This is quite clear, and everyone will admit that the everyday or legal notion of the lack of freedom is thus correctly interpreted, and that a man will be considered quite free . . . if no such external compulsion is exerted upon him.[3]

Schlick adds that the entire vexed free-will controversy in philosophy is so much wasted ink and paper, because compulsion has been confused with causality and necessity with uniformity. If the question is asked whether every event is caused, the answer is doubtless yes; but if it is whether every event is compelled, the answer is clearly no. Free acts are uncompelled acts, not uncaused acts. Again, when it is said that some state of affairs (such as water flowing downhill) is necessary, if "necessary" means "compelled," the answer is no; if it means merely that it always happens that way, the answer is yes: universality of application is confused with compulsion. And this, according to Schlick, is the end of the matter.

Schlick's analysis is indeed clarifying and helpful to those who have fallen victim to the confusions he exposes—and this probably includes most persons in their philosophical growing pains. But *is* this the end of the matter? Is it true that all acts, though caused, are free as long as they are not compelled in the sense which he specifies? May it not be that, while the identification of "free" with "uncompelled" is acceptable, the area of compelled acts is vastly greater than he or most other philosophers have ever suspected? (Moore is more cautious in this respect than Schlick; while for Moore an act is free if it is voluntary in the sense specified above, he thinks there may be another sense in which

---

[2] Susan Stebbing, *Philosophy and the Physicist* (New York: Dover, 1959), p. 212.

[3] *The Problems of Ethics,* trans. Rynin (N.Y.: Prentice-Hall, Inc., 1939), p. 150.

human beings, and human acts, are not free at all.[4]) We remember statements about human beings being pawns of their early environment, victims of conditions beyond their control, the result of causal influences stemming from their parents, and the like, and we ponder and ask, "Still, are we really free?" Is there not something in what generations of sages have said about man being fettered? Is there not perhaps something too facile, too sleight-of-hand, in Schlick's cutting of the Gordian knot? For example, when a metropolitan newspaper headlines an article with the words "Boy Killer Is Doomed Long before He Is Born,"[5] and then goes on to describe how a twelve-year-old boy has been sentenced to prison for the murder of a girl, and how his parental background includes records of drunkenness, divorce, social maladjustment, paresis, are we still to say that his act, though voluntary and assuredly *not* done at the point of a gun, is free? The boy has early displayed a tendency toward sadistic activity to hide an underlying masochism and "prove that he's a man"; being coddled by his mother only worsens this tendency, until, spurned by a girl in his attempt on her, he kills her—not simply in a fit of anger, but calculatingly, deliberately. Is he free in respect of his criminal act, or for that matter in most of the acts of his life? Surely to ask this question is to answer it in the negative. Perhaps I have taken an extreme case; but it is only to show the superficiality of the Schlick analysis the more clearly. Though not everyone has criminotic tendencies, everyone has been moulded by influences which in large measure at least determine his present behavior; he is literally the product of these influences, stemming from periods prior to his "years of discretion," giving him a host of character traits that he cannot change now even if he would. So obviously does what a man is depend upon how a man comes to be, that it is small wonder that philosophers and sages have considered man far indeed from being the master of his fate. It is not as if man's will were standing high and serene above the flux of events that have moulded him; it is itself caught up in this flux, itself carried along on the current. An act is free when it is determined by the man's character, say moralists; but what if

the most decisive aspects of his character were already irrevocably acquired before he could do anything to mould them? What if even the degree of will power available to him in shaping his habits and disciplining himself now to overcome the influence of his early environment is a factor over which he has no control? What are we to say of this kind of "freedom"? Is it not rather like the freedom of the machine to stamp labels on cans when it has been devised for just that purpose? Some machines can do so more efficiently than others, but only because they have been better constructed.

It is not my purpose here to establish this thesis in general, but only in one specific respect which has received comparatively little attention, namely, the field referred to by psychiatrists as that of unconscious motivation. In what follows I shall restrict my attention to it because it illustrates as clearly as anything the points I wish to make.

Let me try to summarize very briefly the psychoanalytic doctrine on this point.[6] The conscious life of the human being, including the conscious decisions and volitions, is merely a mouthpiece for the unconscious—not directly for the enactment of unconscious drives, but of the compromise between unconscious drives and unconscious reproaches. There is a Big Three behind the scenes which the automaton called the conscious personality carries out: the id, an "eternal gimme," presents its wish and demands its immediate satisfaction; the superego says no to the wish immediately upon presentation, and the unconscious ego, the mediator between the two, tries to keep peace by means of compromise.

To go into examples of the functioning of these three "bosses" would be endless; psychoanalytic casebooks supply hundreds of them. The important point for us to see in the present context is that *it is the unconscious that determines what the conscious impulse and the conscious action shall be.* Hamlet,

---

[4] *Ethics,* Chapter 6, pp. 217 ff.
[5] *New York Post,* Tuesday, May 18, 1948, p. 4.

[6] I am aware that the theory presented below is not accepted by all practicing psychoanalysts. Many non-Freudians would disagree with the conclusions presented below. But I do not believe that this fact affects my argument, as long as the concept of unconscious motivation is accepted. I am aware, too, that much of the language employed in the following descriptions is animistic and metaphorical; but as long as I am presenting a view I would prefer to "go the whole hog" and present it in its most dramatic form. The theory can in any case be made clearest by the use of such language, just as atomic theory can often be made clearest to students with the use of models.

for example, had a strong Oedipus wish, which was violently counteracted by superego reproaches; these early wishes were vividly revived in an unusual adult situation in which his uncle usurped the coveted position from Hamlet's father and won his mother besides. This situation evoked strong strictures on the part of Hamlet's superego, and it was this that was responsible for his notorious delay in killing his uncle. A dozen times Hamlet could have killed Claudius easily; but every time Hamlet "decided" not to: a free choice, moralists would say—but no, listen to the superego: "What you feel such hatred toward your uncle for, what you are plotting to kill him for, is precisely the crime which you yourself desire to commit: to kill your father and replace him in the affections of your mother. Your fate and your uncle's are bound up together." This paralyzes Hamlet into inaction. Consciously all he knows is that he is unable to act; this conscious inability he rationalizes, giving a different excuse each time.[7]

We have always been conscious of the fact that we are not masters of our fate in every respect—that there are many things which we cannot do, that nature is more powerful than we are, that we cannot disobey laws without danger of reprisals, etc. We have become "officially" conscious, too, though in our private lives we must long have been aware of it, that we are not free with respect to the emotions that we feel—whom we love or hate, what types we admire, and the like. More lately still we have been reminded that there are unconscious motivations for our basic attractions and repulsions, our compulsive actions or inabilities to act. But what is not welcome news is that our very acts of volition, and the entire train of deliberations leading up to them, are but façades for the expression of unconscious wishes, or rather, unconscious compromises and defenses.

A man is faced by a choice: shall he kill another person or not? Moralists would say, here is a free choice—the result of deliberation, an action consciously entered into. And yet, though the agent himself does not know it, and has no awareness of the forces that are at work within him, his choice is already determined for him: his conscious will is only an instrument, a slave, in the hands of a deep unconscious motivation which determines his action. If he has a great deal of what the analyst calls "free-floating guilt," he will not; but if the guilt is such as to demand immediate absorption in the form of self-damaging behavior, this accumulated guilt will have to be discharged in some criminal action. The man himself does not know what the inner clockwork is; he is like the hands on the clock, thinking they move freely over the face of the clock.

A woman has married and divorced several husbands. Now she is faced with a choice for the next marriage: shall she marry Mr. A, or Mr. B, or nobody at all? She may take considerable time to "decide" this question, and her decision may appear as a final triumph of her free will. Let us assume that A is a normal, well-adjusted, kind, and generous man, while B is a leech, an impostor, one who will become entangled constantly in quarrels with her. If she belongs to a certain classifiable psychological type, she will inevitably choose B, and she will do so even if her previous husbands have resembled B, so that one would think that she "had learned from experience." Consciously, she will of course "give the matter due consideration," etc., etc. To the psychoanalyst all this is irrelevant chaff in the wind—only a camouflage for the inner workings about which she knows nothing consciously. If she is of a certain kind of masochistic strain, as exhibited in her previous set of symptoms, she *must* choose B: her superego, always out to maximize the torment in the situation, seeing what dazzling possibilities for self-damaging behavior are promised by the choice of B, compels her to make the choice she does, and even to conceal the real basis of the choice behind an elaborate façade of rationalizations.

A man is addicted to gambling. In the service of his addiction he loses all his money, spends what belongs to his wife, even sells his property, and neglects his children. For a time perhaps he stops; then, inevitably, he takes it up again. The man does not know that he is a victim rather than an agent; or, if he sometimes senses that he is in the throes of something-he-knows-not-what, he will have no inkling of its character and will soon re-

[7] See *The Basic Writings of Sigmund Freud,* Modern Library Edition, p. 310. (In *The Interpretation of Dreams.*) Cf. also the essay by Ernest Jones, "A Psycho-analytical Study of Hamlet."

lapse into the illusion that he (his conscious self) is freely deciding the course of his own actions. What he does not know, of course, is that he is still taking out on his mother the original lesion to his infantile narcissism, getting back at her for her fancied refusal of his infantile wishes—and this by rejecting everything identified with her, namely education, discipline, logic, common sense, training. At the roulette wheel, almost alone among adult activities, chance—the opposite of all these things—rules supreme; and his addiction represents his continued and emphatic reiteration of his rejection of Mother and all she represents to his unconscious.

This pseudo-aggression of his is of course masochistic in its effects. In the long run he always loses; he can never quit while he is winning. And far from playing in order to win, rather one can say that his losing is a *sine qua non* of his psychic equilibrium (as it was, for example, with Dostoyevsky): guilt demands punishment, and in the ego's "deal" with the superego the superego has granted satisfaction of infantile wishes in return for the self-damaging conditions obtaining. Winning would upset the neurotic equilibrium.

A man has wash-compulsion. He must be constantly washing his hands—he uses up perhaps 400 towels a day. Asked why he does this, he says, "I need to, my hands are dirty"; and if it is pointed out to him that they are not really dirty, he says "They feel dirty anyway, I feel better when I wash them." So once again he washes them. He "freely decides" every time; he feels that he must wash them, he deliberates for a moment perhaps, but always ends by washing them. What he does not see, of course, are the invisible wires inside him pulling him inevitably to do the thing he does: the infantile id-wish concerns preoccupation with dirt, the superego charges him with this, and the terrified ego must respond, "No, I don't like dirt, see how clean I like to be, look how I wash my hands!"

Let us see what further "free acts" the same patient engages in (this is an actual case history): he is taken to a concentration camp, and given the worst of treatment by the Nazi guards. In the camp he no longer chooses to be clean, does not even try to be—on the contrary, his choice is now to wallow in filth as much as he can. All he is aware of now is a

disinclination to be clean, and every time he must choose he chooses not to be. Behind the scenes, however, another drama is being enacted: the superego, perceiving that enough torment is being administered from the outside, can afford to cease pressing its charges in this quarter—the outside world is doing the torturing now, so the superego is relieved of the responsibility. Thus the ego is relieved of the agony of constantly making terrified replies in the form of washing to prove that the superego is wrong. The defense no longer being needed, the person slides back into what is his natural predilection anyway, for filth. This becomes too much even for the Nazi guards; they take hold of him one day, saying "We'll teach you how to be clean!" drag him into the snow, and pour bucket after bucket of icy water over him until he freezes to death. Such is the end-result of an original id-wish, caught in the machinations of a destroying superego.

Let us take, finally, a less colorful, more everyday example. A student at a university, possessing wealth, charm, and all that is usually considered essential to popularity, begins to develop the following personality-pattern: although well taught in the graces of social conversation, he always makes a *faux pas* somewhere, and always in the worst possible situation; to his friends he makes cutting remarks which hurt deeply—and always apparently aimed in such a way as to hurt the most: a remark that would not hurt A but would hurt B he invariably makes to B rather than to A, and so on. None of this is conscious. Ordinarily he is considerate of people, but he contrives always (unconsciously) to impose on just those friends who would resent it most, and at just the times when he should know that he should not impose; at 3 o'clock in the morning, without forewarning, he phones a friend in a near-by city demanding to stay at his apartment for the weekend; naturally the friend is offended, but the person himself is not aware that he has provoked the grievance ("common sense" suffers a temporary eclipse when the neurotic pattern sets in, and one's intelligence, far from being of help in such a situation, is used in the interest of the neurosis), and when the friend is cool to him the next time they meet, he wonders why and feels unjustly treated. Aggressive behavior on his part invites resentment and aggression in turn, but all that he consciously sees is others' behavior toward him—and he considers himself the innocent victim of an unjustified "persecution."

Each of these acts is, from the moralist's point of view, free: he chose to phone his friend at 3 A.M.; he chose to make the cutting remark that he did, etc. What he does not know is that an ineradicable masochistic pattern has set in. His unconscious is far more shrewd and clever than is his conscious intellect; it sees with uncanny accuracy just what kind of behavior will damage him most, and unerringly forces him into that behavior. Consciously, the student "doesn't know why he did it"—he gives different "reasons" at different times, but they are all, once again, rationalizations cloaking the unconscious mechanism which propels him willynilly into actions that his "common sense" eschews.

The more of this sort of thing one observes, the more he can see what the psychoanalyst means when he talks about *the illusion of freedom*. And the more of a psychiatrist one becomes, the more he is overcome with a sense of what an illusion this free will can be. In some kinds of cases most of us can see it already: it takes no psychiatrist to look at the epileptic and sigh with sadness at the thought that soon this person before you will be as one possessed, not the same thoughtful intelligent person you knew. But people are not aware of this in other contexts, for example when they express surprise at how a person whom they have been so good to could treat them so badly. Let us suppose that you help a person financially or morally or in some other way, so that he is in your debt; suppose further that he is one of the many neurotics who unconsciously identify kindness with weakness and aggression with strength, then he will unconsciously take your kindness to him as weakness and use it as the occasion for enacting some aggression against you. He can't help it, he may regret it himself later; still, he will be driven to do it. If we gain a little knowledge of psychiatry, we can look at him with pity, that a person otherwise so worthy should be so unreliable—but we will exercise realism too, and be aware that there are some types of people that you cannot be good to; in "free" acts of their conscious voli-

tion, they will use your own goodness against you.

Sometimes the persons themselves will become dimly aware that "something behind the scenes" is determining their behavior. The divorcee will sometimes view herself with detachment, as if she were some machine (and indeed the psychoanalyst does call her a "repeating-machine"): "I know I'm caught in a net, that I'll fall in love with this guy and marry him and the whole ridiculous merry-go-round will start all over again."

We talk about free will, and we say, for example, the person is free to do so-and-so if he can do so *if* he wants to—and we forget that his wanting to is itself caught up in the stream of determinism, that unconscious forces drive him into the wanting or not wanting to do the thing in question. The analogy of the puppet whose motions are manipulated from behind by invisible wires, or better still, by springs inside, is a telling one at almost every point.

And the glaring fact is that it all started so early, before we knew what was happening. The personality structure is inelastic after the age of five, and comparatively so in most cases after the age of three. Whether one acquires a neurosis or not is determined by that age—and just as involuntarily as if it had been a curse of God. If, for example, a masochistic pattern was set up, under pressure of hypernarcissism combined with real or fancied infantile deprivation, then the masochistic snowball was on its course downhill long before we or anybody else knew what was happening, and long before anyone could do anything about it. To speak of human beings as "puppets" in such a context is no idle metaphor, but a stark rendering of a literal fact: only the psychiatrist knows what puppets people really are; and it is no wonder that the protestations of philosophers that "the act which is the result of a volition, a deliberation, a conscious decision, is free" leaves these persons, to speak mildly, somewhat cold.

But, one may object, all the states thus far described have been abnormal, neurotic ones. The well-adjusted (normal) person at least is free.

Leaving aside the question of how clearly and on what grounds one can distinguish the neurotic from the normal, let me use an illustration of a proclivity that everyone would call normal, namely, the decision of a man to support his wife and possibly a family, and consider briefly its genesis, according to psychoanalytic accounts.

Every baby comes into the world with a full-fledged case of megalomania—interested only in himself, acting as if believing that he is the center of the universe and that others are present only to fulfill his wishes, and furious when his own wants are not satisfied immediately no matter for what reason. Gratitude, even for all the time and worry and care expended on him by the mother, is an emotion entirely foreign to the infant, and as he grows older it is inculcated in him only with the greatest difficulty; his natural tendency is to assume that everything that happens to him is due to himself, except for denials and frustrations, which are due to the "cruel, denying" outer world, in particular the mother; and that he owes nothing to anyone, is dependent on no one. This omnipotence-complex, or illusion of nondependence, has been called the "autarchic fiction." Such a conception of the world is actually fostered in the child by the conduct of adults, who automatically attempt to fulfill the infant's every wish concerning nourishment, sleep, and attention. The child misconceives causality and sees in these wish-fulfillments not the results of maternal kindness and love, but simply the result of his own omnipotence.

This fiction of omnipotence is gradually destroyed by experience, and its destruction is probably the deepest disappointment of the early years of life. First of all, the infant discovers that he is the victim of organic urges and necessities: hunger, defecation, urination. More important, he discovers that the maternal breast, which he has not previously distinguished from his own body (he has not needed to, since it was available when he wanted it), is not a part of himself after all, but of another creature upon whom he is dependent. He is forced to recognize this, e.g., when he wants nourishment and it is at the moment not present; even a small delay is most damaging to the "autarchic fiction." Most painful of all is the experience of weaning, probably the greatest tragedy in every baby's life, when his dependence is most cruelly emphasized; it is a frustrating experience because what he wants is no longer there at all; and if he has been able to some extent to

preserve the illusion of nondependence heretofore, he is not able to do so now—it is plain that the source of his nourishment is not dependent on him, but he on it. The shattering of the autarchic fiction is a great disillusionment to every child, a tremendous blow to his ego which he will, in one way or another, spend the rest of his life trying to repair. How does he do this?

First of all, his reaction to frustration is anger and fury; and he responds by kicking, biting, etc., the only ways he knows. But he is motorically helpless, and these measures are ineffective, and only serve to emphasize his dependence the more. Moreover, against such responses of the child the parental reaction is one of prohibition, often involving deprivation of attention and affection. Generally the child soon learns that this form of rebellion is profitless, and brings him more harm than good. He wants to respond to frustration with violent aggression, and at the same time learns that he will be punished for such aggression, and that in any case the latter is ineffectual. What face-saving solution does he find? Since he must "face facts," since he must in any case "conform" if he is to have any peace at all, he tries to make it seem as if he himself is the source of the commands and prohibitions: the *external* prohibitive force is *internalized*—and here we have the origin of conscience. By making the prohibitive agency seem to come from within himself, the child can "save face"—as if saying, "The prohibition comes from within me, not from outside, so I'm not subservient to external rule, I'm only obeying rules I've set up myself," thus to some extent saving the autarchic fiction, and at the same time avoiding unpleasant consequences directed against himself by complying with parental commands.

Moreover, the boy[8] has unconsciously never forgiven the mother for his dependence on her in early life, for nourishment and all other things. It has upset his illusion of nondependence. These feelings have been repressed and are not remembered; but they are acted out in later life in many ways—e.g., in the constant deprecation man has for woman's

[8] The girl's development after this point is somewhat different. Society demands more aggressiveness of the adult male, hence there are more superego strictures on tendencies toward passivity in the male; accordingly his defenses must be stronger.

duties such as cooking and housework of all sorts ("All she does is stay home and get together a few meals, and she calls that work"), and especially in the man's identification with the mother in his sex experiences with women. By identifying with someone, one cancels out in effect the person with whom he identifies—replacing that person, unconsciously denying his existence, and the man, identifying with his early mother, playing the active rôle in "giving" to his wife as his mother has "given" to him, is in effect the denial of his mother's existence, a fact which is narcissistically embarrassing to his ego because it is chiefly responsible for shattering his autarchic fiction. In supporting his wife, he can unconsciously deny that his mother gave to him, and that he was dependent on her giving. Why is it that the husband plays the provider, and wants his wife to be dependent on no one else, although twenty years before he was nothing but a parasitic baby? This is a face-saving device on his part: he can act out the reasoning "See, I'm not the parasitic baby, on the contrary I'm the provider, the giver." His playing the provider is a constant face-saving device, to deny his early dependence which is so embarrassing to his ego. It is no wonder that men generally dislike to be reminded of their babyhood, when they were dependent on woman.

Thus we have here a perfectly normal adult reaction which is unconsciously motivated. The man "chooses" to support a family—and his choice is as unconsciously motivated as anything could be. (I have described here only the "normal" state of affairs, uncomplicated by the well-nigh infinite number of variations that occur in actual practice.)

Now, what of the notion of responsibility? What happens to it on our analysis?

Let us begin with an example, not a fictitious one. A woman and her two-year-old baby are riding on a train to Montreal in midwinter. The child is ill. The woman wants badly to get to her destination. She is, unknown to herself, the victim of a neurotic conflict whose nature is irrelevant here except for the fact that it forces her to behave aggressively toward the child, partly to spite her husband whom she despises and who loves the child, but chiefly to ward off superego charges of masochistic attachment. Consciously she loves the child, and when she says this she says it sincerely, but she must behave ag-

gressively toward it nevertheless, just as many children love their mothers but are nasty to them most of the time in neurotic pseudo-aggression. The child becomes more ill as the train approaches Montreal; the heating system of the train is not working, and the conductor pleads with the woman to get off the train at the next town and get the child to a hospital at once. The woman refuses. Soon after, the child's condition worsens, and the mother does all she can to keep it alive, without, however, leaving the train, for she declares that it is absolutely necessary that she reach her destination. But before she gets there the child is dead. After that, of course, the mother grieves, blames herself, weeps hysterically, and joins the church to gain surcease from the guilt that constantly overwhelms her when she thinks of how her aggressive behavior has killed her child.

Was she responsible for her deed? In ordinary life, after making a mistake, we say, "Chalk it up to experience." Here we should say, "Chalk it up to the neurosis." *She* could not help it if her neurosis forced her to act this way—she didn't even know what was going on behind the scenes, her conscious self merely acted out its assigned part. This is far more true than is generally realized: criminal actions in general are not actions for which their agents are responsible; the agents are passive, not active—they are victims of a neurotic conflict. Their very hyperactivity is unconsciously determined.

To say this is, of course, not to say that we should not punish criminals. Clearly, for our own protection, we must remove them from our midst so that they can no longer molest and endanger organized society. And, of course, if we use the word "responsible" in such a way that justly to hold someone responsible for a deed is by definition identical with being justified in punishing him, then we can and do hold people responsible. But this is like the sense of "free" in which free acts are voluntary ones. It does not go deep enough. In a deeper sense we cannot hold the person responsible: we can hold his neurosis responsible, but *he is not responsible for his neurosis,* particularly since the age at which its onset was inevitable was an age before he could even speak.

The neurosis is responsible—but isn't the neurosis a part of *him*? We have been speaking all the time as if the person and his unconscious were two separate beings; but isn't he one personality, including conscious and unconscious departments together?

I do not wish to deny this. But it hardly helps us here; for what people want when they talk about freedom, and what they hold to when they champion it, is the idea that the *conscious* will is the master of their destiny. "I am the master of my fate, I am the captain of my soul"—and they surely mean their conscious selves, the self that they can recognize and search and introspect. Between an unconscious that willy-nilly determines your actions, and an external force which pushes you, there is little if anything to choose. The unconscious is just *as if* it were an outside force; and indeed, psychiatrists will assert that the inner Hitler (your superego) can torment you far more than any external Hitler can. Thus the kind of freedom that people want, the only kind they will settle for, is precisely the kind that psychiatry says that they cannot have.

Heretofore it was pretty generally thought that, while we could not rightly blame a person for the color of his eyes or the morality of his parents, or even for what he did at the age of three, or to a large extent what impulses he had, and whom he fell in love with, one *could* do so for other of his adult activities, particularly the acts he performed voluntarily and with premeditation. Later this attitude was shaken. Many voluntary acts came to be recognized, at least in some circles, as compelled by the unconscious. Some philosophers recognized this too—Ayer[9] talks about the kleptomaniac being unfree, and about a person being unfree when another person exerts a habitual ascendancy over his personality. But this is as far as he goes. The usual examples, such as the kleptomaniac and the schizophrenic, apparently satisfy most philosophers, and with these exceptions removed, the rest of mankind is permitted to wander in the vast and alluring fields of freedom and responsibility. So far, the inroads upon freedom left the vast majority of humanity untouched; they began to hit home when psychiatrists began to realize, though philosophers did not, that the domination of the conscious by the unconscious extended, not merely to a few exceptional individuals, but to

all human beings, that the "big three behind the scenes" are not respecters of persons, and dominate us all, even including that *sanctum sanctorum* of freedom, our conscious will. To be sure, the domination by the unconscious in the case of "normal" individuals is somewhat more benevolent than the tyranny and despotism exercised in neurotic cases, and therefore the former have evoked less comment; but the principle remains in all cases the same: the unconscious is the master of every fate and the captain of every soul.

We speak of a machine turning out good products most of the time but every once in a while it turns out a "lemon." We do not, of course, hold the product responsible for this, but the machine, and via the machine, its maker. Is it silly to extend to inanimate objects the idea of responsibility? Of course. But is it any less so to employ the notion in speaking of human creatures? Are not the two kinds of cases analogous in countless important ways? Occasionally a child turns out badly too, even when his environment and training are the same as that of his brothers and sisters who turn out "all right." He is the "bad penny." His acts of rebellion against parental discipline in adult life (such as the case of the gambler, already cited) are traceable to early experiences of real or fancied denial of infantile wishes. Sometimes the denial has been real, though many denials are absolutely necessary if the child is to grow up to observe the common decencies of civilized life; sometimes, if the child has an unusual quantity of narcissism, every event that occurs is interpreted by him as a denial of his wishes, and nothing a parent could do, even granting every humanly possible wish, would help. In any event, the later neurosis can be attributed to this. Can the person himself be held responsible? Hardly. If he engages in activities which are a menace to society, he must be put into prison, of course, but responsibility is another matter. The time when the events occurred which rendered his neurotic behavior inevitable was a time long before he was capable of thought and decision. As an adult, he is a victim of a world he never made—only this world is inside him.

What about the children who turn out "all right"? All we can say is that "it's just lucky for them" that what happened to their unfortunate brother didn't happen to them; *through no virtue of their own* they are not doomed

---

[9] A. J. Ayer, "Freedom and Necessity," *Polemic* (September–October 1946), pp. 40–43.

to the life of unconscious guilt, expiation, conscious depression, terrified ego-gestures for the appeasement of a tyrannical superego, that he is. The machine turned them out with a minimum of damage. But if the brother cannot be blamed for his evils, neither can they be praised for their good; unless, of course, we should blame people for what is not their fault, and praise them for lucky accidents.

We all agree that machines turn out "lemons," we all agree that nature turns out misfits in the realm of biology—the blind, the crippled, the diseased; but we hesitate to include the realm of the personality, for here, it seems, is the last retreat of our dignity as human beings. Our ego can endure anything but this; this island at least must remain above the encroaching flood. But may not precisely the same analysis be made here also? Nature turns out psychological "lemons" too, in far greater quantities than any other kind; and indeed all of us are "lemons" in some respect or other, the difference being one of degree. Some of us are lucky enough not to have a gambling-neurosis or criminotic tendencies or masochistic mother-attachment or overdimensional repetition-compulsion to make our lives miserable, but most of our actions, those usually considered the most important, are unconsciously dominated just the same. And, if a neurosis may be likened to a curse of God, let those of us, the elect, who are enabled to enjoy a measure of life's happiness without the hell-fire of neurotic guilt, take this, not as our own achievement, but simply for what it is— a gift of God.

Let us, however, quit metaphysics and put the situation schematically in the form of a deductive argument.

1. An occurrence over which we had no control is something we cannot be held responsible for.

2. Events E, occurring during our babyhood, were events over which we had no control.

3. Therefore events E were events which we cannot be held responsible for.

4. But if there is something we cannot be held responsible for, neither can we be held responsible for something that inevitably results from it.

5. Events E have as inevitable consequence Neurosis N, which in turn has as inevitable consequence Behavior B.

6. Since N is the inevitable consequence of E and B is the inevitable consequence of N, B is the inevitable consequence of E.

7. Hence, not being responsible for E, we cannot be responsible for B.

In Samuel Butler's Utopian satire *Erewhon* there occurs the following passage, in which a judge is passing sentence on a prisoner:

It is all very well for you to say that you came of unhealthy parents, and had a severe accident in your childhood which permanently undermined your constitution; excuses such as these are the ordinary refuge of the criminal; but they cannot for one moment be listened to by the ear of justice. I am not here to enter upon curious metaphysical questions as to the origin of this or that—questions to which there would be no end were their introduction once tolerated, and which would result in throwing the only guilt on the tissues of the primordial cell, or on the elementary gases. There is no question of how you came to be wicked, but only this—namely, are you wicked or not? This has been decided in the affirmative, neither can I hesitate for a single moment to say that it has been decided justly. You are a bad and dangerous person, and stand branded in the eyes of your fellow countrymen with one of the most heinous known offenses.[10]

As moralists read this passage, they may perhaps nod with approval. But the joke is on them. The sting comes when we realize what the crime is for which the prisoner is being sentenced: namely, consumption. The defendant is reminded that during the previous year he was sentenced for aggravated bronchitis, and is warned that he should profit from experience in the future. Butler is employing here his familiar method of presenting some human tendency (in this case, holding people responsible for what isn't their fault) to a ridiculous extreme and thereby reducing it to absurdity.

Assuming the main conclusions of this paper to be true, is there any room left for freedom?

This, of course, all depends on what we mean by "freedom." In the senses suggested at the beginning of this paper, there are countless free acts, and unfree ones as well. When "free" means "uncompelled," and only external compulsion is admitted, again there are

[10] Samuel Butler, *Erewhon* (Modern Library edition), p. 107.

countless free acts. But now we have extended the notion of compulsion to include determination by unconscious forces. With this sense in mind, our question is, "With the concept of compulsion thus extended, and in the light of present psychoanalytic knowledge, is there any freedom left in human behavior?"

If practicing psychoanalysts were asked this question, there is little doubt that their answer would be along the following lines: they would say that they were not accustomed to using the term "free" at all, but that if they had to suggest a criterion for distinguishing the free from the unfree, they would say that a person's freedom is present *in inverse proportion to his neuroticism*; in other words, the more his acts are determined by a *malevolent* unconscious, the less free he is. Thus they would speak of *degrees* of freedom. They would say that as a person is cured of his neurosis, he becomes more free—free to realize capabilities that were blocked by the neurotic affliction. The psychologically well-adjusted individual is in this sense comparatively the most free. Indeed, those who are cured of mental disorders are sometimes said to have *regained their freedom:* they are freed from the tyranny of a malevolent unconscious which formerly exerted as much of a domination over them as if they had been the abject slaves of a cruel dictator.

But suppose one says that a person is free only to the extent that his acts are *not unconsciously determined at all*, be they unconscious benevolent *or* malevolent? If this is the criterion, psychoanalysts would say, most human behavior cannot be called free at all: our impulses and volitions having to do with our basic attitudes toward life, whether we are optimists or pessimists, tough-minded or tender-minded, whether our tempers are quick or slow, whether we are "naturally self-seeking" or "naturally benevolent" (and *all the acts consequent upon these things*), what things annoy us, whether we take to blondes or brunettes, old or young, whether we become philosophers or artists or businessmen —all this has its basis in the unconscious. If people generally call most acts free, it is rather through not knowing how large a proportion of our acts actually are compelled. Only the comparatively "vanilla-flavored" aspects of our lives—such as our behavior toward people who don't really matter to us—are exempted from this rule.

These, I think, are the two principal criteria for distinguishing freedom from the lack of it which we might set up on the basis of psychoanalytic knowledge. Conceivably we might set up others. In every case, of course, it remains trivially true that "it all depends on how we choose to use the word." The facts are what they are, regardless of what words we choose for labeling them. But if we choose to label them in a way which is not in accord with what human beings, however vaguely, have long had in mind in applying these labels, as we would be doing if we labeled as "free" many acts which we know as much about as we now do through modern psychoanalytic methods, then we shall only be manipulating words to mislead our fellow creatures.

Is "Free Will" a Pseudo-Problem?*

I

In the days when the Verifiability Principle was accepted by its devotees as a secure philosophical truth, one could understand, though one might not agree with, the sweeping claim that many of the traditional problems of philosophy had been shown to be mere "pseudo-problems." It was easy to see how, given the Principle's validity, most of the leading questions which agitated our fore-

* C. A. Campbell, "Is 'Free Will' a Pseudo-Problem?" *Mind*, LX (1951), 441–65, reprinted with the permission of the author and the editor, Gilbert Ryle.

fathers in metaphysics, in ethics, and in theology, automatically became nonsensical questions. What is perplexing, however, is that despite the pretty generally acknowledged deterioration in the Principle's status to that of a convenient methodological postulate, the attitude to these same questions seems to have changed but little. To admit that the Verifiability Principle is not an assured truth entails the admission that a problem can no longer be dismissed as meaningless simply on the ground that it cannot be stated in a way which satisfies the Principle. Whether or not a problem is meaningless is now something that can only be decided after critical examination of the particular case on its own individual merits. But the old antipathies seem in large measure to have survived the disappearance of their logical basis. One gets the impression that for at least many thinkers with Positivist sympathies the "liquidation" of a large, if unspecified, group of traditional philosophic problems is still established fact. If that impression is mistaken, well and good. One may then hope for an early recrudescence of interest in certain problems that have too long suffered the consequences of an unhappy *tabu.* If the impression is correct, a real service would be done to philosophy if it were plainly stated which of the traditional problems are still regarded as pseudo-problems, and what are the reasons, old and new, for passing this sentence upon them. The smoke of old battles, perhaps understandably, darkens the philosophic air, to the considerable inconvenience of all concerned.

Fortunately, however, the obscurity complained of is not totally unrelieved. We do know of one traditional problem that is definitely on the black list of the *avant garde*— the problem of "Free Will": and we do have pretty adequate information about the reasons which have led to its being placed thereon. This, so far as it goes, is satisfactory. A plain obligation now lies upon philosophers who still believe that "Free Will" is a genuine problem to explain just where, in their opinion, the case for the prosecution breaks down. To discharge this obligation is the main purpose of the present paper.

There will be a clear advantage in making our start from the *locus classicus* of the "pseudo-problem" theory, if *locus classicus* there be. And I think that there must be something of the sort. At any rate, the casual, and indeed slightly bored, tones in which so many contemporary philosophers allude to the traditional problem, and their contentment to indicate in only a sketchy manner the reasons why it no longer exists, strongly suggest that *somewhere* the matter has in their eyes been already effectively settled. At least one important "document in the case" is, I suspect, Chapter VII of Moritz Schlick's *Problems of Ethics,* first published in 1931. This chapter, the title of which is "When Is a Man Responsible?" and the first section of which bears the heading "The Pseudo-problem of

Freedom of the Will," presents in concentrated form, but with some show of systematic argument, most of the considerations upon which later writers appear to rely. It will be worth our while, therefore, to try to see just why Professor Schlick is so sure (and he is *very* sure indeed) that "Free Will," as traditionally formulated, is a pseudo-problem, begotten by mere confusion of mind.

II

I shall first summarize, as faithfully as I can, what I take to be the distinctive points in Schlick's argument.

The traditional formulation of the problem, Schlick points out, is based on the assumption that to have "free will" entails having a will that is, at least sometimes, exempt from causal law. It is traditionally supposed, quite rightly, that moral responsibility implies freedom in *some* sense: and it is supposed, also quite rightly, that this sense is one which is incompatible with compulsion. But because it is further supposed, quite *wrongly,* that to be subject to causal or natural law is to be subject to compulsion, the inference is drawn that the free will implied in moral responsibility is incompatible with causal continuity. The ultimate root of the error, Schlick contends, lies in a failure to distinguish between two different kinds of Law, one of which does indeed "compel," but the other of which does *not.*[1] There are, first, *pre*scriptive laws, such as the laws imposed by civil authority, which presume contrary desires on the part of those to whom they are applied; and these may fairly be said to exercise "compulsion." And there are, secondly, *de*scriptive laws, such as the laws which the sciences seek to formulate; and these merely state what does as a matter of fact always happen. It is perfectly clear that the relation of the latter, the natural, causal laws, to human willing is radically different from the "compulsive" relation of prescriptive laws to human willing, and that it is really an absurdity to talk of a species of natural law like, say, psychological laws, *compelling* us to act in this or that way. The term "compulsion" is totally inept where, as in this case, there are no contrary desires. But the traditional discussions of Free Will, confusing descriptive with prescriptive laws, fallaciously

[1] *Problems of Ethics,* Ch. VIII, Section 2. (All references are to the English translation by David Rynin, published in New York in 1939.)

assume "compulsion" to be ingredient in Law as such, and it is contended accordingly that moral freedom, since it certainly implies absence of compulsion, implies also exemption from causal law.

It follows that the problem of Free Will, as traditionally stated, is a mere pseudo-problem. The statement of it in terms of exemption from causal law rests on the assumption that causal law involves "compulsion." And this assumption is demonstrably false. Expose the muddle from which it arises and the so-called "problem" in its traditional form disappears.

But is it quite certain that the freedom which moral responsibility implies is no more than "the absence of compulsion"? This is the premise upon which Schlick's argument proceeds, but Schlick is himself well aware that it stands in need of confirmation from an analysis of the notion of moral responsibility. Otherwise it might be maintained that although "the absence of compulsion" has been shown not to entail a contra-causal type of freedom, there is nevertheless some *other* condition of moral responsibility that *does* entail it. Accordingly Schlick embarks now upon a formal analysis of the nature and conditions of moral responsibility designed to show that the *only* freedom implied by moral responsibility is freedom from compulsion. It was a trifle ambitious, however, even for a master of compression like Professor Schlick, to hope to deal satisfactorily in half-a-dozen very brief pages with a topic which has been so extensively debated in the literature of moral philosophy: and I cannot pretend that I find what he has to say free from obscurity. But to the best of my belief what follows does reproduce the gist of Schlick's analysis.

What precisely, Schlick asks, does the term "moral responsibility" mean in our ordinary linguistic usage?[2] He begins his answer by insisting upon the close connection for ordinary usage between "moral responsibility" and *punishment* (strictly speaking, punishment and *reward*: but for convenience Schlick virtually confines the discussion to punishment, and we shall do the same). The connection, as Schlick sees it, is this. In ordinary practice our concern with the responsibility for an act (he tells us) is with a view to determining *who is to be punished for it.* Now punishment is (I quote) "an educative measure." It is "a means to the formation of motives, which are in part to prevent the wrong-doer from repeating the act (reformation), and in part to prevent others from committing a similar act (intimidation)."[3] When we ask, then, "Who in a given case is to be punished?"—which is the same as the question "Who is responsible?"—what we are really wanting to discover is some agent in the situation upon whose motives we can bring to bear the appropriate educative influences, so that in similar situations in future his strongest motive will impel him to refrain from, rather than to repeat, the act. "The question of who is responsible" Schlick sums up, "is ... a matter only of knowing who is to be punished or rewarded, in order that punishment and reward function as such — be able to achieve their goal."[4] It is not a matter, he expressly declares, of trying to ascertain what may be called the "original instigator" of the act. That might be a great-grandparent, from the consequences of whose behavior vicious tendencies have been inherited by a living person. Such "remote causes" as this are irrelevant to questions of punishment (and so to questions of moral responsibility), "for in the first place their actual contribution cannot be determined, and in the second place they are generally out of reach."[5]

It is a matter for regret that Schlick has not rounded off his discussion, as one had hoped and expected he would, by formulating a precise definition of moral responsibility in terms of what he has been saying. I think, however, that the conclusion to which his argument leads could be not unfairly expressed in some such way as this: "We say that a man is morally responsible for an act if his motives for bringing about the act are such as we can affect favorably in respect of his future behavior by the educative influences of reward and punishment."

Given the truth of this analysis of moral responsibility, Schlick's contention follows logically enough that the only freedom that is required for moral responsibility is freedom from compulsion. For what are the cases in which a man's motives are *not* capable of being favorably affected by reward and pun-

---

[2] *Loc. cit.,* Ch. VII, Section 5.

[3] *Ibid.,* p. 152.
[4] *Ibid.,* p. 153.
[5] *Ibid.,* p. 153.

ishment?—the cases in which, that is, according to Schlick's analysis, we do *not* deem him morally responsible? The only such cases, it would seem, are those in which a man is subjected to some form of external constraint which prevents him from acting according to his "natural desires." For example, if a man is compelled by a pistol at his breast to do a certain act, or induced to do it by an externally administered narcotic, he is not "morally responsible"; or not, at any rate, in so far as punishment would be impotent to affect his motives in respect of his future behavior. External constraint in one form or another seems to be the sole circumstance which absolves a man from moral responsibility. Hence we may say that freedom from external constraint is the only sort of freedom which an agent must possess in order to be morally responsible. The "contra-causal" sort of freedom which so many philosophers and others have supposed to be required is shown by a true analysis of moral responsibility to be irrelevant.

This completes the argument that "Free Will," as traditionally formulated, is a pseudo-problem. The only freedom implied by moral responsibility is freedom from compulsion; and as we have rid ourselves of the myth that subjection to causal law is a form of compulsion, we can see that the only compulsion which absolves from moral responsibility is the external constraint which prevents us from translating our desires into action. The true meaning of the question "Have we free will?" thus becomes simply "Can we translate our desires into action?" And this question does not constitute a "problem" at all, for the answer to it is not in doubt. The obvious answer is "Sometimes we can, sometimes we can't, according to the specific circumstances of the case."

III

Here, then, in substance is Schlick's theory. Let us now examine it.

In the first place, it is surely quite unplausible to suggest that the common assumption that moral freedom postulates some breach of causal continuity arises from a confusion of two different types of law. Schlick's distinction between descriptive and prescriptive law is, of course, sound. It was no doubt worth pointing out, too, that descriptive laws cannot be said to "compel" human behavior in the same way as prescriptive laws do. But it seems to me evident that the usual reason why it is held that moral freedom implies some breach of causal continuity, is not a belief that causal laws "compel" as civil laws "compel," but simply the belief that the admission of unbroken causal continuity entails a *further* admission which is directly incompatible with moral responsibility; viz., the admission that no man could have acted otherwise than he in fact did. Now it may, of course, be an error thus to assume that a man is not morally responsible for an act, a fit subject for moral praise and blame in respect of it, unless he could have acted otherwise than he did. Or, if *this* is not an error, it may still be an error to assume that a man could not have acted otherwise than he did, in the sense of the phrase that is crucial for moral responsibility, without there occurring some breach of causal continuity. Into these matters we shall have to enter very fully at a later stage. But the relevant point at the moment is that these (not *prima facie* absurd) assumptions about the conditions of moral responsibility have very commonly, indeed normally, been made, and that they are entirely adequate to explain why the problem of Free Will finds its usual formulation in terms of partial exemption from causal law. Schlick's distinction between prescriptive and descriptive laws has no bearing at all upon the truth or falsity of these assumptions. Yet if these assumptions are accepted, it is (I suggest) really inevitable that the Free-Will problem should be formulated in the way to which Schlick takes exception. Recognition of the distinction upon which Schlick and his followers lay so much stress can make not a jot of difference.

As we have seen, however, Schlick does later proceed to the much more important business of disputing these common assumptions about the conditions of moral responsibility. He offers us an analysis of moral responsibility which flatly contradicts these assumptions; an analysis according to which the only freedom demanded by morality is a freedom which is compatible with Determinism. If this analysis can be sustained, there is certainly no problem of "Free Will" in the traditional sense.

But it seems a simple matter to show that Schlick's analysis is untenable. Let us test it by Schlick's own claim that it gives us what we mean by "moral responsibility" in ordinary linguistic usage.

We do not ordinarily consider the lower animals to be morally responsible. But *ought* we not to do so if Schlick is right about what we mean by moral responsibility? It is quite possible, by punishing the dog who absconds with the succulent chops designed for its master's luncheon, favorably to influence its motives in respect of its future behavior in like circumstances. If moral responsibility is to be linked with punishment as Schlick links it, and punishment conceived as a form of education, we should surely hold the dog morally responsible? The plain fact, of course, is that we don't. We don't, because we suppose that the dog "couldn't help it": that its action (unlike what we usually believe to be true of human beings) was simply a link in a continuous chain of causes and effects. In other words, we do commonly demand the contra-causal sort of freedom as a condition of moral responsibility.

Again, we do ordinarily consider it proper, in certain circumstances, to speak of a person no longer living as morally responsible for some present situation. But *ought* we to do so if we accept Schlick's essentially "forward-looking" interpretation of punishment and responsibility? Clearly we cannot now favorably affect the dead man's motives. No doubt they could *at one time* have been favorably affected. But that cannot be relevant to our judgment of responsibility if, as Schlick insists, the question of who is responsible "is a matter only of knowing who is to be punished or rewarded." Indeed he expressly tells us, as we saw earlier, that in asking this question we are not concerned with a "great-grandparent" who may have been the "original instigator," because, for one thing, this "remote cause" is "out of reach." We cannot bring the appropriate educative influence to bear upon it. But the plain fact, of course, is that we do frequently assign moral responsibility for present situations to persons who have long been inaccessible to any punitive action on our part. And Schlick's position is still more paradoxical in respect of our apportionment of responsibility for occurrences in the distant past. Since in these cases there is no agent whatsoever whom we can favorably influence by punishment, the question of moral responsibility here should have no meaning for us. But of course it has. Historical writings are studded with examples.

Possibly the criticism just made may seem to some to result from taking Schlick's analysis too much *au pied de la lettre*. The absurd consequences deduced, it may be said, would not follow if we interpreted Schlick as meaning that a man is morally responsible where his motive is such as can *in principle* be favorably affected by reward or punishment—whether or not we who pass the judgment are in a position to take such action. But with every desire to be fair to Schlick, I cannot see how he could accept this modification and still retain the essence of his theory. For the essence of his theory seems to be that moral responsibility has its whole meaning and importance for us in relation to our potential control of future conduct in the interests of society. (I agree that it is hard to believe that anybody *really* thinks this. But it is perhaps less hard to believe today than it has ever been before in the history of modern ethics.)

Again, we ordinarily consider that, in certain circumstances, the *degree* of a man's moral responsibility for an act is affected by considerations of his inherited nature, or of his environment, or of both. It is our normal habit to "make allowances" (as we say) when we have reason to believe that a malefactor had a vicious heredity, or was nurtured in his formative years in a harmful environment. We say in such cases "Poor chap, he is more to be pitied than blamed. We could scarcely expect him to behave like a decent citizen with *his* parentage or upbringing." But this extremely common sort of judgment has no point at all if we mean by moral responsibility what Schlick says that we mean. On *that* meaning the degree of a man's moral responsibility must presumably be dependent upon the degree to which we can favorably affect his future motives, which is quite another matter. Now there is no reason to believe that the motives of a man with a bad heredity or a bad upbringing are either less or more subject to educative influence than those of his more fortunate fellows. Yet it is plain matter of fact that we do commonly consider the degree of a man's moral responsibility to be affected by these two factors.

A final point. The extremity of paradox in Schlick's identification of the question "Who is morally blameworthy?" with the question "Who is to be punished?" is apt to be partially concealed from us just because it is our normal habit to include in the meaning of "punishment" an element of "requital for moral transgression" which Schlick expressly denies to it. On that account we commonly think of "punishment," in its strict sense, as implying moral blameworthiness in the person punished. But if we remember to mean by punishment what Schlick means by it, a purely "educative measure," with no retributive ingredients, his identification of the two questions loses such plausibility as it might otherwise have. For clearly we often think it proper to "punish" a person, in *Schlick's* sense, where we are not at all prepared to say that the person is morally blameworthy. We may even think him morally commendable. A case in point would be the unmistakably sincere but muddleheaded person who at the cost of great suffering to himself steadfastly pursues as his "duty" a course which, in our judgment, is fraught with danger to the commonweal. We should most of us feel entitled, in the public interest, to bring such action to bear upon the man's motives as might induce him to refrain in future from his socially injurious behavior: in other words, to inflict upon him what Schlick would call "punishment." But we should most of us feel perfectly clear that in so "punishing" this misguided citizen we are not proclaiming his moral blameworthiness for moral wickedness.

Adopting Schlick's own criterion, then, looking simply "to the manner in which the concept is used,"[6] we seem bound to admit that constantly people do assign moral responsibility where Schlick's theory says they shouldn't, don't assign moral responsibility where Schlick's theory says they should, and assign degrees of moral responsibility where on Schlick's theory there should be no difference in degree. I think we may reasonably conclude that Schlick's account of what we mean by moral responsibility breaks down.

The rebuttal of Schlick's arguments, however, will not suffice of itself to refute the pseudo-problem theory. The indebtedness to Schlick of most later advocates of the theory may be conceded; but certainly it does not comprehend all of significance that they have to say on the problem. There are recent analyses of the conditions of moral responsibility containing sufficient new matter, or sufficient old matter in a more precise and telling form, to require of us now something of a fresh start.

[6] *Loc. cit.*, Ch. VII, Section 5, p. 151.

In the section which follows I propose to consider some representative samples of these analyses—all of which, of course, are designed to show that the freedom which moral responsibility implies is not in fact a contra-causal type of freedom.

But before reopening the general question of the nature and conditions of moral responsibility there is a *caveat* which it seems to me worth while to enter. The difficulties in the way of a clear answer are not slight; but they are apt to seem a good deal more formidable than they really are because of a common tendency to consider in unduly close association two distinct questions: the question "Is a contra-causal type of freedom implied by moral responsibility?" and the question "Does a contra-causal type of freedom anywhere exist?" It seems to me that many philosophers (and I suspect that Moritz Schlick is among them) begin their enquiry with so firm a conviction that the contra-causal sort of freedom nowhere exists, that they find it hard to take very seriously the possibility that it is *this* sort of freedom that moral responsibility implies. For they are loth to abandon the common-sense belief that moral responsibility itself is something real. The implicit reasoning I take to be this. Moral responsibility is real. If moral responsibility is real, the freedom implied in it must be a fact. But contra-causal freedom is not a fact. Therefore contra-causal freedom is not the freedom implied in moral responsibility. I think we should be on our guard against allowing this or some similar train of reasoning (whose premises, after all, are far from indubitable) to seduce us into distorting what we actually find when we set about a direct analysis of moral responsibility and its conditions.

IV

The pseudo-problem theorists usually, and naturally, develop their analysis of moral responsibility by way of contrast with a view which, while it has enjoyed a good deal of philosophic support, I can perhaps best describe as the common view. It will be well to remind ourselves, therefore, of the main features of this view.

So far as the *meaning,* as distinct from the *conditions,* of moral responsibility is concerned, the common view is very simple. If we ask ourselves whether a certain person is morally responsible for a given act (or it may be just "in general"), what we are considering, it would be said, is whether or not that person is a fit subject upon whom to pass moral judgment; whether he can fittingly be deemed morally good or bad, morally praiseworthy or blameworthy. This does not take us any great way: but (*pace* Schlick) so far as it goes it does not seem to me seriously disputable. The really interesting and controversial question is about the *conditions* of moral responsibility, and in particular the question whether freedom of a contra-causal kind is among these conditions.

The answer of the common man to the latter question is that it most certainly *is* among the conditions. Why does he feel so sure about this? Not, I argued earlier, because the common man supposes that causal law exercises "compulsion" in the sense that prescriptive laws do, but simply because he does not see how a person can be deemed morally praiseworthy or blameworthy in respect of an act which he could not help performing. From the standpoint of moral praise and blame, he would say—though not necessarily from other standpoints—it is a matter of indifference whether it is by reason of some external constraint or by reason of his own given nature that the man could not help doing what he did. It is quite enough to make moral praise and blame futile that in either case there were no genuine alternatives, no open possibilities, before the man when he acted. He could not have acted otherwise than he did. And the common man might not unreasonably go on to stress the fact that we all, even if we are linguistic philosophers, do in our actual practice of moral judgment appear to accept the common view. He might insist upon the point alluded to earlier in this paper, that we do all, in passing moral censure, "make allowances" for influences in a man's hereditary nature or environmental circumstances which we regard as having made it more than ordinarily difficult for him to act otherwise than he did: the implication being that if we supposed that the man's heredity and environment made it not merely very *difficult* but actually *impossible* for him to act otherwise than he did, we could not properly assign moral blame to him at all.

Let us put the argument implicit in the common view a little more sharply. The moral "ought" implies "can." If we say that A morally ought to have done X, we imply that

in our opinion, he could have done X. But we assign moral blame to a man only for failing to do what we think he morally ought to have done. Hence if we morally blame A for not having done X, we imply that he could have done X even though in fact he did not. In other words, we imply that A could have acted otherwise than he did. And that means that we imply, as a necessary condition of a man's being morally blameworthy, that he enjoyed a freedom of a kind not compatible with unbroken causal continuity.

V

Now what is it that is supposed to be wrong with this simple piece of argument?—For, of course, it must be rejected by all these philosophers who tell us that the traditional problem of Free Will is a mere pseudo-problem. The argument looks as though it were doing little more than reading off necessary implications of the fundamental categories of our moral thinking. One's inclination is to ask "If one is to think morally at all, how else than this *can* we think?"

In point of fact, there is pretty general agreement among the contemporary critics as to what is wrong with the argument. Their answer in general terms is as follows. No doubt A's moral responsibility does imply that he could have acted otherwise. But this expression "could have acted otherwise" stands in dire need of analysis. When we analyze it, we find that it is not, as is so often supposed, simple and unambiguous, and we find that in *some* at least of its possible meanings it implies *no* breach of causal continuity between character and conduct. Having got this clear, we can further discern that only in one of these *latter* meanings is there any compulsion upon our moral thinking to assert that if A is morally blameworthy for an act, A "could have acted otherwise than he did." It follows that, contrary to common belief, our moral thinking does *not* require us to posit a contra-causal freedom as a condition of moral responsibility.

So much of importance obviously turns upon the validity or otherwise of this line of criticism that we must examine it in some detail and with express regard to the *ipsissima verba* of the critics.

In the course of a recent article in *Mind*,[7]

---

[7] January, 1948.

entitled "Free Will and Moral Responsibility," Mr. Nowell-Smith (having earlier affirmed his belief that "the traditional problem has been solved") explains very concisely the nature of the confusion which, as he thinks, has led to the demand for a contra-causal freedom. He begins by frankly recognizing that "It is evident that one of the necessary conditions of moral action is that the agent 'could have acted otherwise'" and he adds "it is to this fact that the Libertarian is drawing attention."[8] Then, after showing (unexceptionably, I think) how the relationship of "ought" to "can" warrants the proposition which he has accepted as evident and how it induces the Libertarian to assert the existence of action that is "uncaused," he proceeds to point out, in a crucial passage, the nature of the Libertarian's error:

The fallacy in the argument (he contends) lies in supposing that when we say "A could have acted otherwise" we mean that A, *being what he was and being placed in the circumstances in which he was placed, could have done something other than what he did.* But in fact we never do mean this.[9]

What then *do* we mean here by "A could have acted otherwise"? Mr. Nowell-Smith does not tell us in so many words, but the passage I have quoted leaves little doubt how he would answer. What we really mean by the expression, he implies, is not a *categorical* but a *hypothetical* proposition. We mean "A could have acted otherwise, *if he did not happen to be what he in fact was,* or *if he were placed in circumstances other than those in which he was in fact placed.*" Now, *these* propositions, it is easy to see, are in no way incompatible with acceptance of the causal principle in its full rigor. Accordingly the claim that our fundamental moral thinking obliges us to assert a contra-causal freedom as a condition of moral responsibility is disproved.

Such is the "analytical solution" of our problem offered (with obvious confidence) by one able philosopher of today, and entirely representative of the views of many other able philosophers. Yet I make bold to say that its falsity stares one in the face. It seems perfectly plain that the hypothetical propositions which Mr. Nowell-Smith proposes to substitute for the categorical proposition cannot express "what we really mean" in this

context by "A could have acted otherwise," for the simple reason that these hypothetical propositions have no bearing whatsoever upon the question of the moral responsibility of A. And it is *A* whose moral responsibility we are talking about—a definite person *A* with a definitive character and in a definitive set of circumstances. What conceivable significance could it have for our attitude to A's responsibility to know that someone with a *different* character (or *A* with a different character, if that collocation of words has any meaning), or A in a different set of circumstances from those in which A as we are concerned with him was in fact placed, "could have acted otherwise"? No doubt this supposititious being *could* have acted otherwise than the definitive person A acted. But the point is that where we are reflecting, as we are supposed in this context to be reflecting, upon the question of *A*'s moral responsibility, our interest in this supposititious being is precisely *nil.*

The two hypothetical propositions suggested in Mr. Nowell-Smith's account of the matter do not, however, exhaust the speculations that have been made along these lines. Another very common suggestion by the analysts is that what we really mean by "A could have acted otherwise" is "A could have acted otherwise *if he had willed, or chosen, otherwise.*" This is among the suggestions offered by G. E. Moore in the well-known chapter on Free Will in his *Ethics.* It is, I think, the suggestion he most strongly favored: though it is fair to add that neither about this nor about any other of his suggestions is Moore in the least dogmatic. He does claim, for, I think, convincing reasons, that "we *very often* mean by 'could' merely 'would, *if* so-and-so had chosen.'"[10] And he concludes "I must confess that I cannot feel certain that this may not be all that we usually mean and and understand by the assertion that we have Free Will."[11]

This third hypothetical proposition appears to enjoy also the support of Mr. C. L. Stevenson. Mr. Stevenson begins the chapter of *Ethics and Language* entitled "Avoidability-Indeterminism" with the now familiar pronouncement of his School that "controversy about freedom and determinism of the will ... presents no permanent difficulty to ethics, being largely a product of confusions." A

8 *Loc. cit.,* p. 49.
9 *Loc. cit.,* p. 49.

10 *Ethics,* p. 212.
11 *Loc. cit.,* p. 217.

major confusion (if I understand him rightly) he takes to lie in the meaning of the term "avoidable," when we say "A's action was avoidable" — or, I presume, "A could have acted otherwise." He himself offers the following definition of "avoidable" — " 'A's action was avoidable' has the meaning of 'If A had made a certain choice, which in fact he did not make, his action would not have occurred.' "[12] This I think we may regard as in substance identical with the suggestion that what we really mean by "A could have acted otherwise" is "A could have acted otherwise *if* he had chosen (or willed) otherwise." For clarity's sake we shall here keep to this earlier formulation. In either formulation the special significance of the third hypothetical proposition, as of the two hypothetical propositions already considered, is that it is compatible with strict determinism. If this be indeed all that we mean by the "freedom" that conditions moral responsibility, then those philosophers are certainly wrong who hold that moral freedom is of the contra-causal type.

Now this third hypothetical proposition does at least possess the merit, not shared by its predecessors, of having a real relevance to the question of moral responsibility. If, e.g., A had promised to meet us at 2 P.M., and he chanced to break his leg at 1 P.M., we should not blame him for his failure to discharge his promise. For we should be satisfied that he *could not* have acted otherwise, even if he had so chosen; or *could not,* at any rate, in a way which would have enabled him to meet us at 2 P.M. The freedom to translate one's choice into action, which we saw earlier is for Schlick the *only* freedom required for moral responsibility, is without doubt *one* of the conditions of moral responsibility.

But it seems easy to show that this third hypothetical proposition does not exhaust what we mean, and *some*times is not even *part* of what we mean, by the expression "could have acted otherwise" in its moral context. Thus it can hardly be even part of what we mean in the case of that class of wrong actions (and it is a large class) concerning which there is really no question whether the agent could have acted otherwise, *if* he had chosen otherwise. Take lying, for example. Only in some very abnormal situation could it occur to one to doubt whether A, whose power of speech

was evinced by his telling a lie, was in a position to tell what he took to be the truth *if* he had so chosen. Of *course* he was. Yet it still makes good sense for one's moral thinking to ask whether A, when lying, "could have acted otherwise": and we still require an affirmative answer to this question if A's moral blameworthiness is to be established. It seems apparent, therefore, that in this class of cases at any rate one does *not* mean by "A could have acted otherwise," "A could have acted otherwise *if* he had so chosen."

What then *does* one mean in this class of cases by "A could have acted otherwise"? I submit that the expression is taken in its simple, categorical meaning, without any suppressed "if" clause to qualify it. Or perhaps, in order to keep before us the important truth that it is only as expressions of *will* or *choice* that acts are of moral import, it might be better to say that a condition of A's moral responsibility is that he could have *chosen* otherwise. We saw that there is no real question whether A who told a lie could have acted otherwise *if* he had chosen otherwise. But there is a very real question, at least for any person who approaches the question of moral responsibility at a tolerably advanced level of reflection, about whether A could have *chosen* otherwise. Such a person will doubtless be acquainted with the claims advanced in some quarters that causal law operates universally: or/and with the theories of some philosophies that the universe is throughout the expression of a single supreme principle; or/and with the doctrines of some theologians that the world is created, sustained, and governed by an Omniscient and Omnipotent Being. Very understandably such worldviews awaken in him doubts about the validity of his first, easy, instinctive assumption that there are genuinely open possibilities before a man at the moment of moral choice. It thus becomes for him a real question whether a man could have chosen otherwise than he actually did, and, in consequence, whether man's moral responsibility is really defensible. For how can a man be morally responsible, he asks himself, if his choices, like all other events in the universe, could not have been otherwise than they in fact were? It is precisely against the background of world-views such as these that for reflective people the problem of moral responsibility normally arises.

Furthermore, to the man who has attained

[12] *Ethics and Language,* p. 298.

this level of reflection, it will in *no* class of cases be a sufficient condition of moral responsibility for an act that one could have acted otherwise *if* one had chosen otherwise—not even in these cases where there *was* some possibility of the operation of "external constraint." In these cases he will, indeed, expressly recognize freedom from external constraint as a *necessary condition,* but not as a *sufficient* condition. For he will be aware that, even granted *this* freedom, it is still conceivable that the agent had no freedom to choose otherwise than he did, and he will therefore require that the latter sort of freedom be added if moral responsibility for the act is to be established.

I have been contending that, for persons at a *tolerably advanced level of reflection,* "A could have acted otherwise," as a condition of A's moral responsibility, means "A could have chosen otherwise." The qualification italicized is of some importance. The unreflective or unsophisticated person, the ordinary "man in the street," who does not know or much care what scientists and theologians and philosophers have said about the world, sees well enough that A is morally responsible only if he could have acted otherwise, but in his intellectual innocence he will, very probably, envisage nothing capable of preventing A from having acted otherwise except some material impediment—like the broken leg in the example above. Accordingly, for the unreflective person, "A could have acted otherwise, as a condition of moral responsibility," *is* apt to mean no more than "A could have acted otherwise *if* he had so chosen."

It would appear, then, that the view now favored by many philosophers, that the freedom required for moral responsibility is merely freedom from external constraint, is a view which they share only with the less reflective type of layman. Yet it should be plain that on a matter of this sort the view of the unreflective person is of little value by comparison with the view of the reflective person. There are some contexts, no doubt, in which lack of sophistication is an asset. But this is not one of them. The question at issue here is as to the kind of impediments which might have prevented a man from acting otherwise than he in fact did : and on this question knowledge and reflection are surely prerequisites of any answer that is worth listening to. It is simply on account of the limitations of his

mental vision that the unreflective man interprets the expression "could have acted otherwise," in its context as a condition of moral responsibility, solely in terms of external constraint. He has failed (as yet) to reach the intellectual level at which one takes into account the implications for moral choices of the world-views of science, religion, and philosophy. If on a matter of this complexity the philosopher finds that his analysis accords with the utterances of the uneducated he has, I suggest, better cause for uneasiness than for self-congratulation.

This concludes the main part of what it seems to me necessary to say in answer to the pseudo-problem theorists. My object so far has been to expose the falsity of those innovations (chiefly Positivist) in the way of argument and analysis which are supposed by many to have made it impossible any longer to formulate the problem of Free Will in the traditional manner. My contention is that, at least so far as these innovations are concerned, the simple time-honored argument still holds from the nature of the moral ought to the conclusion that moral responsibility implies a contra-causal type of freedom. The attempts to avoid that conclusion by analyzing the proposition "A could have acted otherwise" (acknowledged to be implied in *some* sense in A's moral responsibility) into one or other of certain hypothetical propositions which are compatible with unbroken causal continuity break down hopelessly when tested against the touchstone of actual moral thinking. It is, I think, not necessary to defend the procedure of testing hypotheses in the ethical field by bringing to bear upon them our actual moral thinking. If there is any other form of test applicable, I should be much interested to learn what it is supposed to be. Certainly "logical analysis" per se will not do. That has a function, but a function that can only be ancillary. For what we are seeking to know is the meaning of the expression "could have acted otherwise" not *in the abstract,* but in the context of the question of man's *moral responsibility.* Logical analysis per se is impotent to give us this information. It can be of value only in so far as it operates within the orbit of "the moral consciousness." One may admit, with some qualifications, that on a matter of this sort the moral consciousness without logical analysis is blind : but it seems to me to be true without any qualification whatsoever that, on the same problem, logical analysis without the moral consciousness is empty.

VI

There are times when what seems to a critic the very strength of his case breeds mistrust in the critic's own mind. I confess that in making the criticisms that have preceded, I have not been altogether free from uncomfortable feelings of this kind. For the arguments I have criticized, and more particularly the analyses of the conditions of moral responsibility, seem to me to be in many cases quite desperately unplausible. Such a state of affairs ought, I think, to give the critic pause. The thought must at least enter his mind (unless he be a total stranger to modesty) that perhaps, despite his best efforts to be fair, he has after all misrepresented what his opponents are saying. No doubt a similar thought will enter, and perhaps find lodgment in, the minds of many readers.

In this situation there is, however, one course by which the critic may reasonably hope to allay these natural suspicions. He should consider whether there may not be certain predisposing influences at work, extrinsic to the specific arguments, which could have the effect of blinding the proponents of these arguments to their intrinsic demerits. If so, he need not be too much disquieted by the seeming weakness of the case against him. For it is a commonplace that, once in the grip of general prepossessions, even very good philosophers sometimes avail themselves of very bad arguments.

Actually, we can, I think, discern at least two such influences operating powerfully in the case before us. One is sympathy with the general tenets of Positivism. The other is the conviction already alluded to, that man does not in fact possess a contra-causal type of freedom; whence follows a strong presumption that no such freedom is necessary to moral responsibility.

About the first of these influences I propose to say very little. I wish merely to indicate how strict adherence to Positivist tenets precludes one in principle from understanding moral responsibility as the ordinary man understands it, and how Positivists are therefore bound, when they attempt to define the conditions of moral responsibility, to say things that seem monstrously unplausible.

That the Positivist—who has certainly not been drawn initially to this way of philosophizing by reflection upon the phenomena of the moral life—should approach the problems of ethical analysis with certain strong prepossessions is only to be expected. The most crucial of these is that (non-tautologous) statements in this field, as in every other field, can have no meaning—or at any rate no cognitive meaning—unless they are, at least in principle, sensibly verifiable. The consequence of that prepossession must be to close the mind in advance, more or less absolutely according to the extent to which the Verifiability Principle is maintained as unshakable dogma, against the common view of the moral ought—which happens also to be the view in terms of which the problem of moral responsibility historically and habitually arises. For on this view the moral ought as apprehended by the moral consciousness is most certainly an object neither of "outer" nor of "inner" sense. One need not wonder, therefore, that the Positivist should recommend analyses of the conditions of moral responsibility, such as the hypothetical propositions offered as the meaning of the expression "could have acted otherwise," which to anyone who understands the moral ought in the ordinary way seem little short of fantastic. By an *a priori* prejudice he has effectively debarred himself from appreciating what ordinary men mean by moral obligation and moral responsibility. I cannot forbear adding that in view of the doom which has so swiftly attended the very various attempts so far made to define moral obligation in Positivist terms, the case for at least a temporary suspension of belief in Positivist presuppositions in the ethical field would appear to be a strong one.

Of far wider and more permanent interest, in my judgment, is the second of the "predisposing influences"—the conviction that there just *is* no contra-causal freedom such as is commonly alleged to be a condition of moral responsibility. A natural desire to "save" moral responsibility issues, logically enough, in attempts to formulate its conditions in a manner compatible with unbroken causal continuity. The consequent analyses may be, as I have urged, very unsatisfactory. But there is no doubt that the conviction that motivates the analysis is supported by reasons of great weight: well-known arguments that are the property of no particular school and which most of us learned in our philosophical cradles. A very brief summary of what I take to be the most influential of these arguments will suffice for the comments I wish to make upon them.

A contra-causal freedom, it is argued, such as is implied in the "categorical" interpretation of the proposition "A could have chosen otherwise than he did," posits a breach of causal continuity between a man's character and his conduct. Now apart from the general presumption in favor of the universality of causal law, there are special reasons for disallowing the breach that is here alleged. It is the common assumption of social intercourse that our acquaintances will act "in character"; that their choices will exhibit the "natural" response of their characters to the given situation. And this assumption seems to be amply substantiated, over a wide range of conduct, by the actual success which attends predictions made on this basis. Where there should be, on the contra-causal hypothesis, chaotic variability, there is found in fact a large measure of intelligible continuity. Moreover, what is the alternative to admitting that a person's choices flow from his character? Surely just that the so-called "choice" is not *that person's* choice at all: that, relatively to the person concerned, it is a mere "accident." Now we cannot really believe this. But if it *were* the case, it would certainly not help to establish *moral* freedom, the freedom required for *moral* responsibility. For clearly a man cannot be morally responsible for an act which does not express his own choice but is, on the contrary, attributable simply to chance.

These are clearly considerations worthy of all respect. It is not surprising if they have played a big part in persuading people to respond sympathetically to the view that "Free Will," in its usual contra-causal formulation, is a pseudo-problem. A full answer to them is obviously not practicable in what is little more than an appendix to the body of this paper; but I am hopeful that something can be said, even in a little space, to show that they are very far from being as conclusive against a contra-causal freedom as they are often supposed to be.

To begin with the less troublesome of the two main objections indicated—the objection that the break is causal continuity which free will involves is inconsistent with the predictability of conduct on the basis of the agent's known character. All that is necessary to meet this objection, I suggest, is the frank recognition, which is perfectly open to the Libertarian, that there is a wide area of human conduct, determinable on clear general principles, within which free will does not effectively operate. The most important of these general principles (I have no space to deal here with the others) has often enough been stated by Libertarians. Free will does not operate in these practical situations in which no conflict arises in the agent's mind between what he conceives to be his "duty" and what he feels to be his "strongest desire." It does not operate here because there just is no occasion for it to operate. There is no reason whatever why the agent should here even contemplate choosing any course other than that prescribed by his strongest desire. In all such situations, therefore, he naturally wills in accordance with strongest desire. But his "strongest desire" is simply the specific *ad hoc* expression of that system of conative and emotive dispositions which we call his "character." In all such situations, therefore, whatever may be the case elsewhere, his will is in effect determined by his character as so far formed. Now when we bear in mind that there are an almost immeasurably greater number of situations in a man's life that conform to *this* pattern than there are situations in which an agent is aware of a conflict between strongest desire and duty, it is apparent that a Libertarianism which accepts the limitation of free will to the *latter* type of situation is not open to the stock objection on the score of "predictability." For there still remains a vast area of human behavior in which prediction on the basis of known character may be expected to succeed: an area which will accommodate without difficulty, I think, all these empirical facts about successful prediction which the critic is apt to suppose fatal to Free Will.

So far as I can see, such a delimitation of the field of effective free will denies to the Libertarian absolutely nothing which matters to him. For it is precisely that small sector of the field of choices which our principle of delimitation still leaves open to free will—the sector in which strongest desire clashes with duty—that is crucial for moral responsibility. It is, I believe, with respect to such situations, and in the last resort to such situations alone, that the agent himself recognizes that moral praise and blame are appropriate. They are appropriate, according as he does or does not "rise to duty" in the face of opposing desires; always granted, that is, that he is free to choose between these courses as genuinely open possibilities. If the reality of freedom be conceded *here,* everything is conceded that the Libertarian has any real interest in securing.

But, of course, the most vital question is, can the reality of freedom be conceded even here? In particular, can the standard objection be met which we stated, that if the person's choice does not, in these situations as elsewhere, flow from his *character,* then it is not *that person's* choice at all.

This is, perhaps, of all the objections to a contra-causal freedom, the one which is generally felt to be the most conclusive. For the assumption upon which it is based, viz., that no intelligible meaning can attach to the claim that an act which is not an expression of the self's *character* may nevertheless be the *self's* act, is apt to be regarded as self-evident. The Libertarian is accordingly charged with being in effect an *In*determinist, whose "free will," in so far as it does not flow from the agent's character, can only be a matter of "chance." Has the Libertarian—who invariably repudiates this charge and claims to be a *Self*-determinist—any way of showing that, contrary to the assumption of his critics, we *can* meaningfully talk of an act as the self's act even though, in an important sense, it is not an expression of the self's "character"?

I think that he has. I want to suggest that what prevents the critics from finding a meaning in this way of talking is that they are looking for it in the wrong way; or better, perhaps, with the wrong orientation. They are looking for it from the standpoint of the *external observer*; the standpoint proper to, because alone possible for, apprehension of the physical world. Now from the external standpoint we may observe processes of change. But one thing which, by common consent, *cannot* be observed from without is *creative activity.* Yet—and here lies the crux of the whole matter—it is precisely creative activity which we are trying to understand when we are trying to understand what is traditionally designated by "free will." For if there should be an act which is genuinely the self's act and is nevertheless not an expression of its character, such an act, in which the self "transcends" its character as so far formed, would

seem to be essentially of the nature of creative activity. It follows that to look for a meaning in "free will" from the external standpoint is absurd. It is to look for it in a way that ensures that it will not be found. Granted that a creative activity of any kind is at least *possible* (and I know of no ground for its *a priori* rejection), there is one way, and one way only, in which we can hope to apprehend it, and that is from the *inner* standpoint of direct participation.

It seems to me therefore, that if the Libertarian's claim to find a meaning in a "free" will which is genuinely the self's will, though not an expression of the self's character, is to be subjected to any test that is worth applying, that test must be undertaken from the inner standpoint. We ought to place ourselves imaginatively at the standpoint of the agent engaged in the typical moral situation in which free will is claimed, and ask ourselves whether from *this* standpoint the claim in question does or does not have meaning for us. That the appeal must be to introspection is no doubt unfortunate. But he would be a very doctrinaire critic of introspection who declined to make use of it when in the nature of the case no other means of apprehension is available. Everyone must make the introspective experiment for himself : but I may perhaps venture to report, though at this late stage with extreme brevity, what I at least seem to find when I make the experiment myself.

In the situation of moral conflict, then, I (as agent) have before my mind a course of action X, which I believe to be my duty; and also a course of action Y, incompatible with X, which I feel to be that which I most strongly desire. Y is, as it is sometimes expressed, "in the line of least resistance" for me—the course which I am aware I should take if I let my purely desiring nature operate without hindrance. It is the course toward which I am aware that my *character,* as so far formed, naturally inclines me. Now, as actually engaged in this situation, I find that I cannot help believing that I *can* rise to duty and choose X; the "rising to duty" being effected by what is commonly called "effort of will." And I further find, if I ask myself just what it is I am believing when I believe that I "can" rise to duty, that I cannot help believing that it lies with me here and now, quite absolutely, which of two genuinely open possibilities I adopt; whether, that is, I make the effort of will and chose X, or, on the other hand, let my desiring nature, my character as so far formed, "have its way," and choose Y, the course "in the line of least resistance." These beliefs may, of course, be illusory, but that is not at present in point. For the present argument all that matters is whether beliefs of this sort are in fact discoverable in the moral agent in the situation of "moral temptation." For my own part, I cannot doubt the introspective evidence that they are.

Now here is the vital point. No matter which course, X or Y, I choose in this situation, I cannot doubt, *qua* practical being engaged in it, that my choice is *not* just the expression of my formed character, and yet *is* a choice made by my *self*. For suppose I make the effort and choose X (my "duty"). Since my very purpose in making the "effort" is to enable me to act against the existing "set" of desire, which is the expression of my character as so far formed, I cannot possibly regard the act itself as the expression of my *character*. On the other hand, introspection makes it equally clear that I am certain that it is *I* who choose: that the act is not an "accident," but is genuinely *my* act. Or suppose that I choose Y (the end of "strongest desire"). The course chosen here is, it is true, in conformity with my "character." But since I find myself unable to doubt that I *could* have made the effort and chosen X, I cannot possibly regard the choice of Y as *just* the expression of my character. Yet here again I find that I cannot doubt that the choice is *my* choice, a choice for which *I* am justly to be blamed.

What this amounts to is that I *can* and *do* attach meaning, *qua* moral agent, to an act which is not the self's character and yet is genuinely the self's act. And having no good reason to suppose that other persons have a fundamentally different mental constitution, it seems to me probable that anyone else who undertakes a similar experiment will be obliged to submit a similar report. I conclude, therefore, that the argument against "free will" on the score of its "meaninglessness" must be held to fail. "Free Will" does have meaning; though, because it is of the nature of a creative activity, its meaning is discoverable only in an intuition of the practical consciousness of the participating agent. To the agent making a moral choice in the situation where duty clashes with desire, his "self" is known

to him as a creatively active self, a self which declines to be identified with his "character" as so formed. Not, of course, that the self's character—let it be added to obviate misunderstanding—either is, or is supposed by the agent to be, devoid of bearing upon his choices, even in the "sector" in which free will is held to operate. On the contrary, such a bearing is manifest in the empirically verifiable fact that we find it "harder" (as we say) to make the effort of will required to "rise to duty" in proportion to the extent that the "dutiful" course conflicts with the course to which our character as so far formed inclines us. It is only in the polemics of the critics that a "free" will is supposed to be incompatible with recognizing the bearing of "character" upon choice.

"But what" (it may be asked) " of the all-important question of the *value* of this 'subjective certainty'? Even if what you say is sound as 'phenomenology,' is there any reason to suppose that the conviction on which you lay so much stress is in fact *true*?" I agree that the question is important; far more important, indeed, than is always realized, for it is not always realized that the only direct evidence there *could* be for a creative activity like "free will" is an intuition of the practical consciousness. But this question falls outside the purview of the present paper. The aim of the paper has not been to offer a constructive defense of free will. It has been to show that the problem as traditionally posed is a real, and not a pseudo, problem. A serious threat to that thesis, it was acknowledged, arises from the apparent difficulty of attaching meaning to an act which is not the expression of the self's character and yet *is* the self's own act. The object of my brief phenomenological analysis was to provide evidence that such an act *does* have meaning for us in the one context in which there is any sense in *expecting* it to have meaning.

VII

My general conclusion is, I fear, very unexciting. It is merely that it is an error to suppose that the "Free Will" problem, when correctly formulated, turns out not to be a "problem" at all. Laboring to reinstate an old problem is dull work enough. But I am disposed to think that the philosophic situation to-day calls for a good deal more dull work of a similar sort.

Ifs and Cans*

Are *cans* constitutionally iffy? Whenever, that is, we say that we can do something, or could do something, or could have done something, is there an *if* in the offing—suppressed, it may be, but due nevertheless to appear when we set out our sentence in full or when we give an explanation of its meaning?

Again, if and when there *is* an *if*-clause appended to a main clause which contains a *can* or *could* or *could have,* what sort of an *if* is it? What is the meaning of the *if,* or what is the effect or the point of combining this *if*-clause with the main clause?

These are large questions, to which philosophers, among them some whom I most respect, have given small answers: and it is two such answers, given recently by English philosophers, that I propose to consider. Both, I believe, are mistaken, yet something is to be learned from examining them. In philosophy, there are many mistakes that it is no disgrace to have made: to make a first-water, ground-floor mistake, so far from being easy, takes one (*one*) form of philosophical genius.[1]

Many of you will have read a short but justly admired book written by Professor G. E. Moore of Cambridge, which is called simply *Ethics.* In it, there is a point where Moore, who is engaged in discussing Right and Wrong, says that if we are to discuss whether any act that has been done was right or wrong then we are bound to discuss what the person concerned *could have* done instead of what he did in fact do. And this, he thinks, may lead to an entanglement in the problem, so-called, of Free Will: because, though few would deny, at least expressly, that a man could have done something other than what he did actually do *if he had chosen,* many people would deny that he *could* (absolutely) have done any such other thing. Hence Moore is led to ask whether it is ever true, and if so in what sense, that a man could have done something other than what he did actually do. And it is with his answer to this question, not with its bearings upon the meanings of *right* and *wrong* or upon the problem of Free Will, that we are concerned.

With his usual shrewdness Moore begins by insisting that there is at least *one* proper sense in which we can say that a man can do something he doesn't do or could have done something he didn't do—even though there may perhaps be *other* senses of can and *could have* in which we cannot say such things. This sense he illustrates by the sentence "I could have walked a mile in 20 minutes this morning, but I certainly could not have run two miles in 5 minutes": we are to take it that in fact the speaker did not do either of the two things mentioned, but this in no way hinders us from drawing the very common and necessary distinction between undone acts that we could have done and undone acts that we could not have done. So it is certain that, at least in *some* sense, we often could have done things that we did not actually do.

Why then, Moore goes on to ask, should anyone try to deny this? And he replies that people do so (we may call them "determinists") because they hold that everything that happens has a *cause* which precedes it, which is to say that once the cause has occurred the thing itself is *bound* to occur and *nothing* else *could* ever have happened instead.

However, on examining further the 20-minute-mile example, Moore argues that there is much reason to think that "could have" in such cases simply means "could have *if* I had chosen," or, as perhaps we had better say in order to avoid a possible complication (these are Moore's words), simply means *"should have if I had chosen."* And if this *is* all it means, then there is after all no conflict between our conviction that we often could have, in this sense, done things that we did not actually do and the determinist's theory: for he certainly holds himself that I often, and perhaps even always, should have done something different from what I did do *if I had chosen* to do that different thing, since my choosing differently would constitute a change in the causal antecedents of my subsequent act, which would therefore, on his theory, naturally itself be different. If, therefore, the determinist nevertheless asserts that in *some* sense of "could have" I could *not* ever have done anything different from what I did actually do, this must simply be a second sense[2] of "could have" different from that

---

* J. L. Austin, "Ifs and Cans," *Proceedings of the British Academy,* XLII (1956), 109–32, reprinted by permission of the British Academy. Footnotes have been renumbered.
[1] Plato, Descartes, and Leibniz all had this form of genius, besides of course others.

[2] About which Moore has no more to tell us.

which it has in the 20-minute-mile example.

In the remainder of his chapter, Moore argues that quite possibly his first sense of "could have," in which it simply means "could or should have if I had chosen," is all we need to satisfy our hankerings after Free Will, or at least is so if conjoined in some way with yet a third sense of "could have" in which sense "I could have done something different" means "I might, for all anyone could know for certain beforehand, have done something different." This third kind of "could have" might, I think, be held to be a vulgarism, "could" being used incorrectly for "might": but in any case we shall not be concerned with it here.

In the upshot, then, Moore leaves us with only one important sense in which it can be said that I could have done something that I did not do: he is not convinced that any other sense is necessary, nor has he any clear idea what such another sense would be: and he is convinced that, on his interpretation of "could have," even the determinist can, and indeed must, say that I could very often have done things I did not do. To summarize his suggestions (he does not put them forward with complete conviction) once again:

1. "Could have" simply means "could have if I had chosen."
2. For "could have if I had chosen" we may substitute "should have if I had chosen."
3. The if-clauses in these expressions state the causal conditions upon which it would have followed that I could or should have done the thing different from what I did actually do.

Moore does not state this third point expressly himself: but it seems clear, in view of the connections he alleges between his interpretation of "could have" and the determinist theory, that he did believe it, presumably taking it as obvious.

There are then three questions to be asked:

1. Does "could have if I had chosen" mean the same, in general or ever, as "should have if I had chosen"?
2. In either of these expressions, is the if the if of causal condition?
3. In sentences having can or could have as main verb, are we required or entitled always to supply an if-clause, and in particular the clause "if I had chosen"?

It appears to me that the answer in each case is No.

1. Anyone, surely, would admit that in general could is very different indeed from should

or would.[3] What a man could do is not at all the same as what he would do: perhaps he could shoot you if you were within range, but that is not in the least to say that he would. And it seems clear to me, in our present example, that "I could have run a mile if I had chosen" and "I should have run a mile if I had chosen" mean quite different things, though unfortunately it is not so clear exactly what either of them, especially the latter, does mean. "I should have run a mile in 20 minutes this morning if I had chosen" seems to me an unusual, not to say queer, specimen of English: but if I had to interpret it, I should take it to mean the same as "If I had chosen to run a mile in 20 minutes this morning, I should (jolly well) have done so," that is, it would be an assertion of my strength of character, in that I put my decisions into execution (an assertion which is, however, more naturally made, as I have now made it, with the if-clause preceding the main clause). I should certainly not myself understand it to mean that if I had made a certain choice my making that choice would have caused me to do something. But in whichever of these ways we understand it, it is quite different from "I could have walked a mile in 20 minutes this morning if I had chosen," which surely says something rather about my opportunities or powers. Moore, unfortunately, does not explain why he thinks we are entitled to make this all-important transition from "could" to "should," beyond saying that by doing so we "avoid a possible complication." Later I shall make some suggestions which may in part explain why he was tempted to make the transition: but nothing can justify it.

2. Moore, as I pointed out above, did not discuss what sort of if it is that we have in "I can if I choose" or in "I could have if I had chosen" or in "I should have if I had chosen." Generally, philosophers, as also grammarians, have a favorite, if somewhat blurred and diffuse, idea of an if-clause as a "conditional" clause: putting our example schematically as "If p, then q," then it will be said that q follows from p, typically either in the sense that p entails q or in the sense that p is a cause of q, though other important variations are possible. And it seems to be

[3] Since Moore has couched his example in the first person, he uses "should" in the apodosis: but of course in the third person, everyone would use "would." For brevity, I shall in what follows generally use "should" to do duty for both persons.

on these lines that Moore is thinking of the *if* in "I can if I choose." But now, it is characteristic of this general sort of *if,* that from "If *p* then *q*" we *can* draw the inference "If not *q,* then not *p,*" whereas we can*not* infer either "Whether or not *p,* then *q*" or "*q*" simpliciter. For example, from "If I run, I pant" we *can* infer "If I do not pant, I do not run" (or, as we should rather say, "If I am not panting, I am not running"), whereas we can*not* infer either "I pant, whether I run or not" or "I pant" (at least in the sense of "I am panting"). If, to avoid these troubles with the English tenses, which are unfortunately prevalent but are not allowed to matter, we put the example in the past tense, then from "If I ran, I panted" it *does* follow that "If I did not pant, I did not run," but it does *not* follow either that "I panted whether or not I ran" or that "I panted" period. These possibilities and impossibilities of inference are typical of the *if* of causal condition : but they are precisely reversed in the case of "I can if I choose" or "I could have if I had chosen." For from these we should not draw the curious inferences that "If I cannot, I do not choose to" or that "If I could not have, I had not chosen to" (or "did not choose to"), whatever these sentences may be supposed to mean. But on the contrary, from "I can if I choose" we certainly should infer that "I can, whether I choose to or not" and indeed that "I can" period : and from "I could have if I had chosen" we should similarly infer that "I could have, whether I chose to or not" and that anyway "I could have" period. So that, whatever this *if* means, it is evidently not the *if* of causal condition.

This becomes even clearer when we observe that it is quite common *elsewhere* to find an ordinary causal conditional *if* in connection with a *can,* and that then there is no doubt about it, as for example in the sentence "I can squeeze through if I am thin enough," which *does* imply that "If I cannot squeeze through I am not thin enough," and of course does *not* imply that "I can squeeze through." "I can if I choose" is precisely different from this.

Nor does *can* have to be a very special and peculiar verb for *ifs* which are not causal conditional to be found in connection with it : all kinds of *ifs* are found with all kinds of verbs. Consider for example the *if* in "There are biscuits on the sideboard if you want

them," where the verb is the highly ordinary *are,* but the *if* is more like that in "I can if I choose" than that in "I panted if I ran" : for we can certainly infer from it that "There are biscuits on the sideboard whether you want them or not" and that anyway "There are biscuits on the sideboard," whereas it would be folly to infer that "If there are no biscuits on the sideboard you do not want them," or to understand the meaning to be that you have only to want biscuits to cause them to be on the sideboard.

The *if,* then, in "I can if I choose" is not the causal conditional *if.* What of the *if* in "I shall if I choose"? At first glance, we see that this is quite different (one more reason for refusing to substitute *shall* for *can* or *should have* for *could have*). For from "I shall if I choose" we clearly cannot infer that "I shall whether I choose to or not" or simply that "I shall." But on the other hand, can we infer, either, that "If I shan't I don't choose to"? (Or should it be rather "If I don't I don't choose to"?) I think not, as we shall see : but even if some such inference can be drawn, it would still be patently wrong to conclude that the meaning of "I shall if I choose" is that my choosing to do the thing is sufficient to cause me inevitably to do it or has as a consequence that I shall do it, which, unless I am mistaken, is what Moore was supposing it to mean. This may be seen if we compare "I shall ruin him if I choose" with "I shall ruin him if I am extravagant." The latter sentence does indeed obviously state what would be the consequence of the fulfillment of a condition specified in the *if*-clause—but then, the first sentence has clearly different characteristics from the second. In the first, it makes good sense in general to stress the "shall," but in the second it does not.[4] This is a symptom of the fact that in the first sentence "I shall" is the present of that mysterious old verb *shall,* whereas in the second "shall" is simply being used as an auxiliary, without any meaning of its own, to form the future indicative of "ruin."

I expect you will be more than ready at this point to hear something a little more positive about the meanings of these curious expressions "I can if I choose" and "I shall if I

[4] In general, though of course in some contexts it does: e.g., "I may very easily ruin him, and I *shall* if I am extravagant," where "shall" is stressed to point the contrast with "may."

choose." Let us take the former first, and concentrate upon the *if*. The dictionary tells us that the words from which our *if* is descended expressed, or even meant, "doubt" or "hesitation" or "condition" or "stipulation." Of these, "condition" has been given a prodigious innings by grammarians, lexicographers, and philosophers alike: it is time for "doubt" and "hesitation" to be remembered, and these do indeed seem to be the notions present in "I can if I choose." We could give, on different occasions and in different contexts, many different interpretations of this sentence, which is of a somewhat primitive and *loose-jointed* type. Here are some:

I can, quaere do I choose to?
I can, but do I choose to?
I can, but perhaps I don't choose to
I can, but then I should have to choose to, and what about *that*?
I can, but would it really be reasonable to choose to?
I can, but whether I choose to is another question
I can, I have only to choose to
I can, in case I (should) choose to, and so on.

These interpretations are not, of course, all the same: which it is that we mean will usually be clear from the context (otherwise we should prefer another expression), but sometimes it can be brought out by stress, on the "if" or the "choose" for example. What is common to them all is simply that the *assertion,* positive and complete, that "I can," is linked to the *raising of the question* whether I choose to, which may be relevant in a variety of ways.[5]

*If*s of the kind I have been trying to describe are common enough, for example the *if* in our example "There are biscuits on the sideboard if you want them." I don't know whether you want biscuits or not, but in case you do, I point out that there are some on the sideboard. It is tempting, I know, to "expand" our sentence here to this: "There are biscuits on the sideboard *which you can (or may) take* if you want them": but this, legitimate or not, will not make much difference, for we are still left with "can (or may) if you

want," which is (here) just like "can if you choose" or "can if you like," so that the *if* is still the *if* of doubt or hesitation, not the *if* of condition.[6]

I will mention two further points, very briefly, about "I can if I choose," important but not so relevant to our discussion here. Sometimes the *can* will be the *can,* and the choice the choice, of legal or other *right,* at other times these words will refer to practicability or feasibility: consequently, we should sometimes interpret our sentence in some such way as "I am entitled to do it (if I choose)," and at other times in some such way as "I am capable of doing it (if I choose)." We, of course, are concerned with interpretations of this second kind. It would be nice if we always said "I *may* if I choose" when we wished to refer to our rights, as perhaps our nannies once told us to: but the interlocking histories of *can* and *may* are far too checkered for there to be any such rule in practice.[7] The second point is that *choose* is an important word in its own right, and needs careful interpretation: "I can if I like" is not the same, although the "can" and the "if" may be the same in both, as "I can if I choose." Choice is always between alternatives, that is, between several courses to be weighed in the same scale against each other, the one to be *preferred.* "You can vote whichever way you choose" is different from "You can vote whichever way you like."

And now for something about "I *shall* if I choose"—what sort of *if* have we here? The point to notice is, that "I shall" is not an assertion of *fact* but an expression of *intention,* verging toward the giving of some variety of undertaking: and the *if,* consequently, is the *if* not of condition but of *stipulation.* In sentences like:

I shall | marry him if I choose
I intend | to marry him if I choose
I promise | to marry him if he will have me

[5] If there were space, we should consider other germane expressions: e.g., "I can do it or not as I choose," "I can do whichever I choose" (*quidlibet*). In particular, "I can whether I choose to or not" means "I can, but whether I choose to or not is an open question": it does *not* mean "I can on condition that I choose and likewise on condition that I don't," which is absurd.

[6] An account on these lines should probably be given also of an excellent example given to me by Mr. P. T. Geach: "I paid you back yesterday, if you remember." This is much the same as "I paid you back yesterday, don't you remember?" It does not mean that your now remembering that I did so is a condition, causal or other, of my having paid you back yesterday.

[7] Formerly I believed that the meaning of "I can if I choose" was something like "I can, I have the choice," and that the point of the *if*-clause was to make clear that the "can" in the main clause was the "can" of right. This account, however, does not do justice to the role of the "if," and also unduly restricts in general the meaning of "choice."

the *if*-clause is a part of the object phrase governed by the initial verb ("shall," "intend," "promise"), if this is an allowable way of putting it: or again, the *if* qualifies the *content* of the undertaking given, or of the intention announced, it does *not* qualify the giving of the undertaking. Why, we may ask, is it perverse to draw from "I intend to marry him if I choose" the inference "If I do not intend to marry him I do not choose to"? Because "I intend to marry him if I choose" is not like "I panted if I ran" in this important respect: "I panted if I ran" does not assert anything "categorically" about me—it does not assert that I did pant, and hence it is far from surprising to infer something beginning "If I did not pant": but "I intend to marry him if I choose" (and the same goes for "I shall marry him if I choose") *is* a "categorical" expression of intention, and hence it is paradoxical to make an inference leading off with "If I do *not* intend."

3. Our third question was as to when we are entitled or required to supply *if*-clauses with *can* or *could have* as main verb.

Here there is one thing to be clear about at the start. There are *two* quite distinct and incompatible views that may be put forward concerning *ifs* and *cans,* which are fatally easy to confuse with each other. One view is that wherever we have *can* or *could have* as our main verb, an *if*-clause must always be understood or supplied, if it is not actually present, in order to complete the sense of the sentence. The other view is that the meaning of "can" or "could have" can be more clearly reproduced by *some other verb* (notably "shall" or "should have") with an *if*-clause appended to *it*. The first view is that an *if* is required to *complete* a *can*-sentence: the second view is that an *if* is required in the *analysis* of a *can*-sentence. The suggestion of Moore that "could have" means "could have if I had chosen" is a suggestion of the first kind: but the suggestion also made by Moore that it means "should have if I had chosen" is a suggestion of the second kind. It may be because it is so easy (apparently) to confuse these two kinds of theory that Moore was tempted to talk as though "should have" could mean the same as "could have."

Now we are concerned at this moment solely with the *first* sort of view, namely that *can*-sentences are not complete without an *if*-clause. And if we think, as Moore was for the most part thinking, about "could have" (rather than "can"), it is easy to see why it may be tempting to allege that it always requires an *if*-clause with it. For it is natural to construe "could have" as a past subjunctive or "conditional," which is practically as much as to say that it needs a *conditional* clause with it. And of course it is quite true that "could have" *may* be, and very often is, a past conditional: but it is *also* true that "could have" may be and often is the *past (definite) indicative* of the verb *can.* Sometimes "I could have" is equivalent to the Latin "Potui" and means "I *was* in a position to": sometimes it is equivalent to the Latin "Potuissem" and means "I *should have been* in a position to." Exactly similar is the double role of "could," which is sometimes a conditional meaning "should be able to," but also sometimes a past indicative (indefinite) meaning "was able to": no one can doubt this if he considers such contrasted examples as "I could do it 20 years ago" and "I could do it if I had a thingummy." It is not so much that "could" or "could have" is ambiguous, as rather that two parts of the verb *can* take the same shape.

Once it is realized that "could have" can be a past indicative, the general temptation to supply *if*-clauses with it vanishes: at least there is no more temptation to supply them with "could have" than with "can." If we ask how a Roman would have said "I could have ruined you this morning (although I didn't)," it is clear that he would have used "potui," and that his sentence is complete without any conditional clause. But more than this, if he had wished to add "if I had chosen," and however he had expressed that in Latin, he would still not have changed his "potui" to "potuissem": but this is precisely what he *would* have done if he had been tacking on some other, more "normal" kind of *if*-clause, such as "if I had had one more vote."[8]

That is to say, the "could have" in "could have if I had chosen" is a past indicative, *not*

---

[8] If the *if*-clause is "if I had chosen," then I *was* able, *was* actually in a position, to ruin you: hence "potui." But if the *if*-clause expresses a genuine *unfulfilled condition,* then plainly I was *not* actually in a position to ruin you, hence not "potui" but "potuissem." My colleague Mr. R. M. Nisbet has pointed out to me the interesting discussion of this point in S. A. Handford, *The Latin Subjunctive,* pp. 130 ff. It is interesting that although this author well appreciates the Latin usage, he still takes it for granted that in English the "could have" is universally subjunctive or conditional.

a past conditional, despite the fact that there is what would, I suppose, be called a "conditional" clause, that is, an *if*-clause, with it. And this is, of course, why we can make the inferences that, as we saw, we can make from "I could have if I had chosen," notably the inference to "I could have" absolutely. Hence we see how mistaken Moore was in contrasting "I could have if I had chosen" with the "absolute" sense of "I could have": we might almost go so far as to say that the addition of the "conditional" clause "if I had chosen" makes it certain that (in Moore's language) the sense of "could have" is the absolute sense, or as I should prefer to put it, that the mood of "could have" is indicative.

It might at this point be worth considering in general whether it makes sense to suppose that a language could contain any verb such as *can* has been argued or implied to be, namely one that can never occur without an *if*-clause appended to it. At least if the *if* is the normal "conditional" *if* this would seem very difficult. For let the verb in question be *to X*: then we shall never say simply "I X," but always "I X if I Y": but then also, according to the accepted rules, if it is true that "I X if I Y," and *also* true (which it must surely sometimes be) that "I do, in fact, Y," it must surely follow that "I X," simpliciter, without any *if* about it any longer. Perhaps this was the "possible complication" that led Moore to switch from the suggestion that "I could have" (in one sense) has always to be *expanded* to "I could have if" to the suggestion that it has always to be *analyzed* as "I should have if": for of course the argument I have just given does not suffice to show that there could not be some verb which has always to be *analyzed* as something containing a conditional *if*-clause: suggestions that this is in fact the case with some verbs are common in philosophy, and I do not propose to argue this point, though I think that doubt might well be felt about it. The only sort of "verb" I can think of that might always demand a conditional clause with it is an "auxiliary" verb, if there is one, which is used solely to form subjunctive or conditional moods (whatever exactly they may be) of other verbs: but however this may be, it is quite clear that *can,* and I should be prepared also to add *shall* and *will* and *may,* are not in this position.

To summarize, then, what has been here

said in reply to Moore's suggestions in his book:

(*a*) "I could have if I had chosen" does not mean the same as "I should have if I had chosen."

(*b*) In neither of these expressions is the *if*-clause a "normal conditional" clause, connecting antecedent to consequent as cause to effect.

(*c*) To argue that *can* always requires an *if*-clause with it to complete the sense is totally different from arguing that *can*-sentences are always to be analyzed into sentences containing *if*-clauses.

(*d*) Neither *can* nor any other verb always requires a conditional *if*-clause after it: even "could have," when a past indicative, does not require such a clause: and in "I could have if I had chosen" the verb is in fact a past indicative, not a past subjunctive or conditional.

Even, however, if all these contentions are true so far, we must recognize that it may nevertheless still be the case that *can, could,* and *could have,* even when used as indicatives, are to be analyzed as meaning *shall, should,* and *should have,* used as auxiliaries of tense or mood with another verb (i.e., so as to make that other verb into a future or subjunctive), followed by a conditional *if*-clause. There is some plausibility,[9] for example, in the suggestion that "I can do X" means "I shall succeed in doing X, if I try" and "I could have done X" means "I should have succeeded in doing X, if I had tried."

It is indeed odd that Moore should have plumped so simply, in giving his account whether of the necessary supplementation or of the analysis of "could have," for the one particular *if*-clause "if I had chosen," which

---

[9] Plausibility, but no more. Consider the case where I miss a very short putt and kick myself because I could have holed it. It is not that I should have holed it if I had tried: I did try, and missed. It is not that I should have holed it if conditions had been different: that might of course be so, but I am talking about conditions as they precisely were, and asserting that I could have holed it. There's the rub. Nor does "I can hole it this time" mean that I shall hole it this time if I try or if anything else: for I may try and miss, and yet not be convinced that I couldn't have done it; indeed, further experiments may confirm my belief that I could have done it that time although I didn't.

But if I tried my hardest, say, and missed, surely there *must* have been *something* that caused me to fail, that made me unable to succeed? So that I *could not* have holed it. Well, a modern belief in science, in there being an explanation of everything, may make us assent to this argument. But such a belief is not in line with the traditional beliefs enshrined in the word *can*: according to *them*, a human ability or power or capacity is inherently liable not to produce success, on occasion, and that for no reason (or are bad luck and bad form sometimes reasons?).

happens to be particularly exposed to the above objections, without even mentioning the possibility of invoking other *if*-clauses, at least in some cases. Perhaps the reason was that *choose* (a word itself much in need of discussion) presented itself as well fitted to bridge the gulf between determinists and free-willers, which *try* might not so readily do. But as a matter of fact Moore does himself at one point give an analysis of "I could have done X" which is different in an interesting way from his usual version, although confusible with it. At a crucial point in his argument, he chooses for his example "The ship could have gone faster," and the suggestion is made that this is equivalent to "The ship *would* have gone faster *if her officers had chosen.*" This may well seem plausible, but so far from being in line, as Moore apparently thinks, with his general analysis, it differs from it in two important respects :

(*a*) the subject of the *if*-clause ("her officers") is different from the subject of the main clause ("the ship"), the subject of the original sentence ;

(*b*) the verb in the *if*-clause following "chosen" is different from the verb in the main clause, the verb in the original sentence. We do not readily observe this because of the ellipsis after "chosen" : but plainly the verb must be, not "to go faster," but "to make her go faster" or, e.g., "to open the throttle."

These two features are dictated by the fact that a ship is inanimate. We do not wish seriously to ascribe free will to inanimate objects, and the "could" of the original sentence is perhaps only justifiable (as opposed to "might") because it is readily realized that some person's free will is in question.

If we follow up the lines of this new type of analysis, we should have to examine the relations between "I could have won" and "I could, or should, have won if I had chosen to 'lob'" and "I could, or should, have won if he had chosen to lob." I will do no more here than point out that the difference between "could" and "should" remains as before, and that the sense of "I could have won," if it really is one, in which it means something of the sort "I should have won if he had chosen to lob" or "to let me win" (the parallel to the ship example), is of little importance—the "if" here is of course the conditional *if*.

It is time now to turn to a second discussion of *ifs* and *cans*. Quite recently my colleague Mr. Nowell-Smith, in another little book

called *Ethics,* also reaches a point in his argument at which he has to examine the sentence "He could have acted otherwise," that is, could have done something that he did not in fact do. His reason for doing so is that, unless we can truly say this of people, we might find ourselves unable to blame people for things, and this would be generally regretted. This reason is not unrelated to Moore's reason for embarking on his earlier discussion, and Nowell-Smith's views show some resemblances to Moore's : perhaps this is because Nowell-Smith, like Moore at the time he wrote his book, is willing, if not anxious, to come to terms with determinism.

Nowell-Smith begins his discussion by saying (p. 274) that " 'could have' is a modal phrase, and modal phrases are not normally used to make categorical statements." I am not myself at all sure what exactly a "modal phrase" is, so I cannot discuss this assertion : but I do not think this matters, because he proceeds to give us two other examples of modal phrases, viz., "might have" and "would have,"[10] and to tell us first what they are not (which I omit) and then what they are :

"Would have" and "might have" are clearly suppressed hypotheticals, incomplete without an "if . . ." or an "if . . . not . . . ." Nobody would say "Jones would have won the championship" unless (*a*) he believed that Jones did not win and (*b*) he was prepared to add "if he had entered" or "if he had not sprained his ankle" or some such clause.

Here (*a*) is actually incorrect—we can say "Jones would (still) have won the championship, (even) if Hagen had entered"—but this does not concern us. (*b*), however, seems to be fairly correct, at least as far as concerns "would have" (in the case of "might have" it might well be doubted).[11] So we have it that, when Nowell-Smith says that "would

---

[10] Also perhaps "may have," for he discusses "It *might* have rained last Thursday" in terms that seem really to apply to "It *may* have rained last Thursday."

[11] I refrain here from questioning it in the case of "would have." Yet "would" is agreed to be often a past indicative of the old verb *will*, requiring no *if*-clause : and I think myself that in, say, "X would have hanged him, but Y was against it" "would have" is likewise a past indicative—indeed it is from this sort of example that we can see how the past tenses of *will* have come to be used as auxiliaries of mood for forming the conditionals of other verbs.

To state what seems to be some grammatical facts (omitting all reference to the use of the words concerned in expressing wishes) :

Could have is sometimes a past indicative, sometimes a past subjunctive of the verb *can*. When it is the main verb and is a subjunctive, it does require a

have" is a "suppressed hypothetical" he means that it requires the addition of an *if*-clause to complete the sense. And he goes on to say that "could have" sentences also (though not so obviously) "express hypotheticals," if not always at least in important cases, such as notably those where we say someone could have done something he didn't actually do: in these cases "could have" . . . is equivalent to "would have . . . if . . . ."

It will be clear at once that Nowell-Smith, like Moore, is not distinguishing between the contention that "could have" *requires supplementation by* an *if*-clause and the quite different contention that *its analysis contains* an *if*-clause.[12] On the whole it seems plain that it is the second (analysis) view that he wishes to argue for: but the argument he produces is that "could have" is (in important cases) like "would have," the point about which is that it needs an *if*-clause to complete it—as though this, which is an argument in favor of the first view, told in favor of the second view. But it cannot possibly do so: and in any event *could have* is liable, as we have already seen, to be in important cases a past indicative, so that the contention that it is like *would have* in requiring a conditional *if*-clause is unfounded.

Nevertheless, it must be allowed that Nowell-Smith may still be right in urging that "could have" *means* "would have if" and that, as he eventually adds, "can" means "will if." What has he to say in support of this?

He propounds two examples for discussion, which I think do not differ greatly, so I shall quote only the first. Here it is:

He could have read *Emma* in bed last night, though he actually read *Persuasion*; but he

could not have read *Werther,* because he does not know German.

This is evidently of the same kind as Moore's 20-minute-mile example. The first thing that Nowell-Smith urges is that such a "could have" statement is not a categorical, or a "straightforward" categorical, statement. And his argument in favor of this view is derived from the way in which we should establish its truth or falsity. No inspection of what the man actually did will, he says, verify directly that he could have done something else (here, read *Emma*) which he didn't do: rather, we should, to establish this, have to show:

(*a*) that he has performed tasks of similar difficulty sufficiently often to preclude the possibility of a fluke, and (*b*) that nothing prevented him on this occasion. For example, we should have to establish that there was a copy of *Emma* in the house.

To refute it, on the other hand, we should have to show either "that some necessary condition was absent" (there was no copy of *Emma*) or "that the capacity was absent." That is, let us say, we have to show on the one hand that he had both the ability and the opportunity to read *Emma,* or on the other hand that he lacked either the ability or the opportunity.

Nowell-Smith seems, at least at first, to be less interested in the matter of opportunity: for he says that we can establish "directly," i.e., by considering what the facts at the time actually were, at least that he did *not* have the opportunity, that is, that something did prevent him, and he does not seem daunted by the obviously greater difficulty of establishing, in order to establish that he *could* have done it, the general negative that *there was nothing* to prevent him. At any rate, it is at first upon our manner of establishing that he had (or had not) the *ability* to do this thing that he did not do that Nowell-Smith fastens in order to support his assertion that the "could have" statement is not categorical. That the man had the *ability* to read *Emma* can*not,* he says, be established "directly," i.e., by observing what happened on that past occasion, but only by considering what prowess he has displayed in the face of similar tasks in the past on other occasions, or displays now when put to the test: the argument that we have perforce to use is an "inductive" one (and, he adds, none the worse for that).

Now let us pass all this, at least for the

---

conditional clause with it. *Can* and its parts are *not* used as auxiliaries of tense or mood to form tenses or moods of other verbs.

Would have, whether or not it is used as a past indicative or subjunctive of the verb *will,* is now commonly used (*should have* in the first person) as an auxiliary for forming the past subjunctive of other verbs: hence if it is the main verb it does in general require a conditional clause with it.

[12] It is true that he uses two different expressions: "would have" *is* a (suppressed) hypothetical, while "could have" sentences *express* hypotheticals. But it does not look as if any distinction is intended, and if it is, the protracted initial analogy between "could have" and "would have" seems irrelevant and misleading. Moreover, discussing the (unimportant) case of "It could have been a Morris," he writes that "it would be absurd to ask under what conditions it *could or would* have been a Morris" (my italics): this seems to show an indifference to the distinction that I am insisting on.

sake of argument.[13] What interests us is to discover why Nowell-Smith thinks that these considerations show that "He had the ability to read *Emma*" is not a categorical statement. I confess I fail to follow the argument:

The very fact that evidence for or against "could have" statements must be drawn from occasions other than that to which they refer is enough to show that "He could have acted otherwise" is not a straightforward categorical statement.

But do we really know what is meant by a "straightforward categorical statement"? Certainly it is not the case that statements made on the strength of inductive evidence are in general not categorical—for example, the statement that the next mule born will prove sterile : this seems categorical enough. Perhaps this example should be ruled out as not in point, on the ground that here there *will some day* be "direct" evidence relevant to the assertion, even if it is not available at the moment. Could the same, I wonder, be said of the inductive conclusion "All mules are sterile"? Or is that not categorical? I know that this has been interpreted by some philosophers to mean "If anything is a mule then it is sterile," but I see no reason to support that curious interpretation.

The situation becomes still more puzzling when we remember that Nowell-Smith is about to generalize his theory, and to assert, not merely that "could have" means "would have . . . if," but also that "can" means "shall or will . . . if." Suppose then that I assert "I can here and now lift my finger," and translate this as "I shall lift my finger if . . .": then surely this will be "directly" verified if the conditions are satisfied and I do proceed to lift the finger? If this is correct, and if the theory is indeed a general one, then there seems to be no point in insisting on the non-availability of "direct" evidence, which is only a feature of certain cases. Incidentally, it is not in fact the case that to say "He could have done it" is always used in a way to imply that he did not in fact do it: we make a list of the suspects in a murder case, all of whom we think could have done it and one of whom we think did do it. True, this is not Nowell-Smith's case : but unless we are prepared to assert that the "could have" in his case differs in meaning from that in the murder case, and so to rule out the latter as irrelevant, we are in danger of having to admit that even "could have" sentences can be "directly" verified in favorable cases. For study of the facts of that past occasion can prove to us that he did it, and hence that our original "He could have" was correct.[14]

However, to proceed. Whether or not we should describe our conclusion here as "categorical" it seems that it should still be a conclusion of the form "he *could* have done so and so," and not in the least a conclusion concerning what he *would* have done. We are interested, remember, in his abilities : we want to know whether he could have read *Emma* yesterday : we ascertain that he did read it the day before yesterday, and that he does read it today : we conclude that he could have read it yesterday. But it does not appear that this says anything about what he *would* have done yesterday or in what circumstances : certainly, we are now convinced, he *could* have read it yesterday, but *would* he have, considering that he had read it only the day before? Moreover, supposing the view is that our conclusion is not of the "could have" but of the "would have if" form, nothing has yet been said to establish this, nor to tell us what follows the "if." To establish that he would have read it yesterday if . . ., we shall need evidence not merely as to his abilities and opportunities, but also as to his character, motives, and so on.

It may indeed be thought, and it seems that Nowell-Smith does at least partly think this, that what follows the "if" should be suppliable from the consideration that to say he could have, in the full sense, is to say not merely that he had the ability, which is what we have hitherto concentrated on, but also that he had the *opportunity*. For to establish *this,* do we not have to establish that certain *conditions* were satisfied, as for instance that there was a copy of *Emma* available? Very well. But

---

[13] Yet I think it is not hard to see that we cannot establish "directly," at least in many cases, that something "prevented" him: he was drugged or dazzled, which prevented him from reading, which establishes that he could not have read—but how do we know that being drugged or dazzled "prevents" people from reading? Surely on "inductive" evidence? And, in short, to be prevented is to be rendered unable.

[14] There are, I should myself think, good reasons for not speaking of "I can lift my finger" as being directly verified when I proceed to lift it, and likewise for not speaking of "He could have done it" as being directly verified by the discovery that he did do it. But on Nowell-Smith's account I think that these would count as direct verifications.

here there is surely a confusion : we allow that, in saying that he could have, I do assert or imply that certain *conditions,* those of opportunity, *were satisfied* : but this is totally different from allowing that, in saying that he could have, I *assert something conditional.* It is, certainly, entirely possible to assert something conditional such as "he could have read *Emma* yesterday if there had been a copy available," *could* being then of course a subjunctive : but to say this sort of thing is precisely not to say the sort of thing that we say when we say "He could have acted otherwise," where "could have" is an indicative— implying, as we now do, that there was no copy available, we imply that *pro tanto* he could *not* have acted otherwise. And the same will be true if we try saying "He would have read *Emma* yesterday if there had been a copy available" : this too certainly implies that he could not in fact have read it, and so cannot by any means be what we mean by saying that he could have read it.

In the concluding paragraph of his discussion, Nowell-Smith does finally undertake to give us his analysis not merely of "could have," but also of "can" (which he says means "will if"). And this last feature is very much to be welcomed, because if an analysis is being consciously given of "can" at least we shall at length be clear of confusions connected with the idea that "could have" is necessarily a subjunctive.[15]

The argument of the last paragraph runs as follows. It is "logically odd" to say something of this kind (I am slightly emending Nowell-Smith's formula, but only in ways that are favorable to it and demanded by his own argument) :

Smith has the ability to run a mile, has the opportunity to run a mile, has a preponderant motive for running a mile, but does not in fact do so.

From this it follows directly, says Nowell-Smith, that "can" means "will if," that is, I suppose, that "Smith can run a mile" *means* "If Smith has the opportunity to run a mile

and a preponderant motive for running it, he will run it."

It seems, however, plain that nothing of the kind follows. This may be seen first by setting the argument out formally. Nowell-Smith's premise is of the form

Not (p and q and r and not -s),

that is

Logically odd (ability + opportunity + motive + non-action).

Now from this we can indeed infer

$p \supset ((q \text{ and } r) \supset s)$,

that is that

If he has the ability, then, if he has the opportunity and the motive, he will do it.

But we can*not infer* the converse

$((q \text{ and } r) \supset s) \supset p$,

or in other words that

If, when he has the opportunity and the motive, he does it, he has the ability to do it.

(I do not say this last is not something to which we should, when so put into English, assent, only that it does not follow from Nowell-Smith's premise : of course it follows merely from the premise that he does it, that he has the ability to do it, according to ordinary English.) But unless this second, converse implication *does* follow, we cannot, according to the usual formal principles, infer that p is *equivalent* to, nor therefore that it means the same as (q and r) $\supset s$, or in words that ability *means* that opportunity plus motive leads to action.

To put the same point nonformally. From the fact that if three things are true together a fourth must also be true, we cannot argue that one of the three things *simply means* that if the other two are true the fourth will be true. If we could argue indeed in this way, then we should establish, from Nowell-Smith's premise, not merely that

"He has the ability to do X" simply means that "If he has the opportunity and the motive to do X, he will do X,"

but also equally that

"He has the opportunity to do X" *simply means* that "If he has the ability and the motive to do X, he will do X,"

and likewise that

"He has a preponderant motive to do X" *simply means* that "If he has the ability and the opportunity to do X, he will do X."

---

[15] It must, however, be pointed out once again that if we are to discuss the assertion that somebody *can* (now) do something, the previous arguments that our assertions are not categorical because they are based on induction and cannot be verified directly, whether they were good or not, must now be abandoned: because of course it *is* possible to verify this "directly" by the method Nowell-Smith has specified in another connection earlier, viz., by getting the man to try and seeing him succeed.

For clearly we can perform the same operations on q and r as on p, since the three all occupy parallel positions in the premise. But these are fantastic suggestions. Put shortly, Nowell-Smith is pointing out in his premise that if a man both can and wants to (more than he wants to do anything else), he will : but from this it does not follow that "he can" *simply means* that "if he wants to he will." Nowell-Smith is struggling to effect a transition from *can* to *will* which presents difficulties as great as those of the transition from *could* to *would* : he puts up his show of effecting it by importing the additional, and here irrelevant, concept of motive, which needless to say is in general very intimately connected with the question of what "he will" do.

When, in conclusion, Nowell-Smith finally sets out his analysis of "Smith could have read *Emma* last night," it is this :

He would have read it, if there had been a copy, if he had not been struck blind, &c., &c., and if he had wanted to read it more than he had wanted to read (this should be "do") anything else.

But so far from this being what we mean by saying he could have read it, it actually implies that he could *not* have read it, for more than adequate reasons : it implies that he was blind at the time, and so on. Here we see that Nowell-Smith actually does make the confusion I referred to above between a statement which implies or asserts that certain conditions *were* fulfilled and a conditional statement, i.e., a statement about what would have happened if those conditions had been fulfilled. This is unfortunately a confusion of a general kind that is not uncommon : I need only mention the classic instance of Keynes, who confused asserting on evidence h that p is probable with asserting that on evidence h p is probable, both of which can be ambiguously expressed by "asserting that p is probable on evidence h," but only the former of which asserts that p is (really) probable. Here similarly there is a confusion between asserting on the supposition (or premise) that he had a copy that he could/would have read it, and asserting that on the supposition that he had a copy he could/would have read it, both of which can be ambiguously expressed by "asserting that he could/would have read it, on the supposition that he had a copy," but only the former of which asserts that he (actually) could have read it.

To some extent, then, we learn from studying Nowell-Smith's arguments lessons similar to those that we learned in the case of Moore. But some are new, as for instance that many assertions about what a man *would have* done or *will do* depend, in critical cases, upon premises about his *motives* as well as, or rather than, about his abilities or opportunities : hence these assertions cannot be what assertions about his abilities *mean*.[16]

On one point I may perhaps elaborate a little further. It has been maintained that *sometimes* when we say "He could have done X" this is a conditional : it requires completion by an *if*-clause, typically "if he had had the opportunity," and so does *not* require us, if we are to establish his truth, to establish that he did in fact have the opportunity. Sometimes on the other hand it is a past indicative, implying that he did have the opportunity : in which case we do, to establish its truth, have to establish that certain conditions were satisfied, but the assertion is *not* to be described as a conditional assertion.

Now while I have no wish to retract this account in general or in all cases, I doubt whether it is the whole story. Consider the case where what we wish to assert is that somebody had the opportunity to do something but lacked the ability—"He could have smashed that lob, if he had been any good at the smash" : here the *if*-clause, which may of course be suppressed and understood, relates not to opportunity but to ability. Now although we might describe the whole sentence as "conditional," it nevertheless manages to assert, by means of its main clause, something "categorical" enough, viz., that he did have a certain opportunity. And in the same way Nowell-Smith's "He could have read *Emma,* if he had had a copy," does seem to assert "categorically" that he had a certain ability, although he lacked the opportunity to exercise it. Looking at it in this way, there is a temptation to say that "could have" has, besides its "all-in" *sense,* several more *restricted senses* : this would be brought out if we said

---

[16] Yet here it must be pointed out once more that it has not been shown that *all* assertions about what he would have done are so dependent, so that this particular argument against the analysis of "could have" as "would have if" is not conclusive: in particular, it does not dispose of the possible suggestion that "could have" means "would have if he had *tried,*" for here considerations of motive may be irrelevant.

"He could have smashed it, *only* he is no good at the smash" or "He could have read *Emma but* he had no copy," where, we should say, "could have" is being used in the restricted senses of opportunity or of ability[17] only, and is a past indicative, not a past conditional.

This view might be reinforced by considering examples with the simple "can" itself. We are tempted to say that "He can" sometimes means just that he has the ability, with *nothing said* about opportunity, sometimes *just* that he has the chance, with nothing said about ability, sometimes, however, that he really actually *fully can* here and now, having both ability and opportunity. Now nobody, I think, would be tempted to say that "can," where it means one of the two lesser things, e.g., "has the opportunity," i.e., "can in the full sense if he has the ability," is grammatically a subjunctive or conditional. Perhaps, then, it was not correct to describe "He could have," either, as always a conditional where it asserts ability or opportunity only, with nothing said about the other, or even where the other is denied to have existed.

The verb *can* is a peculiar one. Let us compare it for a moment with another peculiar verb, *know,* with which it shares some grammatical peculiarities, such as lack of a continuous present tense. When I say that somebody *knows* what the thing in my hand is, I may mean merely that he has the ability to identify it given the opportunity, or that he has the opportunity to identify it if he has the ability, or that he has both. What do we say about *know* here? Certainly we are not prone to invoke the idea of a conditional, but rather that of different senses, or perhaps the still obscure idea of the dispositional. I must be content here merely to say that I do not think that the old armory of terms, such as "mood" and "sense," is altogether adequate for handling such awkward cases. The only point of which I feel certain is that such verbs as *can* and *know* have each an all-in, paradigm use, around which cluster and from which divagate, little by little and along different paths, a whole series of other uses, for many of which, though perhaps not for all, a synonymous expression ("opportunity," "realize," and so on) can be found.

It is not unusual for an audience at a lecture to include some who prefer things to be important, and to them now, in case there are any such present, there is owed a peroration. Why, in short, does all this matter? First, then, it needs no emphasizing that both *if* and *can* are highly prevalent and protean words, perplexing both grammatically and philosophically: it is not merely worth while, but essential, in these studies to discover the facts about *ifs* and *cans*, and to remove the confusions they engender. In philosophy it is *can* in particular that we seem so often to uncover, just when we had thought some problem settled, grinning residually up at us like the frog at the bottom of the beer mug. Furthermore and secondly, we have not here been dissecting these two words in general or completely, but in a special connection which perhaps no one will hold trivial. It has been alleged by very serious philosophers (not only the two I have mentioned) that the things we ordinarily say about what we can do and could have done may actually be consistent with determinism. It is hard to evade all attempt to decide whether this allegation is true—hard even for those who, like myself, are inclined to think that determinism itself is still a name for nothing clear, that has been argued for only incoherently. At least I should like to claim that the arguments considered tonight fail to show that it *is* true, and indeed in failing go some way to show that it is *not*. Determinism, whatever it may be, may yet be the case, but at least it appears not consistent with what we ordinarily say and presumably think. And finally there is a third point. Reflecting on the arguments in this lecture, we may well ask ourselves whether they might not be as well assigned to grammar as to philosophy: and this, I think, is a salutary question to end on. There are constant references in contemporary philosophy, which notoriously is much concerned with language, to a "logical grammar" and a "logical syntax" as though these were things distinct from ordinary grammarian's grammar and syntax: and certainly they do seem, whatever exactly they may be, different from traditional grammar. But grammar today is itself in a state of flux; for fifty years or more it has been questioned on all hands and counts

---

[17] I talk here and throughout of "ability" and "opportunity" only; but I realize that other abstract nouns like "capacity," "skill," and even "right" are equally involved. All these terms need listing and elucidating before we really get to grips with "can."

whether what Dionysius Thrax once thought was the truth about Greek is the truth and the whole truth about all language and all languages. Do we know, then, that there will prove to be any ultimate boundary between "logical grammar" and a revised and enlarged *Grammar*? In the history of human inquiry, philosophy has the place of the initial central sun, seminal and tumultuous: from time to time it throws off some portion of itself to take station as a science, a planet, cool and well regulated, progressing steadily toward a distant final state. This happened long ago at the birth of mathematics, and again at the birth of physics: only in the last century we have witnessed the same process once again, slow and at the time almost imperceptible, in the birth of the science of mathematical logic, through the joint labors of philosophers and mathematicians. Is it not possible that the next century may see the birth, through the joint labors of philosophers, grammarians, and numerous other students of language, of a true and comprehensive *science of language*? Then we shall have rid ourselves of one more part of philosophy (there will still be plenty left) in the only way we ever can get rid of philosophy, by kicking it upstairs.

CHAPTER X

PUNISHMENT

Single is each man born; single he dies; single he receives the reward of his good, and single the punishment of his evil deeds.

Institutes of Menu

The problem of punishment has been discussed for over two thousand years and notoriously little agreement has been reached. In fact, so much confusion still exists that one philosopher has felt the need, at this late date, to write a prolegomenon to the subject.[1] Three questions in particular must be kept separate, for they may be answered in different ways. First, ought we to punish people at all? Second, whom should we punish? Third, what is the proper measure of punishment? Let us look briefly at each of these questions.

In every society there are rules designed to guide conduct. Inevitably there are those who do not follow the rules. How should we react to them? Some urge that we should love rather than hate them, forgive rather than punish. We should "turn the other cheek." Others argue that persons who act in socially undesirable ways are "ill" and that they cannot avoid acting as they do. Antisocial behavior is pathological behavior. Hygiene and not punishment is needed. Most thinkers, however, approve of punishment. Two influential schools of thought among the proponents of punishment are retributivism and utilitarianism.

Retributivists argue that moral guilt requires punishment: retribution is morally desirable. Utilitarians claim that punishment is justified solely by its beneficial consequences to the public. If there were no system of punishment, fewer people would be deterred from socially undesirable conduct. It is desirable to minimize such conduct, and the price is the pain inflicted on punished persons. Punishment is a painful necessity; it is not a positive moral good.

Our second question is: Whom should we punish? For some contemporary theorists this question is trivial. We can never punish the innocent, for what we mean by "punishment" is "inflicting pain for wrongdoing." To say that "only the guilty may be punished" is like saying "only a woman may be a widow." A putative moral principle is a disguised triviality. But does not this definitional maneuver leave unresolved several major questions?

First, consider a legal system in which the relatives of those who have

---

[1] H. L. A. Hart, "Prolegomenon to the Principles of Punishment," *Proceedings of the Aristotelian Society*, LX (1959–60), 1–26.

committed crimes are "punished" for those crimes. Can such a system—call it what you will—be justified? The retributivist would deny that it can. He would charge that on utilitarian grounds it might be. Consequently, utilitarianism as an answer to the question "Whom should we punish?" is a morally deficient position. The retributivist claims that it would be wrong to punish one person for another's crimes and wrong to punish a person if no crime has been committed. He argues that in some circumstances a utilitarian will have to approve of these morally wrong acts.

Second, insisting that it is logically impossible to punish the innocent does not provide us with a justification of excuses in the criminal law. Suppose it is proposed that traditional excuses—infancy, insanity, ignorance, etc.—no longer be allowed. How would retributivists and utilitarians react to such a proposal?

Utilitarians have urged in support of the traditional excuses that infants, lunatics, and the like cannot be deterred by threat of punishment. Consequently, punishing such persons would increase unhappiness without any corresponding decrease in socially undesirable conduct. But is this necessarily so? Can we not imagine cases in which total utility is increased by not allowing certain excuses? Indeed, do not legislators who enact strict liability statutes believe that this is so? Does the utilitarian position fully account for our disapproval of such statutes? And if one adopts utility as a test of the desirability of the institution of punishment, may one reject it as a test of who should be punished?

The retributivist will argue that it is wrong to punish persons who are not morally guilty. If an excusing condition exists, there is no moral guilt. But does such a justification fully account for our disapproval of strict liability and insistence on excuses? Consider a revolutionary in a state in which a revolution is morally desirable. The revolutionary may intentionally violate the laws and not be morally culpable. Now, if in addition to punishing such a person, the state enacts legislation providing for punishment of the insane and of those who act unintentionally, would not our disapproval be even greater? Does the retributivist who relies on the notion of moral guilt account for the additional disapproval of what is done when excuses are not allowed? What, then, does justify disapproval of systems in which human choice is assigned a minor role in determining whether a person is to be punished?

There is, finally, the problem of the measure of punishment. At least two difficult questions arise here. First, what principle should guide us in determining the amount of punishment for particular crimes? Kant suggested the principle of equality. The punishment must in some way "fit" the crime. This view has been ridiculed by pointing to crimes in which the principle could not be applied without some awkwardness. But may there not be some validity to this emphasis on equality? For example, would we approve of life imprisonment for malicious slander if it were demonstrated to us that there was a net benefit to society from this course of action? Would we ever approve of punishing murder with a modest fine or petty theft with death without admitting that we were giving up some basic principle of justice? Second, what justifies our disapproval of a system in which like cases are treated in unlike ways and unlike cases in like ways? Is utility the sole test? Or is there some principle of justice which we should sacrifice to utilitarian considerations only rarely and with reluctance?

The Case of the Speluncean Explorers*

In the Supreme Court of Newgarth, 4300

The defendants having been indicted for the crime of murder were convicted and sentenced to be hanged by the Court of General Instances of the County of Stowfield. They bring a petition of error before this Court. The facts sufficiently appear in the opinion of the Chief Justice.

TRUEPENNY, C. J. The four defendants are members of the Speluncean Society, an organization of amateurs interested in the exploration of caves. Early in May of 4299 they, in the company of Roger Whetmore, then also a member of the Society, penetrated into the interior of a limestone cavern of the type found in the Central Plateau of this Commonwealth. While they were in a position remote from the entrance to the cave, a landslide occurred. Heavy boulders fell in such a manner as to block completely the only known opening to the cave. When the men discovered their predicament they settled themselves near the obstructed entrance to wait until a rescue party should remove the detritus that prevented them from leaving their underground prison. On the failure of Whetmore and the defendants to return to their homes, the Secretary of the Society was notified by their families. It appears that the explorers had left indications at the headquarters of the Society concerning the location of the cave they proposed to visit. A rescue party was promptly dispatched to the spot.

The task of rescue proved one of overwhelming difficulty. It was necessary to supplement the forces of the original party by repeated increments of men and machines, which had to be conveyed at great expense to the remote and isolated region in which the cave was located. A huge temporary camp of workman, engineers, geologists, and other experts was established. The work of removing the obstruction was several times frustrated by fresh landslides. In one of these, ten of the workmen engaged in clearing the entrance were killed. The treasury of the Speluncean Society was soon exhausted in the rescue effort, and the sum of eight hundred thousand frelars, raised partly by popular subscription and partly by legislative grant, was expended before the imprisoned men were rescued. Success was finally achieved on the thirty-second day after the men entered the cave.

Since it was known that the explorers had carried with them only scant provisions, and since it was also known that there was no animal or vegetable matter within the cave on which they might subsist, anxiety was early felt that they might meet death by starvation before access to them could be obtained. On the twentieth day of their imprisonment it was learned for the first time that they had taken with them into the cave a portable wireless machine capable of both sending and receiving messages. A similar machine was promptly installed in the rescue camp and oral communication established with the unfortunate men within the mountain. They asked to be informed how long a time would be required to release them. The engineers in charge of the project answered that at least ten days would be required even if no new landslides occurred. They then asked if any physicians were present, and were placed in communication with a committee of medical experts. The imprisoned men described their condition and the rations they had taken with them, and asked for a medical opinion whether they would be likely to live without food for ten days longer. The chairman of the committee of physicians told them that there was little possibility of this. The wireless machine within the cave then remained silent for eight hours. When communication was re-established the men asked to speak again with the physicians. The chairman of the physicians' committee was placed before the apparatus and Whetmore, speaking on behalf of himself and the defendants, asked whether they would be able to survive for ten days longer if they consumed the flesh of one of their number. The physicians' chairman reluctantly answered this question in the affirmative. Whetmore asked whether it would be advisable for them to cast lots to determine which of them should be eaten. None of the physicians present was willing to answer the question. Whetmore then asked if there were among the party a judge or other official of the government who would answer this question. None of those attached to the rescue camp was willing to assume the role of advisor in this matter. He

* Lon L. Fuller, "The Case of the Speluncean Explorers." Copyright 1949 by Lon L. Fuller. Reprinted from *Harvard Law Review,* LXII (1949), 616–19, with the permission of the author.

then asked if any minister or priest would answer their question, and none was found who would do so. Thereafter no further messages were received from within the cave, and it was assumed (erroneously, it later appeared) that the electric batteries of the explorers' wireless machine had become exhausted. When the imprisoned men were finally released it was learned that on the twenty-third day after their entrance into the cave Whetmore had been killed and eaten by his companions.

From the testimony of the defendants, which was accepted by the jury, it appears that it was Whetmore who first proposed that they might find the nutriment without which survival was impossible in the flesh of one of their own number. It was also Whetmore who first proposed the use of some method of drawing or casting lots, calling the attention of the defendants to a pair of dice he happened to have with him. The defendants were at first reluctant to adopt so desperate a procedure, but after the conversations by wireless related above, they finally agreed on the plan proposed by Whetmore. After much discussion of the mathematical problems involved, agreement was finally reached on a method of determining the issue by the use of the dice.

Before the dice were cast, however, Whetmore declared that he withdrew from the arrangement, as he had decided on reflection to wait for another week before embracing an expedient so frightful and odious. The others charged him with a breach of faith and proceeded to cast the dice. Then when it came Whetmore's turn, the dice were cast for him by one of the defendants, and he was asked to declare any objections he might have to the fairness of the throw. He stated that he had no such objections. The throw went against him and he was then put to death and eaten by his companions.

After the rescue of the defendants, and after they had completed a stay in a hospital where they underwent a course of treatment for malnutrition and shock, they were indicted for the murder of Roger Whetmore. At the trial, after the testimony had been concluded, the foreman of the jury (a lawyer by profession) inquired of the court whether the jury might not find a special verdict, leaving it to the court to say whether on the facts as found the defendants were guilty. After some discussion, both the Prosecutor and counsel for the defendants indicated their acceptance of this procedure, and it was adopted by the court. In a lengthy special verdict the jury found the facts as I have related them above, and found further that if on these facts the defendants were guilty of the crime charged against them, then they found the defendants guilty. On the basis of this verdict, the trial judge ruled that the defendants were guilty of murdering Roger Whetmore. He then sentenced them to be hanged, the law of our Commonwealth permitting him no discretion with respect to the penalty to be imposed. After the release of the jury, its members joined in a communication to the Chief Executive asking that the sentence be commuted to an imprisonment of six months. The trial judge addressed a similar communication to the Chief Executive. As yet no action with respect to these pleas has been taken, as the Chief Executive is apparently awaiting our disposition of this petition of error. . . .

The Right of Punishing and of Pardoning*

Judicial or Juridical Punishment (*poena forensis*) is to be distinguished from Natural Punishment (*poena naturalis*), in which Crime as Vice punishes itself, and does not as such come within the cognizance of the Legislator. Juridical Punishment can never be administered merely as a means for promoting another Good either with regard to the Criminal himself or to Civil Society, but must in all cases be imposed only because the individual on whom it is inflicted *has committed a Crime*. For one man ought never to be dealt with merely as a means subservient to the purpose of another, nor be classified with the objects of the law of property. Against

such treatment his inherent Personality has a Right to protect him, even although he may be condemned to lose his Civil Personality. He must first be found guilty and *punishable*, before there can be any thought of drawing from his Punishment any benefit for himself or his fellow citizens. The Penal Law is a Categorical Imperative; and woe to him who creeps through the serpent-windings of Utilitarianism to discover some advantage that may discharge him from the Justice of Punishment, or even from the due measure of it, according to the Pharisaic maxim: "It is better that *one* man should die than that the whole people should perish." For if Justice and Righteousness perish, human life would no longer have any value in the world. What, then, is to be said of such a proposal as to

* Immanuel Kant, *The Philosophy of Law*, trans. W. Hastie (Edinburgh: T. and T. Clark, 1887), pp. 194–98, 201.

keep a Criminal alive who has been condemned to death, on his being given to understand that if he agreed to certain dangerous experiments being performed on him, he would be allowed to survive if he came happily through them? It is argued that Physicians might thus obtain new information that would be of value to the Commonweal. But a Court of Justice would repudiate with scorn any proposal of this kind if made to it by the Medical Faculty; for Justice would cease to be Justice, if it were bartered away for any consideration whatever.

But what is the mode and measure of Punishment which Public Justice takes as its Principle and Standard? It is just the Principle of Equality, by which the pointer of the Scale of Justice is made to incline no more to the one side than the other. It may be rendered by saying that the undeserved evil which anyone commits on another, is to be regarded as perpetrated on himself. Hence, it may be said: "If you slander another, you slander yourself; if you steal from another, you steal from yourself; if you strike another, you strike yourself; if you kill another, you kill yourself." This is the Right of RETALIATION (*jus talionis*); and properly understood, it is the only Principle which in regulating a Public Court, as distinguished from mere private judgment, can definitely assign both the quality and the quantity of a just penalty. All other standards are wavering and uncertain; and on account of other considerations involved in them, they contain no principle conformable to the sentence of pure and strict Justice. It may appear, however, that difference of social status would not admit the application of the Principle of Retaliation, which is that of "Like with Like." But although the application may not in all cases be possible according to the letter, yet as regards the effect it may always be attained in practice, by due regard being given to the disposition and sentiment of the parties in the higher social sphere. Thus a pecuniary penalty, on account of a verbal injury, may have no direct proportion to the injustices of the slander; for one who is wealthy may be able to indulge himself in this offense for his own gratification. Yet the attack committed on the honor of the party aggrieved may have its equivalent in the pain inflicted upon the pride of the aggressor, especially if he is condemned by the judgment of the Court, not only to retract and apologize, but to submit to some meaner ordeal, as kissing the hand of the injured person. In like manner, if a man of the highest rank has violently assaulted an innocent citizen of the lower orders, he may be condemned not only to apologize but to undergo a solitary and painful imprisonment, whereby, in addition to the discomfort endured, the vanity of the offender would be painfully affected, and the very shame of his position would constitute an adequate Retaliation after the principle of "Like with Like." But how then would we render the statement: "If you *steal* from another, you steal from yourself"? In this way, that whoever steals anything makes the property of all insecure; he therefore robs himself of all security in property, according to the Right of Retaliation. Such a one has nothing, and can acquire nothing, but he has the Will to live; and this is only possible by others supporting him. But as the State should not do this gratuitously, he must for this purpose yield his powers to the State to be used in penal labor; and thus he falls for a time, or it may be for life, into a condition of slavery. But whoever has committed Murder, must *die*. There is, in this case, no juridical substitute or surrogate, that can be given or taken for the satisfaction of Justice. There is no Likeness or proportion between Life, however painful, and Death; and therefore there is no Equality between the crime of Murder and the retaliation of it but what is judicially accomplished by the execution of the Criminal. His death, however, must be kept free from all maltreatment that would make the humanity suffering in his Person loathsome or abominable. Even if a Civil Society resolved to dissolve itself with the consent of all its members— as might be supposed in the case of a People inhabiting an island resolving to separate and scatter themselves throughout the whole world —the last Murderer lying in the prison ought to be executed before the resolution was carried out. This ought to be done in order that everyone may realize the desert of his deeds, and that blood-guiltiness may not remain upon the people; for otherwise they might all be regarded as participators in the murder as a public violation of Justice.

. . .

Against these doctrines, the Marquis BEC-

CARIA has given forth a different view. Moved by the compassionate sentimentality of a humane feeling, he has asserted that all Capital Punishment is wrong in itself and unjust. He has put forward this view on the ground that the penalty of death could not be contained in the original Civil Contract; for in that case, every one of the People would have had to consent to lose his life if he murdered any of his fellow citizens. But, it is argued, such a consent is impossible, because no one can thus dispose of his own life. All this is mere sophistry, and perversion of Right.

No one undergoes Punishment because he has willed to be punished, but because he has willed a *punishable Action*; for it is in fact no Punishment when anyone experiences what he wills, and it is impossible for anyone to will to be punished. To say, "I *will* to be punished, if I murder anyone," can mean nothing more than, "I submit myself along with all the other citizens to the Laws"; and if there are any Criminals among the People, these Laws will include Penal Laws. The individual who, as a Colegislator, enacts *Penal Law,* cannot possibly be the same Person who, as a Subject, is punished according to the Law; for, *qua* Criminal, he cannot possibly be regarded as having a voice in the Legislation. The Legislator is holy. . . .

The End of Punishment*

Washing one's hands of the guilt of others is a way of sharing guilt so far as it encourages in others a vicious way of action. Nonresistance to evil which takes the form of paying no attention to it is a way of promoting it. The desire of an individual to keep his own conscience stainless by standing aloof from badness may be a sure means of causing evil and thus of creating personal responsibility for it. Yet there are circumstances in which passive resistance may be the most effective form of nullification of wrong action, or in which heaping coals of fire on the evil-doer may be the most effective way of transforming conduct. To sentimentalize over a criminal—to "forgive" because of a glow of feeling—is to incur liability for production of criminals. But to suppose that infliction of retributive suffering suffices, without reference to concrete consequences, is to leave untouched old causes of criminality and to create new ones by fostering revenge and brutality. The abstract theory of justice which demands the "vindication" of law irrespective of instruction and reform of the wrong-doer is as much a refusal to recognize responsibility as is the sentimental gush which makes a suffering victim out of a criminal.

Courses of action which put the blame exclusively on a person as if his evil will were the sole cause of wrong-doing and those which condone offense on account of the share of social conditions in producing bad disposition, are equally ways of making an unreal separation of man from his surroundings, mind from the world. Causes for an act always exist, but causes are not excuses. Questions of causation are physical, not moral, except when they concern future consequences. It is as causes of future actions that excuses and accusations alike must be considered. At present we give way to resentful passion, and then "rationalize" our surrender by calling it a vindication of justice. Our entire tradition regarding punitive justice tends to prevent recognition of social partnership in producing crime; it falls in with a belief in metaphysical free will. By killing an evil-doer or shutting him up behind stone walls, we are enabled to forget both him and our part in creating him. Society excuses itself by laying the blame on the criminal; he retorts by putting the blame on bad early surroundings, the temptations of others, lack of opportunities, and the persecutions of officers of the law. Both are right, except in the wholesale character of their recriminations. But the effect on both sides is to throw the whole matter back into antecedent causation, a method which refuses to bring the matter to truly moral judgment. For morals has to do with acts still within our control, acts still to be performed. No amount of guilt on the part of the evil-doer absolves us from responsibility for the consequences upon him and others of our way

* John Dewey, *Human Nature and Conduct* (New York: The Modern Library, 1930), pp. 17–19, reprinted by permission of the publishers, Holt, Rinehart and Winston, Inc., New York.

of treating him, or from our continuing responsibility for the conditions under which persons develop perverse habits.

We need to discriminate between the physical and the moral questions. The former concerns what *has* happened, and how it happened. To consider this question is indispensable to morals. Without an answer to it we cannot tell what forces are at work nor how to direct our actions so as to improve conditions. Until we know the conditions which have helped form the characters we approve and disapprove, our efforts to create the one and do away with the other will be blind and halting. But the moral issue concerns the future. It is prospective. To content ourselves

with pronouncing judgments of merit and demerit without reference to the fact that our judgments are themselves facts which have consequences and that their value depends upon *their* consequences, is complacently to dodge the moral issue, perhaps even to indulge ourselves in pleasurable passion just as the person we condemn once indulged himself. The moral problem is that of modifying the factors which now influence future results. To change the working character or will of another we have to alter objective conditions which enter into his habits. Our own schemes of judgment, of assigning blame and praise, of awarding punishment and honor, are part of these conditions.

Punishment and the Criminal Law*

I

It will not be denied that the nature and function of law require it to be evaluated as a means to an end, but it is well to make the point explicit at the start and to consider some of its implications. No one would contend that legislators and administrators should be given tremendous power over the lives and happiness of other men and be paid to exercise such power because legislation and administration are valuable for their own sake. If they are desirable at all, it is only because they are a means to the achievement of some valuable state of social affairs. Accordingly, the evaluation of a particular legal activity raises two questions: (1) what ends does the activity serve, i.e., what are its actual or probable results in society; and (2) are they ends which men should endeavor to achieve by law, i.e., are they desirable in themselves or as a means to ends desirable but more remote? Similarly, the determination of what kind of legal activity to undertake turns on the ends which ought to be served and the means which are well adapted to serving them. Thus any question about what ought to be done in any of the branches of legal activity is different from and more complex than a question about what has been done, is being done or will be done in any of them.

Questions about the character and results

of a particular legal activity, or about the adaptation of particular means to particular ends, are questions of fact. They can be answered, if they are answerable at all, by the knowledge derived from common experience or from the special experience obtained by historical and sociological investigation. That life imprisonment is well adapted to rendering the persons subjected to it incapable of committing crimes outside of prison, is obviously indicated by common knowledge of what imprisonment involves. Investigations of what occurred during the prohibition era sustains the conclusion that national prohibition gave considerable impetus to the organization of professional criminals. That the severity of the penalties of the early nineteenth-century criminal law was responsible for the refusal of many men to participate in their enforcement, is the inescapable finding of a somewhat more extensive historical investigation. But whether or not the incapacitation of persons convicted of crime, or the organization of professional criminals, or the nullification of penal laws, is desirable, undesirable, or more or less desirable than some alternative state of affairs is a question of value rather than of fact. It is logically impossible to demonstrate that some state of social affairs is good or bad or better or worse than some other state of affairs by facts alone. The syllogism requires a judgment about what is good or bad in social life. The assertion, evaluation, and exploration of such propositions is the province of politics and also of ethics,

* Jerome Michael and Herbert Wechsler, *Criminal Law and Its Administration* (New York: The Foundation Press, 1940), pp. 4–17, reprinted by permission of the publishers. Footnotes have been renumbered.

since what is good in social life cannot be considered apart from what is good in individual life. Both the lawmaker and his critic necessarily employ ethical and political ideas and the more civilized they are the more fully are they conscious that they are doing so.

While this much is clear, what is likely to be unclear is whether the ultimate propositions in ethics and politics, those which concern ends rather than means, can reasonably be asserted as anything more than a personal preference. If they can only be asserted as a personal preference, it is impossible to evaluate law and legal activity on any other ground than their conformity to the personal desires of the individual who makes the judgment. Even in this event, however, judgments of preference may be better or worse in the sense that the individual's appraisal of his own lasting desires may be faulty. He may, for example, either fail to perceive or underestimate his own concern for the welfare of other people. If, on the other hand, the ultimate propositions of ethics and politics can be asserted on some broader basis than personal preference, the reason must be that it is possible, as we think it is, to achieve some grasp of the fundamental and permanent in human desires in general, the specifically human in the capacities of men. This is the groundwork upon which ethical and political thought must build in the articulation of ultimate ends and the ordering of more immediate ends and means.

In the ordering of means and ends one must obviously employ whatever knowledge there is of the adaptation of particular means to particular ends, and the question of adaptation of means to end is, as we have said, a question of fact. That it is a question of fact does not mean, however, that it is easy to answer. To a very considerable degree knowledge of matters of fact, particularly of the crucial sociological and psychological facts of law, consists of opinions the relative validity of which it is difficult or impossible to measure. Hence, even when men agree about remote ends, they frequently disagree about the adaptation of means to these ends and, therefore, about the relative value of intermediate ends. This inadequacy in knowledge of matters of fact marks the limitations of the rôle of reason in the solution of practical problems, and nowhere are these limitations more apparent or more lamentable than in the field

of the criminal law. An understanding of our limitations in this respect is, however, as much a condition of wisdom as an understanding of our rational power. Understanding of our limitations charts the path to decreasing them and guarantees a proper modesty in our expectations. It protects us against actions which are rash and gives us the fortitude to take risks in action which only a thoughtless conservatism decries. But more than this, it enables us to dismiss claims to goodness which can be shown to be unfounded or inferior to competing claims. This is as important a part of the rational process as the assertion of claims which can be shown to be well founded and, which, therefore, compel assent.

II

The major problems of the criminal law are two: what behavior should be made criminal, and what should be done with persons who commit crimes. For reasons already stated, the analysis of these problems should begin with a consideration of ends; and the initial question properly concerns ultimate ends. In this dimension, it has been argued that the ultimate end of the criminal law should be retribution—the punishment of those who will to inflict undeserved evil on others by penalties proportioned to their offenses. This contention has far-reaching implications and its validity must be appraised.

That the retributive position is an ancient one cannot be doubted and it may be that, as Bradley has said, it represents the unstudied belief of most men.[1] Its first systematic development is, however, to be found in the ethical writings of Kant[2] and Hegel[3] and their

[1] Bradley, *Ethical Studies*, 2d ed. (1927), pp. 1–41. "If there is any opinion to which the man of uncultivated morals is attached, it is the belief in the necessary connection of punishment and guilt. Punishment is punishment only where it is deserved. We pay the penalty, because we owe it, and for no other reason; and if punishment is inflicted for any other reason whatever than because it is merited by wrong, it is a gross immorality, a crying injustice, an abominable crime, and not what it pretends to be. . . . Having once the right to punish, we may modify the punishment according to the useful and the pleasant; but these are external to the matter, they cannot give us a right to punish, and nothing can do that but criminal desert. . . . Yes, in despite of sophistry, and in the face of sentimentalism with well nigh the whole body of our self-styled enlightenment against them, our people believe to this day that *punishment is inflicted for the sake of punishment.* . . ." *Id.* at pp. 26–27, 28. . . .
[2] See *The Science of Right,* Part 2, sec. 49; *Philosophy of Law,* trans. Hastie (1887), pp. 194–204.
[3] *The Philosophy of Right,* trans. Dyde (1896), pp. 90–103.

followers, Stammler and Kohler. Kant argued that it is self-evident that the desert of crime is punishment; that justice requires that a man who has willed an unjust act[4] be punished by a penalty which is strictly proportional in nature and intensity to his crime; that a person who does such an act affirms that it is right that people be dealt with in that way and, therefore, he himself should be dealt with in the same way; that if society fails to punish a criminal, it sanctions his principles and thereby becomes *particeps criminis*. Kant denied that any other considerations are relevant; a world in which justice is sacrificed is not worth preserving on other grounds. "Juridical punishment can never be administered merely as a means for promoting another good, either with regard to the criminal himself or to civil society, but must in all cases be imposed only because the individual on whom it is inflicted has committed a crime. For one man ought never to be dealt with merely as a means subservient to the purpose of another . . . Against such treatment his inborn personality has a right to protect him . . . The Penal Law is a Categorical Imperative; and woe to him who creeps through the serpent-windings of Utilitarianism to discover some advantage that may discharge him from the justice of punishment or even from the due measure of it . . ."[5] Hegel states the position somewhat differently. He agrees that punishment is just because it is deserved but, the justice of punishment having been thus established, he, apparently, would permit other factors than the culpability of the offense to be considered in determining the character of the punishment. Later writers introduce even further qualifications while adhering to the basic

point that the end of punishment should be retribution.[6]

The critics of the retributive position deny that it is self-evident that retribution is just, whether one believes in free will (in the sense that purposive behavior is uncaused by antecedent physical, mental, and environmental conditions but is the product of the will which is itself a first cause) or in determinism (in the sense of the rule of cause and effect in the behavior of human beings).[7] They ask what intuitive necessity there is, apart from a con-

---

[4] What actions are unjust depends of course upon Kant's ethical analysis which we cannot examine in detail. It may be useful however to call attention to the following points in his ethical doctrine: (1) Men are rational and have freedom of will; (2) no action can be affirmed to be right or wrong unless it proceeds on a principle of conduct which can be affirmed to be right or wrong for all men in the given situation independent of their special inclinations; (3) no man should use another as a means to some desired end. . . .

[5] *Philosophy of Law*, p. 195. In two cases, however, Kant does not adhere to his own principle. He concedes that punishment may be mitigated if it would "deaden the sensibilities of the People by the spectacle of Justice being exhibited in the mere carnage of the slaughtering bench" and also, apparently, if it would result in an undue depopulation of the State.

[6] Can one who holds the retributive view define the criminal law unambiguously as the body of law, possible and actual, which ought to serve the end of retribution?

[7] Determinists have attacked the retributive theory on the ground that it presupposes a nondeterminist view of human behavior. They have argued that the idea of personal guilt is incompatible with a recognition of the fact that the individual's will to do evil is itself a product of his heredity and environment; that the individual ought not to be held at fault for willing what antecedent conditions caused him to will; and that if there is any fault, it must rest with these antecedent conditions. See, for example, McConnell, *Criminal Responsibility and Social Constraint* (1912), pp. 48 *et seq.* To the extent, and only to the extent, that one who holds the retributive view reasons from his belief in freedom of the will, or that the justice of retribution is, intuitively, dependent upon such freedom (*cf.* Kohler, *Philosophy of Law* (Modern Legal Philosophy ed., 1914), p. 281), is this attack relevant. It is not decisive because if there is any basis, intuitively, for the justice of retribution, there is no logical reason why it may not remain even if determinism be admitted, why, in short, one may not intuit the justice of punishing those who have the capacity to deliberate and choose to do evil, even though one concede that their choices may be determined. The idea of determinism, of the reign of cause and effect in the whole physical order, does not deny the reality of deliberation in the psychological order. Thus Aquinas, following Aristotle, distinguishes between actions which are instinctive and those which follow upon the deliberation; by freedom of the will he means only the capacity to deliberate. Yet he does not reject the conceptions of guilt and sin. Freedom is so defined that there is no conflict with determinism.

On the other hand, some believers in freedom of the will have argued against determinism on the ground that such a view renders punishment inappropriate because it destroys the conception of guilt and, in doing so, the basis of all morality. This argument is completely unfounded. Even were punishment rendered inappropriate by determinism, the truth of determinism would be unaffected; "we cannot prove the existence of anything by the argument that if it did not exist our policies would be unjustified." (M. R. Cohen, *Reason and Nature*, p. 327.) But, beyond this, once retribution is rejected, it is obvious that punishment not only is appropriate in a deterministic world but that it is appropriate only in such a world. For, if retribution is rejected, the whole purpose of inflicting punishment is to control behavior by providing individuals with an additional motive for refraining from criminal conduct—the motive of avoiding punishment, just as the purpose of moral education is to provide them with other motives for right conduct. The basic assumption is that action is governed by motives, that character can be improved by individual effort, which can, in turn, be stimulated. . . .

cern for future actions, that evil be repaid with punishment rather than ignored. "If we give up all utilitarian ideas of social welfare, what necessity is there that the universe should be organized like a penitentiary on the basis of rewards and punishments?"[8] Holmes contended that "it will be seen on self-inspection, that this feeling of fitness [of punishment following wrongdoing] is absolute and unconditional only in the case of our neighbors" and that then it is "only vengeance in disguise."[9] Throughout the history of thought it has been argued in various ways that human punishment is a creature of human law and human law an instrument of the state; that the ultimate end of the state should be the welfare of its members and that both law and legal penalties should serve the same end; and that they are just precisely to the extent that they do serve that end. Since punishment consists in the infliction of pain it is, apart from its consequences, an evil; consequently, it is good and, therefore, just only if and to the degree that it serves the common good by advancing the welfare of the person punished or of the rest of the population. This is the position taken by Plato,[10] Aristotle, Cicero, St. Thomas Aquinas, and the medieval Church, as well as by Hobbes,[11] Beccaria,[12] Bentham,[13] and many others in more modern times. Accord-ing to this view retribution is itself unjust since it requires some human beings to inflict pain upon others, regardless of its effect upon them or upon the social welfare. In any event, it is urged, the retributive theory is incapable of practical application. How can men lacking omniscience measure degrees of guilt in individual cases and apportion pain thereto? How is it possible, moreover, to inflict pain upon the guilty without also inflicting pain upon their innocent relatives and friends? Since the retributive theory requires not only that the guilty be punished but also that the guiltless be not, how . . . is it possible to avoid doing more retributive injustice than justice in any given case?

These considerations seem to us not only to refute the retributive position but also to establish that the criminal law, like the rest of the law, should serve the end of promoting the common good; and that its specific capacity for serving this end inheres in its power to prevent or control socially undesirable behavior. The consequence of rejecting retribution as the ultimate end of the criminal law is that it does not constitute a valid criterion for the evaluation of particular legal provisions, that no legal provision can be justified merely because it calls for the punishment of the morally guilty by penalties proportioned to their guilt, or criticized merely because it fails to do so. This does not mean that legal provisions which may have been instituted to serve the end of retribution are necessarily impolitic. Unless the retributive purpose is deemed to be authoritative for purposes of present administration, the question remains whether the particular provision is well or poorly adapted to the prevention of socially undesirable behavior or to promoting the common good in other ways.[14]

---

[8] M. R. Cohen, *Law and the Social Order*, p. 310.

[9] *The Common Law*, p. 45: "It does not seem to me that anyone who has satisfied himself that an act of his was wrong and that he will never do it again, would feel the least need or propriety, as between himself and an earthly punishing power alone, of his being made to suffer for what he has done, although when third persons were introduced, he might, as a philosopher, admit the necessity of hurting him to frighten others. But when our neighbors do wrong, we sometimes feel the fitness of making them smart for it, whether they have repented or not."

[10] See *Protagoras*, p. 324: ". . . No one punishes the evil-doer under the notion, or for the reason, that he has done wrong—only the unreasonable fury of a beast acts in that manner. But he who desires to inflict rational punishment does not retaliate for a past wrong which cannot be undone; he has regard to the future, and is desirous that the man who is punished, and he who sees him punished, may be deterred from doing wrong again. He punishes for the sake of prevention. . . ." See also *Gorgias*, p. 525; *Republic*, pp. 380, 615; *Phaedo*, p. 113; *Laws*, pp. 854, 862, 934, 957.

[11] *Leviathan* (1651), Part II, c. 30.

[12] *Crimes and Punishments* (1764), *passim*, especially cc. I, II, VII.

[13] "The general object which all laws have, or ought to have, in common, is to augment the total happiness of the community; and therefore in the first place, to exclude, as far as may be, everything that tends to subtract from that happiness; in other words, to exclude mischief . . . But all punishment is mischief; all punishment in itself is evil. Upon the prin-ciple of utility, if it ought at all to be admitted, it ought only to be admitted in as far as it promises to exclude some greater evil." *Principles of Morals and Legislation* (Oxford ed., 1879), p. 170.

[14] Is it possible for one who rejects the retributive view to define the criminal law unambiguously as the body of law, possible and actual, which ought to serve the end of preventing behavior incompatible with the common welfare? Is that not true of much of what is traditionally known as the civil law?

III

The only means which the criminal law can employ to prevent socially undesirable behavior is the treatment of those persons who have engaged or are likely to engage in such behavior. There are many possible methods of treatment and they may serve the end of prevention in different ways. If a person has engaged in behavior of a sort which is undesirable and can be deterred, and if he is subjected to treatment which is generally regarded as unpleasant, other persons may be deterred from engaging in similar conduct by the fear that if they do so they will be similarly treated. Whatever the character of his past behavior, if the person subjected to treatment is himself likely to engage in undesirable behavior in the future, his treatment may serve to prevent him from doing so by incapacitating, intimidating, or reforming him. Accordingly, the determination of the kinds of behavior to be made criminal involves three major problems: (1) What sorts of conduct is it both desirable and possible to deter (2) what sorts indicate that persons who behave in those ways are dangerously likely to engage in socially undesirable behavior in the future; (3) will the attempt to prevent particular kinds of undesirable behavior by the criminal law do less good, as measured by the success of such efforts, than harm, as measured by their other and harmful results. The determination of methods of treating criminals also involves three major problems: (1) What methods are best adapted to the various ends of treatment; (2) to what extent do methods which serve one end of treatment also serve or disserve other ends; (3) if one end of treatment must be preferred over others, either because there are no methods of treatment well adapted to all of them, or for other reasons, what should be the order of preference among them? That there is an intimate relationship between these two sets of problems is clear, since the consequences, desirable and undesirable, of making behavior criminal will to a very considerable extent depend upon the character of the methods employed in the treatment of criminals[15] and since the choice of methods of treatment must depend in part, at least, upon the reasons for making the behavior criminal.[16]

[15] Consider, for example, the differences in the probable consequences of making it a crime to employ minors in industry, to possess a firearm, or to exceed a speed limit, according as the penalty is a small fine or a long term of imprisonment.
[16] Thus, if the primary reason for making particular behavior criminal is that it is deemed to be indicative of a dangerous personality, it is likely to be foolish to devote much attention to deterrence as an object of treatment.

In order to determine the kinds of behavior which it is desirable to deter, the probable results, both good and bad, of behavior of various sorts must be discovered and then estimated as being on the whole socially desirable or socially undesirable. In making behavior criminal three questions must therefore be answered: (1) What consequences of human activity are socially undesirable; (2) what sorts of behavior tend to produce such results; (3) which of the sorts having that tendency are nevertheless socially desirable because their socially beneficial potentialities are greater than their socially dangerous tendencies. It is therefore apparent that, in its broadest aspect, the determination of the behavior to be made criminal, is the problem of the kind of social order we ought to strive for; and that, with respect to particular kinds of conduct, it is the problem whether or not they are conducive to that kind of social order. . . . Even behavior which menaces life or fundamental interests in property may serve ends which are more desirable than the lives or property interests which it endangers. This is especially true, as we shall see, when the threat is remote.

In order to determine the kinds of undesirable behavior which it is possible to deter, the probability that the desire to avoid punishment will be stronger than whatever desires move men to such conduct must be estimated. The determination of the kinds of behavior which indicate that the actors are dangerously likely to engage in socially undesirable behavior in the future involves the even more difficult psychological problem of estimating the potentialities of men for good and evil conduct, of appraising their characters on the basis of their prior behavior. Whatever the purpose of the inquiry, whether to discover what kinds of behavior can be deterred or to discover what kinds of behavior are indicative of bad character, it may be aided by a consideration of other factors than the nature of the behavior itself. What are the relevant factors? Is the knowledge or intention or motive with which a man engages in certain conduct, or the state of his emotions at the time, or his age, or his prior history, pertinent to either of these inquiries? The Anglo-American criminal law, as it now exists, makes some of these factors significant for legal purposes. Are the discriminations reflected in contemporary law justifiable if the purpose of the law is to prevent socially undesirable behavior or only, as some writers assert, if its end is retribution? And if the latter, what discriminations should be made in a system designed to serve nonretributive ends?

That behavior is of a sort which it is desirable and possible to deter or which is indicative of the dangerousness of individuals who engage in it, does not necessarily establish that it should be made criminal. The consequences of making it criminal may be more undesirable than the consequences of the behavior itself. We desire to prevent antisocial behavior in order to improve the conditions of social life; we must take care, therefore that social life is not made worse by the medicine than by the disease.

When we turn to the problems of treatment we find that they are no less complex or difficult. We can be reasonably certain that no methods of treatment can be devised which will deter all potential offenders or reform all actual offenders or, what is even more difficult, do both at once. We do know, of course, that death and life imprisonment are effective methods of incapacitation. We do not know and may never know with certainty what methods of treatment are most efficacious as deterrents or as reformatives or how efficacious any method of treatment is. Common sense tells us that most men fear punishment to an indeterminate and inconstant degree and that the more certain and severe punishment is, the more intensely it is likely to be feared. But the law must rely for its enforcement upon ordinary men acting as complainants, as witnesses, as jurors, and as officials. Common sense also warns us that to varying and uncertain degrees the widespread imposition of drastically severe penalties arouses in many such men a sympathy for the accused which leads them to refuse to participate in inflicting them. When this result occurs nullification ensues, and the effect of the severity of punishment is greatly to magnify its uncertainty and to provoke a general hatred of the law which in a democratic society must inevitably culminate in its change. Accordingly, penalties must be mitigated in most cases to avoid nullification. Common sense further warns us that the infliction of severe punishment short of total incapacitation is likely to result in the return to society of men utterly unfit for a noncriminal life, embittered, and determined to exact their revenge. It cautions us, too,

that, to some extent at least, cruelty or bloodshed inflicted in the name of the law is likely to have the same deleterious effect upon public morals as cruelty or bloodshed inflicted in the name of anything else. Moreover, prisons are relatively few in number and expensive to build and maintain; the government of any considerable number of persons sentenced to life imprisonment is inordinately difficult; and it may be doubted whether any widespread extension of the death penalty would be politically feasible, even if it were wise. There is an additional reason for the mitigation of punishment whenever criminal behavior can be attributed to some grave injustice done the criminal either by some other person or by society as a whole as, for example, when many people are near starvation and men are driven to steal by hunger. As T. H. Green has pointed out,[17] the mitigation of penalties on that ground serves to direct attention to and to increase popular awareness of the original injustice and, thus, may lead to its correction.

On the other hand, while common sense may suggest that lenient or nonpunitive methods of treatment are, in general, better adapted to reformation than severe methods, not all men are corrigible; and the separation of the corrigible from the incorrigible requires psychological judgments which are difficult or impossible to make with any assurance on the basis of the psychological knowledge that we now have; reluctance to delegate to officials the power to make them may, accordingly, be wise. Moreover, the desire for revenge, the belief that retributive punishment is just, and the feeling that examples must be made of those guilty of shocking crimes are to a very considerable degree entrenched in the general population. Too lenient treatment of offenders, however well adapted to reforming them, may therefore lead to lynching, self-help, or indifference about prosecution which may be far worse in their social consequences than the utilization of more severe methods of treatment which satisfy the popular desire for severity though they have no reformative efficacy. This may be what Stephen meant by his famous remark that the criminal law stands to the passion for vengeance in much the same relation as marriage to the sexual

---

[17] *Lectures on the Principles of Political Obligation* (1927), pp. 193–94.

appetite.[18] But, on the other hand, it is urged that the desires for revenge and for retribution are themselves antisocial and, therefore, ought not to be encouraged by law;[19] that if the public mind is unprepared to view the problems of social control dispassionately, it ought to be educated to do so; and that the legal devices adopted by society can and ought to be employed to that end. Apart from these considerations, Bentham believed, and not without reason, that unless punishments are graded in proportion to the social harmfulness of behavior, there is no incentive to the potential offender to engage in less rather than more undesirable behavior.[20] And Beccaria insisted that it is important, not only for the prevention of crime but for social relations in general, that the community should properly evaluate the relative significance of antisocial conduct of various sorts, the degree to which various types of behavior are inimical to the general welfare; and that very lenient treatment of those who engage in exceedingly harmful behavior may lead the community to regard it as less harmful than it is.[21]

But more than this, the deterrence of potential offenders and the incapacitation and the reformation of actual offenders are not the only values which must be considered in determining the ends of treatment. Although criminals ought to be subjected to treatment for the sake of preventing crime and although the deterrence of potential offenders and the incapacitation and reformation of actual offenders are the proximate means to the prevention of crime by the criminal law, the methods employed in treating criminals may in their collateral consequences serve or disserve other social ends and their potentialities in these respects must also be taken into account. By the same token, the position of deterrence, incapacitation, and reformation in relation to one another, as the ends of treatment, cannot be determined solely by reference to the crime-preventive efficacy of a system derived from one ordering of these ends as opposed to another, even when their relative efficacy in this regard can be foretold. The extent to which other desirable ends—such, for example, as the proper expenditure of the national income—will be served or disserved by various alternative policies is an important element in the choice. No program for the determination of methods of treatment, no set of criteria for their evaluation, can ignore this obvious multiplicity of treatment ends.

[18] *General View of the Criminal Law of England* (1863), p. 99 . . .

[19] *Cf.* Holmes, *The Common Law,* pp. 41–42: "If people would gratify the passion of revenge outside of the law, if the law did not help them, the law has no choice but to satisfy the craving itself, and thus avoid the greater evil of private retribution. At the same time, this passion is not one which we wish to encourage, either as private individuals or as lawmakers."

Consider, however, Tarde's hedonistic argument that since people as they are take pleasure in the infliction of pain upon those who have offended, the legal system ought to do its share to provide that pleasure as a means to the happiness of the citizen. *Penal Philosophy,* trans. Howell (1912), pp. 34–36. . . . Compare the following rigorous passages in Stephen, *History of the Criminal Law,* I, 478: "In cases which outrage the moral feelings of the community to a great degree, the feeling of indignation and desire for revenge which is excited in the minds of decent people is, I think, deserving of legitimate satisfaction"; and II, 81–82: "I think it highly desirable that criminals should be hated, that the punishment inflicted on them should be so construed as to give expression to that hatred, and to justify it so far as the public provision of means for expressing and gratifying a healthy natural sentiment can justify and encourage it."

[20] See Bentham, *The Theory of Legislation, Principles of the Penal Code,* Part Three, c. 2.

[21] *Crimes and Punishments,* c. 23 . . .

On Punishment*

* A. M. Quinton, "On Punishment," *Analysis,* XIV (1954), 1933–42, reprinted by permission of the author and the publisher, Basil Blackwell, London.

I. INTRODUCTORY

There is a prevailing antinomy about the philosophical justification of punishment. The two great theories—retributive and utilitarian —seem, and at least are understood by their defenders, to stand in open and flagrant contradiction. Both sides have arguments at their disposal to demonstrate the atrocious consequences of the rival theory. Retributivists, who seem to hold that there are circumstances in which the infliction of suffering is a good thing in itself, are charged by their opponents with vindictive barbarousness. Utilitarians, who seem to hold that punishment is always and only justified by the good consequences it produces, are accused of vicious opportunism. Where the former insists on suffering for suffering's sake, the latter permits the punishment of the innocent. Yet, if the hope of justifying punishment is not to be abandoned altogether, one of these apparently unsavory alternatives must be embraced. For they exhaust the possibilities. Either punishment must be self-justifying, as the retributivists claim, or it must depend for its justification on something other than itself, the general formula of "utilitarianism" in the wide sense appropriate here.

In this paper I shall argue that the antinomy can be resolved, since retributivism, properly understood, is not a moral but a logical doctrine, and that it does not provide a moral justification of the infliction of punishment but an elucidation of the use of the word. Utilitarianism, on the other hand, embraces a number of possible moral attitudes toward punishment, none of which necessarily involves the objectionable consequences commonly adduced by retributivists, provided that the word "punishment" is understood in the way that the essential retributivist thesis lays down. The antinomy arises from a confusion of modalities, of logical and moral necessity and possibility, of "must" and "can" with "ought" and "may." In brief, the two theories answer different questions: retributivism the question "when (logically) *can* we punish?", utilitarianism the question "when (morally) *may* we or *ought* we to punish?" I shall also describe circumstances in which there is an answer to the question "when (logically) *must* we punish?" Finally, I shall attempt to account for this difference in terms of a distinction between the establishment of rules whose infringement involves punishment from the application of these rules to particular cases.

II. THE RETRIBUTIVE THEORY

The essential contention of retributivism is that punishment is only justified by guilt. There is a certain compellingness about the repudiation of utilitarianism that this involves. We feel that whatever other considerations may be taken into account, the primary and indispensable matter is to establish the guilt of the person to be punished. I shall try to show that the peculiar outrageousness of the rejection of this principle is a consequence, not of the brutality that such rejection might seem

to permit, but of the fact that it involves a kind of lying. At any rate the first principle of retributivism is that it is necessary that a man be guilty if he is to be punished.

But this doctrine is normally held in conjunction with some or all of three others which are logically, if not altogether psychologically, independent of it. These are that the function of punishment is the negation or annulment of evil or wrongdoing, that punishment must fit the crime (the *lex talionis*) and that offenders have a right to punishment, as moral agents they ought to be treated as ends not means.

The doctrine of "annulment," however carefully wrapped up in obscure phraseology, is clearly utilitarian in principle. For it holds that the function of punishment is to bring about a state of affairs in which it is as if the wrongful act had never happened. This is to justify punishment by its effects, by the desirable future consequences which it brings about. It certainly goes beyond the demand that only the guilty be punished. For, unlike this demand, it seeks to prescribe exactly what the punishment should be. Holding that whenever wrong has been done it must be annulled, it makes guilt—the state of one who has done wrong—the sufficient as well as the necessary condition of punishment. While the original thesis is essentially negative, ruling out the punishment of the innocent, the annulment doctrine is positive, insisting on the punishment and determining the degree of punishment of the guilty. But the doctrine is only applicable to a restricted class of cases, the order of nature is inhospitable to attempts to put the clock back. Theft and fraud can be compensated, but not murder, wounding, alienation of affection, or the destruction of property or reputation.

Realizing that things cannot always be made what they were, retributivists have extended the notion of annulment to cover the infliction on the offender of an injury equal to that which he has caused. This is sometimes argued for by reference to Moore's theory of organic wholes, the view that sometimes two blacks make a white. That this, the *lex talionis*, revered by Kant, does not follow from the original thesis is proved by the fact that we can always refrain from punishing the innocent but that we cannot always find a punishment to fit the crime. Some indeed would argue that we can never fit punishment to wrongdoing, for how are either, especially wrongdoing, to be measured? (Though, as Ross has pointed out, we can make ordinal judgments of more or less about both punishment and wrongdoing.)

Both of these views depend on a mysterious extension of the original thesis to mean that punishment and wrongdoing must necessarily be somehow equal and opposite. But this is to go even further than to regard guilt and punishment as necessitating one another. For this maintains that only the guilty are to be punished and that the guilty are always to be punished. The equal and opposite view maintains further that they are to be punished to just the extent that they have done wrong.

Finally retributivism has been associated with the view that if we are to treat offenders as moral agents, as ends and not as means, we must recognize their right to punishment. It is an odd sort of right whose holders would strenuously resist its recognition. Strictly interpreted, this view would entail that the sole relevant consideration in determining whether and how a man should be punished is his own moral regeneration. This is utilitarian and it is also immoral, since it neglects the rights of an offender's victims to compensation and of society in general to protection. A less extreme interpretation would be that we should never treat offenders merely as means in inflicting punishment but should take into account their right to treatment as moral agents. This is reasonable enough; most people would prefer a penal system which did not ignore the reformation of offenders. But it is not the most obvious correlate of the possible view that if a man is guilty he ought to be punished. We should more naturally allot the correlative right to have him punished to his victims or society in general and not to him himself.

III. THE RETRIBUTIVIST THESIS

So far I have attempted to extricate the essentials of retributivism by excluding some traditional but logically irrelevant associates. A more direct approach consists in seeing what is the essential principle which retributivists hold utilitarians to deny. Their crucial charge is that utilitarians permit the punishment of the innocent. So their fundamental thesis must be that only the guilty are to be punished, that guilt is a necessary condition of punishment. This hardly lies open to the utilitarian countercharge of pointless and vin-

dictive barbarity, which could only find a foothold in the doctrine of annulment and in the *lex talionis*. (For that matter, it is by no means obvious that the charge can be sustained even against them, except in so far as the problems of estimating the measure of guilt lead to the adoption of a purely formal and external criterion which would not distinguish between the doing of deliberate and accidental injuries.)

Essentially, then, retributivism is the view that only the guilty are to be punished. Excluding the punishment of the innocent, it permits the other three possibilities: the punishment of the guilty, the nonpunishment of the guilty, and the nonpunishment of the innocent. To add that guilt is also the sufficient condition of punishment, and thus to exclude the nonpunishment of the guilty, is another matter altogether. It is not entailed by the retributivist attack on utilitarianism and has none of the immediate compulsiveness of the doctrine that guilt is the necessary condition of punishment.

There is a very good reason for this difference in force. For the necessity of not punishing the innocent is not moral but logical. It is not, as some retributivists think, that we *may* not punish the innocent and *ought* only to punish the guilty, but that we *cannot* punish the innocent and *must* only punish the guilty. Of course, the suffering or harm in which punishment consists can be and is inflicted on innocent people, but this is not punishment, it is judicial error or terrorism or, in Bradley's characteristically repellent phrase, "social surgery." The infliction of suffering on a person is only properly described as punishment if that person is guilty. The retributivist thesis, therefore, is not a moral doctrine, but an account of the meaning of the word "punishment." Typhoid carriers and criminal lunatics are treated physically in much the same way as ordinary criminals; they are shut up in institutions. The essential difference is that no blame is implied by their imprisonment, for there is no guilt to which the blame can attach. "Punishment" resembles the word "murder"; it is infliction of suffering on the guilty and not simply infliction of suffering, just as murder is wrongful killing and not simply killing. Typhoid carriers are no more (usually) criminals than surgeons are (usually) murderers. This accounts for the flavor of moral outrage attending the notion of punishment of the innocent. In a sense a contradiction in terms, it applies to the common enough practice of inflicting the suffering involved in punishment on innocent people and of sentencing them to punishment with a lying imputation of their responsibility and guilt. Punishment *cannot* be inflicted on the innocent; the suffering associated with punishment *may* not be inflicted on them, firstly, as brutal and secondly, if it is represented as punishment, as involving a lie.

This can be shown by the fact that punishment is always *for* something. If a man says to another "I am going to punish you" and is asked "what for?" he cannot reply "nothing at all" or "something you have not done." At best, he is using "punish" here as a more or less elegant synonym for "cause to suffer." Either that or he does not understand the meaning of "punish." "I am going to punish you for something you have not done" is as absurd a statement as "I blame you for this event for which you were not responsible." "Punishment implies guilt" is the same sort of assertion as "ought implies can." It is not *pointless* to punish or blame the innocent, as some have argued, for it is often very useful. Rather the very conditions of punishment and blame do not obtain in these circumstances.

IV. AN OBJECTION

But how can it be useful to do what is impossible? The innocent can be punished and scapegoats are not logical impossibilities. We do say "they punished him for something he did not do." For A to be said to have punished B it is surely enough that A thought or said he was punishing B and ensured that suffering was inflicted on B. However innocent B may be of the offense adduced by A, there is no question that, in these circumstances, he has been punished by A. So guilt cannot be more than a *moral* precondition of punishment.

The answer to this objection is that "punish" is a member of that now familiar class of verbs whose first-person-present use is significantly different from the rest. The absurdity of "I am punishing you for something you have not done" is analogous to that of "I promise to do something which is not in my power." Unless you are guilty I am no more in a position to punish you than I am in a position to promise what is not in my power. So it is improper to say "I am going to pun-

ish you" unless you are guilty, just as it is improper to say "I promise to do this" unless it is in my power to do it. But it is only *morally* improper if I do not *think* that you are guilty or that I can do the promised act. Yet, just as it is perfectly proper to say of another "he promised to do this," whether he thought he could do it or not, provided that he *said* "I promise to do this," so it is perfectly proper to say "they punished him," whether they thought him guilty or not, provided that they *said* "we are going to punish you" and inflicted suffering on him. By the first-person-present use of these verbs we prescribe punishment and *make* promises; these activities involve the satisfaction of conditions over and above what is required for *reports* or *descriptions* of what their prescribers or makers represent as punishments and promises.

Understandably "reward" and "forgive" closely resemble "punish." Guilt is a precondition of forgiveness, desert—its contrary—of reward. One cannot properly say "I am going to reward you" or "I forgive you" to a man who has done nothing. Reward and forgiveness are always *for* something. But, again, one can say "they rewarded (or forgave) him for something he had not done." There is an interesting difference here between "forgive" and "punish" or "reward." In this last kind of assertion "forgive" seems more peculiar, more inviting to inverted commas, than the other two. The three undertakings denoted by these verbs can be divided into the utterance of a more or less ritual formula and the consequences authorized by this utterance. With punishment and reward the consequences are more noticeable than the formula, so they come to be sufficient occasion for the use of the word even if the formula is inapplicable and so improperly used. But, since the consequences of forgiveness are negative, the absence of punishment, no such shift occurs. To reward involves giving a reward, to punish inflicting a punishment, but to forgive involves no palpable consequence, e.g., handing over a written certificate of pardon.

Within these limitations, then, guilt is a *logically* necessary condition of punishment and, with some exceptions, it might be held, a morally necessary condition of the infliction of suffering. Is it in either way a sufficient condition? As will be shown in the last section there are circumstances, though they do not obtain in our legal system, nor generally in extralegal penal systems (e.g., parental), in which guilt is a logically sufficient condition of at least a sentence of punishment. The parallel moral doctrine would be that if anyone is guilty of wrongdoing he ought morally to be punished. This rather futile rigorism is not embodied in our legal system with its relaxations of penalties for first offenders. Since it entails that offenders should never be forgiven it is hardly likely to commend itself in the extralegal sphere.

V. THE UTILITARIAN THEORY

Utilitarianism holds that punishment must always be justified by the value of its consequences. I shall refer to this as "utility" for convenience without any implication that utility must consist in pleasure. The view that punishment is justified by the value of its consequences is compatible with any ethical theory which allows meaning to be attached to moral judgments. It holds merely that the infliction of suffering is of no value or of negative value and that it must therefore be justified by further considerations. These will be such things as prevention of and deterrence from wrongoing, compensation of victims, reformation of offenders, and satisfaction of vindictive impulses. It is indifferent for our purposes whether these are valued as intuitively good, as productive of general happiness, as conducive to the survival of the human race or are just normatively laid down as valuable or derived from such a norm.

Clearly there is no *logical* relation between punishment and its actual or expected utility. Punishment *can* be inflicted when it is neither expected, nor turns out, to be of value and, on the other hand, it can be foregone when it is either expected, or would turn out, to be of value.

But that utility is the morally necessary or sufficient condition, or both, of punishment are perfectly reputable moral attitudes. The first would hold that no one should be punished unless the punishment would have valuable consequences; the second that if valuable consequences would result punishment ought to be inflicted (without excluding the moral permissibility of utility-less punishment). Most people would no doubt accept the first, apart from the rigorists who regard guilt as a morally sufficient condition of pun-

ishment. Few would maintain the second except in conjunction with the first. The first says when you may not but not when you ought to punish, the second when you ought to but not when you may not.

Neither permits or encourages the punishment of the innocent, for this is only logically possible if the word "punishment" is used in an unnatural way, for example as meaning any kind of deliberate infliction of suffering. But in that case they cease to be moral doctrine about punishment as we understand the word and become moral doctrines (respectively, platitudinous and inhuman) about something else.

So the retributivist case against the utilitarians falls to the ground as soon as what is true and essential in retributivism is extracted from the rest. This may be unwelcome to retributivists since it leaves the moral field in the possession of the utilitarians. But there is a compensation in the fact that what is essential in retributivism can at least be definitely established.

VI. RULES AND CASES

So far what has been established is that guilt and the value or utility of consequences are relevant to punishment in different ways. A further understanding of this difference can be gained by making use of a distinction made by Sir David Ross in the appendix on punishment in *The Right and the Good*. This will also help to elucidate the notion of guilt which has hitherto been applied uncritically.

The distinction is between laying down a rule which attaches punishment to actions of a certain kind and the application of that rule to particular cases. It might be maintained that the utilitarian theory was an answer to the question "What kinds of action should be punished?" and the retributive theory an answer to the question "On what particular occasions should we punish?" On this view both punishment and guilt are defined by reference to these rules. Punishment is the infliction of suffering attached by these rules to certain kinds of action, guilt the condition of a person to whom such a rule applies. This accounts for the logically necessary relation holding between guilt and punishment. Only the guilty can be punished because unless a person is guilty, unless a rule applies to him, no infliction of suffering on him is properly called punishment, since punishment is infliction of suffering as laid down by such a rule. Considerations of utility, then, are alone relevant to the determination of what in general, what *kinds* of action, to punish. The outcome of this is a set of rules. Given these rules, the question of whom in particular to punish has a definite and necessary answer. Not only will guilt be the logically necessary but also the logically sufficient condition of punishment or, more exactly, of a sentence of punishment. For declaration of guilt will be a declaration that a rule applies and, if the rule applies, what the rule enjoins—a sentence of punishment—applies also.

The distinction between setting up and applying penal rules helps to explain the different parts played by utility and guilt in the justification of punishment, in particular the fact that where utility is a moral, guilt is a logical, justification. Guilt is irrelevant to the setting up of rules, for until they have been set up the notion of guilt is undefined and without application. Utility is irrelevant to the application of rules, for once the rules have been set up, punishment is determined by guilt; once they are seen to apply, the rule makes a sentence of punishment necessarily follow.

But this account is not an accurate description of the very complex penal systems actually employed by states, institutions, and parents. It is, rather, a schema, a possible limiting case. For it ignores an almost universal feature of penal systems (and of games, for that matter, where penalties attend infractions of the rules)—discretion. For few offenses against the law is one and only one fixed and definite punishment laid down. Normally only an upper limit is set. If guilt, the applicability of the rule, is established no fixed punishment is entailed but rather, for example, one not exceeding a fine of forty shillings or fourteen days' imprisonment. This is even more evident in the administration of such institutions as clubs or libraries and yet more again in the matter of parental discipline. The establishment of guilt does not close the matter; at best it entails some punishment or other. Precisely how much is appropriate must be determined by reference to considerations of utility. The variety of things is too great for any manageably concise penal code to dispense altogether with discretionary judgment in particular cases.

But this fact only shows that guilt is not a logically *sufficient* condition of punishment; it does not affect the thesis that punishment entails guilt. A man cannot be guilty unless his action falls under a penal rule and he can only be properly said to be punished if the rule in question prescribes or permits some punishment or other. So all applications of the notion of guilt necessarily contain or include all applications of the notion of punishment.

An Approach to the Problems of Punishment*

I shall develop, in this article, certain distinctions suggested by recent contributions to the philosophical discussion of punishment, which help to clarify the issues involved. Having separated out what I consider the four central philosophical questions, I shall suggest an approach to them, which, while mainly utilitarian, takes due account, I believe, of the retributivist case where it is

* S. I. Benn, "An Approach to the Problems of Punishment," *Philosophy*, XXXIII (October 1958), 325–41, reprinted with the permission of The Royal Institute of Philosophy, London, and the author; and George Allen & Unwin Ltd., London. This material has been incorporated into *Social Principles and the Democratic State* by R. S. Peters and Stanley I. Benn (London: George Allen & Unwin Ltd., 1959). Footnotes have been renumbered.

strongest, and meets the main retributivist objections.

I make three key distinctions:

(1) Between justifying punishment in general (i.e., as an institution), and justifying particular penal decisions as applications of it;

(2) Between what is implied in postulating guilt as a necessary, and as a sufficient, condition for punishment;

(3) Between postulating guilt in law and guilt in morals, as a condition for punishment.

I distinguish, further, four philosophical questions, to which a complete and coherent approach to punishment would have to provide answers:

What formal criteria must be satisfied in justifying:

(1) Punishment in general, i.e., as an institution?

(2) Any particular operation of the institution?

(3) The degrees of punishment attached to different classes of offense?

(4) The particular penalty awarded to a given offender?

PRELIMINARIES

A. *"Punishment" defined*

Prof. Flew[1] has suggested five criteria for the use of "punishment" in its primary sense, i.e., five conditions satisfied by a standard case to which the word would be applied:

(i) It must involve an "evil, an unpleasantness to the victim";

(ii) It must be for an offense (actual or supposed);

(iii) It must be of an offender (actual or supposed);

(iv) It must be the work of personal agencies (i.e., not merely the natural consequences of an action);

(v) It must be imposed by authority (real or supposed), conferred by the system of rules (hereafter referred to as "law") against which the offense has been committed.

It is not a misuse to talk, for example, of "punishing the innocent," or of a boxer "punishing his opponent"; but since these usages, though related to the primary one, disregard one or more of the criteria ordinarily satisfied, they are extensions, or secondary usages. In considering the justification for punishment, I shall confine the word to the primary sense, unless I indicate otherwise.

B. *The distinction between justifying punishment in general, and justifying the particular application*

There would seem, on the face of it, to be a real difference between utilitarian and retributivist approaches to the justification of punishment, the former looking to its beneficent consequences, the latter exclusively to the wrongful act. It remains to be seen whether the gulf can be bridged. The first

[1] A. Flew, "The Justification of Punishment," *Philosophy*, XXIX, (1954), 291–307.

step is to distinguish between a rule, or an institution constituted by rules, and some particular application thereof. To ask what can justify punishment in general is to ask why we should have the sort of rules that provide that those who contravene them should be made to suffer; and this is different from asking for a justification of a particular application of them in punishing a given individual. Retributivist and utilitarian have tried to furnish answers to both questions, each in his own terms; the strength of the former's case rests on his answer to the second, of the latter's on his answer to the first. Their difficulties arise from attempting to make one answer do for both.

I. *What formal criteria must be satisfied in justifying punishment in general, as an institution?*

The retributivist refusal to look to consequences for justification makes it impossible to answer this question within his terms. Appeals to authority apart, we can provide ultimate justification for rules and institutions, only by showing that they yield advantages.[2] Consequently, what pass for retributivist justifications of punishment in general, can be shown to be either denials of the

[2] Admittedly, a rule might be justified *in the first place* by reference to one more general, under which it is subsumed as a particular application—e.g., "It is wrong to pick flowers from public gardens because it is wrong to steal—and this is a special case of stealing." But this would not be conclusive. It could be countered by making a distinction between private and public property, such that while the more general rule prohibits stealing the former, it does not extend to the latter. Whether the distinction can be accepted as relevant must depend on the reasons for the more general rule, understood in terms of its expected advantages, and on whether to allow the exception would tend to defeat them. Consider "Euthanasia is wrong because it is wrong to kill." It could be argued that the latter does not require the former; that a proper distinction can be made between killings generally, and those satisfying the conditions: (i) that the patient wants to be killed; (ii) that the purpose is to put him out of pain; (iii) that there is no hope for his recovery. Suppose the reason for the general prohibition is to ensure that the life of man shall not be "solitary, poor, nasty, brutish, and short"; then exceptions satisfying the above criteria might be admissible, on the grounds that not only would they not defeat the objectives of the rule, but that advantages would follow from distinguishing on the basis of these criteria, that would otherwise be missed. On the other hand, it might be said that it is *absolutely* wrong to kill—which is to deny the need for justification in terms of purpose or consequences, but is also to deny the need for *any* moral (as opposed to authoritative) justification. But in that case, how are we to decide whether "Thou shalt not kill" does, or does not, extend to a duty "officiously to keep alive"?

need to justify it, or mere reiterations of the principle to be justified, or disguised utilitarianism.

Assertions of the type "it is fitting (or justice requires) that the guilty suffer" only reiterate the principle to be justified—for "it is fitting" means only that it ought to be the case, which is precisely the point at issue. Similarly, since justification must be in terms of something other than the thing in question, to say that punishment is a good in itself is to deny the need for justification. For those who feel the need, this is no answer at all. Given that punishment would not be justified for the breach of *any* rule, but only of legal rules, what is the peculiar virtue of law that makes it particularly fitting for breaches of just this type of rule? Even if we make punishment a definitional characteristic of "a legal system," so that "law" entails "punishment," we are still entitled to ask why we should have rule systems of precisely this sort.

Some retributivists argue that while punishment is a prima facie evil, and thus in need of justification, it is less objectionable than that the wicked should prosper. This is to subsume the rule "Crimes ought to be punished" under a more general rule: either "The wicked ought to be less well off than the virtuous" or "The wicked ought not to profit from their crimes." Now "wickedness" involves assessment of character; we do not punish men for their wickedness, but for particular breaches of law. There may be some ignoble but prudent characters who have never broken a law, and never been punished, and noble ones who have—our system of punishment is not necessarily the worse for that. We may have to answer for our characters on the Day of Judgment, but not at Quarter Sessions. The state is not an agent of cosmic justice; it punishes only such acts as are contrary to legal rules, conformity to which, even from unworthy motives like fear, is considered of public importance. And if we offer the narrower ground, that the wicked ought not to profit from their *crimes,* we are bound to justify the distinction between crimes and offenses against morals in general. What is the special virtue of legal rules that a breach of them alone warrants punishment? It seems that the wicked are to be prevented from prospering only if their wickedness manifests itself in

selected ways; but how is the selection made, unless in terms of its consequences? In any case, if we permit the subsumption of "Crime ought to be punished" under the more general "The wicked ought not to prosper," it would still be proper to seek justification for the latter. It would not help to say "Justice requires it," for this would only deny the right to ask for justification. I see no answer possible except that in a universe in which the wicked prospered, there would be no inducement to virtue. The subsumption, if allowed, would defer the utilitarian stage of justification; it would not render it superfluous.

A veiled utilitarianism underlies Hegel's treatment of punishment, as annulling a wrong. For if punishment could annul the wrong, it would be justified by the betterment of the victim of the crime or of society in general. Not indeed that the argument is a good one; for the only way to annul a wrong is by restitution or compensation, and neither of these is punishment. A man may be sent to prison for assault, and *also* be liable for damages. Similarly with the argument that punishment reaffirms the right. Why should a reaffirmation of right take precisely the form of punishment? Would not a formal declaration suffice? And even if the reaffirmation necessarily involved a need, right, or duty to punish, the justification would be utilitarian, for why should it be necessary to reaffirm the right, if not to uphold law for the general advantage?[3]

Others have treated punishment as a sort of reflex, a reaction of the social order to the crime following in the nature of things, like a hangover.[4] This is to confuse rules with scientific laws. The penal consequences of a breach of a rule follow only because men have decided to have rules of precisely this sort. Laws of nature, unlike rules, need no justification (except perhaps in theology) because they are independent of human choice. To treat punishment as a natural unwilled

[3] Cf. Lord Justice Denning, in evidence to the Royal Commission on Capital Punishment: "The ultimate justification of any punishment is not that it is a deterrent but that it is the emphatic denunciation by the community of a crime." Cmd. 8932, §53 (1953). But "denunciation" does not imply the deliberate imposition of suffering, which is the feature of punishment usually felt to need justification.

[4] Cf. Sir Ernest Barker, in *Principles of Social and Political Theory,* p. 182: "the mental rule of law which pays back a violation of itself by a violent return, much as the natural rules of health pay back a violation of themselves by a violent return."

response to a breach of law is to deny the need for justification, not to justify.[5] Once we agree to have penal rules, any particular punishment might be justified (though not necessarily sufficiently justified) by reference to a rule. But this is to answer a different question from that at present under consideration.

For Bosanquet, punishment was retributive in the sense that, ideally at least, it was the returning upon the offender of "his own will, implied in the maintenance of a system to which he is a party," in the form of pain. It tends to "a recognition of the end by the person punished"; it is "his right, of which he must not be defrauded."[6] Now while a criminal may not seek to destroy the entire social order, and may even agree in principle that law-breakers should be punished, his efforts to elude the police are evidence that he does not will his own punishment in any ordinary sense. He may be unreasonable and immoral in making exceptions in his own favor—but we cannot therefore construct a theory of punishment on a hypothetical will that would be his were he reasonable and moral, for then he might not be a criminal. To say that punishment is his "right" is to disregard one of the usual criteria for the use of that word, namely, that it is something which will be enforced only if its subject so chooses, the corollary being that it operates to his advantage. Only by pretending that punishment is self-imposed can we think of the criminal as exercising choice; and only by treating it as reformative can we regard it as to his advantage. By claiming that punishment tends "to a recognition of the end by the person punished," Bosanquet introduces such a reformative justification; but to that extent the argument is utilitarian.

To sum up: retributive justifications of punishment in general are unsatisfactory for the very reason that they refuse to look to

the consequences of a rule, thereby denying a necessary part of the procedure for justifying it. To look to the consequences does not entail treating the criminal merely as a means to a social end, as critics have asserted; for in weighing advantages and disadvantages, the criminal, too, must "count for one." But equally, he must count "for no more than one." While we must not lose sight of his welfare altogether, we are not bound to treat him as our sole legitimate concern.

Bentham's case is that punishment is a technique of social control, justified so long as it prevents more mischief than it produces. At the point where damage to criminals outweighs the expected advantage to society, it loses that justification. It operates by reforming the criminal, by preventing a repetition of the offense, and by deterring others from imitating it. (These need not exhaust the possibilities of advantage—Bentham included the satisfaction of vengeance for the injured party.)

Not all theories dealing with the reform of criminals are theories of punishment. Prison reformers concerned with moral re-education offer theories of punishment only if they expect the suffering involved in loss of liberty, etc., itself to lead to reformation. Reformative treatment might cure criminal inclinations by relaxing the rigors of punishment; it might nevertheless defeat its purpose by reducing the deterrent effect for others. "Reformation" is in any case ambiguous. A man would be "a reformed character" only if he showed remorse for his past misdeeds, and determined not to repeat them, not through fear of further punishment, but simply because they were wrong. A criminal who decides that "crime does not pay" is merely deterred by his own experience which is as much "an example" to himself as to others.

Sentences of preventive detention, transportation, deportation, and the death penalty may all be examples of punishment operating as a preventive. Punishment might be aimed at preventing repetitions of an offense by the criminal himself where there are good grounds (e.g., a long criminal record) for supposing him undeterrable.

The strongest utilitarian argument for punishment in general is that it serves to deter potential offenders by inflicting suffer-

---

[5] For J. D. Mabbott, too, punishment is a kind of automatic response, though in a different sense. "Punishment is a corollary not of law but of law-breaking. Legislators do not *choose* to punish. They hope no punishment will be needed. The criminal makes the essential choice; he 'brings it on himself.' " ("Punishment," in *Mind,* Vol. 48, 1939, p. 161. He reaffirms the position in "Freewill and Punishment," in *Contemporary British Philosophy,* 3d Series, ed. H. D. Lewis, 1956, p. 303.) But legislators choose to make *penal* rules, and it is this choice that needs justification.

[6] *The Philosophical Theory of the State,* 4th ed. (1923), p. 211.

ing on actual ones. On this view, punishment is not the main thing; the technique works by threat. Every act of punishment is to that extent an admission of failure; we punish only that the technique may retain a limited effectiveness for the future. Thus the problem of justifying punishment arises only because it is not completely effective; if it were, there would be no suffering to justify.

Retributivists do not deny that punishment may act in these ways, nor that it has these advantages. They maintain only that they are incidental; that a system of punishment constructed entirely on these principles would lead to monstrous injustices. These I consider below. It is evident, however, that while *some* sort of justification can be offered within the utilitarian framework, the retributivist is at best denying the need for justification, or offering utilitarianism in disguise. I conclude, therefore, that any justification for punishment in general must satisfy the formal condition that the consequences for everyone concerned of adopting the technique shall be preferable to the consequences of not doing so. If the main advantage arises from a lower incidence of crime (by way of reform, prevention, deterrence, or otherwise), this must be weighed against the penal suffering actually inflicted, and these together must be preferable to a higher incidence of crime, but with no additional suffering inflicted as punishment. This is a frankly utilitarian conclusion. The strength of the retributivist position lies in its answer to the second question, to which I now turn.

II. *What formal criteria must be satisfied in justifying any particular application of the technique of punishment?*

Critics of the utilitarian approach contend that a justification of punishment in terms of deterrence, prevention, and reform could be extended to justify (i) punishing the innocent, providing they were widely believed to be guilty (in the interest of deterrence); (ii) making a show of punishment, without actually inflicting it (again, deterrence, but this time on the cheap); (iii) punishment in anticipation of the offense (in the interests of prevention or reform). These criticisms, if just, would surely be conclusive. They are based, however, on a misconception of what the utilitarian theory is about. "Punishment" implies, in its primary sense, inflicting suffer-

ing only under specified conditions, of which one is that it must be for a breach of a rule. Now if we insist on this criterion for the word, "punishment of the innocent" is a logical impossibility, for by definition, suffering inflicted on the innocent, or in anticipation of a breach of the rule, cannot be "punishment." It is not a question of what is morally justified, but of what is logically possible. (An analogous relation between "guilt" and "pardon" accounts for the oddity of granting "a free pardon" to a convicted man, later found to be innocent.) When we speak of "punishing the innocent," we may mean: (i) "pretending to punish," in the sense of manufacturing evidence, or otherwise imputing guilt, while knowing a man to be innocent. This would be to treat him as *if* he were guilty, and involve the lying assertion that he was. It is objectionable, not only as a lie, but also because it involves treating an innocent person differently from others without justification, or for an irrelevant reason, the reason offered being falsely grounded;[7] (ii) We may mean, by "punish," simply "cause to suffer," i.e., guilt may not be imputed. This would be a secondary use of the word. In that case, it could not be said that, as a matter of logical necessity, it is either impossible or wrong to punish the innocent. To imprison members of a subversive party (e.g., under Defense Regulation 18B) treating them *in that respect* like criminals, though no offense is even charged, would not necessarily be immoral. Critics might describe it as "punishing the innocent," but they would be illegitimately borrowing implications of the primary sense to attack a type of action to which these did not apply. It is only necessarily improper to "punish the innocent" if we pretend they are guilty, i.e., if we accept all the primary usage criteria; in any looser sense, there need be nothing wrong in any given case. For in exceptional conditions it may be legitimate to deprive people of their liberty as part of a control technique, without reference to an offense (e.g., the detention of lunatics or enemy aliens). Similar arguments apply in the case of the show of punishment. A utilitarian justification of punishment cannot be extended to cover lies, or the making of distinctions where there are no relevant differ-

---

[7] Cf. A. Quinton, "On Punishment," in *Analysis*, Vol. 14, reprinted in *Philosophy, Politics, and Society*, ed. P. Laslett, 1956.

ences; it would be impossible merely to pretend to punish *every* criminal—and unless a relevant criterion could be found, there could be no grounds for treating some differently from others.

The short answer to the critics of utilitarian theories of punishment is that they are theories of *punishment,* not of *any* sort of technique involving suffering.

We may now turn to the retributivist position itself. F. H. Bradley asserted "the necessary connection of punishment and guilt. Punishment is punishment, only where it is deserved . . . if punishment is inflicted for any other reason whatever than because it is merited by wrong, it is a gross immorality, a crying injustice, an abominable crime, and not what it pretends to be."[8] Now, we must distinguish between legal and moral guilt. If the necessary connection asserted is between punishment and legal guilt, then this is a definition of "punishment" masquerading as a moral judgment. It would be more accurate to write "Punishment is 'punishment' only when it is deserved," for the sentence is then about the use of a word, not about the rightness of the act. "The infliction of suffering on a person is only properly described as punishment if that person is guilty. The retributivist thesis, therefore, is not a moral doctrine, but an account of the meaning of the word 'punishment.' "[9]

But this is not the only form of retributive thesis. There are at least four possibilities:

(i) That guilt (i.e., a breach of law) is a *necessary* condition of punishment (this is the position just examined);

(ii) That guilt (i.e., a breach of a *moral* rule) is a *necessary* condition of punishment;

(iii) That guilt (*legal*) is a *sufficient* condition of punishment;

(iv) That guilt (*moral*) is a *sufficient* condition of punishment.

Position (iii) is *not* logically necessary, for it does not follow from the definition of punishment; we *cannot* "punish" where there has been no breach, but we can, and often do, let off with a caution where there has. Other conditions besides guilt may have to be satisfied before punishment is wholly justified in a given case.

[8] *Ethical Studies,* 2d ed. 1927, pp. 26–27.
[9] A. Quinton, *op cit.,* in *Analysis,* p. 137, in *Philosophy, Politics, and Society,* p. 86.

The introduction, in (ii) and (iv), of moral guilt puts a new complexion on retributive theory. A person who is morally guilty deserves blame, and the conditions for blameworthiness could be listed. But it is in no sense necessary that a person who is blameworthy should also be punishable. We may blame liars, but unless, e.g., they make false tax returns, or lie to a court of law, we should not feel bound to punish them. If the conditions of blameworthiness cannot be assimilated completely to the conditions for punishment, moral guilt cannot be a sufficient condition for punishment.

Position (ii) might be supported in two ways:

(*a*) A prima facie moral duty to obey law may yield, in the case of an immoral law, to a stronger duty; a breach of law would not then entail moral guilt, and we should question the justice of the punishment.[10]

(*b*) Certain conditions, like unavoidable ignorance or mistake of fact, lunacy, infancy, and irresistible duress, would exonerate from blame; offenses committed under these conditions should not be punishable—and are not in fact punished, though the deterrent effects of the punishment would be no less in these cases than in others. Therefore, in a negative sense at least, the criteria of blameworthiness must be satisfied, if the necessary conditions for punishment are to be satisfied. Punishment is retribution for such moral lapses as the law recognizes.

The first argument (*a*) might be met in two ways. From the judge's standpoint, so long as he continued in office, it would be his duty to enforce the law, whatever his opinion of it.[11] For him, at least, the absence of moral guilt would not be a bar to punishment. Secondly, criticism of a rule is only indirectly criticism of the justice of a punishment inflicted for a breach of it. The utilitarian could argue that a law that is itself mischievous (in Bentham's sense of "mischief") cannot justify the further mischief of punishment; no good can come of it any-

[10] Cf. C. W. K. Mundle, "Punishment and Desert," in *Philosophical Quarterly,* Vol. 4, 1954: "the retributive theory implies that punishment of a person by the state is morally justifiable if, and only if he has done something which is both a legal and moral offense, and only if the penalty is proportionate to the moral gravity of his offense," p. 227.
[11] This is roughly Mabbott's view (*op. cit.*). He is a rare example of a retributivist who dissociates punishment and moral guilt.

way. This is not, therefore, a defense of a retributive theory of punishment so much as a statement of conditions that a rule must satisfy if punishment is properly to attach to it.

The second argument (*b*) is inconclusive. If the technique of punishment operates primarily by deterrence, it can serve its purpose only in respect of deliberate acts. No act committed under any of the above conditions would be deliberate. If, therefore, offenses of these types are left unpunished, the threat in relation to other offenses remains unimpaired, for the sane potential murderer gets no comfort from mercy extended to the homicidal maniac, and other homicidal maniacs will be unaffected either way. Consequently to punish in such cases would be a pointless mischief. In any case, because some of the conditions for blame and punishment coincide, it does not follow that the satisfaction of the former is a necessary condition for the satisfaction of the latter.[12] I shall return to this point later in relation to motive.

Of the four possible interpretations of the retributivist relation of guilt to punishment, it is the first only, whereby guilt in law is a necessary condition for punishment, that is completely persuasive; and this is precisely because it is a definition and not a justification. Consequently, it need not conflict with a utilitarian view.

For a utilitarian to require, for every case of punishment, that it be justified in terms of preventing more mischief than it causes, would be to miss the point of punishment as an institution. Indeed, any rule would be pointless if every decision still required to be justified in the light of its expected consequences. But this is particularly true of penal rules; for the effectiveness of punishment as a deterrent depends on its regular application, save under conditions sufficiently well understood for them not to constitute a source of uncertainty. Legal guilt once established, then, the initial utilitarian presumption

against causing deliberate suffering has been overcome, and a case for a penalty has been made out. But it may still be defeated; for since guilt is not a sufficient condition, there may well be other relevant considerations (e.g., that this is a first offense). The following formal criterion may be postulated, however, which any such consideration must satisfy, namely, that to recognize it as a general ground for waiving the penalty would not involve an otherwise avoidable mischief to society *greater* than the mischief of punishing the offender.

One of the criticisms leveled against utilitarianism is that by relating the justification of punishment to its expected consequences, rather than to the crime itself, it would justify penalties divorced from the relative seriousness of crimes, permitting severe penalties for trivial offenses, if that were the only way to reduce their number. A serious but easily detected crime might warrant lesser penalties than a minor but secret one. This conclusion being intolerable, the retributivist contends that to escape it we must seek the measure of the penalty in the crime itself, according to the degree of wickedness involved in committing it.

Again, I distinguish the justification of rules from the justification of particular applications. To ask "How much punishment is appropriate to a given offense?" is ambiguous: it may refer either to the punishment allotted by a rule to a *class* of acts, or to a particular award for a given act, within that class. The distinction is pointed by the practice of laying down only maximum (and sometimes minimum) penalties in the rule, leaving particular determinations to judicial discretion.

III. *What formal criteria must be satisfied in justifying the degrees of punishment attached to different classes of offense?*

"The only case" (said Kant) "in which the offender cannot complain that he is being treated unjustly is if his crime recoils upon himself and he suffers what he has inflicted on another, if not in a literal sense, at any rate according to the spirit of the law." "It is only *the right of requital (jus talionis)* which can fix definitely the quality and the quantity of the punishment." This is the most extreme retributive position; its essential weakness is present, however, in more mod-

---

[12] A man who had broken a law (say, an import regulation), of the existence of which he was ignorant (but avoidably so), would be liable to punishment. It would be to counsel perfection to say that everyone has a moral duty to know of *every* law that might affect him. I should say, in this case, that the offender had been imprudent, but not immoral, in not ascertaining his legal position. I should impute no moral guilt either for his ignorance or for his breach of the rule; but I should not feel, on that account, that he was an injured innocent entitled to complain that he had been wrongly punished.

erate attempts to seek the determinants of punishment exclusively in the offense itself.

If retaliatory punishment is not to be effected "in a literal sense" (which might well be intolerably cruel, and in some cases physically impossible), but rather "according to the spirit of the law," it involves a sort of arithmetical equation of suffering as impracticable as the hedonistic calculus. Suffering of one sort cannot be *equated* with another, though it may be possible to prefer one to another (or to be indifferent as between one and another). I can certainly say that I would rather see A suffer in one way, than B in another, or that there is really nothing to choose between the two. But this is quite different from saying that A ought to be made to suffer in exactly the same degree as B, whom he has injured; for this involves not a preference enunciated by some third person, but a quasi quantitative comparison of the sufferings of two different people, treated as objective facts. And there is no way of making this comparison, even though the external features of their suffering may be identical. It is even more evidently impossible when the suffering of one is occasioned by, say, blackmail, and of the other by imprisonment.[13]

The difficulty remains in the compromise between a utilitarian and retaliatory position attempted by W. D. Ross. While admitting that the legislator must consider the deterrent ends of punishment in assessing penalties, he maintains that the injury inflicted by the criminal sets an upper limit to the injury that can legitimately be inflicted on him. "For he has lost his prima facie rights to life, liberty, or property, only in so far as these rested on an explicit or implicit undertaking to respect the corresponding rights in others, and in so far as he has failed to respect those rights."[14] But how are we to make this equation between the rights invaded and consequently sacrificed and the amount of suffering so justified—unless there is already available a scale, or rule, fixing the

relation? But then how is the scale to be justified?

J. D. Mabbott admits there can be no direct relation between offense and penalty, but seeks, by comparing one crime with another, to make an estimate of the penalties *relatively* appropriate. "We can grade crimes in a rough scale and penalties in a rough scale, and keep our heaviest penalties for what are socially the most serious wrongs regardless of whether these penalties . . . are exactly what deterrence would require."[15] But what are we to understand by "socially the most serious wrongs"? On the one hand, they might be those that shock us most deeply—we could then construct a shock scale, and punish accordingly. There are some shocking acts, however, that we should not want to punish at all (e.g., some sexual offenses against morality); at the same time, we should be hard put to it to know what penalties to attach to new offenses against, say, currency control regulations, where the initial shock reaction is either negligible, because the rule is unsupported by a specific rule of conventional morality, or where it is of a standard mild variety accompanying any offense against the law as such, irrespective of its particular quality. On the other hand, "the most serious wrongs" may be simply those we are least ready to tolerate. That, however, would be to introduce utilitarian considerations into our criteria of "seriousness." For to say that we are not prepared to tolerate an offense is to say that we should feel justified in imposing heavy penalties to deter people from committing it. But in making deterrent considerations secondary to the degree of "seriousness," Mr. Mabbott implicitly excludes this interpretation.

The retributivists' difficulties arise from seeking the measure of the penalty in the crime, without first assuming a scale or a rule relating the two. Given the scale, any given penalty would require justification in terms of it; but the scale itself, like any rule, must in the end be justified in utilitarian terms. It remains to be seen whether this necessarily opens the way to severe penalties for trivial offenses.

For the utilitarian, arguing in deterrent terms, it is the threat rather than the punishment itself which is primary. Could we rely

---

[13] Hegel virtually admits the impossibility of answering this question rationally (*Philosophy of Right*, § 101) but insists nevertheless that there must be a right answer (§ 214) to which we must try empirically to approximate. But by what test shall we judge whether our shots at justice are approaching or receding from the target?

[14] *The Right and the Good*, 1930, pp. 62–63.

[15] *Op. cit.*, p. 162.

on the threat being completely effective, there could be no objection to the death penalty for every offense, since *ex hypothesi* it would never be inflicted. Unhappily, we must reckon to inflict some penalties, for there will always be some offenders, no matter what the threatened punishment. We must suppose, then, for every class of crime, a scale of possible penalties, to each of which corresponds a probable number of offenses, and therefore of occasions for punishment, the number probably diminishing as the severity increases. Ultimately, however, we should almost certainly arrive at a hard core of undeterrables. We should then choose, for each class of offense, that penalty at which the marginal increment of mischief inflicted on offenders would be just preferable to the extra mischief from which the community is protected by this increment of punishment. To inflict any heavier penalty would do more harm than it would prevent. (This is Bentham's principle of "frugality."[16])

This involves not a quasi-quantitative comparison of suffering by the community and the offender, but only a preference. We might say something like this: To increase the penalty for parking offenses to life imprisonment would reduce congestion on the roads; nevertheless the inconvenience of a large number of offenses would not be serious enough to justify disregarding in so great a measure the prima facie case for liberty, even of a very few offenders. With blackmail, or murder, the possibility of averting further instances defeats to a far greater extent the claims of the offender. One parking offense more or less is not of great moment; one murder more or less is.

In retaliatory theory we are asked to estimate the damage done by the crime, and to inflict just that amount (or no more than that amount) on the criminal; here we are required only to choose between one combination of circumstances and another. The choice may not always be easy; but it is not impossible, or even unusual. For we are well accustomed to choosing between things incapable of quantitative comparison; what is impossible is to assess what one man has suffered from blackmail, and then to impose its equivalent on the blackmailer in terms of a prison sentence. The difference is between

a prescription and a description. To say, as I do above, that the right penalty is that at which the marginal increment of mischief inflicted is just preferable to the mischief thereby avoided, is to invite the critic to choose (or prescribe) one state of affairs rather than another. But to say that the penalty should equal (or should not exceed) the suffering of the victim of the crime is to invite him to prescribe a course dependent not on his own preferences, but on a factual comparison of incomparables, on an equation of objective conditions.

The utilitarian case as I have now put it is not open to the objection that it would justify serious penalties for trivial offenses. For to call an offense "trivial" is to say that we care less if this one is committed than if others are, i.e., we should be unwilling to inflict so much suffering to prevent it, as to prevent others. "Relatively serious crimes" are those relatively less tolerable, i.e., we prefer to inflict severer penalties rather than to suffer additional offenses. If this is so, "Trivial crimes do not deserve severe penalties" is analytic, consequently a utilitarian justification could not be extended to cover a contrary principle.[17]

Some penalties we are unwilling to inflict whatever their deterrent force. We are less ready to torture offenders than to suffer their offenses. And there are people who would rather risk murders than inflict the death penalty, even supposing it to be "the unique deterrent." To kill, they say, is absolutely wrong. Now this may mean only that no circumstances are imaginable in which its probable consequences would make it right, i.e., in which the mischief done would not outweigh the mischief prevented—not that it could *never* be right, only that in any imaginable conditions it would not be. This would not exclude justification by consequences, and is therefore compatible with the view of punishment I am advancing. On the other hand, if the absolutist denies altogether the rele-

---

[16] *Introduction to the Principles of Morals and Legislation*, Chap. XV, §§ 11–12.

[17] We could say "Some trivial crimes deserve serious penalties" if we wished to imply that some crimes are a good deal more serious than they are generally held to be. But the sentence would be better punctuated: "Some 'trivial' crimes . . . ," for they are "trivial" in the view of others, not of the speaker. Consider, in this connection, the difference of opinion between pedestrians and motorists' associations on the gravity of driving offenses—and on the penalties appropriate. A pedestrian might not think a prison sentence too severe a penalty for speeding— but neither is it, for him, a trivial offense.

vance of consequences, he is making an ultimate judgment for which, in the nature of the case, justification can be neither sought nor offered, and which is therefore undiscussible.

I conclude, from this discussion, that any justification for the nature and degree of punishment attached to a given class of offense must satisfy the following formal criterion: that the marginal increment of mischief inflicted should be preferable to the mischief avoided by fixing that penalty rather than one slightly lower. Assuming that the advantages of punishment derive mainly from upholding rules, this means that the conformity secured, weighed against the suffering inflicted, should be preferable to a lower level of conformity, weighed against the suffering inflicted by imposing a lesser penalty. (This entails neither that a very few offenders suffering heavy penalties must be preferred to a larger number of offenders suffering lighter penalties, nor the converse; preferences are not settled by multiplication.)

IV. *What formal criteria must be satisfied in justifying the particular penalty awarded to a given offender?*

Two men guilty of what is technically the same offense (i.e., who have broken the same rule) are not necessarily punished alike. This could be justified only by reference to relevant criteria, other than simple guilt, by which their cases are distinguished. Provocation, temptation, duress, and a clean record may all make a difference. But these are also relevant to the determination of blame. From these considerations arise two possible objections to the view I am advancing:

(*a*) Is it consistent with utilitarianism that in determining the sentence, we should look to the particular conditions of the crime, rather than to the consequences of the penalty? Should we not look forward to the exemplary advantages of the maximum penalty, rather than backward to extenuating circumstances?

(*b*) Since we do look backward, and assess the penalty in the light of criteria also relevant to an assessment of blameworthiness, can we not say that men deserve punishment only in the measure that they deserve blame?

As to (*a*); a rule once accepted, there is no need to justify every application in terms of its consequences; it is necessary to justify in utilitarian terms only the criteria of extenuation, not every application of them. Now precisely because an offense has been committed under exceptional circumstances (e.g., severe temptation, provocation, duress), leniency would not seriously weaken the threat, since offenders would expect similar leniency only in similar circumstances, which are such, in any case, that a man would be unlikely to consider rationally the penal consequences of his act. Given that, the full measure of the penalty would be unjustifiable.[18]

As to (*b*); while some criteria tend to mitigate both blame and punishment, the latter need not depend on the degree of the former. The question of motive is crucial. We generally regard a man as less blameworthy if he breaks a rule "from the highest motives," rather than selfishly or maliciously. A traitor from conscientious conviction may be blamed for wrongheadedness, but, if we respect his integrity, we blame him less than a merely mercenary one. But honest motives will not always mitigate punishment. It may be vital for the effectiveness of government that conscientious recalcitrants (e.g., potential fifth columnists acting from political conviction) be deterred from action. But since strong moral convictions are often less amenable to threats than other motives, they could scarcely be admitted in such cases in extenuation of punishment. On the other hand, if the mischief of the penalty needed for a high degree of conformity exceeds its advantages, it may be reasonable to give up punishing conscientious offenders altogether, provided they can be discerned from the fakes.[19] We

[18] Grading sentences according to the number of previous convictions might be justified by the failure, *ex hypothesi*, of lesser penalties on earlier occasions, to act as deterrents. Possible imitators with similar records may possibly require a similarly severe deterrent example. For most of the rest of us, with little criminal experience, lighter penalties awarded to less hardened offenders are sufficient deterrents. A case can therefore be made for reserving the severest penalties for the class of criminals least easily deterred.

[19] Consider, in this connection, the difficulty of distinguishing the genuine survivor of a suicide pact, who has been unable to carry out his side of the bargain, from the cheat who relies on a counterfeit pact to evade the maximum penalty for murder. (See the Report on Capital Punishment, referred to above §§ 163–176.) The same applies to "mercy-killing": "How, for example, were the jury to decide whether a daughter had killed her invalid father from compassion, from a desire for material gain, from a natural wish to bring to an end a trying period of her life, or from a combination of mo-

no longer punish conscientious objectors to military service, having found by experience that they are rarely amenable to threats, that they are unsatisfactory soldiers if coerced, and that, given a rigorous test of conscientiousness, their numbers are not likely to be so great as to impair the community purpose.

The considerable overlapping of the factors tending to mitigate blame and punishment nevertheless demands explanation. Morality and law are alike rule systems for controlling behavior, and what blame is to one, punishment is to the other. Since they are closely analogous as techniques for discouraging undesirable conduct, by making its consequences in different ways disagreeable, the principles for awarding them largely coincide. But it does not follow that because we usually also blame the man we punish, we should punish in the light of the criteria determining moral guilt. Morality operates as a control not only by prescribing or prohibiting acts, but also by conditioning character (and therefore conduct in general). We blame men for being bad tempered; we punish them only for assault. Furthermore, punishment is administered through formal machinery of investigation, proof, conviction, sentence, and execution; blame by informal and personal procedures which may well take account of evidence of character that might nevertheless be rightly inadmissible in a court of law. To the extent that the techniques are analogous, they may be expected to employ similar criteria; but the analogy cannot be pushed all the way.

CONCLUSION

The quarrel between retributivist and utilitarian is primarily about procedures of justification, about how to go about defending or attacking punishment, in general or in particular, about the formal criteria that together form a schema to which any justification must conform. I have maintained that when what is wanted is a justification of a rule, or an institution, of punishment in general, or of the scale of punishments assigned

to different classes of offense, it must be sought in terms of the net advantages gained or mischiefs avoided. When the particular sentence is in question, the first consideration is guilt, without which punishment in a strict sense is impossible, but which once established constitutes a prima facie case for it. The second consideration must be the legally prescribed limits, within which the penalty must fall. Beyond that, decision must be made in the light of criteria tending to mitigate if not totally defeat the presumption in favor of the maximum penalty. These criteria must themselves be justified in terms of the net advantages, or mischief avoided, in adopting them as general principles.

These are formal principles only. To make out a substantial justification, we must postulate first the sort of advantages we expect from punishment as an institution. I have assumed that its principal advantage is that it secures conformity to rules (though others might conceivably be offered, e.g., that it reformed criminal characters, which could be regarded as a good thing in itself; or that it gave the injured person the satisfaction of being revenged). Further, I have assumed that it operates primarily by way of deterrence. These are in part assumptions of fact, in part moral judgments. I maintain that these being given, the criteria by which the prima facie case for punishment may be defeated, wholly or in part, are generally justifiable in utilitarian terms; that they do not weaken the deterrent threat, that they avoid inflicting suffering which would not be justified by the resultant additional degree of conformity. Further, the total assimilation to the system of punishment of criteria tending to defeat or mitigate blameworthiness, is unjustifiable in theory and is not made in practice. We do not punish men because they are morally guilty, nor must we *necessarily* refrain because they are morally guiltless, nor mitigate the punishment in the same degree for all the same reasons that we mitigate blame. This is not to say that the justifications sought are not *moral* justifications; it is simply that they must be made in the light of criteria different from those governing blame, since however close the analogy may be between the two techniques of control, there are still significant differences between them.

tives?'' (*Ibid.*, § 179). Nevertheless, where we feel reasonably sure that the motive was merciful, we expect leniency. A mercy-killing is not in the same class as a brutal murder for profit, and we may feel justified in tolerating a few examples rather than inflict the maximum penalty on this type of offender.

BIBLIOGRAPHY

CHAPTER I

Ames, J. B. "Law and Morals," *Harv. L. Rev.,* XXII (1908), 97–113.

Andriamanjato, R. *Le Tsiny et le Tody dans la pensée malgache.* Paris: Présence Africaine, 1957.

Bar, K. L. von. *A History of Continental Criminal Law,* trans. Bell. Boston: Little, Brown and Co., 1916.

Barnes, W. H. F., W. D. Falk, A. Duncan-Jones. "Intention, Motive and Responsibility" (symposium), *The Aristotelian Society,* Supp. Vol. XIX (1945), 230–88.

Bentham, J. *An Introduction to the Principles of Morals and Legislation.* Oxford: Basil Blackwell, 1948.

——. *Theory of Legislation.* London: Routledge and Kegan Paul Ltd., 1931.

Bradley, F. H. "Philosophy of Responsibility," *Jour. of Crim. L. and Criminol.,* II (1911), 186–98.

Brandt, R. B. "Blameworthiness and Obligation," in A. I. Melden (ed.), *Essays in Moral Philosophy.* Seattle: Univ. of Washington Press, 1958.

——. *Ethical Theory.* Englewood Cliffs, N.J.: Prentice-Hall, 1959, Chapter 18.

Cohen, M. R. "Moral Aspects of the Criminal Law," *Yale L. Jour.,* XLIX (1940), 987–1026.

Dewey, J., and J. Tufts. *Ethics.* New York: Henry Holt and Co., 1936.

Diamond, A. S. *The Evolution of Law and Order.* London: Watts, 1951.

Feuer, E. S. *Psychoanalysis and Ethics.* Springfield, Ill.: Charles C Thomas, 1955.

Friedrich, C. J. (ed.). *Responsibility.* New York: Liberal Arts Press, 1960.

Ginsberg, M. *The Nature of Responsibility.* London: Clarke Hall Fellowship, 1953.

Green, N. St. J. *Essays on Tort and Crime.* Menasha, Wis.: George Banta Publishing Co., 1933.

Hägerström, A. *Inquiries into the Nature of Law and Morals,* trans. Broad. Stockholm: Almquist and Wiksell, 1953.

Hall, J. *General Principles of Criminal Law,* 2d ed. Indianapolis: The Bobbs-Merrill Co., 1960.

Hart, H. L. A. "The Ascription of Responsibility and Rights," *Proc. Arist. Soc.,* XLIX (1948–49), 171–94.

——. "Legal Responsibility and Excuses," in S. Hook (ed.), *Determinism and Freedom in the Age of Modern Science.* New York: New York Univ. Press, 1958, pp. 81–104.

Hampshire, S. *Thought and Action.* London: Chatto and Windus, 1959.

Hegel, G. F. *Philosophy of Right,* trans. Knox. Oxford: Clarendon Press, 1942.

Hoebel, E. A. *The Law of Primitive Man.* Cambridge, Mass.: Harvard Univ. Press, 1954.

Hogbin, H. I. *Law and Order in Polynesia.* New York: Harcourt, Brace and Co., 1934.

Kant, I. *Critique of Practical Reason,* trans. T. K. Abbott. London: Longmans, Green and Co., 1873.

――――. *Fundamental Principles of the Metaphysics of Morals,* trans. T. K. Abbott. London: Longmans, Green and Co., 1873.

Lamont, W. D. *The Principles of Moral Judgment.* Oxford: Clarendon Press, 1946, Chapter VIII.

Lecky, W. E. H. *History of European Morals.* 2 vols. New York: D. Appleton and Co., 1869.

Lewis, H. D. "Collective Responsibility," *Philosophy,* XXIII (1948), 3–18.

――――, J. W. Harvey, and G. A. Paul. "The Problem of Guilt" (symposium), *Proc. Arist. Soc.,* Supp. Vol. XXI (1947), 175–218.

Llewellyn, K. N., and E. A. Hoebel. *The Cheyenne Way.* Norman, Okla.: Univ. of Oklahoma Press, 1941.

Malinowski, B. *Crime and Custom in Savage Society.* London: K. Paul, Trench, Trubner and Co., Ltd., 1926.

Markby, W. *Elements of Law.* Oxford: Clarendon Press, 1871.

McConnell, R. M. *Criminal Responsibility and Social Constraint.* New York: C. Scribner's Sons, 1912.

Melden, A. I. *Free Action.* London: Routledge and Kegan Paul Ltd., 1961.

Mercier, C. *Criminal Responsibility.* New York: Physicians and Surgeons Book Co., 1926.

Michael, J., and H. Wechsler. *Criminal Law and Its Administration.* Brooklyn, N.Y.: Foundation Press, 1940.

Nowell-Smith, P. H. *Ethics.* Baltimore: Penguin Books, Inc., 1954. Chapters 19–20.

O'Brien, V. P. *The Measure of Responsibility in Persons Influenced by Emotion.* Washington: Catholic Univ. of America Press, 1948.

Petrazycki, L. *Law and Morality,* trans. Babb. Cambridge, Mass.: Harvard Univ. Press, 1955.

Piers, G., and M. Singer. *Shame and Guilt, a Psychoanalytic and Cultural Study.* Springfield, Ill.: Charles C Thomas, 1953.

Radzinowicz, L., and J. W. C. Turner (eds.). *The Modern Approach to Criminal Law.* London: The Macmillan Co., 1948.

Royal Commission on Capital Punishment 1949–53 Report. London: Her Majesty's Stationery Office, 1953.

Ruml, B., K. N. Llewellyn, and R. McKeon. "Crime, Law and Social Science. A Symposium," *Columbia L. Rev.,* XXXIV (1934), 273–309.

Ryle, G. *The Concept of Mind.* London: Hutchinson's Univ. Library, 1949.

Salmond, J. *Jurisprudence.* 11th ed. by Williams. London: Sweet and Maxwell, Ltd., 1957, pp. 396–450.

Sayre, F. B. "Criminal Responsibility for the Acts of Another," *Harv. L. Rev.,* XLIII (1930), 689–723.

Sears, L. *Responsibility, Its Development through Punishment and Reward.* New York: Columbia Univ. Press, 1932.

Skinner, B. F. *Science and Human Behavior.* New York: The Macmillan Co., 1953.

Stephen, J. F. *A History of the Criminal Law of England.* 3 vols. London: Macmillan and Co., Ltd., 1883.

Street, T. A. *Foundations of Legal Liability.* Northport, N.Y.: Edward Thompson Co., 1906.

Stoljar, S. "Ascriptive and Prescriptive Responsibility," *Mind,* LXVIII (1959), 350–60.

Stroud, D. A. *Mens Rea.* London: Sweet and Maxwell, Ltd., 1914.

Tarde, G. de. *Penal Philosophy.* Boston: Little, Brown and Co., 1912.

Wechsler, H. "Challenge of a Model Penal Code," *Harv. L. Rev.,* LXV (1952), 1097–1133.

———, and J. Michael. "A Rationale of the Law of Homicide," *Columbia L. Rev.,* XXXVII (1937), 701–61, 1261–1325.

Wienpahl, P. D. "Concerning Moral Responsibility," *Analysis,* XIII (1953), 127–35.

Wiess, P. "Social, Legal, and Ethical Responsibility," *Ethics,* LVII (1946), 259–73.

Williams, G. *Criminal Law: The General Part.* London: Stevens and Sons Ltd., 1953.

Woodward, J. W. "Psychological Aspects of the Question of Moral Responsibility," *Jour. of Crim. L. and Criminol.,* XXI (1930), 267–96.

CHAPTER II

Anscombe, G. E. M. *Intention.* Oxford: Basil Blackwell, 1957.

Aveling, F. *Personality and Will.* New York: D. Appleton and Co., 1931.

Bain, A. *The Emotions and the Will.* New York: D. Appleton and Co., 1899.

Campbell, C. A. "The Psychology of Effort of Will," *Proc. Arist. Soc.,* XL (1939–40), 49–74.

Croce, B. *Philosophy of the Practical.* London: Macmillan and Co., Ltd., 1913.

Geach, P. T. "Ascriptivism," *Phil. Rev.,* LXIX (1960), 221–25.

Green, T. H. *Prolegomena to Ethics.* Oxford: Clarendon Press, 1883, pp. 97–173.

Hicks, G. D. "The Nature of Willing," *Proc. Arist. Soc.,* XIII (1912–13), 27–65.

Hoernlé, R. F. A. "The Analysis of Volition: Treated as a Study of Psychological Principles and Methods," *Proc. Arist. Soc.,* XIII (1912–13), 156–89.

Leibnitz, G. W. *New Essays Concerning Human Understanding,* trans. A. C. Langley. La Salle, Ill.: Open Court Publishing Co., 1949, pp. 174–220.

Maudsley, H. *Body and Will.* London: K. Paul, Trench, and Co., 1883.

Melden, A. I. *Free Action.* London: Routledge and Kegan Paul, 1961.

———. " 'My Kinaesthetic Sensations Advise Me . . .'," *Analysis,* XVIII (1957), 43–48.

O'Shaughnessy, B. "The Limits of the Will," *Phil. Rev.,* LXV (1956), 443–90.

Pascal, B. *Pensées,* trans. W. F. Trotter. New York: Random House, 1941.

Price, H. H. "Belief and Will," *Proc. Arist. Soc.,* Supp. Vol. XXVIII (1954), 1–26.

Russell, B. *The Analysis of Mind.* London: George Allen and Unwin Ltd., 1921.

Ryle, G. *The Concept of Mind.* London: Hutchinson's Univ. Library, 1949.

Stout, G. F. *Analytic Psychology.* New York: The Macmillan Co., 1909, Volume I.

———. *Manual of Psychology.* New York: Hinds, Noble and Eldredge, 1915, pp. 704–36.

Wells, H. M. *The Phenomenology of Acts of Choice.* Cambridge, Eng.: Cambridge Univ. Press, 1927.

Wittgenstein, L. *The Blue and Brown Books.* Oxford: Basil Blackwell, 1958.

Wyatt, H. G. *The Psychology of Intelligence and Will.* London: K. Paul, Trench, Trubner and Co., Ltd., 1931.

CHAPTER III

Anscombe, G. E. M. *Intention.* Oxford: Basil Blackwell, 1957.

Barnes, W. H. F. "Action," *Mind,* L (1941), 243–57.

Edwards, J. L. J. "Automatism and Criminal Responsibility," *Mod. L. Rev.,* XXI (1958), 375–86.

Fitzgerald, P. J. "Voluntary and Involuntary Acts," in A. G. Guest (ed.), *Oxford Essays in Jurisprudence.* London: Oxford Univ. Press, 1961.

Geach, P. T. "Ascriptivism," *Phil. Rev.,* LXIX (1960), 221–25.

Hall, J. *General Principles of Criminal Law.* 2d ed. Indianapolis: The Bobbs-Merrill Co., 1960.

Hampshire, S. *Thought and Action.* London: Chatto and Windus, 1959.

Hart, H. L. A. "The Ascription of Responsibility and Rights," *Proc. Arist. Soc.,* XLIX (1948–49), 171–94.

Kirchheimer, O. "Criminal Omissions," *Harv. L. Rev.,* LV (1942), 615–42.

Kotarbinski, T. "Concept of Action," *Jour. of Phil.,* LVII (1960), 215–22.

Lewis, C. I. *An Analysis of Knowledge and Valuation.* La Salle, Ill.: Open Court, 1950, pp. 5–9, 365–78.

MacMurray, J., A. C. Ewing, and O. S. Frank. "What Is Action" (symposium), *Proc. Arist. Soc.,* Supp. Vol. XVII (1938), 69–120.

Margolis, J. "Actions and Ways of Failing," *Inquiry,* III (1960), 89–101.

Markby, W. *Elements of Law.* Oxford: Clarendon Press, 1871.

Mead, G. H. *The Philosophy of the Act.* Chicago: Univ. of Chicago Press, 1938.

Melden, A. I. *Free Action.* London: Routledge and Kegan Paul, 1961.

———. *Rights and Right Conduct.* Oxford: Basil Blackwell, 1959.

Mercier, C. *Criminal Responsibility.* New York: Physicians and Surgeons Book Co., 1926.

Miller, J. "The Criminal Act," in M. Radin and A. M. Kidd (eds.), *Legal Essays in Honor of Orrin Kip McMurray.* Berkeley, Calif.: Univ. of Calif. Press, 1935.

Perkins, R. M. "Negative Acts in Criminal Law," *Iowa L. Rev.,* XXII (1937), 659–83.

Pitcher, G. "Hart on Action and Responsibility," *Phil. Rev.,* LXIX (1960), 226–35.

Plato. *Laws,* IX, trans. B. Jowett. London: Oxford Univ. Press, 1920.

Prevezer, S. "Automatism and Involuntary Conduct," *Crim. L. Rev.,* (1958), 361–67, 440–52.

Ritchie, A. M. "Agent and Act in Theory of Mind," *Proc. Arist. Soc.,* LII (1951–52), 1–22.

Ryle, G. *The Concept of Mind.* London: Hutchinson's Univ. Library, 1949.

Snyder, O. C. "Liability for Negative Conduct," *Virginia L. Rev.,* XXXV (1949), 446–80.

Stout, G. F. *Analytic Psychology.* New York: The Macmillan Co., 1909, Volume I.

————. *Manual of Psychology*. New York: Hinds, Noble, and Eldredge, 1915, pp. 704–36.

Wittgenstein, L. *The Blue and Brown Books*. Oxford: Basil Blackwell, 1958.

————. *Philosophical Investigations,* trans. G. E. M. Anscombe. Oxford: Basil Blackwell, 1953.

CHAPTER IV

Alexander, P., and A. MacIntyre. "Cause and Cure in Psychotherapy" (symposium), *Proc. Arist. Soc.,* Supp. Vol. XXIX (1955), 25–58.

Anscombe, G. E. M. *Intention*. Oxford: Basil Blackwell, 1957.

Atkinson, J. W. (ed.). *Motives in Fantasy, Action, and Society*. Princeton, N.J.: Van Nostrand, 1958.

Baier, K. *The Moral Point of View*. Ithaca, N.Y.: Cornell Univ. Press, 1958, Chapter 6.

Barnes, W. H. F., W. D. Falk, and A. Duncan-Jones. "Intention, Motive, and Responsibility" (symposium), *The Aristotelian Society,* Supp. Vol. XIX (1945), 230–88.

Current Theory and Research in Motivation: A Symposium. Lincoln, Neb.: Univ. of Nebraska Press, 1953.

Dilman, I. "The Unconscious," *Mind,* LXVIII (1959), 446–73.

Dingle, H. "The Logical Status of Psychoanalysis," *Analysis,* IX (1949), 63.

Edwards, J. L. J. *"Mens Rea" in Statutory Offences*. London: Macmillan and Co., Ltd., 1955.

Elliot, W. A. "What Is Culpa?" *Juridical Rev.,* LXVI (1954), 6–36.

Evans, J. L. "Choice," *Phil. Quarterly,* V (1955), 303–15.

Falk, W. D. " 'Ought' and Motivation," *Proc. Arist. Soc.,* XLVIII (1947–48), 111–38.

Fingarette, H. " 'Unconscious Behavior' and Allied Concepts; a New Approach to Their Empirical Interpretation," *Jour. of Phil.,* XLVII (1950), 509–20.

Flew, A. "Motives and the Unconscious," in H. Feigl and M. Scriven (eds.), *Minnesota Studies in the Philosophy of Science*. Minneapolis: Univ. of Minnesota Press, 1956, I, 155–73.

Foulkes, S. H. "Psychoanalysis and Crime," *Canadian Bar Rev.,* XXII (1944), 19–61.

Franks, O. C. "Choice," *Proc. Arist. Soc.,* XXXIV (1933–34), 269–94.

Freud, S. *Collected Papers,* trans. Riviere. London: The Hogarth Press, 1957.

————. *The Ego and the Id,* trans. Riviere. London: The Hogarth Press, 1957.

————. *A General Introduction to Psychoanalysis*. London: Boni and Liveright, 1924.

————. *The Psychopathology of Everyday Life,* trans. Brill. New York: The Modern Library, 1938.

Frym, M. "Criminal Intent," *Texas L. Rev.,* XXXI (1953), 260–88.

Geach, P. T. "Ascriptivism," *Phil. Rev.,* LXIX (1960), 221–25.

Glasgow, W. D. "The Concept of Choosing," *Analysis,* XX (1959–60), 63–67.

————. "On Choosing," *Analysis,* XVII (1956), 135–39.

Gotlieb, A. E. "Intention and Knowing the Nature and Quality of an Act," *Mod. L. Rev.,* XIX (1956), 270–75.

Green, T. H. *Prolegomena to Ethics*. Oxford: Clarendon Press, 1883, pp. 97–173.

Hägerström, A. *Inquiries into the Nature of Law and Morals,* trans. Broad. Stockholm: Almquist and Wiksell, 1953, pp. 109–16, 229–347.

Hampshire, S. *Thought and Action*. London: Chatto and Windus, 1959.

Hardie, W. F. R. "Mr. Toulmin on the Explanation of Human Conduct," *Analysis,* XI (1950), 1–8.

Hegel, G. F. *Philosophy of Right,* trans. Knox. Oxford: Clarendon Press, 1942, pp. 75–84.

Hitchler, W. H. "Motive as an Essential Element of Crime," *Dickinson L. Rev.,* XXXV (1931), 105–18.

Holmes, O. W., Jr. *The Common Law*. Boston: Little, Brown and Co., 1881.

Hook, S. (ed.). *Psychoanalysis, Scientific Method, and Philosophy* (symposium). New York: New York Univ. Press, 1959.

Hughes, G. E. "Motive and Duty," *Mind,* LIII (1944), 314–31.

"Intent in the Criminal Law: The Legal Tower of Babel," *Catholic Univ. L. Rev.,* VIII (1959), 31–42.

Levitt, A. "Extent and Function of the Doctrine of Mens Rea," *Ill. L. Rev.,* XVII (1923), 578–95.

Lewis, C. I. *An Analysis of Knowledge and Valuation*. La Salle, Ill.: Open Court, 1950, pp. 5–9, 365–78.

MacIntyre, A. C. *The Unconscious*. London: Routledge and Kegan Paul, 1958.

Maslow, A. H. *Motivation and Personality*. New York: Harper & Brothers, 1954.

Melden, A. I. *Free Action*. London: Routledge and Kegan Paul, 1961.

Michael, J., and H. Wechsler. *Criminal Law and Its Administration*. Brooklyn, N.Y.: Foundation Press, 1940.

Moore, G. E. "Wittgenstein's Lectures in 1930–33, I–II," *Mind,* LXIV (1955), 1-27.

Mueller, G. O. W. "Mens Rea and the Law Without It," *West Virginia L. Rev.,* LVIII (1955), 34–68.

———. "On Common Law Mens Rea," *Minnesota L. Rev.,* XLII (1958), 1043–1104.

Nowell-Smith P. H. "Choosing, Deciding and Doing," *Analysis,* XVIII (1958), 63–69.

Olds, J. *The Growth and Structure of Motives*. Glencoe, Ill.: Free Press, 1956.

Passmore, J. A., and P. L. Heath. "Intentions" (symposium), *Proc. Arist. Soc.,* Supp. Vol. XXIX (1955), 131–64.

Perkins, R. M. "A Rationale of Mens Rea," *Harv. L. Rev.,* LII (1939), 905–28.

Peters, R. S. "Cause, Cure and Motive," *Analysis,* X (1950), 103–9.

———. *The Concept of Motivation*. London: Routledge and Kegan Paul, 1958.

———, D. J. McCracken, and J. O. Urmson. "Motives and Causes," *The Aristotelian Society,* Supp. Vol. XXVI (1952), 139–94.

Radzinowicz, L., and J. W. C. Turner (eds.), *The Modern Approach to Criminal Law*. London: Macmillan and Co., Ltd., 1948.

Remington, F. J., and O. L. Helstad. "Mental Element in Crime—A Legislative Problem," *Wisconsin L. Rev.,* 1952, pp. 644–78.

Russell, B. *The Analysis of Mind*. London: George Allen and Unwin Ltd., 1921.

Salmond, J. *Jurisprudence*. 11th ed. by Williams. London: Sweet and Maxwell, Ltd., 1957, pp. 411–19.

Sayre, F. B. "Mens Rea," *Harv. L. Rev.,* XLV (1932), 974–1026.

Smith, J. C. "Guilty Mind in the Criminal Law," *Law Quarterly Rev.,* LXXVI (1960), 78–99.

Stout, A. K. "Motive and the Rightness of an Act," *Australasian Jour. of Phil.,* XVIII (1940), 18–37.

Stout, G. F. *Analytic Psychology.* New York: The Macmillan Co., 1909, Volume I.

Stroud, D. A. *Mens Rea.* London: Sweet and Maxwell, Ltd., 1914, Chapter I.

Sutherland, N. S. "Motives as Explanations," *Mind,* LXVIII (1959), 145–59.

Teichmann, J. "Mental Cause and Effect," *Mind,* LXX (1961), 36–52.

Turner, J. W. C. "The Mental Element in Crimes at Common Law," in L. Radzinowicz and J. W. C. Turner (eds.), *The Modern Approach to Criminal Law.* London: Macmillan and Co., Ltd., 1948, pp. 195–261.

Walker, K. F. "Motive and Behavior," *Australasian Jour. of Phil.,* XX (1942), 16–29.

Wechsler, H., and J. Michael. "A Rationale of the Law of Homicide," *Columbia L. Rev.,* XXXVII (1937), 701–61, 1261–1325.

White, A. R. "The Language of Motives," *Mind,* LXVII (1958), 258–63.

Wittgenstein, L. *The Blue and Brown Books.* Oxford: Basil Blackwell, 1958.

———. *Philosophical Investigations,* trans. G. E. M. Anscombe. Oxford: Basil Blackwell, 1953.

CHAPTER V

Bingham, J. W. "What Is Legal Negligence?" *Columbia L. Rev.,* IX (1909), 16–37, 136–54.

Bohlen, F. *Studies in the Law of Torts.* Indianapolis: The Bobbs-Merrill Co., 1926.

Demogue, R. "Fault, Risk and Apportionment of Damages," *Ill. L. Rev.,* XIII (1918), 297–311.

Edwards, J. L. J. *"Mens Rea" in Statutory Offences.* London: Macmillan and Co., Ltd., 1955.

Ehrenzweig, A. A. *Negligence Without Fault; Trends Toward an Enterprise Liability for Insurable Loss.* Berkeley, Calif.: Univ. of Calif. Press, 1951.

———. "A Psychoanalysis of Negligence," *Northwestern L. Rev.,* XLVII (1953), 855–72.

Elliot, W. A. "What Is *Culpa?,*" *Juridical Rev.,* LXVI (1954), 6–36.

Fleming, J. G. *The Law of Torts.* Sydney: Law Book Co. of Australia, 1957.

Friedmann, W. G. "Social Insurance and the Principles of Tort Liability," *Harv. L. Rev.,* LXIII (1949), 241–65.

Green, L. "Are Negligence and 'Proximate' Cause Determined by the Same Test?" *Texas L. Rev.,* I (1923), 242–60, 423–45.

———. "The Individual's Protection Under Negligence Law," *Northwestern L. Rev.,* XLVII (1953), 751–77.

———. *Judge and Jury.* Kansas City, Mo.: Vernon Book Co., 1930.

———. "Negligence Issue," *Yale L. Jour.,* XXXVII (1928), 1029–47.

———. *Traffic Victims: Tort Law and Insurance.* Evanston, Ill.: Northwestern Univ. Press, 1958.

Green, N. St. J. *Essays on Tort and Crime.* Menasha, Wis.: George Banta Pub. Co., 1933, pp. 93–111.

Gregory, C. O., and H. Kalven. *Cases and Materials on Torts.* Boston: Little, Brown and Co., 1959.

———. "Trespass and Negligence to Absolute Liability," *Virginia L. Rev.,* XXXVII (1951), 359–97.

Hall, J. *General Principles of Criminal Law.* 2d ed. Indianapolis: The Bobbs-Merrill Co., 1960.

Hart, H. L. A. "Negligence, *Mens Rea* and Criminal Responsibility," in A. G.

Guest (ed.), *Oxford Essays in Jurisprudence*. London: Oxford Univ. Press, 1961.

Holmes, O. W., Jr. *The Common Law*. Boston: Little, Brown and Co., 1881.

James, F., Jr. "The Nature of Negligence," *Utah L. Rev.*, III (1953), 275–93.

———. "Scope of Duty in Negligence Cases," *Northwestern L. Rev.*, XLVII (1953), 778–816.

"Law of Torts—A Symposium," *Northwestern Univ. L. Rev.*, XLVII (1953), 751–893.

Lawson, F. H. "Duty of Care in Negligence: A Comparative Study," *Tulane L. Rev.*, XXII (1947), 111–30.

———. *Negligence in the Civil Law*. Oxford: Clarendon Press, 1950.

"Liability Without Fault Criminal Statutes—Their Relation to Major Developments in Contemporary Economic and Social Policy," *Wisconsin L. Rev.*, 1956, pp. 625–67.

Michael, J., and H. Wechsler. *Criminal Law and Its Administration*. Brooklyn, N.Y.: Foundation Press, 1940.

Montrose, J. L. "Is Negligence an Ethical or a Sociological Concept?" *Mod. L. Rev.*, XXI (1958), 259–64.

Moreland, R. "Rationale of Criminal Negligence," *Kentucky L. Jour.*, XXXII (1943–44), 1–40, 127–92, 221–61.

Morris, C. "Duty, Negligence and Causation," *Univ. of Pa. L. Rev.*, CI (1952), 189–222.

———. "Proof of Negligence," *Northwestern L. Rev.*, XLVII (1953), 817–54.

———. *Studies in Torts*. Brooklyn, N.Y.: Foundation Press, 1952.

Morrison, W. L. "A Re-Examination of the Duty of Care," *Mod. L. Rev.*, XI (1948), 9–35.

Mueller, G. O. W. "Mens Rea and the Law Without It," *West Virginia L. Rev.*, LVIII (1955), 34–68.

Paton, G. W. "Negligence," *Australian L. Jour.*, XXIII (1949), 158–74.

Pollock, F. *Law of Torts*. 15th ed. by P. A. Landon. London: Stevens, 1951.

Prosser, W. L. *Handbook of the Law of Torts*. 2d ed. St. Paul, Minn.: West Publishing Co., 1955.

———. *Selected Topics on the Law of Torts*. Ann Arbor, Mich.: Univ. of Michigan Law School, 1953.

Radzinowicz, L., and J. W. C. Turner (eds.). *The Modern Approach to Criminal Law*. London: Macmillan and Co., Ltd., 1948.

Salmond, J. *Jurisprudence*. 11th ed. by Williams. London: Sweet and Maxwell, 1957, pp. 421–50.

———. *Torts*. 12th ed. by R. F. V. Heuston. London: Sweet and Maxwell, 1957.

Sayre, F. B. "Public Welfare Offenses," *Columbia L. Rev.*, XXXIII (1933), 55–88.

Stroud, D. A. *Mens Rea*. London: Sweet and Maxwell, Ltd., 1914, Chapter VII.

Thayer, E. R. "Liability Without Fault," *Harv. L. Rev.*, XXIX (1916), 801–15.

Turner, J. W. C. "The Mental Element in Crimes at Common Law," in L. Radzinowicz and J. W. C. Turner (eds.), *The Modern Approach to Criminal Law*. London: Macmillan and Co., Ltd., 1948, pp. 192–261.

Williams, G. *Joint Torts and Contributory Negligence*. London: Stevens, 1951.

Winfield, P. H. "History of Negligence in Law of Torts," *Law Quarterly Rev.*, XLII (1926), 184–201.

———. "Myth of Absolute Liability," *Law Quarterly Rev.*, XLII (1926), 37–51.

CHAPTER VI

Anderson, J. "The Problem of Causality," *Australasian Jour. of Phil.,* XVI (1938), 127–42.

Anscombe, G. E. M. *Intention.* Oxford: Basil Blackwell, 1957.

Aristotle, *Metaphysics.*

Ayer, A. J. *The Foundations of Empirical Knowledge.* London: Macmillan and Co., Ltd., 1958, Chapter IV.

Beale, J. H. "The Proximate Consequences of an Act," *Harv. L. Rev.,* XXXIII (1920), 633–58.

Bentham, J. *Theory of Fictions,* ed. C. K. Ogden. London: Routledge and Kegan Paul, 1932.

Bingham, J. W. "Some Suggestions Concerning 'Legal Cause' at Common Law," *Columbia L. Rev.,* IX (1909), 16–37, 136–54.

Bohlen, F. "The Probable or the Natural Consequences as the Test of Liability in Negligence," *Amer. L. Register,* XLIX (1901), 79–88, 148–64.

———. *Studies in the Law of Torts.* Indianapolis, Ind.: The Bobbs-Merrill Co., 1926.

Braithwaite, M. M., B. H. Farrell, and C. A. Mace. "Causal Laws in Psychology" (symposium), *Proc. Arist. Soc.,* Supp. Vol. XXIII (1949), 31–68.

Braithwaite, R. B. *The Nature of Scientific Explanation.* Cambridge, Eng.: Cambridge Univ. Press, 1953.

Burke, N. J. "Rules of Legal Cause in Negligence Cases," *Calif. L. Rev.,* XV (1926), 1–18.

Campbell, R. V. "Duty, Fault and Legal Cause," *Wisconsin L. Rev.,* 1938, pp. 402–25.

Carpenter, C. E. "Concurrent Causation," *Univ. of Pa. L. Rev.,* LXXXIII (1935), 941–52.

———. "Proximate Cause," *Southern Calif. L. Rev.,* XIV (1940), 1–34, 115–53, 416–51; XV (1943), 187–213, 304–21, 427–68; XVI (1943), 1–23, 61–92.

———. "Workable Rules for Determining Proximate Cause," *Calif. L. Rev.,* XX (1932), 229–59, 396–419, 471–539.

Cassirer, E. *Determinism and Indeterminism in Modern Physics,* trans. O. T. Benfey. New Haven: Yale University Press, 1956.

"Causality," in *University of California Publications in Philosophy.* Berkeley, Calif.: Univ. of Calif. Press, 1932.

Cohen, F. S. "Field Theory and Judicial Logic," *Yale L. Jour.,* LIX (1950), 238, 251–56.

"The Conception of Law in Science" (symposium), *Jour. of Phil.,* L (1953), 85–124.

Craik, K. *The Nature of Explanation.* Cambridge, Eng.: Cambridge Univ. Press, 1943.

Dray, W. *Laws and Explanation in History.* London: Oxford Univ. Press, 1957.

Dummett, M. A. E., and A. Flew. "Can an Effect Precede Its Cause?" *Proc. Arist. Soc.,* Supp. Vol. XXVIII (1954), 27–62.

Edgerton, H. "Legal Cause," *Univ. of Pa. L. Rev.,* LXXII (1924), 211–44, 343–75.

Edwards, J. L. J. *"Mens Rea" in Statutory Offences.* London: Macmillan and Co., Ltd., 1955.

Ewing, A. C. "A Defence of Causality," *Proc. Arist. Soc.,* XXXIII (1932–33), 95–128.

Feuer, L. S., and E. M. Albert. "Causality in the Social Sciences" (symposium), *Jour. of Phil.,* LI (1954), 681–706.

Focht, J. L. "Proximate Cause in the Law of Homicide," *So. Calif. L. Rev.,* XII (1938), 19–53.

G. C. T. "Causal Relation Between Defendant's Unlawful Act and the Death," *Michigan L. Rev.,* XXXI (1933), 659–82.

Gardiner, P. *The Nature of Historical Explanation.* London: Oxford Univ. Press, 1952.

Goodhart, A. L. "Appeals on Questions of Fact," *Law Quarterly Rev.,* LXXI (1955), 402–14.

———. *Essays in Jurisprudence and the Common Law.* Cambridge, Eng.: Cambridge Univ. Press, 1931.

Green, L. "Are Negligence and 'Proximate' Cause Determined by the Same Test?" *Texas L. Rev.,* I (1923), 242–60, 423–45.

———. "Are There Dependable Rules of Causation?" *Univ. of Pa. L. Rev.,* LXXVII (1929), 601–28.

———. "Contributory Negligence and Proximate Cause," *North Car. L. Rev.,* VI (1927), 3–33.

———. *Judge and Jury.* Kansas City, Mo.: Vernon Book Co., 1930.

———. *Rationale of Proximate Cause.* Kansas City, Mo.: Vernon Law Book Co., 1927.

Green, N. St. J. *Essays on Tort and Crime.* Menasha, Wis.: George Banta Pub. Co., 1933, pp. 1–17.

Gregory, C. O. "Proximate Cause in Negligence—A Retreat from 'Rationalization,'" *Univ. of Chi. L. Rev.,* VI (1938), 36–61.

Gregory, J. C. "Causal Efficacy," *Proc. Arist. Soc.,* XLIV (1943–44), 1–14.

Hall, J. *General Principles of Criminal Law.* 2d ed. Indianapolis: The Bobbs-Merrill Co., 1960.

———. *Studies in Jurisprudence and Criminal Theory.* New York: Oceana Publications, Inc., 1958, Chapter X.

Hanson, N. R. "Causal Chains," *Mind,* LXIV (1955), 289–311.

Harper, F. V. "Liability Without Fault and Proximate Cause," *Michigan L. Rev.,* XXX (1932), 1001–15.

Hart, H. L. A., and A. M. Honoré. *Causation in the Law.* Oxford: Clarendon Press, 1959.

Hartnack, J. "Some Remarks on Causality," *Jour. of Phil.,* L (1953), 466–72.

Hofstadter, A. "Causality and Necessity," *Jour. of Phil.,* XLVI (1949), 257–70.

Hook, S. (ed.). *Psychoanalysis, Scientific Method and Philosophy* (symposium). New York: New York Univ. Press, 1959.

Hume, D. *An Enquiry Concerning Human Understanding,* ed. L. A. Selby-Bigge. Oxford: Clarendon Press, 1902.

———. *A Treatise of Human Nature,* ed. L. A. Selby-Bigge. Oxford: Clarendon Press, 1888.

James, F., Jr., and R. F. Perry. "Legal Cause," *Yale L. Jour.,* LX (1951), 761–811.

Joseph, H. W. B. *An Introduction to Logic.* London: Oxford Univ. Press, 1916.

Levitt, A. "Cause, Legal Cause and Proximate Cause," *Michigan L. Rev.,* XXI (1922), 34–62, 160–73.

———. "Proximate Cause and Legal Liability," *Century L. Jour.,* LXXX (1920), 188.

"Loss-Shifting and Quasi-Negligence; A New Interpretation of the Palsgraf Case," *Univ. of Chi. L. Rev.,* VIII (1941), 729–45.

Kant, I. *Critique of Pure Reason,* trans. N. Kemp-Smith. London: Macmillan and Co., Ltd., 1950.

Kelsen, H. "Causality and Retribution," in *What Is Justice?* Berkeley: Univ. of Calif. Press, 1957.

———. *Society and Nature.* Chicago: Univ. of Chi. Press, 1943.

Kneale, W. C. *Probability and Induction.* London: Oxford Univ. Press, 1949.

Mace, C. A., G. F. Stout, and A. C. Ewing. "Mechanical and Theological Causation" (symposium), *Proc. Arist. Soc.,* Supp. Vol. XIV (1935), 22–82.

MacLaughlin, J. A. "Proximate Cause," *Harv. L. Rev.,* XXXIX (1925), 149–99.

Malone, W. S. "Ruminations on Cause-in-fact," *Stanford L. Rev.,* IX (1956), 60–99.

Melden, A. I. *Free Action.* London: Routledge and Kegan Paul, 1961.

Michael, J., and H. Wechsler. *Criminal Law and Its Administration.* Brooklyn, N.Y.: Foundation Press, 1940.

Mill, J. S. *A System of Logic.* London: Longmans, Green and Co., 1956, Book III.

Model Penal Code, American Law Institute, Tentative Drafts Nos. 1, 2, 3 ,4.

Montefiore, A. "Determinism and Causal Order," *Proc. Arist. Soc.,* LVIII (1957–58), 125–42.

Morris, C. "Duty, Negligence and Causation," *Univ. of Pa. L. Rev.,* CI (1952), 189–222.

———. "On the Teaching of Legal Cause," *Columbia L. Rev.,* XXXIX (1939), 1087–1109.

———. "Proximate Cause in Minnesota," *Minn. L. Rev.,* XXXIV (1950), 185–209.

———. *Studies in Torts.* Brooklyn, N.Y.: Foundation Press, 1952.

O'Connor, D. J. "Causal Statements," *Phil. Quarterly,* VI (1956), 17–26.

Peaslee, R. J. "Multiple Causation and Damage," *Harv. L. Rev.,* XLVII (1934), 1127–42.

Prosser, W. L. *Handbook of the Law of Torts.* 2d ed. St. Paul, Minn.: West Publishing Co., 1955.

———. "Palsgraf Revisited," *Michigan L. Rev.,* LII (1953), 1–32.

———. *Selected Topics on the Law of Torts.* Ann Arbor, Mich.: Univ. of Michigan Law School, 1953.

Reese, F. S. "Negligence and Proximate Cause," *Cornell L. Quarterly,* VII (1922), 95–115.

Restatement of the Law of Torts, American Law Institute, 1934, and supplements 1948, 1954.

Ryu, P. K. "Causation in Criminal Law," *Univ. of Pa. L. Rev.,* CVI (1958), 773–805.

Russell, B. "On the Notion of Cause," *Proc. Arist. Soc.,* XIII (1912–13), 1–26.

Russell, L. J. "Ought Implies Can," *Proc. Arist. Soc.,* XXXVI (1935–36), 151–86.

———. "The Principle of Causality," *Proc. Arist. Soc.,* XLVI (1945–46), 105–26.

Smith, J. "Legal Cause in Actions of Tort," *Harv. L. Rev.,* XXV (1911), 103–28, 223–52, 303–27.

Teichmann, J. "Mental Cause and Effect," *Mind,* LXX (1961), 36–52.

Terry, H. T. "Proximate Consequences in the Law of Torts," *Harv. L. Rev.,* XXVIII (1914), 10–33.

Warnock, G. J. "Every Event Has a Cause," in A. Flew (ed.), *Logic and Language*. Oxford: Basil Blackwell, 1959, II, 95–111.

Watling, J. "Propositions Asserting Causal Connection," *Analysis,* XIV (1953), 31–37.

Wechsler, H., and J. Michael. "A Rationale of the Law of Homicide," *Columbia L. Rev.,* XXXVII (1937), 701–61, 1261–1325.

Williams, G. "Causation in Homicide," *Crim. L. Rev.* (1957), pp. 429–40, 510–21.

———. *Joint Torts and Contributory Negligence.* London: Stevens, 1951.

Wisdom, J. O. *Causation and the Foundations of Science.* Paris: Hermann, 1946.

Wright, Lord. "Notes on Causation and Responsibility in English Law," *Camb. L. Jour.,* 1955, p. 163.

CHAPTER VII

Anscombe, G. E. M. *Intention.* Oxford: Basil Blackwell, 1957.

Cator, G., and C. E. M. Joad. "Error" (symposium), *Proc. Arist. Soc.,* Supp. Vol. XXVII (1926–27), 213–29.

Edwards, J. L. J. "Criminal Degrees of Knowledge," *Mod. L. Rev.,* XVII (1954), 294–314.

———. *"Mens Rea" in Statutory Offences.* London: Macmillan and Co., Ltd., 1955.

Gow, J. J. "Some Observations on Error," *Juridical Rev.,* LXV (1953), 221–54.

Hall, L., and S. J. Seligman. "Mistake of Law and Mens Rea," *Univ. of Chi. L. Rev.,* VIII (1941), 641–83.

Keedy, E. R. "Ignorance and Mistake in the Criminal Law," *Harv. L. Rev.,* XXII (1908), 75–96.

Kohler, R. E. "Ignorance or Mistake of Law as a Defense in Criminal Cases," *Dickinson L. Rev.,* XL (1936), 113–22.

Krasnowiecki, J. Z. "A Logical Problem in the Law of Mistake as to Person," *Phil. Quarterly,* X (1960), 313–21.

Perkins, R. M. "Ignorance and Mistake in Criminal Law," *Univ. of Pa. L. Rev.,* LXXXVIII (1939), 35–70.

Price, H. H. "Belief and Will," *Proc. Arist. Soc.,* Supp. Vol. XXVIII (1954), 1–26.

———. *Thinking and Experience.* London: Hutchinson's Univ. Library, 1953.

Ryu, P. K., and H. Silving. *"Error Juris*: A Comparative Study," *Univ. of Chi. L. Rev.,* XXIV (1957), 421–71.

Stroud, D. A. *Mens Rea.* London: Sweet and Maxwell, Ltd., 1914, Chapters II and III.

Williams, G. *Criminal Law: The General Part.* London: Stevens and Sons Ltd., 1953.

Winfield, P. H. "Mistake of Law," *Law Quarterly Rev.,* XLIX (1943), 327–42.

CHAPTER VIII

Biggs, J. *The Guilty Mind: Psychiatry and the Law of Homicide.* New York: Harcourt, Brace, 1955.

Board, R. G. "Operational Criteria for Determining Legal Insanity," *Columbia L. Rev.,* LXI (1961), 221–32.

Bromberg, W. *Crime and the Mind.* Philadelphia: J. B. Lippincott Co., 1948.

Cassity, J. H. *The Quality of Murder.* New York: Julian Press, 1958.

Cohen, C. "Criminal Responsibility and the Knowledge of Right and Wrong," *Univ. of Miami L. Rev.,* XIV (1959), 30–56.

Coleman, J. C. *Abnormal Psychology and Modern Life.* Chicago: Scott, Foresman and Company, 1956.

"Criminal Responsibility and Mental Disease: A Panel," *Tennessee L. Rev.,* XXVI (1959), 221–46.

Dession, G. H. "Psychiatry and the Conditioning of Criminal Justice," *Yale L. Jour.,* XLII (1938), 319–40.

East, W. N. *The Roots of Crime.* London: Butterworth, 1954.

Foulkes, S. H. "Psychoanalysis and Crime," *Canadian Bar Rev.,* XXII (1944), 19–61.

Glueck, B. *Studies in Forensic Psychiatry.* Boston: Little, Brown and Co., 1916.

Glueck, S. *Mental Disorder and the Criminal Law.* Boston: Little, Brown and Co., 1925.

Goodwin, J. C. *Insanity and the Criminal.* New York: George H. Doran Co., 1924.

Gotlieb, A. E. "Intention and Knowing the Nature and Quality of an Act," *Mod. L. Rev.,* XIX (1956), 270–75.

Hacker, F. J., and M. Frym. "Legal Concept of Insanity and Treatment of Criminal Impulses," *Calif. L. Rev.,* XXVII (1949), 575–91.

Hall, J. "Mental Disease and Criminal Responsibility," *Columbia L. Rev.,* XLV (1945), 677–718.

Hart, B. *The Psychology of Insanity.* 5th ed. Cambridge, Eng.: Cambridge Univ. Press, 1957.

Henderson, D. K., and R. D. Gillespie. *A Text-Book of Psychiatry.* London: Oxford Univ. Press, 1950.

Hoch, P. H., and J. Zubin (eds.). *Psychiatry and the Law.* New York: Greene and Stratton, 1955.

"Insanity and the Criminal Law—A Critique of *Durham v. U.S.*—A Symposium," *Univ. of Chi. L. Rev.,* XXII (1955), 317–404.

Karpman, B. "Criminality, Insanity and the Law," *Jour. of Crim. L. and Criminol.,* XXXIX (1949), 584–605.

Keedy, E. R. "Insanity and Criminal Responsibility," *Harv. L. Rev.,* XXX (1917), 535–60, 724–38.

Laing, R. D. *The Divided Self; A Study of Sanity and Madness.* London: Tavistock Publications, 1960.

"Law and the Mentality Ill: A Symposium," *Ohio State L. Jour.,* XXI (1960), 1–115.

Lindesay, W. *Psychological Disorder and Crime.* London: C. Johnson, 1953.

Linton, R. *Culture and Mental Disorders.* Springfield, Ill.: Charles C Thomas, 1956.

McConnell, R. M. *Criminal Responsibility and Social Constraint.* New York: C. Scribner's Sons, 1912.

Maudsley, H. *Responsibility in Mental Disease.* New York: D. Appleton Co., 1892.

Mercier, C. *Criminal Responsibility.* New York: Physicians and Surgeons Book Co., 1926, pp. 100–125.

Minty, O. C. D., and F. A. Wilshire. *Mentality and the Criminal Law.* London: Simpkin Marshall, Ltd., 1935.

Neustatter, W. L. *Psychological Disorder and Crime.* London: C. Johnson, 1953.

Nice, R. W. (ed.). *Crime and Insanity.* New York: Philosophical Library, 1958.

Overholser, W. "The Place of Psychiatry in the Criminal Law," *Boston Univ. L. Rev.,* XVI (1936), 322–44.

———. *The Psychiatrist and the Law.* New York: Harcourt, Brace, 1953.

Peskin, M. "Modern Approach to Legal Responsibility, the Psychopath and the M'Naghten Rules," *Jour. of Forensic Medicine,* I (1954), 189–204.

"Psychiatry and the Law—A Symposium," *Temple L. Quarterly,* XXIX (1956), 233–408.

Radzinowicz, L., and J. W. C. Turner (eds.). *Mental Abnormality and Crime.* London: Macmillan and Co., Ltd., 1944.

Roche, P. Q. *The Criminal Mind; A Study of Communication Between the Criminal Law and Psychiatry.* New York: Farrar, Straus and Cudahy, 1958.

Sheldon, W. H. *Varieties of Delinquent Youth.* New York: Harper Brothers, 1949.

Stroud, D. A. *Mens Rea.* London: Sweet and Maxwell, Ltd., 1914, Chapter V.

Sullivan, W. C. *Crime and Insanity.* London: E. Arnold and Co., 1924.

"Symposium on Criminal Responsibility," *Univ. of Kansas L. Rev.,* IV (1956), 349–95.

Waelder, R. "Psychiatry and the Problem of Criminal Responsibility," *Univ. of Pa. L. Rev.,* CI (1952), 378–90.

Weihofen, H. *Insanity as a Defense in Criminal Law.* London: Oxford Univ. Press, 1933.

———. *Mental Disorder as a Criminal Defense.* Buffalo: Dennis, 1954.

———. "Partial Insanity and Criminal Intent," *Ill. L. Rev.,* XXIV (1930), 505–27.

———. "Psychiatry and the Law of Criminal Insanity," *Southwestern L. Jour.,* VI (1952), 47–80.

———. *The Urge to Punish.* New York: Farrar, Straus and Cudahy, 1956.

White, W. A. *Insanity and the Criminal Law.* New York: The Macmillan Co., 1923.

Williams, G. *Criminal Law: The General Part.* London: Stevens and Sons Ltd., 1953.

Woodbridge, F. "Some Unusual Aspects of Mental Irresponsibility in the Criminal Law," *Jour. of Crim. L. and Criminol.,* XXIX (1939), 822–47.

Woodward, J. W. "Psychological Aspects of the Question of Moral Responsibility," *Jour. Crim. L. and Criminol.,* XXI (1930), 267–96.

Zilboorg, G. *The Psychology of the Criminal Act and Punishment.* New York: Harcourt, Brace, 1954.

CHAPTER IX

Adler, M. *The Idea of Freedom.* Garden City, N.Y.: Doubleday, 1958.

Alexander, P., and A. MacIntyre. "Cause and Cure in Psychotherapy" (symposium), *Proc. Arist. Soc.,* Supp. Vol. XXIX (1955), 25–58.

Aveling, F. *Personality and Will.* New York: D. Appleton and Co., 1931.

Ayer, A. J. *Philosophical Essays.* London: Macmillan and Co., Ltd., 1954, Chapter XII.

Bergson, H. *Time and Free Will.* New York: The Macmillan Co., 1910.

Beardsley, E. L. "Determinism and Moral Perspectives," *Phil. and Phen. Research,* XXI (1960), 1–20.

Bradley, R. D. "Free Will: Problem or Pseudo-Problem," *Australasian Jour. of Phil.,* XXXVI (1958), 33–45. Reply by C. A. Campbell, pp. 46–55.

Brandt, R. C. *Ethical Theory.* Englewood Cliffs, N.J.: Prentice-Hall, 1959, Chapter XX.

Broad, C. D. *Determinism, Indeterminism and Libertarianism,* reprinted in *Ethics and the History of Philosophy.* London: Routledge and Kegan Paul Ltd., 1952.

———. *Five Types of Ethical Theory.* New York: Harcourt, Brace and Co., 1934, pp. 192–208.

———, A. S. Eddington, and R. B. Braithwaite. "Indeterminacy and Indeterminism" (symposium), *Proc. Arist. Soc.,* Supp. Vol. X (1931), 135–96.

Carritt, E. F. *Ethical and Political Thinking.* Oxford: Clarendon Press, 1947, Chapter XII.

Cranston, M. *Freedom: A New Analysis.* London: Longmans, Green, 1953.

Danto, A. C., and S. Morgenbesser. "Character and Free Will," *Jour. of Phil.,* LIV (1959), 493–504.

Dilman, I. "The Unconscious," *Mind,* LXVIII (1959), 446–73.

Dingle, H. "The Logical Status of Psychoanalysis," *Analysis,* IX (1949),63.

Ebersole, F. B. "Free Choice and the Demands of Morals," *Mind,* LXI (1952), 234–57.

Ewing, A. C. "Indeterminism," *Rev. of Metaphysics,* V (1951), 199–222.

Farrar, A. *The Freedom of the Will.* London: Black, 1958.

Feuer, L. S. *Psychoanalysis and Ethics.* Springfield, Ill.: Charles C Thomas, 1955.

Fingarette, H. "Psychoanalytic Perspectives on Moral Guilt and Responsibility: A Re-Evaluation," *Phil. and Phen. Research,* XVI (1955), 18–36.

———. " 'Unconscious Behavior' and Allied Concepts; A New Approach to Their Empirical Interpretation," *Jour. of Phil.,* XLVII (1950), 509–20.

Flew, A. G. A. "Determinism and Rational Behavior," *Mind,* LXVIII (1959), 377–82.

———. "Divine Omnipotence and Human Freedom," in A. Flew and A. MacIntyre (eds.), *New Essays in Philosophical Theology.* London: SCM Press, Ltd., 1955, pp. 144–69.

———. "Farewell to the Paradigm Case Argument: A Comment," *Analysis,* XVIII (1957), 34–40.

Foot, P. "Free Will As Involving Determinism," *Phil. Rev.,* LXVI (1959), 439–50.

Foulkes, S. H. "Psychoanalysis and Crime," *Canadian Bar Rev.,* XXII (1944), 19–61.

Freud, S. *Collected Papers,* trans. Riviere. London: The Hogarth Press, 1957.

———. *The Ego and the Id,* trans. Riviere. London: The Hogarth Press, 1957.

———. *A General Introduction to Psychoanalysis.* London: Boni and Liveright, 1924.

———. *The Psychopathology of Everyday Life,* trans. Brill. New York: The Modern Library, 1938.

Green, T. H. *Prolegomena to Ethics.* Oxford: Clarendon Press, 1883, pp. 97–173.

Hampshire, S., W. G. Maclagan, and R. M. Hare. "The Freedom of the Will" (symposium), *Proc. Arist. Soc.,* XXV (1951), 161–216.

Handy, R. "Determinism, Responsibility, and the Social Setting," *Phil. and Phen. Research,* XX (1960), 469–76.

Hardie, W. "My Own Free Will," *Philosophy,* XXXII (1957), 21–38.

Hart, H. L. A. "Legal Responsibility and Excuses," in S. Hook (ed.), *Determinism and Freedom in the Age of Modern Science.* New York: New York Univ. Press, 1958, pp. 81–104.

Hartnack, J. "Free Will and Decision," *Mind,* LXII (1953), 367–74.

Hartshorne, C. "Freedom Requires Indeterminism and Universal Causality," *Jour. of Phil.,* LV (1958), 793–810.

Herbst, P. "Freedom and Prediction," *Mind,* LXVI (1957), 1–27.

Hobart, R. E. "Free Will as Involving Determinism," *Mind,* XLIII (1934), 1–27.

Hook, S. (ed.). *Determinism and Freedom in the Age of Modern Science.* New York: New York Univ. Press, 1958.

———. *Psychoanalysis, Scientific Method and Philosophy* (symposium). New York: New York Univ. Press, 1959.

James, W. "The Dilemma of Determinism," in *Essays in Pragmatism.* New York: Hafner Publishing Company, 1951.

Kant, I. *Critique of Practical Reason,* trans. T. K. Abbott. London: Longmans, Green and Co., 1873.

———. *Fundamental Principles of the Metaphysic of Morals,* trans. T. K. Abbott. London: Longmans, Green and Co., 1873.

Lacey, A. R. "Freewill and Responsibility," *Proc. Arist. Soc.,* LVIII (1957–58), 15–32.

Ladd, J. "Free Will and Voluntary Action," *Phil. and Phen. Research,* XII (1951), 392–405.

Lamont, W. D. *The Principles of Moral Judgment.* Oxford: Clarendon Press, 1946, Chapter VIII.

Landé, A. "Determinism Versus Continuity in Modern Science," *Mind,* LXVII (1958), 174–81.

Lehrer, K. "Can We Know that We Have Free Will by Introspection," *Jour. of Phil.,* LVII (1960), 145–56.

Leibnitz, G. W. *New Essays Concerning Human Understanding,* trans. A. G. Langley. La Salle, Ill.: Open Court Publishing Co., 1949, pp. 174–220.

———. *Philosophical Papers and Letters,* trans. and ed. by L. E. Loember. Chicago, Ill.: Univ. of Chi. Press, 1956, I, 404–10.

———. *Theodicy,* trans. E. M. Huggard. London, 1952.

Levy, H. "Causality and Determinism," *Proc. Arist. Soc.,* XXXVII (1936–37), 89–106.

Mabbott, J. D. "Freewill and Punishment," in H. D. Lewis (ed.), *Contemporary British Philosophy,* 3d Series. London: George Allen and Unwin, 1956, pp. 287–370.

MacIntyre, A. C. "Determinism," *Mind,* LXVI (1957), 28–41.

———. *The Unconscious.* London: Routledge and Kegan Paul Ltd., 1958.

Madden, E. H. "Psychoanalysis and Moral Judgeability," *Phil. and Phen. Research,* XVIII (1957), 68–79.

Mandelbaum, M. "Determinism and Moral Responsibility," *Ethics,* LXX (1960), 204–19.

Matson, W. I. "On the Irrelevance of Free-Will to Moral Responsibility and the Vacuity of the Latter," *Mind,* LXV (1956), 489–97.

Melden, A. I. *Free Action.* London: Routledge and Kegan Paul Ltd., 1961.

Moore, G. E. *Ethics.* Oxford: Oxford Univ. Press, 1949, Chapter VI.

Nowell-Smith, P. H. "Determinists and Libertarians," *Mind,* LXIII (1954), 317–37.

————. *Ethics.* Baltimore: Penguin Books, Inc., 1954, Chapters XIX, XX.

————. "Freewill and Moral Responsibility," *Mind,* LVII (1948), 45–61.

O'Connor, D. J. "Is There a Problem About Free-Will?" *Proc. Arist. Soc.,* XLIX (1948–49), 33–46.

————. "Possibility and Choice," *Proc. Arist. Soc.,* Supp. Vol. XXXIV (1960), 1–24.

Peters, R. S. "Cause, Cure, and Motive," *Analysis,* X (1950), 103–9.

————. *The Concept of Motivation.* London: Routledge and Kegan Paul Ltd., 1958.

Pickford, R. W. "Psychological Aspects of Punishment," *Ethics,* LVIII (1947), 1–17.

Raab, F. V. "Free Will and the Ambiguity of 'Could,' " *Phil. Rev.,* LXIV (1955), 60–77.

Rankin, K. W. "Causal Modalities and Alternative Action," *Phil. Quarterly,* VII (1957), 289–304.

————. "Doer and Doing," *Mind,* LXIX (1960), 361–71.

Raphael, D. D. "Causation and Free Will," *Phil. Quarterly,* II (1952), 13–30.

————. *Moral Judgment.* London: George Allen and Unwin, Ltd., 1955, Chapter X.

Ross, W. D. *Foundations of Ethics.* Oxford: Clarendon Press, 1939, Chapter X.

Russell, L. J. "Ought Implies Can," *Proc. Arist. Soc.,* XXXVI (1935–36), 151–86.

Ryle, G. *The Concept of Mind.* London: Hutchinson's Univ. Library, 1949.

Schlick, M. *Problems of Ethics.* Englewood Cliffs, N.J.: Prentice-Hall, Inc., 1939, Chapter VII.

Scott, K. J. "Conditioning and Freedom," *Australasian Jour. of Phil.,* XXXVII (1959), 215–20.

Sellars, R. W. "Guided Causality, Using Reason and 'Free-Will,' " *Jour. of Phil.,* LIV (1959), 485–93.

Sidgwick, H. *The Methods of Ethics.* London: Macmillan and Co., Ltd., 1922, pp. 56–66.

Spinoza, B. *Ethics.* London: J. M. Dent and Sons, Ltd., 1901.

Stevenson, C. L. *Ethics and Language.* New Haven: Yale Univ. Press, 1944, Chapter XIV.

Stout, A. K. "Freewill," *Australasian Jour. of Phil.,* XVIII (1940) 212–31.

————. "Free Will and Responsibility," *Proc. Arist. Soc.,* XXXVII (1936–37), 213–30.

Stroud, D. A. *Mens Rea.* London: Sweet and Maxwell, Ltd., 1914, Chapter X.

Taylor, R. " 'I can,' " *Phil. Rev.,* LXIX (1960), 78–89.

Toulmin, S. "The Logical Status of Psychoanalysis," *Analysis,* IX (1948), 23–29.

University of California Associates. *Knowledge and Society.* New York: Appleton-Century-Crofts, Inc., 1938, Chapter VI.

Watkins, J. W. N. "Farewell to the Paradigm-Case Argument," *Analysis,* XVIII (1957), 25–33, 41–42.

Weiss, P. "Freedom of Choice," *Ethics,* LII (1941), 186–99.

"What Sort of 'If' Is the 'If' in 'I can *if* I choose'?" *Analysis,* XII (1951–52), 50, 126, 132.

Wilson, J. "Freedom and Compulsion," *Mind,* LXVII (1958), 60–69.

CHAPTER X

Alexander, J. P. "Philosophy of Punishment," *Jour. of Crim. L. and Criminol.,* XIII (1922) 235–50.

Baier, K. "Is Punishment Retributive?" *Analysis,* XVI (1955), 25–32.

Beccaria, C. *An Essay on Crimes and Punishments.* Albany: W. C. Lettle and Co., 1872.

Bentham, J. *An Introduction to the Principles of Morals and Legislation.* Oxford: Basil Blackwell, 1948.

———. *Theory of Legislation.* London: Routledge and Kegan Paul Ltd., 1931, 1950.

Bok, C. *Star Wormwood.* New York: Knopf, 1959.

Brandt, R. B. *Ethical Theory.* Englewood Cliffs, N.J.: Prentice-Hall, 1959, Chapter XIX.

Braybrooke, D. "Professor Stevenson, Voltaire, and the Case of Admiral Byng," *Jour. of Phil.,* LIII (1956), 787–96.

Coddington, F. J. O. "Problems of Punishment," *Proc. Arist. Soc.,* XLVI (1945-46), 155–78.

Cohen, M. R. "Moral Aspects of the Criminal Law," *Yale L. Jour.,* XLIX (1940), 987–1026.

Devlin, P. "Criminal Responsibility and Punishment: Functions of Judge and Jury," *Crim. L. Rev.,* (1954), 661–86.

Ewing, A. C. *The Morality of Punishment.* London: K. Paul, Trench, Trubner and Co. Ltd., 1929.

Flew, A. "The Justification of Punishment," *Philosophy,* XXIX (1954), 291–307.

Gardiner, C. "Purposes of Criminal Punishment," *Mod. L. Rev.,* XXI (1958), 117–29, 221–35.

Green, T. H. "State's Right to Punish," *Jour. of Crim. L. and Criminol.,* I (1910), 19–43.

Hall, J. *General Principles of Criminal Law.* 2d ed. Indianapolis: The Bobbs-Merrill Co., 1960.

———. "Nulla Poena Sine Lege," *Yale L. Jour.,* XLVII (1937), 165–93.

Hart, H. L. A. "Legal Responsibility and Excuses," in S. Hook (ed.), *Determinism and Freedom in the Age of Modern Science.* New York: New York Univ. Press, 1958, pp. 81–104.

———. "Prolegomenon to the Principles of Punishment," *Proc. Arist. Soc.,* LX (1959–60), 1–26.

Hentig, H. von. *Punishment: Its Origin, Purpose and Psychology.* London: W. Hodge and Co. Ltd., 1937.

Hodges, D. C. "Punishment," *Phil. and Phen. Research,* XVIII (1957), 209–18.

Höffding, H. "The State's Authority to Punish Crime," *Jour. of Crim. L. and Criminol.,* II (1912), 691–703.

Kelsen, H. "Causality and Retribution," in *What Is Justice?* Berkeley: Univ. of Calif. Press, 1957.

Lewis, C. S. "Humanitarian Theory of Punishment," *Res Judicatae,* VI (1953), 224–30. Reply by N. Morris and D. Bucke, VI (1953), 231–37. Comment by J. J. C. Smart, VI (1954), 368–71. Reply by C. S. Lewis, VI (1954), 519–23.

Mabbott, J. D. "Freewill and Punishment," in H. D. Lewis (ed.), *Contemporary*

British Philosophy. 3d Series. London: George Allen and Unwin, 1956, pp. 287–310.

———. "Punishment," *Mind,* XLVIII (1939), 152–67.

McConnell, R. M. *Criminal Responsibility and Social Constraint.* New York: C. Scribner's Sons, 1912.

Maclagan, W. G. "Punishment and Retribution," *Philosophy,* XIV (1939), 281–98.

Moberly, W. H. "Some Ambiguities in the Retributive Theory of Punishment," *Proc. Arist. Soc.,* XXV (1924–25), 289–304.

Moore, G. E. *Principia Ethica.* Cambridge, Eng.: Cambridge Univ. Press, 1929, pp. 214–21.

Mundle, C. W. K. "Punishment and Desert," *Phil. Quarterly,* IV (1954), 216–28.

Plato. *Gorgias,* trans. B. Jowett. London: Oxford Univ. Press, 1920.

———. *Laws,* trans. B. Jowett. London: Oxford Univ. Press, 1920.

———. *Protagoras,* trans. B. Jowett. London: Oxford Univ. Press, 1920.

Pufendorf, S. *De Jure Naturae et Gentium.* Oxford: Clarendon Press, 1934, Book 8, Chapter III, pp. 1214 ff.

Radzinowicz, L., and J. W. C. Turner (eds.). *The Modern Approach to Criminal Law.* London: Macmillan and Co., Ltd., 1948.

Rashdall, H. *Theory of Good and Evil.* Oxford: Clarendon Press, 1924, Volume I, Chapter 9.

Rawls, J. "Two Concepts of Rules," *Phil. Rev.,* LXIV (1955), 3–32.

Ross, W. D. "The Ethics of Punishment," *Philosophy,* IV (1925), 205–11.

———. *The Right and the Good.* Oxford: Clarendon Press, 1930, pp. 56–64.

Royal Commission on Capital Punishment 1949–53 Report. London: Her Majesty's Stationery Office, 1953.

Saleilles, S. R. *The Individualization of Punishment,* trans. Jastrow. Boston: Little, Brown and Co., 1911.

Sears, L. *Responsibility, Its Development through Punishment and Reward.* New York: Columbia Univ. Press, 1932.

Sen, Prasanta Kumar. *From Punishment to Prevention.* London: Oxford Univ. Press, 1932.

Spencer, H. "Ethics of Punishment," *Jour. of Crim. L. and Criminol.,* I (1911), 862–76.

Tarde, G. de. *Penal Philosophy.* Boston: Little, Brown and Co., 1912.

Wechsler, H., and J. Michael. "A Rationale of the Law of Homicide," *Columbia L. Rev.,* XXXVII (1937), 701–61, 1261–1325.

Weihofen, H. *The Urge to Punish.* New York: Farrar, Straus, and Cudahy, 1956.

Williams, G. *Criminal Law: The General Part.* London: Stevens and Sons Ltd., 1953.

Willoughby, W. W. "Primitive Justice," *Jour. of Crim. L. and Criminol.,* I (1910), 354–77.

Zilboorg, G. *The Psychology of the Criminal Act and Punishment.* New York: Harcourt, Brace, 1954.